# PSYCHOLOGY

### SIXTH EDITION

 *W · W · NORTON & COMPANY · NEW YORK · LONDON*

# PSYCHOLOGY

## SIXTH EDITION

HENRY GLEITMAN

ALAN J. FRIDLUND

DANIEL REISBERG

W. W. Norton & Company has been independent since its founding in 1923, when William Warder Norton and Mary D. Herter Norton first published lectures delivered at the People's Institute, the adult education division of New York City's Cooper Union. The Nortons soon expanded their program beyond the Institute, publishing books by celebrated academics from America and abroad. By mid-century, the two major pillars of Norton's publishing program—trade books and college texts—were firmly established. In the 1950s, the Norton family transferred control of the company to its employees, and today—with a staff of four hundred and a comparable number of trade, college, and professional titles published each year—W. W. Norton & Company stands as the largest and oldest publishing house owned wholly by its employees.

Editor: Jon Durbin
Assistant Editor: Aaron Javsicas
Project Editor: Kim Yi
Copy Editors: Carol Flechner and Mary Babcock
Editorial Assistants: Tessa Lyons and Andrea Haver
Photo Researcher: Nathan Odell
Production Manager: JoAnn Simony
Book and Cover Designer: Antonina Krass
Layout Artist: Carole Desnoes
Illustrations: Frank Forney
Managing Editor, College: Marian Johnson
Compositor: TSI Graphics
Manufacturer: Quebecor World Versailles

Cover art: Michelangelo Buonarroti. *David* (detail), 1501–04. Galleria dell'Accademia, Florence. Photo: Robert Farber/Corbis.

Further acknowledgments and credits appear on pp. B83–B87, which constitute a continuation of the copyright page.

Library of Congress Cataloging-in-Publication Data
Gleitman, Henry.
    Psychology/Henry Gleitman, Alan J. Fridlund, Daniel Reisberg.—6th ed.
    p. cm.
    Includes bibliographical references and index.
    ISBN 0-393-97767-6
    1. Psychology. I. Fridlund, Alan J. II. Reisberg, Daniel. III. Title.

BF121.G58 2003
150—dc21                                                              2003048792

W. W. Norton & Company, Inc., 500 Fifth Avenue, New York, N.Y. 10110
www.wwnorton.com
W. W. Norton & Company Ltd., Castle House, 75/76 Wells Street, London W1T 3QT

1 2 3 4 5 6 7 8 7 9 0

TO OUR WIVES AND CHILDREN,

Lila, Amy, and Friderike
Ellen, Claire, Jason, Jacob, and Solomon

# CONTENTS IN BRIEF

# CONTENTS

# PART 1 | ACTION 38

# PART 2 | COGNITION 164

# PART 3 | SOCIAL BEHAVIOR 366

PART **5** | INDIVIDUAL
DIFFERENCES  548

versity of Illinois; Morris Moscovitch, University of Toronto; Ulric Neisser, Cornell University; Daniel N. Osherson, Massachusetts Institute of Technology; David Premack, Emeritus, University of Pennsylvania; Miriam W. Schustack, University of California, San Diego; Myrna Schwartz, Moss Rehabilitation Hospital; Michael Turvey, University of Connecticut; Rose T. Zacks, Michigan State University.

## LANGUAGE

Sharon L. Armstrong, Drake University; Anne Fowler, Bryn Mawr College; John Gilbert, University of British Columbia; Roberta Golinkoff, University of Delaware; Barbara Landau, University of Delaware; Elissa Newport, University of Rochester; Ruth Ostrin, Medical Research Council, Cambridge, England; Ted Suppala, University of Rochester; Kenneth Wexler, Massachusetts Institute of Technology.

## SOCIAL PSYCHOLOGY

Emir Andrews, Memorial University of Newfoundland; Solomon E. Asch, late of the University of Pennsylvania; Su Boatright-Horowitz, University of Rhode Island; Joel Cooper, Princeton University; Mary Crawford, West Chester University; Phoebe C. Ellsworth, University of Michigan; Frederick J. Evans, Carrier Foundation, Bellemead, New Jersey; Larry Gross, University of Pennsylvania; Mark Hauser, Harvard University; Michael Lessac; Clark R. McCauley Jr., Bryn Mawr College; Stanley Milgram, late of City College of New York; Martin T. Orne, University of Pennsylvania; Albert Pepitone, University of Pennsylvania; Dennis Regan, Cornell University; Lee Ross, Stanford University; James Russell, University of British Columbia; John Sabini, University of Pennsylvania; Philip R. Shaver, University of California, Davis; R. Lance Shotland, Pennsylvania State University.

## DEVELOPMENT

Justin Aronfreed, University of Pennsylvania; Thomas Ayres, Clarkson College of Technology; Renée Baillargeon, University of Illinois; Edwin Boswell, Ardmore, Pennsylvania; Anne L. Brown, University of Illinois; Adele Diamond, Eunice Kennedy Shriver Center, Waltham, Massachusetts; Carol S. Dweck, Columbia University; Margery B. Franklin, Sarah Lawrence College; Rochel Gelman, University of California, Los Angeles; Frederick Gibbons, Iowa State University; Ellen Gleitman, Devon, Pennsylvania; Susan Scanlon Jones, Indiana University; Ed Kako, University of Pennsylvania; Philip J. Kellman, University of California, Los Angeles; Ellen Markman, Stanford University; Elizabeth Spelke, Massachusetts Institute of Technology; Douglas Wallen, Mankato State University; Sheldon White, Harvard University.

## INTELLIGENCE

Jonathan Baron, University of Pennsylvania; James F. Crow, University of Wisconsin; Daniel B. Keating, University of Minnesota; Robert Sternberg, Yale University.

## PERSONALITY

Hal Bertilson, Saint Joseph's University; Jack Block, Massachusetts Institute of Technology; Nathan Brody, Wesleyan University; Peter Gay, Yale University; Lewis R.

Goldberg, University of Oregon, Eugene; Ruben Gur, University of Pennsylvania; Judith Harackiewicz, Columbia University; John Kihlstrom, University of California, Berkeley; Lester B. Luborsky, University of Pennsylvania; Carl Malmquist, University of Minnesota; James Russell, University of British Columbia; Jerry S. Wiggins, University of British Columbia.

## PSYCHOPATHOLOGY

Lyn Y. Abramson, University of Wisconsin; Lauren Alloy, Temple University; Kayla F. Bernheim, Livingston County Counseling Services, Geneseo, New York; John B. Brady, University of Pennsylvania; Gerald C. Davison, University of Southern California; Leonard M. Horowitz, Stanford University; Steven Matthysse, McLean Hospital, Belmont, Massachusetts; Sue Mineka, Northwestern University; Ann James Premack, Somis, California; Rena Repetti, University of California, Los Angeles; Martin E. P. Seligman, University of Pennsylvania; Larry Stein, University of California, Irvine; Hans H. Strupp, Vanderbilt University; Paul L. Wachtel, College of the City University of New York; Ingrid I. Waldron, University of Pennsylvania; Richard Warner, University of Southern California; David R. Williams, University of Pennsylvania; Julius Wishner, late of the University of Pennsylvania; Lisa Zorilla, University of Pennsylvania.

## INTELLECTUAL HISTORY

Mark B. Adams, University of Pennsylvania; David DeVries, New York University; Claire E. Gleitman, Ithaca College; Alan C. Kors, University of Pennsylvania; Elisabeth Rozin, Upper Darby, Pennsylvania; John Sabini, University of Pennsylvania; Harris B. Savin, Philadelphia, Pennsylvania.

Other colleagues provided guidance on the current edition, and we're grateful for their input.

Lori Badura, University of Buffalo
Michael Bailey, Northwestern University
Tara Callaghan, St. Francis Xavier University
Kimberly Cassidy, Bryn Mawr College
Richard Catrambone, Georgia Institute of Technology
Fernanda Ferreira, Michigan State University
Vic Ferreira, University of California, San Diego
Don Hoffman, University of California, Irvine
John Hollonquist, University College of the Cariboo
Ken Kotovsky, Carnegie Mellon University
Monica Luciana, University of Minnesota
Al Porterfield, Oberlin College
Michael Renner, West Chester University
Leslie Rescorla, Bryn Mawr College
Wendy Rogers, Georgia Institute of Technology
Alex Rothman, University of Minnesota
Avril Thorne, University of California, Santa Cruz
Nancy Woolf, University of California, Los Angeles

Thanks also to Neil Macmillan, who wrote the original version of "Statistics: The Collection, Organization, and Interpretation of Data," an appendix for *Psychology*, with a fine sense of balance between the twin demands of the subject matter and expositional clarity.

Lila R. Gleitman wrote Chapter 9, "Language," and we are deeply grateful for her expertise, her clarity, and her humor. She also read virtually every chapter in earlier editions of the book, and the current edition still shows the benefits of her counsel—on the book's substance, its style, and its broadest goals.

Paul Rozin read every chapter of the fourth edition of this book, and his insightful and wide-ranging comments testify to his extraordinary breadth of knowledge and depth of thought, and continue to influence us. He has helped us see many facets of the field in a new way, especially those that involve issues of evolutionary and cultural development.

Friderike Heuer and Amy Jaffey have also served as advisors, consultants, and critics, helping us to find ways to think about difficult issues and ways to write about them. Their intellectual and personal support have been immeasurably valuable; the book is far better for their input.

Further thanks go to many people at W. W. Norton & Company: JoAnn Simony, who skillfully managed the production of the book; Antonina Krass, whose brilliance as a book designer continues to astound us; Frank Forney, who executed the fine new drawings and illustrations; Nathan Odell, for leaving no stone unturned in researching new photos for this edition; Neil Hoos, for sensitivity, patience, and good advice in the search for chapter and part opening art; Katrina Washington, for care in clearing the text permissions; Carole Desnoes, for her superb layouts; Carol Flechner and Mary Babcock for their careful copyediting; Kim Yi for double-checking every element of the book, while cheerfully working to keep the whole project on schedule; Tessa Lyons and Andrea Haver, who performed their multifarious duties as editorial assistants with skill and grace; Marian Johnson, for steady manuscipt supervision; and April Lange, who once again has provided invaluable editorial guidance on the ancillary program.

We are especially indebted to four highly competent and indefatigable editors, who, while no longer at Norton, played essential roles in the history of this book. One is Cathy Wick, who provided invaluable advice and continual encouragement, and whose personal contact with many psychology instructors throughout the country was of enormous benefit. The second is Margaret Farley, whose care and skill are evident everywhere and whose patience was unflagging no matter how we taxed her. The third is Jane Carter, a person of superb literary taste and judgment, who combines the skills of a first-rate organizer with those of a fine critic. The fourth is Jaime Marshall, an editor who cared deeply about this text, and whose input reflected both that devotion to our project and his remarkably good taste, and who also played a tireless role as therapist, negotiator, and    when needed—taskmaster. We hope they all know how deeply we appreciated them.

In more recent months at Norton, Jon Durbin has guided the smooth completion of this edition, with a firm sense both of the book's original purpose and long-term goals and of the evolution of our field and of our readers. Aaron Javsicas has done an extraordinary job as our editorial midwife, serving simultaneously as efficient manager, skilled coordinator, insightful reader, careful editor, and diplomatic advisor.

Our final thanks go to Norton's former chairman of the board, Donald Lamm, who was responsible for bringing Henry Gleitman and W. W. Norton together over three decades ago. As Gleitman put it in the previous edition, "Age has not withered nor custom staled his infinite variety. His ideas are as brilliant and outrageous as ever; his puns are as bad as ever. And my esteem and affection for him are as great as ever." We all remain greatly indebted to him.

Merion, Pennsylvania
Santa Barbara, California
Portland, Oregon
January, 2003

# PSYCHOLOGY

## SIXTH EDITION

# INTRODUCTION

What is psychology? It is a field of inquiry that is sometimes defined as the science of the mind, sometimes as the science of behavior. It concerns itself with how and why organisms do what they do: why wolves howl at the moon and children rebel against their parents; why birds sing and moths fly into the flame; why we remember how to ride a bicycle twenty years after the last attempt; why humans speak and gesture and make love and war. All of these are kinds of behavior, and psychology is the science in which all of these are studied.

# THE SCOPE OF PSYCHOLOGY

The phenomena that psychology covers are enormous in range. Some border on biology; others touch on social sciences such as anthropology and sociology. Some concern behavior in animals; many others consider behavior in humans. Some of the phenomena studied by psychologists involve aspects of conscious experience; others focus on what people do regardless of what they think or feel. Some investigate humans or animals in isolation; others study what they do when they are in groups. A few examples will offer a glimpse of psychology's scope.

## WATCHING THE LIVING BRAIN

*Functional magnetic resonance images    This figure shows an fMRI image of a healthy human brain. When the image was recorded, the person whose brain this is was looking at a moving pattern of dots; the arrows indicate brain areas that were especially activated in this simple task.*

All that we do, all that we know, and all that we feel are made possible by the functioning of the brain. But what exactly is the relationship between biological mechanisms—specifically, the working of the brain—and psychological phenomena? As one way of approaching this question, investigators in just the last few decades have developed techniques for scrutinizing the rate at which blood flows through different parts of the brain. These techniques rely on the simple fact that, when any part of the body is especially active, more blood flows to it to deliver oxygen and nutrients and to carry away waste products. The brain is no exception to this broader pattern, and investigators use this fact as a basis for determining *which* brain regions are especially involved in particular mental activities. Thus we have learned, for example, that when someone reads silently, certain regions of the brain receive more blood (and are thus more active) than others. A different blood-flow pattern is found when the person reads aloud, and yet another when she watches a moving light (for example, Lassen, Ingvar, & Skinhoj, 1978).

These findings help us to understand how specific functions involve particular brain regions. But the evidence also makes it clear that, for virtually any mental achievement, many brain regions are involved, working together as a closely integrated team. There is no "reading center" or "music center." Instead, we are able to read or understand music or perceive only because of the coordinated actions of many brain sites.

## MEMORY ERRORS

Close examination of the brain has taught us a great deal about how our eyes work, why various drugs have the effect that they do, and so on. But many of the phenomena that interest psychologists are best studied not biologically, but psychologically—by focusing on the person's behavior and thinking rather than on the underlying mechanisms in the nervous system. Consider, for example, the sort of memory an eyewitness to a crime is relying on when she testifies at a trial, reporting what she saw, say, during a robbery.

There are many questions to ask about eyewitness memory, but, in general, we cannot ask these questions from a biological perspective, simply because we so far know little about how these complex memories are represented in the brain. But this has been no obstacle to investigators, and we have actually learned a great deal about how people remember, including what factors (in the person or in the situation) help them to remember and, conversely, what factors lead to "gaps" in what they recall. We also know some of the factors that can sometimes lead an eyewitness to "recall" things that just are not true.

For example, one line of research examines the impact of leading questions. In some studies, the participants view a video and are then asked questions about it, such as "Roughly how fast was the car going when it went past that barn?" In truth, no barn was present in the video, but this leading question can create the memory for a barn—

*The disruption caused by memory loss   Although the movie, Memento, is fictional, it captures some of the huge disruptions in life that are caused by a loss of memory, and conveys just how important memory is for our day-to-day functioning.*

both in the witness's immediate response, when the leading question is asked, and also in his recollection of the video days later. In other studies, similar leading questions have added remembered beards to people who were in fact clean-shaven, have inserted bright yellow school buses that were actually not present, and even created memories for entire events that never occurred.

## INNATE CAPACITIES

Our memories carry the records of all our experiences, and these experiences, in turn, play an enormous role in shaping who we are, how we feel, and how we act. But this does not mean that we are always dependent on experience. Some achievements seem to depend on little beyond the basic capacities that all of us bring into the world when we are born. Take the infant's reaction to heights, for example.

Crawling infants seem to be remarkably successful in noticing the precipices of everyday life. A demonstration is provided by the *visual cliff*. This device consists of a large glass table that is divided in half by a center board. On one side of the board, a checkerboard pattern is attached directly to the underside of the glass; on the other side, the same pattern is placed on the floor three feet below. To adults, this arrangement looks like a sudden drop-off in

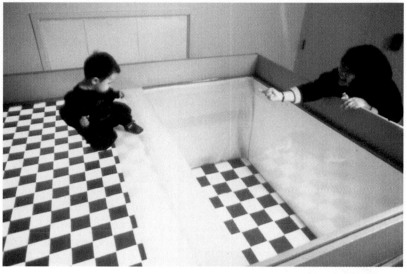

**1.1 The visual cliff** *The heavy sheet of glass will allow the child to crawl anywhere on this apparatus. But the apparent "depth" (conveyed by visual cues) makes the child hesitate to go past the center board.*

the center of the table. Six-month-old infants seem to see it in much the same way. When the infant is placed on the center board and is called by his mother, his response depends on where she is when she beckons. When she is on the shallow side, he quickly crawls to her. But when she calls from the side of the apparent precipice, discretion wins out over valor and the infant stays where he is (see Figure 1.1). This result suggests that, to some extent at least, the perception of depth is not learned through experience, but may be built into us from the very start.

## DISPLAYS AND THE EVOLUTION
## OF COMMUNICATION

So far, all of our examples have dealt with the behavior of individuals. Much of the subject matter of psychology, however, is inherently social. This holds for animals as well as for humans because all animals interact with other members of their species, whether as mates, parents, offspring, or competitors.

A large number of these interactions depends on some kind of communication. An example is courtship in birds. Many species of birds have evolved elaborate bodily structures or rituals by which one sex—usually the male—woos the other. Just what this wooing consists of depends on the species. Some males court by making themselves conspicuous. The peacock spreads its magnificent tail feathers and pirouettes so that all the peahens will notice; the bird of paradise displays his plumage while hanging upside down from a branch; and the frigate bird inflates his red throat pouch. Other males take a more romantic approach. The bowerbird builds a special cabin that he decorates with colored fruit and flowers. The males of other species offer gifts. In all cases, the fundamental message is the same: "I am a male, healthy, and willing peacock (or bird of paradise, or frigate bird, or bowerbird, or whatever), and want you to choose me as your mate" (see Figure 1.2).

These social communications are usually specific to a particular species and have

*Psychology and art*

**1.2** *Courting birds* *Birds have evolved diverse patterns of courtship behavior that are essentially built-in and characteristic of a particular species. (A) The peacock displays his tail feathers. (B) The blue bird of paradise shows off his plumage while hanging upside down. (C) The frigate bird puffs up his red throat pouch.*

**1.3** *Displays* *(A) Threat display of the male mandrill, a large West African baboon. (B) The human smile.*

arisen as a consequence of natural selection—the process that is at the heart of biological evolution. They are ways by which individuals inform one another of their status and current intentions. Some of these communications (including the ones we listed in the previous paragraph) are mating displays. Others are threats ("Back off or else!"; see Figure 1.3A). Still others are attempts at appeasement ("Don't hurt me. I mean no harm!").

Do humans rely on such built-in displays? The evidence suggests that we do, and one example is the smile, a response found in all babies, even in those born blind (who could not have learned to smile by imitation). The smile is often considered a biologically rooted signal by which humans tell each other: "Be good to me. I wish you well" (see Figure 1.3B).

## COMPLEX SOCIAL BEHAVIOR IN HUMANS

In some ways, human social interaction—and the signals we give off in the process—are different from those of other animals. One difference is that human interactions are usually more varied than those of other animals. Peacocks have just one way of courting—they spread their tail feathers and hope for the best. Human males and females are more flexible and much more complex, whether in courtship or in any other social interaction. In part, this reflects the fact that much of human social life is based on one person's appraisal of how another will respond to her actions: "If I do this, . . . he will think this, . . . then I will have to do that . . . ," and so on. These calculations allow humans to weigh options in selecting their social maneuvers; and if one plan fails, they can choose another. Such subtleties are beyond peacocks. If their usual courtship ritual fails, they have no recourse. They will not try to build bowers or buy a dozen roses; all they can do is to fluff their tail feathers again and again.

This description of things makes it sound as if human social behavior is thought-out and sensible—and, in many circumstances, it is. There are other cases, however, in which we seem to act with little thought or reason. This is especially likely when we are in large groups. For example, consider the people who take part in a riot—whether during a political crisis or after a soccer game. The individuals participating in the riot are probably each, on their own, peace-loving, law-abiding, and responsible. But when part of an inflamed group, the individuals are capable of horrible destruction and, in some cases, brutal violence. Why does the crowd act in ways so unlike the individuals that comprise it? For both intellectual and social reasons, this is an important question for psychology.

# A SCIENCE OF MANY FACES

These illustrations document the enormous range of psychology. It is a field of multiple perspectives, a science of many faces, especially when we consider how the field approaches such diverse topics as animal communication and the biological basis for reading. But the field's many faces are just as evident when we consider how psychologists approach a single phenomenon or a single question. This reflects a crucial feature of the current field of psychology: the employment of multiple methods—and multiple types of analysis—for examining virtually every question it considers. To demonstrate this point, let us focus on just one topic—emotion.

Each of us has had a taste of life's emotional highs and lows: the all-consuming happiness of falling in love; the devastating sadness of losing someone we care for; the blinding fury of thinking about someone who has, in our view, treated us horribly. How should we think about these emotions? Are emotional reactions like these inevitable and universal, or are they somehow shaped by culture and personal experience? To what extent are these emotional reactions separate from—and in tension with—our patterns of thinking when we are calm and dispassionate? And to what extent do these reactions influence our calmer, "more rational" thinking?

People have been asking these questions and wondering about the nature of emotion for thousands of years. For most of that time, however, we had no way of testing any claims that were offered, and so no way of knowing which beliefs about emotion were true and which were flatly wrong. However, in the last century or so, careful research has taught us a great deal about emotion, and we can now offer answers to the questions posed in the previous paragraph and to many others as well. To a large extent, this progress has been possible because investigators have drawn on many different research tools and have relied on many different perspectives in approaching this complex topic. Let us look at some of their research.

*Happiness* **We all know the positive feelings that go with life's triumphs.**

## EMOTION AS A SUBJECTIVE EXPERIENCE

Obviously, when we are sad, we feel different than when we are angry, and happiness feels different than fear. But, as an initial step toward understanding emotion, we need to ask what these feelings are all about. In other words, when we feel different emotions, what exactly is it that differs?

In Gilbert and Sullivan's operetta *Patience*, a character notes that the uninitiated may mistake love for indigestion, and there certainly is an element of truth here. We often feel "stirred up" but then have to interpret what it is we are feeling—are we nervous about an upcoming exam, or are we breathlessly anticipating a meeting with our lover? And in some cases, we feel stirred up but haven't the slightest idea why.

Perhaps, then, the feelings that accompany emotion are not straightforward sensations: we do not "feel" our emotions in the same way that we feel an itch or, for that matter, see the color red. Instead, the feelings that seem so central to an emotion are laced with judgments and interpretations.

Evidence for these claims comes from many sources, including a study in which participants were given an injection of a mild stimulant, *epinephrine** (Schachter & Singer, 1962). Some of the participants were warned about the effects of the injection and, when asked later, reported that they were not experiencing any particular emotion, although they did feel "stirred up" by the drug. Other participants were not warned

*Sadness* **Feelings of sadness and anguish can arise from severe loss, or fear of loss.**

---

* This stimulant is the same as the adrenalin made by our adrenal glands, and it is similar to that contained in many commonly used cold remedies such as the medication Sudafed.

about the drug's side-effects and were placed in a room with another person who was clowning around, playing with a hula hoop, and throwing paper airplanes out the window. These participants, like those in the first group, were physiologically stirred up by the injection, but did not know this. Instead, they attributed their agitated state to the situation and reported later that they felt happy. Still other participants, also not warned about the medication, were placed in a room with someone who, instead of acting happy, was annoying and combative. Like the other unwarned participants, they also reported feeling emotionally aroused, apparently attributing their agitation to the setting and not to the drug. Given the setting, it is not surprising that they reported feeling angry, not happy.

In short, when the participants were told the truth about the injection, they used that information to explain their aroused state and testified to feeling no emotion. When they were given no explanation for their stirred-up state, they went looking for one and found it in their immediate situation. As a result, they said that they were either happy or angry (depending on the situation) and believed that the emotion was triggered by the actions of the other person in the room.

Clearly, then, the experiences of "feeling angry" and "feeling happy" are not simple "readouts" of some internal physiological state. Instead, the experiences of emotion are often the product of inference and interpretation, the result of our trying to figure out why we are feeling as we do.

## EMOTION AND COGNITION

Scholars have long debated the relationship between emotions and cognition—our beliefs and memories, and our capacities for judgment and reasoning. Many have proposed that emotions and cognition are separable and perhaps *should* be separated. From this perspective, the Vulcans on *Star Trek* have things right: emotions are best kept isolated from logical thinking.

As the epinephrine study showed, however, we cannot cleanly divide cognition from our emotions. How (or whether) we experience an emotion often depends on an interpretation: an interpretation of our own internal state and certainly an interpretation of the situation we find ourselves in. "Does her message mean she really likes me?" "Did the professor intend that comment as encouragement or as a put-down?" Obviously, our answers to questions like these will have large consequences for our feelings. It is plain, then, that we cannot fully understand emotions without also understanding the intellectual context in which those emotions occur.

In addition, the influence between cognition and emotion sometimes runs in the opposite direction, with our feelings coloring how and what we think. Consider the impact of emotion on our memories. Emotional states are accompanied by many physiological changes inside of us, and some of these changes have the effect of promoting memory, so that we end up remembering emotional events more fully and for a longer time than we do calm or neutral events (Reisberg & Heuer, 2003). Our emotions also influence us when the time comes to recall our experiences. We tend to remember the past as being "emotionally in tune" with the world as we currently experience it, and so, as one illustration, people who are currently sad remember their childhood as being unhappy and their parents as being cold and distant. When these people cheer up, their recollection of childhood changes accordingly (Lewinsohn & Rosenbaum, 1987). In addition, our recall of the past is often self-serving—college students, for example, tend to recall their high-school grades as being better than they actually were (Bahrick, Hall, & Berger, 1996).

Plainly, then, emotion and intellect interact in many ways, and separating them may be impossible. For this reason, an approach to emotion that emphasizes our cognition and how it shapes and is shaped by emotion has helped us understand a great deal about our emotional lives.

*Reason versus passion*   Star Trek's *Vulcans managed to keep emotion from "contaminating" their logical thinking. For humans, this separation of reason and emotion may not be possible—or desirable.*

# EMOTION AND BIOLOGY

Recent research tells us that the *amygdala*—a walnut-sized structure lodged deep within the brain—is central to the link between emotion and cognition (see Figure 1.4). Some of the support for this claim comes from studies of the *fear response*—a pattern shown by many animals (including humans) when they encounter something that has previously been associated with a threatening event. The fear response typically has many elements and can include cringing or freezing as well as tremor and rapid respiration. But this response is disrupted in animals who have suffered damage to the amygdala, even though they seem to have a normal capacity for other sorts of learning (Davis, 1992, 1997; LeDoux, 1994).

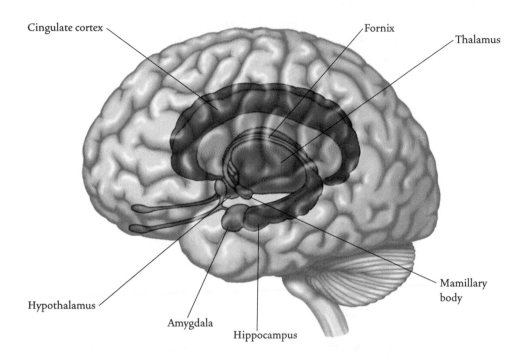

Cingulate cortex · Fornix · Thalamus · Hypothalamus · Amygdala · Hippocampus · Mamillary body

*1.4   The limbic system   The limbic system lies deep within the brain, and so, to reveal the system, this figure pretends that the surrounding brain tissue is semi-transparent. (Thus the figure shows what you would see if you could somehow look through the brain's outer layers, to see the limbic system within.) The limbic system is made up of a number of subcortical structures, including the amygdala, the thalamus, and the hypothalamus.*

*Emotion and the brain   Many brain areas play a crucial role in the creation, experience, and communication of emotion, and the more important ones are highlighted in these MRI scans. The orbitofrontal cortex is highlighted in yellow; the anterior and posterior cingulated cortices are highlighted in blue and green (respectively); the insular cortex is highlighted in purple, and the amygdala is highlighted in red. The left scan shows a side-view of the brain, viewed as if it were sliced vertically, right down the middle. The middle scan shows a frontal view, sliced top to bottom with the slice running just behind the face. The scan on the right also shows a frontal view, but this time sliced top to bottom roughly through the middle of the head.*

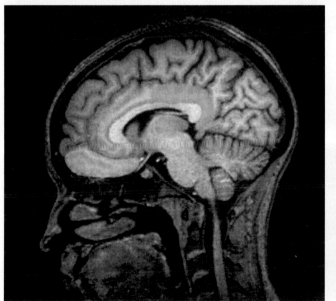
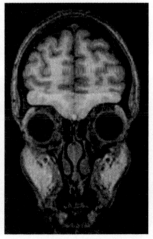
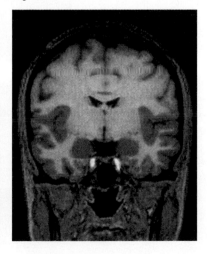

The biological side of emotion also includes changes outside the brain. Whenever we are emotionally aroused, changes take place throughout the body. Digestion is inhibited, and previously stored nutrients are converted to glucose and moved into the bloodstream. Heart rate, blood pressure, breathing rate, and sweating all increase. The smooth-muscle linings of many of the body's arteries constrict to divert the now nutrient-rich blood supply to the muscles that move the limbs. The immune system, which normally identifies germs and destroys them, is temporarily turned off so that we can struggle now and heal later.

These changes have many consequences. The inhibition of digestion plays a large part in producing the "knot in the gut" feeling that many of us experience when we are highly emotional. The heightened blood flow and sweating contribute to the fevered feeling we have "in the heat of the moment." The increased blood glucose reaching the brain contributes to our vigilance now and enhanced memory later for emotional events. In these ways, then, a biological perspective can help us to understand many aspects of emotion.

## EMOTION AND SOCIAL BEHAVIOR

Emotions can be intensely private. No one else can feel our joy or understand precisely what our pain feels like. In many cases, we choose not to share our feelings with others around us, so they may not even know that we are experiencing any emotion at all. But emotion can sometimes have an important social dimension. Often we do share our feelings with others, and doing so helps us to savor the triumphs and to suffer the defeats. Indeed, even if those around us do not react, the fact that we have shared the emotion and "told our tale" may help us deal with our emotional state (see, for example, Pennebaker, 1997; Pennebaker & Graybeal, 2001).

Other aspects of emotion may not seem overtly "social" but may be so nonetheless. For example, our facial expressions are often assumed to mirror our emotional states, so that we spontaneously smile when we are glad and frown when we are angry. But this assumption may be wrong. One study focused on the gold-medal winners at the 1992 Olympics, observing them throughout the awards ceremony. Nearly all of these athletes

*When do we smile?  Research indicates that Olympic athletes show little emotion during most of their award ceremony—even though they report feeling deliriously happy. It is only when they receive their medal and turn to the crowd that their broad smiles appear.*

reported their mood during the ceremony as unambiguously and deliriously happy. Even so, they rarely smiled while waiting to receive the medals or while facing the flag and listening to their national anthem. Only when they received their medal did they smile (Fernandez-Dols & Ruiz-Belda, 1995).

This finding, consistent with other evidence that facial expressions occur mostly when we are in the presence of others and especially when we make eye contact with them, suggests that these expressions are not the inevitable spillover from what we are feeling. Instead, the expressions are communicative, conveying information about our internal state to the people who surround us.

## Emotion and Human Development

Consider the emotion of regret. To experience it, one must have some understanding of how human endeavors unfold, especially how our plans can sometimes work out less well than we had hoped and our decisions sometimes turn out to be unwise. The same with guilt, in which one must understand responsibility and the rules that dictate how we "should" behave.

Other emotions, however, are simpler and may rely less on the acquisition of knowledge about the human condition. Consider, for example, *empathy*—our direct emotional response to another person's circumstances. The seeds of empathy can be found even in newborns only two or three days old. On hearing another newborn's cry, for example, one-day-old infants cry, too, and their hearts beat faster (Sagi & Hoffman, 1976; Simner, 1971). Such infants are less likely to cry in response to nonhuman noises of comparable loudness, including a computer simulation of another infant's crying.

Of course, as the infant grows, empathy grows as well, becoming more attuned to the plight of the other. The child also learns to do more than just empathize: she learns to help and comfort others who are in distress, and to join in the fun with those who are happy. Clearly, then, the child's emotional capacity grows, a process that reminds us of the importance of adding a developmental perspective in any study of our emotional lives.

*Learning to help  Children empathize with others' needs and distress at a very young age. As they grow, however, the children gain skill in actually helping others—both emotionally and pragmatically.*

*Disgust   Humans around the globe all experience disgust, but may show it on their faces in different ways. People in nonliterate cultures, for example, do relatively poorly in identifying the expression of disgust on western faces.*

*Depression   The effects of depression are massively disruptive to the person experiencing the depression, and to those around her.*

## EMOTION AND CULTURE

That newborns show some degree of empathy reminds us that some emotions are not strictly the result of experience, but are instead part of our shared biological heritage. If this is right, then these biologically rooted *basic emotions* should be universal across all cultures.

Are there such universal emotions? The evidence is ambiguous. In one study, American actors posed in photographs designed to convey emotions such as happiness, sadness, anger, and fear. The pictures were then shown to members of different cultures, both literate (Swedes, Japanese, Kenyans) and nonliterate (members of an isolated New Guinea tribe), and the participants were asked to pick the matching emotion label. In other cases, the procedure was reversed (Ekman & Friesen, 1971).

In such studies, participants worldwide—even those in relatively isolated cultures—do reasonably well. But their success depends in part on the particular facial expression they are shown. Smiles are matched to happiness all around the globe, but other emotions are recognized less well.  For example, when asked to pick out the (Western) face showing "disgust," the isolated, nonliterate peoples picked out the predicted face less than 30 percent of the time; when asked to pick out the face showing surprise, they could do this less than 40 percent of the time. It thus remains unclear whether (or which) facial expressions are entitled to the label of "universal." And, sadly, our ability to resolve this issue is fast diminishing. A true test of the universality claim requires data collection from cultures that are fully isolated from each other. With the global expansion of communication and commerce, finding such cultures is increasingly difficult, leaving investigators with no peoples to test.

## EMOTION AND PATHOLOGY

We have now catalogued many different approaches to emotion. As we have seen, our understanding of emotion benefits from both a cognitive perspective and a biological one. An even deeper understanding emerges from including a life-span perspective as well as a perspective that compares emotions worldwide.

Does this exhaust the ways of studying emotion? Far from it. For example, we have considered emotion only as it occurs in normal everyday life. But in many forms of mental illness—*psychopathology*—emotions sometimes veer from normality. People with mental disorders may experience profound emotional suffering: the paralyzing guilt or sadness often associated with depression; the terrors that define the various phobias; the hyperemotionality of mania; and the absence of emotion seen in some forms of schizophrenia. What accounts for this altered emotionality? How can we intervene and restore it to normal? Considering abnormal as well as normal emotions is vital if we are to understand emotion fully and provide the best treatments for mental disorders.

## PERSPECTIVES ON PSYCHOLOGY

Overall, then, the message of this section should be clear: we can profitably explore emotion from many different perspectives, and, indeed, to understand emotion fully, we need to explore it from many perspectives. And what holds for emotion also holds for other psychological phenomena: they, too, must be viewed from many perspectives. Each perspective is valid, but none is complete without the others.

Given the multifaceted character of psychology, it makes sense that the major contributors to our field have come from many different backgrounds. Some had the proper title of "psychologist" with all the appropriate credentials in that discipline; this group includes two of psychology's founding fathers, Wilhelm Wundt of Germany and

William James of the United States. But psychology was not built by psychologists alone. Philosophers have also been among psychology's major contributors, from Plato and Aristotle on. Physicists and physiologists also played important roles and still do. Physicians have contributed greatly, as have specialists in many other disciplines, including genetics, biochemistry, anthropology, linguistics, and computer science.

## THE SCIENCE OF PSYCHOLOGY

With all of this emphasis on psychology's diversity—in the topics we pursue, in the perspectives we take, and in the backgrounds of our contributors—we should acknowledge one theme that unifies our field: a commitment to a *scientific* psychology.

The questions that occupy psychologists have fascinated people for thousands of years. Novelists and poets have plumbed the nature of human emotions in countless settings. Playwrights have spent much time pondering romantic relationships or the relationship between the generations. The ancient Greeks commented extensively on techniques for improving memory and the proper way to rear children. Philosophers, social activists, religious leaders, and many others have all offered their counsel regarding how we should live our lives—how we should run our schools, eliminate violence, improve work productivity, treat mental illness, and so forth.

Against this backdrop, what is distinctive about psychology's contribution to these issues? Our discussion of emotion has already indicated the answer: starting in the late 1800s, psychologists began to do their work within the framework of science—with specific hypotheses that are open to definitive test. In this fashion, we can determine which proposals are well founded and which are not, which bits of counsel are warranted and which are ill advised. Then, when we are reasonably certain about which hypotheses are correct, we can build from there, knowing that we are building on a firm base.

Over the years, psychologists have had different ideas about how we should test hypotheses. In some historical periods, psychologists have argued that all of our hypotheses must be confirmed by biological evidence. During other times, psychologists have argued that the best evidence comes from the study of animals in carefully controlled laboratories. And during still other times, psychologists have claimed that the most compelling evidence comes from the psychoanalyst's case notebook.

In the last half century, however, most psychologists have come to realize that there is no preferred method for collecting data; nor is one form of evidence superior to the rest. As a result, psychologists draw their evidence from many different sources. We rely on observational studies and experiments. Studies are performed in laboratories, in schoolyards, and in the wild. Our evidence includes examination of humans, nonhuman primates, and many other species as well. In short, the methods of the field are eclectic, drawing evidence from any source that can help us in evaluating our hypotheses.

## THE SCIENTIFIC METHOD

The methods of scientific research have served psychology well. We know a great deal about emotion, and also how children develop, why some people suffer from schizophrenia, and much, much, more. The same methods, though, turn out to have other uses as well. In day-to-day life, we often try to draw conclusions from evidence: a friend is in a foul mood; so we think back over recent events, trying to figure out what caused the mood. A sports commentator offers an explanation for why a particular team is

*Wilhelm Wundt*

*William James*

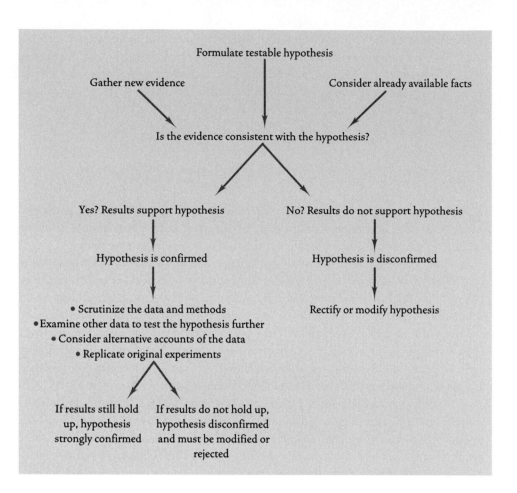

Formulate testable hypothesis

Gather new evidence                     Consider already available facts

Is the evidence consistent with the hypothesis?

Yes? Results support hypothesis          No? Results do not support hypothesis

Hypothesis is confirmed                  Hypothesis is disconfirmed

• Scrutinize the data and methods         Rectify or modify hypothesis
•Examine other data to test the hypothesis further
• Consider alternative accounts of the data
• Replicate original experiments

If results still hold    If results do not hold up,
up, hypothesis           hypothesis disconfirmed
strongly confirmed       and must be modified or
                         rejected

*1.5   The scientific method   **The actual steps a scientist takes, in developing and testing a hypothesis, vary according to the particulars of the case. However, the basic logic is always the same and follows the flow of steps shown here.***

*The right method   **Scientific data must be collected systematically—and, of course, the method for data collection must be an appropriate one for the specific questions being investigated.***

doing well this year; so we try to evaluate this stand by reviewing what we know about that team. On some mornings the car starts easily, but on other mornings it doesn't; so we try to figure out what the problem is (does the car start more easily when the weather is warm? when it is parked in a level spot?). As we will see, the tools of scientific research can be applied to all of these cases, and, in fact, these intellectual tools can be used to improve the process by which we make these and countless other judgments. There is even reason to believe that an understanding of the methods of research can improve our critical thinking in general (Halpern, 1998; Kosonen & Winne, 1995; Nisbett, 1993; Perkins & Grotzer, 1997).

But what is the scientific method, and how is it used within psychology? At its heart, it is a method designed to let us separate truth from fiction or mere conjecture. It is a method that puts our beliefs to the test and allows us to build an understanding of our thoughts, feelings, and actions that rests on a solid foundation. It is a method that provides us with claims that are genuinely reliable and useful.

How is all of this achieved? The scientific method begins with our formulating clear, specific questions that can lead to *testable hypotheses*—hypotheses that allow us to make specific predictions about what we will find, given a particular set of circumstances (Figure 1.5). These predictions are then put to the test. Often this means gathering new data, either by observation or by experiment. Sometimes predictions can be checked by using data already available—perhaps the result of some previous study or the information included in the medical records of U.S. Army recruits or data gathered for the U.S. Census.

No matter where the data come from, there are strict rules regarding how the data should be gathered, summarized, and evaluated. For example, it is not acceptable for scientists to consider only those facts that favor their hypotheses and ignore those that do not. It is also not acceptable to add new assumptions on the spot to explain away facts that do not support the hypothesis. Scientists should also consider only those facts that were collected in a reliable, objective manner. And, of course, fudging or concocting data for any reason—whether for fame and fortune or because of a sincere belief that claiming a certain result will ultimately benefit society—is anathema to science; it is fraud and grounds for expulsion from the profession.

If the facts are not consistent with the prediction, then the hypothesis is *disconfirmed*. In this case, the scientist is obliged to set the hypothesis aside, turning instead to some new hypothesis. The new hypothesis may be wholly different from the previous one, or it may simply involve some minor adjustment. In either case, the scientist does not continue to endorse a hypothesis that has been tested and found wanting.

If, however, the results are consistent with the prediction, then the hypothesis is *confirmed*.* But even at this stage, scientists would hesitate to draw firm conclusions from the evidence. The method used to gather the data and the data themselves must first be made accessible to other members of the scientific community; for psychologists, this usually means giving a presentation at a scientific meeting or publishing an article in a professional journal. This allows other investigators to scrutinize the method and the data to ensure that the hypothesis was evaluated correctly. It also allows others to *replicate* the study—to run the same procedure with a new group of participants. A successful replication (a repetition of the study that yields the same results) assures us that there was nothing peculiar about the initial study and that the study's results are reliable.

Publication of a study also allows other investigators to run alternative experiments in an attempt to challenge the initial findings. Only when the results have been replicated and have survived the challenges are firm conclusions drawn.

*Science takes a long time    Doing science is a slow process, and any scientific achievement builds on the work of other, earlier scientists.*

## DESIGNING A PERSUASIVE EXPERIMENT

Let us examine more closely some of the crucial steps in this process. In the next few sections, we will consider in detail not just how to design an experiment, but also what one has to do in order to make an experiment *persuasive*.

### FORMULATING A TESTABLE HYPOTHESIS

The design of a persuasive experiment begins with a testable hypothesis—a specific claim about what the facts, once observed, will turn out to be. For a hypothesis to be testable, the researcher must be able to specify the results that would confirm the hypothesis as well as those that would disconfirm it. If virtually any set of circumstances could count as supporting the hypothesis, then a scientific test is not possible.

For example, imagine an astrologer who, after consulting the stars, announces: "An important public figure will die in the coming year!" This prediction might make for interesting reading in the supermarket checkout line, but it is too vague to be testable. Who counts as an important public figure? Would the death of Ohio's director of the Department of Motor Vehicles during this time period confirm the hypothesis? How about the death of a once-prominent movie star? Since the astrologer's prediction provides no guidance for making these judgments, we cannot tell whether the data would confirm the prediction or not. As a result, a definitive test of this prediction is impossible.

Similarly, consider the superstition that "bad things always come in threes." Chief among the problems here is the unspecified time interval. Three bank robberies occur-

---

* Note, though, that we say *confirmed*, not *proven*. Sometimes a hypothesis is consistent with an enormous amount of evidence but is challenged when new facts become available. For this reason, scientists never regard a hypothesis as proven correct. A hypothesis that has been confirmed many times and that has avoided refutation again and again is considered *strongly confirmed* and highly likely to be true but still open to refutation if compelling new data come along.

The claims of the psychic   Uri Geller (middle) has persuaded many people that he does indeed have psychic powers. However, systematic tests of his powers (and those of other alleged psychics) often seem to undermine his claims. Psychics can make their claims seem more persuasive by casting the claims in ways that make them untestable.

"I think you should be more explicit here in step two."

Testable claims   A scientific claim must be specific enough to be testable; vague claims cannot be tested.

ring within a single week might seem to confirm this claim. But what if two occur within a week and another occurs a month later? What if the third robbery occurs four months later? Would these cases confirm the hypothesis? The hypothesis as stated provides no guidance on these points, so there is no way to determine whether the data support the hypothesis or not. So this hypothesis, too, is untestable.

Of course, we can modify these hypotheses to come up with testable predictions. For example, a testable version of "bad things come in threes" would stipulate precisely what counts as a "bad thing" and would define "coming in threes." An example might be "If one Oscar-winning actor dies, then two others will die within that same month, followed by a period of at least one month during which no additional Oscar-winning actors die." Of course, this prediction is far clumsier than the original platitude, but, unlike the platitude, it is testable!

## THE NEED FOR SYSTEMATIC DATA COLLECTION

In addition to a testable hypothesis, science also requires systematically gathered data. To see why, let us consider an example.

Many companies sell audiotapes that contain subliminal messages embedded in background music. The message might be an instruction to give up smoking or to curb overeating, or it might be a message designed to build self-esteem or overcome shyness. Even though the message is played so softly that you cannot consciously detect it when listening to the tape, it is nonetheless alleged to provide important benefits—helping you to quit smoking or to stay on a diet, increasing your success in attracting a romantic partner, and so on.

Some *anecdotal evidence*—evidence that has been informally collected and reported— suggests that these subliminal messages can be quite effective. Anecdotal evidence can take many forms: "A friend of a friend said ...," or "In my experience, people ...," or "A scientist on television said. . . . " But these observations are not scientifically persuasive. For one thing, one might worry about the sincerity of these reports: Is that really a scientist or just an actor in a white lab coat? More important, these anecdotes do not allow us to evaluate the data. The anecdotes merely provide one person's description of the data, leaving us with no way to determine whether the description is accurate and whether the data were collected in an appropriate manner. As a result, anecdotal evidence is usually dismissed by scientists for the same reasons that hearsay evidence is dismissed by judges in the courtroom.

It is also worth mentioning that anecdotal evidence usually describes just a single case—for example, a case in which subliminal persuasion seemed to have had a powerful effect. In Chapter 8, we will call these "man who" (or "woman who") stories "I know a man who tried almost everything to give up smoking but finally succeeded by using a subliminal suggestion tape." Such cases, even if well documented, are not persuasive. Perhaps that man is the only one who was helped by such a tape. Or perhaps he would have (at last) given up smoking even without the tape. To evaluate these concerns, scientific studies need data from a broader set of observations.

How can we get beyond these problems? At the least, we need to collect multiple observations to ensure that we are not being influenced by a small number of (perhaps atypical) cases. It is crucial, though, that this collection of observations be done rigorously and systematically. For example, imagine that you have heard from several friends who used the subliminal suggestion tapes in their efforts to quit smoking, some of these friends reporting success and others failure. The problem is that these observations may suffer from a *report bias*—with some observations more likely to be reported than others. After all, a friend who has used the subliminal suggestion tapes and has kicked the cigarette habit is likely to be proud of this achievement and announce it publicly. But a friend who has tried the tapes and has made no progress may be embarrassed by this failure and so report it to no one. This pattern leads to a particular form of report bias called the *file-drawer problem*, so called because studies with encouraging results are often published (or, in less formal settings, simply announced), whereas studies with disappointing results are dumped into a file drawer, never to be seen again. Because of this problem, there is a real chance that informally collected data may be biased, with the success stories being overrepresented in the data and the failures underrepresented.

Even if the file-drawer problem is avoided, another difficulty remains: How should the data be recorded and evaluated? You might simply rely on memory, seeking to recall what various friends said about their experiences with the subliminal suggestion tapes. Then you could count up the successes and failures among these remembered cases. But the accuracy of this approach is far from guaranteed: memory errors are common, and this could compromise your recall of the evidence (see Chapter 7). Memory can also be selective. In Chapter 8, we will consider a pattern known as *confirmation bias*, which would lead you to recall more of the success stories if you expect the subliminal tapes to be effective or more failures if you expect the opposite.

Of course, report biases and memory errors do not happen all the time, and confirmation bias does not always occur. As a result, many of our commonly held beliefs, based on informal data collection, are surely correct. But it is also easy to find cases in which our commonsense assessments of the data are erroneous, which is why people sometimes end up with peculiar superstitions, unfounded beliefs, and so on (for numerous examples, see Gilovich, 1991; Shermer, 1997). Because of cases like these, scientists are probably justified in viewing informal, memory-based data assessment as risky and inadequate for the level of certainty that scientists require.

## SPECIFYING THE DEPENDENT VARIABLE

The problems we have cataloged so far highlight the need for collecting and recording data in a systematic, objective fashion. This means that we need to collect all the data (to avoid the file-drawer problem) and to record the data faithfully (so that there is no chance of memory error). But how do we do this? Let us pursue this question by continuing with our example. Imagine that an investigator wants to evaluate the subliminal self-help tapes scientifically. She selects for the study a tape that is advertised as being able to "increase personal attractiveness" and hypothesizes that the tape will have the advertised effect. How should she run the test?

The investigator first needs some way of measuring attractiveness; without this measure, she will have no way of knowing whether the subliminal tapes work or not. This attractiveness measure will provide the experiment's *dependent variable*, dependent since the investigator wants to find out if this variable depends on some other factor. The *independent variable*, in contrast, is the variable whose effects she wishes to examine. In this example, the independent variable is using or not using the subliminal self-help tape. (Formally, this experiment has just one independent variable with two levels for that variable: self-help tape present or self-help tape absent.)

Often, a dependent variable is a quantity that can be assessed directly—a percent of correct answers on some test, or the number of seconds needed to complete a task. But a quality like attractiveness requires a different sort of yardstick. One option is to use a panel of judges who assess the study's participants on the relevant dimension. The investigator could, for example, videotape the participants during an interview and then show the tape to the judges, who would rate each participant's attractiveness on, say, a seven-point scale. Having the judges evaluate all the participants using the same scale would provide a basis for comparison and so for testing the hypothesis.

Why a panel of judges rather than just one judge? For a variable like attractiveness, there is a possibility that different judges might view things differently. After all, what is attractive to one person may not be attractive to someone else. By using a panel of judges and comparing their ratings, the investigator can check on this possibility. If the judges disagree with one another, then no conclusions should be drawn from the study. But if the judges agree to a reasonable extent—that is, if they show adequate *interrater reliability*—then the investigator can be confident that their assessments are not arbitrary or idiosyncratic.

## USING A CONTROL GROUP

Using the measurement just described, an investigator might gather data in a straight-forward way: she could ask twenty students to listen to the subliminal suggestion tape and then have the judges rate the attractiveness of each student. If all the students turn out to be reasonably attractive, what could she conclude? Perhaps the tapes did help. But perhaps the students were simply attractive to begin with. Or perhaps they appeared attractive due to a boost in self-esteem generated merely by taking part in an experiment. ("Gee, the investigator really cares about me....")

To remove this ambiguity, an investigator needs some basis for comparison in her study. As one option, she might interview and have the judges evaluate each student twice—once before and once after listening to the tape—to determine whether there was any change.

But there is a problem with this procedure. The participants might be uncomfortable during the first interview (before listening to the tape) because the setting and procedure are unfamiliar. They might then be more at ease and confident in the second interview (after listening to the tape) because it is, after all, the second interview. In this case, the experimenter could obtain the predicted result—the participants would seem more attractive after listening to the tape—even if the tape itself had no effect.

One solution to this problem is to use two separate groups of participants. Each group would be interviewed just once—one group after hearing the tape containing the subliminal message and one group after hearing something else. Here, the first group would be the *experimental group* because it is with these participants that the investigator introduces the *experimental manipulation* (in our example, listening to the tape with the subliminal message). The second group would be the *control group* because

"Do you ever have one of those days when everything seems un-Constitutional?"

**Panels of judges**   *Often, investigators need to measure something that is essentially subjective, and this can be done by relying on a panel of judges. By using a panel, rather than just one judge, the investigators can make sure the assessments made by the judges are not arbitrary or idiosyncratic.*

that group provides the basis for comparison that allows the investigator to assess the effects of the experimental manipulation.

*The Proper Treatment for the Control Group*  What should the procedure be for the members of the control group? One possibility is that they would hear no tape at all, whereas those in the experimental group would hear the tape containing the subliminal message embedded in music. In this case, any contrast that the investigator later observes between the two groups might be due to the fact that the experimental group heard the subliminal message, while the control group did not.

But there is also another possibility. Since the subliminal message is embedded in music, perhaps it is the music, and not the message, that influences the experimental group. (Perhaps the participants find it relaxing to listen to music and thus appear more attractive later on because they are more relaxed.) In this case, it helps to listen to the tape, but the result would be the same if there had been no subliminal message at all.

To avoid this ambiguity, the control group must be matched to the experimental group in all respects except for the experimental manipulation. If the experimental group hears music containing the subliminal message, the control group must hear the identical music without any subliminal message. If, for the experimental group, ten minutes elapse between hearing the tape and being interviewed, then the same amount of time must elapse for the control group.

*Placebo Effects and Demand Characteristics*  It is also important for the experimenter to treat the two groups in precisely the same way. If members of the experimental group are told that they are participating in an activity that might increase their attractiveness, then members of the control group should be told the same thing. That way, the two groups will have similar expectations about the procedure. This is crucial since participants' expectations can have a profound effect on a study's results. In Chapter 17, for example, we will discuss the role of placebo effects—effects caused by someone's beliefs or expectations about a drug or therapy. Numerous studies have shown that placebo effects can be strong. For example, patients report considerable pain relief after taking placebos, be they disguised sugar pills or injections of salt water. Similarly, experimental participants might benefit from listening to the subliminal suggestion tapes simply because they believe the tapes will be effective. In this case, it is their belief about the tape, not the tape itself, that is having an effect.

Another factor to consider is that participants usually want to help the investigator—if they believe that the investigator hopes for a particular result, they will try their best to bring about that result. Similarly, participants are often eager to present themselves in the best possible light, and so they try to perform as well as they can on the experimental task. If, therefore, there are cues in the situation signaling that one response is more desirable than another, participants will respond accordingly.

Psychologists call such cues the **demand characteristics** of an experiment. Sometimes the demand characteristics derive from the way questions are phrased ("You do brush your teeth every morning, don't you?"). Sometimes they are conveyed more subtly. Perhaps the investigator inadvertently smiles and is more encouraging when the participants answer in one way rather than another, or perhaps the investigator smiles and is encouraging to members of the experimental group but not to members of the control group.

Investigators take several measures to avoid (or control for) all of these effects. First, they phrase questions and instructions to minimize demand so that no answer or response is identifiable as the preferred or "better" one. In addition, investigators ensure that the members of the experimental and control groups have identical beliefs about the study: investigators phrase their instructions in the same way for both groups and treat the two groups in the same fashion (except for the experimental manipulation).

The best way to ensure identical treatment of both groups is to keep the investigator

*Placebos*  *Placebo effects can be quite powerful, and must be controlled for (typically, by a double-blind design) to ensure that it is the experimenter's manipulation that is having an effect, and not merely the participants' expectations about that manipulation.*

in the dark about which participants are in which group. This is usually accomplished by means of a ***double-blind design***, in which neither the investigator nor the study's participants know who is in the experimental group and who is in the control group. In our example, the investigator's assistant might be the one who decides which participants hear the tape with the subliminal message and which hear the tape without the message. This information would then be revealed to the investigator only after the experiment is completed.

The double-blind design helps ensure that the participants in the two groups will have identical expectations about the procedure; it also helps ensure that the experimenter will not treat the two groups of participants differently. As a result, any difference observed between the two groups can be attributed to the one factor that distinguishes the groups—the experimental manipulation itself. (For more on double-blind designs and the design of control groups, see Chapter 17.)

## CONFOUNDS

A *variant on double-blind testing*

We have highlighted the importance of using well-matched experimental and control groups to ensure that any contrast between these groups is attributable to the independent variable (in our example, the presence or absence of the subliminal message) and not to some other factor. Said differently, it is crucial for an investigator to remove from the procedure any ***confounds***—uncontrolled factors that could influence the results. For example, if those in the experimental group were interviewed early in the morning and those in the control group were interviewed late in the afternoon, then time of day would be a confound: we would have no way of knowing whether differences between the groups were due to experimental manipulation or to time of day. Similarly, if those in the experimental group received encouraging instructions from the experimenter whereas those in the control group received discouraging or neutral instructions, then the manner of instruction would be a confound.

For an experiment to be considered ***internally valid*** (that is, successful at measuring what it purports to measure), all confounds must be removed. An experiment is considered internally valid if it accurately reflects the impact of the independent variable and sensibly measures the dependent variable. Ensuring that the experimental and control groups are treated in exactly the same way (except for the experimental manipulation itself) will go a long way toward eliminating confounds that would otherwise invalidate the experiment's result.

## An Overview of an Experiment's Design

Our example has now grown complicated, but the complexities are unavoidable: a scientific experiment will be convincing only if many safeguards ensure that the data provide an unambiguous test of the investigator's hypothesis. The investigator must start with a clear statement of the hypothesis so that there is no question about what evidence would confirm or disconfirm it. The dependent variables must be well defined so that the results of the experiment can be measured accurately and reliably. The data themselves must be unambiguous and faithfully recorded so that there is no issue of misinterpretation or misremembering. And the evaluation of the data must be complete and thorough.

These steps, ensuring adequate measures and adequate recording of the dependent variable, will leave us with a clear picture of what happened in an experiment. But since we also want to know why the results are as they are, we need another layer of protection. Specifically, we need to eliminate all possible influences on the data other than the influence we care about—the independent variable. In other words, we need to take steps to remove *causal ambiguity* from the experiment—that is, ambiguity about what it was that caused the results actually observed.

As we have discussed, careful matching of the groups as well as removal of confounds are designed to minimize the risk of causal ambiguity. Only when this is done can we draw any conclusions from the data. The logic we are relying on here is straightforward: if the independent variable is the only factor that distinguishes the groups, then this variable must be the cause of any differences we observe. This logic requires us to arrange things so that the independent variable *is* the only distinguishing factor; most of the steps we have described are aimed precisely at this goal (see Table 1.1).

All of these safeguards ensure that our hypothesis receives a definitive test so that, in

---

**TABLE 1.1    SUMMARY OF SUBLIMINAL AUDIOTAPE EXPERIMENT**

| | |
|---|---|
| What is the hypothesis? | A single exposure to a subliminal audiotape will increase an individual's attractiveness. |
| What would confirm or disconfirm the hypothesis? | If a group exposed to a subliminal tape is then judged to be more attractive than a group not exposed, this would confirm the hypothesis. If there is no difference between the groups following the experimental manipulation, this would disconfirm it. |
| What is the independent variable? | The presence or absence of the subliminal message. |
| What is the dependent variable? | Attractiveness as measured by judges' ratings on scale of 1 to 7. |
| Is the dependent variable measured in an objective and systematic fashion? | No direct objective measure is available. But the use of a panel of judges ensures that the measurement is not idiosyncratic, and the use of the scale makes the measurement systematic. |
| Are the groups matched in all respects other than the experimental manipulation itself (that is, are the confounds removed)? | Yes. Both groups must receive identical instructions and are treated identically by the experimenter. Both groups are tested in the same setting. Both groups hear an audiotape, but with one tape containing the subliminal message and one tape not. The timing is identical for both groups—for example, the duration of the audiotape, the interval between the audiotape and the assessment of attractiveness. Ideally, the experiment would be a double-blind—the experimenter, participants, and judges don't know who is in the control group and who is in the experimental group. |
| Are the data analyzed correctly? | The data should be analyzed using the appropriate statistics—see the appendix. |

the end, we know for certain whether the hypothesis is confirmed or not. And with these safeguards in place, what about our example? Are tapes containing subliminal suggestions an effective way to give up smoking, or to increase your attractiveness? Several carefully designed studies have examined the effects of this type of tape, and the results are clear: once the investigator controls for placebo effects, the subliminal messages themselves have no effect (Greenwald, Spangenber, Pratkanis, & Eskenazi, 1991).

## EVALUATING EVIDENCE OUTSIDE THE LABORATORY

We have discussed what scientists must do to ensure that an experiment is persuasive, and so to ensure that their conclusions are justified. But it is not only scientists who want to draw conclusions from evidence. Jesse always takes a large dose of vitamin C whenever she feels a cold coming on and has noticed that her colds are usually mild and brief. She concludes that the vitamins help her. Sol reads his horoscope in the paper every morning and believes that the forecast is usually correct: whenever the stars indicate that he is going to have a day filled with new opportunities, he does! Julie regrets that for months Jacob showed no interest in her. She suspected he was turned off by her shyness, so she tried to act less timid when he was around, and now they are great friends. Julie concludes that her plan was a success. In all of these cases, people are drawing conclusions based on their experiences. Are their conclusions justified?

Notice that Jesse always takes vitamin C. As a result, she has an experimental "group" (herself), which takes vitamin C when coming down with a cold, but no control group (people who take no vitamins). It is possible that her colds would be just as mild without the vitamins, and so her conclusion (that the vitamin C helps) is unwarranted.

Sol does have a comparison—days with a certain astrological prediction and days without such a prediction. But there is an obvious confound in this comparison: Sol reads his horoscope in the morning paper, and so starts the day with expectations based on what he has read. Perhaps, therefore, he is more likely to notice his opportunities if the astrological forecast is good. In this case, the pattern Sol has observed indicates only the power of positive expectations and says nothing about the accuracy of astrology. To see this, let us imagine that the horoscopes were actually generated randomly. An upbeat forecast would still lead Sol to a positive attitude, and this attitude would lead him to notice more opportunities. As a result, the randomly generated forecasts would still be associated with Sol detecting more opportunities.

Julie's comparison (act timid versus act bold) also suffers from a confound. Maybe Jacob is just slow in noticing people, and it wasn't her boldness, but merely the passage of time, that made the difference.

As these examples show, the scientist's concerns also apply to many cases of commonsense reasoning. In the laboratory and in life, control groups are needed if we hope to draw convincing conclusions. In both arenas, we need to rule out confounds if we wish to be certain about the factors leading to a particular outcome. In these ways, the logic of scientific investigation turns out to have a use outside of the laboratory, and, by using this logic, we can avoid drawing unwarranted conclusions. As a result, we can end up with a clearer and more accurate understanding of our personal and social environment.

*Scientific methods outside of the laboratory*
*The methods of science are useful in our day-to-day lives, but this is not because every one of us is an aspiring Einstein.*

# OBSERVATIONAL STUDIES

So far, our discussion has highlighted experimental studies—studies in which an investigator deliberately manipulates some variable and observes the results. In many cases, however, experiments are either impossible or inappropriate. For example, an investigator might wish to find out whether short people are treated differently than tall people. In this case, physical stature is the independent variable, but obviously the investigator cannot manipulate it. She cannot wave a magic wand to make some of her participants tall and some short. Instead, she must use preexisting differences, comparing groups that existed before the investigation was launched.

In the same way, if an investigator wishes to ask at what age children acquire certain social skills, he would presumably want to compare the skills of children at one age with those of children at another age and perhaps then compare the skills of both groups with those of adults. In this case, age would be the independent variable and is something that can easily be assessed (by asking for a birth date) but not something that can be manipulated. Similarly, an investigator might wish to understand how the thought patterns of depressed patients compare with those of the nondepressed. Here, too, we have an independent variable (presence or absence of depression) that cannot be manipulated.

In other cases, an investigator could in principle manipulate the independent variable but must not for ethical reasons. How does physical abuse influence a child's subsequent development? Here, an experiment is possible but ethically repugnant. No investigator would deliberately abuse one group of children while sparing another group, no matter what scientific questions are at stake.

For these reasons, many questions in psychology cannot be pursued through deliberate experimentation. Nonetheless, we can investigate such questions by exploiting differences that already exist. We can compare short individuals with tall ones and in this way begin to understand whether society treats these two groups differently. We can compare younger children with older and depressed individuals with nondepressed. Tragically, many children have been physically abused, and we can compare them with those who have not in order to investigate the effects of this abuse.

In all of these cases, investigators rely on *observational studies* rather than experiments. This terminology reflects the fact that in these studies the investigator observes the key factors, rather than manipulating them directly.

## CORRELATIONAL STUDIES
## AND CAUSAL AMBIGUITY

There are several types of observational studies. But for now, we will focus on *correlational studies* in which the investigator seeks to observe the relationship (or correlation) between two variables—the independent variable (height, age, level of depression, and so on) and some dependent variable. As in an experiment, the investigator seeks to determine whether the dependent variable depends on the independent variable. Given a child's age, for example, can one estimate the sophistication of her social skills? Given an individual with depression, can one predict the pattern of his thoughts?

In many ways, correlational studies are similar to the experiments we have been discussing. In both, the investigator needs to start out with a clearly stated, testable hypothesis. In both, the dependent variable must be well defined and reliably measured. In both, the data must be systematically recorded, evaluated, and analyzed using appropriate statistics. And in both we need to be alert to confounds. If the younger children are observed in their homes and the older children at school, we might wonder whether the observed differences should be attributed to age or to the setting. If short individuals encounter a warm and encouraging interviewer and tall individuals someone cold and discouraging, the results would be uninterpretable. As in an experiment, care must be taken to isolate the independent variable.

## AMBIGUITY ABOUT THE DIRECTION OF CAUSATION

In addition to the similarities between correlational studies and experiments, there is also an important difference: in correlational studies, it is often difficult to determine what is causing what. To illustrate this point, let us consider some observations that we will discuss more fully in Chapter 13. Many investigators have asked how different patterns of child rearing influence a child's personal, social, and intellectual development. For example, does punishing a child shape his personality and behavior? What effect does the lack of punishment have?

Several studies show that more day-to-day aggression is observed among children whose parents regularly use physical punishment than among those whose parents rely on other (nonphysical) forms of discipline (Feshbach, 1970; Parke & Slaby, 1983). This might indicate that physical punishment is a poor child-rearing strategy: it curbs the child's behavior in the short term but has the unhappy consequence of leading to more aggression in the long term. It is also possible, however, that cause and effect are the other way around: it is not the use of physical punishment that causes aggression, but the aggression that leads to (causes) the physical punishment: some children may be more aggressive to begin with, and the parents of these children may quickly discover that severe measures are needed in order to constrain their child's behavior.

This ambiguity in the direction of causality is a common problem in correlational studies. In Chapter 16, for example, we will discuss the fact that schizophrenia is more prevalent among the poor than among the wealthy. Is this because poverty increases the risk of schizophrenia? Or is it because of downward drift, with schizophrenia leading to poverty? (After all, someone suffering from schizophrenia may have difficulty getting and holding a job, managing expenses, and so on.)

This directional ambiguity makes a correlation difficult to interpret. However, the ambiguity can often be resolved by collecting further data. For example, it is sometimes possible to determine which factor arrived on the scene first. Was the person schizophrenic before she became poor, or was she poor before she became schizophrenic? Here, we exploit the simple fact that causes must precede effects, that something cannot be caused by an event that has not yet happened.

*Untangling cause and effect* **Being overweight is correlated with health risk, and so overweight people do have a shorter life expectancy. Many people have interpreted this as cause-and-effect: being overweight causes health problems. But this is not correct. Instead, being overweight is often associated with physical inactivity, and it is the inactivity that causes health problems. If someone is overweight and physically active (as these sumo wrestlers are, for example), then there is little or no risk associated with their much-greater-than-normal weight.**

## THE THIRD-VARIABLE PROBLEM

We have just mentioned some examples in which the direction of causation was unclear. Does schizophrenia lead to poverty or poverty to schizophrenia? Does punishment lead to aggression or aggression to punishment? In other cases, yet another possibility needs to be considered: perhaps a third factor, different from the dependent and independent variables, is causing both. This is the *third-variable problem*.

For example, students who take Latin in high school often get better-than-average

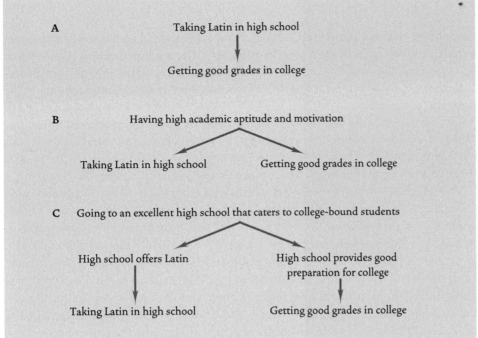

A  Taking Latin in high school
↓
Getting good grades in college

B  Having high academic aptitude and motivation

Taking Latin in high school    Getting good grades in college

C  Going to an excellent high school that caters to college-bound students

High school offers Latin    High school provides good preparation for college

Taking Latin in high school    Getting good grades in college

*1.6  The third-variable problem  Students who take Latin in high school get better grades on average than do their college classmates who did not take Latin. Is Latin the cause of collegiate success (A) or is there some other underlying factor? (B) Maybe what matters is the type of high school student who takes Latin. (C) Alternatively, maybe what matters is the type of school where Latin is offered. Any of these possibilities is compatible with the observation that taking Latin and better grades go together; hence the observation is ambiguous, and no conclusions can be drawn from it.*

grades in college (Figure 1.6). Is there a cause-and-effect relationship here? Does the study of Latin lead to better college performance? Maybe not. We need to ask who takes Latin in high school. In many cases, it is students who are academically ambitious, motivated, and able. As a result, these characteristics may lead both to taking Latin and to better college grades. Similarly, Latin is more likely to be offered in larger, better-funded schools, and probably in schools that primarily serve middle- or upper-middle-class students. Perhaps this feature of the schools is the causal agent here.

The third-variable problem, like the ambiguity about causal direction, makes it difficult to interpret correlational data and leads psychologists to emphasize that correlation does not imply causation. Sometimes correlations do reflect causality: smoking cigarettes is correlated with, and is a cause of, emphysema, lung cancer, and heart disease. But often correlations do not imply causes: for example, the number of ashtrays an individual owns is correlated with that person's health, but not because owning ashtrays is hazardous. Similarly, there is a correlation between how many tomatoes a family eats in a month and how late the children in the family go to bed. But this is not because tomato eating keeps kids awake. Instead, tomato eating and late bedtimes are correlated because both are more likely in the summer.

## "MATCHING" THE EXPERIMENTAL AND CONTROL GROUPS

Correlations cannot by themselves signal a cause-and-effect relationship. To draw a conclusion about cause and effect, we must supplement the correlational result with other data or other arguments. For example, we mentioned considerations of timing. If two variables are correlated (such as poverty and schizophrenia) and we can determine which factor was on the scene first, this can allow us to make causal claims. But, in any case, we do need other arguments to supplement a correlation before we can make claims about causality; this is why investigators generally prefer experiments over correlational studies. But this raises a question: How do experiments escape this ambiguity about causality?

## RANDOM ASSIGNMENT

One answer to this question lies in the fact that experimental and control groups start out identical to each other and come to differ only after the experimental manipulation is introduced. This makes it clear which came first (the manipulation) and which second (the contrast between the groups). As a result, there can be no ambiguity about the direction of causation.

In addition, the third-variable problem does not apply to experimental designs. Since, in a properly controlled experiment, the experimental and control groups start out identical to each other, we do not need to worry about whether some factor besides the independent variable might have influenced the pattern of results.

The key, then, is that in an experiment the two groups started out identical to each other. But how do we know that the two groups are identical? In experiments, participants are assigned randomly to the experimental or control group. Given groups of sufficient size, this *random assignment* makes it very unlikely that all the most able participants, say, would end up in one group and all the least able participants in the other or that all the participants who went to good high schools would end up in one group and all the participants from mediocre high schools would end up in the other. In this fashion, random assignment virtually guarantees that the groups are matched at the outset. If they differ at the end of the experiment, it must be because of the experimental manipulations, leaving no doubt about causality.

## WITHIN-SUBJECT COMPARISONS

The psychologist's tool kit includes one other technique for ensuring that the experimental and control groups match each other at the very start of the experiment. This technique involves using the same people for the two groups, thus guaranteeing that the two groups are identical in their attitudes, backgrounds, motivations, and so forth. An experiment that uses this technique—comparing subjects' behavior in one setting to the same subjects' behavior in another setting—is said to use *within-subject comparisons*, in contrast to the other designs we have been considering so far, which use *between-subject comparisons*.

We earlier considered—and rejected—a within-subject comparison as a means of evaluating the subliminal self-help tapes (page 18). The idea that we considered then was that we could compare the same subjects before and after they heard the self-help tapes, and we rejected this design because it involves an obvious confound: subjects might feel more comfortable or relaxed in the second test merely because it is the second test, and so any contrast between the tests might be due to this factor and not to the self-help tape.

This example illustrates the trade-offs that are inherent in a within-subject comparison. As a major advantage, these comparisons guarantee perfect matching between the groups being compared. As a disadvantage, within-subject comparisons often introduce potential confounds, and so these comparisons can be used only if the confounds are removed.

As an illustration of how a within-subject comparison might be used, consider an experimenter who wishes to find out whether pet dogs respond more consistently to loud commands or soft. To do this, the experimenter would obviously want to give loud commands to one group of dogs and observe their behavior, and soft to another and again observe. As a between-subject comparison, this experiment is easy to design, with two independent groups. In this case, though, a within-subject comparison is both possible and preferable—because it would guarantee precise matching of the two groups.

The problem, though, lies in the fact that if loud commands are first in the sequence, they might be distinctive because they are loud *or* because they are first in the sequence.

If soft commands are first, the problem is the same. The solution to this puzzle is to *counterbalance* the sequence—that is, to use one sequence for half of the subjects and the other sequence for the remainder. That way, any advantage (or disadvantage) associated with being the first test will affect each condition exactly half the time. This ensures that the effect of sequence, whether a large effect or small, will have an equal influence on both conditions and so cannot influence the relationship between the conditions. Said differently, we have not removed the confound, but we have arranged things so that the confound has a balanced effect on both of our conditions (hence, *counterbalance*) and thus cannot compromise the comparison between the conditions.

## STUDIES OF SINGLE PARTICIPANTS

Both correlational studies and experiments (whether within-subject or between-) are generally conducted using groups of participants, rather than single individuals, so that their results might be widely applicable. Under some circumstances, however, psychologists find it useful to study single individuals.

For example, in *case studies*, investigators observe and then describe an individual—one case—in great detail. Historically, case studies have played an enormous role in guiding the development of psychological theory. For example, Sigmund Freud developed most of his ideas based on his detailed observations of individual patients, observations that he reported in books or essays devoted just to one or a few such cases (Chapter 15). Likewise, Jean Piaget's theory was based largely on the study of just three children—his own—although Piaget and his followers went on test his claims with much larger groups of children (Chapter 12).

In recent years, case studies of patients with brain injuries have taught us a great deal about the functioning of the brain and have also illuminated many central psychological questions. Such is the case of H.M., whose memory deficits resulting from neurosurgery for epilepsy are both severe and intriguing (Chapter 7). H.M. may well be the most studied person in the history of psychology, and the pattern of neuropsychological deficits that he shows has provided numerous insights into how normal memory functions. Similarly, the case of Phineas Gage (Chapter 2) was influential in shaping early conceptions of the functions of the brain's frontal lobes. Other important examples of case studies include those of patients with agnosia (Chapters 2 and 6), aphasia (Chapters 2 and 9), and blindsight (Chapter 8).

But case studies of patients with brain injuries have liabilities. For one thing, each patient is unique, with his or her own personality and pattern of aptitudes; each has a specific pattern of brain damage, a specific pattern of signs and symptoms resulting from that damage, and a specific way of attempting to adapt to them. Similar considerations apply to Freud's patients and Piaget's children. Each is unique, with specific traits, skills, and talents. For all these reasons, it is often difficult to know whether the conclusions drawn from a case study can be applied to anyone other than the subject of the original study.

Moreover, many case studies grow out of an extended interaction between the investigator and the participant. Since the published report can represent only a fraction of this long-term observation, questions must be raised about how exactly the data were selected for publication and whether they can be understood outside the con-

*Case studies*   Case studies have been of great value for psychology. The field of developmental psychology, for example, has been enormously influenced by the work of Jean Piaget, who based his claims on the study of just three children—his own.

text of this ongoing relationship. This is certainly true of Freud's case studies as well as the many other case studies described by clinical psychologists.

To remedy some of these deficiencies, psychologists have proposed innovative ways of studying single participants systematically, with all the sophistication of standard experimental methods. In such *single-case experiments*, the investigators manipulate the values of some independent variable, just as they would in an experiment with many participants, and then they assess the effects of this variable by recording the participant's responses (Barlow & Herson, 1984).

For example, consider a school psychologist who must devise a curriculum for a child with a specific learning disability. The psychologist may be able to review previous studies and experiments that suggest the kinds of curricula that tend to benefit children with similar disabilities, but in the end she must develop a curriculum for that child with that disability. Therefore, the single-case experiment is exactly the right approach.

Let's imagine, for example, that the psychologist has noted that the child is especially distractible and easily frustrated while reading but seems more focused and perseveres longer if soft music is playing in the background. To verify this hypothesis, the psychologist can develop a measure of reading attentiveness (the dependent variable)—

## TABLE 1.2   SUMMARY OF A SINGLE-CASE EXPERIMENT

| | |
|---|---|
| What is the *hypothesis?* | This child will read more attentively and for longer when soft music is playing in the background. |
| What would *confirm* or *disconfirm* the hypothesis? | If the child's reading performance is improved when soft music is playing (compared to a condition with no music), this would confirm the hypothesis.<br><br>If the child's reading performance is not improved when soft music is playing (compared to a condition with no music), this would disconfirm the hypothesis. |
| What is the *independent variable?* | The presence or absence of soft music. |
| What is the *dependent variable?* | How long the child reads before expressing frustration. |
| Is the dependent variable measured in an objective and systematic fashion? | How long the child reads can be measured directly and objectively; the experimenter would need to define what counts as "expressing frustration." In addition, the number of observations for each condition must be large enough to ensure that the effect is reliable. |
| Are the conditions matched in all respects other than the experimental manipulation itself (that is, are the *confounds* removed)? | A *double-blind* is not possible because the child can easily hear whether the music is present or not. But the experimenter could be blind to the condition. In any case, the child must receive identical instructions and be treated identically by the experimenter, regardless of whether soft music is playing. Also, both conditions should be assessed in the same setting; the reading material should be comparable in both conditions—equally interesting, equally difficult, and so on; the timing must be identical for the two conditions—for example, length of the material, the duration of breaks between sessions, and so on. |
| Are the data analyzed correctly? | The data should be analyzed using the appropriate statistics—see the appendix. |

perhaps the length of time the child reads before expressing frustration—and vary the occurrence of soft music (the independent variable). On one day the psychologist would measure attentiveness while the child is reading with music, on the next day while the child is reading without music, and so on for several days. After a suitable number of observations, alternating between the conditions, the psychologist can assess the child's average reading attentiveness under each condition. (See Table 1.2.)

Single-case experiments are procedurally just as rigorous, and described just as precisely, as standard group experiments. This rigor reduces the subjectivity that characterizes many case studies and makes replicating the study with other individuals possible. It allows investigators to draw causal inferences. Also, by following up single-case experiments with the proper group experiments, the findings from the single case can be tested on, and generalized to, a wider population.

## TYPES OF DATA

We have now discussed several ways in which psychologists gather data—through group experiments and single-subject experiments, correlational studies and case studies. Each of these approaches can be further subdivided by the type of participant: human participants versus animals, adults versus children. A further subdivision might focus on the setting for the study: some studies are conducted in laboratories, while others are conducted in more natural environments—in schools, for example, or the participants' own homes.

A further division involves the type of data collected. Many studies rely on *self-report data*, with participants asked to describe their feelings, thoughts, attitudes, or behaviors. Other studies use behavioral measures, with no reliance on self-report data. These measures include both what the participants do and how they do it. (For example, how quickly do they answer the investigator's questions; how accurately do they perform an assigned task; how attractive do they appear to others?) Still other studies rely on biological assessments, which can range from brain imaging to chemical analyses of the participants' blood, sweat, and urine. (Chapter 2 provides a broader description of the biological measurements routinely used by psychologists.)

Each of these research paths has its advantages and disadvantages. But psychologists often use them all, even when pursuing a single question. For example, our discussion of depression (Chapter 16) draws on experiments and correlational data, self-report data, behavioral measures, and biological assessments, merging all of these to weave the fabric of what we now know about depression. Similarly, studies of memory (Chapter 7) involve many of these different techniques; indeed, the same could be said for virtually any topic discussed in this book.

## GENERALIZING FROM RESEARCH

So far, we have considered how a hypothesis should be formulated and a study designed and conducted. Then, once the data are collected, they must be analyzed, using proper statistical procedures. (We describe some of those procedures in the appendix.) At that point, the investigator seeks to draw conclusions, usually framed in terms of a confirmation or disconfirmation of the initial hypothesis.

Almost invariably, though, investigators want to generalize from the data. After all, while they have studied just a small number of research participants, they are interested in answering questions that apply to a vast number of people. Likewise, investigators observe research participants for only a brief time but want to understand how people behave (and think and feel) throughout the days of their lives.

Are such generalizations justified? Can we make claims about how people will behave outside of our studies, based on what we observe inside of those studies? This depends on the *external validity* of the study in question. A study is considered externally valid if its participants, stimuli, and procedures adequately reflect the world as it is outside of the investigation. To ensure external validity, the study's participants should be representative of the population to which the results are expected to apply, and the study's stimuli should be representative of the stimuli encountered outside of the laboratory.

## SELECTING PARTICIPANTS

Psychologists usually want their conclusions to apply to a particular *population*: all members of a given group—say, all three-year-old boys, all patients suffering from schizophrenia, all U.S. voters, and, in some cases, all humans. But investigators normally can not study all members of the population. As a result, they have to select a *sample*—that is, a subset of the population they are interested in. Their expectation is that the results found in the sample can be generalized to the population from which the sample is drawn.

Generalizations from a sample to a particular population can only be made if the sample is representative of the population about which one wants to generalize. Suppose a psychologist, using college students, does a study on reading skills. Can the psychologist generalize the results so that they apply to adults in general? The answer is no, for college students probably read more, and more difficult, material than most other adults. As a result, their reading skills may be more sophisticated and are certainly better practiced than those of most noncollege students. Under the circumstances, the safest course may be to restrict the generalizations to the population of college students.

It is easy to find cases in which inadequate sampling led to egregious blunders. The classic example is a 1936 poll that predicted that Franklin D. Roosevelt would lose the presidential election. In fact, he won by a landslide. This massive error was produced by a biased sample: all those polled were selected from telephone directories; but in 1936, having a telephone was much more likely among people of higher socioeconomic status. As a result, the sample was not representative of the voting population as a whole. Since socioeconomic level affected voting preference, the poll was externally invalid, and, as a result, its prediction was false.

*Sample bias*  *A 1936 poll predicted, incorrectly, that Franklin D. Roosevelt (shown here in the car) would lose the presidential election. The poll was misleading because it was based on a biased sample: the people surveyed were all selected from the telephone directory. In 1936, having a telephone was much more likely among people of higher socioeconomic status, and so the sample was not representative of the broader population.*

## RANDOM AND STRATIFIED SAMPLES

To ensure that they can generalize from their sample to the population at large, investigators often use a *random sample*, one in which every member of the population has an equal chance of being picked, as in a jury drawn by lot from all the voters of a given district (assuming that none is disqualified or excuses himself). But for some purposes, even a random sample may not be good enough. While every member of the population may have an equal chance of being selected, the sample may still turn out to be atypical by chance alone. The danger of this happening diminishes as the size of the sample increases. But if we must be satisfied with a small sample (whether because of lack of time or money), other sampling procedures may be necessary.

Suppose we want to take a poll to determine the attitudes of American voters toward legalized abortion. We can expect people's attitudes to differ, depending on their age, sex, and religion. If we need to keep the sample size fairly small, it is important that each subgroup of the population be sampled randomly in proportion to its size. Thus, for example, if 30 percent of the population is below the age of eighteen and 70 percent is above that age, the sample should contain the same proportions. This procedure is called *stratified sampling* and is common when studying psychological traits or attitudes that vary greatly among different subgroups of the population.

## SAMPLING RESPONSES

The distinction between sample and population not only applies to the research participants, but also to their responses. Let us say that an investigator observes his participants on ten occasions. These occasions can then be regarded as a sample of all such occasions, not just the ones actually observed. And here, too, the investigator must make sure that the sample is representative of the broader population. If an investigator wishes, for example, to study physical aggression in children, she must make certain that the children aren't especially tired when she observes them or inhibited by the school principal's presence.

## EXTERNAL VALIDITY

External validity depends on the details of an investigation: how the participants were chosen, how the stimuli or responses were selected, and so on. But external validity also depends on what is being investigated. An investigator interested in the visual system can probably study American college students and draw valid conclusions about how vision works in all humans, whether they are from the United States, Taiwan, or Uganda. This is because the properties of the visual system are rooted in the biology of our species, allowing us to generalize widely. This is obviously different from an example already mentioned—a study of reading skills among college students. In this case, the results of a study of college students might not apply to noncollege students or to people of other cultures.

We should emphasize, though, that questions of external validity must be resolved through research and not be based on assumptions. For example, one might think that the social behavior of college students would be different from that of nonstudents or of people of other cultures. Yet research indicates that some of the principles of social behavior are shared across cultures (Chapters 10 and 11). This research has obvious implications for how we think about external validity in social psychological studies: in some regards, it is appropriate to generalize from studies of college students; in other regards, it is not.

As a related point, external validity usually demands that a study use tasks and stimuli that are representative of those we encounter every day. But in some cases, a study

*External validity   Can we study college students and draw conclusions about the population at large? For some topics, we can. For example, the visual system in college students works in just the same way as it does in any other human. In other ways, college students can be rather strange—and not representative of the population as a whole.*

may be externally valid even if it employs tasks or stimuli that seem unnatural or unrealistic. An important example involves the study of perceptual illusions. We rarely encounter such illusory figures outside the laboratory, but studies using these stimuli are externally valid nonetheless. Investigators can learn about vision by examining how we perceive these unusual figures because the processes we use when perceiving these figures are the same as the processes we use in our everyday perception.

How can we determine whether a study is externally valid? Consider the studies of eyewitness memory that ask how well an observer or victim of a crime will recall that crime. Will he remember the sequence of events or the face of the criminal? Many laboratory experiments have tried to address these questions, but do the principles derived from laboratory studies apply to someone who is angry, afraid, and involved in an event the way an eyewitness is? This is a matter of ongoing debate. One way to resolve the issue is to combine the laboratory studies with case studies of actual eyewitnesses. The case studies are by themselves sometimes difficult to interpret because (among other concerns) life rarely provides well-designed control groups. But we can nonetheless ask whether the results from a case study are, as we would expect, based on the laboratory investigations. If they are, this obviously provides some assurance that our laboratory studies are externally valid. (For discussion of the external validity of eyewitness research, see Loftus, 1993; McCloskey & Egeth, 1983; Ross, Read, & Toglia, 1994; Shobe & Kihlstrom, 1997.)

Questions about external validity are of great importance in all areas of psychology. Are our categories of mental disorder appropriate only in the context of North America and western Europe, or do they apply across cultures (Chapter 16)? Does the pattern of cognitive development seen in healthy, middle-class children describe the cognitive development of children from other socioeconomic groups and other nations (Chapter 13)? Does human reasoning inside the laboratory reflect how people reason in their day-to-day lives (Chapter 8)? Each of these questions is the focus of ongoing research.

# RESEARCH ETHICS

The external validity of an investigation depends on the relationship between the study and its real-world context. This, in turn, requires us to study real people and real animals. And since both people and other animals have rights that must be protected, psychological research must be conducted ethically, in a fashion that protects the rights and well-being of the research participants.

Psychologists take the issue of research ethics very seriously, and virtually every institution sponsoring research—every college and university, every funding agency—has special committees charged with the task of protecting human and animal participants. In the United States, psychological research with human participants must also follow the guidelines established by the American Psychological Association (1981, 1982), one of psychology's most prominent professional organizations. Similar guidelines to protect research participants are in place in many other countries. (See Kondro, 1998, for a discussion about protection of research participants in Canada.)

Research ethics

If laboratory animals are used, the investigator must protect their health and ensure the adequacy of their housing and nutrition. Human participants must not only be protected physically; their privacy, autonomy, and dignity must be fully respected as well. Accordingly, an investigator must guarantee that the data will be collected either anonymously or confidentially and that participants will not be manipulated in a fashion they might find objectionable. Before the study begins, participants must be fully informed about what their task will involve, must be appraised of any risks, and must have the prerogative to leave the study at any time. In short, the investigator must obtain each participant's *informed consent*.

Just as an experiment must begin with informed consent, the experiment must end with a full *debriefing*. If the experiment involved any deception or hidden manipulation, this must be revealed and explained; if the study involved any manipulation of beliefs, mood, or emotion, the investigator must attempt to undo these manipulations. And, ideally, participants should end their participation in a study with some understanding of how it, and their participation in it, may be beneficial to psychological knowledge and human welfare.

It should be noted, though, that these ethical protections—especially the need to obtain informed consent—can produce their own difficulties. In some cases, for example, the validity of a study requires research participants not to be fully informed about the study's design. For example, the participants in the control group cannot be told they are receiving a placebo since placebos only work when recipients believe that they are getting "real" medicine. In the same way, subliminal suggestion audiotapes are alleged to work through unconscious mechanisms. Thus, it may be important that the person hearing the tape not realize exactly what words are spoken on the tape.

Considerations such as these indicate that, in many studies, the need for informed consent can conflict with the procedures needed to ensure the study's validity. How can investigators resolve this conflict, ensuring experimental validity while continuing to honor ethical standards? Overall, it seems clear that greater priority must be given to the ethical considerations, and so, in general, investigators must do everything they can to minimize the use of deception, just as they must do everything possible to minimize risks to research participants. If any risk remains, there must be a clear and persuasive argument that the information to be gained from the experiment really does justify that risk. Similarly, if an experiment involves deception, we need to be certain that the scientific value of the experiment justifies that deception.

Decisions about risk or deception are sometimes difficult, and the history of psychology includes many conflicts over the ethical acceptability of psychological studies (for instance, Baumrind, 1964; Hermann & Yoder, 1998; Korn, 1997; Milgram & Murray, 1992; Savin, 1973; Zimbardo, 1973). This is one of the reasons why decisions about ethical acceptability are usually made not by the investigators themselves, but by a multidisciplinary supervisory committee assigned the task of protecting research participants.

In evaluating any investigation, these committees must understand the investigation in the appropriate social context, and their assessments of the procedure's risks must be tied to the values and scientific knowledge prevailing at the time of the investigation. As a result, studies considered ethical at one time would be considered unacceptable today. For example, in 1911, Edouard Claparède examined a patient's memory by abruptly sticking her with a pin on one day and then determining whether she remembered this episode the next day (for a full description of this study, see Reisberg, 2001), a procedure that would be considered unethical if conducted today, given the important changes that have taken place in our conception of patients' rights. In another example, half a century ago investigators explored the use of radiation to the throat as a treatment for chronic tonsillitis, a procedure that was abandoned when it was found that it greatly increased the risk of thyroid cancer years later. In this case, our assessment of a procedure's risks changed and with it there was a corresponding change in the procedure's ethical status.

In addition, the protection of human and animal rights simply prohibits a number of studies no matter how much might be learned from them. We mentioned earlier that no experimenter would physically abuse research participants to study the effects of this abuse. Likewise, no ethical investigator would expose participants to intense embarrassment or anxiety. Many forms of deception are also considered unacceptable, regardless of the merit of the study. (No investigator, for example, would announce to a participant that his house had burned down just so the investigator could observe the participant's reaction.)

Throughout this chapter, we have emphasized the power of science. By using scientific methods, psychology has made extraordinary advances and has laid a foundation for still further progress over the next millennium. But we must not lose sight of the fact that our science involves living creatures—including our fellow human beings—who must always be respected and protected. We therefore need a science that is as humane as it is rigorous.

## SOME FINAL THOUGHTS: SCIENCE, ART, AND THE INDIVIDUAL

Several times in this chapter, we have argued that a commitment to scientific inquiry has served the field of psychology remarkably well, and this theme will remain in view throughout this book. As we will see, psychologists using the scientific method have learned a great deal, including material that is deeply interesting as well as remarkably useful. Psychology allows us to know an enormous amount about our behaviors, our feelings, and our thoughts, about how humans are distinct from other species, and how we resemble other species. More, it allows us to know these things with some certainty, thanks to the methods of our science. The claims we will offer in this book are not matters of conjecture or opinion, but assertions that are persuasively rooted in well-established facts.

But we should be careful not to overstate what our field knows. There are, to be sure, substantial gaps in our knowledge, and the field of psychology must be understood as an ongoing enterprise, as investigators continue their efforts to fill these gaps and extend what we know. In addition, it is important to mention that some issues and questions may remain forever outside the scientific reach of our field. This point is partially rooted in the fact that science proceeds by focusing on patterns of evidence. It is the patterns that allow us to find out which observations are reliable and which are flukes. It is also the patterns that allow us to disentangle cause-and-effect relationships. Why, for example, did George become depressed? Was it perhaps something in his genetic pattern? We might try to find out by considering other people with similar genetic patterns (perhaps George's relatives). If they, too, are depressed, this would add credibility to our suggestion; if not, this would lead us to seek some new explanation.

Notice, then, that George's case is, by itself, difficult to interpret; we find the interpretation only by placing his personality in the context of other evidence. This is, in fact, the nature of any science: we interpret individual observations by referring to general principles, and those principles, in turn, are derived from the study of many cases.

But what if our goal is to describe the individual cases themselves? Is there any field of endeavor whose primary interest is with the unique George and Mary, so that we understand these individuals entirely on their own terms? Arguably, there is: the great novelists and playwrights have given us portraits of living, breathing individuals who exist in a particular time and place. There is nothing abstract and general about the agonies of Hamlet or the murderous ambition of Macbeth. These are concrete, particular individuals with special loves and fears that are peculiarly theirs. But from these particulars, Shakespeare gives us a glimpse of what is common to all humanity, what Hamlet and Macbeth share with all of us.

Both science and art have something to say about human nature, but they come to it from different directions. Science tries to discover general principles and then apply them to the individual case. Art focuses on the particular instance and then uses this to illuminate what is universal in us all. In a sense, then, science and art are complementary, and to gain insight into our own nature we need both. Consider Hamlet's description:

> What a piece of work is a man! How noble in reason, how infinite in faculty, in form and moving how express and admirable, in action how like an angel, in apprehension how like a god—the beauty of the world, the paragon of animals! (*Hamlet*, Act II, scene ii)

To understand and appreciate this "piece of work" is a task too huge for any one field of human endeavor, whether art, philosophy, or science. What we will try to do in this volume is sketch psychology's considerable contributions toward this end, to show what we have come to know and how we have come to know it. But we do so knowing that our contribution—no matter how substantial—is but one piece of the puzzle and that much still remains to be learned.

# SUMMARY

The phenomena that psychology takes as its province cover an enormous range. Some border on biology; others touch on the social sciences. Some concern behavior in animals; others involve behavior in humans. Some involve humans or animals in isolation; others concern what they do when they are in groups.

## THE SCOPE OF PSYCHOLOGY

1. One important topic is the relation between brain mechanisms and psychological phenomena. One of many techniques for studying this focuses on the rate at which blood flows through different parts of the brain, relying on the fact that when any part of the brain is especially active, more blood flows to it in order to deliver oxygen and nutrients and to carry away waste products.

2. Many of the phenomena that interest psychologists are best studied at the psychological level—by focusing on the person's behavior and thinking, rather than on the underlying mechanisms in the nervous system. An example is provided by work on *eyewitness* memory, as in studies on the role of *leading questions* for subsequent recall.

3. While our experiences play an enormous role in shaping who we are, this does not mean that we are always dependent on prior experience. Many of our achievements seem to depend on little beyond the basic capacities that all of us bring into the world when we are born. An example is the infant's reaction to heights, as shown by studies of the *visual cliff*.

4. Much of the subject matter of psychology is inherently social. This holds for animals as well as humans. In animals, many social interactions depend on built-in communication systems. Examples come from work on built-in displays that are specific to a particular species, as in *mating* or *threat displays*. An important example of such a built-in display in humans is the *smile*.

5. Human social interactions are much more varied than those of other animals. In part, this is because much of human social life is based on one person's appraisal of how another will respond to her actions: but while much of human social behavior is thought-out and sensible, there are other cases in which we seem to act with little thought or reason. This is especially likely when we are in large groups, as for example in riots.

## A SCIENCE OF MANY FACES

Psychologists employ multiple perspectives and multiple methods for examining virtually every question they consider. As one illustration of this pattern, this chapter surveys some of the various perspectives psychologists have brought to bear on the topic of *emotion*.

6. Emotion can be considered as a *subjective experience*. The feelings that accompany emotion are not straightforward sensations like an itch, but typically involve interpretations. One line of evidence comes from studies in which subjects were physiologically aroused by an injection, but they did not know this. Instead, they attributed their physiological arousal to the situation in which they

found themselves. Such findings suggest that we cannot fully understand emotions without also understanding the intellectual context in which those emotions occur.

7. A central link between emotion and cognition is the *amygdala*, as shown in studies of the *fear response*, which is disrupted in animals who have suffered damage to this structure. The biological side of emotion also includes changes outside the brain. Whenever we are emotionally aroused, digestion is inhibited and previously stored nutrients are converted to glucose, while heart rate, blood pressure, and breathing rate increase, and the immune system is temporarily inhibited.

8. Emotions also have an important social dimension. For example, our facial expressions occur mostly when we are in the presence of others, and especially when we make eye contact with them.

9. Still other studies of emotions come from a *developmental perspective*, which have shown that some emotions, such as *regret* and *guilt* develop over time, while others, such as *empathy*, have been observed in newborns. Another approach is the *cultural perspective*, which asks whether there are *emotional universals*, and work on *psychopathology*, which considers emotions in various forms of mental illness.

10. Given the multifaceted character of psychology, it makes sense that some of the major contributors to our field have come from many different backgrounds. While two of psychology's founding fathers, Wilhelm Wundt of Germany and William James of the United States, have the proper title of "psychologist," the field was not built by psychologists alone, and philosophers, physicists, physiologists, and physicians have contributed greatly, as have specialists in many other disciplines, including genetics, biochemistry, anthropology, linguistics and computer science.

## THE SCIENCE OF PSYCHOLOGY

11. The one theme that unifies our field is its commitment to a *scientific* psychology. Psychologists seek evidence from many different sources, relying on experiments as well as observational studies, based on results from humans, nonhuman primates, and other species.

## THE SCIENTIFIC METHOD

12. Psychologists use the *scientific method* to ensure that their claims are correct and reliable. This requires a *testable hypothesis*, which allows the researcher to specify the results that would *confirm* or *disconfirm* the hypothesis. If a hypothesis is tested and found to be inconsistent with the results, it is disconfirmed. If the hypothesis is consistent with the results, it is confirmed. But firm conclusions are drawn only after the hypothesis has survived any challenges and the experiment has been *replicated*.

13. Informally collected anecdotal evidence does not allow a persuasive test of a hypothesis because there is no way to evaluate the data described in the anecdote and no way to know if the observation reported is generalizable. The data drawn from a wider set of observations must be systematically collected and tallied to avoid the *file-drawer problem* and biased recollection.

14. When designing an experiment, an investigator must specify the *dependent* and *independent variables*. The independent variable is the variable whose nature is changed in accord with the *experimental manipulation*. The dependent variable is what the investigator measures to determine whether the experimental manipulation has had the hypothesized effect.

15. The dependent variable should be clearly defined and easily measured. If a direct quantitative assessment of this variable is not possible, the investigator can use a panel of judges to assess it. So long as the *interrater reliability* of this panel is adequately high, the investigator can be confident that the judges' assessments are not arbitrary.

16. An experimental study generally needs both an *experimental group* and a *control group*. The experimental group is subject to the experimental manipulation; the control group provides a basis for comparison, allowing the investigator to determine whether the independent variable had the hypothesized effect. The control group must be matched to the experimental group in all regards except for the experimental manipulation. This matching includes the make-up of the two groups, the procedures used with the two groups, the instructions they receive, and how they are questioned by the investigator.

17. Investigators attempt to minimize *placebo effects* (effects caused by a participant's beliefs and expectations) and *demand characteristics* (cues signaling the desired response). This is often accomplished by means of a *double-blind design*, in which neither the investigator nor the study's participants know who is in the experimental group and who is in the control group.

18. A study is said to be *internally valid* if it successfully evaluates what it purports to evaluate. To ensure validity, all *confounds*—uncontrolled factors that could influence the pattern of results—must be removed.

19. The scientific method can also be applied to many cases of day-to-day reasoning, leading to a clearer and more accurate understanding of our personal and social environment.

## OBSERVATIONAL STUDIES

20. In an *experiment*, the investigator manipulates the independent variable and measures the effect of the manipu-

lation on the dependent variable. In an *observational study*, the dependent and independent variables are observed rather than manipulated.

21. One type of observational study is a *correlational study,* in which the investigator seeks to observe the relationship between the dependent and independent variables. Correlational studies differ from experiments in that correlational studies often suffer from ambiguity with regard to cause-and-effect relationships. In some cases, the *direction of causation* is ambiguous. In other cases, both the dependent and independent variables might be affected by some third variable, a pattern known as the *third-variable problem.* These ambiguities can often be resolved by collecting further data or by a more fine-grained inspection of the evidence. Experiments are generally not ambiguous with regard to the direction of causation because it is clear that the experimental manipulation preceded the experimental effect. In addition, *random assignment* to groups virtually guarantees that the experimental and control groups are identical at the experiment's start.

22. *Case studies* and *single-case experiments* involve only single participants. Case studies have allowed investigators to explore particular phenomena in great depth. But they also have serious liabilities: Since each participant is unique, conclusions are not generally applicable and questions about the selection of data and the effect of the relationship between participant and investigator must be raised. An alternative to the case study is the single-case experiment, which uses *replicable procedures* and reduces subjectivity through experimental rigor.

## TYPES OF DATA

23. Most psychological investigations employ *multiple methods* (experiments, correlational studies, case studies, and single-case experiments) to overcome the shortcomings of each approach. Investigations of a single topic also generally pool different sorts of data, including *self-reported data, behavioral observations,* and *biological assessments.*

## GENERALIZING FROM RESEARCH

24. Generalizing from the results of a study is justified only if the study is *externally valid.* This usually requires that the sample of participants be representative of the population. In many studies, this is ensured by use of a random sample; in some cases, *stratified sampling* is also useful. What makes a study externally valid depends on the particular issue being investigated. Questions of external validity must be resolved through research, not based on commonsense assumptions.

## RESEARCH ETHICS

25. *Research ethics* is an extremely important issue, and many precautions must be taken to protect the physical well being of the research participants as well as their privacy, autonomy, and dignity. But these ethical requirements sometimes collide with procedures needed to ensure a study's validity. In such cases, all risks to the participants must be minimized, and those risks that remain must be fully justified on scientific grounds. At the end of the investigation, the participants must be fully *debriefed.*

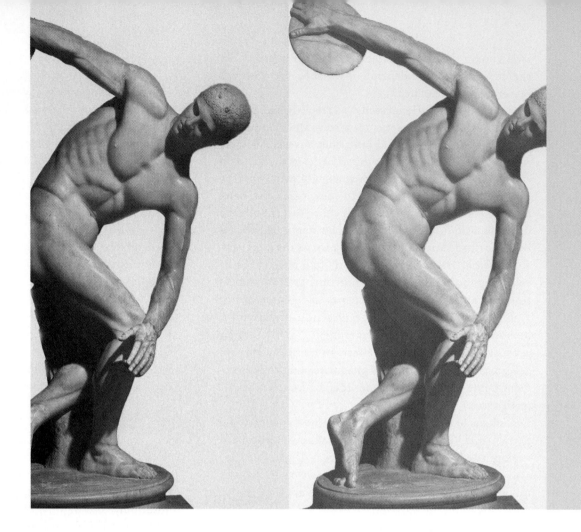

# ACTION

*Why do we act as we do?*

# PART

**1**

*WHY SHOULD PSYCHOLOGISTS STUDY THE BRAIN and the nervous system? Why not leave such bodily details to the biologists and just study the mind? There are several reasons. First, it is a simple historical fact that much in psychology has been learned from the study of how our brains and bodies work. Second, it is important that we aren't just minds; we are minds embodied. Our knowledge about the world enters through our sensory apparatus, we act in the world using our neuromuscular equipment, and we think and reason about the world using the circuitry of our nervous system. This means that psychology cannot be disentangled from biology, and the fullest picture of our behavior requires an understanding of the hardware that enacts it. To be sure, psychologists don't study this hardware as an end in itself but as a way to learn more about the fundamental questions of psychology: What do we humans know? How do we come to know it? What do we want? Why do we act in the ways we do? In this section we present a biological perspective that emphasizes the ways in which the study of our brains, nervous systems, and hormones can help us understand these broad psychological questions.*

CHAPTER

2

# BIOLOGICAL BASES OF BEHAVIOR

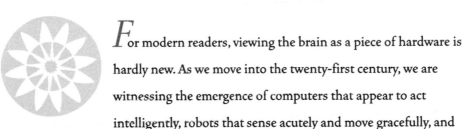

*F*or modern readers, viewing the brain as a piece of hardware is hardly new. As we move into the twenty-first century, we are witnessing the emergence of computers that appear to act intelligently, robots that sense acutely and move gracefully, and combinations of the two that make the possibility of electronic organisms all too real. Suddenly, the notion that an android like *Star Trek*'s Data could become a reality seems plausible, and perhaps even attainable, in the foreseeable future. But such was not always the case. The simple idea that our brain and our body could be thought of as a machine was for many years regarded as unbelievable, even heretical, a state of affairs that changed only four hundred to five hundred years ago.

# THE ORGANISM AS A MACHINE

## MIND AS MECHANISM

The idea that the brain is really some kind of complicated hardware, to be analyzed like any other—by taking it apart, by seeing how the parts connect, and by testing what each of the parts does—was first raised seriously by the French philosopher René Descartes (1596–1650). His proposal provides a framework that we use even today.

Descartes lived in a time that saw the beginning of the science of mechanics. Kepler and Galileo were developing ideas about the movements of the celestial bodies that some thirty years later led to Newton's *Principia* (1687). Radical new views of the universe were put forth. Laws were formulated that could explain natural phenomena ranging from the drop of a stone to the motions of planets. These same laws could be seen operating—rigidly, precisely, immutably—in the workings of ingenious mechanical contrivances that were all the rage in the wealthy homes of Europe: cuckoo clocks that sounded on the hour, water-driven gargoyles with nodding heads, statues in the king's garden that bowed to visitors who stepped on hidden springs. The turning of a gear, the release of a spring—these simple mechanisms could cause all kinds of clever effects. With these intellectual and technical developments in place and with so many complex phenomena explicable in such simple terms, it was only a matter of time before someone asked the crucial question: Could human thoughts and actions be explained just as mechanically?

## DESCARTES AND THE REFLEX CONCEPT

To Descartes, all action, whether human or animal, was essentially a response to some event in the outside world. Something from the outside excites one of the senses; this, in turn, excites a nerve that transmits the excitation to the brain, which then diverts the excitation to a muscle and makes the muscle contract. In effect, the energy from the outside is "reflected" back by the nervous system to the animal's muscles, a conception that gave rise to the term *reflex* (Figure 2.1).

Seen in this light, human and animal actions could be regarded as the doings of a machine. But there was a problem. The same external event could produce one reaction one day and another the day after. Thus, the sight of food might lead us to grab and eat it if we are hungry, but to ignore it altogether if we are not. It seems, therefore, that excitation from the senses could be diverted to one set of muscles on one occasion and an entirely different set on another. This suggests that Descartes' mechanism must have had a central switching system, supervised by some operator who sits in the middle to decide which incoming pipe to connect with which outgoing one.

How did Descartes explain this switching system? A strictly mechanical explanation would have been both difficult and precarious. For one thing, Descartes was deeply concerned over the theological implications of this argument. If all human action was to be explained mechanically, then what role was left for the soul? For another, he was prudent—he knew that Galileo had had difficulties with the Inquisition because his scientific beliefs threatened the doctrines of the Church. So Descartes shrank from taking the last step in his own argument. Instead, he proposed that human mental processes were only semimechanical. Many processes within the brain did function mechanically, but what distinguished us from other animals, what made reason and choice possible, was the soul—operating through the brain, choosing among nervous pathways, and controlling our bodies like a puppeteer pulling the strings on a marionette.

But as theology's grip on science loosened, later thinkers went further. They believed that the laws of the physical universe could ultimately explain all action, whether

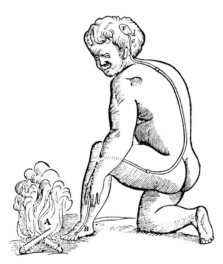

*René Descartes*

**2.1   Reflex action as envisaged by Descartes**
**In this sketch by Descartes, the heat from the fire (A) starts a chain of processes that begins at the affected spot of the skin (B) and continues up the nerve tube until a pore of a cavity (F) is opened. Descartes believed that this opening allowed the animal spirits in the cavity to enter the nerve tube and eventually travel to the muscles that pull the foot from the fire.**

human or animal, so that a scientific account required no further "ghost in the machine"—that is, no reference to the soul. They ruthlessly extended Descartes' logic to human beings, arguing that humans differ from other animals only in being more finely constructed mechanisms.

Descartes' thinking was guided both by theology and by his perception of a key analogy—that between human action and the workings of a machine. Since Descartes' analogy relied on the technology of his day, he envisioned the human "machine" as one in which fluid pressures and levers and gears led eventually to the actions we see. Later theorists could draw on more advanced technology so that by the 1950s many of them would liken the brain to a giant telephone switchboard. More recently, many have suggested that the brain is like a complex computer. In all these cases, though, Descartes' key insight remains: we can explain mental processes in terms of machinery in which some kind of energy (say, electrical or chemical) is transformed, first, into some other form and then eventually into bodily movement. The details of the proposed machine have changed drastically over the years, but the basic idea remains.*

# HOW THE NERVOUS SYSTEM IS STUDIED

Within the human brain, the total number of *neurons*—the individual cells that act as the information processors of the nervous system (Figure 2.2)—has been estimated to be as high as a trillion, with each neuron connecting to as many as ten thousand others (Nauta & Feirtag, 1986). Considering that all these interconnections occur in an organ that weighs only three to four pounds, it is no wonder that the human brain is sometimes said to be the most complex known object in the universe.

How can such an object be studied? Neuroscientists have developed many ways to discover which parts of the brain affect—and are affected by—behavior. Some of these techniques allow us to observe the operations of individual neurons. Others let us eavesdrop on the entire living human brain without seriously disturbing its owner (see Figures 2.3A and B). These techniques are often combined to give the fullest picture of brain function. We discuss them next.

---

* In the final analysis, believing that humans are just machines—of whatever kind—will always be an act of faith (as is believing that we are not just machines) because no one knows how to test for the existence of an intangible (and hence unmeasurable) soul. What is undeniable is that the strategy of regarding humans as machines has fostered dramatic breakthroughs in understanding ourselves and our fellow animals.

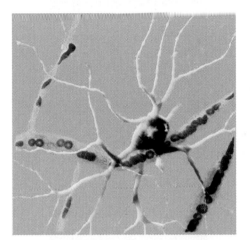

2.2 **Observing the nervous system through a microscope** *A single nerve cell shows as green here; nearby a capillary (pink) contains red blood cells. This nerve cell comes from the retina, the light-sensitive part of the eye.*

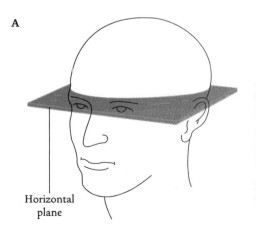

A

Horizontal plane

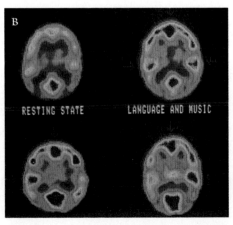

B

RESTING STATE   LANGUAGE AND MUSIC

2.3 **Observing the living brain with PET scans** *(A) Horizontal plane of brain used in taking the PET (positron emission tomography) scan shown in panel B. (B) Four PET scans taken while the participant rests, listens to someone talk, listens to music, or both. These scans indicate the degree of metabolic activity in different parts of the brain, viewed in horizontal cross section with the front of the head on top. Red indicates the most intense activity and blue the least. Listening to speech activates the left side of the brain, listening to music activates the right side, and listening to both activates both sides.*

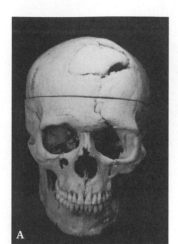

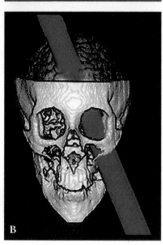

*2.4 Phineas Gage's skull (A) A photograph showing the damage to Phineas Gage's skull. (B) A computer reconstruction showing the path of the rod.*

## CLINICAL OBSERVATION

Probably the first technique to be used for studying the brain was direct *clinical observation* of patients with brain damage or disease. The goal of this technique is to link physical brain abnormality with observable changes in behavior. Sometimes the brain abnormality is self-evident, and any effects on behavior must be evaluated. Such was the celebrated (and grisly) case of Phineas Gage, who in 1848 was working as a construction foreman. While preparing a site for demolition, some blasting powder misfired and launched a three-foot iron tamping rod into his cheek, through the front part of his brain, and out the top of his head (Figure 2.4). Gage lived, though not well. As we will discuss later, he suffered intellectual and emotional impairments that gave valuable clues about the roles of the brain's frontal lobes (Valenstein, 1986).

In other clinical cases, the behavioral effects are known, but the brain damage cannot be assessed until after death. The search for the brain regions responsible for speech is one example. They were first isolated during autopsy by examining the brains of adults who had suffered traumatic losses of speech years before (see pages 57–59 later in the chapter).

Clinical observation is not without its problems, however, the major one being how generalizable it is. For example, would Phineas Gage's case tell us how everyone with frontal lobe damage behaves? Unfortunately, the answer is no: no two people ever suffer exactly the same brain damage, show exactly the same changes in behavior following the damage, or have exactly the same pattern of abilities before the damage. Thus, linking brain areas to behavior often requires more precise investigative techniques.

## INVASIVE TECHNIQUES

Around 1850, investigators began to devise ways to study the brain directly by opening the skull and "invading" the brain matter while the subject was alive (hence, the term *invasive*). Once inside, the investigators could activate or inactivate a given region of the brain and watch for any changes in behavior. Tissue could be stimulated with weak applications of electricity, chemicals, heat, or cold, or it could be *lesioned* (destroyed in place). If the connecting pathways to that tissue were known, then the tissue could be isolated by cutting—technically, *transecting*—the relevant pathways.

Obviously, these invasive techniques engendered a host of ethical quandaries, especially when the humans involved could not give full consent or when disabling, possibly painful, procedures were conducted on animals. Some ethical lapses deserve, and have resulted in, professional censure or criminal prosecution. Nevertheless, when used advisedly, invasive techniques have their place and are invaluable not only in producing basic knowledge, but also in treating a variety of both human and animal disorders.

One other technique should also be mentioned because it allows investigators to create temporary brain dysfunction, permitting them to perform experiments on humans that would not be possible otherwise. This technique—*transcranial magnetic stimulation (TMS)*—involves the creation of a series of strong magnetic pulses at a particular location on the scalp, which causes a temporary disruption in the small brain region directly underneath this scalp area. This technique has been used, for example, to examine whether brain areas ordinarily used for vision are also needed for visual imagery—"seeing" something with the "mind's eye" even though there actually is no visual input (see Chapter 8). It turns out they are: if these brain areas are disrupted via TMS, this causes parallel problems in vision and visual imagery, suggesting that the same brain tissue is involved in both activities (Kosslyn et al., 1999; see also Helmuth, 2001).

# NEUROIMAGING TECHNIQUES

In the last few decades, our understanding of the linkage between brain and behavior has been revolutionized by a number of *neuroimaging techniques*. These provide us with remarkable views of the brain's anatomy (structure) or its physiology (function), with absolutely no invasion of brain tissue and with the brain's owner awake and fully conscious throughout the procedure.

One technique for imaging brain anatomy is the **CT *(computerized tomography)* scan** (or *CAT scan*, an abbreviation for computerized axial tomography), which involves a series of X rays of a brain area taken at different angles and the use of a computer to construct a detailed composite picture.

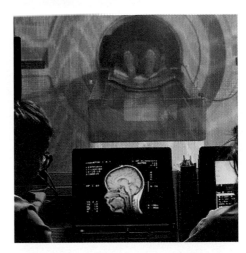

**2.6  Magnetic resonance imaging (MRI)**   A patient goes through the MRI procedure, while a medical specialist watches the image on a screen.

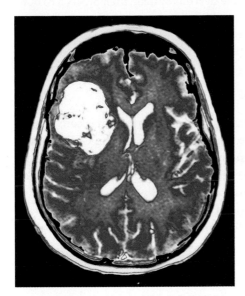

**2.5  Brain cancer   *Magnetic resonance imaging (MRI) scan of a patient's brain showing a cancerous brain tumor (white, area, upper left). The front of the brain is at the top.***

A more widely used neuroimaging technique is **magnetic resonance imaging** (**MRI**, Figure 2.5). MRI scans are safer because they involve no X rays. Instead, MRI scans pass a very-high-frequency alternating magnetic field through the brain. Magnetic sensors detect the resulting reverberations within the brain tissue, and a computer examines these signals for subtle differences that identify the kind of tissue that generated them (for example, blood, nerve fibers, or membranes). These data are then processed by the computer, the result being a magnificently detailed picture of the brain that can show tumors, tissue degeneration, and the blood clots and leaks that may signal strokes (see Figure 2.6).

CT and MRI scans typically allow only anatomical depictions—that is, they can reveal brain structures but not whether those structures are involved in a given behavior. To reveal brain function, experimenters use several techniques. The earliest developed was **electroencephalography** (or **EEG**), which detects tiny electrical currents generated by neurons on the surface of the brain. This procedure only requires affixing tiny metal electrodes to the top and sides of the head.

EEGs can be quite informative but can only indicate activity at the brain's surface. For in-depth, three-dimensional localization of brain function, investigators can use **positron emission tomography** (or **PET**) **scans**. In PET scans, the participant is injected with a safe dose of radioactive sugar that resembles glucose (the only metabolic fuel the brain can use). The brain cells that are more active at any moment will soak up more of this sugar and thus give off more radioactivity, which can be detected and used to derive an image in much the same way as CT and MRI scans. The resulting PET scan can thus tell the physician which regions within the brain are particularly active or inactive, and this may suggest a tumor, lesion, or psychological disorder.

A still newer technique, *functional MRI (fMRI) scanning* (Figure 2.7), adapts standard MRI procedures to detect fast-changing aspects of brain physiology (mostly blood flow and oxygen use) without using any radioactivity. The end result is a three-dimensional image of the brain at work, showing the parts that are most active at any particular moment. Already, neuroscientists have connected fMRIs to three-dimensional virtual-reality displays to give an in-depth view of the brain performing various cognitive tasks and to reveal damage that may require neurosurgical correction.

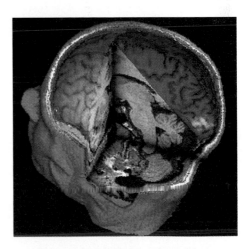

**2.7  functional MRI (fMRI)   *This fMRI scan shows activation in the visual cortex after visual stimulation. The colored activation map is superimposed on a high-resolution anatomical scan, which is rendered in 3-D.***

# THE ARCHITECTURE OF THE NERVOUS SYSTEM

Whether based on clinical observation or invasive or neuroimaging techniques, our investigations have taught us a great deal about the nervous system. In the following sections, we will discuss some of what we have learned. We begin with what we now know about the evolution and development of the nervous system, then proceed to outline the gross structures of the nervous system, and finally turn to how the nervous system communicates with the rest of the body.

## GENES AND THE NERVOUS SYSTEM

The brain is an organ like the heart or the liver, and, like all our organs, it is constructed according to detailed specifications. Thanks to the success of the Human Genome Project (International Human Genome Sequencing Consortium, 2001; Venter et al., 2001), we know that these specifications are contained in the mere 30,000 or so genes contained on the 23 pairs of chromosomes that comprise our genome (that is, the full complement of DNA contained in the nucleus of each of our cells). These genes are responsible for creating the million-odd kinds of molecules that make up our brains and bodies, and for dictating the arrangement of those molecules into cells and those cells into organs. How can such a small number of genes dictate the production of a nervous system that can fly airplanes, cure cancer, and even decode its own genome? The feat is all the more amazing given that the human genome is not strikingly large (roundworms have 19,000, and mustard plants have 25,000) or unique (we share 99.5 percent of our genes with the chimpanzee and 90 percent with the fruit fly).

Discovering the process through which the genes manage to create a human with a human nervous system constitutes an unprecedented challenge, and we only have hints of the principles at work. First, it is now clear that the genes do not act independently. Instead, they collude in various patterns, letting some "speak" but keeping others quiet. Thus, even species with similar genomes can have markedly different patterns of gene expression, which will produce markedly different nervous systems. Second, these patterns of gene expression are very sensitive to environmental factors such as germs, nutrients, and toxins. This means that the genes do not rigidly program the wiring of the developing nervous system so much as they set out guidelines for its completion. Finally, the small size of the genome indicates how wrong it is to say that one or another gene is "for" a particular structure or behavior in the nervous system; rather, overlapping sets of genes are likely to participate in the development of overlapping sets of structures and behavior.

We also know a few specific things about how genes determine the structure of the nervous system, based on studies of organisms like worms, whose nervous systems may contain only a few hundred neurons. First, genes in the fertilized egg turn on and trigger rapid cell reproduction, so that by three days after fertilization the embryo consists of several dozen identical cells. When this clump of cells reaches some critical mass, other genes turn on and give off chemical signals that induce new kinds of cells to develop. This is the start of an unfolding process in which new cell types are created, turning on still other genes that give off signals that induce the next step, and so on. At each step, the new kinds of cells migrate to specific sites within the embryo and then proliferate. Thus, under a genetic timetable, undifferentiated embryo cells become neural stem cells, which eventually develop into neurons or neuron-associated cells.

Finally, once a population of sufficiently differentiated neurons is in place, other genes turn on and give off chemical signals that serve as "beacons," attracting connections that sprout from other neurons. This process of cellular signaling, differentiation, migration, and proliferation is called *neurogenesis*. It happens rapidly, with neurons being generated at a rate of up to 250,000 per minute; in humans, neurogenesis is nearly complete by the fifth month of gestation (Kolb & Whishaw, 2001; Rakic, 1995).

How different are the outcomes of neurogenesis from animal to animal? Just as all animals share a majority of their genes, all nervous systems emerge in the same general way. But, as we shall see, it is the fine print in the genetic contract that gives us a human brain and not that of a rodent or a raptor.

## THE EVOLUTION OF NERVOUS SYSTEMS

All nervous systems, it seems, from the cockroach's to the human's, are offshoots of one basic design. It is the divergences from this design, however, that make the dog uniquely doggish and ourselves uniquely human. Two ways in which nervous systems diverge are in their degree of centralization and in their size. These trends emerge from observations of the nervous systems of many species, a method known as the *comparative approach*.

Nervous systems differ from one another in their degree of regional versus central control. Generally, more complex animals show more central control, whereas in simpler animals, like many invertebrates, regional rule predominates. For example, sea anemones (flowery-looking animals that latch onto the ocean bottom and strain seawater for food) have networks of nerves with no obvious focus of connection. Slightly more complex invertebrates like mollusks (for instance, snails, oysters, clams, squids, and octopuses) have neurons that control individual movements, and these neurons clump together to form *ganglia* (singular, *ganglion*). The ganglia serve primarily to relay messages from the sense organs to the muscles and are usually located near the muscles they control. One mollusk, the sea snail *Aplysia*, has five ganglia that control the animal's entire repertoire of behaviors: sucking food in and out of its siphon, moving its eyes and tentacles, working its sticky foot to enable motion, and managing circulation, gill-breathing, and reproduction (Krasne & Glanzman, 1995; Rosenzweig, Leiman, & Breedlove, 1996; see Chapter 4).

As evolution continued beyond these simple organisms, however, the initial loose federation of ganglia became increasingly centralized, and some ganglia gradually began to control others. The dominant ganglia were those located in the head, and it is not hard to see why. Most organisms, starting with the evolutionarily ancient flatworms, have a body plan organized front to back. Forward movement proceeds head first, making it sensible for receptors for light or chemicals to be situated in the animal's head. Even the lowly flatworm already knows something about what is at its rear, for it was there just a moment ago. What lies ahead, however, is still unknown and often worth exploring. In addition, the worm's head contains its mouth; the terminus of the digestive tube is at the animal's other end. This also makes it useful for the receptors to be located in the head: taste receptors near the beginning of the digestive tube can be used to signal edibility, allowing an animal to sample its food before deciding to eat it.

To integrate the messages from the various receptors in the head, organisms needed to evolve more and more neural machinery. This machinery was best placed close to the receptors, so it, too, needed to be in the head. These ganglionic centers became increasingly complex as organisms evolved and eventually started to coordinate the activity of ganglia elsewhere in the body. Over millions of years of evolution, these centers emerged as the "head" ganglia in status as well as in location. In short, they became the brain.

Although centralization can be advantageous, regional rule has its own virtues. Command hierarchies are slow, and the brains that contain them require a great deal of energy to build and maintain. Much can get done quickly and economically by avoiding a distant, bureaucratic chain of command. For example, cockroaches have brains, but their brains are tiny and mostly dedicated to their compound eyes. What they lack in brains, however, is made up elsewhere—in a chain of large ganglia spanning nearly the length of their body. One of these ganglia connects to nerve endings in the tail and can trigger quick escape when the tail is stimulated by even the faintest air movement. This decentralized reflex is one reason cockroaches are some of Earth's longest survivors and easily defeat even large-brained mammals who wield both rolled-up newspapers and cans of pesticide.

## THE DEVELOPING NERVOUS SYSTEM

In many modern animals, and certainly in all vertebrates, centralized rule is the norm, and the vast majority of the body's neural machinery lies in the brain. This pattern emerges very early in development (see Figure 2.8). The nervous system first begins to appear at about the third week of embryonic life. It starts as a small thickening atop the embryo that runs from the head to (nearly) the tail. Within a few days, the left and right edges of this *neural plate* zip together and fuse lengthwise to form the *neural tube*. By one month of embryonic life, the head end of the neural tube develops three thickenings. These thickenings—which will develop into the *hindbrain* (the thickening nearest the tail), the *forebrain* (that nearest the head), and the *midbrain* (the thickening between the two)—become enclosed by the cranial bones and form the brain. The lower end of the hindbrain marks the beginning of the spinal cord, which we discuss below. But while we separate them in our discussion, the brain and the spinal cord function as one integrated unit, the two together making up the *central nervous system (CNS)*.

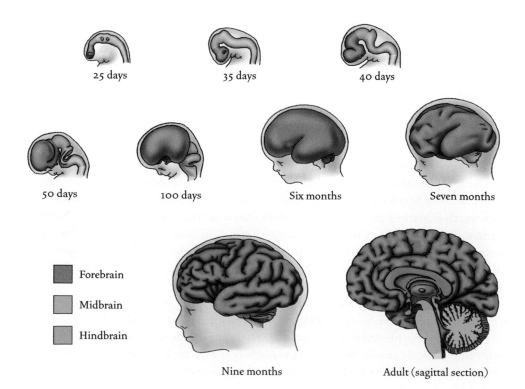

*2.8 Embryonic-fetal development of the human brain*

25 days    35 days    40 days

50 days    100 days    Six months    Seven months

■ Forebrain
□ Midbrain
■ Hindbrain

Nine months    Adult (sagittal section)

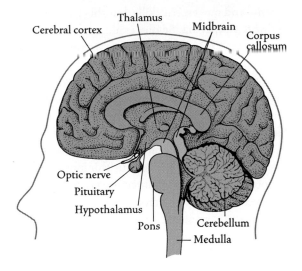

**2.9  The human brain**  **A
diagram of what the brain would
look like if it were cut vertically,
right down the middle. The
hindbrain is shown in light blue,
the midbrain in light green, and
the forebrain in pink. (After
Keeton, 1980)**

## THE MAJOR STRUCTURES OF
## THE CENTRAL NERVOUS SYSTEM

In their embryonic form, the brains of all vertebrate species look remarkably alike, but
they soon diverge in how the different portions develop. For example, birds begin to
develop large midbrains, whereas primates develop large cerebellums and forebrains.
Despite these species-specific differences, one can still make generalizations about the
involvement of each portion in behavior. Here, we focus on the major structures of the
human brain (Figure 2.9). The hindbrain is a good place to start.

### THE HINDBRAIN: MEDULLA, PONS, AND CEREBELLUM

At the bottom of the hindbrain is the *medulla*, which lies directly above the spinal cord.
The medulla is crucial for many basic biological functions. First, it regulates the cardiovascular and respiratory systems, determining each second how rapidly and heavily we
should breathe, how quickly our heart should beat, and how much blood it should
pump. Second, it integrates a number of important reflexes such as swallowing, coughing, and sneezing. Third, it helps us to maintain balance by controlling head orientation and limb positions with respect to gravity.

Just above the medulla the hindbrain thickens, and this thickened area is known as
the *pons*. The pons contains special regions that integrate movements of, and sensations
from, the facial muscles, tongue, eye, and ear. Other regions in the pons are important in
regulating the brain's level of attentiveness and in initiating sleep and dreaming.

The hindbrain's importance in regulating bodily functions is dramatically apparent
in individuals with spinal cord damage that prevents signals from reaching the hindbrain. These individuals frequently lose the ability to regulate blood pressure from
moment to moment and suffer from symptoms that include pounding headaches, nausea and vomiting, and profuse sweating.

Yet another portion of the hindbrain is the *cerebellum*, a massive cauliflowerlike
structure that hangs directly behind the pons and overlaps the medulla. This structure,
which is extraordinarily well developed in primates and especially humans, seems to act
as a specialized computer whose thirty billion or more neurons integrate information
from our gravity-sensing (balance) mechanisms as well as data from the muscles,

joints, and tendons of the body. Some scholars believe that the cerebellum also plays a key role in our learning of new movements and movement skills, but this point remains controversial (see, for example, Hazeltine & Ivry, 2002; Seidler et al., 2002).

The cerebellum has several separate regions. One portion controls overall bodily balance. Damage to this part—whether caused by injury, disease, or the temporary toxin alcohol—results in a wide stance and staggering gait. (This is why traffic officers ask suspected drunk drivers to walk a straight line.) Another portion manages the sequencing and timing of precise skilled movements, whether the execution of a well-practiced tennis swing or an arpeggio on the piano. Damage here can cause tremors during movement and an inability to perform rapidly alternating movements (for example, tapping alternate fingers). The cerebellum's adeptness at sequencing also influences our thinking: cerebellar damage impairs the performance of various cognitive tasks that require exact sequencing, such as mentally reordering lists. This defect seems to play a crucial role in the disordered thinking seen in schizophrenia (Andreasen et al., 1999; and see Chapter 16).

## THE MIDBRAIN

The midbrain is crucial for targeting auditory (sound) and visual stimuli. Portions of the midbrain help regulate body temperature and pain perception, and they cooperate with the pons in controlling the sleeping-waking cycle. Other areas control eye movements and, in floppy-eared animals, causes the animal to prick up its ears when encountering novel or important events. Birds have comparatively large midbrains—it apparently takes lots of fast midbrain machinery to target prey from high above and to swoop down for the catch. Mammals have small midbrains, having shifted much of the control of vision and hearing to their forebrains.

## THE FOREBRAIN

The forebrain comprises everything above the midbrain. Mammals—particularly primates—have the largest forebrains. Indeed, in humans the forebrain is so large that it surrounds and hides from view all of our midbrain and half of our hindbrain. In mammals, the most obvious portion of the forebrain is that part on the surface, which is wrinkled like a prune. This is the mammalian *cortex*, and it is so important that it (and the reason for the wrinkles) will be discussed separately below.

Like the rest of the brain, the forebrain is bilaterally symmetrical. This symmetry is especially obvious on the surface of the cortex, which shows a deep front-to-back cleavage called the **longitudinal fissure**. On either side of this fissure and underneath the cortex lies the rest of the forebrain, including a number of **subcortical structures**. Of these, four are specifically worth mentioning. First, buried deep within the forebrain and shaped like a fist atop the midbrain lies the **thalamus**. The thalamus incorporates a large number of centers that appear to act as relay stations for nearly all the sensory information going to the cortex. A second major structure in this region, lying directly underneath the thalamus, is the **hypothalamus**, which is intimately involved in the control of motivated behavior such as feeding, drinking, maintaining an appropriate body temperature, and engaging in sexual activity (see Chapter 3).

Directly astride the thalamus in each hemisphere lie the **basal ganglia**. They are crucial in regulating muscular contractions during movement (especially smooth movements) and keeping our movements from being jerky. Just how crucial they are is obvious when observing individuals with basal ganglia disorders. One such disorder, **Parkinson's disease**, involves the degeneration of certain cells in the basal ganglia. Sufferers from Parkinson's disease often show a loss of muscle tone, an immobile masklike face, slow movements, and tremors when the limbs are at rest. Parts of the basal ganglia also degenerate in *Huntington's disease*, a progressive, hereditary disorder that can cause jerky limb movements, facial twitches, and uncontrolled writhing of the body. The basal ganglia are also involved in the production of repetitive behavior, and much research suggests that a dysfunction of the basal ganglia may be central to *obsessive-compulsive disorder (OCD)*, a mental illness in which the sufferer is overwhelmed by persistent thoughts and impulses (Chapter 16).

A fourth set of interconnected structures surrounds the thalamus and basal ganglia, and lies directly beneath the cortex. These structures are often grouped together under the term *limbic system* (from the French *limbique*, "bordering"). The limbic system, which includes the amygdala and the hippocampus, has close anatomical ties with numerous parts of the brain, especially the hypothalamus, cortex, and regions controlling the sense of smell (see Figure 1.4 on page 9). It is involved in emotional and motivational activities, and some aspects of learning and memory (see the discussions of the amygdala in Chapter 11 and of the hippocampus in Chapter 7).

## THE CENTRAL NERVOUS SYSTEM'S CONNECTIONS WITH THE BODY

The CNS's connections with the rest of the body are bidirectional. Some nerve fibers, called *afferent nerves*, transmit information from the sense organs to the brain and spinal cord. Other nerve fibers, called *efferent nerves*, transmit their messages from the CNS to the *effectors*, the muscles and glands that are the organs of action.

The spinal cord itself is a major trunk line of nerve fibers—some afferent, some efferent, and others just making local internal connections within the spinal cord. These local connections can initiate or regulate movements on their own and can modulate sensory information as it proceeds to the brain.

But not all nerves between brain and body run through the spinal cord. Separate nerves, twelve pairs in all, enter and exit directly from the hindbrain (from the pons and medulla, specifically—see below) and poke through holes in the skull. These *cranial nerves* have both afferent and efferent functions. They control the movements of the head and neck, carry sensations from them—including vision, olfaction (smell), and audition (hearing)—regulate the various glandular secretions in the head (for example, tears, saliva, and mucus), and control life-sustaining visceral functions such as digestion and excretion.

Together, the cranial nerves and the nerves that connect to the spinal cord—in other words, all the nerve fibers, ganglia, and so forth that lie outside the central nervous system—are called the *peripheral nervous system* (Figure 2.10). Anatomists distinguish between two divisions of the peripheral nervous system, based upon their function. The *somatic division* is the set of nerves that control the skeletal musculature and the transmission of information from the sense organs; the *autonomic division* (typically called the *autonomic nervous system*, or *ANS*) is the set of spinal and cranial nerves that regulate and inform the brain about the viscera (including the heart and lungs, the blood vessels, the digestive systems, the sexual organs, and so on).

A final line of communication between brain and body is indirect, occurring via hormonal secretions. For example, the *pituitary gland*, commonly known as the "master" gland because of its supervisory role among the glands of the body, is actually an extension of the hypothalamus, receiving not only nerve fibers, but also neurochemical channels from it. The brain also has sensors responsive to chemicals circulating in the bloodstream; these chemical receptors are important in regulating states like hunger and thirst. These hormonal connections are discussed further on pages 77–78 and in Chapter 3.

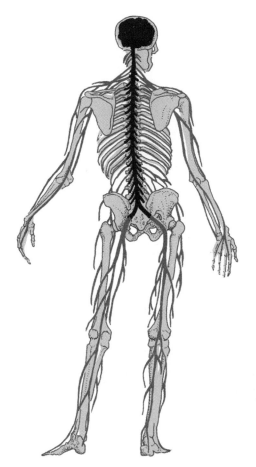

**2.10** *Central and peripheral nervous systems The central nervous system (in dark red) and the peripheral nervous system (in orange). (After Bloom, Lazerson, & Hofstadter, 1988)*

# THE CORTEX

We now turn to the outermost layer of the cerebral hemispheres, the part of the central nervous system known as the *cortex* (or, technically, the *neocortex*—there is an underlying "old cortex" that includes subcortical forebrain structures such as the basal ganglia and the hippocampus; see Figure 2.11).

For primates and other complex mammals, the cortex is the most massive single portion of the brain, accounting for more than half the brain's volume (in humans, 80 percent). Because of this, the cortex has enjoyed the reputation of being the part of the brain that makes us intelligent. But that is only part of the story. Many of the tasks performed in nonmammals by subcortical regions such as parts of the limbic system and the midbrain are performed in mammals by the cortex. These include complex sensory perception and coordinated muscular action. Indeed, this is a clear trend in mammalian brain evolution: as the cortex enlarges, the subcortical structures and the midbrain begin to act more as relay stations or middle managers.

What do the mammals gain from their massive cortex, especially when its functions can be performed by other structures? The answer is flexibility in behavior. The frog that has a fly-sized object waved in front of it will try to swallow it. But we humans are different. If someone waves a chocolate truffle in front of us, there is no guarantee that we will gobble it up. We might decide to do otherwise because we are on a diet or want to save our appetite for dinner. Likewise, a chimpanzee encountering a fresh banana might hide it until all the other chimps who could grab it have left. This flexibility underlies the cleverness that typifies many mammals, most primates, and, now and then, humans.

Remarkably, although the cortex has an enormous volume, it is only 2 to 3 millimeters thick. This is made possible by the cortex's most striking anatomical feature—its many wrinkles (technically, its *convolutions*). If someone could iron the wrinkles out of a human cortex, it would occupy an area of 2,500 centimeters² (about 2 square feet). Housing this structure in uncompressed form would take an odd-sized head indeed (and, just as important, would require much longer nerves to connect all its regions). But all crumpled up, this large surface can be jammed into the limited volume of a human head, one that must remain small enough to pass through a normal-sized birth canal.

Some of the convolutions in the cortex are actually very deep grooves, or *fissures* (see Figure 2.11). The deepest fissure was already mentioned—the longitudinal fissure, which runs from front to back and separates the left and right cerebral hemispheres. Other fissures mark off several large sections of each hemisphere, called *lobes*. There are four such lobes, each named for the cranial bone nearest to it. Within each hemisphere,

*2.11   The cortex of the cerebral hemispheres (A) An actual human brain, shown in side view; the front of the head is towards the left. (B) Side-view drawing, showing its convolutions, fissures, and lobes.*

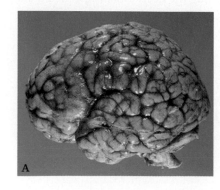

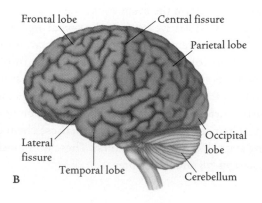

A                    B

the *frontal* and *parietal* lobes form the front and topmost parts of the brain, respectively. The earflap-like *temporal lobes* press up against the frontal lobes. And the *occipital lobe* is the rear-most lobe; it is smoothly adjoined to the temporal and parietal lobes.

## LOCALIZATION OF FUNCTION IN THE CORTEX

We have now identified a number of different brain regions. How does each region contribute to thinking and behavior? This problem is known as *localization of function*, and the predominance of the cortex in the human brain made it the first candidate for localization efforts.

## PROJECTION AREAS

Among the initial discoveries in the study of cortical function was the existence of sensory and motor *primary projection areas*. The *primary sensory projection areas* serve as the receiving stations for information arriving from the eyes, ears, and other sense organs. The *primary motor projection area* is the departure point for signals that enter lower parts of the brain and spinal cord, and ultimately result in muscle movement. The term *projection* is borrowed from cartography because the sensory and motor primary projection areas seem to form maps in which particular regions of the cortex correspond roughly to the parts of the body they represent or influence.

### PRIMARY MOTOR AREA

The discovery of the primary motor projection area dates back to the 1860s, when investigators began to apply mild electric currents to various portions of the cortex of anesthetized animals. The effects were often quite specific. Within the frontal lobe, stimulating one point led to a movement of the forelimb, while stimulating another made the ears prick up, and so forth. These early studies also provided evidence for what neuroscientists call *contralateral control*: stimulating the left hemisphere led to movements on the right side of the body; stimulating the right hemisphere caused movements on the left. Contralateral control appears to operate in nearly all nervous systems. It is also evident anatomically because most of the major efferent pathways from the brain cross over to the opposite side within the hindbrain.

Investigators have produced detailed localization "maps" for motor function in the cortex. Canadian neurosurgeon Wilder Penfield, for example, produced such maps from studies using humans who were suffering from severe epilepsy and needed neurosurgery to remove the diseased cells. For these surgeries, Penfield capitalized on the fact that the brain is remarkably insensitive to pain. (While the brain obviously has an enormous number of nerve cells, it contains very few sensory receptors.) This allowed Penfield to operate on patients under local anesthesia, leaving them fully awake throughout the experience. From surgeries on over four hundred patients, Penfield confirmed that the cortical motor area in humans lies within the frontal lobe. Stimulation there led to movement of

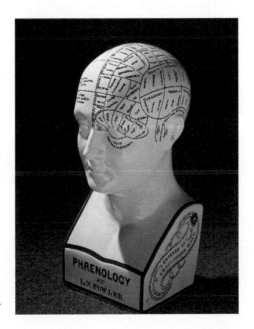

*Early attempts at cerebral localization*
*According to phrenology, a nineteenth-century theory that is now totally discredited, the degree to which people possessed such characteristics as foresight, courage, and the desire to have children could be assessed by looking at the shape of their skulls. The theory assumed that each of these characteristics was associated with a particular part of the brain, and that these brain parts would be enlarged if the individual happened to have more of the characteristic in question (had more foresight, or was more courageous, and so on). These enlarged brain areas would press against the skull, changing the head's shape, and this could be detected by feeling the pattern of bumps on the skull.*

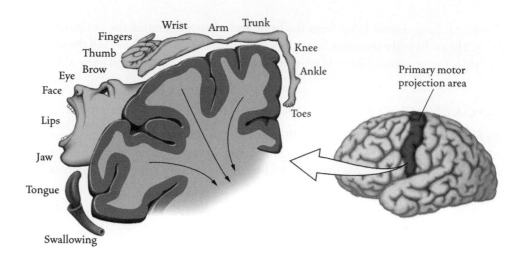

**2.12   The primary motor projection area**
*The primary motor projection area is located at the rearmost edge of the frontal lobe. Each region within the projection area is thought to control the motion of a specific part of the body. The panel on the left shows a cross-sectional slice into the brain, with each body part shown alongside of the brain area that controls its movement.*

specific parts of the body, much to the surprise of patients who had no sense of willing the action or of performing it themselves.

Systematic exploration persuaded Penfield that for each portion of the motor cortex, there was a corresponding part of the body that moved when its cortical counterpart was stimulated, with each hemisphere exhibiting contralateral control. The map generated from such surgery is sometimes depicted graphically by drawing a "motor homunculus," a schematic picture of the body with each part depicted on the motor projection area that controls its movement (see Figure 2.12).

More recent evidence, however, suggests that we may need to refine this conception. Penfield (and most other early investigators) used relatively brief stimuli to trigger responses from the motor cortex; more recent studies have asked what happens if the stimuli are longer (and, indeed, longer in a fashion that better imitates the form of stimulation these brain areas would receive in their normal functioning). This newer evidence suggests that specific brain areas may not correspond to particular parts of the body; instead, specific brain areas may correspond to target locations in space. Thus, stimulation in a particular region might cause someone's hand to move toward a specific destination (a particular location, a particular shape of the hand), no matter what the hand's position was prior to the stimulation (Graziano, Taylor, & Moore, 2002). If this finding is confirmed, it will suggest that the motor cortex maps destinations, not body parts, and pictures like Figure 2.12—long considered "classic" drawings in textbooks—may need revision.

However this issue turns out, one aspect of Figure 2.12 will remain in place: as the picture indicates, equal-sized areas of the body do not receive equal amounts of cortical space. Instead, parts that we are able to move with the greatest precision (for instance, the fingers, the tongue) receive more cortical space than those over which we have less control (for instance, the shoulder, the abdomen). Evidently, what matters is function, the extent and complexity of use (Penfield & Rasmussen, 1950). This generalization seems to apply across species. Unlike the dog, the raccoon is a manual creature that explores the world with its forepaws; neatly enough, the forepaw cortical area in raccoons dwarfs its counterpart in dogs (Welker, Johnson, & Pubols, 1964).

## PRIMARY SENSORY AREAS

Methods similar to Penfield's revealed the existence of sensory projection areas. The primary *somatosensory* area is adjacent to and directly behind the primary motor projection area. This area, located in the parietal lobe in each hemisphere (see Figure 2.13) is the receiving area for sensory information from the skin senses. Patients stimulated at a particular point in this area usually report tingling somewhere on the opposite side

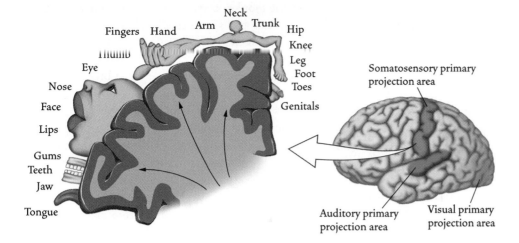

of their bodies. (Less frequently, they report experiences of cold, warmth, or movement.) The somatosensory projection area resembles its motor counterpart in several ways. First, it shows a neat topographic projection, with each part of the body's surface sending its sensory information to a particular part of the cortical somatosensory area. Second, the assignment of cortical space is disproportionate, with the parts of the body that are most sensitive to touch, such as the index finger and the tongue, receiving more cortical space. Finally, sensation—like motor control—is contralateral, with sensory information from each extremity of the body proceeding to the hemisphere on the side opposite to it: the right thumb onto the left hemisphere, the left shoulder onto the right hemisphere, and so on. (Information from the trunk of the body close to the body's midline is represented in both hemispheres.)

Similar primary projection areas exist for vision and for hearing, and are located in the occipital and temporal lobes, respectively (see Figure 2.13). Here, too, the representation is topographical. In the occipital lobe (especially the area known as the "visual cortex"), adjacent brain areas represent adjacent locations in visual space. In the temporal lobes, adjacent areas represent similar ranges of pitch. These projection areas are contralateral as well. For vision, objects seen on the left are processed by the right visual area, while those seen on the right are processed by the left visual area. Similarly, sounds entering the left ear are represented mostly in the right auditory projection area, and vice versa. Patients who are stimulated in the visual projection area report optical experiences, vivid enough but with little form or meaning—flickering lights, streaks of color. Stimulated in the auditory area, patients hear things; but, again, the sensation is meaningless and chaotic—clicks, buzzes, booms, and hums.

## NONPRIMARY (ASSOCIATION) AREAS

The primary projection areas constitute less than one quarter of the human cortex. What about the rest? These areas were originally referred to as "association areas" because they did not seem to show any kind of fixed sensory mapping and were implicated in such higher mental functions as planning, perceiving, remembering, thinking, and speaking. Subsequent research has confirmed that these regions are involved in such higher mental functions, but some of them are now known to function as still further projection areas, over and above the primary ones we have just described.

For example, in front of the primary motor projection area are large nonprimary motor regions that appear critical to initiating and coordinating complex skilled movements. On the sensory side, each sensory modality may have dozens of secondary projection areas located in the temporal and parietal lobes, with each showing topographical and contralateral representation and each involved in processing differ-

**2.13  The primary sensory projection areas** *The primary sensory projection area for the skin senses is at the forward edge of the parietal lobe. Each region within this area receives input from a specific part of the body; the panel on the left shows a cross-sectional slice into the brain, with each body part shown alongside of the brain area that receives input from this body part. The primary projection areas for vision and hearing are located in the occipital and temporal lobes, respectively. These two are also organized in a systematic fashion. For example, in the visual project area, adjacent areas of the brain receive visual inputs that come from adjacent areas in visual space.*

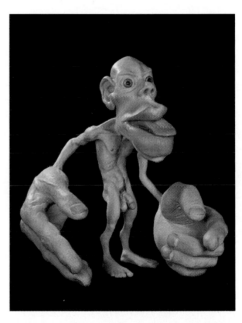

**The sensory homunculus**  *An artist's rendition of what a man would look like if his appearance were proportional to the area allotted by the somatosensory cortex to his various body parts.*

ent aspects of sensation. For example, the monkey cortex has at least twenty-five non-primary projection areas for vision, with each area specialized for different visual qualities such as form, color, or movement (Kolb & Whishaw, 1996). In addition, there are also areas that integrate multiple sensory modalities such as touch and vision so that we can, for example, recognize by sight an object that we have previously only touched.

Collectively, these nonprimary areas serve to organize and relate the various messages that come from the primary sensory projection areas or that go to the primary motor projection areas. To that extent, they do indeed provide the integration and organization that is crucial for the so-called higher mental functions. But despite their involvement in these "higher" functions, we cannot point to any particular brain location and assert that it is the organizing center for, say, planning or visual memory or thinking. These higher tasks seem to depend on control exerted from many different cortical locations.

## DISORDERS OF THE PROJECTION AREAS

Most of our knowledge about cortical functions has come from the study of individuals who have suffered damage to one or more of the projection areas, whether from strokes, tumors, head injuries, or other neurological disorders. By studying the disorders caused by such lesions, *neuropsychologists* have been able to make inferences about the functions of the cortical areas that have been damaged.

### DISORDERS OF ACTION

Some lesions in the frontal lobe of the cortex produce *apraxias*, which are serious disturbances in the initiation or organization of voluntary action. In some apraxias, the patient is unable to perform well-known actions such as saluting or waving good-bye when asked to do so. In other cases, actions that normal persons regard as simple become fragmented and disorganized. When asked to light a cigarette, the patient may strike a match against a matchbox and then strike it again and again after it is already burning; or he may light the match and then put it into his mouth. These deficits are not the result of simple paralysis since the patient can readily perform each part of the action in isolation. His problem is in initiating the sequence or in selecting the right components and fitting them together (Kolb & Whishaw, 2001; Luria, 1966).

Some apraxias may represent a disconnection between the primary and nonprimary motor areas. Although the primary motor area is responsible for producing the movements of individual muscles, the nonprimary motor areas must first organize and initiate the sequence. Evidence for such a disconnection comes from an experiment in which EEG monitoring electrodes were placed on the scalps of participants, who were then asked to press a button in response to various stimuli. The EEG data showed that the neurons in the nonprimary areas fired almost a second before participants actually moved their fingers, suggesting that these areas play a role in preparing that action (Deecke, Scheid, and Kornhuber, 1968). In short, the nonprimary areas seem to be responsible for "Get ready!" and "Get set!" At "Go!" however, the primary motor area takes over (Bear, Connors, & Paradiso, 1996; Roland, Larsen, Lessen, & Skinhøj, 1980).

### DISORDERS OF PERCEPTION AND ATTENTION

In several other disorders, the patient suffers a disruption in the way she perceives the world or attends to it.

*Agnosias* One such group of disorders is the *agnosias*, in which the sufferer cannot identify familiar objects using the affected sensory modality. Patients with visual

WWW

Capgras syndrome

agnosia, for example, can recognize a car key by grasping it but not by looking at it. Some of these patients can identify the separate details of a picture but are unable to identify the picture as a whole (Farah & Feinberg, 2000; Wapner, Judd, & Gardner, 1978, p. 347).

Agnosic patients have similar difficulties when asked to copy drawings. The individual parts are rendered reasonably well, but they cannot be integrated into a coherent whole (see Figure 2.14). Visual agnosia tends to result from damage to the occipital area of the cortex and to the rearmost part of the parietal area that borders the occipital area—that is, the primary and nonprimary projection areas for vision.

One striking and complex kind of agnosia, technically known as *prosopagnosia*, seems to involve areas of both the temporal and parietal lobes. In prosopagnosia, the main difficulty is in recognizing faces. Some of these patients are unable to distinguish familiar faces; others cannot even recognize a face as a face. When walking down the street, one such patient would pat the tops of fire hydrants, which he thought were the heads of little children. On one occasion he mistook his wife's head for a hat (Sacks, 1985; for further discussion, see Chapter 6). But the problems suffered by individuals with prosopagnosia are typically not confined just to faces. They may not be able to identify their own car or particular types of clothing or food. A dairy farmer who could formerly recognize every cow in his herd lost the ability to tell them apart (de Renzi, 2000; Farah & Feinberg, 2000).

*Neglect Syndrome*   In agnosia, the patient can see (or feel or hear) but is unable to make sense of what his senses tell him. In other disorders, the patient's problem is one of attention, and he systematically ignores certain aspects of the world.

A striking example is the *neglect syndrome* (sometimes called *left neglect*), which typically results from damage to certain areas on the right side of the parietal lobe. Its main characteristic is the patient's systematic neglect of the left side: he acts as if it does not exist. When asked to read compound words such as toothpick or baseball, such a patient will read "pick" and "ball," ignoring the left half of each word; when asked to draw the face of a clock, he will squeeze all of the numbers onto the clock's right side (see Figure 2.15). When eating, he will select and eat food only from the right side of his plate. A similar neglect applies to the left side of the patient's own body. When dressing, he will ignore the left shirt sleeve and pants leg; when shaving, he will leave the left side of his face unshaven (Heilman & Watson, 1977; Kolb & Whishaw, 1996).

What accounts for the neglect syndrome? According to some theorists, the reason is essentially a failure of attention, caused by the disruption of a cortical arousal system that orients us to what is new (Heilman & Watson, 1977). Others believe that the person with the neglect syndrome loses the ability to integrate the spatial properties of stimuli or hold the properties in memory (Rafal, 1994; Rafal & Robertson, 1995; Robertson & Manly, 1999).

## DISORDERS OF LANGUAGE

Certain lesions in the cortical nonprimary areas lead to disruptions of the production and comprehension of speech. Disorders of this kind are called *aphasias*. In right-handers, they are almost always produced by lesions (strokes, typically) in the left hemisphere. Disorders of speech take different forms. Which particular form they take depends heavily on the particular sites of brain damage.

Early studies suggested that aphasias could be divided into two broad types: one that seemed primarily to involve the production of speech and one that seemed to involve the comprehension of speech. Aphasias of the first sort were often referred to as *nonfluent aphasias* and typically involved lesions in a region of the left front lobe called *Broca's area* (after the French physician Pierre-Paul Broca, who, in 1861, first noted its relation to speech; see Figure 2.16). In extreme cases, a patient with this disorder

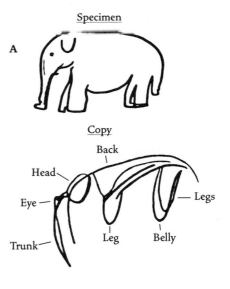

Specimen

A

Copy

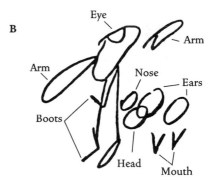

B

2.14   *Drawings by a patient with visual agnosia (A) Trying to copy an elephant. (B) Production when asked to draw a man. (From Luna, 1966)*

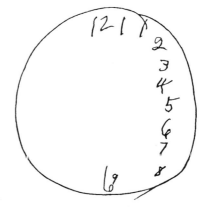

2.15   *Neglect syndrome   A patient with damage to the right parietal cortex was asked to draw a typical clock face. In his drawing the left side was ignored, but the patient still recalled the fact that all twelve numbers had to be displayed; the drawing shows how the patient resolved this dilemma. (From Rosenzweig & Leiman, 1989)*

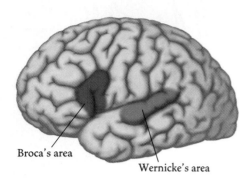

**2.16  Areas of the brain crucial for language**
*Many sites in the brain play a key role in the production and comprehension of language; in right-handed people, these sites are located in the left hemisphere, and are generally located at the lower edge of the frontal lobe and the upper edge of the temporal lobe. Broca's area has long been thought to play a central role in the production of speech (and is alongside of areas that control the speech muscles—see Figure 2.12). Wernicke's area plays a central role in the comprehension of speech (and is alongside of other areas that play a key part in audition—see Figure 2.13).*

becomes virtually unable to utter or write a word. In less severe cases, only a part of the normal vocabulary is lost, but the patient's speech becomes labored and fragmented since finding and articulating each word requires special effort.

A different pattern was associated with the so-called *fluent aphasias,* cases in which patients seem able to produce speech but do not understand what is said to them, though they usually answer anyway. Unlike patients with nonfluent aphasias, those with fluent aphasias talk freely and rapidly; but while they utter many words, they say very little. The sentences they produce are reasonably grammatical, but they are "word salad," largely composed of the little filler words that provide scant information. Fluent aphasias are usually associated with a brain site known as *Wernicke's area,* a region that borders on the auditory primary projection area, named after the nineteenth-century neurologist Carl Wernicke (see Figure 2.16).

This broad distinction—between disorders of production associated with damage to Broca's area and disorders of comprehension associated with damage to Wernicke's area—seems straightforward and nicely parallels the distinction between apraxia (a disorder of action) and agnosia (a disorder of perception). As in apraxia, fluent aphasia is not a problem with the muscles themselves; the patient can move her lips and tongue perfectly well. Instead, the problem is deeper—in producing language itself. Likewise, as in agnosia, nonfluent aphasia is not a sensory problem; there is nothing wrong with the patient's hearing. Instead, the problem lies in the ability to hear—and make sense of—that special stimulus we call "language."

Even with these parallels, however, it has become increasingly clear that this broad distinction does not really capture the nature (and the types) of aphasia. The reason is simple: Like every other mental activity, language use (whether for production or comprehension) involves the coordination of many different steps, many different processes. These include processes needed to "look up" word meanings in one's "mental dictionary," processes needed to figure out the structural relationships within a sentence, processes needed to integrate information gleaned about a sentence's structure with the meanings of the words within the sentence, and so on (see Chapter 9). Since each of these individual processes relies on its own set of brain pathways, damage to those pathways disrupts the process. As a result, the language loss observed in aphasia is often quite specific—with impairment to a particular processing step, followed by a disruption of all subsequent processes that depend on that step. In many cases, this disruption is primarily visible in language production (but not comprehension); in other cases, it is primarily visible in language comprehension (but not production); and in still other cases, the disruption is visible in both activities (see Cabezo & Nyberg, 2000; Peterson et al., 1988; Kimura & Watson, 1989; Demonet, Wise, & Frackowiak, 1993; Habib, Demonet, & Frackowiak, 1996, Kimura & Watson, 1989; Peterson, fox, Posner, Mintun, & Raichle).

*Aphasia and Sign Language*   We have suggested that aphasia is not really a matter of "speaking" or "hearing." Instead, aphasia is the result of disruption in specific processing steps needed for language use. On this view, aphasia should be observed in all of the languages of the world, including those that involve neither speaking nor hearing. For example, what happens to congenitally deaf people who suffer a stroke in the left hemisphere? Many of these persons communicate through sign languages, which are as complex and sophisticated as any of their vocal counterparts (see Chapter 9; Klima & Bellugi, 1979). How is a sign language affected by left-hemisphere brain damage?

The general finding is that, in these cases, the deaf individuals show sign-language deficits that correspond closely to the spoken-language deficits observed in hearing persons. Thus, it appears that the left-hemisphere lesions that produce the aphasias of spoken language affect some mental function that is not specific to the ear-mouth channel. Instead, these lesions seem to disrupt human language itself, no matter what its form. Apparently, then, language depends on some cerebral machinery that is pretty much the same whether the language is produced by tongue and mouth or by hands and fingers (Bellugi, Poizner, & Klima, 1983; Bear et al., 1996; Mayeux & Kandel, 1991).

*Dyslexias*  Dyslexia refers to any reading difficulty not associated with obvious problems such as bad eyesight. Dyslexias occur more often in boys and among left-handed individuals. Common dyslexias include the inability to name letters, to read words or sentences, or to recognize words directly even though they can be sounded out. Each kind of dyslexia may reflect different deficits such as in speech-sound processing or memory for word meanings. Likewise, the different dyslexias are probably associated with different brain regions, and most theories focus on nonprimary areas in the frontal and temporal lobes (Galaburda, 1994; Rosenzweig, Lieman, et al., 1996; see also Shaywitz et al., 1995). Recent studies have linked several forms of dyslexia to genetic markers (Grigorenko, 2001; Grigorenko et al., 1997; Grigorenko, Wood, Meyer, & Pauls, 2000).

## DISORDERS OF PLANNING AND SOCIAL COGNITION

Earlier, we referred to the famous case of Phineas Gage. After his head was shot through by the tamping iron, Gage could still speak and move fairly normally. But something subtler had changed. As the original medical report on Gage stated:

> He is fitful, irreverent, indulging at times in the grossest profanity (which was not previously his custom), manifesting but little deference for his fellows, impatient of restraint or advice when it conflicts with his desires, at times pertinaciously obstinate, yet capricious and vacillating, devising many plans of future operation, which are no sooner arranged than they are abandoned in turn for others appearing more feasible. Previous to his injury … he possessed a well-balanced mind … was energetic and persistent in executing all his plans of operation. In this regard his mind was radically changed, so decidedly that his friends and acquaintances said he was "no longer Gage." (Valenstein, 1986, p. 90)

Just what was different about Gage? It is now known that his problems were typical of what can occur when the frontmost part of the frontal lobe—the *prefrontal area*—is damaged. The prefrontal area is disproportionately large in primates, especially in humans. The effects of prefrontal damage vary, but a number of the same effects are found in many patients (Bradshaw, 2001; Lichter & Cummings, 2001; Milner & Petrides, 1984).

One central manifestation of prefrontal damage is a deficiency in response inhibition. Unable to use rules to control their behavior, patients often break them. This causes many problems for the patients, including difficulties in social interaction and in abiding by the law.

Depending upon the exact site of brain damage, these individuals may appear uninvolved, depressed, and apathetic. Alternatively, they may seem like psychopaths, acting flagrantly and crudely, being sexually promiscuous, and perhaps engaging in criminal conduct. In fact, one hypothesis about actual criminal psychopaths suggests that these individuals may suffer from subtle prefrontal damage (see Chapter 16).

For a time, especially during the 1940s and early 1950s, the effects of prefrontal damage were all too observable because surgery to disconnect the prefrontal areas—*prefrontal lobotomy*—was used to treat individuals with numerous kinds of mental disorders. Although some patients were helped considerably (see da Costa, 1997), the procedure was used indiscriminately, and the result was a cadre of patients—nearly twenty thousand in the United States alone—who were rendered docile but cognitively disabled (Valenstein, 1986). The procedure fell out of favor in the 1950s because of the introduction of drugs like Thorazine, which could control patients' behavior chemically rather than neurosurgically (Weinberger, Goldberg, & Tamminga, 1995; Jasper, 1995).

# DO WE REALLY HAVE TWO BRAINS?

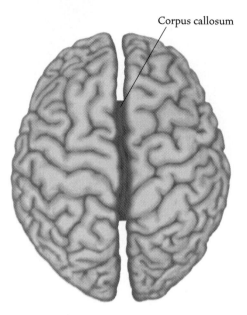

2.17 *The split brain* **To control otherwise intractable epilepsy, neurosurgeons sometimes sever the connections that link the two hemispheres. The largest connection is the corpus callosum. Here, the brain is shown as if viewed from above, the front of the head is at the top of the drawing.**

Corpus callosum

One striking feature of our brains is the dramatic cleavage between the two cerebral hemispheres, and we now know that many of the functions of the two hemisphere are different. This asymmetry of function is called *lateralization*, and its manifestations influence such diverse phenomena as language, spatial organization, and handedness—the superior dexterity of one hand over the other (Springer & Deutsch, 1998).

Despite their superficial similarity, both autopsies and neuroimaging studies show that the two cerebral hemispheres are actually different in both structure and function. Structurally, the convolutions have different patterns, and they develop differently as well, appearing much earlier in infancy on the left than the right. In addition, the portion of the temporal lobe that includes Wernicke's area is larger on the left side in most people. The left and right hemispheres differ in many other ways as well, such as in blood volume, the occipital lobe size, the concentrations of various hormones and other neurochemicals, and the microscopic wiring of their nerve cells (Geschwind & Galaburda, 1985; Geschwind & Levitsky, 1968; Kolb & Whishaw, 1996; Steinmetz, Volksmann, Jancke, & Freund, 1991).

Functionally, the overriding difference between the hemispheres involves language. It has already been noted that in right-handers, aphasia is usually associated with lesions in the left hemisphere. In right-handers, lesions in the corresponding sites in the right hemisphere often lead to difficulties in the comprehension of various aspects of space and form; in many tasks, right-handers with such lesions concentrate on details but cannot grasp the overall pattern.

The results are more ambiguous for the 12 percent or so of the population that are left-handed. About 70 percent of left-handers have speech predominantly lateralized in the left hemisphere; the other 30 percent divide equally between those whose language is represented in both hemispheres and those for whom language seems to be represented just in the right (Rasmussen & Milner, 1977). More generally, there seems to be less lat-

2.18 *A setup sometimes used in split-brain studies* **The participant fixates a center dot and then sees a picture or a word on the right or left side of the dot. He may be asked to respond verbally, by reading the word or naming the picture. He may also be asked to respond without words, for example, by picking out a named object from among a group spread out on a table and hidden from view, so that it can only be identified by touch. Because of the flow of visual information, the word "key" is visible only to the right hemisphere (and is shown on the right occipital lobe—the site of most visual processing). The right hemisphere, in turn, controls the left hand, and so it is with this hand that the participant picks up the key. (After Gazzaniga, 1967)**

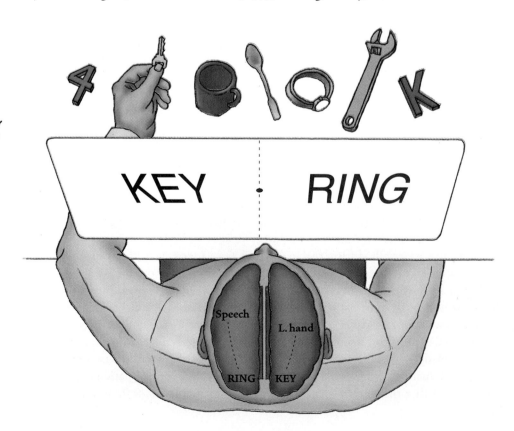

eralization in left-handers than in most right-handers. In line with this view, aphasia in left-handers is sometimes produced by lesions to either hemisphere. But, by the same token, left-handed aphasics have a greater chance for recovery, apparently because the intact hemisphere is better able to assume the responsibilities that formerly belonged to the damaged one (Brain, 1965; Springer & Deutsch, 1998).

## EVIDENCE FROM SPLIT BRAINS

In the normal, intact brain, the two hemispheres are connected by a massive bundle of nerve fibers called the *corpus callosum*. This structure allows the two halves of the brain to communicate so that they can pool their information and function collaboratively. In some cases of severe epilepsy, however, this neurological bridge (and some other subsidiary ones) is cut so that seizures will not spread from one hemisphere to the other (Bogen, Fisher, & Vogel, 1965; Wilson, Reeves, Gazzaniga, & Culver, 1977). Although the surgery relieves the suffering, it has a side effect: the two hemispheres of the brain are now functionally isolated from each other and in some ways act as two separate brains (see Figure 2.17; Gazzaniga, 1967; Sperry, 1974, 1982).

The effect of the split-brain operation is well demonstrated by tasks that pose a question to one hemisphere and require an answer from the other (see Figure 2.18). One method is to show a picture so that the message only reaches one hemisphere. This is done by flashing the picture for a fraction of a second to either the right or the left side of the patient's field of vision. The anatomical pathways of the visual system are such that if the picture is flashed to the right, it is processed by the left hemisphere; if presented to the left, it is processed by the right hemisphere (see Figure 2.19).

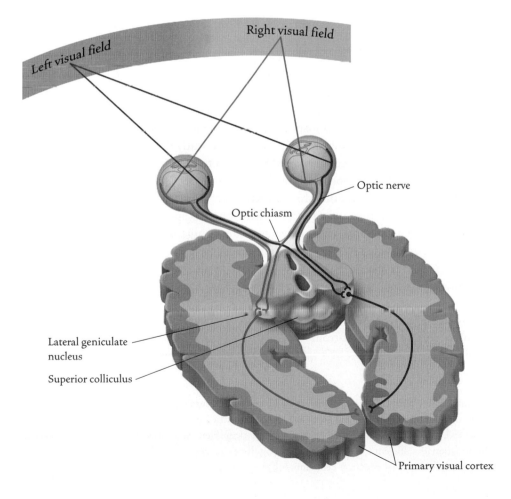

2-19 *Flow of visual information*  *Most of the fibers of the optic nerve pass through the lateral geniculate nucleus and project from there to the primary visual cortex in the occipital lobe. Notice that half of the fibers in the nerve cross from one side to the other; as a result, the left cerebral hemisphere receives visual information from the right side of space, and the right hemisphere receives visual information from the left side of space.*

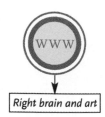

Right brain and art

When the picture is on the right, the patient is easily able to identify what he sees because the information is transmitted to the left hemisphere, which readily formulates a spoken response. The situation is different when the picture is flashed on the left. Now the image is sent to the right hemisphere; but this hemisphere can neither provide a spoken reply nor relay the information to the left hemisphere (which has the language capacity) because the bridge between the two has been cut (Gazzaniga, 1967).

These studies indicate that language is largely the province of the left hemisphere. But this does not mean that language is completely absent in the right hemisphere. A ready example is provided by a split-brain patient who was asked to identify an object in a picture (say, of a planter) that was flashed to the left side (that is, to the right hemisphere). He sometimes ventured a haphazard guess ("Coffee cup?") and then frowned or shook his head immediately afterward. The left hemisphere generated the guess, but the right hemisphere—which saw the object—had evidently understood the question well enough to know that the guess was wrong (Gazzaniga, 1967; for further discussion of right-hemisphere language abilities, see Zaidel, 1976, 1983; Gazzaniga, 1983; Levy, 1983).*

## THE NORMAL BRAIN: TWO MODES OF MENTAL FUNCTIONING

The preceding discussion indicates that language and spatial organization are usually handled in two different areas of the brain. Some psychologists believe that this difference in hemispheric localization coincides with a distinction between two fundamentally different modes of thought: one involving words, the other spatial processes. This distinction certainly accords with everyday observation. Although we often express our thoughts in words, we also mentally envision the world with little benefit from language. Many problems can be solved by either mode. We may find our way to a friend's home by referring to a mental map or by memorizing a verbal sequence such as "first right turn after the third traffic light." But the two modes are not always interchangeable. How a corkscrew works is hard to describe in words; the pros and cons of a political two-party system are impossible to convey without them. (For more on the distinction between words and images, see Chapter 8.)

For some theorists, the verbal-spatial distinction defines the difference in the functioning of the two cerebral hemispheres, with the left hemisphere the "linguist," and the right hemisphere the "map maker." This model neatly fits the fact that performance on various verbal tests is more impaired by lesions to the left hemisphere, while performance on spatial tests is more impaired by lesions to the right hemisphere (Levy, 1974). But other theorists suggest that the distinction between the hemispheres must be conceived differently. In their view, the right hemisphere is specialized for the organization of space, whereas the left hemisphere's specialty is organization in time. Thus, if language functions are found more in the left hemisphere, it is not because of a specialization for language per se. Rather, it is because language, like many other functions, depends crucially on precisely timed sequences of elements. The person who is insensitive to what comes first and what comes second cannot possibly speak or understand the speech of others. *Tap* is not the same word as *pat*, and the sentence "The dog bit the man" is crucially different from "The man bit the dog." To summarize this view, the

---

* Total split-brain procedures are rarely necessary anymore. Neurologists have found that cutting the front three-quarters of the corpus callosum is sufficient either to eliminate the seizures or make them amenable to medication. Interestingly, sparing the back quarter, which preserves the crossover of visual information, is sufficient to wipe out the usual cognitive changes associated with a "split brain" (Woiciechowsky, Vogel, Meyer, & Lehmann, 1997).

right hemisphere is more concerned with what goes where, the left more with what comes when (Bogen, 1969; Tzeng & Wang, 1984).

Although the space-versus-time hypothesis is rather speculative, it fits in well enough with the facts we have described in this chapter. The same is not true of many of the conceptions of hemispheric function written for the general public. Some authors go so far as to equate left-hemispheric function with Western science and right-hemispheric function with Eastern culture and mysticism. In the same vein, others have argued that Western societies overly encourage left-brained functions at the expense of right-brained functions and that we need to make a special effort to train the neglected right hemisphere (see, for example, Ornstein, 1977). One author recommends "Ten Ways to Develop Your Right Brain," one of which involves drowning out the presentation of information with music (Prince, 1978, cited in Springer & Deutsch, 1998). There is, however, no persuasive evidence for any of these popular claims. In many cases, the distinctions being proposed—between the rational and the intuitive, the analytic and the artistic, or the Western and Eastern philosophies of life—are not so clear cut. In other cases, the distinctions fit badly with, or go wildly beyond, the available evidence (Efron, 1990; Levy, 1985).

These popular misconceptions are particularly misleading when they imply that the two cerebral hemispheres, each with its own talents and strategies, endlessly vie for control of our mental life. Instead, each of us has a single brain. Each part of the brain (and not just the cerebral hemispheres) is quite differentiated and so contributes its own specialized abilities to the activity of the whole. But in the end, the complex, sophisticated skills that we each display depend on the whole brain and on the coordinated actions of all its components. Our hemispheres are not cerebral competitors. Instead, they pool their specialized capacities to produce a seamlessly integrated, single mental self.

# BUILDING BLOCKS OF THE NERVOUS SYSTEM: NEURONS AND NERVE IMPULSES

We now have some understanding of the general structures of the nervous system and how they function. How do these structures accomplish their tasks? To answer this question we must first look at the building blocks of which the system is composed— the individual *neurons* and the *nerve impulses* by which they communicate. We will now drop down to this cellular level, discussing the kinds of circuitry that can result from interactions among different nerve cells and the neurochemistry that makes such interactions possible. Along the way, we will show how the analysis of this circuitry has begun to help us understand some aspects of mental illness, the effects of drugs, and the effects of and recovery from brain damage.

## THE NEURON

The neuron is a single cell with three subdivisions: the *dendrites*, the *cell body* (or *soma*), and the *axon* (see Figure 2.20). The dendrites are usually branched, sometimes so much that they resemble a thick, Medusa-like bush. The axon, which extends like a wispy thread, may fork out into several *axonal branches* at its end. The dendrites receive nerve impulses from other neurons; the axon transmits that impulse.

Neurons are very small. Cell bodies vary from 5 to about 100 microns in diameter (1 micron = $^1/_{1,000}$ millimeter). The average hair on your head, in contrast, has a diame-

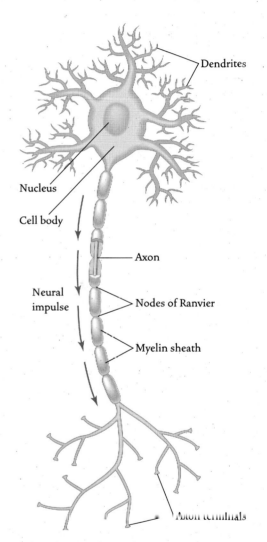

**2.20 The neuron** *A schematic diagram of the main parts of a motoneuron. Part of the cell is myelinated; that is, its axon is covered with sets of segmented, insulating sheaths formed by encircling glial cells.*

ter of about 100 microns. Dendrites are typically short, say a few hundred microns. But, as we will see, axons can be much longer.

The easiest neuron to describe is the motor neuron, or *motoneuron* (Figure 2.20). It provides an efferent pathway that begins within the CNS, exits through the spinal cord or a cranial nerve, winds up on a muscle fiber, and makes that muscle fiber contract. The axon of the motoneuron transmits the nerve impulse initiated at its dendrites to the muscle fiber and, at this *neuromuscular junction*, produces a chemical that triggers the fiber's contraction. Some motoneuron axons are quite long, extending from the head to the base of the spinal cord, others from the spinal cord to the limbs. Our longest axons run from our spinal cords to our legs; these are about a meter long (in the blue whale, the axons to the tail are up to 32 meters long). To get a sense of the cell body relative to the axon in such a motoneuron, imagine a basketball attached to a garden hose that stretches the whole fourteen-mile length of Manhattan.

The muscle contractions initiated by motoneurons are but one kind of efferent control. Other efferent neurons control the endocrine and digestive glands or the smooth muscle fibers that surround the digestive tract and blood vessels.

Still other neurons convey information inward, keeping the nervous system informed about both the external world and the body's internal environment. Some of these are afferent neurons attached to specialized receptor cells that respond to various external energies such as pressure, chemical changes, light, and so on. These receptor cells translate (more technically, *transduce*) these physical stimuli into electrical changes, which then trigger a nervous impulse in other neurons (see Figure 2.21).

Neurons that convey impulses from receptors toward the rest of the nervous system are called *sensory neurons*. Sometimes the receptor is actually a specialized part of the sensory neuron, as in the neurons that are responsible for sensing pressure on the skin. But in many cases, transduction and transmission are separate functions that are entrusted to different cells. In vision and hearing, for example, receptor cells transduce optical stimulation and air pressure, respectively, into electrical changes in the cell, which in turn trigger impulses in sensory neurons that then proceed through the nervous system.

So far we have discussed two kinds of neurons: those that trigger some action (such as the motoneurons) and those that receive information (the sensory neurons). This is consistent with Descartes' simple stimulus-response conception of reflex action (see pp. 42–43), which works well enough for simple actions like knee jerks and eye blinks.

But more complex behavior needs more complex neural circuitry, and indeed the pathways that carry our sensations and produce our actions are typically indirect. In fact, in complex organisms the vast majority of nerve cells are neither sensory neurons nor motoneurons. Rather, they are *interneurons*, neurons that are interposed between

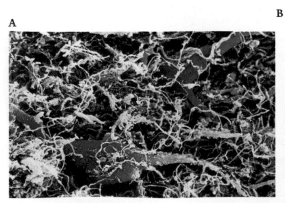
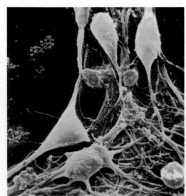
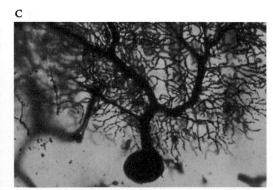

**2.21   *Different kinds of neurons*   It is important to remember that while the text discusses the structure of a motoneuron, neurons actually come in a variety of shapes and sizes. Pictured here are neurons from (A) the spinal cord (stained in red), (B) the cerebral cortex, and (C) the cerebellum.**

two or more other neurons. Interneurons vary widely in both form and function. They often show considerable branching, which produces an enormous number of contacts among different neurons.

In the vast majority of cases, these interneurons transmit their message to yet other interneurons, and these send theirs to still other interneurons. Typically, many thousands of such interneurons must interact before the command is finally issued and sent down the path of the efferent nerve fibers. These interneuronal connections form the *microcircuitry* of the central nervous system. The microcircuitry is where the brain conducts most of its information processing, and the bulk of the brain structures we have reviewed consist of just such microcircuitry.

## GLIAL CELLS: UNSUNG HEROES OF THE NERVOUS SYSTEM

Besides neurons, nervous systems are also full of *glial cells* (from the Greek word for "glue"). In fact, glial cells constitute half of all brain cells, and in some areas of the brain they outnumber neurons by ten to one (Shepherd, 1994). Their functions are crucial to neuronal communication. To begin with, they act as guidewires for growing neurons, much like beanpoles that guide bean shoots in the garden. Later in development, they provide a supportive scaffolding for mature neurons and assist in the repair process when brain tissue is damaged.

Yet another function of glial cells is to increase the speed at which neurons can communicate. The specialized glial cells that accomplish this—found only in vertebrates, which move much faster than invertebrates—are mostly made of the fatty substance known as *myelin*. Beginning shortly after birth, they spiral and wrap their fatty tentacles around neurons that have long axons, such as those that proceed from distant sensory organs or travel to distant muscles. Each spiral creates a myelin "wrapper" around a portion of the axon, and soon the entire length of the axon is covered by a succession of these wrappers. As we will see, the uncoated gaps between the wrappers—the *nodes of Ranvier*—are crucial in speeding up the nerve impulses traveling along these myelinated axons (see Figure 2.22).

The fact that myelin is white explains why brains are made up of both white and gray matter. What anatomists call *white matter* is the myelinated axons traversing long distances either within the brain or to and from the body (hence the need for speed). Conversely, *gray matter* consists of cell bodies, dendrites, and unmyelinated axons and the interneurons that comprise the nervous system's microcircuitry.

All of these functions portray glial cells as constituting a relatively passive support system for the neurons in the brain. Recent evidence, however, is changing this view dramatically. It suggests that glial cells may constitute a second, slow signaling system within the brain. Glial cells are known to be responsive to various electrical, chemical, and mechanical stimuli. They also form networks that communicate with each other using slow internal voltage changes, these changes modulating the activities of neurons nearby. The extent to which glial-cell networks interact with neuronal networks in various brain functions has not yet been determined, but it may be considerable (Gallo & Chitajallu, 2001; Ilno et al., 2001; Newman & Zahs, 1998; Verkhratsky, 1998).

## HOW THE NERVOUS SYSTEM MAKES ITS OWN CIRCUITRY

Within the huge complexity of the brain, it is crucial that each neuron send its neuronal messages to the right targets so that, at the coarsest level, information intended to move the leg does not halt digestion instead. The primary projection areas on the surface of

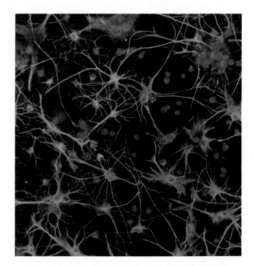

**2.22  Glial cells**  *Glial cells from a rabbit brain.*

the cortex, by themselves, suggest an exquisite mapping of pathways between the brain and the body, and connections within the brain require even more precise navigation. How does each developing neuron come to know its eventual target? How do the micro-circuits that do the brain's information processing organize themselves?

Nerve cells have their origin in the *neural stem cells* lining the neural tube. These cells reproduce rapidly and give rise to other cells that will go on to form neurons and the cells that support them. The fledgling neuronal cells migrate to key areas in the brain-to-be, and, under the influence of various chemicals called *neurotrophic factors*, they differentiate into different kinds of neurons by sprouting axons and dendrites. Some of the budding axons attach themselves to glial-cell guidewires and follow them—at a rate of up to a millimeter per day—to the far reaches of the brain, where they attach themselves to distant neurons. Interneurons proliferate and interconnect. This budding and connecting of neurons occur in spurts as the embryo develops, with wave after wave of axon proliferation interspersed with periods of microcircuitry construction.

All these developmental mechanisms are under genetic control, although they can be distorted by influences like alcohol and other drugs or poor maternal nutrition. They are also affected by normal influences such as circulating hormones generated either by the mother or the fetus itself. For example, testosterone rewires certain parts of the brain according to a masculine pattern, while its absence leads to a feminized wiring pattern. These sex-dependent parts of the brain affect subsequent sexual orientation and reproductive behavior.

This complexity undoubtedly produces wiring errors, but they are minimized through competition among neurons. Many more neurons are created than are needed, and each neuron tries to form far more connections than are required. If a neuron's connections prove either wrong or redundant, that neuron must either withdraw its connections and find suitable targets or be given a message to die (Edelman, 1987; Kolb & Whishaw, 2001; Kuan, Roth, Flavell, & Rakic, 2000; Rubenstein & Rakic, 1999).

It is normal for between 20 and 80 percent of neurons to die as the brain develops, depending upon the region of the brain. This decimation occurs early in development—in humans, about four to six months after conception (Rosenzweig et al., 1999). But this is not to say that the brain is "done" by birth. The connections among the neurons still remain to be wired. Connections are formed and destroyed at an astounding rate in the infant—up to 100,000 per second, according to some estimates (Rakic, 1995). Many connections have yet to be made. For example, in humans the connections within Broca's area show dramatic growth around the age of two, a spurt that coincides with a burst of language ability. Yet another example is the wiring of the pre-frontal areas, whose connections may not be complete until age thirty.

## THE ELECTRICAL ACTIVITY OF THE NEURON

### NEURONAL COMMUNICATION

Neurons communicate by receiving and transmitting nerve impulses. Just how do they do this? How do they transmit signals, influence each other, and cause us to sense, to think, to act? We now know that they do so electrically and chemically. The unraveling of this mystery was hard-won. It required advances both in our knowledge of the anatomy of neurons and in the measurement of tiny quantities of electrical current—the movements of charged particles. One crucial advance was in the production of ever finer microelectrodes, some of which have tips so small (less than 1 micron in diameter) that they can puncture a neuron without squashing it and detect weak electrical currents without disrupting them. A related advance was the invention of a device that could display tiny currents that the microelectrodes could now detect. This device was the *oscilloscope*, which could amplify weak electrical fluctuations and depict them as wavy lines on a fluorescent screen. Every bit as important a contribution was made by natural selection. It gave us the squid, an animal endowed with several giant axons up to 1 millimeter in diameter, which—compared to the smaller neurons found in most other species—could be poked, prodded, and measured much more easily.

## NEURONAL POTENTIALS: THE RESTING AND ACTION POTENTIALS

The neuron is, in most respects, just a cell. It has a nucleus on the inside and a cell membrane that defines its perimeter. In the middle is a biochemical stew of ions, amino acids, proteins, DNA and RNA, and so forth, as well as a collection of smaller structures like Golgi bodies and mitochondria. What makes the neuron a neuron, though, is the peculiarity of its cell membrane. It is irritable. Poke it, shake it, stimulate it electrically or chemically, and the neuronal membrane may destabilize, producing a cascade of changes that form the nerve impulse—that is, make the cell fire. Some neurons even fire on their own, at regular intervals, and seem to act as pacemakers for behavior such as wing flapping, breathing, and sleeping-waking (on this, see Chapter 3). Whether elicited or self-induced, it is this irritability that makes neurons the fast communicators of the nervous system.

Figure 2.23 shows how the neuron's irritability and its effects are studied. Two microelectrodes are used, one inserted into a nerve axon and the other contacting its outer surface. In this manner, any electrical activity near the cell membrane can be detected. As it turns out, there is activity even when the cell is not firing, as shown by a voltage difference between the inside and the outside of the fiber. Like a miniature battery with a positive and a negative connection, the inside of the axon is electrically negative with respect to the outside, with the difference measuring about −70 or so millivolts (a stan-

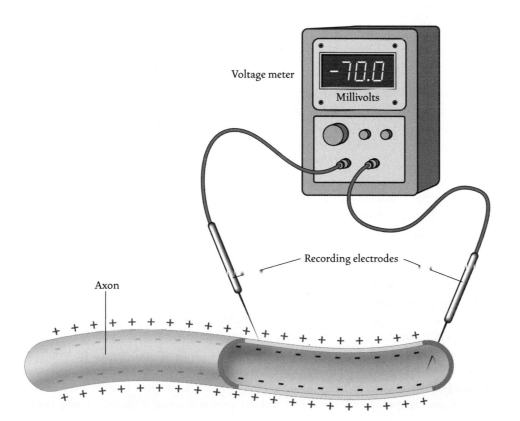

Voltage meter

-70.0

Millivolts

Recording electrodes

Axon

2.23 *Recording the voltage within a neuron* **A schematic drawing of how the impulse is recorded. One electrode is inserted into the axon; the other records from the axon's outside.** (After Carlson, 1986)

2.24    *The action potential*    **Action potential
recorded from the squid's giant axon. (After
Hodgkin & Huxley, 1939)**

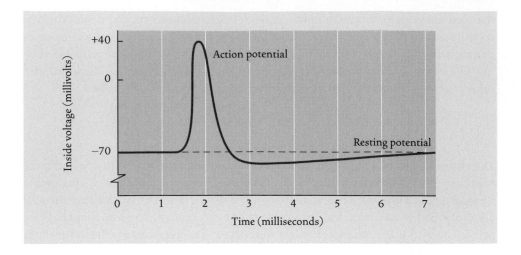

dard AA battery, at 1.5 volts, has over twenty times this voltage). Because this small
negative voltage occurs when the neuron is stable, it has traditionally been called the
neuron's **resting potential**, although, as we shall see, maintaining this voltage takes
work, and in its stable state the neuron is anything but at rest.

What happens when the neuron is irritated and is made to fire? To find out, neuroscientists stimulate the surface of the fiber by means of a third microelectrode, which
applies a brief electrical pulse. This pulse reduces the voltage difference across the membrane. If the pulse is weak, nothing further will happen and the membrane will work to
restore itself to its usual −70 millivolt charge. But if the pulse is strong enough to push
the voltage difference past a critical **excitation threshold** (about −55 millivolts in mammals), something dramatic happens. The voltage difference between the inside and outside of the cell abruptly collapses to zero and, in fact, begins to reverse itself. The inside
of the membrane no longer shows a negative voltage compared to the outside but
instead suddenly swings positive, up to +40 millivolts. This marks the neuron's destabilization, a cataclysm that completely disrupts the cell's membrane. Fortunately, the
chaos is short-lived; the membrane restabilizes itself within about 1 millisecond and
returns to its −70 millivolt state. This entire destabilization-restabilization sequence is
called the **action potential** (Figure 2.24).

*Explaining Neuronal Potentials*    The resting and action potentials are the key to
explaining nearly all neuronal communication. What creates them? Neurobiologists
have concluded that they derive from chemical processes at the neuron's membrane as
well as from the structure of the membrane itself. It turns out that there are electrically
charged particles (ions) dissolved in the fluid both inside and outside the neuronal
membrane. In general, ions are defined as molecules (or single atoms) that have lost or
gained electrons and have thus acquired a positive or negative charge. The membrane
controls which ions are allowed to remain inside the neuron and which ones are shoved
outside. It does this using biochemical portholes, known as **ion channels**, that let certain ions pass through, as well as **ion pumps** that suck ions in or push them out.

It appears that two kinds of ions are crucial for the resting and action potentials:
sodium and potassium. Sodium ions are found mostly outside the neuron and potassium ions mostly inside. When the membrane is stable, positively charged sodium ions
are continually pumped from the inside of the membrane to the outside and kept there,
whereas potassium ions are free to enter or leave the cell. The result is an excess of positively charged ions on the outside, which accounts for much of the voltage difference
known as the resting potential—negative on the inside and positive on the outside (see
Figure 2.25). Maintaining this stable state takes constant work because the membrane
is leaky and the pumps are imperfect. Indeed, probably most of the metabolic energy

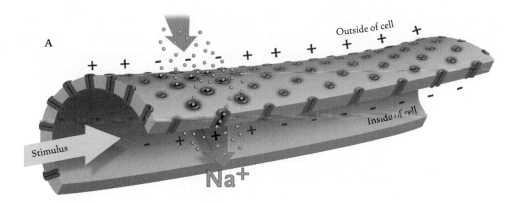

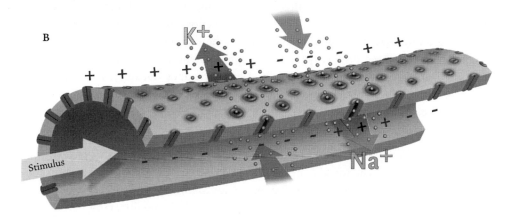

**2.25  Ion channels and the action potential**
*(A) When a stimulus is above threshold, special ion channels of the membrane open, and positively charged sodium ions (Na⁺) surge inside. (B) Immediately thereafter, the gates that admitted Na⁺ close, and the electrical balance is restored, because some other positively charged ions—specifically potassium ions (K⁺)—are now forced out. The whole process is repeated at an adjacent point in the axon. (After Starr & Taggart, 1989)*

used by the brain is expended on maintaining these so-called resting potentials (Rosenzweig et al., 1996).

When the membrane is sufficiently irritated (by reducing the voltage difference to the threshold, for instance), the sodium channels spring open temporarily. Sodium ions flood in, forcing out some potassium ions a moment later. This short-lived excess of positively charged particles on the inside of the membrane produces the positive voltage swing of the action potential. But immediately afterward, the membrane begins to restore itself to stability. The pumps resume their evacuation of sodium to the outside of the neuron, and the gates slam shut to keep it out; meanwhile, potassium ions begin to seep back into the neuron. The result is the resumption of the membrane's stability and the restoration of the resting potential.

*Propagation of the Action Potential*  These electrochemical events explain what happens at a single region of the membrane. Why, then, does this excitation spread to neighboring regions? The reason is that the temporarily positive voltage inside the axon induces the opening of ion channels at adjacent regions, which themselves induce more distant channels to open, and so on. The upshot of this domino-like process is that the impulse—the cascade of events that creates the action potential—moves down the entire length of the axon and throughout the rest of the neuron as well. This is known as the *propagation* of the action potential. The whole thing is like a spark traveling along a fuse except that whereas the fuse is consumed by the spark, the ion channels rapidly reclose and the membrane restores itself within milliseconds. As a consequence, the neuron is soon ready to fire again, and if an above-threshold stimulus is still present, then fire it will (Figure 2.26).

At the microscopic level, the chain reaction that produces the propagation of the action potential seems fairly fast, but it actually travels at a rate of only about 1 meter per second—about average walking speed. If this was the fastest that action potentials could propagate, then all our actions would slow to a crawl and faster-paced acts like

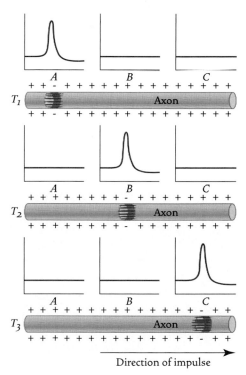

**2.26  The action potential as it travels along the axon**  *The axon is shown at three different moments—T₁, T₂, and T₃—after the application of a stimulus. The voltage inside the membrane is shown at three different points along the axon—A, B, and C. (After Carlson, 1986)*

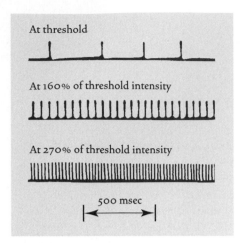

**2.27   Stimulus intensity and firing frequency**
**Responses of a crab axon to a continuous**
**electric current at three levels of current**
**intensity. The time scale is relatively slow. As a**
**result, the action potentials show up as single**
**vertical lines or "spikes." Note that while**
**increasing the current intensity has no effect on**
**the height of the spikes (the all-or-none law) it**
**leads to a marked increase in the frequency of**
**spikes per second. (After Eccles, 1973)**

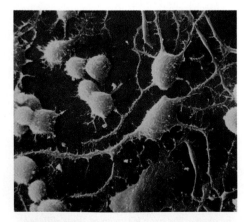

*Interaction among nerve cells   An isolated*
*nerve cell. The cell body is in contact with other*
*cells through numerous extensions. The figure*
*illustrates how nerve fibers cross each other to*
*form an elaborate network.*

speaking and jumping would simply be impossible. Enter the nodes of Ranvier, which, as we mentioned, are the spaces between the glial-cell tentacles that wrap axons with myelin. On these myelinated axons, only the nodes must be destabilized; thus the changes that produce the action potential can skip from node to node. Myelinated axons can propagate their action potentials at speeds up to 120 meters per second (about 260 miles per hour).

The importance of intact myelin is underscored by the deficits suffered when myelination breaks down in the brain. This happens in ***multiple sclerosis (MS)***, a disease in which the body's immune system mistakenly regards the brain's myelin as an intruder and attacks it. The manifestations of MS are highly variable but can include blindness, numbness, and paralysis.

*All-or-None Law*   Once a stimulus is strong enough to destabilize the neuronal membrane, an action potential will propagate. The action potential will be the same size and will be propagated just as rapidly, whether the stimulus just meets threshold or exceeds it by two, three, or twenty times. This phenomenon is sometimes referred to as the ***all-or-none law***. Just as pounding on a car horn does not make it any louder, a stronger stimulus does not produce a stronger action potential. A neuron either fires or does not fire. It knows no in-between.*

*Stimulus Intensity*   Neurons obey the all-or-none law, and stimulus intensity has no effect once the excitation threshold is exceeded. How can we reconcile this fact with our everyday experience? The world is not just black and white, and sounds are not simply on or off. We can obviously see shades of gray (not to mention colors) and tell the difference between the buzz of a mosquito and the roar of a jet engine. How can this be? There are two answers.

First, more intense stimuli can excite greater numbers of neurons. This is because different neurons vary enormously in their excitation thresholds. As a result, a weak stimulus will stimulate all neurons whose thresholds are below a given level, while a strong stimulus will stimulate all of those plus others whose threshold is higher.

The second mechanism applies to individual neurons. When bombarded with a sustained stimulus, most neurons do not just fire once and retire. Instead, they generate a whole stream, or "volley," of action potentials by means of repeated cycles of destabilization and restabilization. In accordance with the all-or-none principle, the size of each of the action potentials remains the same; what changes is the impulse frequency—the stronger the stimulus, the more often the axon will fire. This effect holds until we reach a maximum rate of firing, after which further increases in intensity have no effect (see Figure 2.27). Different neurons have different maximum rates, with the highest in humans on the order of 1,000 impulses per second.

# INTERACTION AMONG NERVE CELLS

## THE SYNAPSE

Neurons are not soloists; they are ensemble players. How do they interact? We can begin with the simplest illustration of such interaction—the reflex. From Descartes on, it was widely believed that reflexes were formed from a long and essentially continuous strand of nervous tissue—in essence, along one neuron. According to this view, the

---

* The all-or-none law holds for the action potential—that is, for conduction along the axon. As we will see shortly, however, the situation is different at the dendrites and cell body, where potentials are graded, being built up or lowered in a continuous rather than an all-or-none fashion.

incoming sensory information triggers a response at one end of this neuron, and then the response is initiated at the other end of the same neuron. But there was a major problem: various studies showed that the time it took from sensation to response (roughly one-fifth of a second) was too long for the route to be direct. The neurons could not be acting like electrical wires because electrical transmission was nearly instantaneous. By the end of the nineteenth century, therefore, most observers were convinced that the neurons must be communicating across some kind of gap. This gap, together with the membranes of the neurons that form it, is called the *synapse*. Once hypothetical, the synapse was confirmed microscopically in 1888 by Spanish neurologist Santiago Ramón y Cajal, who observed synapses in the spinal cord and elsewhere, and called these conjunctions—poetically—"protoplasmic kisses,...the final ecstasy of an epic love story."

Ramón could not guess what the synapse contained, but it was clear what the synapse had to explain. It had to account for various phenomena that emerged from studies of reflexes in dogs, cats, and monkeys conducted by English physiologist Charles Sherrington (1857–1952). First, Sherrington had observed that although a reflex response (such as a limb jerk to mild shock) might not be elicited by a single stimulus, several presentations of the same stimulus might suffice to elicit it. This process, whereby the effects of stimulation accumulate over time, is now called **temporal summation**. Sherrington also found that a reflex response was more likely to be elicited if the animal was stimulated concurrently in several places on its skin rather than just one, a process we now call **spatial summation**.

Finally, Sherrington noted how the limbs have many antagonistic muscle groups that produce opposite actions. For example, in humans the biceps contracts the arm, but the triceps extends it. These muscles usually do not operate independently; normally, when we contract our biceps, the triceps relaxes automatically, and vice versa. This is obviously helpful—there is no point in the muscles working against each other. But Sherrington found that stimulation of a flexor muscle actually made the extensor muscle "extrarelaxed," more relaxed even than when in its normal rest state. From this, Sherrington deduced that the neurons controlling each muscle must have two sets of inputs, some that are excitatory (to produce contractions) and some that are inhibitory (producing superrelaxed states). Thanks to these dual inputs and to the appropriate wiring of the nervous system, the activation of either muscle can actively inhibit the other, and this **reciprocal inhibition** turns out to be crucial in understanding how neurons communicate where they join at the synapse (see Figure 2.28). It was through this mechanism, Sherrington realized, that the effect of a positive (excitatory) influence can be weakened, neutralized, or even reversed by a negative (inhibitory) one.

## THE SYNAPTIC MECHANISM

What at the synapse could account for all these effects? Sherrington and his contemporaries could only guess at the specific mechanism that governs transmission at the synapse. They proposed that neurons communicate with their neighbors via a chemical substance released when the neural impulse reaches the end of the axon. This assumption proved correct, and thanks to developments in electron microscopy and cellular physiology, we now know a lot more about the way in which this transmission occurs.

Let us begin by distinguishing between the **presynaptic neuron**—the cell that sends the message—and the **postsynaptic neuron**—the one that receives it. The actual transmission process begins in the tiny knoblike **axon terminals** of the presynaptic neuron. Within these swellings are numerous tiny sacs, or **synaptic vesicles** ("little vessels"), which are like water balloons filled with neurotransmitters. When the presynaptic neuron fires, some of the vesicles literally burst and eject their contents through the termi-

*Sir Charles Sherrington*

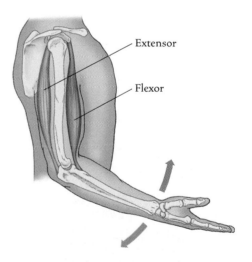

Extensor

Flexor

**2.28 An example of muscle antagonists** *The figure shows how the members of a flexor-extensor pair (biceps and triceps) oppose each other in flexing and extending the forearm. When the flexor contracts (to bend the elbow) the extensor is inhibited, to ensure that it provides no resistance to the flexor. When the extensor contracts (to straighten the elbow) the flexor is inhibited.*

nal's membrane into the *synaptic gap* that separates the two cells. The transmitter molecules then diffuse across this gap and impinge upon the *postsynaptic membrane* (see Figures 2.29 and 2.30A and B). Usually the postsynaptic membrane is part of a dendrite, but it can also be a cell body or even another axon.

Once across the synaptic gap, the transmitters activate specialized molecular receptors in the postsynaptic membrane.* When one of these receptors is activated, it opens or closes certain ion channels in the membrane. For example, some neurotransmitters open the channels to sodium ions. As these ions enter the postsynaptic cell, the voltage difference maintained across

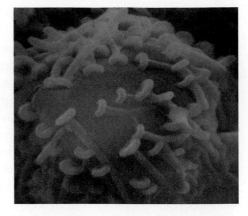

**2.29   The synapse**   *Electron micrograph of the knoblike axon terminals, which contain the synaptic vesicles.*

the membrane is decreased (that is, it shifts in the direction of zero volts), rendering that part of the membrane less stable (see Figure 2.30C and D). As more and more transmitter molecules cross at the synapse, they activate more and more receptors, opening more and more channels, which further reduces the voltage difference. These effects accumulate and spread along the membrane of the postsynaptic neuron. When the voltage difference is reduced enough, the excitation threshold is reached, the action potential is triggered, and the impulse speeds down the postsynaptic cell's axon.

A similar mechanism accounts for inhibition. At some synapses, the presynaptic cell liberates transmitter substances that produce an increased voltage difference across the membrane of the postsynaptic neuron. The heightened voltage difference acts to fortify the membrane against other, destabilizing influences. Since most neurons have synap-

* In contemporary neuroscience, the term *receptor* is used both at the cellular level (referring to neurons that transduce a physical stimulus) and at the molecular level (referring to the synaptic receptors described here).

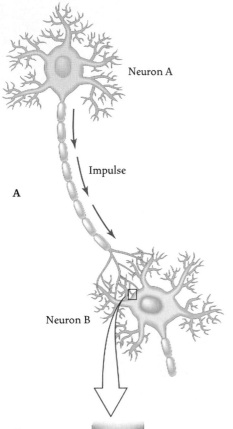

Neuron A

A

Impulse

Neuron B

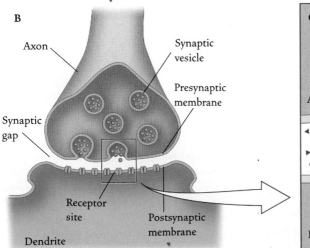

B

Axon

Synaptic vesicle

Presynaptic membrane

Synaptic gap

Receptor site

Postsynaptic membrane

Dendrite

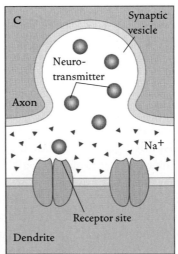

C

Synaptic vesicle

Neurotransmitter

Axon

Na+

Receptor site

Dendrite

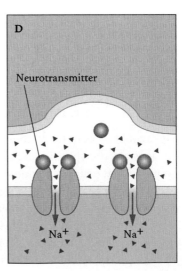

D

Neurotransmitter

Na+      Na+

**2.30**   *Schematic view of synaptic transmission*   **(A) Neuron A transmits a message through synaptic contact with neuron B. (B) The events in the axon knob. (C) The vesicle is released, and neurotransmitter molecules are ejected toward the postsynaptic membrane. (D) Neurotransmitter molecules settle on the receptor site, an ion channel opens, and Na+ floods in. (After Bloom, Lazerson, & Hofstadter, 1988)**

tic connections with neurons that excite them as well as with others that inhibit them, the response of a given postsynaptic cell depends on a final tally of the excitatory and inhibitory "yeas" and "nays" that act upon it. If the net value is excitatory and if this value exceeds the threshold, the cell will fire.

These synaptic mechanisms readily account for Sherrington's discovery that conduction within neurons is governed by different principles than conduction between neurons. Within neurons, conduction occurs via action potentials, which are all-or-none. Between neurons, conduction depends upon levels of neurotransmitters that can accumulate gradually with repeated or concurrent stimulation; and it is this accumulation that lies behind temporal summation, with multiple inputs, arriving across time, adding their effects. Most neurons also receive inputs from many presynaptic cells—in the brain, often from a thousand or more. Thus, the synapse serves as the common final path for all these presynaptic signals, a gathering point at which these inputs can accumulate. This provides a ready account of spatial summation.

What happens to the transmitter molecules after they have affected the postsynaptic neuron? It would not do just to leave them where they are because they might continue to exert their effects long after the presynaptic neuron had stopped firing, thus making any input permanent. There are two mechanisms that prevent such mishaps. First, some transmitters are inactivated shortly after they have been discharged by special "cleanup" enzymes that break them up into their chemical components. More commonly, though, neurotransmitters are not destroyed, but reused. In this process, called *synaptic reuptake*, used neurotransmitter molecules are ejected from the postsynaptic receptors, vacuumed by molecular pumps back into the presynaptic axon terminals, and repackaged into new synaptic vesicles.

These two mechanisms for removing transmitter molecules from the synapse are fast. But, in some cases, the postsynaptic neuron can be bombarded so rapidly with bursts of neurotransmitter that the mechanisms of enzymatic cleanup and reuptake are momentarily overwhelmed. Such rapid-fire stimulation results in a temporary accumulation of neurotransmitter, and it is this that underlies the process of temporal summation.

## NEUROTRANSMITTERS

On the face of it, one might think that the nervous system only needs two transmitters: one excitatory, the other inhibitory. But nature, as is often the case, turns out to be exceedingly generous because in fact there are a great number of different transmitter substances. About a hundred or so have been isolated thus far, and many more are sure to be discovered.

We will mention just a few of these neurotransmitters here. *Acetylcholine (ACh)* is released at many synapses and at the neuromuscular junction (itself a kind of synapse); the release of ACh makes muscle fibers contract. *Serotonin (5HT*, after its formula *5-hydroxy-tryptamine*) is a transmitter that is involved in many of the mechanisms of sleep, mood, and arousal. *Glutamate* is a critical neurotransmitter in the retina of the eye and appears to be important for long-term memory as well as for the perception of pain. *GABA* (or, to give its full name, *gamma-amino butyric acid*) is the most widely distributed inhibitory transmitter of the CNS. Still others are *norepinephrine (NE)* and *dopamine (DA)*, which will be important in later discussions of drug effects and certain mental disorders (see Chapters 3, 16, and 17).

Individual neurons are very selective in what neurotransmitters they will respond to, and one attempt to understand this selectivity is the *lock-and-key model* of transmitter action. This theory proposes that transmitter molecules will only affect the postsynaptic membrane if the molecule's shape fits into certain synaptic receptor molecules much as a key must fit into a lock. But the mere fact that a given molecule fits into the receptor is not enough to qualify it as a transmitter. The key must not just fit into the lock; it

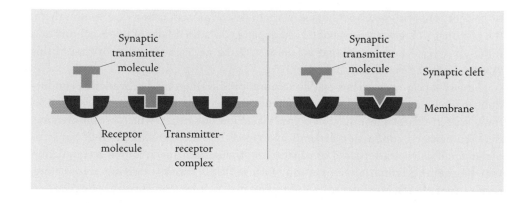

**2.31   Lock-and-key model of synaptic transmission**   *Transmitter molecules will only affect the postsynaptic membrane if their shape fits the shape of certain receptor molecules in that membrane, much as a key has to fit into a lock. The diagram shows two kinds of transmitters and their appropriate receptors. (After Rosenzweig & Leiman, 1982)*

*Curare, the black widow's venom, and paralysis (A) This Cofan man from Colombia is using a curare-tipped dart to hunt. The curare acts as an acetylcholine antagonist: it inhibits this neurotransmitter's action, which leads to paralysis and death. (B) The venom of the black widow spider also affects its victim's acetylcholine level, but instead of inhibiting acetylcholine action, it acts as an acetylcholine agonist, quickly exhausting the victim's supply of this neurotransmitter. For small prey at least, the end is the same: paralysis and death—for humans, a painful but usually nonlethal illness.*

must also turn it (see Figure 2.31). In the language of neurophysiology, the transmitter molecule must produce the changes in membrane potential that correspond to excitatory and inhibitory processes.

## BEYOND LOCK-AND-KEY

Recent findings suggest, however, that neurotransmission is more complicated than the simple lock-and-key model would suggest. Neuroscientists now regard the various transmitters released by the presynaptic neuron as the brain's ***primary messengers***, responsible for neuron-to-neuron communication. But, increasingly, investigators are focusing on various chemical processes that occur within the postsynaptic neuron after it has been stimulated by a primary messenger and that can render the neuron more or less responsive thereafter. These chemical processes regulate such mechanisms as the creation of receptor sites for specific neurotransmitters and the synthesis of the neuron's own neurotransmitter, and they are set in motion by a set of substances known as the neuron's ***second messengers*** (Shepherd, 1994).

Neurons also signal each other using small quantities of dissolved gases. An important gaseous messenger is nitric oxide (NO), which is found in many species and has widespread actions in the brain, especially in the olfactory cortex, hippocampus, and cerebellum (Moroz, 2001). It also has important peripheral effects, including making fireflies flash (Trimmer et al., 2001) and mammalian males have genital erections (NO is enhanced by the erection drug Viagra). Other gases that may act as messengers are carbon monoxide and hydrogen sulfide, which are both involved in regulating hypothalamic responses to stress (Navarra, Dello Russo, Mancuso, Preziosi, & Grossman, 2000).

Finally, neurons involved in the control of very high-speed acts such as eye movements may circumvent chemical neurotransmission altogether. They may communicate via narrow ***electrical synapses***, with the action potential of one neuron directly inducing an action potential in the next (Shepherd, 1994).

While all of these added complexities reflect relatively recent discoveries, it is likely that other additions to the simple lock-and-key model of chemical neurotransmission will be found. The findings we mentioned earlier—that networks of glial cells may constitute a parallel signaling system—are yet another wrinkle. Clearly, the brain may have many other tricks up its metaphorical sleeve.

## DRUGS AND NEUROTRANSMITTERS

The fact that communication between neurons depends on different neurotransmitter substances (and possibly different processes) has wide implications for both psychology and pharmacology because our knowledge of the brain's various neurotransmitters has been crucial to understanding how medications and other drugs—legal and illegal—exert their effects. Overall, drugs can either enhance or impede the actions of a neurotransmitter. Those that enhance a transmitter's activity are technically called *agonists*, a term borrowed from Greek drama in which the agonist is the name for the hero. Drugs that impede such action are *antagonists*, a term that refers to whoever opposes the hero (so to speak, the villain).

Agonists and antagonists exert their influence in numerous ways at the synapse. Some agonists enhance a transmitter's effect by blocking its synaptic reuptake, thus leaving more transmitter within the synapse. Others act by counteracting the cleanup enzyme or by increasing the availability of some neurotransmitter *precursor* (a substance required for the transmitter's chemical manufacture). Conversely, some antagonists operate by speeding up reuptake, others by augmenting cleanup enzymes, and still others by decreasing available precursors. Other drugs affect the synaptic receptors. Some are agonists that activate the receptors by mimicking the transmitter's action. Antagonists of this type prevent the transmitter effect by binding themselves to the synaptic receptor and blocking off the transmitter, thus serving as a kind of putty in the synaptic lock. Table 2.1 shows some common drugs and how they exert their effects.

As the table makes clear, some of the drugs that have substantial effects on the nervous

**TABLE 2.1 SUMMARY OF THE EFFECTS OF COMMONLY USED DRUGS**

| Drug(s) | Neurotransmitter System(s) Affected | Mechanism of Action | Main Effect(s) |
|---|---|---|---|
| Venom of black widow spider | Acetylcholine | Antagonist; blocks transmitter at muscle receptors | Paralysis and death of insect's prey |
| Amphetamines, cocaine* | Dopamine, norepinephrine, epinephrine | Agonist; blocks reuptake into presynaptic neurons | Autonomic arousal, restlessness, insomnia, loss of appetite, sometimes euphoria |
| SSRI antidepressants (e.g., Prozac, Zoloft, Paxil) | Serotonin | Agonist; blocks reuptake into presynaptic neurons | Relief of depression |
| Benzodiazepines (e.g., Xanax, Valium, Klonopin) | GABA (gamma-amino butyric acid) | Agonist | Reduction of anxiety |
| Antipsychotics (Risperdal, Zyprexa) | Dopamine, serotonin | Antagonist; blocks postsynaptic receptors | Control of psychotic thinking (dopamine) and restoration of social engagement (serotonin) in disorders such as schizophrenia |
| Heroin, OxyContin, other opiates | Endorphins | Agonist; mimics transmitter at postsynaptic receptor | Analgesia, sometimes euphoria |
| PCP (phencyclidine, "crystal") | NMDA (N-methyl–D-aspartate) | Antagonist; blocks postsynaptic receptor | Euphoria, psychosis |

* Cocaine, amphetamine, and most other stimulants affect epinephrine and dopamine neurons as well.

system turn out to work either by mimicking or by blocking the actions of neurotransmitters. This has led some scientists to wonder just how many new neurotransmitters might be discovered using existing drugs to probe the brain. The strategy has been successful in several cases. A celebrated example is the discovery of endorphins, which are important in how we perceive and cope with pain (see Chapter 3).

Similar logic led to the discovery of a brain receptor for THC (tetrahydrocannabinol), the active ingredient in marijuana. A team of researchers injected a THC-like chemical into the brains of rats and found that it latched onto receptors located especially in the midbrain and in various limbic structures (Devane, Dysarz, Johnson, Melvin, & Howlett, 1988). Research suggests that all vertebrates may have such *cannabinoid (CB) receptors* (Elphick & Egertova, 2001).

If there are endogenous CB receptors, might the brain produce its own THC-like chemicals? Four years after discovering the first CB receptors, the same team reported isolating a compound produced by the brain itself with many of THC's properties (Devane et al., 1992). The team named this neurotransmitter *anandamide* (from the Sanskrit word *ananda*, for "bliss") because of the giddy euphoria many marijuana users experience. Will anandamide turn out to be the brain's own marijuana, responsible for our natural euphoric moments? Already, some investigators suspect that anandamide may help explain our reactions to a substance that is not usually considered a drug—chocolate. Chocolate contains both anandamide and some closely related compounds, and may produce a mood-elevating effect by activating anandamide neurons (Tomaso, Beltramo, & Piomelli, 1996).

# INTERACTIONS THROUGH THE BLOODSTREAM

Although our discussion of the nervous system has emphasized the neurons and nerve pathways that compose it, two other aspects of the nervous system deserve special mention: blood circulation and the channels of chemical communication within the body.

## BLOOD CIRCULATION

The cells that make up the central nervous system require considerable energy to function and are thus nutrient gluttons. In fact, the brain, which amounts to only about 2 percent of our body weight, consumes about 15 percent of our metabolic energy (Rosenzweig et al., 1996). This makes the circulation of blood—which supplies the brain its diet of oxygen and glucose—particularly crucial. Several arteries enter the brain separately and join up once inside the brain, probably to provide redundancy in the event that any one artery malfunctions.

The cerebral blood vessels not only make sure that the blood supply to the brain is constant; they also make sure that the blood is pure. Since the cells making up the nervous system are quite sensitive to toxins, it is essential to protect them. To accomplish this, the blood vessels within the brain become surrounded by tightly joined cells that act as filters, and together they form the *blood-brain barrier* (Mayhan, 2001). This barrier is remarkably effective. Indeed, it sometimes seems too effective to investigators trying to design medicines to help people with brain disorders. For them the task is twofold—to design an effective medicine, and to design one that can outwit the barrier and reach the brain cells.

# THE ENDOCRINE SYSTEM

An enormous volume of information flows to and from the brain via the nervous system. But the body also has another avenue of internal communication: the *endocrine system* (see Figure 2.32 and Table 2.2). Various *endocrine glands* (such as the *pancreas*, the *adrenal glands*, and the *pituitary*) release certain chemical secretions—*hormones*—directly into the bloodstream, thus affecting structures that are often far removed from their biochemical birthplace. As an example, take the pituitary gland. One of its components secretes a hormone that tells the kidney to decrease the amount of water excreted in the urine, a useful mechanism when the body is short of water. Another part of the pituitary gland controls the thymus gland in the chest, which in turn produces the T-lymphocyte cells so important in fighting widespread systemic infections (including those from the human immunodeficiency virus, or HIV).

On the face of it, the communication and control provided by these endocrine glands seem very different from that provided by the nervous system. In the nervous system, neurotransmitters are sent to particular addresses through highly specific channels. In contrast, the chemical messengers employed by the endocrine system travel indiscriminately throughout the bloodstream, reaching virtually all parts of the body. There is also an enormous difference in the distance these messengers have to travel. While neurotransmitters must only cross the synaptic gap, which is less than $1/10,000$ millimeter wide, the endocrine messengers may have to traverse the entire length of the body. Despite these differences, the two communication systems have a good deal in common

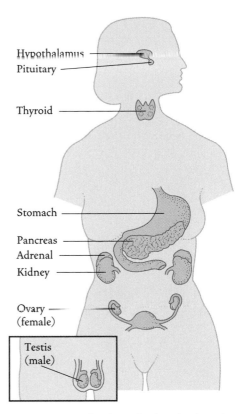

2.32   *Location of major endocrine glands and hypothalamus*

### TABLE 2.2   THE MAIN ENDOCRINE GLANDS AND SOME OF THEIR FUNCTIONS

| GLAND | FUNCTION(S) OF THE RELEASED HORMONES |
|---|---|
| Anterior pituitary | Often called the body's master gland because it triggers hormone secretion in many of the other endocrine glands. |
| Posterior pituitary | Prevents loss of water through kidney. |
| Thyroid | Affects metabolic rate. |
| Islet cells in pancreas | Affects utilization of glucose. |
| Adrenal cortex | Has various effects on metabolism, immunity, and response to stress; has some effects on sexual behavior. |
| Adrenal medulla | Increases sugar output of liver; stimulates various internal organs in the same direction as the sympathetic branch of the ANS (e.g., accelerates heart rate). |
| Ovaries | One set of hormones (estrogen) produces female sex characteristics and is relevant to sexual behavior. Another hormone (progesterone) prepares uterus for implantation of embryo. |
| Testes | Produces male sex characteristics; relevant to sexual arousal. |

because both deliver their messages by the release of chemical substances. In the nervous system, neurotransmitters excite or inhibit the postsynaptic cell; in the endocrine system, hormones affect specially sensitive cells in the target organ.

The relationship between neural and endocrine communication is further underlined by the fact that a number of substances serve both as hormones and as neurotransmitters. For example, norepinephrine is the transmitter released by certain neurons that make blood vessels constrict; it is also one of the hormones secreted by the adrenal gland and has similar results. The adrenal gland's release of norepinephrine and its close relative epinephrine (known commonly as adrenalin) is controlled by nerves that are part of the sympathetic branch of the ANS.

Considering these many relationships, a number of investigators believe that neurons and the cells of the endocrine glands evolved from a common chemical messenger system (LeRoith, Shiloach, & Roth, 1982).

# RECOVERY FROM BRAIN INJURY

We have said a great deal in this chapter about the effects of various brain lesions, and the people suffering from such lesions have been an important source of our current knowledge about brain function. But, of course, this knowledge has been derived from cases that are often tragic, from individuals who have been massively disabled by brain damage from strokes, tumors, head injuries, or infections. Can these people recover? Clearly, this topic is of vital medical importance. The facts about recovery also have considerable scientific importance because they throw further light on how the human brain works.

In some cases, the outcome is favorable, and there is considerable spontaneous recovery from brain damage; a stroke patient with aphasia may regain normal fluency and comprehension after a couple of months, though difficulty in word finding (sometimes called *anomia*) usually remains (Kolb & Whishaw, 1996). In other cases, the recovery is considerably less, and the prospects for improvement are not bright. In all cases, however, the most dramatic gains tend to be made during the first two to three months after the damage has occurred; after a year or so, any further gains tend to be small.

How can we explain these great variations in the degree to which patients recover from brain damage? The first factor is the age at which the lesion occurs. There is more recovery when the damage occurs in early childhood rather than later in life. At least up to age eight, for example, children who become aphasic regain speech function even if their impairment immediately after the brain injury was severe (Woods & Teuber, 1978). For people who become aphasic thereafter, the odds of recovery diminish steadily with age. Second, recovery is greater when brain damage occurs gradually and lesser when the damage occurs suddenly. Thus, a series of small strokes will tend to be less disabling than one large stroke. Third, in the case of aphasia, left-handers do better than right-handers probably because left-handers' normal language processing is not as strictly confined to the left hemisphere.

Whatever the eventual degree of recovery, how is it accomplished? Researchers suggest several mechanisms.

## FINDING ALTERNATIVE STRATEGIES

Some recovery involves a process that is mundane but crucial: the discovery of alternative strategies for circumventing the lost functions. For example, a person who has suffered a right-hemisphere stroke and now loses his way home can make or remember a list of the local street names and the turns to make at each intersection. In this way, he is using verbal coding to replace the abilities he has lost in spatial navigation. Specialists in such *cognitive rehabilitation* have refined many kinds of these techniques, making impressive use of modern technology. Someone who has been paralyzed, for example, can use a wheelchair controlled by eye movements and blinks fed into a computer. In other cases, implanted microprocessors in someone's limbs and sense organs—or in prosthetic replacements—can restore function lost when there was a severing of normal neural connections to the brain. Many more "bionic" replacements of this type are in development.

## NEURAL SUBSTITUTION OF FUNCTION

Not only can a person develop different strategies for circumventing disabilities, it also appears that the brain has a certain flexibility (technically, *plasticity*) of function: the brain can adjust its functioning in a fashion that assigns to the undamaged portions of the brain some of the functions previously controlled by the parts that have been damaged. For example, we have discussed the fact that many language functions are normally supported by the left hemisphere and that damage to this hemisphere often results in aphasia. In some cases, though, aphasic patients recover because their right hemisphere comes to perform some of the tasks originally handled by the left. Evidence of this is provided by patients who show nearly complete recovery of language function subsequent to left-hemisphere lesions; in most of these cases, there is an increase in the blood flow to the right hemisphere, reflecting its increased role (Knopman et al., 1984, cited in Rosenzweig & Leiman, 1989).

The most dramatic cases of neural substitution of function occur when an entire cerebral hemisphere is removed. Such hemispherectomies are sometimes performed in cases of childhood epilepsy that are so severe that neither medications nor more precise neurosurgery is effective. When the left hemisphere is removed early enough, the right hemisphere will assume a good many of the responsibilities of its missing counterpart—even speech. This reassignment to the remaining hemisphere has been confirmed both by neuroimaging studies and by stimulating the remaining hemisphere and verifying movements on the same side of the body (formerly controlled by the absent hemisphere). Remarkably, these children live—literally—with half a brain, but some can function at an almost normal level (Carson, 2000; de Bode & Curtiss, 2000; Kastrup, Leonhardt, Kurthen, & Hufragel, 2000; Snead, 2001).

## REPLACING CONNECTIONS

So far, we have talked about cases in which our nervous system finds ways to circumvent disabilities or to reassign the needed abilities to new, intact areas. Is it also possible for the nervous system to rebuild lost tissue, just as we grow new skin after we get burned? How much the brain can replace its own tissue and restore its lost connections is the focus of a great deal of neurological research, research with profound medical implications.

In the adult nervous systems of mammals, dead neurons cannot ordinarily be replaced. But the brain has other tricks at its disposal. Healthy neurons can form new receptors that increase the sensitivity of the remaining synapses. The axons of healthy neurons adjacent to the damaged cells can also grow new branches, called *collateral sprouts*, that may eventually attach themselves to the synapses left vacant by the cells lost through injury. In addition, neurons that are near death are often saved by the brain's secreting certain *neurotrophic* (neuron-nourishing) *factors*. One neurotrophic factor is pituitary growth hormone (GH), which is normally involved in the maturation of the nervous system and also prevents much of the neuronal death that occurs after brain injury (Scheepens et al., 2001). Another such factor is secreted from glial cells and seems to preserve injured motoneurons (Watabe et al., 2001). One of the most important neurotrophic factors, *nerve growth factor (NGF)*, promotes both neuronal cell growth and sprouting (Bothwell, 1995). Work is under way to determine whether these growth factors can be given clinically to aid in the patient's recovery of function.

## REPLACING NEURAL TISSUE

In addition to facilitating the brain's own reparative mechanisms, investigators are also exploring whether damaged neural tissue can be replaced directly. Brain-tissue implants could potentially reverse many degenerative brain diseases such as Parkinson's disease and Alzheimer's disease (Fine, 1986; Young, 1996). In the case of Parkinson's disease, the results of experiments exploring this prospect have so far been disappointing, but the research effort is sure to continue (Freed et al., 2001; Kordower et al., 1995).

Another group of studies is of potential relevance to Alzheimer's disease, a tragic but common illness that afflicts 5 to 10 percent of all people over age sixty-five and fully 50 percent of those over age eighty, and is characterized by a progressive decline in intellectual functioning. The disease usually begins with problems such as extreme absent-mindedness, forgetting the names of everyday objects like car keys or toothbrushes, and poor judgment involving acts like driving to the store in underwear. As the disorder progresses, the Alzheimer's sufferer may repeatedly wander off and lose his way home, and be unable to recognize close family members. In the disease's final stages, the picture is of disability and vacancy: the sufferer may be bedridden, unresponsive to words, and unable to eat, swallow, or control urination or defecation.

Alzheimer's disease entails devastating structural changes throughout the brain and, in fact, can be diagnosed with certainty only with postmortem inspection of the brain. The degeneration appears to begin at the cellular level, triggered by the expression of a number of "susceptibility" genes. A normal protein created by neurons, *amyloid protein*, begins to be overly secreted in an abnormal form that creates large protein blobs—*amyloid plaques*—that litter the space between neurons. These plaques trigger an immune response in the brain that results in the death of neurons that are innocent bystanders. Also involved is a second protein, *tau protein*, which normally helps sustain the internal structure of the brain's axons. Tau's metabolism somehow goes awry, allowing neurons to degenerate and leave stringy debris called *neurofibrillary tangles*. Together, the plaques and tangles act to block normal neurotransmission, beginning in the base of the temporal lobe, proceeding to the hippocampus (involved in long-term memory), and then spreading throughout the brain, particularly the frontal and parietal lobes (areas crucial to working memory, decision-making, and object recognition). After many years, the brain of the Alzheimer's sufferer is but a shrunken relic of its former self.

Can degenerative changes of this sort be reversed by brain transplants? Early work in rats with various learning and memory deficits showed that brain tissue implanted from other rats could partly improve the rats' performance on the relevant tasks (Björklund & Stenevi, 1984; Gage & Björklund, 1986). Transplant research has yet to achieve clinical application in the treatment of Alzheimer's disease, although work with monkeys is promising (Kordower et al., 1994).

Indeed, for both Parkinson's disease and Alzheimer's disease, researchers have especially high hopes that these diseases can be halted and reversed not by the transplantation of replacement neurons, but by the injection of the same kinds of neural stem cells responsible for building the nervous system originally. Preliminary studies suggest that when such cells are injected into a patch of neurons, the cells are induced to turn into healthy neurons just like their neighbors, taking their shape, producing their neurotransmitters, and filling in for dead neurons (Holm et al., 2001; Isacson, 1999; Philips et al.,

2001; Sawamoto et al., 2001). Even brain injury from stroke may respond to stem-cell therapy. That was the conclusion of one study in which rats who were given strokes that resulted in profound motor impairments showed near-complete resolution of their stroke deficits several months after the cells were implanted (Veizovic, Beech, Stoemer, Watson, & Hodges, 2001). Initial human trials prove promising (Kondziolka et al., 2000).

Such stem-cell studies entail substantial ethical quandaries, given that much of this research has used stem cells taken from aborted fetuses. The issues came to a head in 2001 with the debate over whether using such fetal stem cells would result in a proliferation of embryos—arguably, human lives—being created only to be destroyed for parts. The debate continued in 2002 with extended discussion of whether investigators should be permitted to clone stem cells for therapeutic purposes. The resolution of these ethical (and legal) issues remains uncertain.

## SPINAL CORD INJURY

Perhaps nowhere is interest in recovery of function greater than among those paralyzed by spinal cord injury. Until recently, the outlook for obtaining regeneration of function in such cases was dismal, but there is now some cause for hope. In a dramatic study, researchers in Sweden transected the spinal cords of rats, leaving their hind limbs completely paralyzed. The researchers then spliced the gaps they had created using axons taken from the rats' own peripheral nerves and applied a glue containing a neurotrophic factor. Over the year following the surgery, the rats regained the ability to stand on their hind legs. In contrast, a separate group of rats that were transected but did not receive the nerve splices showed no recovery of hind-limb function. When the researchers inspected the spinal cords of the repaired animals, they found clear evidence that the splices worked: the splices had become functional bridges between the disconnected portions of the spinal cord (Cheng, Cao, & Olson, 1996). The import of this study is considerable, and follow-up research is expected to determine the procedures optimal for recovery (Young, 1996). As in degenerative brain diseases, stem-cell therapy may afford yet another way to restore function in spinal cord injury. Already, researchers have found that neural stem cells from human brains resulted in functional spinal cord repair in rats (Akiyama et al., 2001).

To sum up, scientists investigating the recovery of brain and spinal cord function after injury or disease now believe that they are on the verge of discovering how to reconnect neuronal pathways by using stem-cell implants and various neurotrophic factors. For the first time, there is hope for those who were thought to be hopelessly disabled. The same stem-cell techniques may apply to degenerative brain disorders such as Parkinson's and Alzheimer's diseases. Considering the ever-growing proportion of senior citizens in the population, help can come none too soon.

*Recovery from brain damage* **Actor Christopher Reeve's paralysis resulting from spinal damage has drawn attention and resources to the question of how damage to the spinal cord might be repaired.**

Spinal injury

# SOME FINAL THOUGHTS: SHOULD ALL PSYCHOLOGICAL QUESTIONS HAVE BIOLOGICAL ANSWERS?

We have obviously come a long way since Descartes. Today we know a great deal about the biological foundation on which all human striving rests: the trillion or so neurons whose collective firings make up our human brain. Without these aggregates of neurons, there would be no *Hamlet*, no Great Wall of China, no space travel, no hi-tech medicine. Nor would there be—to mention our darker side—genocide, family violence, or nuclear warfare.

The nervous system and its operation clearly underlie whatever we do and think and feel. But does this mean that all psychological questions are at bottom neurological ones? Does it mean that the answers to all of our questions will ultimately be phrased in terms of action potentials and neurotransmitters?

The answer is no. As this chapter has tried to make clear, many psychological questions lend themselves to physiological answers, but many others do not. Suppose, for example, that a journalist or historian or legal scholar asks why a criminal jury acquitted O. J. Simpson of murder. To answer with a paragraph (or a book) about the jurors' neurons and synaptic connections would be absurd. This neuron-based account might be factually correct, but it would also be unilluminating because the question at stake is ultimately one about reasons, not about neural mechanisms. What is needed is an account phrased in the appropriate terms—the jury's interpretation of the evidence, for example; their personal attitudes toward the defendant; the racial climate of the times; and so on. Any of these answers might prove inadequate or incomplete, but at least they are aimed at the right level of explanation. In contrast, a statement about neuronal firings in the frontal cortex of each juror seems off the mark. This is not because we simply do not know enough yet about the nervous system. Even if we could analyze all the neuronal firings in all the jurors throughout the trial, this analysis would not provide adequate answers for the journalist, the historian, or the legal scholar—let alone the ordinary person on the street.

What holds for historians asking questions about a particular event holds for psychologists asking about the mind. When psychologists ask about how humans and animals act, perceive, think, remember, and feel, they often want answers at a level different from that offered by a neurophysiologist. Of course, they are aware that all our actions take place within a framework set by our nervous system. But even so, they believe that many psychological explanations are more appropriately offered in other terms. Just how such psychological explanations are formulated will be the topic of subsequent chapters.

# SUMMARY

## THE ORGANISM AS A MACHINE

1. Since Descartes, many scientists have tried to explain human and animal movement within the framework of mechanisms usually modeled after the technology of the time. For Descartes, this involved the reflex concept: a stimulus excites a sense organ, which transmits excitation upward to the spinal cord or brain, which in turn relays the excitation downward to a muscle or gland, and thus produces action.

## HOW THE NERVOUS SYSTEM IS STUDIED

2. Neuroscientists have developed numerous ways to investigate the links between brain and behavior. The traditional techniques included human clinical observation and also *invasive techniques,* usually performed on animals. Invasive techniques may involve *stimulation,* the creation of a *lesion,* or *transection.* Some invasive procedures, such as *transcranial magnetic stimulation (TMS),* produce brain dysfunctions that are only temporary. An early noninvasive technique is *electroencephalography (EEG).* More recent techniques involve *neuroimaging,* which make it

possible to diagnose and study lesions in the brains of living patients, as well as to study the brain activities of normal participants. They include *computerized tomography (CT)*, *magnetic resonance imaging (MRI)*, and *positron emission tomography (or PET) scans*. A still newer technique is *functional MRI (fMRI) scanning*.

## THE ARCHITECTURE OF THE NERVOUS SYSTEM

3. Across species, brains vary in their degree of central versus regional control, with more complex animals showing more centralized control. All vertebrates have brains that develop early in embryonic life. The brain begins as a simple tube that develops three thickenings, which mature to form the *hindbrain* (including the *pons*, *medulla*, and *cerebellum*), the *midbrain*, and the *forebrain*. The forebrain is well-developed in primates, especially humans, and includes the *thalamus*, *hypothalamus*, and structures such as the *cerebral hemispheres*, the *basal ganglia*, and the *limbic system*.

4. The brain and spinal cord together form the *central nervous system (CNS)*. The CNS connects with the body in two main ways: through the *afferent* and *efferent* nerves of the *peripheral nervous system* (both the *somatic* and *autonomic divisions*) and (indirectly) through the bloodstream, by virtue of the brain's control of hormonal secretions and internal receptors that monitor hormone levels in the blood.

## THE CORTEX

5. The *cerebral cortex* is generally believed to underlie the most complex aspects of behavior. The *primary projection areas* of the cortex act as receiving stations for sensory information or as dispatching centers for motor commands. Early studies of the primary motor projection area indicated that the brain exhibits *contralateral* control (the right side of the body is primarily controlled by the left side of the brain and vice versa).

6. The *primary sensory projection areas* for vision, hearing, and the bodily senses are respectively located in the *occipital*, *temporal*, and *parietal lobes*. The *primary motor projection area* is in the frontal lobe. It controls single muscle actions, while the adjoining nonprimary motor projection areas coordinate complex acts involving multiple muscles. The remaining regions of the cortex seem to link multiple kinds of sensations (for example, sights with sounds).

7. Certain lesions of the frontal lobe lead to *apraxias*, serious disturbances in the organization of voluntary action, some of which may be produced by disconnection between the primary and nonprimary motor areas. Other lesions produce *agnosias*, the disorganization of perception and recognition. One kind of agnosia is *prosopagnosia*, in which the main difficulty is in recognizing faces. A related disorder is the *neglect syndrome* whose main characteristic is the patient's systematic neglect of the left side.

8. Still other lesions cause *aphasias*, profound disruptions of language, which may involve speech production, speech comprehension, or both. A lesion in *Broca's area* leads to nonfluent aphasia; one in *Wernicke's area* leads to fluent aphasia. These lesions evidently affect some mental function that is not specific to the ear-mouth channel, as shown by the fact that congenitally deaf people who suffer a stroke in the left hemisphere show sign-language deficits that correspond closely to the spoken-language deficits observed in hearing persons.

9. *Prefrontal lesions* can produce deficits in planning and problem solving that have important consequences for social behavior.

## DO WE REALLY HAVE TWO BRAINS?

10. The two hemispheres of the human brain are somewhat different in both structure and function. In most right-handers, the left hemisphere handles the bulk of the language functions, while the right hemisphere is more relevant to spatial comprehension. One source of evidence for this difference in hemispheric function, or *lateralization*, comes from the study of split-brain patients in whom the main connection between the two hemispheres, the *corpus callosum*, has been surgically cut. Many studies of normal participants, often using neuroimaging, such as PET and fMRI scans, also show that speech tasks produce predominantly left-hemisphere activity, whereas right-hemisphere predominance occurs on spatial tasks.

## BUILDING BLOCKS OF THE NERVOUS SYSTEM: NEURONS AND NERVE PULSES

11. The basic unit of communication in the nervous system is the *neuron*, whose primary components are the *dendrites*, *cell body*, and *axon*. Some are motor neurons (*motoneurones*) that form an *efferent pathway*, which extends from the CNS, winds up on a muscle fiber and makes that fiber contract. Others are *sensory neurons* that convey information from receptors to the CNS. But the vast majority of neurons are interneurons, which act as middle men, typically connecting to yet other interneurons, that form the *microcircuitry* of the nervous system.

12. In addition to the neurons, the nervous system contains *glial cells* that are crucial for enabling neurons to find the right connections during development, and they may

constitute a separate, slow signal system throughout the nervous system.

13. The main function of a neuron is to produce a nerve impulse, an electrochemical disturbance that is propagated along the membrane of the axon when the cell's normal *resting potential* is disrupted by a stimulus whose intensity exceeds the *excitation threshold*. This stimulus produces a brief destabilization and restabilization of the cell membrane, which constitutes the *action potential*.

14. The resting and action potentials derive from chemical processes at the neuron's membrane. There are electrically charged particles (*ions*) dissolved in the fluid both inside and outside the neuronal membrane. Biochemical portholes, *ion channels,* let some of these ions pass through and hold others back. Two kinds of ions are of primary relevance: *sodium* and *potassium*. When the membrane is stable, there is an excess of positively charged ions on the outside, resulting in the voltage difference of the *resting potential*—negative on the inside and positive on the outside.

15. When the membrane is sufficiently irritated, the sodium channels spring open temporarily. Sodium ions flood in, forcing out some potassium ions a moment later. This short-lived excess of positively charged particles on the inside of the membrane produces the positive voltage swing of the *action potential*. This excitation spreads to neighboring regions because the temporarily positive voltage inside the axon induces the opening of ion channels at adjacent regions, which themselves induce more distant channels to open, and so on. This domino-like process produces the *propagation* of the action potential all along the axon. In vertebrates, the axons are encased in *myelin sheaths* with gaps (the *Nodes of Ranvier*) in between them, and the action potential can skip from node to node, achieving much greater impulse speeds. In *multiple sclerosis (MS)*, the myelin breaks down resulting in such symptoms as blindness and paralysis.

16. The action potential obeys the *all-or-none law:* Once threshold is reached, further increases of stimulus intensity have no effect on its magnitude. But the nervous system can nevertheless distinguish between different intensities of stimuli, all of which are above threshold. One means for doing this is *frequency:* The more intense the stimulus, the more often the neuron fires.

## INTERACTION AMONG NERVE CELLS

17. To understand how neurons communicate, investigators have studied *reflex action,* which is necessarily based on the activity of several neurons. Conduction within neurons has been shown to obey different laws than conduction between neurons (that is, at their *synapses*). Evidence included the phenomena of *spatial* and *tempo-ral summation.* Further studies argued for a process of *inhibition,* as shown by *reciprocal inhibition* found in flexor-extensor muscle pairs. Further work showed that a reflex can be activated either by increasing excitation or by decreasing inhibition, with an algebraic summation at the synapse.

18. To understand the bio-chemical processes that underlie synaptic transmission we begin with the distinction between the *presynaptic neuron*—the cell that sends the message—and the *postsynaptic neuron*—the one that receives it. The axon terminals of the presynaptic neuron contain numerous tiny sacs, the *synaptic vesicles,* which contain *transmitter molecules.* When the presynaptic neuron fires, some of the vesicles eject their contents into the *synaptic gap,* which diffuse across this gap and activate specialized molecular receptors in the postsynaptic membrane. These open or close certain ion channels, changing the voltage difference—either decreasing or increasing it. When the voltage difference is sufficiently decreased, it leads to excitation, and the action potential is triggered. When it is increased, it leads to inhibition, and fortifies the membrane against further destabilizing influences. The ultimate response of a given postsynaptic cell depends on a final tally of the excitatory and inhibitory "yeas" and "nays" that act upon it.

19. Some transmitters are inactivated shortly after they've been discharged by special "cleanup" enzymes that break them up into their chemical components. More commonly, neurotransmitters are not destroyed but reused, by a process of *synaptic reuptake*.

20. Important examples of neurotransmitters include *acetylcholine serotonin, glutamate, GABA, norepinephrine, epinephrine,* and *dopamine*.

21. The *lock-and-key model* of transmitters proposes that transmitter molecules will only affect the postsynaptic membrane if the molecule's shape fits into certain synaptic receptor molecules—much as a key must fit into a lock. More recent studies suggest some additional complications, for example, by distinguishing between *primary messengers,* responsible for neuron-to-neuron communication, and *second messengers,* which affect a number of processes that occur *within* the postsynaptic neuron after it has been stimulated by a primary messenger.

22. The fact that communication between neurons depends on different neurotransmitter substances has wide implications for both psychology and pharmacology. Drugs can either serve as *agonists,* enhancing a neurotransmitter's effect, or as *antagonists,* impeding its effect. Some agonists enhance a transmitter's effect by blocking its synaptic reuptake, others act by counteracting the cleanup enzyme or by increasing the availability of some neurotransmitter *precursor.* Conversely, some antagonists operate by speeding up reuptake, others by augmenting cleanup enzymes,

and still others by decreasing available precursors. Yet other drugs affect the synaptic receptors, by mimicking the transmitter's action.

## INTERACTIONS THROUGH THE BLOOD STREAM

23. Blood circulation also plays a vital role in the functioning of the brain and as an instrument of communication. Not only does the blood bring energy to the nutrient-hungry brain, it also carries the hormones secreted by the endocrine glands to the various target organs throughout the body.

## RECOVERY FROM BRAIN INJURY

24. Recovery from cerebral lesions varies considerably from one patient to another, depending in part on the age of the victim and the nature of the injury. Some recovery can be produced by *collateral sprouting*, whereby healthy neurons adjacent to the region of injury grow new branches. In addition, some functions of the damaged regions may be taken over by other, undamaged parts of the brain. Recent work on the transplanting of neurons, neuronal stem cells, and on spinal cord repair offers hope that neurobiologists may be able to replace damaged tissue and restore function in patients with *neurodegenerative* disorders such as *Parkinson's disease* and *Alzheimer's disease*.

CHAPTER

*3*

# MOTIVATION

*I*n this chapter, we examine some of the motives that characterize human behavior. Our focus here will be on relatively simple motives such as temperature regulation, hunger, and sex. These are often called biological motives since they depend on built-in physiological mechanisms that are critical for the individual's personal survival and the perpetuation of his genes. This is in contrast to other, more complex motives such as the need for friendship and love, which are often subsumed under the category of social motives.

Some biological motives can be understood as attempts at self-regulation—for example, the organism's tendency to maintain a temperature that stays within certain limits and nutrient levels adequate for providing energy. Others are attempts at self-preservation, such as the body's response to pain or preparation for threat. Yet another biological motive is sex, which is our means of genetic preservation. Finally, there is a need for sleep, which is sometimes thought to reflect the need for self-restoration.

These motives differ from each other in many ways, but they share certain properties—including an essential one: the property of making some acts more probable than others. For example, when we are hungry, we are more likely to eat than to wash our hair or read a book. When we are thirsty, we are more likely to drink than to run around the block. These motives are also all able to tune our perceptions: when we are hungry, we become more alert to food-related stimuli like the smell of popcorn or the sight of a package of cookies across the room. And when we finally do eat, our hunger makes us more likely to savor the taste.

This property of motives, making some behaviors and perceptions more probable, is sometimes called *potentiation*. The term reflects the fact that motives do not directly imply a change in behavior; instead, they increase the potential for action. Put another way, motives direct our behavior, and in this chapter we discuss how this comes about.

# MOTIVATION AS DIRECTED ACTION

Most human and animal actions are directed. We do not simply walk, reach, shrink, or flee; we walk or reach *toward* some objects, and shrink or flee *from* others. Sometimes what we approach or avoid is physically present, as when a dog fetches a ball or runs from a honking car. At other times, the object of an action is not yet present, but exists only in the organism's expectations—as, for example, when a hawk circles in search of prey or a lizard changes color to camouflage itself in case a predator ventures by.

Such directed actions seem difficult to reconcile with Descartes' notion (Chapter 2) that animals (and, in great part, humans) are automatons whose actions are mere sensorimotor reflexes. This view is problematic when we wish to understand actions that are directed toward some goal since the organism seems to be responding to a stimulus that is not actually present.

A different problem arises even when the action is directed toward an object that is present. Consider the dog fetching the ball. Dogs do not fetch robotically, moving the same muscles each time. Rather, the movements they make in their approach depend upon the ball—where it is in relation to them; whether it is in motion, and, if so, where it is likely to land; and whether they need to scoop the ball off the ground or grab it in the air.

In an important sense, then, the dog's behavior is determined by the ball's. If the ball veers left or right, the dog turns to follow. If the ball goes over a fence, the dog tries to jump the fence or sneak around it. How can we arrange for a mechanism that provides this flexibility?

*Sony's robot dog, Aibo   Unlike the machines of Descartes' time, modern machines are capable of enormous flexibility in their behavior.*

## CONTROL SYSTEMS

The machines of Descartes' time were designed to move only in prescribed, repetitive patterns. Today's machines, in contrast, can tailor their behavior to their environment, which lets them act flexibly—chasing balls, even. They do this by monitoring their environment and adjusting their actions to match their assigned tasks, just as dogs keep their eye on the ball and move in line with the ball's trajectory.

How can we make a machine gear its actions to its circumstances? The trick lies in the use of *feedback*. As a machine operates, it changes its environment, whether that change is mechanical, electrical, thermal, or whatever. If we can make these changes alter the further oper-

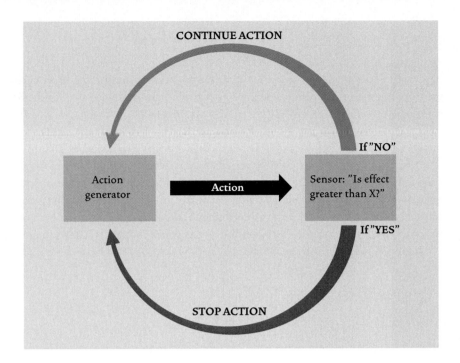

*3.1 Negative feedback   In negative feedback systems, the feedback slows, stops, or reverses the action that produces it. A sensing device indicates the level of a certain stimulus. If that level exceeds a certain setpoint, the action stops. The effect is self-regulation.*

ation of the machine—that is, "feed back" upon it—we have a **control system** based on feedback.

The most useful kind of control-system feedback is **negative feedback**, in which the feedback stops, or even reverses, the response of the machine that produced the original change (Figure 3.1). A simple example is the system that controls most home heating systems. A thermostat turns on the heater when the house's temperature falls below a given setting. The heater then causes the house's temperature to rise, and this provides the negative feedback signal to the thermostat: when the house reaches the preset temperature, the thermostat turns the heater off.

We might loosely say that this arrangement gives the thermostatically controlled heater a "goal": the heater acts as if it "desires" to maintain a particular temperature. Similar negative feedback systems exist at all levels of most nervous systems. Many examples of goal-directedness using negative feedback involve the organism's regulation of its own internal environment.

## HOMEOSTASIS

Descartes' account of behavior (Chapter 2) emphasizes the role of the external environment. Stimuli within the environment impinge on our senses, which trigger reactions in our muscles. Some two hundred years after Descartes, another Frenchman, physiologist Claude Bernard (1813–1878), emphasized that the organism possesses not only an external environment, but an internal one as well—the organism's own bodily fluids. Bernard noted that even with great fluctuations in the outside environment, there is a striking constancy in these fluids—in the concentrations of various salts, dissolved oxygen levels, the quantities of nutrients like glucose, and in their pH (that is, their acidity). In addition, many creatures (including all birds and mammals) maintain a relatively constant body temperature as well. All these conditions fluctuate within narrow limits—critically narrow—because otherwise the organism is at severe risk. These examples of internal equilibrium reflect a process known as **homeostasis** (literally, "equal state"), a process so awe-inspiring in both its complexity and effectiveness that it was said to reflect a "wisdom of the body" (Cannon, 1932).

# TEMPERATURE REGULATION

A clear example of homeostasis and the role of feedback in maintaining it is provided by temperature regulation. Natural selection has provided animals with two kinds. Some animals, called *ectotherms*, maintain their body temperatures using externally directed behavior (usually, choosing to be in the sun or shade). This method works well for organisms with relatively slow metabolisms such as reptiles. For birds and mammals—*endotherms*, as they are known—things are different. Since their metabolisms are most efficient only at elevated temperatures, they need an additional repertoire of internal adjustments to maintain stable body temperatures. Some of these adjustments involve large-scale bodily changes such as gaining weight and growing insulating fur in preparation for the cold months, and losing both over the warm months. Other adjustments involve smaller but equally important changes in how the body conserves or loses heat.*

## TEMPERATURE CONTROL BY INTERNAL ADJUSTMENT

Endothermic animals generally have fast metabolisms that generate considerable heat within their bodies. If this heat accumulates to the point at which their body temperature becomes too high, various reflexive reactions come into play to exhaust the excess heat. One such reaction is peripheral *vasodilatation*, a widening of the skin's capillaries. This sends warm blood to the body's surface and results in heat loss by radiation. Other reactions that lead to cooling are sweating (in humans) and panting (in dogs), both of which produce heat loss by evaporation.

The opposite pattern comes into play when the animal's internal temperature dips too low. Sweating and panting stop, and there is *vasoconstriction*, a contraction of the capillaries that squeezes blood away from the cold periphery and keeps it instead in the body's warmer core. Other reflexive reactions include a ruffling of the fur to create a thick envelope of protective air and the stimulation of certain fatty cells throughout the body to speed up their metabolism and build up heat.

Like all homeostatic adjustments, these reflex reactions are directed at maintaining physiological constancy. Heat is exhausted when the core body temperature goes too high and conserved when the temperature drops too low. In this regard, these adjustments perform functions analogous to a thermostatically controlled heater or air conditioner; in all cases, these mecha-

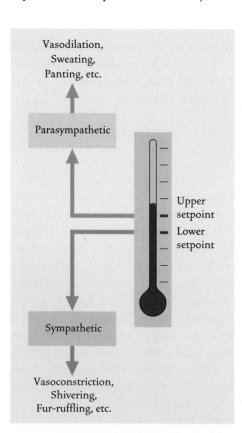

3.2 *Reflexive temperature regulation in mammals* **When the temperature deviates from an internal setpoint, various reflexive reactions occur to restore the temperature.**

* Endothermic animals used to be called "warm-blooded," in contrast to ectotherms, which were said to be "cold-blooded." But these terms are misleading because the internal temperatures of endotherms and ectotherms are about the same. What distinguishes the two is the capacity for internal thermoregulation.

nisms act to maintain some optimal temperature *setpoint*—a point that defines a kind of target value for temperature (see Figure 3.2).

## TEMPERATURE CONTROL BY EXTERNALLY DIRECTED BEHAVIOR

Along with the automatic, reflexive homeostatic mechanisms we have just described, endotherms also control their temperature with voluntary action. This is especially true in very young animals, who have immature thermoregulatory systems and typically huddle together or stay next to their mothers to keep warm. This snuggling can become precarious for the mother, however; she must limit the duration of this snuggling lest she overheat (Leon, Coopersmith, Beasley, & Sullivan, 1990). Other kinds of thermoregulatory behavior are also available. One borrowed from ectotherms is lounging in the sun to keep warm or lurking in the shade to stay cool. Another strategy is nest building, which, among its other advantages, provides an insulating layer around the inhabitants. We humans, of course, have our own variations on these techniques: we wear coats, use blankets, and snuggle with partners during the winter. Conversely, we wear light clothing and shower or swim more during the summer. All these actions serve the same goal—preserving the internal environment, whose constancy is so crucial to survival.

*Ectotherms* **Some animals maintain their body temperature using external behavior, such as choosing to be in the sun to warm up, or in water to cool down.**

## THE AUTONOMIC NERVOUS SYSTEM AND TEMPERATURE CONTROL

What regulates our internal temperature? The most direct control is exerted by the *autonomic nervous system (ANS)*. In general, this is the part of the peripheral nervous system that sends commands to the *glands* and to the *smooth muscles** of the viscera (internal organs) and blood vessels. The ANS has two broad divisions or branches: the *sympathetic branch*, which tends to "rev up" bodily activities in preparation for vigorous action, and the *parasympathetic branch*, which tends to restore them to normal after the action has been completed (Cannon, 1929).

These divisions of the ANS often act reciprocally. Thus, excitation of the sympathetic branch leads to a speeding up of heart rate and a slowing down of peristalsis (rhythmic contractions) of the intestines (we should not be digesting while we are on the run). Parasympathetic activation has the opposite effects: cardiac slowing and speeded-up peristalsis. The same relationship is seen in temperature regulation. The sympathetic branch acts to conserve internal heat; it triggers vasoconstriction, shivering, and fur ruffling. In contrast, the parasympathetic branch helps to exhaust heat and cool off the organism; it stimulates panting, sweating, and vasodilatation (see Figure 3.9, p. 102).

*Endotherms* **Some animals have internal mechanisms that help to maintain a stable body temperature.**

## SENSING THE INTERNAL ENVIRONMENT: THE HYPOTHALAMUS

What governs the ANS itself? A crucial brain region is the *hypothalamus*, which is located at the base of the forebrain (see Figure 3.3). This brain structure represents the apotheosis of anatomical miniaturization; it contains over twenty clusters of neurons that regulate many of the biological motives, yet in humans it is only about the size of a pea.

Among its other functions, the hypothalamus appears to contain a thermostatlike control mechanism that detects when the body is too cold or too hot. This was shown

---

* The individual fibers of these muscles look smooth when observed under a microscope, in contrast to the fibers of the skeletal muscles, which look striped.

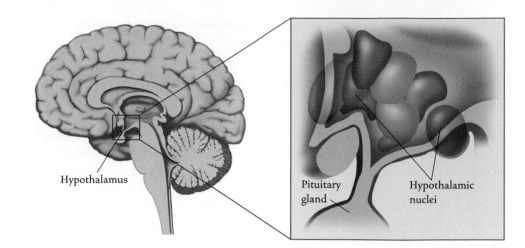

3.3    *The hypothalamus*

Hypothalamus

Pituitary gland

Hypothalamic nuclei

in cats that had an electrode implanted in their anterior hypothalamus. When the electrode was heated gently, the cats panted and vasodilated as though they were too hot and needed to cool themselves, even though their body temperature was well below normal (Magoun, Harrison, Brobeck, & Ranson, 1938).

In many cases, the hypothalamus also regulates externally directed behavior such as moving into the sun, huddling, nesting, or even putting on a jacket. In one experiment, rats in a cold chamber learned to press a bar for a brief burst of heat (Weiss & Laties, 1961; see Figure 3.4). The question was whether rats with this skill would press the bar if their brains were cooled rather than their bodies. To find out, cold liquid was run through a tiny cannula (tube) implanted near the anterior hypothalamus (Satinoff, 1964). The answer was clear: even when the outside temperature was normal, the rats turned on the heat lamp when only their brains were cooled.

*Thermoregulation*, then, is a delicate balancing act, with both internal reflexes and overt actions being called into play as needed to preserve a stable body temperature. A similar balancing act is evident in other kinds of homeostatic regulation. An example is thirst. We continually lose water—primarily through urination, but also through respiration, sweating, defecation, and, occasionally, vomiting and bleeding. Our bodies must therefore monitor this water level carefully, taking steps to replace what is lost and conserve what remains when supplies are low. We do this using reflexive adjustments such

3.4    *Performing a learned response to keep warm    A rat kept in a cold environment will learn to press a lever that turns on a heat lamp for a few seconds after each lever press.*

*"This looks like a good spot."    (Drawing by Chas. Addams; © 1987, The New Yorker Magazine, Inc.)*

as commanding the kidneys to retain water instead of excreting it. Just as in thermoregulation, though, this internal readjustment can only preserve our water balance up to a point, and further correction requires an external action: drinking—in humans, an average of two to three quarts of water per day.

The same coordination of internal and external adjustments also applies to an even more complex system of self-regulation: maintaining the body's nutrient levels by feeding.

# HUNGER

All animals have to eat, and much of their lives revolves around food—searching for it, hunting it, ingesting it, and doing their best not to become food for others. All of these acts are related crucially to homeostasis because each serves the broader purpose of maintaining appropriate nutrient supplies in the animal's internal environment. But what are the mechanisms that determine when humans and animals eat or stop eating?

*Battling dehydration*    **Tom Hanks searches for**
**water in the 2000 film Castaway.**

## BODY WEIGHT, NUTRITION, AND ENERGY

Through the process of digestion, nutrients are extracted from food and then converted when needed into energy that supplies body heat, enables the muscles to contract, and, in general, supports all of our life functions (Rosenzweig, Leiman, & Breedlove, 1996). Animals with big brains also devote considerable energy—up to 20 percent—to the maintenance of neuronal potentials.

Animals vary greatly in how fast they need to "burn" food—that is, in their *basal metabolic rate*—in order to gain the energy and raw materials they need. With their faster metabolisms, endotherms, who eat almost constantly, need much more food than ectoderms, who sometimes go for weeks or months between meals. In addition, smaller animals generally have faster metabolisms than larger ones, which means that they have to eat proportionately more food to maintain their normal body weight.

When food is freely available, adult animals usually eat just about the right amount to satisfy their immediate nutritional needs yet keep their weight roughly constant. The "right amount" here refers not to the volume of food, but to the number of calories—and hence, the metabolic energy it can provide. This was demonstrated in a study in which rats had the caloric levels of their food adulterated using nonnutritive cellulose. The more diluted the food, the more the rats ate, in a quantity that kept the total caloric content roughly constant (Adolph, 1947).

What if no food is around?  Here, too, we see the operation of homeostasis because animals immediately lower both their metabolic rates and their activity level, allowing them to fulfill their bodily needs while maintaining their normal body weight for as long as possible (Keesey & Powley, 1986). (We will discuss the obvious implications of this for dieting humans below.)

## THE SIGNALS FOR FEEDING

What makes us hungry and want to eat? What makes us sated and want to stop? Most of us don't step on a scale, check our body weight, and then decide how much to eat (certainly, nonhuman animals don't). Instead, we maintain our body weight by our response to numerous internal signals. Some signals indicate the state of the short-term energy reserves we need for emergencies and other bursts of activity; others indicate the state of the long-term reserves we need for sustained exertion.

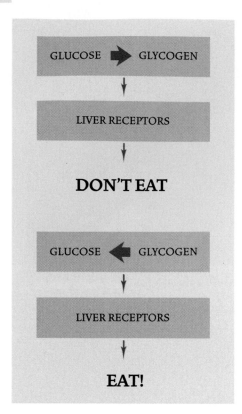

3.5  *The relation between the glucose-glycogen balance in the liver and eating*

## GLUCOSE SIGNALS

A major source of information on our nutritional needs is the liver, which has the crucial job of monitoring and controlling the major nutrient used for short-term energy: the blood sugar known as *glucose*.

Immediately after a meal, glucose is plentiful. While some is used right away, much is converted to *glycogen* (often called animal starch) and various fatty acids, which are stored for later use. Later, when this stored energy is needed, the process will be reversed, and the glycogen and fatty acids will be turned back into usable glucose.

The liver manages this reversible conversion process and informs other organs in which direction the metabolic transaction is going, from glucose cash to glycogen deposits or vice versa. If the balance tips toward storage (supply currently exceeds demand so that the excess can be converted into glycogen), the liver sends a satiety signal and the animal stops eating. If the balance tips toward glucose production (demand exceeds supply so that reserves are being used), the liver sends a hunger signal and the animal eats (Figure 3.5). The evidence for the liver's role comes from hungry dogs that had glucose injected into the vein that goes directly to the liver. The dogs stopped eating. When the glucose was injected anywhere else, eating was unaffected (Friedman & Stricker, 1976; Russek, 1971).

Notice, though, that this regulatory system must deal with a considerable time lag. Imagine that the liver waited until glucose supplies were low and only then gave the signal to start eating. Since food metabolism takes time, many minutes would elapse between the "Need glucose!" signal and the time that the glucose finally arrived. Nutrient supplies would be exhausted, and the animal could die. To avert this calamity, the liver anticipates the body's needs so that the nutrient supplies are replenished well before they are needed.

How does the liver manage to do this? It does so by monitoring blood glucose levels and looking for a characteristic pattern of fluctuation. When an organism has not eaten for a while, the level of glucose in the blood begins to drop. Before this level drops too far, the liver takes action, drawing some glycogen out of storage and converting it to glucose. As a result, the blood glucose level bounces back to normal. The result of this sequence of events is an easily identifiable pattern—a gradual drop in blood glucose, usually lasting many minutes, followed by a quick rise, resulting from the liver's compensatory action.

This slow-drop/quick-rise pattern does not indicate that the energy account is empty; it just means that the organism is drawing on its reserves, making it a good time to make a deposit. When this blood glucose pattern occurs in rats, the animals start to eat (Campfield & Smith, 1990a, b). When it occurs in humans, they say they are hungry and want something to eat (Campfield & Rosenbaum, 1992).

Let's emphasize, though, that the liver—as important as it is—is only one component in regulating food intake. The brain also contains cells sensitive to glucose levels in the blood, these cells concentrated, once again, in the hypothalamus. Evidence for such *glucoreceptors* comes from studies in which the hypothalamus was injected with a chemical that made its cells insensitive to glucose. The result was ravenous eating. This treatment presumably silenced the glucoreceptors; their silence was then interpreted by other brain mechanisms as indicating a fuel deficiency, which in turn led to feeding (Miselis & Epstein, 1970).

## SIGNALS FOR SATIETY

We have now discussed why an animal starts eating. What causes it to stop? The receptors in the brain cannot be the reason because they do not respond until we are well into digesting our meal. So what does stop us from eating?

*Peasant Wedding Feast    (Painting by Peter Brueghel the Elder, 1568)*

The common belief is that we eat until we are full. This is partly true. An animal will stop eating when its stomach is only partially full, but only if it has ingested something nutritious. On the other hand, if its stomach is filled with an equal volume of nonnutritive bulk, the animal will continue to eat. Apparently, the stomach walls contain receptors sensitive to the nutrients dissolved in the digestive juices. These receptors signal the brain that nutrient supplies are on their way, and the result is satiety (Deutsch, Puerto, & Wang, 1978).

Further satiety signals come from the duodenum, the first part of the small intestine. When food passes from the stomach into the intestines, the duodenum begins to release a hormone from its mucous lining. There is good evidence that this hormone—*cholecystokinin*, or *CCK*—sends "stop eating" messages to the brain (Gibbs & Smith, 1984). When CCK is injected into the abdominal cavity of hungry rats and dogs, they stop eating (Stacher, Bauer, & Steinringer, 1979; see also Chen, Deutsch, Gonzales, & Gu, 1993; Weller, Blass, Gibbs, & Smith, 1995). One might think that this would lead to a powerful dietary aid, but, unfortunately, humans given this hormone experience abdominal cramping, nausea, and sometimes vomiting (Miaskiewicz, Stricker, & Verbalis, 1989), and the appetite-suppression effect in rats seems also to be due to nausea (Chen et al., 1993).

## SIGNALS FROM FATTY TISSUE

Because they cannot be sure that food will be available the next time they need energy, animals do not just eat for the moment. Instead, they eat enough to satisfy both their current needs and to create a store of potential nutrients for later. Part of this store is for the short term, so food is converted to glycogen, which can quickly be converted to glucose when needed. Another store is needed for the long haul, and for this animals use the fat, or *adipose cells*, distributed throughout their body. These cells absorb the fatty acids created by the liver and swell in the process. When the animal's glycogen supplies are exhausted, it must turn to these longer term reserves. Fatty acids are drained from the adipose cells into the bloodstream and then converted into glucose.

Adipose tissue used to be regarded only as a kind of inert storage, but we now know that it plays a role in governing hunger. Fat cells, when full, secrete the chemical *leptin* into the bloodstream, where it is sensed by receptors in the hypothalamus and areas near the brain's ventricles (Maffei et al., 1995; McGregor et al., 1996). Leptin seems to provide a signal indicating that there is plenty of fat in storage and no need to add more, and it increases energy expenditure and oxygen consumption as well. Leptin appears to work by inhibiting the actions of another neurochemical, *neuropeptide Y*

*The importance of leptin    Cells in the adipose tissue, when full, secrete the chemical leptin, signalling that there is plenty of fat in storage and no need to add more. The mouse shown on the left is deficient in leptin, and so its brain never receives this feedback signal from the adipose tissue. As a result, the animal eats and eats, with the result shown in the photo.*

**(NPY)**, manufactured in the hypothalamus and the gut. NPY itself turns out to be the most potent appetite stimulant yet discovered (Gibbs, 1996), so potent that, when it is injected into the brain, it can make even fully sated rats resume eating (Stanley, Magdalin, & Leibowitz, 1989). Leptin secretion, then, is the negative feedback holding NPY in check.

## SIGNALS FROM THE OUTSIDE

Humans and animals obviously eat because their bodies need food. But they also eat for other reasons. For example, external stimuli—say, the smell of pizza—can often induce us to eat. The time of day is also important; animals are more likely to eat at their habitual mealtime. Yet another influence is the company of fellow eaters. A hen who has had her fill of grain will eagerly resume her meal if joined by other hens that are still hungry (Bayer, 1929).

The effectiveness of these external cues is not constant; it depends on the internal state of the organism. If we have just eaten an enormous meal or if we are enduring the stomach flu, even the tastiest dessert will no longer be tempting. These commonsense claims are confirmed in studies of waking monkeys implanted with microelectrodes in their hypothalamus. Certain neurons fired when the animal was shown a peanut or a banana, but these cells only fired when the monkey was hungry. When the animal was first fed to satiety and then shown the same foods, the hypothalamic neurons did not respond at all. It would seem that at least in the hypothalamus, the eye is not bigger than the stomach (Mora, Rolls, & Burton, 1976; Rolls, 1978).

That food is more appealing when we are hungry illustrates once again how all motives work—by potentiating certain responses. After all, animals have no way of knowing exactly what their bodies need at any particular moment; neither they nor most of us have ever read a text on digestive physiology. Thankfully, natural selection has led us to have nervous systems that know, and they make hunger a state that leads us not only to eat, but to eat with some level of discrimination.

## HYPOTHALAMIC CONTROL CENTERS

With all the different signals for food intake, it seems reasonable to suppose that there is a place in the nervous system where all the signals are integrated and a final decision is made to eat or not to eat. For many years, the best candidate was the hypothalamus, which was already known to contain controls for temperature regulation and water balance.

An early theory held that the hypothalamus contained separate "go" and "stop" centers for eating. In this *dual-center theory*, the "go" center was in the lateral region of the hypothalamus, while the "stop" center was in the ventromedial region. Certain kinds of evidence supported this theory. Rats whose lateral hypothalamus (the supposed "go" center) was lesioned stopped eating and starved to death unless force-fed for a few weeks after the surgery (Teitelbaum & Epstein, 1962; Teitelbaum & Stellar, 1954). Conversely, rats with lesions to the ventromedial region (the supposed "stop" center) ate voraciously and finally reached a final weight three times as great as before surgery. Tumors in this hypothalamic region, although very rare, have the same effect on humans (Hoebel & Teitelbaum, 1976; Miller, Bailey, & Stevenson, 1950; Teitelbaum, 1955, 1961; see Figure 3.6).

Despite the initial appeal of the dual-center theory of feeding, research on the neurochemicals involved in feeding has shown it to be far too simple. For example, lesions of the ventromedial hypothalamus (the supposed "stop" center) were found to heighten the rate of fat storage and not appetite per se (Stricker & Zigmond, 1976). In addition, the lateral hypothalamus was considered the "go" center. True, certain neurochemicals

*Inborn aversions?   (This Far Side cartoon by Gary Larson is reprinted by permission of Chronicle Features, San Francisco, California, all rights reserved.)*

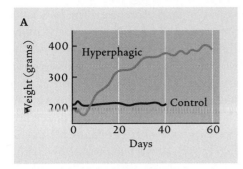

3.6   Hyperphagia   (A) Curve showing the weight gain of hyperphagic rats after an operation creating a hypothalamic lesion. The weight eventually stabilizes at a new level. (B) Photograph of a rat several months after the operation. This rat weighed over 1,000 grams.

called *orexins* initiate eating when they are injected into the brain, and they are secreted in the lateral hypothalamus (Sakuriam et al., 1998). But the consummate appetite stimulant NPY exerts its strongest effects outside the lateral hypothalamus, which suggests that this region cannot be the main "feeding" center (Leibowitz, 1991).

These (and other) results indicate that, while the hypothalamus is critical for the control of eating, other mechanisms are also crucial. In essence, it appears that there are multiple hunger and satiety systems, some specialized for short-term energy needs, others for long-term storage. These systems are not situated in just a few centers, but are located throughout the body and at multiple sites in the brain.

## OBESITY

Natural selection has provided organisms with multiple mechanisms for regulating their food intake, and, in most circumstances, these mechanisms work smoothly. They do not always operate perfectly, however, and many of the factors we have already discussed contribute to a problem partially created by the affluence of modern industrialized society—obesity. The problem is worldwide, with the World Health Organization now classifying obesity as a global epidemic (Ravussin & Bouchard, 2000).

Obesity is sometimes defined as a body weight that exceeds the average for a given height by 20 percent. Judged by this criterion, about 35 percent of American women over the age of twenty are obese, as are 31 percent of men over age twenty. By this same criterion, about 25 percent of American children and adolescents are also obese (Stern et al., 1995). Even using a looser criterion, a huge number of individuals still want to be thinner, and their desperation offers a ready market for a vast number of trendy diet foods and food additives. Although people often say that losing weight is for their "health" (and for a few, admittedly, it is), far more important are social standards of physical attractiveness. There are no fat teen heartthrobs or sex symbols (Stunkard, 1975).

There are many reasons why people become obese. In some cases, the cause is a bodily condition sometimes related to genetic factors. In others, it is simply a matter of how many calories they eat versus how many they expend.

### BODILY FACTORS IN OBESITY

Do fat people simply overeat? At bottom, this question betrays the moralistic view our society takes toward obesity. If obesity is just overeating, then it is the individual's

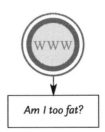

Am I too fat?

"fault" if she is obese, with *obesity* just a medical term for slothfulness. The facts tell a different story, one in which obesity cannot be explained so easily or moralistically. Instead, factors entirely out of a person's control can predispose that person to get fat, even if he eats no more (and exercises no less) than his slender next-door neighbor. What are these factors? Some of the important factors center on the *efficiency* of each person's digestive apparatus, with some people simply extracting more calories from any given food. Similarly, people differ in their overall metabolic level; if, as a result, less nutrient fuel is burned up, then more is left for fatty storage (Astrup, 2000). In still other individuals, too much of the nutrient intake may be converted into fat, leaving too little to burn as metabolic fuel. These and other constitutional differences in metabolic efficiency may help explain why some people gain weight so easily while others struggle to keep it on (Friedman, 1990a, b; Sims, 1986).

## GENETIC FACTORS IN OBESITY

Where do these constitutional factors come from? Part of the answer is genetics, and our genetic makeup greatly influences our predisposition to obesity. Evidence comes from studies of identical twins reared apart, whose weights are as similar as when they are reared together (Price & Gottesman, 1991). In addition, one kind of severe human obesity seems due to a defect in a gene that regulates the manufacture of leptin in both mice and men (Reed et al., 1996).

It would be false, however, to claim that a genetic pattern causes obesity because, here and everywhere else, genes can only express themselves within a suitable environment. After all, on a near-starvation diet, anyone, regardless of his or her genetic makeup, will lose weight. But our genes can certainly predispose us to obesity. This is evident in the results of a study of twelve pairs of male identical twins. Each of these men was fed about 1,000 calories per day above the amount required to maintain his initial weight. The activities of each participant were kept as constant as possible, and there was very little exercise. This regimen continued for one hundred days. Needless to say, all twenty-four men gained weight, but the amounts they gained varied substantially, from about ten to thirty pounds. Also varying was where on their bodies the weight was deposited. For some participants, it was the abdomen; for others, it was the thighs and buttocks. The important finding was that the amount each person gained was very similar to the weight gain of his twin (see Figure 3.7). The twins also tended to deposit the weight in the same place. If one gained in the abdomen, so did his twin; if another deposited the fat in his thighs and buttocks, his twin did, too. These findings demonstrate that people differ in how their body machinery handles excess calories and that this metabolic pattern is inherited (Bouchard, Lykken, McGue, Segal, & Tellegen, 1990).

Does such metabolic inefficiency indicate some sort of genetic defect? Not for proponents of the "thrifty gene" hypothesis. They note that many of our ancestors lived in times when food supplies were unpredictable and famines frequent, and those who had inefficient metabolisms and, as a result, stored more fat would have had a survival advantage (Fujimoto et al., 1995; Groop & Tuomi, 1997; Ravussin, 1994). However, this tendency, which helped us in ancestral environments, does not serve us well now, especially those of us belonging to affluent cultures where obtaining food—high-calorie food, at that—simply means a trip to the supermarket.

## DIETING AND THE WEIGHT SETPOINT

The constitutional factors just described allow some people to eat whatever they want and never gain a pound, while others place severe restrictions on what they eat and still gain weight. In addition, it is likely that people differ in their weight *setpoints*, the target weights their bodies work homeostatically to maintain. These setpoints

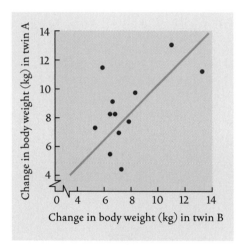

**3.7 Similarity of weight gains in identical twins** *Weight gains for twelve pairs of identical twins after 100 days of the same degree of overfeeding. Each point represents one twin pair, with the weight gain of twin A plotted on the vertical axis and the weight gain of twin B plotted on the horizontal axis. Weight gains are plotted in kilograms (1 kg = 2.2 lbs). The closer the points are to the diagonal line, the more similar the weight gains of the twins are to each other.*

may be "hard wired" and may in part be genetically determined (see also Foch & McClearn, 1980).

That we have such setpoints is suggested by the fact that obese people who go on crash diets return rapidly to their starting weight as soon as they go off their diet. Moreover, dieters do not lose nearly as much weight as would be expected based on their reduced caloric intake. The reason is that the body compensates for the caloric loss by reducing its basal metabolic rate, partly by slowing the rate at which stored fat is utilized (Guesbeck et al., 2001). As a result, the body makes fuller use of (and so gains the same nutrients from) a diminished food intake.

The situation is worse with "yo-yo" dieting, in which people repeatedly go on diets, break them, regain their starting weight, and then start dieting again (Carlson, 1991). Although the evidence is inconsistent, it appears that there may be further metabolic adaptation with each successive diet, such that it takes longer to achieve the desired weight each time (Brownell, Greenwood, Stellar, & Shrager, 1986). This may occur in part because the metabolic adaptation persists long after the person goes off the diet.

## THE TREATMENT OF OBESITY

In extreme cases, obesity is a health hazard that must be treated medically, if psychotherapy or behavioral interventions do not work. Certainly, such "morbid" obesity usually leads to early death, and for the worst cases physicians resort to surgical procedures such as stapling the stomach (to limit its capacity) or removing segments of the small intestine (to reduce caloric absorption from food). Much more commonly, physicians prescribe various appetite-suppressing medications. These can produce dramatic weight loss, but they all have side effects that, in rare circumstances, can be lethal. Moreover, these medications clearly illustrate the degree to which our bodies defend a weight setpoint because the medications are effective only as long as they are taken. When they are stopped, ravenous hunger ensues and the lost weight rapidly returns.

Apart from cases of morbid obesity, the relation between overweight and life expectancy is actually a matter of debate (Fitzgerald, 1981; see Figure 3.8). Determining the direct role of obesity is especially difficult because obesity is associated with inactivity, which itself is a health risk. Indeed, one study tracked over 25,000 men and 7,000 women for eight years and found that obese men who were physically fit had lower mortality rates than men of normal weight who were sedentary. A similar (although smaller) result was found for women (Kampert, Blair, Barlow, & Kohl, 1996).

Some authors argue, therefore, that problems of obesity may often be more social and aesthetic than medical. This is especially so for women, who are much likelier than men to believe they are overweight (Gray, 1977; Fallon & Rozin, 1985). Seen in this light, being slender is strictly a social ideal, one held by only some societies at that. Other cultures set quite different standards. The women painted by Rubens, Matisse, and Renoir were considered beautiful in their day; by comparison, today's supermodels would have been judged then to be undernourished and unappealing.

Of course, the forces sustaining a society's ideal body weight are formidable including a barrage of media images promoting thinness as an ideal. This makes it immensely difficult for overweight individuals simply to accept themselves as they are. They might understand that there is nothing sacred about a society's ideal body weight and that there is no law (or any medical reason) requiring each individual to match this ideal. But this knowledge is a puny defense against a world of weight-obsessed peers and parents, Hollywood screen idols, and fashion advertisements, all celebrating a level of thinness that is, for many of us, unnatural and unhealthy (for further discussion, see Smith, 1996).

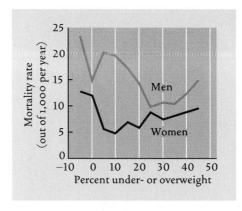

3.8   *Relation of obesity to mortality*   **The figure presents the mortality rate in a sample of 5,209 people in Massachusetts. The figure shows that being overweight does not increase overall mortality risk, at least not for overweight percentages that are less than 50.**

*Thin is beautiful—or is it?*   **The Boston organization Boycott Anorexic Marketing is a group of women who believe that the glamorization of ultrathin models in advertising tends to encourage the development of eating disorders in young women. To call attention to this relationship, such groups sometimes annotate the ads of those they see as culprits.**

# ANOREXIA NERVOSA

In some cases, the desire to be thin may be so extreme that it leads to eating disorders whose health implications are serious indeed. One such condition is *anorexia nervosa*, which in industrialized societies afflicts up to 1 percent of young people, almost all of them female. Its defining feature is "the relentless pursuit of thinness through self-starvation, even unto death" (Bruch, 1973, p. 4). The disorder typically begins in midadolescence and is most common in societies in which food is plentiful but thinness is the ideal of attractiveness (American Psychiatric Association, 1994).

Anorexics are intensely and continually preoccupied by the fear of becoming fat. They eat only low-calorie food, if they eat at all. In addition, they may induce vomiting to purge whatever they do eat and may use laxatives to speed weight loss. Moreover, they often engage in strenuous exercise, sometimes for many hours per day. This regimen leads to drastic weight loss, sometimes reaching body weights that can dwindle to as little as 50 percent of what would be considered normal. Further symptoms include the cessation of menstruation, hyperactivity, sleep disorders, and avoidance of sex.

For up to 40 percent of those with anorexia nervosa, treatment—which can range from outpatient care all the way to forced hospitalization and intravenous feeding—is successful. Less happily, the largest percentage of patients suffers chronically. Most tragically, in about 10 percent of the cases, the end result of this self-starvation is death (Andreasen & Black, 1996).

What leads to anorexia nervosa? Hypotheses abound. Some authorities believe that the primary causes are psychological and reflect our modern obsession with slimness (Logue, 1986). In other patients, the main cause may be a fear of sexuality or a defiance of one's parents and a fierce desire to wrest some degree of personal autonomy and control (Bruch, 1978, p. 61).

More biologically oriented authors believe that the problem lies in some disruption of regulatory pathways in the hypothalamus. One reason is that anorexics tend to have imbalances in certain neurotransmitters as well as in reproductive and growth hormones. One clue that the hormonal problems may be primary is provided by the fact that about one-fifth of anorexic females cease menstruation before they lose any weight (Andreasen & Black, 1996). A genetic predisposition also appears likely. Between 6 and 10 percent of female siblings and relatives of anorexics also have anorexia nervosa. For identical twins, if one twin has anorexia nervosa, the other has more than a 50 percent chance of being anorexic herself (Andreasen & Black, 1996). Perhaps most striking is the fact that individuals with anorexia nervosa are much likelier than nonanorexic controls to have relatives with *obsessive-compulsive disorder* (*OCD*; see Chapter 16), a disabling mental condition that tends to run in families. Certainly, the anorexic's compulsive self-starvation and obsessive preoccupation with calories and body image resemble OCD in many ways, and investigators are increasingly viewing anorexia nervosa as but one variant of a spectrum of OCD-related disorders (Bellodi et al., 2001).

# BULIMIA NERVOSA

Another, more common, eating disorder is *bulimia nervosa*, characterized by repeated eating binges followed by attempts to purge oneself of the food by self-induced vomiting or the taking of laxatives. Bulimia nervosa is fairly common among college students; in one survey, it was found in 19 percent of the women and 5 percent of the men. Unlike those with anorexia nervosa, individuals with bulimia have roughly normal weights. Still, they suffer both physically and emotionally from repeated binging and purging. The binges may produce disruptions of electrolyte balance that can ultimately result in heart and kidney disease as well as urinary infections. And their self-induced vomiting often

*Changing conceptions of the relation between body weight and attractiveness   An underlying cause of many eating disorders in Western women is their belief that being slender is beautiful. And certainly our modern culture does celebrate thinness: compare (A) The* Three Graces, *painted by the Flemish master Peter Paul Rubens in 1639 with (B) Gisele Bundchen, a contemporary supermodel regarded by many as beautiful, but vastly thinner than the women who appeared beautiful at other time periods.*

causes erosion of their fingernails and tooth enamel. Since most bulimic individuals also suffer from serious depression, antidepressant medications such as Prozac are typically successful not only in relieving the depression, but in halting most of the binge-and-purge behavior (Fluoxetine Bulimia Nervosa Collaborative Study Group, 1992).

Together, the eating disorders show us that, although tight homeostatic adjustments regulate food intake, social and psychological factors can override these mechanisms and result in grave bodily harm, even death.

# THREAT

Our emphasis so far has been on motives that are largely based on internal, homeostatic controls. A disruption of the internal environment impels the organism to act in a way that ultimately restores internal balance. As we have seen, though, these so-called internally regulated motives are not entirely regulated from within. The sight of food can cause us to eat even when we are not hungry; the anticipation of winter can trigger nest building even before it gets cold.

Other motives take this one step further since their primary triggers are largely external. An example is our reaction to intense threat. In this case, the instigation is the threatening event or object—but a major component of the adjustment is largely internal as the body prepares to escape, retaliate, or negotiate.

## THREAT AND THE AUTONOMIC NERVOUS SYSTEM

What are the biological mechanisms that underlie our reactions to threat? We have already discussed the fact that the autonomic nervous system is divided into two branches: sympathetic and parasympathetic (p. 91). According to American physiologist Walter B. Cannon (1871–1945), these branches serve two broad and different functions. The parasympathetic branch handles the vegetative functions of ordinary life: the conservation of bodily resources, reproduction, and the disposal of wastes. In effect, these reflect an organism's operations during times of peace—a low and steady heart rate, peristaltic movements of stomach and intestines, secretions by digestive glands, and the like. In contrast, the sympathetic branch has an activating function. It summons the body's resources in times of crisis and gets the organism ready for vigorous action (Cannon, 1929).

The complementary actions of the two autonomic divisions are seen in many bodily activities. For example, parasympathetic excitation slows down the heart rate and reduces blood pressure. Sympathetic excitation, as we have mentioned, has the opposite effect and also inhibits digestion and sexual activity. In addition, it stimulates the inner core of the adrenal gland, the adrenal medulla, to pour epinephrine (adrenaline) and norepinephrine into the bloodstream. These have essentially the same effects as sympathetic stimulation—they accelerate the heart rate, speed up metabolism, and so on. As a result, the sympathetic effects are amplified even further (see Figure 3.9 on p. 102).

## THE EMERGENCY REACTION

Cannon argued that intense sympathetic arousal serves as an emergency reaction that mobilizes the organism for a crisis—for "flight or fight," as he described it. Consider a grazing zebra, placidly maintaining homeostasis by nibbling at the grass and vasodi-

**3.9** *The sympathetic and parasympathetic branches of the autonomic nervous system The parasympathetic system (shown in red) facilitates the vegetative functions of the organism: It slows the heart and lungs, stimulates digestive functions, permits sexual activity, and so on. In contrast, the sympathetic system (shown in blue) helps ready the organism for emergency: It accelerates the heart and lungs, liberates nutrient fuels for muscular effort, and inhibits digestive and sexual functions. Note that the fibers of the sympathetic system are interconnected through a chain of ganglionic fibers outside of the spinal cord. As a result, sympathetic activation has a somewhat diffuse character; any sympathetic excitation tends to affect all of the viscera rather than just some. This is in contrast to the parasympathetic system, whose action is more specific and which operates through the vagus nerve, a cranial nerve that emerges from the skull and permeates the chest and abdomen.*

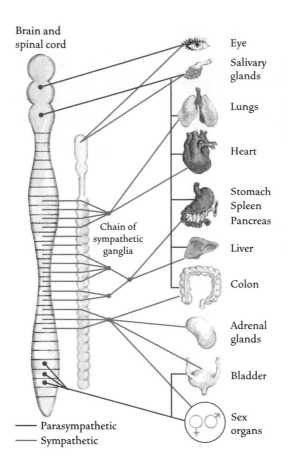

**PARASYMPATHETIC SYSTEM**
Constriction of pupil
Secretion of tears
Salivation
Slowing of heart action
Constriction of respiratory passages
Stomach contraction; secretion of
    digestive fluids
Intestinal peristalsis
Contraction of bladder
Erection

**SYMPATHETIC SYSTEM**
Dilation of pupil
Inhibition of tear glands
Inhibition of salivation
Acceleration of heart action
Opens respiratory passages
Inhibits stomach contractions and
    digestive secretion
Inhibits intestinal peristalsis
Relaxes bladder
Inhibits erection

latating in the hot African sun. Suddenly it sees a lion closing in for the kill. Escape will require pronounced muscular exertion, with the support of the entire bodily machinery, and this is exactly what intense sympathetic activation provides. Because of this activation, more nutrient fuel is available to the muscles and can be delivered rapidly through wide-open blood vessels. At the same time, waste products are jettisoned and all less-essential organic activities are brought to a halt.

Cannon produced considerable evidence suggesting that a similar autonomic reaction occurs when the pattern is one of attack rather than of flight. A cat about to tangle with a dog shows accelerated heartbeat, piloerection (its hair standing on end, normally a heat-conserving device), and pupillary dilation—all signs of sympathetic arousal, signs that the body is girding itself for violent muscular effort (Figure 3.10).

It soon became apparent, however, that Cannon's fight-or-flight formulation was too simple because organisms respond to threat in many different ways. For example, rats try to escape when threatened but fight when finally cornered. Some animals stand perfectly immobile so that predators are less likely to notice them. Other animals have more exotic means of self-protection: some species of fish pale when threatened, which makes them harder to spot against the sandy ocean bottom. This effect is produced by the direct action of adrenal epinephrine on various pigments in the animal's skin (Odiorne, 1957).

In fact, it is relatively rare that threatening encounters result immediately in fight or flight for either participant. Instead, there is usually a period of heightened vigilance during which each animal senses the behavioral signals given by the other. These signals—whether paling, piloerection, or paralysis, vocalizations or facial expressions—serve as cues to the signaler's status and intentions (see Chapter 11). This allows for a kind of negotiation in which the ultimate outcome might be fight or flight, but might just as well be playing or mating (Hinde, 1985; Smith, 1977). Regardless of the outcome, these situations require immediate action, and Cannon's emergency reaction comes into play in all of them.

## DISRUPTIVE EFFECTS OF AUTONOMIC AROUSAL

The emergency system we have been discussing has undoubted biological value, but strong arousal of the sympathetic branch of the ANS can also be disruptive and even damaging. This is especially clear in humans. In our day-to-day lives, we rarely encounter emergencies that call for violent physical effort. But our biological nature has not changed just because the modern world contains no saber-toothed tigers. We are plagued instead by chronic stressors like traffic jams, ornery bosses, and agonizing world crises. And although we often feel impelled to defend ourselves against these threats of the modern world, physical action is frequently inappropriate, ineffective, or illegal. Nonetheless, we are stuck with the same emergency reactions that our ancestors had, and so we keep ourselves armed physiologically against situations we cannot really control. The resulting bodily wear and tear can take a serious toll.

The disruptive effects of threat upon our digestion or sexual responses are common knowledge. During periods of acute anxiety, diarrhea or constipation are widespread, and it is difficult to achieve or maintain sexual arousal. This is hardly surprising since our digestive functions and many aspects of our sexuality (for example, erections in males and vaginal lubrication in females) are largely controlled by the reciprocal branch of the ANS, the parasympathetic nervous system, and are thus inhibited by intense sympathetic arousal. The aftereffects of threat can also be disabling, causing disorders such as stomachaches and headaches. If the threat continues, the prolonged stress responses result in chronic suppression of the immune system, which can make us vulnerable to infection by pathogens like bacteria and viruses.

**3.10 Sympathetic emergency reaction** *A cat's response to a threatening encounter.*

# PAIN

We have seen how organisms respond to threats of various sorts. Many of these threats have acquired their significance through learning (see Chapter 4). Others seem to produce the emergency reactions we have described without any prior experience. An important example of such a built-in trigger is pain.

## PAIN AS AN AID TO SURVIVAL

It seems paradoxical, but the sensation of pain has considerable survival value. This fact is highlighted by the rare cases of individuals born with a virtual insensitivity to pain. They often die young, having suffered numerous injuries and showing considerable scarring (Manfredi et al., 1981). As a child, one such individual bit off the tip of her tongue while chewing, incurred serious burns when kneeling on a heater, and dislocated her hips and vertebrae because she did not shift her weight appropriately or turn over in her sleep. Finally, she developed massive infections that caused her death at the age of twenty-nine (Melzack, 1973).

## PAIN RELIEF THROUGH ENDORPHINS

Pain serves as a call to action, leading us to withdraw from a flame, run cold water on a burn, or put less weight on a sprained ankle (Bolles & Fanselow, 1982). But if the pain

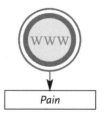

Pain

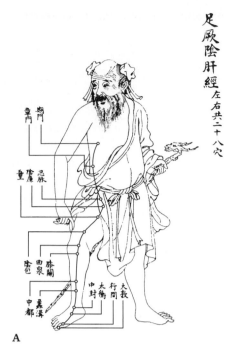

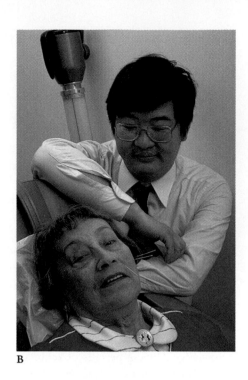

*3.11 Acupuncture  Acupuncture is a complex system of treatment that grew up in ancient China and was based on the idea that disease is a disturbance of vital energies that circulate in particular channels. Their balance was to be restored by manipulating metal needles at special points along these channels. (A) From a seventeenth-century Chinese treatise illustrating the liver tract with twenty-eight special points. (B) A contemporary dental patient receiving treatment in place of novocaine.*

A

B

continues, it may interfere with whatever needs to be done. Fortunately, organisms have evolved means of alleviating some of their own pain.

There are many stories of athletes who suffer injuries but do not feel the pain until the game is over; similar accounts are told of soldiers in battle or parents rescuing their children from accidents. These stories suggest that internal mechanisms are available that can produce *analgesia*, or pain relief. Various laboratory experiments support this conclusion. Rats subjected to various forms of stress, such as being forced to swim in cold water, become less sensitive to pain (Bodnar, Kelly, Brutus, & Glusman, 1980). Similar analgesia under stress has been shown in humans, who experience analgesia from mild electric shock to the back or limbs. Analgesia also occurs in acupuncture, an ancient Chinese treatment in which needles are inserted in various parts of the body (see Figure 3.11; Mann, Bowsher, Mumford, Lipton, & Miles, 1973); this procedure seems to suppress pain in animals as well as humans (Nathan, 1978).

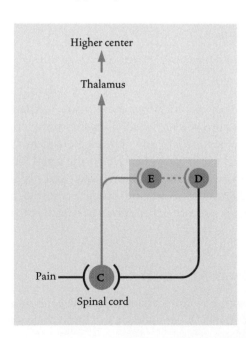

*3.12  Pain and pain relief  Highly schematic diagram of a proposed neural circuit to explain certain pain relief phenomena, with green indicating excitation and red indicating inhibition. Pain stimuli excite neurons in the spinal cord (C) that carry pain information upward to the thalamus. But they also excite endorphin-releasing neurons (E) in the midbrain, which, through several intermediate steps, excite descending neurons (D) that inhibit the pain pathway in the spinal cord.*

Higher center

Thalamus

E · · · D

Pain — C

Spinal cord

What mechanisms underlie these effects? The answer may be found in brain chemistry. It has long been known that the experience of pain can be dulled or eliminated by drugs such as morphine and other opiates. These drugs are typically delivered from outside the body, but on occasion the brain is its own pharmacist. When assailed by various kinds of stress (including pain), the brain produces its own painkillers, which it then administers to itself. These are the *endorphins* (a contraction of *endogenous*—that is, internally produced—and *morphine*), a group of neurotransmitters that are chemically very similar to opiates. Like opiates, endorphins modulate pain messages going to the brain through nerve tracts in the spinal cord (see Figure 3.12). It appears, then, that the opiate compounds prescribed by physicians work by mimicking the body's own analgesics, although, in fact, some of the brain's endorphins are considerably more powerful than any current opiate medication (Bloom, 1983; Olson, Olson, & Kastin, 1995; Snyder & Childers, 1979).

# SEX

Sex is clearly a biological motive and is just as rooted in our physiology as are temperature maintenance, hunger, thirst, and the response to external threat. In some ways, however, sex is different. To begin with, sexual behavior is necessary not for personal survival, but for the survival of our genes. Furthermore, unlike the other biological motives, sex is inherently social, and in humans its pursuit is intertwined with all manner of cultural patterns and attitudes (we discuss social aspects of sexual behavior later, in Chapters 11 and 13). For now, we focus on sex as a biological motive of individual organisms, with only a cursory glance at its social ramifications.

## HORMONES AND ANIMAL SEXUALITY

Sexual behavior in animals is all about arranging for the union of sperm and ova, and this can proceed only after male and female have met, courted, and determined each other to be a suitable mate. At that point, at least for terrestrial mammals and birds, the male generally introduces his sperm cells into the genital tract of the female, where the ova are fertilized. The sperm has to encounter a ready ovum, and then the fertilized egg can develop only if it is provided with the appropriate conditions. The sequence of events necessary for these events requires a complex hormonal feedback system between the brain and the reproductive organs.

### HORMONAL CYCLES

Timing is everything. Except for primates, mammals mate only when the female is in heat, or *estrus*. The female rat, for example, goes through a fifteen-hour estrus period every four days. At all other times, she will resolutely reject any male's advances. If he nuzzles her or tries to mount, she will kick and bite him. But during estrus, the female responds quite differently to the male's approach. She first retreats in small hops, then stops to look back and wiggles her ears (McClintock & Adler, 1978). Eventually, she stands still, her back arched, her tail held to the side—a willing sexual partner.

What brings about this change in the female's behavior? The mechanism is an interlocking system of hormonal and neurological controls that involves the pituitary gland, the hypothalamus, and the ovaries. There are three phases. During the first, *follicles* (ova-containing sacs) in the ovary mature under the influence of pituitary secretions. The follicles produce the sex hormone *estrogen*. As the concentration of estrogen in the bloodstream rises, the hypothalamus responds by directing the pituitary to change its secretions. In consequence, follicle growth is accelerated until the follicle ruptures and releases the mature ovum.

This triggers the second phase, during which the animal is in estrus. Estrogen production peaks and stimulates certain structures in the hypothalamus, which make the animal sexually receptive.

The third phase is dominated by the action of another sex hormone, *progesterone*, which is produced by the ruptured follicle. Its secretion leads to a thickening of the uterine lining, a first step in preparing the uterus to receive the embryo. If the ovum is fertilized, there are further steps in preparing the uterus. If it is not, the thickened uter-

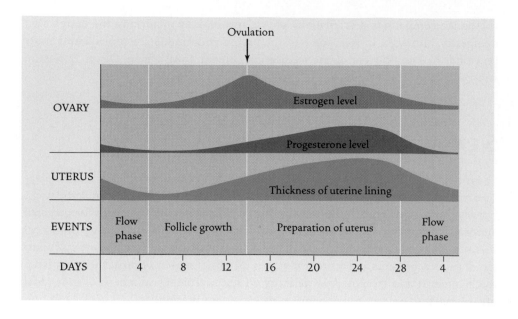

**3.13 The main stages of the human menstrual cycle** *The figure shows estrogen and progesterone levels and thickness of the uterine lining during the human menstrual cycle. The cycle begins with the growth of a follicle, continues through ovulation and a maximum estrogen level, is followed by a phase during which the uterus becomes prepared to receive the embryo, and ends with a flow phase during which the thickened uterine lining is sloughed off.*

ine walls are reabsorbed, and another cycle begins. In humans and some primates, this thickening of the uterine wall involves too much extra tissue to be easily reabsorbed; the thickened uterine lining is therefore sloughed off as *menstrual flow* (Figure 3.13).

## HORMONAL CHANGES AND BEHAVIOR

These and other hormonal changes affect behavior dramatically. When female rats have their ovaries removed, they soon lose all sexual interest and capacity, as do male rats when castrated. But sexual behavior is quickly restored in the male by appropriate injections of *testosterone* and in the female mainly by estrogen (the female also needs, and secretes, a small amount of testosterone).

Many investigators believe that the behavioral effects of these hormones are mediated by receptors in the hypothalamus. This hypothesis has been tested by injecting tiny quantities of various hormones into different regions of the hypothalamus. Such studies reveal, for example, that a spayed female cat will go into estrus when estrogen is implanted (Harris & Michael, 1964) and that castrated males will resume sexual behavior after doses of the appropriate male hormones (Davidson, 1969; Feder, 1984; McEwen et al., 1982).

Hormones affect behavior, but the effect can also be the other way around. What an animal experiences and what it does can substantially affect it hormonally. In some animals, the female's courtship behavior can trigger the release of testosterone in courting males. In animals such as rodents, the female's sexual receptivity is triggered by chemicals contained in the male's urine. In other cases, copulation itself produces reproductive readiness. For example, the female rat secretes some progesterone during the normal cycle but not enough to permit the implantation of the fertilized ovum in the uterus. The critical dose is secreted only as a reflex response to sexual stimulation. This leaves the sexually aroused male rat with two reproductive functions: supplying sperm and providing the mechanical stimulation necessary for hormonal secretion. Should he ejaculate too quickly and thus leave the female inadequately stimulated, all is lost, for no pregnancy results (Adler, 1979; Rosenzweig et al., 1999).

## HORMONES AND HUMAN SEXUALITY

Compared to other animals, humans are much less automatic in their sexual activities, much more varied, and much more affected by prior experience. This difference is especially marked when we consider the effects of sex hormones. In rats and cats, sexual behavior is highly dependent upon sex hormone levels; castrated males and spayed females stop copulating a few months after the removal of their gonads (Figure 3.14). In humans, on the other hand, sexual activity may persist for years, even decades, after castration or ovariectomy, provided that the operation was performed after puberty (Bermant & Davidson, 1974).

The liberation from hormonal control is especially clear in human females. The female rat or cat is chained to an estrus cycle that makes her receptive during only one period, but women can respond sexually at virtually all points of their menstrual cycle. They still show some variation within that period, with sexual desire and activity tending to peak during the middle of the cycle, when ovulation occurs (Bancroft, 1986; Hamburg, Moos, & Yalom, 1968). But these effects are not very pronounced; they probably represent vestiges of an estrus cycle, left behind by waves of evolutionary change.

Although we humans are not at the mercy of our hormones, they still have their effects. Testosterone injections into men or women who have abnormally low hormone levels will generally increase their sex drive (Davidson, 1986; Rosenzweig et al., 1999). An important demonstration concerns the effects of testosterone administration on gay men. The testosterone-injected gay male becomes more sexually active; but, contrary to a common misconception, these injections have no impact on his sexual orientation—the augmented sexual desire is directed toward other men, just as before (Kinsey, Pomeroy, & Martin, 1948).

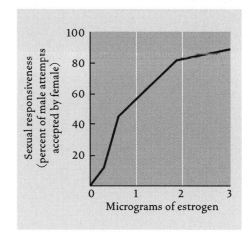

**3.14 Estrogen and sexual behavior** *The effect of estrogen injections on the sexual responsiveness of female rats was measured by the number of male attempts at mounting that were accepted by the female. The females' ovaries had been removed, so they could not produce estrogen themselves. Sexual behavior was measured eight days after the hormone treatment began.*

## The Phases of the Human Sexual Response

Scientific investigations of how humans respond sexually began as early as the 1890s, when such studies were regarded as unspeakably scandalous. Even anonymous surveys of people's sexual behavior were incendiary (but sold many copies) as late as the 1950s (Kinsey, 1948, 1952). Today, much of what we know about human sexual response dates from the 1960s, when two medical investigators, William Masters (1915–2001) and Virginia Johnson (b. 1925), sought to help sufferers of sexual problems by bringing these people into the laboratory and asking them to engage in sex. Their studies began the field of sexual medicine, which has taught us a great deal about human sexuality and has led to numerous kinds of sex therapies.

In the couples they observed, Masters and Johnson found a predictable pattern to human sexual arousal, one that occurs in four stages. The first stage, known as *excitement*, begins when a couple are in a sexual context and engage in light touching, hair stroking, kissing, nuzzling, gentle hugging, and so on. At this stage, the parasympathetic branch of the autonomic nervous system initiates *vasocongestion* of (diversion of blood to) the body's erectile tissues, which include the genitals, nipples, and even tissues inside the nose. Vasocongestion of the genitals produces the most salient signs of sexual arousal: in males, erection of the penis; and in females, the lubrication of the vagina and the swelling of the labia and clitoris. Meanwhile, the sympathetic branch produces its own changes: a quickening of respiration and heart rate, and increased blood pressure. This excitement stage requires, paradoxically, that the couple be relaxed; any distraction or interruption can kill such passion instantly.

After a few minutes, the couple enters the *plateau* stage. The physiological changes begun during the excitement stage are intensified. Fuller body contact is desired, full embrace replaces gentle hugging, and deep, rhythmic caresses to the breasts, genitals, and other areas supplant light touch. Muscles throughout the body may become tense, and the skin of the breasts, stomach, and beyond may become flush with blood and redden (the *sex flush*). In the male, the erection becomes more rigid, and the testes retract within the scrotum. In the female, the clitoris becomes erect but recedes, making it look smaller, while increased vasocongestion lengthens the vagina and makes it rigid and tunnellike in preparation for insertion of the penis.

The culmination of the plateau stage is the *orgasm*, a seizurelike episode that usually lasts only a few seconds. In males, orgasm is experienced as an inevitable reflex during sexual intercourse, one that is difficult to postpone; in contrast, females may need sustained stimulation, especially direct stimulation of the clitoris, to achieve it. Orgasm in both sexes is characterized by involuntary muscle contractions throughout the body, especially in the limbs, toes, and anal muscles. Heart rate, blood pressure, and breathing rate soar momentarily. Finally, there occur rhythmic contractions—between 3 and 15 of them every 0.8 seconds—of the urethra in the male (thus expelling semen) and of the vagina and uterus in the female. These contractions are probably triggered by the pulsed release of *oxytocin*, a hormone manufactured mostly in the hypothalamus, which plays an important role not only in sexual pleasure, but also in nesting, birthing, breast feeding, and mother-infant bonding (Carter, 1992). Direct nipple stimulation in women is known to trigger the release of oxytocin and cause uterine contractions (Amico & Finley, 1986). Although this mechanism mainly promotes lactation and nursing, it can also increase orgasmic intensity.

Orgasm is usually—but not always—accompanied by ecstatic pleasure and an immediate reduction of sexual tension. This signals the onset of the *resolution* stage. Males immediately lose their excitement (but can regain it, within minutes in young males and hours and even days for older ones). Some females show the same pattern, while others with sufficient stimulation can proceed almost immediately to another orgasm. Interestingly, the excitement and plateau stages are not necessary preludes to orgasm. Orgasm without sexual arousal can occur with sufficient physical stimulation, and some medications taken for depression have been reported to cause spontaneous orgasms while yawning (Klein, 1989).

## THE FUNCTION OF THE ORGASM

What is the orgasm for? In males, the answer is obvious: it is necessary for the ejaculation of sperm and seminal fluid. The female orgasm is tougher to explain. Some investigators believe that it promotes fertilization. They point to the fact that during the contractions of orgasm, the female's cervix dips down toward the rear of the vagina, putting it in contact with any semen that might be present and increasing the odds of fertilization. Evidence suggests that a woman who has an orgasm from 1 to 45 minutes after receiving semen retains more sperm than if no orgasm occurred. This allows females to be selective about the males with whom they reproduce; to reduce—but not eliminate—the odds of conception, she simply makes sure she does not have an orgasm (Baker & Bellis, 1993, 1995).

In our discussion of human sexual response, we have focused here on its neurology and physiology. Obviously, there is much more to human sexuality than these clinical descriptions. But just as glucoreceptors, leptin, and the liver underlie the epicurean pleasures to be had at a four-star restaurant, so do analogous physiological mechanisms underlie all the grander aspects of sexuality: attraction, courtship, love, commitment, and, finally, reproduction and the nurturance of the young. We will discuss these issues, together with insights gleaned from the study of nonhumans, in subsequent chapters.

# SLEEP AND WAKING

We turn next to a different sort of motivation: the need for sleep. Sleep is actually just one phase of what researchers called the *sleep-wake cycle*, a daily rhythm that reflects a continuum of both brain and bodily arousal ranging from alert hypervigilance to the near-total deactivation of deep sleep.

## WAKING

The sympathetic branch of the autonomic nervous system is the arousal system for many processes in the body. Another set of arousal systems alerts the brain itself, waking the animal if it is asleep or bringing an already-awake animal to full alertness. These arousal systems involve structures in the mid- and hindbrain, which send pathways that ascend to the rest of the brain (Aston-Jones, 1985).

Apart from these subcortical structures, the brain's state of arousal is also regulated by the cortex. That the cortex can rouse itself is seen with some complex stimuli whose recognition requires cortical involvement—a baby's cry, the smell of burning wood, the sound of our own name—that are more likely to wake us than others, regardless of their intensity. Furthermore, signals from the cortex can excite subcortical structures, which then reciprocate and activate the cortex further. This arc—cortex to lower systems to cortex—is involved in many phenomena of sleep and waking. We sometimes have trouble falling asleep because we cannot "shut off" our thoughts. Here, cortical activity triggers the subcortical arousal system, which activates the cortex, which again excites the lower-level subcortical system, and so on.

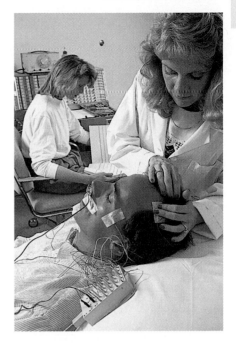

*Observing sleep    All-night EEG recordings of patients in sleep labs have revealed the several stages of sleep.*

## SLEEP AND PHYSIOLOGICAL ACTIVITY

The same circuits that enhance arousal can also lower it—for example, when we listen to the drone of a monotonous lecturer or fixate on the median line of the highway while driving late at night. Such minimal stimulation can cause our arousal levels to drop so low that we are tempted to nod off into a state that seems the very opposite of high arousal—sleep. What can we say about this state in which we spend about one-third of our lives?

Eavesdropping on the brain of waking or sleeping participants is possible because, as we saw in Chapter 2, the language of the nervous system is partly electrical. When electrodes are placed at various points on the scalp, they pick up electrical fluctuations that result from the activity of the millions of neurons in the cortex just underneath. In absolute terms, these voltage changes are very small, so they are fed through highly sensitive amplifiers before being graphed on a scrolling paper chart or displayed directly on a computer screen (Figure 3.15). The resulting record is an *electroencephalogram*, or *EEG*, a picture of voltage changes over time occurring at the surface of the brain.

EEG records can be obtained either from an awake participant or a sleeping one. Figure 3.16 shows an EEG record from an awake participant in a relaxed state with eyes closed. The record shows alpha waves, a regular waxing and waning of electrical potential, at some eight to twelve cycles per second (Hz). This *alpha rhythm* is characteristic of this state (awake but resting) and is found in most mammals. When the participant attends to some stimulus with his eyes open or when he has his eyes closed but is thinking actively (for instance, doing mental arithmetic), the picture changes. Now the alpha rhythm is blocked, and the participant mainly shows a *beta rhythm*: the voltage is lower, the frequency is much higher (12 to 14 Hz), and the pattern of ups and downs is nearly random.

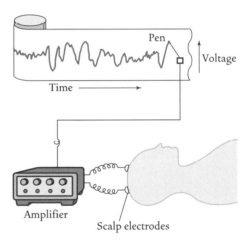

*3.15    Schematic diagram of an EEG recording    A number of scalp electrodes are placed on a research participant's head. At any one time, there are small differences in the electrical potential (that is, the voltage) between any two of these electrodes. These differences are magnified by an amplifier and are then used to activate a recording pen. Since the voltage fluctuates, the pen goes up and down, thus tracing a brain wave on the moving paper. The number of such waves per second is the EEG frequency.*

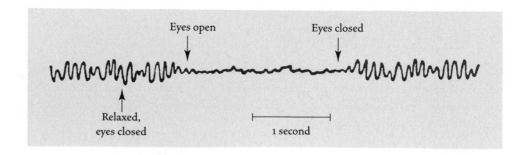

Eyes open                    Eyes closed

Relaxed,
eyes closed

1 second

3.16    *Alpha waves and alpha blocking*

EEG records can also tell us about the brain's state during sleep. Sleep researchers most often obtain continuous, all-night recordings not only of brain waves, but also of other kinds of physiological activity that are informative about both sleep and wakefulness, including respiration rate, heart rate, muscle tension, and eye movements.

## THE STAGES OF SLEEP

Such physiological recordings demonstrate that there are two distinct kinds of sleep: *slow-wave sleep* and *REM sleep*. Let us begin with slow-wave sleep. At bedtime, as a person begins to relax in bed and becomes drowsy, his EEG pattern tends to slow from its jittery waking frequency and develops an accentuated alpha rhythm. He is now in a light, dozing sleep from which he is easily awakened and in which he experiences fleeting daydreamlike imagery; this is the lightest stage, or Stage 1, of slow-wave sleep (Figure 3.17).

After a few minutes in Stage 1, the participant passes a "point of no return" in which he feels himself drop off to sleep (perhaps with a few muscle twitches). This signals the start of Stage 2 of slow-wave sleep. Over the next hour, as his sleep deepens, he passes from Stage 2 to Stages 3 and 4 of slow-wave sleep. His heart rate and respiration slow, and his eyes drift slowly and no longer move in tandem. His EEG shows fluctuations of increasingly higher voltage and lower frequency (Stages 2 through 4 in Figure 3.17). At this point he is virtually immobile, curled up in semifetal position, and hard to wake up. Indeed, trying to wake up a person from slow-wave sleep takes sustained effort; the person will protest, appearing disoriented, mumbling incoherently, or thrashing around even if shaken or shouted at. Some people enter such a confused half-sleep, half-awake state spontaneously, and this accounts for slow-wave sleep disturbances such as sleepwalking and childhood night terrors (Hauri, 1977).

The sleeper will typically spend about 90 to 100 minutes in uninterrupted slow-wave sleep, shifting up and down among Stages 2, 3, and 4. After that, his quality of sleep changes dramatically. His heart rate and respiration rate quicken, almost as if he were awake and exercising. His EEG returns to the high-frequency activity associated with wakefulness (Jouvet, 1967). His eyes stop rolling lazily and begin jittering back and forth under his closed eyelids. According to all these physiological signs, he should be awake and alert. But he does not wake up, and his skeletal muscles show sudden flaccidity—his jaw goes slack, and he moves from a semifetal position to a sprawl, with arms and legs draped haphazardly. And despite the active EEG, in this sleep stage he is

3.17    *The stages of sleep    The figure shows EEG records taken from the frontal lobe of the brain during waking, slow-wave sleep, and REM sleep.*

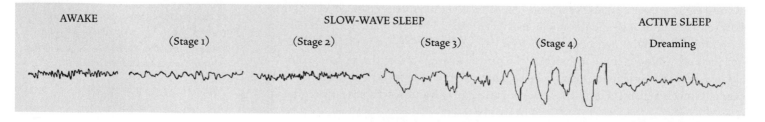

| AWAKE | SLOW-WAVE SLEEP | | | | ACTIVE SLEEP |
|---|---|---|---|---|---|
| | (Stage 1) | (Stage 2) | (Stage 3) | (Stage 4) | Dreaming |

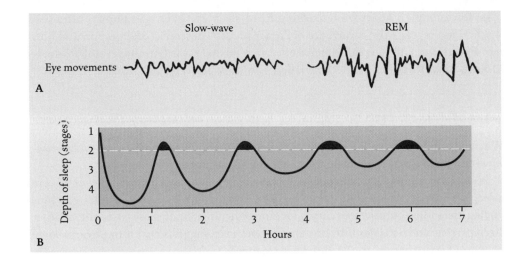

A

B

*3.18   REM and slow-wave sleep   (A) Eye movements during slow-wave and REM sleep. (B) The alternation of slow-wave and REM sleep periods throughout the night (REM periods are in color). Rapid eye movements begin as the person repeatedly emerges from deeper sleep to the level of Stage 2. More vivid and visual dreams are recalled after awakening from REM sleep.*

least sensitive to external stimulation (Williams, Tepas, & Morlock, 1962). But if awakened, he leaps to attention instantly. This odd state is REM sleep, named for the participant's rapid eye movements (Figure 3.18). Participants in this state are both physiologically activated and muscularly inactivated, and because of this contrast, REM sleep is often called *paradoxical sleep*.

This first REM period of a night's sleep usually lasts only about 5 minutes, after which people switch back to slow-wave sleep. After another 90 to 100 minutes, a second REM period ensues. This pattern continues, with alternating slow-wave and REM sleep periods. The average night's sleep includes four to five REM periods that last longer each time, with the final REM period of the night lasting up to 45 minutes. Because REM sleep is so physiologically active, these latter REM periods can be strenuous, explaining why people who decide to "sleep in" and ignore the alarm clock often wake up extratired: they have exhausted themselves REMing. They may also be more susceptible to the frightening but harmless state known as *sleep paralysis* (Hauri, 1977), in which the muscular paralysis of REM sleep persists for a few moments past awakening, leaving the person conscious but temporarily unable to move.

## SLEEP AND BIOLOGICAL RHYTHMS

The complex nature of sleep and its component stages shows that sleep is in large part a clock-driven process (see Figure 3.19), one that resembles a number of other biological rhythms that seem to depend on internal timers. Some of these biological rhythms extend over a whole year, such as the seasonal patterns that determine migration, mating, and hibernation in many animals. Other rhythms are much shorter, such as the moment-to-moment rhythms of respiration and heartbeat. The sleep-wake rhythm is intermediate in length, spanning about a twenty-four-hour day and, therefore, called a *circadian rhythm* (from the Latin *circa*, "nearly," and *dies*, "day"). This rhythm probably originates from clock circuits in the hypothalamus and pineal gland, whose operation involves the hormone *melatonin*; these clocks appear to be set by inputs from the optic nerve that tell the system whether it is day or night (Morgan & Boelen, 1996). Indeed, the debilitating effects of jet lag are due to disruption of these clocks, caused by the traveler's seeing her mornings or evenings suddenly arrive too early or too late. Clinical studies also implicate the role of melatonin in sleep cycles, and this hormone is often useful as an insomnia treatment (Kayumov, Brown, Jindal, Buttoo, & Shapiro, 2001).

The intervals between REM sleep periods seem to indicate a separate cycle, called the *ultradian rhythm* (for one occurring many times per day). Although the ultradian rhythm is 90 to 100 minutes in humans, it varies widely by species (7 minutes in guinea

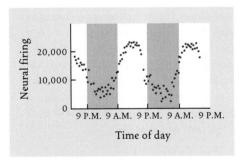

*3.19   The ticking of the brain's biological clock Activity of single cells in the superchiasmatic nucleus of a rat's hypothalamus. The regular day-night fluctuations in the firing rate of these cells demonstrate that the brain has a built-in biological clock; in fact, biological clocks similar to the one described here can also be found in several other brain regions.*

pigs, for example). Apart from clocking REM sleep episodes, the human ultradian rhythm may regulate the occurrence of daydreams, the processes of digestion and hormone secretion, and the performance of certain mental tasks (Armitage, Hoffmann, & Moffitt, 1992; Kripke, 1982; Rechtschaffen, 1998; Rosenzweig et al., 1999).

## THE FUNCTIONS OF SLEEP

Why does sleep show such a complex architecture? What functions are served by slow-wave and REM sleep? Surprisingly enough, the answers are still unknown.

Is sleep beneficial at all? Certainly, it comes at a great cost, given that when we are asleep we do not engage in more productive activities such as eating, drinking, reproducing, defending ourselves, or caring for our young. In light of these costs, the fact that sleep persists and occupies fully one-third of our lives suggests that it must carry some benefits (Rechtschaffen, 1998). But what are they?

### SLEEP DEPRIVATION

One way to assess the benefits of sleep is to observe what ills befall us without it. This is the logic of sleep-deprivation experiments in which humans and animals are kept awake for days on end. The results confirm that the desire for sleep is powerful indeed. If deprived of sleep, we seek it just as we crave food when we are famished. When sleep is finally possible, we typically collapse wherever we can and try to regain the sleep we have lost.

Sleep-deprived people do not just desire sleep; they need adequate amounts of both slow-wave and REM sleep. If sleepers are awakened during REM periods throughout the night and thus prevented from getting a normal amount of REM sleep, they will try to make up the lost REM sleep on subsequent nights (Figure 3.20). This **REM rebound** is commonly seen after taking, and then withdrawing from, medications that selectively suppress REM sleep—a group that includes some commonly prescribed sleeping medications. The same compensation holds for selective deprivation of Stages 3 and 4 of slow-wave sleep. If lost one night, they are made up on another (Webb, 1972).

Is sleep deprivation damaging? Some have suggested that REM sleep deprivation induces drug-like hallucinations and other psychotic phenomena, but investigators now believe these reports are either exaggerated or erroneous. Nonetheless, REM sleep is essential for physical health. The main evidence comes from animal studies, and the message of these studies is clear. Prolonged sleep deprivation—or just REM sleep deprivation—can lead to illness and even death (Rechtschaffen & Bergmann, 1995). The main reason seems to be that sleep deprivation leads to a compromised immune system, leaving the animal susceptible to bacterial invasion (Everson & Toth, 2000).

In addition to its direct effects on health, sleeplessness also creates other risks and, in humans, is associated with automobile and workplace accidents, for example. Fortunately, insomnia is easily treated in most people, but few of us—only about 5 percent in some surveys—actually seek professional help (Dement & Mitner, 1993; Kupfer & Reynolds, 1997; National Commission on Sleep Disorders, 1993). Many cases of insomnia respond readily to simple sleep regimens: making the bedroom quiet and dark; keeping bedtimes and waking times constant; refraining from vigorous exercise, stressful thinking, or stimulants like caffeine or nicotine after the evening meal. Even alcohol, which makes most of us sleepy, actually produces troubled, fragmented sleep and results in less total sleep time (Hauri & Linde, 1991).

How much sleep do we need? The answer varies from person to person and certainly varies with age. Infants take brief naps throughout the day, with 50 percent of their sleep devoted to REM periods (they average sixteen hours of sleep a day, eight of those REM sleep). It is not until four to six months of age that infants begin to consolidate

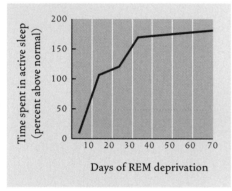

**3.20   The effect of lost REM sleep   The figure shows an increase in the time cats spend in REM sleep after various periods of REM-sleep deprivation. The animals were deprived of REM sleep (but not non-REM sleep) for from 5 to 72 days by being awakened as soon as their EEG indicated the beginning of a REM period. On the day when the animals were finally allowed to sleep undisturbed, there was an increase in the proportion of time spent in REM sleep rather than non-REM sleep.**

their sleep into one nighttime period. As children age, they need less sleep, and less of that sleep is spent in REM periods. Adolescents average eight hours per night, two of which are REM sleep. Senior citizens, on the other hand, average six hours per night, of which only one hour is spent in REM (Rosenzweig et al., 1999). Many sleep researchers, however, believe that six hours is not enough and suggest that the six-hour figure—in seniors or anyone—represents undiagnosed yet treatable insomnia (Dement & Vaughan, 1999).

These numbers, of course, are just averages; some people sleep more and a few much less. One researcher found a seventy-year-old nurse who rarely slept more than about one hour per night! She was nonetheless attentive and cheery, and apparently suffered no ill effects from what would, for most people, constitute acute sleep deprivation (Meddis, 1977).

## SLEEP AS A RESTORATIVE PROCESS

Sleep-deprivation experiments demonstrate the need for sleep, but they do not tell us why. One possibility is that sleep is restorative, a period during which some vital substance is replenished in the nervous system. But if sleep is restorative, it is unclear what is being restored. The energy savings associated with sleep are modest—the brain shows no overall decrease in neuronal activity, and many physiological activities increase during sleep, particularly during REM sleep (Rechtschaffen, 1998).

*Restoration and Slow-Wave Sleep*  Some researchers believe that any restoration is probably to be observed only during slow-wave sleep (especially Stages 3 and 4) since people show longer periods of slow-wave sleep under conditions such as physical fatigue, where there is a greater need for bodily recuperation. For example, marathon runners sleep longer during the two nights after the race, with this increase made up largely of slow-wave sleep (Shapiro, Bortz, Mitchell, Bartell, & Jooste, 1981). Despite these observations, it has still been difficult to pinpoint exactly what is restored (see, for example, Horne, 1988; and then Benington & Heller, 1995).

*Restoration and REM Sleep*  We are equally in the dark about why we have REM sleep. According to one conjecture, the fact that infants have the most REM sleep is no accident because the heightened brain activity seen during REM sleep may help forge the correct neuronal connections in the developing brain; on this, there is no evidence one way or the other. Another possibility is that REM sleep helps the sleeper consolidate whatever she learned during the day. These theories, even if partly correct, are incomplete. They have no problem explaining why so many nonhuman animals experience REM sleep, but they do not explain why some animals that are adept at learning—cetaceans like the whales and dolphins—show no REM sleep. (These aquatic animals are surface breathers that would die if they experienced REM-induced muscle paralysis; therefore, when they sleep, the cerebral hemispheres take turns at wakefulness and slow-wave sleep.) Overall, the evidence that REM sleep is related to learning and memory is weak, and some investigators doubt whether there is any relationship at all (Vertes & Eastman, 2000).

Another explanation for REM sleep holds that the eye movements reflect visual information processing. On this view, eye movements in REM sleep correspond to dream content, with the dreamer in effect "watching" the dream action (Dement & Kleitman, 1957). This view is now discredited for several reasons, among them the fact that the movements of the eyes during REM periods are appreciably slower than when awake. Moreover, in dreaming the eyes are frequently uncoordinated and misaligned by as much as 30 degrees (Aserinsky, Lynch, Mack, Tzankoff, & Hurn, 1985; Zhou & King, 1997).

Perhaps the best current explanation of REM sleep is also the most mundane. It may simply be to move the eyes, which in land mammals (but not aquatic ones like cetaceans) require a constant supply of fresh, circulating tears to lubricate and aerate the moist, crystalline corneas—especially when the lids are closed during sleep (Maurice, 1998). The same might hold for the tumescence of genital tissue (erections in the penis, arousal and lubrication in the vagina) that occurs during REM periods. Perhaps blood must periodically surge into these tissues to keep them operative. But the aeration explanation remains conjecture, and, remarkably, the function of REM sleep, like the function of sleep itself, remains a matter of debate.

## DREAMS

Overall, then, we are still ignorant about what sleep is really for (for discussion, see Webb, 1979, 1982; Horne, 1988). The same situation applies to one of the most salient features of sleep—namely, dreaming.

### DREAMING IN SLOW-WAVE AND REM SLEEP

It is a myth that people dream only in REM sleep. We actually dream in both slow-wave and REM sleep. When sleeping participants are awakened from REM sleep, up to 80 percent report that they were dreaming; in slow-wave sleep, the figure is about 60 percent. The two kinds of sleep also differ somewhat in the kinds of dreams people report after awakening from each. Almost all REM sleep reports are of pictorial dreaming, visual episodes that include the dreamer as a character and that seem real at the time. In contrast, when awakened from slow-wave sleep, people tend to give only sparse summaries, noting that they were only "thinking about something" or that their dreams were "boring." They rarely relate the kind of colorful, event-filled drama we usually consider a dream (Armitage et al., 1992; Cartwright, 1977; Foulkes, 1985).

Does this mean that we actually dream more or differently in REM sleep than in slow-wave sleep? This is often assumed but is difficult to prove because all of the evidence has come from what research participants report after they have been awakened. Since participants awakened from slow-wave sleep tend to be more sluggish and disoriented while those awakened from REM sleep are almost instantly alert, perhaps the different kinds of dream reports indicate the state of the sleeper upon awakening more than the nature of the dreaming itself.

Using dream reports may underestimate slow-wave-sleep dreaming in yet another way. In slow-wave sleep, people sometimes sleepwalk, talk in their sleep, have night terrors, and even engage in sex, and may remember nothing when they are awakened. These actions require some kind of mental activity that we might justifiably call "dreaming," but they often go unreported upon awakening and thus remain uncounted as dreams.

Studies of dream reports have also revealed other surprises. They disprove the notion of *dream condensation*, the idea that events in a dream flash instantaneously before us. To the contrary, events in dreams seem to take just about as long as they would in real life (Dement & Kleitman, 1957; Dement & Wolpert, 1958).

Quantitative studies of dream reports also disprove the notion that dreams are typically bizarre. Instead, dreams reflect current life preoccupations, whether expressed directly or metaphorically (Domhoff, 2000). We may simply remember our bizarre dreams more than our mundane ones because we think about them more during or after the dream itself (see Chapter 7 for a discussion of such biases in recall). At the same time, dreams are not merely instant replays of daily events. Life changes from day to day, but people's dream reports reveal remarkably similar themes year after year, even over decades (Domhoff, 1966). Dreams also tend to contain more bad outcomes than good ones, more negative emotions than positive ones, and more aggressive interactions than friendly ones—in one estimate, murders in dreams occur for 2 out of every 100 dream characters, far exceeding real-life homicide rates (Hall & Van de Castle, 1966).

## DO DREAMS HAVE A FUNCTION?

Why do we dream? Historically, dreams were often considered prophetic, dream analysis being standard practice among fortune-tellers. More recently, several theorists have argued that dreams reflect the sleeper's personal problems. The most influential account was that of Sigmund Freud, who maintained that we all harbor a host of primitive and forbidden wishes and motives, which the mind usually keeps unconscious. In dreams, however, our self-censorship is relaxed just a bit, and these impulses may break through to consciousness; if they do, it is only in a masked and censored form because if we experienced them uncensored, we could not remain peacefully asleep. For Freud, this explains why our dreams so often seem strange and senseless. In his view, the oddity is only on the outside; beneath the surface lie the disguised meanings and the cleverly hidden, unacceptable wishes that might awaken us and preclude sleep (Freud, 1900).

Other researchers subscribe to a more biological view, the *activation-synthesis hypothesis*. This hypothesis holds that dreaming during REM sleep is the product of a cerebral cortex that is activated by specific sites in the brainstem while remaining largely shut off from environmental input. Thus, memory images become more prominent and less realistic because there is no waking here-and-now to anchor them (Hobson, 1988; Hobson & McCarley, 1977; Hobson, Pace-Schott, & Stickgold, 2000).

Neither theory has fared well. Freud's was correct in appreciating that dreams often reflect the sleeper's ongoing emotional concerns, but there is little evidence to support his more ambitious claim that much of dreaming is disguised wish fulfillment (Fisher & Greenberg, 1977, 1996; and see Chapter 15 for a discussion of the empirical status of psychoanalytic theory).

Evidence is also turning against the activation-synthesis hypothesis largely because it so closely associates dreaming with both brainstem activation and REM sleep. As we have seen, the association is poor. Dreaming is now believed to be common during slow-wave sleep, when the brainstem is relatively quiescent. Moreover, although children have two to three times the REM sleep of adults each night, they report many fewer REM-sleep dreams than adults (Foulkes, 1999). Finally, neuropsychological studies show that dreaming persists even when the brainstem sites critical for cortical activation during REM sleep are lesioned. In contrast, lesions in certain cortical areas can readily reduce or abolish dreaming; in fact, the brain sites that seem most critical for dreaming involve not the brainstem, but parts of the frontal lobe and the limbic structures of the temporal lobe (Solms, 1997).

So why do we dream? We are left with no good explanation. The best one so far may be that dreams are an accidental by-product of the evolution of consciousness (Domhoff, 2001; Flanagan, 2000; Foulkes, 1983). Perhaps our thinking only stops in coma or death, and dreams merely represent the failure to suppress the mental activity that must occur while we are awake.

*Jacob's Dream*   **Dreams have often been regarded as a gateway between everyday reality and a more spiritual existence. An example is the biblical patriarch Jacob, who dreamed of angels descending and ascending a ladder between heaven and earth.**

# WHAT DIFFERENT MOTIVES HAVE IN COMMON

In this chapter, we have dealt with a number of motives that impel us to action—hunger, thirst, threats, and so on. Some of these motives, such as hunger, serve to maintain the internal environment. Others, such as threats, are triggered by factors in the external environment and serve the goal of self-preservation. For a few others—the main example is sleep—the functions are still unknown. All of these motives are very different, as are the goals toward which they steer the organism—food, water, mates, coping with predators or enemies, a good night's sleep.

Motivation
and art

Despite these differences, the motives have much in common. They all potentiate behavior and organize what we do, what we see, and what we feel. Indeed some investigators believe that our motives all share one basic physiological process: the search for an optimal level of general stimulation or *arousal*.

## AROUSAL AND THE PSYCHOLOGY OF REWARD

According to an influential theory proposed some fifty years ago by Clark L. Hull (1884–1952), organisms seek an optimal level of arousal that is essentially zero. In developing this *drive-reduction theory*, Hull and his students drew on the observation that many motives seem directed at the reduction of some internal state of bodily tension, which Hull called a *drive*. Hunger drives an animal to behave in such a way that would diminish its hunger (eating); likewise, pain drives an animal to find some way to alleviate the pain (for example, leaving the briar patch). For Hull, each of these acts was rewarding precisely because it reduced the drive that instigated it. By extension, he inferred that what organisms strive for is the reduction of all drives—total "peace and quiet," an absolute minimum of arousal and stimulation.

Was Hull right? Do organisms really aim for zero stimulation? The contention is difficult to sustain, given many of the experiences that people actively seek, like the taste of sweets, sexual foreplay, athletic workouts, and roller-coaster rides. These are physiologically arousing, and in many cases (like the roller coaster) they are sought because they are arousing. Such stimulation seeking can be seen even in the rat, who prefers to drink artificially sweetened water than plain water, even though the sweetener has no caloric value and does not quell hunger (Sheffield & Roby, 1950). Likewise, a cat given a paper bag won't just lie next to it: he will make it part of a game in which he darts in and out of the bag. A dog given a toy will fling it himself and then fetch it.

Research on curiosity and manipulation forces the same conclusion. Monkeys will go to considerable lengths to figure out how to open latches mounted on a wooden board (see Figure 3.21), even if opening them gets the animal nothing.

**3.21 Curiosity and manipulation** *Young rhesus monkeys trying to open a latch. The monkeys received no special reward for their labors but learned to open the devices "just for the fun of it."*

The act of solving the puzzle seems to be its own reward. In this regard, monkeys act much like human beings, who buy jigsaw puzzles, break things to see how they are put together, pursue so-called "extreme sports," watch violent or erotic films, and in countless other ways seek stimulation, rather than minimizing it (Zuckerman, 1979; see Chapter 15).

### DRUGS AND ADDICTION

Ordinarily, people seek to adjust their arousal levels through the expected routes: eating when hungry, sleeping when tired, looking for interesting people or exciting situations when bored. In some cases, though, our desire for stimulation can lead us to seek drastic changes in arousal through the use—and abuse—of drugs.

*Drugs That Change Arousal Level*  Two major classes of drugs are used to change arousal level: *depressants*, which reduce arousal, and *stimulants*, which heighten it.

The depressants include sedatives such as barbiturates, antianxiety agents like Xanax, Valium, Klonopin or alcohol, and analgesics like the opiates (opium, heroin, OxyContin, and morphine).* Their general effect is to depress the activity of all the neurons in the central nervous system. That alcohol is a depressant drug may seem surprising since many of us have seen drunks who are loud and aggressive; they are hardly lethargic or depressed. But this paradox is resolved if we recognize that the drunken person's hyper-excitability is a case of impaired control of his behavior. After just a drink or two, the inhibitory synapses in the brain seem to be depressed, but at these (relatively) low doses, the excitatory ones are not yet affected. As a consequence, the individual may act without his usual inhibitions, speaking bombastically, gesturing aggressively, and inter-acting extraflirtatiously. Many traffic accidents, homicides, and cases of rape and domestic abuse are tragic consequences of this release from inhibition. If the drinker keeps at it, however, the depressive effects will spread to all his cerebral centers. Now the excitement of lowered inhibitions gives way to a general slowdown of activity. His atten-tion and memory will blur, his movements will become clumsy and his speech inarticu-late, until finally he falls down and loses consciousness.

The effects of the behavioral stimulants such as amphetamine and cocaine are notably different. These drugs produce effects like rapid heart rate and high blood pres-sure, insomnia, lowered appetite, and—perhaps as a result of internal stimulation—behavioral quieting. This last finding has led to the widespread prescription—and, to some observers, the overprescription—of low doses of amphetamine-like stimulants such as Dexedrine, Cylert, Adderall, and Ritalin to treat individuals suffering from hyperactivity or attention deficit disorders (Andreasen & Black, 1996).

Stimulants also heighten mood. With cocaine in particular, the mood elevation can be intense—a euphoric "rush" or "high," accompanied by feelings of enormous energy, sexuality, and increased self-esteem, which led some turn-of-the-twentieth-century physicians such as Sigmund Freud to tout cocaine as a miracle drug that produced boundless energy, exhilaration, and euphoria with no untoward side effects. This is unfortunately far from true, for the initial euphoria is bought at a considerable cost. Amphetamines and cocaine often produce addictions that can become the user's pri-mary focus in life. In addition, chronic use of these drugs can lead to deranged states that resemble certain kinds of schizophrenia in which there are delusions of persecu-tion, irrational fears, and hallucinations (Siegel, 1984). Some of the chemical cousins of these drugs have other toxic effects; methamphetamine, for example, is a powerful *neu-rotoxin* that can obliterate neurons.

*Tolerance, Withdrawal, and Loss of Control* Many drugs other than ampheta-mines and cocaine are addictive. What does this mean? *Addiction* is characterized by several important features. First, the addict acquires an increased *tolerance* for the drug, so that she requires ever larger doses to obtain the same effect. Second, when the drug is withheld, she suffers from various *withdrawal symptoms.* In general, these symptoms are the opposite of the effects of the drug itself (Solomon, 1980; Solomon & Corbit, 1974). For example, heroin produces relief from pain, relaxation, and sleepiness, but heroin addicts deprived of their drug are extremely irritable, are restless and anxious, and suffer insomnia. The stimulants show the same kind of contrast: cocaine and amphetamines produce elation and energy, but withdrawal from them leads to pro-found depression and fatigue. The same holds for many of the physical symptoms pro-duced by these drugs: chronic opiate use tends to cause marked constipation. (They have been used for centuries to relieve diarrhea and dysentery.) But when they are with-drawn, then a typical consequence is acute diarrhea (Julien, 1985; Solomon, 1980; Solomon & Corbit, 1974; Volpicelli, 1989).

**Extreme sports** *The popularity of these sports is testimony to the fact that people seek arousal.*

**Horror movies** *People seek thrills in many places—including the movies. (Pictured here: Jamie Lee Curtis in* Halloween H2O.)

* Strictly speaking, the opiates belong to a separate class since, unlike alcohol and other sedatives, they serve as narcotics (that is, pain relievers) and act on separate opiate receptors. In addition, one of their number—heroin—seems to be able to produce an unusually intense euphoric "rush," sometimes likened to intense sexual excitement, when taken intravenously.

Perhaps most important in defining addiction is the loss of control experienced by the addict. Addicts often endure many negative consequences as a result of their addictions, including disease, job loss, separation or divorce, and imprisonment. Yet they are unable to stop taking the drugs. They may repeatedly seek treatment and still be afflicted with drug cravings that prove uncontrollable. This loss of control over one's drug taking is at the heart of addiction, and many researchers believe that the compulsive drug seeking of the addict represents a brain that has been altered, even "hijacked," by the drug. What exactly is this alteration? To answer this, investigators have focused increasingly on certain areas of the brain that may constitute its "reward centers."

## THE BIOLOGY OF REWARD

The motives we have discussed involve the organism's seeking some optimal state. Satisfying hunger, slaking thirst, comsummating sexual desire—all of these *feel* good. Do these feelings share anything more than positivity? Might they also share a physiological commonality? Does some activation of a certain brain region explain "pleasure," whether that pleasure is from having sex, listening to great music, or eating a hot-fudge sundae? Investigators have tried to answer this question by studying the rewarding effects of stimulating various regions in the brain.

This general area of study had its beginnings in 1954, when James Olds and Peter Milner discovered that rats would learn to press a lever if they were rewarded with only a brief burst of electrical stimulation in certain regions of the hypothalamus and limbic system (Olds & Milner, 1954; see Figure 3.22). Similar rewarding effects of self-stimulation have been demonstrated in a wide variety of other animals, including cats, dolphins, monkeys, and human beings. To obtain such stimulation, rats will press a lever at rates up to 7,000 presses per hour for hours on end. When forced to choose between food and self-stimulation, hungry rats will often opt for self-stimulation, even though it literally brings starvation (Spies, 1965).

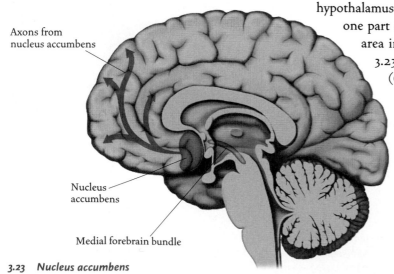

**3.22   Self-stimulation in rats   The rat feels the stimulation of a pulse lasting less than a second.**

## THE DOPAMINE HYPOTHESIS OF REWARD AND DRUG EFFECTS

What is the physiological basis for this self-stimulation effect? A number of investigators believe that the key lies in some dopamine-releasing pathways in the brain. It is known that self-stimulation is most effective when applied to a bundle of nerve fibers called the **medial forebrain bundle (MFB)**. These fibers course from the midbrain to the hypothalamus and appear to trigger activity of other cells that extend from one part of the midbrain—the **ventral tegmental area**, or **VTA**—to an area in the forebrain known as the **nucleus accumbens** (see Figure 3.23), whose pathways rely on dopamine as a neurotransmitter (Gallistel, Shizgal, & Yeomans, 1981; Garris et al., 1999; Stellar & Stellar, 1985; Wise & Rompre, 1989; ).

Indeed, the activation of fibers originating in the nucleus accumbens may be the neurological equivalent of "Good—let's have it again." This may help explain some of the phenomena of drug addiction. Both cocaine and amphetamine enhance the levels of dopamine at synapses throughout the brain. Cocaine does so by blocking dopamine reuptake (so that the transmitter persists longer); amphetamine does the same and also enhances the release of dopamine at the axon terminal.

It is clear that dopamine plays a crucial role in reward and addiction, and we have identified some of the brain struc-

Axons from
nucleus accumbens

Nucleus
accumbens

Medial forebrain bundle

**3.23   Nucleus accumbens**

tures involved. Despite this growing knowledge, there is still much to ask about the nature of this reward and of pleasure itself. Does only one neural mechanism really underlie the full range of human pleasures? When we are awed by the ceiling of the Sistine Chapel, do the same circuits fire as when we eat ice cream? Does our exultant pride at seeing our child take his first steps trigger the same pathways as the taste of lemonade on a summer's day? We await a comprehensive theory of pleasure that can explain all pleasurable experiences: ecstasy and serenity, pride and dedication, amazement and admiration, an orgasm and a cocaine high. As yet, it is unclear whether neuroscience can give us all the answers, but it has given us a good start.

## SOME FINAL THOUGHTS: THE INSEPARABILITY OF BIOLOGY AND LEARNING

This chapter has been concerned with motives that arise from largely innate mechanisms. These are motives concerned with the biological goals we must attain in order for us—or our genes—to survive. Some of these, such as temperature regulation and hunger, are largely based on conditions that arise from within the organism; others, such as the response to threat, are reactions to stimuli from outside. But in all cases, it is clear that when we look at these motives in detail, we find that our motivated behavior depends not only on our biology, but also on what we know and have learned about our environment. For example, all humans eat, but some humans refuse to eat insects while others find them quite tasty, and this is a preference (in either direction) that is learned. The same is true for other motives, such as what catches our curiosity, what threatens us, or what arouses us sexually. In all these cases, our experience is interwoven with our biology, and the resulting fabric, both complex and seamless, is our very selves.

In the next chapter we will begin our discussion of just how this weave is formed, starting with the process by which we gain information about our environment and how to navigate it—the process of *learning*.

## SUMMARY

In this chapter, our focus is on relatively simple motives, such as temperature regulation, hunger, and sex. These are often called *biological motives*, in contrast to more complex motives such as the need for friendship and love, often subsumed under the category *social motives*.

### MOTIVATION AS DIRECTED ACTION

1. Motives ready the organism to engage in a particular behavior; they *potentiate* certain perceptions and behaviors rather than others, impelling the organism toward or away from some goal.

### TEMPERATURE REGULATION

2. One biological mechanism that permits directed action is *negative feedback*, in which the system "feeds back" upon itself to stop its own action. Built-in negative feedback is responsible for many reactions that maintain the stability of the organism's internal environment, or *homeostasis*.

Special cells in the hypothalamus sense various aspects of the body's internal state, such as *temperature*. If this is above or below certain *setpoints*, a number of reflexes controlled by the *sympathetic* and *parasympathetic divisions* of the *autonomic nervous system* are triggered (for example, shivering). In addition, externally directed actions (such as moving into or out of the sun) are also brought into play.

## HUNGER

3. The biological motive that has been studied most extensively is *hunger*. Many of the signals for feeding and satiety come from the internal environment. *Feeding signals* include nutrient levels in the bloodstream (which probably affect *glucose receptors* in the brain) and metabolic processes in the liver (especially the *glucose-glycogen* balance). Satiety signals include messages from receptors in the stomach, the small intestine (particularly a satiety hormone called *cholecystokinin*, or *CCK*), and the adipose tissue, which secretes *leptin*. Other feeding and satiety signals are external, including the *palatability* of the food.

4. According to the *dual-center theory*, the control of feeding is lodged in antagonistic hunger and satiety centers in the hypothalamus. As evidence, this theory points to the effects of lesions that produce either a complete refusal to eat or a vast increase in food intake. However, this theory has been supplanted by findings suggesting a greater role for the digestive organs and adipose tissue in hunger, as well as multiple hunger and satiety pathways in the brain.

5. One feeding-related disorder is *obesity*. Some cases are produced by various constitutional factors, including increased metabolic efficiency. The obesity seen in some people may represent the operation of "thrifty genes" that code for slower metabolisms, which are optimal for sparse diets but deleterious for modern abundance. Another account of obesity derives from the *setpoint* hypothesis, which asserts that overweight people simply have a higher internal setpoint for weight.

6. Other eating disorders are *anorexia nervosa*, in which there is a pattern of relentless and sometimes lethal self-starvation, and *bulimia nervosa*, which is characterized by normal weight despite repeated binge-and-purge bouts.

## THREAT

7. In contrast to hunger, which is largely based on controls from within, a number of motives are instigated externally. An example is the preparatory reaction to *threat*. Its biological mechanisms include the operations of the *autonomic nervous system (ANS)*. The *parasympathetic* branch of the ANS serves the vegetative functions of everyday life, such as digestion and reproduction. It slows the heart rate and reduces blood pressure. The *sympathetic* branch activates the body and mobilizes its resources in response to emergencies. It increases the available metabolic fuels and accelerates their utilization by increasing the heart rate and respiration. Intense sympathetic activity is an *emergency reaction* that makes us vigilant and able to deal with the momentary contingencies imposed by threatening situations.

8. The *sympathetic emergency reaction* is not always adaptive. It can produce temporary disruptions of digestive and sexual functions, and causes suppression of the immune system that leaves us vulnerable to infection.

## PAIN

9. Among the stimuli that set off the sympathetic emergency reaction is *pain*, which is of considerable survival value as a signal to react to danger. But since continued pain may interfere with appropriate action, counteracting processes intervene to alleviate it. One pain mechanism involves the *endorphins*, a group of opium-related neurotransmitters secreted within the brain that act to block the transmission of pain messages.

## SEX

10. Sexual motivation is necessary not for personal survival, but for the survival of our genes through reproduction. Both male and female behavior are under strong hormonal control and regulation by the hypothalamus, although human sexual behavior appears quite flexible and amenable to change through experience.

11. Studies of the physiology of human sexual response show four phases of sexual arousal: the first two are *excitement* and *plateau*, accompanied by increasing levels of *vasocongestion* of erectile tissues in the penis, vagina, and clitoris. The third phase is *orgasm*, a seizure-like episode characterized by involuntary muscle contractions throughout the body, rhythmic contractions of the urethra (in the male) and the vagina and uterus (in the female), and semen ejaculation by the male. The final phase is *resolution*, in which the excitement and vasocongestion subside. The orgasm in the male is necessary for ejaculation; in females, it may increase the odds of conception by increasing semen flow into the cervix.

## SLEEP AND WAKING

12. While the sympathetic nervous system arouses many processes in the body, several cortical and subcortical structures activate the brain. These waking systems are opposed by antagonistic processes that lead to sleep. During sleep, brain activity changes, as shown by the *electroen-*

*cephalogram*, or *EEG*. Each night, we oscillate between *slow-wave sleep*, during which the cortex is less active and bodily functions are relatively quiescent, and *REM sleep*, characterized by considerable cortical and bodily activity, rapid eye movements (or REMs), and a near-complete flaccidity of the trunk and limb muscles. Since participants in this state are both physiologically activated and muscularly inactivated, REM sleep is sometimes called *paradoxical sleep*. The muscular paralysis of REM sleep may persist for a few moments past awakening, leading to the state of *sleep paralysis*, in which the person is conscious but temporarily unable to move.

13. The sleep-wake cycle is a *circadian rhythm*, which probably originates from clock circuits in the hypothalamus and pineal gland, whose operation involves the hormone *melatonin*. The intervals between REM sleep periods seem to indicate a separate cycle, called the *ultradian rhythm*, about 90–100 minutes in humans.

14. *Sleep-deprivation* studies confirm that the desire for sleep is very powerful. If deprived of REM sleep, people will try to make up the lost REM sleep on subsequent nights—showing a *REM rebound*. The same compensation holds for selective deprivation of Stages 3 and 4 of slow-wave sleep. Prolonged sleep deprivation—or just REM sleep deprivation—can lead to illness and even death. Some theorists have suggested that sleep is *restorative*. But, as yet, it is unclear just what is restored.

15. Experimental studies of sleep have disproved some widely held beliefs about dreaming. Contrary to what was once assumed, people dream throughout both slow-wave and REM sleep. In addition, there is no evidence for *dream condensation*, since events in dreams take just about as long as they would in real life.

16. Do dreams have a function? According to Sigmund Freud, they represent unconscious wishes that break through during sleep but only in a masked and censored form. According to the *activation synthesis hypothesis*, dreaming during REM sleep is the product of a cerebral cortex activated by specific sites in the brainstem while remaining largely shut off from environmental input, so that memory images become less realistic because there is no waking here-and-now to anchor them. Another hypothesis holds that dreams help to promote *memory consolidation*, helping to establish new learning in long-term storage. But there is little evidence in support of any of these views. While Freud was correct in asserting that dreams often reflect the sleeper's ongoing emotional concerns, there is little confirmation for his claim that much of dreaming is disguised wish fulfillment. Evidence is also turning against the activation-synthesis hypothesis, largely because it so closely associates dreaming with REM sleep and brainstem activation, contrary to many lines of evidence. And the memory-consolidation hypothesis also remains controversial. So, thus far, the function of dreams, if any, is unknown.

## WHAT DIFFERENT MOTIVES HAVE IN COMMON

17. According to *drive-reduction theory*, all built-in motives act to reduce stimulation and arousal. Today, most authors discount that generality, and instead note that organisms often *seek* stimulation, such as the taste for sweets, sexual foreplay, and the satisfaction of curiosity.

18. One way of adjusting one's arousal level is by the use and abuse of drugs. Some drugs act as *depressants*, including alcohol and the opiates. Others, such as amphetamines and cocaine, act as *stimulants*. In many individuals, repeated drug use leads to *addiction*, accompanied by a loss of control over drug taking, the need for more of the drug to achieve the same effect—increased *tolerance*, and *withdrawal effects* if the drug is withheld.

19. That there may be "pleasure centers" in the brain is supported by evidence that stimulation of certain areas leads to specific reward effects, as shown by the facts of cranial *self-stimulation* in a wide variety of animals, including human beings. Self-stimulation is most effective when applied to a group of nerve fibers called the *medial forebrain bundle* (*MFB*). The MFB triggers the activity of other cells that extend to the *nucleus accumbens*, which relies on *dopamine* as a neurotransmitter. Some investigators suggest that the activation of this structure is the neurological equivalent of "Good—let's have it again!" This hypothesis may help to explain some phenomena of drug addiction, since both cocaine and amphetamines enhance the levels of dopamine at synapses throughout the brain.

# LEARNING

*M*uch of our discussion so far has centered on the neural equipment that each of us has, equipment shaped largely by our biological inheritance. But much of what we do goes beyond these built-in mechanisms and depends instead on experience acquired during our lifetime. In other words, organisms learn. A human being learns to grasp a baby bottle, to read and write, to love or hate his neighbors. In other animals, the role of learning may be less dramatic, but it is enormously important for them, too.

In the preceding chapters, we discussed Descartes' conception of the organism as a reflex machine. In this view, behavior depends on built-in links between one set of neural messages, triggered by stimuli outside the organism, and another set sending commands to the muscles or glands. One problem with this conception is that it provides no obvious mechanisms for behavior change. It is obvious, though, that behavior does change as organisms learn new behavior, acquire new skills, and, in general, adapt to their circumstances.

Can we accommodate this potential for learning and still preserve the simple architecture envisioned by Descartes? Some investigators, called *learning theorists*, believe that we can. The organism is born, they argue, with a limited repertoire of hard-wired reflexes. But this set can be supplemented through learning. In some cases, the learning creates new connections between stimuli so that, for example, the sight of the mother's face may come to signify the taste of milk. In other cases, the learning involves new connections between acts and their consequences, as when a toddler learns that touching a heater can cause a burn. In all cases, though, the basic arrangement of things stays the same, with identifiable stimuli eliciting identifiable responses. The intellectual challenge for this view lies in discovering how exactly these bits of "rewiring" come about.

The learning theorist's perspective continues to contribute to our understanding of learning, but the greatest blossoming of this perspective occurred during the first part of the twentieth century, especially in the United States. This was, in part, a reflection of the intellectual and political climate of the times: during this period, society was deeply committed to the belief that humans were extraordinarily malleable and perhaps infinitely perfectible, given the proper environment and the right education. Under the circumstances, it was not surprising that learning became one of the great concerns of American psychology.

How should learning be studied? Initially, most learning theorists believed that basic laws governed all learning, regardless of what is learned or who does the learning—whether it is a dog learning to sit on command or a college student learning calculus. To be sure, some examples of learning seem quite complicated, but these, it was argued, are actually made up of simpler bits of learning, just as complex chemical compounds are made up of basic elements. Given this belief, it was only natural that the early investigators first tried to understand learning in simple situations and in nonhuman creatures such as dogs, rats, and pigeons. In this way, the investigators hoped to strip the learning process down to its essentials in order to reveal both the basic elements of learning and the principles that governed them. With this done, the elements could then be recombined as needed to account for more complex cases.

As we will see, the early learning theorists never succeeded in finding one set of laws that covered all cases of learning in all organisms. But their search for these laws did lead to a series of important discoveries that form the foundation of much of what we know about learning today. These same discoveries also provide the basis for a number of therapeutic techniques, including the desensitization procedures often used in treating phobias and the behavior modification techniques used to treat some eating disorders as well as many other problems. We will return to these uses of learning principles in later chapters. First, let us lay the foundation.

## HABITUATION

Perhaps the simplest form of learning is *habituation*. This term refers to the decline in an organism's tendency to respond to a stimulus once the stimulus has become familiar. A sudden noise usually startles us; but the second time the noise is heard, the startle will be diminished, and the third time, it will hardly be evoked. After that, the noise will be ignored altogether: we will have, at this point, become fully habituated to it.

One of the benefits of habituation is that it narrows the range of stimuli that elicit alarm. Since a sudden and unfamiliar stimulus may well indicate danger, it makes sense to give our full attention to it. But there is usually no point in scrutinizing something familiar, especially since this would probably distract us from more important activities. Habituation solves this problem by allowing organisms to ignore the familiar, which in turn allows them to focus instead on more important and informative events (Shalter, 1984; Wyers, Peeke, & Herz, 1973).

Habituation plainly relies on memory. The animal must somehow compare what it now hears and sees with what it has previously heard and seen. To the extent that the current stimulus matches what is in memory, it is judged to be familiar and so not worth attending. "Same noise as before? No need to respond. But what's that movement? That wasn't there before. I'd better check it out." In this fashion, habituation, as simple as it seems, relies on what the organism remembers about its previous experiences and thus surely counts as an example of learning.

*Habituation With repeated exposure, organisms grow accustomed to a stimulus, and cease responding to it, just as these buffaloes have ceased responding to the oncoming cars.*

# CLASSICAL CONDITIONING

In habituation, an organism learns to recognize an event as familiar but does not learn anything new about that event. Much of our learning, however, does involve new information, and often this information is concerned with the relationship among events or between an event and a particular behavior. Learning theorists (and many other investigators) talk about these relationships in terms of associations, proposing that much learning can be understood as the formation (or strengthening) of associations or the weakening of already existing associations. Thus we learn, for example, to associate thunder with lightning, a smile with friendly behavior, and tigers with zoos.

The importance of associations in learning and thinking has been emphasized since the days of the ancient Greek philosophers, but the experimental study of these associations did not begin until the end of the nineteenth century. A major contribution was the work on conditioning performed by the great Russian physiologist Ivan Petrovich Pavlov (1849–1936).

## PAVLOV AND THE CONDITIONED REFLEX

Pavlov had already earned a Nobel prize for his research on digestion before he began to study conditioning. In that earlier work, Pavlov was exploring the neural control of various digestive reflexes, and many of his laboratory studies focused on the secretion of saliva in dogs.

Pavlov knew from the start that salivation is typically triggered by food (especially dry food) placed in the mouth. In the course of his research, however, a new fact emerged: the salivary reflex could be set off by a range of other stimuli as well, including stimuli that were at first totally neutral. Dogs that had been in the laboratory for a while would salivate not only to the taste and touch of meat in the mouth, but also in response to the mere sight of meat, or to the sight of the dish in which the meat was ordinarily placed, or to the sight of the person who usually brought the meat, or even to the sound of that person's footsteps. Pavlov decided to study these effects in their own right because he recognized that they provided a means through which the reflex concept could embrace learned as well as innate reactions.

To study this learning, Pavlov created simple patterns for the animal to detect and learn about. For example, he would repeatedly sound a bell and always follow it with

*Ivan Petrovich Pavlov* **Pavlov (center) in his laboratory, with some colleagues and his "best friend."**

food. Later, he observed what happened when the bell was sounded alone, without any food being given (Pavlov, 1927; Figure 4.1).

The result was clear: repeated pairings of the sound of the bell with food led to salivation when the sound of the bell was presented by itself (that is, unaccompanied by food). To explain this finding, Pavlov proposed a distinction between *unconditioned* and *conditioned reflexes*. Unconditioned reflexes, he argued, were a product of the organism's biology and largely independent of any learning. Food in the mouth, which unconditionally elicits salivation, would be one example. In contrast, conditioned reflexes were acquired through learning—that is, they were conditional upon the animal's experience.

Pavlov proposed that every unconditioned reflex is based on a hardwired connection between an *unconditioned stimulus (US)* and an *unconditioned response (UR)*. Likewise, a conditioned reflex involves a connection between a *conditioned stimulus (CS)* and a *conditioned response (CR)*. The connection between CS and CR, however, is learned, not innate. Thus, the CS (in our example so far, the bell) is initially a neutral stimulus—it does not elicit the CR. The CS comes to elicit the CR (in this case, salivation) only after some presentations of the CS (again, the bell) followed by the US (in this case,

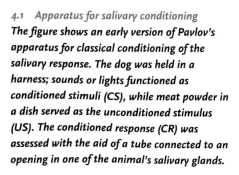

**4.1** *Apparatus for salivary conditioning* **The figure shows an early version of Pavlov's apparatus for classical conditioning of the salivary response. The dog was held in a harness; sounds or lights functioned as conditioned stimuli (CS), while meat powder in a dish served as the unconditioned stimulus (US). The conditioned response (CR) was assessed with the aid of a tube connected to an opening in one of the animal's salivary glands.**

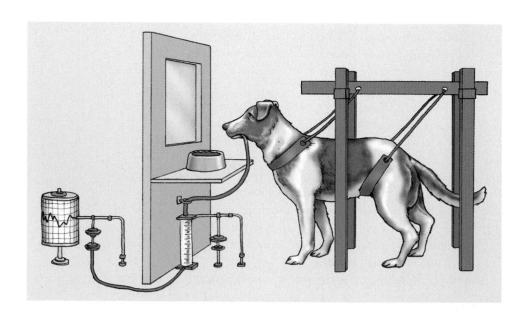

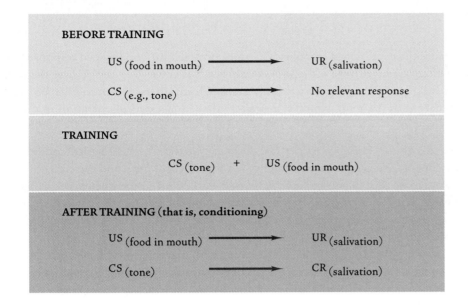

**BEFORE TRAINING**

US (food in mouth) ⟶ UR (salivation)

CS (e.g., tone) ⟶ No relevant response

**TRAINING**

CS (tone) + US (food in mouth)

**AFTER TRAINING** (that is, conditioning)

US (food in mouth) ⟶ UR (salivation)

CS (tone) ⟶ CR (salivation)

*4.2 Relationships between CS, US, CR, and UR in classical conditioning*

food in the mouth). These various relationships are summarized in Figure 4.2 and constitute the basis of what is now known as *classical conditioning*.*

Early research on classical conditioning focused on dogs salivating to the sound of bells, to lights, and to the ticking of metronomes. But the scope of conditioning turns out to be much wider than this, encompassing a vast range of cases—both inside and outside the laboratory. This form of conditioning is found in species as diverse as ants and anteaters, cats and cockroaches, pigeons and people. Crabs have been conditioned to twitch their tail spines, fish to thrash about, and octopuses to change color, using the appropriate US in each case. Responses conditioned in studies with humans include the galvanic skin response (where the US is typically a loud noise or rap on the knee) and reflexive eye blink (with the US consisting of a puff of air on the open eye; Kimble, 1961).

Outside of the laboratory, classical conditioning touches many aspects of our everyday lives. Numerous feelings and urges, for example, are probably the result of classical conditioning. We tend to feel hungry at mealtime and less in between; this probably reflects a conditioning process in which the CS is a particular time of day and the US is the presentation of food (which normally is paired with that time of day). Another example is sexual arousal, which can often be produced by a special word or gesture the erotic meaning of which is very private and is surely learned.

We will say more about these cases and the great breadth of classical conditioning's effects in later sections. For now, we simply note that this is a phenomenon with wide application and of correspondingly great importance.

## THE MAJOR PHENOMENA OF CLASSICAL CONDITIONING

Pavlov was able to document, fully and accurately, many of the central phenomena of classical conditioning; his findings laid the foundation for subsequent theories in this domain. We begin, therefore, by describing some of Pavlov's basic findings.

---

* The adjective *classical* is used, in part, as dutiful tribute to Pavlov's eminence and historical priority, and, in part, as a way of distinguishing this form of conditioning from *instrumental conditioning*, to which we will turn later.

Initially, the conditioned stimulus (CS) does not elicit the conditioned response (CR). But after several pairings with the unconditioned stimulus (US), the CS (say, the sound of a bell) is able to elicit the CR (salivation). Clearly, then, presenting the US (food) together with (or, more typically, just after) the CS is a critical operation in classical conditioning.

*Measuring the Strength of the CR*    How can we test whether classical conditioning is occurring? We need to test the strength of the CR as it forms, and there are a number of ways to do this. One is *response amplitude*—in Pavlov's experiments, the amount of saliva secreted when the CS was presented without the US. Another measure is *probability of response*—the proportion of trials in which the CR occurs when the CS is presented alone.

How does the strength of a CR change as learning progresses? Figure 4.3 shows an idealized *learning curve* in which the strength of the CR (*y*-axis) is plotted against successive learning trials (*x*-axis). The pattern of these data is clear: the strength of the CR is initially zero, grows rapidly, and then levels off at some nonzero level. This pattern is not only easily demonstrated with dogs salivating in response to the sound of bells but also with other organisms, other CSs, and other CRs. This is, in short, a highly typical pattern for virtually all instances of classical conditioning.

*Second-Order Conditioning*    Once the CS-US relationship is solidly established, the CS can serve to condition yet further stimuli. To give one example, Pavlov first conditioned a dog to salivate to the beat of a metronome, using meat powder as the US. Once this was done, he presented the animal with a black square followed by the metronome beat, but without ever introducing the food. This pairing of black square and metronome beat was repeated several times, and soon the sight of the black square alone was enough to produce salivation. This phenomenon is called *second-order conditioning*. In effect, the black square had become a signal for the beat of the metronome, which in turn signaled the appearance of food.

## EXTINCTION

Classical conditioning can have considerable adaptive value. Imagine a wolf that has often found many mice to eat at a particular site. It would serve the wolf well to learn about this conjunction of mice and location; that way, the wolf would know where to find a good meal the next time it is hungry. But it would be unfortunate if this connection, once established, could never be undone. The mice might leave the area or might all be eaten up, and the wolf would now waste time and energy revisiting this barren spot.

Fortunately, though, classical conditioning can be undone, as Pavlov showed, using a procedure not so different from the one that established the conditioning in the first place. To be precise, Pavlov demonstrated that the CR will gradually disappear if the CS is repeatedly presented by itself—that is, without the US. In Pavlov's terms, the CS-US link undergoes *extinction*. Figure 4.4 presents an extinction curve from a salivary extinction experiment, with response strength measured along the *y*-axis, while the *x*-axis indicates the number of extinction trials—that is, trials with a CS, but no US. As the extinction trials proceed, the dog salivates less and less. In effect, the dog has learned that the CS is no longer a signal for food.

Extinction itself can also be undone. One means is through *reconditioning*—that is, by presenting further learning trials. Reconditioning typically proceeds more quickly than the initial conditioning did: the speed of relearning, in other words, is faster than the original speed of learning. This remains true even if the extinction trials were continued until the animal stopped responding to the CS altogether. Apparently, extinc-

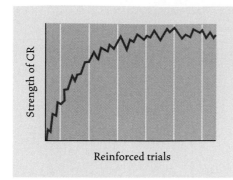

**4.3   An idealized learning curve    Strength of the CR is plotted against the number of reinforced trials. The curve presents the results of many such studies, which by and large show that the strength of the CR rises with increasing number of trials, but each trial adds less strength than the trial just before it.**

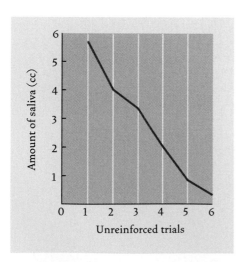

**4.4   Extinction of a classically conditioned response    The figure shows the decrease in the amount of saliva secreted (the CR) with increasing number of extinction trials—that is, trials on which the CS is presented without the US.**

tion does not work by "erasing" the original learning; after extinction, the animal does not return to its original "naive" state. Instead, the animal retains some memory of the learning, and this memory provides it with a head start in the reconditioning trials.

Similar conclusions about extinction can be drawn from the phenomenon of ***spontaneous recovery***. This phenomenon is observed in animals who have been through an extinction procedure and then left alone for a rest interval. After this rest period, the CS is again presented, and now the CS will often elicit the CR—even though the CR was fully extinguished earlier.

According to one view of this effect, the extinction trials lead the animal to recognize that a once-informative stimulus is no longer informative. The bell used to signal that food would be coming soon, but now, the animal learns, the bell signals nothing. However, the animal still remembers that the bell was once informative, and so when a new experimental session begins, the animal checks to see whether the bell will again be informative in this new setting. Thus, the animal resumes responding to the bell, producing the result we call spontaneous recovery (Robbins, 1990).

## GENERALIZATION

So far, our discussion has been confined to situations in which the animal is trained with a particular CS—the sound of a bell or metronome, for example—and then later tested with that same stimulus. In the real world, however, things are more complicated than this. The master's voice may always signal food, but his exact intonation will vary from one occasion to another. The sight of an apple tree may well signal the availability of fruit, but apple trees vary in size and shape. These facts demand that animals be able to respond to stimuli that are not identical to the original CS; otherwise, the animals will obtain no benefit from their earlier learning.

It is not surprising, therefore, that animals show a pattern called ***stimulus generalization***—that is, they respond to a range of stimuli, provided that these stimuli are sufficiently similar to the original CS. For example, a dog might be conditioned to respond to a yellow light. When tested later on, that dog will respond most strongly if the test light is still yellow. However, the dog will also respond (although a bit less strongly) to an orange light. The dog will probably also respond to a red light, but the response will be weaker still. In general, the greater the difference between the new stimulus and the original CS, the weaker the CR. Figure 4.5 illustrates this pattern, called a ***generalization gradient***. The peak of the gradient (the strongest response) is typically found when the test stimulus is identical to the stimulus used in training; the response gets weaker and weaker (and so the curve gets lower and lower) as the stimuli become more dissimilar.

## DISCRIMINATION

Stimulus generalization is obviously beneficial but can be carried too far. A tiger may be similar to a kitten, but someone who generalizes from one to the other is likely to regret it. What he must do instead is discriminate—and not try to pet the tiger.

The phenomenon of ***discrimination*** is readily demonstrated in the laboratory. A dog is first conditioned to salivate to a CS—for example, the sight of a black square. After the CR is well established, trials pairing the black square with the US are randomly interspersed with trials with another stimulus—say, the sight of a gray square—and no US. This continues until the animal discriminates perfectly, always salivating to the black square (referred to, generally, as the CS$^+$) and never to the gray (referred to as the CS$^-$). Of course, the dog does not reach this point immediately. During the early trials, it will be confused—or, more precisely, it will generalize rather than discriminate and salivate equally to both the CS$^+$ and the CS$^-$. However, these errors gradually become fewer and fewer until perfect discrimination is achieved.

In understanding this pattern, however, it is important to realize that the animal

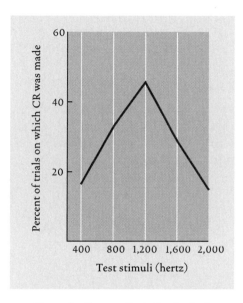

**4.5  Generalization gradient of a classically conditioned response**   *The figure shows the generalization of a conditioned blinking response in rabbits. The CS was a tone of 1,200 hertz, and the US was electric shock. After the conditioned response to the original CS was well established, generalization was measured by presenting various test stimuli, ranging from 400 hertz to 2,000 hertz and noting the percent of the trials on which the animals gave the CR. The figure shows the results, averaged over several testing sessions.*

learns the significance of both the CS⁺ and the CS⁻. It learns, of course, that the CS⁺ signals the approach of the US. What about the CS⁻? One might think that the animal learns that this stimulus conveys no information—after all, this stimulus is not followed by the US. But there *is* information here: the CS⁻ signals a period in which the US is likely not to arrive. If the US is a loud noise, then the CS⁻ signals the start of a period of time that will be noise-free. If the US is food, then the CS⁻ indicates that food is not coming soon.

In essence, then, the CS⁻ takes on a significance opposite to that of the CS⁺. It means "no noise," or "no food," or, in general, "no US." Correspondingly, the animal's response to the CS⁻ tends to be the opposite of its response to the CS⁺. If the US is a noise blast, then the CS⁺ elicits fear, and the CS⁻ seems to inhibit fear. If the US is food, then the CS⁺ elicits salivation, and the CS⁻ causes the animal to salivate less than it ordinarily would. Thus, the CS⁻ takes on the role of *inhibitor*—it inhibits the response elicited by the CS⁺ in that procedure.

## EXTENSIONS OF CLASSICAL CONDITIONING

Thanks to the various facts just mentioned, classical conditioning has an easily identifiable profile; it is a form of learning, in other words, that reliably shows the features we have just described. This allows us to use this profile to ask whether phenomena outside of the laboratory involve classical conditioning or not. For example, many emotional reactions clearly show this profile, which is a strong indication that these reactions are, in fact, attributable to classical conditioning. Let us pursue this point by looking specifically at conditioned fear.

### CONDITIONED FEAR

In many procedures, the conditioned response involves a single act such as salivating or blinking. Sometimes, though, the CR is more complex. For example, we have mentioned procedures in which the US is an aversive stimulus such as a loud noise. In these procedures, the CS will come to elicit a multifaceted response, including changes in the animal's behavior as well as in its internal state (heart rate, hormone secretions, and so on). In short, the animal will become fearful and will do all the things that animals do when they are afraid.

Many studies have examined these conditioned emotions, especially fear. Often, these studies employ the *conditioned emotional response (CER)* procedure. In this procedure, a rat, say, is first taught to press a lever for a food reward. After a few training sessions, it learns to press at a steady rate, and now fear conditioning can start. While the animal is pressing the lever, a CS is presented—perhaps a light or a tone that will stay on for, say, three minutes. At the end of that period, the CS stops, and the rat receives a brief electric shock (the US). This causes the rat to freeze and suspend its lever pressing. But soon the rat starts pressing again, and the CS-US sequence is repeated: another tone and another shock. Again, this causes an interruption in the rat's lever pressing. But after a moment, the rat returns to lever pressing, and the cycle is repeated, with yet another CS-US pairing (Estes & Skinner, 1941; Kamin, 1965).

In this procedure, the fear response is superimposed on an ongoing activity—namely, the pressing of the lever. This is crucial because it allows us to measure the fear. Early in training, the animal essentially ignores the CS, so that when the CS is presented, the animal's lever pressing continues without interruption. Later on, the animal learns that the CS signals the approach of the US (the shock). At this stage, the CS (and the anticipation of the shock) keeps the animal from its chore of lever pressing, so that it presses less often during the CS (while afraid) than otherwise. By measuring this *response suppression*, we can measure the strength of the conditioning (see Figure 4.6).

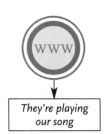

They're playing
our song

This technique can be used for many purposes, including the study of inhibitory learning. In one experiment, a tone (the CS$^+$) was associated with shock, and a light (the CS$^-$) was associated with absence of shock and thus signaled a period of relative safety. After some learning, the CS$^+$ elicited fear from the animal, but the CS$^-$ (the "safety signal") inhibited fear. All of this was evident in the animal's lever pressing: response rates went down during the CS$^+$ (this is the standard pattern of response suppression) but up during the CS$^-$. Clearly, then, the CS$^-$ had taken on a meaning opposite to that of the CS$^+$ and had an opposite effect on the animal's lever pressing (Reberg & Black, 1969).

Is human fear (or, for that matter, other emotions) shaped in the same manner? In many cases, they probably are. A frightful experience in a particular room can lead to fear of that room; falling off a bicycle can lead to fear of bike riding. These cases are easily understood in terms of classical conditioning. Some psychologists have also proposed that the irrational fears we call *phobias* can be understood in the same terms, although other investigators are skeptical (Schwartz & Robbins, 1995). No matter how this debate is resolved, most researchers agree that classical conditioning can usefully be employed in the treatment of phobias, a point to which we will return in Chapter 17.

## THE RELATION BETWEEN CR AND UR

The phenomenon of fear conditioning brings us to an important question: What is the relation between CR and UR? In Pavlov's original studies, the CR and UR seem similar: his dogs salivated both when they heard the CS and when they experienced the US. But, in fact, the CR and UR are rarely identical. When meat is placed in the mouth (the US), a dog's salivation is more copious and much richer in digestive enzymes in comparison to salivation in response to a tone or bell (CS).

The difference between CR and UR is even more pronounced in the case of fear conditioning. When exposed to electric shock, the animal jumps and squeals, and its heart beats faster; this is the UR. When the same animal hears or sees a CS that signals the shock, its response (the CR) is different: the animal freezes, tenses its muscles, and its heartbeat slows. This is not an escape-from-shock reaction; it is, instead, a manifestation of fearful anticipation.

All of this makes good biological sense. An animal cannot eat a tone that has been paired with food, and no tissue damage is produced by a light that has been paired with shock. Therefore, it would make no sense for the animal to treat the CS and US in the same fashion. Instead, the animal seems to treat the CS as a "Get ready!" signal, an indication that the US is about to arrive. Viewed in this way, the CR is nothing more than the animal's preparation for the US. If the sound of a bell has been reliably followed by food, then the sound now signals that the animal should moisten its mouth, so that it will be ready to eat when the food does arrive. If the sight of a light has been followed by a shock, then it is a signal that the animal should stop moving around and stay at "full alert" so that it will be ready to jump when the shock begins (see Zener, 1937; Holland, 1984; Hollis, 1984).

## CONDITIONING AND DRUG EFFECTS

Preparation for a US can take many forms. Consider, for example, a person who has received many doses of insulin, a hormone that depletes blood sugar. After a number of these injections, the individual begins to respond to the various stimuli that accompany the insulin injections such as the mere sight of the needle. The reaction to these stimuli, though, is the opposite of the response to the insulin itself: when these stimuli are presented (with no insulin injection), the blood-sugar level goes up.

In conditioning terms, the US in this case is the insulin, and the UR is the individual's built-in response to it—that is, the decrease in blood sugar. The CS is the sight of

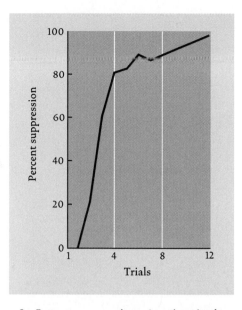

4.6 *Response suppression   A rat is trained to press a lever at a steady rate to gain food. The figure plots the extent to which this response is suppressed after successive presentations of a three-minute light (CS) that is immediately followed by electric shock (US). After twelve such trials, suppression is at 100 percent, and the animal doesn't respond at all during the three minutes when the CS is presented.*

*Drug addiction and learning    According to some authors, classical conditioning plays a key role in drug addiction. The drug itself is the US; the various cues that precede the US (the sight of the needle, for example) form the CS; the CR is a compensatory response aimed at counteracting the drug's effects.*

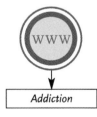

Addiction

the needle (or some other stimulus that generally accompanies the injection), and, apparently, the CR is an increase in blood-sugar level.

This CR makes sense as preparation for the upcoming US. In general, various mechanisms within the body try to maintain a stable, unchanging internal environment. (In Chapter 3, we discussed these as ways of maintaining homeostasis.) Insulin disrupts this stability by dropping blood-sugar levels. How, therefore, might stability be preserved? By increasing blood-sugar levels through some other mechanism just as the insulin arrives. This increase will offset the insulin-produced decrease, leading to no change overall and, thus, to stability.

The body's preparation for insulin, therefore, can be thought of as a *compensatory reaction*, preparation for the physiological effects to come. As a rough analogy, this is similar to a bear's stuffing itself just before it begins its winter hibernation: the animal takes in a calorie overload so that it will be all set for the upcoming calorie shortfall. Of course, in the bear's case, this compensatory response is deliberate and relies on external food sources. In the case of the insulin reaction, the response is automatic and entirely dependent on internal mechanisms.

Classical conditioning plays a crucial role in creating and sustaining these compensatory mechanisms. For hormones and many drugs, these mechanisms are activated because of repeated pairings between some CS (for example, the sight of the needle) and the US (the drug). The mechanisms can be eliminated by a conventional extinction procedure. We can also observe a generalization gradient, if we vary the CS. In short, these effects show the full profile of classical conditioning, strongly suggesting that conditioning is in fact the mechanism behind them (Siegel, 1977, 1983, 1989; Siegel & Allan, 1998; but also see Baker & Tiffany, 1985; Poulos & Cappell, 1991).

# INSTRUMENTAL CONDITIONING

Habituation and classical conditioning are two forms of simple learning, each one important in its own right. Another form of learning is *instrumental conditioning* (also called *operant conditioning*). As an example of instrumental conditioning, consider the tricks people teach their pets. When your dog learns how to "shake hands" in order to get a dog biscuit, it has learned an instrumental response in that the response leads to a sought-after effect—in this case, getting the biscuit.

Instrumental conditioning is different from classical conditioning in several ways. The most important is that, in instrumental learning, reinforcement (that is, the delivery of reward) depends upon the proper response. For your dog, no "handshake" means no biscuit. This is not true for classical conditioning. There, the US is presented regardless of what the animal does—the meat powder, for example, arrives whether the animal salivates to the sound of a metronome or not. Another difference concerns the selection of the response. In instrumental learning, the response must be selected from a (sometimes large) set of alternatives. The dog's job is to select the handshake from among the numerous other things a dog could do. Not so in classical conditioning. There, the response is forced, for the US unconditionally evokes it: in response to meat, the animal salivates; this is not a matter of choice.

## THORNDIKE AND THE LAW OF EFFECT

The experimental study of instrumental learning began a century ago as a consequence of the debate over Darwin's theory of evolution by natural selection. Supporters of Darwin's theory emphasized the continuity among species, both living and extinct: despite their apparent differences, a bird's wing, a whale's fin, and a human arm, for example, all have the same basic bone structure. This continuity buttressed the claim that these diverse organisms all descended from common ancestors. But opponents of Darwin's theory pointed to something they perceived as the crucial discontinuity among species: the human ability to think and reason, an ability that animals did not share.

In response, Darwin and his colleagues argued that there was continuity of mental prowess across the animal kingdom. Yes, humans are smarter in some ways than other species, but the differences might be smaller than we sometimes think. In support of this idea, Darwinian naturalists collected stories about the intellectual achievements of various animals (see Darwin, 1871). These painted a flattering picture, as in the reports of cunning cats who scattered bread crumbs on the lawn in order to lure birds into their reach (Romanes, 1882).

In many cases, however, it was unclear whether these reports were genuine or just bits of folklore. If genuine, it was unclear whether the reports had been elaborated or polished by the loving touch of a proud pet owner. What was needed, therefore, was more systematic, more objective, and better-documented research. That research was made possible by a method described in 1898 by Edward L. Thorndike (1874–1949).

## CATS IN A PUZZLE BOX

Thorndike's method was to set up a problem for an animal—in his experiments, usually a hungry cat. The cat was placed inside a box with a door that it could open only by performing some simple action such as pulling a loop of wire or pressing a lever (Figure 4.7). Once outside this *puzzle box*, the cat was rewarded with a small portion of food. Then it was placed back into the box for another trial so that the procedure could be repeated over and over until the task of escaping the box was mastered.

On the first trial, the typical cat struggled valiantly, meowing, clawing, and biting at the bars. This continued for several minutes until finally, by pure accident, the animal hit upon the correct response. Subsequent trials brought gradual improvement. The moments of struggle grew shorter, and the animal took less and less time to produce the response that unlocked the door. By the time the training sessions were completed, the cat's behavior was almost unrecognizable from what it had been at the start. Placed in the box, it immediately approached the wire loop, yanked it with businesslike dispatch, and hurried through the open door to enjoy the well-deserved reward.

If one merely observed the cat's sophisticated final performance, one might well credit the animal with reason or understanding. But Thorndike argued that the problem was solved in a very different way. For proof, he examined the *learning curves*. He plotted how much time the cat required on each trial to escape from the puzzle box and charted how these times changed over the course of learning. Thorndike found that the resulting curves declined quite gradually as the learning proceeded (Figure 4.8). This is not the pattern one would expect if the cats had achieved some understanding of the problem's solution. If they had, their curves would show a sudden drop at some point in the training, when the cat finally got the point. ("Aha!" muttered the insightful cat, "it's the lever that lets me out," and henceforth howled and bit no more.) Instead, these learning curves suggest that the cats learned to escape in small increments, with no evidence at all of understanding and certainly no evidence of any sudden insight into the problem's solution.

## THE LAW OF EFFECT

In Thorndike's view, the cats' initial responses to this situation were likely to be a result of prior learning or perhaps some built-in predisposition. As it happened, however, nearly all of these initial responses led to failure. Therefore, as the trials proceeded, the

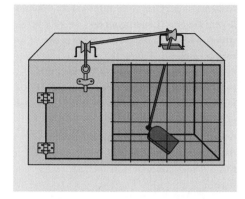

**4.7  Puzzle box**  *This box is much like those used by Edward Thorndike. The animal steps on a treadle attached to a rope, thereby releasing the latch that locks the door.*

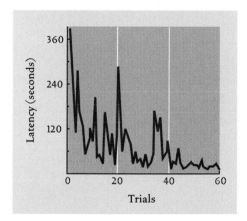

**4.8  Learning curve of one of Thorndike's cats**  *To get out of the box, the cat had to move a wooden handle from a vertical to a horizontal position. The figure shows the gradual decline in the animal's response latency (the time it takes to get out of the box). Note that the learning curve is by no means smooth but has rather marked fluctuations. This is a common feature of the learning curves of individual subjects. Smooth learning curves are generally produced by averaging the results of many individual subjects.*

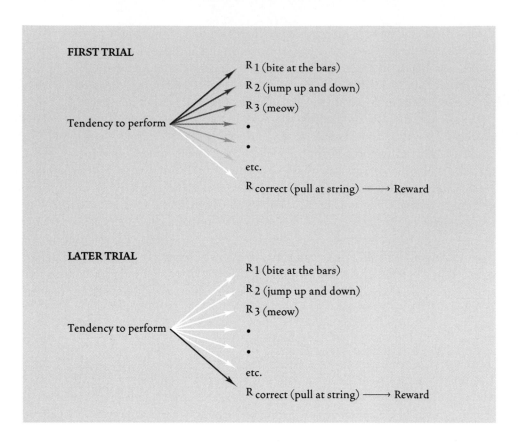

4.9  *The law of effect   The figure is a schematic presentation of Thorndike's theory of instrumental learning. On the first trial, the tendency to perform various incorrect responses (biting the bars, jumping up and down) is very strong, while the tendency to perform the correct response (pulling the string) is weak or nonexistent. As trials proceed, the strength of these responses changes. The incorrect responses become weaker and weaker, for none of these responses is immediately followed by reward. In contrast, there is a progressive strengthening of the correct response because this is followed more or less immediately by reward.*

tendency to produce these responses gradually weakened. In contrast, the animal's tendency to produce the correct response was initially weak but, over the trials, gradually grew in strength. In Thorndike's terms, the correct response was gradually "stamped in," while futile ones were correspondingly "stamped out."

What is it that causes some responses to get strengthened and others weakened as learning proceeds? Thorndike's answer was the *law of effect*. Its key proposition is that, if a response is followed by a reward, that response will be strengthened. If a response is followed by no reward (or, worse yet, by punishment), it will be weakened. In general, strength of a response is adjusted according to that response's consequences (Figure 4.9).

In this view, we do not need to postulate any sophisticated intellectual processes to explain the cat's performance. We do not need to assume that the animal noticed a connection between act and consequence or that it was trying to attain some goal. If the animal made a response and reward followed shortly, that response was more likely to be performed later.

Thorndike's proposal suggests a clear parallel between how an organism learns during its lifetime and how species evolve, thanks to the forces of natural selection. In both cases, variations that "work"—behaviors that lead to successful outcomes, or individuals with successful adaptations—are kept on. In both cases, variations that are less successful are weakened or dropped. And, crucially, in both cases the selection does not involve any guide or supervisor to steer the process forward. Instead, the selection depends only on the consequences of actions or of adaptations and on whether these serve the organism's biological needs or not.

## SKINNER AND OPERANT BEHAVIOR

Thorndike initiated the experimental study of instrumental behavior, but the psychologist who shaped the way in which most modern learning theorists think about

**4.10 Animals in operant chambers** (A) A rat trained to press a lever for water reinforcement. (B) A pigeon pecking at a lighted key for food reinforcement. Reinforcement consists of a few seconds' access to a grain feeder that is located just below the key.

the subject is B. F. Skinner (1904–1990). Skinner was one of the first theorists to insist on a sharp distinction between classical and instrumental conditioning. In classical conditioning, the animal's behavior is elicited by the CS; salivation, for example, is set off by an event outside of the organism. But in instrumental conditioning, Skinner argued, the organism is much less at the mercy of the external situation. Its reactions are emitted from within, as if they were what we ordinarily call voluntary. Skinner called these instrumental responses *operants*: they operate on the environment to bring about some change that leads to some consequence, and whether that consequence is positive or negative influences whether the operant is more or less likely to be emitted in the future. This is reminiscent of Thorndike's view, and, in fact, Skinner endorsed Thorndike's proposal of the law of effect, insisting that the tendency to emit an operant is strengthened or weakened by the behavior's consequences (Skinner, 1938).

Skinner believed, however, that Thorndike's procedure for studying learning was inefficient. Rather than placing animals in a puzzle box, Skinner sought a procedure in which the instrumental response could be performed repeatedly and rapidly. Many of his studies, therefore, employed an experimental chamber (popularly called the "Skinner box") in which a rat presses a lever or a pigeon pecks at a lighted key (Figure 4.10). In these situations, the animal remains in the presence of the lever or key for, say, an hour at a time, pressing or pecking at whatever rate it chooses. All of the animal's responses are automatically recorded, and stimuli and reinforcement are typically controlled by a computer. The usual measure of response strength is the *response rate*—that is, the number of responses per unit of time.

## THE MAJOR PHENOMENA OF INSTRUMENTAL CONDITIONING

Many of the central phenomena of instrumental learning parallel those of classical conditioning. One example concerns the acquisition of a learned response. In classical conditioning, learning trials typically involve the presentation of a CS, followed by a US. In instrumental conditioning, learning trials typically involve a response by the organism followed by a reward or reinforcer. The reinforcement often involves the presentation of something good, such as grain to a hungry pigeon. Alternatively, reinforce-

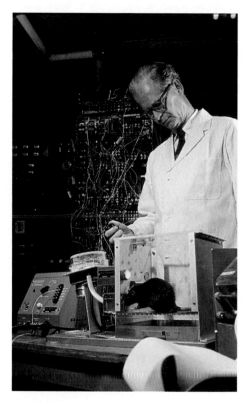

B. F. Skinner

ment may involve the termination or prevention of something bad, such as the cessation of a loud noise.

In both forms of conditioning, though, the more such pairings there are, the stronger the learning. And if these pairings are discontinued so that the CS is no longer followed by the US or the response by a reinforcer, extinction is observed.

## GENERALIZATION AND DISCRIMINATION

The instrumental response is not elicited by external stimuli, but is, in Skinner's terms, emitted from within. But this does not mean that external stimuli have no role. They do exert considerable control over behavior, serving as *discriminative stimuli*. Suppose a pigeon is trained to hop on a treadle to get some grain. When a green light is on, hopping on the treadle will pay off. But when a red light is on, treadle hopping will gain no reward. Under these circumstances, the green light becomes a positive discriminative stimulus and the red light a negative one (usually labeled $S^+$ and $S^-$, respectively). The pigeon will swiftly learn this pattern and so will hop in the presence of the first and not in the presence of the second.

Let us be clear, though, about the relationship among these stimuli. A $CS^+$ tells the animal about events in the world: "No matter what you do, the US is coming." The $S^+$, on the other hand, tells the animal about the impact of its own behavior: "If you respond now, you'll get rewarded." The $CS^-$ indicates that no US is coming, again independent of what the animal does. The $S^-$, in contrast, tells the animal something about its behavior—namely, that there is no point in responding right now.

Despite these differences, generalization and discrimination function similarly in classical and instrumental conditioning. One example is the generalization gradient. We saw earlier that, if trained with one CS (perhaps, a high tone) but then tested with a different one (a low tone), the CR will be diminished. The greater the change in the CS, the greater the drop in the CR's strength. The same pattern can be observed in instrumental conditioning. In one experiment, pigeons were trained to peck at a key illuminated with yellow light. Later, they were tested with lights of varying wavelengths, and the results show an orderly generalization gradient (Figure 4.11). As the test light became less similar to the original $S^+$, the pigeons were less inclined to peck at it (Guttmann & Kalish, 1956).

## SHAPING

The law of effect tells us that once a response has been made, then reinforcement will act to strengthen it. But what causes the animal to perform the desired response in the first place? Some responses are no problem: Pecking is the sort of thing pigeons do all the time, providing frequent opportunities for the animal trainer to reinforce (and thus encourage) this response; likewise for rats pressing and manipulating easily reachable objects in their environment.

But what about more complex responses? For example, we could place a lever so high that the rat must stretch up on its hind legs to reach it. Now the rat might never press the lever on its own. Nonetheless, it can learn this response if its behavior is suitably *shaped*. This is accomplished by a little "coaching," using the method of *successive approximations*.

How should we train a rat to press the elevated lever? First, we must teach the animal to collect its food rewards. At random intervals, a click sounds, and a food pellet drops into a little cup. Initially, the rat might be afraid of this sound, but habituation quickly quells this fear so that, before long, the rat approaches the food tray and collects the pellet as soon as it hears the click. Shaping can now begin. At first, we reinforce the animal merely for walking into the general area where the lever is located. As soon as the rat is there, we deliver food: the rat hears the click and devours the pellet. Very soon, the rat

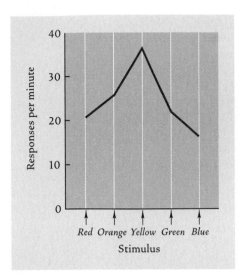

**4.11  Stimulus generalization of an instrumental response**  *Pigeons were originally reinforced to peck at a yellow light. When later tested with lights of various colors, they showed a standard generalization gradient, pecking more vigorously at colors more similar to yellow (such as green and orange) than at colors farther removed (such as red and blue).*

will have learned to remain in this neighborhood virtually all the time, allowing us to increase our demand: when the rat is in this neighborhood, sometimes it is facing one way, sometimes another; from this point on, though, the rat is reinforced only if it is in the area and facing the lever. This response also is soon mastered, and so again we increase our demand: now the rat is reinforced only if it is facing the lever and stretching its body a little bit upward. We continue in this fashion, reinforcing the rat only when it stretches all the way up to the lever, then when it actually touches the lever, and so on. Step by step, we move the rat toward the desired response. Throughout, the guiding principle is immediacy of reinforcement. If we want to reinforce the rat for standing up on its hind legs, we must do it the instant after the response; even a one-second wait may be too long for by then the rat may have fallen back on all fours, and if we reinforce it at that point, we will reinforce the wrong response.

By means of this technique, animals have been trained to perform all kinds of complex behavior (see Figure 4.12), and closely related techniques have been used in therapeutic settings with humans. For example, behavior-modification techniques are often used to shape the behavior of the hospitalized mentally ill. Initially, the hospitalized patients are rewarded merely for getting out of bed. Then, once that behavior is established, the requirement is increased so that, perhaps, the patients have to move around a bit in their room and then, later, to step out of the room and go to breakfast or to get their medicine. In this fashion, the behavior therapist can gradually lead the patients into a fuller, more acceptable level of functioning.

**4.12 Show-business animals** *Nhat is a four-year-old monkey performing with the Hanoi Circus, who was trained using techniques closely related to the ones described here—a process of gradual shaping, leading to the desired response.*

## CONDITIONED REINFORCEMENT

So far, our examples of reinforcers have included food, water, and termination of electric shocks. But instrumental learning is not always reinforced by events of such immediate biological consequence. For example, piano teachers rarely, if ever, reinforce their students with food or by turning off a shock; a nod or the comment "Good" is all that is usually required. How does Thorndike's approach explain why the word *good* is reinforcing?

Thorndike or Skinner would answer that a stimulus acquires reinforcing properties if it is repeatedly paired with another reinforcer. In this way, a stimulus can become a ***conditioned reinforcer*** and will then function just as any other reinforcer would.

Numerous experiments demonstrate that neutral stimuli can acquire reinforcing properties in this way. For example, chimpanzees in one study were first trained to insert poker chips into a vending machine to acquire grapes. Having learned this, they then learned to operate another device that delivered poker chips (Cowles, 1937; see Figure 4.13). Examples of this kind indicate that the critical factor in establishing a stimulus as a conditioned reinforcer is its association with a primary reinforcer, and so this effect will increase the more frequently the two are paired. Conversely, a conditioned reinforcer gradually loses its power if it is repeatedly presented alone, unaccompanied by some primary reinforcement.

Training your dog

All of this argues that conditioned reinforcement is established by a process that is similar to, if not identical with, classical conditioning. In short, conditioned reinforcers (tokens, smiles, nods) are similar to CSs. In both cases, these initially neutral stimuli become associated with a biologically impor-

**4.13 Conditioned reinforcement in chimpanzees** *Chimpanzee using a token to obtain food after working to obtain tokens.*

tant event; once this is accomplished, the CS or the conditioned reinforcer takes on motivational significance.

## WHAT IS A REINFORCER?

If all reinforcers were stimuli that met basic biological needs such as food, water, or warmth, or stimuli that have been associated with these biologically important stimuli, then reinforcement might be explained in terms of the homeostatic mechanisms described in Chapter 3. Reinforcers, in essence, would always be stimuli that help an organism satisfy its biological needs.

However, much evidence indicates that this suggestion is far too simple. Pigeons, for example, will peck in order to gain *information* about the availability of food (see, for example, Bower, McLean, & Meachem, 1966; Hendry, 1969). Monkeys will work merely to open a small window through which they can see a moving toy train (Butler, 1954). And, in general, animals will respond simply to gain the opportunity to engage in some other, more preferred activity—for instance, press a lever in order to run inside an exercise wheel (Premack, 1965; but also Timberlake & Allison, 1974; Timberlake, 1995).

These (and many other) examples make reinforcement difficult to define. Some reinforcers meet biological needs, but many do not. As a consequence, this term is generally defined only after the fact. Is a glimpse of a toy train reinforcing? We can find out only by asking whether an animal will work to obtain this glimpse. Remarkably, no other more informative definition of a reinforcer is currently available.

*Behavioral Contrast*  The issues are just as complicated when we consider the *magnitude* of a reinforcer. It is no surprise that an animal will respond a little bit for a small reward, but will respond more (more quickly, more strongly) for a large reward. What counts as small or large, however, depends on the context. If a rat is used to getting sixty food pellets for a response, then sixteen pellets will seem measly, and the animal will respond only weakly for this puny reward. But if a rat is used to getting only four pellets for a response, then sixteen pellets will seem like a feast, and the rat's response will be fast and strong (see, for example, Crespi, 1942). Thus, the effectiveness of a reinforcer will depend to a large extent on what other rewards are available and on what other rewards have been recently available. This pattern is often referred to as *behavioral contrast*.

*Intrinsic Motivation*  Behavioral contrast may provide a partial explanation for another phenomenon called *intrinsic motivation*, easily demonstrated in many species but quite striking in humans. In an early study of this phenomenon, nursery-school children were given an opportunity to draw pictures. The children seemed to enjoy this activity and produced drawings at a steady pace even though no reinforcers for this activity were in view. Apparently, they were drawing because the activity was fun or, put differently, because drawing was its own reward. The reward was intrinsic to the activity, not separate from it.

In this study, though, the experimenters added an extrinsic reward: the children were now presented with an attractive "Good Player" certificate for producing their pictures. Then, sometime later, the children were again given the opportunity to draw pictures, but this time with no provision for "Good Player" rewards. Remarkably, these children now showed considerably less interest in drawing than they had at the start, choosing instead to spend their time on other activities (see, for example, Lepper, Greene, & Nisbett, 1973; see Kohn, 1993, for a review of subsequent related studies).

At one level, these data illustrate the power of behavioral contrasts. At the start of the study, the intrinsic reward involved in drawing was by itself sufficient to motivate the children. Later on, though, this same reward seemed puny when compared to the (greater) prize that consisted of the intrinsic reward plus the "Good Player" certificate.

As a consequence, the seemingly smaller reward was now insufficient to motivate continued drawing.

More fundamentally, though, these results imply that there may be two different types of reward. One type is merely tacked on to a behavior and is under the control of the experimenter. The other is intrinsic to the behavior and is independent of the experimenter's (or anyone else's) intentions. Moreover, some authors have suggested that intrinsically motivated behaviors—behaviors that we do for their own sake—may have a special status. Think about an artist who continues in her creative endeavors even though her art wins her no tangible rewards. Think about a scientist who perseveres in testing an unpopular hypothesis despite the criticism of skeptical colleagues, or an individual who insists on taking a firm moral stance despite the financial incentives tempting him toward a morally dubious alternative. In all of these cases, important human activities seem to be sustained only by intrinsic motivation, with no accompanying extrinsic reinforcement. Indeed, the scientist and the moralist stay the course despite extrinsic rewards favoring an alternative course of action. Cases such as these lead one to wonder how many activities are intrinsically motivated, and whether intrinsically motivated acts have a special status, as these examples suggest. These are crucial questions to pursue if we are to understand the nature of reinforcement and reward, and, indeed, the nature of human motivation.

We note, though, that there has been considerable controversy attached to these issues. Some scholars have questioned, for example, whether cases like the ones we have mentioned truly involve intrinsic motivation. Perhaps reinforcers are involved but are not obvious. (Perhaps the artist is banking on being recognized in ten or twenty years; perhaps the scientist is hoping for ultimate vindication and the chance to say, "I told you so!") In light of these questions, it seems certain that investigators will continue to debate the nature of intrinsic motivation, including whether it exists as a special kind of motivation, somehow different from the motivations more easily studied in the learning laboratory. (For discussion, see, for example, Deci, Koestner, & Ryan, 1999a, b; Eisenberger, Pierce, & Cameron, 1999; Lepper, Henderlong, & Gingras, 1999).

## SCHEDULES OF REINFORCEMENT

Let us return, though, to the issue of how extrinsic reinforcements work since, on anyone's account, extrinsic reinforcement plays a huge role in governing human (and other species') behavior. We do, after all, work for money, buy lottery tickets in hopes of winning, and act in a fashion that we believe will bring us praise. How do these extrinsic rewards govern our behavior?

Note that, in these examples, reinforcement comes only occasionally: we are not paid after every task we perform at work; we rarely (if ever) win the lottery; we do not always get the praise we seek. In fact, this is the usual pattern outside the laboratory. The fisherman does not hook a fish with every cast, and even a star tennis player occasionally loses a match. It is, in other words, a fact of life that our efforts are usually reinforced only some of the time. This is known as *partial reinforcement*.

In the laboratory, partial reinforcement can be arranged in different ways. Reinforcement might be delivered after a certain number of responses are made or after some interval has passed. These different patterns can each be described in terms of a *schedule of reinforcement*. In essence, the schedule defines the rules that determine when and under what conditions a response will be reinforced.

*Ratio Schedules*   One example of such a rule is the *fixed-ratio (FR) schedule*, in which the research participant must produce a specified number of responses in order to receive each reward. The number of responses required determines the number following "FR": if two responses are required for each reinforcement, the schedule is FR 2; if three or four responses are required, then the schedule is FR 3 or FR 4; and so on. Such schedules can generate very high rates of responding, especially if the ratio is high. But to reach these high rates, the ratio must increase gradually, beginning with FR 1 (each response is rewarded) and then slowly increasing the requirement.

Even higher rates of responding, however, can be produced by a *variable-ratio (VR) schedule*, in which reinforcement still comes after a certain number of responses but the number of responses needed varies from one reinforcement to the next. VR schedules are typically described in terms of the average number of responses required so that a VR 10, for example, is a schedule in which, on average, the animal receives a reward for every ten responses. However, within this schedule, it might turn out that the first five responses were enough to earn one reward, but fifteen more were needed to earn the next.

In a VR schedule, there is no way for the animal to know which of its responses will bring the next reward. Perhaps one more response will do the trick, or perhaps it will take a hundred more. This uncertainty helps explain why VR schedules produce such high levels of responding in humans and in other creatures. Although this is easily demonstrated in the laboratory, more persuasive evidence comes from any gambling casino. There, the slot machines pay off on a VR schedule, with the "reinforcement schedule" adjusted so that "responses" occur at a very high rate, ensuring that the casino will be lucrative for its owners and not for its patrons.

*Interval Schedules* Ratio schedules are based on numbers of responses. Interval schedules are based on time. In a *fixed-interval (FI) schedule*, reinforcement becomes available only after a certain interval has passed since the last reinforcement. Responses during that interval are not rewarded. Once the interval is completed, the very next response earns a reward. An example of an FI schedule is looking in the mailbox. No matter how many times you check the box, your effort will go unrewarded if you look before the mail has been delivered. But once the mail has been delivered, your very next response is certain to be reinforced. Since most mail delivery occurs daily, this would be a schedule of FI 24 hours.

A *variable-interval (VI) schedule* differs from an FI schedule in the same way that a VR schedule differs from an FR schedule. For a VI schedule, reinforcement occurs on average only after some specified interval. However, the actual interval varies unpredictably from trial to trial. An example from everyday life would be an employer who requires periodic drug tests of her employees. These might be administered, on average, every month, but to preserve the element of surprise, the timing of each drug test is unpredictable.

*Partial Reinforcement and Extinction* The various schedules of reinforcement, as we have now seen, have different influences on behavior. But one of the most important effects of partial reinforcement is seen only during extinction because, quite reliably, partial reinforcement leads to slower extinction, a fact that was first documented many years ago (Humphreys, 1939) but has been confirmed many times since then (see Figure 4.14).

On the face of it, this result is paradoxical. If each reinforcement increases the strength of the instrumental response, then a greater number of reinforcements should lead to a more strongly established behavior. We might expect, therefore, that an organism reinforced 100 percent of the time would continue to respond longer than one reinforced only 33 percent of the time. But the opposite is true. Why? Speaking informally, we might say that the partially reinforced animal has learned that not every effort leads to success; it has learned that "if at first you don't succeed, try, try again." This animal might not even notice initially that extinction trials have begun since it has responded without reinforcement many times before.

Consistent with this idea, studies show that it is more difficult to extinguish a response that was established with an irregular sequence of reinforcements. With a regular sequence, the animal knows when reinforcement will be delivered; so the absence

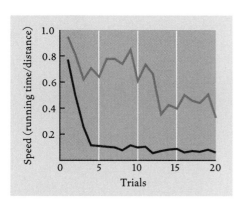

**4.14   The partial-reinforcement effect   The** figure shows runway speeds during extinction trials on two groups of rats. One group had previously been reinforced on every trial; the other had only been reinforced on 30 percent of the trials. The figure shows that the group trained under full reinforcement (in red) stops running considerably before the group that was trained under partial reinforcement (in green).

of reinforcement can be surprising and informative. With an irregular sequence, though, the delivery of reinforcement cannot be predicted; so the absence of reinforcement is less informative, and extinction is correspondingly slowed.

## THE BREADTH OF INSTRUMENTAL CONDITIONING

Instrumental conditioning—just like classical conditioning—can be observed in a wide variety of organisms and settings. Rats can be trained to press levers, cats to pull on wire loops, and chimps to operate vending machines. Other examples are easy to enumerate, and instrumental conditioning has been observed in species as simple as honeybees and as complex as humans.

The breadth of instrumental conditioning is also visible in the many applications of these techniques in nonlaboratory settings. We have already mentioned the role of behavior modification in therapeutic settings; and behavior modification is also widely used both in hospitals for the mentally ill and in one-on-one therapy. (We will return to these applications of instrumental conditioning in Chapter 17.) Similarly, many prisons use instrumental conditioning to shape prisoners' behavior, and parents often employ similar techniques to teach their children good manners, household chores, and interpersonal skills. In short, then, these techniques are extensively used and very useful, and provide an effective means for altering or maintaining specific patterns of behavior.

## PUNISHMENT AND AVOIDANCE LEARNING

Our discussion so far has centered on cases of reward, in which responding brings something good. But what about punishment, in which a response is followed by some aversive stimulus—perhaps a startling noise for laboratory rats or a stern "No!" for a naughty child? These stimuli, just like rewards, have a powerful effect in shaping behavior.

*Punishment* In cases of **punishment**, a response is followed by an aversive stimulus, which will make that response less likely to occur on subsequent occasions. As with rewards, though, the timing of the punishment is crucial. Consider a dog that has developed the unfortunate habit of chewing on shoes. Since the pet owner may discover the misdeed hours later and yell at the dog then, it's likely that this punishment will not produce the hoped-for learning because the animal has no way of connecting the crime with the punishment. Nor does the punishment teach what response is desired in place of the punished act. For punishment to have its desired effect, it must be administered shortly after the unwanted response is performed, and then, if at all possible, the correct response should be elicited and reinforced.

Other factors also influence the impact of punishment. Evidence suggests, for example, that more intense punishers (a more painful shock, a louder burst of noise) are more effective in suppressing behavior than less intense punishers. One might conclude, therefore, that, to maximize the effect of punishment, the punishing stimulus should be as intense as possible. Obviously, though, ethical considerations must enter our discussion here. An intense punishment might well be judged cruel, even if that punishment is effective in stopping an animal from some destructive (or self-destructive) behavior. The trade-off between cruelty and effectiveness must be evaluated in any case involving punishment.

Common sense suggests one way to deal with this trade-off, but, in this context, common sense actually leads us astray. Imagine a parent who wishes to stop her child from engaging in some dangerous behavior—perhaps bicycling in traffic without a helmet. To avoid issues of cruelty, the parent might begin with some relatively mild punishment for this behavior, hoping that that is sufficient. If it is not, the parent might

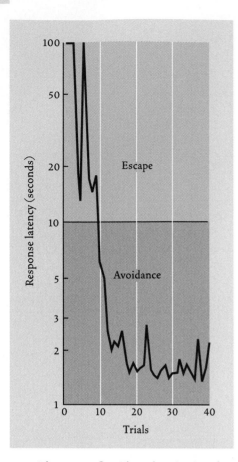

**4.15 The course of avoidance learning in a dog** *The figure shows response latencies of one animal in a shuttle box (where latency is the time from the onset of CS to the animal's response). A warning stimulus indicated that shock would begin 10 seconds after the onset of the signal. For the first nine trials the dog escaped. It jumped over the hurdle after the shock began. From the tenth trial on, the dog avoided: it jumped before its 10 seconds of grace were up.*

slowly escalate the punishment, continuing until she finds the minimal level of punishment (and so the minimal level of cruelty) that will achieve the goal.

Attractive as this strategy might be, the evidence suggests it is ill advised: punishments that are introduced in mild form and then gradually intensified turn out to be markedly less effective than punishments that are introduced at "full strength" from the start. The hypothetical parent we have just described, therefore, will probably end up delivering more punishment than she might have had she used a strong punishment from the start. (For evidence on this point, see, for example, Azrin & Holz, 1966; Church, 1969. For further discussion of the principles that influence the effectiveness of punishment, and the sometimes complex interplay between the use of punishment and ethical considerations, see Schwartz, Wasserman, & Robbins, 2002.)

*Escape and Avoidance* In punishment, an aversive stimulus is used to weaken an unwanted behavior. But aversive stimuli can also be used to strengthen a response. Consider *escape responses*, for example; these allow an animal to get away from, or terminate, an aversive situation. *Avoidance responses* have an even better outcome: they prevent the aversive stimulus from occurring in the first place. Clearly, from the animal's point of view, both escape and avoidance bring about a good result. It is no surprise, therefore, that escape and avoidance responses are often swiftly learned. As an example of escape, a rat can easily be trained to press a lever in order to turn off an electric shock. As an example of avoidance, a dog can readily learn to jump from one chamber to another whenever it hears a tone that signals impending shock. If it jumps within some grace period, it will manage to avoid the shock entirely (see Figure 4.15).

*Aversive Conditioning and the Law of Effect* The effects of punishment are easily accommodated by the law of effect. As we have already noted, good consequences strengthen the tendency to produce a behavior, and bad consequences weaken it. Likewise, an escape response is followed by the termination of something bad, and this serves as a reward, making that same response more likely in the future.

But the interpretation of avoidance learning is more difficult. Consider a dog who jumps back and forth in order to avoid an electric shock. In the early stages of learning, the dog did not jump until after the shock had begun, and so each jump was rewarded by the termination of shock. Eventually, however, the dog learned to jump early enough so that it now avoids the shock altogether. On the face of things, this means that the reinforcement for jumping (the termination of the shock) is no longer being delivered, and this should lead to extinction of the response. Yet the animal continues to jump. Why is this?

Of course, each of the dog's jumps is followed by absence of shock, which probably reinforces the jumping response. But let us be clear about what this involves. The dog must know that there is a real threat of shock in this situation, otherwise absence of shock would not be rewarding. To understand this, consider the fact that each of the dog's jumps is also followed by the absence of a violent explosion, just as it is followed by the absence of shock. But there is no reason to believe that explosion avoidance is why the animal continues to jump. Since there was never any reason to fear (or even to think about) explosions in this situation, the absence of explosions provides no relief, no release from fear, and, therefore, no reward.

Hence, it is not absence of shock itself that is the reward. This absence is rewarding only when shock is realistically threatened, and only in that context is the absence of shock a relief and a reward. To explain avoidance learning, therefore, we need somehow to acknowledge that the animal not only knows what threats are present in a situation, but also knows what will happen if it does not respond. It is these complexities that demand an account fuller than that provided simply by the law of effect. This account is readily developed within a more cognitive approach to learning.

# COGNITIVE LEARNING

There is no question that classical and instrumental conditioning reveal important forms of learning, observable in many species and many settings. But what is it that the organism is learning? Our discussion up to now has suggested that the essential thing about classical and instrumental conditioning is that both procedures modify behavior. In classical conditioning, a new response (the CR) is created. In instrumental conditioning, responses are strengthened or weakened by the mechanical effects of reinforcement.

From the earliest days of learning theory, however, there was an alternative view of conditioning that asserted that learning is not the change in behavior as such, but is instead the acquisition of new knowledge. One of the most prominent exponents of this view was Edward C. Tolman (1886–1959). As Tolman saw it, the response an animal acquires in the course of a learning experiment is crucial because it provides us with an indication that new knowledge has been gained. But it is the cognition, and not the response, that is the essence of what is learned (Dickinson, 1987).

*Edward C. Tolman*

Tolman's view is supported by many results. For example, in one experiment, rats were ferried from one end of a large room to another, riding in transparent trolley cars. During these rides, the rats' behavior did not change, but there was learning nonetheless: later tests showed that the rats had learned the layout and the general features of the room (Gleitman, 1963)—they had acquired what Tolman called a "cognitive map" that represents what is where and what leads to what (Tolman, 1948). Thus, learning cannot be equated with behavior change because here the passenger rats showed the former without the latter.

## A COGNITIVE VIEW OF CLASSICAL CONDITIONING

Classical conditioning can also be understood in cognitive terms—in terms of what the animal knows rather than what it does. This is reflected in the fact that an animal in a conditioning procedure usually does not respond to the CS just as it did to the US. Instead, as we have mentioned, the CR and UR are usually different from each other and may, in fact, be exact opposites. It seems, therefore, that the CS does not become a substitute for the US, but instead becomes a signal that the US will soon follow, leading the animal to make appropriate preparations for the US (Rescorla, 1988; Tolman, 1932).

### TEMPORAL RELATIONS BETWEEN THE CS AND THE US

This emphasis on the CS as a signal helps us understand many aspects of classical conditioning. For example, what is it that produces the conditioning? What causes the CS to become associated, in an animal's mind, with the US? Pavlov believed that the key was *temporal contiguity*—that is, the mere fact that the two events, CS and US, occurred together in time. But the mechanism is actually more complicated.

Consider, for example, the fact that the rate at which conditioning develops depends on how the CS and US are related to each other in time. Conditioning is best when the CS precedes the US by some optimum interval.* If the interval between the CS and US is increased beyond this optimum, the effectiveness of the pairing declines sharply. In addition, presenting the CS and US simultaneously is much less effective in establish-

---

* The precise value of the optimum interval depends on the particulars of the situation; it usually varies from about half a second to about ten seconds. In one form of classical conditioning, learned taste aversion, the CS-US is very long and may be an hour or more. This phenomenon poses obvious difficulties for a contiguity theory of conditioning—and much else besides—and will be discussed in a later section (see pp. 150–152).

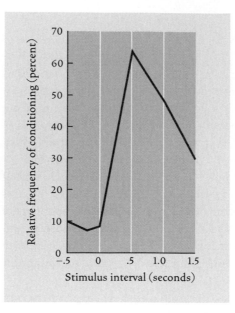

4.16   *The CS-US interval in classical conditioning*   *The figure shows the results of a study of the effectiveness of various CS-US intervals in humans. The CR was a finger withdrawal response, the CS a tone, and the US an electric shock. The time between CS and US is plotted on the horizontal axis. Negative intervals mean that the US was presented before the CS (backward pairing), a zero interval means that the two stimuli were presented simultaneously, and a positive interval means that the CS began before the US (forward pairing). The vertical axis indicates the degree of conditioning.*

ing an association, and the backward procedure is even worse (Rescorla, 1988; see Figure 4.16.).

These facts make perfect sense if we understand the CS as a signal, allowing the organism to prepare for the US. To see how this works, imagine a mountain road that contains a dangerous hairpin turn. How should drivers be warned about this turn? The ideal warning would be a "Caution" sign just before the turn (analogous to forward pairing with a short CS-US interval; see Figure 4.17.). This sign would be informative and would give the driver time to prepare for the relevant maneuver. But it is important that the sign not appear too far in advance of the turn. As an extreme example, imagine a "Caution" sign appearing 100 miles before the turn (analogous to forward pairing with an extremely long CS-US interval). In this case, the driver might not connect the sign with what it signifies or, just as bad, might have forgotten about the sign altogether by the time she approaches the curve. Things would be worse still, though, if the sign were prominently displayed right in the middle of the hairpin turn because now the sign's warning comes too late to be of any use (simultaneous pairing). Worst of all, the driver would suspect a degree of malevolence if she discovered the sign placed on the road 100 feet beyond the turn (backward pairing), although she would probably be grateful that she did not find it at the bottom of the ravine.

## CONTINGENCY

It seems useful, therefore, to think of the CS as a signal that the US is soon to arrive. But what is a "signal"? Consider a dog in a conditioning experiment. Several times, it has heard a metronome and, a moment later, received some food powder. But many other stimuli were also present. Simultaneous with the metronome, the dog heard some doors slamming and some voices in the background. It saw the laboratory walls and the light fixtures hanging from the ceiling. At that moment, it could also smell a dozen different scents and could feel a similar number of bodily sensations.

What, therefore, should the dog learn? If it relies on mere contiguity, then it will learn to associate the food powder with all of these stimuli—metronomes, light fixtures, and everything else that is on the scene. After all, these were all present when the US was introduced.

We have already suggested, though, that the CR is an act of preparation for the upcoming US. It would seem, then, that what the animal needs is the ability to predict

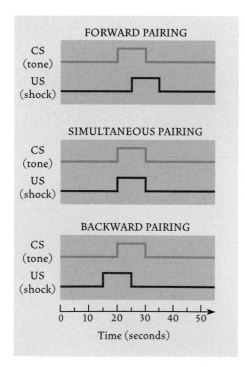

4.17   *Some temporal relationships in classical conditioning*

the US so that it knows when to prepare and when not to bother. For this purpose, an association between the US and, say, the light fixtures would be of no value: the fixtures were on the scene just before the food powder arrived, but they were also on the scene during the many minutes in which no food was on its way. Likewise for the smells and most of the sounds in the laboratory: although these were associated with food, they were also associated with the absence of food. Therefore, none of these provides any information or allows any prediction about when food is going to arrive.

What the animal needs is some event that reliably occurs when food is about to appear and that does not occur otherwise. And, of course, the metronome beat in our example is the stimulus that satisfies these requirements since it never beats in the intervals between trials when food is not presented. Therefore, if the animal hears the metronome, it is a safe bet that food is on its way. If the animal cares about signaling, it should learn about the metronome and not about these other stimuli, even though they were all contiguous with the target event.

*Contingency versus Contiguity*  Are animals sensitive to these patterns? A variety of research indicates that they are. In one experiment, rats were exposed to various combinations of a tone (CS) and a shock (US). The tone was never a perfect predictor of shock but, even so, was a signal that shock was likely to arrive soon. Specifically, presentation of the tone signaled a 40 percent chance that a shock was about to arrive.

For some of the rats in this experiment, shocks also arrived 40 percent of the time without any warning. For these rats, the tone really provided no information; the rats' expectations about things to come should have been the same with the tone or without it. This situation led to no conditioning, and the rats learned to ignore the tone.

For other rats in the experiment, things were different. For these rats, the tone still signaled a 40 percent chance of shock and also as before, shocks still arrived occasionally with no warning. For these animals, though, the likelihood of a shock was smaller (below 40 percent) when there was no tone than when there was a tone. In this case, the tone was an imperfect predictor of things to come but still provided some information: shock is more likely following the tone than otherwise. And in this situation, the rats did develop a conditioned response and became fearful whenever the tone was sounded.

Because of the way this experiment was set up, both groups of rats experienced the same number of tone-shock pairings, and so the degree of contiguity between tone and shock was the same for both groups. What differed between the groups, though, was whether the tone was informative or not, and it is the information value, apparently, that matters for conditioning. In addition, notice that the tone was never a perfect predictor of shock: tones were *not* followed by shock 60 percent of the time. Even so, conditioning was observed; apparently, an imperfect predictor is better than no predictor at all (Rescorla, 1967, 1988; but see also Papini & Bitterman, 1990).

The *Absence of Contingency*  When the probability of a shock following a tone is equal to the probability of a shock without a tone, one might think there is nothing to be learned since, in this situation, the tone provides no information about things to come. But the animal does learn something in this situation: it learns that there is danger in this setting and, crucially, it learns that it can never feel safe.

To see how this works, consider two contrasting situations. In the first, the CS signals that shock is likely to follow. When the CS appears, the animal will become fearful. But when there is no CS, the animal can relax because now shock is less likely. The absence of the CS has become a safety signal, an inhibitor of fear (see pp. 129–130).

In the second situation, no stimulus predicts when shock will occur—there is no CS to elicit fear. But, from the animal's point of view, this makes things worse, not better. Without the CS, there is no safety signal, and, as a result the animal must be afraid all the time.

The difference between signaled and unsignaled shock may be related to a distinction frequently made between fear and anxiety. According to some theorists, fear is a state elicited by a specific situation or object, whereas anxiety is chronic, is objectless, and occurs in many situations. A number of authors suggest that such unfocused anxiety is in part produced by unpredictability—in essence, by an absence of safety signals (Schwartz et al., 2002; Seligman, 1975).

## THE ROLE OF SURPRISE

Apparently, animals are influenced by the probabilities inherent in a series of events, but they are obviously not standing by with a calculator, tallying trials on which the CS was followed by a US and dividing this by the number of trials on which the US occurred alone. How, then, do animals learn? And how are they influenced by these probabilities?

Researchers have suggested that learning depends on mechanisms that involve simple trial-by-trial adjustments in the strength of association between CS and US. With these mechanisms, there is no need for the animal to compute any sort of overall tally, comparing probabilities in one situation to probabilities in another. Nonetheless, such mechanisms ensure that the animal will end up sensitive to, and influenced by, the pattern of probabilities.

While there is some disagreement over the details, most researchers agree that a critical ingredient driving this process is the extent to which the US is surprising (that is, unexpected). If the US is unsurprising, then the animal's expectations were in line with reality, and so there is no point in adjusting those expectations. But when surprises occur, it is time to adjust: if a CS has been paired with a US in the past but now appears alone, this will be a surprise and will lead to a weakening of the CS-US connection; conversely, if the animal has not associated a CS with a US and now the two are paired, this will also be a surprise and so will lead to a strengthening of the association (Kamin, 1968; Rescorla & Wagner, 1972; but see also Miller, Barnet, & Grahame, 1995; Pearce & Bouton, 2001).

The role of surprise is clearly visible in a series of studies performed by Leon Kamin, who discovered a phenomenon called the *blocking effect*. Kamin's basic experiment was run in three stages. In Stage 1, the rats heard a hissing noise that was followed by a shock. As one might expect, this noise became a CS for conditioned fear. In Stage 2, the shock was preceded by two stimuli presented simultaneously: one was the same hissing noise used in Stage 1; the other was a light. In Stage 3, the light was presented alone to see whether it would also produce a conditioned fear reaction. The results show that it did not. Even though the light had been paired many times with the shock, no learning took place. Why? Because the light provided only redundant information: the animal already knew that a shock was coming; the hissing noise told it so. Since no new information was associated with the light, no surprise was evoked by the light, and, therefore, there was no learning.

Humans are similarly alert to redundancy. Consider the once common practice among many U.S. radio stations of announcing the day's temperature in both Fahrenheit and Celsius. Initially, educators hoped that this would teach listeners to use the Celsius scale—listeners would learn that an announcement of 1° Celsius meant a cold day; an announcement of 25° Celsius meant a warm one. But this learning never happened: listeners got all the information they needed from the familiar Fahrenheit numbers and so ignored, and learned nothing about, the Celsius numbers. (For more on blocking in humans, see Kruschke & Blair, 2000.)

# A COGNITIVE VIEW
# OF INSTRUMENTAL CONDITIONING

The cognitive perspective provides many insights into classical conditioning, helping us to understand both what is learned and what produces the learning. A similar cognitive account applies to instrumental conditioning.

## COGNITIONS ABOUT ACT-OUTCOME RELATIONSHIPS

According to the law of effect, responses are strengthened if they are followed by positive consequences (a reinforcer) and weakened if they are followed by negative consequences (a punishment). This implies that learning always involves a change in behavior, with some responses "stamped in" and others "stamped out." But, as mentioned earlier, it turns out that learning can take place even in the absence of any behavioral change. This fact makes no sense if learning is simply a matter of the strengthening or weakening of responses, but makes perfect sense if we conceive of learning in a different way: as the acquisition of knowledge.

Many studies, for example, demonstrate the reality of *latent learning*—the acquisition of new knowledge without a corresponding change in behavior. A classic example is an experiment in which rats were allowed to explore a maze without any reward for ten days. There was no detectable change in their behavior during these days, but latent learning was nonetheless taking place: the rats were learning how to navigate the maze's corridors. This became obvious on the eleventh day, when food was placed in the maze's goal box for the first time. The rats learned to run to this goal box, virtually without error, almost immediately. The knowledge they had acquired earlier now took on motivational significance, and so the animals swiftly displayed what they already knew (Tolman & Honzik, 1930).

Animals also acquire knowledge about the specific relationships between their actions and the outcomes of those actions—in other words, they acquire knowledge that can be referred to as an *act-outcome representation* (Tolman, 1932). This knowledge can then be demonstrated in many ways. In one study, rats were trained to make two different responses, each of which produced a different reward. On some days, their experimental chamber contained a standard Skinner-box lever that projected from one wall. If the animals pressed this lever, they were rewarded with a food pellet. On other days, instead of the lever, a chain dangled from the ceiling. If the rats pulled this chain, they were rewarded with a few drops of sugar water.

After a few days of training, the rats were busily lever-pressing and chain-pulling, indicating that instrumental learning had been effective. But what was it that had been learned? One possibility is that the rats had simply acquired a tendency to perform these two responses. Another is that they acquired some knowledge—that bar pressing leads to food pellets and chain pulling leads to sugar water.

To decide between these alternatives, the experimenters changed the attractiveness of one of the rewards. They allowed the rats to drink some of the sugar water, but then gave them injections of a mild toxin. This created a taste aversion for the sugar (but not for the pellets), so that the rats no longer found the sugar water desirable. (For more on taste aversions, see pp. 150–152.) What effects would this have when the animals were next given the chance to press a lever or pull a chain? The results showed that the rats continued to press the lever to obtain food but they no longer pulled the chain. Clearly, the animals had learned which response led to which reward (Colwill & Rescorla, 1985; Rescorla, 1991, 1993a, b; see Figure 4.18).*

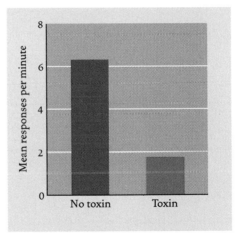

4.18 *Act-outcome cognitions* **The figure shows the results on the final test of an experiment in which two different responses were reinforced by two different food rewards. Once this learned relationship was established, one of the two rewards was paired with a toxin. There was a marked decline in the response leading to the reward that was devalued by the toxin (in green) as compared with the response leading to the reward that was not devalued (red).**

---

* For half the rats, a taste aversion was established for the pellets rather than the sugar water. When subsequently tested, these rats pulled the chain (which led to the sugar water) and did not press the lever (which led to the pellets).

## CONTINGENCY IN INSTRUMENTAL CONDITIONING

We have seen that classical conditioning depends on the information value of the CS as a predictor for the US. A similar relationship holds for instrumental conditioning except that here the issue is how well an animal's actions predict whether a certain outcome will occur. If the act is lever pressing and the outcome is a food pellet, then the rat must learn the probability of getting a pellet after lever pressing versus the probability of getting it after not lever pressing. If the first probability is greater than the second, getting food is contingent upon lever pressing. If the two probabilities are equal, there is no contingency—lever pressing and getting pellets are independent.*

*Response Control in Infants*  One line of evidence for the importance of contingency in instrumental conditioning comes from studies of human infants. In one study, the infants were placed in cribs above which a colorful mobile was suspended. Whenever the infants moved their heads, they closed a switch in their pillows; this activated the overhead mobile, which spun merrily for a second or so. The infants soon learned to shake their heads about, making their mobiles turn. They evidently enjoyed this, smiling and cooing at their mobiles, clearly delighted to see the mobiles move.

A second group of infants was exposed to a similar situation, but with one important difference: their mobile turned just as often as the mobile for the first group, but it was moved for them, not by them. This turned out to be crucial. After a few days, these infants no longer smiled and cooed at the mobile, nor did they seem particularly interested when it turned. This suggests that what the first group of infants liked about the mobile was not that it moved, but that they made it move. Clearly, then, infants can distinguish between response-controlled and response-independent outcomes—they can detect when a contingency is present and when it is absent. And infants, just like adults, desire some control over their environment. Even a two-month-old infant wants to be the master of her own fate (Watson, 1967; see Figure 4.19).

*Helplessness in Dogs*  The mobile-turning infants illustrate the joy of mastery. Another highly influential series of studies demonstrates the despair of no mastery at all. The focus of these studies is on **learned helplessness**, an acquired sense that one has lost control over one's environment, with the sad consequence that one gives up trying (Seligman, 1975).

The classic experiment on learned helplessness used two groups of dogs, A and B, which received strong electric shocks while strapped in a hammock. The dogs in group A

---

* If the second probability is greater than the first, then getting the pellet is contingent upon *not* pressing the lever. This kind of contingency is common whenever one wants the learner to refrain from doing something, for example: "I'll give you a cookie if you stop whining."

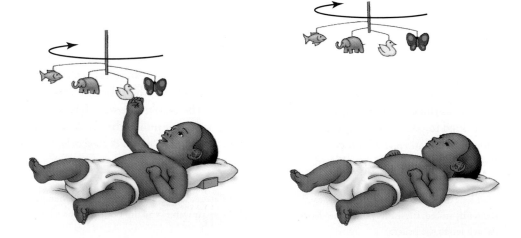

4.19  *Response control*  **Infants who can make a mobile move smile and coo at it, while those who have no control over its motion stop smiling.**

were able to exert some control over their situation. They could turn the shock off whenever it began simply by pushing a panel that was placed close to their noses. The dogs in group $B$ had no such power. For them, the shocks were inescapable. But the number and duration of these shocks were the same as for the first group. This was guaranteed by the fact that, for each dog in group $A$, there was a corresponding animal in group $B$ whose fate was yoked to that of the first dog. Whenever the group $A$ dog was shocked, so was the group $B$ dog. Whenever the group $A$ dog turned off the shock, the shock was turned off for the group $B$ dog. Thus, even though the physical suffering meted out to both groups was identical, what differed was what the animals could do about it. The dogs in group $A$ were able to exercise some control; those in group $B$ could only endure.

What did the group $B$ dogs learn in this situation? To find out, both groups of dogs were next presented with a standard avoidance learning task in which they had to jump from one compartment to another to avoid a shock (Figure 4.20). The dogs in group $A$ learned this task easily. During the first few trials, these dogs ran about frantically when the shock began but eventually scrambled over the hurdle into the other compartment. Better still, they soon learned to jump before their grace period was up and so avoided the shock entirely. Things were different, though, for the dogs in group $B$, the dogs who had previously experienced the inescapable shock. Initially, these dogs behaved much like any others, running about, barking, and so on. But they soon became much more passive. They lay down, whined, and simply took whatever shocks were delivered. They neither avoided nor escaped; they just gave up trying. In the first phase of this experiment, they really had been objectively helpless; there truly was nothing they could do. But in the shuttle box, their helplessness was only subjective, for there was now a way in which they could make their lot bearable. But they never discovered it. They had learned to be helpless (Seligman & Maier, 1967).

*Helplessness and Depression*    Martin Seligman (b. 1942), one of the discoverers of the learned-helplessness effect, asserts that a similar mechanism underlies the development of certain kinds of depression in humans. Like the helpless dog, Seligman argues, the depressed patient has come to believe that his acts are uniformly futile. And Seligman maintains that, like the dog, the depressed patient has reached this morbid state because of an exposure to a situation in which he really was helpless. While the dog received inescapable shocks in its hammock, the patient found himself powerless in the face of bereavement, some career failure, or serious illness (Seligman, Klein, & Miller, 1976). In both cases, the outcome is the same—a belief that there is no contingency between acts and outcomes and so no point in trying. (For more on the strengths and the limitations of this theory of depression, see Chapter 16.)*

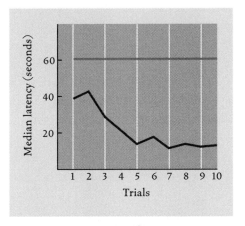

**4.20    Learned helplessness    *The figure shows the shuttle-box performance of two groups of dogs. On each trial, the animal could escape or avoid a shock. If it jumped within ten seconds after the CS, it avoided the shock altogether; if it did not jump within sixty seconds, the trial was terminated. The figure shows how quickly the animals jumped. The animals in Group A (red) had previously received electric shocks that they could escape by performing an instrumental response. The animals in Group B (green) received the same shocks, but were unable to do anything about them.***

# VARIETIES OF LEARNING

Humans are, of course, capable of behaviors and cognitions far more complex than those produced by other animals. But the perspective we have been exploring suggests that these complex behaviors are learned and maintained by the same rules that govern

---

* Before moving on, we should mention that studies of learned helplessness in dogs—like many studies we have mentioned in this chapter—raise ethical questions. Is it ethically acceptable to deliver electric shock to animals? Is it acceptable given the fact that, in some circumstances, the shock produces a depressionlike state in the animals? These are difficult and worrisome questions, but the link between these studies and human depression may provide an answer. It was thought that these studies would help us to understand human depression and lead to more effective forms of treatment for, or even prevention of, depression. These considerations persuade many investigators that the animal work, as troubling as it is, is necessary as a means of working toward the goal of diminishing human suffering.

a rat's lever pressing or a pigeon's key pecking, rules that emphasize, for example, the role of contingency, the importance of discrimination, and so on.

This perspective has much to recommend it. Some principles of learning do seem remarkably general, and we have commented in this chapter on the many parallels between human and nonhuman behavior. Recognition of this generality has helped us to gain insights into human depression by studying helplessness in dogs; it has also increased our understanding of human drug addiction, thanks to research on classical conditioning in rats. Different species share many biological traits and, it seems, many psychological traits.

But it is also clear that there are sometimes differences from one species to the next in how learning proceeds, differences often best understood by taking an evolutionary perspective on learning (see, for example, Roper, 1983; Bolles & Beecher, 1988; Rozin & Schull, 1988).

## BIOLOGICAL CONSTRAINTS ON LEARNING: BELONGINGNESS

In the early days of learning theory, there was a widespread belief that animals are capable of connecting any CS to any US (in classical conditioning) and of associating virtually any response with any reinforcer (in instrumental conditioning). A dog could be taught that a tone signaled the approach of food or that a flashing light or a particular smell did. Likewise, a rat could be trained to press a lever to get food, water, or access to a sexually receptive mate.

This broad claim is sometimes called the *equipotentiality principle*—the idea that there is an "equal potential" for producing any association we might choose. But much evidence speaks against this idea. Instead, each species seems predisposed to form some associations and not others. The predispositions put *biological constraints* on that species' learning, governing what the species can learn easily and what it can learn only with difficulty. These associative predispositions are probably hardwired and help each species adjust to the requirements of the environment in which it evolved (Rozin & Kalat, 1971, 1972; Seligman & Hager, 1972).

### CS-US RELATIONS IN CLASSICAL CONDITIONING

One set of predispositions about learning and, with it, one important constraint on learning derive from the fact that, from an animal's point of view, some stimuli belong together and some do not—a pattern clearly contrary to the equipotentiality principle. Much of the evidence for this phenomenon of *belongingness* comes from an effect we have already mentioned: *learned taste aversion* (Domjan, 1983; Garcia & Koelling, 1966).

*Belongingness and Learned Taste Aversions*  Rats are remarkably adept at learning to avoid foods that, in the past, have made them sick. This is why it is so difficult to exterminate wild rats with poison: the rat takes a small bite of the poisoned food, becomes ill, generally recovers, and from that point forward avoids that particular flavor. Since the animal never returns for a second "dose" of the poison, it avoids the fate the exterminator had hoped for.

Similar effects are easily observed in the laboratory. The subjects, usually rats, are presented with a given flavor such as water containing the artificial sweetener saccharin. After drinking some of this sweetened water, they are exposed to X-ray radiation—not enough to injure them, but enough to make them ill. After they recover, if they are given a choice between, say, plain water and the saccharine solution, they will refuse to drink the sweetened water even though they preferred this sweet-tasting drink prior to their illness.

This sort of learned taste aversion seems to be based on classical conditioning. The CS is a certain flavor (here, sweetness), and the US is the sensation of being sick. In this case, though, the classical conditioning is rapid: one pairing of CS and US is enough to establish the connection between them. Researchers call this *one-trial learning*.

In addition to how rapidly they are acquired, learned taste aversions are also remarkable for their specificity. In one early study, thirsty rats were allowed to drink sweetened water through a drinking tube. Whenever the rats licked the nozzle of this tube, a bright light flashed and a clicking noise sounded. Thus, the sensations of sweetness, bright light, and loud noise were always grouped together; if one was presented, all were presented. Some time later, one group of these rats received an electric shock to the feet. A second group was exposed to a dose of X rays strong enough to produce illness.

Notice, then, that we have two different USs—illness for one group and foot shock for the other. In addition, both groups have received a three-part CS: sweet + bright + noisy. The question is: How will the animals put these pieces together—what will get associated with what?

To find out, the experimenters tested the rats in a new situation. They gave some of the rats water that was saccharin-flavored but unaccompanied by either light or noise. Rats who had received foot shock showed no inclination to avoid this water; apparently, they did not associate foot shock with the sweet flavor. However, rats who had been made ill with X rays refused to drink the sweet water even though the light and noise were absent. They associated their illness with the taste (Table 4.1).

Other rats were tested with plain, unflavored water accompanied by the light and sound cues that were present during training. Now the pattern was reversed. Rats who had become ill showed no objection to this water; they did not associate illness with sights and sounds. Rats who had been shocked refused it; in their minds, pain was associated with bright lights and loud clicks (Garcia & Koelling, 1966).

These results clearly undermine the equipotentiality principle. For the rat, taste goes with illness, sights and sounds with externally induced pain. And for this species, this pattern makes good biological sense. Illness, for many creatures, is likely to have been caused by some untested or perhaps tainted food. And in the wild, the rat selects its food largely on the basis of flavor. With this setup, it is sensible for rats to avoid tastes they associate with illness; this will ensure that they do not resample harmful berries or tainted meat. There is survival value in the rat's tendency to ask itself, whenever it has a stomachache, "What did I eat?"

Using this logic, one might expect species that choose foods using other attributes to make different associations. For example, many birds make their food choices largely on appearance; how will this affect the data? In one study, quail were given blue, sour water to drink and were then poisoned. Some of the birds were later tested with blue, unflavored water; others were tested with water that was sour but colorless. The results

### TABLE 4.1    BELONGINGNESS IN CLASSICAL CONDITIONING

| Training | In all groups: CS = saccharine taste + light + sound | | | |
|---|---|---|---|---|
| US: | Shock | | X-ray illness | |
| Test: water with | Saccharine taste | Light + sound | Saccharine taste | Light + sound |
| Results | No effect | Aversion | Aversion | No effect |

*Learned food aversions in birds*   *In contrast to rats and humans, whose learned food aversions are usually based on taste and odor, most birds rely on visual cues. The figure shows the reaction of a bird who has just eaten a monarch butterfly, which contains distasteful and poisonous substances. The distinctive wing pattern of this butterfly provides the cue for an immediately acquired food aversion, for after one such mistake the bird will never again seize another monarch.*

showed that the quail had developed a drastic aversion to blue water, but they drank just about as much sour water as they had before being poisoned. Here, the learned aversion was evidently based on color rather than taste (Wilcoxin, Dragoin, & Kral, 1971).

Clearly, what belongs with what depends upon the species. Birds are generally disposed to associate illness with visual cues. Rats (and many other mammals) associate illness with taste. In each case, this bias makes the animal more prepared to form certain associations and far less prepared to form others (Seligman, 1970).

*Taste Aversion in Humans*   Imagine a person who enjoys a delicious bowl of strawberry ice cream. Unfortunately, this person also has the flu and, later that night, becomes acutely nauseated. He knows he has the flu (there are, after all, many other symptoms). And he knows that the ice cream itself was innocent (after all, the rest of his family ate the same dessert without ill effects). But despite the knowledge, this individual is likely to develop a taste aversion, just as a rat would. The mere thought of strawberry ice cream is now utterly revolting, a reaction that may last for years (Logue, 1986).

## BIOLOGICAL CONSTRAINTS ON INSTRUMENTAL CONDITIONING

Clearly, then, the CS-US relationship in classical conditioning is far from arbitrary. A CS belongs with certain USs and not with others. Similarly for instrumental learning: from an animal's point of view, certain responses belong with some rewards and not others (Shettleworth, 1972).

Consider a pigeon pecking away in a Skinner box. Pigeons can easily be taught to peck a lit key in order to obtain food or water. But it is exceedingly difficult to train a pigeon to peck in order to escape or avoid electric shock (Hineline & Rachlin, 1969). In contrast, pigeons can easily be taught to hop or flap their wings in order to get away from shock, but it is difficult to train the pigeon to produce these same responses in order to gain food or water.

These patterns, although contrary to the equipotentiality claim, make good biological sense. The pigeon's normal reaction to danger is hopping away or breaking into flight, and so the pigeon is biologically prepared to associate these responses with aversive stimuli such as electrical shock. Pecking, in contrast, is distant from the pigeon's innate defense pattern, making it difficult for the pigeon to learn pecking as an escape response (Bolles, 1970). Conversely, since pecking is what pigeons do naturally when they eat, the pigeon is biologically prepared to associate this response with food or drink; it is no wonder, then, that pigeons easily learn to make this association in the psychologist's laboratory.

## ADAPTIVE SPECIALIZATIONS OF LEARNING

These examples make it clear that animals come biologically prepared to make certain associations and not others. Apparently, then, we need to "tune" the laws of learning on a case-by-case basis to accommodate the fact that a given species learns some relationships easily, others only with difficulty, and still others not at all.

This "tuning" would build some flexibility into the laws of learning, but it would also allow us to retain the idea that there *are* general laws, applicable (with the appropriate tuning) to all species and to all situations. Many theorists, though, believe we must go further than this. In their view, some types of learning in some species follow their own specialized rules and depend on specialized capacities found in that species and few others. If this is right, we will need to do more than "adjust" the laws of learning.

Instead, we may need some new laws, laws that are specific to the species that does the learning and also to what it is that gets learned (Gallistel, 1990; Roper, 1983).

## DIFFERENCES IN WHAT DIFFERENT SPECIES LEARN

One striking example of specialized learning involves the Clark's nutcracker, a bird that makes its home in the American Southwest. In the summer, this bird buries thousands of pine nuts in various hiding places over an area of several square miles. Then, throughout the winter and early spring, the nutcracker flies back again and again to dig up its thousands of caches. The bird does not mark the burial sites in any special way. Instead, it relies on memory—a remarkable feat that few of us could duplicate.

The Clark's nutcracker has a number of anatomical features, not shared by other birds, that support its food-hoarding activities—for example, a special pouch under its tongue that it fills with pine nuts when flying to find a hiding place. The bird's extraordinary ability to learn a huge number of geographical locations and then to remember these locations across the next few months is probably a similar evolutionary adaptation. Like the tongue pouch, this learning ability is a specialty of this species: related birds, such as jays and crows, do not store food in this way, and, when tested, they have a correspondingly poorer spatial memory (Olson, 1991; Shettleworth, 1983, 1984, 1990).

Many phenomena of animal learning—in birds, fish, and mammals—reveal similar specializations. In each case, the organism has some extraordinary ability not shared even by closely related species. In each case, the ability has obvious survival value. And in each case, the ability seems interestingly narrow: the nutcracker has no special skill in remembering pictures or shapes; instead, its remarkable memory comes into play only in the appropriate context—hiding and then relocating buried pine nuts. Similarly, many birds show remarkable talent in learning the particular songs used by their species. This skill, however, can be used for no other purpose: a zebra finch easily masters the notes of the zebra-finch song but is utterly inept at learning any other (nonmusical) sequence of similar length and complexity.

Truly, then, these are specialized learning abilities, possessed just by one or a few species and applicable just to a particular task crucial for their members' survival (Gallistel, 1990; Marler, 1970; we will have much more to say about specialized learning abilities in humans in Chapters 9 and 12).

*The Clark's nutcracker*

## SIMILARITIES IN WHAT DIFFERENT SPECIES LEARN

The evolutionary perspective raises an interesting question for us. Different species live in different environments, need different skills, and may need to learn in different ways. But if this is the case, why are there so many similarities in learning from one species to the next? To put this in more concrete terms, rats and pigeons do not gather food the way a honeybee does; they do not communicate with their fellows the way the bee does; they also have nervous systems that are vastly different from the bee's. So it would not be surprising to discover that they learn in different ways as well. And yet, as we have repeatedly noted, the major phenomena of conditioning are found in honeybees just as they are in rats and pigeons (Couvillon & Bitterman, 1980).

We can understand the specialized forms of learning with reference to a species' ecological niche and its evolutionary history. But how should we think about the fact that there are also general forms of learning, shared from one species to the next?

One answer to this question lies in the fact that various creatures, while inhabiting very different niches, all live in the same physical world. Thus, all are subject to the laws of gravity. All require energy in order to survive. And all need to learn certain things. In our shared world, for example, it pays to be prepared for things that are soon to happen; thus, a porpoise, a porcupine, and a person all increase their chances of survival if they can learn to anticipate—and prepare for—upcoming events. This preparation is made possible by the fact that some events are predictable from other events, and so it is no wonder that many species have learned to exploit that predictability and are, therefore, capable of classical conditioning.

Similarly, since, in the world we all share, important outcomes are often influenced by one's behavior, it pays for all species to repeat actions that have worked well in the past and to abandon actions that have not been successful. Hence, we might expect natural selection to favor mechanisms that would allow creatures to learn about the consequences of their actions and to adjust their future acts accordingly. It is these mechanisms that allow instrumental conditioning.

In this fashion, there are straightforward, pragmatic reasons why principles of learning are (and perhaps must be) shared from one species to the next. Thus, while our account of learning must include some important species-specific differences in how learning proceeds, it must also include some general principles such as those governing classical and instrumental conditioning. Organisms do differ in their learning capacities, but we can also find important principles—often rather specific ones—that describe learning in an extraordinary range of species and settings.

# THE NEURAL BASIS FOR LEARNING

It seems, then, that all organisms need to learn roughly the same lessons—about the relationships between their actions and subsequent events, and about the relationships among the different events they experience. This shared need leads to principles of learning that apply with equal force to ants, bats, cows, dolphins, and humans.

But even though different species need to learn the same lessons, they do not have to learn these lessons in the same fashion. It, therefore, seems plausible that the biological mechanisms that allow this learning will vary from species to species, and at least some evidence suggests that this is, in fact, the case.

In all cases, learning involves changes in how neurons function, both internally and in their communication with each other. In other words, learning depends on *neural plasticity*—a capacity for neurons to change the way they function as a consequence of experience. How neurons achieve this, though, varies from one group of animals to another, so that one type of plasticity may be particularly important for mammals, whereas other types are crucial for reptiles, amphibians, or invertebrates (Macphail, 1996; Woolf, 1998).

## CHANGES IN SYNAPTIC EFFICIENCY: PRESYNAPTIC FACILITATION

Part of what we know about neural plasticity comes from the study of the marine mollusk *Aplysia*. *Aplysia* has a simple nervous system, with a mere twenty thousand neurons or so (compared to the trillion or so in the human brain), and, therefore, is a good candidate for detailed scrutiny and analysis.

*Aplysia's* behavior is also rather simple. Mostly, this animal just crawls and eats seaweed. If threatened by a touch or a poke, though, *Aplysia* retracts both its gill, which is usually spread across its back, and its tubular siphon, which sucks in water and circulates it over the gill. What makes *Aplysia* especially valuable to investigators, though, is the fact that this animal is capable of a simple form of learning. In each learning trial, the animal is first touched lightly on its siphon and then, a moment later, shocked on its tail. Initially, the light touch is not enough to trigger a response (retraction of the gill and siphon), but the tail shock is. After a number of these pairings, however, the animal will respond to the light touch alone. It has developed a new response—in effect, a CR.

Close studies of *Aplysia's* nervous system indicate that this learning is made possible largely by changes inside sensory neurons—specifically, the sensory neurons triggered directly by the light touch on the animal's siphon. The pairings between tail shock and the light touch actually cause these neurons to increase the amount of neurotransmitter they release each time they fire, and this is why, at the end of the learning, these neurons are able to trigger the response of gill contraction all by themselves.

Note, then, that learning in this case has its effect on the sending side of the synapse and is, therefore, said to involve **presynaptic facilitation.** These changes do not change the intensity of the action potential itself; as we noted in Chapter 2, action potentials are either produced or not—they do not vary in size. What is changed, though, as a result of learning is the immediate consequence of the action potential—that is, how much neurotransmitter is released.

## LONG-TERM POTENTIATION

Other forms of neural plasticity involve postsynaptic changes—that is, they influence the receiving side of the synapse.

One particularly important mechanism for postsynaptic plasticity is **long-term potentiation (LTP)** (Bliss & Lomo, 1973; Martinez & Derrick, 1996)—"potentiation" because the mechanism involves an increase in the responsiveness of a neuron (an increase in the neuron's potential for firing) and "long term" because this potentiation lasts for days, perhaps even weeks.*

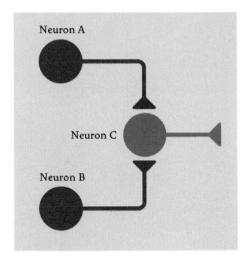

LTP is of special interest to investigators for two reasons. First, the longevity of this potentiation suggests that it may actually serve as the neural basis for memory. Second, LTP has been observed in a wide range of organisms, making it a plausible candidate for a mechanism that supports learning in all vertebrates and perhaps in other life forms as well.

LTP's main effect is to increase the sensitivity of the postsynaptic neuron as a consequence of repeated stimulation. Thus, if neuron A (in Figure 4.21) fires rapidly, over and over, within a brief period of time, neuron C will become more responsive to A than it was initially. As a result, C will now be more "prepared" for A's signal than it had been in the past; in effect, C will "remember" that A was a prominent source of information in the past and will be ready to "listen" to A more in the future.

This potentiation can also spread to other neurons with synapses on neuron C, such as neuron B in Figure 4.21. For example, let us say that neuron A fires repeatedly within a short period of time. As a result, the receptors on neuron C that receive the neurotransmitter from neuron A will become more sensitive. This is the potentiation effect. But C also has other receptors that receive input from other neurons. These receptors, too, will become more sensitive, provided that these other neurons fire at the same time as neuron A. In other words, the spread of potentiation is *activity dependent* and will spread to neuron B only if B was active at the same time as the neuron that caused the potentiation in the first place—in this case, neuron A (Levy & Steward, 1979; McNaughton, Douglas, & Goddard, 1978).

It appears, therefore, that LTP provides a cellular mechanism through which associations—in our example, the association between A's and B's activity—can be detected and recorded in the brain (Kandel & Hawkins, 1992; Martinez & Derrick, 1996).

**4.21 Long-term potentiation** *If neuron A fires over and over, neuron C will become more responsive to A than it was initially. This is the potentiation effect. If neuron B tends to fire at the same time as neuron A, then it too will benefit from this potentiation.*

---

* Another important building block of learning is *long-term depression (LTD)*, through which the postsynaptic neuron becomes less sensitive as a function of experience.

Because of this, many researchers regard LTP as one of the primary mechanisms in the brain that make learning possible. This claim has been controversial, though, and the debate continues about the role that LTP plays in more complicated forms of learning (see, for instance, Martinez & Derrick, 1996; Gallistel, 1995).

## STRUCTURAL CHANGES PRODUCED BY LEARNING

Presynaptic facilitation and LTP both involve changes in how a synapse functions; both, in other words, involve alterations in synaptic efficiency. In contrast, another form of neural plasticity—and perhaps the key form in mammals—involves structural changes: specifically, the creation of entirely new synapses. These changes seem to take place largely on the dendrites of the postsynaptic neurons. The dendrites grow new *dendritic spines*, little knobs attached to the surface of the dendrites (Moser, 1999; Woolf, 1998), which are the "receiving stations" for most synapses. Thus, growing more spines almost certainly means that, as learning proceeds, the neuron is gaining new synapses, new lines of communication with its cellular neighbors.

As with LTP, debate continues about how this increase in dendritic spines contributes to learning. However the debate unfolds, though, these structural changes, produced by learning, convey an important double message. On the one side, these changes may be unique to mammals and thus may underscore the importance of an approach to learning that draws data from the study of many different species. We obviously cannot assume, say, that the mechanisms observed in *Aplysia* are the same as those that allow humans to learn new facts about China or new skills. On the other side, there is a close resemblance between the specific chemical mechanisms that underlie presynaptic facilitation in *Aplysia* and those that lead to the growth of dendritic spines in mammals (Atkins, Selcher, Petraitis, Trzaskos, & Sweatt, 1998). This is a powerful reminder that even though species differ broadly in how they learn, they also have much in common.

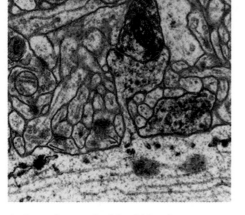

*A photomicrograph of dendritic spines.*

# COMPLEX COGNITION IN ANIMALS

Let us pull away from these microscopic events and return to a larger issue that we introduced earlier: the fact that animals often know something without manifesting this knowledge in their actions. What is the nature of this knowledge? How is it maintained and used? These will become crucial questions in Chapters 7 and 8, when we turn more fully to the topics of memory and thinking. But we can also examine the intellectual capacities relevant to the tasks we have already considered in this chapter. (For further discussion of the role of memory in these learning tasks, see Tarpy, 1997.)

## COGNITIVE MAPS

In our earlier discussion of latent learning, we mentioned Tolman's claim that an animal can create a cognitive map, a mental representation of spatial layout that indicates what is where and what leads to what. This spatial knowledge can be quite complex. Some of the evidence comes from studies of rats in radial-arm mazes—mazes with a central platform from which a number of pathways fan outward, like spokes in a wheel (Figure 4.22). In one experiment, each arm of the maze contained a food pellet. A hungry rat was placed on the center platform and allowed to move about freely. It generally

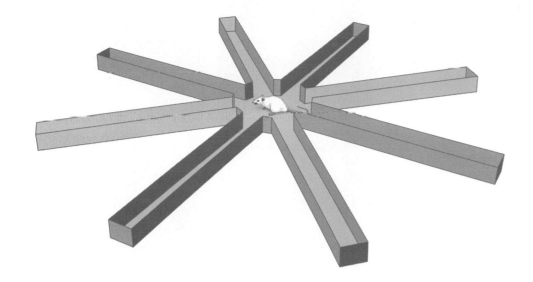

4.22 *A radial-arm maze* **One pellet is placed at the end of each arm, so the rat earns the greatest reward for the least effort by choosing each arm once.**

explored a bit, then chose one of the arms, ran to its end, found the food pellet, and ate it. After a while, the rat returned to the maze's center.

What would the rat do next? Its optimal strategy is not to revisit the arm it just left because this arm is now empty. Instead, the rat should visit each arm just once, in this way getting the most food for the least effort. To accomplish this, though, the rat has to learn the maze's layout and to remember where it had been and where it had not. This was no problem for the rat, and performance in this task was nearly perfect: given a radial maze of 8 arms, on average the rats chose 7.9 different arms in 8 choices (Olton, 1978, 1979; Olton & Samuelson, 1976), a score of 99 percent accuracy.

What rats can do, chimpanzees can do even better. Proof comes from a chimpanzee version of an Easter-egg hunt. The experimenter carried one animal at a time along an irregular route across a large open area. The experimenter's assistant accompanied them on this tour, and as they moved along, the assistant hid pieces of fruit at various locations. The chimpanzee was not allowed to do anything during this tour but merely watched as the bits of food were hidden. Nonetheless, the moment the chimp was set down and allowed to move on its own, it dashed from one hiding place to the next, locating and eating the fruit. It had obviously learned—and remembered—the eighteen locations after just one trial of passive observation (Menzel, 1973, 1978; for evidence of cognitive maps in other creatures, including invertebrates, see Gallistel, 1994; Gould, 1990).

## INSIGHTFUL BEHAVIOR

A cognitive map is more than a figure of speech: there really is some representation of spatial layout in the animal's mind. Once again, therefore, our account of learning cannot rely only on descriptions of behavior and behavior change. Instead, we must make reference to cognition—complex cognition—occurring within the animal. The role of cognition is equally clear in another domain: the study of insightful learning.

Recall Thorndike's argument that nonhuman animals solve problems only through trial and error: The law of effect strengthens behaviors produced on the successful trials and weakens behaviors on the failed trials. This claim was soon challenged by the German psychologist Wolfgang Köhler (1887–1967).

Köhler contended that some animals, at least, can behave intelligently. True, Thorndike's cats had shown little sign of understanding the puzzle box, but perhaps cats are not the best subjects for determining the upper reaches of animal intellect. Animals more closely related to human beings, such as chimpanzees, might be a better

*Wolfgang Köhler*

158

**4.23  Tool using in chimpanzees**  *(A) Using a stick as a pole to climb up to a banana. (B) Using a stick as a club to beat down a banana. (C and D) Erecting three- and four-story structures to reach a banana. (From Kohler, 1925)*

choice. Even more important, Köhler believed that Thorndike had loaded the dice in favor of blind trial and error by giving his cats problems that were impossible to solve in any other way. After all, the strings and pulleys were hidden from the animal's view; therefore, even an intellectual supercat could hit on the idea of yanking the wire that pulled the door latch only by chance; there was no other way to solve this problem. To Köhler the real question was whether animals would behave intelligently when the conditions were optimal—when all of the ingredients of the solution were visibly present.

Köhler's procedure was simple. A chimpanzee was placed in an enclosed play area. Somewhere out of its reach was a food treat (usually a piece of fruit such as a banana); to obtain this treat, the ape had to employ some nearby object as a tool. The animals had no problem with this task. They learned to use sticks as rakes to haul in bananas placed on the ground just outside the cage but beyond the reach of their arms. They also learned to use these sticks as clubs, to knock down fruit hung too high overhead. Some chimpanzees used the sticks as climbing poles as well. They stood it upright under the banana, frantically climbed up its 15-foot length, and grasped their reward just as the stick toppled over (a considerable intellectual as well as gymnastic feat, demonstrating the virtues of a healthy mind in a healthy body). The chimpanzees also learned to use boxes as "climb-upon-ables," dragging them under the banana and then stepping atop them to claim their prize. Eventually they even became builders, piling boxes on top of boxes and finally erecting structures that went up to four (shaky) stories, as Köhler spurred them on to ever-greater architectural accomplishments by progressively raising the height of the lure (Figure 4.23).

Occasionally the apes became toolmakers as well as tool-users. For example, when in need of a stick, they might break a branch off a nearby tree. Even more impressive was one feat by a particularly gifted chimpanzee, Sultan, who was faced with a banana far out of his reach. There were two bamboo sticks in his cage, but neither of them was long enough to rake in the lure. After many attempts to reach the banana with one stick or another, Sultan finally hit upon the solution. He pushed the thinner of the two sticks into the hollow inside of the thicker one and then drew the banana toward himself, his reach having now been extended by the length of two sticks (Figure 4.24).

Köhler argued that these achievements were not the result of trial and error nor the product of some mechanical strengthening of response tendencies. On the contrary, the animals behaved as if they had attained insight into the problem and into the relationship crucial for solving the problem. In support of this conclusion, Köhler offered

**4.24  Tool making in chimpanzees**  *Sultan making a double stick.*

several observations. To begin with, the insightful solution often came suddenly, sometimes after a pause during which the chimpanzee only moved its head and eyes, as if studying the situation. In addition, once each problem had been solved, the animals could smoothly and easily solve it again and again, as if they knew what they were doing. This stands in marked contrast to Thorndike's cats, who went on fumbling for many trials, even after their first success.

But the most convincing evidence for Köhler's claims came from tests in which the situation was changed somewhat, in order to determine what skills the animals would transfer from the original task to the new setting. Such *transfer of training tests* are, in general, a useful means of finding out what has been learned in a situation. Teachers use just this approach to find out what their students have understood. Consider a young child who quickly answers "7" when confronted by the symbols "3 + 4 = ?" Has he really grasped the notion of addition? A simple test might be to present him with another problem, "4 + 3 = ?" If he is now bewildered, he presumably has learned merely to give a specific answer to a specific question. But if his reply again is "7," he may be on the way to genuine arithmetic insight.

Köhler used similar tests with his chimpanzees. For example, he took animals who had previously learned to use a box as a platform and presented them with yet another high lure but now with all the boxes removed from the scene. The animals were untroubled by this. They were quick to find other objects, such as a table or a small ladder, which they promptly dragged to the proper place, allowing them to climb up and grab the fruit. On one occasion, Sultan did something even more impressive: he came over to Köhler, pulled him by the arm until he was under the banana, and then showed that in a pinch even the director of the Prussian anthropoid station would do as a climb-upon-able.

In one sense, this pattern of transfer might seem to be just another example of stimulus generalization. We know that a dog who has been conditioned, say, to salivate to a tone of 1,000 hertz will also salivate to a tone of 1,500 hertz. Köhler argued, though, that the transfer displayed by his chimpanzees was different from this. Stimulus generalization ordinarily depends on perceptual similarity. An animal will generalize its prior learning to a novel stimulus if that stimulus looks or sounds or feels like the stimulus used in training. But things are different with the chimpanzees. When Sultan figured out that he could reach the high banana by climbing on Köhler, this was not because Köhler looked like the climbed-upon box used during training. Instead, the key relationship was conceptual. Sultan saw that, despite their perceptual differences, boxes and human experimenters were alike in just the crucial way: each was capable of supporting Sultan's weight, allowing him to climb. This attention to conceptual elements and the ability to focus on just the attributes that matter, ignoring the perceptual differences, were for Köhler the mark of genuine understanding.

## COMPLEX PERCEPTUAL CONCEPTS IN ANIMALS

Köhler was duly impressed by his apes' attention to conceptual categories—for example, the category of climb-upon-ables. But perceptually based categories can also grow complex. For instance, pigeons in one study were trained to peck a key whenever a picture of water was in view, but not to peck otherwise. Some of the water pictures showed flowing water; some showed still water. Some showed large bodies of water photographed from far away; some showed small puddles photographed close up. Despite this diversity, pigeons rapidly mastered this discrimination task and so seemed to have grasped the category *water* (Herrnstein, Loveland, & Cable, 1976). Similar procedures have shown that pigeons can discriminate between pictures showing trees and pictures not showing trees, with (as before) considerable diversity in the tree pictures actually shown. Thus, pigeons can learn to peck in response to a picture of a leaf-covered tree or a tree bare of leaves, but they will not peck in response to a picture of a telephone pole or a picture of a celery stalk. Likewise, pigeons can learn to peck whenever they are shown a picture of a particular human, whether photographed from one angle and close up, from a very different angle and wearing different clothes, or from far away (see, for example, Herrnstein, 1979; Lea & Ryan, 1990).

Some investigators conclude from these studies that pigeons have the concept *water*, or *tree*, and so on. If they do, it is likely to be a concept very different from the concept humans hold. Humans recognize pictures of water, but they also understand a great deal about water and about the relationship between water and many other concepts. What the pigeons have learned to do is complex, to be sure, but it is a far cry from the sort of concepts we hold. (For further discussion of concepts, see Reisberg, 2001.)

## SOME FINAL THOUGHTS: LEARNING THEORY AND BEYOND

Where, then, does all of this leave us? The investigations begun by Pavlov and Thorndike more than a hundred years ago have led to many important discoveries, and it is now clear that some principles of learning do apply to every species we have studied. At the same time, though, we have been forced to move beyond the conceptions offered by Pavlov and Thorndike in two crucial ways. First, there are also, as we have seen, important differences in how species learn. At the least, these differences concern how prepared different species are to make certain associations. More strongly, these differences may involve truly distinctive forms of learning, with different species having their own specialized capacities.

Second, it has become clear that we cannot understand learning even in simple species without considering what the animal knows as well as what it does. This point has helped launch an active area of research into "animal cognition," a field that examines the intellectual capacities of species as diverse as pigeons and chimpanzees, and that considers animals' understanding both of perceptual categories such as *water* or *tree* and more abstract concepts such as *same* and *different* (Cook, Cavoto, & Cavoto, 1995; Giurfa et al., 2001; Premack, 1976, 1978; Premack & Premack, 1983; Reiss & Marino, 2001; Wasserman, Hugart, & Kirkpatrick-Steger, 1995; Zentall, 2000).

Of course, psychology must deal with both action and knowledge. In our discussion of animal learning we have straddled both, for the field represents a kind of bridge between these two major concerns. We will now cross the bridge completely and move on to the study of cognition as a topic in its own right.

# SUMMARY

An influential perspective on learning, especially in the United States, was *learning theory*, which regards learning as the wiring and rewiring of connections between bits of behavior. In this view, learning should be understood in terms of simple laws that hold for all animals.

## HABITUATION

1. The simplest form of learning is *habituation*, a decline in the response to stimuli that have become familiar through repeated exposure. In habituation the organism simply learns that it has encountered the stimulus before.

## CLASSICAL CONDITIONING

2. In *classical conditioning*, first studied by Ivan Pavlov, animals learn about the association between one stimulus and another. Prior to conditioning, an unconditioned stimulus (US, such as food) elicits an unconditioned response (UR, such as salivation). After repeated occasions in which the US follows a conditioned stimulus (CS, such as a buzzer), this CS alone will begin to evoke the conditioned response (CR, here again, salivation), which is often similar to the UR.

3. The strength of conditioning is assessed by the readiness with which the CS elicits the CR. This strength increases with the number of reinforced trials, that is, with occasions on which the CS is followed by the US. When a CS-US relation is well established, the CS can be preceded by a second, neutral stimulus to produce *second-order conditioning*.

4. *Unreinforced trials* (when the CS is presented without the US) lead to *extinction*, a decreased tendency of the CS to evoke the CR. Some contend that *spontaneous recovery* shows that the CR is masked, not abolished, by extinction.

5. The CR can be elicited not only by the CS but also by stimuli that are similar to it. This effect, *stimulus generalization*, increases the more the CS resembles the new stimulus. To train the animal to respond to the CS but not to other stimuli, one stimulus (CS⁺) is presented with the US, while another (CS⁻) is presented without the US. The more similar the CS⁺ is to the CS⁻, the more difficult this *discrimination* will be.

6. Classical conditioning can involve many responses other than salivation, including fear, as assessed by the *conditioned emotional response (CER)* procedure. The CR is never identical, and sometimes not even similar to the UR, which suggests that the CS serves as a signal and not a substitute for the US. In some cases, the CR is not just different from the UR but is its very opposite. One example is found in the development of drug tolerance. According to some authors, this is partially caused by a compensatory reaction conditioned to stimuli that habitually accompany drug administration.

## INSTRUMENTAL CONDITIONING

7. When training an animal using classical conditioning, the US occurs regardless of whether the animal performs the CR. When training an animal using *instrumental conditioning* (also called *operant conditioning*), a reward or *reinforcement* is only delivered upon performance of the appropriate instrumental response.

8. According to Thorndike, instrumental learning reflects no understanding and is based instead on a gradual strengthening of the correct response and a weakening of the incorrect one. To account for this, he proposed his *law of effect*, which states that the tendency to perform a response is strengthened if it is followed by a reward (reinforcement) and weakened if it is not.

9. During the past seventy years or so, the major figure in the study of instrumental conditioning was B. F. Skinner, one of the first theorists to distinguish sharply between classical conditioning, in which the CR is elicited by the CS, and instrumental (or operant) conditioning, in which the instrumental response, or operant, is emitted from within. *Operants* are strengthened by reinforcement, but their acquisition may require some initial *shaping*, through a method of *successive approximations*.

10. While some reinforcers are stimuli whose reinforcing power is unlearned, other *conditioned reinforcers* acquire their power from prior presentations with stimuli that already have that capacity. One of the factors that determines the strength of instrumental conditioning is the *delay of reinforcement*: the more quickly the response is followed by the reinforcer, the stronger the response.

11. During *partial reinforcement*, the response is reinforced only some of the time. Responses that were originally learned under partial reinforcement are harder to extinguish than those learned under *continuous reinforcement*, that is, when the response was always reinforced. The rule that determines when a reinforcer is given is called a *schedule of reinforcement*. In *ratio schedules*, reinforcers are deliv-

ered after a number of responses that may be fixed (as in FR-2 or FR-5; with FR-1 designating continuous reinforcement), or variable (as in VR-1, VR-5, and so on). In *interval schedules,* reinforcers are delivered for the first response made after a given interval since the last reinforcement, say 1 or 5 minutes, which again can be fixed or variable (FI-1, FI-5, or VI-1, V-5, and so on).

12. Reinforcers can include the presentation of *appetitive stimuli* (e.g., food) or the termination or prevention of *aversive stimuli* (e.g., electric shock). Aversive stimuli can weaken or strengthen instrumental responding, depending on the relation between the aversive stimulus and the response. In *punishment training,* the response is followed by an aversive stimulus; as a result, responding decreases or is extinguished. In *escape learning,* the response stops an aversive stimulus that has already begun; in *avoidance training,* the response stops the aversive stimulus from starting in the first place.

## COGNITIVE LEARNING

13. Pavlov, Thorndike, and Skinner believed that the essence of both classical and instrumental conditioning was that they modified action. Cognitive theorists such as Köhler and Tolman believed that when humans and animals learn, they acquire new bits of knowledge, or *cognitions.* According to many theorists, what is learned in classical conditioning is an association between two events, the CS and the US, such that the CS serves as a signal for the US. One line of evidence comes from studies of the effect of the *CS-US interval.* The general finding is that conditioning is more effective when the CS precedes the US by some optimal, usually short, interval.

14. A number of investigators have asked how the animal learns that the CS is a signal for the US. The evidence shows that CS-US pairings alone will not suffice; there must also be trials in which the absence of the CS predicts the absence of the US. This allows the animal to discover that the US is contingent (depends) on the CS. The discovery of this *contingency* seems to depend on the extent to which the US is unexpected or surprising, as shown by the phenomenon of *blocking.*

15. Unlike Thorndike and Skinner, who argued that instrumental learning involves the strengthening of an instrumental response, cognitive theorists believe that it is based on learning what is where, and what leads to what. Evidence for this view comes from early work on *latent learning,* and subsequent studies in which animals were trained to perform two responses that lead to two different outcomes, after which one of the outcomes is made less desirable. Subsequent tests indicate that the animals learned which response led to which result.

16. Contingency is as crucial to instrumental conditioning as it is to classical conditioning. In instrumental conditioning, the relevant contingency is between a response and an outcome. When there is no such contingency, the organism learns that it has no *response control.* Threatening conditions in which there is no response control may engender *learned helplessness,* which often generalizes to other situations. According to some authors, some facets of learned helplessness may be related to depression in humans.

## VARIETIES OF LEARNING

17. According to Pavlov, Skinner, and other early learning theorists, the connections established by classical and instrumental conditioning are essentially arbitrary: just about any CS can become associated with any US, and just about any response can be strengthened by any reinforcer. This *equipotentiality principle* is challenged by the fact that certain conditioned stimuli are more readily associated with some unconditioned stimuli than with others, as shown by studies of *learned taste aversions.* These studies suggest that animals are biologically prepared to learn certain relations more readily than others. Similar effects occur in instrumental conditioning, with some responses more readily strengthened by some reinforcers than by others.

18. According to some investigators, certain forms of learning are *species-specific;* they cite evidence that some animals can readily learn what others cannot. Various birds, for example, have specialized adaptations that include remarkable memory for hoarded food, song learning, and navigational abilities, whereas other, closely related birds lack these abilities.

## THE NEURAL BASIS FOR LEARNING

19. In recent years, investigators have made considerable progress in understanding the neural bases for learning. One possible neural mechanism is *presynaptic facilitation.* Another involves *postsynaptic changes* such as *long-term potentiation (LTP)* that increases in the responsiveness of a neuron, which may last for several days and has been suggested as a mechanism that underlies association. Still another possibility is that learning, especially in mammals, is based on *structural changes* in the nervous system, based on the growth of *dendritic spines,* which act as "receiving stations" for synapses and open new lines of communication with their cellular neighbors.

## COMPLEX COGNITION IN ANIMALS

20. Cognitive theorists point out that animals are capable of complex cognitions. Evidence comes from work on *spatial memory* in rats and chimpanzees, which shows that these animals can form elaborate *cognitive maps.*

Further work concerns the ability to abstract conceptual relationships. Early evidence came from Köhler's studies of insightful learning in chimpanzees, who showed remarkable transfer to novel situations. Later work showed that some chimpanzees can acquire certain *higher-order concepts,* such as same-different.

# COGNITION

*How do we know what we know?*

# PART 2

*THE APPROACH TO PSYCHOLOGY that we have considered so far emphasizes action, what organisms do and how they do it. We now turn to a different perspective, one that asks what organisms know, how they come to know it, and how they use what they know to direct their own actions or to guide the actions of others.*

*Many kinds of animals are capable of knowledge, but in our species, knowing (or cognition) is immensely complex. We know about the world directly around us, perceiving objects and events that are in our here and now, like the rose that we can see and smell. We also know about events in our past. The rose may fade, but we can recall what it looked like when it was still in bloom. Our knowledge can also be transformed and manipulated by thinking, as we somehow sift and analyze our experiences to emerge with new and often abstract notions. We can, for example, think of the faded rose petals as but one stage in a reproductive cycle, which in turn reflects the procession of the seasons. We can also communicate our knowledge to others by the use of language, a uniquely human capability that allows us to transmit vast quantities of information, with each of us building on the discoveries of the preceding generations. In this chapter and the next four, we will examine all of these forms and uses of knowing.*

# SENSORY PROCESSES

To survive, we must know the world around us, for most objects in the world are charged with meaning: some are food; others are mates; still others are mortal enemies. The ability to distinguish among these—say, between a log and a crocodile—can be a matter of life and death. To make these distinctions, we have to use our senses. We must do our best to see and hear the crocodile so that we can recognize it for what it is before it sees, hears, smells, and (especially) tastes us. But how exactly do our senses function? How accurate and how complete is the sensory information we receive from our eyes, ears, and other sensory organs? And to what extent is our perception of the world *objective*—true to the sensory information we receive, with a minimum of interpretation? Conversely, to what extent is our perception influenced by our biases, expectations, and perhaps even our hopes? It is to these questions that we now turn.

# THE ORIGINS OF KNOWLEDGE

The study of sensory experience grows out of an ancient question, and it is a question closely tied to the broad issues we just mentioned: Where does human knowledge come from? One suggestion is straightforward: our senses receive and record information, much as a camera receives light or a microphone receives sound. In this view, our eyes and ears are sensitive to the relevant information, just as film (for example) is sensitive to light. According to this approach, however, the collection of information is a relatively passive affair. The camera, after all, does not choose which light beams to receive, nor does it do much interpretation of the light it detects. Instead, it simply records the light available to it. Likewise, a tape recorder does not interpret the speech or appreciate the music; again, in a passive fashion, it simply records. Could this be the way vision and hearing work?

## AN EARLY VIEW—THE EMPIRICISTS

Many philosophers have argued that our senses are passive in this way, and this position is associated with the philosophical view known as *empiricism*. One major proponent of this position, the English philosopher John Locke (1632–1704), argued that, at birth, the human mind is simply a blank tablet, a *tabula rasa*, on which experience leaves its mark.

*John Locke*

> Let us suppose the mind to be, as we say, a white paper void of all characters, without any ideas:—How comes it to be furnished? Whence comes it by that vast store which the busy and boundless fancy of man has painted on it with an almost endless variety? Whence has it all the materials of reason and knowledge? To this I answer, in one word, from experience. In that all our knowledge is founded; and from that it ultimately derives itself. (Locke, 1690)

### DISTAL AND PROXIMAL STIMULI

In understanding Locke's position, though, we need to be clear about exactly what the information is that the senses receive. Consider what happens, for example, when we look at another person some distance away. We are presumably interested in what the person looks like, who he is, and what he is doing. These are all facts about the *distal stimulus*, the real object (in this case, the person) in the world outside of us. (The distal stimulus is typically at some distance from the perceiver, hence the term *distal*.)

As it turns out, though, we have no direct access to the distal stimulus. Instead, our only information about the distal stimulus lies in the energies that actually reach us— the pattern of light that is reflected off of the person's outer surface, collected by our eyes, and cast as an image on the *retina*, the light-sensitive tissue at the rear of each eyeball. This is the *proximal* (or "nearby") *stimulus*. If there were no proximal stimulus, if the light reflecting off of this person were somehow blocked or interrupted on its way to us, the person would be invisible to us. The same holds for the other senses as well. We can smell a rotten egg (the distal stimulus) only because of the hydrogen sulfide molecules in the air that flows over the sensory cells in our nasal cavities (the proximal stimulus).

The distinction between distal and proximal stimuli raises difficult questions for the empiricist. If the senses are the only portals we have to the outside world, and the proximal stimuli are the only messengers allowed to pass through these gates, then how can we ever know the true qualities of the distal stimulus? To see why this is a problem, consider a concern raised by another empiricist philosopher, George Berkeley (1685–1753). Berkeley pointed out that we cannot tell the size of a physical object from the size of its

*Bishop George Berkeley*

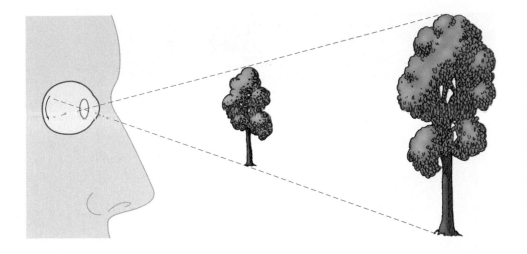

THE ORIGINS OF KNOWLEDGE 169

**5.1 Distal and proximal stimuli** *The two trees are distal stimuli, real objects in the world outside. One is small and close to the viewer; one is larger and more distant. But the proximal stimuli they give rise to—the images they cast on the retina—are identical. This highlights the potential ambiguity of the proximal stimulus.*

retinal image. A tree that we are looking at might be a miniature plant nearby or a giant one in the distance (see Figure 5.1); either of these (or a vast number of other stimuli, appropriately sized and positioned) could lead to the same retinal image. By the same token, since the retina is a two-dimensional (flat) surface, Berkeley argued that our vision cannot directly inform us about the three-dimensional world. How, then, does perception of depth proceed? In actual life, we seem to have little difficulty in telling how far away an object is from us, and we can generally perceive the size of an object with some accuracy. How can these observations be reconciled with the empiricist view?

## SENSATIONS

The empiricists claimed that knowledge comes from the senses, but these give us access to the proximal stimulus, not the distal. How, therefore, do we know the distal world? In addition, the empiricist view invites another concern: The empiricists assumed that all knowledge is constructed out of simple sensory experiences, or *sensations*—the sensation of green or brown, for example, or the sensation of loud or sweet. These are the building blocks out of which all complex experiences and all complex ideas are constructed. But can this description do justice to the richness of our perceptual world? The fact is that what we see is not mere patches of green and brown. Instead, we see trees and coffee cups, the people around us, and the familiar surroundings of our lives. What, then, glues the pieces of the mosaic together so that we end up not with sensations but with coherent and meaningful objects?

## THE ROLE OF ASSOCIATION

To all of these questions, the empiricists offered a single answer: learning. They argued that prior experience plays a crucial role in creating the meaningfulness and organized character of our perceptual world. The key mechanism of this learning was held to be *association*, the process through which one sensation is linked to another. The basic idea was very simple: if two sensations occur together often enough, eventually one of them will evoke the idea of the other. According to the empiricists, this associative linkage is the cement that binds the separate components of the perceptual world together.*

---

* It is obvious that the notion of association was at the root of many of the theories of learning we discussed in the last chapter. For example, Pavlov's conceptions of classical conditioning are in many ways derived from the views of the early associationists.

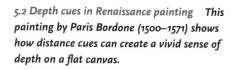

*5.2 Depth cues in Renaissance painting*   **This painting by Paris Bordone (1500–1571) shows how distance cues can create a vivid sense of depth on a flat canvas.**

An example is provided by the empiricists' account of how we use various *distance cues* to perceive the three-dimensional layout of the world (Figure 5.2). There are actually many such cues, including linear perspective, relative size, and texture gradients, and these cues can convey a vivid sense of depth. (For more on these cues, see Chapter 6.) But how exactly does perspective convey depth? To the empiricists, the explanation is a matter of prior association. We see the visual cues of perspective, and a moment later we reach for or walk toward the object we are viewing. This experience creates an association in the mind between the visual cue and the appropriate movement, so that eventually the visual cue alone will produce the memory of the movement and thus the experience of depth.

## THE ACTIVE PERCEIVER

The empiricists acknowledged that the perceiver must supplement her sensory inputs with associations. Other scholars, however, have suggested that the perceiver plays a far more active role than this. This position was taken, for example, by a group often known as the *nativists*, who argued that many aspects of perceptual experience depend critically on our ability to categorize and interpret the incoming sensory information. The ability to understand the sensory input, they claimed, is what makes perception possible in the first place; without this ability, there can be no perception. This ability must be in place, therefore, before any perceptual experience can occur, and so it cannot possibly be derived from perceptual experience. Instead, it must be part of our natural (innate) endowment.

*Immanuel Kant*

This general position has a long ancestry, but it is often attributed to the German philosopher Immanuel Kant (1724–1804). Kant argued that knowledge cannot come from sensory input alone; there must also be certain preexisting categories according to which this sensory material is ordered and organized. Indeed, it is these categories, according to Kant, that make the sensory input interpretable; without them, there would be no experience. What are these preexisting categories? Kant claimed that the categories of space, time, and causality order all of our experience, so that there is no way in which we can see the world except in terms of these categories. The categories, in his view, were built into the very structure of the mind, part of our biological heritage.

PSYCHOPHYSICS

The dispute between the empiricists and the nativists is, in the broadest of terms, a dispute over the nature, origins, and trustworthiness of all our knowledge, and so it is no surprise that this dispute focused investigators' attention on the role of the senses and prodded them to explore just how the senses function. This functioning can be pursued in several different ways, but one central perspective is that of *psychophysics*, the study of the specific relationship between the properties of the (physical) stimulus and the (psychological) sensory experience the stimulus ultimately gives rise to. For example, what physical attribute of light gives rise to the experience of hue, and so leads us to see a stimulus as red rather than green? What changes in our perception of a sound as the frequency of the sound waves changes? The goal of psychophysics is to answer questions just like these.

## Measuring Sensory Intensity

In order to relate qualities of the stimulus to qualities of perception, we need first to measure the physical stimulus. This is easy enough; we can readily find out how many pounds this bowling ball weighs or how hot this water is in degrees centigrade. But how can we make the corresponding psychological measurements needed to assess the sensory experience of the subject? How can we quantify how something tastes, sounds, or smells?

Gustav Theodor Fechner (1801–1887), the founder of psychophysics, argued that sensations and the stimuli that produce them belong to two totally different realms—the first belong to the mental world, the second to the physical world. Therefore, they cannot be directly compared to each other. But it is possible, Fechner noted, to make comparisons within each of these realms. Even if sensations cannot be compared to physical stimuli, they can at least be compared to each other, and this can provide a basis for measuring them.

Consider the sensation of visual brightness produced by a patch of light projected onto the eye. We can ask, what is the minimal amount by which the intensity of this light must be increased so that the observer experiences a sensation of brightness just greater than the one he had before? This minimal change in the stimulus defines the observer's *difference threshold*—the smallest stimulus change that the observer can reliably detect—and if the stimulus is changed by this amount, it creates what psychophysicists call a *just-noticeable difference*, or *jnd*. The jnd is a psychological entity, because it describes an observer's ability to discriminate. But it is expressed in the units of the physical stimulus that produced it. It would seem, therefore, that Fechner had found an indirect means to relate sensory magnitude to the physical intensity of the stimulus.

### THE WEBER FRACTION AND FECHNER'S LAW

To Fechner, measuring jnds was only the means to a larger goal; his ultimate aim was to formulate a general law relating physical stimulus intensity to psychological sensory magnitude. He believed that such a law could be built on a proposal made in 1834 by the German physiologist E. H. Weber (1795–1878). Weber had proposed that the size of the difference threshold (that is, the size of a jnd) is a constant fraction of the stimulus we are comparing to. Suppose, for example, that we can just tell the difference between 100 and 102 candles burning in an otherwise dark room. This does not indicate, Weber argued, that in general we are sensitive to differences of just 2 candles. What matters instead, he suggested, is the proportional difference—in this case, a difference of 2 percent. On this logic, we would not be able to distinguish 200 candles from 202 (a 2-candle difference but only a 1 percent change) or even 203. But we should be able to distinguish 200 candles from 204, or 300 from 306—in each case a 2 percent difference.

Fechner referred to this relationship as *Weber's law*, a label by which we still know it. Put algebraically, this law is usually written as

$$\frac{\Delta I}{I} = c.$$

$I$ is the intensity of the standard stimulus, the one to which comparisons are being made; $\Delta I$ is the amount that must be added to this intensity in order to produce a just-noticeable increase; $c$ is a constant (in our example, it was .02, or 2 percent). The fraction $\Delta I/I$ is referred to as the *Weber fraction*.

Fechner and his successors performed numerous studies to determine whether Weber's law holds—that is, whether the sensory apparatus is sensitive to percentage changes rather than absolute changes. The evidence suggests that this claim is correct for all of the sensory modalities, across most of the range of intensities to which an organism is sensitive. It seems that the nervous system is geared to notice relative differences rather than absolute ones.

Weber's law provides us with several advantages. Among them, it allows us to compare the sensitivities of different sensory modalities. Suppose we want to know whether the eye is more sensitive than the ear. We cannot compare jnds for brightness and loudness directly; the first is measured in millilamberts, the second in decibels, and there is no way to translate the one into the other. But we can compare the Weber fractions for the two modalities. If the fraction is small, then we know that the sense modality is able to make fine discriminations; put differently, relatively little must be added to the standard for a difference to be detected. And the smaller the Weber fraction, the more sensitive the sense modality. Using these comparisons, we can show that we are much keener at discriminating brightness (we are sensitive to differences of merely 2 percent or less) than loudness (here we are largely insensitive to differences less than 10 percent); the Weber fractions needed for this comparison, and fractions for other sense modalities, are presented in Table 5.1.

By making a number of further assumptions, Fechner generalized Weber's finding to express a broad relationship between the sensory experience and the physical intensity of a stimulus. The result was *Fechner's law*, which states that the strength of a sensation grows as the logarithm of stimulus intensity:

$$S = k \log I.$$

$S$ stands for psychological (that is, subjective) magnitude; $I$ is the physical intensity of the stimulus; and $k$, a constant whose value depends on the value of the Weber fraction.

This law has been challenged on several grounds and does not hold up perfectly in all circumstances. For our purposes, though, the law does provide a remarkably consistent and rather accurate characterization of the relationship between stimulus intensity and subjective impression.

## DETECTION AND DECISION

The goal of psychophysics is to chart the relationship between an individual's perceptions and various characteristics of the physical stimulus. However, the physical characteristics of the stimulus are not the only factors that determine what the research participant does or says in a psychophysical experiment. The participant is also influenced by her expectations (conscious or unconscious) for how the experiment will unfold—for example, expectations about whether the experimenter will present the target stimulus often or only rarely. Similarly, the participant is guided by her perception of the "payoffs" built into the situation. Will the experimenter think she is insensitive or uncooperative if she misses many of the signals? If so, she might try to minimize her number of misses by adopting a rule of, "If in doubt, say, 'Yes, I

**TABLE 5.1    REPRESENTATIVE (MIDDLE-RANGE) VALUES FOR THE WEBER FRACTION FOR THE DIFFERENT SENSES**

| SENSORY MODALITY | WEBER FRACTION ($\Delta I/I$) |
|---|---|
| Vision (brightness, white light) | 1/60 |
| Kinesthesis (lifted weights) | 1/50 |
| Pain (thermally aroused on skin) | 1/30 |
| Audition (tone of middle pitch and moderate loudness | 1/10 |
| Pressure (cutaneous pressure "spot") | 1/7 |
| Smell (odor of India rubber) | 1/4 |
| Taste (table salt) | 1/3 |

SOURCE: Geldard, 1962.

heard the tone.'" Or might she be more concerned that the experimenter will think she is careless and impulsive? If so, she might adopt the opposite rule and so proceed with the idea, "If in doubt, say, 'No, I didn't hear it.'"

The early psychophysicists believed that such factors could largely be disregarded. But a more recent approach to psychophysical measurement insists that they cannot. This is **signal-detection theory**, an approach that provides an influential and broadly useful way of thinking about how people make decisions both in the psychophysics laboratory and in a wide range of other contexts. Indeed, this approach, developed to study elementary sensations, has been applied to cases as diverse as jury decision making, the memory effects of hypnosis, and the diagnosis of mental disease.

## SIGNAL DETECTION

In a signal-detection procedure, the experimenters present a target stimulus on some trials but no stimulus on other trials. This allows them to ask how often the participant gives each of the four possible types of response. One type is a **hit**, with the participant saying, "Yes, I detected the target" when there really was one. A second response type is a **false alarm**, with the participant saying, "Yes, I detected the target" when there was none. A third response type is a **correct negative**: saying "no target" when in truth there was none. The final type is a **miss**: saying "no target" even though one was actually presented (see Table 5.2).

To see how this information can be used, consider two research participants. Lynn is cautious in her responding and says, "Yes, I heard the tone" only when she is sure. However, Lynn also has exquisitely sensitive hearing, and, as a result, her hit rate (saying yes when the stimulus is present) is high. Charles, in contrast, is almost deaf but

**TABLE 5.2    THE FOUR POSSIBLE OUTCOMES OF THE DETECTION EXPERIMENT**

| | STIMULUS PRESENT | STIMULUS ABSENT |
|---|---|---|
| RESPONDS YES | Hit | False alarm |
| RESPONDS NO | Miss | Correct negative |

quite casual in his responding, and so he tends to say yes whenever he is in doubt. His hit rate is also high, and he reliably says yes when the stimulus is present. But this is not because Charles is accurate; it is merely because his casual attitude leads him to say yes most of the time.

If we looked only at hit rates, we would have no way to distinguish the sensitive Lynn from the deaf Charles. But, fortunately, we have more information than just the hit rates. Charles, always inclined to say yes, also produces many false alarms (saying yes when the stimulus is absent). His responses, in other words, tend to be in the top two cells of Table 5.2. Lynn, in contrast, will produce few false alarms. With her acute hearing, she will probably realize when the stimulus is truly absent and will produce many correct negatives. Lynn's responses, in other words, will accumulate in the top-left and bottom-right cells of Table 5.2.

This sets the pattern for a signal-detection analysis. In general, if individuals differ in how sensitive they are to the signal, then they will differ in their proportions of correct and incorrect responses—their total number of hits and correct negatives relative to their total number of misses and false alarms. But if they differ in their criterion for responding (for example, whether they say "yes" when in doubt, or "no"), then they will differ in their proportions of yes and no responses. As a result of all this, we can assess both a research participant's sensitivity to the signal and his criterion for responding, by looking at all four types of response and calculating the relative numbers of each.

## EXTENSIONS TO OTHER FIELDS

Signal-detection theory has applications to many areas outside of psychophysics. It is relevant whenever a person must decide between two alternatives but cannot be sure of the outcome. As one example, consider the situation of a juror trying to evaluate the evidence in a criminal trial. The juror might believe that prisons are cruel, horrible, and inhumane places, with little chance of reforming prisoners. From this perspective, a false alarm (voting guilty when the defendant is actually innocent) would have terrible consequences, and so the juror would be determined to avoid this error. As a result, a juror with these beliefs will vote guilty only if the quantity of evidence is considerable.

Another juror might see things differently. She might be deeply concerned about cases in which the justice system has set guilty people free, allowing them to break the law again. For this juror, a miss (voting not guilty when the defendant is actually guilty) would be an unacceptable prospect; this would lead her to vote to acquit the defendant only if she were absolutely certain of the defendant's innocence. As a result, the juror is willing to vote guilty with a more modest quantity of evidence.

As a different example, consider medical testing. Here, too, a signal is present or absent (the person has the disease or does not), and the test indicates either yes, the disease is present or no, it is not. And here too there are four possible outcomes, as in Table 5.3, each with its own consequences. For example, a false alarm on an HIV test will bring horrible anxiety to someone who is in fact healthy, but a miss might lead someone to neglect life-prolonging medical treatment and to infect others.

Signal-detection theory provides a powerful research tool in exploring cases like these. For example, does a particular set of instructions by a judge increase the quality of a jury's decision making, or do the instructions simply create a bias in the jury, making jurors more inclined to vote guilty? Signal-detection theory allows us to ask a question like this in a systematic fashion, with the theory leading us to separate measurements for how the instruction influences the jury's sensitivity to the trial evidence and how it influences the jury's voting criteria.

In addition, applications of signal-detection theory remind us that, in virtually all decisions, some errors are inevitable. These errors can be either misses or false alarms, and, for any given test, there is always a trade-off between the two. In order to minimize

**TABLE 5.3    HIV DETECTION**

|  | HIV Is Present | HIV Is Absent |
|---|---|---|
| Test says "HIV present" | Hit—Person will probably seek (and benefit from) treatment | False alarm—Person will suffer horrible anxiety. |
| Test says "No HIV" | Miss—Person will fail to receive treatment | Correct negative—Person will need no treatment, and not be anxious |

the number of misses (for example, to minimize the number of guilty people that we fail to convict, or the number of people with HIV whose tests fail to detect the virus), we could lower the cutoff used in our evaluation (how much incriminating evidence we insist on before voting guilty, or how high a test result has to be before we announce that the disease is present). This would decrease the misses but would also increase the number of false alarms (innocent people who we found guilty, or people without HIV whose tests yield a false positive). Conversely, in order to minimize the number of false alarms, we could shift the cutoff in the opposite direction, but this would certainly increase the number of misses. Just which trade-off is chosen has to depend on the particulars of the case, and the costs and benefits associated with the different errors and correct responses. (For more on how signal detection can be applied to other domains, including medical diagnosis, see, for example, McFall & Treat, 1999; Swets, Dawes, & Monahan, 2000.)

## SENSORY CODING

Signal-detection measurements have provided us with a powerful tool for measuring a perceiver's sensitivity to a stimulus input. These measurements are used when investigators are trying to find out whether a sensory input can be detected at all (and this is the origin of the label *signal detection*). The same types of measurements are used when investigators are examining the perceiver's sensitivity to differences among stimuli. (In that case, the difference is the signal to be detected.) But in all cases, signal-detection techniques provide a crucial research tool for students of psychophysics.

Sensory psychologists, however, want to understand more than just the specific relationship between the physical properties of the stimulus and the sensory experience it gives rise to. They also want to learn something about the events within the nervous system that make this experience possible. As a start, how is the physical stimulus—a molecule floating in the air, in the case of smell; a beam of light, in the case of vision; a change in air pressure, in the case of hearing—converted, or *transduced*, into a neural signal? Second, in the transduction step and then in the subsequent neural events, how does the nervous system manage to represent the qualities of our various sensory experience? For example, how does the nervous system register the fact that we saw the porcupine's quills but did not feel them? How does the nervous system register the fact that the flute's note was high, not low, or that the wine was dry, not sweet, or that the pizza tasted like pizza and not like brussels sprouts? These are questions of *sensory coding*.

In general, a code is a set of rules through which information is transformed from one format into another. An example is the code a fax machine uses to transform the patterns on a printed page into a sound-based pattern that can be transmitted through a telephone line. In the same way, the nervous system encodes (that is, translates) the various properties of the proximal stimulus into neural impulses so that these can be transmitted to the brain.

We will consider some of the details of these codes in subsequent sections, when we survey what is known about some of the sense modalities. But here we will start with some general points. One of these concerns the code for *psychological intensity*, such as changes in loudness and brightness. In general, the code for intensity used by the nervous system is the rate of firing by the neurons in a sensory system: the more intense the stimulus, the greater the rate of firing. Recall that neurons cannot fire more strongly or less strongly; as we discussed in Chapter 2, either a neuron fires or it does not. But neurons can fire more or less often, and this seems to be the cue that usually indicates how intense the stimulus was. In addition, stimulus intensity is also encoded via the sheer number of neurons that are triggered by the stimulus: the more intense the stimulus, the more neurons it activates, and the greater the psychological magnitude.

Another broad question concerns the code for *sensory quality*—the difference in the neural code that tells us we are hearing rather than seeing, or tasting something sweet rather than smelling something rotten. These sensations are obviously produced by very different stimuli, but this is not what is crucial for the nervous system. What matters, instead, is which nerves are being stimulated. Stimulation of the optic nerve (whether the stimulation comes from light or some other source) causes the sense of seeing; this is why strong pressure on the eyeballs leads us to see rings or stars (to the chagrin of boxers and the delight of cartoonists) just as light does. Similarly, stimulation of the auditory nerve (whether the stimulation comes from sound or something else) causes the sense of hearing. This is why people sometimes experience "ringing in their ears" in the absence of any environmental sound—some illness or injury is causing stimulation of the auditory nerve.

A great deal of evidence supports these claims, including the fact that it is possible, in the laboratory, to stimulate the visual system directly through electric currents; this stimulation invariably causes the feeling of "seeing." All of this fits well with the *doctrine of specific nerve energies*, which was first formulated in 1826 by Johannes Müller (1801–1858). According to this doctrine, the differences in sensory quality—the difference between seeing and hearing, between hearing and touch, and so on—are not caused by differences in the stimuli themselves but by the different nervous structures that these stimuli excite.

But what about qualitative differences within a sense modality? For example, blue, green, and red are qualitatively different even though all three are visual sensations. How are differences of this sort encoded? The answer depends on which differences and which sensory modality we are considering. In some cases, these differences are best described by an idea that stays close to Müller's insight: This idea is often referred to as *specificity theory*, and is the notion that different sensory qualities (sweet versus sour, red versus green) are signaled by different neurons, just as the different sense modalities (vision versus pressure) are signaled by different nerves. On this conception, the nervous system acts as if these quality-specific neurons were somehow "labeled" with their quality, so that the nervous system registers the presence of "pain" whenever there is an incoming signal in the "pain neurons," registers the presence of "hot" whenever there is a signal coming from the "hot neurons," and so on. (This conception is sometimes referred to as the labeled-line theory, for obvious reasons.)

The alternative position is *pattern theory*. According to this view, what matters for sensory quality is a pattern of activation across a whole set of neurons. In taste, for example, certain neurons in the tongue fire whenever one is tasting "sweet," but that is not because these neurons reliably signal the sensation of sweetness. These same neurons also fire when one is tasting "sour." Clearly, then, the difference between "sweet" and "sour" is not a matter of which neurons are firing. Instead, what differs between

How many tastes?

"sweet" and "sour" is the pattern of activation—which neurons are firing more and which less at any given moment—across the set of sensory neurons. The significance of each particular neuron's activity, therefore, can only be understood in relation to the broader pattern, and it is this pattern that gives rise to the sensory qualities.

Thus, it seems that overall there is no single answer to the question of how sensory coding is achieved. The difference among senses (taste versus sight, hearing versus smell) is certainly signaled by "labeled lines," and so activity in the optic nerve causes the sensation of seeing, activity in the auditory nerve causes the sensation of hearing, and so on. Some qualitative differences within each modality may also be signaled by "labeled lines" (for example, the sensation of pain), but, as we will see, for other sensory qualities, the nervous system uses a pattern code.

# THE FUNCTIONING OF THE SENSES

It is often said that humans have five sense modalities—vision, hearing, touch, taste, and smell. In truth, though, we have several more than this. To begin with, there is *kinesthesis*, a collective term for information that comes from receptors in the muscles, tendons, and joints and that informs us about our movements and the orientation of our body in space. Another is the *vestibular sense*, whose receptors are in a cavity within the inner ear and signal movements of the head. Yet another group are the **skin senses**. Whereas Aristotle believed that all of the senses from the skin could be subsumed under the broad rubric of *touch*, we now know that there are at least four different skin receptors that give rise to the sensations of pressure, warmth, cold, and pain.

We know a great deal about each of these senses, including what they have in common and what makes each of them different from the others. In this chapter, though, we will focus on the two sense modalities that are unquestionably the most important sources of information for us—namely, hearing and vision.

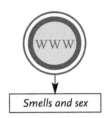

*Smells and sex*

# HEARING

Our sense of hearing provides us with much information about the world, but, crucially, our sense of hearing is central for our communication—whether it occurs through someone's tone of voice, a whistle, a moment of laughter, or, of course, language. How do we hear?

## SOUND

What is the stimulus for hearing? Outside in the world some physical object is moving—perhaps an animal scurrying through the underbrush or a set of vocal cords vibrating. This movement agitates the air particles that surround the moving object, causing these particles to jostle other particles, which in turn jostle still other particles. The actual movement of these particles is slight (about one-billionth of a centimeter) and short-lived (the particles return to their original position in a few thousandths of a second), but the motion is enough to create a momentary pressure moving outward from the moving object, similar to the ripples set in motion by a stone thrown into a pond.

If the movement continues for even a short time, it will create a series of pressure variations in the air, and when these **sound waves** hit our ears, they initiate a set of further changes that ultimately trigger the auditory receptors. The receptors then trigger various neural responses, which eventually reach the brain and lead to the experience of hearing.

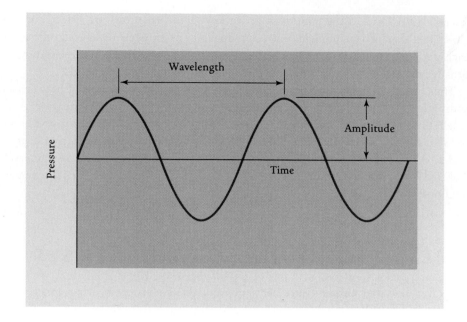

5.3   *The stimulus for hearing*   *A vibrating object creates a series of pressure pulses in the molecules surrounding it; these pulses then spread outward like ripples in a pond into which a stone has been thrown. To describe this pattern, it is useful to measure the air pressure at a single point in space. The pressure of a sound wave waxes and wanes, as shown here. The extent of the pressure determines the height of the wave; the timing between points of maximum pressure determines the wavelength.*

Sound waves vary in many ways, but, in the simplest case, they take the form shown in Figure 5.3. Here we have plotted measurements of how the air pressure produced by a sound wave changes moment by moment, and, as the figure shows, the pressure waxes and wanes in an orderly fashion. In fact, the pattern corresponds to the plot of the trigonometric sine function, which is why this wave is referred to as a *sine wave*. To describe the wave, we need to specify two things. First is the *amplitude*, the amount of pressure exerted by each air particle on the next. Since this pressure is constantly changing as the sound wave moves along, the amplitude we actually measure is the maximum pressure achieved, at the crest of the sound wave. Second, we need to specify the *frequency* of the wave—that is, how many crests there are in each second, or, correspondingly, how many times in each second the wave reaches its maximum amplitude (Figure 5.4).

Amplitude and frequency are physical dimensions of the sound wave itself, but they correspond reasonably well to the psychological dimensions of loudness and *pitch*. Roughly speaking, a sound will be heard as louder as its amplitude increases and more high pitched as its frequency goes up.

*Amplitude and Loudness*   The range of amplitudes to which humans can respond is enormous, so investigators find it useful to measure these intensities with a logarithmic scale, which compresses this huge range into a more convenient form. Thus, sound intensities are measured in *decibels* (Table 5.4), and psychologically, perceived loudness doubles each time the intensity of a sound increases by 10 decibels (Stevens, 1955).

5.4   *Simple wave forms vary in frequency and amplitude*   *These curves show the sine waves for a weak and a strong 100-hertz tone (relatively low in pitch) and a weak and a strong 1,000-hertz tone (comparatively high in pitch).*

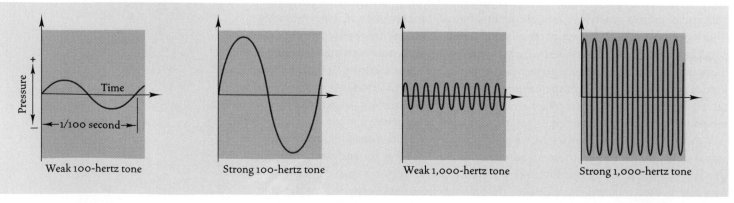

Weak 100-hertz tone        Strong 100-hertz tone        Weak 1,000-hertz tone        Strong 1,000-hertz tone

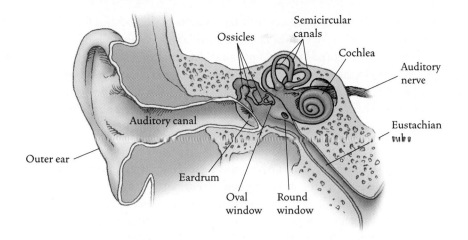

**5.6 The human ear** *Air enters through the outer ear and stimulates the eardrum, which sets the ossicles in the middle ear in motion. These in turn transmit their vibration to the membrane of the oval window, which causes movement of the fluid in the cochlea of the inner ear.*

the vibration pattern to the oval window to which it is attached. The movements of the oval window then give rise to waves in the fluid that fills the cochlea, causing (at last) a response by the receptors (Figure 5.6).

Why do we have this roundabout method of sound transmission? Sound waves reach us through the air, and the proximal stimulus for hearing is made up of minute changes in the air pressure. But the inner ear (like most body parts) is filled with fluid—cochlear fluid to be exact. Therefore, in order to hear, the changes in air pressure must cause changes in fluid pressure. This is a problem, because fluid is harder to set in motion than air is. To solve this problem, the pressure waves must be amplified on their way toward the receptors, and this is accomplished by various features of the ear's organization. For example, the outer ear itself is shaped in a fashion that serves as a "sound scoop," funneling the pressure waves toward the auditory canal. Within the middle ear, the ossicles work as levers, using leverage to increase the sound pressure. Finally, the eardrum is about twenty times larger than the portion of the oval window that is moved by the ossicles. As a result, the fairly weak force provided by sound waves acting on the entire eardrum is transformed into a much stronger pressure concentrated on the (smaller) oval window.

## TRANSDUCTION IN THE COCHLEA

Throughout most of its length the cochlea is divided into an upper and lower section by several structures, including the *basilar membrane*. The actual auditory receptors are called *hair cells*, and these cells—some fifteen thousand of them in each ear—are lodged between the basilar membrane and other membranes above it (Figure 5.7).

**5.7 Detailed structure of the middle ear and the cochlea** *(A) Movement of the fluid within the cochlea deforms the basilar membrane and stimulates the hair cells that serve as the auditory receptors. (B) Cross section of the cochlea showing the basilar membrane and the hair cell receptors.*

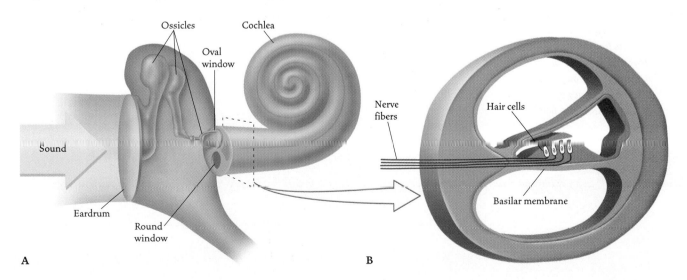

A B

Motion of the oval window produces pressure changes in the cochlear fluid that in turn lead to vibrations of the basilar membrane. As the basilar membrane vibrates, its deformations bend the hair cells, and it is this physical deformation that triggers the neural response. But how do the movements of the hair cells lead to the sensory properties of auditory experience? Much of the work in this area has focused on the perception of pitch, the sensory quality that depends on the frequency of the stimulating sound wave.

*Basilar Place and Pitch*    Sound waves arriving at the ear cause the entire basilar membrane to vibrate, but the vibration is not uniform. Some regions of the membrane actually move more than others, and where this region of greatest movement is located depends on the frequency of the incoming sound. For higher frequencies, the region of greatest movement is at the end of the basilar membrane closer to the oval window; for lower frequencies, the region of greatest movement is closer to the cochlear tip.

These points were anticipated more than a century ago by Hermann von Helmholtz (1821–1894), who proposed the *place theory* of pitch perception. This theory proposes that the nervous system is able to identify a sound's pitch simply by keeping track of where the movement is greatest along the length of the basilar membrane. More specifically, stimulation of hair cells at one end of the membrane leads to the experience of a high tone, whereas stimulation of hair cells at the other end leads to the sensation of a low tone.

Confirmation for these claims, however, did not come until a half-century later, in a series of classic studies by Georg von Békésy (1899–1972), whose work on auditory function won him a Nobel prize in 1961. Working with preserved specimens of both human and animal cochleas, Békésy was able to remove part of the cochlear wall so that he could observe the basilar membrane through a microscope while the oval window was being vibrated by an electrically powered piston. He found that this stimulation led to a wavelike motion of the basilar membrane (Figure 5.8). As he varied the frequency of the vibrating stimulus, the pattern of the membrane's motion changed, and, in particular, the point of greatest movement shifted in an orderly fashion, just as Helmholtz had proposed (Békésy, 1957).

*Sound Frequency and Frequency of Neural Firing*    However, the place theory of pitch faces a major difficulty. As the frequency of the stimulus gets lower and lower, the pattern of movement that it produces on the basilar membrane gets broader and broader. At frequencies below 50 hertz, the movement produced by a sound stimulus deforms the entire membrane just about equally (although, see Khanna & Leonard, 1982; Hudspeth, 1989). Therefore, if we were using the pattern of the basilar's movement as our cue to a sound's frequency, we would be unable to discern these low frequencies. But that is not the case; humans, in fact, can discriminate frequencies as low as 20 hertz. Apparently, then, the nervous system must have some means for sensing pitch in addition to basilar location.

The second means for sensing pitch is likely to be tied to the firing frequency of the

*Hermann von Helmholtz*

**5.8    The deformation of the basilar membrane by sound    (A)** In this diagram, the membrane is schematically presented as a simple, rectangular sheet. In actuality, of course, it is much thinner and coiled in a spiral shape. **(B)** The relation between sound frequency and the location of the peak of the basilar membrane's deformation. The peak of the deformation is located at varying distances from the stapes (the third ossicle, which sets the membrane in motion by pushing at the oval window). As the figure shows, the higher the frequency of the sound, the closer to the stapes this peak will be.

A

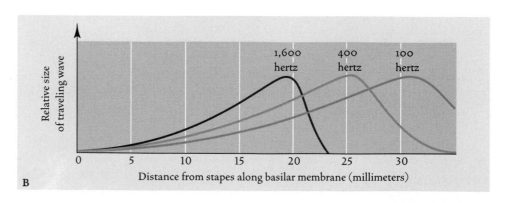

B

auditory nerve, a hypothesis referred to as *frequency theory*. For lower frequencies, the frequency of a stimulus tone may be directly translated into the appropriate number of neural impulses per second. This information would then be relayed to higher neural centers that somehow interpret this information as pitch.

Current evidence indicates that both of these mechanisms—the one identified by place theory and the one identified by frequency theory—contribute to pitch perception. It appears that higher frequencies are coded by the place of excitation on the basilar membrane, and lower frequencies by the frequency of the neural impulses. Place of excitation plays little role in the perception of frequencies below 500 to 1,000 hertz, while impulse frequency has little effect for tones above 5,000 hertz. In the middle range, between 1,000 and 5,000 hertz, both mechanisms are operative, and in this range the discrimination of pitches is particularly accurate (Goldstein, 1989; Green, 1976).

# VISION

It is easy to argue that vision is more important to us than any other sense modality. This is reflected in the enormous cortical area devoted to vision; it is also evident in the fact that we trust vision more than we trust our other senses. This trust is detectable in some of our common expressions, such as "seeing is believing." It can be demonstrated more formally in experiments which show that, when the senses provide discrepant information (through some experimenter's trick), we rely on what we see rather than what we hear or feel.

In describing vision we will focus on three broad issues. First, what are the structures for gathering the stimulus, and how do they work? Second, what is the nature of the transduction process through which the physical energy of the stimulus is converted into a neural signal? Third, what is the nature of the coding processes through which we are able to discriminate the millions of shapes, colors, and patterns of movement that make up our visual world?

## THE STIMULUS: LIGHT

Many objects in our environment are sources of light, including the sun, a candle, or even a glow worm. Most objects, however, do not emit light on their own; instead, they are sources of light only if some external light source illuminates them. They then reflect some portion of the light cast on them, and this is what reaches our eye.

Whether emitted or reflected, though, the stimulus energy we call *light* travels in a wave form that is analogous to the pressure waves that are the stimulus for hearing. To describe these waves, we need two measurements, just as we did with sound: First, light waves can vary in their amplitude, which (just like with sound) is measured as the maximum displacement of the wave away from its baseline; a light wave's amplitude is the major determinant of perceived brightness. Second, light waves can also vary in their frequency—how many times per second the wave reaches its maximum amplitude. As a matter of convenience, though, investigators typically describe light waves using the mathematical inverse of frequency—*wavelength*, the distance between the crests of two successive waves. Wavelengths are measured in nanometers (millionths of a millimeter) and are the major determinant of perceived color.

As it turns out, the wavelengths to which our visual system is sensitive are only a tiny part of the broader electromagnetic spectrum. Light with a wavelength longer than 750 nanometers is invisible to us, although we do feel these longer infrared waves as heat. Likewise, light with a wavelength shorter than 360 nanometers is also invisible to us, although many other organisms (bees, for example) can perceive these ultraviolet wavelengths. Therefore, the light we see consists only of the wavelengths between these two boundaries; this is the *visible spectrum*, with wavelengths close to 360 nanometers usually perceived as violet, wavelengths close to 750 nanometers perceived as red, and the range in between perceived as the rest of the colors in the rainbow.

## GATHERING THE STIMULUS: THE EYE

Eyes come in many forms. Some invertebrates have simple eyespots sensitive merely to light or dark, while others have complex multicellular organs with pinhole apertures or crystalline lenses. In vertebrates, the actual detection of light is done by cells called *photoreceptors*, located on the *retina*, a layer of tissue lining the back of the eyeball. Before the light reaches the retina, however, several mechanisms are needed to control the amount of light reaching the photoreceptors and, above all, to ensure a clear and sharply focused *retinal image*.

The human eye is sometimes compared to a camera, and in its essentials this analogy holds up well enough (Figure 5.9). Both eye and camera have a *lens*, which suitably bends (or refracts) light rays passing through it, thus projecting an image onto a light-sensitive surface behind—the film in the camera, the retina in the eye. (In the eye, refraction is accomplished by both the lens and the *cornea*, the eye's transparent outer coating.) In the camera, the image is focused by changing the position of the lens; in the eye, this is accomplished by a set of muscles that change the shape of the lens, contracting to curve the lens further when focusing on an object close by and relaxing to flatten out the lens when focusing on an object at a distance. Finally, both camera and eye are able to govern the amount of entering light. In the camera, this function is performed by the lens aperture; in the eye, it is performed by the *iris*, a smooth, circular muscle that surrounds the pupillary opening and that contracts or dilates under reflex control as the amount of illumination changes.

## THE VISUAL RECEPTORS

Once light reaches the retina, we leave the domain of optics and enter the domain of neurophysiology, because it is at the retina that the physical stimulus energy is transduced into a neural impulse. The retina contains two kinds of receptor cells, the *rods* and the *cones*; the names of these cells reflect their different shapes. The cones are plentiful in the *fovea*, a small, roughly circular region at the center of the retina, but then become less and less prevalent as one moves away from the fovea into the retina's periphery. The opposite is true of the rods; they are completely absent from the fovea but frequent in the periphery. In all, there are some 120 million rods and about 6 million cones in the normal human eye.

**5.9 Eye and camera** *The eye has a number of similarities to a camera. Both have a lens for bending light rays to project an inverted image on a light-sensitive surface at the back. In the eye a transparent outer layer, the cornea, participates in this light bending. The light-sensitive surface in the eye is the retina, whose most sensitive region is the fovea. Both eye and camera have a focusing device; in the eye, the lens can be thickened or flattened. Both have an adjustable iris diaphragm. Finally, both are encased in black to minimize the effects of stray light; in the eye this is done by a layer of darkly pigmented tissue, the choroid coat.*

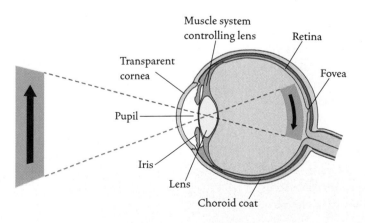
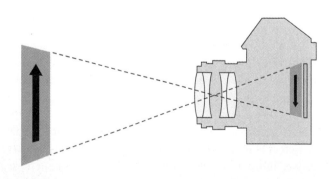

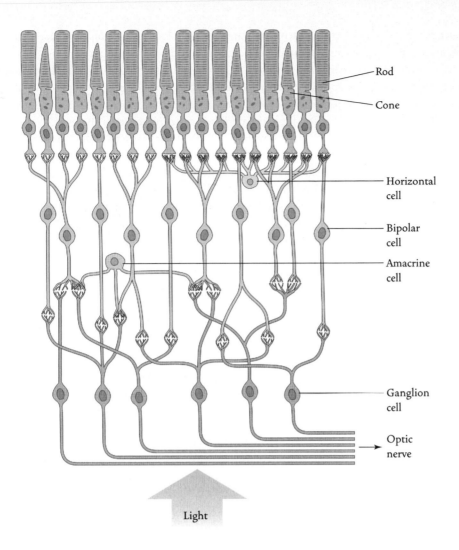

5.10 *The retina*  *There are three main retinal layers: the rods and cones, which are the photoreceptors; the bipolar cells; and the ganglion cells, whose axons make up the optic nerve. There are also two other kinds of cells, horizontal cells and amacrine cells, that allow for lateral (sideways) interaction. As shown in the diagram, the retina contains an anatomical oddity. As it is constructed, the photoreceptors are at the very back, the bipolar cells are in between, and the ganglion cells are at the top. As a result, light has to pass through the other layers (they are not opaque so this is possible) to reach the rods and cones, whose stimulation starts the visual process.*

The rods and cones do not report to the brain directly. Instead, their message is relayed by several other layers of cells within the retina (Figure 5.10). The receptors stimulate the *bipolar cells*, and these in turn excite the *ganglion cells*. The ganglion cells collect information from all over the retina, and the axons of these cells converge to form a bundle of fibers that we call the *optic nerve*. Leaving the eyeball, the optic nerve carries information, first, to an important way station in the thalamus, called the *lateral geniculate nucleus*, and then to the cortex. Where the optic nerve leaves the eyeball, there is no place for photoreceptors, and so this region of the eyeball cannot give rise to visual sensations; appropriately enough, it is called the *blind spot* (Figure 5.11).

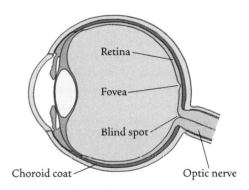

5.11 *Fovea and blind spot*  *The fovea is the region on the retina in which the receptors are most densely packed. The blind spot is a region where there are no receptors at all, this being the point where the optic nerve leaves the eyeball.*

## THE DUPLEX THEORY OF VISION

The fact that rods and cones differ in structure, number, and placement on the retina suggests that they also differ in function. Almost a hundred years ago, this notion led to the development of the *duplex theory of vision*, a theory that by now has the status of established fact. The idea is that rods and cones handle different aspects of the visual task. The rods are the receptors for night vision; they operate at low light intensities and lead to *achromatic* (colorless) sensations. The cones serve day vision; they respond at much higher levels of illumination and are responsible for sensations of color. The utility of this duplex arrangement becomes clear when we consider the enormous range of light intensities encountered by organisms like ourselves that transact their business during both day and night. In humans, the ratio between the stimulus energy at absolute threshold and that transmitted by a momentary glance at the sun is 1 to 100,000,000,000. Natural selection has allowed for this incredible range by a biological division of labor, with two separate receptor systems responsible for dim-light and bright-light vision.

The enormous sensitivity of the rods, however, comes at a price. The rods are much worse than the cones at discriminating fine detail; *acuity*, the ability to perceive detail, is much greater in the cones. This is a major reason why we move our eyes whenever we wish to inspect an object. To "look at" a stimulus means to move the eyes so that the target's image falls on the foveas of both eyes. It is at the fovea that the cones are most closely bunched, so acuity is greatest when a stimulus is in foveal view.

Conversely, consider the fact that sailors, wishing to perceive a faint star in the night sky, know that they should not look directly toward the star but instead should look slightly to the left or right of the star's position. This ensures that the star's image will fall in the periphery, where the rods are most prevalent. This strategy sacrifices the ability to discern detail but, by relying on the more sensitive rods, maximizes sensitivity to dim light.

## SPECTRAL SENSITIVITY

Further evidence for the duplex theory comes from the study of *spectral sensitivity*. As we have mentioned, the human eye is insensitive to light waves shorter than 360 nanometers or longer than 750 nanometers. What is its sensitivity to the wavelengths in between? To answer this question, we can ask subjects to detect a faint test light of a specific intensity and wavelength. Then we can do the same with another test light at a slightly different wavelength, and then with another test light at still a new wavelength. If we continue in this fashion, we can determine in a systematic way how the eye's sensitivity varies as a function of wavelength. If we project these lights onto the rod-free fovea, this procedure will allow us to determine the sensitivity of the cones to each individual wavelength. If we project the lights onto the retina's periphery, we can do the same for the rods.

The results of this sort of experiment are usually summarized in terms of a *spectral sensitivity curve* in which sensitivity is plotted against wavelength. As the curve in Figure 5.12 shows, maximal sensitivity for the rods is toward the short-wave region, with a peak at about 510 nanometers. (This wavelength, if presented to the cones, appears green; it appears gray if presented to the color-blind rods.) The curve for the cones is lower overall, reflecting the cones' lesser sensitivity to light. In addition, the cones' region of maximal sensitivity is toward the longer wavelengths, with a peak at about 560 nanometers (seen as yellowish green). For rods, the blues are easier to detect than the yellows and reds (although, again, all appear gray to the rods); for cones, the opposite is the case.

## VISUAL PIGMENTS

The rods and cones can be distinguished functionally (by what they do) and anatomically (by their shapes). They can also be distinguished chemically. Inside each photoreceptor is a *visual pigment*, a chemical that is sensitive to light, and it is the pigment that allows the transduction of light energy into a neural signal. When light enters the receptor, the light energy changes the chemical form of the visual pigment, setting off a chain of events that leads, ultimately, to an electrical signal. In this fashion, the light energy is translated into the language of the nervous system. The pigment itself is then reconstituted by other mechanisms so that it will be ready to react when the next opportunity arises.

The visual pigment inside the rods is *rhodopsin*. The cones contain three different pigments, but their exact chemical composition remains uncertain. Still, the fact that they have three pigments rather than one is crucial to the cones' ability to discriminate colors, a topic to which we will turn shortly.

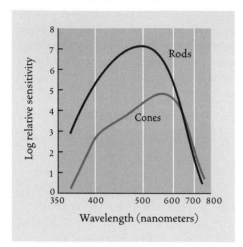

**5.12 Sensitivity of rods and cones to light of different wavelengths** *Sensitivity was measured by determining the threshold for different frequencies of light projected on retinal areas rich in rods or cones. Sensitivity was then computed by dividing 1 by the threshold (the lower the threshold, the greater the sensitivity). Since sensitivity varied over an enormous range, the range was compressed by using logarithmic units. Note first that the cones, overall, are less sensitive than the rods. Note also that the point of maximal sensitivity is different for the two receptor systems. The cone maximum (560 nanometers) is closer to yellow, the rod maximum (510 nanometers) closer to green.*

# THE IMPORTANCE OF CHANGE: ADAPTATION

One might think of the rods and cones as mere detectors of light, passively receiving and recording the stimulus. Many observations, however, show that the visual system, even at this early stage, is not at all passive. The visual system actively shapes and transforms the stimulus input (as, indeed, do all sensory systems). This activity begins at the receptor level and continues at all subsequent levels, owing to the fact that the components of the visual system interact constantly and never function in isolation from each other.

One kind of interaction concerns the relation between the signal a neuron is now receiving and the signal it received a moment ago. The nature of this interaction is straightforward: vision, like all the sensory systems, reacts strongly to change, and, if there is no change, then the visual system gradually stops reacting.

The visual system's "nonreaction" to an unchanging stimulus is readily demonstrated in the laboratory, but it can also be shown informally. Hold the text so that Figure 5.13 is roughly six inches from your eye and stare at the figure's center, trying not to move your eyes at all. After 15 or 20 seconds, portions of the yellow circles will probably fade into a much paler yellow, and the circles may disappear altogether. (The moment you move your eyes, the circles are restored.)

What does the organism gain by this sort of sensory adaptation? Stimuli that have been around for a while have already been inspected; any information they offer has already been detected and analyzed. It is sensible, therefore, to give these already-checked inputs less sensory weight. What is important is change, especially sudden change, because this may well signify food to a predator and death to its potential prey. Adaptation is the sensory system's way of ensuring these priorities, by pushing old news off the neurophysiological front page.

# INTERACTION IN SPACE: CONTRAST

We have been discussing the importance of change with regard to temporal relationships—what is the sensory information now as compared to the information a moment ago? For our visual system, though, the pattern of change also involves spatial relationships—what is the sensory input here as compared to there? If, for example, one looks at a uniformly colored region (so that there is no change in view), the neural response is literally smaller than it would be when looking at a patterned field. In addition, patterns of spatial change also influence what we see, so that the appearance of a stimulus within a uniform field is often different from the appearance of the same stimulus within a varied field.

The visual system's sensitivity to spatial relationships can be demonstrated in many ways. For example, it has long been known that the appearance of a gray patch depends on its background. The identical gray will look much brighter on a black background than it will on a white background. This is *brightness contrast*, an effect that increases as the intensity difference increases between two contrasting regions (Figure 5.14).

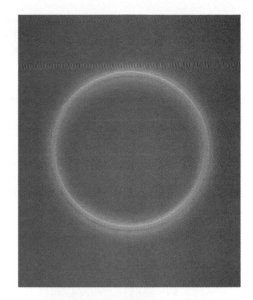

**5.13   Stabilized retinal images   Hold this picture about 6–8 inches from your eyes, and stare at the center of the ring without moving your eyes at all. For most people, the ring will fade away after a few seconds. In this case, the figure is not perfectly stabilized on the retina (because, even when you try to hold your eyes still, they will jitter a little). However, the gradual edges within the figure guarantee that small eye movements produce very little change in the visual stimulus. With no change, the visual system soon detects no input. The moment you make a larger eye movement, though, your eye does receive new information, and so the ring reappears.**

**5.14 Brightness contrast   Four (objectively) identical gray squares on different backgrounds. The lighter the background, the darker the gray squares appear.**

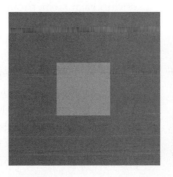

**5.15**  *The effect of distance between contrasting regions*   The white lines in the grid are physically homogenous, but they do not appear to be—each of the "intersections" seems to contain a gray spot. The uneven appearance of the white strips is caused by contrast. Each strip is surrounded by a black square, which contrasts with it and makes it look brighter. But this is not the case at the intersections, which only touch upon the black squares at their corners. As a result, there is little contrast in the middle of the intersections. This accounts for the gray spots seen there.

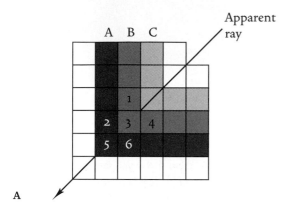

A

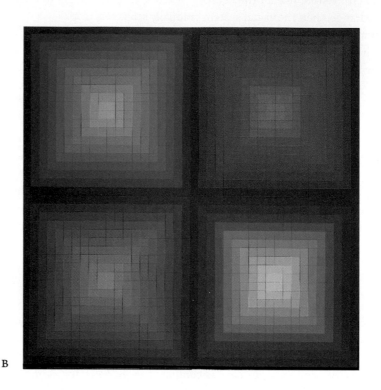

B

**5.16**  *Contrast*   *(A) The figure focuses on three of the frames of the painting in (B) to show how the luminous rays are created. Consider squares 1, 3, and 4. Squares 1 and 4 each have an entire side next to the brighter frame C above them. As a result of brightness contrast, they look darker than square 3, which suffers little contrast, for it touches on the brighter frame only at its corner. For the same reason, squares 2 and 6 seem darker than square 5. Since this happens for all the squares at the corners, the observer sees four radiating luminous diagonals. (B) Arcturus (1966) by Victor Vasarely.*

Contrast is also a function of the distance between the two contrasting regions—the smaller that distance, the greater the contrast (Figure 5.15). This phenomenon gives rise to a number of visual illusions and has been used by some contemporary artists to create striking effects (see Figure 5.16).

## ACCENTUATING EDGES

Contrast effects have another consequence: They serve to accentuate the edges between different objects in our visual world, allowing us to see these edges more clearly. Consider Figure 5.17A, which contains strips of grays that range from very dark to very light. Within each strip, though, the brightness is constant. That is, the figure shows a uniform dark gray strip, then a uniform slightly lighter strip, then another uniform slightly lighter strip, and so on. This pattern is summarized by Figure 5.17B, in which the actual light intensities for each strip have been plotted against stimulus position.

But the appearance of Figure 5.17A is different from what one might expect based on the pattern shown in Figure 5.17B. At the border between each strip and the neighboring one, there seems to be a band. On the dark side of each juncture, an even darker band is seen; on the bright side of the juncture, a brighter band is visible. This pattern is summarized in Figure 5.17C, which shows *perceived* brightnesses (as opposed to the physical brightnesses, shown in Figure 5.17B).

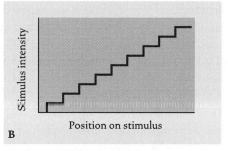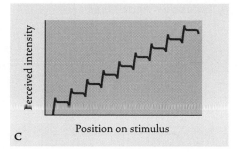

**5.17** *Mach bands* *(A) The series of gray strips is arranged in ascending brightness, from left to right. Physically, each strip is of uniform light intensity, as shown graphically in (B), which plots position against physical light intensity. But the strips do not appear to be uniform. For each strip, contrast makes the left edge (adjacent to its darker neighbor) look brighter than the rest, while the right edge (adjacent to its lighter neighbor) looks darker. The result is an accentuation of the contours that separate one strip from the next. The resulting appearance—the way the figure is perceived—is described graphically in (C).*

These illusory bands are called ***Mach bands***, after the nineteenth-century physicist Ernst Mach who discovered them. They are produced by the same contrast effects we discussed before. When a light region borders a darker region, contrast makes the light region look even lighter; when a dark region borders a light region, contrast makes the dark region look darker still. In both directions, contrast accentuates the difference between the two adjacent regions and in this way highlights the edge where the two regions meet.

This process helps vision overcome certain optical imperfections in the eye. Because of these imperfections, the retinal image is often fuzzy, even though the external stimulus is outlined sharply. Contrast corrects this fuzziness, for the visual system re-creates, and even exaggerates, boundaries by the same mechanisms that generate Mach bands.

## LATERAL INHIBITION AND BRIGHTNESS CONTRAST

The effects just described are clearly helpful for the visual system: they enhance the differences between adjacent regions, making it easier for the visual system to locate the edges that define an object's shape. But what is the physiological mechanism that produces these effects?

At many levels in the visual system, activity in one region tends to inhibit responding in the adjacent regions. This tendency is called ***lateral inhibition***—it is, in essence, inhibition exerted sideways. This effect is well documented and can be confirmed, for example, by recordings from single cells in the visual system. These recordings clearly show that neighboring regions in the retina tend to inhibit each other. Similar effects can also be observed at higher levels in the visual system.

To put this concretely, when any visual receptor is stimulated, it transmits its excitation to other cells that eventually relay this signal to the brain. But the receptor's excitation also has a further effect. It stimulates neurons that extend sideways along the retina. These lateral cells make contact with neighboring cells and inhibit their activation.

To see how this works, consider Figure 5.18. Receptor cell *A* is positioned so that it receives light reflected from a dark gray patch. This incoming light causes the cell to respond, and this response is then transmitted upward to the brain. Receptor cell *B* also receives light from a dark gray patch and so, initially, is stimulated in just the way cell *A* is. But the excitation from cell *B* will not be passed upward to the brain unimpeded. Cell *B* is next to cell *C*, which receives its light from a brightly illuminated patch and so is intensely excited. *C*'s excitation stimulates yet another cell, *D*, whose effect is inhibitory, blocking the excitation that *B* sends upward. Cell *D*, in other words, carries the lateral inhibition.

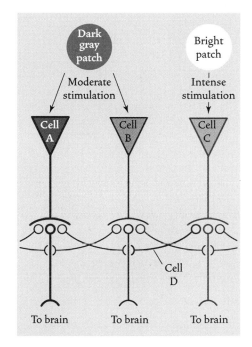

**5.18** *Lateral inhibition and contrast* *Two receptor cells, A and B, are stimulated by the same dark gray patch. A's excitation is transmitted to the brain unimpeded. But B is adjacent to cell C, which is intensely stimulated by a bright patch. C's excitation is transmitted to the brain, but C also excites a lateral cell, D, which exerts an inhibitory effect on the message being sent by B. As a result, A and B, receiving the same inputs, send different messages to the brain.*

In short, receptors *A* and *B* are exposed to the same stimulus but do not send the same signal to the brain. Cell *B* is hushed by its excited neighbor and, as a result, sends a weaker signal to the brain than does cell *A*. This is the basis for brightness contrast, and it has the effect of sending the brain a visual message that is, in a sense, an exaggeration. Whenever a dark region is next to a lighter one, the dark one seems darker, and the light one seems lighter.

Lateral inhibition is important for its own sake, but it also illustrates a broader point. At the very beginning of this chapter, we asked whether the sensory mechanisms were best thought of as passive recorders of the stimulus input, or whether these mechanisms somehow organize and interpret that input. Our answer to these questions is not yet fully in view, but we are getting some powerful indications of what the answer must be: owing to lateral inhibition, the visual system seems to be refining the stimulus information from the very start, emphasizing some aspects of the input (the edges) and understating other aspects (areas that are being uniformly stimulated). Lateral inhibition arises from mechanisms just a synapse or two into the visual system, but, even at this level, our nervous system is far from passive and is doing more than merely receiving and recording the incoming stimulus.

## COLOR

It is clear, then, that interaction among sensory elements can shape the sensory input and can serve to highlight elements such as boundaries and moments of change that are of particular interest to the organism. This pattern of interaction is also evident when we consider a different aspect of vision, namely, the perception of color.

### CLASSIFYING THE COLOR SENSATIONS

A person with normal color vision can distinguish over seven million different color shades. These many colors can be classified in terms of a few simple dimensions.

*The Dimensions of Color* **Hue** is the attribute that distinguishes blue from green from red, and it is the attribute that is shared by, say, a bright orange, a middle orange, and a dark orange. This term corresponds closely to the way we use the word *color* in everyday life. Hue varies with wavelength (Figure 5.19) so that a wavelength of 465 nanometers is perceived as **unique blue**, a blue that is judged to have no trace of red or green in it; a wavelength of about 500 nanometers is perceived as **unique green** (green with no blue or yellow); a wavelength of 570 nanometers is perceived as **unique yellow** (yellow with no green or red).

**Brightness** is the dimension that differentiates black (low brightness) from white (high brightness), with various shades of gray in between. Black, white, and all of the grays are the **achromatic colors**; these have no hue. But brightness is also a property of the **chromatic colors** (purple, red, yellow, and so forth). Thus, ultramarine blue is darker (has a lower brightness) than sky blue, just as charcoal gray is darker than pearl gray (Figure 5.20).

**5.19**  *The visible spectrum and the four unique hues*  **The visible spectrum consists of light waves from about 360 to 700 nanometers.**

*Saturation* is the "purity" of a color, the extent to which it is chromatic rather than achromatic. The more gray (or black or white) that is mixed with a color, the less saturation it has. Consider the various blue patches in Figure 5.21. All have the same hue (blue), and all have the same brightness. The patches differ only in one respect: the proportion of blue as opposed to that of gray. The more gray there is, the less saturated the color. When the color is entirely gray, saturation is zero. Red and pink differ largely in saturation, so that pink looks like a washed-out red.

*The Color Circle, Color Disk, and Color Solid* Consider the colors that look most chromatic—that is, colors whose saturation is maximal. If we arrange these on the basis of perceptual similarity, the result is the so-called *color circle*, in which red is followed by orange, orange by yellow, yellow-green, green, blue-green, blue, and violet, until the circle finally returns to red (Figure 5.22).

The color circle embodies the perceptual similarities among the different hues. For each of these hues, a range of saturations is possible, and these can all be depicted as a *color disk*, shown in Figure 5.23.

For each of these combinations of hue and saturation, a range of different brightnesses is also possible, requiring another dimension in our representation. The resulting three-dimensional form summarizing these perceptual attributes is called the *color solid* (Figure 5.24). By specifying a position within this solid, we can identify each of the seven million colors that humans can discriminate.

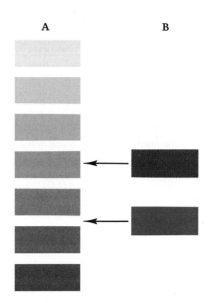

**5.20 Brightness** *Colors can be arranged according to their brightness. (A) This dimension is most readily recognized when we look at a series of grays, which are totally hueless and vary in brightness only. (B) But chromatic colors can also be classified according to their brightness. The arrows indicate the brightness of the blue and dark green shown here in relation to the series of grays.*

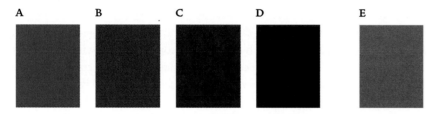

**5.21 Saturation** *The four patches A–D are identical in both hue and brightness. They differ only in saturation, which is greatest for A and decreases from A to D. The gray patch, E, on the far right matches all the other patches in brightness; it was mixed with the blue patch, A, in varying proportions to produce patches B, C, and D.*

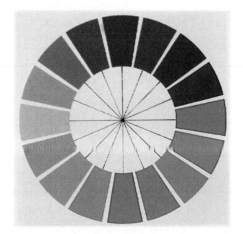

**5.22 The color circle** *The relationship between maximally saturated hues can be expressed by arranging them in a circle according to their perceptual similarity. Note that in this version of the color circle, the spacing of the hues depends on their perceptual properties rather than the wavelengths that give rise to them.*

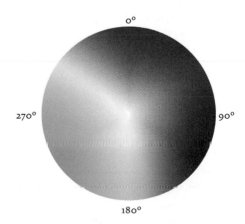

**5.23 The color disk** *The two dimensions of a disk allow the representation of hue and saturation. The hues are positioned at the disk's perimeter. Fully saturated colors are shown at the edge of the disk, completely unsaturated (achromatic) colors at the center.*

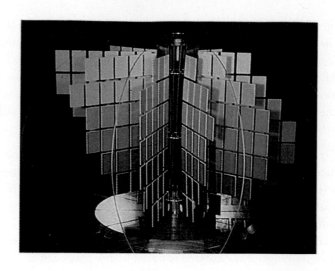

**5.24** *The color solid*    *To represent all colors, one needs three dimensions. Brightness is represented by the central axis, going from darkest (black) to brightest (white). Hue is represented by angular position relative to the color circle. Saturation is the distance from the central vertical axis: the maximal saturation that is possible varies from hue to hue; hence, the different extensions from the central axis. The inside of the solid is shown here by taking individual slices, each of which illustrates, for a single hue, the variations in brightness and saturation.*

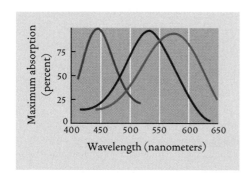

**5.25** *Sensitivity curves of three different cones in the primate retina*    *The retinas of humans and monkeys contain three different kinds of cones, each with its own photopigment that differs in its sensitivity to different regions of the spectrum. One absorbs more of the shorter wavelengths (and is thus more sensitive to light in this spectral region), a second more of the middle wavelengths, a third more of the longer ones. The resulting sensitivity curves are shown here.*

## THE PHYSIOLOGICAL BASIS OF COLOR VISION

What is the physiological basis of color vision? We will consider this issue by subdividing it into two questions: How are wavelengths transduced into receptor activity? And how is the receptor output coded so that it yields the psychological attributes of color, such as the experience of blue or yellow?

### COLOR RECEPTORS

Normal human color vision depends on three different kinds of cones; this is why our color vision is called *trichromatic*. Each of the three cone types responds to a very broad range of wavelengths in the visible spectrum, but their sensitivity curves differ in that one cone type is most sensitive to wavelengths in the short-wave region of the spectrum, the second to wavelengths in the middle range, and the third to wavelengths in the long range (Bowmaker & Dartnall, 1980; MacNichol, 1986; see Figure 5.25).

As we have already noted, all three cone types respond to some extent to a wide range of wavelengths. Therefore, we cannot discriminate among wavelengths simply by noting which cones are responding—generally all are. What is crucial is the relative rates of response by the three cone types. For an input of 480 nanometers, for example, the "short-preferring" and "middle-preferring" cones will respond equally, and their response will be approximately double the response of the "long-preferring" cones. It is this pattern of response that specifies the wavelength; other patterns indicate other wavelengths.

### THE YOUNG-HELMHOLTZ THEORY

These observations are broadly consistent with a view proposed in the late nineteenth century by Thomas Young and Hermann von Helmholtz. According to the *Young-Helmholtz theory*, stimulation by red light strongly activates the long-preferring receptors and only weakly activates the other two receptors; they argued that it is this combination that gives rise to the experience of red. Similarly, stimulation by blue light strongly activates the short-preferring receptors and only weakly activates the other two; this is what gives rise to the perception of blue. And, finally, stimulation by green light strongly excites the medium-preferring receptors and only weakly activates the other receptors; this gives rise to the perception of green. All other colors are then derived from mixtures of these three primary experiences.

Young first proposed this view in 1802; Helmholtz's refinements of the theory arrived in 1866. Today, these claims fit reasonably well with what we know about receptor function and the spectral sensitivities of the three cone types. The claims also fit well with some basic facts about color mixing. Artists have known for years that three pigments can be mixed together to produce a wide variety of colors; better still, three different-colored lights can be mixed (in appropriate proportions) to produce any of the colors we can perceive. (This is how a television or computer monitor produces all of the colors that appear on the screen.) These observations strongly suggest a system of color vision based on three basic elements, just as the Young-Helmholtz theory suggests.

## COMPLEMENTARY HUES

The trichromatic analysis of color vision allows us to explain how we discriminate between lights of different wavelengths. For each wavelength, there is an identifiable pattern in the relative firing rates of the three cone types. If there is strong firing only from the short-preferring cones, the wave length is likely to be around 430 nanometers. Equal firing from the short-preferring and medium-preferring cones, with only modest firing from the long-preferring cones, indicates that the wavelength is 480 nanometers. And so on for other wavelengths.

In addition, the Young-Helmholtz theory asserts that three colors—red, green, and blue—have special status, since each maximally stimulates one of the three receptors. This fits with the fact that these colors do look relatively pure to most observers, in contrast to a color such as purple, say, which looks like a mixture of primary colors (in this case, red and blue).

But other facts seem not to fit with the Young-Helmholtz view. For example, most observers agree that yellow looks like a primary color—that is, it does not look like a mixture. But this fact has no explanation within trichromatic theory, since, in this theory, yellow is not considered a primary color (Bornstein, 1973).

Trichromatic theory also does not explain the fact that, in important ways, colors come in pairs. For example, every hue has a *complementary color*—another hue that, if mixed with the first in appropriate proportions, produces gray. (This is true, at least, if we mix together lights of the appropriate colors; things work a bit differently if we mix paints or crayons or some other pigments, rather than lights; see Figure 5.26.)

The "pairing" of colors is also evident in the phenomenon known as *simultaneous color contrast*, the chromatic counterpart of brightness contrast. *Color contrast* refers to the fact that any chromatic region in the visual field tends to induce its complementary

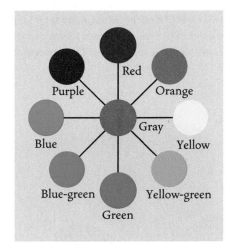

*Complementary hues* *Any hue will yield gray if additively mixed (in the correct proportion) with a hue on the opposite side of the color circle. Such hue pairs are complementaries. Some complementary hues are shown here linked by a line across the circle's center. Of particular importance are the two complementary pairs that contain the four unique hues: red-green and blue-yellow.*

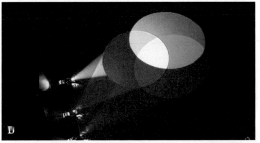

*5.26* *Different ways to mix color* *Most of the colors we perceive are not "pure" hues—composed of just one wavelength; instead, most are mixes of different hues. Actually, there are two ways to mix colors. When an artist mixes pigments or when color filters are placed on top of each other (A), this is subtractive mixture. In this case, each pigment or each filter absorbs its own set of wavelengths, and the only wavelengths that emerge are the ones absorbed by none of the pigments or filters. Said differently, each pigment or filter "subtracts" its set of wavelengths from the initial set, and the perceived color depends on what is left over after this subtraction. That is why a (subtractive) mixture of three sufficiently different colors produces dark gray. When lights are mixed together (B), in contrast, this is additive mixture. Now, each light contributes its own wavelengths, and the resulting mix can be thought of as the "sum" of these contributions. In this case, a mixture of appropriately chosen colors produces white.*

**5.27 Color contrast** *The gray patches on the blue and yellow backgrounds are physically identical. But they do not look that way. To begin with, there is a difference in perceived brightness: The patch on the blue looks brighter than the one on the yellow, a result of brightness contrast. There is also a difference in perceived hue, for the patch on the blue looks somewhat yellowish, while that on the yellow looks bluish. This is color contrast, a demonstration that hues tend to induce their antagonists in neighboring areas.*

**5.28 Negative afterimage** *Stare at the center of the figure for a minute or two, and then look at a white piece of paper. Blink once or twice; the negative afterimage will appear within a few seconds, showing the rose in its correct colors.*

color in adjoining areas. For example, a gray patch will tend to look bluish if surrounded by yellow, yellowish if surrounded by blue, and so on (Figure 5.27).

A similar phenomenon involves temporal relationships, rather than spatial ones. Here, too, we see the apparent "pairing" of colors, with each member of a complementary pair able to induce the other member of the same pair. Concretely, suppose that we stare at a green patch for a while and then look at a white wall. We will see a *negative afterimage* of the patch, in this case, a reddish spot (Figure 5.28). In the same fashion, a brief glance at a brightly lit red bulb will make us see a dark greenish shape when we subsequently look at a white screen. Likewise, staring at a blue patch will produce a yellow afterimage, a glance at a yellow bulb will produce a blue afterimage, and so on. In general, negative afterimages have the complementary hue of the original stimulus—in essence, the afterimage will be the "opposite" color of the stimulus (and this is why these afterimages are called *negative*).

## THE OPPONENT-PROCESS THEORY

What produces this pairing of hues? And why is it that yellow looks relatively pure to the human eye and not at all like a mixture? These observations can be accounted for by the *opponent-process theory*, first suggested by Ewald Hering but then developed in crucial ways by Leo Hurvich and Dorothea Jameson. This theory begins with the fact that we have three cone types, as we have already discussed. The output from these cone types, however, is then the input for another layer of neural mechanisms, which recode the signal into three opponent-process pairs: red-green, blue-yellow, and black-white. These pairs are said to involve an "opponent process" because the two members of each

*Leo Hurvich and Dorothea Jameson*

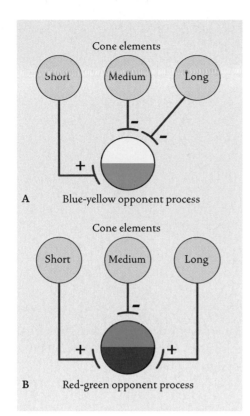

**A**    Blue-yellow opponent process

**B**    Red-green opponent process

**5.29    From receptors to opponent-process pairs    A simplified presentation of a neural system in which the three receptor elements feed into two color opponent-process pairs. (A) The blue-yellow system is excited by the short-wave receptors and inhibited by the medium- and the long-wave receptors. If excitation outweighs inhibition, the opponent-process signals blue; if inhibition outweighs excitation, it signals yellow; if excitation and inhibition are equal, there is no signal at all and we see gray. (B) The red-green system. This is excited by both the short-wave and the long-wave receptor elements, and is inhibited by the medium-wave elements. If excitation outweighs inhibition, the system signals red; if inhibition outweighs excitation, it signals green; if excitation and inhibition are equal, there is no signal and we see gray.**

pair are antagonists: excitation of one member automatically inhibits the other (Figure 5.29) (Hurvich & Jameson, 1957).

*The Two Hue Pairs*    According to the opponent-process theory, the experience of hue depends on two of the opponent-process pairs—red-green and blue-yellow. Each of these opponent-process pairs can be likened to a balance. If one arm (say, the blue process) goes down, the other arm (its opponent, yellow) necessarily goes up. The hue we actually see depends on the positions of the two balances (Figure 5.30). If the red-green balance is tipped toward red and the blue-yellow balance toward blue (excitation of red and blue with concomitant inhibition of green and yellow), the perceived hue will be violet. If the red-green system is in balance, and the blue-yellow system tips toward blue, unique blue is perceived (that is, blue with no trace of red or green). The three other unique hues are coded in a similar fashion. (For example, unique red is perceived when the blue-yellow system is in balance, and the red-green system tips toward red.) If both hue systems are in balance, there will be no hue at all, and the resulting color will be seen as achromatic (that is, without hue).

## THE PHYSIOLOGICAL BASIS OF OPPONENT PROCESSES

When first proposed, the opponent-process mechanism was only an inference, based on the perceptual phenomena of color vision. This inference was subsequently confirmed, however, by single-cell recordings (see Chapter 2), which show that some neurons, in the retina and higher up, behave very much as the opponent-process theory would lead one to expect.

As an example, consider studies of the visual pathway of the rhesus monkey, whose color vision seems to be very similar to ours. Some of the cells in this pathway behave as though they were part of a blue-yellow system. If the retina is stimulated by blue light, these cells fire more rapidly. If the same area is exposed to yellow light, the firing rate is

Light of 450 nanometers

Hue: Blue + Red = Violet

**5.30    The opponent-process hue systems    The diagram shows how opponent-process theory interprets our response to light of a particular wavelength. In the example, the light is in the short-wave region of the visible spectrum, specifically, 450 nanometers. This will affect both the blue-yellow and red-green systems. It will tip the blue-yellow balance toward blue, and the red-green balance toward red. The resulting hue will be a mixture of red and blue (that is, violet).**

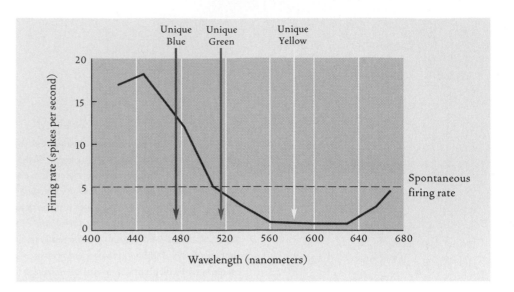

*5.31   Opponent-process cells in the visual system of a monkey   The figure shows the average firing rate of blue-yellow cells to light of different wavelengths. These cells are excited by shorter wavelengths and inhibited by longer wavelengths, analogous to the cells in the human system that signal the sensation "blue."*

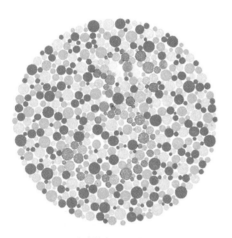

*5.32   Testing for color blindness   A plate used to test for color blindness. To pick out the number in the plate, an observer has to be able to discriminate certain hues. Persons with normal color vision can do it and will see the number 3. Persons with red-green color blindness cannot do it.*

inhibited (Figure 5.31). Other cells show a similar antagonistic pattern when stimulated by red light or green (De Valois, 1965). All of this is exactly what one might expect if these cells embody the mechanisms proposed by the opponent-process theory.

## COLOR BLINDNESS

Most mammals have some degree of color vision (Jacobs, 1993), as do most humans. A small proportion of the population, however, does not respond to color as the rest of us do. The vast majority of these cases are men; some form of color-vision defect is found in 8 percent of all males as compared to only .03 percent of females.

Deficiencies in color vision come in various forms. Some involve a missing visual pigment, others a defective opponent process, and many involve malfunction at both levels (Hurvich, 1981). Most common is a confusion of reds with greens; least common is total color blindness in which no hues can be distinguished at all. Interestingly, these problems are rarely noticed in everyday life, and color-blind people can spend many years without even realizing that they are color blind. They call stop signs "red," just as anyone else does, and grass "green." And, presumably, they spend much of their lives believing that others perceive colors just as they do. Their color blindness can be confirmed, therefore, only with special tests, similar to the one shown in Figure 5.32.

How does the world look to someone who is color blind? This question long seemed unanswerable, since most color-blind individuals have no way to compare their experience to that of an individual with normal color vision, and so no way to describe the difference. However, one unusual person (one of the rare women with a color-vision defect) was red-green color blind in one eye but had normal color vision in the other. She was able to describe what she saw with the defective eye by using the color language she had learned to use with her other eye. As she described it, with the color-blind eye she saw only grays, blues, and yellows. Red and green hues were altogether absent, as if one of the opponent-process pairs were missing (Graham & Hsia, 1954).

## PERCEIVING SHAPES

The perception of color is important to us—whether in enhancing our appreciation of art or, more practically, in allowing us to distinguish a ripe fruit from one that is green. But other aspects of perception are at least as important. After all, a color-blind individ-

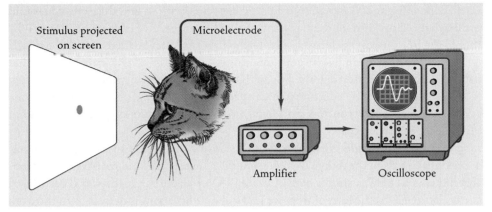

5.33    *Recording from the visual system of a cat*
*The experimental setup for recording neural responses from the visual system of a cat. An anesthetized cat has one eye propped open so that visual stimulation can be directed to particular regions of the retina. A microelectrode picks up neural impulses from a single cell in the optic system, amplifies them, and displays them on an oscilloscope.*

ual can live a perfectly normal life. But not so an individual who is unable to discriminate among shapes or forms, or an individual unable to recognize a square or a circle. These individuals (known as *visual agnosics*) are dramatically impaired in their functioning. We need to ask, therefore, how the visual system achieves the perception of shape. This achievement turns out to be quite complex; so while we begin addressing it in this chapter, the issues discussed here will carry over into Chapter 6.

## FEATURE DETECTORS

How do we perceive the contours that outline and define the shape of any particular form? The process begins with specialized detector cells that respond to certain characteristics of the stimulus and to no others—so some respond to curves, others to straight edges, some to contours angled upward, others to contours angled downward, and so forth.

How have these cells been discovered? Recordings from single nerve cells (see Chapter 2) have allowed electrophysiologists to examine how particular cells in the visual system respond to certain stimuli. In these studies, a microelectrode is placed into the optic nerve or, in some studies, the brain of an anesthetized animal. (Special care is taken to protect the well-being of the animal, both for ethical reasons and to allow the investigators to assess how neurons function in an intact, healthy organism.) The eye of the animal is then stimulated by visual inputs of varying brightness and different shapes, at different locations (Figure 5.33). In this fashion, the investigator can learn which stimuli evoke a response (either an increase or a decrease in firing rate) from that cell.

Typically, results show that a cell responds maximally to an input of a certain shape and size at a certain position. This defines the *receptive field* for that cell—the region of a particular shape, size, and location within the visual field to which that cell responds (see Figure 5.34).

For example, certain ganglion cells in a frog's optic nerve respond intensely to a

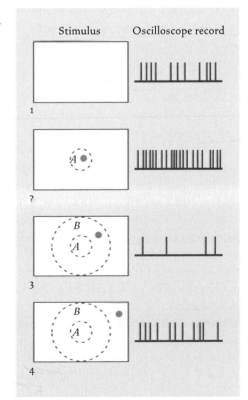

5.34    *Receptive fields on the cat's visual system*
*Using the setup shown in Figure 5.33, stimuli are presented to various regions of the retina. The panels show the firing frequency of a particular ganglion cell. Panel 1 shows the baseline firing rate when no stimulus is presented anywhere. Panel 2 shows the effect when a stimulus is presented anywhere within an inner, central region A on the retina. When stimulated in A, the cell's firing rate goes up. Panel 3 shows what happens in response to a stimulus presented anywhere within the ring-shaped region, B, surrounding region A. Stimulation in B causes the cell's firing rate to go down. Panel 4, finally, shows what happens when a stimulus is presented outside of either A or B, the regions that together comprise the cell's receptive field. Now there is no significant change from the cell's normal baseline.*

small, dark object that is moved into a particular retinal region and then moved around within that region. Stimuli that lack any of these features have little or no effect. Why should the frog possess such fussy cells? Ordinarily, the stimulus that excites these cells is a flying insect—a stimulus of some importance to the frog. It is no wonder, then, that natural selection has provided the frog with this prewired sensory mechanism—often called a "bug detector"—which responds specifically to buglike objects that move in a buglike manner, with a concomitant disregard for all other stimuli (Lettvin, Maturan, McCulloch, & Pitts, 1959).

In the frog and in many other animals, this sort of visual analysis is carried out largely by specialized cells in the retina. In higher animals, such as cats and monkeys (and probably humans as well), a similar sort of analysis takes place, but in the visual cortex and not in the retina itself. Much of what we know about this analysis derives from the work of two physiologists, David Hubel and Torsten Wiesel, who won the Nobel prize for their work. They found that cells in the cat's visual cortex were each "tuned" for a particular type of stimulus. Some cells, for example, fired maximally only when the visual input was a line or an edge of a specific orientation at a specific retinal position. One such cell might respond to a vertical line at one position in the visual field, while another cell might respond to a line tilted to 45 degrees at the same position; still another cell might respond to a vertical line at some other position. In this fashion, the visual field is blanketed by receptive fields, so that lines of any orientation at any position will be detected by the appropriately tuned cell (Hubel & Wiesel, 1959, 1968).

Other cells in the cat's visual cortex are a bit more sophisticated: They, too, fire only in response to a line or edge of a particular orientation, but they are largely indifferent to the line's specific location within the visual field (Figure 5.35). Cells like these serve as *feature detectors*, detecting certain elements within the visual pattern. Other cells, deeper within the visual system, presumably then assemble these now detected elements in order to detect larger configurations and more complex patterns.

Consistent with this suggestion, Hubel and Wiesel were able to locate other cells that responded only to more complicated inputs. For example, some cells responded maximally in response to corners, or angles of certain sizes. Other cells responded to movement patterns—firing maximally only when movement of the appropriate velocity, in the appropriate direction, is in view.

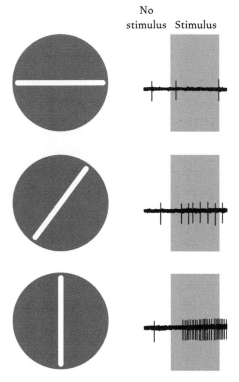

**5.35** *Feature detectors in the visual system of the cat*  **The response of a single cortical cell when stimulated by a slit of light in three different orientations. This cell was evidently responsive to the vertical. A horizontal slit led to no response, a tilted slit led to a slight response, while a vertical slit led to a marked increase in firing.**

No stimulus    Stimulus

## DETECTORS FOR COMPLEX FORMS

How does the visual system organize all these features into the countless and highly complex objects that we can recognize? After all, as we mentioned earlier in the chapter (in our discussion of the empiricists), the world we perceive is not filled with swarms of unassembled features; instead, we perceive whole objects—things that look coherent and that are often familiar and meaningful for us. If the visual system begins by detecting simple features—horizontal and vertical lines, bits of curve and color—how are these pieces assembled to create the complex forms that surround us?

In some cases, the answer to this question may be straightforward: there are simply more detectors. For some complex shapes, particularly those that have special significance for a species, there are cells within the visual system with the sole job of detecting this or that particular stimulus. The "bug detector" in the frog provides one example, and similar cells, of suitable design and sophistication, have also been documented in more complex creatures. For example, certain cells in a monkey's cortex have been shown to respond to pictures of a monkey's face but not at all to nonface stimuli. Other cells seem to respond almost exclusively to pictures of a monkey's hand, whether the hand appears with an open palm or clenched fist, with the fingers pointed up or pointed down (Desimone, Albright, Gross, & Bruce, 1984).

It seems highly unlikely, though, that such built-in mechanisms could account for all the forms that higher animals—especially humans—perceive and recognize. Simple creatures like frogs are able to recognize only a few patterns, making it plausible that they might have specialized detectors for each one. In contrast, humans easily discriminate among a multitude of patterns, and this simple fact speaks powerfully against the idea that we might have specialized detectors for each of them—triangles, squares, apples, apple pies, champagne bottles, cabbages, kings—the list is endless.

Given what we know about "monkey's hand detectors" and the like, perhaps we do possess some cells that do for us what the bug detector does for the frog. But there is little doubt that the vast majority of the forms we recognize are assemblies of lower-level features glued together by experience. As we will see in the next chapter, these lower-level feature detectors are the raw material out of which we construct the infinity of shapes we perceive and recognize. But the way we glue the output of these detectors together is surprisingly complex and will be one of our main concerns in Chapter 6.

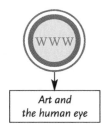

Art and
the human eye

## SOME FINAL THOUGHTS: FROM SENSATION TO PERCEPTION

We have looked at the way in which two sensory systems respond to external stimuli, how they transduce the proximal stimulus and convert it into a neural impulse, how they code the incoming message into the various dimensions of our sensory experience, and how activity in any part of these sensory systems interacts with the activity of other parts. All of this has led us to some understanding of how we come to see bright yellow-greens and hear high-pitched sounds. But it has not yet addressed the question with which we started. How do we come to know about the objects and events outside—not just bright yellow-greens but grassy meadows, not just high-pitched sounds but singing birds? That the sensory systems contribute the raw materials for such knowledge is clear enough. But how do we get from the sensory raw materials to a knowledge of the world outside? This question is traditionally dealt with under the heading of perception, the topic to which we turn next.

## SUMMARY

How do our senses function, and how accurate and complete is the sensory information we receive from them? To what extent is our perception of the world *objective*—true to the sensory information we receive, with a minimum of interpretation? Conversely, to what extent is our perception influenced by our biases, expectations, and hopes?

### THE ORIGINS OF KNOWLEDGE

1. The study of sensory processes grew out of questions about the origin of human knowledge. John Locke and other adherents of *empiricism* argued that all knowledge comes through stimuli that excite the senses. We can distinguish two kinds of stimuli. One is the *distal stimulus*, an object or event in the world outside. The other is the *proximal stimulus*, the pattern of physical stimulus energies that impinges on a given sensory surface. The only way to get information about distal stimuli is through the proximal stimuli these give rise to. This leads to theoretical problems, for we perceive many qualities—depth, constant size, and shape—that are not given in the proximal stimulus. *Empiricists* try to overcome such difficulties by asserting that much of perception is built up through learning by *association*. This view has been challenged by *nativism*, a

view espoused by Immanuel Kant and others who believe that the sensory input is organized according to a number of *built-in categories*.

2. The path to sensory experience or sensation begins with a proximal stimulus. This is *transduced* into a nervous impulse by specialized *receptors*, is usually further modified by other parts of the nervous system, and finally leads to a *sensation*. *Psychophysics*, a branch of sensory psychology, tries to relate the characteristics of the physical stimulus to both the quality and intensity of the sensory experience. The founder of psychophysics, Gustav Fechner, studied sensory intensity by determining the ability of subjects to discriminate between stimulus intensities. The *difference threshold* is the change in the intensity of a given stimulus that is just large enough to be detected, producing a *just-noticeable difference, or jnd*. According to *Weber's law*, the jnd is a constant fraction of the intensity of the standard stimulus. Fechner generalized Weber's law to express a wider relationship between sensory intensity and physical intensity. This is *Fechner's law*, which states that the strength of a sensation grows as the logarithm of stimulus intensity.

3. A way of disentangling sensory sensitivity and response bias is provided by *signal-detection theory*. In a typical detection experiment, the stimulus is presented on some trials and absent on others. In this procedure, there can be two kinds of errors: a *miss* (saying a stimulus is absent when it is present) and a *false alarm* (saying it is present when it is absent). Their relative proportion is partially determined by *expectation* and by a *payoff matrix*. An individual's *sensitivity* to the stimulus is assessed by the proportion of hits and correct negatives relative to his number of misses and false alarms. His criterion for responding (e.g., saying "yes" when in doubt, or "no") is measured by the proportions of yes and no responses.

4. This general approach has applications to many other situations in which one has to decide between two alternatives but cannot be certain of the outcome, as in cases of juror decisions ("innocent" or "guilty"), or medical diagnosis ("yes, there is a tumor," "no, there is no tumor").

5. *Sensory codes* are the rules by which the nervous system translates the properties of the proximal stimulus into neural impulses. Some codes are for *psychological intensity*, such as changes in loudness and brightness. Such changes are usually coded by the rates of firing by the neurons, and also by the sheer number of neurons triggered by the stimulus. Other codes are for *sensory quality*. According to the *doctrine of specific nerve energies*, such differences in sensory quality (e.g., the difference between seeing and hearing) are not caused by differences in the stimuli themselves but by the different nervous structures that these stimuli excite. In some cases, qualitative differences within a *sensory modality* are best described by *specificity theory*, which holds that different sensory qualities (sweet versus sour; red versus green) are signaled by different neurons, just as the different sense modalities (vision versus pressure) are signaled by different nerves. An alternative position is *pattern theory*, which holds that certain sensory qualities arise because of different patterns of activation across a whole set of neurons.

## THE FUNCTIONING OF THE SENSES

6. Different sense modalities have different functions and mechanisms. One group of senses provides information about the body's own movements and location. Skeletal motion is sensed through *kinesthesis*, bodily orientation by the *vestibular* organs located in the inner ears. The various skin senses inform the organism of what is directly adjacent to its own body. There are at least four different skin sensations: *pressure*, *warmth*, *cold*, and *pain*.

## HEARING

7. The sense of hearing, or audition, informs us of pressure changes that occur at a distance. Its stimulus is a disturbance of the air that is propagated in the form of sound waves. These can vary in *amplitude* and *frequency*, and may be simple or complex.

8. Sound waves set up vibrations in the eardrum that are then transmitted by the *ossicles* to the *oval window*, whose movements create waves in the *cochlea* of the inner ear. Within the cochlea is the *basilar membrane*, which contains the auditory receptors that are stimulated by the membrane's deformation. According to the *place theory*, the sensory experience of pitch is based on the place of the membrane that is most stimulated, each place being especially responsive to a particular wave frequency and generating a particular pitch sensation. According to the *frequency theory*, the experience of pitch depends on the firing frequency of the auditory nerve. But since very low frequency waves deform the whole membrane just about equally, modern theorists believe that both the place of deformation and firing frequency of the auditory nerve are important. It turns out that the perception of higher frequencies depends on the place stimulated on the basilar membrane, while perception of lower frequencies depends on neural firing frequency.

## VISION

9. Vision is our primary distance sense. Its stimulus is light, which can vary in *intensity* and *wavelength*. Many of the structures of the eye, such as the *lens* and the *iris*, serve to control the amount of light entering the eye and to fashion a proper proximal stimulus, the *retinal image*. Once on the retina, the light stimulus is transduced into a neural

impulse by the visual receptors, the *rods* and *cones*. *Acuity* is greatest in the *fovea*, where the density of the receptors (here, cones) is greatest.

10. According to the *duplex theory of vision*, rods and cones differ in function. The rods operate at low light intensities and are insensitive to differences in hue. The cones function at much higher illumination levels and are responsible for sensations of color. Further evidence for the duplex theory comes from differences in the receptors' *spectral sensitivity*.

11. The first stage in the transformation of light into a neural impulse is a photochemical process that involves the breakdown of various visual pigments that are later resynthesized. The pigment in the rods is *rhodopsin*. The cones contain three different pigments but the chemical composition of these pigments is still unknown.

12. The various components of the visual system do not operate in isolation but interact constantly. The visual system actively shapes and transforms the stimulus input (as, indeed, do all sensory systems). One kind of interaction concerns the relation between the signal a neuron is now receiving and the signal it received a moment ago. An example is *sensory adaptation*.

13. Interaction also occurs in space between neighboring regions on the retina. This is shown by *brightness contrast*, an effect that increases as the intensity difference increases between two contrasting regions. Brightness contrast tends to accentuate edges, as in the case of *Mach bands*.

14. The physiological mechanism that underlies these effects is *lateral inhibition*. When any visual receptor is stimulated, it transmits its excitation to other cells that eventually relay this signal to the brain. But the receptor's excitation also stimulates lateral neurons, which make contact with neighboring cells and inhibit the activation of these neighbors. Lateral inhibition shows that the visual system is refining the stimulus information from the very start, emphasizing some aspects of the input and understating others.

15. Visual sensations have a qualitative character—they vary in *color*. Color sensations can be ordered by reference to three dimensions: *hue, brightness,* and *saturation*. The *color circle embodies the perceptual relations among the differ-*

ent hues; the *color solid* summarizes the perceptual relations among all three of the color dimensions.

16. Normal human color vision is *trichromatic*, depending on three cone types, which are respectively most sensitive to wavelengths in the short-, middle-, and long-wave regions of the visible spectrum. These facts are consistent with a view proposed in the late nineteenth century by Thomas Young and Hermann von Helmholtz. Their claims fit reasonably well with what we know about the spectral sensitivities of the three cone types, and some basic facts about color mixing. But other facts do not seem to fit, including the fact that yellow does not look like a mixture, and that colors come in pairs as shown by the phenomena of *complementary colors, simultaneous color contrast,* and *negative afterimages*.

17. These problems are addressed by the *opponent-process theory*, proposed by Hurvich and Jameson. This theory assumes that the output of the three cone types constitutes the input for a further layer of neural mechanisms, which recode the signal into three *opponent-process* pairs: *red-green, blue-yellow,* and *black-white*. The two members of each pair are antagonists, so that excitation of one member automatically inhibits the other. Further evidence for the opponent-process view comes from single-cell recordings of rhesus monkeys and some phenomena of color blindness.

18. Shape perception depends on specialized *detector cells* that respond to certain characteristics of the stimulus and to no others, such as curves and straight edges. These detectors have been discovered by single nerve cell recordings taken while the eye of the animal is stimulated by visual inputs. Results show that certain cells respond maximally to an input of a certain shape and size at a certain position, which defines their *receptive field*. An example is the "bug detector" in a frog's retina. In cats and monkeys, such detectors are found in the visual cortex, "tuned" for a particular type of stimulus, such as a line or an edge of a specific orientation, which serve as *feature detectors*, detecting certain elements within the visual pattern. Other cells, deeper within the visual system, will then presumably assemble these elements in order to detect larger configurations and more complex patterns.

CHAPTER

6

# PERCEPTION

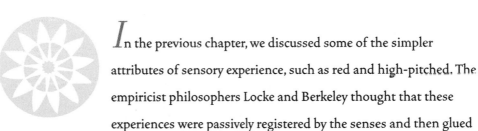In the previous chapter, we discussed some of the simpler attributes of sensory experience, such as red and high-pitched. The empiricist philosophers Locke and Berkeley thought that these experiences were passively registered by the senses and then glued together, by means of associations, to form more complex perceptions. As they saw it, the creation of these associations was in turn also a passive affair: two ideas were associated in the mind, they argued, merely because these ideas had been experienced together in the past. Associations, like the sensations themselves, are imposed on us from the outside.

But the eye is much more than a camera, the ear more than a microphone. From the very start, both sensory systems actively transform their stimulus inputs, emphasizing areas of difference or contrast within the input and minimizing areas of uniformity.

This active organization of the stimulus input is impressive enough when we consider the experience of simple sensory attributes. It becomes even more dramatic when we turn to the broader question of how we apprehend objects and events in the world around us—how we see, not just something bright or something red, but a bright red apple.

## THE COMPLEXITY OF PERCEPTION

One might think that there is nothing simpler than perceiving. One opens one's eyes and sees the world, effortlessly recognizing the objects that are in view. Where, therefore, is the mystery, the complexity, that needs to be explained? But there is complexity here. One problem lies in how we manage to grasp the meaning of the visual input. Having perceived the apple, how do we manage to interpret it as an edible fruit—one that grows on trees, keeps the doctor away, caused the expulsion from Eden, and so on? As it turns out, though, these are not the most basic questions for the student of perception. The deeper issue is not why we see a particular kind of object, but rather why we see any object at all. Suppose we show the apple to someone who has never seen this type of fruit before. He will not know what it is or what it is for, but he will certainly see it as some round, red thing of whose tangible existence he has no doubt—in short, he will perceive it as an object.

How do we accomplish this feat? After all, the apple is known to us (at least visually) only through the proximal stimulus it projects onto our retina, and this proximal stimulus is two dimensional and constantly changing. It gets smaller or larger depending on our distance from the apple; it stimulates different regions of the retina each time we move our head or eyes. How do we see past these continual variations in the proximal stimulus to perceive the constant properties of the external object? For that matter, how do we manage to identify the apple's boundaries, treating all of the apple's parts as one unit, separate from those of the banana right beside it? How do we compensate for the fact that part of the apple's form is hidden from view by the edge of the fruit bowl? These

*The problem of perception   How do we come to perceive the world as it is—to see the flags as smaller than the boat, to see the wall extending continuously behind the people that block some portion of it from view, and so on?*

achievements, simple as they seem, turn out to be impressively complicated, and they are achievements without which perception cannot proceed.

In short, before we can decide whether the object we are looking at is an apple (or a baseball or a human head or whatever), we must organize the sensory world into a coherent scene in which there are real objects (such as apples) and real events. Likewise, before we can take a walk down a hallway, we need to perceive the layout of the hallway—which obstacles are nearby and which are far off, whether the people we see are standing still or moving across our path. To accomplish all of this, we have to answer three important questions about whatever it is we see (or hear or feel) in the world outside: Where is it? Where is it going? And, most important, what is it? Each of these questions is crucial, since our very existence demands that we act differently toward a potential mate than toward a lamppost, toward a tiger far away than one nearby, and toward a car streaking toward us than one zooming away.

Our discussion will begin with the question of where the object is and in particular how we determine whether it is nearby or far away.

# THE PERCEPTION OF DEPTH: WHERE IS IT?

The image that falls on the retina has only two dimensions, but we obviously are able to perceive a three-dimensional world. This capacity is crucial for us—without it, our ability to move around would be horribly compromised. How could we walk if we did not know how far away the various obstacles were? How could we reach for the coffee cup if we did not know how far it was from us—or whether it was within reach at all? Questions like these have led investigators to a search for *depth cues*, features of the stimulus situation that might indicate how far an object is from the observer, or how far it is from other objects in the world.

## BINOCULAR CUES

One important cue for depth comes from the fact that we are binocular creatures— that is, we have two eyes. Our eyes obviously look out onto the world from slightly different positions, and, as a result, each eye has a slightly different view of the world. This difference between the two eyes' views is called *binocular disparity*, and it provides important information about depth relationships in the world (Figure 6.1).

Binocular disparity can induce the perception of depth even if no other distance cues are present. For example, the bottom panels of Figure 6.1 show the views that would be received by each eye while looking at a pair of nearby objects. If we separately present each of these views to the appropriate eye (for example, by drawing the views on two cards and placing one card in front of each eye), we can obtain a striking impression of depth. (The popular child's toy, the Viewmaster, works in the same way, presenting two slightly different pictures to the two eyes; many years ago, the stereopticon viewer used the same principle.)

## MONOCULAR CUES

Binocular disparity is a powerful (and probably innate) determinant of perceived depth. Yet we can perceive depth even with one eye closed, and so, clearly, there must also be cues for depth perception that come from the image obtained with one eye alone. These are the *monocular depth cues*.

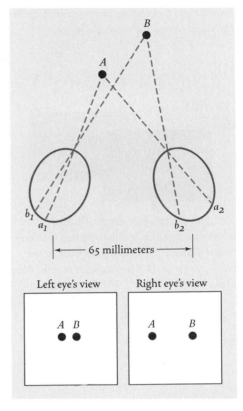

**6.1 Retinal disparity** *Two points, A and B, at different distances from the observer, present somewhat different retinal images. In the left-eye's view, the image cast by A and that cast by B are close together; in the right-eye's view, the images are further apart. This disparity between the views serves as a powerful cue for depth.*

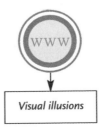

Visual illusions

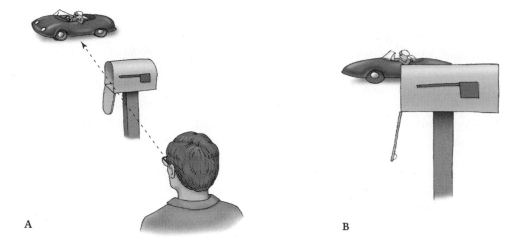

**6.2 Pictorial cues** *The observer is looking at the sports car, but the mailbox blocks part of his view (A). Panel B shows how this will appear from the observer's point of view. The fact that the mailbox blocks the view is a simple but powerful cue that the mailbox must be closer to the observer than the sports car is.*

A                                                                    B

**6.3 Interposition with simple displays** *Depth cues can also be demonstrated with very simple displays. Because of interposition, the red rectangle in the figure appears to be in front of the blue one.*

Some of the monocular depth cues have been exploited for centuries by artists in order to create an impression of depth on a flat surface—that is, within a picture. Hence, these cues are called *pictorial cues*. In each case, these cues exploit simple principles of physics. For example, imagine a situation in which an observer is trying to admire a sports car, but a mailbox stands between them (Figure 6.2A). In this case, the mailbox will inevitably block the view, because it obstructs the path of the light traveling from the car to the observer. This is a fact about the physical world, but it also provides us with a cue that we can use in judging distance, a cue known as *interposition* (Figure 6.2B). In our example, this cue tells the observer that the mailbox is closer than the car; in the case shown in Figure 6.3, it tells us that the red rectangle is closer than the blue.

**6.4 Linear perspective as a cue for depth**

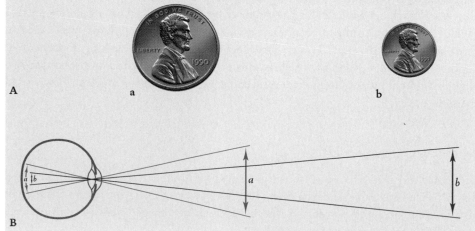

**6.5 Relative size** *(A) All other things being equal, the larger of two otherwise identical figures will seem to be closer than the smaller one. This is a consequence of the simple geometry of vision illustrated in (B). Objects a and b are equal in size, but because they are at different distances from the observer, they will project retinal images of different sizes.*

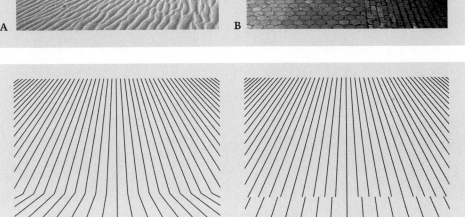

6.6 *Texture gradients as cues for depth*
*Uniformly textured surfaces produce texture gradients that provide information about depth: as the surface recedes, the size of the texture elements decreases, and the density of these elements increases. Such gradients may be produced by sand ripples (A), or stones in a courtyard (B).*

6.7 *The effect of changes in texture gradients Such changes provide important information about spatial arrangements in the world. Examples are (A) an upward tilt at a corner; and (B) a sudden drop.*

In the same way, distant objects necessarily produce a smaller retinal image than nearby objects of the same size; this is a fact about optics. But this physical fact again provides us with information we can use, and, in particular, provides the basis for the cues of *linear perspective* and *relative size* (Figures 6.4 and 6.5).

A related sort of pictorial cue is provided by *texture gradients*. Consider what meets the eye when we look at cobblestones on a patio or patterns of sand on a beach. The retinal projection of the sand or the cobblestones shows a pattern of continuous change, with the elements of the texture growing smaller and smaller as they become more and more distant. This pattern of change by itself can reveal the spatial layout of the relevant surfaces (Figure 6.6), and if, in addition, there are discontinuities in these textures, this too can tell us a great deal about how the surfaces are laid out in depth (Figure 6.7; Gibson, 1950, 1966).

## THE PERCEPTION OF DEPTH
## THROUGH MOTION

Whenever we move our heads, the images projected by the objects in our world necessarily move across the retina. For reasons of geometry, the projected images of nearby objects move more than those of more distant ones. The direction of motion across the retina depends on where we are pointing our eyes. Points closer to us than the target of our gaze appear to be moving in a direction opposite to our own, while points farther away appear to be moving in the same direction we are. This entire pattern of motion in the retinal images provides a further depth cue, called *motion parallax* (Helmholtz, 1909; see Figure 6.8).

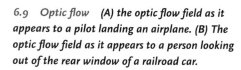

6.8  *Motion parallax*  *As the bicyclist moves forward, her position changes relative to stationary objects in her environment. As a result, these objects are displaced (and therefore seem to move) relative to her and each other. The rate of displacement is indicated by the red arrows: the thicker these arrows, the more quickly the objects seem to move. The direction of the observer's movement is indicated by the blue arrows. (For simplicity's sake, we assume that, as the bicyclist moves forward, she keeps her eyes fixed on the horizon.)*

Position 2 ◄———————— Viewer ———————— Position 1

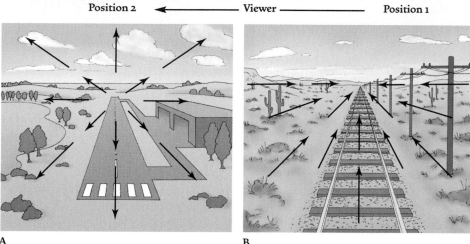

6.9  *Optic flow*  *(A) the optic flow field as it appears to a pilot landing an airplane. (B) The optic flow field as it appears to a person looking out of the rear window of a railroad car.*

A                                B

A different motion cue is produced when we move toward or away from objects. As we approach an object, its image gets larger and larger; as we move away, it gets smaller. In addition, as we move toward an object, the pattern of stimulation across the entire visual field changes, resulting in a pattern of *optic flow*, which provides crucial information about depth and also plays a large role in the coordination of our movements (Gibson, 1950, 1979; Figure 6.9).

## THE ROLE OF REDUNDANCY

We have noted that the pictorial cues for depth derive from simple facts of geometry and optics. The same is true for the other depth cues. The information we call binocular disparity, for example, derives in a straightforward fashion from the position of the two eyes and the fact that light travels in a straight path. It is just a fact of our world, therefore, that these cues are available to us as potential sources of information about distance and depth.

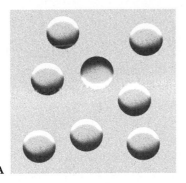 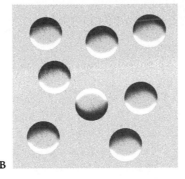

**A**          **B**

*More monocular cues to depth: light and shadow* **Observers are sensitive to many different depth cues, including depth from shading. (A) shows eight circular objects. To most viewers the one in the middle looks concave, indented, whereas the other seven look as if they are bulging out. (B) shows the same figure rotated 180 degrees. Now the middle object looks convex, while the other seven seem concave. The reason is the location of the shadows. When the shadow is at the bottom, the object looks convex; when at the top, the object looks concave. This makes good biological sense, since light almost always comes from above.**

What is perhaps surprising, however, is that we make use of all these cues (as well as some others we have not described). Why did natural selection favor a system influenced by so many cues, especially since the information provided by these cues is often redundant? After all, what we can learn from linear perspective is often the same as what we can learn from motion parallax. Why then should we be sensitive to both?

The most likely answer is that different distance cues become important in different circumstances. For example, binocular disparity is a powerful cue, but it is informative only for objects relatively close by. (For targets farther than thirty feet away, the two eyes receive virtually the same image.) Likewise, motion parallax tells us a great deal about the spatial layout of our world, but only if objects are moving. Texture gradients are informative only if there is a suitably uniform texture in view. So while these various cues are often redundant, each can provide information in circumstances in which the others cannot. By being sensitive to all, we are able to judge depth in nearly any situation we encounter.

# THE PERCEPTION OF MOVEMENT: WHAT IS IT DOING?

It is one thing to see someone attractive across a crowded room; it is quite another to see that person smile and walk toward you. Plainly, then, we want to know what an object is and where it is located, but we also want to know what it is doing. Put another way, we want to perceive events as well as objects. And to do this, we must be able to perceive movement,

## RETINAL MOTION

One might think that we see things move because they produce an image that moves across the retina. In fact, some cells in the visual cortex do seem responsive to such movements on the retina. These cells are *direction specific*, firing if a stimulus moves across their receptive field from, say, left to right but not if the stimulus moves from right to left. (Other cells, of course, show the reverse pattern.) These cells are therefore well suited to act as *motion detectors* (see, for example, Vaultin & Berkeley, 1977).

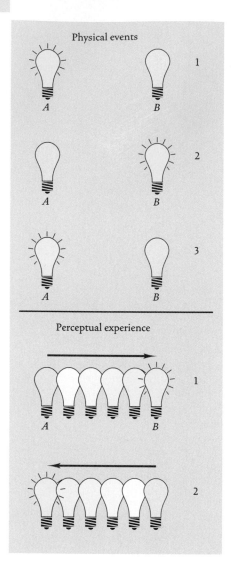

Physical events

*A*    *B*    1

*A*    *B*    2

*A*    *B*    3

Perceptual experience

*A*    *B*    1

2

**6.10  Apparent movement**  *The sequence of optical events that produces apparent movement. Light A flashes at time 1, followed by light B at time 2, then back to light A at time 3. If the time intervals are appropriately chosen, the perceptual experience will be of a light moving from left to right and back.*

## APPARENT MOVEMENT

Further evidence makes it clear, however, that retinal motion is only part of the story. Suppose we turn on a light in one location in the visual field, then quickly turn it off, and after an appropriate interval (somewhere between 30 and 200 milliseconds) turn on a second light in a different location. The result is *apparent movement.* The light appears to travel from one point to another, even though there was no stimulation—let alone movement—in the intervening region (Figure 6.10). This phenomenon is perceptually overwhelming; given the right intervals, it is indistinguishable from real movement (Wertheimer, 1912). It is an effect that has numerous technological applications and is why, for example, people and objects seen in movies seem to move. (Movies, of course, actually consist of a sequence of appropriately timed still pictures.)

This phenomenon underscores the fact that motion can be perceived even when there is no motion of an image across the retina. Instead, all we need is an appropriately timed change in position. Something is here at one moment and there at the next. If the timing is right, the nervous system interprets this as evidence that this something has moved.

## EYE MOVEMENTS

A further complication arises from the fact that our eyes are constantly moving, and this creates a continuous series of changes in the retinal image, even when we are inspecting a static scene. Given this fact, why do we perceive the world as stationary? One hypothesis is that the perception of motion depends on the relative positions of the objects in our view. If we move our eyes while looking at a chair, the retinal image of the chair is displaced, but so is the image of the lamp alongside the chair, the image of the floor beneath both chair and lamp, and so on. As a result, there is no movement of one object relative to the others, and perhaps this is what signals the world's stability.

But this cannot be the entire story. As Hermann von Helmholtz showed a century ago, movement will be seen if the eyes are moved by muscles other than their own. To experience this, close one eye and jiggle the outside corner of the other eye (gently!) with a finger. Now the entire world will seem to move around, even though all relationships within the image remain intact. This shows that the perceptual system can sense "motion" even when there are no changes in the spatial relationships on the retina. So we must look elsewhere to explain the fact that we perceive a stable visual world.

A different hypothesis is that the nervous system somehow compensates for the retinal displacements that are produced by voluntary eye movements. The idea here is that when the brain signals the eye muscles to move, it computes the retinal displacement

*Apparent movement created by a series of stills*

that such a movement would produce and then cancels out this amount of movement in interpreting the visual input (Figure 6.11). If, for example, the brain orders the eyes to move 5 degrees to the left, it anticipates that, as a result, the retinal image will shift 5 degrees to the right. This anticipation is then used as a basis for cancelling out the image motion that really does occur as a result of the eye movement, leaving no motion signal overall. (Think of the process algebraically: 5 degrees right of anticipated change minus 5 degrees right of actual change, yielding zero change overall; that zero change, of course, is what is perceived.) In this way, we perceive stationary objects as stationary, even though our eyes are moving (Bridgeman & Stark, 1991).

Proof for this claim comes from studies in which a number of heroic experimenters had themselves injected with drugs that cause temporary paralysis of the eye muscles. They reported that, under these circumstances, the world did appear to jump around whenever they tried to move their eyes, just as the canceling-out theory would predict. The brain ordered the eyes to move, say, 10 degrees to the right, and therefore anticipated that the retinal image would shift 10 degrees to the left. But the eyes were unable to comply with the command, and so no retinal shift took place. In this setting, the normal cancellation process failed, and as a result, the world was seen to jump with each eye movement. (Algebraically, this is 10 degrees left of anticipated change minus no degrees of actual change, yielding 10 degrees left overall. It is this 10-degree overall difference that was interpreted by the visual system as a motion signal.) These studies provide persuasive confirmation of the canceling-out theory (see Matin, Picoult, Stevens, Edwards, & MacArthur, 1982).

## ILLUSIONS OF MOTION

Clearly, then, the perception of motion depends on several factors. Movement of an image across the retina stimulates motion detectors in the visual cortex (and elsewhere in the brain), and this certainly contributes to movement perception. However, the activity of these detectors by itself does not lead to a perception of movement, because the nervous system also needs to compensate for changes in eye or head position, in order to determine whether motion across the retina is produced by an object's movement in the environment or merely by a change in our viewing position. In addition, as we have seen, we can also perceive motion without any motion across the retina; that is the case of apparent motion.

But even with all of this said, a further step is required, because we not only detect motion but also interpret it.

*The Barber-Pole Illusion* Think about an ordinary barber pole. The pole actually rotates from left to right, but we perceive the stripes on the pole as moving upward. Similarly, a spinning spiral shape drawn on a flat surface appears to be moving toward us (or away from us, depending on the direction of spin). These illusions derive from the way the perceptual system interprets the relationship between the view in front of our eyes right now and the view we had just a moment ago. Specifically, the perceptual system must solve the *correspondence problem*, the problem of determining which elements of our current view correspond with which elements were in our view a moment before (Wallach, Weisz, and Adams, 1956; Wallach, 1976).

*Induced Motion* A different sort of perceptual interpretation is illustrated by the phenomenon of *induced motion*. Consider a ball rolling on a billiard table. We see the ball as moving and the table at rest. But why not the other way around? To be sure, we see the ball getting closer and closer to the table's edge, but, at the same time, we also see the table's edge getting closer and closer to the ball. Why, therefore, do we perceive the movement as "belonging" entirely to the ball, while the table seems to be sitting still?

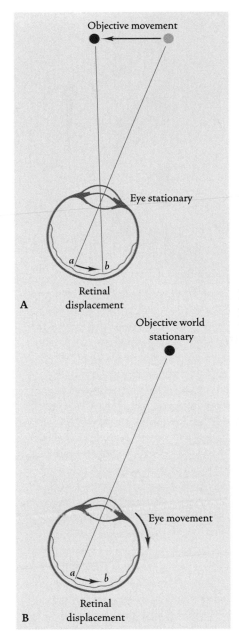

**6.11** *Compensation for eye movements* In (A) an object has moved from right to left, as a result, its retinal image has shifted from location a to location b. In (B) there is no motion in the world; instead, the eye has moved from left to right. But here, too, the object's retinal image shifts from location a to location b. Based only on the retinal information, the displacements in (A) and (B) seem identical. But our brains allow for the displacements caused by changes in eye position. So in (B) the brain would decide that there had been no movement because the motion of the eye was precisely equal (and opposite) to the displacement on the retina.

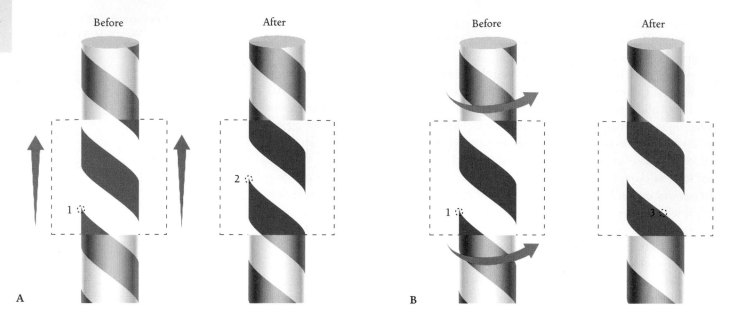

Before · After · Before · After

A · B

One might guess that we see this pattern as we do simply as a result of learning. Perhaps experience has taught us that balls generally move around while tables stay put. But the evidence indicates that what matters is a more general perceptual relationship between the two stimuli: the object that encloses the other tends to act as a frame, which is seen as stationary. In the case of the billiard table, the table serves as a frame against which the ball is seen to move.

In our example, perception and physical reality coincide, because the frame provided by the table is truly stationary. But what happens when the objective situation is reversed? In one study, research participants were shown a luminous rectangular frame in an otherwise dark room. Inside the frame was a luminous dot. In actual fact, the rectangle moved to the right while the dot stayed in place. But the subjects saw something else. They perceived the dot as moving to the left, in the direction opposite to the frame's motion. Participants had correctly perceived that the dot was moving closer and closer to the rectangle's left edge and farther from its right edge. But they misperceived the source of this change. The physical movement of the frame had induced the perceived movement of the enclosed shape (Figure 6.12).

The induced-motion effect is familiar from everyday life as well. The moon seems to sail through the clouds; the base of a bridge seems to float upstream, against the flow of the river's current. In both cases, the surrounded object is seen as moving, and the frame is seen as still—exactly as in the laboratory findings. A related (and sometimes unsettling) phenomenon is *induced motion of the self*. If the participant stands on the bridge that he perceives as moving, he perceives himself moving along with it. The same effect occurs when sitting in a train that is standing in a station. If a train on the adjacent track pulls out, we tend to feel ourselves moving even though we (and the train we are in) are stationary.

**6.12 Induced movement** *Research participants in an otherwise dark room see a luminous dot surrounded by a luminous frame. When the frame is moved upward, participants perceive the dot moving downward, even though it is objectively stationary.*

# FORM PERCEPTION: WHAT IS IT?

So far, we have considered how we know where an object is and where it is going. But we have not yet considered what is probably the most important question of all: How do we perceive and recognize what an object is? In vision, our primary means for recognizing an object is through the perception of its form. To be sure, we sometimes rely on color (a violet) and occasionally on size (a toy model of an automobile), but in the vast majority of cases, form is our major avenue for identifying what we see. The question is how? How do we recognize the myriad forms and patterns that are present in the world around us—triangles and ellipses, skyscrapers and automobiles, elephants and giraffes?

One simple hypothesis (ultimately derived from the work of the early empiricists) is that we have some sort of checklist in our memory for each of the objects we are able to recognize. Does the object have four legs and a very long neck? Is it yellow and brown? If so, it is likely to be a giraffe. Does the object have four straight sides of equal length? If so, then it is a square.

But a bit of reflection shows that things cannot be quite so simple. One problem is the variability of most stimuli: We recognize giraffes from the side or from the front, whether we see them close up or from far away, whether they are lying down or standing up (Figure 6.13). Do we have a different checklist for each of these views? Or do we somehow have a procedure for converting these views into some sort of "standardized view," which we then compare to a checklist? If so, what might that standardization procedure be? Similarly, we often have only partial views of the objects around us, yet we recognize them nonetheless. We see television newscasters as intact human beings, even though we never see their legs; we identify the form in Figure 6.14 as a square, even though one corner is hidden.

A related point is that we can recognize a form even if its component parts are

**6.14 Recognizing partially occluded figures** *We have no trouble recognizing the square, even though one of its corners is hidden. This further supports the argument that we do not have a checklist or template for every object we recognize.*

**6.13 The variability of stimuli we recognize** *We recognize giraffes from the side or from the front, whether we see them close up or from far away. This makes it unlikely that we have a checklist or template for recognizing giraffes; we would need a different template for each of the possible views.*

altered. The shapes in Figure 6.15 are all triangles. They differ in size, in color, in whether they are made up of solid or dotted lines. But this seems not to matter for our perception of the overall shape. The same phenomenon can be observed with sounds: a melody remains the same even when all of its notes are changed by *transposition* to another key, and the same rhythm will be heard whether played on a kettledrum or a glockenspiel.

Observations such as these were crucial for **Gestalt psychology**, a school of psychology whose adherents believed that *organization* is an essential feature of all mental activity. They insisted that a form is not perceived by somehow summing up all its individual components. Instead, they argued that a form is perceptually experienced as a coherent, intact **Gestalt**, a whole that is different from the sum of its parts. (The word *Gestalt* is derived from a German word that means "form" or "entire figure.") Thus, the triangularity of the shapes in Figure 6.15 is not a property of any of the shape's elements; we see that in the fact that we can change the elements in countless ways while preserving our sense of what the shape is. Our sense of the shape, therefore, must derive from the properties of the whole form, taken as a coherent unit.

The Gestalt psychologists clearly had an important point. There is little doubt that a form is not just the sum of its parts. Three angles alone do not make a triangle, no more than a mouth, a nose, and two eyes suffice to make a face. Instead, these forms are defined by the relationships among their elements, and so, to specify the nature of these forms, we need to specify how exactly the parts are bound together. This is a problem to which we will return later in the chapter. First, though, we need to consider what else is known about the broader issue of form perception.

*6.15  Transposition    The perceived form (the triangle) remains the same even if the form is transposed (i.e., created out of an entirely new set of elements).*

## THE ELEMENTS OF FORM

Even with the insights of the Gestalt psychologists acknowledged, most investigators believe that the recognition of a form begins with the detection of *primitive features*, which are as the building blocks of visual perception. This claim is based in part on the physiological findings we discussed in the previous chapter. Various cells in the brain do seem to act as feature detectors, responding selectively to certain elements of visual form. In addition, a number of findings indicate that these simple features do have special priority in our perception of form.

### FREE-FLOATING PRIMITIVES

In an influential series of studies, Anne Treisman argued that primitive visual features can be perceived in an immediate, effortless fashion. One does not have to search the display or analyze its pattern to locate and identify these features. Instead, the features just "pop out" (Treisman, 1986a, b, 1988).

One way of demonstrating this is by means of a *visual search task* in which participants have to indicate whether a certain target is or is not present in a display. When the target is an *O* amidst a field of *V*s, participants find it very quickly (see Figure 6.16). What's more, the number of *V*s in which the *O* is embedded has very little effect on the search time: Participants can locate an *O* hidden within a dozen *V*s almost as quickly as they can locate an *O* sandwiched between only two *V*s. This indicates that the visual system does not have to inspect each of the figures to determine whether it has the relevant properties. (If it did, the larger number of figures would require more time.) Instead, the difference between the *O*s and *V*s jumps out immediately. The same holds for differences in color, orientation, or direction of movement (Treisman & Gelade, 1980; Treisman & Souther, 1985; for a broad review of the relevant evidence, and also some interesting exceptions to this pattern, see Wolfe, 1994).

Of course, the objects we perceive are made up of more than one visual feature. A leaf

*Anne Treisman*

on a tree has a certain shape and position, as well as a certain color, and it is not enough merely to detect all these features individually; they also need to be assembled into the correct packages. We need to perceive that it is the round apple that is red and the leaf that is green, and not the other way around.

Unlike the identification of single features, perceiving a combination of features is not immediate or automatic. Treisman and her collaborators showed their subjects displays that contained items such as a red *F* and a green *X* for about 200 milliseconds, and then asked them to report what they saw. On a fair proportion of the trials, the subjects reported **illusory conjunctions**, such as having seen a green *F* or a red *X*. It seems that subjects were able to perceive the features of this display but were not able to figure out how these features were related to each other. Apparently, then, the coordination of features requires a separate step that occurs after the features are identified.

Confirmation for these claims comes from an individual who had suffered damage to the parietal cortex on both sides of the brain. When looking at a display, this person is able to report accurately what features are present, and can search successfully for targets defined by a single feature. However, the patient fails miserably when asked to search for targets defined by a combination of features and, while still looking at the display, is completely unable to report which features are part of the same object (Robertson, Treisman, Friedman-Hill, & Grabowecky, 1997; also see Cohen & Rafal, 1991; we return to patients like this one, and what we have learned from them, when we consider the role of attention in perceiving). This case provides strong support for the idea that different mechanisms are needed, first, for the detection of features, and then, second, for the integration of these features to form complex wholes; in this patient, the second process is disrupted while the first is perfectly intact.

## PERCEPTUAL SEGREGATION

So far we have considered only the initial steps of form perception: deciding which features are present and how these features go together. The next step is to organize the overall scene, a process known as **visual segregation**.

Suppose the observer looks at the still life in Figure 6.17. To make sense of the picture, the perceptual system must somehow group the elements of the scene appropriately. For one thing, it has to determine what is focal (in this case, the fruit and the bowl) and what can be ignored (at least for now) as background. And since some pieces of fruit will be blocking others, the perceiver must also figure out what goes with what. Portion *B* (one

**6.16 Pop-out in visual search** *An O embedded in an array of Vs pops out immediately. Here, the visual system does not have to inspect each figure in turn to determine whether it is the target. Instead, it conducts a parallel search, inspecting all of the items simultaneously.*

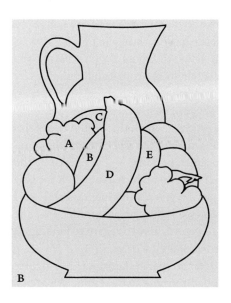

**6.17 Perceptual segregation** *(A) A still life. (B) An overlay designating five different segments of the scene shown in (A). To determine what an object is, the perceptual system must first decide what goes with what: Does portion B go with A, with C, D, or E? Or with none of them?*

6.18 *Figure and ground* *The first step in seeing a form is to segregate it from its background. The part seen as figure appears to be more cohesive and sharply delineated. The part seen as ground seems more formless and to extend behind the figure.*

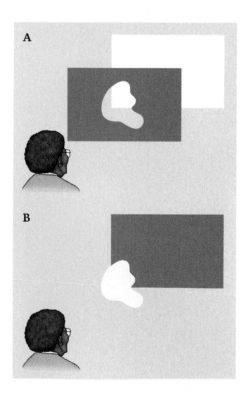

6.19 *Edges belong to the figure* *If we perceive Figure 6.19 as a blue rectangle with a hole in it (A), the edge marks the contour of the hole. The situation is reversed in (B). Now the edge demarcates the white blob, not a break in the blue background. In this sense, the edge belongs to the figure, not the ground.*

half of the apple) must be united with portion *E* (the other half of the apple), even though they are separated by portion *D* (a banana). Portion *B* should not be united with portion *A* (a bunch of grapes), even though they are adjacent and approximately the same color. The bit of the apple hidden from view, or occluded, by the banana must somehow be filled in, so that we perceive an intact apple rather than two apple slices.

This process of visual segregation is sometimes called *perceptual parsing*. It performs the same function for vision that parsing performs for speech. When someone talks to us, our eardrums are exposed to a sound stream that is essentially unbroken. What hits the ears is a sequence of sounds such as

*Thestudentsaidtheteacherisverysmart.*

The listener parses the sound pattern by grouping some sounds together with others, forming individual words, and then parses further by grouping the words into phrases, as in:

*"The student," said the teacher, "is very smart."*

In many cases, the listener may even discover that there are alternate ways of parsing, as in:

*The student said, "The teacher is very smart."*

Reparsing can also change the identities of the individual words. In one often-mentioned example, a bit of song lyric by Jimi Hendrix is sometimes perceived as "kiss this guy," even though Hendrix actually sings "kiss the sky." The possibility for ambiguity highlights the fact that the parsing is not determined entirely by the stimulus but also depends on the listener's contribution. The speech stream itself actually contains no pauses between words and certainly contains no commas.

To understand any bit of speech, the listener must first parse the stimulus itself—only then can she identify the words and the phrases. And what holds for speech also holds for objects in the visual world. Visual segregation (or perceptual parsing) is the first step in organizing the world we see.

## FIGURE AND GROUND

A crucial step in visual segregation is the separation of the object from its setting, so that the object is seen as a coherent whole, separate from its background. This separation of *figure* and *ground* allows us to recognize (as focal) the familiar shapes of an apple or banana, but the same process also occurs with figures that have no particular meaning. Thus, in Figure 6.18, the white splotch appears as the figure and is typically perceived as in the foreground relative to the blue region (which is seen as the ground). The edge between the blue and white regions is perceived as part of the figure, defining its shape. The same edge does not mark a contour for the blue region but merely marks the point at which this region drops from view (Figure 6.19).

Let us emphasize, though, that this differentiation of figure and ground, like all aspects of parsing, is contributed by the perceiver and is not a property of the stimulus itself. This is most evident when the perceiver discovers that there is more than one way to parse a given stimulus, as with Figure 6.20, which can be seen either as a white vase or as two blue faces in profile. These *reversible figures* make it clear that the stimulus itself is neutral with regard to parsing. What is figure and what is ground is in the eye of the beholder.

After we parse the input into figure and ground, different kinds of processing are applied to these two regions. We are sensitive to fine detail within the figure, but our

**6.20  Reversible figure-ground pattern**
*The classic example of a reversible figure-ground pattern. It can be seen as either a pair of silhouetted faces or a white vase.*

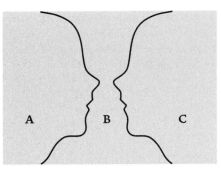

*6.21  Fine detail is more readily seen in the figure than the ground  Research participants looked at the vase-profiles figure and had to determine whether lines that were briefly flashed at points A, B, or C were tilted or vertical. If the vase was seen as the figure, they did much better when the stimuli were presented at B than at A or C. If the profiles were seen as the figure, they did much better when the lines were presented in A or C rather than in B.*

perceptual analysis of the ground seems to employ a cruder analysis, appropriate to the perception of larger areas (Julesz, 1978). This was evident in one experiment in which subjects were briefly shown vertical or tilted lines, flashed in various positions on the vase-profiles figure (see Figure 6.21). Subjects were much more accurate in judging the orientation of the lines when they were projected onto an area the subjects happened to see as the figure; they were less accurate when the line was projected onto an area they perceived as the ground (Weisstein & Wong, 1986).

## PERCEPTUAL GROUPING

If we happen to see a cat walking behind a picket fence, the stimulus that strikes our eye is not the image of an intact cat. Instead, at any moment, we might see a bit of the cat's head here, a bit of its body there, and a bit of its tail for good measure. Somehow, though, we fuse these bits together and perceive the animal as a whole. Likewise, we perceive the left half and right half of the apple as parts of the same whole, and the top half of a blouse as united with the bottom, even if the two parts are separated by a striped pattern in the fabric. This *grouping* of a figure's parts seems a trivial achievement, but grouping, like the assignment of figure-ground, is often ambiguous. The resolution of this ambiguity once again signals that grouping is an achievement of the perceiver and not a property of the stimulus.

Several of the factors that guide visual grouping were first described by Max Wertheimer, the founder of Gestalt psychology. Wertheimer regarded these grouping factors as the laws of *perceptual organization* (Wertheimer, 1923; for a more recent and complex treatment, though, see Palmer, 2002). One factor he identified is *proximity*: the closer two figures are to each other, the more they tend to be grouped together perceptually (see Figure 6.22A). Another factor is *similarity*. Other things being equal, we group together figures that resemble each other. So in Figure 6.22B, we group blue dots with blue dots, red with red. Similarly, we are likely to group verticals with verticals and diagonals with diagonals. However, more complex properties such as shape, are less effective guides to grouping, presumably because shape depends on more complex relations among the stimuli (Beck, 1982; see Figure 6.23). Not surprisingly, the stimulus attributes that support grouping tend to be the same features that pop out from a complex display. This is just what we would expect if parsing is an early step in visual organization and so dependent on the feature information available at that early stage.

*6.22  Grouping by proximity and similarity We perceive the six lines in (A) as three pairs, grouping the lines by proximity. We perceive the dots in (B) as organized into rows on the left and columns on the right, grouping by similarity.*

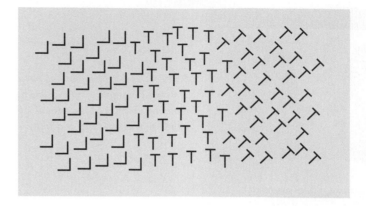

**6.23    The effect of orientation and shape on perceptual grouping    The demarcation between the upright Ts and the tilted Ts is more easily seen than that between the upright Ts and the upright Ls.**

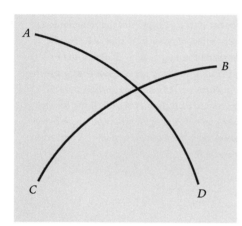

**6.24    Good continuation    The line segments in the figure will generally be grouped so that the contours continue smoothly. As a result, segment A will be grouped with D and segment C with B, rather than A with B and C with D.**

Our visual system also seems to organize patterns in a fashion that suggests a preference for contours that continue smoothly along their original course (Figure 6.24). This principle of *good continuation* prevails even when pitted against prior experience (Figure 6.25), and is why camouflage can be an effective means of hiding a creature from view (Figure 6.26).

A dramatic extension of this principle is visible in *subjective contours*, contours that are perceived even though they do not physically exist (Figure 6.27). Some theorists interpret subjective contours as a special case of good continuation. In their view, the contour is seen to continue along its original path, even, if necessary, jumping a gap or two to achieve this continuation (Kellman & Shipley, 1991).

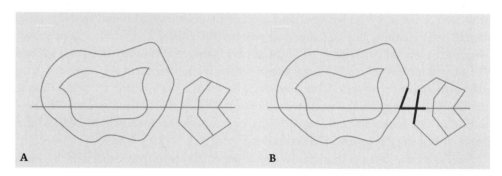

**6.25    Good continuation pitted against prior experience    In (A), virtually all viewers see two complex patterns intersected by a horizontal line. Hardly anyone sees the hidden 4 contained in that figure—and shown in (B)—despite the fact that we have encountered 4s much more often than the two complex patterns, which are probably completely new.**

**6.26    Camouflage    The principles of perceptual organization play a key role in explaining why camouflage is effective. Good continuation and similarity help the praying mantis (A) to look like a twig, and the katydid (B) to look like a leaf.**

## BIDIRECTIONAL ACTIVATION

Top-down processing guides our perception in many ways. But top-down processing cannot work on its own: it is bottom-up processing that keeps us in touch with the stimulus input, ensuring that our perceptions stay faithful to the world around us.

It would appear, therefore, that perceptual processing must occur in both directions at once, guided both by the stimulus input and by our understanding and expectations. As an illustration of how this works, let us take a problem in word recognition (see Figure 6.30). Suppose a perceiver is shown a three-letter word in dim light. In this setting, the visual system might register the fact that the word's last two letters are *AT*, but, at least initially, the system has no information about the first letter. How, then, would it choose among *MAT*, *CAT*, and *RAT*? Let us suppose that the perceiver has just been shown a series of words, including several names of animals (*dog, mouse, canary*). This experience will activate the detectors for these words, and this activation is likely to spread out to the memory neighbors of these detectors, including (probably) the detectors for *CAT* and *RAT*. (See Chapter 8 for further discussion of spreading activation.) Activation of the *CAT* or *RAT* detector, in turn, will cause a top-down activation of the detectors for the letters in these words, including *C* and *R*.

While all of this is going on, the bottom-up analysis is continuing, so that by now the system might have registered the fact that the left edge of the target letter is curved (see Figure 6.30B). This bottom-up effect will cause partial activation of the detector for the letter *C*; this partial activation will join up with the activation *C* has already received from *CAT*, so that the *C* detector becomes fully activated. Then, once *C* is activated, this will feed back to the *CAT* detector, activating it still further.

All these steps involve mechanisms through which detectors within the feature net can activate each other. But many feature-net proposals also incorporate inhibitory mechanisms. In these models, activation of the *CAT* detector, in turn, would inhibit the detectors for competing words—for example, the detectors for *RAT* or *MAT* (McClelland, Rumelhart, & Hinton, 1986). This makes it all the more likely that the *CAT* detector's response will be stronger than the response from any other detector, leading, finally, to a (correct) detection of the word.

In effect, then, the initial activation of *CAT* serves as a knowledge-driven "hypothe-

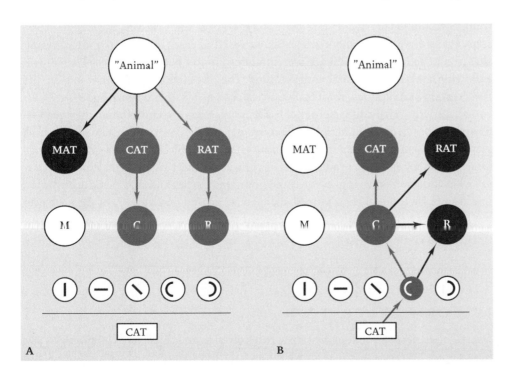

6.30 *Bidirectional activation*   **(A) *Top-down processing*.** Activation of the concept Animal activates the words CAT and RAT (among others), which then activate their constituent letters, including the first-position letters C and R. It also inhibits incompatible words such as MAT. Activation is indicated in green; inhibition in red. **(B) *Bottom-up processing*.** Some milliseconds later, further perceptual analysis of the first letter of the stimulus word has activated the feature curved-to-the-left, which partially activates the letter C. This adds to the activation of the word CAT and inhibits the letter R and the word RAT. The result is that the word CAT is more intensely activated than all other words and will reach recognition threshold. Activation is again in green and inhibition in red. To keep things simple, many mutually inhibitory effects (e.g., between the words CAT and RAT) are not shown in the figure.

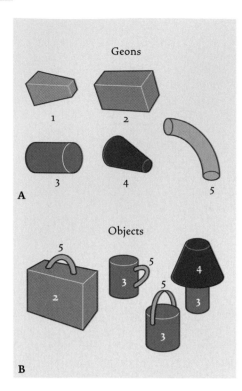

**6.31    Some proposed geometric primitives**
**(A) Some geons. (B) Some objects that can be created from these geons.**

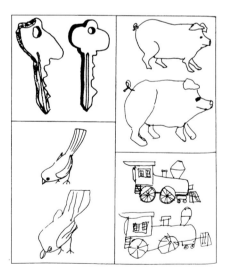

**6.32    Drawings by a patient with associative agnosia**    *While the patient could see the models well enough to reproduce them fairly accurately, he was unable to recognize these objects.*

sis," making the visual system more receptive to the relevant "data" from the feature detectors. The arriving data confirm the hypothesis, leading to the suppression of alternative hypotheses. Overall, we are left with a set of processes in which detectors at every level of the hierarchy—from above, below, and both sides—influence each other until a single detector finally wins out.

## AN INTERMEDIATE STEP: PERCEPTUAL COMPONENTS

It is easy to construct a feature net for targets as simple as letters or numerals. But what about the vast variety of three-dimensional objects that surround us? For these, theorists believe that the recognition process must be more complex. In particular, object recognition may involve some intermediate levels of analysis, levels concerned with object parts broader than the features we have discussed so far.

A model proposed by Irving Biederman, for example, relies on some thirty geometric components that he calls *geons* (short for "geometric ions"). These are three-dimensional figures such as cubes, cylinders, pyramids, and the like. Just about all objects can be analyzed perceptually into some number of such geons. To recognize an object, therefore, we first identify its features and then use these to identify the component geons and their relationships. We then consult our visual memory to see whether there is an object that matches up with what we have detected (Biederman, 1987; see Figure 6.31).

## FROM GEONS TO MEANING

Geons and their relationships give us a complete description of an object's geometry in three dimensions. Thus, in Biederman's system, we can describe, say, the structure of a lamp in terms of a certain geon (number 4 in Figure 6.31) on top of another (number 3). But that is not enough to tell the system that the object is a lamp, that it is an object that casts light, can be switched on and off, and so on. For those things, we need some further steps, because, while the geon description does a fine job of representing the object's geometry, it says nothing about the object's meaning.

As with most other aspects of perception, those further steps seem effortless to us most of the time. We see a chair and almost immediately know what it is, what it is for, and where it probably belongs. We see a picture of George W. Bush and cannot avoid thinking about his presidency and our evaluation of it. But—easy as they seem—these steps are far from trivial, and, remarkably, we can find cases in which the visual system succeeds in achieving an accurate structural description but fails in these last steps—endowing the perceived object with meaning. The cases involve patients who have suffered certain brain lesions, specifically cortical lesions leading to visual agnosia (Farah, 1990). Patients with this disorder can see but cannot recognize what they see (see Chapter 2, p. 57). Some patients can perceive objects well enough to draw recognizable pictures of them but are unable to identify either the objects or their own drawings. One patient, for example, produced the drawings shown in Figure 6.32. When asked to say what these were drawings of, he could not name the key and said that the bird was a tree stump. He evidently had formed adequate structural descriptions of these objects, but his ability to process what he saw stopped there; what he perceived was stripped of its meaning (Farah, 1990).

## THE PROCESSING SEQUENCE IN FORM PERCEPTION

Overall, then, it seems that many steps are involved in an achievement as simple as seeing an apple and recognizing it for what it is. The first step is visual segregation: seeing the apple as a figure against the ground of whatever else is in the visual field and seeing it as a unified whole, even if it is partially obscured by other objects in the field. After this come several steps in pattern recognition: lower-level features stimulate detectors that come together to stimulate higher-level detectors; these in turn are built up into geons that are then assembled to form a structural description of the object. The final steps involve the perception of the actual object.

We have described these processing steps as if they always occur one after another and in this precise bottom-up order. In actuality, these steps often occur simultaneously rather than in sequence. To use the technical terms, the processing may be parallel rather than serial. If the steps do occur serially (that is, in sequence), their order may sometimes be the reverse of the one we described; this was evident in our discussion of the interaction between top-down and bottom-up processing. In any case, our account plainly is going to need all of these processing steps—even for the simplest examples of perception.

## THE PERCEIVER'S ACTIVE ROLE

Whatever the sequence of the processing stages, one thing should be clear from our discussion so far: the perceiver plays an enormously active role in organizing and interpreting the stimulus input. This is a direct consequence of the fact that the stimulus information we receive is often ambiguous: If we observe a dot getting closer to a frame's edge, is that because the dot is moving or the frame is moving? Is Figure 6.20 (p. 217) a picture of a vase on a blue background, or a pair of profiles on a white background? Is Figure 6.33A a wire cube aligned with the solid cube shown in Figure 6.33B, or is it aligned with the one shown in Figure 6.33C? For that matter, does Figure 6.14 (p. 213) show a complete square that is more distant than (and so partly hidden from view by) the circle? Or does the figure show a square with a "bite" taken out of it, perhaps closer to us than the circle?

Ambiguities of this sort are easy to find, but our perception typically resolves the ambiguity so that we easily and quickly perceive Figure 6.20 either as a vase or as profiles, and likewise perceive Figure 6.33A as similar either to Figure 6.33B or to C. In these ways, our perception quite routinely goes beyond the information given to us, apparently adding a layer of interpretation and organization.

The perceiver's active contribution is also evident in other ways. Consider our discussion of how top-down processes interact with bottom-up processes. In the examples we discussed earlier, the perceiver's knowledge that *CAT* is a type of animal helped the perceiver to detect this word; similarly, the knowledge that *THE* is a common word, while *TAE* is not, systematically influenced how the ambiguous pattern in Figure 6.29 (p. 220) was perceived.

Plainly, then, the perceiver plays a large part in shaping and guiding perception, but one might worry that all of this activity undermines the objectivity of our perception: If we are making inferences and interpretations as we perceive, won't that lead us to be less accurate than we would be if we simply "stuck to the facts"? This is a sensible worry, and, in truth, we are vulnerable to a number of illusions and perceptual confusions. Fortunately, these perceptual errors occur rarely in our day-to-day lives—usually because there are multiple sources of information available to us as we move around in the world, and so an error in interpreting one source of information is likely to be corrected by some other information. Even so, errors do occur and provide further evidence for the perceiver's active interpretive role.

Why did evolution allow a perceptual system that is occasionally open to error? The answer may be that there is no other option, because the inferences and assumptions we make, as part of our perceiving, are, quite simply, necessary. We cannot escape the

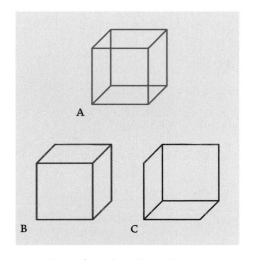

**6.33 The Necker cube** *The ambiguous Necker cube, shown in (A), can either be perceived as aligned with the cube shown in (B) or the one in (C).*

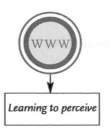

Learning to perceive

fact that the perceptual input often is ambiguous, demanding some sort of interpretation. And there is no question that top-down processes, supplementing the visual input with other things we know, make our perception vastly more efficient. This suggests that the occasional errors, and the occasional departures from objectivity, are just the price we must pay for an enormously effective visual system.

## THE LOGIC OF PERCEPTION

We will have more to say about the perceiver's active role in later sections. Let us first, though, consider how we should conceive of this role. How should we think about the ways in which the perceiver interprets and analyzes the perceptual input? Investigators have different views on this issue. Some emphasize the "logic" of perception and focus on what it is that the perceiver accomplishes. Other investigators focus on the specific biological mechanisms through which these accomplishments are actually carried out.

For example, Irvin Rock argued that we can usefully describe the perceiver as if she were engaged in a peculiar form of problem solving, asking, in essence, "What is this object now before me?" Expectations, prior knowledge, and early analyses of the stimulus all lead to a "hypothesis" about the object's identity, and then this hypothesis is checked against the evidence. That is, her perceptual system analyzes the stimulus further, seeking information that might confirm or disconfirm the hypothesis. If the stimulus information does not fit the hypothesis, a new hypothesis is generated, and it too must be tested against the "data."

This process, Rock argued, is governed by a series of logical principles. First, our solution of the perceptual puzzle must provide a coherent explanation for all the information contained within the stimulus. Second, it must try to avoid contradictions, such as perceiving a surface to be both opaque and transparent. Third, it must try to avoid interpretations of the world that depend on accident or coincidence.

An illustration of these principles comes from the study of apparent movement. We have already described (p. 210) the standard demonstration of this form of movement. Viewers are first shown a light at one position; then, a moment later, that light disappears, and a second light appears at a nearby position (see Figure 6.10). If the timing is right, viewers do not perceive these as two stationary lights, coming one after the other. Instead, they perceive a single light moving from the first position to the second.

To the perceiver, this interpretation of the display is quite reasonable. Why does the

*Perceptual problem solving* **What is this a picture of? In cases like this, perception really does feel like problem solving, as the perceiver develops "hypotheses" about the picture and checks them against the "data." Some investigators have suggested, though, that perception always has the quality of problem solving: it always involves the checking of hypotheses against the data, even when the perception feels effortless and immediate.**

disappearance of the first light coincide with the second light's appearance? If there are two lights, then this is an odd coincidence that needs to be explained. But if there is just a single light moving between two points, then there is no coincidence, and the pattern of stimulation makes perfect sense.

But now let us add a complication. What if an obstacle is placed between the lights, apparently blocking the path between position 1 and position 2 (Figure 6.34); does this interfere with the perception of movement? It does not. Instead, viewers are likely to perceive motion in three dimensions: the light seems to hop in front of the obstacle, as it zooms from its starting point toward its goal. And again this is reasonable: it explains why one light disappears at just the moment that another appears, while avoiding the contradiction of a light passing through a solid obstacle.

Is the perceptual apparatus literally proceeding through these logical steps, weighing each consideration in turn? Surely not. Still, we can generally predict accurately how a display will be perceived by considering how this process of logical consideration might unfold. This implies that the perceptual processes somehow respect these principles, giving perception its logical character.

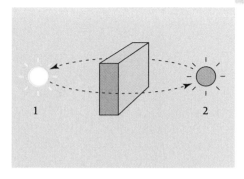

**6.34   The logic of apparent movement**
*Adding an obstacle to block the path between the two lights in an apparent-movement display leads perceivers to see the light as zipping smoothly around the obstacle from position 1 to position 2.*

# FORM PERCEPTION AND THE NERVOUS SYSTEM

How is the logic of perception made possible by the nervous system? And how does the nervous system manage to go through all the steps we have described swiftly enough so that we perceive the approaching bus in time to jump out of its path, or the slice of apple pie soon enough to grab it before our younger brother or sister does? To answer questions like these, experimental psychologists have worked closely with neuroscientists in analyzing the anatomical and functional components of the visual system. Thanks to their efforts, we can trace many of the neurological steps that make vision possible, beginning when individual photons of light excite retinal receptors and continuing, neuron by neuron, tissue layer by tissue layer, upward into the brain.

## EARLY STAGES OF VISUAL PROCESSING

As we saw in the previous chapter, the rods and cones pass their signals to the bipolar cells, which relay them to the ganglion cells (see Figure 5.10, p. 185). The axons of the ganglion cells form the optic nerve, which leaves the eyeball and begins the journey toward the brain. But even at this early stage, the neurons are specialized in important ways, with different cells responsible for detecting different aspects of the visual world.

The ganglion cells can be broadly classified into two categories: the smaller ones are called *parvo cells*, and the larger are called *magno cells*. (The terminology derives from the Latin words for "small" and "large.") Parvo cells, far outnumbering the magno cells, blanket the entire retina. Magno cells, in contrast, are found largely in the retina's periphery. Parvo cells appear to be sensitive to color differences (to be more precise, to differences in hue), while magno cells, which are color blind, respond to changes in brightness. (For more on the difference between hue and brightness, see Chapter 5.)

There is good reason to believe that magno and parvo cells play rather different roles within the sequence of visual processing. Parvo cells seem crucial for the perception of pattern and form, in part because their small receptive fields allow them to distinguish fine differences in position. In contrast, magno cells probably play a central role in the detection of motion and the perception of depth. Unlike their parvo counterparts, the magno cells do not continue to fire if the light stimulus remains unchanged. Instead,

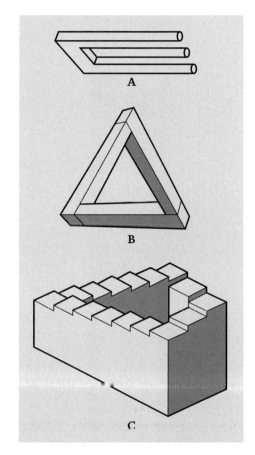

*Impossible figures   We have emphasized how "logical" the perceptual system seems to be, but we should emphasize that there are limits on that logic. As an illustration, consider the so-called impossible figures—perceived as if they show three-dimensional objects although contradictions within the figure guarantee that they couldn't be three-dimensional.*

they fire when the stimulus appears and then again when it disappears. As a result, they are particularly sensitive to motion-produced changes in the visual scene.

## VISUAL PROCESSING IN THE BRAIN

This pattern of neural specialization continues and sharpens as we look more deeply into the nervous system. The relevant evidence comes largely from the single-cell recording technique that we described in Chapter 5 (pp. 196–198), a technique that lets investigators determine which specific stimuli elicit a response from a cell and which do not. This has allowed investigators to explore the visual system cell by cell by cell, and has provided us with a rich understanding of the neural basis for vision.

### PARALLEL PROCESSING IN THE VISUAL CORTEX

In the last chapter, we described cells in the visual cortex that are sensitive to simple characteristics such as the tilt of a line or its position. As we've seen, these cells fire most strongly in response to a line or edge of a specific orientation and position. Other cells in the visual cortex are a bit more sophisticated; they are also sensitive to the input's orientation but are less sensitive to its position. Additional cells are sensitive to whether the target is moving or not, and still other cells respond to yet more complex features, including corners, angles, and notches.

This proliferation of cell types suggests that the visual system relies on a "divide-and-conquer" strategy, with different cells—and, indeed, different areas of the brain—each specializing in a particular kind of analysis. Moreover, these different analyses go on in parallel: cells analyzing the forms within the visual input do their work at the same time that other cells are analyzing the motion and still others the colors. Using single-cell recording, investigators have been able to map where these various cells are located in the visual cortex and also how they communicate with each other; one such map is shown in Figure 6.35.

Why this heavy reliance on parallel processing? We have already mentioned one reason. Parallel processing allows greater speed, since (for example) brain areas trying to discern the shape of the incoming stimulus do not need to wait until the motion analysis or the color analysis is complete. Instead, all of the analyses can go forward simulta-

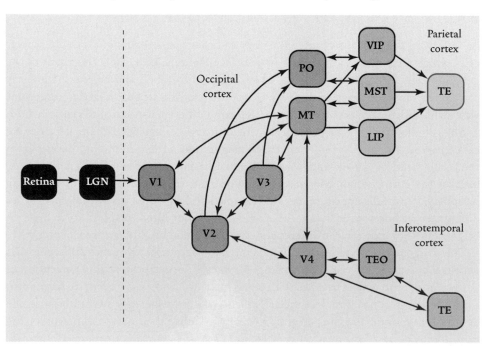

**6.35  The visual processing pathways**
*The visual system relies heavily on parallel processing, with different brain areas engaged in their own specific analyses. Information from the LGN is primarily sent to Area V1, but from there, information is sent along several different pathways.*

neously, with no waiting time. Another advantage of parallel processing lies in the benefits gained from mutual influence among multiple systems. These benefits derive from the fact that sometimes our understanding of a form's shape depends on our understanding of its motion, while sometimes the reverse is true, and our understanding of motion depends on shape. Parallel processing makes both sorts of influence possible, with each type of analysis able to inform the other. Put differently, neither the shape-analyzing system nor the motion-analyzing system gets priority over the other. Instead, the two systems work concurrently and "negotiate" a solution that satisfies both (Van Essen & DeYoe, 1995).

## THE "WHAT" AND "WHERE" SYSTEMS

Evidence for specialized neural processes, all operating in parallel, continues as we move beyond the visual cortex. As Figure 6.36 indicates, information from the visual cortex (at the back of the head) is transmitted to two other important brain areas, in the temporal cortex and the parietal cortex. The pathway that carries information to the temporal cortex is often called the *"what" system* and plays a major role in the identification of visual objects, telling us whether the object is a cat, an apple, or whatever. The second pathway, which carries information to the parietal cortex, is often called the *"where" system*; it tells us where an object is located—above or below, to our right or left (Ungerleider & Haxby, 1994; Ungerleider & Mishkin, 1982).

There has been some controversy over how exactly we should conceive of these two systems (see, for example, Carey, 2001; Milner & Goodale, 1995; Sereno & Maunsell, 1998), but there is no question that the systems are distinct from each other and serve different functions. Evidence for this point comes from many sources, including studies of brain-damaged monkeys. The animals are given two tasks. One is a visual identification task, in which the monkey must learn to reach for one shape rather than another, for a cube, say, rather than a pyramid. The other task involves visual location, so that, for example, the monkey must learn to reach for a cube when it appears on the animal's left but not when it appears on the animal's right.

Monkeys who have suffered damage to the occipital-temporal pathway (that is, to the "what" system) show serious impairment on the identification task but do perfectly well on the location task. The reverse is true for monkeys with damage to the occipital-parietal pathway (the "where" system); they are impaired on the location task but behave normally on the identification task (Mishkin, Ungerleider, & Macko, 1983).

Similar observations have been made in humans. Patients with lesions in the occipital-temporal pathway show visual agnosia (see Chapter 2). They may be unable to recognize common objects, such as a cup or a pencil, and are often unable to recognize the faces of relatives and friends (although if the relatives speak, the patients recognize them by their voices). On the other hand, these patients show little disorder in visual

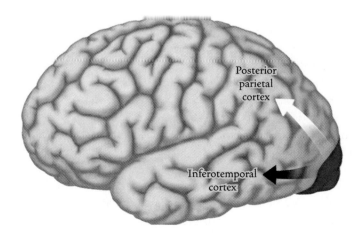

*6.36 The "what" and "where" pathways Information from the primary visual cortex (located at the back of the head) is transmitted both to the inferotemporal cortex (the so-called "what" system) and to the posterior parietal cortex (the "where" system).*

orientation and reaching. The reverse pattern is observed with patients who have suffered lesions in the occipital-parietal pathway—they have difficulty in reaching but no problem in object identification (A. R. Damasio, Tranel, & Damasio, 1989; Farah, 1990; Goodale, 1995; Newcombe, Ratcliff, & Damasio, 1987).

## THE BINDING PROBLEM

It appears, then, that the visual system consists of an intricate network of subsystems, each specialized for a particular task. It seems clear that natural selection has favored a division-of-labor strategy for vision, with individualized processes responsible for each aspect of the whole.

This division into specialized subsystems allows us to perceive an extraordinary range of stimuli with extraordinary speed. But this structure of the visual system raises a problem. How do we integrate these disparate pieces of information into one whole? When we see a ballet dancer in a graceful leap, the leap itself is registered by the magno cells, while the recognition of the ballet dancer depends on parvo cells. How are these pieces put back together? Likewise, when we reach for a coffee cup but stop midway because we see that the cup is empty, the reach itself is guided by the occipital-parietal system (the "where" system); the fact that the cup is empty is perceived by the occipital-temporal system (the "what" system). How are these two streams of processing coordinated?

If we begin with a visual system that analyzes the scene into its constituents, how do we reunite the constituents to allow the perception of intact objects? Neuroscientists call this the *binding problem*—how the nervous system manages to bind together elements that were initially detected by separate systems. We are only beginning to understand how the nervous system solves this problem, and it is a matter of intense interest to contemporary researchers. The evidence is accumulating, however, that the brain uses a special rhythm to identify which sensory elements belong with which. Specifically, imagine two groups of neurons in the visual cortex. One group of neurons fires maximally whenever a vertical line is in view. Another group of neurons fires maximally whenever a stimulus is in view moving from left to right. Let us also imagine that, right now, a vertical line is presented, and it is moving in the right way. As a result, both groups of neurons are firing strongly. But how does the brain encode the fact that these attributes are bound together, different aspects of a single object? How does the brain differentiate between this stimulus and one in which the features being detected actually belong to different objects—perhaps a static vertical and a moving diagonal?

The visual system seems to encode this difference by means of neural synchrony. If the neurons detecting a vertical line are firing in synchrony with those signaling movement, then these attributes are registered as belonging to the same object. If they are not in synchrony, the features are not bound together. Moreover, the synchrony is made possible by the fact that the neurons are firing at roughly the same rate—about 40 times per second, a rate called a *gamma-band oscillation* (Csibra, Davis, Spratling, & Johnson, 2000; Elliott & Müller, 2000; Fries, Reynolds, Rorie, & Desimone, 2001; Gray, Koenig, Engel, & Singer, 1989; Singer, 1996).

Of course, we do not know yet whether neural synchrony causes the perception of bound attributes. The evidence so far is correlational: when attributes are perceived as bound, synchronous firing is observed in the visual system; when attributes are not perceived as bound, the firing is not synchronized. But, even so, the evidence suggests that we may need to broaden our account of how neurons code various aspects of the sensory world. In Chapter 5, we considered coding in terms of which neurons were firing (so that activity in the optic nerve is experienced as seeing, activity in the auditory nerve is experienced as hearing) and also in terms of patterns of activity (so that a particular pattern is experienced as red, another as green, and so on). It now appears that we also need to consider coding in terms of *when* the neurons are firing, with some timing patterns associated with binding (that is, the experience of coherent objects).

# PERCEPTUAL SELECTION: ATTENTION

Synchronized neural firing, therefore, may be the nervous system's way of representing the fact that different attributes are bound together—that is, parts of a single object—But what causes this synchrony? How do the neurons become synchronized in the first place? We do not know yet, but we do know one factor that plays an essential role: attention.

Attention actually plays several different roles in perception. One role is preparation: We are better able to perceive when we are paying attention. Attention also allows us to select some aspects of a scene for consideration while ignoring others. We focus on the figure, not the ground, and if several figures are present, we choose the one to which we will attend. And as we will see, attention also helps us knit together the sensations we receive to create a unified and coherent perceptual experience.

## SELECTION THROUGH ORIENTATION

When a stimulus interests us, we turn our head and eyes to inspect it. Similarly, we actively explore the world with our hands, and we position our ears for better hearing. Other animals do the same, exploring the world with paws or lips or whiskers or even a prehensile tail. These various forms of *orienting* serve to adjust the sensory machinery and to provide one of the most direct means of selecting input—a means through which we focus on the stimuli we care about and disregard those we do not.

In humans, movements of the eyes provide the major means of orienting. Peripheral vision informs us that something is going on, say, in the upper-left section of our field of vision. But our peripheral acuity is not good enough to tell us precisely what it is. To find out, we move our eyes so that the region in which the activity is taking place falls into the visual field of the fovea. In fact, motion in the visual periphery tends to trigger a reflex eye movement, making it difficult not to look toward a moving object.

## CENTRAL SELECTION

Eye movements are important, but they are not our only means of selecting what we will pay attention to and what we will ignore. The selective control of perception also draws on central processes, which determine both which inputs we will consider and what we will do with those inputs.

### SELECTIVE LOOKING

A widely used method for studying visual attention is the visual search procedure, discussed earlier in this chapter. In this task, a research participant is briefly shown an array of letters, digits, or other visual forms and asked to indicate as quickly as he can whether a particular target is present.

*Searching for Feature Combinations* As we noted earlier (pp. 214–215), visual search seems almost effortless if the target can be distinguished from the field on the basis of just one feature—for example, searching for a vertical among a field of horizontals or for a green target amidst a group of red distracters. In such cases, the target pops out from the distracter elements, and search time is virtually independent of the number of items in the display.

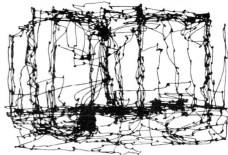

*Eye-movement records when looking at pictures*
**This picture (top) was looked at for ten minutes. With the picture is the record of the eye movements during this period (bottom). As the records show, most of the eye movements are directed toward the most visually informative regions. As a result, the eye-movement record is a crude mirror of the main contours of the picture.**

The situation is different, though, when the target is defined by a combination of features; for example, if the task involves searching for a red *O* among distracters that include green *O*s and red *V*s. Now it is not enough to search for redness or for the *O*'s roundness; instead, the participant must search for a target with both of these features. Under these conditions, the search process is usually serial rather than parallel. Search times are longer and increase with the number of items in the display. (For some exceptions and complications, see Wolfe, 1994.)

Notice the trade-off that is in place here. When we are searching for just a single feature, our search is remarkably efficient, and we can search through a dozen stimuli just as quickly as we can search through one. When we are searching for a more complex target, our search is much less efficient, and we have to search through the stimuli one by one. But, in return, our attention on a single stimulus reduces our chances for confusion about how the stimulus features within the display are assembled. By focusing a mental spotlight on just a single item, the perceiver avoids any risk of confusion about which elements belong with which stimulus (Treisman, 1988; see Figure 6.37).

This view implies that attention plays a central role in solving the binding problem—the problem of figuring out which elements in the stimulus information belong with which. Consistent with this idea, evidence suggests that individuals who suffer from severe attention deficits (because of brain damage in the parietal cortex) are particularly impaired in tasks that require them to judge how features are conjoined to form complex objects (Cohen & Rafal, 1991; Eglin, Robertson, & Knight, 1989; Robertson et al., 1997). Similarly, we earlier suggested that the nervous system identifies how features are bound together through a pattern of synchronized firing, with "bound-together" feature detectors firing in synchrony, at a gamma rhythm. It turns out that this synchronized firing is observed when an animal is attending to a specific stimulus, but is not observed in neurons activated by an unattended stimulus. This finding obviously strengthens the claim that attention plays a key role in solving the binding problem.

*Priming*    What does it mean to say that we focus a mental spotlight on a stimulus? How is this selection achieved? And does this focusing provide other benefits in addition to the (considerable) gain just described—namely, a step toward solving the binding problem?

Part of the answer lies in something we have already discussed: priming and top-down processing. If the circumstances lead the perceiver to expect, say, the word *CAT*, then the appropriate detectors will be partially activated. As a result, when the expected input actually arrives, it will be processed more efficiently: since the detectors are primed, they need only slight additional activation to trigger a response. Notice, though, that the priming is selective. An individual who expects to see the word *CAT* will be unprepared for anything else. So if the stimulus turns out to be the word *BOG*, for example, it will be processed less efficiently. If the unexpected stimulus is weak (perhaps flashed briefly or only on a dimly lit screen), then it may not trigger a response at all. It is in this fashion that priming provides a further benefit—sparing us from distraction by selectively facilitating the perception of expected stimuli but simultaneously hindering the perception of anything else.

**6.37** *Searching for feature combinations*  **In Panel A, it's easy to find the red figure, since it can be distinguished from the background on the basis of a single feature (color). In Panel B, it's easy to find the O, because it too can be distinguished on the basis of a single feature (in this case, shape). In Panel C, however, it takes some time to locate the red O, because now the target is defined in terms of a conjunction of features (color + shape).**

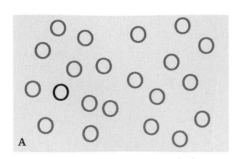

A

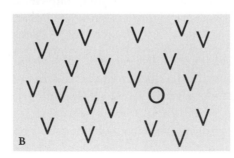

B

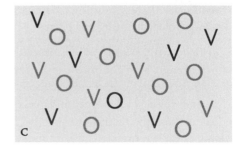

C

Priming not only can enhance the recognition of a particular stimulus but can also prepare the perceiver for a broad class of stimuli—for example, any stimulus that appears in a particular location. In some experiments, participants are asked to point their eyes at a dot on a computer screen. A moment later, an arrow appears for an instant in place of the dot and points either left or right. Then, a fraction of a second later, the stimulus is presented. If it is presented in the location toward which the arrow pointed, the participants respond more quickly than they do without the prime. If the stimulus appears in a different location (so that the prime was actually misleading), participants respond more slowly than they do with no prime at all. Clearly, the prime influences how we allocate our processing resources.

This spatial priming is not simply a matter of cuing eye movements. In most studies, the interval between the appearance of the prime and the arrival of the target is too short to permit a voluntary eye movement.* But even so (when it is not misleading), the arrow makes the task easier. Evidently, priming affects an internal selection process, as if the mind's eye moves even though the eyes in the head are stationary (Egeth, Jonides, & Wall, 1972; Eriksen & Hoffman, 1972; Gleitman & Jonides, 1976; Jonides, 1980, 1983; Posner, Snyder, & Davidson, 1980).

## PERCEPTION IN THE ABSENCE OF ATTENTION

As we have seen, attention accomplishes several things for us. It orients us toward the stimulus so that we can gain more information. It helps bind the input's features together so that we can perceive a coherent object. And it primes us so that we can perceive more efficiently and so that, to some extent, we are sheltered from unwanted distraction.

If attention is this important, with so many effects, then one might guess that perceiving would be seriously compromised in the absence of attention. Recent studies indicate that this is correct. If research participants are focused on just one aspect of a visual display, they are remarkably insensitive to what is going on in the display outside of the attended elements—that is, to elements they are not paying attention to. In one study, for example, participants watched a video screen in which one group of players, dressed in white shirts, were tossing a ball back and forth. Interspersed with these white-shirted players, and visible on the same video screen, a different group of players, in black shirts, also were tossing a ball. But, when participants were focusing on the white-shirted players, that was all they noticed. They were oblivious to what the black-shirted players were doing, even though they were looking right at them. Indeed, in one remarkable experiment, the participants even failed to notice when someone wearing a (black) gorilla suit strolled right through the middle of the scene (Neisser & Becklen, 1975; Simons & Chabris, 1999).

In a related study, participants were asked to stare at a dot in the middle of a computer screen while trying to make judgments about stimuli presented a bit off their line of view. During the moments in which the to-be-judged stimulus was on the screen, the dot at which the participants were staring momentarily changed to a triangle and then back to a dot. When asked about this a few seconds later, though, the participants insisted that they had seen no change in the dot. When given a choice whether the dot had changed into a triangle, a plus sign, a circle, or a square, they chose randomly. Apparently, with their attention directed elsewhere, the participants were essentially "blind" to a stimulus that had appeared directly in front of their eyes (Mack & Rock, 1998).

*How do you hide a 200-pound gorilla?* **In this experiment, subjects were instructed to keep track of the ball players in the white shirts. Intent on their task, the subjects were oblivious to what the black-shirted players were doing, even though they were looking right at them. They also failed to see the person in the (black) gorilla suit, strolling through the scene.**

* That interval is usually about 100 milliseconds, while an eye movement takes about 150 to 200 milliseconds to execute.

## SELECTIVE LISTENING

Attention, therefore, is plainly crucial for vision, and, in some circumstances, it seems, we are effectively blind to unattended stimuli. Attention is just as important for the other sensory modalities, including hearing. You may be at a noisy party, but you still manage to focus on just the voice of your conversational partner. Many other voices are audible, but these are somehow consigned to a background babble. This pattern, referred to as the *cocktail party effect*, is easily studied in the laboratory by asking research participants to attend to one of two simultaneously presented verbal messages. The usual procedure is *dichotic presentation*, in which the participant wears stereo headphones and receives different messages in each ear. To guarantee selective attention, the individual is asked to *shadow* the to-be-attended message. This means that she has to repeat it aloud, word for word, as it comes over the appropriate earphone. Under these conditions, the irrelevant message tends to be shut out almost entirely. She can hear speechlike sounds but notices little else. She is generally unable to recall the message that came by way of the unattended ear. In one classic study, research participants did not even notice whether the speaker on the unattended ear shifted into a foreign language or read a passage backward (Cherry, 1953).

**Attentional limits** *We are usually quite effective in focusing on a single task while shutting out distracters. One thing we cannot do, however, is focus on many tasks simultaneously; when we try, our performance suffers. This has been documented in many studies showing that driving performance (e.g., speed of reacting to red lights) is impaired when the driver is simultaneously on the phone.*

However, participants are not totally deaf to the unattended message. If the voice reading the message changes from a male's to a female's, or if it changes pitch, they notice it immediately. Occasional words from this message are also perceived. For example, research participants seem generally oblivious to the content of the unattended message but may register their own name if it is mentioned. Even with this salient stimulus, however, the effects of attention are visible: Only one-third of individuals notice their name, pronounced clearly in the unattended message; the majority do not (Moray, 1959).

# PERCEIVING CONSTANCY

We have now considered a rich set of perceptual mechanisms, mechanisms that, in their normal operation, provide us with accurate information about the world around us. We have acknowledged that the perceptual system can lead us astray, as in illusions of distance or movement, but this occurs relatively rarely. By and large, the processes of perception serve us well as messengers about the real world outside.

However, there is still a layer of complexity here. To see the real world is to see the properties of distal objects: their color, form, size, and location; their movement through space; their permanence or transience. But as we have noted before, organisms cannot gain experience about the distal stimulus directly; instead, all information about the external world comes to us only from the proximal-stimulus patterns that distal objects project onto our senses. And this creates a problem, because the same distal object can produce many different proximal stimuli. Its retinal image will get larger or smaller, depending on its distance from us. Its retinal shape will change, depending on its slant relative to our viewing perspective. The amount of light it projects onto our retinas will increase or decrease depending on the illumination that falls on it.

Under the circumstances, it may seem surprising that we ever manage to see the real

**6.38   Shape constancy**   *When we see a door at various slants from us, it appears rectangular despite the fact that its retinal image is often a trapezoid.*

properties of objects at all. But see them we do. We are somehow able to distinguish changes in the proximal stimulus brought about by shifts in our viewing circumstances from changes created by an actual alteration in the world. We manage, in other words, to achieve *perceptual constancy*. Thus, an elephant looks large even at a distance, a postcard looks rectangular even though its retinal image is a rectangle only when it is viewed directly head on, and a crow looks black even in sunlight. In all of these cases, we manage to transcend the vagaries of the proximal stimulus so that we can react to the world as it truly is. How do we accomplish this feat?

## SIZE AND SHAPE CONSTANCY

*Size constancy* describes the fact that the perceived size of an object is the same whether it is nearby or far away. A house at the end of the street looks larger than a mailbox close by, even though the former produces a much smaller retinal image than the latter. An analogous phenomenon is *shape constancy*, which refers to the fact that we perceive the shape of an object more or less independently of the angle from which we view it. A rectangular door will look rectangular even though most of the angles from which we regard it will produce a trapezoidal retinal image (see Figure 6.38).

### HIGHER-ORDER INVARIANTS

How do we achieve these constancies? One explanatory approach was offered by James J. Gibson (1950, 1966, 1979). He believed that the vital characteristics of an object, such as its size, shape, and distance from the observer, are directly signaled by the visual stimulus. However, the relevant information is not the size or shape of the retinal image as such; instead, the information that allows constancy is contained in *higher-order invariants*, unchanging stimulus patterns that usually involve the relationship between the size (or shape) of the retinal image and other attributes of the stimulus.

*James J. Gibson*

The size of the retinal image, for example, necessarily varies as the distal object changes its distance from the observer. But this does not mean that there is no size information in the stimulus that hits the eye. One reason is that objects are usually seen against a background that provides a basis for comparison with the target object. The dog, sitting nearby on the kitchen floor, is half as tall as the chair and hides eight of the kitchen's floor tiles from view. If we take several steps back from the dog, none of these relationships changes, even though the sizes of all the retinal images are reduced (Figure 6.39). Size constancy, therefore, can be achieved by focusing not on the images themselves but on the unchanging relationships, relationships that provide direct, higher-order information about the stable properties of the world.

Evidence suggests that these relationships do contribute to size and shape constancy, so that we are better able to judge size when comparison objects are in view, or

6.39 *An invariant relationship that provides information about size* (A) *and* (B) *show a dog at different distances from the observer. The retinal size of the dog varies with distance, but the ratio between the retinal size of the dog and the retinal size of the textural elements (e.g., the floor tiles) is constant.*

when the target we are judging sits on a surface that has a uniform visual texture (like the floor tiles in our example). But these relationships do not account for the whole story. Size constancy is found even when the visual scene provides no basis for comparison (if, for example, the object to be judged is the only object that is in view), provided that other cues (such as binocular disparity or motion parallax) signal the distance of the target object. This finding suggests the need for a different theory, and, in particular, one that makes use of this distance information.

## UNCONSCIOUS INFERENCE

We can accurately judge size even if the stimulus information provides no basis for comparison between the target object and other elements of the scene. Invariant size relationships, therefore, cannot explain all cases of size constancy. But what can? Many results point to the importance of distance information. As we just noted, size judgments tend to be accurate if cues indicating the distance of the target object are available to the observer. To a large extent, it does not matter which distance cues are present, and, in particular, it does not matter if the cues are contained within the visual scene itself (as linear perspective is) or are brought to the scene by the viewer (as binocular disparity is). But the number of cues does matter: as the number of distance cues available decreases, the accuracy of size constancy declines (Chevrier & Delorme, 1983; Harvey & Leibowitz, 1967; Holway & Boring, 1947).

A direct demonstration of the role of these cues comes from the fact that, if one of these distance cues is altered, indicating that the target object has moved farther away, the perception of size changes. This is true even if the relationship between the target and the background remains constant, a result that simultaneously points to the importance of distance information and argues against the view that our perception of a constant world depends on higher-order relationships in the stimulus input.

How is this distance information used? An influential hypothesis was formulated by Hermann von Helmholtz. Helmholtz started with the fact that there is a simple inverse relationship between distance and retinal image size. Thus, if an object doubles its distance from the viewer, the size of its image is reduced by half. If an object triples its distance, the size of its image is reduced to a third of its initial size (Figure 6.40).

This relationship makes it possible for perceivers to achieve constancy by means of a simple calculation. First, the perceiver needs to know the size of the image on the retina. Second, the perceiver needs to know how far away the object is (and, presumably, this information is provided by the distance cues we have already discussed). These two bits of information can then be combined via a process that somehow multiplies the size of the retinal image by the distance of the object from the viewer, and it is

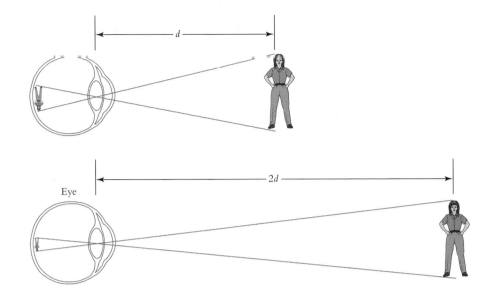

**6.40 The relationship between image size and distance** *If an object moves to a new distance, the size of the retinal image cast by that object changes. A doubling of the distance causes the retinal image size to be reduced by half. If the distance is tripled, the retinal image size is cut to one-third of its initial size.*

this calculation that leads to size constancy. Imagine an object that, at a distance of 10 feet, casts an image 4 millimeters across. The same object, at a distance of 20 feet, casts an image of 2 millimeters. In both cases, the product—10 × 4 or 20 × 2—is the same. Of course, Helmholtz knew that we do not make conscious calculations of this sort. But he believed that some such process—or something that produces the same result—was going on outside of our awareness, and so he called it *unconscious inference* (Helmholtz, 1909).

The heart of Helmholtz's view is that we somehow take distance into account in judging size. Likewise, for shape constancy, we somehow take the slant of the surface into account and make appropriate adjustments in our interpretation of the retinal image's shape. As we have already noted, much evidence indicates that this sort of adjustment is, in fact, an important element of our perception. As a result, many contemporary theorists agree that a taking-into-account process must be involved in size constancy and that some sort of unconscious inference must be drawn by our perceptual system (see, for example, Rock, 1977, 1983, 1986; Hochberg, 1981, 1988).

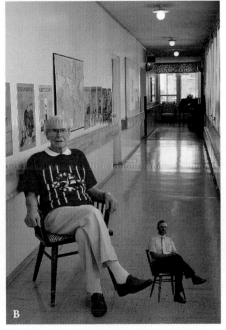

*Perceived size and distance* **(A) The actual image of the two men in the picture—which corresponds to the size of their retinal image—is in the ratio of 3 to 1. But this is not the way they are perceived. They look roughly equal in size, but at different distances, with one three times farther off than the other. In (B) there are no cues that indicate that one man is farther away than the other—on the contrary, the picture indicates that they are equally distant from the viewer. With this misinformation about distance, the men now look very different in size. The figure was constructed by cutting the more distant man out of the picture and pasting him next to the other man, with the apparent distance from the viewer equal for the two.**

# SOME FINAL THOUGHTS: SEEING, KNOWING, AND THE PERCEIVER'S ACTIVE ROLE

We began this chapter by noting the apparent simplicity of perception. The perceiver certainly does not feel as if she is doing any work or any analysis in order to perceive. Instead, she simply opens her eyes and sees, effortlessly recognizing the objects that are in view and instantly seeing where those objects are and what they are doing.

From this chapter and the last, however, we have seen that perception is complex. That it seems effortless is simply because we are all immensely practiced at the task of perceiving, and because our nervous systems are exquisitely well prepared to support this task. In this final section, let us revisit some of this complexity.

## PROXIMAL AND DISTAL STIMULI REVISITED

We began Chapter 5 by distinguishing between the distal stimulus (the object or event in the world that we wish to perceive) and the proximal stimulus (the energies that actually reach us from the distal stimulus), and, as our discussion proceeded, the contrast between the two has sharpened and grown. The proximal stimulus for vision is the pattern of light energies arriving at the retina, and is different in many ways from the world as we actually perceive it. For one thing, the proximal stimulus is two dimensional and not organized in any fashion—there is nothing in the light energies, for example, to indicate whether this color patch belongs to the same object as that, or whether they are parts of different objects. As another difference, the proximal stimulus changes whenever our viewing circumstances change, for example, if the sun comes out from behind a cloud, or if we move to a new viewing position. Let us also recall that there are two sets of proximal stimuli, one supplied by each eye, and yet we typically do not see double. Instead, we fuse the two images, and, indeed, this helps us to perceive depth. In addition, the proximal stimulus contains some elements that we must somehow "see past," in order to achieve an unobscured view of the world. For example, the proximal stimulus goes dark every time a person blinks, but this does not cause a perception of flicker in the world once or twice every second.

These points all serve to remind us that the visual system does indeed go beyond the information given (Bruner, 1973), and that the perceiver makes a substantial contribution at every step of the sequence from proximal stimulus to conscious perception. This contribution is evident when we consider the underlying biology (for example, see pp. 225–229), and also when we consider what the perceiver actually accomplishes: in parsing the input into groups; in identifying some of those groups as "figure"; in organizing the figure in depth; in choosing among alternative interpretations, to find the most logical one; in taking distance into account, in order to assess size; and so on. There can be no question, therefore, that the perceiver plays a crucial role—transforming a proximal stimulus, which in many ways is impoverished, into a perception of the distal stimulus that is coherent, complete, and precise—and, in general, extraordinarily accurate.

## SEEING AND KNOWING

This emphasis on the perceiver's active role, however, draws us to one final issue. Common sense tells us there is a difference between seeing and knowing: "I know that shirt is blue, but in this light it looks green." "Those stripes make me look fatter than I really am." "I know we've been cleaning up for hours, but it looks like we've barely started." In each of these cases, there is a distinction between appearances and what we know to be real.

In this chapter, though, we have blurred this line between seeing and knowing. We know, for example, that *CAT* is a common word, and this influences how we perceive

Figure 6.29. We know that solid objects cannot move through each other, and this influences how we perceive the motion pattern described in Figure 6.33. But, at the same time, there are limits on this pattern of results, and, in some regards, what we perceive seems well insulated from what we know or what we expect. This is evident in the so-called impossible figures (p. 225)—know these figures cannot possibly show three-dimensional forms, but we perceive them as if they were three dimensional anyhow. Likewise, we know that the "triangle" in Figure 6.27 really isn't there, but this knowledge does not alter our perception.

Of course, there must be limits on how knowledge and expectations influence what we see. After all, the mechanisms of perception evolved to serve an essential function: providing us with accurate and up-to-date information about the world around us. We obviously need this information to navigate through situations that are objectively dangerous (such as driving in heavy traffic), but the need is just as great in the ordinary circumstances that fill our lives: we cannot walk across a room unless we know what objects surround us and where they are. Plainly, then, perception must provide us with a relatively accurate portrait of the world around us—otherwise, we could not function.

However, the need for perception to be accurate takes nothing away from the fact that the interplay between perception and knowledge is complex, both in the ordinary workings of perception and in a very special setting: the representation of reality in art. Consider Figure 6.41, a wall painting from Egypt created some three thousand years ago. Why did the artist depict the figures as he did, with eyes and shoulders in front view and the rest of the body in profile? His fellow Egyptians were surely built as we are. But if so, why didn't he draw them "correctly"? The answer seems to be that Egyptian artists drew not what they could see at any one moment or from any one position, but rather what they believed was the most enduring and characteristic attribute of their model. They portrayed the various parts of the human body from the vantage point that shows each in its most distinguishable manner: the front view for the eyes and shoulders, the profile for the nose and feet. The fact that these orientations are incompatible was evidently of no concern; what mattered was that all of the components were represented as the artist knew them to be (Gombrich, 1961).

This example, drawn from the arts, reminds us that perception and conception, seeing and knowing—even if different from each other—interact in complex ways. In a real sense, therefore, we must connect our discussion of perception to our discussion of what we know, what we remember, and how we think. We turn to these latter topics in the next chapter.

**6.41   Horemhab offering wine to Annubis, ca. 1339–1304 B.C.E.   The conventions of Egyptian art required the main parts of the human body to be represented in their most characteristic view. Thus, heads are shown in profile, arms and legs from the side, but eyes are depicted in full-face view, as are shoulders and chest.**

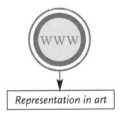

Representation in art

# SUMMARY

## THE COMPLEXITY OF PERCEPTION

1. The fundamental problem of perception is how we come to apprehend the objects and events in the world around us. One problem lies in how we grasp the meaning of the visual input. Another question is why we see any object at all. How do we see past the continual variations in the *proximal stimulus* to perceive the constant properties of the *distal stimulus,* the external object? To answer these questions, we must consider the way in which we see *depth, movement, and form.*

## THE PERCEPTION OF DEPTH: WHERE IS IT?

2. The visual world is seen in three dimensions even though only two of these are given in the image that falls upon

the eye. This fact has led to an interest in *depth cues.* Among these are *binocular disparity* and *monocular depth cues* (sometimes called *pictorial cues*) such as *interposition* and *linear perspective, relative size,* and *texture gradients.* Another source of information is provided by the motion of our heads and bodies. This leads to *motion parallax* and various patterns in the *optic flow,* all of which provide information about how far objects are from each other and from us. Many of these depth cues are redundant. This redundancy is helpful, because different distance cues become important in different circumstances (e.g., binocular disparity is only informative for objects relatively close by).

## THE PERCEPTION OF MOVEMENT: WHAT IS IT DOING?

3. What accounts for the perception of *movement*? One might think that we see things move because they produce an image that moves across the retina. In fact, there are cells in the visual cortex that respond to such movements on the retina, and function as *direction-specific motion detectors.* But retinal motion is only part of the story as shown by the phenomenon of *apparent movement,* in which a change in location without any actual movement produces a perception of movement.

4. The nervous system also needs to compensate for changes in eye or head position, to determine whether motion across the retina is produced by an object's movement in the environment or merely by a change in our viewing position. Further complications arise because we not only detect motion; we also interpret it, as shown by the barber-pole illusion and by the phenomenon of *induced motion.*

## FORM PERCEPTION: WHAT IS IT?

5. In vision, our primary means for recognizing an object is through the perception of its *form.* How do we do this? A simple memory checklist hypothesis is insufficient, in part because we recognize objects under various viewing conditions. As pointed out by *Gestalt psychology* we can also recognize forms even if many of their component parts are altered, as in the case of *transposition.*

6. Many modern investigators believe that form perception begins with the detection of *primitive features,* which can be identified by the fact that they "pop out" in a *visual search task.* In the early stages of processing, these features are detected but not related to each other, as shown by *illusory conjunctions.*

7. Unlike the identification of single features, perceiving a combination of features is not immediate or automatic. Instead, the coordination of features requires a separate step that occurs after the features are identified. Some confirmation comes from a study of a patient who suffered damage to the parietal cortex on both sides of the brain. When looking at a display, this person is able to report accurately what features are present, and can search successfully for targets defined by a single feature, but is unable to find targets defined by a combination of features. The demonstrates that there are separate mechanisms for the *detection* of features, and for the *integration* of these features to form complex wholes.

8. Before the perceiver can recognize a form, he must first engage in a process of *visual segregation* and *parse* the visual scene (also called *perceptual parsing*). This involves the segregation of *figure* and *ground,* which are not inherent in the proximal stimulus but are imposed by the perceptual system, as shown by *reversible figures.* Further segregation produces perceptual *grouping,* which depends upon factors such as *proximity, similarity,* and *good continuation.* According to some theorists, the phenomenon of *subjective contours* is a special case of good continuation.

9. *Pattern recognition* involves two kinds of processes. One is *bottom-up* (or *data-driven*) processing, which starts with the stimulus and subjects it to an analysis that begins with lower-level units (such as slanted lines) that then activate higher-level units (such as geometrical figures). The other is *top-down* (or *knowledge-driven*) processing, which is based on expectations and hypotheses, as shown by *perceptual context effects* and *priming.* These top-down processes are able to prime lower-level detectors, so that they will respond even to weak inputs. Bottom-up and top-down processes work together, resulting in a process that allows lower-level units to activate higher-level units and also higher-level units to activate lower-level ones.

10. To account for the recognition of ordinary, three-dimensional objects, theorists have proposed that pattern recognition also involves an intermediate level of analysis, in which features are assembled into object parts. One proposal is that these parts are *geons,* which are then assembled to form a structural description of the object.

11. These various processing steps often occur simultaneously rather than in sequence—in *parallel,* rather than in a *serial* pattern.

12. Top-down processes provide *perceptual hypotheses* that are then tested by bottom-up processes. The result is sometimes described as *perceptual problem solving,* with the observer's perceptions apparently guided by a number of logical principles, including a principle that all the information within the stimulus must be explained, and an avoidance of interpretations that depend on accident or coincidence.

## FORM PERCEPTION AND THE NERVOUS SYSTEM

13. The neural processes that underlie perception involve a number of specialized subsystems. On the retina, two types of ganglion cells are sensitive to different aspects of the visual input: *parvo cells* are sensitive to color differences and seem crucial for the perception of pattern and form; *magno cells* are color blind and play an essential role in the detection of motion and the perception of depth. In the visual cortex, different types of cells each respond to specific aspects of the stimulus. This pattern of neural specialization continues and sharpens at further levels of the nervous system. These different analyses go on in parallel, with the cells analyzing the forms within the visual input doing their work at the same time that other cells are analyzing the motion and still others analyzing the colors.

14. Information from the visual cortex is transmitted to two other important brain areas; one in the temporal cortex, often called the *"what" system*, the other in the parietal cortex, often called the *"where" system*. The "what" system is crucial for the identification of visual objects, the "where" system tells us where a stimulus is located.

15. The division into the various specialized neural subsystems allows us to perceive an extraordinary range of stimuli with extraordinary speed. But this sub-specialization raises a problem. How do we integrate these disparate pieces of information into one whole? This question, called the *binding problem*, continues to be a subject of intense research. There is some evidence that the binding is accomplished by means of *neural synchrony*: if (for example) the neurons detecting a *vertical* line are firing in synchrony with those signaling *movement*, then these attributes are registered as belonging to the same object. Synchronized neural firing, therefore, may be the nervous system's way of representing the fact that different attributes are bound together and, are parts of a single object. But how do the neurons become synchronized in the first place? One factor plays an essential role: namely, *attention*.

## PERCEPTUAL SELECTION: ATTENTION

16. Perception is selective. This selection is partially achieved by *orienting*, as in the case of *eye movements*. It is also achieved by a central process, *selective attention*. Methods for studying attention include *selective looking*, as demonstrated in visual search tasks, and *selective listening*, as shown by *dichotic presentation* in which the subject shadows one message while ignoring another.

## PERCEIVING CONSTANCY

17. The ultimate function of perception is to help the organism apprehend the outside world as it really is. This is illustrated by the *perceptual constancies* in which the perceiver responds to certain permanent characteristics of the *distal object* despite various contextual factors—including *illumination*, *distance*, and *orientation*—that lead to enormous variations in the proximal stimulus. In *size* and *shape constancy*, the perceiver responds to the actual size and shape of the object more or less regardless of its distance and orientation, in part by drawing *unconscious inferences* about its size and shape based on distance away and angle of regard.

# MEMORY

*A*s we move through our lives, we are dependent both on the information provided by our senses and on the information supplied by memory. We need to know what objects and events surround us right now, but we also need to relate these things to our experiences last year, last month, and even just moments ago. For this recollection, we need memory.

Perceiving and remembering are obviously different activities, but, as we will see, many of the principles we needed in our discussion of perception will be just as useful in our discussion of memory. For example, in the last two chapters we emphasized the active role of the perceiver in organizing and interpreting the incoming sensory information, and in filling in gaps in a way that allows one to perceive a complete and coherent world based on input that is often incomplete or ambiguous. Many of the same lessons apply to memory. Here, too, the individual plays an active part, organizing and interpreting and filling in gaps to supplement the bits supplied by recollection. As with perception, this active role usually serves us well. It provides us with memories that are typically accurate and complete, and a process of remembering that is remarkably efficient, allowing us to locate the information we need, within the vast warehouse of memory, with incredible speed. But as with perception, these interpretive steps can open the door for memory errors and illusions, even when we feel certain that our memories are absolutely correct.

Memory is a topic of central interest to psychologists, and it is not difficult to see why. All the facts that we know and the skills that we possess are recorded in our memories, and so without memory there would be no knowledge and no skills. Every time we recall an episode from our past, we are relying on memory, and so, without memory, there would never be any recollection of prior events. If we are able to navigate to the store, humming a song as we go, recognizing friends along the way, it is because we remember the route and the song, and remember our friends' faces. Indeed, knowing that our friends are our friends (perhaps because we recall how they have helped us in the past) is dependent on memory, as is knowing who our foes are. For that matter, memory is also the basis for the sense of who we are that each of us carries. Are you proud of who you are? If so, it is probably because you remember your past achievements. Are you embarrassed about who you are? If so, it is probably because you recall your shortcomings. If you feel happy about your life, or sad, you are probably being influenced by your memory of positive things you have experienced, or negative. In all of these cases, your perception of yourself and your life—and with that, your mood and your self-esteem—is dependent on memory. Putting all of these pieces together, therefore, it is no wonder that psychologists regard the study of memory as a topic of enormous importance, relevant to a broad range of concerns.

# ACQUISITION, STORAGE, RETRIEVAL

How do psychologists study memory? The first step is to realize that memory is not a single entity and that there is no single set of memory processes. Instead, the term *memory* is a blanket label for a large number of processes that work together to create a bridge between our past and our present. Let us start by examining what the various types of memory have in common.

Any act of remembering implies success at three aspects of the memory process. First, in order to remember, one must have learned. This seems an obvious point, but it deserves emphasis because many failures of memory are, in fact, failures in this initial stage of *acquisition*. For example, imagine meeting someone at a party, being told his name, and moments later realizing that you no longer know it! This embarrassing (but common) experience is probably not the result of ultrarapid forgetting. Instead, it is likely to stem from a failure in acquisition. You were exposed to the name but barely paid attention to it and, as a result, never learned it in the first place.

The next aspect of remembering is storage. To be remembered, an experience must leave some record in the nervous system (the *memory trace*); it must be squirreled away and held in some enduring form for later use. One question to be asked here is how a memory's content is actually recorded in the brain tissue. How, for example,

*Using memory   Games (like the card game "Memory") obviously depend on what we remember. But memory also matters for a wide range of other functions—including functions that seem, on first inspection, not to depend on remembering at all.*

does an assembly of neurons manage to record the fact that you had lunch with Jill yesterday, and felt good about how the meal went? So far, scientists know relatively little about this issue, and it will probably be many years before we can address this sort of question.

Another question to be asked about storage concerns where in the brain the memories are recorded. Interestingly, the evidence suggests that individual memories are not stored in specific brain sites. Instead, any individual memory is distributed across a large section of brain tissue, with different bits of the memory stored in widely scattered locations, and the entire memory represented only through the pattern of activity across a vast number of brain cells.

The final phase of remembering is *retrieval*, the point at which we draw information from storage and use it in some fashion. One way to retrieve material is through *recall*. This is the process in which we draw information from memory in response to a cue or question. Trying to answer a question like "What is Sue's boyfriend's name?" or "Can you remember the last time you were in California?" or "What is 'classical conditioning'?" requires recall.

A different way to retrieve information is through *recognition*. In this kind of retrieval, we are presented with a name, fact, or situation and are asked if we have encountered it before. "Is this the man you saw at the bank robbery?" or "Was the movie you saw called *Memento?*" would be a question requiring recognition. When recognition is tested in the laboratory, research participants are usually asked to pick out the previously encountered item from a group of options ("Which of these pictures is the one you saw earlier?"). This format resembles a multiple-choice test, and in fact, multiple-choice testing in the classroom puts a premium on the ability to recognize previously learned material. In contrast, essay or short-answer examinations emphasize recall.

# ENCODING

People commonly speak of memorizing new facts, or, more broadly, of learning new material. However, psychologists prefer the term *memory acquisition*, using it to include cases of deliberate memorization and *incidental learning*, learning that takes place without any intention to learn and often without the awareness that learning is actually occurring. (You know that grass is green and the sky is blue, and you probably can easily recall what you had for dinner yesterday, but you did not set out to memorize these; the learning, therefore, was incidental.)

Crucially, memory acquisition is not a simple matter of "copying" an event or a fact into memory, the way a camera copies an image onto film. Instead, acquisition requires some attention to the to-be-remembered material, and some intellectual engagement with that material—thinking about it in some way. It is then the product of this engagement—what you thought about during the to-be-remembered event—that is stored in memory. In a sense, then, memory acquisition involves a translation process, translating the raw input into an intellectual record of the input. Investigators call this process *memory encoding*.

## THE STAGE THEORY OF MEMORY

Memory has often been compared to a storehouse. This conception goes back to ancient Greek philosophers who compared memories to objects that are put into storage compartments, held for a while, and then searched for at a later time (Crowder, 1985; Roediger, 1980). In more modern terms, this conception compares memory to a computer hard-drive: memories are saved onto the drive, reside there until needed, and are then retrieved when you want to make use of them.

The *stage theory of memory*, developed roughly forty years ago, builds on this conception, but at the heart of the theory is the idea that there is not just one memory warehouse. Instead, there are several storage systems, each with different properties (Atkinson & Shiffrin, 1968; Broadbent, 1958; Waugh & Norman, 1965), and it is the "movement" through these various systems that provides the "stages" in the stage theory.

Why would we need several kinds of memory? Think about the relationship between your desktop and your bookshelves. Your shelves hold many books and thus a great deal of information. But this information is not instantly available to you; if you want to check on some fact, you probably need to spend a few moments searching for the right book, and then hunting through that book to find the information you need. If you are actively working with some information (writing a paper, for example, or studying for an exam), you probably want it to be more accessible than this, and so you spread the relevant books out on your desktop. Now the information is immediately available to you, but with a clear limit: your desktop has a fixed size, and so only a few books can be displayed at any one time; the rest must remain on the shelves.

Each of these modes of storage, therefore, has its own advantages and disadvantages, and each of us has learned to use the two together in order to gain the benefits of both. We want to retain a great deal of information for the long term, but we do not want to be distracted by that information right now, and we do not want that information to hide from view the information we are working with at that moment. For this purpose, our shelves provide effective storage. But we also want to maximize the accessibility of information we are currently working with, and, for this, we use the desktop—limited in size, but putting the information we need right at our fingertips.

The stage theory proposes a similar architecture for memory, distinguishing between working memory (called *short-term memory* in the original theory) and long-term memory. *Working memory* holds information for short intervals—that is, while we are working with it. *Long-term memory*, in contrast, stores materials for much longer, sometimes for as long as a lifetime.*

## THE STORAGE CAPACITY OF WORKING AND LONG-TERM MEMORY

Working memory and long-term memory differ in many important ways. One difference is in the *storage capacity* of each. The capacity of long-term memory is enormous. The average college student remembers the meanings of 80,000 words, thousands of autobiographical episodes, millions of facts, hundreds of skills, the taste of vanilla, and the smell of lemon. All of this and much more are stored in long-term memory.

In contrast, the capacity of working memory is exceedingly limited. Traditionally, this capacity has been measured by a *memory span* task in which the individual hears a series of items and must repeat them, in order, after just one presentation. If the items are randomly chosen letters or digits, adults can repeat seven items or so without error. With longer series, errors are likely. This has led to the assertion that working memory's capacity is seven items, give or take one or two. In fact, many tasks, not just memory span, show this limit of seven plus-or-minus two items, leading psychologists to refer to this as the *magic number* (after Miller, 1956). Given the assumption that a wide range of tasks must rely on working memory, it is perhaps unsurprising that this limit—presumably, a reflection of the small size of this memory—sets a boundary on performance in a variety of settings. (For more on the measurement of working memory, see Chapter 15.)

---

* The original theory asserted that an additional stage—a sensory register in which sensory material is held for a second or two—precedes the others (Atkinson & Shiffrin, 1968; Sperling, 1960).

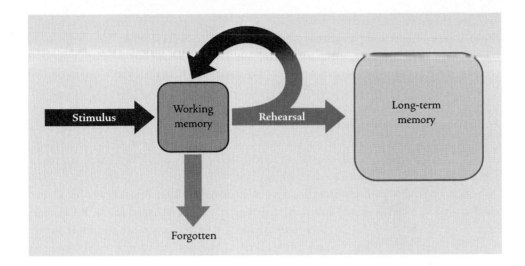

7.1 *The relation between working memory and long-term memory as envisaged by stage theory* The figure is a schematic representation of the relation between the two memory systems as stage theorists conceive of them. Information is encoded and enters working memory. To enter the long-term store, it must remain in working memory for a while. The means for maintaining it there is rehearsal. (Adapted from Waugh & Norman, 1965)

## WORKING MEMORY AS A LOADING PLATFORM

What is the relation between working memory and long-term memory? The stage theory asserts that the road to long-term memory necessarily passes through working memory. Seen in this light, working memory could be regarded as a loading platform, sitting at the entrance to the huge long-term warehouse.

*Transfer into Long-Term Memory*  If working memory is the loading platform for long-term memory, then what is it that moves information off of the platform and into more permanent storage? One key factor, according to the stage theory, is memory *rehearsal*, a process through which items are kept in working memory for an extended period of time, increasing the likelihood that these items will be transferred to long-term storage (see Figure 7.1).

To see how rehearsal matters, consider how the stage model accounts for some classic results obtained with list-learning procedures. In these procedures, research participants hear a series of unrelated words, each presented just once, one word at a time. At the end of the list, the participants are asked to recall the items in any order they choose (this is why the participants' task is called *free recall*). If the list contains just six or seven items, participants are likely to remember them all. But, if the list is longer, the participants will not remember all the words and there is a clear pattern for which ones they recall and which ones they do not: words presented at the beginning of the list are quite likely to be recalled; this is called the *primacy effect*. Likewise, the last few words presented are also likely to be recalled; this is the *recency effect*. The likelihood of recall is appreciably poorer for words in the middle of the list (see Figure 7.2).

What creates this pattern? As the to-be-remembered words are presented, the participant pays attention to them, and this ensures that a representation of each word is placed in working memory. Bear in mind, though, that working memory is limited in size, and so, as participants try to keep up with the list presentation, the newly arriving words will bump the previous words out of this memory. Therefore, as participants proceed through the list, their working memories at each moment will contain just the half-dozen words that arrived most recently.

On this account, the only words that do not get bumped out of working memory are the last few words on the list, since obviously no further input arrives to displace these words. Hence, when the list presentation ends, these few words are still in working memory and are easily retrieved. This is why participants remember the end of the list so accurately—the pattern we called the recency effect.

In contrast, the items recalled from the beginning of the list must be retrieved from long-term memory. (This must be the case, since these words were displaced from

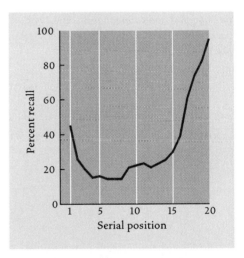

7.2 *Primacy and recency effects in free recall* Research participants heard a list of twenty common words presented at a rate of one word per second. Immediately after hearing the list, participants were asked to write down as many of the words on the list as they could recall. The results show that position in the series strongly affected recall: the words at the beginning (primacy effect) and at the end (recency effect) were recalled more frequently than those in the middle. (After Murdock, 1962)

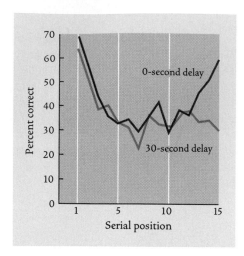

**7.3   The recency effect and working memory**
*Research participants heard several fifteen-word lists. In one condition (red), free recall was tested immediately after they heard the list. In the other condition (green), the recall test was given after a thirty-second delay during which rehearsal was prevented. The delay left the primacy effect unaffected but abolished the recency effect, indicating that this effect is based on retrieval from working memory. (After Glanzer & Cunitz, 1966)*

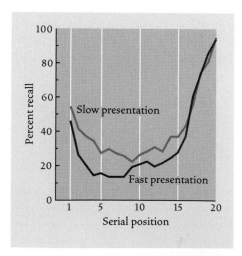

**7.4   The primacy effect and long-term storage**
*The figure compares free-recall performance when item presentation is relatively slow (two seconds per item) and fast (one second per item). Slow presentation enhances the primacy effect but leaves the recency effect unaltered. The additional second per item presumably allows more time for rehearsal, which leads to long-term storage. (After Murdock, 1962)*

working memory and so cannot be retrieved from that store.) What, then, produces the primacy effect? One hypothesis is that individuals have more opportunity to rehearse the earliest items in the list, increasing the likelihood that these items will be transferred into long-term storage. To see why, let us say that the first word on the list is *camera*. When research participants hear this word, they can focus their full attention on it, silently rehearsing "*camera, camera, camera, . . .*" When the second word arrives, they will rehearse that one too, but they will now have to divide their attention between the first word and the second one ("*camera, boat, camera, boat, . . .*"). Attention will be divided still further after hearing the third word ("*camera, boat, zebra, camera, boat, zebra, . . .*"), and so through the list.

Notice, then, that earlier words get more attention than later ones. At the list's start, participants can lavish attention on the few words they have heard so far. But as they hear more and more of the list, they must divide their attention more and more thinly, since they have more words to keep track of. This provides our account of the primacy effect: earlier words receive more attention than later words and so are more likely to make it into the long-term warehouse. As a consequence, they are more likely to be recalled later.

Supporting evidence for these interpretations comes from various manipulations that affect the primacy and recency effects. For example, what happens if we require research participants to do some other task immediately after hearing the words but before recalling them? This other task will briefly require the use of working memory, but this should be enough to displace this memory's current contents. Those contents, of course, are the hypothesized source of the recency effect, and so, according to our hypothesis, this task, even if it lasts just a few seconds, should disrupt the recency effect. And it does. If participants are required to count backward for just thirty seconds between hearing the words and recalling them, the recency effect is eliminated (see Figure 7.3).

Other manipulations produce a different pattern—diminishing the primacy effect but having no effect on recency. An example is the rate at which items are presented. If this rate is relatively fast, participants have less time for rehearsal. As a result, there is less transfer to long-term storage. We therefore should expect a reduced primacy effect (since primacy depends on retrieval from long-term memory) but no change in the recency effect (because the recency items are not being retrieved from long-term memory). This is exactly what happens (see Figure 7.4).

## RECODING TO EXPAND THE CAPACITY OF WORKING MEMORY

As we have seen, working memory has a limited capacity: it can handle only a small number of packages at any one time. However, what these packages contain is, to a large extent, up to us. If we can pack the input more efficiently, we can squeeze more information into the same number of memory units.

*Recoding into Larger Chunks*   As an example, consider an individual who tries to recall a series of digits that he heard only once:

$$149162536496481$$

If he treats this as a series of fifteen unrelated digits, he will almost surely fail. But if he recognizes that the digits form a pattern, specifically

$$1\ 4\ 9\ 16\ 25\ 36\ 49\ 64\ 81$$

his task becomes much easier. He only has to remember the underlying relationship, "the squares of the digits from 1 to 9," and the fifteen components of the series are easily re-created.

*The role of chunking in remembering a visual display*  **Could you possibly remember all the figures in this bewildering array? You might, if you knew Netherlandish proverbs of the sixteenth century, for that is what the painting depicts. To mention only some, there is (going from left to right): a man who "butts his head against the wall," another who is "armed to the teeth," and two women of whom "one spins while the other winds" (malicious gossips). Going further right, we see a woman who "puts a blue cloak over her husband" (deceives him), and a man who "fills the hole after his calf was drowned." Recognizing these scenes as illustrations of familiar proverbs will organize the visual array and thus help you to remember its many parts.**

In this example, the person repackages the material to be remembered, *recoding* the input into larger units that are often called chunks. Recoding makes the material much easier to remember and allows the person to remember much more, because working memory's capacity is measured in chunks, rather than in bits of information.

Much of the recoding of memory items, or **chunking**, happens quite automatically. For example, consider memory for sentences. If we have to recall a list of random words (*chair, line, smoke, page,...*), we are unlikely to remember more than six or seven of them. But we can often recall a fairly long sentence after only a single exposure. This fact holds even for sentences that make little sense, such as *The enemy submarine dove into the coffee pot, took fright, and silently flew away.* This dubious bit of naval intelligence consists of fourteen words, but it clearly contains fewer than fourteen memorial packages: the enemy submarine is essentially one unit, took fright is another, and so on. (For more on chunking, see Gobet et al., 2001.)

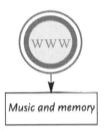

Music and memory

## A CHANGED EMPHASIS: ACTIVE MEMORY AND ORGANIZATION

The stage theory dominated memory research for several decades. But as time went on, there was a reevaluation. The evidence indicated that the theory had described the "architecture" of memory in roughly the right way. But what it failed to encompass was the enormously important role of the learner—her strategies and goals and, above all, the previous knowledge that she brings to the learning situation.

### WORKING MEMORY AS AN ACTIVE PROCESS

One shortcoming of the stage theory lies in how it explained the transfer of information from the short-term loading platform into the long-term warehouse. According to the theory, this transfer depends to a large extent on how long the information sits on the platform. The longer it sits there, the greater the probability of its being transferred. This implies that rehearsal promotes memory for a simple reason: it keeps information in working memory longer, increasing the likelihood of transfer into more permanent storage.

*The work in working memory*  *Working memory is crucial for virtually any task, because it is in this memory that you hold materials or ideas you are working on right now.*

It turns out, however, that entering long-term memory is not this automatic and depends on more than the mere passage of time. The evidence comes from studies of *maintenance rehearsal*, a strategy that keeps information in working memory but with little long-term effect. As an everyday example, consider what happens when you look up a telephone number. You need to retain the number long enough to complete the dialing, but you have no need to memorize the number for later use. In this circumstance, you are likely to employ maintenance rehearsal: you repeat the number to yourself while you dial. But what happens if the line is busy? A moment later, you try to dial the number again but realize you have already forgotten it. Maintenance rehearsal kept the number in working memory long enough for you to dial it the first time but failed to establish it in long-term memory. As a result, the number is forgotten after just a few seconds.

Many laboratory studies have confirmed the claim that maintenance rehearsal provides poor preparation for subsequent recall (e.g., Craik & Watkins, 1973). More compelling evidence, though, comes from a study of everyday remembering. To understand this study, let us start by asking how often the typical American has seen a penny. Perhaps fifteen thousand times (roughly twice a day for twenty years)? In each of these encounters, though, there was no reason to scrutinize the penny, no reason to think about the penny's appearance. On the logic we have just developed, people's memory for the penny should be quite poor. And it is. In one study, participants were asked whether Lincoln's profile, shown on the heads side of the penny, faced to the right or to the left. Only half of the participants got this question right, exactly what one would expect if they were merely guessing. This provides striking confirmation of the fact that memory requires mental engagement with a target and not mere exposure (Nickerson & Adams, 1979).

## THE WORK IN WORKING MEMORY

The fact that maintenance rehearsal does not promote long-term retention tells us that the transfer to long-term memory is not automatic; instead, some sort of work is involved in making this transfer happen. By the same token, it seems that working memory is not just a passive receptacle in which materials rest on their way to long-term storage. Instead, we should conceive of working memory in more active terms, terms that reflect the work that is being done there.

This point highlights the contrast between the stage theory and most contemporary views of memory. Current theorists emphasize the fact that long-term memories are formed by an active process in which the individual's own way of encoding and organizing the material plays a major role. As a result, they regard working memory not so much as a temporary storage platform but rather as a mental workbench on which various items of experience are sorted, manipulated, and organized. According to this view, how well information will be retained in memory does not depend on a simple transfer from one storage container to another. Instead, it depends on how this material is processed (that is, encoded and recoded). The more elaborate the processing, the greater the likelihood of recall and recognition.

Considerations of this sort provide one of the reasons why working memory is now named as it is, in place of the older term *short-term memory* (see, for example, Crowder, 1982). The newer term appropriately draws our attention to the activity and processing made possible by working memory, rather than treating this memory merely as a box in which information is passively held.

Perhaps, therefore, the appropriate metaphor for working memory is not really a loading platform that can hold only so many parcels. It is, rather, an overworked operative at the memory workbench, an operative who can pack only so many parcels—can do only so much chunking and organizing—at any one time. It is as if he (or she or it) has only so many mental hands (Baddeley, 1976, 1986).

## PROCESSING AND ORGANIZING:
## THE ROYAL ROAD INTO MEMORY

Our discussion invites some obvious questions. If memories are formed by an active process, then what is that process? If some forms of encoding or rehearsal are more helpful than others, what identifies the more effective strategies?

*Depth of Processing*  One influential position hypothesizes that success in remembering depends on the depth at which the incoming information is processed (Craik & Lockhart, 1972). For verbal materials, **shallow processing** refers to encoding that emphasizes the superficial characteristics of a stimulus, such as the typeface in which a word is printed. In contrast, **deep processing** refers to encoding that emphasizes the meaning of the material.

Many experiments suggest that deep processing leads to much better recall. In one study, research participants were told that the researchers were studying perception and speed of reaction and then were shown forty-eight words. As each word was presented, the participants were asked a question about it. For some words, they were asked about the word's physical appearance ("Is it printed in capital letters?"); this should produce shallow encoding. For others, they were asked about the word's sound ("Does it rhyme with train?"); this should engender an intermediate level of encoding. For the remainder, they were asked about the word's meaning ("Would it fit into the sentence: The girl placed the _____ on the table?"); this presumably would lead to deep encoding. After the participants had gone through the entire list of words, they were given an unexpected task: they were asked to write down as many of the words as they could remember. The results were in line with the **depth-of-processing hypothesis**. The participants recalled very few of the words that called for shallow processing (typeface); words that required an intermediary level (sound) were recalled a bit better; and words that demanded the deepest level (meaning) were recalled best of all (Craik & Tulving, 1975).

Other experiments have applied this approach to nonverbal stimuli, such as faces. Here, too, instructions for deep processing (for example, thinking about the personality of the person being viewed) promoted memory (Bloom & Mudd, 1991; Reinitz, Morrissey, & Demb, 1994; Shapiro & Penrod, 1986; Sporer, 1991). However, we should note that it is sometimes difficult to apply the depth-of-processing hypothesis to other, more complex cases, largely because the central term, *depth*, is not well defined (see, for example, Baddeley, 1978). Even so, this approach does provide a useful rule of thumb: the more attention we pay to the meaning of what we hear and see and read, the better we will remember it.

*The Role of Understanding*  The depth-of-processing hypothesis emphasizes the importance of meaning in producing good memory: if we pay attention to the meaning of materials we encounter, we are more likely to remember those materials. But it is not just the search for meaning that matters. Instead, memory is promoted by *finding* the meaning, that is, by finding an understanding of the to-be-remembered materials.

Support for this claim comes from many sources. In some studies, experimenters gave participants material to read that is difficult to understand, and then, immediately after, probed them to see whether (or how well) they understood the material. Some time later, the experimenters tested the participants' memory for this material. The result was straightforward: the better the understanding, the better the memory later on.

Other studies manipulated whether the to-be-remembered material is understandable or not. For example, in one experiment the following tape-recorded passage was presented:

*Active encoding    Placing information into long-term storage requires active attention, and some sort of intellectual engagement with the to-be-remembered material. Passive exposure or rote repetition are largely ineffective in promoting long-term retention. All of this has obvious implications for students hoping to remember the material they learn in their classes!*

The procedure is actually quite simple. First you arrange things into different groups depending on their makeup. Of course, one pile may be sufficient depending on how much there is to do. If you have to go somewhere else due to lack of facilities that is the next step; otherwise you are pretty well set. It is important not to overdo any particular endeavor. That is, it is better to do too few things at once than too many. In the short run this may not seem important, but complications from doing too many can easily arise. A mistake can be expensive as well. The manipulation of the appropriate mechanisms should be self-explanatory, and we need not dwell on it here. At first, the whole procedure will seem complicated. Soon, however, it will become just another facet of life. It is difficult to foresee any end to the necessity for this task in the immediate future, but then one never can tell. (From Bransford & Johnson, 1972, p. 722)

Half of the people heard this passage without any further information as to what it was about, and, when tested later, their memory for the passage was poor. The other participants, though, were given a clue that helped them to understand the passage—they were told, "The paragraph you will hear will be about washing clothes." This clue, allowing them to make sense of the material, dramatically improved later recall (Bransford & Johnson, 1972).

A picture we saw in the previous chapter (p. 224) can be used to make a similar point with a nonverbal stimulus. This picture is immensely difficult to remember unless one detects the pattern. But if the pattern is detected, the picture becomes meaningful, and then it is effortlessly remembered (Wiseman & Neisser, 1974).

Before moving on, we should note that there is a powerful message here for anyone hoping to remember some body of material—for example, a student trying to learn material for the next quiz. Study techniques that emphasize the meaning of the to-be-remembered material, and that involve efforts toward understanding the material, are likely to pay off with good memory later on. Memory strategies that do not emphasize meaning will provide much more limited effects.

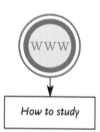

How to study

## MNEMONICS AND MEMORY CONNECTIONS

Why is it that attention to meaning improves memory? Why does understanding aid subsequent recall? Many investigators believe that the key lies in memory connections linking one memory to the next. In understanding something—a story, perhaps, or a picture or an event—we grasp how each element of the material is linked to the others: this caused that; this is in place despite that; this has to balance that; and so on. In essence, then, we can think of understanding as largely a matter of seeing these connections, and the more connections seen, the deeper the understanding.*

When the time comes to recall something, these connections serve as *retrieval paths*. If, in your understanding of an event, you saw that Jane's smile caused Tarzan to howl, then, later, thinking of Jane's smile will bring Tarzan's howl into your thoughts. The connection you saw early on will lead you from one memory to the other, as if the connection were a pathway along which your thoughts could travel.

Support for this idea comes from a practical endeavor whose roots go back to ancient times—the development of techniques for improving memory. These techniques are called *mnemonics*, and, as it turns out, virtually all mnemonics build on the same base:

"You simply associate each number with a word, such as 'table' and 3,476,029."

* Let us note that this appeal to memory connections raises many questions. How are these connections realized in the brain? Is there just one type of memory connection or a variety of types, each serving its own role? And, above all, how are more complex assemblies of ideas created? Are they made up simply of many ideas linked, pair by pair, via simple associations? Or is there some sort of order and organization to the pattern of connections? These questions present difficult and controversial issues. For now, though, we can hold these issues to the side, and focus simply on the essential idea that memories can be (somehow) connected to each other and that these connections have a number of functional consequences, as we describe in the next several pages.

to remember well, it pays to establish memory connections, and, if those connections are established, then substantial remembering is almost guaranteed.

*Mnemonics through Verbal Organization*  The ancients were well aware that it is easier to remember verbal material if it is organized, with each word or phrase linked to others within the material that is being memorized. Verse, with word sequences that maintain a fixed rhythm or rhyme, provides one way to achieve this organization, and many cultures at many times have exploited this fact. Without the use of verse, preliterate societies might never have transmitted their oral traditions intact from one generation to the next. Homeric bards could recite the entire *Iliad*, but could they have done so had it been in prose? Even in modern times, verse is still used as an effective mnemonic ("Thirty days hath September, April, June, and November").

*Mnemonics Based on Visual Imagery*  Other mnemonics involve the deliberate use of mental imagery. One such technique is the **method of loci**, which requires the learner to visualize each of the items she wants to remember in a different spatial location (locus). In recall, each location is mentally inspected and the item that was placed there in imagination is retrieved.

The effectiveness of this method is easy to demonstrate. In one study, college students had to learn lists of forty unrelated concrete nouns. Each list was presented once for about ten minutes, during which the students tried to visualize each of the forty objects in one of forty different locations around their college campus. Tested immediately, they recalled an average of thirty-eight of the forty items; tested one day later, they still managed to recall thirty-four (Bower, 1970, 1972; Higbee, 1977; Roediger, 1980; Ross & Lawrence, 1968). In other studies, participants using the method of loci were able to retain seven times more than their counterparts who learned in a rote manner.

In order for imagery to be helpful, however, the image must link the to-be-remembered materials to each other or to other things the person knows—and so here, too, we see the importance of memory connections. To make this concrete, consider a person who has to learn a list of word pairs and who chooses to use imagery as an aid. He might construct mental pictures that bring the items into some kind of relationship, linking them in some way. For example, to remember the pair *eagle-train*, he might imagine an eagle winging to its nest with a locomotive in its beak. Alternatively, he might only imagine the eagle and the locomotive side by side, not interacting. Evidence indicates that images of the first (interacting) sort produce much better recall than nonunifying images (Wollen, Weber, & Lowry, 1972). A similar effect is found when the test items are pictures, rather than words. Pictures with interacting parts are remembered much more effectively than are pictures with their constituents merely side by side and not interacting (Figure 7.5).

A                    B

7.5  *Interactive and noninteractive depictions*  **Research participants shown related elements, such as a doll sitting on a chair and waving a flag (A), are more likely to associate the words doll, flag, and chair than participants who are shown the three objects next to each other but not interacting (B). (After Bower, 1970)**

*The Usefulness of Mnemonics in Everyday Life*  There are actually many different types of mnemonic systems, and these systems are quite useful in memorizing a list of foreign vocabulary words or the unfamiliar materials sometimes encountered in the psychology laboratory. But what about memorizing more meaningful materials, such as a philosopher's argument or a pattern of evidence favoring a particular historical claim? Here, too, mnemonics will be effective, but it is probably a mistake to use mnemonics with such materials, because the mnemonics, powerful as they are, will not lead to the sort of memory most people want.

Why is this? Mnemonics are an effective tool for memorization because they lead the memorizer to focus on a relatively narrow set of memory links—the fact that the locomotive is in the eagle's beak, or the fact that September rhymes with November. With attention lavished on these few links, it is no surprise that the relevant memory connections end up well established and able to serve as efficient retrieval paths later on.

The problem, though, is that people often want more than a narrow set of links; instead, they want a rich network of connections, tying the to-be-learned material to many other beliefs and ideas. During learning, seeking these connections will help them understand the material by placing it into a broader mental context. During retrieval, these same connections will provide a variety of different retrieval paths, all leading to the target material. This will allow the person to recall the material from multiple perspectives and in multiple contexts, which in turn will allow more flexible retrieval, certainly helping people to use the material they have learned.

All of these gains, though, depend on finding multiple memory connections—precisely what mnemonics do not accomplish. Thinking about the eagle with the locomotive in its beak does nothing to promote one's understanding of the fragile ecosystem within which eagles live, or the locomotive's role in moving freight. During retrieval, this image will be quite helpful if one is asked, "What word went with *eagle*?," but may be of little value in responding to some other memory cue.

In short, then, mnemonics are useful for memorizing material that, by itself, has no internal organization. But if the material to be learned is meaningful or already organized, the best approach is to seek an understanding of the material when it is being learned. This will lead to the best memory as well as to flexibility in how the target information can be retrieved.

# RETRIEVAL

When we learn, we transfer new information from working memory into our long-term store of knowledge. But successful encoding is not enough. We must also be able to retrieve the information when we need it; otherwise, what we have learned will be useless to us. The importance (and potential difficulty) of retrieval is obvious to anyone who has ever experienced a "block" on a familiar name. We may know the name (have encoded and stored it) but be unable to retrieve it when trying to introduce an old friend to a new one. In such cases, the memory trace is said to be inaccessible.

Often retrieval seems effortless. You are asked your middle name and instantly respond. Sometimes, though, retrieval is more difficult, requiring effort and a deliberate search for retrieval cues. You walk out of the shopping mall and cannot remember where you parked your car. But then you recollect that your first stop was at the drugstore, and this seems to trigger the memory of squeezing the car into a narrow space in the lot near the store.

In still other cases, retrieval initially seems impossible, as though the target information was truly lost. But then some **retrieval cue** is presented and suddenly the memory returns. A return to your hometown, for example, after a long absence, may unleash a flood of recollection, as the sights and sounds of the place effectively trigger the relevant memories. A word, a smell, a visit from a school friend not seen for years—any of these may summon memories you thought were utterly lost.

## THE RELATION BETWEEN ORIGINAL ENCODING AND RETRIEVAL

What makes a retrieval cue effective? Why do some reminders succeed, while others have no effect? One important factor is whether the cue re-creates the context in which the original learning occurred. For example, if an individual focused on the sounds of words while learning them, then he will be well served by reminders that focus on sound ("Was there a word on the list that rhymes with *log*?"); if he focused on meaning while learning, then the best reminder would be one that again draws his attention toward meaning ("Was one of the words a type of fruit?"; Fisher & Craik, 1977).

Why should this be? Our earlier discussion of memory connections provides the answer. Learning, we suggested, can be thought of as a process of creating (or strengthening) memory connections that link the to-be-remembered material to other things you already know. When the time comes for retrieval, these same connections serve as retrieval paths, leading you back to the desired information.

If, therefore, an individual focused on the sounds of words during learning, this established a corresponding set of memory connections—a connection, for example, between *dog* and *log*. That connection will be useful later if the person is asked the question about rhymes: if he thinks about *log*, the connection will guide his thoughts to the target word, *dog*. But this connection will play little role in other contexts. If he is asked, "Did any of the words on the list name animals with sharp teeth?," the path from *log* to *dog* is irrelevant; what he needs with this cue is a retrieval path leading from *sharp teeth* to the target.

This is why retrieval is most likely to succeed when the cues and context during retrieval match those in place during the initial encoding. The shared context will allow a person to make best use of the connections established earlier; a change in context, in contrast, can render these connections irrelevant (no matter how well established they are). This principle is often referred to as *encoding specificity*, marking the fact that ideas and events are encoded from a particular perspective and within a particular context (Hintzman, 1990; Tulving & Osler, 1968; Tulving & Thomson, 1973). The optimal retrieval cue, therefore, is one that re-creates that perspective and that context.

The effects of encoding specificity can be observed with virtually any manipulation that changes an individual's perspective on the to-be-remembered materials. We have already considered direct manipulations of a person's approach to the materials—instructing the person to focus on meaning during learning, and then providing rhyme cues later on. Similar effects can be produced with shifts in physical context. A dramatic illustration of this point is provided by a study of scuba divers who had to learn a list of unrelated words either on a boat or underwater. The divers were later tested for recall in either the same or the alternate environment in which they had learned. The results showed a clear-cut context effect:

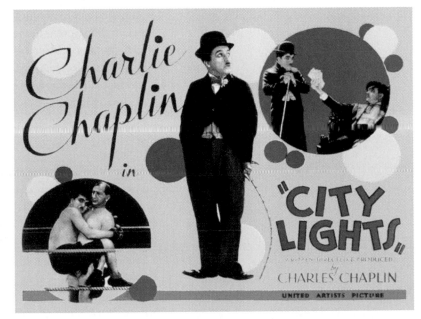

*Retrieval cues in the movies*  *The 1931 film* City Lights *tells the story of a millionaire who, after a night of drinking, befriends a tramp (played by Charlie Chaplin). The next morning the temporarily sober millionaire does not recognize the tramp, but greets him as an old friend when he gets drunk again the following night. While nowhere as extreme as this, such state-dependent memory effects have been observed in the laboratory.*

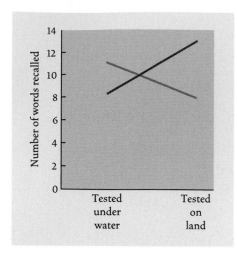

14
12
10
8
6
4
2
0

Number of words recalled

Tested    Tested
under     on
water     land

**7.6  The effect of changing the retrieval situation**   *Scuba divers learned a list of thirty-six unrelated words above water (red) or twenty feet underwater (green) and were then tested above or underwater. The figure shows that retention was better when the retrieval situation was the same as that in which encoding took place. (Godden & Baddeley, 1975)*

what was learned in the water was best recalled in the water, likewise for what was learned on deck (Godden & Baddeley, 1975; see Figure 7.6).

Similar effects can be obtained without going underwater. One experimenter asked students to read an article similar to the ones they routinely read in their college classes; half read the article in a quiet setting, and half read it in a noisy environment. When given a short-answer test later on, those who read the article in quiet did best if tested in quiet; those who read it in a noisy environment did best if tested in a similar environment (Grant et al., 1998).

Does this mean that students should make a practice of studying in the same environment in which they will be tested, so that they can gain from these effects when the time comes for an exam? The answer is no, because what really matters here is the mental context and not the physical environment. This is evident in a study in which participants were presented with a long list of words. A day later the experimenter brought them back for an unexpected recall test that took place in either the same room or a different one, one that varied in size, furnishings, and so on. Recall was considerably better for those who were tested in the same physical environment. But the investigator found a simple way of overcoming this context effect. A different group of participants was brought to the new room, but just prior to the recall test they were asked to think about the room in which they had learned the lists—what it looked like, what it made them feel like. By doing so, they mentally re-created the old environment for themselves. On the subsequent recall test, these participants performed just as well as those for whom there was no change of rooms. It appears, therefore, that a change in physical context influences memory because it usually brings with it a corresponding change in mental perspective. If one changes physical context without changing one's mental perspective, the physical relocation has little or no effect (Smith, 1979; Smith & Vela, 2001).

## ELABORATIVE REHEARSAL

The results we have just described point toward an obvious suggestion: memory encoding should be particularly effective if the encoding involves multiple connections. That way, there will be many different paths leading to the sought-after information, making the information easy to find from a variety of different starting points.

Direct support for this claim comes from studies of *elaborative rehearsal*, an activity in which the learner looks for multiple connections within the to-be-remembered material or connections between this material and other things she already knows. (This is in contrast to maintenance rehearsal, in which, as we discussed, material is simply held in a more or less passive fashion in working memory.) Elaborative rehearsal enhances learning because each step of elaboration builds another path by which the material can be accessed. The more such paths that are created, the easier retrieval will be.

In one study, research participants read sentences in which one word was missing. Some of the sentences were rather simple, such as "He cooked the _____." Others were more complex, such as "The great bird swooped down and carried off the struggling _____." The task was to decide whether a given target word (such as *chicken*) could appropriately fit into the sentence frame. After sixty such trials, the participants were unexpectedly asked to recall as many of the target words as they could. In line with the elaborative rehearsal hypothesis, the more complex sentence frames led to better recall. The richer encoding contexts presumably built more and better retrieval paths (Craik & Tulving, 1975).

## IMPLICIT MEMORY

Up to now, we have only considered methods of retrieval in which the research participant is asked questions that refer to her prior experience. She may be tested for recall:

"Tell me the name of one of your former high-school teachers." Or she may be asked for recognition: "Was Mr. Halberdum one of your former high-school teachers?" These tests are said to rely on *explicit memory*. But we are also influenced by *implicit memory*, a term referring to cases in which we are affected by some past experience without realizing that we are in fact remembering. Implicit memory is also referred to as "memory without awareness" and has been a subject of intense research scrutiny (see Schacter, 1987, 1992; Brainerd, Reyna, & Mojardin, 1999; Richardson-Klavehn & Gardiner, 1998; Roediger, 1990).

## IMPLICIT MEMORY EFFECTS

Participants in one study were first shown a number of words. Later, they were given two tests of memory. The first was a test of explicit memory, employing a standard recognition procedure. The second was a test of implicit memory in which their task was simply to identify words that were flashed very briefly on a computer screen. Participants had no idea that many of the words in this identification task were taken from the list of words they had seen during the procedure's initial step.

The data from the word-identification task showed a pattern referred to as *repetition priming*: words that had been on the original list were identified more readily than words that had not. Impressively, this priming effect was observed even for words that the participants failed to recognize as familiar in the recognition task. In other words, there was no relationship between the results of the explicit memory test (standard recognition) and the results of the implicit memory test (word identification). Thus, research participants showed evidence of implicit memory for items that they did not consciously—that is, explicitly—remember (Jacoby & Witherspoon, 1982).

Many other procedures also show this pattern of memory without awareness. In fragment-completion tasks, for example, participants are shown partial words (such as C___O___O___I___E) and asked to complete them to form actual words (CROCODILE). Success in this task is much more likely if the target word was encountered recently; this advantage is observed even without conscious recollection of the encounter (Graf & Mandler, 1984; Jacoby & Dallas, 1981; Tulving, Schacter, & Stark, 1982).

Similar effects can be demonstrated with pictures, melodies, or sentences. In each case, it seems that an encounter with a stimulus leaves us better prepared for that stimulus the next time we meet it. This preparation can then influence us in many ways, quite independently of whether we can recall the earlier encounter with that stimulus or not. As an illustration of how far this pattern can reach, consider the so-called illusion of truth. In the relevant studies, participants hear a series of statements and have to judge how interesting each is. For example, "The average person in Switzerland eats about twenty-five pounds of cheese each year," or "Henry Ford forgot to put a reverse gear in his first automobile."* Later on, the same participants are presented with some more sentences but now have to judge the credibility of them, rating each on a scale from "certainly true" to "certainly false." Needless to say, some of the sentences in this "truth test" were repeats from the earlier presentation; the question for us is how the judgments of sentence credibility are influenced by the earlier exposure.

The result of these studies is a propagandist's (or advertiser's) dream: sentences heard before are more likely to be accepted as true, or, in other words, familiarity increases credibility (Begg, Anas, & Farinacci, 1992; Brown & Halliday, 1980). To make this worse, the effect emerges even when participants are explicitly warned in advance not to believe the sentences in the first list. That is, sentences plainly identified as false when they are first heard still create the illusion of truth, and so these sentences are

---

* The first statement, by the way, is false; the average is closer to eighteen pounds. The second statement is true.

subsequently judged to be more credible than sentences never heard before. How could this be? With no conscious recollection of the earlier encounter, participants have no way to know which of the sentences of the truth test they encountered on the first list. Therefore, it does not help them to know that the sentences on that first list were all false. With no conscious memory of the earlier encounter, participants have no way to protect themselves from the illusion.

### DISTINGUISHING IMPLICIT FROM EXPLICIT MEMORY

Implicit memories are distinct from explicit memories in several ways. As we have seen, people can be implicitly influenced by events they cannot recall. In addition, some forms of brain damage impair explicit memory but spare implicit memory, whereas other forms of brain damage have the opposite effect. (See the discussion of amnesia later in the chapter.)

Implicit and explicit memories also seem to function differently. For example, we have seen that performance on a recall test (a test of explicit memory) is improved if participants pay attention to the meaning of the to-be-remembered material during encoding. Tests of implicit memory generally do not show this pattern; similar implicit-memory effects can be observed after shallow encoding or deep encoding (Graf, Mandler, & Haden, 1982; Jacoby & Dallas, 1981; for some complications, though, see, for example, Brown & Mitchell, 1994; Thapar & Greene, 1994).

Another difference concerns the effect of rather peripheral aspects of the stimulus. These aspects have little impact on explicit memory. Suppose, for example, a research participant is shown a series of words and is asked which of these were in a set he was shown earlier. If one of the original words was GIRAFFE, it will not matter if the test word looks the same (GIRAFFE) or different (*giraffe*). His response will be the same in either case.

Things are different, though, in many tests of implicit memory. If a participant initially sees GIRAFFE, then she will show a priming effect if asked to complete the fragment: G__R__F__E. But she will show little (or no) priming effect if tested with g__r__f__e. Apparently, implicit memory effects are often specific to a particular stimulus format and thus, once again, distinguishable from explicit memory effects.

All of these considerations combine to suggest that explicit and implicit memory tasks tap different kinds of memory. But how exactly we should distinguish the two is a matter of debate. Some authors suggest that the crucial distinction is one of consciousness, with implicit memories unconscious and explicit memories conscious. Others suggest that the crucial distinction lies in the fact that implicit memories are automatic—they influence our judgment whether we want them to or not. Explicit memories, in contrast, are controllable—we can choose whether or not we will use information contained in the memory. Still other authors argue that the key lies in the type of content preserved by each memory, with implicit memory providing a repository for skills and procedures, whereas explicit memory stores so-called declarative knowledge (knowledge we can talk about, or declare). Currently, it is unclear which of these conceptualizations is correct. But it is fully clear that implicit memories can be distinguished from explicit memories and that they influence us in a surprisingly wide range of circumstances.

# WHEN MEMORY FAILS

In popular usage, the word *forgetting* is employed whenever memory fails. But, in truth, memory failures have many causes, and so we probably do not want to label them all with the same term. Some failures arise from faulty encoding; others arise at the moment of recall. In this section, we will discuss three aspects of memory failure. One

*Cartoon by Abner Dean*

concerns the passage of time: why is it easier to remember the recent past than it is to remember events from long ago? A second concerns memory error—cases in which events are misremembered, so that the past as recalled differs from the past as it actually unfolded. The third topic concerns memory failure of a more extreme sort, as we consider what happens to memory in patients with certain kinds of brain damage.

## FORGETTING

Common sense tells us that yesterday's lecture is easier to recall than last week's, and last week's better than last year's. In general, the longer the time between learning and retrieval—that is, the longer the *retention interval*—the greater the chance of forgetting. Many studies have documented this simple fact. In addition, research has shown that the passage of time erodes memory accuracy for things as diverse as past hospital stays, our eating or smoking habits in past years, car accidents we experienced, our consumer purchases, and so on (Jobe, Tourangeau, & Smith, 1993). The classic demonstration of this pattern, though, was offered more than a century ago by Hermann Ebbinghaus (1850–1909). Ebbinghaus systematically studied his own memory in a series of careful experiments, examining his ability to retain lists of nonsense syllables, such as *zup* and *rif*.\* Ebbinghaus was the first to plot a *forgetting curve* by testing himself at various intervals after learning (using different lists for each interval). As expected, he found that memory did decline with the passage of time. However, the decline was uneven, sharpest soon after the learning and then more gradual (Ebbinghaus, 1885; see Figure 7.7).

## DECAY

What accounts for the pattern observed by Ebbinghaus? The most venerable theory holds that memory traces simply *decay* as time passes, like mountains that are eroded by wind and water. The erosion of memories is presumably caused by normal metabolic processes that wear down memory traces until they fade and finally disintegrate.

One line of support for this theory exploits the fact that, like most chemical reactions, many metabolic processes increase their rates with increasing temperature. If these metabolic reactions are responsible for memorial decay, then forgetting should increase if body temperature is elevated during the retention interval. This prediction is difficult to test with humans (or any other mammal), because internal mechanisms keep the temperature of our bodies relatively constant (see Chapter 3). However, this prediction was tested with animals such as goldfish whose bodies tend to take on the temperature of their surroundings. By and large, the results are in line with the hypothesis: the higher the temperature of the tank in which the fish were kept during the retention interval, the more forgetting took place (Gleitman & Rozin, as reported in Gleitman, 1971).

Other findings, however, make it clear that decay cannot provide the entire explanation of forgetting. For example, several experiments compared recall after an interval spent awake with recall after an equal interval spent sleeping. If the passage of time were all that mattered for forgetting, then performance would be the same in these two cases. But it was not. The group that slept during the retention interval remembered

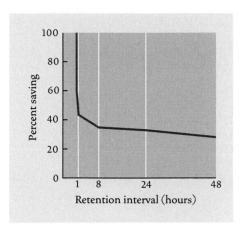

**7.7  Forgetting curve    The figure shows retention after various intervals since learning. Retention is here measured in percent saving, that is, the percentage decrease in the number of trials required to relearn the list after an interval of no practice. If the saving is 100 percent, retention is perfect—no trials to relearn are necessary. If the saving is 0 percent, there is no retention at all, for it takes just as many trials to relearn the list as it took to learn it initially. (After Ebbinghaus, 1885)**

---

\* Ebbinghaus used nonsense syllables in order to study learning that was uncontaminated by prior associations. Modern psychologists, however, are skeptical about this approach. First, Ebbinghaus's nonsense syllables may not have been so meaningless after all. While *zup* is not an English word, it surely resembles several (e.g., *soup*). Second, the influence of prior associations is not a nuisance to be removed from studies of memory; instead, this influence is an important part of learning and remembering.

more than the group that stayed awake (for example, see Jenkins & Dallenbach, 1924). Presumably, the group that stayed awake experienced interference—new ideas and events somehow interfered with their recall. This finding suggests that events and activities, and not the mere passage of time, are crucial for forgetting. (For other evidence comparing the effects of time to the effects of interference, see Reisberg, 2001.)

## INTERFERENCE

It seems, then, that memory is vulnerable to some sort of interference, with the newly arriving information somehow interfering with the previously learned material. But what produces this interference? One hypothesis is that the forgotten material is neither damaged nor erased; it is simply misplaced. By analogy, consider someone who buys a newspaper each day and then stores it with others in a large pile in the basement. Each newspaper is easy to find when it is still sitting on the breakfast table; it can still be located without difficulty when it is on top of the basement stack. After some days, though, finding the newspaper becomes difficult. It is somewhere in the pile but may not come into view without a great deal of searching. And, of course, the pile grows higher and higher every day; that is why the interference increases as the retention interval grows longer.

Memory interference is easily demonstrated in the laboratory. In a typical study, a control group learns the items on a list (A) and then is tested after a specified interval. The experimental group learns the same list (A), but, in addition, they must also learn the items on a second list (B) during the same retention interval. The result is a marked inferiority in the performance of the experimental group. List B seems to interfere with the recall of list A (Crowder, 1976; McGeoch & Irion, 1952).

Of course, not all learning produces interference. If it did, we all would remember less and less as we learned more and more (a powerful argument, if true, against continuing education!). Instead, interference emerges only under certain circumstances. No interference is observed, for example, between dissimilar sorts of material—learning to skate does not interfere with one's memory for irregular French verbs. In addition, interference occurs only if the things to be remembered are essentially incompatible. The newly learned material will not interfere if it is consistent with earlier-learned material. In fact, just the opposite occurs: the subsequent learning helps memory, rather than hindering it.

## RETRIEVAL FAILURE

We have suggested that interference does not "erase" memories; it simply renders them difficult to locate. With a suitable cue or prompt, these memories might be recovered. Could this be true of all forgetting? Or is some forgetting truly a matter of erasure (and thus permanent loss)? This is currently a matter of some controversy. It is clear, however, that much forgetting does involve *retrieval failure*: the memories are misplaced but not erased.

This idea certainly fits several of our earlier claims. For example, we mentioned earlier that elaborative rehearsal leads to better memory (less forgetting) than maintenance rehearsal, and this is easy to understand in terms of retrieval failure: elaborative rehearsal involves the establishment of multiple memory links, with each link providing a retrieval path leading to the target memory. With multiple retrieval paths, retrieval failure is less likely.

We also noted that memories can often be triggered by returning to the context (mental or physical) in which learning took place. Prior to that return, the target information might not be recalled—an apparent case of forgetting. But then, once the right retrieval cues are available, the memory resurfaces, making it clear that the problem was retrieval failure and not a genuine memory loss.

*The child's world is in many ways different from the adult's* **According to some authors, childhood amnesia is partially produced by the enormous change in the retrieval cues available to the adult.**

Other phenomena can also be explained in these terms. Consider the fact that adults are usually unable to recall events that took place before their third or fourth birthday, a phenomenon known as *childhood amnesia* (Sheingold & Tenney, 1982; Waldfogel, 1948; see Figure 7.8). This amnesia may derive from the fact that the world of the young child is different in many important ways from the world he will occupy some ten or fifteen years later. It is a world in which tables are hopelessly out of reach, chairs can be climbed on only with great effort, and adults are giants in size and gods in ability. The child's memories, therefore, are formed and encoded within this context, and it is a context massively different from the circumstances of an adult. This virtually guarantees that the adult's perspective during retrieval, and the set of available retrieval cues, will be different from the perspective and cues in place during encoding, and it is this shift in context that leads to the observed amnesia (Neisser, 1967; Schachtel, 1947).

Other factors also contribute to childhood amnesia. For example, the hippocampus and prefrontal cortex, structures crucial for establishing coherent autobiographical memories, are not fully mature until the child is three or four years old (Nadel & Zola-Morgan, 1984; Newcombe, Drummey, Fox, Lie, & Ottinger-Alberts, 2000). Thus, the very young child lacks the neural equipment needed to record memories in a full and orderly fashion. Another factor is that very young children have not yet developed the necessary schemas within which experiences can be organized, encoded, and rehearsed (Pillemer, 1998; White & Pillemer, 1979).

In addition, it is striking that individuals differ in the severity of their childhood amnesia, with some people remembering more, and more detailed, early memories, and other people unable to recall much before their fourth or even fifth birthday. Some of these differences are tied to cultural background. European adults are able to report earlier memories than Asian adults, and New Zealand Maoris are able to report earlier memories still (MacDonald, Uesiliana, & Hayne, 2000). There is also a gender difference, with women generally able to report earlier memories than men (Fivush & Schwarzmueller, 1998; MacDonald et al., 2000).

What causes these differences? One factor might be the types of conversations that the child engages in, at a very early age, with her caregivers. Those conversations help the child learn how to report on an event and how to link the elements of an event into a coherent narrative. These skills then help the child not only in reporting her memories but also in encoding subsequent events—guiding her attention during the event and helping her grasp its meaning as the event unfolds (see Chapter 12).

Overall, then, it is clear that childhood amnesia (like most forms of forgetting) is caused by several different factors. The change in cues, between the child's world and the adult's, must be part of our account, but other mechanisms also play an important role.

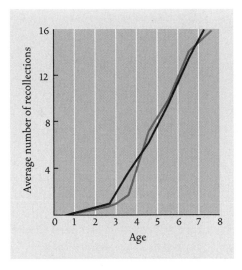

**7.8  Number of childhood memories  College students were asked to recall childhood experiences. The figure plots the average number of events recalled as a function of the age at which they occurred for men (green) and for women (red). Women recall a bit more at the earliest ages, which may reflect the fact that the maturation of girls is generally ahead of that of boys. (Data from Waldfogel, 1948)**

## THE TIP-OF-THE-TONGUE PHENOMENON

The idea that *forgetting* is often produced by retrieval failure has many implications. It suggests that forgetting sometimes is "reversible" (once the proper retrieval cues are located) and that some forms of encoding (those providing more retrieval paths) make forgetting less likely. It also suggests that forgetting can be incomplete. In other words, we can sometimes retrieve some aspects of a memory but not others. This pattern is perhaps most clearly exemplified by the *tip-of-the-tongue phenomenon*.

At times, when we are trying to remember a word, or perhaps someone's name, we reach a point at which we are totally certain we know the word but cannot quite recall it. We feel as if the searched-for memory is on the tip of the tongue, tantalizingly close but inaccessible nonetheless.

In one study of this phenomenon, college students were given the dictionary definitions of uncommon English words such as *apse*, *sampan*, and *cloaca*. The students were asked to supply the words that fit these definitions. In some cases, they simply did not

**Instructions**

Here are the dictionary definitions of twelve uncommon words. Please look at each definition in turn. Try to think of the word. There are several possibilities:

1. You may be pretty sure that you know the word. Or you may be quite sure that you don't know it. In either case, just move on to the next definition on the list.

2. You may feel that you know the word but can't recall it just now. In fact, it may be "on the tip of your tongue." If so, quickly do the following:

   a. Guess the first letter of the word.

   b. Try to think of one or two words that sound similar to the one you're trying to find.

Follow this procedure as you go through the whole list of definitions. Then turn to the next left-hand page for the list of the words that fit these definitions.

**Definitions**

1. A blood feud in which members of the family of a murdered person try to kill the murderer or members of his family
2. A dark, hard, glassy volcanic rock
3. A secretion from the sperm whale used in the manufacture of perfume
4. An Egyptian ornament in the shape of a beetle
5. The staff of Hermes, symbol of a physician or of the medical corps
6. A navigational instrument used in measuring altitudes of celestial bodies

**7.9  The tip-of-the-tongue phenomenon** *This figure may provide an opportunity to demonstrate how something can be close to being retrieved from memory but not quite. (Adapted from Foard, 1975)*

know the words; these trials were of no interest to the researchers. Instead, the experimenters were concerned with the occasions on which participants could not recall the target word but felt certain that they were on the verge of finding it (see Figure 7.9). Whenever this happened, participants were asked to venture some guesses about what the target word sounded like. These guesses turned out to be closely related to the target. Participants guessed the target's initial letter over 50 percent of the time and were generally able to guess the number of syllables. When asked to supply some other words that they thought sounded like the target, they were usually in the correct phonological neighborhood. Presented with the definition "a small Chinese boat," participants in the tip-of-the-tongue state offered these sound-alikes: *saipan, Siam, Cheyenne,* and *sarong*—all similar to the actual word, *sampan* (Brown & McNeill, 1966; Koriat & Lieblich, 1974; for a more recent account of why this phenomenon occurs, see James & Burke, 2000).

## WHEN FORGETTING SEEMS NOT TO OCCUR

The emphasis on retrieval failure, rather than erasure, also implies that memories may last for a long, long time. In fact, a number of studies have documented cases of remarkably little forgetting, even after very long intervals.

*Long-Lasting Memories*  If a student studied Spanish in high school, will she remember it five or ten or even fifteen years later? In one study, nearly 800 participants were given a Spanish reading-comprehension test; all of the participants had studied Spanish either in high school or in college. Not surprisingly, participants who had finished their Spanish classes just one week earlier did quite well on the test. Performance grew worse for those who had not studied Spanish for the past year, or for the past two or three years (Figure 7.10). Remarkably, though, performance then leveled off, and students who had taken their Spanish classes thirty years before remembered almost as much as students whose classes were just three years ago. In essence, if the memories were established well enough to last three years, then they seemed to be virtually lifelong. (Performance levels did drop at retention intervals of forty and fifty years, but this may reflect the generalized effects of aging, rather than forgetting per se.)

It should also be noted that the degree of forgetting varied somewhat from one participant to the next, but in a predictable way: students who had received As in their Spanish classes forgot less than students who had received Bs and Cs (Bahrick, 1984). This pattern was observed even though the students had earned these grades a half-century ear-

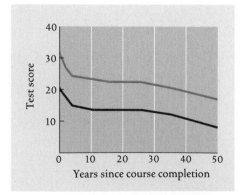

**7.10  Forgetting a foreign language  The** *figure shows performance on a Spanish reading-comprehension test administered from zero to fifty years after taking Spanish in high school or college. The results from persons who had earned an A in the course are shown in green; the results from persons who had earned a C are shown in red. (After Bahrick, 1984)*

lier! Similar findings come from a study on the retention of knowledge acquired in an advanced psychology course. Here, too, the basic concepts were retained for at least twelve years (Conway, Cohen, & Stanhope, 1991; also see Bahrick & Hall, 1991; Bahrick, Hall, Goggin, Bahrick, & Berger, 1994).

These results seem to conflict with Ebbinghaus's forgetting curve, described earlier in the chapter. In Ebbinghaus's case, forgetting grew worse and worse as time passed. In contrast, Bahrick's and others' data show some initial forgetting, but then the memories endure without change for many years. This invites a question about why some materials achieve this relatively permanent storage—why, in Bahrick's terms, some memories move into *permastore*—whereas other materials do not. Several factors contribute. We have already mentioned the importance of the initial learning: material learned extremely well in the first place is much more likely to reach permastore. In addition, recall that Ebbinghaus's forgetting curve was derived from studies using nonsense syllables, whereas the studies discussed here involve meaningful, structured information. This, too, matters for permastore, with inherently structured materials more likely to achieve this permanence than are, say, items on a shopping list (Neisser, 1989).

*Flashbulb Memories* Most examples of permastore involve general knowledge, not memories tied to a specific episode or event. But can episodic memories be similarly immune to forgetting? Much of the evidence relevant to this question derives from studies of so-called *flashbulb memories*, extremely vivid and long-lasting memories that typically concern events that were highly distinctive, unexpected, and strongly emotional (Brown & Kulik, 1977). Sometimes flashbulb memories concern personal events, such as an early-morning telephone call that tells of a parent's death. Others may involve news of national importance; many people have flashbulb memories of the *Challenger* space-shuttle disaster, the fall of the Berlin Wall, the reading of the O. J. Simpson verdict, or the news of Princess Diana's death.

One striking feature of flashbulb memories is their focus on immediate and personal circumstances. For example, many people remember exactly where they were when they first heard about the Simpson verdict, what they were doing at the time, who was with them, what words were spoken, and so on. This personalized focus, together with the level of detail and longevity of these memories, has led some authors to argue that there must be some special "flashbulb mechanism," distinct from the mechanisms that lead to the creation of other, more mundane memories (Brown & Kulik, 1977; but see also Winograd & Neisser, 1993).

The full pattern of evidence, however, suggests that such a special mechanism does not exist. For one thing, as vivid as they are, flashbulb memories are sometimes incorrect, straying from the actual facts in crucial ways (see, for example, Neisser, 1982a, 1986; McCloskey, Wible, & Cohen, 1988; Thompson & Cowan, 1986). In addition, much of what is remembered may have been rehearsed in subsequent conversations with others, and it is likely to be this rehearsal, rather than some special encoding mechanism, that produces the memories' longevity.

It should be said, though, that some episodic memories do seem extraordinarily accurate and virtually permanent; this is most likely for events that were deemed highly consequential for the rememberer at the time the event occurred (see, for example, Conway et al., 1994). Thus, even for episodic memories, some sort of (relatively) permanent storage does seem possible—at least for this special set of episodes.

## CONCEPTUAL FRAMEWORKS AND REMEMBERING

So far, our discussion of memory failures has focused on cases in which we are simply unable to recall a name or recognize a face. But memory can also let us down in another way, because sometimes we are certain we remember an event, but end up giving a

*Flashbulb memories* **The classic example of a flashbulb memory is the assassination of John F Kennedy in November 1963. Virtually any American (and most Europeans) who were at least nine or ten years old on that date still remember the day vividly. The attack on the World Trade Center, on September 11, 2001, is the sort of shocking and highly consequential event that seems very likely to create a flashbulb memory, with the expectation that people will still remember this day clearly even decades from now.**

report of the past that is simply mistaken. In such cases, we are not lying about what happened; instead, we are misremembering, sincerely offering our best recollection but, in the process, providing an account that happens to be false. How does this sort of memory failure occur?

## MEMORY DISTORTIONS

Classic experiments on memory errors were performed by the British psychologist Frederic Bartlett sixty years ago. Bartlett presented his subjects with stories drawn from the folklore of Native Americans, and for his British subjects, many elements of these stories seemed rather strange. In the subjects' recollection of these stories, though, the tales became less strange. Parts of the tale that had made no sense to the subjects (such as the supernatural elements) either were left out of the subjects' recall or were reinterpreted along more familiar lines. Similarly, subjects often added elements so that plot events that had initially seemed inexplicable now made sense (Bartlett, 1932).

What happened here? Bartlett's subjects quite naturally tried to understand these stories by relating them to other things they knew and understood. In the process, they ended up creating connections in their memories, weaving together the actual elements of the stories with various aspects of their knowledge. This weaving together was helpful: it allowed the subjects to comprehend the materials they were hearing by linking the unfamiliar materials to a more familiar framework. But, at the same time, this weaving together caused troubles later on: it made it difficult for subjects to keep track of which elements were actually in the stories and which were merely associated with the story via their understanding of it. This is what produced the memory errors.

*Learning to remember*   *How well will the children remember the story they are hearing? The answer depends in large part on how well they understand the story. Aspects they understand will be well remembered. Aspects they do not understand may be forgotten, or they may be altered in memory to bring them into better alignment with the children's understanding.*

*The Effect of Schemas and Scripts*   Many studies have replicated and extended Bartlett's findings, showing in many contexts that memory is strongly affected by an individual's conceptual framework. In study after study, elements that fit neatly within that framework were easily remembered; elements that were somewhat at odds with the framework were distorted in memory or omitted; and elements that were absent but typically present in events of that type were added to the event in memory. For example, participants in one study were told about a person's visit to the dentist and then later asked to recall what they had been told. Many participants falsely remembered hearing about the patient checking in with the receptionist and looking at a magazine in the waiting room, even though these details were not mentioned in the original account (Bower, Black, & Turner, 1979). In a different experiment, participants waited briefly in a professor's office and, seconds later, were asked to recall the contents of the office. One-third of the individuals "remembered" seeing books in the office, even though none were present (Brewer & Treyens, 1981). In this case, the error is a substantial one (bookshelves are large; the participants were actually in the office; the recollection took place just moments after leaving the office) but, again, is entirely in line with subjects' expectations of what "should" be in a professor's office.

In all these cases, memory is plainly and strongly affected by the research participants' broad knowledge of the world and by the conceptual framework they brought to the situation. Following Bartlett, many psychologists describe these frameworks as *schemas*, a cognitive framework that summarizes what we know about a certain type of event or situation. Schemas reflect the simple fact that many aspects of our experience are redundant—professors' offices do tend to contain many books, patients visiting the dentist do generally check in with a receptionist, and so on—and schemas provide a convenient summary of this redundancy. This summary, in turn, can help us in interpreting and supplementing the details of our remembered experience. When we encounter an event (whether it is a trip to the dentist or a story from another culture), we seek to understand it by relating it to a schematic frame. Then, when we try to remember the event, we can rely on that same frame to guide our recall. In most cases, this will help us, but, as we have seen, it can also lead to memory error.

*Eyewitness Testimony*  The evidence indicates that our memories are accurate far more often than not. Even so, memory errors do occur, and sometimes the errors are large. And, troublingly, the errors can occur in circumstances in which an enormous amount depends on someone's recollection—for example, in legal cases hinging on an eyewitness's memory.

Police investigators, judges, and juries all rely on the accuracy of eyewitness testimony, but witnesses (like anyone else) do make memory errors. For example, the details of an accident that occurred months ago may have dimmed over time, and, as the witness tries to recall this past event, he may fill in the gaps by inferences of which he is quite unaware. Even if the inferences are faulty, the witness may be entirely confident that his recollection is accurate, and this confidence may persuade a jury to take the testimony quite seriously. As it turns out, though, many studies have shown that a witness's confidence in the truthfulness of his testimony is nearly worthless as an indicator of accurate memory. Mistaken witnesses can be just as confident, and can offer testimony that is just as detailed and emotional, as accurate witnesses (Reisberg, 2001). Therefore, in using a witness's confidence to judge the witness's credibility, juries are relying on an index of virtually no value.

*Elizabeth Loftus*

What should jurors pay attention to in order to evaluate an eyewitness's testimony? As one crucial consideration, they should take into account how the memory evidence was "collected" and, specifically, how the witness was questioned, both in court and in interviews prior to the courtroom appearance. This issue has been examined in a series of studies by Elizabeth Loftus and her associates. In one experiment, research participants watched a film of a car accident. Immediately afterward they were asked a number of questions. Some were asked, "Did you see the broken headlight?" Others were asked, "Did you see a broken headlight?" This small difference in wording had a large impact, and participants questioned about "the headlight" were much more likely to report having seen one than subjects asked about "a headlight," whether the film actually showed a broken headlight or not (Loftus & Zanni, 1975).

Another study showed that leading questions asked during one interrogation can change how an event is reported in subsequent interviews. Again, participants were shown film segments of a car accident. Shortly afterward some of them were asked leading questions, such as "Did you see the children getting on the school bus?" (This question is leading because it is phrased in a way that presupposes a state of affairs —namely, that there was a school bus.) A week later, all participants were asked a direct (and unbiased) question, "Did you see a school bus in the film?" In actual fact, there was no bus. But when compared to controls, those who were originally asked the leading question were three to four times more likely to say that they had seen one (Loftus, 1975; for similar data with children, see Ceci & Bruck, 1995; Bruck & Ceci, 1999).

The memory errors observed in these experiments are not small: we mentioned "memories" for buses that were not there and headlights that were not broken. In other studies, researchers have planted memories for buildings that do not exist and, indeed, memories for entire events that never occurred. While it is worth emphasizing that, in general, our memories are quite accurate—especially if appropriate, nonleading cues are provided—errors plainly do occur; they can be substantial in magnitude, and, in some contexts, they can be frequent. The implications of this for the courts, or for any process that depends on memory-based testimony, are clear and deeply troubling.

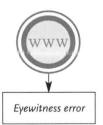

Eyewitness error

*What Produces Memory Errors?*  We have mentioned two broad types of memory errors. In one case, knowledge of a general sort intrudes into one's recollection of a specific event—for example, one's knowledge about dentists' offices shapes what one remembers about a particular visit to the dentist. In a second case, knowledge acquired on one occasion becomes mixed up with recollection of some other occasion, so that the bus mentioned by an interviewer gets added to one's recollection of the earlier film.

In some ways, however, these two types of memory error are quite similar to each other. In both cases, the person is correctly recalling information that is associated in memory with the to-be-remembered event. A bus *was* mentioned in connection with the to-be-remembered film, and so the memory of (seeing) the film is likely to be connected in some way to the memory of (hearing about) a bus. Likewise, checking in with the receptionist was probably part of the subjects' understanding of the dentist office story, and so the idea of a receptionist is connected, via this understanding, to the memory of the story.

In a sense, then, subjects would be correct if they simply asserted, "I recall that there was something about a bus somehow associated with this film," or "There was something about checking in somehow associated with this story." The recall involves a memory error, though, because subjects say more than this—they say that the bus was part of the original episode (although we know that it was not) and likewise for checking in and the dentist story. Both of these errors, therefore, arise largely from a confusion about whether the remembered element was part of the actual episode as it was experienced, or whether the element was drawn from some other source. For this reason, these errors are often referred to as *source confusion*, and, in fact, this term can be applied to most memory errors. Because of source confusion, our memory errors import elements of general knowledge into specific episodes, and import elements of one episode into our recall of other clearly related episodes.

## THE LIMITS OF MEMORY

Clearly, memory is fallible. Can this fallibility be overcome? Moreover, if a great deal of forgetting involves retrieval failure, can retrieval be improved? It turns out that there are things we can do to promote accurate remembering, both to increase the total amount of information someone recalls and to avoid some memory errors. For example, interview techniques have been developed that help eyewitnesses to crimes to remember more, relying on principles we have already discussed. Among other steps, these techniques help the witness to get back into the "mind set" she was in during the original crime; this *context reinstatement* makes memory retrieval more likely (pp. 252–254). Investigators have also developed better procedures for collecting *eyewitness identifications*, with a goal of maximizing the chance that the witness will identify the culprit from a police lineup, but minimizing the chance that the witness will mistakenly identify someone who is innocent. These suggestions have been taken quite seriously by law enforcement agencies and have been adopted as required procedures in some jurisdictions—potentially a major contribution by psychology to the criminal justice system! (For discussion of these procedures by the U.S. Department of Justice, see Technical Working Group for Eyewitness Evidence, 1999. For discussion of the implementation of these changes by the state of New Jersey, see Kolata & Peterson, 2001. For a broad discussion of research in this domain, see Saywitz & Geiselman, 1998; Giles, Gopnik, & Heyman, 2002; Wells & Olson, 2002.)

*Memory, Hypnosis, and the Courtroom*  Law enforcement agencies seem well served by memory-promoting techniques that have grown naturally out of what psychologists have learned so far—techniques, for example, that seek to reduce retrieval failure or that carefully avoid leading a witness. Some people, however, have proposed more exotic means of improving memory, including the use of *hypnosis*. The idea is that

*(Drawing by Chas. Addams, © The New Yorker Collection, 1979)*

someone—for example, an eyewitness to a crime—can be hypnotized, given the suggestion that he is back at a certain time and place, and asked to tell what he sees. On the surface, the results of this procedure—in a police station or in laboratory studies—are quite impressive. A hypnotized witness mentally returns to the scene of the crime and seems able to recall exactly what was said by the various participants; a hypnotized college student mentally returns to childhood and appears to relive her sixth birthday party with childlike glee.

These hypnotized people are usually convinced that they are actually reexperiencing these events, and so they have full confidence in the accuracy of their recall. But after investigation, these hypnotically evoked memories often turn out to be false. In one courtroom case, a witness recalled seeing the suspect during an assault, but investigation confirmed that he was out of the country at the time (Orne, 1979). Similar points apply to the description of childhood events elicited under hypnosis: convincing details contained within these reports often turn out to be false when later checked against available records (Lynn, Lock, Myers, & Payne, 1997; Spanos, Burgess, Burgess, Samuels, & Blois, 1999).

Moreover, the mental return to childhood itself turns out to be mere—though unwitting—pretense. In one study, participants were asked to draw a picture while mentally "regressed" to the age of six. At first glance, their drawings looked remarkably childlike. But when compared to the participants' own childhood drawings made at that very age, it is clear that they are much more sophisticated. They represent an adult's conception of what a childish drawing is, rather than being the real thing (see Figure 7.11; Orne, 1951). Similarly, these hypnotized adults answer questions and perceive the world, not as children would, but as they believe children would. When their (adult) beliefs about children are incorrect, then their simulation is correspondingly off the mark.

How can we explain these results? First of all, it is clear that hypnosis does not have the near magical memory-enhancing powers sometimes attributed to it (Barber, 1969; Hilgard, 1977; Orne & Hammer, 1974). It does not enable us to relive our past any more than we can while we are awake (nor, for that matter, does it permit feats of agility or strength of which we are otherwise incapable). What hypnosis does do is make people unusually ready to believe in another person, the hypnotist, and (within certain limits) to do what he asks of them. If he asks them to remember, they will do their very best to oblige. They will doggedly stick to the task and rummage through their minds to find any possible retrieval cue. And so would we all, whether hypnotized or not, if we really wanted to remember badly enough. But what if we don't succeed? If we are not hypnotized, we will eventually concede failure. But hypnotized people will not. The hypnotist has told them to recall and has assured them that they can recall. And so, to please the hypnotist, they produce "memories"—by creatively adding and reconstructing on the basis of what they already know. As we have seen, such reconstructions are a common feature in much so-called remembering. The difference is that under hypnosis subjects become unusually confident that their memories are real.

Evidence for this interpretation comes from a study of the susceptibility of those under hypnosis to leading questions. The experimenter employed the familiar technique of showing participants videotapes of an event and later asking them to recall certain details, in some cases while hypnotized and in others while not. Some of the probes were leading questions, while others were more objective in phrasing. As we have seen, such leading questions lead to errors even without hypnosis. But they lead to even more errors in hypnotized subjects than in controls. When asked whether they had seen "the license plate . . . " (which in fact was not visible), some of the hypnotized subjects not only said yes but actually volunteered partial descriptions of the license plate number. Findings of this sort cast serious doubts on the use of hypnosis in real-life judicial settings (Putnam, 1979; Smith, 1983), and, indeed, courts in America almost invariably reject testimony that has been "facilitated" by hypnosis.

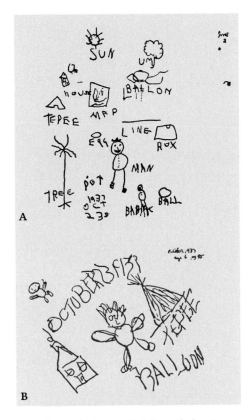

**7.11** *Remembering studied through drawings done while under hypnosis* **(A)** *Drawings done at age six.* **(B)** *Drawings done while the participant was hypnotized and told that he was six years old. Note some interesting differences between the pictures, for example, the tepee, which is much more detailed in (B), the spelling of balloon, and a sense of overall design present in (B) but altogether lacking in (A). (From Orne, 1951)*

*The Tape-Recorder Theory of Memory*   In addition to what these findings tell us about hypnosis, they also have implications for what is sometimes called the *tape-recorder* (or, to update it, the videotape-recorder) *theory of memory*. According to this view, the brain contains a virtually indelible record of all we have ever heard or seen or felt. The only trick is to find a way to turn the recorder back to some desired portion of the tape. The evidence indicates, however, that this suggestion is exceedingly implausible. To be sure, there is much in memory that, under ordinary circumstances, we cannot retrieve. (This is guaranteed by the fact that much forgetting is attributable to retrieval failure.) Nonetheless, all the evidence indicates that information will be recorded in memory only if we paid some attention, only if we engaged that information somehow, during our initial encounter with it. Without this engagement or attention, there is no memory record to be recovered. Likewise, we have seen that some information reaches the status of permastore and so can be remembered years and years after learning it. But information reaches this state only if it is extremely well learned in the first place; most information is not that well entrenched.

Let us also note that every technique ever proposed for "playing back" memories does not work as advertised. Hypnosis is one example of these techniques, but the evidence is similar in other cases (including, for example, drugs alleged to improve memory). Under the circumstances, it appears that the tape-recorder theory is simply false. We do not retain every bit of sensory information we have ever encountered. Some never enters long-term storage, some enters but then is lost, and some, it seems, may be altered to fit later incoming material (Loftus & Loftus, 1980; Neisser, 1982b).

*Are There Repressed Memories?*   A special problem that has received much public attention concerns what have been called *repressed memories*. Claims about repression appear in many contexts, but in recent years, repression has been most widely discussed in connection with the recovery of traumatic childhood memories, often memories involving sexual abuse. In these cases, people often report that the traumatic memories were pushed out of consciousness—that is, repressed—for many years, sometimes for as long as two or three decades. The memories then surface much later, often while the person is being treated by a therapist for some problem not obviously connected to the alleged childhood events.

Are these memories accurate—that is, a true description of what really happened? This question has serious social and legal significance. If the memories are accurate, then they provide evidence for horrible wrongdoing and, indeed, for criminal prosecution. If, however, the memories are factually incorrect, then we must worry about the terrible consequences of these false accusations; we also need to worry about how these large-scale and painful false memories could ever come to be.

It is certainly clear that incest and childhood sexual abuse are far more prevalent than many people suppose. We also know that events—particularly emotionally significant events—are stored in memory for a very long time, perhaps permanently. Thus many memories of childhood abuse are likely to be entirely accurate. Still, we must be extremely careful in interpreting these memories of abuse, particularly those that were "repressed" for many years and then "recovered." As one broad concern, many investigators are skeptical about whether the phenomenon of repression exists at all (see, for example, Holmes, 1990; Loftus, 1993, 1997; Shobe & Kihlstrom, 1997). Highly emotional events, they argue, tend to be better remembered than more mundane occurrences—exactly the opposite of the (alleged) repression pattern. Thus, rape victims are often haunted for years by the memory of their hideous experience; survivors of the Holocaust find it difficult to avoid thinking about the horrors they endured. (We return to these long-lasting memories in Chapter 16, when we discuss post-traumatic stress disorder.)

In addition, it is sadly plausible that memories "recovered" after a period of amnesia are, in many cases, false, fabricated through mechanisms we have already discussed. Thus, for example, we know that the possibility for error is greater in remembering the distant past than it is in remembering recent events. Likewise, we know that close questioning of a witness can create "memories" for entire events that never occurred, particularly if the questions are asked over and over (see, for example, Ofshe, 1992; Ceci, Huffman, & Smith, 1994; Hyman, Husband, & Billings, 1995; Loftus, 1997; Zaragoza & Mitchell, 1996). We also know that false memories, when they occur, can be recalled just as fully, just as confidently, and, indeed, with just as much distress as memories for actual events.

It is also worth noting that many of these recovered memories emerge only with the assistance of a therapist who is genuinely convinced that the client's psychological problems stem from childhood abuse. Often, the therapist believes that these problems can be dealt with only if the client faces them squarely and uncovers the buried memories of that abuse (for example, Bass & Davis, 1988). To help this process along, the therapist may rely on a variety of techniques aimed at improving memory, including hypnosis, drugs alleged to promote recollection, and guided imagination. In these cases, the therapist's intentions are good, but the techniques used magnify the risk of memory error. As we have noted, hypnosis and "memory-promoting" drugs (such as ambybarbitol sodium, commonly referred to as sodium amytal) do little to promote accurate recall, but they clearly do increase the risk of false memories. And while guided imagery is an effective way to increase recall, it is also a powerful source of false memories.

A therapist who is convinced that abuse took place may also ask suggestive questions that further increase the chances of memory fabrication. Even if the therapist scrupulously avoids leading questions, she can shape the client's memory in other ways—by giving signs of interest or concern if the client hits on the "right" line of exploration, by spending more time on topics related to the alleged memories than on other issues, and so forth. In these ways, the climate within the therapeutic session can subtly guide the client toward finding exactly the "memories" the therapist expects to find.

None of this is said to minimize the social and moral problems produced by childhood sexual abuse and incest. These offenses do occur and can have severe lifelong consequences for the victim.* But here, as in all cases, the veracity of our recollection cannot be taken for granted. We must always be careful in interpreting what seems like a memory of a long-past event, and that caution must be increased if the memory emerged through someone's (for example, a therapist's) suggestions and hypnosis. (For further discussion of this difficult issue, see Bass & Davis, 1988; Conway, 1997; Freyd, 1996, 1998; Holmes, 1990; Kihlstrom, 1993; Loftus, 1993; Pendergast, 1995; Schacter, 1996.)

## THE LIMITS OF DISTORTION

Memory, it seems, is not a passive repository for our experience, recording the days of our lives and then permitting playback of these records later on. Instead, memory depends on a highly active set of processes, starting with the interpretation inherent in the initial encoding and continuing through the processes of reconstruction and interpretation used unwittingly to fill gaps in what we recall. There are numerous ways in which a memory can be distorted, but such distortions do not always occur—far from it. After all, we

---

* Some writers contend that people who were abused as children can develop a variety of symptoms, including eating disorders, inabilities to form close relationships, a variety of anxieties, and so on (e.g., Bass & Davis, 1988). But each of these symptoms can readily arise from other sources—that is, with no history of abuse. Therefore, we cannot interpret any symptom, or any pattern of symptoms, as evidence that abuse must have occurred at some prior point in an individual's life. In addition, it is important to note that we are a resilient species, and some children who have been abused emerge without subsequent symptoms (Kendall-Tackett, Williams, & Finkelhor, 1993). Let us be clear, though, that this takes nothing away from the ugliness of this offense: abusing a child, sexually or otherwise, is a horrible deed and a criminal offense, whether the child develops subsequent symptoms or not.

do remember many details of our experiences, and we can retain these details for a very long time. Even when errors do occur, some forms of testing, and some retrieval hints, seem capable of enabling recovery of the original record (Alba & Hasher, 1983).

In short, our memory is neither wholly distorted nor wholly accurate. The tape-recorder theory of memory is false, but so is the suggestion that everything we remember is changed and distorted. In these regards, memory is much like perception. Both are affected by processes that work from the top down as well as by those that start from the bottom up. Perception without any bottom-up processing (that is, without any reference to stimuli) would amount to continual hallucination. Memory without bottom-up processing (that is, without any reference to memory traces) would amount to perpetual delusion, with the remembered past continually being constructed and reconstructed to fit the schemas of the moment. Thus, in both of these domains, bottom-up processes must play a crucial role.

The use of schemas—that is, top-down processing—clearly has a cost, for it can lead to distortions of memory. But it also confers great benefits. Our cognitive machinery is limited, and there is only so much that we can encode, store, and retrieve. Thus, we are forced to schematize, bringing order to the world we perceive and think about. Our mental shortcuts therefore serve us well, helping us to understand and remember, and this should be kept in mind when we realize that these same shortcuts occasionally backfire, leading to illusions and error.

## DISORDERED MEMORIES

Our discussion so far has largely centered on people with normal memories. But over the last century, some intriguing questions about memory have been raised by studies of people with drastic defects in memory caused by various kinds of damage to the brain (Mayes, 1988; Squire, 1987; Squire & Shimamura, 1996).

### ANTEROGRADE AMNESIA

Certain lesions in the temporal cortex (specifically, in the hippocampus and nearby subcortical regions) produce a memory disorder called *anterograde amnesia* (*anterograde* means "in a forward direction"). These lesions can result from several different causes, including stroke and physical trauma. One of the most common causes, though, is a specific type of malnutrition associated with chronic alcoholism; in this case, the amnesia is one of the central symptoms of an illness called *Korsakoff's syndrome*. No matter what the cause, however, what defines anterograde amnesia is, in essence, an inability to learn anything new—an inability to form new memories.

To make this concrete, consider a patient known as H.M., perhaps the most famous and best-studied case of anterograde amnesia. Many of the specifics of H.M.'s case are unique—his amnesia was a tragic side effect of neurosurgery undertaken to treat severe epilepsy (see Figure 7.12). But the pattern of his memory loss is representative of the general profile of this amnesia. Following his surgery, H.M. had a normal memory span and so, apparently, a normal working memory. But he seems incapable of adding any new information to his long-term storage. He remembers no events that took place after his surgery. He is unable to recognize people he first met after his surgery, even if he sees them often (for example, the hospital staff). He can participate in a conversation (thanks to his intact working memory), but, if the conversation is interrupted for a few minutes, he has no recollection that the conversation ever occurred.

Observations like these suggest that H.M.'s long-term storage is completely closed to new memories, but his recollection of events prior to the operation remains largely intact, especially for events that happened more than a year or so before the surgery. His

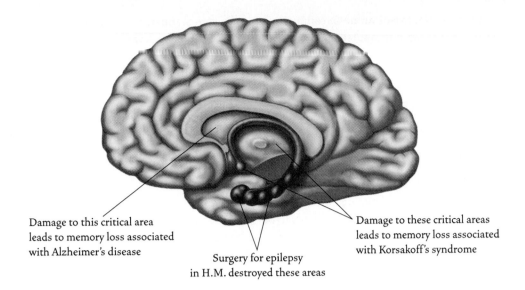

Damage to this critical area
leads to memory loss associated
with Alzheimer's disease

Surgery for epilepsy
in H.M. destroyed these areas

Damage to these critical areas
leads to memory loss associated
with Korsakoff's syndrome

**7.12** *Regions of the brain where damage can cause memory loss* *A cutaway section of the human brain showing regions of the hippocampus and associated structures whose destruction caused H.M.'s massive memory deficits. Patients with Korsakoff's syndrome tend to have lesions in regions that lie higher up, including the thalamus, while patients with Alzheimer's disease show damage in the base of the forebrain. (Adapted from Mishkin & Appenzeller, 1987)*

broad intellectual functioning also seems largely unimpaired. He can, for example, still read, write, and comment intelligently on the (distant) events that he does remember.

As one can easily imagine, this amnesia has had a devastating effect on H.M.'s life—including some effects that one might not think of as involving memory. For example, H.M. had an uncle whom he was very fond of. When first told that his uncle had died, he was deeply moved, but then he forgot all about this sad news. Some time later, he asked again when his uncle would come to visit, and was told again of his uncle's death. His grief was as intense as before, and, indeed, each time he hears this sad news, he is hearing it for the first time—with all the shock and all the pain (Corkin, 1984; Hilts, 1995; Marslen-Wilson & Teuber, 1975; Milner, 1966; Milner, Corkin, & Teuber, 1968).

H.M. has also offered some unsettling comments about his own state:

> Right now, I'm wondering, Have I done or said anything amiss? You see, at this moment everything looks clear to me, but what happened just before? That's what worries me. It's like waking from a dream; I just don't remember. (Milner, 1966)

And on another occasion:

> Every day is alone in itself, whatever enjoyment I've had, and whatever sorrow I've had. (Milner et al., 1968; for more on H.M.'s case, see Hilts, 1995)

## RETROGRADE AMNESIA

An opposite set of deficits occurs in **retrograde amnesia** (*retrograde* means "in a backward direction"), in which the patient suffers a loss of memory for some period prior to the brain injury. A brief period of retrograde amnesia can sometimes follow a blow to the head; longer periods of amnesia, lasting weeks or even years, can result from brain tumors, diseases, or strokes (Conway & Fthenaki, 1999; Kapur, 1999; Mayes, 1988). Retrograde amnesia can occur either by itself or, in some cases of brain damage, together with anterograde amnesia (Cipolotti, 2001; Nadel & Moscovitch, 2001).

What accounts for retrograde amnesia? According to some authors, one cause is a problem with **trace consolidation**, a process by which newly acquired memory traces gradually become firmly established. This might explain why this amnesia primarily affects memories that were formed shortly before the injury. These memories would not have had time to consolidate and would thus be more liable to destruction (Weingartner & Parker, 1984).

Whether retrograde amnesia can be explained in this manner, however, is still unde-cided. One trouble is that retrograde amnesia often extends back for several years prior to the injury. If so, consolidation could not explain the deficit unless one assumes—as a few authors do—that consolidation is an exceedingly drawn-out process, occurring over very long time periods (Hasselmo, 1999; McGaugh, 2000; Squire, 1987; Squire & Cohen, 1979, 1982).

## WHAT AMNESIA TEACHES US

The study of amnesic patients is important in its own right. These are, after all, individuals whose lives have been deeply disrupted, leading one to ask, What can we do to help them? At the present time, there seems to be no way to reverse anterograde amnesia, but there are ways in which these patients can be helped to lead productive lives (see, for example, Glisky, Schacter, & Tulving, 1986). The prognosis is different for retrograde amnesia. Generally, this form of amnesia dissipates with the passage of time, although, in many cases, some of the memory loss is permanent (Campbell & Conway, 1995).

In addition, amnesic patients can teach us a great deal about the nature of memory. In this section, we consider some of the lessons learned from the study of amnesia.

### WHAT TYPE OF MEMORY IS SPARED IN AMNESIA?

Many investigators have argued that patients with anterograde amnesia cannot acquire any long-term memories at all. But further study demonstrates that this is not true. These patients can, for example, learn to trace the correct path through a maze and get faster each time they redo the same maze. They can also acquire skills such as learning to read print that has been mirror-reversed (see Figure 7.13). H.M. plays the piano, and each time he plays a piece, he plays it more skillfully than he did the last time, all the while insisting that he has never seen the music before. In these and many other cases, the patients benefit from practice, and so they must have retained something from their previous experience—even though each time they are brought back into the testing situation, they insist that they have never seen the apparatus or the test materials before (Corkin, 1965; Cohen & Squire, 1980; Schacter, 1996; Weiskrantz & Warrington, 1979).

What can we make of these findings? Apparently, some sorts of memory are spared in anterograde amnesia, but what is it that divides the memories that are spared from those that are disrupted? Some authors believe that the crucial distinction is between *procedural* and *declarative knowledge*. Procedural knowledge is knowing *how*: how to ride a bicycle or how to read mirror writing. Declarative knowledge, in contrast, is knowing *that*: that there are three outs in an inning, that automobiles run on gasoline, that March has thirty-one days. Declarative knowledge also includes episodic memory—the knowledge that you had chicken for dinner yesterday or that you woke up late this morning.

Procedural and declarative knowledge are surely different from each other, and one can have procedural knowledge in a domain without any corresponding declarative knowledge. Professional baseball players know how to swing a bat, but few can explain just what it is that they know. Conversely, most physicists probably know (and can describe) the underlying mechanics of a baseball swing, but few will be able to perform competently when given a bat and asked to hit a ball (especially one thrown at ninety miles per hour). The physicists, it seems, have declarative knowledge without the corresponding procedural knowledge.

Many neuroscientists argue that procedural and declarative memories depend on different neural systems and that only one of these systems is disrupted in amnesiac patients. As a result, the amnesiacs perform normally on most tasks of skill-learning but fail miserably on any task requiring the acquisition of declarative knowledge (Cohen & Squire, 1980; Squire, 1986).

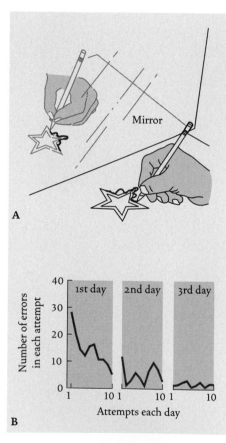

**7.13** *An example of what amnesiacs can learn (A) In mirror drawing, the research participant has to trace a line between two outlines of a figure while looking at her hand in a mirror. Initially, this is very difficult, but after some practice the individual gets very proficient at it. The same is true for amnesiacs. The graphs in (B) show H.M.'s improvement on this task over a period of three days. (Milner, Corkin, & Teuber, 1968)*

A somewhat different description of amnesia centers on the distinction between explicit and implicit memory (see pp. 254–256). Anterograde amnesiacs generally show their disruption on any task requiring explicit recollection of the past, and so they cannot answer a question like "Do you remember?" or "Do you recognize?" (at least not if the question pertains to events that occurred after the cerebral damage). The patients perform normally, however, on tests of implicit memory. To put this in concrete terms, the patients will fail completely if they are shown a number of words and later asked to recall or recognize them. The results are quite different, though, if the patients are shown a list of words and later tested implicitly—say, with a word-fragment completion task. For example, the patients might be shown __ L __ P __ A __ T or B __ O __ C __ S __ and asked to complete these fragments to form English words. This task is quite difficult if the patient has not been primed in any way. But if the patient was previously shown a list containing the words ELEPHANT and BOOK-CASE, he is likely to complete the fragments properly. Apparently, the patient does have some memory of seeing these words, and that memory facilitates performance with the word-fragment task (Diamond & Rozin, 1984; Graf, Mandler, & Squire, 1984; Schacter, 1996; Warrington & Weiskrantz, 1978).

Which, then, is the better account? Does anterograde amnesia disrupt declarative knowledge while sparing procedural? Or does it disrupt explicit memory while sparing implicit? The evidence at this point is equivocal. As one complication, these distinctions overlap. Procedural knowledge is often implicit; declarative knowledge is generally explicit. In addition, it may turn out that different cases of amnesia require different explanations. Anterograde amnesia is probably not a single disorder, so which conception provides the better account may vary from patient to patient (Squire & Cohen, 1984). With either explanation, though, these cases of brain damage provide powerful reasons for distinguishing at least two types of memory, and continued research on amnesia is certain to sharpen our understanding of this distinction.

## OTHER TYPES OF MEMORY

We have been focusing on a distinction that hinges on how a memory is revealed—implicitly or explicitly; in what the subject does (procedural knowledge) or what he says (declarative knowledge). But memories can also be distinguished according to the type of information contained within the memory, and here, too, the distinction can be illuminated by the study of amnesia.

For example, a patient known as Gene sustained a serious head injury in a motorcycle accident, damaging large areas of his frontal and temporal lobes, including his left hippocampus. As a result, he can recall no events at all from any time in his life. "Even when detailed descriptions of dramatic events in his life are given to him—such as the derailment, near his house, of a train carrying lethal chemicals that required 240,000 people to evacuate their homes for a week," Gene remembers nothing (Schacter 1996, p. 150; Tulving, Schacter, McLachlan, & Moscovitch, 1988). But he does remember some things. He remembers that he owned two motorcycles and a car, that his family has a summer cottage where he has spent many weekends, and the names of classmates in a school photograph (Schacter, 1996). In short, Gene's episodic memory is massively disrupted, but his memory for generic information, including information about repeated events in his life, is intact.

Other patients show the reverse pattern. One such patient had suffered damage to the front portion of her temporal lobes as a result of encephalitis. As a consequence, she has lost her memory of many common words, important historical events, famous people, and even the fundamental traits of animate and inanimate objects. "However, when asked about her wedding and honeymoon, her father's illness and death, or other specific past episodes, she readily produced detailed and accurate recollections" (Schacter, 1996, p. 152).

Cases like these make it clear that episodic memory is truly different from generic memory, and the two are supported, it seems, by distinct brain systems. As a result, damage in some brain sites disrupts episodic memory, leaving generic memory untouched; damage in other sites has the opposite effect (for more on this point, see Tulving, 2002). But we should not think of these brain sites as the seat of memory, or, worse, as the "memory centers." This is because remembering involves many steps and many processes, starting with the moment of encoding and ending with the recollection of the target information some time later. These various steps involve different regions of the brain, so that, in the end, many different brain sites play a role in remembering.

As an illustration of this multipart organization, consider the nature of memory retrieval. Some aspects of retrieval are swift and effortless—the sought-after information simply "pops" into mind. This form of remembering is called *associative retrieval* and applies both to generic memory ("Who was the first president of the United States?") and to episodic memory (as, for example, when a song or a smell calls a particular event to mind). Other aspects of retrieval, however, require some effort. This *strategic retrieval* is needed whenever we must actively search for a memory ("How did you spend your summer vacation in 1999?") or whenever we must sort through various memories to locate the correct one ("Let's see . . . was that the summer I went hiking or the summer I worked at the bookstore?").

These two aspects of retrieval draw on different brain areas. Some of the evidence for this claim comes from brain-imaging studies (such as PET scans) that show much greater activation in the prefrontal cortex (especially in the right hemisphere) during strategic retrieval and greater activation in the hippocampus (and nearby temporal lobe structures) during automatic retrieval (Conway, 1996; Conway & Fthenaki, 1999; Conway & Pleydell-Pearce, 2000; Moscovitch, 1995; Schacter, 1996). This pattern is then confirmed by studies of patients with different types of amnesia: Damage to the right prefrontal cortex, for example, is associated not just with memory loss but also with a peculiar pattern of memory error. The errors, referred to as *confabulations*, are sincerely offered, but utterly false, recollections. One patient recalled confidently that he and his wife had been married for only four months, when in fact they had been married for over thirty years. Remarkably, this same patient correctly remembered that he and his wife had four children, the youngest of whom was twenty-two (Moscovitch, 1995).

Why does prefrontal damage lead to confabulation? One proposal is that this kind of brain damage disrupts strategic retrieval. This leaves the patient unable to distinguish which thoughts are fantasies and which are genuine memories, which remembered elements derived from this episode and which are from that one. As a result, the patient's thoughts are "filled with all kinds of mnemonic flotsam and jetsam—fragments of experience that are not anchored to a proper time and place, and thus enter into peculiar alliances and marriages with one another" (Schacter, 1996, p. 121).

Other brain areas also play a crucial role in memory. We have just mentioned the role of the prefrontal cortex in memory retrieval; this same brain site is also essential for the operation of working memory. Damage to this area, therefore, impairs all of the tasks we earlier described as relying on working memory (also see Chapter 8). Likewise, a brain structure called the *amygdala* plays an important part in memory for emotional events. Damage to this structure has many effects; among them, the affected individual seems incapable of fear conditioning (Bechara et al., 1995; for more on fear conditioning, see Chapter 4; for more on the amygdala's role, see Chapter 11). Other forms of remembering seem to rely on still other brain areas. Damage to the occipital and temporal lobes can disrupt an individual's ability to retrieve specifically visual memories, such as the remembered face of a friend or the appearance of a previously visited landscape (also see Supèr, Spekreijse, & Lamme, 2001); damage elsewhere can disrupt the ability to remember words of certain types; and so on (see, for example, Schacter, 1996).

It is thus perfectly clear that no one brain area "handles" the job of remembering. Instead, remembering (like most cognitive operations) requires the close collaboration of many brain sites, each performing its own specific function.

## SOME FINAL THOUGHTS: THE INTERPLAY AMONG PERCEPTION, MEMORY, AND THINKING

In looking back over this chapter, we are again struck by the intimate pattern of relationships among perception, memory, and thinking. It is often unclear where one ends and another begins. To give just one example, consider how people use reconstruction and inference to fill "gaps" in the memory record. In essence, they supplement what they actually remember about an event by drawing on their general knowledge about how such events typically unfold. Examples like this make it clear that much of memory involves thinking. And as we saw previously, the same is true of perception. There, too, the perceiver becomes a thinker as she tries to solve perceptual problems and make sense out of ambiguous or impossible figures. In the next chapter, we will turn to the topic of thinking in its own right.

# SUMMARY

Memory is not a single entity and there is no single set of memory processes. Instead, the term memory is a blanket label for a large number of processes that work together to create a bridge between our past and our present.

## ACQUISITION, STORAGE, RETRIEVAL

1. Any act of remembering implies success at three aspects of the memory process. First is *acquisition*, the process of gathering information and placing it into memory. The next aspect of remembering is *storage*, the holding of information in some enduring form in the mind for later use. The final phase of remembering is *retrieval*, the point at which we draw information from storage and use it in some fashion. One way to retrieve material is through *recall*; another is through *recognition*.

## ENCODING

2. *Memory acquisition* includes cases of deliberate memorization and also *incidental learning*. Acquisition requires some

amount of attention to the to-be-remembered material, which involves a translation process, *memory encoding*.

3. According to the *stage theory of memory*, there are several memory systems. The most important of these are *working memory* (originally called, *short-term memory*), in which information is held while one is actively working on it, and *long-term memory*, in which information is stored for much longer periods.

4. The *storage capacity* of long-term memory is enormous; however a search is sometimes required to locate information in this store. In contrast, the capacity of working memory is quite limited, and many tasks show this limit to be about seven plus-or-minus two items, the so-called *magic number*. However, items can be recoded (through *chunking*) so that more items can be packed into working memory. Chunked materials are also easier to recall from long-term memory. Working memory holds information for short intervals; long-term memory stores materials for much longer, sometimes for as long as a lifetime.

5. The stage theory asserts that the road to long-term memory necessarily passes through working memory, so that working memory can be regarded as a *loading platform*, sit-

ting at the entrance to the huge long-term warehouse. According to stage theory, items are transferred from working memory to long-term memory by means of *rehearsal*.

6. Studies of *free recall* show *primacy* and *recency effects*, and these effects fit well with the predictions of stage theory. Primacy reflects the fact that early items in a presentation receive more attention, and so are more likely to be transferred to long-term storage. Recency reflects the fact that just-heard items are likely to be still in, and can be retrieved from, working memory.

7. According to stage theory, rehearsal keeps information in working memory longer, increasing the likelihood of transfer into more permanent storage. But later work on *maintenance rehearsal* shows that entering long-term memory is not automatic, and merely maintaining items in working memory, with no further engagement with the materials, is a poor way to promote long-term storage. Long-term storage is instead promoted by *elaborative rehearsal*, an active process in which the individual's own way of encoding and organizing the material plays a major role. This has led to the view that working memory is not so much a temporary storage platform but is rather a kind of *mental workbench*.

8. According to the *depth-of-processing hypothesis*, successful remembering depends on the depth at which the incoming information is processed, where shallow processing refers to encoding that emphasizes the superficial characteristics of a stimulus (such as its type face), and deep processing refers to encoding that emphasizes the meaning of the material.

9. Consistent with the depth-of-processing perspective, we remember best material that we have understood, but why does understanding aid subsequent recall? Many investigators believe that the key lies in memory connections that link one memory to the next. At the time of recall, these connections serve as *retrieval paths*. Support for this idea comes from many sources, including the efficacy of *mnemonics*, techniques for improving memory. These mnemonics guide a person toward forming memory connections, and these connections can provide dramatic improvement in memory. Some mnemonics, including the ancient *method of loci*, utilize imagery. However, imagery is effective in promoting memory only if the visualized items are imagined in some interaction—linking the items to each other, just as one would expect if imagery is a means of promoting memory connections, and if it is the connections that improve recollection.

RETRIEVAL

10. Unless we can retrieve the material we learned, whatever we've learned will be useless to us. If we cannot retrieve,

the memory trace is said to be inaccessible. Inaccessible memories, however, can often be made accessible by an appropriate *retrieval cue*. Whether a retrieval cue is useful or not depends in large part on the extent to which the cue re-creates the context in which the original learning occurred, a phenomenon referred to as *encoding specificity*. One reason why certain forms of encoding (for example, organization and understanding) are so effective is that they help pave the way for later retrieval by establishing many retrieval paths leading to the target material. This same idea explains the effect of elaborative rehearsal, which, unlike maintenance rehearsal, helps in remembering because it provides appropriate retrieval paths.

11. In tests of *explicit memory*, participants are overtly asked about something they know or experienced. In contrast, *implicit memory* refers to cases in which there is an effect of some past experience without the person being aware that they are remembering at all—or even that there was a relevant past experience. Methods for studying implicit memory include *word identification*, *repetition priming*, and *fragment completion*. Implicit memory effects may explain the fact that familiarity increases credibility, the so-called *illusion of truth*. Explicit and implicit memory can be distinguished in several ways, including the fact that explicit memory (but not implicit) benefits from deep processing; and the fact that implicit memory (but not explicit) is often influenced by peripheral aspects of the stimulus, such as the typeface of a word.

WHEN MEMORY FAILS

12. Other things being equal, forgetting increases the longer the *retention interval*. This point was first demonstrated by Ebbinghaus, who plotted the *forgetting curve* of associations between *nonsense syllables*. The causes of forgetting are still a matter of debate. One theory holds that traces gradually decay over time. Decay cannot be the sole cause of forgetting, however, as shown by the fact that more is forgotten after an interval spent awake than after an equal interval spent sleeping. If the passage of time were all that mattered for forgetting, then performance would be the same in these two cases.

13. Another view argues that the fundamental cause of forgetting is *interference* produced by other memories. Evidence comes from studies which show that learning a second list of words leads to a marked inferiority in memory for a first list.

14. Yet another theory asserts that forgetting is caused primarily by changes in retrieval cues at the time of recall. This position fits with much evidence, and is sometimes used to explain the phenomenon of *childhood amnesia*. According to one hypothesis, this amnesia arises because children's memories are formed and encoded within a context

that is massively different from that which they will later encounter as adults. A different hypothesis about this amnesia, however, is that various cerebral structures are not fully mature until the child is three or four years old. Still another hypothesis is that very young children have not yet developed the necessary schemas within which experiences can be organized, encoded, and rehearsed.

15. Much forgetting clearly involves retrieval failure—cases in which memories are misplaced, but not erased. Various phenomena can be explained in these terms, including the role of elaboration rehearsal and the effects of reinstating the mental or physical context in which learning took place. Another is a case of conscious memory search in which we reach a point in which we are certain we know the target information and can recall some features of that information, but we cannot recall the target information itself. This is the *tip-of-the-tongue phenomenon*.

16. Under some circumstances, forgetting does not seem to occur, as in the case of a second language well-learned in school. Such material seems to reach a status called *permastore*, in which it is retained for many decades. According to some authors, certain episodic memories, including *flashbulb memories*, may also be very long-lasting. However, some of these episodic memories, even though confidently recalled, turn out to be inaccurate.

17. In some cases memory failure involves *memory distortions*, in which we give a report of the past that is mistaken. The classic study of this phenomenon was performed by Bartlett, in which subjects were asked to recall stories from the folklore of other cultures. The data indicated that the subjects reconstructed the stories to fit their own cultural notions, and so recalled them in a distorted form—although a form that made the stories easier for the subjects to understand. Later studies showed similar effects, and have led psychologists to argue that many events and experiences are understood (and remembered) with reference to general knowledge structures called *scripts* or *schemas*.

18. Memory errors can also arise when an element experienced in one context is misremembered as having occurred in a different context. This point has been elaborated by studies of eyewitness testimony, which show that what is remembered can be extensively shaped by the questions posed to an eyewitness. *Leading questions* asked during one interrogation can change how an event is reported in subsequent interviews. The resulting errors are examples of *source confusion*, in which a witness is mistaken about the source of a particular remembered element. In addition, there is evidence that a witness's confidence in the truthfulness of his testimony is of very little value as an indicator of accurate memory.

19. *Hypnosis* is sometimes offered as a means of improving memory accuracy. However, evidence indicates that hypnosis does nothing to improve memory and can actually increase the risk of memory error. These results throw serious doubt on the so-called *tape-recorder theory of memory*.

20. There has been considerable controversy over the status of *repressed memories*. Evidence suggests that enormous caution is required in assessing these memories, especially if the memories emerged with the help of close questioning, hypnosis, or drugs alleged to promote recall.

21. Certain injuries to the brain, particularly to the hippocampus and surrounding regions, can produce disorders of memory. In *anterograde amnesia*, the patient's ability to fix material in long-term memory is reduced. In *retrograde amnesia*, the loss is for memories prior to the injury and is sometimes attributed to a disruption of *trace consolidation*. An important current issue is why patients with severe anterograde amnesia can acquire certain long-term memories (learning a maze, benefiting from repetition priming) but not others (remembering that they have seen the maze or heard the word before). According to one hypothesis, the crucial distinction is between *procedural* and *declarative knowledge*; according to another, it is that between *implicit* and *explicit retrieval*.

22. Some brain-imaging studies show much greater activation in the prefrontal cortex during strategic retrieval and greater activation in the hippocampus during *automatic retrieval*. This has been confirmed by studies of patients with different types of amnesia. Further work has implicated the *amygdala* in memory for emotional events.

# THOUGHT AND KNOWLEDGE

*I*n ordinary language, the word *think* has a wide range of meanings. It may be a synonym for *remember* (as in "I can't think of her name") or for *believe* (as in "I think sea serpents exist"). It may also refer to a state of vague reverie, as in "I'm thinking of nothing in particular." These various uses suggest that the word has become a blanket term to cover many different psychological processes.

But *think* also has a narrower meaning, best conveyed by such words as *reason* and *reflect.* Psychologists who study thinking are mainly interested in this sense of the term, which they call **directed thinking**—the mental activities we use whenever we try to solve a problem, judge the truth of an assertion, or weigh the costs and benefits in an important decision.

In each of these activities, we draw constantly on the foundation of what we already know. If the situation is one we have encountered before, then we can take into account how we reasoned or decided the last time we were in this setting. If the situation is unfamiliar but resembles others we have encountered, then we can draw on more general knowledge: to make a new kind of pie, we call on our broad knowledge of cooking; to manage a difficult social situation, we rely on what we know in general about diplomacy and politeness.

Even in a completely new situation, though, knowledge is still necessary to give meaning to our thoughts. Without a knowledge base, for example, we could not think about dogs, because we would not know what dogs are, and likewise for any other thought—whether it is about dogs, trees, soccer matches, or Supreme Court justices. In any of these cases, our knowledge provides the material we are able to think about, and so it seems entirely sensible that we begin our discussion of thinking with a consideration of knowledge.

*Thinking*    (Saint Jerome, by Guido Reni)

# ANALOGICAL REPRESENTATIONS

Many (perhaps all) of the components of our knowledge can be regarded as **mental representations** of the world and of our experiences in it. These representations are the main elements of thought. They are like the many external representations we encounter in ordinary life, the signs and symbols that stand for something else, such as maps, blueprints, menus, price lists, stories—the list is very long. In all these cases, the representation is not the same as what it stands for; instead, it signifies the real thing. We do not literally drive on the map, nor do we eat the menu.

Psychologists, philosophers, and computer scientists have found it convenient to distinguish between two broad classes of representations, the analogical and the symbolic.* **Analogical representations** capture some of the actual characteristics of (and are thus analogous to) what they represent. In contrast, **symbolic representations** bear no such relationship to the item they stand for. As we will see, human thought uses both kinds of representations.

Consider a picture of a mouse. The picture is in some ways quite different from the real animal; the picture consists of marks on paper, whereas the actual mouse is flesh and blood. In this sense, the picture represents a mouse rather than actually being one. Even so, the picture has many similarities to the creature it represents, so that, in general, the picture looks like a mouse: the mouse's eyes are side by side in reality, and they are side by side in the picture; the mouse's ears and tail are at opposite ends of the creature, and they are at opposite ends in the picture. It is properties like these that make the picture an analogical representation.

In contrast, take the word *mouse*. Unlike a picture, the word in no way resembles the mouse. It is an abstract representation, and the relation between the five letters *m-o-u-s-e* and the little animal that they represent is entirely arbitrary.

The same distinction holds for mental representations. Some of our mental representations are images that reflect more or less directly many of the attributes of the objects or events they represent. Other mental representations are more abstract, just like words in a language. We will begin our discussion by considering analogical representations: mental images and the related topic of spatial thinking.

---

* Many psychologists and computer scientists use the term *digital* for what we here call *symbolic*. This is because computers usually encode such symbolic, nonpictorial representations in a discrete, all-or-none fashion by various combinations of the digits 0 and 1.

*Some representations are pictorial, others are abstract*
*(A) A photograph of the artist Dora Maar. (B) A Cubist portrait of Madame Maar by Pablo Picasso. Note that while Picasso's rendering is by no means literal, there is enough of a pictorial similarity to the model that the portrait is still recognizable as a human figure. While this painting is a pictorial representation, the model's name—Dora Maar— is not. It stands for her, but it is not like her, for both names and words are abstract representations rather than pictorial ones.*

# MENTAL IMAGES

Imagine someone standing with her arms hanging loosely at her sides. Will her hands be higher than her hips or lower? Most people faced with this question will retrieve the relevant information from a mental image, easily discerning in the image that her hands will fall below her hips (but above her knees). Observations like these suggest that some of our knowledge is based on analogical representations called *mental images*. We seem to inspect these images with "our mind's eye," and read information from these images much as we would read information off of a picture. Similar claims have been made for other senses—including "mental sounds" we hear with the "mind's ear," or "mental objects" we feel with the "mind's fingers." But far more is known about *visual imagery* than about imagery in these other modalities, and so our focus will be on visual images.

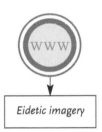

Eidetic imagery

## PICTURELIKE ASPECTS OF VISUAL IMAGERY

One might think that the most obvious way to study mental imagery is via *introspection*, a process through which each of us could "look within" to observe (and then report on) the contents of our thoughts. With introspection, each of us could examine our own mental images, and, in that way, we could begin the endeavor of describing what these images are like, what information they contain, and so on. This was, as it turns out, the earliest method used to study mental imagery (Galton, 1883), but most modern psychologists are wary of introspective data—not just for imagery, but in general (see, for example, Nisbett & Wilson, 1977). One problem is that many aspects of our mental lives proceed without our conscious awareness, and, for these, introspection is (by definition) of no value: when we look within, we cannot detect ideas or processes that are unconscious! Even for conscious contents (like mental images), we often lack the vocabulary to describe the details or quality of our thoughts, and this obviously diminishes the precision and value of the introspective report. Worst of all, though, when

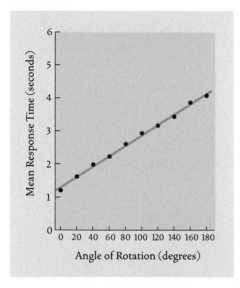

ORIENTATION

Normal          Backward

| | | | |
|---|---|---|---|
| 0° | 300° | 0° | 300° |
| 60° | 240° | 60° | 240° |
| 120° | 180° | 120° | 180° |

**8.1   Mental rotation   Normal and backward versions of one of the characters used in the mental rotation study, showing the orientations in which it appeared as a test stimulus. (Adapted from Cooper & Shepard, 1973)**

**8.2   Data from a mental rotation experiment Research participants need to imagine a form rotating into an upright position in order to make a judgment about that form. The greater the degree of rotation required, the longer the response time. (After Shepard & Metzler, 1971)**

someone does find words to report on their own mental states, the words are often hard to interpret. If someone claims, for example, to have particularly vivid imagery, can we take that at face value? Perhaps his imagery is rather cloudy, but he regards it as vivid because he has never experienced anything more. Another participant, also claiming to have vivid imagery, might actually be able to call up much more detailed images. Such ambiguities make introspective self-reports of uncertain value.

These concerns have led researchers to seek more objective means of studying mental imagery. Their experiments typically ask research participants to do something with the image—to manipulate it in some fashion or to "read off" certain information from the image. The results of these studies indicate that, to a remarkable extent, visual images do function just like mental pictures.

In *mental rotation* experiments, for example, participants are shown a letter or a number, either in its normal version or mirror-reversed (that is, *R* or *Я*). In addition, the figures are tilted so that participants might encounter an *R* rotated by, say, 180 degrees or an *Я* rotated by, say, 60 degrees (see Figure 8.1). Their task is to press one button if the stimulus is normal, another if it is mirror-reversed.

As the orientation of the letters changes from upright (that is, 0-degree rotation) through 60 degrees to 180 degrees, participants' response times for making this decision steadily increase (Figure 8.2). Apparently, they perform this task by imagining the test stimulus rotating into an upright position; only then can they judge it as normal or mirror-reversed. And it seems that mental rotation, just like actual movement, takes time: the more the character has to be rotated, the longer it takes (Cooper & Shepard, 1973; Shepard & Cooper, 1982).

Another line of evidence comes from studies on image scanning. In a classic study, research participants were first shown the map of a fictitious island containing various objects: a hut, a well, a tree, and so on (see Figure 8.3). After memorizing this map, the participants were asked to form a mental image of the entire island. The experimenter then named two objects on the map (say, the hut and the tree), and the participants had to imagine a black speck zipping from the first location to the second. The results showed that the time needed for this speck to "travel" from location to location was directly proportional to the distance between the two points. Of course, this is just what one would expect if participants were scanning a physical map with their eyes. That the same holds true when they scan a mental image with the mind's eye highlights the remarkable parallels between mental images and visual stimuli, between imaging and perceiving (Kosslyn, Ball, & Reisser, 1978).

**8.3   Image scanning   Research participants were asked to form a mental image of a map of an island and then to imagine a speck zipping from one location to another. (After Kosslyn, Ball, & Reisser, 1978)**

Clearly, then, visual images do share many properties with pictures. In particular, it seems that the spatial characteristics of a scene or object are directly represented in the image, so that the image truly depicts the scene just as a picture does, rather than describing it in some symbolic fashion. Thus, if two points are close together in the to-be-represented scene, they will be functionally close together in the image; if they are far apart, they will be functionally far apart in the image. Likewise for the spatial relationship of being "between." If point *B* in the scene is between points *A* and *C*, this relation will be preserved in the image, and so one cannot mentally scan from point *A* to point *C* without passing through point *B*.

It is perhaps unsurprising, therefore, that images function just like pictures in many settings. For example, we discussed the role of mnemonic imagery in Chapter 7: apparently, we can "discover" elements in a mental image and thus be reminded of them, just as we can with a picture. Similarly, mental images can help people solve problems, including problems that require creative solutions (Finke, 1993; Finke, Ward, & Smith, 1992).

In addition, much evidence indicates that the process of visualization draws on many of the same brain areas as the processes needed for actual vision. Some of the evidence for this claim comes from neuroimaging techniques, using the procedures described in Chapter 2. These studies make it clear that many of the same brain regions (primarily in the occipital lobe) are active during both visual perception and visual imagery. Moreover, the exact pattern of brain activation during imagery depends on the type of image being maintained. For very detailed images, the brain areas that are especially activated tend to be those crucial for the perception of position and spatial relationships. In contrast, when people are asked to imagine movement patterns, high levels of activation are observed in brain areas that are sensitive to motion in ordinary perception (Behrmann, 2000; Farah, 1988; Goebel, Khorram-Sefat, Mucklin, Hacker, & Singer, 1998; Thompson & Kosslyn, 2000).

Evidence also comes from studies of individuals with brain damage. Lesions that disrupt vision also seem to disrupt visual imagery and vice versa. Often these disruptions are quite specific. For example, patients who, because of a stroke, lose the ability to perceive color often seem to lose the ability to imagine scenes in color; patients who lose the ability to perceive fine detail also seem to lose the ability to visualize fine detail (Farah, 1988; Isha & Sagi, 1995; Miyashita, 1995).

Still further evidence comes from a procedure that produces a "temporary lesion" in an otherwise healthy brain. The technique of transcranial magnetic stimulation (TMS) creates a series of strong magnetic pulses at a specific location on the scalp; these pulses cause a short-lived disruption in the brain region directly underneath this scalp area (see Chapter 7). In this fashion, it is possible to disrupt the primary visual cortex in a normal brain. Not surprisingly, using TMS in this way causes problems in vision. It also causes parallel problems in visual imagery, providing a powerful argument that this brain region is crucial both for the processing of visual information and for the creation and maintenance of visual images (Kosslyn et al., 1999).

All of these findings point to considerable overlap between visualizing and perceiving, and between mental pictures and actual pictures. But alongside this overlap, there are also important contrasts here, for while images are picturelike, they are not pictures. Evidence for this view comes from a study in which research participants were shown a figure that they had never seen before. This figure is normally ambiguous: if it is seen as oriented toward the left, it looks like the head of a duck; if oriented toward the right, it looks like the head of a rabbit (Figure 8.4). The picture was then removed and the participants were asked to form a mental image of the figure. They were then asked to inspect the image and describe what it looked like. All "saw" either a duck or a rabbit with their mind's eye, and some said they saw it very vividly. They were then asked

*8.4  Images are not pictures*  **The rabbit-duck figure, first used in 1900 by Joseph Jastrow. (For details see text.)**

whether their image might look like something else. Not one of the participants came up with a reversal, even after hints and considerable coaxing. The results were very different, though, when, a minute later, they drew the figure and looked at their own drawing. Now everyone came up with the perceptual alternative. These results seem to indicate that a visual image is not a picture. It is, as we have said, a depiction, and in this regard it is very much like a picture. But, unlike a picture, an image seems to be already organized and interpreted to some extent and, as a result, has lost the potential for easy reinterpretation (Chambers & Reisberg, 1985; for further discussion, see Reisberg & Heuer, 2002).

We should mention that, in this last regard, mental images are just like *percepts*, the mental representations of the world around us that are produced during ordinary perceiving. In Chapter 6, we noted that our perception "goes beyond the information given" in the stimulus information, so that our perception of the world contains elements of organization and interpretation that are not present in the sensory input. Apparently, the same is true for mental images. Like percepts, images show us directly what the imaged object or scene looks like (that is, both depict the object or scene). But like percepts, images do so in a fashion that organizes the information and, in the process, removes the ambiguity (and so the potential for reinterpretation) that is present, say, in the picture shown in Figure 8.4.

## SPATIAL THINKING

We began the chapter by distinguishing between analogical and symbolic forms of representation. As we have now seen, though, the distinction between these two is sometimes blurred: mental images not only are analogical but also contain elements of organization and interpretation that are probably symbolic in their nature. A similar blurring is evident when we consider some forms of *spatial thinking*, the kind of thinking we use when we want to determine a shortcut between two locations or when we mentally try to rearrange the furniture in the living room.

### MENTAL MAPS THAT ARE BOTH ANALOGICAL AND SYMBOLIC

There is no question that some instances of spatial thinking draw on *mental maps* that have many pictorial qualities (see, for example, Jonides & Baum, 1978). In other cases, though, spatial thinking involves a mix of processes that are analogical and others that are symbolic. In one study, research participants were asked to indicate the relative locations of San Diego, California, and Reno, Nevada (Figure 8.5). The participants judged San Diego to be west of Reno, although it is actually farther east. Similarly, they judged Montreal, Canada, to be farther north than Seattle, Washington, although the reverse is true. These results suggest that they were not basing their answers on mental maps at all. Instead, they seemed to be reasoning in this fashion:

> *California is west of Nevada.*
> *San Diego is in California.*
> *Reno is in Nevada.*
> *Therefore, San Diego is west of Reno.*

The knowledge being used here ("San Diego is in California") is clearly symbolic, not pictorial. Moreover, these symbolic formulations can (and in this case do) lead to error. Even so, most of us often store spatial information in such a rough-and-ready conceptual way. To the extent that we do store some geographical information under category rubrics, our spatial knowledge cannot be exclusively—or even largely—picturelike (Stevens & Coupe, 1978).

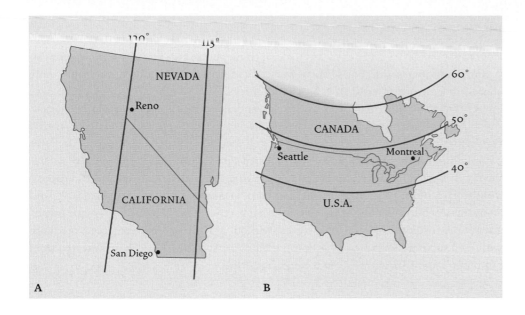

**8.5  Conceptual mental maps**  *Research participants tend to judge San Diego to be west of Reno and Montreal to be north of Seattle. But these judgments are in error. (A) A map of California and Nevada with lines of longitude (angular distance from an arbitrary reference point in Greenwich, England), which shows that, in fact, San Diego is east of Reno. (B) A map of the United States and southern Canada with lines of latitude (angular distance from the equator), which shows that Seattle is slightly north of Montreal. (Stevens & Coupe, 1978)*

# SYMBOLIC REPRESENTATIONS

Plainly, then, some of our thinking—and perhaps most of it—is symbolic, not analogical, in nature. But what are the symbols that constitute this form of thinking, and how do these symbols specify what ideas or objects in the world they are symbols of? The attempt to address these questions is relatively recent, at least in psychology. But other disciplines—including philosophy, logic, and linguistics—have wrestled with these issues for many years, and their progress provides crucial groundwork for psychological research in this domain.

## SYMBOLIC ELEMENTS

Investigators have generally argued that we must distinguish two aspects of our symbolic thinking: First, there are concepts, the things we think about, and, second, there are ways of assembling concepts into more complex thoughts and beliefs.

### CONCEPTS

The term *concept* describes a mental class or category. An example is *dog*, which includes *poodle, beagle, dachshund*, and *Alsatian*. Other concepts designate qualities or dimensions. Examples are length and age. Still other concepts are relational, such as *taller than*.

There is some disagreement among scholars about how exactly concepts are represented in the mind. Some have suggested that the representation is relatively abstract—perhaps a list of features that characterize the concept. Others have suggested more concrete modes of representation—for example, some memory record of the various individuals within the relevant category, with these records collectively representing the entire concept. Still others have suggested that our concepts are represented only in relationship to each other, so that our mental representation of *airplane*, for example, is intimately connected to our representations of *travel* and of *distance* and so on. We will return to these issues in Chapter 9 (see also Reisberg, 2001). Alongside of these disagreements, though, one point is clear: concepts are the building blocks of our symbolic knowledge.

## PROPOSITIONS

Concepts provide the basic elements that we think about, but, in order to represent our (sometimes complex) ideas and beliefs, we need a means of combining concepts into more complicated structures. One means of combination is by association, and some have argued that a great deal of our thinking can be understood in these terms. Others suggest, though, that associative links may be inadequate as a means of representing the organized regularities of our thoughts, and have suggested instead that our thoughts take the form of *propositions*. These are statements that relate a subject (the item about which the statement is being made) and a predicate (what is being asserted about the subject). Propositions can be true or false. For example, "Solomon loves toads," "Jacob plays lacrosse," and "Squirrels eat burritos" are all propositions. But just the words "Susan," or "is squeamish" are not propositions—the first is a subject without a predicate; the second is a predicate without a subject. (For more on how propositions are structured, and the role they play in our thoughts, see, for example, Anderson, 1993, 1996.)

## KNOWLEDGE AND MEMORY

When we think, we often form new concepts and formulate new beliefs. But many concepts and beliefs are already stored in memory, where they constitute our accumulated knowledge, the "database" that sustains and informs our thoughts. How is this knowledge organized in memory, and how is it retrieved?

### GENERIC MEMORY

In the previous chapter, we said a great deal about how information is stored in, and then retrieved from, memory. Many of the examples we considered in the earlier chapter were concerned with episodic memory. This term refers to the stored records of particular events (episodes) in one's own life, memory for what happened when and where. This contrasts with *generic memory*, which is memory that contains the knowledge that each of us holds, independent of any particular episodes, and certainly independent of where or when we acquired that bit of knowledge. Thus, for example, our generic memories tell us that Paris is the capital of France, that three is the square root of nine, and that sugar is an ingredient of most cookies. Rarely, though, do we remember how or when we acquired these bits of knowledge; if we did, our recollection of these occasions would be episodic, not generic.

For each person, generic memory contains an extraordinary wealth of knowledge, including countless facts about the world, knowledge of what objects look like, friends' names and the spatial layout of one's hometown, the lyrics for perhaps a hundred songs, the plots from dozens of TV shows, and on and on and on. Within this huge archive, one of the important components is *semantic memory*, which concerns the meanings of words and concepts. As some authors conceive it, our entire vocabulary is in this store: every word, together with its pronunciation, all of its meanings, its relations to objects in the real world, and the way it is put together with other words to make phrases and sentences.

Given the huge size of generic memory, how do we ever find the information we seek within this vast library? Clearly, there must be some sort of organizational system; otherwise, the hunt for an entry might last for days. But what is that system?

### NETWORK MODELS OF GENERIC MEMORY

Several investigators have proposed *network models* of generic memory. Within these networks, words or concepts are represented by *nodes*, while the associations between the concepts are indicated by *associative links* or associative connections (see Figure 8.6). These connections serve as retrieval paths, and so they provide the means through which we locate information in storage: we follow these paths from one node to the next. But these same connections are also part of the knowledge representation—and so the link from, say, *Abe Lincoln* to *president* is not just a retrieval path; that link actually represents part of our knowledge about Lincoln.

Links within the network can represent many different kinds of relationships, including relationships based on hierarchical position (as in *canary-bird*) or based on similarity of meaning (*apple-orange*) or on well-learned associations (*peanut butter-jelly*). According to some proposals, groups of links can also be organized in a fashion that allows them to represent propositions (Figure 8.7, Anderson, 1993, 1996). In addition, the links among these concepts can vary in strength, so that two frequently associated terms (*white-house*) will be connected via a strong linkage, whereas less frequently associated terms (*father-niece*) will be connected via a weak linkage or perhaps connected only indirectly (with links, perhaps, from *father* to *uncle* and then from *uncle* to *niece*).

In this sort of model, the nodes representing a specific idea are activated whenever a person is thinking about that idea. This activation then spreads to neighboring nodes, through the associative links, much as electrical current spreads through a network of wires. The spread of activation will be stronger (and will occur more quickly) between nodes that are strongly associated. Moreover, the activation will dissipate as it spreads outward, so little or no activation will reach the nodes more distant from the activation's source (Collins & Loftus, 1975).

One line of evidence in support of these ideas comes from experiments on *semantic priming*. In the classic study in this area, participants were presented with two strings of letters, one printed above the other (Meyer & Schvaneveldt, 1971). Three examples are:

|        |        |        |
|--------|--------|--------|
| *nurse* | *nurse* | *narde* |
| *butter* | *doctor* | *doctor* |

The participants' job was to press a "yes" button if both sequences were real words (for example, *nurse-butter* or *nurse-doctor*) and a "no" button if either was not a word (for example, *narde-doctor*). Our interest is in the two pairs that required a "yes" response. (In these tasks, the "no" items serve only as *catch trials*, ensuring that participants really are doing the task as they were instructed to do.)

Response times in this task were reliably shorter when the two words were related in meaning (as in *nurse-doctor*) than when they were unrelated (*nurse-butter*). Presumably, the sight of the word *nurse* activated the node for this concept. Once the node was acti-

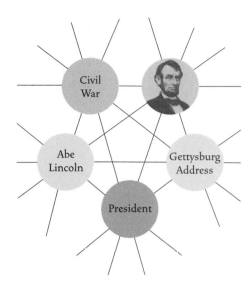

**8.6 Associative connections** *Many investigators propose that our knowledge is represented through a network of associated ideas, so that the idea of "Lincoln" is linked to "Civil War" and "President," and so on.*

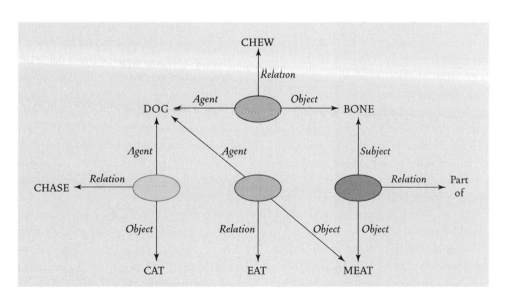

**8.7 Propositions** *One proposal is that your understanding of dogs—what they are, what they are likely to do—is represented by an interconnected network of propositions. In this figure, each proposition is represented by an ellipse, and is the meeting place for the elements that are brought together in the proposition. Thus, this bit of memory network contains the propositions "dogs chew bones," "dogs chase cats," and so on. A complete representation about your knowledge of dogs would include many other propositions as well. (After Anderson, 1990)*

vated, activation spread out from this source to the other nodes nearby. This warmed up the nearby nodes, including the node for *doctor*. If *doctor* was then the next word to be dealt with, the warm-up led to easier activation of its node and thus to a faster response.

## PARALLEL DISTRIBUTED PROCESSING

Theorists have offered several different proposals for how a network model might function, and one major difference among these proposals concerns the nature of the representation for individual ideas. According to some theorists, human knowledge is best understood through models relying on *local representations*, in which each concept— say, the concept *fire engine*—is represented by a particular node or set of nodes. When these nodes are activated, one is thinking about fire engines, and when one is thinking about fire engines, these nodes are activated.

Other theorists argue for a different type of model, one relying on *distributed representations*. In these models, each concept is represented, not by a single node, but by a pattern of activation across the entire network. To take a highly simplified case, the concept *fire engine* might be represented by a pattern in which nodes *A*, *D*, *H*, and *Q* are firing, whereas the concept *ambulance* might be represented by a pattern in which nodes *D*, *F*, *L*, and *T* are firing. In this case, node *D* is not only part of the pattern that represents *fire engine* but also part of the pattern that represents *ambulance* and many other concepts as well. Thus, the *D* node, by itself, does not represent anything; the significance of this node is only interpretable in the broader context of other nodes' activities.

This difference in representational format has important consequences for how the network functions. Imagine being asked, "What equipment would you find in an ambulance?" Presumably, you would answer this question by starting with thoughts about ambulances, and this would trigger other thoughts—about stretchers, oxygen tanks, and so on. With distributed representations, this must involve a process in which all of the nodes representing *ambulance* manage collectively to activate the broad pattern of nodes representing (say) *oxygen tank*. In the (simplified) terms we used a moment ago, node *D* might trigger node *H* at the same time that node *F* triggers node *Q*, and so on, leading ultimately to the activation of the *H-Q-S-Y* combination that represents *oxygen tank*. In short, then, a network using distributed representations must employ processes that are similarly distributed, so that one widespread activation pattern (for example, that for *ambulance*) can have broad enough effects to evoke a different (but equally widespread) pattern. Moreover, the steps bringing this about must occur simultaneously—in parallel—with each other, so that one entire representation can smoothly trigger the next entire representation. That is why this sort of model is said to involve *parallel distributed processing*, or **PDP** for short. Models of this type are also described as *connectionist*, highlighting the fact that the functioning of these models depends on having just the right connections among all the various nodes at just the right strengths.

In a *connectionist model*, all processes are distributed across the entire network, including the processes that control the model's functioning. In other words, there is no centralized control mechanism to ensure that all works smoothly, no supervisor to adjust the connections if things go offtrack. The model is, in essence, the ultimate grassroots enterprise, with all operations entirely under local control. To make this concrete, consider an espionage story in which, say, a master spy works out an ingenious plot to overthrow the government. The plot involves one hundred different operatives, but to ensure secrecy, the master spy has made certain that none of the operatives knows anything about the overall plan. Each knows only her own little part—just that small bit that she has been instructed to do. And now chance enters: immediately after instructing the last operative, the master spy dies of a heart attack. This will not, however, terminate the scheme. All of the operatives have their orders and need no further supervision; the plot will presumably run by itself, even after the master spy's death.

Notice the peculiar status of the master spy's plan in this situation. As long as the master spy was alive, the overall plot was represented in his thoughts—there was, therefore, a local representation of the entire scheme. After the master's death, there is no local representation of the plan. There is surely none in the minds of the individual operatives, since each knows only a tiny part of the whole. Still, in a way, the overall plan continues to exist, and it would be seen if only we could view all the operatives simultaneously and understand how the actions of each fit into the whole. The plan is thus represented in a distributed fashion, manifest in the collective and simultaneous activity of all the operatives. And whether we perceive it or not, the plan will go forward, because of the distributed pattern of the operatives' actions (Reisberg, 2001).

In some ways this seems a peculiar proposal, and one might think that we give up a lot by not including, within the network, any sort of centralized control system. Nonetheless, many investigators find connectionist proposals extremely promising. They note, for example, that the brain and nervous system seem to rely on parallel distributed processing, with virtually all of our intellectual achievements dependent on broad patterns of activity spread over many brain areas. They argue, therefore, that connectionist models, relying on distributed processing, are biologically more plausible than networks relying on local representations and local processing.

In addition, it turns out that connectionist models have impressive computational power, and working models of this type have been devised for many cognitive operations, including pattern recognition, memory processes, and aspects of thinking and language (Churchland & Sejnowski, 1992; McClelland & Rumelhart, 1986; Rumelhart, 1997). Indeed, proponents of this approach believe that eventually all cognitive operations will be described in these terms. They argue that, in general, the complex phenomena of mental functioning are best understood as the result of many smaller events, much as an avalanche is produced by the movement of many small stones and rocks. Each of these smaller events is computationally simple, but that is okay, since each is responsible only for a fraction of the overall achievement, much as each of the operatives in the spy story was responsible only for a bit of the overall scheme.

These proposals, however, have led to considerable debate, with some researchers strongly advocating net or connectionist models (see, for example, Churchland & Sejnowski, 1992; Christiansen, Chater, & Seidenberg, 1999; McClelland & Seidenberg, 2000) and others claiming that these models are sharply limited in what they can accomplish (see, for example, Fodor, 1997; Pinker, 1999). How this debate will turn out remains to be seen. This is an exciting area of research, and new advances are coming at a rapid rate.

# THE PROCESS OF THINKING: SOLVING PROBLEMS

So far, we have said a lot about the building blocks of thought and knowledge, but what about the more dynamic aspects of thought—the flow of ideas that we move through when we are drawing a conclusion or weighing factors to make a decision? We turn now to these issues, starting with the question of how thought proceeds in a particular area: problem solving.

## ORGANIZATION IN PROBLEM SOLVING

How do we proceed when we are trying to repair a broken bicycle or, for that matter, a damaged relationship? How do we move forward when searching for a job or for a

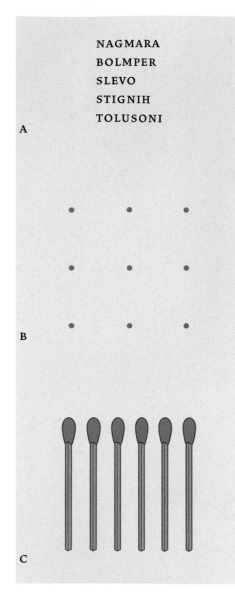

NAGMARA
BOLMPER
SLEVO
STIGNIH
TOLUSONI

A

B

C

*8.8  Examples of problems  (A) Anagrams. Rearrange the letters on each line to form a word. (B) Nine-dot problem. Nine dots are arranged in a square. Connect them by drawing four continuous straight lines without lifting your pencil from the paper. (C) Matchstick problem. Assemble all six matches to form four equilateral triangles, each side of which is equal to the length of one match. (For the solutions to all three problems, see p. 294.)*

topic for the term paper due on Friday? In each case, our situation has an *initial state* (we need a paper topic, or the bicycle is not working) and a *goal state* (we have selected a topic, or the bicycle is fine), and our task is to find a path that will bring us from the former to the latter.

Our search for a path forward, in solving a problem, is heavily influenced by how we understand the problem. At the minimum, this understanding involves knowing what the goal state is, and often this is not self-evident. For example, let us say that you want to do something fun next summer. In this case, your understanding of the goal state is rather vague, providing little guidance in your search for a specific plan. Alternatively, how should we solve the problem of global warming? Here, too, we do not know exactly what the goal state involves—it might be a situation in which we have found a way to burn less fossil fuel, or it might be a situation in which we have found a way to remove pollutants already in the atmosphere, or it might take some other form altogether.

Psychologists call problems like these *ill-defined problems*, because, at the start, we do not know exactly what our goal is, nor do we know what our options might be for reaching the goal. In contrast, a problem like solving an anagram (what English word can be produced by rearranging the letters *subufoal*?) is a *well-defined problem*. Here, we know from the start that the goal will involve just these eight letters and will be a word in the English language; other examples of well-defined problems are shown in Figure 8.8.

It is no surprise that well-defined problems are easier, because, with them, we know where we are going and we know what possibilities to consider as means of getting there. It is entirely sensible, therefore, that people often try to solve ill-defined problems by first making them well defined—that is, by seeking ways to clarify and specify the goal state. In many cases, this effort involves adding extra constraints or extra assumptions. ("Let me assume that my summer of fun will involve spending time near the ocean," or "Let me assume that my summer travel can't cost more than $500.") This will narrow the set of options—and, conceivably, may hide the best ones from view—but, for many problems, defining them more clearly helps enormously in the search for a solution (Schraw, Dunkle, & Bendixen, 1995).

## HIERARCHICAL ORGANIZATION

Having a clear definition of a problem's goal helps the problem solver know which options are worth considering and which are not. For example, in solving an anagram, you will not waste time in adding extra letters or turning some of the letters into numerals—these steps are incompatible with your goal. (The solution to the earlier example, by the way, is *fabulous*.)

Having a clear goal can also help in other ways. For example, consider a taxi driver trying to choose a route to the airport. The driver already knows what her options are— she can go straight at this intersection, or turn left or turn right. Her choice among these options, though, is guided by the goal. Perhaps she knows that a left turn will bring her to the freeway's on-ramp, but this by itself will not cause her to turn. Instead, she is likely to ask, "Will this path bring me where I want to go?" If the freeway heads in the wrong direction, or if the driver remembers road construction along that route, she is likely to seek an alternative path. Notice, then, that the problem's goal provides a constant reference point against which one's options can be evaluated.

Understanding a problem, though, involves more than just understanding the problem's goal. To see this, consider an often effective problem-solving strategy called *means–end analysis*. To use this strategy, one asks, "What is the difference between my current state and my goal?" Then, with that difference defined, one asks, "What means do I have available for reducing this difference?" Thus, for example: "I want to get to the store. What's the difference between my current state and my goal? One of distance.

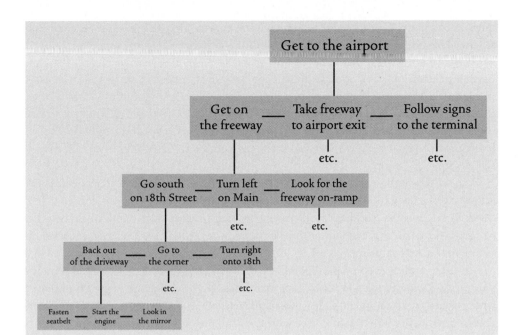

**8.9 Problems and subproblems**   *It is helpful to replace an initial problem with a series of subproblems. By solving these, the initial problem is also solved. Subproblems, in turn, can be broken down into still-smaller subproblems, creating a hierarchical structure.*

What changes distance? My automobile. My automobile won't work. What is needed to make it work? A new battery. Where do I get a battery?" And so on (after Newell & Simon, 1972).

A means-end analysis can replace the initial problem (for example, getting to the store) with a series of subproblems (for example, getting the car to work), and, with that, the initial goal gets replaced by a series of subgoals. If this process is repeated (with subproblems being broken down into still smaller subproblems), it can create a hierarchical structure like the one shown in Figure 8.9.

Understanding a problem in terms of this sort of hierarchical structure brings a number of advantages. For one, the subproblems are, by definition, smaller than the initial problem, and so they are likely to be more easily dealt with than the original problem. In addition, the subproblems are often quite straightforward. For example, the taxi driver might realize that her best path to the airport is indeed the freeway, and so the larger problem ("get to the airport") can be replaced with a simpler and much more familiar routine ("take the freeway"). This routine in turn is composed of still simpler *subroutines*, such as "go to the on-ramp at Front Street," "accelerate when the light turns green," or even "maneuver through traffic." In this fashion, a series of modular units can be assembled into the larger-scale solution to the initial problem (see Figure 8.9).

This reliance on subroutines can lead to great efficiency. The modular units are often well practiced, and this allows the problem solver to focus attention on the larger-scale plan, rather than worry about the details of how the plan is to be implemented. In fact this is one of the reasons why problems that seem impossible for the novice are absurdly easy for the expert: even when the expert is facing a novel problem, she is likely to rely on a number of familiar subroutines that are already available as "chunks" in memory. Thus, the expert taxi driver gives little thought to maneuvering through traffic and so can focus her thoughts on the more general task of navigation. The novice driver must focus on the maneuvering, and, preoccupied with this, may miss his exit.

## EXPERTS

Having a set of well-practiced subroutines is an important part of "expertise," but there is more to expertise than this. In fact, experts have several different advantages when compared to those of more modest skill. For one, experts simply know more in their domain of expertise, and some theorists have suggested that this is why someone usually needs a full decade to acquire expert status, whether the proficiency is in music, software design, chess, medicine, or any other domain. Ten years is simply the time needed to acquire a large enough knowledge base so that the expert has the necessary facts near at hand and the necessary subroutines well practiced and available (Hayes, 1985). In addition, an expert's knowledge is heavily cross-referenced, so that each bit of information has associations with many other bits. As a result, not only do experts know more, they also have faster, more effective access to what they know (Bédard & Chi, 1992).

Crucially, though, experts also have a different sort of knowledge than novices do, knowledge focused on higher-order patterns. As a consequence, experts can, in effect, think in larger units, tackling problems in big steps rather than small ones. In other words, experts can proceed subroutine by subroutine, rather than needing to assemble all the procedural steps from scratch.

Consider studies of chess players (Chase & Simon, 1973a, b; de Groot, 1965). In one study, players at different levels of expertise (including two former world champions) were posed various chess problems and asked to select the best move. All of the masters chose continuations that would have won the game, while few of the other players did. Why? Many theorists believe that the reason lies in the way the players organized the problem. The chess masters structured the chess position in terms of broad strategic concepts (for example, *a king-side attack with pawns*) from which many of the appropriate moves follow naturally. In effect, the masters have a "chess vocabulary" in which these complex concepts are stored as single memory chunks, each with an associated set of subroutines for how one should respond to that pattern. Some investigators estimate, in fact, that the masters may have as many as 50,000 of these chunks in their memories, each representing a strategic pattern (Chase & Simon, 1973a).

Memory chunks can be detected in many ways, including the pattern of a player's eye movements as she inspects the board, and in the way that players remember a game. For example, players of different ranks were shown chess positions for five seconds each and then asked to reproduce the positions a few minutes later. Grandmasters and masters did so with hardly an error; lesser players performed much worse (see Figure 8.10). This difference in performance was not due to the chess masters having better visual memory. When presented with bizarre positions, unlikely ever to arise in the course of a game, they recalled them no better than novices did, and in some cases, they remembered these bizarre patterns less accurately than did novices (Gobet & Simon, 1996a, b, but also see Gobet & Simon, 2000; Lassiter, 2000). The superiority of the masters, therefore, was in their conceptual organization of chess, not in their memory for patterns as such.

**8.10** *Memory for chess positions in masters and average players* **(A) An actual chess position that was presented for five seconds after which the positions of the pieces had to be reconstructed. Typical performances by masters and average players are shown in (B) and (C) respectively, with errors indicated in red. (After Hearst, 1972)**

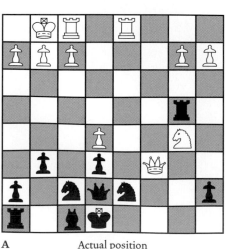

A        Actual position

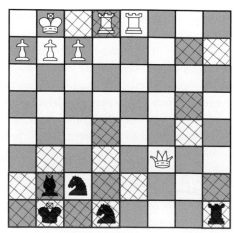

B    Typical master player's performance      C    Typical average player's performance

We should say again that chess masters, like experts in general, have other advantages in addition to their huge vocabulary of chess chunks. For example, they are also better in evaluating chess positions and look further ahead in their mental calculations (Charness, 1981; Holding, 1985; Holding & Reynolds, 1982). But chunks, and their associated subroutines, clearly play a major role in this mental skill, just as they do in a wide range of other skills (see, for example, Allard, Graham, & Paarsalu, 1980).

## AUTOMATICITY

The reliance on familiar routines has many advantages. As we have discussed, it allows the problem solver to focus on the more strategic aspects of a problem, rather than on the details. The patterns supplied by memory can also serve to organize the problem from the very start, highlighting useful subgoals. This is evident, for example, in the fact that novices in physics tend to focus on the surface form of the problems they encounter and so might group together, say, all the problems involving springs or all the problems involving inclined planes. Experts, in contrast, instantly perceive the deeper structure of each problem, and so they group the problems, not according to surface features, but according to the physical principles relevant to each problem's solution. Clearly, then, the experts are more sensitive to the higher-order patterns, and this calls their attention to the strategies needed for solving the problem (Chi, Feltovich, & Glaser, 1981; also Cummins, 1992; Reeves & Weisberg, 1994).

This reliance on routine can even become so well practiced, so familiar, that the routine is executed without much thought. The routine, in other words, becomes automatic and so is performed with minimal attention. Often this is just what one wants, since this frees up attention for other aspects of the task. In some circumstances, though, this *automaticity* can create its own problems: automatic actions, once set in motion, are sometimes difficult to turn off or modify.

A striking example of this is known as the *Stroop effect*, named after its discoverer (Stroop, 1935). To demonstrate this effect, research participants are asked to name the colors in which groups of letters are printed (Figure 8.11). If the letters are random sequences (*fwis, sgbr*) or irrelevant words (*chair, tape*), this task is rather easy. If, however, the letters form color names (*yellow, red*), the task becomes much harder. Thus, a participant might see *red* printed in green ink, *blue* in brown ink, and so on. His task, of course, is simply to name the ink color, and so he should say "green, brown" in the example trials just mentioned. But in this setting, the participant cannot help but read the words, and this produces a strong competing response: he is likely to respond very slowly, because while trying to name the ink colors, he is fighting the tendency to read the words themselves aloud. (For more on automaticity, see Stolz & Besner, 1999; Bargh & Ferguson, 2000; Pashler, Johnston, & Ruthruff, 2000.)

| A | B |
|---|---|
| ZYP | RED |
| QLEKF | BLACK |
| SUWRG | YELLOW |
| XCIDB | BLUE |
| WOPR | RED |
| ZYP | GREEN |
| QLEKF | YELLOW |
| XCIDB | BLACK |
| SUWRG | BLUE |
| WOPR | BLACK |

**8.11  The Stroop effect**  *The two lists, A and B, are printed in five colors—black, red, green, blue, and yellow. To observe the Stroop effect, name the colors (aloud) in which each of the nonsense syllables in list A is printed as fast as you can, continuing downward. Then do the same for list B, calling out the colors in which each of the words of the list is printed, again going from top to bottom. This will very probably be easier for list A than for list B, a demonstration of the Stroop effect.*

## OBSTACLES TO PROBLEM SOLVING

No matter how hard we try, some problems—whether an infuriating crossword puzzle or a demoralizing job dispute—seem downright intractable. Can our knowledge about how problem solving works help us in approaching these complex problems?

We have already mentioned one crucial factor: problem solvers, be they novices or experts, bring certain assumptions and habits with them whenever they approach a problem. Some of these assumptions are sensible and productive. For instance, a taxi driver—even a beginner—does not waste time wondering whether a magic carpet might be the fastest transport to the airport; and even a novice cook realizes that pickles are an unpalatable topping for the morning's pancakes. Likewise, assumptions play a crucial (and enormously helpful) role in transforming an ill-defined problem into a well-defined one. But, even so, these background assumptions can sometimes lead us

**TABLE 8.1   THE THREE-CONTAINER PROBLEM**

| Desired quantity of water (quarts) | VOLUME OF EMPTY JAR (QUARTS) | | |
| --- | --- | --- | --- |
| | A | B | C |
| 99 | 14 | 163 | 25 |
| 5 | 18 | 43 | 10 |
| 21 | 9 | 42 | 6 |
| 31 | 20 | 59 | 4 |

astray—if, for example, they are simply wrong or just inappropriate to the present situation. In either case, the would-be problem solver may end up a victim of his own often unnoticed assumptions, misled by a powerful *mental set*.

A well-known study illustrates this point and shows how people can become fixated on one approach to a task and correspondingly unable to think of the task in any other way. The participants in this study were told that they had three jars, A, B, and C. Jar A held exactly 21 quarts; jar B held exactly 127 quarts; jar C held exactly 3 quarts. The participants' job was to use these three jars to obtain exactly 100 quarts from a well.

Participants required a few minutes to solve this problem, but they generally did solve it. The solution is to fill B (127 quarts) completely and then pour out enough water from B to fill A. Now 106 quarts remain in B (127–21). Next, pour enough water out of B, to fill up C (3 quarts), leaving 103 quarts in B. Finally, dump out C and fill it again from B, leaving the desired amount—100 quarts—in B (Figure 8.12).

Participants then did several more problems, all of the same type. The numerical values differed in each problem (Table 8.1), but in each case, the solution could be obtained by the same sequence of steps: fill B, pour from it into A, then pour from B into C, empty out C, and pour again from B into C. In each case, in other words, the desired amount could be reached by the arithmetical sequence of B–A–2C.

After five such problems, the participants were given two critical tests. The first was a problem that required them to obtain 20 quarts, given jars whose volumes were 23, 49, and 3 quarts. The participants cheerfully solved this problem using the same sequence—49–23–(2 × 3). They reliably failed to notice that there is a simpler method available for this problem, one that requires only a single step (Figure 8.13).

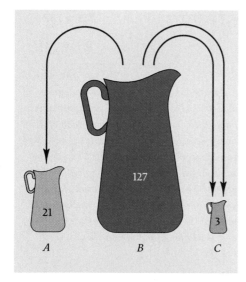

**8.12** *The standard method for solving the three-container problem* **(After Luchins, 1972)**

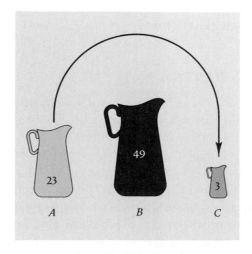

**8.13** *A simpler method for solving certain three-container problems (After Luchins, 1972)*

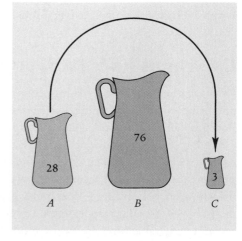

**8.14** *A case where only the simple method works (After Luchins, 1972)*

8.15 *Horse-and-rider problem* *The task is to place B on A in such a way that the riders are properly astride the horses. (For solution, see p. 296.) (After Scheerer, Goldstein, & Boring, 1941)*

The participants were next asked to obtain 25 quarts, given jars of 28, 76, and 3 quarts. Note that here the only method that will work is the direct one, that is, $28 - 3 = 25$ (Figure 8.14). But the mental set was so powerful that many subjects failed to solve the problem altogether. They tried the old procedure, but this did not lead them to the goal $(76 - 28 - [2 \times 3] \neq 25)$, and they could not hit on an adequate alternative! The set had made them so rigid that they became mentally blind (Luchins, 1942; for other, related examples, see Figure 8.8B and Figure 8.15).

We should perhaps mention that the participants in this study were not being foolish: once they found a way to solve a problem, it's entirely sensible that they did not go looking for another, alternate path. If, for example, you know how to scramble an egg, isn't it sensible to use the same tried-and-true technique each time, rather than complicating your life by seeking a new procedure for each breakfast? The worry, though, is that this pattern—sensible as it generally is—can cause difficulties, as it did in the water jar problem, slowing, and sometimes even preventing, successful problem solving.

## OVERCOMING OBSTACLES TO SOLUTIONS

Problem-solving sets generally help us, but clearly they can also cause difficulties, leading us to ask, how can these sets be overcome? Similarly, we have emphasized the importance of subgoals and familiar routines, but what can we do if we fail to perceive the subgoals or are unfamiliar with the relevant routine?

### WORKING BACKWARD

One useful method for solving problems is to work backward, starting with the goal or final state and seeking a path back toward the starting point. For example, consider the following problem:

> Water lilies double in area every twenty-four hours. On the first day of summer, there is one water lily on a lake. It takes sixty days for the lake to become covered with water lilies. On what day is the lake half covered?

This problem can be tackled in the following fashion. On day 1, there is one lily; on day 2, there are two; on day 3, there are four; and so on. With sufficient patience, this will lead to the conclusion that, on day 60, there will be 580 million billion lilies; half of this is 290 million billion, which would have been reached on day 59. There is, however, a simpler path, one that skips all the calculations: if the lake is fully covered on day 60, it must be half covered on the day before, since lilies double in area every day, which means that the answer is day 59 (after Sternberg & Davidson, 1983; see Figure 8.16).

A

B

8.16 *The water-lily problem* *Water lilies double in area every twenty-four hours. On the first day of summer, there is one water lily, as in (A). On the sixtieth day, the lake is all covered, as in (B). On what day is the lake half-covered?*

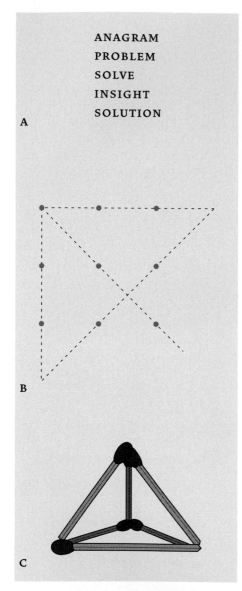

ANAGRAM
PROBLEM
SOLVE
INSIGHT
SOLUTION

A

B

C

*Answers    See Figure 8.8, p. 288. (A) Solution to anagrams. (B) Solution to the nine-dot problem. The problem is solved by going outside of the square frame in which the dots are perceptually grouped. The lines have to be extended beyond the dots as shown. Most participants fail to hit on this solution because of a perceptual set imposed by the square arrangement. (C) The matchstick problem. To arrange six matches into four equilateral triangles, the matches have to be assembled into a three-dimensional pyramid. Most participants implicitly assume the matches must lie flat. (After Scheerer, 1963)*

Working backward is an effective strategy when one does not know how to reach a goal or cannot discern a problem's structure. It is interesting, therefore, that experts use this strategy less often than novices. That is because experts more easily see the problem's structure right from the start, and so they can leap right into the problem's solution. When experts are stumped, though, or when they are working on unfamiliar problems, they are just as likely to use the working-backward strategy as anyone else (Bédard & Chi, 1992; Bhaskar & Simon, 1977; Gick, 1986).

## FINDING AN APPROPRIATE ANALOGY

Another crucially important tool for solving difficult problems is to work by analogy, since many problems are similar to each other. A school counselor is likely to find that the problem he hears about today reminds him of one he heard a few months back, and his experience with the first can help with the second. Similarly, scientists seeking to understand some new phenomenon often benefit from thinking back to other similar phenomena. In fact, analogies have often played an important role in the history of science, with scientists expanding their knowledge of gases by comparing the molecules to billiard balls or enlarging their understanding of the heart by comparing it to a pump, and the like (Gentner & Jeziorski, 1989).

The benefits of analogy are also evident in the laboratory. In one study, research participants were given this problem, devised by Duncker (1945):

> Suppose a patient has an inoperable stomach tumor. There are certain rays that can destroy this tumor if their intensity is great enough. At this intensity, however, the rays will also destroy the healthy tissue that surrounds the tumor (e.g., the stomach walls, the abdominal muscles, and so on). How can the tumor be destroyed without damaging the healthy tissue through which the rays must travel on their way?

This problem is quite difficult, and in this experiment, 90 percent of the participants failed to solve it. A second group, however, did much better. Before tackling the tumor problem, they read a story about a general who hoped to capture a fortress. He needed a large force of soldiers for this, but all of the roads leading to the fortress were planted with mines. Small groups of soldiers could travel the roads safely, but the mines would be detonated by a larger group. How, therefore, could the general move all the soldiers he would need toward the fortress? He could do this by dividing his army into small groups and sending each group via a different road. When he gave the signal, all the groups marched toward the fortress, where they converged and attacked successfully.

The fortress story is similar in its structure to the tumor problem. In both cases, the solution is to divide the "conquering" force so that it enters from several different directions. Thus, to destroy the tumor, several weak rays can be sent through the body, each from a different angle. The rays converge at the tumor, inflicting their combined effects just as desired (Figure 8.17).

With no hints, instructions, or analogous cases, 90 percent of the participants failed to solve the tumor problem. However, if they were given the fortress story to read and told that it would help them, most (about 80 percent) did solve it. Obviously, the analogy was massively helpful. But it was not enough merely to know about the fortress story; participants also had to realize that the story is pertinent to the task at hand. And, surprisingly, they often failed to make this discovery. In another condition, participants read the fortress story but were not given any indication that this story was relevant to their task. In this condition, only 30 percent solved the tumor problem (Gick & Holyoak, 1980, 1983).

Given how beneficial analogies can be, is there anything we can do to encourage their use? Evidence suggests that people are more likely to use analogies if they are encour-

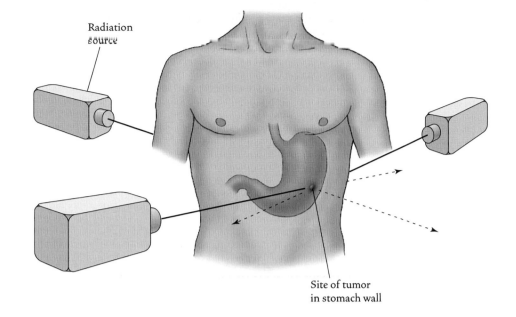

Radiation
source

Site of tumor
in stomach wall

*8.17  Solution to the ray-tumor problem*
*Several weak rays are sent from various points*
*outside so that they meet at the tumor site.*
*There the radiation of the rays will be intense,*
*for all the effects will summate at this point.*
*But since they are individually weak, the rays*
*will not damage the healthy tissue that sur-*
*rounds the tumor. (After Duncker, 1945)*

aged to focus on the underlying dynamic of the analogies (for example, the fact that the fortress problem involves converging forces) rather than their more superficial features (for example, the fact that the problem involves mines). Focusing on the underlying dynamic calls attention to the features shared by the problems, helping people to see the relevance of the analogies and helping them to map one problem onto another (Blanchette & Dunbar, 2000; Catrambone, 1998; Cummins, 1992; Dunbar, Blanchette, & Mail, 2001; Needham & Begg, 1991).

## RESTRUCTURING

As we have seen, whether a problem is solved or not often depends on how the problem is interpreted at the very start. Much depends, for example, on the problem solver's interpretation of the goal (pp. 287–288) and on whether the problem solver perceives the problem's various subgoals (pp. 288–289). The problem solver's interpretation also influences the prospects for finding a useful analogy: if she understands the problem in terms of its underlying dynamic, she may be led to a helpful analogy and thus to a solution. If she understands the problem in terms of its surface elements, an analogy may not come to mind, making the problem appreciably more difficult.

All of this suggests that there will be times when the problem solver will be well served by changing her interpretation of a problem, moving from an understanding that somehow hinders performance toward one that somehow helps. This suggestion is certainly in line with common experience. Some of the problems we encounter initially seem quite difficult. Later, however, we might discover an alternative way to conceptualize the problem, breaking the mental set that inhibited us, and soon after, we come up with the answer. Sometimes, this *restructuring* of a problem can be quite sudden, experienced as a flash of insight, with an accompanying exclamation of "Aha!" (You may have experienced something similar when you finally solved the nine-dot, matchstick, or horse-and-rider problems Figures 8.8B, 8.8C, and 8.15.)

It should be said, though, that these flashes of insight, as one moves from one understanding to another, are not uniformly beneficial. Sometimes, these (apparent) insights turn out to be false alarms, because the new interpretation or new approach simply leads

*Solution to horse-and-rider problem* **Solving the horse-and-rider puzzle (see Figure 8.15, p. 293) requires a change of perceptual set. Part B must be rotated 90 degrees over the middle of A, and then placed as above. (After Scheerer, Goldstein, & Boring, 1941)**

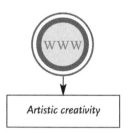

Artistic creativity

to yet another dead end (Metcalfe, 1986; Metcalfe & Weibe, 1987). Perhaps, then, the "Aha" experience cannot be understood as "I see the solution!" Instead, the experience merely implies, "I've discovered a new approach!" Whether this approach will turn out to be productive can only be decided after the fact. One way or another, though, these changes in the way a problem is defined are often essential for breaking out of an unproductive set and moving toward one that may lead to a solution.

## CREATIVE THINKING

The restructuring of a problem also plays an important role in those special discoveries we consider creative. In general, scholars call the solution to a problem creative if that solution is both new and valuable or useful. Creativity is evident in the scientific discoveries of Marie Curie, the artistic innovations of Martha Graham, and the literary achievements of Toni Morrison. But creativity is also visible—albeit on a modest scale—in many ordinary achievements, ranging from a new conversational ploy to an improved recipe or a novel argument in a term paper.

What leads to these creative achievements? Many factors contribute, but one pattern figures prominently in reports by the creators themselves when they describe how their insights or discoveries arose. In case after case, these accounts indicate that critical insights arrive rather abruptly, typically at unexpected times and places. Often, the thinker has been working steadily on the problem for some time but making relatively little progress. She then sets the problem aside in order to rest or to engage in some other activity. It is during this other activity that the insight emerges—not while at the writer's desk or the composer's piano, but while riding in a carriage (Beethoven, Darwin), while stepping onto a bus (the great mathematician Poincaré), or in the most celebrated case of all, while sitting in a bathtub (Archimedes; see Figure 8.18).

This pattern has often been attributed to a process of *incubation* (Wallas, 1926). The idea here is that the thinker believes she has set the problem aside but is actually continuing to think about it unconsciously. Some authors have suggested that this unconscious incubation is actually more creative and less constrained than conscious thought, and this is why solutions to vexing problems so often appear during periods when, on the surface, the thinker is paying attention to some altogether different matter.

Many researchers, however, are skeptical about these claims. One reason is that time away from a problem does not reliably promote its solution. In some studies it does; in other studies it does not. Of course, everyday reports of creativity do emphasize these unexpected insights, but it is conceivable that this simply reflects a bias in reporting. A sudden inspiration while sitting in a bathtub is surprising and worth mentioning to one's friends; progress while working steadily along at one's desk may not be. As a result, the former—even if rare—becomes part of our cultural lore, whereas the latter, perhaps more common, does not.

Even when time away from a problem is beneficial, incubation may not be the reason. As an alternative, time away from a problem may simply allow fatigue and frustration to dissipate, and this by itself may be helpful. In addition, the time away may allow the problem solver to shake off unproductive mental sets (Anderson, 1990; Smith & Blankenship, 1989; Wickelgren, 1974). With the passage of time, the thinker can forget, or lose interest in, the lines of attack that initially seemed attractive. Moreover, a drastic change of retrieval cues (the bus or the bathtub) will make reinstatement of this earlier frame of mind less likely. This obviously increases the likelihood that a different, and possibly more productive, set will be selected. Of course, the chances of this occurring are greater if one is totally familiar with all the ins and outs of the problem, and especially if one has the talents of a Beethoven or an Archimedes. Unfortunately, just taking a bath is not enough.

**8.18  Archimedes in his bathtub**  *A sixteenth-century engraving celebrating a great example of creative restructuring. The Greek scientist Archimedes (287–212 B.C.) tried to determine whether the king's crown was made of solid gold or had been adulterated with silver. Archimedes knew the weight of gold and silver per unit volume but did not know how to measure the volume of a complicated object such as a crown. One day, in his bath, he noticed how the water level rose as he immersed his body. Here was the solution: The crown's volume can be determined by the water it displaces. Carried away by his sudden insight, he jumped out of his bath and ran naked through the streets of Syracuse, shouting "Eureka! I have found it!" (Engraving by Walter H. Ryff.)*

## RESTRUCTURING AND HUMOR

Restructuring is, as we have seen, crucial for insightful problem solving. But the same process also plays a role in a very different context: humor. Indeed, problem solving and humor have several things in common. For example, jokes typically require some insight, since a joke will not strike us as funny unless we get the point. Conversely, insights sometimes have a comical aspect, especially when one recognizes how absurdly simple a problem's solution really is.

In addition, both insight and humor often involve a dramatic shift from one cognitive organization to another (see, for example, Suls, 1972, 1983; see Figure 8.19). In a joke, an expectation is created during the joke's setup, only to be dashed by the punch line. This is why so many jokes involve a set of three (three sheep, three lawyers, or some such). The first in the trio establishes the precedent. The second shows that the pattern is continuing. And the third unexpectedly alters the pattern, but in a fashion that makes perfect sense (H. Gleitman, 1990).

As an example, consider the story about a doctor, a lawyer, and an engineer all of whom are scheduled for execution on a guillotine. As they step up to the scaffold, each is given a choice of lying face up or face down. The doctor goes first, and believing that one should confront one's fate directly, he opts to lie face up. The blade drops but then screeches to a stop just a foot above the doctor's throat. Amid the gasps of the crowd, the doctor is released.

The lawyer goes next. She is sure that legal precedent would lead to her own release were the blade to stop for her just as it had for the doctor, so she also lies face up. Again the blade stops short, and the lawyer is released.

Now it is the engineer's turn. He figures that his best bet is to go with whatever worked

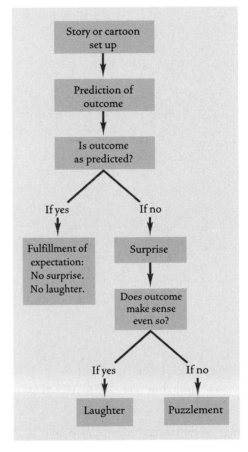

**8.19**  *A cognitive analysis of the appreciation of humor*  *The joke or cartoon sets up an expectation. The experience of humor arises (1) if this expectation is not fulfilled and (2) if the outcome nevertheless makes sense. (After Suls, 1972)*

*Visual humor*  *In many cases, humor poses a puzzle to be solved. In this particular cartoon, the puzzle arises from the fact that there's nothing odd or comical about a machine with an "Out of Order" sign. Yet the viewer knows that this drawing is being presented as a joke—so there must be some other meaning to be discovered. The puzzle is solved when the reader realizes that there is another way to understand the phrase "out of order."*

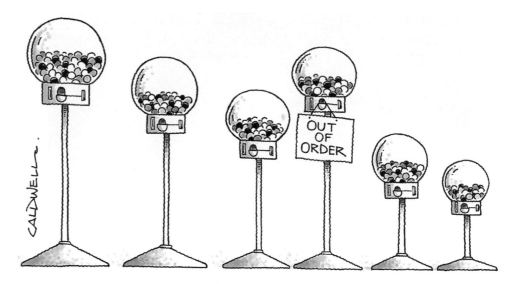

before. So he lies face up and sees the blade overhead. But then, just before the blade drops, he turns to the executioner and says, "Wait! I think I see what your problem is up there."

The ending to this story is unexpected but nonetheless makes perfect sense. The engineer can't resist solving an engineering problem, even if it kills him. And both elements are crucial. If the ending were entirely predictable (the blade simply stops again), there would be no joke. If the ending made no sense ("...just before the blade drops, he turns to the executioner and says, 'Can I have a blindfold?'"), the result would be puzzlement, not humor. Thus, the punch line works only if the comical ending can be fit into a framework that makes sense of the entire narrative.

Let us note, though, that, while cognitive restructuring is an important condition for the production of humor, it is clearly not the whole story; other elements are also needed. In many cases, for example, it is also important that the "solution" to the "puzzle" posed by the joke be simultaneously sensible and absurd. In still other cases, it is important that the joke's outcome provide a relatively harmless outlet for wishes that cannot be indulged directly, as in sarcastic wit or "dirty" jokes. In these cases, though, it is crucial that the point of the joke be emotionally acceptable to the listener. Jokes about Hitler's extermination camps or about rape are appalling to everyone. We can get away with jokes about the assassination of Julius Caesar, but joking about a contemporary assassination would be unpardonable.

# THE PROCESS OF THINKING: REASONING AND DECISION MAKING

The ability to solve problems is an extraordinary human skill. We just considered how this skill allows us to get jokes, but it also allows far more—great inventions, extraordinary artistic achievements, remarkable feats of diplomacy. Less impressive, but more often, our capacity for solving problems allows us to deal with the challenges we meet in our day-to-day lives, whenever we have a goal and need to spend a moment thinking about how to reach that goal.

However, problem solving is only one type of thinking. Just as important is our capacity for *reasoning*, in which we start with observations or beliefs and draw conclusions from them. Like problem solving, our capacity for reasoning is responsible for marvelous human achievements—in science, the arts, and the social world. More commonly, though, in ways that we will see, reasoning plays a crucial role in allowing us to function in, and make sense of, our ordinary existence.

Reasoning can take several different forms. In one form, we begin with a set of facts—perhaps events we have read about, or actions we have observed for ourselves—and ask what general conclusions follow from these facts. This is called *inductive reasoning*, a process that leads us from individual observations to more general claims. As examples, consider the reasoning you would have to go through to answer questions like these: Are American automobiles less reliable than imports? Does playing "hard to get" help out in fostering a romance? Is using an analogy a good means of solving problems? In each case, these questions request general claims that might be derived from a suitable set of specific observations.

Another form of reasoning is *deductive reasoning*. For this, we begin with some sort of general claim and ask what other assertions follow from it. What steps should you take if your child is ill? To answer, you might begin with general beliefs you have about illness and medicine, and deduce from these particular ideas about how to treat your child. Similarly, you suspect that Andrea likes you, but you are not certain. To check on this idea, you might try the following deduction: if she likes you, she will say yes with enthusiasm if you ask her out. This provides an obvious means for confirming (or disconfirming) your suspicion.

How do people reason in any of these settings? For many years, scholars assumed that people used rules similar to the laws of formal logic. Today, however, this assumption is widely questioned. Perhaps the laws of logic tell us how people should think, but they probably do not correspond to how people really do think. In addition, we need to ask, How well do people reason? Do people draw conclusions that are sensible and justified, or ones that are foolish? As we will see, errors in reasoning are easy to observe (and will provide us with important clues about the strategies people use while reasoning). But these errors sit side by side with high-quality and accurate reasoning, so we will need to understand both why humans make reasoning errors and why their reasoning is so often correct.

## DEDUCTIVE REASONING

Many studies on deductive reasoning have examined people's ability to evaluate simple arguments called *syllogisms*. A syllogism contains two premises and a conclusion, and the question is whether the conclusion follows logically from the premises; Figure 8.20 offers several examples. Syllogisms are relatively simple in their form and seem rather straightforward. It is disheartening, therefore, that research participants make an enormous number of errors in evaluating syllogisms. To be sure, performance varies in response to several factors, and some syllogisms are easier than others. Participants are more accurate, for example, if the syllogism is set in concrete terms, rather than in terms of abstract symbols. Nonetheless, across all the syllogisms, mistakes are frequent, with error rates sometimes as high as 70 or 80 percent (Gilhooly, 1988).

Moreover, participants' errors are not the result of mere carelessness. Instead, when solving syllogisms, people rely on systematic strategies that often lead them astray. For example, participants are more likely to judge a conclusion to be valid if the conclusion strikes them as plausible—quite independent of whether the conclusion follows logically from the stated premises (Klauer, Musch, & Naumer, 2000). Thus, they are more likely to endorse the conclusion "All artwork should be cherished" in Figure 8.20, than they are to endorse the conclusion "All artwork can be turned into clocks." Both of these conclusions are warranted by their premises, but the first is plausible, and thus it is more likely to be accepted as valid.

In some ways, this reliance on plausibility is a sensible strategy: participants are doing their best to assess the syllogisms' conclusions based on all they know. At the same time, however, this strategy implies a profound misunderstanding of the rules of logic. With this strategy, people are willing to endorse a bad argument if it happens to

All M's are B.
All D's are M's.
Therefore all D's are B.

All X's are Y.
Some A's are X's.
Therefore some A's are Y.

All A's are not B's.
All A's are G's.
Therefore some G's are not B's.

All artwork is valuable.
All valuable things should be cherished.
Therefore all artwork should be cherished.

All artwork is made of wood.
All wooden things can be turned into clocks.
Therefore all artwork can be turned into clocks.

*8.20 Examples of categorical syllogisms* All of the syllogisms shown here are valid—that is, if the two premises are true, then the conclusion must be true.

Deductive reasoning *(© Sidney Harris.)*

lead to conclusions they already believe are true, and willing to reject a good argument if it leads to conclusions they already believe are false.

## THE SELECTION TASK

Studies of syllogistic reasoning paint a grim portrait of our capacity for logical reasoning, and the data are similar in many of the studies in which participants are asked to reason about **conditional statements**, logical statements of the familiar "if,...then..." format. In some of these studies, participants are given logical arguments written out, and need to evaluate them (see Figure 8.21; Evans, Newstead, & Byrne, 1993; Rips, 1990); in other studies, participants are given a problem called the **selection task**. In this task, the participants are shown four cards, like those shown in Figure 8.22. They are told that these cards may or may not follow a simple rule: "If there is a vowel on one side of the card, there must be an even number on the other side." Their task is to figure out which cards to turn over in order to determine whether the cards do, in fact, follow this rule.

Performance on this task is generally miserable. Roughly half the participants make the mistake of turning over the "A" and the "6" cards. Another 33 percent make the mistake of turning over just the "A" card. Only 4 percent of the participants correctly select the "A" and the "7" cards, or, said differently, fully 96 percent of the participants get this problem wrong (for example, Wason, 1966, 1968).

But performance is not always this poor; participants actually do quite well in some versions of the selection task. For example, participants in one study were shown the four cards pictured in Figure 8.23, and were told that each card identified the age of a customer at a bar and what that customer was drinking. Their task was to evaluate this rule: "If a person is drinking beer, then the person must be over 19 years of age." This problem is logically identical to the original selection task, but performance was vastly better—three-fourths of the participants correctly chose the cards "drinking a beer" and "16 years old" (Griggs & Cox, 1982).

Why do people do so well on some versions of the selection task but perform atrociously on other (logically equivalent) versions of the task? This is currently a matter of debate. One proposal comes from an evolutionary perspective on psychology. It begins with the suggestion that our ancient ancestors did not have to reason about whether or not all *As* are *Bs*, nor did they have to reason about vowels and even numbers. Instead, our ancestors had to worry about issues like social interactions, including issues of

---

1. If the switch is turned on, then the light will go on.
   The switch is turned on.
   Therefore: The light goes on.
2. If the switch is turned on, then the light will go on.
   The switch is not turned on.
   Therefore: The light goes on.
3. If the switch is turned on, then the light will go on.
   The light does not go on.
   Therefore, the switch is not turned on.

**8.21** *A logic exercise    In each case, does the conclusion follow from the premise?*

---

**8.22** *The selection task    Each card has a letter on one side and a number on the other side. Which card(s) must be turned over to check this rule: "If a card has a vowel on one side, it must have an even number on the other side"? The correct answer, offered by very few participants, is to turn over the A and the 7. If the A (a vowel) has an odd number on the reverse side, this would break the rule. If the 7 has a vowel on the reverse side, this too would break the rule. No matter what is on the other side of the 6, however, a vowel or consonant, this would be consistent with the rule. (After all, the rule did not say that only vowels have even numbers on the reverse side.) Likewise, no matter what is on the reverse side of the J, this would be consistent with the rule. (The rule says nothing about what is on the reverse side of a consonant card.)*

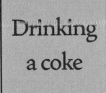

**8.23** *Variant of the selection task* *Each card has a drink on one side, and an age on the other. Which cards would you have to turn over to check this rule: "If the person is drinking beer, then the person must be over 19 years of age"? This task is formally identical to the standard selection task, but turns out to be much easier.*

betrayal and cheating: "I asked you to gather firewood; have you done it, or have you betrayed me?" "None of our clan is supposed to eat more than one share of meat; is Joe perhaps cheating and eating too much?" If our ancestors needed to reason about these issues, then individuals who were particularly skilled in this reasoning would have had a survival advantage, and so, little by little, they would have become more numerous within the population, while those without the skill would die off. In the end, only those skillful at social reasoning would be left, and we, as their distant ancestors, inherited their skills. This is why we perform badly with problems like the "classic" selection task (for which we are evolutionarily unprepared) but perform well with the drinking-beer problem, since it involves cheating (a problem for which we are prepared) (Cosmides, 1989; Cummins & Allen, 1998; Gigerenzer & Hug, 1992).

A different approach to the selection task emphasizes the sorts of reasoning we each must learn to do in order to function in our day-to-day lives. Our daily routines provide little or no practice in reasoning about *A*s and *B*s. However, we often have to reason about permission ("If I want to do X, I better get permission"), obligation, certain cause-and-effect relationships, and so on. As a result, we have developed *reasoning schemas* for these various problems, and we reason well if a laboratory task elicits one of these pragmatic schemas, but not otherwise. The drinking-beer problem involves permission; and so it calls up our well-practiced skills in thinking about permission. The same problem cast in terms of vowels and even numbers has no obvious connection to pragmatic reasoning, and it calls up no schema, leading to poor performance (Cheng & Holyoak, 1985; Cheng, Holyoak, Nisbett, & Oliver, 1986).

Choosing among these hypotheses has been difficult, in part because the hypotheses overlap in their predictions of when deductive performance will be good and when it will be poor. (For yet another perspective on why performance with the selection task is so uneven, see Ahn & Graham, 1999.) Even so, one thing is clear: our performance with these problems is heavily influenced by the content of the problem (drinking beer versus vowels and even numbers), and, in this regard, the rules governing our reasoning seem quite different from the rules of logic. That is because logic depends only on the form of the problem, and not the problem's content. This is one of the reasons why logic is so powerful—it can be applied to any content. But powerful or not, logic does not mesh with the way humans reason. Instead, how we reason plainly depends on what we are reasoning about.

## INDUCTIVE REASONING

We have been discussing deductive reasoning, in which we reason from the general to the particular. In other words, deduction usually begins with a general rule ("All people

"There it comes again."

*Induction*    *(Illustration by Henry Gleitman.)*

are mortal") and asks how it applies to a particular case ("Pat Smith is a person"). Much of the reasoning we engage in, however, is inductive, in which the process is reversed. Here we reason from the particular to the general. We consider a number of different instances and try to determine—that is, induce—what general rule covers them all.

Induction is at the heart of the scientific enterprise, because the object of science is to determine what common principles underlie seemingly disparate events. To do this, scientists formulate hypotheses—tentative assertions about the regularities of the world—and then seek to test them. But hypotheses are also developed by nonscientists, as they seek to understand (and to predict or maybe even influence) a pattern of events. We observe the behavior of a moody friend and seek hypotheses for his moodiness. We cannot get the car to start and seek hypotheses about what might be wrong. The hypotheses we come up with may not be correct, but they nonetheless constitute our attempts to comprehend an individual case by viewing it as just one instance within a more general pattern.

## FREQUENCY JUDGMENTS

How do we form hypotheses—about the behavior of a friend, the misbehavior of an automobile, or the likely future actions of a politician? In many cases, we are strongly influenced by the pattern of past evidence. How often has the politician kept his promises? How frequently has lack of sleep been the source of a friend's bad moods? How often has the car's performance been improved by pumping the gas pedal? How often has pumping the gas failed to work?

Questions like these often provide the basis for our hypotheses. We ask ourselves how frequently an event has occurred, as a way of determining how likely that event will be in the future. In this fashion, hypotheses—both in the scientific world and in our day-to-day lives—depend on frequency estimates, estimates of how often we have encountered an event or an object.

Evidence suggests that we often make frequency estimates by means of a simple strategy. We try to think of specific cases relevant to our judgment—examples of politicians keeping their word or of friends feeling awful after a sleepless night. If these examples come easily to mind, we conclude that the circumstance is a common one; if the examples come to mind slowly, or only with great effort, we conclude that the circumstance is rare.

This strategy is referred to as the *availability heuristic*, because the judgment uses availability as the basis for assessing frequency. The term *heuristic* is borrowed from computer science and rests on a distinction between two types of strategies. Some strategies, called *algorithms*, are procedures guaranteed to solve a problem or answer a question, if a solution or answer is possible at all. However, algorithms are sometimes cumbersome to use, requiring considerable effort or considerable time. That is why a different sort of strategy—a heuristic—is often useful. *Heuristics* are strategies that often work, but with no guarantee of success. This lack of guarantee, however, is simply the price one pays for the real gain that comes with using a heuristic: efficiency. Said differently, heuristics are usually successful shortcuts, and, if a heuristic is well chosen, the gain it offers in efficiency is large enough to make up for the fact that it will occasionally fail—lead to error or to no answer at all.

Of course, there is an algorithm that we could use for making frequency judgments: we could scour the relevant records and count up all of the cases. To find out if a politician keeps his word, for example, we could do the relevant research, cataloguing all of the promises and then examining subsequent performance. This score card would give us the information we seek, but would probably take a long time to compile. Perhaps, then, a heuristic—and, in particular, the availability heuristic—would be preferable, doing a quick check of memory for pertinent cases and then rendering a judgment based on how easily the relevant cases come to mind.

The availability heuristic usually serves us well. For example, are most of your close friends male or female? If the first six friends who come to mind are men, or if they are four women and two men, you will draw the obvious conclusion and probably be correct. In other circumstances, though, this strategy can lead to error. In one study, research participants were asked this question: Considering all the words in the language, does *R* occur more frequently in the first position of the word (*rose, robot, rocket*) or in the third position (*care, strive, tarp*)? Over two-thirds of the participants said that *R* is more common in the first position, but in fact the reverse is true, and by a wide margin.

The reason for this error is availability. The participants made their judgments by trying to think of words in which *R* is the first letter, and these came easily to mind. They next tried to think of words in which it is the third letter, and these came to mind only with some effort. They then interpreted this difference in availability as if it reflected a difference in frequency—and there is the error. The difference in ease of retrieval merely shows that our memorial dictionary, like a printed one, is organized according to the starting sound of each word, which makes it easy to search for words with a particular starting letter. Thus words like *rose* and *rocket* are fewer in number, but easier to find, than words like *care* or *strive* or *tarp*. This creates an availability bias, which is then directly reflected in participants' frequency judgments (Tversky & Kahneman, 1973).

In the *R*-word task, it seems entirely sensible that people would use a shortcut (the heuristic), rather than the much more laborious algorithm of counting through the pages in a dictionary. The algorithm would guarantee the right answer but would also be much more work than the problem is worth. In addition, the error in this case is entirely harmless—nothing hinges on these assessments of spelling patterns. The problem, though, is that people rely on the same shortcut, using availability to assess frequency, even in cases that are much more consequential. What are the chances that the stock market will go up tomorrow or that a certain psychiatric patient will commit suicide? The stockbrokers and psychiatrists who make these judgments regularly base their decisions on an estimate of probabilities. In the past, has the market generally gone up after a performance like today's? In the past, have patients with these symptoms generally been dangerous to themselves? These estimates, too, are likely to be based on the availability heuristic, and so (for example) the psychiatrist's judgment may be poor if she vividly remembers a particular patient's repeated bluffs about suicide. This easily available recollection may bias the psychiatrist's frequency judgment, leading to inadequate precautions in the present case.

A different example comes from the public's perception of crime rates. Throughout the last decade, crime rates have declined in many American cities, but fear of crime has nonetheless been increasing. This is probably due to the fact that, even though the actual number of crimes has dropped, media coverage of crimes has increased. As a result, memories of crimes are more available to people, leading to an increased estimate of frequency and, in turn, to increased fear.

The same pattern is evident in studies in which people have been asked which is the more common—death by homicide or death by stroke? death from car crashes or death from stomach cancer? People generally identify the first cause in each pair as the more common, although the opposite is the case. (Death by stroke is ten times more likely than death by homicide.) These are not trivial matters, since an error in judgment here could have a bearing on what precautions someone takes, or on how the government allocates resources for prevention of these hazards. What produces these errors? The estimates are again clearly influenced by the media: murders and car crashes make front-page stories and so are commonly encountered and easily remembered. This provides an availability advantage that, in turn, biases people's estimates (Slovic, Fischoff, & Lichtenstein, 1982).

EXTRAPOLATING FROM AVAILABLE OBSERVATIONS

The availability heuristic is used in a wide range of settings, including cases in which we are trying to make judgments of considerable importance. It is troubling, therefore, that this generally helpful strategy can, on occasion, lead to error. The same can be said for another common strategy, one that we employ when seeking to generalize from the information we have gathered.

Many of the categories we encounter are uniform in important ways. People do not vary much in their number of fingers or their number of ears. Birds uniformly share the property of having feathers, and hotel rooms share the property of having beds. This uniformity may seem trivial, but it actually plays an important role: it allows us to extrapolate from our experiences, so that we know what to expect the next time we see a bird or enter a hotel room.

Such extrapolation based on assumed uniformity is generally sensible, but we overuse this strategy, extrapolating from our experiences even when it is clear we should not. In other words, we fall prey to the *representativeness heuristic*, the strategy of assuming that each case is representative of its class. Because of this assumption, we are willing to apply what we know about a category (for example, the category of birds, or hotel rooms) to each new case we meet, even if it is obvious that the new case is unusual. Similarly, we are willing to draw conclusions about the entire category from just a single (assumed-to-be-representative) observation, even when this is clearly inappropriate.

This pattern is evident, for example, whenever someone offers or is persuaded by a "man who" or "woman who" argument: "What do you mean that cigarettes cause cancer? I have an aunt who smokes cigarettes, and she's perfectly healthy at age eighty-two!" Such arguments are often presented in debates, and even on editorial pages, and take their force from our extraordinary willingness to generalize from a single case. We act as though the category of all cigarette smokers is uniform, so that any one member of the category (including the speaker's aunt) can be thought of as representative of the group, allowing us to draw conclusions about the group, and, in the process, draw conclusions that are unjustified and (in this example) potentially dangerous.

In the laboratory, research participants extrapolate from a single case even when they are explicitly warned that the case is in no way typical. In one study, participants watched a videotaped interview with a prison guard. Some had been told in advance that the guard was quite atypical, chosen for the interview because of his extreme views. Others were not given this warning. After watching the videotape, participants were asked their views about the prison system, and their views were plainly influenced by the interview they saw. Having heard an interview with a harsh, unsympathetic guard, participants were inclined to believe that, in general, prison guards are severe and inhumane. Remarkably, though, participants who had been told clearly that the guard was atypical were just as willing to draw the same conclusion. Their use of the representativeness heuristic in this case seems to have overruled the warning (Hamill, Wilson, & Nisbett, 1980; Kahneman & Tversky, 1972, 1973; Nisbett & Ross, 1980).

It is easy to be impressed and dismayed by the errors caused by these heuristics. We should therefore re-emphasize that, in general, they serve us well. If a category is frequent in the world, then examples of that category will generally be easily available to us. Therefore, frequency judgments based on availability will often be correct. Likewise, many of the categories we encounter are uniform in important regards, and so extrapolations based on assumed representativeness will often be warranted. In addition, both of these strategies are quick and easy to use, so if they do sometimes lead to error, this may be balanced by the efficiency they afford.

In addition, it is important to note that we do not always rely on these strategies in making our judgments. In some settings, we do seem to realize that a member of a particular category is atypical, and so we hesitate to draw conclusions about the entire category based on observations of just a few instances. In other settings, we seem alert to the fact that a large sample of data is more informative than a small sample. Several hypotheses have been offered for why we sometimes are sensitive to these factors and sometimes not, but at the moment, there is no consensus on these points (Gigerenzer & Hoffrage, 1995, 1999; Kahneman & Tversky, 1996; Mellers, Hertwig, & Kahneman, 2001; Nisbett, Krantz, Jepson, & Kurda, 1983; also see pp. 306–307).

## CONFIRMATION BIAS

The fact remains, however, that we do use these heuristics in many circumstances, including cases in which we are making judgments of considerable importance. It is also undeniable that, while these shortcuts generally serve us well, they can also lead to substantial error. One might hope, therefore, that these errors will soon be corrected as more information becomes available. Thus, we might initially be led to a false belief by a "man who" story, but as we gain experience, encountering more and more evidence that does not fit this belief, we will be led to revise our view. In other words, hearing about one eighty-two-year-old cigarette-smoking aunt might convince us that smoking is not hazardous, but then hearing about other (more typical) smoking victims will set us straight.

However, a different pattern works against such self-correction. This pattern, called *confirmation bias*, actually takes several different forms, but, in general, it is a tendency to take evidence consistent with one's beliefs more seriously than evidence inconsistent with those beliefs. One manifestation of this bias shows up whenever people seek out new information to test their beliefs. They tend to seek information that will confirm their views, rather than information that might challenge them. Similarly, if people are given evidence that is consistent with their beliefs and information that is inconsistent, they tend to believe the former and discount the latter. We are impressed by the quality of evidence when it supports our views, and such evidence strengthens our commitment to our beliefs; evidence that counts against our views, in contrast, is greeted with skepticism—subjected to hard criticism, reinterpreted, or in some cases, ignored outright.

Confirmation bias can be observed in many settings. For example, many compulsive gamblers believe they have a "winning strategy" that will, in the end, bring them great wealth. Their empty wallets, and the overall pattern of their wins and losses, provide powerful evidence against this belief, but the belief is maintained even so. How is this

*Confirmation bias* **In the Salem witch trials, the investigators believed the evidence that fit with their accusations, and discounted (or re-interpreted) the evidence that challenged the accusation. Here we see Daniel Day-Lewis as John Proctor and Winona Ryder as Abigail Williams in a 1996 film version of** The Crucible, **Arthur Miller's play about the witch trials.**

possible? In this case, confirmation bias takes the form of influencing how the gamblers think about their past wagers. Of course, they remember their wins quite vividly, using those memories to bolster the belief that they have a surefire strategy. What about their past losses? These also are remembered, but usually not as losses. Instead, they are categorized as "near wins" ("We would have won if not for the ref's bad call!") or as chance events ("It was just bad luck that I got a two of clubs instead of an ace!"). In this way, confirming evidence is taken at face value, but disconfirming evidence is discounted, leaving the gamblers' erroneous beliefs intact (Gilovich, 1991; for examples of how confirmation bias is studied in the laboratory, see Wason, 1960, 1968; Schulz-Hardt, Frey, Lüthgens, & Moscovici, 2000; Tweney, Doherty, & Mynatt, 1981).

Confirmation bias can be a genuine obstacle to understanding, because, in many ways, disconfirmations are more helpful in the search for truth than confirmations. One disconfirmation shows that a hypothesis is false, but countless confirmations cannot really prove that it is true. Nonetheless, confirmation bias is a powerful phenomenon, not only in the laboratory but also in real-world behavior—including the behavior of gamblers, politicians, and even scientists (Mahoney, 1976; Mahoney & DeMonbreun, 1981; Tweney, 1998; Mitroff, 1974).

What accounts for confirmation bias? One idea is that humans have a powerful tendency to seek order in the universe. We try to understand what we see and hear, and to impose some organization on it. The organization may not be valid, but it is often better than none at all, for without some such organization we would be overwhelmed by an overload of information. But the benefits provided by an organization do not come free, for our confirmation bias makes it quite difficult for us to escape a false belief once it is acquired.

## THE EFFECT OF EDUCATION

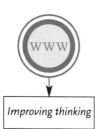

Improving thinking

We have mentioned that humans often reason quite well. There are, for example, circumstances in which they make correct choices in the selection task, and situations in which they rise above the simple heuristics we have been discussing. The fact remains, though, that people often do rely on these simple strategies and this can often lead to error. This causes us to ask whether anything can be done to improve the quality of people's reasoning so that errors can be avoided. In fact, the evidence on this issue provides grounds for optimism. As one point, it turns out that the likelihood of judgment errors depends on how exactly the evidence is presented to subjects, and so we can diminish the errors simply by presenting the evidence in the proper way. For example, people make many errors when asked to think about probabilities ("If you have this surgery, there is a .2 chance of side effects"), but are much less likely to make errors when thinking about frequencies ("Two out of ten people who have this surgery experience side effects"). There is some controversy about why exactly this shift in data format has its effect, but there is no doubt that we can improve human judgment by presenting the facts in the "right way" (Gigerenzer & Hoffrage, 1995, 1999; Lewis & Keren, 1999; Mellers, Hertwig, & Kahneman, 2001; Mellers & McGraw, 1999).

In addition, training in the elementary principles of statistics seems to make some judgment errors less likely, so that after statistics training, students are more alert both to the problems of drawing a conclusion from a small sample and to the possibility of bias within a sample. The benefits of training can also be derived from courses—such as those in psychology—that provide numerous examples of how sample size and sample bias affect any attempt to draw conclusions from evidence (Fong, Krantz, & Nisbett, 1986; Fong & Nisbett, 1991; Lehman, Lempert, & Nisbett, 1988; Lehman & Nisbett, 1990).

These educational experiences provide students with new knowledge and new strategies, which, in turn, improve their ability to think about evidence. Just as important, though, this education seems to build on intuitions that students already possess. What are these intuitions? Students certainly do not need a statistics course to teach them, for example, that accidents sometimes happen. (Sometimes, just by chance, a tossed coin will come up heads four times in a row.) Likewise, they do not need a course to tell them that accidents do not keep happening. (If the same coin comes up heads thirty times in a row, they will start to suspect a trick!)

These intuitions about accidents are widely shared and, in many circumstances, do help students to think sensibly about sample size. If an astrologer correctly predicts the score of tomorrow's football game, they might not be impressed—perhaps it was just a lucky prediction. (Accidents do happen.) But if the astrologer were able to predict game after game after game, this would be remarkable, and probably not attributable to luck. (Accidents do not keep happening.)

One might hope that these intuitions would protect people from erroneous reasoning—they might protect them, for example, from taking a "man who" argument seriously. (If someone says that cigarette smoking is okay because they have a friend who smokes and is healthy, the proper response should be that this friend is just a single case, and might be a fluke. After all, accidents happen.) In many circumstances, though, people fail to see the connection between these sensible intuitions and the particular case they are considering, and this leaves them vulnerable to the errors we have been discussing. This vulnerability is decreased, however, by some statistical training. After training, students seem to be able to apply their statistical intuitions to a broader set of cases, and, as a result, the training increases the likelihood that they will reason correctly about evidence, accidents, and sampling whenever they confront a new problem—be it in the laboratory or in their lives (Fong & Nisbett, 1991; Nisbett et al., 1983).

## DECISION MAKING

Both induction and deduction allow us to form new judgments and to form new beliefs. However, we want to do more than this; we also want to put our beliefs into action. In some cases, doing so is a simple matter of marching forward toward one clear goal. In many other cases, though, we have more than one path available to us, and we must choose which one to take. How do we make these choices? This question is illuminated by research on decision making.

### FRAMING EFFECTS

Two factors are obviously relevant to any decision. First, we should consider the possible outcomes of the decision and choose the most desirable one. Would you rather have 10 dollars or 100 dollars? Would you rather pay 5 dollars or 10 dollars to see the same movie? In each case, we effortlessly choose the option with the greatest benefit (100 dollars) or the lowest cost (the 5-dollar movie). Second, we should consider the risks. Would you rather buy a lottery ticket with one chance in a hundred of winning, or a lottery ticket for the same prize with one chance in a thousand of winning? If one of your friends liked a movie and another did not, would you want to go see it? What if five of your friends had seen the movie and all liked it, would you want to see it then? In these cases, we are attracted by the options that give us the greatest likelihood of achieving the things we value (increasing our odds of winning the lottery or seeing a movie we will enjoy).

Our decisions are clearly influenced by both of these factors—the attractiveness of the outcome and the likelihood of achieving that outcome. But our decisions are also heavily influenced by something that should not guide us, namely, how exactly a question is phrased or how our options are described. In many cases, these changes in the *framing* of a decision can reverse our decisions, turning a strong preference in one direction into an equally strong preference in the opposite direction. Take, for example, the following problem:

> Imagine that the United States is preparing for the outbreak of an unusual disease, which is expected to kill 600 people. Two alternative programs to combat the disease have been proposed. Assume that the exact scientific estimate of the consequences of the two programs is as follows:
>
> If Program A is adopted, 200 of these people will be saved.
>
> If Program B is adopted, there is a one-third probability that 600 people will be saved and a two-thirds probability that no people will be saved.
>
> Which of the two programs would you favor?

Given these alternatives, a clear majority—72 percent—opted for Program A, and, in many ways, this preference is easy to understand or to justify. But now consider what happens when participants are given the exact same problem but with a different formulation of their options. Participants were again told that if no action is taken, the disease will kill 600. They were then asked to choose between the following options:

> If Program A is adopted, 400 people will die.
>
> If Program B is adopted, there is a one-third probability that nobody will die and a two-thirds probability that 600 people will die.

Given this formulation, a huge majority—78 percent—chose Program B. To them the certain death of 400 people was less acceptable than a two-thirds probability that all 600 people would die (Tversky & Kahneman, 1981). But of course the options here are identical to the options in the first version of this program—400 dead, out of 600, is equivalent to 200 saved, out of 600. The only difference between the problems lies in how the alternatives are phrased, but this shift in framing has an enormous impact, turning a majority vote for A into an equally strong majority for B (Kahneman & Tversky, 1984).

Similar framing effects are easy to observe in other settings, including cases outside of the laboratory, and these effects follow a simple pattern: in general, people try to make choices that will minimize or avoid losses—that is, they show a tendency called *loss aversion*. If, therefore, the disease problem is framed in terms of losses (for example, people dying), people are put off by this, and, if they can, they will choose to gamble in hopes of diminishing the loss (thus, they choose Program B, which involves a gamble).

Loss aversion also leads people to hold tight to what they have, so they will not lose it. Thus, once they have a gain, they will take no chances with it; in this situation, they will scrupulously avoid gambling. If, therefore, the disease problem is framed in terms of a gain (for example, lives saved), people want to take no chances with this, and choose the sure bet (Program A).

Loss aversion is a strong and sensible inclination, and so is people's hesitancy to risk what they already have. Unfortunately, though, these inclinations leave people open to self-contradiction and inconsistency. This is evident in the disease problem but shows up in many other contexts as well. Thus, physicians are more willing to endorse a program of treatment that has a 50 percent success rate than they are to endorse a program with a 50 percent failure rate—they are put off by the emphasis on the negative outcome. Similarly, people generally refuse to play a fair game of "heads, you get a dollar; tails, I get a dollar." In this case, they are more impressed by the potential loss than they are by the potential gain, so the game seems unattractive. Likewise, research participants make one choice in the problem shown in the top half of Figure 8.24 and the opposite choice in the problem shown in the bottom half of the figure—again, they will gamble in hopes of avoiding a loss but will hold tight to retain a gain.

> 1. Assume yourself richer by $300 than you are today. You have to choose between:
>    A. a sure gain of $100, and
>    B. a 50 percent chance to gain $200 and a 50 percent chance to gain nothing.

> 2. Assume yourself richer by $500 than you are today. You have to choose between:
>    A. a sure loss of $100, and
>    B. a 50 percent chance to lose nothing and a 50 percent chance to lose $200.

*8.24 Framing effects The outcomes of these two choices are identical. In both cases, option A leaves you with $400, while option B leaves you with a 50–50 chance between getting $300 and getting $500. Despite this fact, 72 percent of research participants selected option A in choice 1, and 64 percent selected option B in choice 2. Once again, the way the outcomes were framed reversed the choices the participants made.*

## REASONING ERRORS IN CONTEXT

We have considered an impressive list of slips, errors, and inconsistencies in human thinking. How is this possible? Could humans really be this prone to error? If so, then how has humanity managed to achieve what it has in mathematics, philosophy, and science?

One response to these questions is already in view. We have suggested that our strategies for reasoning and judgment, even though open to error, do reach sensible conclusions more often than not. In addition, we have seen that, with training, people can be led to better reasoning strategies. A single course in statistics, it seems, can improve one's ability to think about a range of day-to-day judgments. Further courses in scientific method or in logic can magnify these effects (Lehman et al., 1988; Lehman & Nisbett, 1990).

It is also important to remember that the great intellectual achievements of humanity have been supported by a powerful set of intellectual tools, including techniques of formal data gathering and analysis, tools that are immune to many of the errors we have catalogued here. In addition, many discoveries depend on a *community* of researchers working on related projects. Errors committed by the majority may still be detected by a minority, and this may be enough to keep us all on track. Similarly, an individual scientist may well be biased toward confirmation and so may not seek evidence that could disprove her hypothesis. But other scientists may prefer different hypotheses and so will be quite glad to disprove the first researcher's claims. This adversarial relation is an important part of scholarly research and serves us well, rooting out error and rendering confirmation bias—a powerful force for the individual—irrelevant for the community.

Still, research on thinking and decision making may yet force us to rethink certain key issues about humanity, our intellectual prowess, and, indeed, the nature of rationality. On the surface, rationality might seem to mean avoiding error, but perhaps it is actually rational to tolerate some error if the alternative is spending vastly too much time on each judgment encountered. Better to be right most of the time than to spend life paralyzed in thought. Likewise, rationality might seem to entail avoiding self-contradiction. But perhaps other forces outweigh the need for self-consistency. Perhaps the avoidance of loss, for example, is so powerful a consideration that it is rational to accept some contradiction rather than occasionally losing our shirts.

"But we just don't have the technology to carry it out."

*(© 1976 by Sidney Harris, American Scientist magazine.)*

# THE THINKING BRAIN

In this chapter, we have covered a number of topics—the mental representation of knowledge, problem solving, induction and deduction, and decision making. Let us emphasize, though, that the study of these topics is not unique to psychology. Philosophers have much to say about the nature of knowledge, logicians about deduction, economists about decision making. And while psychologists are deeply interested in processes of thought, neuroscientists are focusing on the neural processes that make thought possible. It is therefore fitting that all of these various topics are often studied from a multidisciplinary perspective, under the rubric of *cognitive science*.

We close this chapter with two illustrations of the power of this multidisciplinary approach to the study of knowledge, its acquisition, and its use. First, we consider briefly the biological basis for some of the processes described in this chapter, and, second, we turn to the relation between cognition and consciousness.

## LOCALIZATION OF THOUGHT

In important ways, the processes of thought depend on the entire brain. A person could not think without the many midbrain and hindbrain structures that maintain life while the process of thought is going on. But many sites within the forebrain are more directly involved. If a person is thinking about visually presented materials, then sites relevant to the visual system (mostly in the occipital lobe) will be heavily activated; if a person is shifting attention from one aspect of a visual scene to another, this shift in attention to a large extent involves sites in the parietal cortex. If a person is engaged in linguistic tasks, then brain areas crucial for language use—including Broca's area (in the left frontal lobe) and Wernicke's area (near the juncture between the temporal and parietal lobes)—will be heavily involved. (See Chapter 2 for further discussion of all these anatomical regions.)

In addition to these other brain sites, evidence also indicates that the prefrontal cortex (the brain tissue just behind the forehead) plays a crucial role in many aspects of thought. Chapter 2 presented some of the evidence for this claim. Patients with damage in the prefrontal area often show profound deficits in strategy formation and are particularly unable to deal with novel situations—that is, situations requiring the design and initiation of some new plan or response. These patients frequently show a pattern known as *perseveration*—they persevere in producing the same response over and over and over, even though they remember perfectly well that the task requires them to change their response (see, for example, Bianchi, 1922; Luria, 1966; Diamond & Goldman-Rakic, 1989; Milner, 1963).

The role of the prefrontal cortex is also highlighted by studies of the neural basis of working memory. Recall that working memory is best understood as a process or activity, not as a passive repository for remembered material. In Chapter 7, we described working memory as the "workbench" on which various items of experience are sorted, manipulated, and organized. Clearly, then, there is an intimate tie between working memory and thought—working memory holds the materials one is currently thinking about. And working memory, it seems, depends heavily on the prefrontal cortex.

Evidence for this claim comes from studies of both humans and nonhuman animals (generally monkeys). These studies show that areas of the prefrontal cortex are strongly activated whenever the research participant must think about a stimulus seen just moments earlier, remember a sequence of letters, or make judgments about words ("Is this the name of a vegetable?"). But while there is a consensus that prefrontal areas are crucial for all these tasks, there is debate over how the prefrontal areas themselves are organized. Some researchers claim that portions of the prefrontal cortex are specialized for different types of materials, with one portion dealing with spatial position, another dealing with details of an object's appearance. Other researchers claim that some portions of the prefrontal cortex are pivotal in the retrieval of information from long-term storage, whereas other portions are crucial for the design and coordination of new actions. How these disagreements will be resolved remains to be seen. A conclusion awaits the arrival of new data and, conceivably, new techniques for studying and localizing brain activity (Cohen et al., 1997; Courtney, Ungerleider, Keil, & Haxby, 1997; Duncan & Owen, 2000; Rao, Rainer, & Miller, 1997; Wickelgren, 1997).

## COGNITION AND CONSCIOUSNESS

In perceiving, we do not merely gain the knowledge that the apple is red; instead, we experience redness. In imagery, we do not merely activate the belief that Monet's *Water Lilies* is beautiful; instead, our experience in contemplating the relevant mental picture resembles the one we have when examining the actual painting. And in remembering, we do not merely recall the past; instead, we are aware of trying to remember something and then are aware of our own recollection. What can we say about these various aspects of conscious experience?

When scientific psychology first started out, late in the nineteenth century, these observations, and the study of consciousness in general, were central concerns of the newly created field. The early psychologists did their best to describe and analyze their conscious experiences, but since different psychologists came up with very different descriptions, they were led to different, sometimes contradictory, claims. Moreover, there was no way to resolve these disputes. In general, researchers iron out their disagreements by examining each other's data and by considering each other's evidence. But there is no way to do this in the study of consciousness. There is no way for one researcher to share another's experience, and so no way to find out, for example, whether their experiences are the same or different. As a result, psychologists early in the twentieth century concluded that consciousness could not be studied scientifically and, for many years, abandoned the study of consciousness to philosophers (see, for example, Block, Flanagan, & Guzeldere, 1997; Chalmers, 1996; Dennett, 1991; Flanagan, 1994; Rosenthal, 1993; Searle, Dennett, & Chalmers, 1997).

As the previous chapters have suggested, however, psychologists are now ready to join forces with their colleagues in philosophy to tackle the issue of consciousness once again. To be sure, there are many questions about consciousness that we still cannot answer. What exactly is consciousness? How is it possible for a biological mechanism, namely, the human brain, to be conscious at all? Are other organisms conscious in the same sense we are? Could computers be conscious? Even with these questions acknowledged, though, psychologists have made considerable progress in this broad arena, owing, in large measure, to two lines of research: the first line examines the neural correlates of conscious experience; the second focuses on how our mental processes unfold in the absence of consciousness.

### THE NEURAL CORRELATES OF CONSCIOUSNESS

When someone is consciously thinking about the sound of a trumpet, what is the status of his brain? Which areas are more active, and which are less active, in comparison to, say, a time when the person is consciously thinking about the taste of bananas, or not thinking about anything in particular? Questions like these concern the brain states that occur whenever certain conscious states occur; they are questions, in other words, about the **neural correlates** of consciousness, and it seems likely that identifying these neural correlates will be the first step toward asking how neural activity makes conscious experience possible.

Over the last decade or two, much progress has been made in identifying potential correlates, but, even so, work in this area remains tentative and most claims remain controversial. Some investigators argue that consciousness depends on particular activation patterns spread over a very large number of neurons (see, for example, Libet,

1993, 2000). Other investigators suggest that there may literally be "consciousness neurons" distributed throughout the brain (Crick & Koch, 1995). They hypothesize that activity of these neurons (or at least a subset of them) is necessary for conscious experience (there can be no conscious experience without these neurons being activated) and sufficient for conscious experience (if these neurons are activated, there will be a conscious experience). (For a discussion of where these consciousness neurons might be, see Bogen, 1995; Crick and Koch, 1995; for broad reviews of this research, see Chalmers, 1998; Atkinson, Thomas, & Cleeremans, 2000; Dehaene & Naccache, 2001; Taylor, 2002.)

Choosing among these options awaits further research, and probably new experimental paradigms and technological developments. Even so, we are already building an impressively precise characterization of the "conscious brain," and, with that, a powerful base from which to test hypotheses about the nature of consciousness.

## MENTAL PROCESSES THAT GO ON BELOW THE SURFACE

Investigators have also learned a lot about consciousness by studying what happens when consciousness is absent. More specifically, many studies have shown that a lot of our mental activity can be done without conscious awareness or control. These findings allow us to begin characterizing what can—and perhaps what cannot—be done without consciousness, and in this fashion we can gain important clues about just what it is that consciousness contributes to our mental functioning.

Before proceeding, however, we should say a bit about the word *unconscious*. The popular understanding of this term has been shaped mightily by the ideas of Sigmund Freud. Freud believed that certain ideas or memories were "repressed"—that is, actively kept out of consciousness—because they were threatening or anxiety provoking (see Chapter 15). These painful or threatening ideas, however, continued to exist in the mind, or so Freud claimed, and resided in what he called the unconscious.

The mechanisms we are discussing here, however, are of a different sort. Much as one rides in a car without a moment's awareness of the engine's functioning, thought can proceed without any awareness of the vast and intricate mental machinery that makes

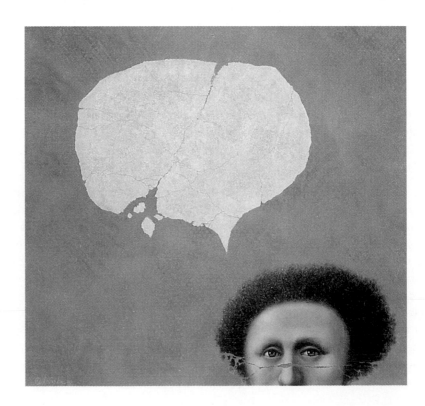

*Nonconsciousness*  **Some hints of what consciousness is about come from studies of mental processes that go on in the absence of consciousness. (Figure 14, 1982, by Alfredo Castañeda.)**

thought possible. The workings of this machinery, therefore, are simply nonconscious—outside our awareness. In contrast to the Freudian conception, these unconscious contents are in no sense threatening, nor are they actively suppressed. Instead, these contents are the "support apparatus," the underlying processes and mechanisms that make conscious experience possible. This "cognitive unconscious" is rich and complicated, but it is dramatically different from the unconscious hypothesized by Freud.

*Perception without Awareness*  When we look at the world, we see familiar objects—a chair, a dog, a friend, and so on. We respond appropriately to them all: we do not sit on the dog, throw a bone to the friend, or ask the chair how it is doing. Obviously, therefore, each stimulus triggers the relevant memories and knowledge. But we are generally unaware of the steps involved in these achievements. Without our conscious supervision, we separate figure from ground and compute distances in order to achieve constancy (Chapter 6), and we search through memory for pertinent information (Chapter 7). All we are aware of is the product of these operations—the world as it is consciously perceived.

Apparently, then, the processes that make perceiving possible can go forward without conscious supervision. This is evident in the ordinary perceiving that we do moment by moment, but is dramatically underscored by the phenomenon of **blindsight**, a pattern observed in some patients who suffer from damage to the occipital cortex (the main "receiving area" in the brain for visual information; see Chapter 2). These patients report that they can see nothing in large parts of their visual field, and, consistent with these reports, they fail to react to visual stimuli—even bright flashes of light—when they appear in the affected regions.

But this reported blindness is misleading. In some experiments, researchers presented stimuli to the patients' affected field and asked them to guess what the stimuli were—*X*s or *O*s, circles or squares. The patients complained that this task was absurd: they are blind, so how could they guess? When the investigators persisted, however, the patients did venture a guess, and these guesses were surprisingly accurate. It would appear, then, that these patients can see (or, more precisely, can perceive some aspects of the visual world), even though they have no conscious experience of seeing (Cowey & Stoerig, 1992; Rodman, Gross, & Albright, 1989; Weiskrantz, 1986). There has been much discussion of the neural connections that make this possible, but whatever its neurological base, this phenomenon makes it clear that perception can take place without our being aware of it. Perceiving, it seems, does not require conscious supervision, nor does it necessarily yield a conscious experience.

*Memory and Understanding without Awareness*  What holds for perception holds for other cognitive processes as well. We have already seen, for example, that we often rely on inferences to fill in gaps in our recollection (see Chapter 7). Usually, these inferences occur unwittingly, and this is one of the reasons why it is difficult to distinguish between the elements of a recollection that are truly based on what we experienced in an earlier episode and the elements that are based on our reconstruction or surmise. This same lack of awareness crops up whenever we listen and understand. Here, too, we routinely consult our memories without any awareness that we are doing so.

Consider the sentence:

*Susan put the vase down too firmly on the table and it broke.*

In this sentence, what does "it" refer to? The sentence is actually ambiguous, but most of us see only one meaning: "it" has to be the vase, not the table. To draw this conclusion, we rely on our knowledge that vases are often fragile, whereas tables generally are not. Hence, we interpret the sentence in a fashion guided by our knowledge, knowledge supplied to us by memory. However, we are not conscious of the fact that we are relying on memory; indeed, we are typically unaware that the sentence was ambiguous in the first place. Instead, we are conscious only of the product of these operations—our understanding of the sentence's meaning.

Similar claims can be made for all the sentences we hear or read. To understand them, we must construct their meaning from pieces we retrieve from memory, and we do so without awareness. In fact, it is crucial that these memory consultations go on underground. If we consciously registered every ambiguity we encountered and paused to search our memories, seeking the best resolution of each, we would probably never get to the end of any paragraph.

*Action without Awareness*  People can also act without awareness. For example, we all know how to tie our shoes, but most of us have forgotten the exact sequence of steps needed to accomplish this feat. We intend to tie our shoes and, before we know it, the task is done. We tie our shoes, it seems, without being aware that we are doing so.

More complex tasks can also be done in this unconscious fashion, so that many of our actions are performed on "autopilot." In most cases, this results from extended practice with the task, and this invites us to ask how practice creates this automaticity. One proposal is that, with practice, fewer decisions are required as one steps through a complex task. The well-practiced shoe tier does not have to choose what to do next after the first loop is formed. Instead, she can simply draw on the memory of what she has done many times before. A complete subroutine has been stored in memory, encapsulating all of the steps of the procedure, and so once the routine is launched, no decisions are needed—she simply repeats the familiar steps. (For theoretical proposals on how such subroutines are formed, see Logan, 1988; Boronat & Logan, 1997; Logan, Taylor, & Etherton, 1996; Shiffrin, 1997.)

## WHAT IS CONSCIOUSNESS GOOD FOR?

Overall, then, it is clear that much of our mental life goes on behind the scenes, out of sight. We seem to be largely unaware of the processes by which we perceive, remember, and think. What we are aware of instead are the products that emerge from these processes (Nisbett & Wilson, 1977). But if all this can be accomplished without awareness, then what is consciousness good for?

Nonconscious processing is fast and efficient—whether it involves shoelace tying, perceiving, or drawing a conclusion from evidence. Some of this efficiency, we have suggested, derives from the fact that automatized actions rely on familiar routines, allowing us to run off an already encoded sequence of steps, rather than attending to each new decision. By relying on familiar routines, we ensure that we will approach the task on this occasion just as we approached it on previous occasions. But this efficiency comes at a price: as we described earlier in the chapter, automatized actions are often relatively inflexible.

This inflexibility leads to an obvious suggestion: perhaps we need consciousness in order to break away from automaticity, to pay attention to our performance on precisely those tasks for which we must preserve flexibility. For these, we must remain mindful of what we are doing, so that we can choose, step-by-step, how our actions will unfold. Consciousness, in other words, plays its role whenever we must avoid becoming victims of habit and whenever we have reason to give up the efficiency afforded us by nonconscious processing.

Some tasks, by their nature, require a succession of conscious decisions. For these, conscious processing may be mandatory. Other tasks require some degree of fine tuning to make our actions appropriate to the present decision. To take an ordinary example, if we simply relied on habit, we might find ourselves habitually telling the same joke over and over each time we had an opportunity. Unfortunately, this might lead to our telling the joke a second or a third time to the exact same audience. To avoid this embarrassment, we need to rise above our habits to remember, and reflect on, when we last told the joke and to whom (see Jacoby, Kelley, Brown, & Jasechko, 1989).

The data we have reviewed also suggest another role for conscious experience. Blindsight patients apparently can perceive some aspects of their world, but they nonetheless do not take action based on what they see—they do not reach for desirable targets, do not duck to avoid bumping into things. Similarly, amnesic patients clearly retain many aspects of their past, but they also take no action based on what they remember and will not, for example, respond to an investigator's direct questions about their memories (Graf, Mandler, & Haden, 1982, provides a particularly clear case of this pattern).

How should we think about these observations? Perhaps our conscious experience plays a role in determining our willingness to act. We decide that a memory is a memory, and not a chance association, because of how we experience that memory, and so we take action based on that memory (compare with Mitchell & Johnson, 2000). Likewise, we decide that a perception is genuine, and not a fleeting impression, because of the conscious experience of that perception. Without this experience, we might gain the information contained within the perception but be incapable of acting on this information.

These last points clearly rest on conjectures, and, so far, research has provided only the earliest of steps on our path toward understanding consciousness. But we should not be surprised by this, since the mysteries surrounding consciousness have, after all, perplexed some of the greatest minds in human history. Even so, we are making progress in this arena, and psychologists and neuroscientists are increasingly turning their attention to these issues. It seems plausible, therefore, that research will continue to provide crucial clues about one of the greatest puzzles of all time.

# SOME FINAL THOUGHTS:
# THE DOMAINS OF COGNITION

In describing perception, we often cross over the border into memory. This is evident in many cases, including that how we perceive familiar objects is guided by how we perceived them in the past. But perception also shades into thinking: we look at an ambiguous picture and eventually solve the perceptual puzzle that it poses—as (for example) when we recognize in the picture the image of a dalmatian dappled by sunlight (see p. 224).

In the same way, it is not at all clear where memory leaves off and thinking begins. Much of remembering seems like problem solving. We may try to recall to whom we lent a certain book, conclude that it has to be Jane, for we know no one else who is interested in the book's topic, and then suddenly have a vivid recollection of the particular occasion on which she borrowed it (and the way she swore that she'd return it right away). But if remembering is sometimes much like thinking, thinking can hardly proceed without reference to the storehouse of memory. Whatever we think about—which route to take on a vacation trip, how to fill out a tax form—requires retrieval of items from various memory systems.

All of this shows that there are no exact boundaries separating perception, memory, and thinking. These areas are not sharply separated intellectual domains but are simply designations for somewhat different aspects of the general process of cognition. We will now turn to the one aspect of cognition that we have so far discussed only in passing—language. It, too, is intertwined with the other domains of cognition, but unlike perception, memory, and thinking, which are found in many animals, language seems unique to human beings.

# SUMMARY

All thought draws on knowledge we already possess. The components of knowledge can be regarded as *mental representations*, which are either *analogical* or *symbolic*. *Analogical representations* capture some of the actual characteristics of what they represent; thus a picture of a mouse (an analogical representation) shares some features with an actual mouse—the thing that is represented. Symbolic representations bear no such relationship to what they represent (e.g., there is no resemblance between the word "mouse" and the thing it represents).

## ANALOGICAL REPRESENTATIONS

1. An important example of analogical representation in thinking is provided by *mental images*. Visual images have many picture-like properties, as is shown by studies of *mental rotation* and *mental scanning*. However, other evidence indicates that visual images—like our visual perceptions—are not a simple re-embodiment of some stimulus but are already organized and interpreted in ways that the corresponding picture is not.

2. Neuroimaging techniques have shown many of the same brain regions (primarily in the occipital lobe) are active during both visual perception and visual imagery. Related findings come from work on brain damage: lesions that disrupt vision also seem to disrupt visual imagery and vice versa. In addition, temporary disruptions of brain function produced by *transcranial magnetic stimulation* (*TMS*) seem to produce parallel difficulties in perceiving and visualizing, adding to the argument that imagery and perception rely on many of the same brain areas.

3. *Spatial thinking* is both symbolic and analogical as shown by studies on *mental maps*.

## SYMBOLIC REPRESENTATIONS

4. The elements of symbolic thought are *concepts* and *propositions*. Many of these are stored in *generic memory*, where they constitute the "database" for our thoughts. A *concept* in essence defines a mental category. Some theorists regard concepts as relatively abstract (so that they might be represented in the mind by means of a list of characterizing features), while others believe that concepts are represented in a more concrete fashion (such as a record of the various items within the category). Other investigators suggest that concepts are represented only in relationship to each other.

5. One means of combining concepts is through *propositions*, which relate a *subject* and a *predicate* and can be true or false.

6. An important component of generic memory is *semantic memory*, whose organization has been described by various *network models*. Such network hypotheses receive support from studies of *semantic priming*. What is contained within the network? One proposal is that knowledge is locally represented, but many theorists prefer models relying on distributed representations. These models must rely on *parallel distributed processing*, with individual concepts represented, not by some definable number of nodes within a network, but by the state of the network as a whole.

## THE PROCESS OF THINKING: SOLVING PROBLEMS

7. *Problem solving* is a *directed activity* in which all steps are considered as they fit into the overall structure set up by the task. This structure is typically hierarchical, with goals, subgoals, and so on. Some important problem solving techniques involve changing *ill-defined problems* into *well-defined* ones and the use of *means-end analysis*, which replaces an initial problem with a series of *subproblems*.

8. Increasing competence at any directed activity goes with an increase in the degree to which the *subroutines* of this activity have become *chunked* and *automatized*. This chunking is visible in many forms of expertise, and is one of the things that differentiates masters and novices in many endeavors. Automatic actions, once set in motion, are sometimes difficult to turn off or modify, as in the case of the *Stroop effect*.

9. Problem solving is not always successful. One reason may be a strong, interfering *mental set*. A set can be overcome, though, in several different ways. One is working backward from the goal; another is trying to find an analogy. Sometimes the solution to a difficult problem requires a radical restructuring by means of which a misleading set is overcome. Such restructurings may be an important feature of much creative thinking. Accounts by prominent writers, composers, and scientists suggest that restructuring often occurs after a period of *incubation*, although the nature of incubation—if it exists at all—has been a sub-

ject of dispute. Restructuring may also play a role in humor, which often occurs when an unexpected cognitive organization turns out to make sense after all.

## THE PROCESS OF THINKING: REASONING AND DECISION MAKING

10. *Inductive reasoning* leads from individual observations to more general claims. In *deductive reasoning* one starts with a general claim, and asks what other assertions follow from it.

11. Many studies of how people reason have looked at people's ability to evaluate *syllogisms*. The results showed that participants are more likely to judge a conclusion to be valid if the conclusion strikes them as plausible—quite independent of whether the conclusion follows logically from the stated premises. Overall, performance tends to be quite poor, as it is also in the *selection tasks*, in which participants have to evaluate *conditional statements*.

12. In inductive reasoning, the thinker tries to induce a general rule from particular instances. An initial, tentatively held induction is a *hypothesis*.

13. Inductions often involve the estimation of frequencies and then extrapolations from these estimates. For these steps, people often make use of *heuristics*, cognitive shortcuts that serve us well enough, even though they may also lead to serious errors. One such rule of thumb is the *availability heuristic*: estimating the frequency of an event by how readily examples of such an event come to mind. Another rule of thumb is the *representative heuristic*: assuming that a case is representative of its class. A number of studies have pointed to another problem—a powerful *confirmation bias* that makes participants seek evidence that will confirm their hypotheses rather than look for evidence that would show their hypotheses to be false.

14. Despite these demonstrations of poor-quality reasoning and judgment, people perform well in other reasoning tasks. For example, most people have sensible intuitions about the role of sample size. These intuitions often lead people to realize that a small sample should not be trusted (its pattern might be the result of accident) and

that a larger sample is more likely to be informative (since, with a larger sample, the likelihood of an accidental pattern is smaller). The problem, though, is that people often fail to apply these statistical intuitions. Courses in statistics and courses in psychology seem to diminish such errors, making it easier for people to apply the knowledge that they have.

15. In decision making, people are not only sensitive to the benefit or loss and risk associated with each option. They are also sensitive to the way the options are framed. If an option is framed as a gain, people will usually choose to avoid all risk, holding tightly to what they have. If the same option is framed as a loss, however, people generally will seek out gambles (and take risks) in hopes of diminishing their (potential) loss.

## THE THINKING BRAIN

16. Thinking can be localized in many different parts of the brain. The occipital cortex is active when people are thinking about visual events or forming a mental image. *Broca's* and *Wernicke's areas* are active when people are thinking about linguistic materials. The prefrontal cortex is active in many aspects of thought and may provide the neural basis for working memory.

17. In recent years, psychologists have paid increasing attention to the problem of consciousness. Most of the progress in this area has come from studying psychological processes that operate when consciousness is absent. One example is *blindsight*, which occurs in people who have lost some portion of their visual cortex but can nevertheless perform many visual discriminations without being conscious that they can do so. Similar nonconscious processing occurs during innumerable occasions of everyday life when people retrieve memories without realizing they are doing so. Yet another everyday occurrence of nonconscious processing is the performance of automatized tasks. These phenomena suggest that consciousness functions as a monitor that lets us rise above habit and routine and allows us to tune our actions more appropriately to the specific circumstances.

TA MATETE

# LANGUAGE

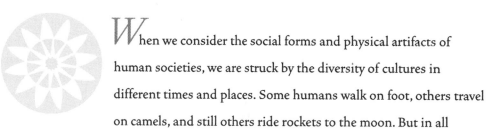When we consider the social forms and physical artifacts of human societies, we are struck by the diversity of cultures in different times and places. Some humans walk on foot, others travel on camels, and still others ride rockets to the moon. But in all communities and all times, humans are alike in having language. This crucial psychological connection, *between having language and being human*, has always intrigued those who are interested in the nature of the human mind. Indeed, to philosophers such as Descartes, language is the mental function that most clearly distinguishes humans from the other beasts, and is "the sole sign and only certain mark of thought hidden and wrapped up in the body." In this chapter, we will provide a general picture of human language and its learning, as well as its relation to the communication systems of other intelligent animals including chimpanzees and dolphins.

# THE BASIC UNITS OF LANGUAGE

Languages consist of a hierarchy of building blocks or units, which combine and recombine to form higher and higher level categories. At the bottom are units of sound such as *c*, *t*, and *a*, which at a level above combine into such words as *cat*, *act*, and *tact*. These words combine in turn into such phrases as *a fat cat*, and the phrases then combine into such sentences as *A fat cat acts with tact* and *That's the act of a tacky cat*. (See Figure 9.1, which illustrates this hierarchy of linguistic categories.) Each language gets by with a small inventory of sound units and a limited (though large) inventory of words, but because of the flexibility with which these units combine and recombine, each person can express and understand innumerable new thoughts. We now take up each of these levels of organization in turn.

## THE SOUND UNITS

To speak, we force a column of air up from the lungs and out through the mouth, while simultaneously moving the various parts of the vocal apparatus from one position to another (see Figure 9.2). Each of these movements shapes the column of moving air and thus changes the sound produced. The human speech apparatus can produce hundreds of different speech sounds clearly and reliably, but each language makes systematic use of only a small number of these units. For example, consider the English word *bus*, which can be pronounced with more or less of a hiss in the *s*. This sound difference, though audible, is irrelevant to the English-language listener, who interprets what was heard to mean "a large vehicle" in either case. But some sound distinctions do matter, for they signal differences in meaning. Thus, neither *but* nor *fuss* will be taken to mean "a large vehicle." This suggests that the distinctions among *s*, *f*, and *t* sounds are relevant to the perception of English, while the difference in hiss magnitude is not. The sound categories that matter in a language are called its **phonemes**. In English, *s* and *f* are different phonemes, whereas a long hiss and a short hiss are simply variations on a single phoneme. English uses about forty different phonemes.* Other languages select their own sets. For instance, German uses certain guttural sounds that are never heard in English, and French uses some vowels that are different from the English ones (Ladefoged, 1975).

---

* The English alphabet provides only twenty-six symbols (letters) to write these forty phonemes, and so often the same symbol is used for more than one phoneme. Thus, the letter *O* stands for two different phonemes in *hot* and *cold*, an "ah" sound and an "oh" sound. This fact—that the written and spoken symbols do not quite match—contributes to the difficulty of learning how to read English

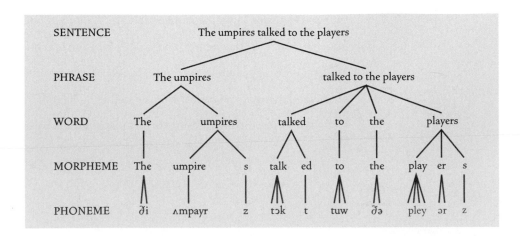

**SENTENCE**    The umpires talked to the players

**PHRASE**    The umpires    talked to the players

**WORD**    The    umpires    talked    to    the    players

**MORPHEME**    The    umpire    s    talk    ed    to    the    play    er    s

**PHONEME**    ðiˌ    ʌmpayr    z    tɔk    t    tuw    ðə    pley    ər    z

*Adam gives names to the animals* **The belief that knowledge of word meanings sets humans above animals goes back to antiquity. An example is the biblical tale (illustrated in this painting by William Blake), which shows Adam assigning names to the animals. According to some ancient legends, this act established Adam's intellectual superiority over all creation, including even the angels.**

**9.1** *The hierarchy of linguistic units* **Language is hierarchical, with sentences at the top. Sentences are composed of phrases, which in turn are composed of words. Words are made up of morphemes, the smallest units of language that carry meaning. The units of sound that compose morphemes are phonemes. Equivalent gestural units exist for sign languages.**

The phonemes are combined and sequenced to create words. Not every phoneme sequence occurs in every language. Sometimes these gaps are accidental. For instance, as it happens there is no English word *pilk*. But other gaps are systematic effects of the language design. As an illustration, could a new breakfast food be called *Pritos*? How about *Glitos* or *Tlitos*? Each of these would be a new sequence in English, and all can be pronounced, but one seems wrong: *Tlitos*. English speakers sense intuitively that English words never start with *tl*, even though this sequence is perfectly acceptable in the middle of a word (as in *motley* or *battling*). So the

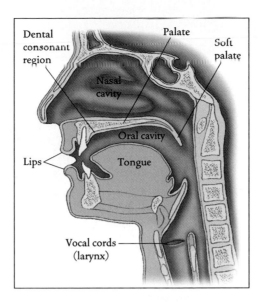

Dental consonant region
Palate
Soft palate
Nasal cavity
Oral cavity
Lips
Tongue
Vocal cords (larynx)

**9.2   The human vocal tract**   *Speech is produced by air flow from the lungs that passes through the larynx (popularly called the voice box) containing the vocal cords and from there through the oral and nasal cavities, which together make up the vocal tract. Different vowels are created by movements of the lips and tongue, which change the size and shape of the vocal cavity. Consonants are produced by various articulatory movements that temporarily obstruct the air flow through the vocal tract. (After Lieberman, 1975)*

new breakfast food will be marketed as tasty, crunchy *Pritos* or *Glitos*. Either of these two names will do, but *Tlitos* is out of the question. The restriction against *tl* beginnings is not a restriction on what human tongues and ears can do. For instance, one Northwest Indian language is named Tlingit, obviously by people who are perfectly willing to have words begin with *tl*. This shows that the restriction is a fact about English specifically. Few of us are conscious of this pattern, but we have learned it and similar patterns exceedingly well, and we honor them in our actual language use.

Languages differ in several other ways at the level of sound (Mehler et al., 1996). There are marked differences in the **rhythm** in which the successive syllables occur, and differences in the use and patterning of **stress** (or accent) and **tone** (or pitch). For instance, in languages such as Mandarin Chinese or Igbo, two words that consist of the same phoneme sequence, but which differ in tone, can mean entirely different things (Cutler, Mehler, Norris, & Segui, 1986; Dupoux et al., 1997; Jusczyk, Cutler, & Redanz, 1993). Languages also differ in how the phonemes can occur together within **syllables**. Some languages, such as Hawaiian and Japanese, do not allow clusters of consonants in their syllables and words; rather, they regularly alternate a single consonant with a single vowel. Thus, we can recognize words like *Toyota* and *origami* as sounding Japanese when they come into English usage. In contrast, syllables with many consonants at the beginning and end are common in English; for example, the first syllables in the words *flinging* or *strengthen* (Cutler & Otake, 1994; Frederici & Wessels, 1993; Pallier, Christophe, & Mehler, 1997).

*The distinctive sound of Hawaiian*   **The names of these two tropical fish—the** Humuhumunukunukapua'a *and the* Hinalea 'Akilolo—*sound foreign to the English listener in part because of the regular alternation between consonant and vowel. English, in contrast, has many words in which two or more consonants occur next to each other—for instance shrimp, lobster, and flounder.*

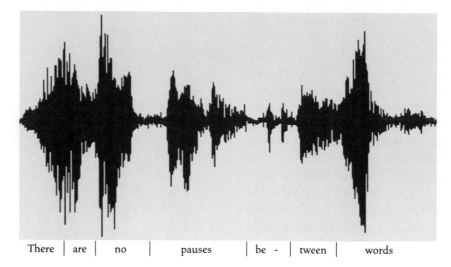

| There | are | no | | pauses | be - | tween | words |

**9.3   The actual sound pattern of speech**   *This figure shows the moment-by-moment sound amplitudes produced by a speaker uttering the sentence "There are no pauses between words." Notice that there is no gap between the sounds carrying the word* are *and the sounds carrying* no. *Nor is there a gap between the sounds carrying* between *and the sounds carrying* words. *Therefore listeners must figure out where one word ends and the next begins, a process known as segmentation.*

Speech can be understood at rates of up to 250 words per minute without significant loss of comprehension (Foulke, 1971). The normal rate of speech is closer to 180 words per minute, which converts to about 14 phonemes per second. These phonemes are usually fired off in a continuous stream, without gaps or silences in between to mark the boundaries of morphemes and words. Indeed, the utterance of one phoneme often runs right into the utterance of the next (Figure 9.3). This is true for successive phonemes within a single word and also for sucessive words within a phrase, so that sometimes it is hard to know whether one is hearing "that great abbey" versus "that gray tabby" or "The sky is falling" versus "This guy is falling" (Liberman, Cooper, Shankweiler, & Studdert-Kennedy, 1967).

## MORPHEMES AND WORDS

At the next level of the linguistic hierarchy (see Figure 9.1), fixed sequences of phonemes and syllables are joined into morphemes. The *morphemes* are the smallest language units that carry bits of meaning. Examples of morphemes are *talk, tree,* and the *ed* morpheme that marks the past tense. Some words consist of a single morpheme, such as *and, run,* and *bake,* while others contain more than one, for example, *nightfall* and *downstairs.* Certain morphemes cannot stand alone and must be joined with others to make up a complex word. We mentioned *ed;* other examples are *er* (meaning "one who") and *s* (meaning "more than one"). When these are joined with the morpheme *bake* (meaning "to cook by slow heating") into the complex word *bakers* (bake + *er* + *s*), the meaning becomes correspondingly complex ("ones who cook by slow heating").

### CONTENT MORPHEMES AND FUNCTION MORPHEMES

Morphemes such as *bake* and *man* that carry the main burden of meaning are called *content morphemes*. The morphemes that not only add details to the meaning but also serve various grammatical purposes (such as the suffixes *-er* and *-ed* and the connecting words *and* and *which*) are called *function morphemes*. Recent evidence shows that this distinction of morpheme types, existing in all languages, is reflected in the sound

"Boy, he must think we're pretty
stupid to fall for that again."

*(Courtesy of Leigh Rubin, Creators
Syndicate, Inc. © 1990 Leigh Rubin)*

characteristics of the language, so that content and function morphemes are pronounced somewhat differently (Shi, Morgan, & Allopenna, 1998). There is also much evidence that these two classes of words and morphemes are psychologically distinctive. For example, very young children often omit function morphemes in their first primitive English utterances (R. Brown & Bellugi, 1964; Gerken, Landau, & Remez, 1990; L. R. Gleitman & Wanner, 1982). Adults learning a second language have significantly greater trouble achieving native-like performance with the function morphemes and words than with the content morphemes and words (J. S. Johnson & Newport, 1989). Often, in brain injury, a person's ability to process function morphemes is compromised, while the content words remain intact or close to intact; the reverse condition also sometimes occurs. (See Chapter 2 for a discussion of aphasia.) Recordings of activity in the brain also reveal that content and function morphemes are processed in different ways during normal language activities (C. M. Brown, Hagoort, & ter Keurs, 1999).

## PHRASES AND SENTENCES

Just as a morpheme is an organized grouping of phonemes and a word is an organized grouping of morphemes, so a *phrase* is an organized grouping of words (*the, black,* and *cat* combine to yield the phrase *the black cat*), and a *sentence* is an organized grouping of phrases (*the black cat* and *runs rapidly away* combine to yield *The black cat runs rapidly away*). As is the case for the lower levels of the linguistic hierarchy, here too there are constraints on the sequences that are allowed. "House the is red" and "Where put you the pepper?" do not sound acceptable (or grammatical) as combinations. One might think that the distinction between grammatical and ungrammatical sentences is just a matter of meaningfulness—whether the combination of words and phrases has yielded a coherent idea or thought. But this is not so. Some nonsentences have meaning ("Me Tarzan; you Jane"). And many apparently grammatical sentences are entirely uninterpretable ("Colorless green ideas sleep furiously"). This sentence makes no sense because abstract ideas have no color and green things are not colorless. But it seems well formed in a way that the following word string does not: *Sleep green furiously ideas colorless*. Conformance with some rulelike system rather than meaningfulness seems to be behind the notion of grammaticality—regularities of formation that have a flavor much like that of the rules of arithmetic or of chess. Much as you cannot (as a competent chess player) move Queen from Knight Pawn 3 to King Pawn 6 or (as a competent calculator) add 2 and 2 to yield 5, in much this sense you can't say, "House the is red" to yield a sentence in English. These constraints on how words and phrases can combine into sentences are called the *rules of syntax* (from Greek meaning, "arranging together").

**Noam Chomsky**

The study of syntax has been one of the principal concerns of linguists and psycholinguists over the last several decades, with much of the discussion organized around the ideas and theories of Noam Chomsky (Chomsky, 1965, 1981, 1995). As Chomsky emphasized, this interest in the rules governing word combination is not surprising if one wants to understand the fact that we can say and understand a virtually unlimited number of new things, all of them "in English." To make infinite use of the finite number of words in one's vocabulary, one must understand the patterning that underlies their combination. Here we take a very preliminary look at the way that English is organized syntactically.*

### PHRASE STRUCTURE

Consider the simple sentence "The zebra bit the giraffe." The sentence seems naturally partitioned into two major subparts or phrases, a noun phrase (*the zebra*) and a verb phrase (*bit the giraffe*). Linguists depict this partitioning of the sentence by means of a tree diagram, so called because of its branching appearance:

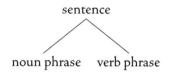

This notation is a useful way of showing that sentences can be thought of as a hierarchy of structures (see Figure 9.1, p. 320). Each sentence can be broken down into phrases, and these phrases into smaller phrases. Thus, our verb phrase redivides as a verb (*bit*) and a noun phrase (*the giraffe*).

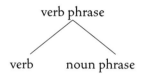

These subphrases in turn break down into the component words and morphemes. The descending branches of the tree correspond to the smaller and smaller units of sentence structure. The whole tree structure is called a ***phrase structure description*** of the sentence. Figure 9.4 shows the phrase structure of this example sentence.

The phrase structure description is a compact and efficient way of describing our implicit knowledge of how sentences are organized. Part of this efficiency is achieved by defining phrases in a way that is independent of where they appear within the sentence. The makeup of a noun phrase, for example, must always follow the same pattern of words whether the noun phrase is at the start or the end of a sentence: articles such as *a* and *the* come first; any adjectives come next; then the noun; and so forth. As a result, these rules define groups of words as if they are modules that can be plugged in anywhere that the sentence calls for a phrase of the specified type. Consider as an instance the hypothetical sentence *The ball big rolled away.* Anyone who rejects this as a sentence of English is guaranteed also to reject *He chased the ball big* and *The ant was squashed under the ball big.* This is because the phrase *the ball big* does not follow the

---

* From another perspective, several psycholinguists have recently provided plausible arguments for a "nonsymbolic" redescription of these linguistic design features via distributed patterns or neural nets (J. Allen & Seidenberg, 1999; Christiansen & Chater, 2001; Dell et al., 1999; Elman, 1991; Rumelhart & McClelland, 1986; Smolensky, 1999). Some of these arguments are to the effect that such networks can simulate the structural relations between words and phrases, without the "rules" of symbolic grammars. Others point to neuroscientific findings as supporting one of these approaches over the other.

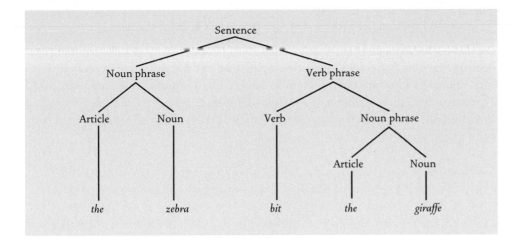

*The structure of the sentence* The zebra bit the giraffe *This tree is called a phrase structure description because it shows how the sentence can be analyzed into phrase units. Notice particularly that there are two noun phrases in this sentence. The first one (the zebra) is the subject of this sentence. The second one (the giraffe) is inside the verb phrase (bit the giraffe). A description of this kind also shows the word class types (e.g., article, noun, verb) of which each phrase consists. Finally, the tree shows the words of the sentence (the bottom row in the tree).*

English-language rules for noun phrases, and so is illegitimate no matter where it occurs in the sentence. By the same token, anyone who accepts the sentence *I kissed a girl who is allergic to coconuts* is guaranteed to accept *A girl who is allergic to coconuts was chased by a moose* and *He hid the flowers behind a girl who is allergic to coconuts*. That is because once the phrase *a girl who is allergic to coconuts* is accepted as a noun phrase, it can be plugged into any position within the sentence that calls for a noun phrase.

Crucially, phrase structure organization also allows us to describe dependencies at a distance within sentences. For instance, the agreement of number between the main (or head) noun (*committees, swindlers, brothers, men*) and the verb form *are* (rather than *is*) continues to hold no matter how great the distance between them:

| | |
|---|---|
| *Committees* | *are meeting.* |
| *Those swindlers with moustaches* | *are meeting.* |
| *Those brothers of the king of North Dakota* | *are meeting.* |
| *These tall men sitting on the plaza drinking cokes with Tony* | *are meeting.* |

That is, if we count word by word, the distance between the plural noun and its verb grows and grows as we move from the first of these sentences to the last. But if we count by phrases, then the helping verb *are* is always the same distance away from its governing plural noun-phrase; that is, it is just a single phrase away.

The role of phrase structure is evident in many aspects of language use. For example, one investigator asked subjects to memorize strings of nonsense words. Some of the strings had no structure at all, such as *yig wur vum rix hum im jag miv*. Other strings, however, also included various function morphemes, providing a structure: *the yigs wur vumly rixing hum im jagest miv*. One might think that sequences of the second type would be harder than the first to memorize, for they are longer. But in fact the opposite is true. The function morphemes in the second version allowed the listeners to organize the sequence in terms of a phrase structure, with the consequence that the structured sequences were appreciably easier to remember (W. Epstein, 1961; see also Levelt, 1970). (This is obviously related to the examples of memory chunking that we discussed in Chapter 7. Memory is reliably improved whenever we are able to organize individual pieces of information, combining them into one higher-level unit that can then be treated as just a single chunk to memorize.) Figure 9.5 shows that phrase structure organization aids reading just as it aids listening.

*Phrase structure organization aids the reader* *The panel on the left (blue) shows a sentence written so that its phrases and major words mostly appear on their own lines of print. This makes reading easier because the sentence has been pre-organized so that the eye can move phrase by phrase down the page. In the panel on the right (green), the sentence has been rewritten so that bits of more than one phrase often appear on a single line. Reading is now slower and may contain more errors because the phrasal organization has been visually disrupted. (Courtesy John Trueswell)*

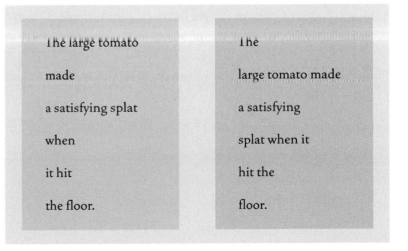

| | |
|---|---|
| The large tomato | The |
| made | large tomato made |
| a satisfying splat | a satisfying |
| when | splat when it |
| it hit | hit the |
| the floor. | floor. |

## THE REAL COMPLEXITY OF LANGUAGE DESIGN

Let us now look at a more complex example of sentence organization, for after all, even ordinary language users fluently utter, write, and understand many sentences forty, fifty, and even a hundred morphemes in length. The example below appeared in the "Letters to the Editor" column of a popular TV magazine (quoted in L. R. Gleitman & Wanner, 1982), so we can hardly protest that it was the creation of some linguistic Einstein or literary giant:

> *How Ann Salisbury can claim that Pam Dawber's anger at not receiving her fair share of acclaim for* Mork and Mindy's *success derives from a fragile ego escapes me.*

Leaving aside the peculiar interests of this correspondent, we must be impressed with the intricacy and systematicity with which he or she put the pieces of this sentence together. For example, the structure signaled by the first word of this sentence (*How*) requires that the twenty-eighth word (*escapes*) must have an *s* at its end. How does the writer know this? For that matter, how do we readers recognize this same requirement and so conclude that the sentence is grammatical? Surely not by memorizing a table of relations between "all first words of sentences" and "all twenty-eighth words of sentences," but rather via appreciating combinatorial regularities of enormous generality and power. Much of this power comes from the fact that the same regularities that apply to the simplest sentences apply in the same way to the complex sentences, with just a little tinkering around the edges. The complex sentences are built up by using and reusing the same smallish set of syntax rules, but each tagged with a bit of information (often supplied by the function morphemes—such as *how, for, ing,* and *s* in the Ann Salisbury example sentence) to signal just how they are being organized into the complex whole (Chomsky, 1981b; Z. Harris, 1951; Jackendoff, 2002; Joshi, 2002). Thus, just as for the noun phrases we discussed earlier, the simplest sentence forms can be snapped together to create large complexes, using function morphemes for the nails and glue.

## AMBIGUITY IN WORDS AND SENTENCES

Very often a single use of language can be interpreted in more than one way. Linguists are very fond of collecting such ambiguities in case one interpretation comes out hilarious. Sometimes these ambiguities are of word meaning (for example, such newspaper headlines as "Children's Stools Useful for Garden Work"; "Red Tape Holds up Bridge"; or "Prostitutes Appeal to Pope"), while others concern how phrases are grouped

*How structure can affect meaning  On being asked what a Mock Turtle is, the Queen tells Alice, "It's the thing Mock Turtle Soup is made from." Needless to say, this is a misanalysis of the phrase* mock turtle soup *as (mock turtle) (soup)—a soup that is not really made out of turtles (and is in fact usually made out of veal). (Lewis Carroll,* Alice in Wonderland, *1969, p.73)*

*9.6  Ambiguity of structure  Two interpretations of the sentence "Smoking volcanoes can be dangerous."*

together ("Drunk Gets 6 Months in Violin Case"; "Police Are Ordered to Stop Drinking on Campus"). It is important to realize how pervasive the phenomenon of ambiguity is in everyday speech and writing. Many very short and apparently simple sentences are really ambiguous. For instance, "Smoking cigarettes can be dangerous" could be a warning that to inhale cigarettes could harm your health, or a warning that if you leave them smouldering in an ashtray, your house might burn down (Figure 9.6).

# HOW LANGUAGE CONVEYS MEANING

So far, our survey of language has concentrated attention on the forms of language. Here we turn to the topic of meaning. As we shall see, form and meaning crucially link together in the linguistic organization of thought.

## THE MEANINGS OF WORDS

Word meanings are of many different kinds. Some words such as *Madonna* and *Batman* describe individuals in the real and imaginary world; others such as *dog* and *unicorn* are more general and describe categories of things. Yet other words describe substances (*water, Kryptonite*), properties (*green, imaginary*), quantities (*some, zillions*), actions (*run, transform*), states of mind (*knowing, hoping*) or being (*am, seem*), and manners of doing (*carefully, musically*). A moment's thought reveals that the kind of meaning is well correlated with the so-called parts of speech, with things and stuff generally labeled by nouns, acts and states by verbs, properties by adjectives, and manners by adverbs. These correlations between meaning and word class accord with the representation of language in the brain; for example, nouns and verbs are retrieved with differently distributed neural systems and can be independently compromised in brain injury (Bates, Chen, Tzeng, Li, & Opie, 1991; Caramazza & Hillis, 1991; Luzzatti et al., 2001).

### THE DEFINITIONAL THEORY OF WORD MEANING

At first glance, the words of a language seem to be like little atoms of meaning, each distinct from all the other words. But several theories of word meaning assert that only a handful of words in a language describe elementary, "simple" ideas or concepts. The rest are more like molecules: they are composites of more elementary atoms of meaning. Thus, according to such theories, words like *yellow* and *round* might indeed name simple ideas or concepts that derive their meaning from our physiological reactions to their instances. But many other words seem more complex in the sense that while yellowness is part of their meaning, it is by no means their whole meaning: *canary, yolk,* and *banana* are obvious instances (Hume, 1739; Jackendoff, 2002; Katz & Fodor, 1963; Locke, 1690). This kind of observation is central to a ***definitional theory of word meaning***, which states that words are organized in our minds much as they are in standard dictionaries. This approach starts out with the fact that there are various meaning relationships among different words and phrases. Some words are similar in meaning (*wicked-evil*); others are opposites (*wicked-good*); still others seem virtually unrelated (*wicked-ultramarine*). According to the definitional proposal, these relationships can be explained by assuming that words are bundles of ***semantic features*** or meaning-atoms (Katz, 1972; Katz & Fodor, 1963). As an example, take the word *bachelor*. This word clearly has something in common with *uncle, brother, gander,* and *stallion*. As speakers of English, we know that all of these words carry the notion [maleness]. This point is forcefully made by considering various sentences that most English speakers will regard

*Can a white rose be red?* **The Queen had ordered the gardeners to plant a red rose bush, but they planted a white one by mistake. They're now trying to repair their error by painting the white roses red. On the definitional theory of meaning, this seems reasonable enough. For the expressions** red rose bush **and** white rose bush **differ by only a single feature— red** versus **white. But if so, why are they so terrified that the Queen will discover what they did?**

as odd (or, to use the technical term, anomalous). Thus, the sentence *My_____ is pregnant* is false (or at least peculiar) if the missing word is any of the members of the *bachelor*-related group listed below:

$$My \quad \begin{matrix} uncle \\ brother \\ gander \\ stallion \\ bachelor \end{matrix} \quad is\ pregnant.$$

Further thought shows that *bachelor* contains additional features, such as [single] and [adult]. This explains why the following sentences would also be anomalous in meaning:

*My sister is married to a bachelor.*
*I met a two-year-old bachelor yesterday.*

On the definitional view, therefore, the full meaning of each word is a set of features that are essential for membership in the class. Thus, *bachelor* might be composed of the set of semantic features [single], [human], [adult], and [male]. If some creature is missing any one of these necessary features (for example, if the creature was a married human adult male, or an unmmarried adult male duck), it could not correctly be called "a bachelor." And this set of features is also sufficient for bachelorhood—the man in question might be tall or short, flirtatious or shy, English or Greek, and so on, but none of this affects his status as a bachelor. These semantic features constitute the definition of each word, and according to this theory, we carry such definitions in our heads for each of the words in our vocabulary.*

## THE PROTOTYPE THEORY OF MEANING

The definitional theory faces several problems. For one thing, once we have gone beyond such relatively formal words as *bachelor*, it is surprisingly hard to come up with definitions that cover all the uses of a word or that seem to do it justice at all. For instance, consider the (proposed) definition of *bird* in Figure 9.7. This definition seems promising but, in fact, not all birds are covered with feathers (neither baby birds nor plucked birds have feathers, yet they are birds all the same). The author of the definition in the figure seems to acknowledge this problem by hedging on the feathers issue, writing "more or less covered with feathers." And the picture helps in some ways, filling in what the words miss, but notice that the picture is far too particular to describe the range of real birds; it hardly seems appropriate for the emus or the albatrosses (for discussion, see Armstrong, Gleitman, & Gleitman, 1983; Fodor, 1983; Huttenlocher & Hedges, 1994; Prinz, 2002; Rey, 1996).

A further problem for definitional theory is that some members of a meaning category appear to exemplify that category better than others do. Thus, a German shepherd seems to be a more typical dog than a Pekinese, and an armchair seems to be a better example of the concept of furniture than a reading lamp. This seems to be at odds with

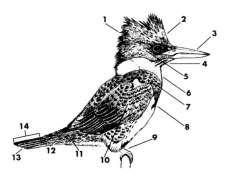

**9.7** *Is this the entry for bird in your mental dictionary?* "bird . . . n. . . . [ME, fr. OE bridd] . . . 2: Any of a class (Aves) of warm-blooded vertebrates distinguished by having the body more or less completely covered with feathers and the forelimbs modified as wings. . . . "bird 2 (kingfisher): 1 crest, 2 crown, 3 bill, 4 throat, 5 auricular region, 6 breast, 7 scapulars, 8 abdomen, 9 tarsus, 10 upper wing coverts, 11 primaries, 12 secondaries, 13 rectrix, 14 tail" (Merriam-Webster's Collegiate Dictionary, Tenth Edition)

---

* It is important to distinguish between the word and its semantic features. Thus, [male] may be a semantic feature or atom that constitutes part of the meaning of such words as *stallion* and *brother*. But there is also a word *male*. It is the kind of word that consists of only the single semantic feature [male]. At a lower level of language, a related phenomenon exists. The English indefinite article *a* is a word (the one that appears in the phrase *a cat*), but it is also a phoneme. That is, *a* is the rare case of a word which, at the level of sound, contains only one phoneme rather than a sequence of phonemes. In the same sense, *male* is the relatively rare case, according to definitional theory, of a word that contains only a single semantic feature, [male].

*Diversity within categories* **The enormous diversity of instances within categories is one reason why categories are difficult to define. These creatures differ in many regards (e.g., whether they fly or swim, how large they are, the shapes and colors of their feathers, and so forth), but all are instances of the category** bird.

the analysis we have described thus far, whose aim was to specify the necessary and sufficient attributes that define a concept. When a dictionary says that a bachelor is "an adult human male who has never been married," it claims to have said it all. Whatever fits under the umbrella of this definitional feature list is a bachelor. Whatever does not, is not. But if so, how can one bachelor be more bachelor-like (or one dog more doglike) than another?

Observations like these have led some investigators to argue for an alternative view, called prototype theory (Medin, Goldstone, & Gentner, 1993; Rosch, 1973b; Rosch & Mervis, 1975; E. E. Smith & Medin, 1981). The facts that prototype theory tries to account for can easily be illustrated. Consider again the category *bird*. Are there features that characterize all birds and that characterize birds only? One might think that being able to fly is a feature of all birds, but it is not. (Ostriches can't fly.) Instead, one might suppose that having feathers is a feature of all birds, but as we have noted, neither baby birds nor plucked birds have feathers. And not everything that lays eggs (turtles), or flies (airplanes, helicopters), or has feathers (hats, down comforters, quill pens) is a bird. With all these failures of the definition in mind, perhaps it is wrong to suppose that we can ever find a set of necessary and sufficient features for the concept of *bird*. But if not, then the definitional theory is not correct.

According to the prototype theory, the meaning of many words is described as a set of features, just as in the definitional theory, but not a necessary and sufficient set. Instead, the concept is held together by what some philosophers call a *family resemblance structure* (Wittgenstein, 1953). Consider the ways that members of a family resemble each other. Joe may look like his father to the extent that he has his eyes; he may look like his mother by virtue of his prominent chin. His sister Sue may look like her father to the extent that she has his nose, and she may smile just like her mother. But Joe and Sue may have no feature in common (he has his grandfather's nose and she has Aunt Fanny's eyes), and so the two of them do not look alike at all. Even so, they are both easily recognized as members of the family, for they each bear some resemblance to their parents (see Figure 9.8).

Several investigators believe that the same pattern holds for many of our common concepts, such as *bird*, *chair*, and so forth. We have already noted that some members of a category seem more prototypical than others, so that a German shepherd seems more typically doggy than a Pekinese. This is presumably because the shepherd has many of the features associated with the "dog family" while the Pekinese has fewer. Similarly, we have discussed the difficulties of finding necessary and sufficient conditions for con-

**9.8** *The Smith brothers and their family resemblance* **The Smith brothers are related through family resemblance, though no two brothers share all features. The one who has the greatest number of the family attributes is the most prototypical. In the example, it is Brother 9 who has all the family features: brown hair, large ears, large nose, moustache, and eyeglasses. (Courtesy of Sharon Armstrong)**

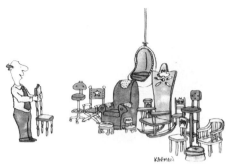

"Attention, everyone! I'd like to introduce the newest member of our family."

*(Drawing by Kaufman; © 1977 The New Yorker Magazine, Inc.)*

cepts such as *bird*; this too is compatible with the family resemblance idea, because, as we mentioned, it is entirely possible that no features will be shared by all members of a family and reasonably likely that no features will be unique to that family.

How is knowledge about a family resemblance structure represented in the mind? According to some psycholinguists, we carry in memory a mental *prototype* for each of our concepts—a prototypical bird, a prototypical chair, and so on (Gentner, 1983; Goldstone, Lippa, & Shiffrin, 2001; Rosch, 1973b; Rosch & Mervis, 1975; E. E. Smith & Medin, 1981; Tversky, 1977). These prototypes are generally derived from our experiences, so that each prototype provides something like a mental average of all the examples of the concept the person has encountered. In the case of birds, people in our culture have presumably seen far more robins than penguins. As a result, something that resembles a robin will be stored in their memory system and will then be associated with the word *bird*. When the person later sees a new object, she will judge it to be a bird to the extent that it resembles the prototype in some way. A sparrow resembles it in many ways and so is judged to be a "good" bird; a penguin resembles it just a little and hence is a marginal bird; a rowboat resembles it not at all and hence is judged to be no bird.

We have already mentioned some of the evidence consistent with this view: the fact that some category members are reliably judged to be better members than others, and the difficulty in specifying necessary and sufficient conditions for a category. Other evidence comes from numerous laboratory studies. For example, when people are asked to come up with examples of some category, they generally produce instances that are close to the presumed prototype (for example, robin rather than ostrich). A related result concerns the time required to verify category membership. Study participants respond more quickly to the sentence *A robin is a bird* than to *An ostrich is a bird*. This is perfectly sensible. A robin resembles the bird prototype and so the similarity is readily discerned, allowing a fast response. For an ostrich, one must spend a moment searching for birdy features, so verification is correspondingly slower (Rosch, 1978).

## COMBINING DEFINITIONAL AND PROTOTYPE THEORIES

**Prototypes and definitions** Robin Williams playing the role of Mrs. Doubtfire might resemble the typical grandmother, but as a male, he is surely not a real grandmother. In contrast, Loni Anderson is far from the prototype but is, in reality, a grandmother.

The prototype view helps us to understand why robins are better birds than ostriches. But the definitional theory explains why an ostrich is nevertheless recognized as a bird. The prototype view helps us understand why a trout is fishier than a sea horse, but the definitional theory seems important if we are to explain why a sea horse is far fishier than a whale (which, of course, is not a fish at all, though it has some fishy properties). Perhaps we can combine both views of meaning rather than choosing between them.

Consider the word *grandmother*. For this term, there are necessary and sufficient features, so here the definitional theory seems just right: a grandmother is a female parent of a parent. But there may also be a prototype: a grandmotherly grandmother is a person who bakes cookies, is old and gray, and has a kindly twinkle in her eye. When we say that someone is grandmotherly, we are surely referring to the prototypical attributes of grandmothers, not to genealogy. And, in many circumstances, we use this prototype, rather than the definition. For example, we are likely to rely on our grandmother prototype for picking a grandmother out of a crowd, for predicting what someone's grandmother will be like, and so on. But in other circumstances, we rely on the definition: if we know some kindly lady who is gray and twinkly but never had a child, we may think of her as grandmotherly but not as a grandmother.

It appears, therefore, that people have two partly independent mental representations of *grandmother*, and the same is probably true for most other words as well. They know about prototypical attributes associated with the term and probably store a list (or perhaps a picture) of such attributes as a handy way of picking out likely grandmother candidates. But they also store defining grandmother features (for example, mother of a parent). These definitional features determine the limits of the term *grandmother* and tell one how to use the prototype appropriately (Armstrong, Gleitman, & Gleitman, 1983; Landau, 1982; G. Miller & Johnson-Laird, 1976; E. E. Smith & Medin, 1981; for a recent discussion, Prinz, 2002).

## WORD MEANINGS IN "FOLK THEORIES" OF THE WORLD

One more element of word meaning must be discussed before leaving this topic, for in many ways our understanding of words is embedded in a web of beliefs that is much broader than either the theory of definitions or the theory of prototypes can describe. We seem to have well-developed ideas (sometimes called "folk theories") of why objects or properties are the way they are, and therefore how they could and could not change without becoming something altogether different (Carey, 1985; Keil, 1989; Locke, 1690; MacNamara 1982). Objects can change a good deal in their particulars, of course, and still be appropriate for the same labeling. For instance, lawnmowers that are now made out of steel and plastics might one day be constructed from the kinds of exotic metals that today are only used in spacecraft. They can still be legitimately called "lawnmowers" all the same. But some materials such as shaving cream or ice simply could never be considered for lawnmowers, because they could not support the essential function (something capable of cutting grass) of such a device. We never have to experience any of these proposed lawnmower changes to know which ones will be acceptable and which ones will not. In this sense, our knowledge of what things are constrains what they could ever be (for another example, see Figure 9.9).

> 1. *Alfred is an unmarried adult male, but he has been living with his girlfriend for the last twenty-three years. Their relationship is happy and stable. Is Alfred a bachelor?*
>
> 2. *Bernard is an unmarried adult male, and he does not have a partner. Bernard is a monk living in a monastery. Is Bernard a bachelor?*
>
> 3. *Charles is a married adult male, but he has not seen his wife for many years. Charles is earnestly dating, hoping to find a new partner. Is Charles a bachelor?*
>
> 4. *Donald is a married adult male, but he lives in a culture that encourages men to take two wives. Donald is earnestly dating, hoping to find a new partner. Is Donald a bachelor?*

**9.9 Word meanings are "theories"** *Your answers to the questions shown here—and with that, your understanding of "bachelor"— depends on a web of beliefs about who is marriageable and who is not. (After Fillmore, 1982)*

## THE MEANINGS OF SENTENCES

Sentences have meanings too, over and above the meanings of the words they contain. This is obvious from the fact that two sentences can be composed of all and only the same words and yet be meaningfully distinct. For example, "The giraffe bit the zebra"

*A grammar lesson at the Mad Hatter's tea party* **The meanings of English sentences change when the same words appear in different places, so grammatical patterns are of great importance for communication.**

> March Hare: "You should say what you mean."
> Alice: "I do—at least I mean what I say—that's the same thing, you know."
> Hatter: "Not the same thing a bit! Why, you might just as well say that 'I see what I eat' is the same thing as 'I eat what I see'!"
> March Hare: "You might just as well say that 'I like what I get' is the same thing as 'I get what I like.'"
> (From Lewis Carroll, Alice in Wonderland, 1971)

and "The zebra bit the giraffe" describe different events, a meaning difference of some importance, at least to the zebra and the giraffe.

The basic sentences we use introduce some topic (the subject of the sentence) and then make some comment, or offer some information, about that topic (the **predicate** of the sentence). Thus, when we say, "The giraffe bit the zebra," we introduce the giraffe as the topic, and then we propose or predicate of the giraffe that it bit the zebra. Accordingly, sentence meanings are often called **propositions**: to say that the giraffe bit the zebra is to propose of the giraffe that it bit the zebra.

In effect, a proposition describes a miniature drama in which the verb is the action and the nouns are the performers, each playing a different **semantic role**. Thus, in the sentence *The zebra bit the giraffe*, the zebra plays the role of doer or agent who causes or instigates the action, the giraffe is the done-to, and biting is the action itself. The job of a listener who wants to understand a sentence, then, is to determine which actors are portraying the various roles in the drama and what the plot (the action) is (Grimshaw, 1990; Healy & Miller, 1970). We now see how the syntactic structuring of the sentence links up to the semantic structure of who-did-what-to-whom. In the syntactic tree (see Figure 9.10), a different, fixed position is provided for each such role in a sentence (M. Baker, 1998; Fillmore, 1968; Grimshaw, 1990; Jackendoff, 2002). This allows us to decide who is the perpetrator and who is the victim of the biting act. To see how this system works, refer back to Figure 9.4, which shows the phrase structure of this sentence. We can "read" the semantic roles off of this tree by attending to its geometry. The doer of the action is the noun phrase that branches directly from the root sentence of the tree (a position known as "the subject of the sentence," namely, *the zebra*). The "done-to" is the noun phrase that branches off of the verb phrase in the tree, namely, *the giraffe*. So different noun phrases have different semantic roles, or functions, marked out by the syntax of the sentence.

Notice that the position of the words in this simple sentence of English is providing the semantic role information; indeed, word order is of central importance in this regard, in English and many other languages. However, there is another type of information, used in the English pronoun system, that can signal these roles regardless of serial position in the sentences. For instance, regardless of how the pronouns are serially positioned, the sentences *He had always admired her intelligence* and *Her intelligence is what he had always admired* mean the same thing. It is the particular form of a pronoun (*he* versus *him*, *she* versus *her*), rather than serial position, that assigns the semantic role. The second of these sentences is somewhat awkward or stilted in English, but still understandable. Many other languages use something analogous to our pronoun system as the primary means for signaling semantic roles, for all of the nouns as well as the pronouns. These are the so-called **case markers**, which usually occur as function morphemes, very often as suffixes at the ends of noun content morphemes. When such case markers occur regularly in a language to mark the semantic roles, the word order itself can be much more flexible than it is in English. In Finnish, for example, the words meaning "zebra" and "giraffe" change their serial order in "Seepra puri kirahvia" and "Kirahvia puri seepra," but in either order it is the giraffe (*kirahvia*) who needs the medical attention. It is the suffix *-a* (rather than *-ia*) that in both sentences identifies the zebra as the aggressor in this battle (Kaiser & Trueswell, 2002).

The sentence types within a language vary in their syntactic form in ways that derive from differences in their plots (verbs) and thus in the number and kinds of actors needed to depict the whole event. For acts of snoring, there will be just one actor (it only takes one to snore, as many of us know from sleepless nights in a snorer's company), so we hear sentences like *John snores*, but not *John snores Bill*. For biting, as we just saw, two actors—the doer and the done-to—are required. Thus, the syntax of *snore* and *bite* differs because of an aspect of their different meanings—how many actors each

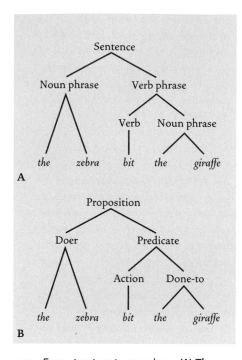

**9.10   From structure to meaning**   *(A) The structure of the sentence "The zebra bit the giraffe." (simplified); (B) The drama of who-did-what-to-whom as reconstructed by the listener from the structure in (A).*

requires to depict the event. We can see another such distinction for verbs like *give*, which describes the transfer of objects from one entity to another, thus requiring three semantic roles—one each for the giver, the given, and the getter (for example, "The child gives a bone to the dog"). Finally, some verbs such as *think* can express a relation between an entity and a whole proposition (rather than just a relation between two entities). We express this with a sentence inside a larger sentence (for example, "John thinks *Mary is a mongoose*"). In these ways, then, sentences are a reflection of the variety of ways in which people conceptualize events, scenes, and relations (Fisher, Gleitman, & Gleitman, 1991; L. R. Gleitman, 1990; Grimshaw, 1990; Jackendoff, 1972; Naigles & Kako, 1993; Levin, 1993; Willliams, 1994).

## COMPLEX SENTENCE MEANINGS

We just saw that in very simple sentences, the phrase structure straightforwardly reflects the compositional meaning of who-did-what-to-whom. But the sentences we encounter in everyday conversation are usually much more complicated than these examples. Many factors contribute to this complexity. Sometimes, we phrase our sentences in a fashion that allows us to emphasize aspects of the scene other than the doer ("It was THE GIRAFFE who got bitten by the zebra"). Sometimes we wish to question ("Who bit the giraffe?") or command ("Bite that giraffe!") rather than merely to comment on the passing scene. And often we wish to express our attitudes toward certain states of affairs ("I was DELIGHTED TO HEAR THAT the zebra bit the giraffe"), or to relate one proposition to another, and so will utter two or more of them in the same sentence ("The zebra that arrived from Kenya bit the giraffe" or "This is the dog that chased the cat that followed the rat that lived in the house that Jack built"). Added complexity of meaning is mirrored by corresponding complexities in the sentence structures themselves. Function morphemes now occur to guide the listener to the particular ways that the sentences are being combined (for example, the *who* and *that* which signal the boundaries between the propositions within a single sentence). The done-to may be mentioned before the doer (as in passive-voice sentences such as *The giraffe was bitten by the zebra*, but requiring the telltale markers *was, en,* and *by*); some words may be omitted, as the *you* in imperative sentences; and so forth. Indeed these complex sentences are harder to decipher and understand than the simpler ones. But even so, listeners usually manage to grasp the basic sentence drama of who-did-what-to-whom even though this scenario is hidden and disguised in the complex sentence.

## HOW WE UNDERSTAND

How then do we manage to understand each other? We describe here several factors that listeners use to home in on the real intents of speakers.

### THE FREQUENCY WITH WHICH THINGS HAPPEN

Very often listeners are able to assess the wild implausibility of one or another interpretation that is made available by the particular wording of a sentence. For example, no sane reader is really in doubt over the punishment meted out to the perpetrators as described in the headline "Drunk Gets Six Months in Violin Case." But in less extreme cases, the correct reading is not immediately obvious. Most of us have had the experience of being partway through a written paragraph or sentence and realizing that somewhere we went wrong; then our eyes whip back so that we can start afresh. For example, we may make a word-grouping error, as in reading a sentence that begins *The fat people eat . . .* The natural inclination is to take *the fat people* as the subject noun phrase and *eat* as the beginning of the verb phrase (Bever, 1970). But suppose the sentence continues:

*The fat people eat accumulates on their hips and thighs.*

Now one must go back and reread. (Notice that this sentence would have been much easier if, as is certainly allowed in English, the author had placed the function word *that* before the word *people*: *The fat that people eat accumulates on their hips and thighs*.) The partial misreading is termed a **garden path** (in honor of the cliché phrase). Because of the misleading content or structure at the beginning of the sentence, the reader is led toward one interpretation, but must then retrace her mental footsteps to find a grammatical and understandable alternative. Psycholinguists have their ways of detecting when people are experiencing a garden path during reading. One method is to use a device called an eye-tracker, which allows us to record the motion of the reader's eyes across the page of print. Slowdowns and visible regressions of these eye movements tell us where and when the reader has gone wrong and is restarting the reading of the passage (Rayner, Carlson, & Frazier, 1983). Using this kind of technique, one group of investigators looked at the effects of plausibility on readers' expectations of the structure they were encountering. Suppose that the first three words of a test sentence are

*The detectives examined . . .*

Participants in experiments who read these words quickly commit to assuming that *The detectives* is the subject and that *examined* is the main verb—but in this case they are merrily wandering down the garden path. They are expecting the sentence to end with a noun phrase like *the evidence*. So when they dart their eyes forward and instead discover

*. . . by the reporter . . .*

they are flummoxed. They pause and then reread the sentence. To make sense of the phrase *by the reporter*, they must revise their first guess that *examined* is the main verb. Technically speaking, *examined* in this sentence is an instance of the so-called passive participle, and *revealed* is the real main verb of the sentence, as they discover when they read further:

*. . . revealed the truth about the robbery.*

*Interpreting two complex sentences* **(A) With the sentence** The detectives examined by the reporter revealed the truth about the robbery: *we see that the reporter is examining (interviewing) the detectives to find out about the crime.* **(B) With the sentence** The evidence examined by the reporter revealed the truth about the robbery: *here we see the reporter himself examines the tell-tale evidence (ladder, footsteps, drops of blood) to find out about the crime.*

A

B

The noticeable pause at *by the reporter* showed that participants found out that they had been led down the garden path and now had to rethink what they were reading. Of course, the experimenters could have made these readers' life easier by putting the function morphemes *who were* between *detectives* and *examined*. Then there would have been no garden path experience and the word *by* would have come as no surprise to the readers. But the devilish motive of the experimenters in designing these test sentences was to find out what makes sentences hard, not to make the readers' life easier.

What was it exactly that led the participants off course with this sentence? Was the difficulty just that passive sentences are less frequent, in general, than active sentences? To find out, the experimenters also presented sentences that began

*The evidence examined . . .*

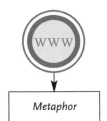

Metaphor

Now the participants experienced little or no difficulty, and read blithely on as the sentence ended as it had before (*. . . by the reporter revealed the truth about the robbery*). Why? Again the sentence requires the reader to interpret *examined* as a passive participle, but in this case the readers experienced no difficulty in doing so (and did not slow down or reread after the word *by*). So the cause of the delay for the prior sentence (*The detective examined. . . .*) cannot just be that passive participles are hard in general. The answer has to do with the plausible semantic relation among the words. The noun *detectives* is a "good subject" of verbs like *examined* because, as we all know, detectives do examine things—such as ladders leaning against second-story windows, love letters hidden in secret drawers, spots of blood on the snow, and documents. But evidence is not capable of examining anything, while it is quite capable of being examined. *Evidence* is a good object of examination but a poor subject of examination. Therefore, the participant who has finished reading *The evidence examined . . .* is not a bit surprised that the next word that comes up is *by*. This is the function morpheme that signals that a passive participle is on its way—just what the reader expected given the meanings of the first three words of the sentence. Evidently, the process of understanding makes use of word meanings and sentence structuring as mutual guides. We use the meaning of each word (*detectives* versus *evidence*) to guide us toward the intended structure, and we use the expected structure (active versus passive) to guess at the intended meanings of the words (MacDonald, Perlmutter, & Seidenberg, 1994; Trueswell, Tanenhaus, & Garnsey, 1994).

## WHAT IS HAPPENING RIGHT NOW?

A striking fact about humans and their language use is that they can think and talk about the future, the past, and the altogether imaginary. We devour books on antebellum societies that are now gone with the wind, and tales that speak of a Darth Vader galaxy that we hope we will never experience. But we should not overdo this revelation about the partial independence of language use from the events of the moment. Much of our conversation is focused on more immediate concerns, and in these cases the listener can often see what we are referring to and can witness the actions we are describing. When people talk of present things and events, the incoming linguistic information (the sentence as it is unfolding in time) affects how we fix our attention on the visual world. For example, in one experiment, on viewing the array of four objects pictured in Figure 9.11, participants listening to a sentence like "Now I want you to eat some cake" turn their eyes toward the cake as soon as they hear the verb *eat* (Altmann & Kamide, 1999). After all, it is unlikely that the experimenter will be requesting the participants to ingest the toy train. This is an effect that words in a sentence can have in focusing our attention on only certain aspects of the world in view.

**9.11** *Understanding a sentence in its situational context* **As soon as the subject hears "Now I want you to eat . . ." his eyes turn toward the only edible thing in sight: the cake.**

"Put the frog <u>on the napkin</u> in the box."

A                                    B

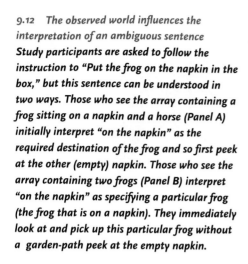

**9.12** *The observed world influences the interpretation of an ambiguous sentence* **Study participants are asked to follow the instruction to "Put the frog on the napkin in the box," but this sentence can be understood in two ways. Those who see the array containing a frog sitting on a napkin and a horse (Panel A) initially interpret "on the napkin" as the required destination of the frog and so first peek at the other (empty) napkin. Those who see the array containing two frogs (Panel B) interpret "on the napkin" as specifying a particular frog (the frog that is on a napkin). They immediately look at and pick up this particular frog without a garden-path peek at the empty napkin.**

Just as powerful are the reverse phenomena: effects of the visually observed world on how we interpret a sentence. This effect is often demonstrated by showing how people can avoid being led down the garden path by a sentence if they look sensibly at the world (Altmann & Steedman, 1988; Crain & Steedman, 1985). Consider the array of toy objects in Figure 9.12A. These include a little frog sitting on a napkin and another napkin that does not have a toy on it. When study participants look at such scenes and hear the instruction "Put the frog on the napkin into the box," most of them experience a garden path, thinking at first that "on the napkin" is where a frog should be put, and only later realizing that this phrase tells them about the frog itself, with the real destination being the box. This reaction shows up in the participants' eye movements: on hearing "napkin," participants look to the empty napkin, as if this was the destination of the "put" instruction, but then they look around in a confused manner when they hear "into the box." Participants rapidly recover from this confusion, as we know from the fact that they go on to execute the instruction correctly, picking up the frog and putting it in the box.

But now consider the array of objects in Figure 9.12B. It differs from Figure 9.12A because now there are two frogs, only one of which is on a napkin. This has a noticeable effect on subjects' eye movements. Now, on hearing the same instruction, most of them look to the frog on the napkin when they hear "napkin," and then show no signs of confusion on hearing "into the box." What caused the difference in reaction? In the array of 9.12A, with only one frog, a listener does not expect the speaker to specify it further by saying "the green frog" or "the frog to the left" or "the frog on the napkin," for there would be no communicative point in doing so. Though such descriptions are true of that particular frog, there is no need to say that much—it is entirely obvious and therefore is superfluous to mention. So the idea, when looking at Figure 9.13A, that the speaker is further specifying an already unique frog never crosses the listeners' minds, until they hear that another destination is mentioned. By saying "the frog," enough has been said to carry out the command (Grice, 1975). But when looking at the array in Figure 9.13B, the listener could not uniquely carry out the experimenter's instruction without further specification of exactly which frog was intended. Therefore, the listener expected to be verbally informed that it was "the frog on the napkin" (or "the frog on the plate"), and acted as though that was how the instruction was to be interpreted (Tanenhaus, Spivey-Knowlton, Eberhard, & Sedivy, 1996; Trueswell, Sekerina, Hill, & Logrip, 1999).

There is every reason to believe that these laboratory effects are closely analogous to what happens in the real world of talking and listening. When we hear, "These missionaries are ready to eat" or "Smoking volcanoes can be dangerous," it is the extralinguistic context that saves us from continual confusions and misunderstandings.

## CONVERSATIONAL INFERENCE: FILLING IN THE BLANKS

The actual speech acts that pass between people are merely hints about the thoughts that are being conveyed. Talking would take just about forever if speakers literally had to say all, only, and exactly what they meant. Rather, the communicating pair takes the utterance and its context as the basis for making a series of complicated inferences about the meaning and intent of the conversation, and therefore the relevance of what is said. Let us look at a piece of ordinary conversation that requires the listener to understand when part of the logic behind the speaker's remark is left unsaid:

> A: Do you own a Cadillac?
> B: I wouldn't own *any* American car.

It would be an uncooperative listener indeed (or a fool) who then responds:

> A: I didn't ask you about American cars. Do you own a Cadillac?

A normal speaker A would fill in the blanks with no trouble at all; that is, she would supply some intervening context of plausible inferences that would explain how her query might sensibly have prompted speaker B's retort. Speaker A's implicit and just about automatic interpretation might go something like this: Speaker B must have been thinking as follows: Speaker A must know that a Cadillac is an American car. I will tell her that I do not drive a Cadillac in a way that will respond to her question with a *no* but will simultaneously tell her something else: that I dislike all American cars. Such leaps from a speaker's utterance to a listener's interpretation are commonplace. Listeners do not usually wait for everything to be said explicitly. On the contrary, they often supply a chain of inferred causes and effects that sometimes were not intended to be discovered (or weren't even meant) by the speaker. Here is an example of a hypothetical lovers' quarrel:

> SHE: I'm leaving you.
> HE: Who is he?

As we can see, the powerful reasoning abilities of communicating pairs are useful for disentangling the enormous ambiguity of everyday speech and the unspoken thoughts that intervene between the words (H. H. Clark, 1978; Levinson, 1983; Sperber & Wilson, 1986).

## HOW COMPREHENSION WORKS

It appears from our discussion that the process of language comprehension is marvelously complex, influenced by syntax, semantics, the extralinguistic context, and inferential activity, all guided by a spirit of communicative cooperation. But how are all these factors integrated? One hypothesis is that the listener first uses the syntax of a sentence to uncover its structure; this leads to an initial hypothesis about the sentence, which is then checked against other sources of information (Frasier & Fodor, 1978). The alternative hypothesis is that all of these sources of information interact from the very start, with the listener using every clue "incrementally" and "immediately" as soon as the words become available during the saying of a sentence. This issue has been a matter of considerable debate, but evidence is accumulating to support the position that these factors interact from the start (Altmann & Steedman, 1988; Carlson & Tanenhaus, 1988; Carpenter, Miyake, & Just, 1995; MacDonald, Pearlmutter, & Seidenberg, 1994; Marslen-Wilson, 1975; Stowe, 1987; Trueswell & Tanenhaus, 1994). No matter how this debate is resolved, it is clear that several kinds of cues work together to ensure that the listener is not drowned in confusion by the pervasive ambiguity of word, phrase, and sentence structure.

# THE GROWTH OF LANGUAGE IN THE CHILD

Our survey of language has revealed it to be of such startling complexity that one might doubt whether mere children could acquire it. But as we will see now, not only can they acquire language, but they are vastly better at doing so than even the wisest and most knowledgeable adults. From the very first moments after birth, infant ears and minds are open to detect the sounds of language and to organize them into words. They recognize many words before they can even walk. The rate of word learning rapidly accelerates to about three a day in toddlers, to five or eight or so a day in the preschool years, and to ten to fifteen words a day throughout childhood and early adolescence (Carey, 1978; P. Bloom, 2000). The upshot is a vocabulary of about 10,000 words by age five and 75,000 to 100,000 by adulthood. Late in the second year of life, toddlers start to put the words together into little sentences—"Throw ball!" "No mommy eat!"—and soon are eagerly acquiring the rules of grammar that, in later school life, we all came to dread. In sum, whatever their circumstances—intelligent or dull, otherwise motivated or apathetic, encouraged by their parents or ignored, exposed to Hindi or to English—children learn the language of their environment in a few short years, with virtuoso syntax a common occurrence by age four to five. An example of this proficiency—and of how well the child can shape language to achieve his or her social and material goals—is a telephone query from a five-year-old boy (of course, to his doting grandmother): "Remember that toy that you told me on the phone last night that you would buy me?" How is this rapid, ornate learning possible?

*Language is learned in ordinary social interactions*

## THE SOCIAL ORIGINS OF LANGUAGE LEARNING

Prelinguistic children have nonverbal ways of making contact with the minds, emotions, and social behaviors of others. Neonates' heart rate quickens or slows according to whether they hear a human speaking in a tone that is excited or soothing, or disapproving versus approving. Babies do not have to learn these emotive qualities of language any more than a puppy has to learn by experience which barks or growls from adult dogs are playful and which are threatening. This was shown by recording German mothers talking to their infants and then replaying the audiotape to babies who had heard only English or French up until then. The recording was presented while the baby was playing with a novel toy. When infants hear the approving German sentence, they go right on playing; but on hearing the disapproving tone, though in a totally unfamiliar language, they drop the toy like a hot potato (Fernald, 1993). Thus, language appears to be social and interpersonal in its very origins. In order to learn to speak and understand, the infant begins with an implicit understanding that "the other" is a fellow human being who lives in the same, mutually perceived world (Bates, 1976; Mandler, 2000).

Particularly interesting in this regard are findings about word learning. Suppose that a child is shown a fascinating new toy and allowed to explore it. Suppose at this very moment the child's mother says excitedly, "That's a blicket! Wow, a blicket!" Will the child by a process of automatic association now think that the name for this new toy is "blicket"? The answer is no. First, the child appears to seek evidence that the speaker was attending to the toy too. One investigator put mothers and their eighteen-month-old children in exactly this situation. When the children heard the mother saying, "That's a blicket!," they immediately turned and glanced into the mother's eyes (just as an adult would). Following the direction of the mother's gaze, these infants evidently set out to determine if the mother herself was looking at the toy in the child's hands (and thus, probably, referring to it and not something else when she said "blicket"). If the mother was looking at this toy, then, when tested later on, the children showed that they had learned the "blicket" label for the new toy. But if the mother had been looking elsewhere—say, into a bucket whose contents were not visible to the child—the children did not assign this new word as the toy's name. In short, even children under two years old use social context as a critical guide in language learning. They do not form word-to-meaning associations if the social context of language use does not guide them to do so (Baldwin, 1991; see also Meltzoff, 1995).

Armed with this social understanding, babies find their way into the world of linguistic communication. Even as they learn to build castles out of alphabet blocks and to stack up colorful rings on a stake, so they search out and organize the building blocks of the human language that they hear spoken around them and to them.

## DISCOVERING THE BUILDING BLOCKS OF LANGUAGE

Recent neuroscientific findings show that infants are ready for language learning at birth or almost immediately thereafter (Dehaene-Lambertz, Dehaene, & Hertz-Pannier, 2002; Mehler et al., 1988). One group of investigators recorded changes in the blood flow in two-day-old babies' brains in the presence of linguistic stimulation. Half of the time the babies were hearing recordings of normal human speech, and the other half of the time they were hearing that speech played backward. Blood flow in the babies' left hemisphere increased for the normal speech but not for the backward speech (Peña, Kovacic, Dehaene-Lambertz, & Mehler, in press). Because the left hemisphere of the brain is the major site for linguistic activity in humans, this evidence suggests that the special responsiveness to language-like signals is already happening close to the moment of birth.

### THE RHYTHMIC FOUNDATIONS OF LANGUAGE LEARNING

Recall that languages vary in their significant sounds (phonemes and syllables), tones, rhythms, and melodies, enough so that most of us can guess very well whether a speaker is uttering Japanese or German or French speech even if we do not understand a word of any of these languages. The amazing fact is that newborn infants can do almost as well. Babies' responsiveness can be measured by an ingenious method which takes advantage of the fact that, while newborns can do very few things voluntarily, one of their earliest talents—and pleasures—is sucking at a nipple. In one study, a nonnutritive nipple (or "pacifier") was connected to a recording device such that every time the baby sucked, a bit of French speech was heard coming from a nearby loudspeaker. The four-day-old French babies rapidly discovered that they had the power to elicit this speech just by sucking, and they sucked faster and faster to hear more of it. After a few minutes, however, they apparently got bored (or habituated to the stimulus—see Chapter 4), and therefore the sucking rate decreased. Now the experimenter switched the speech coming from the microphone from French to English. Did the infant notice? The answer is yes. When the switch was made, the infants' interest was reawakened, and they began sucking faster and faster again (they dishabituated). To perfect the experimental proof, the same recordings were flown to the United States, and the experiment was repeated with four-day-old American babies, with the same result. American newborns also can and do discriminate between English and French speech.

*Detecting phonetic distinctions* **This two-and-a-half year-old baby's head is covered with a geodesic sensor net, which picks up signals from the brain. The baby, seated in a carrier on the mother's lap, faces a loudspeaker emitting meaningless syllables, and watches a video of moving colored objects. When repeated spoken syllables were changed to new, different ones, there were significant changes in the event-related potential signals (ERP's), showing that the baby had noticed the change.**

Indeed by two months old, not only do infants make these discriminations, now they become patriotic and listen longer when their own native language is being spoken (Mehler et al., 1988; Nazzi, Bertoncini, & Mehler, 1998; see also Fernald, 1985). What is it about the native language that is attracting these infants? It cannot be the meanings of words, because they as yet do not know any word meanings. Evidently the first feature that babies are picking up about their native tongue has to do with its particular melody, specifically, the characteristic rhythms of speech in that language. Remarkably then, only a few days past birth we see infants already hard at work, preparing the ground for language learning by selectively listening for the sweet music of the mother tongue (Morgan, 1996; Peña, Bonatti, Nespor, & Mehler, 2002; Ramus, Nespor, & Mehler, 1999).

By the age of one or two months, still long before infants show any sign of understanding anything said to them, they become keenly sensitive to distinctions between phonemes. This was shown in habituation experiments like the ones we just discussed. After the baby is habituated to, say, the sound "ba," as measured by decreasing sucking rate, the sound "pa" is substituted. Will the baby notice this difference despite the fact that "pa" is acoustically quite close to "ba"? The answer is yes (see Figure 9.13) (Eimas, Siqueland, Jusczyk, & Vigorito, 1971).

Initially, infants respond to just about all sound distinctions made in any language, and so Japanese babies can detect the distinction between "la" versus "ra" as easily as American babies, despite the fact that this contrast is not phonemic in Japanese (and not readily discerned by adult Japanese speakers). However, these perceptual abilities erode if they are not exercised, and so infants lose the ability to make distinctions that are not used in their language community. Thus, Japanese infants gradually stop distinguishing between "la" and "ra." Symmetrically, American infants soon cease distinguishing between two different *k* sounds that are perceptually distinct to Arabic speakers (see Figure 9.13; Jusczyk, Friederici, Wessels, Svenkerud, & Jusczyk, 1993; Werker, 1991, 1995; see also Kuhl, Williams, Lacerda, Stevens, & Lindblom, 1992). How quickly does this erosion of the ability to notice foreign sound contrasts take place? By the age of twelve months, just as true speech begins in the average child, sensitivity to foreign contrasts has diminished significantly (Werker & Tees, 1984). In essence, then, every normal baby is born with the capacity and inclination to notice all sound contrasts made in any human language. After all, this had better be the case, as the baby does not arrive on earth with a passport telling him which language he is going to have to acquire. But as the baby approaches the first birthday—just the time when word learning begins in full force—the baby recalibrates so as to listen specifically for the particulars of the language to which he is being exposed.

## BUILDING THE MORPHEME AND WORD UNITS FROM THE SEPARATE SOUNDS AND SYLLABLES

To learn a language, infants must do more than detect its rhythms and phonemes and syllables. They must find the boundaries of morphemes and words. Often it is a challenge to do so, as we see from errors that children sometimes make. For instance, English toddlers often reach their arms up to their mothers and fathers, plaintively crying out, "Ca-ree-oo." Of course, the children have learned to say this from hearing caregivers ask them, "Do you want me to carry you?," but they mean "Carry me." The evidence is that they are not mixed up as to the words *you* and *me,* nor do they have an urge to lift and transport their parent. Rather they assume that there is a three-syllable word that means "pick me up" and that is pronounced *carreeoo.* These kinds of errors often persist unnoticed for years. For instance, one seven-year-old, carefully writing her first story about a teacher, spelled out "Class be smissed!," showing that she had falsely thought there was a word boundary within the word *dismissed* (L. R. Gleitman, Gleit-

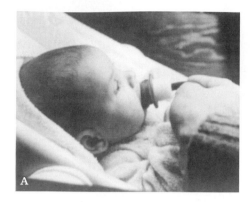

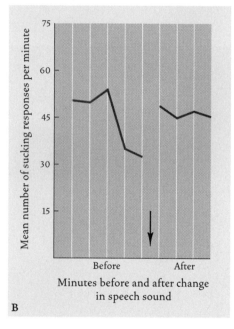

**9.13**  *Sucking rate and speech perception in the infant*  *(A) An infant sucks to hear "ba" or "ga." (Photograph courtesy of Philip Morse, Boston University) (B) The graph shows the sucking rate of four-month-olds to "ba" or "ga." The infants soon become habituated, and the sucking rate drops. When a new stimulus is substituted ("ga" for "ba" and "ba" for "ga"), the infant dishabituates and sucks quickly once again. Similar results have been obtained for one-month-olds. The point of the shift is indicated by the arrow. (From Eimas et al., 1971)*

man, & Shipley, 1972). As we noted earlier, the problem is that phonemes and syllables run right into each other and even overlap in speech. Unlike the case for writing, where words are written with gaps (white spaces) demarcating their borders, words are not uttered with gaps of silence between them. The right question, then, is not, How come learners make some mistakes in finding word boundaries? but rather, How come they get these right most of the time? The answer appears to be that infants keep a mental record of which syllables occur right next to each other with unusual frequency. For instance, the syllables *rab* and *it* often occur next to each other; this is because together they form the word *rabbit*. But *stub* followed by *it* is much much rarer, just because there does not happen to be such a word in English as *stubbit*. Of course on the rarest of occasions, one just might hear the syllable *stub* followed by the syllable *it* (as in the weird interchange: "Why do you always keep your big toe bandaged?" "Because otherwise I might *stub it*").

Beginning well before infants understand any meaningful words at all, they seem to be sensitive to these frequencies, busily recording cases of unusually frequent syllable sequences and using this information to decide which such sequences are actual words of the language. This process has been demonstrated experimentally. In one study, eight-month-old infants heard a two-minute tape recording that sounded something like "bidakupadotigolabubidaku." These syllables were spoken in a monotonous tone, with no difference in stress from one syllable to the next and no pauses in between any of the syllables. But there was a pattern. The experimenters had decided in advance to designate the sequence "bidaku" as a word. Therefore, they arranged the sequences so that if the infant heard "bida," then "ku" was sure to follow (just as, in ordinary circumstances, hearing "stuh" is a good predictor that one is about to hear "mik"). For other syllables and syllable pairs, there was no such pattern of regular sequencing. For instance, "daku" (the end of the nonsense word *bidaku*) would sometimes be followed by "go" (that is, "dakugo"), sometimes by "pa," and so on. Remarkably, the babies detected this pattern. In a subsequent test, the babies showed no evidence of surprise if they heard the string "bidakubidakubidaku." From the babies' point of view, these were simply repetitions of a word they already knew. However, the babies did show surprise if they were presented with the string "dakupadakupadakupa." This was not a "word" they had heard before, although of course they had heard each of its syllables many times. Thus, the babies had learned the vocabulary of this made-up language. They had detected the statistical pattern of which syllables followed which, despite their rather brief, entirely passive exposure to these sounds and despite the absence of any supporting cues such as pauses or shifts in intonation (Aslin, Saffran, & Newport, 1998; Marcus, Vijayan, Bandi Rao, & Vishton, 1999; Saffran, Aslin, and Newport, 1996). Other studies varying such properties as stress and tone showed that babies can respond to these cues as well.

## THE GROWTH OF WORD MEANING

Children begin to understand a few words that their caregivers say during the first year of life. Actual talking begins sometime between the ages of about ten and twenty months. Almost invariably, children's first utterances are one word long. Some first words refer to simple interactions with adults, such as *hi* and *peekaboo*. Others are names, such as *Mama* and *Fido*. Most of the rest are simple nouns, such as *duck* and *spoon*, with a smattering of action verbs such as *give* and *push*. And as every parent soon discovers, one of the earliest words learned is a resounding *No!* (Caselli, Bates, Casadio, & Fenson, 1995; Gentner & Boroditsky, 2001; Huttenlocher, Smiley, & Charney, 1983). Missing almost altogether in novice English speech are the function words and suffixes, such as *the*, *and*, and *-ed*. These are among the most frequent items the child hears, but even so they are rarely uttered by beginners. This may be in part because their grammatical functions have not yet become relevant in the child's rudimentary language system. But another factor is that these function words as pronounced in English are difficult to perceive, since they are usually not stressed in parental speech and are uttered in a relatively low pitch (Cutler, 1994; Gerken, 1996; L. R. Gleitman, Gleitman, Landau, & Wanner, 1988; Kelly & Martin, 1994).

How do children discover the meanings of words? The obvious answer appears to be that, once they have noticed a recurrent sound pattern—for example, the pattern "rabbit"—they now look around the world to see which object or event is characteristically in view when that pattern of sound is heard. Aha! Rabbit! (Locke, 1690; for modern discussions, see Grimshaw, 1981; Pinker, 1984). But is such a procedure of matching up words to their extralinguistic circumstances really as easy as that? Although matching words to the world must ultimately be the way children search out the meanings, there are many reasons to suppose that the child's path to word learning is strewn with problems. For instance, every time the child views a rabbit, she views something furry, something alive, something about the size of a breadbox, rabbit ears, the whole sentence-like idea of "There goes a rabbit!," and (if you want to stretch your imagination), a bunch of undetached rabbit parts. Children's imaginations are very good indeed. So how come none of them comes to think that the sound "rabbit" refers, not to rabbits, but rather to ears, to furriness, or to undetached rabbit parts (Anthony, 2000; Chomsky, 1959; L. R. Gleitman, 1990; Quine, 1960; see Figure 9.14)?

By repeated observations one would expect children to get much of this confusion of words and things all sorted out. For instance, if the child is lucky, she may one day hear her father say, "rabbit!" while she is viewing an earless rabbit or a rabbit whose ears are hidden among the cabbages. This might get the word *rabbit* sorted out from the word *ear*. But even so, one might expect that, because of these ambiguities in the world, young children would often be confused for some time about what a word means. Yet, in fact, children are impressively accurate in their understanding of word meaning (P. Bloom, 2000), and the errors that do occur are short-lived. By the time the child has a one-hundred-word vocabulary, he is almost always correct in using words to refer to things and events in much the way that adults do. In addition, the sheer pace of vocabulary learning (as we mentioned, about ten words a day) suggests that the children are not often fumbling around with false guesses. Several investigators believe that these phenomenal feats of learning are instances of children's amazing ability to take in, organize, and store information of just about any kind. They point to the fact that children remember newly introduced facts ("My uncle gave me this toy") as well as they remember newly introduced words ("This toy is called a fogril"; P. Bloom, 2000; Markson & Bloom, 1997). However, other investigators believe that the learning of words is

**9.14  Symmetrical problems for child learners and investigators of child language**  *(A) The child's helpful mother points out a rabbit, saying, "rabbit." The child sees a rabbit but also sees an animal, an ear, and the ground beneath the rabbit. Which one does the mother mean by the word rabbit? (B) The mother's (and the investigator's) problem in understanding young children's speech is much the same. The child may say "rabbit" when she observes a rabbit, but for all the mother knows the child may have made an error in learning and thus may mean something different by this word.*

special, a feature of behavior that is tied to language itself. They point to the fact that children generalize the use of new words, such as *fogril*, to new instances—for instance, to other toys that look like or function like the first one they were shown, whereas they do not generalize from the factual information in the same way (Booth & Waxman, 2002).

## PERCEPTUAL AND CONCEPTUAL PROPERTIES OF CHILD LANGUAGE

The very first examples of language use (at roughly the age of ten months) seem to involve direct labeling of objects in current view without the inclination or ability to talk about things and events that are absent from view (L. Bloom, 1993). At about the ages of twelve to sixteen months, infants begin to search for an absent object whose name is mentioned (Huttenlocher, 1974). The ability to use words in the absence of their referents is firmly in place at about eighteen months (Tomasello, Strosberg, & Akhtar, 1996). One group of investigators has examined this issue by following twenty-four-month-old children's gaze when they listen to spoken language, for example, "Where's the doggie?" There are three conditions in this experiment. In the first condition, the child is actually looking at a picture of a dog on a screen over to the left when he or she hears the question. In the second condition, the child is looking at another picture (say, of a cat) to her right, but (because there were opportunities to look from side to side in advance) the child knows that the dog picture can be viewed if she shifts her eyes leftward. In the third condition, there is no dog picture—rather, a picture of a cat to the right and, say, one of a doll to the left. If the child was already looking at a picture of a dog (the first condition), naturally enough, her eyes do not shift in response to this question. In the second condition, she will rapidly shift her gaze toward the dog picture. But the big question is what the child will do in the total absence of dogs or dog pictures. If she really can think about absent objects, she ought to go right on searching to make sense of the utterance "Where is the doggie?" when a dog is not anywhere in sight. And this is precisely what happens. Apparently even the smallest toddlers can understand language "decontextualized"—that is, divorced from the immediate evidence of the senses (Swingley & Fernald, 2002). We next ask how the child learns the word meanings in the first place.

*Whole Objects at the Basic Level*  Word learning is heavily influenced by the ways the child is disposed to think about and categorize objects and events in the world (Rosch, 1973a; Fodor, 1983; Keil, 1989). This is reflected, for example, in the fact that young children acquire the basic-level words for whole objects (*dog*) before learning the superordinates (*animal*) or subordinates (*Chihuahua*) (Rosch, 1978). One might think this happens just because the basic-level words are used most frequently to children. But differential frequency does not seem to be the whole explanation. In some homes, the words *Spot* or *Rex* (specific names) are used much more often than *dog* (a basic level term) for obvious reasons. And it is true that in this case the young learner will use the word *Spot* before she learns to utter *dog*. But she first learns it as a basic-level term all the same. This is shown by the fact that she will utter *Spot* to refer to the neighbor's dog as well as her own. She overgeneralizes *Spot* just enough to convert it from a specific name to the basic level of categorization, evidently, the most natural level for carving up experience (Mervis & Crisafi, 1978; Shipley, Kuhn, & Madden, 1983). Evidence comes from experimental attempts to teach new words to children. The method is to point to a new object and label it with a new (nonsense) word. Thus, the experimenter might point toward an object and say, "That is a biff." To what new objects will the child apply this new label? He generally will not use *biff* to describe other objects that happen to be made of the same material, size, or color. Instead, he uses *biff* to describe objects having the same shape as the entire original (Landau, Smith, & Jones, 1988; Soja, Carey, & Spelke,

1991). Apparently, then, learners naturally understand this new term as a label for the entire object (Markman, 1989; Markman & Hutchinson, 1984).

*All the Words Have Different Meanings*   In many contexts, children act as if they believe that no word can have a synonym. Said differently, they seem to assume that any one concept can have only one word that refers to it (E. V. Clark, 1987; Hirsh-Pasek & Golinkoff, 1996). Evidence again comes from experiments on new-word learning. This time, the investigators showed some preschoolers familiar objects, ones that the children already had a word for, such as a pewter cup. Other children were shown unfamiliar objects, such as pewter ice tongs. In both cases the investigator said, "This is my blicket." Thereafter the children were shown numerous new objects (some cups, some tongs, and some other things) made of various substances (red enamel cups and tongs, pewter cups and tongs, and so on). The investigator asked, "Show me more blickets." Children who had been shown the tongs now picked out all the tongs. But children who had been shown the cup now picked out all the pewter things. What accounts for the difference? We have already seen that children have an initial bias toward interpreting words as labels for whole objects; this should lead them to interpret *blicket* (a label they have not heard before) as another word for the cup. But the whole-object tendency is overruled in this setting. The children already know the word *cup* and so, given their bias against synonyms, they conclude that *blicket* must refer to something else—in this case, a specific property of the original cup, the substance (pewter) that it is made of (Markman, 1994; Markman & Wachtel, 1988).

*The Conceptual Framework of Word Meaning: Folk Theories of the Very Young Child*   Earlier we discussed the idea that word meanings are constrained by implicit "folk theories" of what makes things the way they are and so how they can and cannot change. Even children as young as three and four years seem to have acquired this "essentialist" view of concepts and, therefore, of the meanings of words. In one experiment documenting this point, preschool children were asked whether it would be possible to turn a toaster into a coffeepot. The children thought about this for a while, then said it would be possible, provided that one could widen the holes in the top of the toaster, somehow seal the bottom (so the coffee would not leak out), and so on. Things were different, though, when the children were asked whether one could, with suitable adjustments, turn a skunk into a raccoon. They understood that one could dye the skunk's fur, and teach it to climb trees and, in general, to behave in a raccoon-like fashion. Even so, the children steadfastly denied that by such adjustments one would have created a raccoon. A skunk who looks, sounds, and acts just like a raccoon might be a peculiar skunk, but it is a skunk nonetheless. According to these children, to be a racoon one must be "made out of raccoon stuff" and, in particular, have raccoons for one's mommy and daddy (Keil, 1986). Similarly, young children cannot be persuaded that statues of people are "real" because, as they insist, "the statue doesn't have real feet" and isn't "made out of people stuff" (Massey & Gelman, 1988; see also Gopnik & Meltzoff, 1997; Gelman & Lucariello, 2002; Gelman & Wellman, 1991; Keil, 1989; Rattermann & Gentner, 1998).

*Using Words and Sentences to Learn More Words*   Children also use the structure of the language as a way of guiding their word learning (P. Bloom, 1996; Brown, 1957; L. R. Gleitman, 1990; L. R. Gleitman & H. Gleitman, 1997; Hall et al., 2000; Landau & Gleitman, 1985; Landau & Stecker, 1990). In one study, three- and four-year-olds were shown a picture in which a pair of hands was performing a kneading sort of motion with a mass of red confetti-like material that was overflowing a low, striped container (Figure 9.15). Some of the children were asked, "In this picture, can you show me sebbing?" The children responded by making the same kneading motions with their hands. Other children were asked, "In this picture, can you show me a seb?"

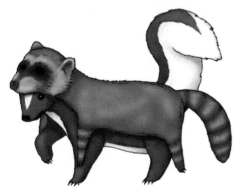

*Can a skunk turn into a raccoon?*

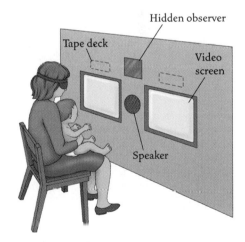

9.15 *Word classes and word meanings*
*When asked "In this picture can you see any*
*sebbing?" (verb), children pointed to the*
*hands; when asked "Can you see a seb?" they*
*pointed to the bowl; and when asked "Can you*
*see any seb?" they pointed to the confetti.*
*(Adapted from Bown, 1957)*

In response, the children pointed to the container. Still other children were asked, "Can you show me some seb?" These children pointed to the confetti (R. Brown, 1957). The evidence of word class (for example, *seb* + *ing* indicates that *seb* is a verb) for word meaning (verbs usually describe actions) influenced their understanding of what the new word referred to in the picture.

It seems then that children's learning proceeds in two directions at once. On the one hand, they use their growing knowledge of word classes within the language to guide their discovery of what a particular new word means. It is almost as if the child were saying to herself, "Because this new word was just used as a noun, it probably describes a thing." And symmetrically, they use their knowledge of individual words to predict how those words can be used: "Because this Woodstock toy is now an instrument for hitting me on the head, I can use it as a verb and tell my friend to 'Stop woodstocking me or go home!' "; (P. Bloom, 2000; E. V. Clark, Gelman, & Lane, 1985; Pinker, 1984). Using both kinds of evidence, children efficiently find their way into knowledge of tens of thousands of words and the ways these words can be used in sentences (Bowerman, 1982; Gillette, Gleitman, Gleitman, & Lederer, 1999; L. R. Gleitman, 1990).

One might think that the ability to take word classification (that is, whether a word is a noun or verb or adjective) into account in learning its meaning would be a process that begins quite late, with rather sophisticated children of three and four years old. But the rudiments of word-class sensitivity have been shown for children under two (Katz, Baker, & MacNamara, 1974). A perhaps even more surprising phenomenon is infants' sensitivity to how function words are used in English, even when these words are conspicuously absent from the children's own speech. These quite abstract items such as *of, ing, by, been,* and so forth hardly seem like child's play, suggesting that any child who is not a budding Noam Chomsky or Noah Webster would ignore them altogether. Yet the fact is that toddlers as young as fifteen months have been shown to be sensitive not only to the requirement for function words in a sentence (Gerken, Landau, & Remez, 1990; Shipley, Smith, & Gleitman, 1967; Slobin, 1982), but also to which function morphemes must go together in a sentence. This holds even when these dependencies operate at a distance. Fifteen-month-olds recognize, for example, that the word *is* requires that *ing* be added after the verb; for example, that *John is baking* is normal, but that *John can baking* is odd or "wrong." This is despite the fact that most children of this age are incapable of uttering even such foreshortened versions as *John baking* or *Mommy singing.* By eighteen months, the infants can recognize the dependency between *is* and *ing* even if the distance between them is increased, as in *John is quietly baking* versus the unacceptable *John can quietly baking* (Santelman & Jusczyk, 1998).

Perhaps most remarkably of all, syntax, and the way it links up with meaning, are understood in a rudimentary way by children far in advance of their being able to produce whole sentences. One experiment documenting this fact involved children aged about seventeen months. The children sat on their mothers' laps and watched two video screens, one to their left and one to their right (Figure 9.16), each screen showing a different event. On the screen to the left, Big Bird is tickling Cookie Monster, and on

9.16 *Set-up for the selective looking*
*experiment* *The child sits on the mother's lap*
*and listens to a taped sentence, while two video*
*screens show two cartoon characters performing*
*different actions. A hidden observer notes which*
*screen the child is looking at. The mother wears*
*a visor that covers her eyes to make sure she*
*does not see which screen shows which action*
*and thereby give inadvertent clues to the child.*
*(Adapted from Roberta Golinkoff)*

**9.17** *Stimuli for the selective looking experiment   One screen shows Big Bird tickling Cookie Monster, the other shows Cookie Monster tickling Big Bird.*

the screen to the right Cookie Monster is tickling Big Bird (Figure 9.17). Half the children heard a voice saying, "Oh look! Big Bird is tickling Cookie Monster." The other children heard the reverse sentence ("Oh look! Cookie Monster is tickling Big Bird"). Hidden observers recorded which screen the children turned their attention to. The finding was that the toddlers looked primarily at the screen that matched the sentence they heard. This is despite the fact that these children themselves spoke only in single-word utterances (Hirsh-Pasek, Golinkoff, Fletcher, DeGaspe-Beaubien, & Cauley, 1985; see also Landau & Gleitman, 1985; Naigles, 1990).

## THE PROGRESSION TO ADULT LANGUAGE

Typically, children's speech progresses very rapidly by the beginning of the third year of life. Utterances now become longer (Figure 9.18), and the children can say little sentences. Function words begin to appear. By five years the average child sounds much like an adult in the forms of his or her speech. There is enormous variation in the words and sentences children hear from their caretakers and their peers, but all the same, before they have reached the first grade, just about all of them use complex and grammatical sentences to express their thoughts. This occurs despite the fact that they cannot explicitly describe this knowledge or even bring it to consciousness—and thus may do badly indeed when asked by their teacher to "diagram" or "parse" a sentence.

Clearly children do not get to this state of knowledge by memorizing all the sentences that are said to them. For one thing, we know that people, even little children, can understand sentences that are quite novel and even bizarre, such as "There is a unicorn hiding behind your left ear," the very first time they hear them. More generally, a good estimate of the number of English sentences less than twenty words in length is $2^{30}$ (a bit more than a billion). A child memorizing a new sentence every five seconds, starting at birth, working at this twenty-four hours a day, would have mastered only 3 percent of this set by his fifth birthday, making the learning-by-memorizing strategy seem hopelessly implausible. It follows that children learn the grammar of their language by extracting patterns ("rules" or perhaps networks of connections) that they simply apply in new ways to say whatever they want to, rather than memorizing whole sentences.

We can get some insight into how the child goes about building language structure by looking at the relatively simple case of word building: how the learners figure out which morphemes can be joined together to form complex words. As so often, "errors" that the youngsters make along the way reveal something of the processes involved in acquiring the adult system.

We will use here the example of the English suffix *-ed*, indicating the past tense. When children start using past tense verbs, often they say them correctly at first. They

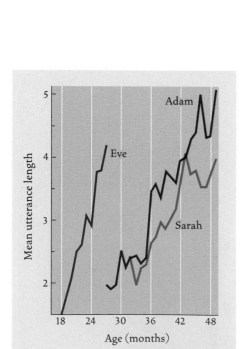

**9.18** *The average length of the utterances produced by three children   The mean utterance length in three children between one-and-a-half and four years of age. The utterance length is measured in morphemes, where* **dolls** *counts as two morphemes (doll + s). Note the variations among the children, who were all within a normal range. (After Brown, Cazden, & Bellugi-Klima, 1969)*

use the suffix *-ed* as an adult would, applying it to regular verbs, but not to irregular ones. Thus, the child says "walked" and "talked" and also (correctly) uses irregular forms such as *ran, came,* and *ate*. By the age of four or five, however, these same children start to treat the irregular verbs as though they were regular. Thus, they sometimes say "runned," "bringed," and "holded" (Marcus et al., 1992; Pinker & Ullman, 2002; Prasada & Pinker, 1993). And these are not simply errors of carelessness or slips of the tongue, as can be seen in the following exchange:

CHILD: My teacher holded the baby rabbits and we patted them.
MOTHER: Did you say your teacher *held* the baby rabbits?
CHILD: Yes.
MOTHER: What did you say she did?
CHILD: She holded the baby rabbits and we patted them.
MOTHER: Did you say she held them tightly?
CHILD: No, she holded them loosely. (Bellugi, 1971)

This kind of error offers evidence that children do not learn language solely, or even mostly, by imitation. Few adults would say "holded" or "eated," and the mother in the quoted exchange repeatedly offers the correct form of the verb for imitation. In fact, parents are often aghast at these errors. A half-year earlier, their child was speaking correctly but now is making errors. Apparently, he is regressing! So parents often try to correct these errors, but to no avail: the child holds firm, despite the correction.

But if not the result of imitation, then what is it that leads children to produce "errors" where there was correctness before? Many investigators argue that the young child starts out by memorizing the past tense of each verb, learning that the past tense of want is *wanted*, the past tense of *climb* is *climbed*, and so on. But this is a highly inefficient strategy. It is far more efficient to detect the pattern: simply add the *-ed* suffix to a verb every time you are speaking of the past. But once the child detects this pattern, it is apparently quite easy to get carried away, and so *overregularization errors* are produced. The errors will drop out only when the child takes the further step of realizing that, while there is a pattern, there are also exceptions to the pattern. (For an alternative view, see McClelland & Patterson, 2002; for discussion, see Pinker & Prince, 1988).

# LANGUAGE LEARNING IN CHANGED ENVIRONMENTS

Under normal conditions, language seems to emerge in much the same way in virtually all children. They progress from babbling to one-word speech, advance to two-word sentences, and eventually graduate to complex sentence forms and meanings. This progression can be observed in children in Beijing learning to speak Chinese, as well as in children in Athens learning to speak Greek. This uniformity from one child to the next, from one language to the next is certainly consistent with the claim that language development is rooted in our shared biological heritage. But is this pattern truly universal? What happens when children grow up in environments radically different from those in which language growth usually proceeds? Examining these cases may help us to understand the biological roots of human language and will also allow us to ask which aspects of the early environment are essential for language learning.

## WILD CHILDREN

In 1920, Indian villagers discovered a wolf mother in her den together with four cubs. Two were baby wolves, but the other two were human children, subsequently named

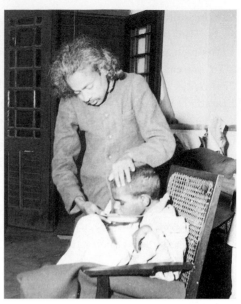

**9.19   A modern wild boy**   *Ramu, a young boy discovered in India in 1976, appears to have been reared by wolves. He was deformed, apparently from lying in cramped positions, as in a den. He could not walk, and drank by lapping with his tongue. His favorite food was raw meat, which he seemed to be able to smell at a distance. After he was found, he lived at the home for destitute children run by Mother Theresa in Lucknow, Utter Pradesh. He learned to bathe and dress himself but never learned to speak. He continued to prefer raw meat and would often sneak out to prey upon fowl in the neighbor's chicken coop. Ramu died at the age of about ten in February 1985. (New York Times, Feb. 24, 1985)*

Kamala and Amala. No one knows how they got there or why the wolf adopted them.* Brown (1958) tells us what these children were like:

> Kamala was about eight years old and Amala was only one and one-half. They were thoroughly wolfish in appearance and behavior: Hard callus had developed on their knees and palms from going on all fours. Their teeth were sharp edged. They moved their nostrils sniffing food. Eating and drinking were accomplished by lowering their mouths to the plate. They ate raw meat.... At night they prowled and sometimes howled. They shunned other children but followed the dog and cat. They slept rolled up together on the floor.... Amala died within a year but Kamala lived to be eighteen.... In time, Kamala learned to walk erect, to wear clothing, and even to speak a few words. (p. 100)

The outcome was much the same for the thirty or so other wild children about whom we have reports. When found, they were all shockingly animal-like. None of them could be rehabilitated to use language normally, though some, including Kamala, learned to speak a few words (Figure 9.19).

## ISOLATED CHILDREN

Clearer data come from a number of other children who were raised by humans but under conditions that were hideously inhumane, for their parents were either vicious or deranged. Sometimes, such parents will deprive a baby of all human contact. For example, "Isabelle" (a code name used to protect the child's privacy) was hidden away, apparently from early infancy, and given only the minimal attention necessary to sustain her life. No one spoke to her (the mother was deaf and also emotionally indifferent).

At the age of six, Isabelle was discovered by other adults and brought into a normal environment. Of course, she had no language, and her cognitive development was below that of a normal two-year-old. But within a year, she learned to speak, her tested intelligence was normal, and she took her place in an ordinary school (K. Davis, 1947; R. Brown,

---

* There has always been some controversy attached to these reports (see, for example, Ogburn & Bose, 1959; and Candland, 1993). One concern is that Amala and Kamala may have been retarded and for this reason were abandoned. Thus, the pattern of their development may be due to retardation and not to isolation from other humans. Given this ambiguity, it is important to emphasize that our claims about language acquisition rest on a broad pattern of data and not just on the reports about wolf children.

1958). Thus, Isabelle at seven years, with one year of language practice, spoke about as well as her peers in the second grade, all of whom had had seven years of practice.

But rehabilitation from isolation is not always so successful. "Genie," discovered in California about thirty years ago, was fourteen years old when she was found. Since about the age of twenty months, apparently, she had lived tied to a chair; she was frequently beaten and never spoken to but sometimes was barked at, because her father said she was no more than a dog. Once discovered, Genie was brought into foster care and taught by psychologists and linguists (Fromkin, Krashen, Curtiss, Rigler, & Rigler, 1974). But Genie did not become a normal language user. She says many words and puts them together into meaningful propositions as young children do, such as "No more take wax" and "Another house have dog." Thus, she has learned certain basics of language. Indeed, her semantic sophistication—what she means by what she says—is far beyond that of young children. Yet even after years of instruction, Genie has not learned the function words that appear in mature English sentences, nor does she combine propositions together in elaborate sentences (Curtiss, 1977).

Why did Genie not progress to full language learning? The best guess is that the crucial factor is the age at which language learning began. Genie was discovered after she had reached puberty, while Isabelle was only six when she was discovered. As we shall see later, there is some reason to believe that there is a critical period for language learning. If the person has passed this period, language learning proceeds with greater difficulty.

## LANGUAGE WITHOUT SOUND

The work on wild and isolated children argues that the child will learn language only if she has some contact with, and some interaction with, other humans. But what aspects of this contact are crucial? An obvious hypothesis is that the child must hear the speech of others to detect the patterns and learn the rules. However, this hypothesis is false. Deaf people do not hear others speaking; they are never exposed to ordinary (auditory) conversation. Yet they do learn a language, one that involves a complex system of gestures. In the United States, the deaf usually learn *American Sign Language* (or *ASL*), but many other sign languages also exist. Plainly, language can exist in the absence of sound.

Are these gestural systems genuine languages? One indication that they are is that these systems are not derived by translation from the spoken languages around them but are independently created within and by communities of deaf individuals (Klima et al., 1979; Senghas, 1995). Further evidence comes from comparing ASL to the structure and development of spoken languages. ASL has hand shapes and positions of which each word is composed, much like the tongue and lip shapes that allow us to fashion the phonemes of spoken language (Stokoe, 1960). It has morphemes and grammatical principles for combining words into sentences that are similar to those of spoken language (Supalla, 1986; see Figure 9.20).

Finally, babies born to deaf users of ASL (whether or not the babies themselves are deaf) pick up the system from these caregivers through informal interaction rather than by explicit instruction, just as we learn our spoken language (Newport & Ashbrook, 1977).* And they go through the same steps on the way to adult knowledge as do hearing children learning English. Given all of these considerations (and some others), it is hard to avoid the conclusion that ASL and other gestural systems are true languages (Klima et al., 1979; Newport, 1984, 1990; Supalla & Newport, 1978).

* In fact, the expert sign-language translators seen on television are usually hearing children of deaf parents. They grow up in a bilingual environment, with ASL learned from their parents and English learned by contact with hearing children and adults, so they achieve perfect knowledge of both and thus are the best translators.

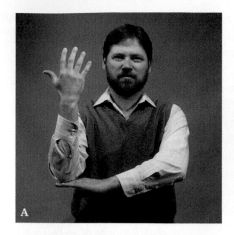

**9.20   Some common signs in ASL   (A) The sign for** tree. *One difference between ASL and spoken language is that many of the signed words physically resemble their meanings. This is so for* tree, *in which the upright forearm stands for the trunk and the outstretched fingers for the branches. But in many cases, such a resemblance is not present. Consider (B), which is the modern sign for* help, *whose relation to its meaning seems as arbitrary as that between most spoken words and their meanings. Even so, such a relation was once present, as shown in (C), a nineteenth-century sign for help. At that time, the sign was not arbitrary; it consisted of a gesture by the right hand to support the left elbow, as if helping an elderly person cross a street. (B) grew out of (C) by a progressive series of simplifications in which signs tend to move to the body's midline and use shorter, fewer, and more stylized movements. All that remains of (C) is an upward motion of the right palm. (Frishberg, 1975; photographs of and by Ted Supalla)*

Thus, language does not depend on the auditory-vocal channel. When the usual modes of communication are denied to humans of normal mentality, they come up with an alternative that reproduces the same contents and structures as other language systems. It appears that language is an irrepressible human trait: deny it to the mouth and it will dart out through the fingers.

## LANGUAGE WITHOUT A MODEL

Let us revise our hypothesis: in order to learn language, one needs some exposure to language. This requires contact with other humans, but it does not require auditory contact. Being able to see the gestures of others is enough to enable one to detect the patterns and thus to learn the rules and semantic content of the system.

But is this entirely correct? What if children of normal mentality were raised in a loving and supportive environment but not exposed to either speech or signed language? Researchers found six children who were in exactly this sort of situation (Feldman, Goldin-Meadow, & Gleitman, 1978; Goldin-Meadow, 2000; Goldin-Meadow & Feldman, 1977). These children were deaf, so they were unable to learn spoken language. Their parents were hearing and did not know ASL. They had decided not to allow their children to learn a gestural language, because they shared the belief (held by some educators) that deaf children should focus their efforts on learning spoken language through special training in lip-reading and vocalization. This training often proceeds slowly at first, so for some time these children did not have access to spoken English.* Not yet able to read lips, unable to hear, and without exposure to a gestural language, these children were essentially without any linguistic input.

---

* The degree of success with lip-reading and vocalization of English, as well as reading acquisition, by deaf children is variable, with the level attained closely related to the degree of deafness. Even the slightest hearing capability helps enormously. But there is growing evidence that the most natural alternative for profoundly deaf children is to learn and use sign language, for in this manual-visual medium they have no language handicap at all.

Without any access to language, these children did something remarkable: they invented a language of their own. For a start, the children invented a sizable number of gestures that were easily understood by others. For example, they would flutter their fingers in a downward motion to express snow, twist their fingers to express a twist-top bottle, and so on (Figure 9.21; for earlier related observations, see Fant, 1972; Tervoort, 1961). But in addition, this spontaneously invented language showed many parallels to ordinary language learning. The children began to gesture one sign at a time at approximately the same age that hearing children begin to speak one word at a time, and progressed to more complex sentences in the next year or so. And in these basic sentences, the deaf children placed the individual gestures in a serial order, according to semantic role—again, just as hearing children do.

More recent evidence has shown just how far deaf children can go in inventing a language if they are placed into a social environment that favors their communicating with each other. In Nicaragua until about the early 1980s, deaf children from rural areas were widely scattered and usually knew no others who were deaf. Based on the findings just mentioned, it was not surprising to discover that all these deaf individuals developed home-made gestural systems to communicate with the hearing people around them, each system varying from the others in an idiosyncratic way. In the early 1980s, a school was created just for deaf children in Nicaragua, and they have been bussed daily from all over the countryside to attend it. Just as in the American case, the school authorities have tried to teach these children to lip-read and vocalize. But on the bus and in the lunchroom, and literally behind the teachers' backs, these children (aged four to fourteen in the initial group) began to gesture to each other. Bit by bit their different home signs converged on conventions that they all used, and the system grew more and more elaborate. The emerging gestural language of this school has now been observed over two generations of youngsters, as new four-year-olds arrive at the school every year. These new members not only learn the system but also elaborate it and improve on it, with the effect that in the space of twenty years a language system of considerable complexity and semantic sophistication has been invented and put to communicative use by these children (Kegl, Senghas, & Coppola, 1999; Saffran, Senghas, & Trueswell, 2001). Perhaps it is true that Rome was not built in a day, but for all we know, maybe Latin was! In sum, if children are denied access to a human language, they go to the trouble to invent one for themselves.

## CHILDREN DEPRIVED OF ACCESS
## TO SOME OF THE MEANINGS

The extraordinarily robust nature of language development is also apparent when we consider language learning in the absence of vision. Imagine a child who hears, "Look! There's a big dog!" or "Do you see that man playing the guitar?" Surely, the child will find it easier to grasp the meaning of these phrases if he can observe the dog or the guitar player, using the perceptual experience to help decode the linguistic input. This would seem to suggest that language learning would proceed slowly or be somehow limited in a blind child. A blind child would seem to be cut off from many of the learning opportunities available to the sighted child, with fewer chances to observe the referents of words or to observe the action being discussed. Remarkably, though, the evidence shows that blind children learn language as rapidly and as well as sighted children. One particularly striking example is vision-related words like *look* and *see*, which blind children use as early (two years old) and as systematically as sighted children. Of course, there are differences in how blind and sighted children understand these words. A young sighted listener asked to "Look up!" will tilt her face upward (even if her vision is blocked by a

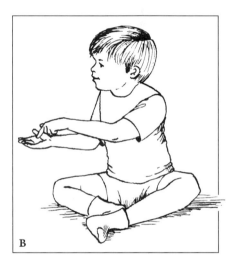

9.21 *Self-made signs in a deaf boy never exposed to sign language* **A two-sign sequence. (A) The first sign means "eat" or "food." Immediately before, the boy had pointed to a grape. (B) The second sign means "give." The total sequence means "give me the food." (Goldin-Meadow, 1982; drawing courtesy Noel Yovovich)**

**9.22    The meaning of "look"**
**(A) A blindfolded, sighted three-year-old tilts her head upward in response to "Look up!" for to her the word look means "perceive by eye."**
**(B) A congenitally blind three-year-old raises her arms upward in response to "Look up!" for to her the word look means "perceive by hand."**
**(Drawings by Robert Thacker)**

A                                    B

*Learning language requires a receptive human mind*    **Ginger gets plenty of linguistic stimulation but is prepared by nature only to be man's best friend. (This Far Side cartoon by Gary Larson is reprinted by permission of Chronicle Features, San Francisco, California.)**

blindfold). For this child, *look* clearly refers to vision (Figure 9.22A). A congenitally blind child, when told to "Look up!," produces a different—but entirely sensible—response. Keeping her head immobile, the blind youngster reaches upward and searches the space above her body with her hands (Figure 9.22B). Thus, each of these children understands *look* differently. But both children realize that the term is an instruction to search a bit of the world by use of the sense organs (Landau & Gleitman, 1985; see also Andersen, Dunlea, & Kekelis, 1993; Bigelow, 1987; Mulford, 1986; Urwin, 1983).

Once again, we see that language emerges in all of its complexity and on schedule despite a dramatic shift away from the standard circumstances of learning. This provides further support for the claim that language is a truly basic factor in human nature. Prepared as the human child is to acquire a language, its learning can proceed despite significant sensory deprivation.

# LANGUAGE LEARNING WITH CHANGED ENDOWMENTS

As we just saw, language learning can proceed in the face of severe environmental deprivations, so long as the learner has a normal human brain. But what happens if the nature of the learners themselves is changed? Since language learning and use are determined by brain function, changing the brain should have strong effects (L. R. Gleitman, 1986; Lenneberg, 1967; Menyuk, 1977).

There are many indications that the nature and state of the brain have massive consequences for language functioning. In Chapter 2 we discussed the evidence of aphasia, in which damage in the brain's left hemisphere can have devastating and highly specific impacts on speech and comprehension. Further evidence comes from individuals with an apparently inherited syndrome known as *specific language impairment*. Individuals with this syndrome are generally slow to learn language and throughout their lives have difficulty in understanding and producing many sentences. Yet these individuals seem normal on most other measures, including measurements of intelligence (Gopnik & Crago, 1993; Pinker, 1994; van Der Lely & Christian, 2000).

We can also find cases with the reverse pattern: disruption of all mental capacities except language. Individuals with this pattern (called Williams syndrome) are severely mentally retarded (with IQ scores of 60 or lower; see Chapter 14) but are still capable of

P A R T

3

IN THE PRECEDING CHAPTERS, WE ASKED what organisms do, what they want, and what they know. In pursuing these questions, we have largely considered organisms as isolated individuals abstracted from the social world in which they live. But many aspects of behavior are impossible to describe by considering a single organism. Courtship, sex, parental care, competition, and cooperation do not take place in a vacuum. They are not merely actions; they are interactions in which each participant's behavior affects, and is affected by, the behavior of others.

In humans, the role of social factors is crucial, and most of our motives—whether the desire for love and esteem, the drives to achieve, to dominate or cooperate, and, in some cases, unhappily, to inflict pain—are social. Even motives that at first glance may appear asocial, such as hunger, thirst, and temperature maintenance, are enormously affected by long-standing social practices and traditions. Thus, we eat food that is produced by a complex agricultural technology based on millennia of human discovery, and we eat it delicately, with knife and fork—or chopsticks—according to the court etiquette of long-dead kings and emperors.

The study of social behavior is the study of lives inextricably intertwined with those of others, both living and dead. It is the study which proves that, to quote John Donne's famous sermon, "no man is an island, entire of itself."

CHAPTER

10

# COGNITION AND
# SOCIAL BEHAVIOR

We have discussed how organisms perceive, remember, and think about their world. We have also considered language, the quintessential human capacity that allows us to talk about the world, tell stories about it, report on it, and so on. But so far we have said little about an obviously central fact about humans, and, indeed, about many species: that we live in a world populated with others of our kind and spend all of our days interacting with them.

In important ways, our social interactions set the pattern of our lives—what we do and who we are. Many of the things we accomplish are possible only because of these interactions, and many of the things we value—for example, friendship and love—are aspects of the social world. But how do social interactions proceed? How do we come to understand the people around us, and what guides us toward one sort of social interaction with them or another (i. e., helping them or not, being influenced by them or not, liking them or not)?

In this chapter and the next, we address these social psychological questions. In this chapter, we will consider how people perceive, think about, and remember the social world. Our focus, in other words, will be on social cognition. In Chapter 11, we turn to the role of feelings, emotions, and passions in governing our social behavior and our social selves.

# THE SOCIAL SELF

Whenever we interact with other people, the nature of the interaction—how we behave, how we perceive the others and react to them—depends on many factors. One factor, obviously, is our personality—whether we are friendly or hostile, reserved or outgoing. (For more on personality, see Chapter 15.) Another crucial factor is our sense of self: who we want to be, how we wish to be perceived, and how we perceive ourselves. These aspects of our *self-concept* play a powerful role in governing how we present ourselves, how we interpret others' reactions to us, and how we in turn respond to them.

The self—who we are and who we think we are—plainly influences social interactions. But the reverse is also true, and there is no question that the social world influences—and, some would say, defines—who we think we are. Each of us is influenced by how others treat us and how they respond to our actions. Their behavior causes us to adjust our social role, and, in many cases, to reshape how we think about ourselves. Indeed, some authors cast this more strongly, suggesting that what each of us considers to be "me" is in large part derived from what others have taught us and how they have reacted to us. The self that each of us knows, in other words, is what William Cooley, many years ago, called a "looking glass self," defined largely through what we have learned in our interactions with others (Cooley, 1902). For all these reasons, our understanding of the unit we call "us" must be based on an understanding of the unit we call "me," and so we begin our study of social psychology by discussing the self. (For more on the broad influences of the "self," see Ellemers, Spears, & Dossje, 2002.)

## KNOWING OURSELVES

Every one of us knows a great deal about ourselves—we know our own likes and dislikes; we know our hopes and aspirations; we know what we have done in the past, and

**Social interaction** *Our social interactions depend on many aspects of the relationship between who we are, and who the person is with whom we are interacting. As one small part of this relationship, if the other person is too different from us, we may not be able to communicate. If the person is too similar to us, we may not be able to sustain the relationship.*

how we wish to behave in the future. We also seem to have some amount of insight into the reasons for our various attitudes and behaviors. We know—and could, potentially, explain—why we like some people but detest others. When we do something, we believe we know the cause.

Where does this self-knowledge come from? On the face of it, the answer seems obvious: each of us is able to look within ourselves, or *introspect*, consulting our memory for the critical events that inspired us or the thought processes that guided us, and thus we gain the relevant self-knowledge. But, in fact, things are not as simple as that. A great deal of evidence suggests that the path to self-knowledge is not so direct, because many of the factors and processes that influence us are outside of our conscious awareness and therefore are not open to introspection. (For more on these limits of consciousness, see Chapter 8.) But this does not mean we are stymied when we try to figure out why we made a particular decision, or why we like or dislike something. We do know ourselves, but indirectly—not via introspection, but instead by means of a process of inference and interpretation (c.f. Nisbett & Wilson, 1977).

This indirect, inferential path to self-knowledge is the main theme of *self-perception theory*, which asserts that we come to know ourselves in precisely the same way we come to understand other people (Bem, 1972). How is it that we understand others? We observe their behaviors and then draw inferences about why they acted as they did. Those inferences are guided by certain beliefs that we have about the relation between behaviors and internal states. (We believe people eat because they are hungry, that people cry because they are sad, and so on.) The inferences are also guided by certain "interpretive habits" that we all seem to have, and we will say more about these habits later in the chapter. The point for now, though, is that the path to understanding ourselves may be the same: we observe our own behavior and draw inferences about the sources of our actions, typically with no realization that the self-knowledge is merely interpretive and inferential.

## BEHAVIORS SHAPE ATTITUDES

This inferential base for self-knowledge can be revealed in many ways, including studies of the relationship between attitude and behavior. Common sense argues that attitudes cause behavior, that our actions stem from our feelings and our beliefs. This may be true at times, so that (for example) people in favor of a strong military are unlikely to demand cuts in the defense budget, and environmentalists are unlikely to vote for a candidate who promises to loosen pollution controls. But under many circumstances, the cause-and-effect relation is reversed, and our feelings or beliefs seem to be the result of our actions, and not their cause.

A demonstration comes from the *foot-in-the-door technique* (originally devised by door-to-door salesmen). In one study, suburban homeowners were asked to comply with an innocuous request, to put a three inch square sign advocating auto safety in a window of their homes. Two weeks later, a different experimenter came to visit the same homeowners and asked them to grant a much greater request, to place an enormous billboard on their front lawn that proclaimed "Drive Carefully" in huge letters. The results showed that whether people granted this larger request was heavily influenced by whether they had earlier agreed to the smaller request (that is, to display the small sign). The homeowners who had complied with the small request were much more likely to give in to the greater one (Freedman & Fraser, 1966; although, for some limits on this technique, see Chartrand, Pinckert, & Burger, 1999).

One interpretation of this (and similar findings) is a change in self-perception (Snyder & Cunningham, 1975). Having agreed to put up the small sign, the homeowners now thought of themselves as active citizens involved in a public issue. "Why

*Self-perception and attribution    In the movie* **Donnie Brasco,** *an undercover FBI agent infiltrates the mob. As his involvement deepens, he grows uncertain of his own allegiances. (Al Pacino and Johnny Depp in the 1997 film.)*

*Self-perception among active citizens*
*Students of Emerson Elementary School in Nebraska hoped to collect 911 cans of food in remembrance of the attack on September 11, 2001. Will the small step of donating a can of food to this drive change how the donors perceive themselves, and, with that, their willingness to be more active citizens in general?*

did I put up the sign? No one forced me to do it. I guess, therefore, that this is an issue that I care about." Thus, they interpreted their own actions as revealing a conviction that previously they did not know they had, and, given that they now thought of themselves as active, convinced, and involved, they were ready to play the part on a larger scale.

Fortunately, for the neighbors, the billboard was never installed—after all, this was an experiment. But in real life we may not be so easily let off the hook. The foot-in-the-door approach is a common device for persuading the initially uncommitted and is used both to peddle encyclopedias and to harden political convictions. Extremist political movements, for example, rarely demand strong actions from new recruits. Instead, they begin with small requests like signing a petition or giving a distinctive salute. But these may lead to a changed self-perception that ultimately readies the person for more drastic acts.

## SELF-PERCEPTION AND COGNITIVE DISSONANCE

In the foot-in-the-door technique, people are led to take a small and innocuous step, such as putting a small sign in their window. What happens, though, if someone initially is led to take a step that is not at all innocuous, a step that instead is contrary to their beliefs or values? This sort of thing does, after all, happen in our day-to-day lives. Sometimes an employee must act as if she likes a boss she detests. Sometimes a polite dinner guest must pretend to enjoy a meal when, in truth, her host is insufferably boring. What does this conflict do to their subsequent attitudes and self-perception?

This issue has been explored in a number of studies of forced compliance,* with some of the earliest (and now classic) studies carried out by social psychologist Leon Festinger and his associates. In one experiment, participants were asked to perform several extremely boring tasks, such as packing spools into a tray and then unpacking them, or turning one screw after another for a quarter turn. When they were finished, they were induced to tell the next participant that the tasks were really very interesting. Half the participants were paid generously for lying in this way (they were given $20); the others were given just $1 for telling this lie.

When later asked how enjoyable they really found the tasks, the well-paid participants said that the tasks were in fact boring, and they understood fully that they had lied to the other participants. In contrast, the poorly paid participants claimed that the monotonous, menial tasks were fairly interesting, and indicated, therefore, that they had, in fact, told the other participants the truth (Festinger & Carlsmith, 1959).

What produces this odd pattern? According to Festinger, the well-paid liars knew why they had mouthed sentiments they did not endorse: $20 cash was reason enough. The poorly paid liars, however, had experienced *cognitive dissonance*, a disconcerting emotional state that occurs when two beliefs that we hold are plainly inconsistent with each other, or when there is a conflict between what we believe and what we actually do. In Festinger's experiment, the poorly paid participants had misled other people without good reason; they had received only a paltry payment. Taken at face value, this made them look like casual and unprincipled liars, a view that conflicted with how they wanted to see themselves. How, therefore, could they reconcile their behavior with their self-concept? One plausible solution was to reevaluate the boring tasks. If they could change their minds about the tasks and decide they were not so awful, then there was no lie and hence no dissonance. Apparently, this is the

---

* The term *forced compliance* was coined to describe the phenomenon when it was first demonstrated experimentally (Festinger & Carlsmith, 1959). It is a bit of a misnomer, however, since the participant is not really forced to lie about his attitudes but is instead persuaded or coaxed. Modern social psychologists prefer the more accurate—if clumsier—designation *counterattitudinal advocacy*.

solution that the participants selected—bringing their attitudes into line with their behavior.

Many other studies have yielded similar results (see, for example, Rosenfeld, Giacalone, & Tedeschi, 1984; Cialdini, Trost, & Newsom, 1995). Closely related findings emerge in studies of people who must make considerable sacrifices to attain a goal. Most of us would find it difficult to tolerate the idea that we had worked for many years to achieve something trivial. To make our own efforts seem sensible, therefore, our only choice is to value what we attained. Thus, dissonance theory predicts that goals will be valued more if they were harder won. Experimental support comes from various laboratory studies on justification of effort. Thus, for example, participants who were admitted to a group after going through an unpleasant screening test put a higher value on their new membership than did participants who did not undergo this screening (Aronson & Mills, 1959; Gerard & Mathewson, 1966).

*Justification of effort    Newly accepted members of a group tend to value their group membership even more if their initiation was especially harsh, as in the case of soldiers who have gone through boot camp.*

This result helps to explain why many organizations have difficult or aversive entrance requirements. For example, many American college fraternities have hazing rituals that are typically unpleasant and, in some cases, humiliating or worse. But while these rituals may be objectionable, they do serve a function: they lead the new fraternity members to place a higher value on their membership. They know what they have suffered through to achieve membership, and it would create dissonance for them to believe that they suffered for no purpose. This dissonance is eliminated, though, if they become convinced that their membership is really valuable. In that case, their suffering was, in their view, "worth it."

What is the nature of the dissonance that produces these effects? Is it merely a logical discrepancy that people dispassionately try to resolve? It seems to be more than that, because people in dissonance studies actually show physiological signs of conflict that indicate real turmoil (Elkin & Leippe, 1986). In many cases, this turmoil reflects the fact that the dissonance poses a challenge to our favorable self-concept. After all, it is not exactly smart to endure great pain to achieve small gain (Aronson, 1969; Cooper & Fazio, 1984; Elliot & Devine, 1994; Steele & Liu, 1983). But if we reevaluate the gain, then our efforts to reach the gain are justified, and the challenge to our self-concept is removed.

A challenge to our self-concept is also central in the forced compliance tasks. In this case, the challenge is to our view of ourselves as basically honest and decent. It is this self-view that leads us to feel guilty about lying to someone about our attitudes. If we can manage to change our own views just a bit ("The task really wasn't so bad . . ."), we can assuage our guilt about duping our victim. Consistent with this view, there is no dissonance (and no change in attitude) if participants feel no guilt—if, for example, they thought the person they lied to was unconvinced by their lies, or if they did not like him anyway (Cooper, Zanna, & Goethals, 1974; for more on why dissonance works as it does, see Wood, 2000).

## DO ATTITUDES PREDICT BEHAVIOR?

The studies we have just reviewed suggest that, when our behavior conflicts with our attitudes, something has to give, and, in many cases, it is our attitudes that are apt to change. Of course, the underlying assumption here is that our attitudes and our behavior have something to do with one another. Otherwise, there would be no conflict between saying a task was fun and believing that it was not, or working hard to achieve a goal that we felt was worth only little.

This assumption is well rooted in common sense, and we sneer at hypocrites who do not behave in accord with their principles. But is this assumption really warranted? Does our behavior truly reflect our attitudes? This topic has received wide attention and generated considerable controversy. As social psychologists use the term, an *attitude* is a stable set of mental views and assessments about some idea, object, or person (Eagly & Chaiken, 1993). An attitude not only involves beliefs (for example, "Nuclear power is not safe"; "The death penalty is a deterrent to crime"), but also involves feelings and evaluations—assessing something as good or bad, harmful or beneficial, likable or dislikable (Ajzen, 2001). Social psychologists measure attitudes in a number of ways, but they usually rely on questionnaires on which participants can indicate the extent to which they endorse certain statements. A typical survey question might ask the participant to rate how he feels about the statement, "Nuclear power plants are worth the risks," using a scale from +10 (total agreement) to −10 (total disagreement). The person's responses to a number of statements about a given topic will then provide an assessment of that person's attitude toward that topic. (For some complications associated with this means of assessing attitudes, see Cacioppo & Berntson, 1994; Ajzen, 2001; Schwarz, 1999; Thompson, Zanna, & Griffin, 1995.)

Do attitudes, measured in this way, actually predict behavior? The early verdict on this point was dismaying. In a widely cited study conducted in the 1930s (when there was considerable anti-Asian sentiment), Richard LaPiere traveled throughout the United States with a Chinese couple and stopped at over fifty hotels and motels and at nearly two hundred restaurants. All but one hotel gave them accommodations, and no restaurant refused them service. Some time afterward, the very same establishments received a letter asking whether they would house or serve Chinese persons. Ninety-two percent of the replies were "no" (LaPiere, 1934). This result pointed to major inconsistencies between people's stated attitudes and their actual behavior.

In light of these results, some social psychologists began to wonder whether the attitude concept is particularly useful. If attitudes do not predict behavior, what is the point of studying them at all (Wicker, 1969)? Later studies, however, showed that this worry was too sweeping, and that under many circumstances attitudes do indeed predict behavior. Thus, voter preferences as expressed in preelection interviews indicate fairly well how people will vote. In one study, 85 percent of the people interviewed voted in line with their previously expressed preference. For the most part, those who shifted had initial preferences that were rather weak (Kelley & Mirer, 1974).

Apparently, then, we should not ask, Do attitudes predict behavior? Sometimes they do, and sometimes they do not. What we need to ask instead is, *When* do attitudes predict behavior? Several determining factors have come to light. One is the strength of the attitude. As we might expect, people are more likely to behave in a manner consistent with their strong attitudes than with their weak ones (Bassili, 1993, 1995; Kraus, 1995; for a more detailed analysis of what makes an attitude strong, see Prislin, 1996).

Another factor lies in the immediate situational pressures. When LaPiere's partici-

*Strong attitudes and behavior*  **In political demonstrations, it is highly likely that the participants have attitudes consonant with their political actions. Pro-choice partisans are unlikely to support a pro-life demonstration, or vice versa. In this case, the consistency of attitudes and behaviors is sensible, because the attitudes are strong ones.**

pants gave their "no's" in their letters, they were most likely envisioning their own (negative) stereotypes of Asian customers who might enter their establishments. But in fact, LaPiere's Chinese couple consisted of two young students who were well dressed and attractive. These students probably did not fit the negative stereotype, and the obligation to be courteous hosts made refusal difficult and embarrassing.

Whether attitudes predict behavior is also a function of whether the attitude is simply one isolated belief or is instead enmeshed in a web of other, related attitudes (Ajzen, 2001; Prislin & Ouellette, 1996); in general, behavior is more consistent with enmeshed attitudes than with isolated ones. It also matters how specifically the attitude is defined in the first place. The less specific one's definition, the less likely it is to predict a particular bit of behavior. One study analyzed the relation between general attitudes toward environmentalism and a particular action: being a volunteer for the Sierra Club. The investigators found no relation. But when they tested the specific attitude toward the Sierra Club as such, those who strongly endorsed the club were much more likely to volunteer (Weigel, Vernon, & Tognacci, 1974; for a similar study, see Davidson & Jaccard, 1979).

## IMPLICIT ATTITUDES

There is one further—and crucial—reason why the attitudes we express do not always predict the way we behave. It is because some of our behavior is shaped by *unconscious* attitudes, attitudes that we do not realize we have. Social psychologists find it useful, in fact, to distinguish between *explicit attitudes*, attitudes we are aware of and could, for example, express in response to a survey question, and *implicit attitudes*, attitudes that are revealed only indirectly, by how we behave in certain special settings.

In one experiment, for example, participants were shown various words (*he, she, it, do, all,* and so on) and, for each, simply had to judge whether the word was a pronoun or not. Immediately before each pronoun was presented, though, the participants were very briefly shown a prime word, which the participants were told to ignore as best they could. As it turns out, some of the prime words were the names of occupations typically held by women (*nurse, secretary*); other primes named occupations typically held by men (*doctor, mechanic*). How would this affect the results? If the participants believed that secretaries are likely to be women, then seeing the word *secretary* might prime them to think about females, and this might in turn prepare them to perceive other stimuli associated with females—for example, the pronoun *she*. Consistent with this claim, responses to *she* were faster than responses to *he* when these pronouns were preceded by the name of a stereotypically female occupation. The pattern of response times reversed (and so responses to *he* were faster than those to *she*) if the prime was the name of a stereotypically male occupation, such as *mechanic* (Banaji & Hardin, 1996, Experiment 2).

These results suggest that people tend to associate certain professions with certain genders, whether they wish to or not. The implicit associations are unconscious and, in fact, are quite separate from conscious beliefs. The data show no relationship between the strength of these associations and whether someone explicitly (consciously) believes gender should play a role in a person's choice of occupation (Banaji & Hardin, 1996, Experiment 1; also Banaji & Greenwald, 1995). These associations, in other words, can be demonstrated with equal ease in someone who is profoundly sexist and someone who is fully egalitarian in his politics.

Similar results reflect people's implicit associations regarding racial issues. In the Implicit Associate Test (IAT, Greenwald, McGhee, & Schwartz, 1998; Greenwald et al., 2002), white students are asked to make two types of judgments, with the type of judgment randomly varying from trial to trial. In one of the judgments, the students must indicate whether a face they see on the computer screen is that of a black person or a white person; the students respond by pressing one of two computer keys, with one key indicating "black" and the other, "white." In the other judgment, subjects must indicate whether a word they see on the screen is a "good word" (for example, *love, joy, honest, truth*) or a "bad word" (for example, *poison, agony, detest, terrible*). Again, they respond via two keys, with one key indicating "good" and the other "bad."

Importantly, the same two keys are used for both judgments. In one configuration, one key indicates "black" (on the face trials) and "bad" (on the word trials); the other key indicates "white" and "good." This configuration yields consistently faster responses than the opposite arrangement, with one key indicating "black" and "good" and the other indicating "white" and "bad." The different results suggest that subjects arrive in the experiment already primed to associate each race with an evaluation, and respond more slowly when the experiment requires them to break that association (e.g., Cunningham, Preacher, & Banaji, 2001; Greenwald, McGhee, & Schwartz, 1998; Greenwald et al., 2002).

Of course, not everyone shows this data pattern, and, of those who do, not everyone shows it to the same degree. Put differently, the connection between "white" and "good" and between "black" and "bad" is stronger in some people's minds and less strong in others'. This is, in fact, useful for us, because it allows us to use the IAT as a tool for measuring degree of prejudice. Is the measurement valid? Many studies suggest it is. For example, IAT scores are reliably correlated with explicit measures of racial prejudice (see Greenwald & Nosek, 2001; McConnell & Leibold, 2001). In addition, the IAT can be used to predict behavior. In one study, white students interacted with a black experimenter, and their behavior during the interaction was assessed by trained judges. The behaviors were reliably judged to be more negative for the students whose IAT scores had indicated stronger negative attitudes toward blacks (McConnell & Leibold, 2001).

These results make it clear that people are primed to make certain associations, and that, in some cases, these associations actually run contrary to their explicitly held beliefs. These unconscious associations, in turn, can influence people's subsequent actions, their emotions, and their evaluations of an event or object (see, for example, Bargh & Chartrand, 1999). At the very least, this adds to our earlier argument that much self-knowledge is indirect, since these implicit associations are, as we have noted, unconscious and so not available to introspection. In addition, social psychologists are just beginning to explore how these implicit attitudes color our behavior and our per-

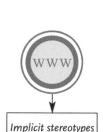

Implicit stereotypes

*Implicit stereotyping* **Participants were shown a series of pictures, some of them showing Caucasian faces, some showing African-American faces, some showing tools, and some showing weapons. Participants were instructed to ignore the face stimuli, to press one button if the stimulus was a weapon, and a different button if the stimulus was a tool. The results showed faster responses if a weapon was preceded by a black face. Apparently, seeing the black face led these (white) subjects to think about weapons, priming their perception of the gun.**

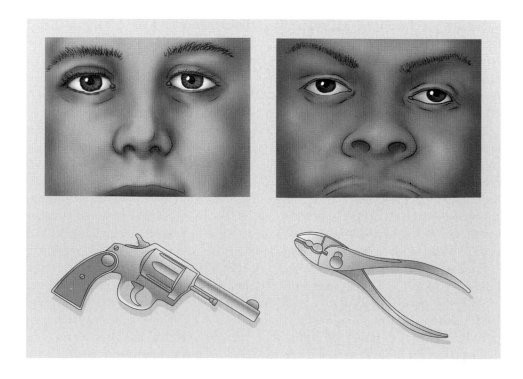

ceptions of the world, and this is currently an area of intense research activity (Bargh & Chartrand, 1999; Kihlstrom et al., 2000; Payne, 2001; for discussion of how emotional evaluations guide our behaviors and decision making, often without our being aware of it, see Bechara et al., 1997; Damasio, 1994).

# SELF-CONCEPT AND SELF-DEFENSE

If self-knowledge is indirect and the result of our interpretations of our own actions, then we must ask, How accurate is our self-knowledge? Are our interpretations usually correct? In fact, we all know ourselves reasonably well, but with an important qualification, because it turns out that, in interpreting our own actions, we tend to err on the side of self-flattery. Nowhere is this clearer than in studies of the *above-average effect*, a tendency people have to perceive themselves as better than average.

## THE ABOVE-AVERAGE EFFECT

It is a matter of statistical logic that half the population is above average in height, weight, and various other attributes, and half the population is below. But people seem to believe otherwise. When people in North America or Europe compare themselves to others, the vast majority judge themselves to be better than average on a number of favorable characteristics (see Harter, 1990; as we will see later, the results are different if we test people in most Asian countries). Thus, in 1976–77, the College Board asked one million high-school students to rate their own leadership ability. Twenty-eight percent thought they were merely average, but 70 percent said they were above average, and only 2 percent felt they were below average. Even more impressive, all the students claimed they were above average in their ability to get along with others; 60 percent thought they were in the top 10 percent on this dimension. In athletic ability, 34 percent judged themselves to be "average," 60 percent rated themselves above average, and 6 percent below. Similar findings have been obtained in people's judgments of talents ranging from managerial skills to driving ability (see Dunning, Meyerowitz, & Holzberg, 1989). And it is not just high-school students who show these effects. One study of university professors found that 94 percent believed they were better at their jobs than their colleagues (Gilovich, 1991).

What is going on here? Part of the cause lies in the way we search our memories, in order to decide whether we have been good leaders or bad, good drivers or poor ones. Evidence suggests that this memory search is often selective, showcasing the occasions in the past in which we have behaved well and neglecting the occasions in which we have done badly (Kunda, 1990; Kunda et al., 1993).

In addition, people seem to capitalize on the fact that the meanings of these traits— effective leader, good at getting along with others, and so on—are often ambiguous. This allows each of us to interpret a trait, and thus to interpret the evidence, in a fashion that puts us in the best-possible light. Take driving ability. Suppose Henry is a slow, careful driver. He will tend to think that he is better than average precisely because he is slow and careful. But suppose Jane, on the other hand, is a fast driver who prides herself on her ability to whiz through traffic and hang tight on hairpin turns. She too will think that she is better than average because of the way she has defined "driving skill." As a result, both Henry and Jane (and indeed most drivers) end up considering themselves above-average. By appropriately redefining success or excellence, each of us can conclude that we are the ones who are successful (Dunning & Cohen, 1992; Dunning, Meyerowitz, & Holzberg, 1989; for yet another contributing factor, see Kruger, 1999).

## THE SELF-SERVING BIAS

The self-flattery we are all prone to is also evident in other ways, including the fact that people tend to take credit for successes but deny responsibility for failures. The tennis player explains a loss by complaining that his serve was off and that the sun was in his eyes, but takes a win as proof of his skill and stamina. The student who fails a course says that the exam was unfair and happened to cover just the material she did not study, but she believes that a good grade is a tribute to her talent and hard work.

Such self-serving interpretations are well documented by studies in which participants were asked to perform various tasks and then given fake information about how well they had done. The tasks have ranged from sensory or perceptual discriminations (see, for example, Luginbuhl, Crowe, & Kahan, 1975; Stevens & Jones, 1976), to purported measures of social sensitivity (Miller, 1976; Sicoly & Ross, 1977), to competitive games played against fictitious opponents (Snyder, Stephan, & Rosenfield, 1976). In all cases, the participants attributed their successes to their abilities, while blaming their failures on the overwhelming task or plain bad luck.

### EXTENDING THE SELF TO INCLUDE OTHERS

The same self-serving bias is extended to the people and groups that we identify in some way as "ours": our family members, our social and political groups, and even our hometown sports teams. For happily married couples, each member of the couple regards the spouse's success as reflecting his or her talents and character, while attributing the failures to temporary circumstances (Hall & Taylor, 1976; Holtzworth-Munroe & Jacobson, 1985). The same holds for people's favorite political candidate: if a candidate does poorly in a debate, her supporters will chalk it up to her having an off day, while her opponents will insist that it only proves their own candidate is the better one (Winkler & Taylor, 1979).

A related effect is produced by friendship. Friendship engenders a kind of interdependence in which the operative unit is "us" rather than "me." This was shown in a study that asked pairs of volunteers to take a collaborative test. If the participants were strangers, they each showed self-serving interpretations of the outcomes, taking credit for successes but blaming the other for failures. If the volunteers were friends, then the partners shared the credit for both successes and failures (Campbell et al., 2000).

## IMPRESSION MANAGEMENT

Our self-service also takes one further—and very important—form: we each have a sense of who we are and what we are like, but we also are aware of the fact that others have a sense of who we are, and, in many circumstances, we do what we can to shape this perception and to guide how others view us. For this purpose, we rely on strategies of *impression management*, a term coined by the sociologist Erving Goffman (Goffman, 1959; see also Schlenker, 1980). As Goffman saw it, much of social interaction is like a theatrical performance in which the actors are "putting on a front." Some "play hard to get," others contrive to look "casual," still others try to appear "above it all." Many of these impressions go along with social or professional roles. The medical student soon discovers that there is more to becoming a doctor than acquiring certain skills. He must also learn how to instill confidence and develop a proper bedside manner. These social skills have many functions, including the fact that, as patient after patient calls him "Doctor" and treats his pronouncements with reverence, the would-be healer gains confidence in his own role, and therefore becomes better able to carry out that role.

Goffman pointed out that many of these social performances are jointly produced. The doctor's image is maintained not only by his own behavior but also by that of vari-

**Self-serving bias** *The self-serving bias can extend to others we see as members of our group, as shown by the different points awarded to a diver at a swim meet by two coaches from opposing teams. Which of the two judges do you think is the diver's own coach?*

ous aides, nurses, and patients as well. Further support comes from the audience itself. We often go to considerable lengths to preserve another person's self-presentation, to allow her to "save face." If we want to break off an encounter at a party, we pretend that we are going to the bar for another drink. The other person may very well know that we have no intention of returning, and we may know that she knows, but this does not matter. Both participants tactfully play along. This kind of tact can reach consummate heights as in the case of the legendary English butler who accidentally surprised a lady in her bath and hurriedly mumbled, "I beg your pardon, Sir."

In addition, we all have a repertoire of social maneuvers that we employ in order to put ourselves in the best possible light (Leary & Kowalski, 1990; Schlenker & Weigold, 1992). Many of these maneuvers provide cover for us, protecting us if we run into an awkward situation. For example, participants in one study were asked to present material that was likely to be offensive to their audience (for example, an argument opposing affirmative action, delivered to African Americans). These participants insulated themselves from the potential awkwardness by employing a number of distancing behaviors, including verbal disclaimers and a number of nonverbal displays—rolling their eyes to express sarcasm or grimacing to convey disgust (Fleming & Rudman, 1993).

Similarly, if we anticipate failure or embarrassment, we often take steps to protect ourselves in advance. One such strategy is known as *self-handicapping*, in which one arranges an obstacle to one's own performance. This way, if failure occurs, it will be attributed to the obstacle and not one's own limitations (Higgins, Snyder, & Berglas, 1990; Jones & Berglas, 1978). Thus, if Sam is afraid of failing next week's biology exam, he might spend more time than usual watching television. Then, if he fails the exam, it will look like he did not study hard enough rather than that he is stupid.

## EMBARRASSMENT

In obvious ways, the maneuvers we employ to defend our self-concept can also be seen as attempts at avoiding embarrassment, a condition whose causes prove to be complex and varied (Miller, 1996). One factor may be public failure, a loss of esteem in the eyes of others that produces a loss of esteem in our own eyes (Modigliani, 1971). But that cannot be the whole story, because we can become embarrassed without any loss of esteem, as when our friends ask the waiters to sing "Happy Birthday" to us in a crowded restaurant. In addition, we are sometimes embarrassed even when our own self-concept is not involved, such as when we are embarrassed for another person (see Miller, 1987). This might happen when we watch a friend speak up in class, forget what she was saying, and become flustered for what seems an eternity. Of course, she is horribly embarrassed and would crawl into a hole if she could. But the fact is that we are also embarrassed for her and want to join her in that hole.

How can we explain such experiences of embarrassment? According to one account, they are partially caused by the disruption of a social interaction that no one knows how to repair (Parrott, Sabini, & Silver, 1988). As Goffman noted, all social intercourse is based on various "scripts" that provide a general frame within which each participant plays his part. If that script is completely disrupted—as, for example, when an actor forgets his lines and cannot ad lib—the performance comes to a sudden stop. It is this awkward, what-do-we-do-next disruption that leads to embarrassment.

*Embarrassment*   **In many films, the comedy comes from watching the embarrassment of others—something we would find intolerable in real life. In movies, though, the embarrassment is at a "safe distance." This plays an important part in** American Pie, *a* **film that centers around a succession of embarrassments for a group of teens.**

Fortunately, though, embarrassment is usually not the calamity we feel it to be. A variety of evidence shows that when we commit a social blunder, others judge us much less harshly than we do ourselves—a blessed exception to the self-serving bias. That we condemn ourselves so unmercifully may simply reflect our egocentrism at the moment. When we are embarrassed, we think only about ourselves and our failings, while those around us see a moderated view of the entire situation. Our horror lies in our myopia (Savitsky, Epley, & Gilovich, 2001).

# PERSON PERCEPTION

Impression management reflects our concerns over how others perceive us. But at the same time that others are forming an impression of us, we are forming an impression of them. How we do this is a question of person perception.

## FORMING IMPRESSIONS

In the course of ordinary life we encounter many other people. The vast majority of them are anonymous extras in each of our private dramas, people we see on the way to school or work, at the grocery, or the gym. We may never know their names or see them again. But a number of others have bigger roles, as bit players (a traffic cop we ask for directions), supporting cast (a casual acquaintance), and costars (friends, lovers, bosses, enemies). In our interactions with these people, we inevitably are "sizing them up." We observe their behavior and reach conclusions about what they are "really like"—and they do the same about us.

## PERSON PERCEPTION AS DISCERNING PATTERNS

Many theorists have suggested that the processes we use to understand another person are analogous to the ways we perceive the various attributes of physical objects. Consider visual form. This is a perceptual whole that depends on the relation among the elements of which the form is composed; thus, a triangle can be composed of dots or crosses and still be perceived as the same triangle (see Chapter 6). According to Solomon Asch, a similar principle describes our conceptions of other people. In his view, these conceptions of others are not a simple aggregate of the attributes we perceive them to have. Instead, they form an organized whole whose elements are interpreted in relation to the overall pattern (Asch, 1952).

### CENTRAL TRAITS

Asch explored this idea in studies in which participants were given a list of attributes said to describe a single person. The participants' task was to write a short sketch about that person and then to rate that person on a checklist of antonyms (*generous* versus *ungenerous*, *good-natured* versus *irritable*, and so on).

In one study, some participants were given a list of seven traits: *intelligent, skillful, industrious, warm, determined, practical, cautious.* Other participants received the same list except that *cold* was substituted for *warm.* The resulting sketches were quite different. The warm person was seen as "driven by the desire to accomplish something that would be of benefit," while the cold person was described as "snobbish . . . calculating and unsympathetic." The checklist results were in the same direction. The warm person was seen as generous, happy, and good-natured, but the cold person was characterized by the corresponding antonyms (Asch, 1946).

According to Asch, the warm/cold trait acted as the focus around which the total impression of the person had crystallized. To use his term, it was a *central trait* that determined the perception of the whole. Other traits seemed to be of lesser importance. For example, it made little difference whether the list of traits included *polite* or *blunt*.*

## FIRST IMPRESSIONS

Some traits, it seems, set up a framework within which we understand other traits and color how we perceive them. In the same fashion, the first information we get about people creates its own framework and guides our interpretation of their other attributes.

The power of first impressions is easy to demonstrate. In another experiment, Asch had one group of participants give their impressions of a person who was intelligent, industrious, impulsive, critical, stubborn, and envious. Another group of participants received the same list, but in reverse order (envious, stubborn, . . . and so on). The results indicate that it pays to put one's best foot forward. If the list began on a positive note, it set up a favorable evaluative tone that seemed to override the subsequent negative words; the opposite effect occurred when the unfavorable traits came first (Asch, 1946; although for some alternative interpretations, see Ostrom, 1977; Schneider, Hastorf, & Ellsworth, 1979).

# PERSON PERCEPTION AND COGNITIVE SCHEMAS

Whereas Asch likened person perception to visual perception, current social psychologists tend to draw instead on modern theories of memory and thinking. In their view, our impressions of others are cognitive constructions based on various *schemas*, sets of organized expectations about the way different behaviors hang together. If we believe that someone is outgoing and gregarious, we will also expect him to be talkative. He may or may not be, but what we perceive is tainted by our schema of what an outgoing and gregarious person is like. Such schemas about persons are sometimes called *implicit theories of personality* (Bruner & Tagiuri, 1954; Schneider, 1973).

That we use such schemas to "fill in the blanks" in our perceptions of others is apparent in a study in which participants read different lists of attributes. One described a person said to be an extrovert; another, a person who was an introvert. After a delay, the participants were given a new list and asked to indicate which traits on this (new) list they had seen in the earlier presentation. All the participants gave some "false alarms" and checked off words that were not on the original list. But the particular words they checked off depended on whether the earlier list had described an introvert or an extrovert. For the "extrovert," participants remembered seeing words like *spirited* and *boisterous,* even though these were not on the original list. For the "introvert," participants falsely remembered seeing words like *shy* and *reserved* (Cantor & Mischel, 1979).

Phenomena of this kind suggest that *social cognition*—that is, thinking about other people—works much like cognition in general. Suppose we briefly looked into a toolbox and were then asked which tools we had seen. We would be far more likely to misremember seeing a hammer than a baby bottle, assuming neither was actually in the

*First impressions* **In the movies, it is common for two figures to hate each other initially but grow to love each other, as Han and Leia did. In real life, however, this pattern is quite rare, and our first impression of someone often dominates all our subsequent perceptions of them.**

---

* The question of why and when some traits are central and others are not has received considerable attention. According to Julius Wishner, the effect is partially dependent on the observer's beliefs about which traits go with others (Schneider, 1973; Wishner, 1960).

chest (see Chapter 7). This is because our memory is guided by our preconception—our cognitive schema—of a toolbox, and this schema includes a hammer, just as our schema for an "extrovert" includes attributes like *spirited* and *boisterous*.

## SCHEMAS AS SOCIAL SHORTCUTS

There is more information in our world than we could ever manage to remember or think about, and this is why schemas are so important: they provide mental shortcuts that allow us to circumvent our limited cognitive capacities. By using schemas, we can supplement our incomplete perceptions and memories with inference, filling in the gaps in what we have seen or what we can remember.

Without such schemas, every one of our social interactions, however incidental, would leave us buried in thought. We would be unable to cope with the constant succession of people we meet, greet, and deal with every minute of every day. Without the ability to make snap social judgments, we would be unable to make any sense of our social world.

But, while schemas provide shortcuts that are quick and efficient, they also leave us vulnerable to error, because sometimes our preconceptions turn out to be wrong, and we end up trying to navigate the social terrain with a bad map. In many cases, this is a small price to pay for the gains associated with using schemas, and, for that matter, the errors produced are often easily corrected. But there is also no doubt that using schemas can lead to more serious errors, with important social consequences.

## GROUP STEREOTYPES AND ILLUSORY CORRELATION

The cost of schematic thinking is particularly clear in the case of social *stereotypes*, in which schemas are simplified and applied to whole groups, so that we talk about Greeks, Jews, or African Americans (or Generation Xer's, baby boomers, and liberals or conservatives) as if they were all alike. Such stereotypes often have deep historical roots and are transmitted to each new generation both explicitly ("Never trust a _____ ") and implicitly (via jokes, caricatures, and the like). Our reliance on social schemas then provides a powerful mechanism helping to maintain these stereotypes. In using schemas, we are guided as much by inference as we are by the facts we actually encounter, and this obviously makes it easier to maintain a mistaken belief (since the belief is never checked against the facts). In addition, even if we are alert to the facts—and pay attention to the individual Jews, individual African Americans, individual baby boomers that we encounter—schemas can still bias how we interpret these facts.

One example lies in our perception of *illusory correlations*. Many characteristics of the world naturally go together—clouds and rainfall, picnics and ants, smoke and fire—and our sensitivity to these correlations helps us to understand the cause-and-effect fabric of our world. But we also see correlations where they do not exist. We form such illusory correlations because we note and remember certain co-occurrences more than others, in part because they are the ones that are expected. Having then recorded this biased set of observations into memory, it is no surprise that we draw a biased and inaccurate conclusion, perceiving a relationship that really is not there.

For example, let us assume that we hold the common view that the English are reserved. Suppose we now meet two Englishwomen: Anne, who is reserved, and Elyse, who is gregarious. Other things being equal, we are more likely to recall that Anne is English than Elyse, because Anne fits our schema while Elyse does not. As a result, our stereotype is reinforced, and we may continue to see a correlation where actually there is none (or overestimate a correlation that is in fact quite low). Various laboratory studies support this conclusion, showing both a "noticing bias" toward cases that confirm our view and a corresponding bias in the conclusions we draw about the cases we encounter (see Hamilton & Rose, 1980).

*In-groups*   *In-groups are often defined in terms of racial or ethnic background, but loyalty to a sports team can also define an in-group. The group members sometimes emphasize their affiliation with elaborate (and some might say bizarre) costumes.*

*"They're All Alike"*   Our tendency to rely on stereotypes is further reinforced by the so-called *out-group homogeneity effect*, which describes how we perceive "us" (the in-group) versus "them" (the out-group). Take the assertions "All Asians are alike" or "All Germans are alike." The first is almost invariably made by a non-Asian, the second by a non-German. The same holds for assertions such as "All women are alike," "All men are alike," "All blacks are alike," and "All whites are alike." Members of a group tend to see members of other groups as more alike than members of their own.

*Group Stereotypes and In-group Favoritism*   Illusory correlations help us understand why people often have false beliefs about other groups. But what about another, and rather troubling, fact about stereotypes—namely, the fact that they are so often derogatory (Sabini, 1995; Hewstone, Rubin, & Willis, 2002)?

One reason for this fact comes from the various forms of self-serving bias discussed earlier in the chapter. As we have seen, people generally find a positive interpretation of their own behavior and discount information detrimental to their self-concept. To the extent that we identify with a group we belong to ("I'm a lifelong Democrat" or "Proud to be Irish!"), then we will apply the same tendency to the group, with the others (the out-groups) suffering by comparison.

This favoritism seems to be in large part inadvertent, as demonstrated by a study in which participants were shown repeated pairings of pronouns with nonsense syllables. Some of the pronouns were self-referential (*we, us, ours*), while the remainder referred to others (*they, them, theirs*). Participants were then asked to rate the pleasantness of each nonsense syllable. The syllables that had been paired with the self-referential pronouns were rated more pleasant (Perdue et al., 1990). Numerous other findings also show that we quickly endorse and easily remember positive information about our own group and negative information about other groups, especially if that information matches our preexisting group stereotypes (Fiske, 1998).

Does this sort of inadvertent favoritism influence actual stereotypes? We have already seen evidence that it does, in our discussion of implicit attitudes and implicit associations. Even among people who explicitly hold egalitarian views, we can detect patterns of priming that are prejudiced against one group or another—against women, African Americans, and so on (Blair & Banaji, 1996; Chen & Bargh, 1997; Kawakami, Dion, & Dovidio, 1998; Wittenbrink, Judd, & Park, 1997).

The power of stereotypes is obviously troubling, as stereotyping can plainly lead to various forms of discrimination (and worse). This makes it all the more important for investigators to pursue another issue—namely, what we can do to combat stereotyping and prejudice. As it turns out, prejudice can be reduced, through a number of steps. Some sorts of intergroup contact have a powerful effect, especially if the contact is sustained over a long period of time, involves active cooperation toward a shared goal, and provides equal status for all participants (e.g., Pettigrew, 1998). There are also steps we can take to enhance the likelihood that a prejudiced person will develop a more individualized perception of the members of another group, and so lose the "they're all alike" attitude (Dovidio & Gaertner, 1999). Given the importance of these issues, it is surely encouraging that investigators are finding means to combat prejudice, and it is in some ways urgent that this research continue.

# ATTRIBUTION

Whenever we rely on schemas, we are interpreting others' behaviors within a particular framework. In fact, virtually all social perception involves some amount of interpretation, as we seek to draw conclusions about what a person is "really like."

Why is interpretation necessary? It is because most of the social behavior we encounter is actually ambiguous. If Mary smiles at you, is it a sign of affection? Or was she merely in a good mood? Or is she generally polite, smiling at everyone? Your conclusions about Mary—and your likely actions toward her in the future—will be very different, depending on which of these interpretations you choose. Similar ambiguities arise in interpreting a friend's remark, a shove in the subway, or a candidate's warm handshake. In each case, we observe a behavior, but the conclusions we will draw, the actions we will take in turn, depend on how we construe that behavior.

"I've heard that outside working hours he's really a rather decent sort."

## ATTRIBUTION AS A RATIONAL PROCESS

Social psychologists refer to the process through which we interpret behavior as *causal attribution*, and how we form these explanations of behavior (that is, to what do we attribute it?) is one of social psychology's central concerns (see, for example, Heider, 1958; Jones & Nisbett, 1972; Kelley, 1967; Kelley & Michela, 1980). According to Harold Kelley, one of the first investigators in this area, the process through which such decisions are reached is analogous to the way in which a scientist tracks down the cause of a physical event (Kelley, 1967)—by isolating those conditions under which the event occurs, and those in which it does not.

This means that, to answer the question, "Why did Mary smile at me?" you have to consider the various circumstances in which the smiling occurs. Does Mary consistently smile in social settings? Would most other people smile in the same circumstances? If the answer to both of these questions is yes, her smile is probably best understood as a result of the situation. But if other people do not smile in this setting, or if Mary does not smile when greeting others, then another attribution is called for (Heider, 1958; Kelley, 1967).

To put this differently, causal attribution is often concerned with whether the behavior should be understood as a product of the situation or as a product of the person's traits or predispositions. The latter two terms refer to a person's tendency to act in a certain way so persistently that it is considered part of that individual's basic character. People's predispositions include their typical way of interpreting events (such as people who generally are optimists, pessimists, romantics, cynics, or whatever); they also include their typical pattern of behavior (being friendly, cunning, or self-indulgent).

# ERRORS IN THE ATTRIBUTION PROCESS

How accurately do people discern when behaviors should be attributed to someone's predispositions, and when to the situation? In truth, we are not all that accurate, and one of the contributions of social psychologists has been to discover when and why we are apt to make errors in causal attribution.

## THE FUNDAMENTAL ATTRIBUTION ERROR

A major source of error comes from a tendency to ascribe people's behavior to their nature and not to their situation—even when there is ample reason to believe the situation is, in fact, playing a crucial role. This bias is so pervasive that it has been called the *fundamental attribution error* (Ross, 1977; see Sabini, Siepmann, & Stein, 2001, for a current interpretation). Thus, the person on welfare is often judged to be lazy (a dispositional attribute) when he may really be unable to find work (a situational attribute). Much the same holds for our interpretation of public affairs. We look for heroes and scapegoats and tend to praise or blame political leaders for acts over which they had little control.

This overemphasis of dispositional factors is dramatized by an experiment that had college students participate in a simulated TV quiz show. Students were run in pairs and drew cards to decide who would be the "quiz master" and who the "contestant." The quiz master had to make up questions, drawn from any area in which she had some expertise; the contestant had to try to answer them. Some of the questions were extremely difficult (for example, "What do the initials *W. H.* stand for in the poet W. H. Auden's name?"), and so it is unsurprising that the contestants' score for correct answers was quite low, averaging only 40 percent.

The entire mock game show was witnessed by a student audience. When later asked to rate the two participants, these observers judged the quiz masters to be considerably more knowledgeable than the contestants. After all, the quiz masters seemed to have a wealth of factual knowledge, allowing them to generate these challenging questions. The contestants, on the other hand, failed to answer these questions. Obviously, therefore, they did not know facts that the quiz masters did, and so the contestants were judged to be less knowledgeable.

Of course, this comparison was rigged, because the quiz masters could choose any question, any topic, that they wished. Hence, if a quiz master had some obscure knowledge on just one topic, he could focus all his questions on that topic, avoiding the fact that he had little knowledge in other domains. The contestants, on the other hand, were at the mercy of whatever questions their quiz masters posed. And, in fact, it would have been an impressive coincidence if the special area of expertise selected by the quiz master was also an area of expertise for the contestant. No wonder, then, that the contestants did so poorly.

This was, in short, a situation plainly set up to favor the quiz master, and so any interpretation of the quiz master's "superiority" needs to take this situational advantage into account. But the observers consistently failed to do this. They knew that the roles in this setting—who was quiz master, who was contestant—had been determined by chance, for they witnessed the entire procedure. Even so, they could not help regarding the quiz masters as more knowledgeable than the contestants—a tribute to the power of the fundamental attribution error (Ross, Amabile, & Steinmetz, 1977).

## THE ACTOR-OBSERVER BIAS

The tendency to underrate the importance of situational factors occurs primarily when we try to understand the behavior of others. The results are quite different when we ourselves are the actors rather than the observers. If someone else trips, we think she is

*Challenges to attribution* **In deciding why someone is behaving as they are, we need to decide whether their behavior is shaped primarily by the circumstances, or primarily by who they are. Was Jesse Ventura a wild and aggressive fellow in the wrestling ring because that is what he is really like, or because that is the sort of behavior appropriate for (and elicited by) the wrestling ring?**

careless or clumsy. But when we ourselves trip, we say the floor is slippery. If someone else does poorly on a test, we are astonished by his ignorance. But if the poor grade is our own, we conclude that the test must have been either too hard or unfair.

These contrasts illustrate the *actor-observer difference* in attribution. When we are the observers, we tend to emphasize dispositional factors and may fall prey to the fundamental attribution error. But when we are the actors, we usually show the opposite pattern and conclude that the responsibility lies not with us but in the external situation (Jones & Nisbett, 1972).

*A Cognitive Interpretation: Different Information*   What accounts for this actor-observer difference? One interpretation is simply that we know ourselves better than we know anyone else. Let us say that on one evening you undertip a waiter in a restaurant. Does this imply that you are stingy by nature? You may testify that you are not, because you know that, on other evenings, in other restaurants, you have tipped generously. You conclude, therefore, that you are not generally stingy, and so the fact that you undertipped this evening must be due to extenuating circumstances—perhaps the waiter was rude, or perhaps you were distracted by the dinner conversation and miscalculated the percentage.

Things are obviously different for the people observing you, because most likely they have not seen you before in this sort of situation. For them, therefore, this one instance of undertipping weighs heavily, and they have no evidence to counter the idea that your behavior is typical. As a result, the causal attribution will emphasize disposition (you are stingy) over the situation.

The suggestion, then, is that the actor-observer difference is a simple consequence of how much we know about ourselves, relative to how much others know about us. Some evidence in line with this hypothesis comes from a study which shows that the tendency to make dispositional attributions is somewhat less when the person we are describing is a close friend rather than a mere acquaintance (Nisbett et al., 1973). As predicted, more knowledge about a person leads to more attention to the situation.

*A Perceptual Interpretation: Different Perspective*   There is another factor that contributes to the difference between actors and observers: the two have different physical perspectives. To the observer, what stands out perceptually is the actor and her actions. The situation that elicits these actions is seen much less clearly, in part because the stimuli to which the actor responds are not as readily visible from the observer's vantage point. The reverse holds for the actor. She is not focused on her own behavior. One reason is that she cannot see her own actions very clearly (some, such as her own

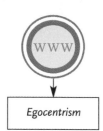

Egocentrism

**10.1   The actor-observer difference**   *A schematic figure of a study on the effect of visual perspective on the actor-observer difference. Two actors (actually confederates) were engaged in a conversation and observed from three vantage points: from behind Actor A, from behind Actor B, and from midway between them. The results showed that the observer who watched from behind Actor A believed that B controlled the conversation, while the observer behind Actor B thought the reverse. The observer who watched from midway between the two believed that both were equally influential. (After Taylor & Fiske, 1975)*

Actor A         Actor B

facial expressions, are literally invisible to her). What she attends to is the situation around her—the place, the people, and how she interprets them all. If we assume that whatever serves as the main center of attention (the figure rather than the ground) is more likely to be seen as the cause for whatever happens, then the differences in attribution follow: dispositional for the observer (who thus commits the fundamental attribution error), situational for the actor (Heider, 1958).

That the vantage points of actor and observer affect causal attribution was shown in a study that had two strangers meet and converse while each was being videotaped. When the videotape was replayed to the participants later, only one of them was on camera (on the pretense that the other's camera had malfunctioned). As a result, one of the participants saw just what he had seen before: his fellow conversationalist. But the other saw something different: himself. When asked to describe his own behavior, the participant who saw the videotape of his partner gave the usual pattern of attribution—he said that his own actions were caused by the situation. For the participant who now saw himself, his reversed perspective led to a reversal of the usual actor-observer difference. Having watched himself, he described his own behavior dispositionally (Storms, 1973; for a related result see Figure 10.1).

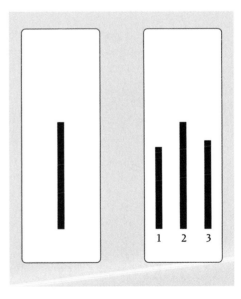

*Soloman E. Asch (1907–1997)*

# CONFORMITY AND THE SOCIAL CONSTRUCTION OF REALITY

Earlier in this chapter, we argued that many aspects of who we are—including our attitudes about ourselves and others—are shaped by social interactions. But psychologists have also suggested that social interactions have a still more powerful effect: guiding our most basic perceptions of reality. After all, much of what we know about the world, we know because of others. As a result, we look at the world not just through our own eyes but also through the eyes of others, and we form our beliefs on the basis of what we have heard them say or what they have written.

In fact, our very notion of physical reality is at least in part a matter of mutual agreement. This point was made very dramatically in a classic study performed by Solomon Asch (Asch, 1956). In Asch's experiment, nine or ten participants were brought together in a laboratory room and shown pairs of cards placed a few feet in front of them. On one card was a black line, say, 8 inches long. On the other card were three lines of different lengths, say 6, 8, and 7 inches (Figure 10.2). The participants were asked to make a simple perceptual judgment, to pick which of the three lines on the one card was equal in length to the single line on the other card.

The three lines were clearly different, and one of them was an exact match to the original line, so the task was absurdly simple. But there was a catch. There was actually only one real participant. All of the others were the experimenter's secret confederates, whose seats were arranged so that most of them would call out their judgments before the real participant had his turn.

In the first few trials, these confederates each called out the correct response and the real participant followed suit. After the initial trials, however, the confederates shifted strategy and unanimously rendered false judgments on most of the trials thereafter. For example, they might declare that a 6-inch line equaled an 8-inch line and likewise for the subsequent trials. Given the predicament that the clear evidence of his senses was now contradicted by everyone around him, what was the participant to think, and what would he do?

Asch found that the chances were less than one in four that the participant would be fully independent and stick to his guns when the group disagreed with him. Most participants yielded to the group on at least some occasions, in clear disregard of the evidence

**10.2 The stimulus cards in Asch's social pressure experiment** *The cards are drawn to scale. (Asch, 1956)*

*The participant in a social pressure experiment* (A) *The true participant (left) listens to the instructions.* (B) *On hearing the unanimous verdict of the others, he leans forward to look at the cards more carefully.* (C) *After twelve such trials, he explains that "he has to call them as he sees them."*

of their senses. When interviewed after the experiment, virtually all of the yielding participants made it clear that the group did not really affect how they saw the lines. No matter what everyone else said, the 8-inch line still looked longer than the 6-inch line. But no matter how clear their perception seemed to be, the participants reported that, as they called out their judgments, they had agonized about whether they were right or not, began to fear for their vision and sanity, and were exceedingly embarrassed at expressing their deviance in public (Asch, 1952, 1956; Asch & Gleitman, 1953; for a more recent survey of related studies, and how this result may be shaped by the cultural surroundings, see Bond & Smith, 1996).

Why were the participants so deeply distressed by this situation? The answer is that Asch's procedure had violated what was for the participants (and most of us, too) an inviolable premise: that however we may differ, we all share the same physical reality. Under the circumstances, it is small wonder that the participants in Asch's studies were alarmed by a discrepancy they had never previously encountered. They probably felt as if a vital prop had been knocked out from under them, a prop so basic that they never even realized it was there.

## SOCIAL REFERENCING
## AND SOCIAL COMPARISON

In the Asch study, the participant had to pit the clear evidence of his own senses against the verdict of a unanimous group. Suppose, though, that our own perceptions are not

*Social comparison   The two museum visitors don't seem quite sure what to make of Marisol's sculpture* The Family *and compare reactions.*

so clear-cut. What would happen, for example, if we were Asch's participants, but Asch made the lines differ by only a small amount? If left to our own devices, we would reexamine the lines or try to measure them with a ruler. If we could not do that, then it is only reasonable to listen to what others say and to use their judgments in lieu of further information provided by our own eyes or hands. If the others disagreed with our not-very-confident impression, it should be easy for us to back down and to change our own answer on their say-so.

Several studies have shown that this is precisely what occurs in an Asch-type experiment in which the discrimination is fairly difficult. There is more yielding and very little emotional disturbance (Crutchfield, 1955). This general line of reasoning also explains why people seek the opinion of others whenever they are confronted by a situation that they do not fully understand. To evaluate the situation, they need more information. If they cannot get it firsthand, they will try to compare their own reactions to those of others (Festinger, 1954; Suls & Miller, 1977).

This pattern of relying on others in the face of uncertainty can also be observed in young children, and even infants. Infants who confront a scary situation and do not know whether to advance or retreat will glance toward their caretaker's face. If she smiles, the infant will tend to advance; if she frowns, he will tend to withdraw and return to her (Rosen, Adamson, & Bakeman, 1992; Walden & Baxter, 1989). This early phenomenon of social referencing may be the prototype for what happens all our lives, a general process of validating our reactions by checking on how others are behaving, a process known as *social comparison*.

## PERSUASIVE COMMUNICATIONS

In the Asch experiment, each of the confederates simply announced his decision and then sat silently as the other confederates announced their views. In most social settings, though, people do more than this. They offer justifications of their views, with the intent of persuading others that their views are correct. Likewise, they challenge the opposing views, in hopes of persuading the dissenters to shift position. What is the impact of all of this? How responsive is each of us to persuasion?

A number of social psychologists have tried to understand the effectiveness (or ineffectiveness) of *persuasive communications*, messages that openly try to convince us to stop smoking, to outlaw abortion, to favor capital punishment, or, on a humbler level, to choose one brand of toothpaste over another. Not surprisingly, many factors govern whether these messages have their desired effect, including the person who sends the message and the message itself (Cialdini, Petty, & Cacioppo, 1981; McGuire, 1985).

*The Message Source* One factor that determines whether someone will change your mind on a given issue is who that someone is. Naturally, communications have more of an effect if they are delivered by a credible source rather than by someone with no credentials. Thus, a recommendation for a new allergy medicine is more effective if ascribed to the *New England Journal of Medicine* rather than a popular mass-circulation magazine; a positive review of an obscure poem is more likely to lead to appreciation of the poem if the review is attributed to a famous poet such as T. S. Eliot rather than to a fellow student (Aronson, Turner, & Carlsmith, 1963; Hovland & Weiss, 1952).

Credibility is important, but so is trustworthiness. Would-be persuaders have a much harder time persuading us if we believe that they have something to gain from it. Conversely, persuaders are more effective when they argue for a position that seems to go against their own self-interest. In one study, students were shown statements that argued either for or against the strengthening of police power; the statements were attributed either to a prosecuting attorney or to a criminal. Statements in favor of stronger law enforcement had more effect when attributed to the criminal rather than the prosecutor; the reverse was true for statements favoring weaker law enforcement (Walster, Aronson, & Abrahams, 1966). In the same fashion, when a car salesman tells you he would like to sell you a car, but that another make of car would suit you better, you are likely to believe him. (Unless you believe that the other car dealership he recommends belongs to his brother-in-law.)

*The Message*  However important the messenger, the message she delivers is more important. What determines whether the message will be persuasive? According to Petty and Cacioppo (1985) there are two routes to persuasion. In the first, the *central route to persuasion*, we follow the message carefully and think through its arguments. We take this route if the issue is one that matters to us and if we are not distracted by other concerns. Here, content and information are what matter, and strong arguments will prevail over weak ones.

Things are different, though, if the message comes by way of the *peripheral route to persuasion*. We take this route if we do not care much about the issue, or if the message is garbled because of background noise, or if we are somehow distracted. In such circumstances, content and arguments matter little. What counts instead is who presents the message and how and where it is presented (Petty & Cacioppo, 1985; Petty, Wegener, & Fabrigar, 1997; Petty & Wegener, 1998; for a closely related view, see Chaiken, Liberman, & Eagly, 1989; Chaiken, Wood, & Eagly, 1996; Eagly & Chaiken, 1993; for more on the factors that lead us to rely on the peripheral route rather than the central one, see Wood, 2000). Similarly, we are more apt to be persuaded by the good looks of an attractive spokesperson if we are not paying much attention to the message itself (Shavitt et al., 1994).

The central route to persuasion involves reasoned thought. But what does the peripheral route involve? According to some authors, this route provides one more example of the mental shortcuts that we so often take. After all, there are only so many things we can pay attention to, and so we use some rules of thumb, or *heuristics*, to help us decide whether to accept or reject the message (Chaiken, 1987; Eagly & Chaiken, 1984). Such heuristics may include some reliance on the nature of the speaker (for example, his apparent expertise, likability, or good looks) and on some superficial features of the arguments being presented, such as their sheer length or number, regardless of how good they are. Such heuristics in reacting to persuasive communications are reminiscent of heuristics in reasoning and decision making; both are mental shortcuts we resort to simply because our time and cognitive capacities are limited (see Chapter 8 for a further discussion of heuristics).

The peripheral route to persuasion may involve other mechanisms as well. Some authors believe, for example, that something like classical conditioning is involved, such that a message or product becomes associated in the minds of the audience with another object or outcome (see Chapter 4; Cacioppo et al., 1993). In other cases, persuasion may involve the priming of implicit attitudes or implicit memories (see Chapter 7; also Greenwald & Banaji, 1995).

*Appealing to reason*   *Often, advertisements try to sell a product merely by associating it with a popular activity or an attractive person. Sometimes, though, ads do try to* persuade *us, giving us information that might influence our choices in the marketplace.*

## CONFORMITY AND BEYOND

If the world worked solely by persuasion, then it would be a world of calm advocacy and reasoned communication. But people change their minds and behavior not just because of persuasion; they also conform, pure and simple, without giving much thought to it. Why do people conform? There are many reasons. As we have indicated, sometimes the information we have received is ambiguous or incomplete, and so we turn to others on the belief (or, sometimes, the hope) that they have information we do not have. This holds for any difficult judgment, whether it is sensory, social, or moral. If we are near-

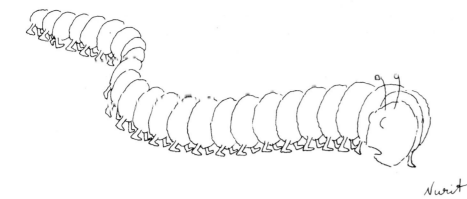

"Twenty-two is out of step. Pass it on."

*(© 1974, Saturday Review, cartoon by Nurit Karlin)*

sighted and are not wearing glasses, we will ask others to read distant street signs; if we are not sure of what to wear (or what to say, or who to vote for), we watch what others do to get some clues for how we should act. This makes it easy to understand why people are less likely to conform if they believe they are more competent and knowledgeable in some area than others are (see, for example, Wiesenthal et al., 1976; Campbell, Tesser, & Fairey, 1986).

Another reason for going along with the crowd has less to do with information and more to do with appearances. Consider the original Asch study in which a unanimous majority made a grossly incorrect judgment. The participant saw the world as it is, but if she said what she believed, she could not help but be embarrassed; after all, the others would probably think that she was a fool and would even laugh at her. Under the circumstances, many participants preferred to disguise what they really believed and go along. That something of this sort is going on was shown in another variant of the experiment in which the participant came late while the experiment was already in progress. The experimenter told him that since he arrived late, it would be simpler for him to write his answers down in private rather than to announce them out loud. Under these circumstances, few participants bent to the group pressure and, instead, stuck with their own (private) judgments (Asch, 1952; for more on how publicly expressed views may or may not differ from private ones, see, for example, Cowan & Hodge, 1996; Lambert et al., 1996; Wood, 2000).

## MAJORITIES AND MINORITIES

A unanimous majority evidently exerts a powerful effect on a solitary individual, an effect that makes it very difficult for the individual to stray from the majority's position. What happens, though, when the individual is no longer alone? An answer to this question comes, once again, from Asch's studies of conformity. In one variation of his experiment, Asch had one of the confederates act as the participant's ally; all of the other confederates gave wrong answers while the ally's judgments were correct. Under these conditions, the pressure to conform largely evaporated, and the participant yielded rarely and was not particularly upset by the odd judgment offered by (the majority of) the confederates.

Note, however, that this study is ambiguous. Was the pressure to conform reduced because the participant had an ally, sharing his views? Or was the pressure reduced merely because the consensus was broken, so that the participant was no longer alone in questioning the majority view? To find out, another variation of the study was conducted in which the confederate again deviated from the majority, but did not do so by giving the correct answer. On the contrary, he gave an answer that was even further from the truth than was the group's. Thus, on a trial in which the correct answer was 6¼ inches and the majority answer was 6¾ inches, the confederate's answer might be 8 inches. This response was obviously not arrayed on the side of the participant (or of truth!), but it helped to liberate him even so. The participant now yielded very much less than when he was confronted by a unanimous majority. What evidently mattered was the group's unanimity, and once this was broken, the participant felt that he could speak up without fear of embarrassment (Asch, 1952). Similar studies have been performed in other laboratories with essentially similar results (Allen, 1975; Allen & Levine, 1971; Nemeth & Chiles, 1988).

One person who shares our view can sustain us against all others. But if we cannot find a supporter, the next best thing is to find another person who also opposes the majority, even if his opposition is for different reasons than our own. Thus, totalitarian systems have good reason to stifle dissent of any kind. The moment one voice is raised in dissent, the unanimity is broken, and then others may (and often do) find the courage to express their own dissent, whatever its form.

*The effect of a consistent minority*  **A steadfast minority can gradually create genuine changes in what people think and feel as in the case of the American civil rights movement. A scene from the 1965 march from Selma to Montgomery.**

## OBEDIENCE

Other people, it seems, influence our behavior in many ways. They may persuade us, through both the central and the peripheral route. They induce us to conform, for both cognitive and motivational reasons. But there is also another way that others influence our behavior: they instruct us, or even command us, and in many circumstances we obey those commands. The student obeys the teacher, the automobile driver obeys the policeman, the soldier obeys the general. In some cases, this obedience is far-reaching, leading people to violate their own principles and do things they previously felt they should not do. What produces this sort of obedience?

Before we explore this issue, we should note that obedience, by itself, is neither a good nor a bad thing. After all, a certain degree of obedience is a necessary ingredient of social life. In any society, some individuals need to have authority over others, at least within a limited sphere. Someone needs to direct traffic; someone needs to tell people when they should put their garbage out at the curb for collection; someone needs to instruct children and get them to do their homework. In each of these cases, it is entirely appropriate that the relevant person be granted authority, and that people obey their instructions.

At the same time, though, it is clear that obedience in some circumstances can lead to hideous outcomes. The atrocities of the last century—the Nazi death camps, the Cambodian massacres, the so-called ethnic cleansing in Bosnia—could not have been committed without the obedience of tens or hundreds of thousands and the acquiescence of many more. How could such obedience have come about?

In trying to answer this question, some psychologists have taken a dispositional approach and explored whether people in general, or perhaps just some people, are obedient by nature. Other psychologists, using a situational approach, have studied how obedience is promoted or controlled by aspects of the social situation and our interpretation of it.

### OBEDIENCE AND PERSONAL PREDISPOSITION

What makes people obey and become accomplices to the unspeakable crimes that stain human history? One interpretation is that some personalities are more prone to obey than others, that the crucial determinant is within the person rather than in the situation.

An influential version of the person-centered hypothesis was proposed shortly after World War II by investigators who believed they had discovered a personality type predisposed toward totalitarian dogma and thus toward blind obedience. Such so-called *authoritarian personalities*, it was proposed, are prejudiced against various minority groups and hold certain sentiments about authority, including a general belief that the world is best governed by a system of power and dominance in which each of us must submit to those above us and show harshness to those below. These authoritarian attitudes can be revealed (and measured) by a tendency to agree with statements such as "Obedience and respect for authority are the most important virtues children should learn," "Most of our social problems would be solved if we could somehow get rid of the immoral, the crooked, and feeble-minded people," and "People can be divided into two distinct classes: the weak and the strong" (Adorno et al., 1950).

This work on the authoritarian personality has been the subject of considerable criticism (for review, see Snyder & Ickes, 1985), but while the investigators probably overreached in their conclusions, they did focus attention on an important set of relationships between social and political attitudes (Brown, 1965; Fiske, 1998). Minority prejudice probably does tend to go together with authoritarian sentiments, and people with such sentiments do show a number of political characteristics that might be expected: they tend to be more obedient to authority, vote for law-and-order candidates, accept the attitudes of those in power, and tout the virtues of stern childhood discipline (Elms & Milgram, 1966; Izzett, 1971; Poley, 1974).

## OBEDIENCE AND THE SITUATION

Can the notion of the authoritarian personality, and, more broadly, a person-centered hypothesis, explain the atrocities of recent times? Are the perpetrators of genocides simply a different breed, perhaps people who are, by their nature, all too ready to obey? Or might they be different from the rest of us in some other way—perhaps as moral monsters or similarly deranged? Although some of them probably are (Dicks, 1972), the frightening fact is that many seem to be quite ordinary people. What is horrifying about the commanders in the Nazi death camps or the brutal leaders of the Bosnian massacres is what they do and not who they are. In a well-known account of the trial of Adolf Eichmann, the man who supervised the deportation of six million Jews and other minorities to the Nazi gas chambers, historian Hannah Arendt noted a certain "banality of evil": "The trouble with Eichmann was precisely that so many were like him, and that the many were neither perverted nor sadistic, that they were, and still are, terribly and terrifyingly normal" (Arendt, 1965, p. 276).

If it does not take monsters to perpetrate monstrosities, then perhaps what makes apparently normal people capable of such horrors is the situation in which they find themselves. Under some social systems—Hitler's Germany, Stalin's Russia, Afghanistan under the Taliban—the conditions for compliance or tacit acceptance may well be so powerful that an outsider might pause to wonder whether "there but for the grace of God go I." But can we actually document the power of these situational factors?

*The Milgram Studies*   The importance of the situation in producing obedience was hammered home by the results of what may be the best-known study in social psychology, conducted by Stanley Milgram (1963; see Blass, 2000, for an examination of its substantial impact). Milgram drew his participants not from a group of violent felons, but from a local newspaper advertisement offering $4.50 per hour to persons willing to participate in a study of memory. The respondents, who represented a broad range of incomes and educations, arrived at a laboratory control room where a white-coated experimenter told them that they would be participating in a study of how punishment affected human learning.

The participants were run in pairs and drew lots to determine who within each pair would be the "teacher" and who the "learner." The task of the learner was to master a list of associations. The task of the teacher was to read out the cue word for each association, to record the learner's spoken answer, and—most important—to administer

*Obedience*   *The commandant of a concentration camp in Germany stands amid some of his prisoners who were burned or shot as the American army approached the camp during the last days of World War II. Most Nazis who held such positions insisted that they were "just following orders."*

**10.3   The obedience experiment   (A) The**
*"shock generator" used in the experiment.*
*(B) The learner is strapped into his chair and*
*electrodes are attached to his wrist.*
*(C) The teacher receives a sample shock.*
*(D) The teacher breaks off the experiment.*
*(© 1965 by Stanley Milgram. From the film*
*Obedience, distributed by Penn State Audio-*
*Visual Services.)*

punishment whenever the learner answered incorrectly. The learner was led to a cubicle, where the experimenter strapped him in a chair, to "prevent excess movement," and attached shock electrodes to his wrist—all in full view of the teacher. After the learner was securely strapped in place, the teacher returned to the control room and was seated in front of an imposing-looking shock generator that had 30 switches on it, each labeled with a voltage ranging from 15 volts for the leftmost switch to 450 volts at the opposite end. Below each of the levers there were ominous labels that ranged from "Slight Shock" to "Danger: Severe Shock" to a final, undefined "XXX" (Figure 10.3).

The procedure then began. The teacher presented the cue words, and if, on a given trial, the learner answered correctly, the teacher simply moved on to the next trial. But if the learner made a mistake, the teacher had to give the learner a shock before proceeding. The first shock given was the lowest voltage on the scale, but with each successive error, the teacher was required to increase the punishment by one step, proceeding (if needed) through the entire range of available punishments. To ensure that the teacher understood what the learner was experiencing, the teacher was also administered a sample shock that gave him an unpleasant jolt—and it was only 45 volts, just the third step in the 30-step punishment series.

Needless to say, the shock generator never delivered any shocks (except for the test jolt given to the teacher), and, to make sure the teacher did not discover this, the learner was kept out of sight in a separate cubicle, and all communication between teacher and learner was conducted over an intercom. The initial drawing, deciding who was teacher and who was learner, was also rigged so that the learner was always a confederate, played by a mild-mannered, middle-aged actor. The point of the experiment, then, was not to study punishment and learning at all; that was just a cover story. It was actually to determine how far the participants would go in obeying the experimenter's instructions.

Within the procedure, the learner made a fair number of (scripted) errors, and so the shocks that were to be delivered to the learner kept getting stronger and stronger. By the time 120 volts was reached, the victim shouted that the shocks were becoming too painful. At 150 volts he demanded that he be let out of the experiment. At 180 volts, he cried out that he could no longer stand the pain, sometimes yelling, "My heart, my heart!" At 300 volts, he screamed, "Get me out of here!" and said he would not answer any more. On the next few shocks there were agonized screams. After 330 volts, there was unbroken silence.

The learner's responses—from complaints to tormented cries—were all predetermined and well rehearsed. But the real participants—the teachers—did not know that, so they had to decide what to do. When the victim cried out in pain or refused to go on, the participants usually turned to the experimenter for instructions, a tragic form of social referencing. In response, the experimenter told the participants that the experiment had to go on, indicated that he took full responsibility, and pointed out that "the shocks may be painful but there is no permanent tissue damage."

How far did subjects go in obeying the experimenter? The results were astounding: about 65 percent of Milgram's subjects—both males and females—continued to obey the experimenter to the bitter end. This proportion was unaffected even when the learner complained of a heart condition. This is not to say that the obedient participants had no moral qualms—quite the contrary. Many of them were seriously upset. They bit their lips, twisted their hands, sweated profusely—but obeyed even so. Similar results were obtained when the study was repeated with participants from other countries such as Australia, Germany, and Jordan (Kilham & Mann, 1974; Mantell & Panzarella, 1976; Shanab & Yahya, 1977).

Is there a parallel between obedience in these artificial laboratory situations and obedience in horrific real-world situations? In some ways, there is no comparison, given the enormous disparities in scope and degree. But Milgram believed that some of the underlying psychological processes may be the same in all of these cases.

*Being Another Person's Agent* For Milgram, one of the crucial factors was the fact that all of us are brought up in a world in which there is a continual stress on obedience to legitimate authority, first within the family, then in school, and finally in the legitimate institutions in the adult world. As a result, we all become used to acting as agents performing actions that others mandate—with the others taking the responsibility. The good child does what she is told; the good employee may question his boss but will go along in the end; the good soldier learns not even to question why. They all come to see themselves as acting at others' behest and feel that they are just an agent who executes another's will: the hammer that strikes a nail, not the carpenter who wields it.

The feeling that one is a mere instrument with little or no sense of personal responsibility can be promoted even further. One way is by increasing the psychological distance between one's own actions and their end result. To study this possibility, Milgram ran a variation of his procedure in which two "teachers" were involved: one a confederate who administered the shocks, and the other—actually, the real participant—who had to perform subsidiary tasks such as reading the words over a microphone and recording the learner's responses. In this new role, the participant was still an essential part of the experiment, because if he stopped, the victim would receive no further shocks. In this variation, though, the participant was more removed from the impact of his actions, like a minor cog in a bureaucratic machine. After all, he did not do the actual shocking! Under these conditions, over 90 percent of the participants went to the limit, continuing with the procedure even at the highest level of shock (Milgram, 1963, 1965; see also Kilham & Mann, 1974).

If obedience is increased by decreasing an individual's sense of personal responsibility, does the opposite hold as well? To answer this question, Milgram decreased the psychological distance between what the teacher did and its effect on the victim. Rather than being out of sight in an experimental cubicle, the victim was now seated directly adjacent to the teacher. Instead of merely pressing a lever, the teacher also had to press the victim's hand down on a shock electrode, by force if necessary. (The teacher's own hand was encased in an insulating glove "to protect it from the shock"; see Figure 10.4). Now compliance dropped considerably, in analogy to the fact that it is easier to drop bombs on an unseen enemy than to plunge a knife into his body when he looks you in the eye. Even so, 30 percent of the subjects still obeyed to the end. (For further discussion of this and related issues, see Miller, 1986.)

*Cognitive Reinterpretations* In addition to emphasizing his role as merely another's agent, the obedient person has still other ways to reinterpret the situation, to diminish any sense of culpability. One of the most common approaches is to put on psychic blinders and try to ignore the fact that the victim is a living, suffering fellow being. According to one of Milgram's participants, "You really begin to forget that there's a guy out there, even though you can hear him. For a long time I just concentrated on pressing the switches and reading the words" (Milgram, 1974, p. 38). This **dehumanization of the victim** is a counterpart to the obedient person's self-picture as a tool of another's will, someone "who has a job to do" and who does it whether he likes it or not. The obedient person, in other words, sees himself as an instrument, not an agent, and sees the victim as an object, not a person. In this way, both have become dehumanized (Bernard, Ottenberg, & Redl, 1965).

The dehumanization of the opponent is common in war and mass atrocity. Victims are rarely described as people, but instead are referred to as bodies, objects, and numbers. The process of dehumanization is propped up by euphemisms and bureaucratic jargon. The Nazis used terms such as "final solution" (for the mass murder of six million people) and "special treatment" (for death by gassing); the nuclear age contributed "fallout problem" and "preemptive attack"; the Vietnam War gave us "free-fire zone" and "body count"; other wars gave "ethnic cleansing" and "collateral damage"—all dry,

10.4  *Obedient teacher pressing the learner's hand upon the "shock electrode"* **(© 1965 by Stanley Milgram. From the film** Obedience, **distributed by Penn State Audio-Visual Services.)**

*Dehumanizing the opponent*  **In wartime, propaganda posters routinely dehumanize the opponent, as this World War I poster turns the German enemy into a gorilla savaging the innocent maiden. This dehumanization helps motivate the populace in support of the war effort and also diminishes any sense of guilt about acts of aggression conducted against the enemy.**

official phrases that are admirably suited to keep the thoughts of blood and human suffering at a reasonably safe distance.

By dehumanizing the victim, moral qualms are pushed into the background. But for all except the most brutalized, though, these qualms cannot be banished forever. To justify continued obedience, such queasy feelings must be suppressed, and one powerful way to do this is by reference to some higher, overriding moral ideology. In Milgram's study, the participants convinced themselves that science had to be served regardless of the victim's cries; in Nazi Germany, the goal was to cleanse humanity by ridding it of Gypsy and Jewish "vermin." In a related kind of self-justification, the fault is often projected on the victims; they are considered subhuman, dirty, evil, and if they suffered—well, they only have themselves to blame.

*The Slippery Slope* One's abdication of personal responsibility—through distancing or dehumanizing—is achieved not instantly, but incrementally, in gradual steps. This is why obedience is often obtained through a variation on the foot-in-the-door technique we outlined earlier. Thus, the authority figure starts by requesting some inconsequential deed that entails no moral qualms. This is then followed by commands which escalate so gradually that each step seems only slightly different from the one before. This escalation, obvious in Milgram's study, creates a slippery slope that subjects slide down unawares. The same slippery slope was part of the indoctrination of Nazi death-camp guards, and it is a vital part of military training everywhere. Draftees go through "basic training" not only to survive in combat but also to acquire the habit of instant and unquestioning obedience. Before basic training, few raw recruits would point their guns at other people and shoot to kill. By the end of basic training, obedience to the command to shoot comes almost automatically.

*Milgram's Study, the Person, and the Situation* Modern social psychologists generally interpret Milgram's results as a pointed reminder of the power of the situation, with the situation in this case able to lure people into actions that—on calm reflection—they find horrific. But his results also make another point—namely, the degree to which we seem to misunderstand the sources of our own actions. We all surely know that some of our behaviors are governed by situational cues; we all know that virtually everyone stops at a red light and is solemn at funerals. But we all seem to carry the belief that there are clear limits on what a situation can make us do. We are convinced that we would not be like Milgram's teachers, willing to administer such high levels of shock. Each of us instead believes that we have a basic sense of right and wrong that no amount of coercion—even someone putting a gun to our head—could get us to violate.

In fact, Milgram collected data to document this intuition. Before he published his results, he described his study to several groups of experts, including a group of forty psychiatrists. All of them predicted that he would encounter a great deal of defiance in his procedure, with at most only 2 percent of the teachers willing to go to the maximum shock intensity. As we now know, their predictions were way off the mark.

In a sense, then, Milgram's results provide yet another example of the fundamental attribution error—our belief that what people do is largely caused by who they are, and, with that, our consistent underestimation of the power of the situation to determine our behavior. At the same time, though, we should not overstate this point. The fact that two-thirds of Milgram's subjects were fully obedient and did use the maximum shock intensity provides a powerful reminder that what we do is heavily influenced by the circumstances in which we find ourselves (including the instructions that we receive from "authorities"). At the same time, it is no less important that one-third of his subjects did not obey the commands they received. The power of the situation is considerable, but it need not be overwhelming.

*The Zimbardo Prison Study* One might hope that Milgram's obedience study is just an isolated case, locating the one special circumstance in which situational pressures

*Prison conditions*    *Why are prisons as they are?*
*Why are prison guards so often aggressive and*
*prisoners so often rebellious? Does the reason lie*
*in the personalities of each group? Or is it in*
*their circumstances?*

can lead us to behave in a fashion that departs wildly from our values and our expectations. Sadly, though, other results show the same pattern and add to the argument that the situation is indeed powerful in shaping who we are and how we behave. One often-mentioned example is the prison study, conducted by Philip Zimbardo (Haney, Barks, & Zimbardo, 1973; Zimbardo, 1973; also Haney & Zimbardo, 1998).

Many authors have commented on the brutal conditions that exist in many American prisons (and the prisons of numerous other countries as well). In far too many prisons, the guards use harsh punishment and cruel coercion to force the prisoners to act as the guards wish. The prisoners, in turn, loathe the guards and seek any opportunity to rebel or, better still, to hurt the guards. What produces this explosive situation? A dispositional account would emphasize the personalities of the sort of people who seek out careers as prison guards or the personalities of convicted criminals. It turns out, though, that here too a situational account may be preferable: guards and prisoners act as they do, not because of who they are, but because of the role they are made to play, and thus the situation they are in.

In his study, Zimbardo recruited ordinary college students and randomly assigned them to be either "guards" in a pretend prison or "prisoners." Few instructions were given, and few constraints were placed on the students' behavior. What rapidly evolved, however, was a set of behaviors remarkably similar to those observed in actual prisons—with cruelty, inhumane treatment, and massive disrespect evident in all the participants. The behaviors observed were sufficiently awful that Zimbardo terminated the procedure earlier than intended, before things got really out of hand. One way or the other, though, these data underscore just how far decent and sensible people can be led toward acting in a manner that none of us (including the participants themselves) find acceptable. The power of the situation is indeed great (Zimbardo, 1978).

# SOCIAL IMPACT: THE CONVERGENCE OF SOCIAL FORCES

In most cases of obedience, people's behavior is not governed just by their response to a single individual. In Milgram's experiment, for example, participants were obedient to the commands of a white-coated experimenter, an apparent authority figure who spoke with all the authority of science. In a sense, then, participants were not capitulating to the instructions of an individual; instead, they were obeying the voice of an entire institution. In the same way, our response to a policeman is not simply our obedience to a man with a badge; rather, the force of the policeman's commands comes from the full weight of the criminal justice system. Likewise, a military commander speaks for the society he defends; teachers speak with the voice of the educational establishment. And a member of the clergy speaks for God. In each case, challenging the authority's power would be far more than a personal affront; it would be a challenge to the entire system that granted these figures authority in the first place. In light of this, it is no wonder that each of them has considerable power over what we do and how we act.

How should we think about these cases of "obedience to an institution"? Or, as a simpler case, how does it matter if we hear a command, or even a persuasive argument, from two people rather than one? The answers to these questions are addressed by Bibb Latané's **social impact theory** (Latané, 1997), which suggests that all forms of social influence can be understood by thinking of the individual as exposed to a field of social forces that converge on her, much as a number of light bulbs cast light on a target surface. How much light will be cast depends on the number of bulbs, the strength of each one, and how close the bulbs are to the target. According to Latané, the impact of social forces converging on one individual works in a similar manner. The total impact will depend on the number of people who affect the target individual, how socially strong (in age, status, or power) each of these people is, and how close they are to her in space or time (see Figure 10.5).

Evidence for the role of these factors includes work on stage fright: performers are more anxious when anticipating playing before audiences of higher than of lower status (Latané & Harkins, 1976). There is also evidence for the role of immediacy: performing for a live audience produces more stage fright than performing for one that watches a video monitor in another room (Borden, 1980). Numbers also matter: the larger the audience, the greater the stage fright. Indeed, the effects of numbers can be demonstrated in many social situations, and quite consistently—the larger the crowd, the greater its impact.

What happens if social influence is spread out over more than one target? According to Latané, this will diffuse the impact, and the more targets there are, the less social impact will hit any one of them (see Figure 10.6). Evidence again comes from a study of stage fright in participants at a college talent show. The acts at the show had from one

**10.5** *Convergence of social forces*   *(Freely adapted from Latané, 1981)*

**10.6** *Diffusion of social impact*   *(Freely adapted from Latané, 1981)*

near-cut. What would happen, for example, if we were Asch's participants, but Asch made the lines differ by only a small amount? If left to our own devices, we would reexamine the lines or try to measure them with a ruler. If we could not do that, then it is only reasonable to listen to what others say and to use their judgments in lieu of further information provided by our own eyes or hands. If the others disagreed with our not-very-confident impression, it should be easy for us to back down and to change our own answer on their say-so.

Several studies have shown that this is precisely what occurs in an Asch-type experiment in which the discrimination is fairly difficult. There is more yielding and very little emotional disturbance (Crutchfield, 1955). This general line of reasoning also explains why people seek the opinion of others whenever they are confronted by a situation that they do not fully understand. To evaluate the situation, they need more information. If they cannot get it firsthand, they will try to compare their own reactions to those of others (Festinger, 1954; Suls & Miller, 1977).

This pattern of relying on others in the face of uncertainty can also be observed in young children, and even infants. Infants who confront a scary situation and do not know whether to advance or retreat will glance toward their caretaker's face. If she smiles, the infant will tend to advance; if she frowns, he will tend to withdraw and return to her (Rosen, Adamson, & Bakeman, 1992; Walden & Baxter, 1989). This early phenomenon of social referencing may be the prototype for what happens all our lives, a general process of validating our reactions by checking on how others are behaving, a process known as *social comparison*.

## PERSUASIVE COMMUNICATIONS

In the Asch experiment, each of the confederates simply announced his decision and then sat silently as the other confederates announced their views. In most social settings, though, people do more than this. They offer justifications of their views, with the intent of persuading others that their views are correct. Likewise, they challenge the opposing views, in hopes of persuading the dissenters to shift position. What is the impact of all of this? How responsive is each of us to persuasion?

A number of social psychologists have tried to understand the effectiveness (or ineffectiveness) of *persuasive communications*, messages that openly try to convince us to stop smoking, to outlaw abortion, to favor capital punishment, or, on a humbler level, to choose one brand of toothpaste over another. Not surprisingly, many factors govern whether these messages have their desired effect, including the person who sends the message and the message itself (Cialdini, Petty, & Cacioppo, 1981; McGuire, 1985).

*The Message Source* One factor that determines whether someone will change your mind on a given issue is who that someone is. Naturally, communications have more of an effect if they are delivered by a credible source rather than by someone with no credentials. Thus, a recommendation for a new allergy medicine is more effective if ascribed to the *New England Journal of Medicine* rather than a popular mass-circulation magazine; a positive review of an obscure poem is more likely to lead to appreciation of the poem if the review is attributed to a famous poet such as T. S. Eliot rather than to a fellow student (Aronson, Turner, & Carlsmith, 1963; Hovland & Weiss, 1952).

Credibility is important, but so is trustworthiness. Would-be persuaders have a much harder time persuading us if we believe that they have something to gain from it. Conversely, persuaders are more effective when they argue for a position that seems to go against their own self-interest. In one study, students were shown statements that argued either for or against the strengthening of police power; the statements were attributed either to a prosecuting attorney or to a criminal. Statements in favor of stronger law enforcement had more effect when attributed to the criminal rather than the prosecutor; the reverse was true for statements favoring weaker law enforcem[ent] (Walster, Aronson, & Abrahams, 1966). In the same fashion, when a car salesman te[lls] you he would like to sell you a car, but that another make of car would suit you better, you are likely to believe him. (Unless you believe that the other car dealership he recommends belongs to his brother-in-law.)

*The Message* However important the messenger, the message she delivers is more important. What determines whether the message will be persuasive? According to Petty and Cacioppo (1985) there are two routes to persuasion. In the first, the **central route to persuasion**, we follow the message carefully and think through its arguments. We take this route if the issue is one that matters to us and if we are not distracted by other concerns. Here, content and information are what matter, and strong arguments will prevail over weak ones.

Things are different, though, if the message comes by way of the **peripheral route to persuasion**. We take this route if we do not care much about the issue, or if the message is garbled because of background noise, or if we are somehow distracted. In such circumstances, content and arguments matter little. What counts instead is who presents the message and how and where it is presented (Petty & Cacioppo, 1985; Petty, Wegener, & Fabrigar, 1997; Petty & Wegener, 1998; for a closely related view, see Chaiken, Liberman, & Eagly, 1989; Chaiken, Wood, & Eagly, 1996; Eagly & Chaiken, 1993; for more on the factors that lead us to rely on the peripheral route rather than the central one, see Wood, 2000). Similarly, we are more apt to be persuaded by the good looks of an attractive spokesperson if we are not paying much attention to the message itself (Shavitt et al., 1994).

The central route to persuasion involves reasoned thought. But what does the peripheral route involve? According to some authors, this route provides one more example of the mental shortcuts that we so often take. After all, there are only so many things we can pay attention to, and so we use some rules of thumb, or *heuristics*, to help us decide whether to accept or reject the message (Chaiken, 1987; Eagly & Chaiken, 1984). Such heuristics may include some reliance on the nature of the speaker (for example, his apparent expertise, likability, or good looks) and on some superficial features of the arguments being presented, such as their sheer length or number, regardless of how good they are. Such heuristics in reacting to persuasive communications are reminiscent of heuristics in reasoning and decision making; both are mental shortcuts we resort to simply because our time and cognitive capacities are limited (see Chapter 8 for a further discussion of heuristics).

The peripheral route to persuasion may involve other mechanisms as well. Some authors believe, for example, that something like classical conditioning is involved, such that a message or product becomes associated in the minds of the audience with another object or outcome (see Chapter 4; Cacioppo et al., 1993). In other cases, persuasion may involve the priming of implicit attitudes or implicit memories (see Chapter 7; also Greenwald & Banaji, 1995).

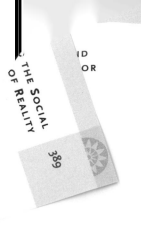

*Appealing to reason* **Often, advertisements try to sell a product merely by associating it with a popular activity or an attractive person. Sometimes, though, ads do try to persuade us, giving us information that might influence our choices in the marketplace.**

## CONFORMITY AND BEYOND

If the world worked solely by persuasion, then it would be a world of calm advocacy and reasoned communication. But people change their minds and behavior not just because of persuasion; they also conform, pure and simple, without giving much thought to it. Why do people conform? There are many reasons. As we have indicated, sometimes the information we have received is ambiguous or incomplete, and so we turn to others on the belief (or, sometimes, the hope) that they have information we do not have. This holds for any difficult judgment, whether it is sensory, social, or moral. If we are near-

*Social loafing* **In a tug-of-war, everyone seems to pull as hard as he can, but the total force exerted by the group tends to be less than would be the sum of the members' solo efforts.**

to ten performers, and the stage fright these performers experienced depended on the number of coperformers in the act: the greater their number, the less stage fright any one member of the act felt (Jackson & Latané, 1981; see Figure 10.7).

A different example of diffusion of social impact comes from a phenomenon called *social loafing*. This describes the fact that when individuals work as a group on a common task, all doing the same thing, they often generate less effort than they would if they worked alone (Karau & Williams, 1995). An example is pulling at a rope. In one study, one man working alone pulled with an average force of 139 pounds, while groups of eight pulling together only averaged 546 pounds—only about 68 pounds per person (Latané, Williams, & Harkins, 1979). There is an old adage: "Many hands make light the work." The trouble is that they do not make it as light as they should.

We should note, though, that—interestingly—groups can also have the opposite effect, producing an effect known as *social facilitation*. In the presence of others, we often do better on a task than we otherwise would, something that can be demonstrated with both physical tasks and mental ones (Bond & Titus, 1982; Zajonc, 1965; Zajonc & Sales, 1966). Why is it that the presence of a group sometimes helps performance and sometimes hurts it? An explanation was first offered by Robert Zajonc (1965), who suggested that the presence of others promotes performance of well-practiced or habitual activities but impedes performance of complex or unfamiliar activities. This is probably because the presence of others causes some degree of arousal in us, and arousal itself aids performance with some tasks but interferes with others. In either case, though, the main message is clear: our performance is plainly influenced by the social surround, even when our activity seems to be one that has no overt social component.

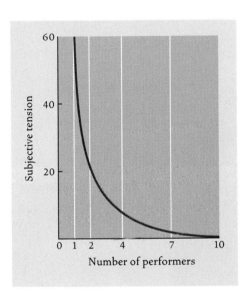

**10.7** *Diffusion of social impact and performance anxiety* **Ratings of nervousness obtained prior to a college talent show from persons who performed alone or with two, four, seven, or ten others. (After Jackson & Latané, 1981)**

# LEADERSHIP

The words we have used to describe social influence—conformity, persuasion, obedience—all have negative connotations. Conformity squashes creativity, persuasion is brainwashing, obedience permits totalitarianism. Yet each has its place, ensuring the smooth functioning of society and leading to good outcomes at least as often as bad.

Another kind of social influence that can be used for good or evil is one in which a single individual exerts his or her influence on a number—sometimes a very large number—of others. This influence is called leadership.

Leaders are found in a multitude of social contexts, including politics, the military, business and commerce, sports teams, and even the family (Hollander, 1985; Bass,

1990). Leadership can be exercised in groups as large as China or as small as a neighborhood gang. Leaders can be ultimate authorities or intermediaries in a chain of command (such as a colonel reporting to a general). Finally, leaders can exert their influence through force of personality ("charisma"), by inspiring through their own personal conduct (Mother Teresa), or by building absolute obedience (Saddam Hussein). Considering these many differences, is there anything one can say about leadership in general?

## GREAT PERSON OR SOCIAL FORCES

From one perspective, history is essentially created by exceptional individuals who, for better or worse, determine the course of human events. In the nineteenth century, the proponents of this *great-person theory* often cited the case of Napoleon Bonaparte—a political and military genius, they argued, whose brilliant mind and unyielding will overcame all opposition for over two decades (see, for example, Carlyle, 1841).

From another perspective, however, the success or failure of individuals like Napoleon is determined by the times in which they lived. Thus, for the great Russian novelist Leo Tolstoy, Napoleon's initial successes were caused by circumstance: the ineptitude of the opposing generals, the zeal of the French soldiers, the huge armies under his command. When Napoleon finally failed, it was not because his genius deserted him, but because of the ferocious Russian winter, the long supply lines, and so on (Tolstoy, 1868).

The same controversy has arisen in analyses of many other events, including current ones. Would there have been a Bolshevik Revolution if Vladimir Lenin had remained exiled from Russia? Would the British have sued for peace with Hitler if Churchill had died before 1940? Would the terrorism of September 11, 2001 have been averted if Osama Bin Laden had been killed earlier? The controversy also occurs when we consider intellectual and cultural leadership. Would natural selection have prevailed in nineteenth-century biology without Darwin? Would American women have gotten the vote by 1920 without Susan B. Anthony? The two poles of the argument have surfaced again and again: one stressing the genius of the leader, the other the historical context (Burns, 1978; Hook, 1955; Jennings, 1972; Weisberg, 1986).

Notice, though, that this debate among historians is directly analogous to the person-situation duality we have already discussed: accounts framed in terms of the leader's qualities are analogous to explanations of behavior cast in terms of a person's dispositions; appeals to the historical setting can be aligned with explanations cast in terms of the situation. In the context of leadership, one way to address these issues is to ask whether all (or most) successful leaders share any distinguishing personal characteristics. The great-person theory would predict that they do, so that a Napoleon would have probably achieved leadership even if he had never entered the military. The alternative view, in contrast, implies that there are no special qualities that identify a leader. Napoleon, in effect, just happened to be in the right place at the right time; if someone else with very different qualities had been in his role, the outcome would have been the same. What evidence can social psychology offer in choosing between these positions? Are there identifiable "leadership qualities"?

## LEADERSHIP IN THE LABORATORY

Using a variety of different techniques, social psychologists have tried to identify personal characteristics that might predict whether someone will be perceived as a leader and whether he or she will be effective in this role. In some studies, psychologists have examined leadership in real-world settings, collecting data, for example, from some-

*Leadership   How should we think about Joan of Arc's leadership? Was it created by her circumstances (as suggested by the context-rich painting in the top panel) or by her own special qualities as a person (bottom panel)?*

one's subordinates, peers, and supervisors in the workplace. Other studies have been carried out in the laboratory, with small groups of four to six given a joint task that has to be solved by discussion. Thus, group members might be told that they are explorers stranded 200 miles from their base camp, and, in order to get back to the base, they must jettison some of their equipment (tent, tools, and so on). Each member first tells the others which item he would jettison first, which second, and so on. Then the group comes up with a consensus list. To assess leadership perception, each member is rated by all others on how much he influenced the group. To assess leadership performance, each member's initial list is compared with the group's consensus list, and the extent to which a member's list resembles the final list provides an index of his effectiveness as a leader (Bottger, 1984; Cammalleri et al., 1973).

The next step in these studies is to see whether leadership perception and performance are related to any other personal characteristics. And, in fact, these studies do reveal some relevant traits. People who are seen as leaders tend to be more outgoing and more dominant than those not considered leaders (see, for example, Kenny & Zaccaro, 1983; Lord, DeVader, & Alliger, 1986). Leaders also tend to be more intelligent, although practical and creative intelligence seems much more involved than traditional IQ measures of intelligence (Riggio & Murphy, 2002, see Chapter 14).

However, the studies also indicate that these "leadership traits" play only a weak role, because, in study after study, the situation is also crucial. Thus, a prominent leader is much more likely to emerge if the situation is one that allows this (potential) leader considerable authority. It also helps if the task to be performed is clear-cut, and the group members get along with each other and with the leader. If any one of these conditions is not met, it is unlikely that anyone—no matter what his or her traits—will take on the role of, and be recognized as, a great leader.

The particular situation also matters in shaping the particular traits that someone needs to become a good leader, and this is why a person who is an effective leader in one situation may be much less effective in another setting. Concretely, the qualities that make for leadership on a corporate board of directors are different from those that make for leadership in a Scout troop or a street gang. (For a detailed proposal on the proper matchup between leaders and situations, see Fiedler, 1978.)

# GROUP DECISION MAKING

In many groups, a leader plays a pivotal role in guiding the group to a certain belief or in persuading group members to make a certain decision. Even in the absence of a leader, however, group settings can have a powerful influence on how members think and how they reach decisions. One manifestation of this influence is revealed in a phenomenon known as *group polarization*, a tendency for decisions made by groups to be more extreme than the decisions that would have been made by any of the group members working on their own. This pattern can be revealed in student workgroups, in committees working on a project, or (crucially) in juries making courtroom decisions. Often, the polarization takes the form of a so-called *risky shift*, in which groups appear more willing to take risks, more willing to take an extreme stance, than the group members would individually (see, for example, Bennett, Lindskold, & Bennett, 1973; Schroeder, 1973; Morgan & Aram, 1975). However, group polarization can also take the opposite form. If the group members are slightly cautious to begin with or slightly conservative in their choices, then these are the tendencies that are magnified, and the group's decision will end up appreciably more cautious than the decisions that would have been made by the individuals alone (Levine & Moreland, 1998; Moscovici & Zavalloni, 1969).

What produces group polarization? As is usually the case, several factors contribute.

One factor lies in the simple point that, during a discussion, individuals often state, restate, and restate again what their views are, and this helps to strengthen their commitment to these views (Brauer, Judd, & Gliner, 1995). Another factor involves the sort of confirmation bias that we introduced in Chapter 8. This term refers to the fact that people tend to pay more attention to, and more readily accept, information that fits with (confirms) their views, in comparison to their (relatively hostile) scrutiny of information that challenges their views. How does this shape a group discussion? In the discussion, people are likely to hear sentiments on both sides of an issue. Owing to confirmation bias, the arguments that support their view are likely to seem clear, persuasive, and well informed. Arguments on the other side of the issue, however, will seem weak and ambiguous. This allows people then to draw the conclusion that the arguments favoring their view are strong, while the arguments opposing it are weak. No wonder, then, if all of this simply strengthens their commitment to their own prior opinion (for the classic example of this pattern, see Lord, Ross, & Lepper, 1979).

Another factor leading to group polarization hinges on two topics we have already mentioned. On the one hand, people generally try to conform with the other members of the group, both with regard to their behavior and with regard to the attitudes they express. But, in addition, people want to stand out from the crowd so that they look good and can be judged "better than average." How can they achieve both of these goals—conforming and excelling? They can do this by taking a position that is at the group's "leading edge"—similar enough to the group's position so that the demands of conformity have been honored, but "out in front" of the group in a fashion that makes the person seem distinctive. Of course, this same logic applies to everyone in the group, and so everyone will seek to take positions and express sentiments at the group's leading edge. As a result, this edge will become the majority view! In this fashion, the group's sentiments at the start will be sharpened and made a step or two more extreme—exactly the pattern of group polarization.

Group decision making also reveals another pattern often dubbed *groupthink* (Janis, 1982). This pattern is particularly likely when the group is highly cohesive, faced by some external threat, and closed to outside information or opinions. In this setting, there is a strong tendency for group members to do what they can to promote the sense of group cohesion, and, as a result, doubts or disagreements are downplayed, the "moral" or "superior" status of the group's arguments is celebrated, enemies are stereotyped ("our opponents are stupid" or "evil"), the likelihood of success is markedly overestimated, and risks or challenges to the group are discounted or ignored.

That groupthink exists is clear, and, arguably, groupthink has been the source of a number of disastrous decisions, including the United States' decision to invade the Bay of Pigs in Cuba in the early 1960s (Janis, 1971) and the calamitous decision to launch the space shuttle *Challenger* in 1986, despite the day's cold temperature (Moorhead, Ference, & Neck, 1991). What is less clear, however, is when exactly the groupthink pattern emerges, and whether it always leads to bad outcomes (Aldag & Fuller, 1993; Esser, 1998; Tetlock et al., 1992).

# CROWD BEHAVIOR AND PANDEMONIUM

We have now considered many forms of social influence, including persuasion, conformity, leadership, and obedience. There is one further kind of social influence, though, that many observers believe belongs in a class by itself, with its own rules and its own logic: crowd behavior. Certainly, under some circumstances people in crowds behave differently from the way they do when alone. In riots or mobs, they are aggressive with

*Panic*  **On March 9, 1996, a riot broke out at a cricket match in Bangalore, India, when a large crowd tried to force its way though a narrow stadium entrance. The photo gives a glimpse of the resulting panic.**

**TABLE 10.1    PAYOFF MATRIX FOR
THE PRISONER'S DILEMMA**

|  |  | Prisoner B: | |
| --- | --- | --- | --- |
|  |  | STAYS SILENT | CONFESSES |
| Prisoner A: | STAYS SILENT | 1 year for A<br>1 year for B | 20 years for A<br>No jail for B |
|  | CONFESSES | No jail for A<br>20 years for B | 8 years for A<br>8 years for B |

ferent consequence, or payoff, for each of the prisoners, as shown in the payoff matrix in Table 10.1.

Given this payoff matrix, what should the prisoners do? Prisoner A may reason this as follows. If B confesses, it would be better for A if he confesses too (and so get eight years in jail), rather than being the one to keep silent (in which case, he would get twenty years in jail). In terms of Table 10.1, B's confession pushes us into matrix's right column, and here A is better off in the bottom cell than in the top.

On the other hand, if B keeps silent, it is still better if A confesses (and gets no punishment) rather than keeping silent as well (in which case they will both get a year in jail). Again, in terms of the table, B's *silence* keeps us in the matrix's left column, and here, once more, A is better off in the bottom cell than in the top.

In short, then, if B confesses, A is better off if he confesses too. If B does not confess, A is better off if he confesses. In either case, the conclusion is clear: A should confess. Of course, Prisoner B would go through the same logic and reach the same conclusion: either A will confess or he will not; in either case, B is better off if he confesses. With both prisoners therefore persuaded by the same logic, both will end up giving the district attorney the confession that she wants.

This situation is peculiar. If each prisoner, on his own, sensibly and logically reasons through this problem, then both will confess, and both will spend eight years in jail. But, of course, this is much less desirable (from the prisoners' point of view) than the outcome in which neither confesses, and so each spends only one year in jail. In a sense, then, the prisoners have logically chosen a course of action, each guided by their own self-interest, that leads to a "wrong outcome" for both of them.

## THE PRISONER'S DILEMMA AND PANIC

The logic of the prisoner's dilemma applies to many kinds of social interactions, including panic. In most cases of panic, the essential ingredients are the same as in the prisoner's dilemma. Each person in the burning theater, for example, has two choices: she can wait her turn to get to the exit, or she can rush ahead. As in the case of the prisoners, the outcome she can expect from each choice depends partially on what others in the theater do. If she rushes to the exit and everyone else does too, they will all probably suffer severe injuries and run some risk of death. If she takes her turn and others do the same, the outcome is better; they will all probably escape. Just as in the prisoner's dilemma, though, the best outcome for the individual is produced if she ruthlessly pushes herself ahead of the others while they continue to file out slowly. In this case she will escape unscathed, but the odds of the others escaping are slimmer. And, of course, the opposite case is the worst possible outcome: if she waits her turn while everyone else runs ahead, then they may very well get out without injury while she dies in her

**TABLE 10.2   PAYOFF MATRIX FOR AN INDIVIDUAL AND OTHERS IN A BURNING AUDITORIUM**

| | | Others (O): | |
|---|---|---|---|
| | | TAKE TURNS | RUSH AHEAD |
| Individual (I): | TAKES TURN | Minor injuries for I<br>Minor injuries for O | Increased chance of death for I<br>No injuries for O |
| | RUSHES AHEAD | No injuries for I<br>Increased chance of death for O | Severe injuries for I<br>Severe injuries for O |

seat. These sets of decisions and their associated outcomes represent another version of the prisoner's dilemma, and they are shown in the payoff matrix of Table 10.2.

Given this situation, most people probably will opt to rush ahead rather than wait their turn. As in the case of the two prisoners, this solution is grossly maladaptive, and individuals making decisions about what is good for them (individually) end up producing an outcome that is bad for all. But from the point of view of each person making these choices, the decision is, sadly enough, quite rational.

## SOCIAL DILEMMAS

In the classic prisoner's dilemma only two criminals are involved in the choice. But as the panic scenario illustrates, the dilemma can be expanded to include any number of individuals, each of whom has to decide whether to cooperate or to defect. Thus, the prisoner's dilemma and its payoff structure can be applied to many serious social and economic issues (Dawes, 1980).

Consider the social dilemma posed by industrial pollution. The payoff matrix for this case is shown in Table 10.3, with each company making a decision about whether or not to install antipollution devices, and with each then bearing the consequences of the choice—both good (a competitive advantage) and bad (a degraded environment). The analogy between this situation and the prisoner's dilemma should be clear, and it

**TABLE 10.3   PAYOFF FOR POLLUTION DEVICES**

| | | Other companies (O) | |
|---|---|---|---|
| | | INSTALL ANTIPOLLUTION DEVICES | DO NOT INSTALL ANTIPOLLUTION DEVICES |
| Company (C) | INSTALLS ANTI-POLLUTION DEVICES | All gain cleaner air | Air only moderately improved, O gains a competitive advantage |
| | DOES NOT INSTALL ANTIPOLLUTION DEVICES | Air only moderately improved, C gains a competitive advantage | No improvement to air quality; no company gains a competitive advantage |

should be equally clear that, in this case, companies may be led to make the choice that is best for them, but worst for society as a whole. Given this outcome, we are led to ask, Is there anything we can do to encourage individuals or companies to make the socially beneficial decision—for example, averting panic or avoiding pollution? One option is to adjust the payoff matrix to favor the outcomes that we desire. This is largely what the district attorney did to encourage the prisoners to confess. In the case of social dilemmas, we can adjust the payoff matrix by imposing penalties such as taxes or fines on companies that pollute, or we can enhance the appeal of altruistic behavior through education. In addition, we can also redefine the situation in a fashion that avoids the sort of adversarial your-interest-versus-mine pattern that gives rise to the prisoner's dilemma in the first place. This involves teaching the ultimate benefits of cooperation, ensuring open communication among individuals, and taking steps to increase people's trust that others will not exploit them (see, for example, Orbell, van de Kragt, & Dawes, 1988; Komorita & Parks, 1999; Rapoport, 1988).

# CULTURE AND SOCIAL INFLUENCE

Until fairly recently, many of the social phenomena we have reviewed in this chapter— the ways we make social comparisons, tend to conform, or attempt to explain the behavior of others—have been presumed to reflect basic properties of social cognition, and, as such, we expected them to be found among all peoples and in all cultures. Within the last few decades, however, social psychology experiments conducted around the world have made it clear that many of these phenomena are not universal and instead depend on the norms, values, and teachings of each culture. These results have led investigators to ask just how it is that cultural differences can lead to differences in how people interact, perceive each other, and in general think about the social world.

## COLLECTIVISM VERSUS INDIVIDUALISM AND VIEWS OF THE SELF

Many authors believe that one important distinction among cultures and ethnic groups lies in whether they are *collectivist* or *individualist* (Triandis, 1989, 1994). Collectivist societies include many of the societies of Latin America and most of the cultures of Asia and Africa. Individualist societies include the dominant cultures of the United States, Western Europe, Canada, and Australia. Of course, none of these countries is completely uniform in its culture, and people from New Jersey, say, may well have different values and perspectives than people in Arizona. Nonetheless, the countries are homogeneous enough on these issues so that we can meaningfully speak of them as being (predominantly) collectivist or (predominantly) individualist. (For more on the cultural variation within nations, see, for example, Vandello & Cohen, 1999.)

What does this distinction amount to? These two kinds of societies actually differ in many ways (Fiske et al., 1998). In collectivist societies, people are considered to be fundamentally interdependent, and the emphasis is on obligations within one's family and immediate community. These primary groups determine what is expected and what is frowned on, and provide the major motives and rewards; any efforts to individuate or stand out from one's social group are considered disruptions of the group's harmony.

In individualist societies, on the other hand, people are viewed as independent, separable entities whose actions are driven by internal needs, desires, and emotions. In these societies, the emphasis is on the ways a person can stand out through achieving private goals. There are still obligations, of course, to family and to community, but individuals have some leeway in how (or whether) they fulfill these obligations. Thus, one's important life choices—of occupation, friends, and spouse—are much less affected by the wishes of family and neighbors, for the ultimate goal is to be true to oneself and not to conform.*

Thus, students from individualist California are more likely to agree with statements that emphasize self-reliance, such as "Only those who depend on themselves get ahead in life," than are students from collectivist Hong Kong or Costa Rica. In contrast, students from Hong Kong and Costa Rica will be more likely to agree with statements that affirm a concern for one's family and close friends, such as "I would help within my means if a relative told me he (she) is in financial difficulty" and "I like to live close to my friends" (Triandis et al., 1988).

The collectivism-individualism difference offers a fresh perspective on many of the social psychological phenomena we have reviewed, with much of the relevant evidence coming from studies that have used participants from diverse cultures; here, we summarize some of the main results of such cross-cultural studies.

## CULTURAL CONTEXT OF ABOVE AVERAGE

Recall that, illogically, about 70 percent of American high-school students consider themselves above average in their leadership ability as well as on a host of other traits. For the above-average effect to occur, most of the students must have been motivated to see themselves as better than their peers, not only standing apart from their group but also, in a self-serving manner, standing over it.

What is so good about being better than one's peers? This question is rarely asked by members of individualist cultures, who are thoroughly accustomed to the premium their culture places on self-aggrandizement. But for members of collectivist cultures, self-aggrandizement brings disharmony, and this is unacceptable. On this basis, we might expect not to find the above-average effect in collectivist cultures, and the evidence bears this out. In one study, American and Japanese college students were asked to rank their abilities in areas ranging from mathematics and memory to warm-heartedness and athletic ability. The American students showed the usual result: on average, 70 percent rated themselves above average on each trait. But among the Japanese students, only 50 percent rated themselves above average, indicating no self-serving bias at all (Markus & Kitayama, 1991).

## ATTRIBUTIONS ABOUT CAUSES OF BEHAVIOR

We have noted that people show a powerful bias in how they interpret the behavior of others, generally explaining others' behavior in terms of internal dispositions rather than properties of the situation. Note, though, that this tendency reflects an emphasis on the individual—we seem to believe that people do what they do because of their individual traits, their specific styles, their particular habits—and a corresponding de-emphasis on the context. Phrased in this way, it should be clear that this explanatory bias is much more consistent with an individualist society's view than a collectivist society's. We might expect, therefore, that this bias would be diminished, and perhaps even reversed, in a collectivist society, one in which people focus more on the context (including the situation) and less on the individual.

Evidence in support of this expectation comes from a study in which participants

*Culture differences between east and west*    **It is only in the last decade or two that psychologists have taken heed of how cultures differ in their social organization. Ironically, these differences may be eroded in the near future as contact and commerce between east and west blur the differences between them. Here Den Fujita, the founding president of McDonald's in Japan, bites into a Big Mac.**

---

* Of course, both individualists and collectivists have families to which they have strong ties. But in a collectivist society, the family is normally greatly extended. Typical individualists, on the other hand, take family to mean the nuclear family: two parents and their children. Individualists often feel deep affection for their parents, but they do not feel obliged to live with them or close to them after they have started their own families.

were asked to explain the actions of the main characters in brief stories. Some of the participants were American adults and others were Hindu adults from India. The results showed that the Americans were much more likely to explain the behavior in terms of the characters' personal qualities rather than in terms of the situation, a result entirely consistent with findings we reviewed earlier in the chapter. Indian participants, on the other hand, showed the reverse pattern and were twice as likely to explain the behavior in terms of social roles and other situational factors. For example, one of the stories described a motorcycle accident in which the passenger, but not the driver, was injured. Following the accident, the driver dropped the injured passenger off at the hospital, but then, rather than staying with his friend, proceeded to work. How should one think about these actions? The Americans were surprised by the driver's actions and labeled the driver "obviously irresponsible" or "in a state of shock." The Indians had a different view and typically explained that it was the driver's duty to be at work or that the passenger's injury must not have looked serious (Miller, 1984; see also Smith & Bond, 1993; Fiske et al., 1998).

Another study examined Chinese and American newspaper accounts of two murders that occurred in the United States. The American accounts were prominently about personal qualities: the murderer was mentally unstable or had a "very bad temper" or a "psychological problem." In the Chinese accounts, the murders were blamed on the availability of guns or social isolation or interpersonal rivalry (Morris & Peng, 1994).

Cross-cultural investigators are quick to point out, however, that the use of dispositional rather than situational factors to explain behavior (and vice versa) is a cultural tendency, not an absolute. Indeed, even the most collectivist cultures retain the notion of personal traits and dispositions, just as the most individualist cultures retain the notion that situations can explain behavior. The cultural differences therefore lie in large part in the extent to which each member of the culture pays attention to the situations in which behavior occurs. For members of collectivist cultures, people's actions occur in an interlocking social matrix, and so it is natural (but not inevitable) that the actions one observes will be understood with reference to this matrix. For members of individualist cultures, actions tend to be seen as an outgrowth of an individual's dispositions, so there is little need to look further in explaining the behavior that one sees (Fiske et al., 1998). In addition, people in collectivist cultures tend to believe that a person's disposition is more malleable and less permanent than do people in individualist cultures, and this too contributes to their deemphasis on dispositional qualities in explaining the behavior that they see (Choi, Nisbett, & Norenzayan, 1999; for some complications, though, see Norenzayan & Nisbett, 2000; Nisbett & Norenzayan, 2002; Norenzayan, Choi, & Nisbett, 2002).

## IN-GROUPS AND OUT-GROUPS

Members of collectivist and individualist societies also differ in other ways. (For a discussion of just how far-reaching these differences may be, see Nisbett et al., 2001.) As an example, consider the effects of group pressure. On the face of it, one might expect that collectivists, who are more attentive to the group than the individual, will be more likely to conform with a group's judgments or actions. But it turns out that this depends on the nature of the group. Members of collectivist societies are more likely than individualists to agree or conform with members of their *in-group*, a group to which they are tied by traditional bonds. In contrast, they are less affected than individualists by members of the *out-group*, with whom they share no such bonds (compare with Bond & Smith, 1996).

A related phenomenon concerns the permanence of an individual's social bonds. Collectivists belong to relatively few in-groups, but their bonds to them are strong and long lasting. It is no accident that in Japan (a collectivist society), workers tend to remain for many years in the company they started out with, wearing the company's col-

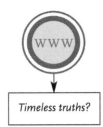

Timeless truths?

ors and singing company songs, such as "A Bright Heart Overflowing with Life Links Together Matsushita Electric" (Weisz, Rothbaum, & Blackburn, 1984).*

In contrast, members of individualist cultures belong to a whole set of overlapping in-groups, but their relation to these groups is more fragile and less enduring. In part, this is a consequence of their different values. To the individualist, what matters most is the freedom to pursue personal goals and preferences. As these change, so do social relationships. Members of individual cultures also think about their in-group differently than their out-group, and are more responsive to influences from the in-group than the out-group. But, given the impermanence of these groups, as the individual moves from one status to another, it is understandable that people in individualist cultures show somewhat less of a distinction between in-group and out-group than do members of collectivist cultures.

## SOME FINAL THOUGHTS: SOCIAL BEHAVIOR AND REASON

The great lesson of social psychology is that we are not the autonomous, self-driven individuals we conceive ourselves to be. Instead, we are inexorably intertwined within a complex web of social and cultural influences that help form our sense of self, mold our values and attitudes, and sway both our private and public actions. In this chapter, we documented many kinds of social influence, from the social referencing of the infant to the pandemonium of the panicky crowd.

Our primary emphasis in this chapter was on the role of cognition within the social sphere—what we believe, and how we perceive others in our social surrounding. But on looking back, we must note that many of the phenomena we have considered in this chapter involve the operation of both cognition and motivation, or to use two old-fashioned terms, reason and passion. Consider the effect of forced compliance: is it caused by a force toward cognitive consistency (that is, dissonance reduction) or by an attempt to minimize guilt? Or take the actor-observer bias in attribution: is it produced by such cognitive factors as differential information and distinct perspectives or by the self-serving bias?

Both reason and passion determine what we think and feel and do. As we try to make sense of our social world, we try to be rational, but our cognitive strategies often lead us to rely on various mental shortcuts and schemas that may result in errors and biases. Since we are people with motives, passions, and a need to maintain self-esteem, these biases are often shaped by what we hope to see, so that we are sometimes wishful thinkers rather than rational ones.

In the next chapter we approach head-on the "passion" side of the human equation. We examine human emotions: what they are, what they mean, and how they affect our behavior. We take a special look at love and sexual attraction, and at the darker side of human nature: violence and aggression. Our survey will also require that we take into account our "biosocial" side: the bodily mechanisms that underlie the passions and their expression, and how they evolved. We shall see that, even here, our cognition operates jointly with motivation to determine how we act and what we experience.

---

* There has been some discussion in recent years over whether the increasing globalization of the economy may undercut this pattern. If the same employer is doing business in Tokyo and in Detroit, there is some likelihood that employees will be treated in much the same way in the two countries, potentially homogenizing the employees' attitude toward their employer. Even with this complication, however, there is no question that this homogenization sits atop a substantial difference in employees' initial view of their relation to their employer.

# SUMMARY

## THE SOCIAL SELF

1. How we interact with other people depends on many factors. One is our *self-concept.* Every one of us seems to know a great deal about ourselves. One possibility is that this knowledge comes from *introspection.* But the evidence indicates that the path to self-knowledge is not so direct because many of the processes that influence us are outside of our *conscious awareness.* According to *self-perception theory* we come to know ourselves not via introspection, but in the same way we come to understand other people—by means of a process of inference and interpretation.

2. Evidence comes from studies that show that under some circumstances our feelings or beliefs seem to be the result of our actions, and not their cause. Examples are provided by studies of the *foot-in-the-door technique,* which seem to reveal a change in *self-perception.* Related findings come from studies of *forced compliance* and studies of *justification of effort.* According to many theorists, these effects can be understood as attempts to avoid *cognitive dissonance,* a disconcerting emotional state that occurs when two beliefs that we hold are plainly inconsistent with each other, or when there is a conflict between what we believe and what we actually do.

3. Cognitive dissonance seems to be more than a logical discrepancy. This is because people in dissonance studies show physiological signs of conflict, suggesting that the dissonance poses a challenge to our favorable self-concept.

4. An *attitude* is a stable set of mental views and assessments about some idea, object, or person; attitudes involve beliefs as well as feelings and evaluations. Social psychologists usually measure attitudes by the use of questionnaires, on which participants can indicate the extent to which they endorse certain statements. While early findings suggested that attitudes, measured in this way, don't actually predict behavior, later work showed that they do if the strength of the measured attitude is strong enough and if the attitude is defined specifically.

5. An additional reason why the attitudes we express sometimes conflict with the way we behave is that while some of our attitudes are *explicit* and could, for example, be expressed in response to a survey question, others are *implicit attitudes,* revealed only indirectly. Such implicit attitudes include the implicit association that "white" is associated with "good," and "black" with "bad," something revealed in the *Implicit Associate Test.*

## SELF-CONCEPT AND SELF-DEFENSE

6. When asked to compare themselves to others on various favorable characteristics, the vast majority of North American and European participants judge themselves to be better than average—the so-called *above-average effect.* This effect illustrates a *self-serving bias,* which has been observed in a number of other situations, including a wide-spread tendency to take credit for successes but deny responsibility for failures. The same self-serving bias is extended to the people and groups that we identify in some way as "ours," such as our social and political groups.

7. A similar self-serving tendency leads to various strategies of *impression management* and maneuvers such as *self-handicapping* that protect us if we anticipate failure. Some of these strategies can also be seen as attempts to avoid embarrassment.

## PERSON PERCEPTION

8. According to Solomon Asch, our conceptions of other people are not a simple aggregate of the attributes we perceive them to have. Instead, our impressions form an organized whole whose elements are interpreted in relation to the overall pattern. Evidence for this view comes from studies of first impressions. More recent theorists emphasize social *schemas,* sometimes called *implicit theories of personality.* Such schemas provide *mental shortcuts* for interpreting and categorizing others' behavior. These short cuts are quick and efficient, but also leave us vulnerable to error, because sometimes our preconceptions turn out to be wrong. The cost of schematic thinking is particularly clear in the case of social *stereotypes,* in which schemas are simplified and applied to whole groups. In part, such over-simplified schemas are the result of *illusory correlations,* which are produced because we note and remember certain co-occurences more than others.

## ATTRIBUTION

9. Social psychologists call the process by which we interpret behavior *causal attribution.* This attribution is often concerned with whether a given behavior is a product of the situation, or a product of the person's *traits* or *predispositions.* Often, though, we make errors in attribution, including the *fundamental attribution error,* a tendency to

ascribe people's behavior to their nature and not to their situation. Another common attribution pattern is the *actor-observer difference:* as observers, we tend to over-rate dispositional factors, as actors, we over-rate the external situation.

## CONFORMITY AND THE SOCIAL CONSTRUCTION OF REALITY

10. The fact that our notion of physical reality is at least in part a matter of mutual agreement, is highlighted in Asch's classic study on *conformity,* in which participants followed the judgments of a unanimous majority rather than follow the evidence provided by their own eyes. When a group's *unanimity* was broken, yielding decreased greatly. Further work showed that yielding increases when the discrimination becomes more difficult, because then participants are likely to rely more on *social comparison.*

11. Studies of *persuasive communications* have shown that their effectiveness depends on many factors. One is the credibility of the *messenger* and the *message source.* If the message is delivered via the *central route to persuasion,* then the content and information of the message are crucial. If the message comes via the *peripheral route to persuasion,* what matters is who presents the message and how and where it's presented.

12. What leads to blind *obedience?* According to some investigators, the crucial determinant is within the person rather than in the situation, as in the case of so-called *authoritarian personalities.* Later work, especially the Milgram studies, emphasized situational rather than dispositional factors. Milgram showed that about 65 percent of his subjects continued to obey the experimenter to the bitter end, electrically shocking (or so they believed) the so-called learner at the extreme setting, even when he complained of a heart condition. In Milgram's view, the crucial factor leading to this obedience was that the participants regarded themselves as *another person's agent.* He showed that obedience increased as the psychological distance between one's own actions and their end result is increased, and decreased as that psychological distance is diminished. Some alternative interpretations focus on *cognitive reinterpretations,* such as *dehumanization of the victim.* It is also important that obedience is achieved gradually, leading the obeying individual down a slippery slope.

13. Several groups of experts had predicted that Milgram would encounter a great deal of defiance in his procedure, providing yet another example of our consistent underestimation of the power of the situation to determine our behavior. Related results come from Zimbardo's prison study, which also highlights the importance of the role people are made to play.

## SOCIAL IMPACT: THE CONVERGENCE OF SOCIAL FORCES

14. *Social impact theory* tries to understand all social influence as a field of social forces that converge upon the individual. The total impact will depend on the number of people who affect the target individual, how socially strong these people are, and how close they are to the target in space or time. Evidence comes from work on *stage fright.* Such studies also show that if the social influence is spread out over more than one target, the impact will *diffuse.* Further evidence of diffusion comes from work on *social loafing.* A related phenomenon is *social facilitation* and *inhibition.* The presence of others promotes performance of well-practiced or habitual activities, but impedes performance of complex or unfamiliar activities.

## LEADERSHIP

15. *Leadership* can be exercised in a multitude of social contexts. According to the *great-person theory,* history is created by exceptional individuals, such as Napoleon. From another perspective, the success or failure of individuals like Napoleon is determined by the times in which they lived. This debate is analogous to the person-situation duality in social psychology. Experimental studies by social psychologists have tried to identify personal characteristics relevant to leadership. The results have shown that "leadership traits" can be assessed, but may be less important than situational factors such as the kind of group and the nature of the task the group is assigned.

## GROUP DECISION MAKING

16. Groups can also influence how we think and how we make decisions. *Group polarization* is the tendency for decisions made by groups to be more extreme than the decisions that would have been made by any of the group members working on their own, as in the case of a *risky shift.* Another pattern found in studies of group decision is *groupthink,* which may occur when the group is highly cohesive, faced by some external threat, and closed to outside information or opinions.

## CROWD BEHAVIOR AND PANDEMONIUM

17. What accounts for such crowd behaviors as riots or mobs? One hypothesis holds that the crowd incites the individual to lose his individuality and become essentially irrational. In this view, the key to crowd behavior is *deindividuation,* which tends to disinhibit impulsive actions that are normally under restraint.

18. Another position stresses the crowd members' cognitive appraisals of the total situation, as in the case of panic. This analysis is often understood with reference to the game-theory analysis of the *prisoner's dilemma*, whose logic applies to many kinds of social interactions, including panic. As in the case of the two prisoners, this solution is grossly maladaptive: individuals each making decisions guided by their own self-interest end up producing an outcome that is bad for all.

The prisoner's dilemma and its payoff structure can be applied to many serious social and economic issues, resulting in such social dilemmas as industrial pollution.

## CULTURE AND SOCIAL INFLUENCE

19. Within the last few decades, it has become clear that many of the phenomena studied by social psychology are not universal and depend instead on the norms, values, and teachings of one's culture. One important distinction among cultures and ethnic groups is whether they are *collectivist* or *individualist*. In collectivist societies (including those of Latin America and most of the cultures of Asia and Africa), people are considered to be fundamentally interdependent, and the emphasis is on obligations within one's family and immediate community. In individualist societies (such as the United States, western Europe, Canada, and Australia), the emphasis is on the ways a person can stand out by achieving private goals.

20. The collectivism-individualism difference offers a fresh perspective on many of the social psychological phenomena we have reviewed. An example is the above-average effect, which is found in individualist cultures but not in collectivist ones. Another concerns the fundamental error of attribution, which is more likely to be found in individualist than in collectivist societies.

21. Other differences concern the effects of *in-groups* and *out-groups*. Members of collectivist societies are more likely to conform with members of their in-group, but are less affected than individualists by members of the out-group. A related phenomenon concerns the *permanence of an individual's social bonds*. Collectivists belong to relatively few in-groups, but their bonds to those are strong and long lasting. In contrast, members of individualist cultures belong to a whole set of overlapping in-groups, but their relation to these groups is more fragile and less enduring.

CHAPTER

*11*

# BIOLOGY, EMOTION, AND SOCIAL BEHAVIOR

*I*n the previous chapter, we discussed social behavior predominantly from the standpoint of social cognition: how we form impressions of other people, for example, and how we interpret why people do what they do. Here we approach other kinds of social behavior, those governed more by passion than by reason. These kinds of behavior are rooted in what Charles Darwin called our "social instincts," basic ways that we have evolved to interact with one another. These general types of behavior include sex and love, parenting, aggression, altruism, and emotion. All have counterparts within the animal kingdom, yet we humans have distinct versions of each. As we will see, however, even these biologically fundamental kinds of interactions cannot occur without a good dose of cognition, and so we emphasize at the start that our distinction between passion and reason—like so many other dichotomies within psychology—will not hold up as neatly as one might wish.

# THE BIOLOGICAL ROOTS OF SOCIAL BEHAVIOR

*Charles Darwin*

Was Charles Darwin correct in arguing that human social behavior is guided by social instincts similar to the inborn tendencies that shape other species' actions? To pursue this question, we first need to be clear on what these social instincts might be, and, with that, we need to be clear on how biological forces might be expected to shape our social behavior.

In his theorizing about evolution, Darwin began with the fact that within each species there are variations from one individual to the next—for example, one cheetah has longer legs than another, one fish is a darker color than another, and so on. Many of these variations are a function of the animal's genetic makeup and so will be inherited by its descendants. But, of course, this inheritance will happen only if the animal actually has descendants, and, as a matter of fact, most organisms do not live long enough to reproduce. Only a few seedlings grow up to be trees; only a few tadpoles achieve froghood. Darwin pointed out, though, that the issues of who survives and who reproduces are far from random. The longer-legged cheetah is likely to be a faster runner and so is more likely to catch its prey than its slower fellow. As a result, it is more likely to survive long enough to reproduce and leave offspring who inherit its long legs. Likewise, the darker-colored fish may be better camouflaged against the river's bottom and so is more likely to escape predators. Again, this will help the darker-colored fish to survive long enough to reproduce, increasing the likelihood that the genes promoting this coloration are represented in the next generation.

Darwin pointed out that this process of selection, if repeated generation after generation, would eventually produce large changes in a species. If dark-colored fish are more likely to survive and breed than are lighter-colored ones, then they will have more descendants, and so, after a few generations, many, and perhaps most, of the surviving fish will be the descendants of dark-colored ancestors and probably will be dark-colored themselves. In this fashion, a survival advantage for a genetically-rooted trait will lead, over the generations, to a change in the entire species.

Of course, not all variations within a species are beneficial in this way, and so not all variations will lead to a reproductive advantage. For example, if there are few predators, the light-colored fish may fare as well as the dark ones. Even if predators are numerous, the dark-colored fish will benefit only if the river bottom is dark. If the river bottom is sandy, then it might be the light-colored fish who are better camouflaged. In short, then, we should not think of evolution as favoring the "better" or "more advanced" organism. Instead, evolution merely favors the organism that is better suited to the environment currently in place—and if the environment changes (for example, a sandy river bottom becomes muddy), then the pattern of selective advantages will change as well.

## PERSONAL AND GENETIC SURVIVAL

Evolution by *natural selection* sometimes is described with the phrase "survival of the fittest," but, in truth, this phrase is misleading. Personal survival as such is not what evolution is about. Personal survival matters, of course, but only insofar as that survival leads to reproductive success, so that the organism can pass its genes along to the next generation. From an evolutionary perspective, an animal that manages to outlive all its competitors but leaves no offspring has not flourished. Thus, what really matters for evolution is not personal survival, but the survival of one's genes, because it is via one's genes that future generations (and so the evolution of the species) will be shaped.

This emphasis on genetic survival and, with it, an emphasis on reproductive success, helps us understand some otherwise puzzling facts. For example, the magnificent tail feathers of the peacock are actually cumbersome to drag around and may diminish the peacock's chances of escaping predators. Even so, the tail does contribute to a peacock's evolutionary fitness. This is because the peacock has to compete with his fellow males for access to the peahen; the larger and more magnificent his tail, the more likely it is that she will respond to his sexual overtures. From an evolutionary point of view, the potential gain evidently offsets the possible loss; as a result, long tail feathers eventually flourished in the males.

This logic does not merely apply to an organism's physical traits: it also applies to an animal's behavior. Many behaviors, it turns out, are rooted in an animal's genetic makeup and so will be inherited by the animal's offspring. If these behaviors happen to contribute to the animal's reproductive success, then animals with these behaviors will have more offspring, and a larger proportion of the next generation will inherit the genes that led to the behavior in the first place. In this fashion, natural selection will lead to an evolution of how animals behave just as it leads to an evolution of the animals' anatomy.

Genetic survival  *The peacock's long tail feathers are a cumbersome burden that may decrease his chances of escaping predators and, thus, his own personal survival. But this cost is more than offset by his increased chances of attracting a sexual partner, thereby assuring survival of his genes.*

# SOCIAL BEHAVIOR AND REPRODUCTION

What behaviors are most likely to be shaped by evolution in this way? The answer should be obvious: social behaviors, particularly those associated with the process that is central for evolution—namely, reproduction.

## ADVERTISING FOR A MATE

Not all organisms reproduce sexually (with a male and female each contributing half the genetic material), but among those that do, one of the first tasks in reproduction is for the organism to find a potential mate. Accomplishing this usually requires an animal to advertise his or her availability, and, with that, the animal must somehow announce his or her sex (so that the males' availability is noticed by females, and vice versa). Many animals have anatomical structures whose function seems to be nothing other than this sexual advertising—for example, the tail feathers of the peacock or the comb and wattle of the rooster (see Figure 11.1). These structures are often crucial to mating. In one species of widow birds, the males have long tail feathers, up to twenty inches long. To study the importance of this trait, an unsympathetic investigator cut the tails on some males and placed feather extensions on others. After a suitable period, the investigator counted the number of nests in each bird's territory. The males whose tails were cosmetically extended had more nests than did the unaltered males, who in turn had more nests than their unfortunate fellows whose tails had been shortened (Andersson, 1982). It evidently pays to advertise.

In humans, our structural displays of sex differences are less pronounced, but they are present nonetheless. One example is likely to be the female breast, whose adipose tissue does not really increase the infant's milk supply. According to some theorists, the breast evolved for signaling purposes. As we began to walk erect and lost our reliance on smell (an important source of sexual information for other mammals), members of our species needed some other ways of displaying their sex. The prominent breasts of the human female, it is proposed, may be one such announcement.

11.1  Advertising one's sex  *The comb and wattle of this barred rock rooster proclaim that he is a male.*

11.2 *Courtship rituals* **(A) The male bower bird tries to entice the female into an elaborate bower decorated with berries, shells, or whatever else may be available, such as colored clothespins. (B) The male tern courts by feeding the female. (C) A male waterlilly frog calls to a female.**

## BEHAVIORAL ADVERTISEMENTS

Many animals advertise both their sex and their readiness to mate via their behaviors. In some species, these behaviors take the form of *courtship rituals*, particular behaviors that provide an important means of announcing one's reproductive intentions (Figure 11.2). Some of these courtship rituals are quite elaborate, sometimes involving alternating bouts of approach and withdrawal, of coy retreat and seductive flirtation. What accounts for these apparent oscillations between yes and no? Each animal has reason to approach the other, but each also has reason to fear the other: is the approach amorous or aggressive? This tension between attraction and threat must be resolved, and the alternating approaches and withdrawals presumably serve this purpose.

## ATTRACTION

Humans are, of course, biological creatures, and, on that basis, our behaviors, too, perhaps including some aspects of courtship, might well be shaped by our genes. On the other hand, one might think the culture-based learning we each do during our lifetime plays a far-larger role in governing when, how, and with whom we mate. After all, there is no question that culture does have an influence. It is cultural change, and not ultrarapid evolution, that has altered the average age of parenting over the last few decades. It is cultural differences, not biological contrast, that made people with facial tattoos so attractive among the New Zealand Maori a century ago, but rather off-putting to many Westerners.

As a step toward tackling these themes, we might begin by asking what commonalities there are among the diverse peoples of the world with regard to their mate preferences and their courtship patterns. If we find no commonality, this would be a powerful argument that human mating is not heavily governed by the biology that our species obviously shares. But if we do find commonality, we might well ask where this commonality comes from—and whether, in particular, it is a part of our biological heritage.

## PHYSICAL ATTRACTIVENESS

There is little doubt that physical appearance is immensely important in determining a person's attractiveness (or at least his or her initial attractiveness). The vast sums of money spent on cosmetics, fashion and beauty magazines, diets, and various forms of plastic surgery are one kind of testimony; our everyday experience is another. Under the circumstances, one may wonder whether there is any need to document this experimentally, but in any case, such documentation does exist.

In one study, freshmen were randomly paired at a dance and later asked how much they liked their partner and whether he or she was someone they might want to date. What mainly determined each person's desirability as a future date was his or her physical attractiveness (Walster, Aronson, Abrahams, & Rottman, 1966). Similar results were found among clients of a commercial video-dating service who selected partners

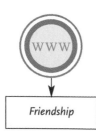

Friendship

*In the eye of the beholder?   Evidence suggests that people across cultures agree on certain aspects of what makes a face attractive, but there are also points of disagreement. Things that some cultures consider enormously attractive, such as the elongated necks of the Padaung Karen hilltribe women in Thailand, or the patterns of face paint among the Huli Wigmen of Papua New Guinea, may not be appealing to perceivers from other cultures.*

based on files that included a photograph, background information, and details about interests, hobbies, and personal ideals. When it came down to the actual choice, the primary determinant was the photograph (Green, Buchanan, & Heuer, 1984).

Physically attractive individuals also benefit from the common belief that what is beautiful is good, because people tend to associate physical attractiveness with a variety of positive personality traits, including dominance, good social skills, intelligence, happiness, and good mental health (see Dion, Berscheid, & Walster, 1972). This is, in fact, part of a larger pattern sometimes referred to as the "halo effect," a term that refers to our tendency to assume that people who have one good trait are likely to have others (and conversely that people with one bad trait are likely to be bad in other regards as well). In some ways, the belief that underlies the halo effect becomes a self-fulfilling prophesy, and so it is no surprise that people who are physically attractive are also more popular and sexually experienced. However, here as elsewhere, the "halo" probably extends farther than it should. For example, people often assume that individuals who are attractive will also be more intelligent than average, but there is, in truth, no correlation between attractiveness and intelligence (Eagly, Ashmore, Makhijani, & Longo, 1991; Feingold, 1992; Jackson, Hunter, & Hodge, 1995).

## MATCHING FOR ATTRACTIVENESS

Physical attractiveness is clearly desirable, but if we all set our sights on only the most beautiful people, the world would soon be depopulated—there are simply not enough supermodels to go around. People, therefore, must be choosing their partners on some more sensible basis. Perhaps we covet the most attractive of all possible mate but temper our desires with a down-to-earth perception of our own desirability and attractiveness. As a consequence, we seek partners who are roughly at the same level of attractiveness that we are; this will ensure that we reach as high as we can in our romantic aspirations, while simultaneously minimizing the chance of rejection. Much evidence favors this *matching hypothesis*, which states, simply, that there will be a strong correlation between the physical attractiveness of the two partners (Berscheid, Dion, Walster, & Walster, 1971). Everyday observations confirm this hypothesis ("They make such a fine couple!"), and so do many empirical studies (Berscheid & Walster, 1974; Feingold, 1988; White, 1980).

## WHAT IS PHYSICALLY ATTRACTIVE?

Just what is it that makes someone physically attractive? To be sure, this is to some extent a matter of "personal taste," and so it varies from one perceiver to the next. (Attractiveness is, as they say, in the eye of the beholder.) However, there is more agreement about attractiveness than this bit of common wisdom would suggest. People of

*Attractiveness    How attractive are these indi-
viduals? Research indicates that there will be
reasonable consensus on this judgment, with
the evaluation of attractiveness heavily dependent on whether the faces are "average" in several dimensions.*

different cultures by and large, seem to agree about which faces are attractive, and so do people of different generations (Cunningham, Roberts, Barbee, Druen, & Wu, 1998). Evidence also indicates that infants prefer to look at faces that adults consider attractive, suggesting that the allure of these faces is not learned (Langlois et al., 1987).

Across ages, generations, and cultures, attractive people are almost always those with clear skin, shiny hair, and no visible deformities. Faces that are symmetrical are usually considered more attractive than those that are not, and, generally speaking, "average faces" (those of average width, average eye size, and so on) are more attractive than faces that deviate from the average (see, for example, Grammer & Thornhill, 1994; Fink & Penton-Voak, 2002; Mealey, Bridgstock, & Townsend, 1999; Rhodes, Proffitt, Grady, & Sumich, 1998; Rhodes, Sumich, & Byatt, 1999; Thornhill & Gagestad, 1999).

However, some departures from the average increase attractiveness, and these departures seem to be ones that exaggerate important features found in the average face. The average female, for example, has big eyes, full lips, and a small chin. A female face will be more attractive, therefore, if it has slightly larger-than-average eyes, fuller-than-average lips, and so on—in essence, a caricature of the average. Similarly, the average male has a strong chin, a large jaw, and prominent brows; a male face will be more attractive if these features are slightly exaggerated (Fink & Penton-Voak, 2002).

Of course, it is not just faces we find attractive but bodies as well, and here too there are some consistencies in people's preferences. As with faces, symmetry and being near average contribute to the attractiveness of someone's body. This is probably why, for example, individuals who are symmetrical in the size of their hands or feet tend to begin having sex at an earlier age and have more sex partners during their lifetime (Thornhill & Gangestad, 1994).

What about body size? This seems to be a regard in which preferences vary from one culture to the next and from one time period to the next, but even here there may be consistency in the preferred proportions. One line of research has focused on the waist-to-hip ratio, which is simply the waist circumference divided by the hip circumference. Numerous studies indicate that women are perceived to be more attractive if their ratio is approximately 7:10. If, therefore, a culture favors slender women, then someone with a 24½-inch waist and 35-inch hips will be considered attractive. If a culture favors larger women, then someone with a 32-inch waist and 46-inch hips might be the ideal. In both cases, the 7:10 ratio is preserved (Furnham, Tan, & McManus, 1997; Henss, 2000; Singh, 1993; Singh & Luis, 1995; but see Tassinary & Hansen, 1998).

## THE BIOLOGICAL BASIS FOR ATTRACTIVENESS

Why is it that people find symmetrical faces attractive and a certain waist-to-hip ratio appealing? Some scholars believe the answer lies in our evolutionary past. The apparently attractive waist-to-hip ratio in women, for example, may be indicative of a mature pelvis and an adequate supply of fat, both showing a readiness for pregnancy and so signaling a fertile partner. In addition, a relatively low ratio (with relatively more fat on the hips than the abdomen) indicates higher estrogen levels and, with that, better overall health and greater fertility (Singh, 1993, 1994). Any male with a preference for this shape, therefore, would maximize his chances for reproductive success, and so natural selection would favor individuals with this preference—a plausible source of the preference in the present day.

What about the preference for average, or symmetrical, faces? This, too, may have evolutionary roots. A number of health problems will lead to asymmetrical faces, or faces that depart widely from the average, and so facial symmetry and proximity to the average may indicate the absence of these problems. Hence, any of our ancestors who were attracted to these features would have been more likely to end up with healthy partners, increasing their chances of healthy offspring (Thornhill & Gangestad, 1999). Thus, natural selection would favor an organism that found average and symmetrical faces attractive.

We note, though, that some scholars are skeptical about these evolutionary claims. As one concern, there is room for doubt about whether facial attractiveness truly is an indicator of health (Kalick, Zebrowitz, Langlois, & Johnson, 1998), and, if it is not, then we need to rethink the evolutionary argument just offered. In addition, it is possible that our preference for symmetrical and average faces derives from an entirely different source—namely, our general aesthetic preference for balance, a preference that not only guides how we think about faces but also leads us to prefer average wristwatches over unusual ones, and average birds over peculiar ones (Halberstadt & Rhodes, 2000). Untangling these issues awaits more data. (See Hosken, 2001, for further discussion of the controversies surrounding symmetry and mating success.)

## PROXIMITY

Physical attractiveness is important, but it is not the only thing that draws two people together. We also need to consider the aspects of someone's personality or behavior that make them likable or not, charismatic or not, attractive or not. People often regard these issues as something of a mystery. "There's no accounting for tastes," they say, or they ask with a tone of bewilderment, "What does she see in him?" But even so, there are a number of surprisingly simple factors that play a large role in making someone attractive, and one of the most important of these is sheer proximity. The statistics are impressive. For example, of all the couples who took out marriage licenses in Columbus, Ohio, during the summer of 1949, more than half were people who lived within sixteen blocks of each other when they went out on their first date (Clarke, 1952). Proximity also predicts who will stay engaged and get married; the farther apart the two live, the greater the chance that the engagement will be broken (Berscheid & Walster, 1978).

Why should proximity be so important? Obviously, you cannot like someone you have never met, and the chances of meeting that someone are much greater if he is nearby. But it is worth noting that the effects of proximity are not always positive. The results of a study on a condominium complex showed that the people who lived there developed most of their friendships with others who lived there. However, it turns out that the people they disliked also lived in the same complex (Ebbesen, Kjos, & Kohecni, 1976). It seems, then, that proximity often provides only the opportunity for social interactions; it does not by itself determine their quality.

In one regard, though, proximity may foster liking. Proximity allows familiarity to develop, and there is a good deal of evidence that people in general tend to like what is more familiar, whether it is a word in a foreign language, a melody, or a brand name, and the more often it is seen or heard, the better it will be liked (Brickman & D'Amato, 1975; Moreland & Zajonc, 1982; Zajonc, 1968).

Does familiarity have an impact on attraction? In one study, people shown photographs of strangers' faces judged the strangers to be more likable the more often they saw them (Jorgensen & Cervone, 1978). Another study applied this general idea to the comparison of faces and their mirror images. Which will be better liked? If familiarity is what is critical, then our friends should prefer an unaltered view of our face to its mirror image, since they have seen the first much more often than the second. But we ourselves should prefer the mirror image, which for us is by far the more familiar. The results fit the familiarity hypothesis (Mita, Dermer, & Knight, 1977; see Figure 11.3).

"Do you really love me, Anthony, or is it just because I live on the thirty-eighth floor?"

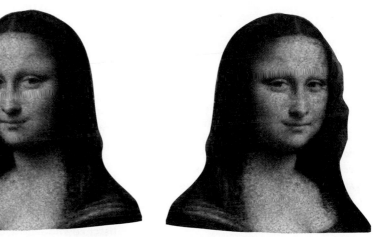

*11.3   Familiarity and liking*   *The figure shows two versions of a rather well-known lady. Which do you like better—the one on the right or the one on the left?* *(Please turn to p. 423.)*

## SIMILARITY

Do people like others who are similar to themselves, or do they prefer those who are very different? To pit one proverb against another, is it that "Birds of a feather flock together" or—perhaps like magnets or static electricity—"Opposites attract"?

Here, the birds have more to teach us than magnets or static electricity, because people tend to be attracted to others who are like themselves on attributes such as race, ethnic origin, social and educational level, family background, income, and religion, as well as behavioral patterns like gregariousness and drinking and smoking habits. One widely cited study showed that engaged couples in the United States tend to be similar along all of these dimensions (Burgess & Wallin, 1943). These findings provide evidence for **homogamy**, a powerful tendency for like to choose like. Another study showed that homogamy influences a couple's stability; couples who remained together after two-and-a-half years were more similar than those who had broken up (Hill, Rubin, & Peplau, 1976). Moreover, married couples tend to be similar on nearly all personality dimensions (Caspi & Herbener, 1990). This association may be in part a two-way street, given that couples may become more alike over time by virtue of their continual interaction; indeed, some evidence suggests that they grow more similar in their verbal skills, degree of open-mindedness, and even their physical appearance (Gruber-Baldini, Schaie, & Willis, 1995; Zajonc, Adelmann, Murphy, & Niedenthal, 1987; but see Caspi, Herbener, & Ozer, 1992).

What produces homogamy? One possibility is that similarity really does lead to mutual liking. Another is that the similarity one observes between people in a relationship is just a by-product of proximity, since, after all, "few of us have an opportunity to meet, interact with, become attracted to, and marry a person markedly dissimilar from ourselves"? (Berscheid & Walster, 1978, p. 87). For this reason, the effect of proximity could produce the observed pattern of similarity. The choice between these interpretations is not obvious, but, in truth, the choice may not matter much. In either case, like pairs with like, and few heiresses ever marry the butler, except in the movies.

*Homogamy*  **American Gothic by Grant Wood, 1930.**

*Birds of a feather*  **People tend to select romantic partners who are much like themselves in important regards. It is only in the movies that love routinely blossoms between people of very different cultural or educational backgrounds. (A still from Notting Hill, starring Hugh Grant and Julia Roberts.)**

## WHO CHOOSES WHOM?

The study of attractiveness considers both what makes a male attractive and what makes a female attractive. In most animal species, however, the two sexes play very different roles in seeking and selecting a partner. It is usually the female who makes the final choice of whether to mate or not. The biological reason is simple—the female shoulders the major costs of reproduction. If she is a bird, she supplies not only the ovum but also the food supply for the developing embryo. If she is a mammal, she carries the embryo within her body and later provides it with milk. In either case, her biological burden is vastly greater than the male's. This burden can be measured in many ways, including the sheer amount of time that each sex must invest in its offspring. If a doe's offspring fails to survive, she has lost a whole breeding season. In comparison, the stag's loss is minimal—a few minutes of his time and some easily replaced sperm. No wonder, then, that females are choosy in picking their mates. For the female, reproduction is a serious business with heavy biological costs (Bjorklund & Shackelford, 1999; Trivers, 1972).

There are a few interesting exceptions. One is the sea horse, whose young are carried in a brood pouch by the male (see Figure 11.4). In this animal, the male makes the greater reproductive investment, and he exhibits greater sexual discrimination than the female. The same story applies to phalaropes, arctic seabirds whose eggs are hatched and whose chicks are fed by the males. Here, a greater part of the biological burden falls on the male, and we should expect a corresponding increase in his sexual choosiness. This is just what happens. Among the phalaropes, the female does the wooing. She is brightly plumaged and aggressively pursues the careful, dull-colored male (Williams, 1966).

## HUMAN MATE CHOICE

What about humans? In our species, both males and females are selective in choosing their sexual partners, and mating happens only when both partners consent. However, the two sexes differ in the criteria they use in making their choices. According to a number of surveys, the physical attractiveness of the partner seems more important to men than to women. It also appears that men generally prefer younger women, whereas women prefer older men. Yet another difference concerns the social and financial status of the partner, which seems to matter much more to women than it does to men. The data also indicate that these male-female differences are not unique to our own society but are found throughout the world, in countries as diverse as China, India, France, Nigeria, and Iran (Buss, 1989, 1992; Buss & Barnes, 1986). Quite interestingly, though, the two sexes agree on one point: across cultures, both men and women value kindness and intelligence in their prospective mates (Buss, 1992).

These results are open to many interpretations. According to David Buss, the investigator who uncovered many of these results, the best explanation is evolutionary. If our male ancestors preferred attractive women, Buss argues, this would have increased their reproductive success, because attractive women are likely to be healthy and so likely to be fertile. As a result, natural selection would favor males with this preference, and thus the preference would become widespread among the males of our species. Likewise for the woman's age. The younger she is, the more reproductive years she is likely to have ahead of her, and so a male selecting a younger partner could plausibly look forward to more offspring. Again, this would increase the male's reproductive success, be favored by natural selection, and so become common for the species.

The female's preferences are also easy to understand from this perspective. Because of her high investment in each child, she is better off having just a few offspring and doing all she can to ensure the survival of each. A wealthy and high-status mate would help her reach this goal, because he would be able to provide the food and other resources her children need. Thus, there would be a reproductive advantage associated with a preference for such a male, and so a gradual evolution toward all females in the species having this preference (Bjorklund & Shackelford, 1999; Buss, 1992).

These findings, however, can also be interpreted in other ways. One plausible alternative is that human females prefer wealthy, high-status males not because of some hardwired, genetically rooted preference, but simply because they have learned, across their lifetimes, the social and economic advantages they will gain from such a mate. Why is status of mate more important for females than for males? It may be because, in many cultures, women soon learn that their professional and educational opportunities are limited, and so "marrying wealth" is their best strategy for gathering resources for themselves and their young.

If this culture-based account is correct, then mating preferences may well be different in different cultures, and some evidence suggests this is the case. More specifically, and consistent with the culture-based account, women seem less concerned with their potential mate's status if they happen to live in a culture that provides more opportunities for women; in this case, "marrying wealth" is not a woman's only chance for economic and social security, and, correspondingly, a potential husband's resources become less important in mate selection (Kasser & Sharma, 1999; also see Eagly & Wood, 1999).

In short, then, there seems to be considerable consistency in mating preferences and a clear contrast between the criteria males and females typically use; this consistency can be confirmed within a culture, across cultures (to an impressive extent), and, appar-

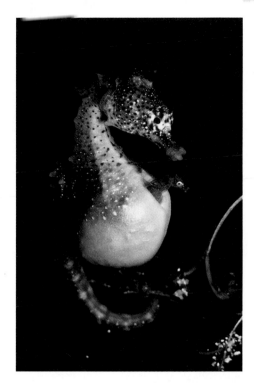

11.4 Male sea horse "giving birth"

*Revisiting Figure 11.3 The familiarity-leads-to-liking hypothesis would predict a preference for the left panel—a retouched photograph of the Mona Lisa (see p. 421). The panel on the right is a mirror image of that photograph, which is presumably the less familiar of the two.*

ently, across generations. But there are also some variations in these mate-selection preferences that are clearly attributable to the cultural context. Do these variations indicate that mating preferences are set in the first place by the cultural context and so are dependent on that context? Or do they indicate merely that the cultural context is able, in some settings, to override the biologically rooted pattern? This is a difficult question to resolve, and until the evidence becomes clearer, the issue remains open.

## MATING SYSTEMS

In many species, the partners remain together after mating, for a breeding season or even longer. In those cases, their arrangement often involves *polygamy*, several members of one sex mating with one individual of the other. And if polygamous, the arrangement either involves *polygyny*, with several females mating with one male, or, more rarely, *polyandry*, with several males mating with one female. Still other animals demonstrate *monogamy*, with a reproductive partnership based on a more or less permanent tie between one male and one female.

What accounts for these different mating systems? A clue comes from a difference in the patterns found in mammals and birds. Some 90 percent of all birds are monogamous: they mate and stay together throughout a breeding season. In contrast, more than 90 percent of all mammals are polygynous, with one male mating with a number of females. Evolutionary biologists explain this contrast through a kind of evolutionary economics, all hinging on what an organism can do to maximize its reproductive success. Consider the problem faced by birds. In many species, successful incubation requires both parents: one to sit on the eggs, the other to forage for food to nourish the bird that is sitting. After hatching, finding food for a nestful of hungry chicks may still require the full-time efforts of both birds. Under the circumstances, monogamy makes reproductive sense for both the male and the female: each mate needs its partner's continuing help; otherwise, no chicks—and therefore, none of their genes—will survive.

The situation is quite different for most mammals. Here, there is no issue of tending the nest, because there is no nest. Instead, the fetus grows within the mother's uterus, allowing her to continue foraging for food during the offspring's gestation. Then, after birth, only the mother can secrete the milk needed to feed the young. Thus, strictly in terms of physical needs, the father is unnecessary after conception. The young can often survive under the mother's care alone, and the male's genes will be carried into the next generation nonetheless.

How should a male behave in these circumstances? Recall that, in evolutionary terms, a successful organism is one that perpetuates its genes through successive generations. The most successful organism, therefore, is the one that has the greatest number of thriving and fertile offspring. How to achieve this goal? If the young can survive without his parental care, then the male can maximize his reproductive success by mating with as many females as possible. The end result is polygyny, with each male seeking to mate with a number of females.

These facts have an interesting anatomical consequence. To succeed, polygynous males must be physically distinctive—to attract a female, and to win in the competition with other males. Consistent with this, polygyny is almost always accompanied by *sexual dimorphism*, a pronounced difference in the size or bodily structures of the two sexes. In fact, the more polygynous the species, the more dimorphic it tends to be, with the males larger and often more ornamented than the females, as shown by the peacock's tail, the stag's antlers, and the male sea lion's disproportionate size (Figure 11.5A). Polyandrous species, such as the spotted sandpiper bird, also show sexual dimorphism, but here the females are bigger, more aggressive, and more territorial (Oring, 1985). In monogamous species, such as the titi monkey, there is no such sexual dimorphism (Figure 11.5B).

**Birds as monogamous**  *Birds tend to mate and stay together during a mating season as both parents are needed for successful incubation of their young. Here, a black-bowed albatross male courts a female on the nest that will serve as home for their offspring.*

11.5 *Sexual dimorphism* **Polygynous species tend to be dimorphic. (A) A Hooker's sea lion bull with his harem. Note the bull's markedly larger size. (B) In titi monkeys, which are monogamous, males and females are very similar in size and form.**

## HUMAN MATING SYSTEMS

Are humans biologically inclined toward monogamous relationships? Evolutionary theorists begin by observing that humans are moderately dimorphic: on average, the human male is about 10 percent larger and five inches taller than the female. This suggests that humans would have a tendency toward polygyny. And, as it turns out, most traditional cultures do allow polygyny; only 16 percent of those studied require monogamous marital arrangements, with just one spouse to each partner (Ford & Beach, 1951).*

Most modern societies frown on polygamy, but, nonetheless, at least some evidence suggests that men express a desire for a greater number of sexual partners than women do (see, for example, Symons, 1979). Evolutionary theorists believe that these differences between the sexes are ultimately rooted in our biological nature, and that men want greater sexual variety because for them it is reproductively adaptive. Their investment in each child (in terms of time or resources) is small, and so they can "afford" to have a large number of children. Indeed, it is in their interest to have many children, because this will maximize their genes' representation in the next generation, and, of course, the more women they mate with, the more children they are likely to father.

In contrast, women need to evaluate potential sexual partners more cautiously, because they are more interested in a stable familial relationship. With their much greater parental investment in each offspring, women cannot afford to have child after child after child. As a result, they need to ensure the well-being of each child, and so they have a huge stake in finding the best possible father for their young—one who will provide resources and support.

Here again, though, the evolutionary account is controversial. Some critics have suggested that sexual attitudes reflect cultural values rather than biological preprogramming, with the male's attitudes shaped by social conditions in which young boys are often taught that sexual conquests prove their "manliness," while girls are taught to value home, family, and a single dependable partner.

In addition, the data themselves are controversial. It is true that, on average, men seem to desire more sexual partners than women—in one study, the difference seemed quite large, with men expressing a desire for 7.7 sexual partners over the next thirty years, and women expressing a desire for only 2.8 over the same time period (Pedersen, Miller, Putcha-Bhagavatula, & Yang, 2002). However, this result may be misleading,

---

* Note that this 16 percent figure applies to 185 different cultures, indicating that 30 of these cultures were monogamous. Of course, the percentage would be much higher if it were based on individuals rather than cultures, since the monogamous modern cultures (including our own) are much more populous than most of the cultures described in the anthropological literature.

because, on other measures, men and women appear much more alike. Almost half of the men in this study indicated that their ideal number of sexual partners would be just one, in a fashion apparently contrary to the evolutionary logic we have described. Moreover, virtually all of the men in this study (98.9 percent) indicated that they hoped to settle down with one mutually exclusive sexual partner at some point in their life, ideally within the next five years. Virtually all women in the study (99.2 percent) expressed the same wish (Pedersen et al., 2002).

Overall, then, we can find a difference between men and women, in the direction predicted by an evolutionary account. But other results (for example, the strong preference for settling down with just one partner) run contrary to the evolutionary predictions, suggesting that, here, as always, cultural values and expectations play at least as strong a role as biology.

# LOVE

We have now commented on the ways animals (including humans) select their mates, and how many mates animals want to have. But what about the *relationship* between the two animals in a mating pair? Many animals show lasting bonds with their mates, but for humans this bonding often takes on a special meaning and a special importance, something we celebrate with the term *love*. In fact, love involves many elements: a feeling, a physiological upheaval, a desire for sexual union, a set of living and parenting arrangements, a sharing of resources (from bank accounts to friends), a mutual defense and caretaking pact, a merging of extended families, and more. So complex is human loving that, according to some authorities, psychologists might have been "wise to have abdicated responsibility for analysis of this term and left it to poets" (Reber, 1985, p. 409). Wise or not, psychologists have tried to say some things about this strange state of mind that has puzzled both sages and poets throughout the ages.

Psychologists have found it useful to distinguish different kinds of love and have proposed many different categorization schemes. While these schemes differ in important ways, most psychologists would agree that there are at least two broad types of love. One is *romantic*—or passionate—*love*, the kind of love that one "falls into," that one is "in." The other is *companionate love*, a less violent state that emphasizes companionship and mutual trust and care.

## ROMANTIC LOVE

Romantic love has been described as essentially passionate: "a wildly emotional state [in which] tender and sexual feelings, elation and pain, anxiety and relief, altruism and jealousy coexist in a confusion of feelings" (Berscheid & Walster, 1978). And in contrast to the stereotype that men are "rational" and women "emotional," males tend to fall into this state more often and more quickly, while women tend to fall out of love more easily (Hill et al., 1976).

The tumultuous emotions of romantic love are sharply focused on the beloved, who is almost always seen through a rosy haze. The lover constantly thinks about the beloved and about their next time together, sometimes to the point of obsession. Given this giddy mixture of erotic, irrational passion and fantasy, it is understandable why Shakespeare felt that lovers have much in common with both madmen and poets. Lovers are a bit mad because their emotions are so turbulent and their thoughts and actions so obsessive; they are a bit poetic because they do not see their beloved as he or she really is, but as an idealized fabrication of their own desires and imaginings.

*Romantic love    Shrek and Princess Fiona experience the adventures and misadventures of romantic love.*

## ROMANTIC LOVE AS AN EXCITING ADVENTURE

According to some authors, romantic love involves two distinguishable elements: a state of physiological arousal and a set of beliefs and attitudes that leads the person to interpret this arousal as passion. What leads to the arousal itself? One obvious source is erotic excitement, but other forms of stimulation may have the same effect. Fear, pain, and anxiety can all heighten general arousal and so can, in fact, lend fuel to romantic passion. One demonstration of this comes from a widely cited experiment in which men were approached by an attractive young woman who asked them to fill out a questionnaire (allegedly to help her with a class project); she then gave them her telephone number so they could call her later if they wanted to know more about the project. The study was conducted in Capilano Park, just north of Vancouver, British Columbia. The park is famous for its narrow, wobbly suspension bridge, precariously suspended over a shallow rapids 230 feet below. Some of the men in the study were approached while they were on the bridge itself. Others were approached after they had already crossed the bridge and were back on safe and solid ground.

Did the men actually call the young woman later (ostensibly to discuss the experiment, but really to ask her for a date)? The likelihood of their making this call depended on whether they were approached while they were on the bridge or later, after they had crossed it. If they filled out the questionnaire while crossing the bridge—at which point they might well have felt some fear and excitement—the chances were almost one in three that the men would call. If they met the young woman when they were back on safe ground, the chances of their doing so were very much lower (Dutton & Aron, 1974; but see also Kenrick & Cialdini, 1977; Kenrick, Cialdini, & Linder, 1979).

What is going on here? Being on the bridge would make almost anyone feel a little jittery—it would, in other words, cause a state of arousal. The men who were approached while on the bridge detected this arousal, but they seem to have misinterpreted their own feelings, attributing their elevated heart rate and sweaty palms not to fear, but to their interest in the woman. Then, having misread their own state in this fashion, they followed through in a sensible way, telephoning a woman whom they believed had excited them.

This account obviously emphasizes the "interpretive" aspects of romantic love, with the men understanding their feelings in a certain way and then acting in accord with this understanding. But what is it that leads to this interpretation of the arousal and not some other? One crucial factor is the set of ideas that each of us has about what love is and what falling in love feels like. These ideas have been fashioned by a historical heritage that goes back to Greek and Roman times (with tales of lovers hit by Cupid's arrows), were revived during the Middle Ages (with knights in armor slaying dragons to win a lady's favor), and were finally mass-produced by the Hollywood entertainment machine (with a final fade-out in which boy and girl embrace to live happily ever after).* This complex set of ideas about what love is, together with an appropriate potential love object—one who is attractive, of the right age, more or less available, and so on—constitutes the context that may lead us to interpret physiological arousal as love.

*The Rocky Course of Romantic Love*    These comments may help us understand why romantic love seems to thrive on obstacles. Shakespeare tells us that the "course of true love never did run smooth," but if it had, the resulting love probably would have been lacking in ardor. The fervor of a wartime romance or an illicit affair is probably fed

*Knights and damsels in distress    Many of our ideas about love are shared by our cultural heritage. The knight rescuing the damsel in distress, for example, is a centuries-old idea, but still well represented in popular movies. (Tobey Maguire and Kirsten Dunst in a scene from Spider-Man.)*

---

* While various Hindu myths and Chinese love songs make it clear that romantic love is found in other times and places than our own, it is unlikely that any other cultural epoch has taken it quite as seriously as ours does; thus, love as a precondition for marriage is a relatively new and Western concept (see, for example, De Rougemont, 1940; Grant, 1976; Hunt, 1959).

*The rocky course of love    Frustrations and difficulties often seem to add fuel to a romance—sometimes with wonderful consequences, and other times with a tragic ending. (Hayden Christensen and Natalie Portman as Anakin Skywalker and Padme Amidala.)*

in part by danger and frustration, and many a lover's passion becomes all the more intense for being unrequited. In all these cases, there is increased arousal, whether through fear, frustration, or anxiety. This arousal continues to be interpreted as love, a cognitive appraisal that fits in perfectly with our ideas about romantic love, since, after all, these ideas include both the rapture of love, and the agony.

An interesting demonstration of this phenomenon is the so-called ***Romeo-and-Juliet effect*** (named after Shakespeare's doomed couple, whose parents violently opposed their love). This term describes the fact that parental opposition tends to intensify the couple's romantic passion rather than to diminish it. In one study, couples were asked whether their parents interfered with their relationship. The greater this interference, the more deeply the couples fell in love (Driscoll, Davis, & Lipeitz, 1972). The moral is that if parents want to break up a romance, their best bet is to ignore it. If the feuding Montagues and Capulets had simply looked the other way, Romeo and Juliet might well have become bored with each other by the end of the second act.

## ROMANTIC LOVE AND JEALOUSY

In fairy tales, the two lovers come blissfully together and live happily ever after. In real life, though, this does not always happen, because the course of romantic love is often thwarted. In some cases there is a rival, and one's true love turns out not to be true. The frequent result is jealousy.

Jealousy is, of course, found in both men (as in Shakespeare's Othello) and women (Hell has no fury like a woman scorned, to paraphrase William Congreve). But there is at least some suggestion that the basis for this jealousy is different in men and in women. Men, it is alleged, care more about sexual loyalty than emotional loyalty; it is worse, in their view, if their partner is sleeping with someone else than it is if their partner is merely emotionally engaged with someone else. For women, it is alleged, this pattern reverses, with greater concern about emotional disloyalty than about sexual transgressions.

Like many other findings we have presented in this chapter, this pattern can be understood from an evolutionary perspective. In evolutionary terms, it should not matter very much for a woman if her mate has sex with others. This will not take anything away from her own offspring and her own chances of (genetic) survival. What she does need, though, in order to foster her own offspring is her mate's resources, and so it is worrisome for her if he starts devoting those resources to other women (and to their children). That, of course, is more likely to happen if he becomes emotionally attached to someone else, and this is why it is her mate's emotional disloyalty that is threatening to the woman's evolutionary self-interest.

What about men? If a man devotes his resources to a woman and her children, he needs to be sure that these children carry his genes—otherwise, he has spent his resources to promote another male's legacy. If his mate loves someone else, that is okay—provided that her love does not lead her to have sex with that someone else.

Evidence consistent with these evolutionary claims comes from studies in which men and women were asked to imagine themselves in a romantic relationship in which an infidelity takes place. They were then asked to indicate whether they would be more upset if their partner had a sexual relationship with another person or if their partner fell in love with that other person. In several such studies the results were in line with the evolutionary hypothesis: women said that they would be more upset by a mate's emotional infidelity, and men by a mate's sexual infidelity (Buss, Larsen, Westen, & Semmelroth, 2001).

However, this hypothesis and the results supporting it have been seriously criticized. One critic pointed out that these studies relied only on hypothetical scenarios. Would the results have been the same if the infidelities were real rather than merely imagined?

To find out, the investigator focused on people who had had an actual experience with a mate cheating and asked them how they felt about the infidelity. There was no gender difference whatsoever in the people's reactions. Contrary to the evolutionary hypothesis, both men and women were more upset by an emotional than a sexual infidelity (Harris, 2002; for corroborating data, see DeSteno, Bartlett, & Salovey, 2002). In short, then, there are differences in how men and women *think about* some (not all) sorts of infidelity, in a fashion consistent with evolutionary theorizing. The available evidence, though, suggests that how men and women *react to* infidelity is rather similar. (However, for some other data, apparently favoring the evolutionary perspective on mating and, in particular, on "poaching" on another's mate, see Schmitt & Buss, 2001; for other concerns about the evolutionary perspective, see Miller, Putcha-Bhagavatula, & Pedersen, 2002.)

## COMPANIONATE LOVE

It is widely agreed that romantic love tends to be a short-lived bloom. That wild and tumultuous state, with its intense emotional ups and downs, with its obsessions, fantasies, and idealizations, rarely, if ever, lasts forever. Eventually there are no further surprises and no further obstacles, except those posed by the inevitable problems of ordinary life. The adventure is over, and romantic love ebbs. Sometimes it turns into indifference or active dislike. Other times—and hopefully more often—it transforms into a related but gentler state of affairs—companionate love. This type of love is sometimes defined as the "affection we feel for those with whom our lives are deeply intertwined" (Berscheid & Hatfield, 1978, p. 176). In companionate love, the similarity of outlook, mutual caring, and trust that develop through day-to-day living become more important than the fantasies and idealization of romantic love, as the two partners try to live as happily ever after as it is possible to do in the real world. This is not to say that the earlier passion does not flare up occasionally. But it no longer has the obsessive quality that it once had, in which the lover is unable to think of anything but the beloved (Caspi & Herbener, 1990; Hatfield, 1988; Neimeyer, 1984).

*Companionate love*    Eventually, the wild and tumultuous state of romantic love passes. In many cases, though, it is replaced by companionate love, the "affection we feel for those with whom our lives are deeply intertwined."

# PARENTING

There is another bond whose biological foundations are just as basic as those between males and females—the relation between mother and child, and in many animals, the relation between father and child as well. Most fish and reptiles lay eggs by the hundreds and then abandon them. In contrast, most birds and mammals invest in quality, not quantity; they have many fewer offspring but display a strong parental attachment to them. Of course, this makes it more likely that these offspring will survive, because the parent feeds them, cleans them, shelters them and protects them, trying in all these ways to ensure that most of their brood reach the point of self-sufficiency and reproductive readiness.

*Orangutan mother and child*

## THE INFANT'S ATTACHMENT TO THE MOTHER

During this period of dependency, most young birds and mammals become strongly attached to their mother. Ducklings follow the mother duck, lambs follow the mother ewe, and infant monkeys cling tightly to the mother monkey's belly. In each case, separation from the mother leads to considerable stress: the young animals give piteous distress calls and quack, bleat, or cry continuously until the mother returns. The biological function of this attachment is a simple matter of personal survival. This holds for humans as well as other animals, because there is little doubt that in our early evolutionary history a motherless infant would have died an early death, from exposure, starvation, or predation.

The mechanisms that lead to this attachment will be discussed later (see Chapter 13). For now, we will only say that the infant's attachment to the mother goes far beyond the biological functions, the alleviation of hunger, thirst, and pain. This is reflected in the fact that infants—be they birds, monkeys, or humans—show great separation distress even when they are perfectly well fed and housed.

## THE MOTHER'S ATTACHMENT TO THE INFANT

From the infant's point of view, the biological function of the mother-child bond is a matter of survival. As it turns out, the function is the same from the mother's point of view, although, for her, the survival is genetic rather than personal: unless her young survive to reproduce, her genes will perish. It seems virtually certain, therefore, that natural selection would favor individuals who act like proper parents, caring for and protecting their young. Such parents, of course, would have a greater chance of transmitting their genes to subsequent generations, including any genes that promoted a predisposition toward parental behavior. On this basis, it seems highly likely that such behaviors are rooted in the parents' biology.

In many species, the parents' caretaking behaviors are elicited by specific signals from the young. In some types of birds, for example, the hatchlings open their mouths as wide as they can as soon as the parent arrives at the nest. This gaping response is their means of begging for food (see Figure 11.6), and the parents respond appropriately. In fact, some species of birds have special anatomical features that draw attention to these signals, essentially guaranteeing a proper parental reaction. An example is the cedar waxwing, whose bright red mouth lining evidently provides a further signal to the parent: "I'm young, hungry, and a cedar waxwing!"

Child care among humans takes much longer than it does among cedar waxwings, with most human children not becoming self-sufficient until they are well into their teens. Human caretaking is also more varied and complex, but it too has biological foundations. This is evident, for example, in the way humans talk to their young, with virtually all parents using a special singsong pitch whenever they talk to their infants. This so-called *Motherese* occurs quite spontaneously and in every culture that has been studied, and probably represents a biologically determined communication style. It is triggered whenever an adult interacts with an infant (Newport, Gleitman, & Gleitman, 1977; and see Chapter 9). It is also used with other small and dependent creatures, including small pets such as puppies and lapdogs (Hirsh-Pasek & Treiman, 1982). This peculiar form of communication probably serves several important purposes. Among them, it keeps the infant's attention focused on the social interaction; it may also help communicate aspects of the adult's intentions toward the child (Fernald, 1992).

The human infant also has a set of skills and capacities that promote these early social interactions. One is an essentially innate signal system through which he tells the mother that he is in distress: he cries. Similar distress calls are found in many animals, for when the young chirp, bleat, mew, or cry, the mother immediately runs to their aid and comforts them.

Many biologists believe that natural selection has further equipped the infant with a set of stimulus features that function as innate releasers of parental, and especially maternal, feelings. The cues that define "babyness" include a large protruding forehead, large eyes, an upturned nose, chubby cheeks, and so on. Endowed with these distinctive properties, the baby looks cute and cuddly to adult humans, something to be picked up,

**11.6 Innate triggers** *In many species, the parents' care-taking behaviors are elicited by specific signals from the young — such as when adult cedar waxwings see the bright red mouth lining of their hatchlings.*

11.7    *The stimulus features of "babyness"* *"Cute" characteristics of the baby schema are common to humans and a number of animals. (A) These include a rounded head shape, protruding forehead, and large eyes below the middle of the head. (B) The Disney character Mickey Mouse became "cuter" over the years by subscribing more and more to the baby schema, with his eyes and head becoming larger.*

fussed over, and taken care of. The situation is similar for the young of various animals who share aspects of the same babyness schema. In all cases, some argue, these stimulus characteristics help ensure that adults will react to the infant in just the right protective, nurturing fashion (Lorenz, 1950). These same tendencies, though, are open to exploitation, and many commercial enterprises have devoted themselves to the deliberate manufacture of cuteness. Dolls and Walt Disney creatures are designed to be babied by children, while certain lapdogs are especially bred to be babied by adults (Figure 11.7; see Fridlund & MacDonald, 1998).

Nature has provided human infants with yet another trick to disarm even the stoniest of parental hearts: the smile. In some fashion, smiling may begin within the first month; it is often considered a built-in signal by which humans tell each other, "I wish you well. Be good to me." There is reason to believe that both the giving of this signal (smiling) and the response to it are either innate or learned very early. Infants who are born blind smile under conditions that also produce smiling in sighted children, as when they hear their mother's voice. They obviously could not have learned this response by imitating what they see, and this strongly suggests an innate basis for this simple, but very important, human gesture.

# AGGRESSION

We have now considered many of the social motives that bring humans together—attraction, love, parenting. There is one social motive, though—namely, *aggression*—that seems to work in the opposite direction, driving humans apart or driving them to fight with each other. Does aggression have biological underpinnings? To address this question, we again turn to the *comparative method*, studying nonhumans as well as humans to see whether there are commonalities that reflect some shared biological heritage.

## AGGRESSION AND PREDATION

Studying aggression requires first that we divorce it from predation. To be sure, both involve violence, but that is where the commonality ends. Predators hunt and kill for food, but they do so quite dispassionately. A predator about to pounce on its prey shows none of the signs of anger. The dog who is on the verge of catching a rabbit never growls, nor does it have its ears laid back (Lorenz, 1966). Predation and aggression are also quite different neurologically. In the cat, rat stalking (predatory attack) and arched-back hissing (aggression or self-defense) are elicited by the stimulation of two different areas of its hypothalamus (Wasman & Flynn, 1962). Predatory attack is an outgrowth of the hunger motive and not of aggression: the hypothalamic site whose stimulation gives rise to rat stalking also elicits eating (Hutchinson & Renfrew, 1966).

## MALE AGGRESSION AND HORMONES

Both predatory attacks and defensive fighting are relatively common in the animal world, but, even if we hold these to the side, many cases of animal combat remain. In other words, aggression is widespread among animals, and there is probably no species that has foresworn aggression altogether. Fish chase and nip each other; lizards lunge and push; birds attack with wing, beak, and claw; deer lock antlers; and rats adopt a boxing stance and eye each other warily until one finally pounces on the other (see Figure 11.8).

In most of these cases, the individuals we identify as aggressive are male, because, among vertebrates, the male is by far the more physically aggressive sex. In some mammals, this difference in combativeness is apparent even in childhood play. Young male rhesus monkeys, for instance, engage in much more vigorous rough-and-tumble play than their sisters (Harlow, 1962). Among humans, boys worldwide are more physically aggressive than girls (Geary & Bjorklund, 2000; and see Chapter 13), and as adults, male murderers outnumber females by a ratio of 10:1 (Anderson & Bushman, 2002).

But this gender difference only holds for physical aggression. Women are also aggressive, but usually not physically. Their aggression is typically indirect, via social attacks of one sort or another. They attack by means of subtle insults or the spreading of rumors; they take steps to isolate someone from friends and allies. If we focus on these sorts of aggression, then it is women, not men, who are the aggressive sex (Oesterman et al., 1998).

Why is physical aggression so much more prevalent in men? Biological factors are clearly relevant, because aggression is partially influenced by hormones, particularly by the sex hormone *testosterone*. High testosterone levels in the bloodstream are associated with increased physical aggressiveness; low levels, with less. This correlation has been observed in many different species, including fish, lizards, turtles, birds, rats, mice, and monkeys (Davis, 1964; Siegel & Demetrikopoulos, 1993). However, we emphasize that with humans the relationship between testosterone and physical aggression is much weaker, and some studies have not found it at all (Book, Starzyk, & Qunisey, 2001). In any case, it would be inaccurate to say simply that for any species testosterone causes aggression, because in fact it can be both a cause and an effect. Thus, testosterone administered externally can increase subsequent aggressiveness, but successful aggressive encounters can cause increased secretion of testosterone (Dabbs, 1992; Rosenzweig, Leiman, & Breedlove, 1996; Sapolsky, 1998).

Some further biological mechanisms concern the neurotransmitter serotonin. Low serotonin levels are generally associated with impulsive aggression in monkeys (Higley, Suomi, & Linnoila, 1990) and with interpersonal assaults, self-injurious behavior, and even violent suicides in humans (Dolan, Anderson, & Deakin, 2001; New, Trestman, Mitropovlov, & Benishay, 1997; Rosenzweig et al., 1996). But research in monkeys shows that higher serotonin levels are also associated with the individual's place in the group's dominance hierarchy, and levels of serotonin in a single animal can rise or fall depending on its position in the hierarchy. Drug-induced serotonin increases can also

**11.8 Aggressive fighting** *Male rats generally fight in fairly stereotypical ways, including (A) a "boxing" position that often escalates into (B) a leaping, biting attack. (From Barnett, 1963)*

raise an animal's status. Thus, serotonin plays a complex role here. It plays a role in inhibiting impulsive aggression (and so this aggression increases when the inhibition is removed). And it serves somehow to enhance the wider range of strategic "social skills" necessary to achieve and maintain dominance (Brammer, Raleigh, & McGuire, 1994; Raleigh et al., 1991, 1992; Shively, Fontenot, & Kaplan, 1995).

## TERRITORIALITY

What do humans and other animals fight about? Their struggles are generally about a scarce resource, whether it be a food source, a water hole, a mate, or a job position. To secure such resources, many animals stake out a claim to a particular *territory*—one that includes or will lead to the desired resource—and then they defend that territory as their exclusive preserve.

Many species, including many types of birds, fish, and mammals, stake out and defend territories. For example, in the spring, male songbirds endlessly patrol their little fiefdoms and furiously repel all male intruders who violate their borders. Contrary to the poet's fancy, the male bird who bursts into full-throated song is not giving vent to inexpressible joy, pouring out his "full heart in profuse strains of unpremeditated art" (Shelley, 1821). Instead, his message is prosaic and double-edged. It is a warning to other males: "Don't trespass!" And it is an invitation to unattached females, who on their flybys are appraising his song for tips to his vigor and thus his mateworthiness: "Am fit, have territory, will share."

In animals, territoriality promotes reproductive success in an obvious way: a male able to secure a resource-filled territory provides well for his offspring, and likewise for a female who selects a male with ample resources in his domain. In addition, territoriality helps to keep aggressiveness within bounds. Good fences make good neighbors, at least in the sense that they keep the antagonists out of each others' hair (or fins or feathers). One mechanism that accomplishes this is rather simple. Once a territory is established, its owner has a kind of home-court advantage in further disputes (Krebs, 1982). On his home ground he is courageous; if he ventures beyond it, he becomes timid and is readily repulsed. As a result, there may be occasional border skirmishes but few actual conflicts.

### HUMAN TERRITORIALITY

In a variety of ways, humans also stake out territories, announcing their ownership both of certain spaces and of certain material objects. Even within the home, individual family members each have their private preserves—their own rooms or corners, their places at the dinner table, and so on. In more public places, territorial claims are more temporary, such as a seat on a train, whose possession we mark with a coat or a book if we have to leave for a while.

The power of human territorial behavior is illustrated by the phenomenon of *personal space*, the physical zone surrounding us whose intrusion we guard against (Figure 11.9). The desire for a protected personal space can be demonstrated in many settings, including, say, the New York City subways. On these subways, passengers sit on long benches and carefully choose their seats so as to leave the greatest possible distance between themselves and their nearest neighbor. The same pattern can be observed when people choose seats in a movie theater, or arrange their blankets on the beach.

A desire to maintain some minimal personal space is probably universal, but the physical dimensions of this space are affected by the standards of a particular culture. In North America, acquaintances stand two to three feet apart during a conversation; if one moves closer, the other feels crowded or pushed into unwanted intimacy. For Latin

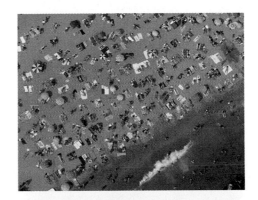

**11.9   Personal space   In many public spaces, humans arrange themselves in remarkably uniform spatial patterns, as if each is respecting the territory of the others. This is certainly visible whenever people spread out their blankets on the beach.**

Americans, the acceptable distance is much less. Under the circumstances, misunderstanding is almost inevitable. The North American regards the Latin American as overly intrusive; the Latin American in turn feels that the North American is unfriendly and cold (Hall, 1966).

Once again, though, we need to confront the issue that has already emerged many times in this chapter. Does human territoriality arise from the same sources as the territoriality observed in other species? More specifically, is human territoriality somehow prescribed by our genes, a product of natural selection? Or is it the product of cultural rules, acquired through learning during the individual's lifetime and therefore (presumably) open to modification if further experience overrules this learning?

On this matter, just as in other settings, these questions elicit controversy. On the one side, there are similarities between human territoriality and the songbird's (or the wolf's or the baboon's). These imply a shared (biological) base for this behavior. But, on the other side, there are also important contrasts, and these contrasts indicate a role of culture and of learning in shaping human territoriality. Some of the clearest evidence involves the variation we observe in how humans express their territoriality, variation that is difficult to understand in strictly evolutionary or genetic terms (since all humans have, in this regard, roughly the same genes and the same evolutionary past).

What is this variation? Members of all human societies resist being crowded to some extent (Evans, Lepore, & Allen, 2000) but, within this broad framework, societies differ markedly in how they view space and how they apportion it. In some societies, individuals own certain spaces; in other societies, ownership is communal, rather than private. Within a society, some individuals fiercely protect their real estate, while others are indifferent to the exclusiveness of their surroundings. These differences are difficult to reconcile with claims of a biologically fixed territorial imperative, and they remind us that, like almost everything human, territoriality begins in biology but is elaborated and transformed by culture (Rivano-Fischer, 1987).

## CONSTRAINTS ON AGGRESSION

A certain amount of aggressiveness is likely to increase an animal's evolutionary fitness. For example, a more aggressive songbird will probably secure a larger and more desirable territory. But aggression also has serious biological costs. Combat is dangerous and can lead to death or injury. In addition, it distracts the animal from other vital pursuits. The male who is continually fighting with his sexual rivals will have little time (let alone energy) left to gather food or to mate with the female after his competitors have fled (Enquist & Leimar, 1990). Thus, natural selection favors aggression only within limits.

As one limit, animals seem keenly sensitive to the strength of their enemy. If the enemy seems much stronger (or more agile or better armed or armored) than oneself, the best bet is to proclaim a cease-fire or to concede defeat quickly, or better yet, never to start the battle at all. Animals therefore use a variety of strategies to proclaim their strength, with a goal of winning the battle before it starts. They roar, they puff themselves up, they strut, they offer all sorts of threats, all with the aim of appearing as powerful as they possibly can (see Figure 11.10). Conversely, once an animal determines that it is the weaker one, and likely to lose a battle, it uses a variety of strategies for avoiding a bloody defeat, usually involving specific conciliatory signals, such as crouching or exposing one's belly (see Figure 11.11).

Another major constraint on aggression, found in many species, is a *dominance hierarchy*, in which each member of the group has an assigned status that determines who has access to mates, who gets first turn at the food supply, who gets the best nest site, and so on. With all of these issues settled by one's place in the hierarchy, fighting over them is much reduced, and thus overall aggression is decreased. (For more on how this

**11.10 Threat displays** *(A) Some species threaten by making themselves appear larger and more impressive. (B) Other species threaten by shouting at the top of their lungs, like howler monkeys, who scream at each other for hours on end.*

dominance is established, see Cheney & Seyfarth, 1990; de Waal, 1982; Hrdy & Williams, 1983; Packer, 1977; Silk, 1986; Smith, 1981; Walters & Seyfarth, 1986).

## PATTERNS OF HUMAN AGGRESSION

Humans, no less than other species, will engage in aggression in order to secure resources, maintain dominance, or defend their territory. But human aggression often occurs under particular circumstances that usually revolve around our specific capacity for symbolism, because, in the end, many instances of human aggression result from symbolic exchanges (for example, insults to our honor or our beliefs), rather than palpable threats to our welfare.

Certain kinds of social interactions are especially likely to provoke aggression in humans. Most important among these are frank provocations that include both physical aggression or obstruction, and other less direct attacks, such as social slight, insults, and verbal assaults (Geen, 2001). Often, these provocations lead immediately to violence, but sometimes the violence emerges only after a delay, as retaliation for the earlier grievance. In some cases, the delay can be quite long, with someone eventually exploding into violence in response to a long-festering insult. When the retaliation does occur, it is often aimed at the provocateur. However, sometimes it is directed toward an innocent bystander—as, for example, in the case of a parent yelling at his child after being scolded severely by his boss (Pedersen, Gonzales, & Miller, 2000).

Of course, not all individuals respond to provocation with violence. Some turn the other cheek; some find nonviolent means of asserting themselves or their privileges. What determines how someone responds? For many years, investigators believed that aggression was more likely to come from people with relatively low self-esteem, on the argument that such individuals were particularly vulnerable to insult and also likely to have few other means of responding. More recent work, however, suggests that the opposite is the case, that social provocations are more likely to inspire aggression if the person provoked has unrealistically high self-esteem (Baumeister, 2001; Baumeister, Smart, & Boden, 1996). Such a person is particularly likely to perceive the provocation as a grievous assault, challenging his inflated self-image, and, in many cases, violence will be the result.

In addition, whether someone turns to aggression or not is influenced heavily by the culture in which he was raised. Some cultures prescribe violence, often via rules of chivalry and honor that demand certain responses to certain insults. Gang violence in many U.S. cities can be understood partly in this way, and so can many cases of larger-scale violence (for example, some of the fighting among the warlords of Somalia). Within the United States, social psychologists Richard Nisbett and Dov Cohen have

*Red deer stag roaring*

**11.11** *Ritualized fighting* **Two South African** *wildebeest males in a harmless ritualized duel along an invisible but mutually defined border between their territories.*

described what they call a "culture of honor" in the southern states, a culture that, in their view, has features that make it prone to violence (Nisbett & Cohen, 1996). They begin with the fact that the homicide rate in the South is reliably higher than in the North, and they argue that the difference cannot be attributed to differences in population density, socioeconomic factors, climate, or a history of slavery. Rather, they argue that the southern states share a culture that inculcates the idea that men must learn to "fight or even to kill to defend their reputations as honorable men."

The investigators supported their thesis with a set of experiments involving University of Michigan students who had grown up either in the North or in the South (Cohen, Nisbett, Bowdle, & Schwartz, 1996). In each experiment, a six-foot-three-inch, 250-pound accomplice of the experimenters "accidentally" bumped into the participant in a hallway and then verbally insulted him. Compared to those reared in the North, participants brought up in the South were more upset by the incident (their stress hormones were more elevated), were more primed for aggression (their testosterone levels were higher), and showed more bravado in their subsequent behavior (they were less likely to step aside when walkng on a collision course with a second accomplice). We should note that this research has been controversial (see, for example, Raper, 1997), but, even so, it provides a clear example of how certain cultural values might, in some circumstances, end up fostering violence.

This mention of honor also draws our attention to another issue. For obvious reasons, discussions of aggression usually showcase the evils that aggression can produce, and, unfortunately, these evils are easy to catalog: shootings in high schools, the devastation of war, the senseless violence of many crimes, the numerous cases of genocide our species has attempted. But we should also add that aggression is sometimes initiated by motives that are not so dark: the defense of honor, or the wish to defeat an awful enemy. It is certainly possible to argue that, even in these cases, the aggression is unacceptable—this is, after all, the position of "conscientious objectors" who refuse military service under any circumstances. Whatever one makes of this moral position, though, the psychological point should be clear: aggression can arise from a variety of motives, some of which are obviously condemnable, but some of which may not be.

## AGGRESSION AND THE MEDIA

One other influence on aggression has been prominently discussed, by scientific investigators, by political figures, by journalists. This is the influence allegedly arising from the violence that is so often portrayed in the television shows we watch and the movies we see. And there is no question that these entertainment media are violent. Prime-time television programs contain, on some accounts, an average of five violent acts per hour, as characters punch, kick, shoot at, and sometimes murder each other. Saturday-morning children's shows are even worse—some estimate as many as twenty-five violent acts per hour. Overall, investigators have estimated that the average child observes more than 10,000 acts of TV violence every year (see, for example, Anderson & Bushman, 2001).

Does this exposure to violence promote violence in the viewer? Some of the pertinent evidence comes from studies of violence levels within a community before and after television was introduced, or before and after the broadcast of particularly gruesome footage of murders or assassinations. These studies consistently show that assault and homicide rates increase after these exposures (Berkowitz & Macauley, 1971; Centerwall, 1989; Joy, Kimball, & Zabrack, 1986). Other studies indicate that children who are not particularly aggressive become more so after viewing TV violence (Belson, 1978; Eron & Huesmann, 1980, 1985; Huesmann, Lagerspetz, & Eron, 1984; Huesmann & Miller, 1994).

These studies leave little doubt that there is a strong correlation here, such that those who view violence are likely to be violent themselves. But does this correlation reveal a

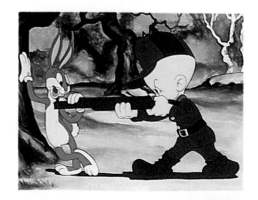

*Television violence  Children's television cartoons contain, by some estimates, twenty-five violent acts per hour, as characters punch, kick, shoot, stab, or crush each other.*

cause-and-effect relationship, in which the viewing actually causes someone to be more violent themselves? Many investigators believe it does (Anderson & Bushman, 2001, 2002). Indeed, the evidence persuaded six major professional societies (including the American Psychological Association, the American Medical Association, and the American Psychiatric Association) to issue a joint statement noting that studies "point overwhelmingly to a causal connection between media violence and aggressive behavior in some children" (Joint Statement, 2000, p. 1).

Other investigators, however, remain skeptical about this causal claim and have suggested that, in at least some cases, the causal connection is the reverse: people who are inclined toward violence may be the ones who seek out violent television, so that being more violent causes one to view more violence, and not the other way around. Another concern comes from the fact that not all studies show a relationship between viewing violence and being violent, and at least some texts suggest that this is because the effect of viewing violence may be small, short-lived, or both (for a review see Green, 1998). There is substantial disagreement about these specific points, just as there is about the overall issue, and, given the urgency of the issue—with regard both to the level of violence in our world and to the amount of violence in the media—one can only hope that a consensus is reached soon.

Video game
violence

# ALTRUISM AND SELF-SACRIFICE

All of the behaviors we have considered so far are relatively easy to understand in evolutionary terms, because they all serve an animal's genetic self-interest in an obvious fashion: an aggressive animal fights for resources that will serve it (or its offspring), mates select a mate that will increase their chances of having healthy descendants, and so on. But there are some circumstances in which animals stray from this pattern and seem to act in a manner not consistent with their own self-interest; indeed, they act as if they were unselfish altruists. How should we understand such behaviors?

It is, of course, well known that many animals go to considerable lengths to defend their offspring. Various birds, for example, have evolved the strategy of feigning injury in order to draw a predator away from their nests (see Figure 11.12). The bird drags one wing or paddles in circles in order to appear vulnerable to the predator. Then, when the predator turns to approach this seemingly easy target, the bird moves a little farther away. This process continues, with the bird continuing the pretense and drawing the predator farther and farther from the nest.

On the face of it, such acts appear heroically unselfish, because the parent is putting itself in considerable danger, making itself relatively vulnerable to the predator. If we examine the behavior biologically, though, this strategy actually is self-serving and not at all altruistic (Wilson, 1975). To see this, imagine that the mother bird played it safe and flew off, rather than putting herself at risk to protect her young. This mother is likely to survive, but, as we have noted repeatedly, from an evolutionary perspective what counts is not personal survival but genetic survival. The mother's genes are more likely to perish if she flies off to safety, leaving the predator to eat her chicks. As a result, she will have fewer offspring to whom she has passed on her genes, including the very gene or genes that predispose her toward maternal indifference.

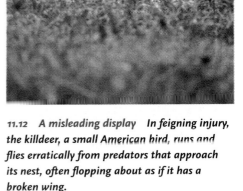

**11.12 A misleading display** *In feigning injury, the killdeer, a small American bird, runs and flies erratically from predators that approach its nest, often flopping about as if it has a broken wing.*

## ALTRUISM IN ANIMALS

Seen in this light, parental self-sacrifice can easily be understood in evolutionary terms. A similar analysis can be applied to altruistic acts that benefit individuals other than

**11.13   Alarm call**   *Ground squirrels give alarm calls when they sense a nearby predator. Such alarm calls are more likely to be given by females than males. The females usually have close relatives living nearby. As a result, their alarm call is more likely to benefit genetically related rather than unrelated individuals, which suggests that it is based on kin selection.*

one's own offspring.* A case in point is provided by the alarm calls given by many species at the approach of a predator (see Figure 11.13). For example, when a robin sees a hawk overhead, it gives an alarm call, a special cry that alerts all members of the flock and impels them to seek cover. All robins emit this call when in danger, and they do so even if raised in complete isolation from their fellows. And there is no doubt that this alarm call benefits all robins who hear it. They crouch low and hide, so their chances of escape are enhanced. But the bird who sounds the alarm may not reap these rewards—that bird is busy crying out rather than hiding. In fact, the alarm call may place the calling bird in greater danger by revealing its location to the hawk (although see Blumstein, 1999; Clutton-Brock, et al., 1999). Why, therefore, does the robin play the hero instead of quietly stealing away and leaving its fellows to their fate? There are several possible factors.

## KIN SELECTION

Let us assume that our heroic robin is unlucky, is seized by the hawk, and dies a martyr's death. While this act may have caused the robin to perish as an individual, it may well have served to preserve some of that bird's genes. This may be true even if none of the birds in the flock are the hero's own offspring. They may be relatives who carry some of its genes, brothers and sisters who share half of the same genes, or nieces and nephews who share one-fourth. If so, the alarm call may have saved several relatives who carry the alarm-calling genes and who will pass them on to future generations of robins. From an evolutionary standpoint, the alarm call has survival value—if not for the alarm caller or its offspring, then for the alarm-calling genes (Hamilton, 1964; Maynard-Smith, 1965).

According to this view, altruistic behavior will evolve if it promotes the survival of the individual's kin. This *kin-selection hypothesis* predicts that unselfish behavior should be more common among relatives than among unrelated individuals, and there is some evidence that this is indeed the case. Certain deer snort loudly when alarmed, which alerts other deer nearby. This behavior is much more likely among groups of does, who tend to be related, than among groups of bucks, who are less likely to be related. Similar behavior is seen in roosters and a wide range of other species (Hirth & McCullough, 1977; Marler, Duffy, & Pickert, 1986a, b; Sherman, 1977).

## RECIPROCAL ALTRUISM

There is another mechanism that might lead to biologically unselfish acts—*reciprocal altruism*. Some animals, and we may well be among them, may follow a built-in Golden Rule: do unto others as you would have them do unto you (or unto your genes). If one individual helps another, and that other later reciprocates, the ultimate result is a benefit to both. For example, male baboons sometimes help each other in aggressive encounters, and the one who received help on one occasion is more likely to come to the other's assistance later (Packer, 1977; but see Bercovitch, 1988).

Reciprocity among animals is also evident in other contexts—for example, grooming. Monkeys and apes often sit in pairs while one meticulously picks vermin out of the other's fur (Figure 11.14). We can certainly see that the animal being groomed benefits. It gets cleaned in areas that may be hard to reach. And it may also find being groomed relaxing—the primate version of a back rub. But it is not clear what the animal doing the gooming gets out of it—until later, when the reciprocity comes into view, and the groomer becomes the groomed.

In addition, grooming is one of the ways of cementing a social bond in primates. It

---

* In fact, modern biological usage reserves *altruism* for just those cases in which the good deed benefits neither the doers nor their own offspring.

occurs most commonly among kin (mothers and children, brothers and sisters, cousins, and so on), although it may also occur among unrelated individuals. But whether they are kin or unrelated, animals who groom most often are also the most closely bonded by other measures of primate togetherness: they sit together, forage for food together, and form coalitions against common antagonists (Boyd & Silk, 1997; Walters & Seyfarth, 1986; for more on the possible evolutionary roots of altruism, see McAndrew, 2002).

## RECIPROCITY AND HUMAN ALTRUISM

A built-in predisposition toward reciprocity may well be an important source of the behaviors we call altruistic: "I help you now so that you'll help me later." But reciprocity may also have a wider reach, and, in fact, a number of theorists believe that a principle of *social exchange* underlies many of the ways people deal with others. According to this view, each partner in a social interaction gives something to the other and expects to receive something in return. Just what is exchanged depends on the interaction. If the relationship is primarily economic, as between buyers and sellers or employees and employers, the exchange will involve goods or labor for money. If it is between friends, lovers, or family members, the exchange will involve valued intangibles such as esteem, loyalty, and affection.

According to social-exchange theory, many human relationships have this underlying give-and-take quality and so can be understood as *exchange relationships*. This is why, if one partner gives and receives nothing in return, the relationship will disintegrate sooner or later (Kelley & Thibaut, 1978). Similarly, people who make a habit of not reciprocating are often excluded from social interactions, and some researchers believe that we possess a predisposition for recognizing good and bad reciprocators, and that this exclusion is a basis for stigmatization (Kurzban & Leary, 2001).

The social-exchange perspective is essentially economic and so quite appropriate to the realm of material transactions. But what about social interactions in which the exchange involves such "commodities" as praise or loyalty or love? Here it is difficult to put a value on the things being exchanged, in order to determine whether the exchange is fair or not. How, therefore, can we apply the exchange perspective?

This question has made it a matter of debate whether the social-exchange approach does apply to all social interactions. There is no question, though, that it does apply to many, and one important example is the operation of the *reciprocity principle*, a basic rule that affects many aspects of social behavior. We feel that we somehow must repay whatever we have been given: a favor for a favor, a gift for a gift, a smile for a smile. The reciprocity rule is extremely powerful and pervasive. As one author points out, our sense of social indebtedness is so deeply ingrained that it has been built into the vocabulary of several languages: thus, "much obliged" is a virtual synonym for "thank you" (Cialdini, 1984).

Behavior in accord with this principle is found in virtually all cultures and societies—both past and present. In the Trobriand Islands, for example, inland islanders give vegetables to the fishermen on the shore, who will later repay the gift with fish, a further gift that in turn calls for a vegetable repayment, and so on—a reciprocity system in which "neither partner can refuse, neither may stint, neither may delay" (Malinowski, 1926). Such exchanges often yield mutual gain, as in the case of the farmers and the fishermen who obtain nutritional benefits. But over and above such material advantages, the gift exchange has a further social function. It creates a web of mutual obligations that knits the members of a society together. In fact, there are a number of societies in which gift giving creates a ritualized cycle of obligations that are never completely canceled; any one gift represents a repayment for a previous gift with a little bit extra, an extra just enough to require still another gift in return, and so on (Gouldner, 1960).

**11.14 Reciprocity** *One common example of reciprocity among animals is in their grooming. Monkeys and apes sit for hours while one picks vermin out of the other's hair; then they exchange roles, and so the groomer becomes the groomed.*

*Reciprocity among people    Reciprocity is easily visible in circumstances based on a barter system. In 2002, the Argentine group Global Bartering Network offered barter as a protest against (and perhaps an alternative to) their country's economic crisis.*

How can we explain the fact that so much of human social life is governed by the reciprocity rule? According to Leda Cosmides and John Tooby, human exchange rules are just a further elaboration of a widespread pattern of reciprocal altruism in the animal kingdom. The idea is that reciprocity benefits both parties to a transaction and can aid the survival of offspring. This being so, natural selection will favor genotypes that predispose individuals toward reciprocity. In fact, Cosmides and Tooby believe that much of human intelligence evolved to help in understanding the uses and principles of social exchange. In their view, we did not become social because we are intelligent. Instead, we became intelligent because we are social (Cosmides & Tooby, 1992).

## RECIPROCITY AND PERSUASION

The power of the reciprocity principle also provides an important tool for persuasion (Cialdini, 1984, 1993). As Robert Cialdini notes, someone doing us a favor necessarily leads to a sense of indebtedness. We feel that we must repay the donor, even if we never wanted his gift in the first place. As a result, we are sometimes manipulated into compliance—saying yes or buying some merchandise or making donations, all despite the fact that we never really wanted to.

*The Reciprocal-Concession Effect*  The power of reciprocity is visible in many settings, including bargaining. The seller states his price. The potential buyer says no. Now the seller makes a concession by offering the item (the house, the car, or whatever) at a lower price. This exerts pressure on the buyer to increase her offer; since the seller offered a concession, she feels that she ought to give a little too.

This pattern is well known to many salespeople but can also be demonstrated experimentally. In one study, an experimenter approached people walking on a university campus and first made a very large request—asking them to work as unpaid volunteer counselors in a juvenile detention center for two hours a week over a two-year period. Not a single person agreed. The experimenter then made a much smaller request: that they accompany a group of boys or girls from the juvenile detention center on a single two-hour trip to the zoo. When this smaller request came on the heels of the large request that had been refused, 50 percent of the people consented. In contrast, only 17 percent of the people acceded to the smaller request when it was not preceded by the larger demand. Apparently, the experimenter's concession (abandoning his large request and moving to the smaller one) made the people feel that they should make a concession of their own, saying yes even though they were initially inclined to say no (Cialdini et al., 1975).

*Reciprocity and Self-Disclosure*    Clearly, the reciprocity principle can be used to persuade people to give of their time or money. But it can also be used to persuade people to give of themselves. Take *self-disclosure*, revealing something personal about oneself. In some ways, telling another person something about your own life is a bit like giving a present, and, just as with other gifts, self-disclosure is influenced by reciprocity: if a person hears an intimate secret, he generally feels obliged to disclose a bit about himself in return (see Miller & Kenny, 1986).

This reciprocity of disclosure plays an important role in the development of friendships, and, as the relationship deepens, the self-disclosures become more frequent and intimate (Altman, 1973; Hansen & Schuldt, 1984; Jourard, 1964; Rubin, Hill, Peplau, & Dunkel-Schetter, 1980). Moreover, another's self-disclosure usually enhances our liking for him; we tend to perceive him as trusting and therefore more worthy of our trust (see Collins & Miller, 1994). Trust, it seems, is one more arena in which reciprocity operates—with someone giving of trust perceived as deserving of trust!

The exchange of information about oneself is also like the exchange of goods in another way: if someone we barely know gives us an expensive gift, we are embarrassed; if someone returns a small favor with a huge one, we feel awkward. The same is true for the exchange of information. Unexpectedly intimate disclosures by strangers or even casual friends can be embarrassing and disruptive to the relationship (Miller, 1990). Intimacy takes time, as the friends need to cycle through larger and larger disclosures before they feel comfortable sharing their deepest secrets.

The pattern of self-disclosure does not just depend on the status of the relationship—it also depends on sex, because men and women differ in their patterns of self-disclosure. By and large, women are more willing to reveal themselves to other women than men are to men, at least in Western culture (Morton, 1978). According to some authors, what matters to women—and is the basis for many woman-to-woman friendships—is sharing emotions. In contrast, the basis for male friendships is often the sharing of some common activity, playing basketball together or watching TV (Sherrod, 1989; Maccoby, 2002). But these differences are clearly affected—and very probably produced—by cultural factors. Thus, Chinese students in Hong Kong were, overall, more self-disclosing than a comparable group of Americans and showed none of the gender difference common in our own culture (Reis & Wheeler, 1991; Wheeler, Reis, & Bond, 1989).

A final point: So far, we have only discussed the positive aspects of reciprocity—a gift for a gift, a smile for a smile. But there is a negative side as well, as promulgated in the Babylonian Hammurabi's code: an eye for an eye, a tooth for a tooth. Some such tendency toward retaliation surely exists in every human culture, and it may be the result of the same biological tendencies that lead to reciprocity in other contexts. It is comforting to know, however, that few modern societies insist on the literal one-for-one reciprocity legislated by Hammurabi. If an accident victim loses two teeth, the guilty party may be forced to pay damages (or even to go to jail), but he will not be sent to a dentist to have two of his own teeth extracted.

## FAIRNESS

The concept of reciprocity is intimately related to the notion of fairness, and, indeed, reciprocity can often be a basis for fairness: if you do for me what I have done for you, then we will each, in the end, have received the same treatment. That equity is, for many people, one of the key aspects of fairness. But fairness can also be understood in larger terms—not just in terms of what two people do for each other, but in terms of how large groups behave, how institutions are set up, and how societal resources are allocated. In discussion of these broad topics, there is no question that people say that fairness and its related concept, justice, are enormously important considerations. They say that they usually try to act fairly, that they want to be treated fairly by others, and that they want societal rules to be fair. But do people actually behave in accord with these principles?

Several studies have probed this issue by means of the so-called *ultimatum task*. The task involves two people who are told that they are going to share a cash prize, but the two have to figure out for themselves how they will share it. One of the people in the pair—let us call him the "divider"—is asked to decide how the prize should be divided, and so the divider can, if he wishes, decide on a 50-50 split, or a 90-10 split, or any other split he chooses. But then it is the other player's turn. The second person—call him the "decider"—cannot alter the divider's proposal. What he can do is to either accept the proposal (in which case, the money is divided as the divider proposed) or reject the proposal altogether (in which case, neither player gets anything). Notice, then, that the divider offers the decider a strict, "take-it-or-leave-it" proposal; this is how the ultimatum task gets its name.

From a standpoint of crass economic self-interest, what should the players do? The divider should presumably make an offer that leaves him with most of the money, and offer the decider just a few pennies. And the decider should accept this offer, on the simple logic that he is better off with a few pennies than with nothing—and nothing is what he will get if he turns the offer down.

In truth, though, players in this situation do not act in this self-interested fashion. Those in the divider's role typically offer a fair division of the cash, even though they could logically get away with keeping more and giving away less. Those in the decider's role tend to reject the offers that are not fair, apparently preferring nothing over the prospect of a small pittance based on an inequitable division (Bazerman, 1998; Guth, Schmittberger, & Schwarze, 1982; Medin, Schwartz, Blok, & Birnbaum, 1999).

However, it is important to note that participants are not always fair in this and similar laboratory tasks. If the task is described in a way that implies it is a personal or ethical choice, behavior governed by fairness is likely; if the same task is described in a fashion that makes it sound like a business decision, self-interest is likely to count for more than fairness (see, for example, Larrick & Blount, 1997).

A further factor that determines whether we will or will not act fairly toward someone is who that someone is. As we have discussed, many relationships are governed by reciprocity, and this ensures some measure of fairness. But fairness in such relationships ultimately rests on self-interest (your good deeds mean that I now owe you something, and so you will benefit in the end). And, of course, calculations of self-interest can change, as new considerations enter the scene (if, for example, some other person rewards you heavily for not being fair to me), and so provide a potentially fragile base for fairness.

Other sorts of relationships, though, seem different. In *communal relationships*—with close friends, for example, and, in some circumstances, work partners—the "self" is expanded to include the "other," so that the operative unit now becomes "we." In such relationships, another's gains are seen as our own, and so there is no keeping track of who owes what to whom, nor will we be easily led away from fairness by other payoffs (Borden & Levinger, 1991; Clark & Mills, 1979, 1993; Fiske & Tetlock, 1997; Mills & Clark, 1994). In communal relationships, there is no tension between self-interest and fairness because the two have been merged.

## HELPING

In communal relationships, humans are virtually certain to respond to each other's needs, because the other's needs are their needs. In exchange relationships, the logic is somewhat different, but the outcome is often the same, and the many demonstrations of reciprocity seem to suggest that humans necessarily, inevitably, respond to each other—

reciprocating good deeds with good deeds of their own, returning intimacy with intimacy, and punishing bad actions with other bad actions directed to the evildoer.

We need to balance all of this, however, with the fact that sometimes humans choose not to interact with each other and, troublingly, often fail to help each other even in circumstances of obvious distress. In fact, there is ample evidence that people often fail to help others who are in need. The widespread indifference of pedestrians to beggars and the homeless all around them is by now a daily fact of American city life. The classic example of public apathy to a stranger's plight, though, is the case of Kitty Genovese, who was attacked and murdered one early morning in 1964 on a street corner in Queens, New York. The assault lasted over half an hour, during which time Genovese screamed and struggled while her assailant stabbed her repeatedly until she finally died. It later came out that thirty-eight of her neighbors had watched the episode from their windows, but none of them had come to her aid. No one even called the police (Rosenthal, 1964). Why this appalling inaction?

## THE BYSTANDER EFFECT

*Kitty Genovese*

One factor may be a lack of altruistic motivation. Perhaps people in a big city simply do not care about the fate of strangers, no matter how terrible it may be. But according to Bibb Latané and John Darley, the failure to help is often produced by the way people understand the situation (Darley & Latané, 1968). It is not that people do not care, but that they do not understand what should be done. Here, as in many other contexts, social action (and interaction) is heavily affected by social cognition.

*Ambiguity*   Consider the passerby who sees a man lying unconscious on a city street. How can he tell whether the man is ill or drunk? The situation is ambiguous. A similar confusion troubled some of the witnesses to the Genovese slaying. They later reported that they were not quite sure what was transpiring. Perhaps it was a joke, a drunken bout, a lovers' quarrel. If it were any of these, intervention might have proved very embarrassing.

*Pluralistic Ignorance*   The situation is further complicated by the fact that the various witnesses to the Genovese tragedy realized that many others were seeing just what they did. As they watched the drama on the street unfold, they saw the lights go on in many of the windows of adjacent buildings, and this created a situation in which there was *pluralistic ignorance*. Each of the witnesses was uncertain whether there really was an emergency, and looked to the others, trying to decide. Their reasoning was simple: if my neighbors do not react, then apparently they have decided there is no emergency, and, if no emergency, there is no reason for me to react.

The problem, of course, is that the identical reasoning was going on in each of their neighbor's thoughts. Each was waiting for the others to do something, and, if one had acted, all would have taken this as a signal that action was indeed warranted. Tragically, though, each failed to realize that the others were in the same ambiguous situation as they were themselves. As a result, each misinterpreted the others' inactivity, thinking that their neighbor's nonresponse reflected an informed decision, when, in truth, it derived from the same uncertainty that they were experiencing. In the end, all remained inactive, and Genovese received no help.

*Diffusion of Responsibility*   The fact that each observer knew that others observed the same event made it difficult to realize that the event was an emergency. But this fact had yet another consequence. It made intervention less probable even for the witnesses who did recognize (or at least suspect) that the situation was an emergency, because these persons were now faced with a *diffusion of responsibility*. They knew that many people could respond to the emergency, and saw no reason why they should be the ones. "Yes, something needs to be done, but why should I be the one to do it—and, with so many witnessing the event, surely someone else will have already called 9-1-1" (or "… gone down to investigate" or "… called the building's security guard").

Why would people be so ready to push the burden of action onto others? Many simply do not want to get involved in a violent or criminal episode; others are afraid of the criminal; still others are apprehensive about dealing with the police. In any case, the conflict between their desire to help and the desire to mind their own business is all too often resolved in favor of inaction, and it is inaction with no sense of guilt: "My doing nothing won't be a problem; someone else will surely do what needs to be done." The obvious problem, though, once again, is that everyone who views the emergency is likely to think the same thought, and, as a result, no one does anything (see Figure 11.15).

We have framed these arguments in commonsense terms, but many experiments indicate that this sort of reasoning does, in fact, occur in many bystanders to a crisis or emergency. In one experiment, participants were asked to join in what they thought was a group discussion about college life with either one, three, or five other people. The participants were placed in individual cubicles and took turns talking to each other over an intercom system. In actuality, though, there was only one participant; all the other "discussants" were voices on a previously recorded tape. The discussion began as one of these other "discussants" described some of his personal problems, which included a tendency toward epileptic seizures in times of stress. When he began to speak again during the second round of talking, he feigned a seizure and gasped for help. What was at issue is what would happen next: would the actual participant take action to help this other person apparently in distress?

The answer was powerfully influenced by the "crowd size." If the participant believed that he had been having just a two-way discussion (so that there was no one else around to help the person in distress), he was reasonably likely to leave his own cubicle in order to help. But if the participant thought it was a group having the discussion, a diffusion of responsibility was observed, and the larger the size of the group that the

**11.15**   *The bystander effect*

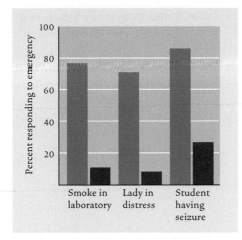

11.16 *Group inhibition of bystander intervention in emergencies* **When people are alone (in green) they are more likely to respond in an emergency than when they are—or think they are—with others (in red), in part because of diffusion of felt responsibility. (Data from Darley and Latané, 1968; Latané and Darley, 1968; Latané and Rodin, 1969)**

participant thought he was in, the less likely he was to come to the victim's assistance (Darley & Latané, 1968; see Figure 11.16).

The *bystander effect* has been demonstrated in numerous other situations. In some, an actor posing as a fellow participant seems to have an asthma attack; in others, someone appears to faint in an adjacent room; in still others, the laboratory fills with smoke. Whatever the emergency, the result is always the same: the larger the group the subject is in (or thinks he is in), the smaller the chance that he will take any action—in dramatic accord with the diffusion-of-responsibility hypothesis (Latané & Nida, 1981; Latané, Nida, & Wilson, 1981).

## THE COSTS OF HELPING

Apparently, people often do not recognize that a need for help exists, and, even when they do, they may not act because they think that others will. But suppose the situation is not at all ambiguous and that responsibility for helping is not diffused. Will people then help a stranger in distress?

One factor that determines whether people will or will not help is the physical or psychological cost to the prospective helper. The greater that cost, the smaller the chance that he will in fact help. In some cases, the cost is physical danger. In others, it is simply time and effort. In one study, students had to go from one campus building to another to give a talk. They were told to hurry, since they were already late. As they rushed to their appointments, these students passed by a shabbily dressed man who lay in a doorway groaning. Only 10 percent stopped to help the victim. Ironically enough, the students were members of a theological seminary, and the topic of their talk was the

*Helping* **The text describes many of the reasons why people often fail to help each other, but, happily, the fact remains that there are circumstances in which we do help one another. One powerful example comes from the outpouring of assistance that emerged in the minutes and then days following the attack on the World Trade Center. Many police officers and fire fighters performed heroically in immediately helping the victims of the attack; in the days following, many made generous donations to help the victims.**

parable of the Good Samaritan who came to the aid of a man lying injured on a road-side. It appears that if the cost—here in time—is high enough, even theological students may not behave altruistically (Darley & Batson, 1973).

What is costly to one potential helper may not be equally so to another. Take physical danger. It is probably not surprising that bystanders who intervene in cases of assault are generally much taller, stronger, and better trained than bystanders who do not intervene, and they are almost invariably men (Eagly & Crowley, 1986; Huston, Ruggiero, Connor, & Geis, 1981).

# EMOTION

We have now covered a lot of ground, discussing many aspects of how people behave in their dealings with others—whether the others turn out to be a child, a romantic partner, or a bitter enemy. But alongside this emphasis on what people do, we also need to ask how they feel, because there is no doubt that people attach strong feelings to many of their social actions: being with a child makes us happy; with an enemy, angry, or perhaps afraid. How should we think about these powerful emotional feelings?

## EMOTIONAL EXPERIENCE: INTERPRETATIONS OF INTERNAL STATES

In Chapter 1, we argued that the feelings that accompany emotion are not straightforward sensations—we do not "feel" our emotions in the same way, we suggested, that we feel an itch or see the color yellow. Instead, our emotions are clearly affected by processes of interpretation and judgment (see, for example, Schachter & Singer, 1962; Mandler, 1975, 1984). We saw one example of this in our discussion of attraction (p. 427), and we will return to that particular example shortly. First, though, let us set the context.

### THE JAMES-LANGE THEORY

Many nineteenth-century psychologists tried to catalog various emotional experiences much as they had classified the different sensations provided by the senses (such as *red, sour, A-flat*), but their efforts were not very successful. People simply reported too many emotional experiences, and the classifications that were proposed did not seem to do justice to the richness of these subjective feelings. In addition, there were disagreements about the precise meaning of emotional terms. How does *sadness* differ from *weariness* or *dejection*? Different people reported different shades of meaning, and there seemed to be little hope of agreement as long as the description was confined to the subjective experience alone.

William James proposed a different approach to the problem. To James, the crucial facet of emotion was that it is an aspect of what a person does. In fear, we run; in grief, we weep. The commonsense interpretation is that the behavior is caused by the emotion. James, however, stood common sense on its head and maintained that the causal relation is actually the opposite of what we normally suppose; in his view, we are afraid because we run:

> Common-sense says, we lose our fortune, are sorry and weep; we meet a bear, are frightened and run; we are insulted by a rival, are angry and strike. The hypothesis here ... is that we feel sorry because we cry, angry because we strike, afraid because we tremble....
> (James, 1890, v. 2, p. 449)

This is the core of what is now known as the *James-Lange theory of emotions*. (Carl Lange was a European contemporary of James who offered a similar account.) In effect,

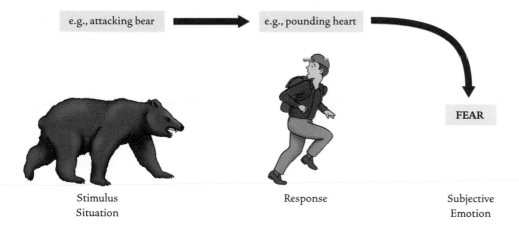

e.g., attacking bear → e.g., pounding heart

FEAR

Stimulus
Situation

Response

Subjective
Emotion

11.17 *The sequence of events as conceived by the James–Lange theory of emotions* According to the James–Lange theory, the subjectively experienced emotion is simply our awareness of our own response to the anger- or fear-arousing situation. We see a dangerous object (an attacking grizzly bear will do as well as any other); this triggers a bodily response (running, pounding heart), and the awareness of this response is the emotion (here, fear).

the theory asserts that emotion begins when we perceive a situation of an appropriate sort—see the bear or hear the insult. But our perception of these events is, as James put it, "purely cognitive in form, pale, colorless, destitute of emotional warmth." What turns this perception into genuine emotion is our awareness of the bodily changes that are produced by these arousing stimuli. These changes might consist of skeletal movements (running) and visceral reactions (pounding heartbeat), although later adherents of the James-Lange theory emphasized the visceral responses and the activity of the autonomic nervous system that underlies them (Figure 11.17).

This theory has been the focus of considerable controversy. One major attack on it was presented by Walter B. Cannon, a pioneer in the study of the physiology of homeostasis (see Chapter 3). Cannon pointed out that the nervous and glandular secretions that comprise our sympathetic reactions are too slow to account for the quickness of our emotional reactions. Moreover, he contended that our sympathetic reactions to arousing stimuli are too diffuse and general to account for the wide range of human emotional experience. Take the relation between rage and fear. These two emotions appear to be accompanied by just about the same autonomic discharge, he claimed, and yet we are easily able to distinguish between them. Therefore, Cannon concluded, the identity of these emotions cannot be shaped primarily by their physiological accompaniments, and so the James-Lange theory must be wrong (Cannon, 1927).

Cannon's argument also seemed to gain support from early studies in which participants received injections of epinephrine, triggering broad sympathetic activation with all its consequences—nervousness, palpitations, flushing, tremors, and sweaty palms. According to the James-Lange theory, these responses should be among the internally produced stimuli that give rise to the intense emotions of fear and rage. But in fact the participants did not experience these emotions. Some simply reported the physical symptoms. Others said they felt "as if" they were angry or afraid, a kind of "cold emotion," not the real thing (Landis & Hunt, 1932; Marañon, 1924). Apparently, the visceral reactions induced by epinephrine are by themselves not sufficient for emotional experience.

More recent evidence suggests, however, that autonomic activity may not be as broad and diffuse as Cannon contended. Some studies of autonomic activity show clear differences in the autonomic patterns that accompany such emotions as anger and fear (see, for example, Ax, 1953; Ekman, Levenson, & Friesen, 1983; Funkenstein, 1956; Schwartz, Weinberger, & Singer, 1981; Sinha & Parsons, 1996). And people across cultures report bodily sensations that differ depending on the emotion: they generally report a quickened heartbeat and tense muscles when both angry and fearful, and they feel hot or flushed strictly when angry, but cold and clammy when afraid (Mesquita & Frijda, 1992).

However, even with these refinements, the fact remains that—just as Cannon argued—

emotions are not easy to distinguish through their associated bodily responses. This, combined with Cannon's other argument regarding the speed of our sympathetic reactions, leaves most contemporary investigators convinced that there is little support for the contention that our behavior alone (whether skeletal or visceral) can account for our emotional experience.

## THE ATTRIBUTION-OF-AROUSAL THEORY

The James-Lange theory emphasizes the role of feedback from the musculature and the autonomic nervous system in shaping the experience of emotion. As we have seen, this account has not fared well, but a related conception, focusing on cognitive factors, does appear more promising. In agreement with the James-Lange theory, this conception assumes that bodily action and bodily arousal play an important role, and, without these, there is no emotion. However, this theory does not assume that the identity of the emotion depends on the specific quality of the arousal; instead, the theory focuses on how the individual interprets the circumstances she is in, and, with that, it focuses on what the source is to which she *attributes* the arousal.

In fact, we encountered this attribution-based account earlier, in our discussion of romantic love. There we saw that the arousal produced by fear (specifically, the fear that results from standing on a high and narrow bridge) can enhance (and perhaps be mistaken for) feelings of attraction. How could this be? As Cannon noted, the arousal one feels when afraid is diffuse and difficult to define; from the point of view of the aroused person, the arousal is ambiguous with regard to its nature and its source. The aroused person, therefore, is likely to seek other information to guide the interpretation of the arousal, and that other information is readily provided by the environment: if a heterosexual male feels excited while standing next to an attractive female, it is entirely sensible that he will attribute his excitement to her, and so he will attribute his jitters to romantic or sexual interest.

Many experiments provide support for this **attribution-of-arousal theory**, a theory that argues in general that bodily arousal provides only the raw materials for an emotional experience (see Figure 11.8). To turn this undifferentiated raw material into a spe-

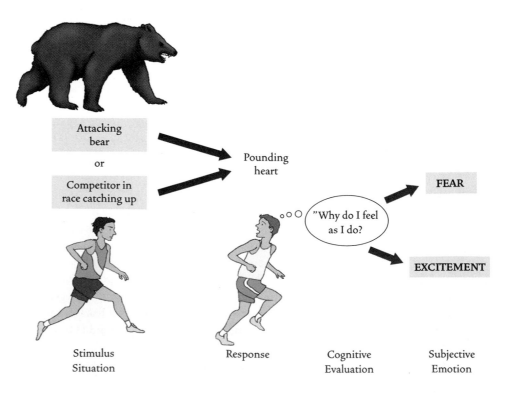

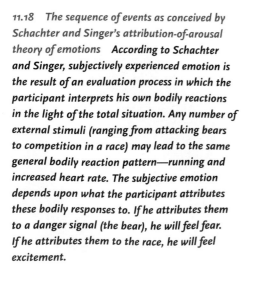

**11.18** *The sequence of events as conceived by Schachter and Singer's attribution-of-arousal theory of emotions* **According to Schachter and Singer, subjectively experienced emotion is the result of an evaluation process in which the participant interprets his own bodily reactions in the light of the total situation. Any number of external stimuli (ranging from attacking bears to competition in a race) may lead to the same general bodily reaction pattern—running and increased heart rate. The subjective emotion depends upon what the participant attributes these bodily responses to. If he attributes them to a danger signal (the bear), he will feel fear. If he attributes them to the race, he will feel excitement.**

Attacking bear

or

Competitor in race catching up

Pounding heart

"Why do I feel as I do?"

FEAR

EXCITEMENT

Stimulus Situation          Response          Cognitive Evaluation          Subjective Emotion cific emotional experience, there must also be a cognitive appraisal and interpretation, one that attributes the arousal to some emotional event (Schachter, 1964; Schachter & Singer, 1962; Mandler, 1984, 1998).

The classic demonstration of this mechanism comes from an experiment that we described briefly in Chapter 1. In that experiment, participants were injected with a drug that they believed to be a vitamin supplement but that was really epinephrine, a mild stimulant. Some participants were informed of the drug's real effects and were told, for example, that they might feel a little jittery or that their palms might sweat a bit. Others were not told about these effects; they were told merely that the drug might have some side effects, such as numbness or itching. Then, after the drug was administered, both groups of participants sat in the waiting room for what they thought was to be a test of vision.

Another person was also in the waiting room and was, in truth, a confederate of the experimenter. In one version of the procedure, he sat there sullen and irritable, making angry remarks, and eventually stormed out of the room. In another version, he was ebullient and frivolous; he threw paper planes out of the window, played with a hula hoop, and tried to engage the participant in an improvised basketball game with paper balls. Of course, all of this was the actual experiment; the vision test the participants were expecting never took place (Schachter & Singer, 1962).

How would the participants react to this situation? Schachter and Singer reasoned that the participants who had been correctly informed about the physiological consequences of the injection would show less of an emotional response than those who had been misinformed. These informed participants would (correctly) attribute their tremors and palpitations to the drug rather than to the external situation—and so there was no ambiguity attached to their symptoms, no mystery to be solved. More specifically, there was no reason for them to attribute their aroused state to emotion, and so no reason why their arousal should contribute to a feeling of emotion.

In contrast, the participants not informed about the symptoms were confronted with a puzzle: why were they all stirred up? With no reason to attribute their agitation to the drug, they were likely to assume instead that their internal reactions were caused by something outside—the elation of the euphoric confederate or the sullenness of the angry one. In essence, they would reason, "I'm stirred up, and it's a happy setting, and so I suppose I'm stirred up because it's a happy setting, and so I suppose I must be happy." Of course, this reasoning would not be conscious, but it would influence them nonetheless.

These predictions fit with the data reasonably well. The informed participants did report less emotion than the uninformed participants, because only the latter were likely to attribute their aroused state to an internal feeling. More, the uninformed participants exposed to the euphoric confederate did report that they felt happy, and, to a lesser degree, participants exposed to the angry participant reported that they felt angry.

*Carry-over of Arousal* In our day-to-day lives, the arousal we feel does not come from an experimenter's injected epinephrine, but from our own—produced and secreted by our adrenal glands. What makes us secrete epinephrine and thus lay the ground for the construal of emotion? Nearly any stressor will do it, whether from an earthquake, a dog barking, or our realizing that we forgot to pay the phone bill.

Epinephrine, once released into the bloodstream, continues to affect us for a while. As a consequence, the arousal we feel in a situation need not be due to that situation; it can be left over from a previous one, and, in fact, some bodily aftereffects of fear or anger or even physical exercise remain for quite a bit longer than we might expect. Such aftereffects may lead to *excitation transfer* (Zillman, 1983, 1996), in which the arousal produced in one setting is attributed to, and thus influences, an entirely different setting. In one study, some participants first engaged in a bout of strenuous physical activity on an exercise bicycle. A few minutes after they finished pedaling, they were given a number of mild electric shocks, allegedly as a punishment delivered by another participant in the study. When they were subsequently given a chance to retaliate, they were more aggressive (that is, administered more severe shocks) than controls who also had been bicycling, but who received the punishment shocks only after their heart rate and blood pressure returned to base levels. A similar effect was found for sexual excitement in response to erotic films; here, too, arousal was enhanced by preceding physical exercise (Cantor, Zillman, & Bryant, 1975; Zillman, Katcher, & Milavsky, 1972).

The explanation for both of these results readily follows from Schachter and Singer's proposal. Shortly after exercise, participants are still aroused, still feeling the effects of the exercise-produced epinephrine. But this arousal actually lasts longer than participants expect it to, and so, after a while, the participants do not know why they are aroused—they are (mistakenly) convinced that the exercise could not still be the cause. Therefore, they seek some other source and probably will attribute their arousal to their current situation, rather than their previous exercise. If they have just been provoked, they will attribute the arousal to anger and feel angrier as a result than they otherwise would have. If they have just seen an erotic stimulus, they will attribute the arousal to it and find it sexier than they otherwise would (Valins, 1966).

*The Role of the Amygdala*    The Schachter and Singer proposal has provoked considerable criticism and remains controversial (Marshall & Zimbardo, 1979; Maslach, 1979; Reisenzein, 1983; Schacter & Singer, 1979). Nonetheless, their theory reminds us that our conception of emotion must include at least two elements: the bodily arousal itself and the cognitive appraisal of the circumstances attending that arousal. We have commented on the bodily underpinnings of the arousal, but what about the appraisal? What biological structures support it, and what structures support the integration of arousal and appraisal that emerges as the emotion itself?

As we mentioned in Chapter 1, the *amygdala*, a small structure in the limbic system, plays an essential role in emotional appraisal (see Figure 1.4 in Chapter 1; p. 9). When the amygdala is damaged (through accident, stroke, or surgery), this appraisal process is severely disrupted. Thus, rats with lesions in the amygdala no longer show any signs of fear in response to stimuli previously associated with electric shock or some other aversive stimulus (Davis, 1992, 1997; LeDoux, 1994). Similarly, human patients with damage to the amygdala do not acquire conditioned fear responses, even though they can (calmly) recall which visual or auditory stimuli were paired with the unconditioned stimulus (Bechara et al., 1995).

The amygdala may also have other specialized roles that contribute to its functioning as a regulator of emotions. For example, there is some suggestion that the amygdala plays an essential role in governing how we pay attention to and recognize emotional expressions on people's faces (Öhman, 2002). The amygdala may also help to keep us vigilant in any circumstance that involves ambiguity and, therefore, a possible threat (Whalen, 1998). In addition, the amygdala may also influence how we attend to and later remember emotional events we experience (Buchanan & Adolphs, 2003).

## EMOTIONAL EXPRESSIONS

Not only does each of us experience emotion and interpret emotion in others; we also express our own emotion. In fact, humans have a sizable repertoire of verbal and non-verbal means for these expressions, with some of the most obvious ones conveyed by the face. These facial expressions—our smiles, frowns, laughs, gapes, grimaces, snarls, and winks—are intimately tied to our social lives and have been of special concern to psychologists studying emotion.

## THE UNIVERSALITY OF EMOTIONAL EXPRESSIONS

Much of our current interest in facial expressions is due to Charles Darwin (Darwin, 1872b), who hypothesized that humans possess a set of universal facial expressions that are vestiges of basic adaptive patterns shown by our evolutionary forerunners. He argued, for example, that our "anger" face, often expressed by lowered brows, widened eyes, and open mouth with exposed teeth, reflects the facial movements our ancestors would have made when biting an opponent. Similarly, our "disgust" face, often manifested as a wrinkled nose and protruded lower lip and tongue, reflects how our ancestors rejected odors or spit out foods. (For elaborations, see Ekman, 1980, 1984; Fridlund, 1994; Izard, 1977; Tomkins, 1963.)

*Cross-cultural Studies of Facial Expression* In arguing that these facial expressions are part of our primate heritage, Darwin noted their similarities to many of the displays made by monkeys and apes, and he believed that the expressions would be identical, reflecting identical emotions, among humans worldwide, even "those who have associated but little with Europeans" (Darwin, 1872b, p. 15). It was almost a century later, though, that researchers began to test this universality claim using rigorous experimental methods, and only a tiny number of studies have used the participants most crucial for testing it: members of relatively isolated, non-Western cultures (Ekman, 1973; Ekman & Oster, 1979; Fridlund, Ekman, & Oster, 1983; Izard, 1971; Russell, 1994). Why is this group crucial? If research participants, no matter where they live, have been exposed to Western movies or television, their responses might only indicate the impact of these media and thus provide no proof of the universality claim.

In one of these studies, which we briefly mentioned in Chapter 1, American actors were photographed while they posed in a fashion that conveyed emotions such as happiness, sadness, anger, and fear. These pictures were then shown to members of various modern, literate cultures (Swedes, Japanese, Kenyans) and to members of an isolated, nonliterate New Guinea tribe. All were asked to pick the emotion label that matched each photo. In other cases, the procedure was reversed. For example, the New Guinea tribesmen were asked to portray the facial expressions appropriate to various situations, such as happiness at the return of a friend, grief at the death of a child, and anger at the start of a fight (see Figure 11.19). Photographs of their performances were then shown to American college students, who were asked to judge which situation the tribesmen had been asked to convey (Ekman & Friesen, 1975).

In these studies, all the participants, including those in relatively isolated cultures, did reasonably well (Russell, 1994; see Figure 11.20, on p. 452). They were able to supply the appropriate emotion label when given the photographs, or to describe a situation that might plausibly have elicited the expression shown in the photo. But their success was not uniform. It varied according to which particular facial expression they were shown. Smiles, which are generally matched with "happy" terms and situations, produced much greater consistency in identification than did all the other expressions (Russell, 1994; and see discussions by Ekman, 1994; Izard, 1994; Russell, 1995). Other emotions are less well recognized. For example, if asked to pick out the Western face showing "disgust," nonliterate people chose the correct face only 30 percent of the time.

The greater-than-chance worldwide performance in these matching tasks was seized on by some investigators as proving the universality of emotional expressions. But critics have indicated several problems with the studies (Fridlund, 1994; Russell, 1994), and, as a result, we must regard these data as suggestive of universality in facial expressions, but surely inconclusive. And, unfortunately, this issue may stand unresolved forever, for the simple reason that Western culture has now penetrated virtually every corner of the globe, so that the truly "non-Westernized" research participants needed for a definitive study may no longer exist.

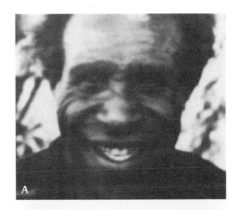

**11.19** *Attempts to portray emotion by New Guinea tribesman* **Acting out expressions appropriate to various situations: (A) "Your friend has come and you are happy"; (B) "You see a dead pig that has been lying there for a long time."**

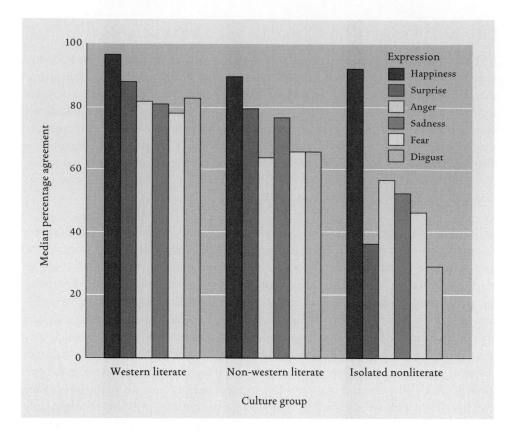

**11.20   Success at matching facial expressions to labels for six emotions   The graph shows results for literate Westerners (twenty studies), and non-Westerners who were either literate (eleven studies) or relatively isolated and nonliterate (three studies). (From Russell & Fernandez-Dols, 1997, p. 15).**

## CULTURAL VARIATIONS IN FACIAL EXPRESSIONS

Even if some facial expressions do turn out to be universal, it is clear that the public use of facial expressions is affected by culture. A widely studied example comes from research in which American and Japanese participants were presented with a harrowing documentary film of a primitive puberty rite. As they watched the film, their facial expressions were recorded with a hidden camera, and the results showed the facial reactions of Americans and Japanese to be virtually identical. But when the participants watched the film while being interviewed by a white-coated experimenter, the results were quite different. In this context, the Japanese looked more polite and smiled more than did the Americans (Ekman, 1972, 1977; for further discussion, see Fridlund, 1994).

These results probably reflect *cultural display rules*, learned but deeply ingrained conventions, often obeyed without awareness, that govern what facial expressions may or may not be shown in what contexts (Ekman, 1985; Ekman & Friesen, 1986; Ekman, Friesen, & O'Sullivan, 1988). Certainly, the fact that the Japanese may have indicated politeness toward the investigator rather than revulsion toward the film is consistent with the primacy accorded interpersonal harmony in Japanese culture (Markus & Kitayama, 1994).

## FACIAL EXPRESSIONS AS COMMUNICATIONS

So far we have treated facial expressions as though they were the natural and spontaneous outcome of an underlying emotional state. Of course, in many cases, we are able to hide or fake an emotional reaction; however, in general, when we are happy, we smile; when sad, we cry. But there is an alternative view. Recall that Darwin proposed a connection between our facial expressions and the communicative displays of our primate relatives. Similarly, some researchers contend that our facial expressions are primarily communicative. Seen in this light, facial expressions are not so much a revelation of an inner state as they are a message to others about actions we may take or wish them to take. Just as the monkey's fear grin signals submission (Van Hooff, 1972), adherents of the communicative-display position argue that the pouty face signals that we want to be comforted or embraced; the angry face, that we want others to take us seriously, obey us, or back off; and so forth. The smile does not necessarily mean that we are happy, but rather that we want to play or be friends (see, for example, Fridlund, 1991, 1994, 1997; Mandler, 1984, 1997; Patterson, 1983).

Advocates of this communicative view offer several lines of evidence. First, it is simply not true that facial expressions are the inevitable and natural result of someone's feeling a particular emotion. This is illustrated, for example, by a study of gold medalists at the 1992 Olympic Games. As we noted in Chapter 1, the medalists were observed as they waited behind the podium for their medals, then while they received them from the presenters, and finally, while they stood and faced the flag and listened to the national anthem. The gold medalists reported their mood during the entire awards ceremony as extremely happy, but for most of the ceremony, they did not smile (Fernandez-Dols & Ruiz-Belda, 1995; see Figure 11.21). They only smiled when they received their medal and looked at the Olympic official who awarded it, or glanced at their fellow medalists.

Further evidence comes from the fact that facial expressions are far more likely to occur when we are in the presence of others, especially if we make eye contact with them. In one study, bowlers were observed when they made spares or strikes. The bowlers did not smile at the moment of their success. Their smiles came later, when they turned around in the lane and met the gaze of their friends (Kraut & Johnston, 1979). What holds for adult bowlers also holds for ten-month-old infants playing with toys while their mothers watch on the sidelines. They smile most often when they turn to watch their mothers watching them (Jones, Collins, & Hong, 1991; for data on preschoolers, see Schneider & Josephs, 1991; Fridlund & Duchaine, 1996).

Related findings were obtained in a study in which participants viewed amusing videotapes in one of four contexts: while sitting with a friend, while believing that a friend was also watching in an adjacent room, while believing that a friend was in an adjacent room but taking a test, and while alone. Compared to solitary viewing, participants smiled much more when they viewed the videotape with a friend, but they smiled just as much when they merely believed that the friend was viewing the tape (Fridlund, 1991). Such audience effects have been demonstrated for many different facial expressions and in many different situations (Chovil, 1991; Hess, Banse, & Kappas, 1995; Jakobs, Fischer, & Manstead, 1997; Jakobs, Manstead, & Fischer, 2001; Wagner & Smith, 1991; but see Jakobs, Manstead, & Fischer, 1996).

Of course, considering facial expressions as signals or solicitations does not exclude a role for emotion. Facial expressions do signify what is going on inside of us, and, with or without an audience, we are unlikely to laugh when afraid or snarl when happy. In essence, then, facial expressions are controlled from both the outside and the inside, with our inner state determining which emotion we might signal and our social surroundings determining whether the signal is sent or not.

**11.21   Facial expressions do not necessarily indicate our emotions**   As we pointed out in Chapter 1, Olympic athletes rate standing on the podium in their medals as among the very happiest moments in their lives, yet few smile—until they shake the presenter's hand. (Morocco's Khalid Skah, gold medalist in the 10,000-meter race at the 1992 Olympics.)

## ARE THERE BASIC EMOTIONS?

So far, we have focused on a relatively narrow set of emotions: fear and anger, happiness and sadness. This reflects a belief on the part of many investigators that these are among the *basic emotions*, coherent patterns of feelings, internal physiological changes, outward expressions, and behavior (such as approach or avoidance) that are hardwired, adaptive, automatic, and the result of natural selection (see, for example, Ekman, 1992; Izard, 1991, 1994).

Other investigators, however, question this premise. For one thing, the number of emotions held to be "basic" varies from one theorist to another (Ortony & Turner,

1990). One account lists only two—pain and pleasure (Mowrer, 1960); another lists six—surprise, anger, sadness, disgust, fear, and contempt (Ekman, 1984); others list from eight to eighteen and may include emotions like shame, guilt, arrogance, and indifference (see, for example, Frijda, 1986; Izard, 1971, 1991). And one critic noted that lust, by any reasoning, should be a—perhaps *the*—basic emotion, yet it is found on no such list (Mandler, 1997).

Nor is there any consensus on what would make an emotion "basic." On one account, an emotion is basic if it can be linked to an identifiable facial expression (Ekman, 1984). A second account stipulates that a basic emotion must have its own hardwired neural circuitry (see, for example, Izard, 1977). The difficulty with these two accounts is that their criteria yield different lists. As we saw in Chapter 3, the states of hunger and thirst have their own dedicated neural circuitry and might therefore be considered emotions, but they have no associated facial expressions. In contrast, many consider sadness to have an identifiable facial expression, yet there is little evidence for any neural circuitry specifically dedicated to this emotion.

In a third approach, what makes an emotion basic is that it cannot be reduced to any combination of other emotions. This approach, reminiscent of that used to establish primary colors, has the advantage of clarifying the complexity of our emotional lives. For example, we can distinguish among resignation, regret, grief, and despair as well as satisfaction, jubilation, rapture, and serenity. Are these two groups of emotions simply shades of sadness and happiness, respectively? Some theorists have suggested so. In one theory, jealousy is not basic because it can be regarded as a mix of fear and anger; nor is anxiety because it reflects a complex interaction of fear, guilt, sadness, and shame (Izard, 1991).

Although this account is plausible, it is difficult to prove. The example of jealousy shows why. If we are jealous of another's success, we very well may be both angry about it and fearful of what that success might mean for us. But it is equally true that, if we are accosted by a stranger, we may be both fearful that he will hurt us and angry that he has intruded on us in the first place. In this case, we are again both angry and afraid, but surely not jealous. Explaining why fear and anger might produce jealousy in the first instance but not in the second is likely to be quite complex, and this complexity suggests why the evidence that some emotions are actually composites of other, more basic ones is weak at best (Ortony & Turner, 1990; for yet another idea on how emotions might be categorized, see, for example, Barrett & Russell, 1999).

## COMPLEX EMOTIONS

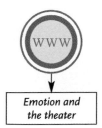

*Emotion and
the theater*

An alternative approach to understanding the full range of human emotions is more cognitive. Adherents of this position contend that some emotions can be distinguished by the level of symbolic processing they require. Embarrassment, for example, seems to require knowledge of both one's social role and one's social standing. Further examples are such emotional experiences as pity, anger, guilt, and regret, all of which depend on a complex appraisal of why we or someone else failed or succeeded in some endeavor, an analysis that even the cleverest chimpanzee would find impossible.

### PITY, ANGER, AND GUILT

Consider the emotions of pity, anger, and guilt. Each of them is aroused by some misfortune. According to Bernard Weiner, which particular emotion is felt depends on our perception of how this misfortune came about. If we hear that Mary failed an important exam because she went to a party the night before, we feel a bit angry (all the more so if we really like her, wanted her to do well, and perhaps even helped her study for the exam). But if she failed the exam because she had been ill all semester, we are more likely to pity her. In the first case, we feel that the failure was Mary's own fault; in the second, we feel that she failed but could not help it (Weiner, 1982).

A similar analysis applies when the emotional target is not someone else, but ourself. Here, too, what matters is whether we could or could not control the outcome. If it was controllable, we feel guilt (which in a sense is anger directed at ourself). If it was not controllable, we feel self-pity.

Still further complexities are introduced by the fact that, in humans, certain emotions, such as righteous anger and guilt, involve an appreciation of a moral order. Imagine that you are waiting in line to buy a pair of World Series tickets. By the time you reach the ticket office, you find out that there are no more tickets left; the person just in front of you bought the very last pair. Do you get angry at him? You may get angry about your bad luck and curse the fates, but you will not get angry at him. You somehow recognize that his position in the line gave him the right to the tickets. The situation would be very different if he had pushed himself ahead of you. In that case you would become fiercely angry because you would perceive his act as a moral transgression (Averill, 1978; Sabini & Silver, 1982).

Of course, anger also has a biological basis, perhaps similar to the aggression one sees in nonhumans (see pp. 431–435). But for humans, anger is often much more than this. We have seen that it can involve the appreciation of another person's intentions and capacities. Beyond that, it also involves some sense of moral rights and transgressions. At this point, it is not rage, but outrage. Given all that, it clearly transcends its biological roots.

## REGRET

Yet another complex emotion is regret, a reaction produced by comparing the outcomes of whatever one did with what one might have done. It is the emotion of the "might have been."

We have all had the experience of almost achieving some desired goal but just missing out. Somehow such near misses are much more painful than attempts that do not come close at all. The person who gets a lottery ticket that differs from the winning number by just one digit feels much worse than the one whose number is way off the mark. The same holds for the golfer whose putt rims the hole but does not drop in, or the actor who almost landed the lead role. This general phenomenon has been docu-

*Anger at moral transgression*  **Waiting in line to avoid righteous anger.** (© The New Yorker Collection 1960, 1988 Chas. Addams from Cartoonbank.com. All rights reserved.)

*Regret*  **The sadness of "It might have been."** (© The New Yorker Collection 1956, 1984 Chas. Addams from Cartoonbank.com. All rights reserved.)

mented in a number of studies in which participants were presented with various scenarios and had to indicate their reactions. One example concerns a missed plane:

> Mr. Crane and Mr. Tees were scheduled to leave the airport on different flights, at the same time. They traveled from town in the same limousine, were caught in a traffic jam, and arrived at the airport thirty minutes after the scheduled departure time of their flights.
>
> Mr. Crane is told that his plane left on time. Mr. Tees is told that his flight was delayed, and left five minutes ago.
>
> Who is more upset? (Kahneman & Tversky, 1982, p. 203)

The virtually unanimous answer was Mr. Tees, who suffered the near miss. But why should this be so, considering that the objective situation of the two men was identical, since they both missed their planes? Kahneman and Tversky believe the near miss is more upsetting because it is much easier to imagine circumstances that would have prevented the problem: if only the limousine had made just one more traffic light, if only the baggage had been unloaded a bit more quickly, if only....

A number of further findings represent variations on the same general theme. In one study, participants read about two people who died of exposure after surviving a plane crash in a remote area. One victim, they learned, made it to within a quarter mile of safety; the other came within seventy-five miles. They were then asked to determine how much the victims' families should be compensated. The participants recommended a considerably higher sum for the family of the victim who came quite close than for the family of the victim who perished farther away. They evidently felt that the fate of the first victim, the one who came so close, was worse (more "unfair" so to speak) than that of the second. In their imaginary reconstructions, they found it easier to construct a mental simulation for undoing the first victim's fate than for undoing the second's: if he had only known how close he was, if he had just been able to take a few more steps....

A similar account may explain why misfortunes that are caused by some exceptional departure from routine seem especially regrettable. That someone died on the Titanic is terrible enough, but it appears even more terrible if he only got his ticket because of a last-minute cancellation by someone who suddenly fell ill. It is apparently easier to create a mental script for undoing an unusual circumstance than to imagine how more usual patterns of events can be altered (Kahneman & Miller, 1986; also see Gilovich & Medvec, 1995; Gilovich, Medvec, & Kahneman, 1998).

## CULTURE AND EMOTION

Basic emotions are generally assumed to be closely tied to our biology, rooted in our evolutionary past and shaped by hardwired patterns in our nervous system. If so, then basic emotions are a trait of our species and should be found in all cultures. We have already considered the cross-cultural universality of facial expressions, but what about the emotions themselves?

It is notable that the common lists of basic emotions used in cross-cultural research were all constructed by Westerners, because, in fact, cultures differ widely in their emotion lexicons, the vocabularies available to describe emotions. Obviously, the words used by different peoples to denote emotions may tell us little about their inner, emotional lives. But if certain emotions are truly basic and universal, then one might expect all cultures to have developed a vocabulary that would allow them to name these allegedly universal feelings.

Instead, across cultures one finds no common list of basic emotions. Some cultures appear to have no words for emotions that many Westerners consider basic; thus, the people who live on the western Pacific Island of Ifaluk lack a word for "surprise," and the Tahitians lack a word for "sadness." Other cultures have words that describe common emotions for which we have no special terms. Thus, the Ifaluk often feel an emotion they call *fago*, which involves a complex mixture of compassion, love, and sadness experienced in relationships in which one person is dependent on the other (Lutz, 1986, 1988). And the Japanese report a common emotion called *amae*, which is a desire to be dependent and cared for (Doi, 1973; Morsbach & Tyler, 1986). The German language reserves the word *Schadenfreude* for the special pleasure derived from another's misfortune.

But putting these issues of vocabulary aside, how are the emotions felt by members of various cultures? Some evidence suggests commonality. We have already mentioned the common reports of bodily reactions while experiencing anger and fear. It also seems that certain events lead to pretty much the same emotions the world over; examples are bereavement and the anticipation of physical danger (Frijda & Mesquita, 1994; Mesquita & Frijda, 1992). Furthermore, the ways that people appraise emotional situations are similar across many cultures (Ellsworth, 1994; Scherer, 1997). Thus, Westerners can likely sympathize with the feelings of people who experience *fago* or *amae* or *Schadenfreude* and may sometimes experience such feelings themselves, even if they do not have a name for them.

Alongside these commonalities, though, there are probably also important differences in how people in various cultures experience emotion. Recall, for example, the contrast between individualist and collectivist cultures both in the social roles of their members and in how their members explain the behavior of others. Given these dramatic differences, some observers question whether emotional experience could ever be identical across cultures, especially for complex emotions that require so much symbolic processing. For example, can we feel Western-style guilt if we believe that the situation determined our actions? Can we feel Eastern-style shame if we believe that we are ultimately beholden to no one? Acquiescence, obligation, self-criticism, and submersion of the self within the group are intimately associated with "good" feelings in collectivist cultures and "bad" feelings in individualist ones (Kitayama, Markus, & Matsumoto, 1995; Markus & Kitayama, 1994). And given the difference between individualist and collectivist cultures in attributions about behavior, members of individualist cultures may be more likely to "look inside" and attend to their physiological reactions when they are emotional, whereas members of collectivist cultures may tend to "look outside" and attend to their ongoing social relations (Paez & Vergara, 1995). These contrasts raise the possibility that, in diverse cultures, emotions not only may have different names but also may feel different (see Schweder, 1994). On this issue, the jury is still out.

# SOME FINAL THOUGHTS: SOCIAL BEHAVIOR AND PASSION

In this and the preceding chapter we asked how the individual interprets the social world in which he lives and how he interacts with the other people in it.

Where does all of this leave us in our broad account of why people think, act, and feel the way they do in social settings? Three points seem worth highlighting, and each involves a duality that might initially seem a useful way of framing the facts, but which, in the end, cannot be maintained as a strict "either-or" dichotomy.

*Biology versus Culture* The first duality is that between biologically based accounts of our social behavior, framed in terms of natural selection, and learning-based interpretations, emphasizing the role of culture. Over and over we have asked which of these accounts does a better job of explaining human social behavior, but, in the end, it seems that both accounts seem promising, and both capture important truths. There is no question that we have an enormous amount in common with other animals—in our general anatomy, in our genetics, and in our shared evolutionary history. Even in cases in which our history has been separate from, say, that of deer or fish or birds, we have still been subjected to the same sorts of selective pressures, guiding how our species has evolved. It is surely no surprise, therefore, that we can find many parallels between human social behavior and that of other species.

At the same time, there is no question that human social behavior is flexible and subject to cultural learning in ways that other species' behavior is not. We are, of course, biological creatures, but we are also creatures embedded in a network of complex, sophisticated, and powerful cultural influences, and our social behavior plainly reflects those influences.

*Reason versus Passion*  A similar assessment applies to the duality that divided this chapter from the previous one. In Chapter 10, our emphasis was on the cognitive factors that guide social behavior—the beliefs, the interpretations, and the assumptions that we all make about our social world. In this chapter, we turned to less "intellectual" concerns, focusing on passion, rather than reason.

But as we have seen, this distinction is hard to maintain. Most social behaviors are influenced by both reason and passion. Our willingness to help, for example, is influenced both by an unreflective compulsion toward reciprocity, and also by our intellectual assessment of the situation ("Is it really an emergency?" "Are others available to help?") The same mixing of factors can be identified in virtually every other topic we have discussed. We are neither entirely reasoned creatures nor wholly governed by passion, and so any account of our social action must acknowledge both poles of the duality.

*Self versus Other*  Finally, what can we say about human nature? Are we selfish individuals or basically good and decent? Here, too, the either-or choice will not serve us well. We have discussed human aggression, but noted that it is sometimes motivated by such positive things as honor and a defense of important values. We have likewise discussed altruism, but noted the cases in which humans fail to help others, and also considered how altruism may derive from various and subtle forms of self-service. We have discussed fairness, but noted that people are sometimes—but not always—fair.

Perhaps we should close this section, though, by emphasizing that, whatever human nature might be in general, there can be no question that we are capable of extremities of evil and good. The evils that people have committed are all too easy to catalog—assaults, murders, torture, and genocide. But the good is just as important—whether it takes the form of a major act of heroism or the small bits of kindness people show each other all the time. To be sure, the acts of human kindness and pure altruism do not occur as often as we would wish. The true miracle, though, is that they occur at all.

Many kinds of social behavior are governed more by passion than by reason, by what Darwin called the "social instincts," which include sex and love, aggression, altruism, and emotion, all of which have counterparts within the animal kingdom.

## THE BIOLOGICAL ROOTS OF SOCIAL BEHAVIOR

1. Personal survival as such is not what evolution is about. What ultimately matters is *genetic survival,* which in turn depends on *reproductive success.* This applies to an animal's *behavior* as well as its physical traits, particularly behaviors that are central for its reproduction.

## SOCIAL BEHAVIOR AND REPRODUCTION

2. To find a potential mate, an animal must usually *advertise* his or her availability and his or her sex. This may be accomplished by anatomical structures. Many animals (including humans) also advertise both their sex and their readiness to mate via their behaviors, such as *courtship rituals.*

3. To what extent do cultural features determine mating preferences in humans? We begin by asking whom people find *attractive.* One obvious factor is *physical attractiveness.* Its role is apparent from ordinary observation and has been confirmed by various studies (e.g., studies of commercial dating services.) Evidence for the *matching hypothesis* comes from a strong correlation between the physical attractiveness of the two partners. People of different cultures tend to agree on the factors that make someone attractive, including symmetrical faces and certain bodily proportions (such as a specific waist-to-hip ratio). According to some theorists, the preference for these features lies in our evolutionary past (e.g., facial symmetry may indicate greater health), but such claims are controversial.

4. Another factor determining attractiveness is *proximity,* which often provides the opportunity for social interactions. In addition, proximity allows familiarity to develop, and people tend in general to like what's more familiar. Another factor is *similarity,* for people tend to be attracted to others who are like themselves, sometimes resulting in *homogamy.*

5. In most animal species it is the female who makes the final choice of whether to mate or not. The biological reason is that the female shoulders the major costs of reproduction. In a few exceptions (the sea horse, the phalarope), much of the biological burden falls on the male, with a consequent increase in his sexual choosiness. Do these patterns apply to humans as well? There is evidence that human men and women differ in the criteria they use in making their choices, with men preferring younger women and women preferring older men. According to some theorists the explanation is evolutionary (i.e., younger women have more reproductive years ahead of them, and wealthy, high-status males are better able to provide resources for a woman's children). An alternative interpretation looks for cultural rather than genetically rooted factors (i.e., if professional and educational opportunities are limited in a given culture, "marrying wealth" is the woman's best strategy for gathering resources for herself and her young).

6. Different *mating systems* in animals include *polygamy,* in which several members of one sex mate with one individual of the other sex. The polygamous arrangement may involve *polygyny,* which is usually accompanied by *sexual dimorphism.* Here, several females mate with one male. A much less common form of polygamy is *polyandry,* in which several males mate with one female. Still other animals demonstrate *monogamy,* with a reproductive partnership based on a more or less permanent tie between one male and one female. Most birds are monogamous, while the majority of mammals are polygynous. The biological reason is that in birds, successful incubation and feeding the young requires the full-time efforts of both parents; in contrast, mammalian young can often survive under the mother's care alone.

7. Evolutionary theorists suggest that humans have a tendency toward polygyny, given that they are moderately dimorphic. Some evidence indeed suggests that men express a desire for a greater number of sexual partners than women do. But here too an evolutionary account is controversial, for some critics argue that sexual attitudes reflect cultural values rather than biological pre-programming.

## LOVE

8. Psychologists have found it useful to distinguish two different kinds of love. One is *romantic love,* the other is *companionate love.* Romantic love generally involves a state of physiological arousal, and the interpretation of this as passion. It has been suggested that this interpretation is based on a set of ideas that each of us has about what love

is, based on a long cultural heritage. The physiological arousal may be increased by various dangers and frustrations, as exemplified by the *Romeo-and-Juliet effect. Jealousy* is found in both men and women, but its basis has been said to be different in the two sexes. Men, it is alleged, are more concerned about sexual loyalty than emotional loyalty, and women show the reversed pattern. Some theorists have tried to account for this on evolutionary grounds, but both this hypothesis and the results supporting it have been seriously criticized. Romantic love may be transformed into companionate love, in which similarity of outlook, mutual caring, and trust become more important than the idealization of romantic love.

## PARENTING

9. Most young birds and mammals go through an initial period of dependency during which they become strongly *attached* to their mother. Attachment is also evident in humans, but, in our species, caretaking is vastly more complex. Humans show many specializations that promote this caretaking, including the special way parents talk to their young, in *Motherese,* and also the parents' sensitivity to a number of stimuli that seem to trigger parental feelings, including the features of "babyness" and the smile.

## AGGRESSION

10. *Aggression* has to be distinguished from *predation.* Among vertebrates, the male is by far the more physically aggressive sex, but this is a difference that only holds for *physical* aggression; females often show social aggression. To secure resources, many animals defend some territory, which promotes reproductive success. Human territorial behavior is illustrated by phenomena such as *personal space.* Aggressiveness has biological costs, leading to some constraints on aggression, including *dominance hierarchies.* But while there are similarities between human territoriality and that of animals, there are also important contrasts which indicate the role of culture.

11. Human aggression often occurs because of various provocations that include physical aggression and other less direct attacks, such as slights and insults, and verbal assaults. Whether someone turns to aggression or not is influenced by the culture (a possible, though controversial example is what has been described as a *"culture of honor"* in the southern U.S. states.). In addition, *media violence* may promote aggression in viewers. There is considerable evidence that assault and homicide rates increase after such exposures, but there is some question about the nature of the cause-and-effect relationship between media violence and aggression in the viewer.

## ALTRUISM AND SELF-SACRIFICE

12. *Altruism* in animals is demonstrated by such acts as *alarm calls* given by many species. Interpretations of the biological basis of this and similar behavior include *kin selection* and *reciprocal altruism.* Evidence for the latter includes *grooming* in primates, which may be a ways of cementing a social bond.

13. Some social psychologists believe that there is a built-in predisposition toward *reciprocity* in humans, which may underlie a principle of *social exchange* in many of the ways people deal with others. The *reciprocity principle* is found in virtually all cultures and societies. This principle has been shown to be an important tool for persuasion, as in *bargaining* and *self-disclosure.* The reciprocity principle has a negative side as well, as in tendencies toward *retaliation.* This principle can often be a basis for *fairness,* as experimentally studied by means of the *ultimatum task.*

14. People often fail to help others who are in need. The classic example is the case of Kitty Genovese. Social psychologists have tried to understand such failures to help. They have shown that the *bystander effect* is partially produced by social cognition. One factor is the *ambiguity* of the situation, another is *pluralistic ignorance,* yet another is *diffusion of responsibility.* Another factor is the *cost* of helping.

## EMOTION

15. What accounts for the nature of *emotional experience?* An influential interpretation is the *James-Lange theory of emotions,* which asserts that emotion consists of the awareness of the bodily changes that are produced by arousing stimuli. A major attack on this theory was presented by Walter Cannon, who argued that sympathetic reactions are too slow to account for the quickness of emotional reactions, and that sympathetic reactions to arousing stimuli are too diffuse to account for the wide range of human emotional experience. Some support for these arguments came from studies in which participants received injections of epinephrine, which led to "as if" rather than real emotions.

16. A more recent conception of emotion is the *attribution-of-arousal theory,* which argues that while bodily arousal provides the raw materials for an emotional experience, there must also be a *cognitive appraisal* that attributes the arousal to some emotional event. Evidence for this view comes from a study in which participants who were not informed about the physiological consequences of an injection attributed their arousal to the situation in which

they found themselves, experiencing elation or anger depending on what that situation was. Related findings come from work on *excitation transfer*.

17. Studies of the biological structures that support the *integration* of arousal and appraisal have focused on the *amygdala*. Patients with damage to the amygdala do not acquire conditioned fear responses, even though they can recall which stimuli were paired with the unconditioned stimulus; they also seem largely unable to interpret facial expressions.

18. The study of facial expressions was initiated by Charles Darwin, who hypothesized that humans possess a set of universal facial expressions that are vestiges of basic adaptive patterns shown by our evolutionary forerunners. He supposed that these facial expressions are identical among humans worldwide. Some recent investigators have shown photographs of American actors portraying various emotions to members of isolated nonliterate cultures, and asked them to pick the emotion label that "matched" each photo. The participants did reasonably well but their success varied according to the particular facial expression they were shown, with smiles producing much greater consistency in identification than all the other expressions. Some critics believe that while these results are suggestive of *universality* in facial expressions, they are as yet inconclusive. Cultural *display rules* govern what facial expressions may or may not be shown in what contexts.

19. According to the *communicative view*, facial expressions represent a message to others about actions we may take or wish them to take, rather than a "read out" of some inner state. Evidence comes from the fact that facial expressions are far more likely to occur when we are in the presence of others, especially if we make eye contact with them.

20. According to many investigators, there are a few *basic emotions* (e.g., surprise, anger, sadness, disgust, fear, and contempt), but the number of emotions held to be "basic" varies from one theorist to another. One problem comes from the fact that the full range of human emotions includes those that are more cognitive, including such complex feelings as pity, anger, guilt, and regret. Further problems come from cross-cultural differences (i.e., acquiescence, obligation, self-criticism, and submersion of the self within the group are intimately associated with "good" feelings in collectivist cultures and "bad" feelings in individualist ones).

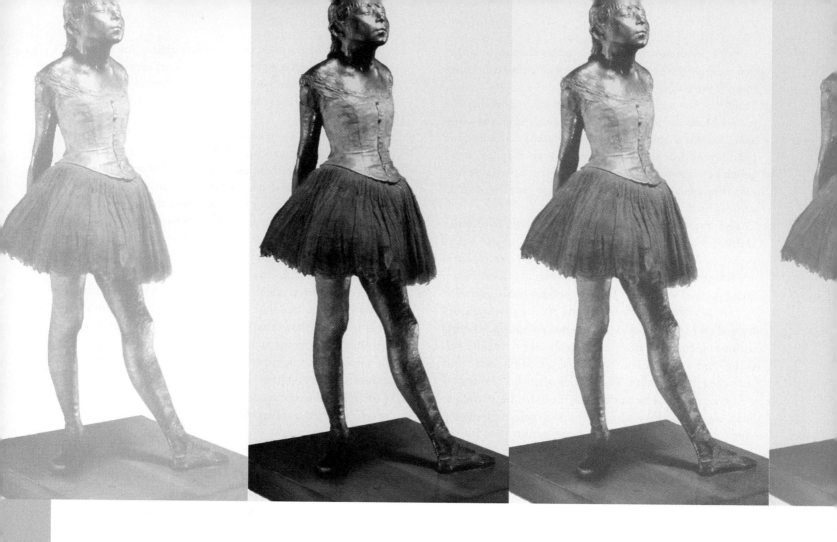

# DEVELOPMENT

*How do we develop throughout life?*

PART

4

*SO FAR, WE HAVE CONSIDERED TWO different kinds of psychological explanation. The first is concerned with mechanism—how something works. The second focuses on function—what something is for. But there is also another approach to explanation in psychology, one that focuses on development. This approach deals with questions of history and trajectory—it asks how a given state of affairs came into being and how it is likely to progress.*

*In the next two chapters, we consider this developmental perspective on psychological phenomena. We will ask how we come to reason and think, how we feel and act as we now do—how it is that we are no longer children but have become adults in mind as well as in body.*

CHAPTER

*12*

# PHYSICAL AND COGNITIVE DEVELOPMENT

*O*ver the course of their lives, humans (and most other creatures) develop in a variety of ways. Some changes involve physical development, the maturation of various bodily structures; others involve motor development, the progressive attainment of various motor skills. Still other changes involve cognitive development, the growth of intellectual functioning, and social development, changes in the ways we perceive and deal with others.

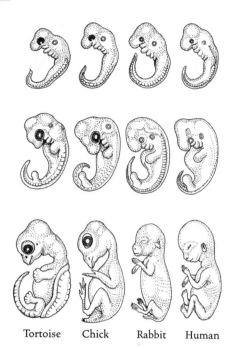

*Differentiation during embryonic development*
**The figure shows three stages in the embryonic development of four different vertebrates— tortoise, chick, rabbit, and human. At the first stage, all of the embryos are very similar to each other. As development proceeds, they diverge more and more. By the third stage, each embryo has taken on some of the distinctive characteristics of its own species.**

Tortoise    Chick    Rabbit    Human

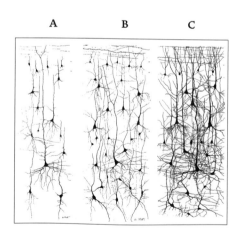

A          B          C

**12.1    *Growth of neural interconnections***
**Sections of the human cortex in (A) a newborn, (B) a three-month-old, and (C) a fifteen-month-old.**

# WHAT IS DEVELOPMENT?

## DEVELOPMENT AS GROWTH

Among all these kinds of development, perhaps the most obvious is physical growth. Organisms grow as they change from a fertilized egg to an embryo, then a fetus, then to a neonate and thereafter, increasing in both physical dimensions (for example, height) and psychological ones (for example, vocabulary size).

### GROWTH BEFORE BIRTH

The voyage toward becoming a human being begins at conception, when a sperm and egg cell unite to form the fertilized egg. This egg divides and redivides repeatedly, producing a cellular mass that attaches itself to the wall of the uterus. Two weeks after conception the mass of cells (now called an *embryo*) begins to differentiate into separate cell layers. Two months after conception, the mass of cells has grown to about one inch in length and is now called a *fetus*. In the next month, the fetus grows to about three inches in length and begins to resemble a miniature baby, with some functioning organ systems and a number of early reflexes, including sucking movements when the lips are touched. In another four months (that is, seven months after conception), the fetus has grown to sixteen inches, has a fully developed reflex pattern, can cry, breathe, swallow, and has a good chance of survival if it should be delivered at this time.

### GROWTH AFTER BIRTH

Nine months after conception the human fetus is ready to leave the uterus to enter the outer world. *Ready*, however, is a relative term. Most other animals can walk shortly after birth and can take care of themselves almost immediately. Humans, in contrast, are extraordinarily helpless at birth and utterly dependent on others and remain so for many months.

The immaturity of the human infant can be documented in many different ways. Consider the nervous system. The infant's neurons begin to mature in the later stages of prenatal growth, and their axons and dendrites form increasingly complex interconnections with other nerve cells (Schacher, 1981). But the brain is far from mature at birth. Figure 12.1 shows sections of the human cortex in a newborn, a three-month-old, and a fifteen-month-old child (Conel, 1939, 1947, 1955). As the figure clearly shows, there is tremendous growth across this period in the number of neural interconnections. If one simply counts the number of synapses per cortical neuron, this number is ten times greater for a one-year-old than it is for a newborn (Huttenlocher, 1979).

Likewise, consider brain size. In most mammals, the newborn's brain is nearly adult sized, but not in primates and most especially not in humans. Human newborns have achieved only 23 percent of their adult cranial capacity at birth and have still only reached 75 percent of it even by the age of two and a half years (Catel, 1953, cited in Gould, 1977).

The growth of the child—in brain size and complexity, and also overall physical growth—continues for many years. This growth is not continuous; rather, it comes in spurts, with each period of accelerated growth lasting only a few months. This is obvious for growth of the body (see Figure 12.2), but is also true for the child's brain. It, too, grows in fits and starts, with the spurts beginning around ages two, six, ten, and fourteen and continuing for about two years each (H. T. Epstein, 1978). Each of these spurts leaves the brain up to 10 percent heavier than it was when the spurt began.

What happens during these growth spurts? The answer is complex. Although the newborn has nearly all the neurons it will ever have, these neurons continue to establish new functional connections and with-draw malfunctioning or unneeded ones (see Chapter 2). At first, the formation of new connections outpaces the disconnections, and so the number of synapses appears to reach a maximum when the child is around two years old. After the age of two, however, the pruning of synapses exceeds the formation of new ones, ultimately leaving the adult with only half the number of synapses the child had at two. What, then, explains the brain's weight gain with each growth spurt? In part, the gain is due to the growth of glial cells, some of which are responsible for the myelin sheaths that surround the axons that must travel long distances in the brain and spinal cord (see Chapter 2). Such myelination begins just after birth and lasts through puberty and beyond (Kolb & Whishaw, 1996).

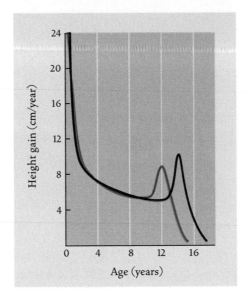

**12.2** *Physical growth* *Height gains for British boys (red) and girls (green) from birth until nineteen years of age. Physical growth continues for almost twenty years after birth with a special spurt at adolescence. (From Tanner, 1970)*

## THE SLOW PACE OF HUMAN GROWTH

Compared to the rate of development in most other animals, human development is amazingly slow, and one might think that this would be a great disadvantage for our species. After all, human parents are burdened with years of childcare and must devote a great quantity of resources to raising their children. This stands in marked contrast to, say, lions, whose male cubs are chased off from the pride by the age of two or three.

Actually, though, the slow pace of human development is not a disadvantage at all. The immaturity of the human infant, and the slow pace of development, do make an extended period of dependency inevitable, and, in some ways, this is inconvenient (for child and parent alike). But this long period of dependency is tailor-made for a creature whose major specialization is its capacity for learning and whose basic invention is culture—the ways of coping with the world that each generation hands on to the next. Human infants, in other words, have a great deal to learn and a huge capacity for learning. Under these circumstances, there is much to be gained by a decade (or two) of living at home.

*Capacity for learning* *Learning from culture is not accomplished overnight. A ten-month-old baby is trying to master the intricacies of eating with a spoon.*

## THE NEWBORN'S EQUIPMENT

We have emphasized the immaturity of human infants, but it is also true that newborns arrive in the world with some very important capacities. In Chapter 9, we considered their biologically given predisposition for language learning. What other skills do infants bring with them into the world? We begin with their motor and sensory capacities.

*The Infant's Response Capacities* Initially, infants have little ability to control their motor apparatus. They thrash around awkwardly and cannot even hold up their heads. But they also have a number of important reflexes that help them through this period of helplessness. An example is the grasp reflex—when an object touches an infant's palm, he closes his fist tightly around it. If the object is lifted up, the infant hangs on and is lifted along with it, supporting his whole weight for a minute or more. Reflexes of this sort are sometimes regarded as a primitive heritage from our primate ancestors, whose infants had to cling to their mothers' furry bodies.

Other infantile reflexes pertain to feeding—for example, the *rooting reflex*. When her

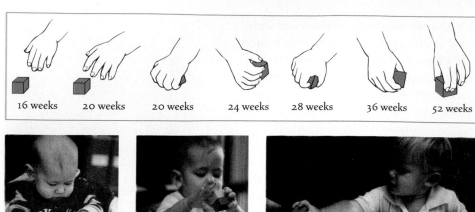

| 16 weeks | 20 weeks | 20 weeks | 24 weeks | 28 weeks | 36 weeks | 52 weeks |

*The development of manual skills* **The diagram shows the progressive differentiation in the infant's use of the hand. At sixteen weeks of age, he reaches for the object but can't hold on to it. At twenty weeks, he grasps it using the hand as a whole, with no differentiated use of the fingers. Between twenty-four and thirty-six weeks, the fingers and thumb become differentiated in use, but the four fingers operate more or less as a whole. Photos illustrate the same point at twenty-three, twenty-eight, and fifty-eight weeks.**

23 weeks     28 weeks     58 weeks

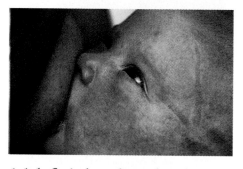

*A vital reflex in the newborn* **The sucking reflex is initiated when an appropriate object is inserted three or four centimeters into the mouth.**

cheek is lightly touched, a baby's head turns toward the source of stimulation, her mouth opens, and her head continues to turn until the stimulus (usually a finger or nipple) is in her mouth. When this point is reached, sucking begins.

Many infantile reflexes disappear after a few months. In some cases, the reflex is replaced by a more directed response. Thus, infants stop reflexive grasping when they are about three or four months old, but this does not mean that they never grasp again. Of course they will. But when they do (at about five months), they do so because they want to—their grasp has become voluntary rather than reflexive. Likewise, newborns placed in water begin to swim by dog-paddling, but they lose this capability shortly after birth and must be taught to swim years later. Such voluntary actions have to wait until various parts of the brain have matured sufficiently. But until that point, the infantile reflexes serve as a temporary substitute.

*The Infant's Sensory Capacities* While newborns' motor capacities are initially very limited, their sensory channels function nicely from the start. They can discriminate between tones of different pitch and loudness and, as it turns out, also show an early preference for their mother's voice in comparison to that of a strange female (Aslin, 1987; DeCasper & Fifer, 1980). Newborns also can see: they are quite nearsighted and unable to focus on objects more than about four feet away, but they can readily discriminate brightness and color, and they can track a moving stimulus with their eyes (Aslin, 1987; Bornstein, 1985). In addition, they can touch, smell, and taste (Crook, 1987).

All in all, infants seem well equipped to sense the world they enter. But are they able to interpret what they see, hear, or touch? This is a disputed issue, and whether infants have some built-in ability to interpret the world, or must develop one as they grow, is a question we will consider in a later section.

# THE PHYSICAL BASIS OF DEVELOPMENT

What produces the many changes that constitute development? One important factor is the genetic blueprint that each organism inherits; another factor is its environment—both before and after it is born.

# THE MECHANISM OF GENETIC TRANSMISSION

An organism's genetic makeup is encoded in the *genes*, the units of hereditary transmission. These genes provide a set of instructions that determine growth and steer the organism's development from fertilized cell to mature animal or plant. Most genes are stored within the *chromosomes* in the cell's nucleus, with each chromosome holding a thousand or more of these genetic commands. In organisms that reproduce sexually, the chromosomes come in pairs; one member of each pair is contributed by the mother, the other by the father (see Figure 12.3).

Scientists have been striving for decades to identify the exact sequence of genes on each chromosome, and in early 2001 they announced a complete draft of this sequence. Remarkably, the set of human genes was much smaller than anticipated, consisting of a mere 30,000 or so genes.

Work on this gene sequence continues as scientists strive to fill in some gaps in the sequence and to clarify some ambiguities about the order of placement of some of the genes. Even so, there is every expectation that the draft will permit a much more detailed and sophisticated understanding of physical and psychological development and also of the disease processes that can derail development.

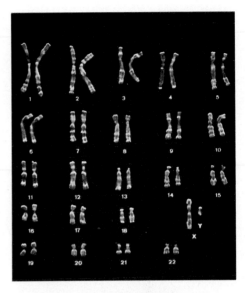

**12.3   The human chromosome pairs**
*The figure shows the twenty-three pairs of chromosomes in a human male. The twenty-third pair determines the individual's sex. In males, one member of this pair is an X chromosome, the other a Y chromosome. In females, both are X chromosomes.*

## SEX DETERMINATION

Certain facts about human genetics, however, have been known for many years. For example, we have long known that the genetic commands that determine whether a given animal will be male or female are inscribed in a pair of sex chromosomes. In males, one of the members of this pair is called an **X chromosome**; the other is somewhat smaller and is called a **Y chromosome**. In females, both members of the pair are X chromosomes. This setup guarantees that the sex of a child will depend mostly on the father. The mother has only X chromosomes to contribute, and so every egg cell contains an X chromosome. Sperm cells contain either an X chromosome or a Y chromosome. Depending on which of the two kinds joins up with the egg cell, the resulting fertilized egg (or zygote) will end up with an XX pair (and develop into a female) or an XY pair (a male).

## DOMINANT AND RECESSIVE GENES

Chromosomes, we have noted, come in pairs, and the same is true for genes. Each gene occupies a specific position within its chromosome, and so, for each gene, there is a partner gene, located at the corresponding position on the other member of the chromosomal pair. The two genes in each pair—one contributed by each parent—may or may not be identical. Consider eye color. If both genes in the pair specify the same eye color (both coding for blue or both for brown), the eye color will follow suit. But suppose they are different. In humans, the gene for brown eyes is *dominant*; it will exert its effect regardless of whether the other member of the gene pair calls for brown or blue eyes. In contrast, the gene for blue eyes is *recessive*. This recessive gene will lead to blue eyes only if the gene in the corresponding locus of the paired chromosome also calls for blue eyes. Or, to put this differently, the baby's eyes will be blue only if both parents contributed a genetic instruction for blue; if either parent contributed an instruction for brown, the eyes will be brown.

Many other human traits are also based on a single gene pair, with one trait dominant and the others recessive. The list includes dark hair, dimples, and thick lips (all dominant), and baldness, red hair, and straight nose (all recessive). A single gene pair also determines red-green color blindness and susceptibility to poison ivy (both recessive).

*Genetic effects on behavior*

"It's true. You were actually born a beautiful princess but you were given to us to be brought up . . . and there's not a damned thing you can do about it!"

**Nature versus nurture** *Cartoonists apparently have strong views about the role of environment and inheritance in shaping who we are.*

## POLYGENIC INHERITANCE

So far, we have considered only the characteristics governed by a single gene pair. More typically, though, an organism's attributes are influenced by many gene pairs—a pattern known as *polygenic inheritance*. Thus, one gene pair might influence an early stage of development for a particular attribute, while a different pair influences an intermediate stage, and still another pair influences a later stage. Alternatively, the various gene pairs influencing a trait might all be active simultaneously, with each pair controlling some aspect of the body's inner workings, but with all the pairs collectively shaping the manifested trait.

In all cases, though, it is worth emphasizing that the genes do not directly control the observable traits. In truth, there is no gene that directly determines eye color, and certainly no gene that literally governs height or intelligence. Instead, what each gene truly controls is the production of a specific protein or enzyme; these then combine to regulate a specific biochemical sequence within the developing organism. It is this sequence that eventually determines the organism's manifest traits.

Notice, therefore, that the link between the genetic blueprint (the *genotype*) and the organism's actual characteristics (the *phenotype*) is indirect. Genes guide the biochemical processes that eventually lead to the characteristics we observe in an individual. But many other factors also influence these same biochemical processes, and so many other forces shape the complex developmental sequence. Thus, genetic influences on development are profoundly important, but it is meaningless to speak of a characteristic as being entirely determined by the genes. Instead, genes are simply one factor within the set of factors that determine each aspect of the developing organism. (We will return to these issues, and the role of genetic factors in development, in Chapter 14.)

## ENVIRONMENTS AT DIFFERENT POINTS IN DEVELOPMENT

Clearly, development involves both heredity and environment. But the relation between the two is subtler than may be apparent at first, because what is meant by environment changes continually as development proceeds.

### THE ENVIRONMENT BEFORE BIRTH

*Early Embryonic Development* Some of the cells in the embryo will eventually become the organism's brain; others will become the gallbladder or the bones of the foot. But every cell in the embryo has the same genes, and so presumably all receive the same genetic instructions. How, therefore, does each cell manage to develop appropriately?

In part, the fate of each cell is determined by its cellular neighbors—the cells that are adjacent to it and form its physical environment. Evidence comes from studies of salamander embryos. Early in their development, salamanders have an outer layer of tissue that gradually differentiates. Cells in this layer will become teeth if they make contact with certain other cells in the embryo's mouth region. Without this contact, cells in this layer instead become skin. This is demonstrated by surgically rearranging cells in the embryo's outer layer. If these cells had stayed in their initial position, they would have developed into the skin. Transplanted into the embryo's mouth region, these cells became teeth (Spemann, 1967).

*The Development of Sexual Structures* In an early stage of embryonic development, each cell's environment consists of its cellular neighbors. Somewhat later, development is affected by another kind of environment—the organism's own bodily fluids, especially its blood. Moreover, the bloodstream of mammalian embryos is intimately

*The creation of Eve    According to the Bible, Eve was created after Adam. But biologically, the order is reversed. (Panel from the Sistine Chapel ceiling, by Michelangelo, 1508–1512.)*

connected to the mother's blood supply, and so this too becomes part of the embryo's environment.

An example of the influence exerted through the bloodstream is the development of sexual structures and behavior. What determines whether an individual is biologically male or female? As we mentioned earlier, someone is genetically male if he is chromosomally XY and genetically female if she is XX. But the full story is more complicated than that. After about six weeks of gestation, the human embryo has primordial *gonads* that as yet give no indication of the baby's sex. A week or so later, the chromosomes initiate the differentiation of ovaries and testes. In a genetic male, the XY chromosome pair leads to the formation of testes. Once formed, these produce *androgens* (male sex hormones) such as testosterone, and it is the presence of these hormones in the bloodstream that steers the differentiation of the external genitals.

The pattern is different for females. The formation of the female's external genitals depends on hormones only indirectly. As long as no androgens circulate in the bloodstream, the fetus will develop the appropriate female organs. Thus, the basic genetic plan for humans, shared by both sexes, seems to call for the building of a female.* If it is left undisturbed (that is, if no androgens are present), the plan runs its course. To build a male, the developmental path has to be diverted by the appropriate hormones. It would seem that biologically—if not biblically—speaking, Adam was created from Eve (Money, 1980; Money & Ehrhardt, 1972).

Thus, the chromosome pairs define an individual's genetic sex. But the way in which that sex is actually shaped depends on the organism's internal environment—the presence or absence of male hormones in its bloodstream.

## THE ENVIRONMENT AFTER BIRTH

After birth, the range of environmental events affecting development broadens appreciably and now includes many aspects of the surrounding physical, social, and cognitive

* In birds, the basic plan is male, with females the result of special hormonal intervention (Shepherd, 1994).

worlds. We will have much more to say about specific environmental influences later in this chapter, but for now let us simply note the rich diversity of this set of influences. They include the nutrients (and toxins) that enter the child; the behavior of other people, which the child observes, learns from, and sometimes imitates; the explicit instructions that the child receives from others; and the feedback the child receives, after trying this or that behavior and observing its consequences. Obviously, these factors are all important in guiding the child's learning and development.

Which aspects of the environment weigh most heavily, though, depends on the child's age. Imagine a three-month-old who hears her parents shout, "Surprise!" as they show her a new toy. In all likelihood, the baby will cry in fear, because all she hears is a loud noise. At the age of three years, the same shout will probably produce joyous squeals of anticipation, because now the sound has meaning and that meaning is vastly more important than its acoustic intensity.

## SENSITIVE PERIODS

We have just noted that a child's reaction to an event (or any other environmental influence) depends on her age. Some developmental theorists, however, believe this idea should be framed in much stronger terms. They argue that there are *critical periods* in development during which certain events will have an enormous impact; outside of these critical periods, the same events will have little or no influence.

The idea of critical periods was derived from embryology, where it refers to the development of tissue differentiation. We previously saw that parts of a salamander embryo's outer tissue, if transplanted early in development, may become skin or teeth, depending on what cells they are adjacent to. But at a later time, this flexibility is gone. If the cells destined to be teeth are transplanted at this point, they still become teeth. For these cells, the critical period has passed, and the path of their development is already set (Spemann, 1967).

Many psychologists believe that similar critical periods exist for key developments after birth, but the boundaries of these periods are not as rigidly fixed as are the critical periods in embryological development. As a result, these windows of opportunity are often called *sensitive periods*, to indicate that this is a time in which the organism is especially sensitive to a particular influence. An example is the attachment of the young of many species to their mother, an attachment that is much more readily formed at an early age (see Chapter 13). In humans, a related example is the acquisition of language, which, as we have seen, is also easier at younger ages (see Chapter 9).

## THE GENETIC ROOTS OF COGNITIVE CAPACITIES

Clearly, then, the interaction between genes and environment is complex. The genes provide the initial blueprint for the developing organism, but the environment plays a large role in determining how the genetic pattern is expressed. The genetic pattern in turn makes the organism sensitive to some factors in the environment, but less sensitive to others. Notice, therefore, that the influence here runs in both directions, with the environment shaping how the genetic patterns unfold and the genetically rooted patterns shaping the organism's sensitivity to the environment. The exact nature of this two-way influence changes as the organism grows, with different genes expressing themselves at different development stages and different environmental factors having a role at different stages.

Even with these complexities, the fact remains that genes do have an enormous impact on the developing organism—not just in guiding physical development, but also in guiding cognitive and social development. With regard to cognition, we have already seen that our capacity for language is rooted in the biology of the human brain, and therefore in our genetic pattern (Chapter 9). In upcoming chapters, we will explore

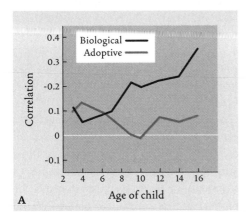

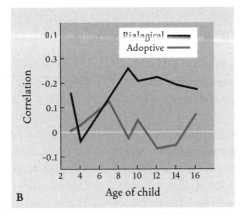

A — Age of child

B — Age of child

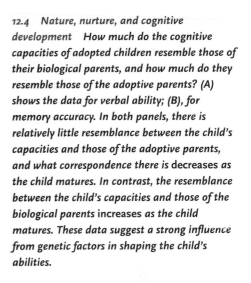

12.4 *Nature, nurture, and cognitive development* How much do the cognitive capacities of adopted children resemble those of their biological parents, and how much do they resemble those of the adoptive parents? (A) shows the data for verbal ability; (B), for memory accuracy. In both panels, there is relatively little resemblance between the child's capacities and those of the adoptive parents, and what correspondence there is decreases as the child matures. In contrast, the resemblance between the child's capacities and those of the biological parents increases as the child matures. These data suggest a strong influence from genetic factors in shaping the child's abilities.

some of the biological roots of intelligence (Chapter 14) and genetic influences on personality (Chapter 15).

For now, though, a single example will be useful in underscoring the importance of genetics in shaping human development. One way to explore the genetic roots of a capacity is by comparing the abilities of adopted children to those of their adoptive parents and those of their biological parents. To the extent that the ability is shaped by genetics, we would expect the child's ability to resemble the abilities of his biological parents. Conversely, to the extent that the ability is shaped by environmental factors (including the child's day-to-day experiences), we would expect the child's ability to resemble the ability of his adoptive parents, since they, after all, play a central role in shaping and choosing those experiences.

Data pertinent to these claims are available from several sources, and the pattern of the data is clear. There is relatively little resemblance between the intellectual capacities of the child and those of the adoptive parents. Moreover, what correspondence there is decreases as the child matures, and so the correlations between child and adopted parents essentially drop to zero by the time the child enters the teenage years (Figure 12.4A shows the data for verbal ability; Figure 12.4B shows the data for tests of memory accuracy; Plomin, Fulker, Corley, & DeFries, 1997).

The pattern is different, however, if we compare the capacities of adopted children with those of their biological mothers (whom the children have never met). Here there is a reasonable correspondence, and the correspondence increases as the children enter their teenage years.* These data suggest, therefore, that genes play a large role in shaping intellectual capacities; that is why people with similar genetic patterns (for example, a parent and her biological offspring) end up with similar scores. In Chapter 14, we will return to these findings and have more to say about what these data suggest about the nature and origins of intelligence. For now, though, our point is straightforward: genes do not influence us directly; they influence us, as we have said, only through a complex interaction with a variety of environmental factors. Nonetheless, the genetic profile that each of us inherits is crucial in shaping many aspects of who we are and who we become. This essential point must be understood if we are to understand the broader issue of how each of us develops across our childhood and, indeed, across our life span.

*The benefits of starting young* It seems likely that innate abilities contribute to Tiger Woods' extraordinary talent on the golf course. Even so, years and years of practice have also played a crucial role. He first held a golf club at age two, became devoted to the sport and practiced incessantly. In 1997, when he was only twenty-one, he won the Masters, a major tournament, by twelve strokes, setting the new tournament record of eighteen under par.

* We should mention that these adoption studies almost certainly underestimate the role of environment in shaping intelligence. As one large concern, these studies look only at the adoptive parents' cognitive abilities and how those are related to the child's abilities. Other aspects of the family environment (for example, the adoptive parents' attitudes about education, or how encouraging the parents are for the child) may have a substantial influence but are not considered in most adoption studies. Therefore, while the study described here does speak to the importance of genetic factors, it has little to say about environmental factors. For more on how the environment does shape intelligence, see Chapter 14.

*Jean Piaget*

# COGNITIVE DEVELOPMENT

There is no question that each of us has to learn a great deal from the world. We observe. We imitate. We interpret what we have observed, and then extrapolate from that base. How do these processes unfold?

For many decades, the exploration of these issues was focused on theoretical claims developed by the Swiss psychologist Jean Piaget (1896–1980). As we will see, many of Piaget's claims have been disputed, and most of his theoretical proposals have come under serious attack. Even so, we cannot begin the study of cognitive development without first considering Piaget's views, since the data he uncovered, the methods he developed, and the way he framed the issues have played an enormous role in shaping the way all subsequent investigators have approached the subject.

Piaget believed that there were profound differences between a child's thinking and an adult's. In development, he argued, the child does not just learn more or add new skills to her repertoire. Instead, development involves drastic changes in every aspect of the child's intellectual capacities.

Piaget proposed that there are four main stages of intellectual growth. They are the period of *sensorimotor intelligence* (from birth to about two years), the *preoperational period* (two to seven years), the period of *concrete operations* (seven to eleven years), and the period of *formal operations* (eleven years and on). The age ranges are approximate, however, and successive stages are often thought to overlap and blend into one another.*

## SENSORIMOTOR INTELLIGENCE

According to Piaget, the child's mental life during the first few months consists of nothing but a succession of fleeting, disconnected sensory impressions and motor reactions. There is no distinction between stable objects and transient events, and no differentiation between the "me" and the "not me." The critical achievement of the first two years is the development of these distinctions.

### OBJECT PERMANENCE

Consider an infant holding a rattle. At the moment, the infant might be looking at the rattle, but this looking at is not part of the rattle's identity. If the infant looked away, the rattle would still exist. Likewise, the infant is now holding the rattle, but this too is incidental; the rattle's continued existence is in no way dependent on its being held.

According to Piaget, infants understand none of this. For infants, the only world that exists is the world of their own sensations. Therefore, infants are aware of looking at the rattle but have no conception of the rattle itself existing as a permanent, independent object. If infants look away from a rattle (and thus stop seeing it), then the rattle ceases to exist. It is not just "out of sight, out of mind." More strongly, it is "out of sight, out of existence." In this way, Piaget claims, infants lack a sense of *object permanence*—the understanding that objects exist independent of our momentary sensory or motoric interactions with them.

What led Piaget to this view? He observed that infants typically look at a new toy with evident delight, but if the toy disappears from view, they show little concern (see Figure 12.5). At a slightly later age, infants might show some signs of distress when the toy dis-

---

* These stages roughly correspond to the categories employed by modern developmental psychologists, regardless of their stand on Piaget's theory: infancy (from birth to about two and a half years), early childhood (two and a half to six years), middle childhood (six to eleven years), and adolescence and beyond (twelve years and up).

appears, but still make no effort to retrieve it. This is true even if it seems perfectly obvious where the toy is located. For example, an experimenter might drape a light cloth over the toy, while an infant is watching. In this situation, the toy is still easily within reach and its shape is still (roughly) visible through the folds of the cloth. The child watched it being covered just moments earlier. But still the infant makes no effort to retrieve it. According to Piaget, this is because the toy, no longer visible, has ceased to exist in the mind of that child.

At about the age of eight months, infants do start to search for toys that have been hidden or that have fallen out of their cribs. Apparently, an eight-month-old knows that objects endure even when they are out of view. But the child's searching for the toy shows a peculiar limitation, and this indicated to Piaget that the child still lacks a mature concept of object permanence.

This limitation is easy to demonstrate. Suppose a nine-month-old sees an experimenter hide a toy monkey under a cover located, say, to the child's right. The child will happily push the cover off and snatch up the monkey. The experimenter now repeats the process a few times, always hiding the monkey under the same cover to the child's right. Again and again the child pulls the cover off and retrieves the monkey. But now the experimenter introduces a slight change in the procedure. Very slowly and in full view of the child, she hides the toy in a different place, say, under a cover to the child's left. The child closely watches her every movement—and then does exactly what he did before. He searches under the cover on the right, even though he saw the experimenter hide the toy in another place just a moment earlier.

This phenomenon is often called the **A–not–B effect**, where *A* designates the place where the object was first hidden and *B* the place where it was hidden last. Why does this peculiar error occur? According to Piaget (1952), the nine-month-old still has not grasped the fact that an object's existence is independent of his own actions. Thus, the child believes that his reaching toward place *A* (where he found the toy previously) is as much a part of the monkey as the monkey's tail. In effect, the child is not really searching for a monkey; he is searching for the-monkey-that-I-find-on-the-right. No wonder, then, that the child continues searching on the right (Flavell, 1985; P. L. Harris, 1987).

According to Piaget, the notion that objects exist on their own even when they are not seen, heard, felt, or reached for is a major accomplishment of the sensorimotor period. This notion emerges as infants gradually integrate their motor reactions with the information provided by the different sensory modalities—vision, hearing, touch, and bodily movement—eventually grasping the fact that there is one spatial framework in which all the world's objects—themselves included—exist. What makes this possible is their increasingly sophisticated *schemas*.

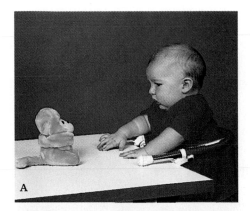

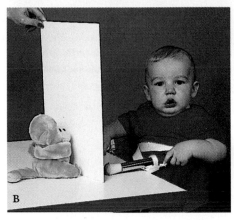

**12.5 Object permanence** *(A) A six-month-old looks intently at a toy. (B) But when the toy is hidden from view, the infant does not search for it. According to Piaget, this is because the infant does not as yet have the concept of object permanence.*

## SENSORIMOTOR SCHEMAS

Newborns start life with a rather limited repertoire of built-in reactions, such as sucking, swallowing, and, after a few days, certain orienting responses such as head and eye movements. In Piaget's view, these action patterns provide the first mental categories, or schemas, through which infants organize their sensory world: the world is understood, in other words, as consisting of the suckables, the swallowables, and so on.

Across the first few months of life, though, the child refines and extends these schemas and also learns how to integrate these schemas into more complex ways of dealing with the world. What makes this possible, according to Piaget, are two processes that in his view are responsible for all cognitive development: *assimilation* and *accommodation*. In assimilation, children use the mental schemas they have already formed to interpret (and act on) the environment; in other words, objects in the environment are assimilated into the schema. But the schemas also change as the child gains experience in interacting with the world; the schemas accommodate to the environment.

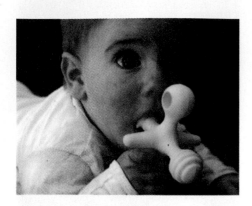

*Assimilation and accommodation*   *The three-month-old has assimilated the rattle into her sucking schema and has accommodated the schema so that it now includes the rattle as a suckable object.*

For example, the schema for sucking initially applies only to the nipple. But with time, infants start to suck other objects, such as a rattle. Piaget (1952) would say that by doing this they have assimilated the rattle into their sucking schema. But the process does not stop there. After all, rattles are not the same as nipples; while both are suckable, they are not suckable in quite the same way, and so the sucking schema must adjust to (that is, accommodate) the new object. This refinement in the sucking schema now allows the child to apply the schema even more broadly—that is, the child is better able to assimilate objects into the schema. But this will demand still further refinement—further accommodation. As this process continues, the schemas gradually become more and more differentiated. At the same time, the increasing skill acquired with each schema allows the infants to use more than one schema at a time—reaching while looking, grasping while sucking—and this allows them to coordinate these individual actions into one unified exploratory schema. Notice that these developments break the connection between an object and a specific way of acting on that object, or a specific way of experiencing that object. Now, the child can relate to an object in a more flexible way, and, crucially, this liberation of the object from a specific action helps propel the child toward an understanding that the object's existence is independent of the child—that is, it helps propel him toward object permanence and a mature understanding of what an object is.

## BEGINNINGS OF REPRESENTATIONAL THOUGHT

According to Piaget, the last phase of the sensorimotor period (about eighteen to twenty-four months) marks a momentous change in intellectual development. Children begin to conceive of objects and events that are not immediately present. These early mental representations may be internalized actions (anticipating how one might throw an object that is not currently in view) or images (remembering what the object looked like) or even words. But in any case this ability to represent objects in one's mind is a crucial step on the path toward abstract symbolic thought.

    This capacity for mental representation grows out of the achievements we have already discussed. In order to attain a full concept of object permanence, for example, the child must be able to think about (represent) an object in a fashion that is emancipated from the immediate here and now of sensorimotor experience. The child must be able to think about an object seen earlier, even if it is not visible at the moment. Thus, the achievement of object permanence must go hand in hand with the capacity for mental representation.

# THE PREOPERATIONAL PERIOD

With the emergence of representational thought, two-year-olds have taken a gigantic step forward. But, according to Piaget, their mental world is still a far cry from the world of adults. Two-year-olds have learned how to represent the world mentally but have not yet learned how to interrelate these representations in a coherent way. The achievement of the next five years, therefore, is the emergence of a reasonably well-ordered world of ideas. In Piaget's view, this requires a new and more sophisticated set of schemas that he called **operations**. These allow the internal manipulation of ideas according to a stable set of rules. In his view, genuine operations do not appear until about seven or so, hence the term *preoperational* for the period from two to about seven years.

## FAILURE OF CONSERVATION

A revealing example of preoperational thought is seen in the young child's apparent failure to conserve quantity. This failure can be demonstrated in many ways; one proce-

A

B

**12.6 Conservation of liquid quantity** *(A) A child is asked by the experimenter, "Do we both have the same amount of juice to drink?" the child says yes. (B) The experimenter pours the juice from one of the beakers into a new, wider beaker. When now asked, "Which glass has more juice?" the child points to the thinner one.*

dure uses two identical glasses, *A* and *B*, which stand side by side and are filled with the same amount of colored liquid. A child is asked whether there is more juice in one glass or the other, and the experimenter obligingly adds a drop here, a drop there until the participant is completely satisfied that there is "the same to drink in this glass as in that." Four-year-olds can easily make this judgment.

The next step involves a new glass, *C*, which is shorter but wider than *A* and *B* (see Figure 12.6). While the child is watching, the experimenter pours the entire contents of glass *A* into glass *C*. She now points to *B* and *C*, and asks, "Is there more juice in this glass or in that or are they the same?" For an adult, the question is almost too simple to deserve an answer. The amounts are obviously identical, since *A* was completely emptied into *C*, and *A* and *B* were made equal at the outset. But four- or five-year-olds do not see this. They insist that there is less juice in *C*. When asked for their reason, they explain that the liquid comes to a much lower level in C. They seem to think that the juice has somehow decreased in quantity as it was transferred from one glass to another. They are too impressed by the visible changes in liquid level to realize that there is an underlying constancy in quantity.

By the time children are about seven years old, they respond much like adults. They hardly look at the two glasses, for their judgment needs little empirical support. "It's the same. It seems as if there's less because it's wider, but it's the same." The experimenter may continue with other glasses of different sizes and shapes but the judgment remains what it was: "It's still the same because it always comes from the same glass." (Also see Figure 12.7.)

A related phenomenon is conservation of number. The child is first shown two rows of quarters. The child agrees that both rows contain the same number of coins. The experimenter now rearranges one row by spacing the quarters out more. Prior to age five or six, children generally assert that there are now more coins in this row because "they're more spread out" (see Figure 12.8). From about six on, there is conservation; the child has no doubt that there are just as many coins in the tightly spaced row as there are in the spread-out line.

Why do preschool children fail to conserve? According to Piaget, part of the problem is their inability to interrelate the different dimensions of a situation. To conserve liquid quantity, for example, the children must first comprehend that there are two relevant factors: the height of the liquid column and the width of the glass. They must then appreciate that an increase in the column's height is accompanied by a decrease in its width. Thus, the children must be able to attend to both dimensions concurrently and relate the dimensions to each other. This is the capacity that they lack, since it requires a higher-order schema that reorganizes initially discrete perceptual experiences into one conceptual unit.

In Piaget's view (1952), children gain this capacity only when they begin to focus on the transformations from one experience into another, rather than on the individual experiences themselves. Children see that these transformations are effected by actions that are reversible, such as pouring the contents of one glass into another and then

**12.7 Conservation of mass** *Preschoolers also fail to conserve mass. This child is shown two clay balls which he adjusts until he is satisfied that there is the same amount of clay in both. The experimenter takes one of the balls and rolls it into a "hot dog." When now asked which has more clay, the child points to the hot dog.*

**12.8 Conservation of number** *When the two rows of coins are evenly spaced, the child correctly says that both rows contain the same number of coins. When one row is spaced more widely, the child says that it has more coins.*

back again. This reversible action eventually becomes internalized, so that they can think about the liquid being poured back and forth with no overt action. The result of this reversible mental operation is conservation of quantity.

### EGOCENTRISM

Piaget argued that preoperational children are also limited in how they understand the social world. Here, too, the children focus on one dimension at a time and are locked into their own perspective on a situation. They do not understand another person's point of view and do not even recognize that another person's point of view may be different from their own.

Piaget used the term *egocentrism* to describe this characteristic of preoperational thought. As Piaget used the term, it does not imply selfishness. Instead, the children simply have not yet grasped that there are other selves, with their own needs, beliefs, and perspectives.

## CONCRETE AND FORMAL OPERATIONS

By the age of three or four (early in the preoperational period), children have learned how to represent the world mentally. By age seven or so, they have learned how to interrelate these representations. They now grasp the fact that changes in one aspect of a situation are compensated for by changes in some other aspect. They are able to transform their own mental representations in a variety of ways and thus understand what would happen if the water were poured back into its original glass and why the spacing of a row of coins does not affect its number.

But according to Piaget, children's intellectual capacities are still limited in an important way: they have gained skill in a variety of mental operations, but they apply these operations only to relations between concrete events (hence, the term *concrete operations*). Thus, children are able to think about a wide range of concrete cases, but lack skill in thinking abstractly.

For example, eight- and nine-year-olds can easily see that 4 is an even number and 4 + 1 is odd. Similarly, they understand that 6 is even, while 6 + 1 is odd, and likewise for 8 and 8 + 1. But the same children fail to see the inevitability of this pattern; they fail to see that the addition of 1 to any even number must always produce a number that is odd. According to Piaget, the comprehension of this abstract and formal relationship requires formal operations, operations of a higher order, which emerge at about the age of eleven or twelve years.

Once children have entered the period of formal operations, their ability to reason and solve problems takes a large step forward. Their thought can now embrace the possible as well as the real; they can now entertain hypothetical possibilities and can deal with what might be no less than what is.

# WHAT IS THE COGNITIVE STARTING POINT?

The account offered by Piaget—children's initial achievement of sensorimotor intelligence and then their progress through preoperational thought, concrete operations, and, finally, formal operations—has been enormously influential. Piaget's theories have shaped the ways in which psychologists, educators, and even parents conceptualize children's intellectual growth. The phenomena discovered by Piaget are quite striking and seem to provide key insights into children's intellectual capacities and, sometimes, their intellectual limitations.

At the same time, though, Piaget's claims have not gone unchallenged. We now turn, therefore, to some of the responses to Piaget's claims. Our presentation will be centered on two claims that, in some ways, are at the heart of Piaget's theory. First, Piaget's evidence seems to indicate that young children are limited in striking ways—with infants lacking an object concept, preschoolers unable to conserve, and so on. More recent studies, however, show that these intellectual limits sit side by side with pockets of impressive competence, making young children seem in some ways more advanced than Piaget suggested.

Second, Piaget plainly envisioned the child as passing through a series of discrete stages, so that the capacities of the infant are truly different from those of the preoperational child, and those in turn are truly different from those of a child in the stage of concrete operations. As we will see, however, the right sorts of tests reveal that the boundaries between stages are not so clear-cut, and, under the right circumstances, a sensorimotor infant will display skills that, according to Piaget, were only available to her preoperational sibling, and so on.

These various findings leave Piaget's theory in an interesting status. On the one hand, the data patterns revealed by Piaget—the limits of what children can do in many circumstances, the apparently large leaps forward that take place (roughly) at age two, and again at age four or five—must be explained, and so we cannot abandon Piaget's insights altogether. On the other hand, Piaget was plainly mistaken in some of his specific claims and, potentially, in his broad theoretical approach, and we will need to revise his conception in important ways. Let us examine how these arguments unfold.

## SPACE AND OBJECTS IN INFANCY

Many investigators have argued that Piaget seriously underestimated the intellectual capacities of infants. Their minds, these investigators claim, are not a mere jumble of sensory impressions and motor reactions. Instead, infants arrive with primitive concepts of space, objects, number, and even the existence of other minds. These are, of course, the same concepts that adults use to organize their world, implying—contrary to Piaget—that the infants' world is not so different from the adults'.

### THE EFFECT OF OCCLUSION

Consider Figure 12.9A, which shows an object partially occluding (hiding from view) another object behind it. Adults viewing this scene will surely perceive it as a child behind a gate. They are completely certain that when the gate is opened, they will see a whole child (Figure 12.9B) and would be utterly astounded if the opened gate revealed a child with gaps in her body (Figure 12.9C).

Do infants perceive partially hidden objects in the same way? If so, this would be evidence that their perceptual experience is not as fragmented as Piaget had proposed. More precisely, it would indicate that infants have at least a primitive concept of objects, and an appreciation of the fact that an object's parts stay connected regardless of whether the object is entirely visible or not.

To pursue these questions, many experiments employ *habituation procedures*. In one such study, infants were shown a rod that moved back and forth behind a solid block that occluded the rod's central portion (Figure 12.10A). This display was kept in view, with the rod continuing to move back and forth, until the infants became bored with it (that is, habituated) and stopped looking at the display. The investigators then presented the infants with either of two test displays. One was an unbroken rod that

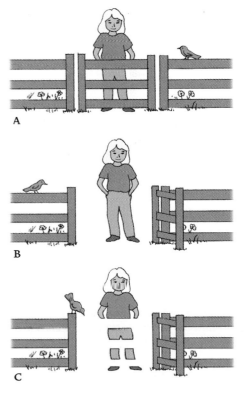

**12.9 The perceptual effect of occlusion** *(A) A child occluded by a gate is perceived as a whole person behind a gate, so that she will look like (B) when the gate is opened, rather than being perceived as (C), a child with gaps in her body.*

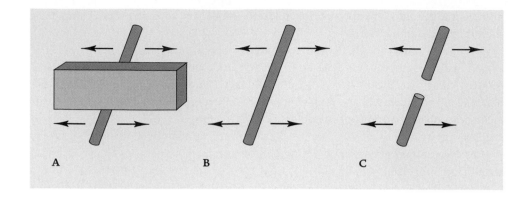

**12.10　The perceptual effect of occlusion in early infancy**　*Four-month-olds were shown a rod that moved back and forth behind an occluding block as shown in (A). After they became habituated to this display and stopped looking at it, they were shown two new displays, neither of which was occluded. In (B) the rod that moved back and forth was unbroken. In (C) it was made of two aligned rod pieces that moved back and forth together. The infants spent much more time looking at (C) than at (B).*

moved back and forth (Figure 12.10B). The other consisted of two aligned rod pieces that moved back and forth in unison (Figure 12.10C).

If these infants had perceived the original stimulus as a complete, unitary rod, then Figure 12.10B would show them nothing new, whereas Figure 12.10C would seem novel. This pattern would be reversed if the infants had perceived only the pieces of the original stimulus. In this case, Figure 12.10C would show them nothing new and Figure 12.10B would be the novel display.

Since these infants had already become habituated to (bored with) the original stimulus, a novel stimulus should attract their attention and hold it longer. Thus, we can measure how long the infants looked at the display to find out which the infants consider novel, and once we know what the infants consider novel, then we will know how they perceived the original display.

The evidence in this study is clear. The four-month-old infants spent more time looking at the broken rod than at the complete rod. Apparently, they found the broken rod more novel, which tells us that they had perceived the original stimulus as not broken. Instead, they had perceived the parts of the rod in the original stimulus as connected to each other (just as adults would). This suggests that some notion of a real physical object exists even at the age of four months (Kellman & Spelke, 1983; Kellman, Spelke, & Short, 1986; but also see Jusczyk, Johnson, Spelke, & Kennedy, 1999; for more on how infants identify the objects in their environment, including the physical object we call a human body, and on how they discern the boundaries of those objects, see, for example, Meltzoff & Moore, 1995; Xu & Carey, 1996).

How much do infants understand about the objects in the world around them? Do they have any knowledge about the physical properties shared by all solid objects? Do they understand, for example, that two objects cannot occupy the same space at the same time?

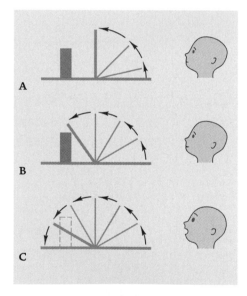

**12.11　Knowing about objects**　*A four-and-a-half-month-old infant is looking at a stage on which he sees an upright box. In front of the box is a screen that initially lies flat and then starts to rotate upward (A). In the first condition (B), the screen stops rotating as soon as it hits the box. In the second condition (C), when the screen is at a point high enough to hide the box, the box is surreptitiously removed and the screen continues to rotate backward. The infant seems to find this quite surprising as shown by the fact that he continues to look at the stage much longer than he did in the first condition.*

To answer these questions, four-and-a-half-month-olds were shown a miniature stage in the middle of which was a box. In front of the box was a screen that was hinged on a rod attached to the stage floor. Initially, that screen was laid flat so that the box behind it was clearly visible, but the screen was then rotated upward like a drawbridge, hiding the box from view (Figure 12.11A). There were two conditions. In one condition, the screen rotated backward until it reached the box, stopped, and then rotated forward again, returning to its initial position (Figure 12.11B). In the other condition, the screen rotated backward until it reached the occluded box and then kept on going as though the box were no longer there. Once it finished the full 180-degree arc, it reversed direction and swiveled all the way forward, at which point the box was revealed again (the box being surreptitiously removed and replaced as required; see Figure 12.11C; Baillargeon, 1987; Baillargeon, Spelke, & Wasserman, 1985).

To adults, the first of these conditions makes perfect physical sense. Since two objects cannot occupy the same space at the same time, the screen necessarily stops when it encounters the box. But the second event is radically different. The box seems to be blocking the screen's path, as the screen rotates backward. Therefore, the screen should not be able to rotate all the way back. When the screen does rotate all the way, it appears to have passed through the box—a physical impossibility.

Do infants react to these events in the same way? The answer seems to be yes. The four-month-olds evidently found the second condition more surprising (and, presumably, more puzzling) than the first condition, just as adults would. This was revealed by the fact that they spent much more time looking at the stage in the second condition than they did in the first. Apparently, these young infants had some notion of object permanence and continued to believe in the box's existence (and its ability to block the motion of other objects) even when it was entirely hidden from view. In addition, young infants evidently do have some notion of the principles that govern objects in space, including the fact that two objects (here, the screen and the box) cannot occupy the same space at the same time.

## THE INFANTS' UNDERSTANDING OF *SUPPORT*

Apparently, infants know more about the world than Piaget gave them credit for. At the same time, though, there are also limits on what infants know, and, correspondingly, there is much intellectual growth during the first year of life. The various situations depicted in Figures 12.12 demonstrate some of these limits. In each case, what will happen if the hand lets go of the red block? According to most adults, the block will drop in the first three situations; only in situation D will the red block maintain its position once it is let go.

Infants believe otherwise. In one study, infants were shown events similar to the ones depicted in Figure 12.12. In some cases, the red block, once it lost its support, fell to the tabletop. In other cases, the experimenters had secretly arranged for a hidden support for the block, and so, when let go, it simply held its position. The question is, which of these outcomes will be surprising to the infant, and which outcomes will simply show the event unfolding as (the infant believes) it should? Surprise in this case is again measured by looking time, on the assumption (supported in many other studies) that infants will look for a longer time at events they find surprising or puzzling, and will look only briefly at events they find ordinary.

The results show a clear developmental trajectory. At the age of three months, infants act as if they believe that any physical contact will provide support. They therefore are surprised if the red block does *not* fall in situation A, but they are surprised if it *does* fall in situation B.

By roughly five months, infants have learned that contact is not by itself enough to provide support. They now know that the support has to be underneath the target object. Therefore, they expect the red block to fall in situation B, but not in situation C.

By roughly six months, infants have learned that the support has to be underneath the target and appropriately positioned, and now their reaction to these displays is similar to that of adults: they expect all the red blocks to fall except for the one in situation D (Baillargeon, 1994; for related data, see, for example, Baillargeon & Wang, 2002; Hespos & Baillargeon, 2001a, 2001b; Needham & Baillargeon, 1993; Spelke, 1999; for a broad review of infants' object knowledge, see Mareschal, 2000).

Thus, we see once again that infants begin to understand the physical world at ages far earlier than Piaget claimed. Even so, infants still have much to learn, and one crucial task for developmental psychologists is to explore how the relevant knowledge is acquired.

## OBJECT PERMANENCE AND THE SEARCH PROCESS

These (and other) results suggest that, by the time the infant is eight or nine months old, she has a reasonable grasp of how the physical world works and, with that, an adequate understanding of what a solid object is. But, in this case, how can we explain Piaget's own findings, findings that led him to conclude that infants lack a concept of

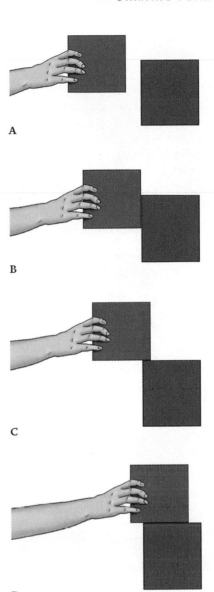

**12.12  Developing a sense of support  Even
very young infants seem to know a lot about the
physical world, but they also have much to
learn. At the age of three months, infants act as
if they believe that any physical contact will
provide support—and so the red block in (B) will
hold its position even if the hand lets go. By
roughly five months, infants have learned that a
support has to be underneath the supported
object. Therefore, they act as if the red block in
(B) will fall if let go, but not the red block in (C).
By roughly six months, infants have learned that
the support has to be appropriately positioned,
and so they expect the red block in (B) or (C) to
fall when let go, but not the red block in (D).**

**12.13** *A dissociation between what the infant knows and what the infant does* *(A) A seven-month-old looks at a toy that has just been placed in B, one of the two wells. (B) He continues to look at well B after both wells are covered. (C) When finally allowed to reach for the toy, he uncovers well A, in which he found the toy on a previous trial, rather than well B, in which he saw the toy being placed. In this particular sequence, he actually still looks at B while uncovering A, suggesting a dissociation between what the infant knows and what he does.*

object permanence? How, in particular, can we explain the fact that an eight- or nine-month-old consistently fails in retrieving objects that are out of sight?

Most modern investigators suggest that—contrary to Piaget—infants do believe that objects continue to exist, even when hidden from view. At the same time, though, infants are exceedingly inept at searching for these objects, and that is why Piaget observed the peculiar failures that he did.

To illustrate this, we can use the A-not-B effect, which (as we have discussed) refers to the infant's tendency to search at a place where he previously found a toy rather than at a place where he has just seen the toy hidden. What accounts for this effect? If the infant has just reached toward *A* several times, then the reaching-toward-*A* response is well primed. To reach toward *B*, therefore, the infant must override this newly acquired habit, and that is the problem. The infant does know where the toy is, but he is unable to inhibit the momentarily potent reach-toward-*A* response. In line with this hypothesis is the fact that many infants look at *B* at the same time that they reach for *A*, as if they knew where the object was but could not tell their arms what they had learned with their eyes (see Figure 12.13; Baillargeon & Graber, 1987).

Some investigators believe that the ability to override a dominant action depends on the maturation of certain areas in the prefrontal cortex, a region just in front of the motor projection area. Evidence comes from studies on monkeys with lesions in this area; they show a pattern very similar to the A-not-B error shown by human infants (A. Diamond, 1988, 1989; A. Diamond & Goldman-Rakic, 1989; also see Zelazo & Frye, 1998; for a somewhat different account of the A-not-B error, see L. B. Smith, Thelen, Titzer, & McLin, 1999).

In short, Piaget was almost certainly mistaken about infants' understanding of object permanence. Young infants do understand that there are objects out in the world and that these objects (and their parts) continue to exist even when out of view. What infants lack is a full understanding of how to deal with those objects—for example, how to find them when they are hidden.

## NUMBER IN INFANCY

Infants also have unexpected competence in other domains. For example, Piaget argued that children younger than six years have little understanding of number. After all, children do not conserve number until then, and so might say (for example) that a row of four buttons, all spread out, has more buttons in it than a row of four bunched closely together. This certainly sounds like they have failed to grasp the concept of numbers.

But more recent experiments have shown that children much younger than six do have some numerical ability. In one study, infants only six months old were shown a series of slides that displayed different sets of objects. The specific items shown varied from one slide to the next, but each slide contained exactly three objects. One slide, for example, might show a comb, a fork, and a sponge; another might show a bottle, a brush, and a toy drum; and so on. Each slide also differed in the spatial arrangement of the items. They might be set up with two on top and one below, or in a vertical column, or with one above and two below.

With all these variables, would the infants be able to detect the one property shared by all the slides—the fact that all contained three items? To find out, the experimenters used the habituation technique. They presented these sets of threes until the infants became bored and stopped looking. Then they presented a series of new slides in which some of the slides showed two items, while others continued to show three. The infants spent more time looking at the slides that displayed two items rather than three. Evidently, the infants were able to step back from all the particulars of the various slides and detect the one abstract property that all the slides had in common. In this regard, at

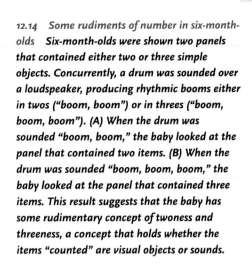

**12.14** *Some rudiments of number in six-month-olds* **Six-month-olds were shown two panels that contained either two or three simple objects. Concurrently, a drum was sounded over a loudspeaker, producing rhythmic booms either in twos ("boom, boom") or in threes ("boom, boom, boom"). (A) When the drum was sounded "boom, boom," the baby looked at the panel that contained two items. (B) When the drum was sounded "boom, boom, boom," the baby looked at the panel that contained three items. This result suggests that the baby has some rudimentary concept of twoness and threeness, a concept that holds whether the items "counted" are visual objects or sounds.**

least, the infants had grasped the concept of "threeness" (Starkey, Spelke, & Gelman, 1983, 1990; for related evidence, see Figure 12.14).

Further studies indicate that these young infants even grasp the rudiments of certain arithmetical relations. For example, infants also have the rudiments of addition. In one study five-month-olds were shown a toy mouse on a small stage. After the infants had looked at this scene for a while, a screen came up from the floor and hid the mouse from view. The infants then saw the experimenter's hand appear from the side, holding another mouse and placing it behind the screen. The final step was the test. The screen was lowered to reveal either one mouse or two. If the infants had some notion of addition, they should expect to see two mice and be surprised to see only one. In fact, this surprise is just what happened. The infants continued to look at the single mouse as if wondering why the other one was not there. Analogous results were found in a pint-sized subtraction task in which the experimenter presented two mice at first and then took one away. Here, the infants looked longer when they saw two mice as if surprised that none had been removed (Wynn, 1992, 1995).

Investigators have a range of views on just what it is that young infants know about numbers and arithmetic relations (Butterworth, 1999; Clearfield & Mix, 1999; Gallistel & Gelman, 2000; Spelke, 2000). Across all of these views, though, it is clear that even young infants do grasp some of the fundamental principles on which arithmetic is based, and so, once again, have a competence that is neither revealed by Piaget's own tasks nor reflected in his theory.

## SOCIAL COGNITION IN INFANCY:
## THE EXISTENCE OF OTHER MINDS

The social world provides yet another domain in which young children are surprisingly competent. It is certainly true that much of what we know about other individuals is acquired through learning, and it is self-evident that a three-year-old's capacity for getting along with others is less sophisticated than that of a nine-year-old, which is in turn less sophisticated than that of an eighteen-year-old. But there is reason to believe that this development begins with knowledge and skills that are detectable at a very young age, and may even be innate.

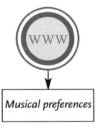

Musical preferences

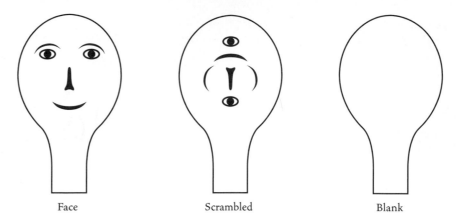

**12.15    Rudimentary face recognition in newborns    Newborn babies look longer at a pattern showing a schematic face than at a scrambled or a blank pattern.**

Face          Scrambled          Blank

## INFANTS RESPOND TO FACES

Infants come into the world with a built-in predisposition to look at human faces. In one study of newborns just a few minutes old, the experimenter moved several patterns in front of the child's eyes. The infants turned their heads and looked longer at the pattern when it was of a schematic rather than a scrambled face (Goren, Sarty, & Wu, 1975; M. H. Johnson, 1993; see Figure 12.15).

Infants do more than look at faces; they also imitate them. In an extraordinary study, investigators sat face to face with infants less than twenty-one days old and made faces at them. The investigators stuck out their tongues at the infants or opened their mouths as wide as possible. How would the infants respond? Careful scrutiny of the infants' faces showed that infants responded by imitation. When the investigators stuck out their tongues, the infants did too. When the investigators' mouths gaped wide open, so did the babies' (Meltzoff & Moore, 1977; Figure 12.16). Clearly, therefore, human babies within the first month of life are attuned to and responsive to faces.

The imitation observed in this experiment is actually quite impressive. The infants have no way of observing their own faces, nor do they have a history, in their first days of life, of sitting at a mirror, practicing their facial movements. It seems, therefore, that infants are born with a capacity to translate the facial expressions they see (in the inves-

**12.16    Imitation in neonates    In a remarkable study, investigators sat face-to-face with infants just a few days old. When the investigators stuck out their tongues, the infants did the same. When the investigators opened their mouths wide, or pursed their lips, the infants did too. The capacity for imitation, it seems, is in place even for very young babies!**

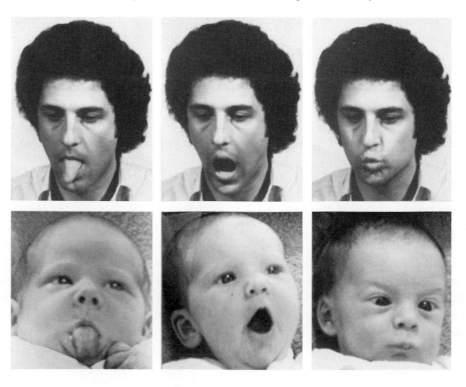

tigators) into muscle movements that will produce a comparable expression on their own faces. This is by itself remarkable in what it reveals about a baby's ability to intercoordinate sensory information and motor actions. That to the side, though, the fact of imitation makes it clear that, from birth, infants are ready to begin one kind of nonverbal communication—a first but crucial step on the path toward social competence (Meltzoff & Moore, 1998; but also see S. S. Jones, 1996).

## A SHARED WORLD

Infants also seem to recognize rather early that others live in the same physical world that they do, and so can see more or less what they see, hear what they hear, and so on. This is revealed by work on shared attention. For example, nine-month-olds tend to look in the direction of their mothers' gaze (Scaife & Bruner, 1975). And soon this capacity expands. In one study, infants between twelve and eighteen months old were held in their mothers' laps while the mothers looked at a particular toy. But while the mothers looked toward the toy, the children were held with their heads facing their mothers, so that they could not see the target of the mothers' gaze. All they could see were their mothers' eyes. Evidently, that was enough—as soon as the mothers loosened their hold, the infants squirmed around and looked at just the toy the mothers had looked at a moment before (Butterworth & Cochran, 1980; Butterworth & Jarrett, 1991).

As a related point, infants also seem to understand the world they observe in terms of others' goals, and not just their actions. In one study, six-month-old infants saw an actor reach for, say, a ball that was sitting just to the left of a teddy bear. (The left-right position of the toys was reversed for half of the infants tested.) The infant watched this event over and over, until she became bored with it. At that point, the position of the toys was switched, so now the teddy bear was on the left. Then the infant was shown one of two test events. In one, the actor again reached for the ball (although, given the switch in position, this was the first time the infant has seen a reach toward the right). In the other condition, the actor again reached for the object on the left (although, given the switch, this was the first time the infant has seen a reach toward the bear).

If, in the initial observation, the infant was focusing on behavior ("reach left"), then the reach-for-ball test event involves a change, and so will be a surprise. If, however, the infant was focusing on the goal ("reach for ball"), then it is the reach for the teddy bear that involves a change, and will be a surprise. And, in fact, the latter is what the data show: six-month-olds are more surprised by the change in goal than they are by the change in behavior (A. L. Woodward, 1998). Apparently, and contrary to Piaget, they understand that the object reached for is separate from the reach itself, and they are sophisticated enough in perceiving others' actions that they understand the actions in terms of their intended goals and not merely in terms of their physical movements. (For still other evidence making it clear that young children are sensitive to others' intentions, desires, and emotions, see Meltzoff, 1995; Meltzoff, Gopnik, & Repacholi, 1999.)

# COGNITIVE DEVELOPMENT IN PRESCHOOLERS

Overall, infants know and understand much more than Piaget realized. But what about the process of development from then on? Central to Piaget's conception is the idea that cognitive development goes through several qualitatively distinct stages. Is this view correct? No one doubts that there is mental growth and that children change in the way they think as they get older. But is this growth best described as a progression through successive stages?

## THE MEANING OF MENTAL STAGE

Piaget used the term *stage* in the same way that the term is used in embryology. Embryological stages tend to be discrete rather than continuous. The difference between a tadpole and a frog, for example, is not just a matter of "more this" or "less that." Instead, there is a qualitative difference between the two, with different breathing mechanisms, different food needs, and so on. To be sure, the change from one to the other takes a while, but by the time the creature is a frog, its tadpole days are emphatically over.

Piaget claimed that the same discontinuities characterize cognitive development, such that the cognitive capacities that mark one period of development are completely absent at prior periods. Is this correct? In the case of conservation of quantity or number, the stage hypothesis implies that the capacity to conserve should be totally absent at an early age—say, five years and younger—and then emerge virtually full blown when the curtain finally opens on the next act of the developmental drama—namely, the period of concrete operations.

Many modern investigators disagree with this claim and deny that cognitive development occurs in such all-or-none steps. As they see it, cognitive achievements such as conservation have primitive precursors that appear several years earlier than the Piagetian calendar would predict. If we identify these precursors and chart their development, we will see that children's growth is far more gradual than Piaget envisioned. As a result, the contrast between six-year-olds and four-year-olds, or between ten-year-olds and five-year-olds, may be less dramatic than Piaget believed (Gelman, 1978; Gelman & Baillargeon, 1983).

As illustrations, we will consider two areas of cognitive growth during the preschool period—number and social cognition—from the perspective of some of these modern investigators.

## NUMERICAL SKILLS IN PRESCHOOLERS

We have seen that infants can abstract the properties of twoness and threeness, and we have suggested that this provides the starting point for the development of numerical abilities. What happens in the years following infancy?

### COUNTING

Some precursors of the skill of counting appear as early as two and a half years. At this age, children may not know the conventional sequence of number terms, but they have grasped the idea of what the counting process is all about. Thus, one two-year-old consistently counted "one, two, six," and another used "one, thirteen, nineteen." But what is important is that they used these series consistently and realized that each of these number tags has to be applied to just one object in the to-be-counted set. They also realized that the tags must always be used in the same order and that the last number applied is the number of items in the set. Thus, the child who counted "one, thirteen, nineteen" confidently asserted that there were thirteen items when he counted a two-item set, and nineteen items when he counted a three-item set. This child is obviously not using the adult's terms but surely does seem to have mastered some of the key ideas on which counting rests (Gallistel & Gelman, 2000; Gelman & Gallistel, 1978).

### NUMERICAL REASONING

A child who can count has taken a big step, but there is more to numerical understanding than counting. The child must also grasp some principles of numerical reasoning—

the ideas of "more than" and "less than," simple principles of arithmetic, and so on. Preschoolers gradually acquire these conceptual basics. When comparing two sets of items, for example, if the number of items is small enough, three- and four-year-olds can correctly point to the set that is smaller or larger (Gelman, 1982; Gelman & Gallistel, 1978).

If preschool children have these skills, then why do they fail the Piagetian tests for conservation of number? We have already described the standard Piagetian finding: when preschoolers are asked to compare two rows, each containing, say, four toy ducks, they often say that the longer row contains more ducks, in an apparent confusion of length and number. How can we reconcile this with the demonstrations of the preschooler's numerical competence?

In part, the problem may lie in how the children were questioned in Piaget's studies. In these procedures, the child is typically questioned twice. First, the two rows of items are presented in an evenly spaced manner, so that both rows are the same length. When asked, "Which row has more or do they both have the same?" the child quickly answers "The same!" Now the experimenter changes the length of one of the rows—perhaps spreading the items out a bit more or pushing them more closely together—and asks again, "Which row has more or do they both have the same?"

Why is the same question being asked again? From the point of view of the child, this may imply that the experimenter did not like his first answer and so, as adults often do, is providing him the opportunity to try again. This would obviously suggest to the child that his first answer must have been wrong, and so he changes it.

Of course, this misinterpretation is possible only because the child is not totally sure of his answer. Hence, he is easily swayed by this subtle hint from the experimenter. However, if the number of items in the row is small enough, the child will not be confused and so will resist the hint. And with small numbers of items, children do show evidence of conserving at appreciably younger ages (M. Siegal, 1997).

Thus, here, as in other cognitive realms, the achievements of later periods are built on foundations established much earlier. If we look carefully enough, we see that the accomplishments of the concrete-operational period do not come out of the blue but have preludes in much earlier childhood years. Thus, it would seem that there is more continuity in development than Piaget asserted, with no neat demarcations between stages and no sharp transitions. The stages of cognitive development are not as all-or-none as the changes from tadpole to frog (let alone from frog to prince).

## SOCIAL COGNITION IN PRESCHOOLERS: DEVELOPING A THEORY OF MIND

Similar conclusions emerge when we consider other aspects of early development, including the development of a child's understanding of the social world.

Much of the recent discussion has focused on what some theorists call the child's *theory of mind*. In general, this term refers to the set of interrelated concepts and beliefs that we all employ whenever we try to make sense of our own behavior or that of others (Fodor, 1992; Leslie, 1992; D. Premack & Woodruff, 1978; Wellman, 1990).

An adult's theory of mind has many elements. Each of us knows that other people have beliefs, that their beliefs may be true or false, and that their beliefs may differ from our own, which may also be true or false. We know that other people have desires and that these desires may also differ from our own. We also know that other people sometimes know things that we do not and that we sometimes know things that they do not.

These beliefs may not sound complex or profound, but they are an essential resource for us all, providing a crucial knowledge base that we rely on in virtually all of our day-to-day social functioning. It is these beliefs that allow us to understand the behavior of

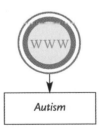

Autism

other people and, within certain limits, to predict how people will behave in the future. Without these beliefs—that is, without a theory of mind—we would be bewildered by much of the action going on around us and incapable of acting appropriately in most social situations.

## EGOCENTRISM REVISITED

What about children? Do they have a theory of mind? Do they have any understanding of the actions (or thoughts) of other individuals?

If tested in the right way, even very young children reveal some of this understanding. For example, if two-year-old Mario is told that Lisa wants a cookie, then he will correctly predict that Lisa will look for a cookie and that she will be happy if she finds one (see, for example, Wellman & Wooley, 1990). These are hardly earth-shaking insights into Lisa's actions, but they do indicate that the toddler is beginning to understand why other people do the things they do and feel the things they feel.

In the same fashion, in one study eighteen-month-olds watched as experimenters made "yuk" faces after tasting one food and smiled broadly after tasting another. The experimenters then made a general request to these toddlers for food, and the children responded appropriately—offering the food that the experimenter preferred, even if the children themselves preferred the other food. Here, too, we see indications that young children understand both the relationship between desires and actions and the crucial fact that other people have desires different from their own (Repacholi & Gopnik, 1997; for more on the child's theory of mind, see Gopnik & Meltzoff, 1997).

## TRUE AND FALSE BELIEFS

The child's task becomes more difficult when it comes to beliefs. Suppose you tell three-year-old Alicia that Johnny wants to play with his puppy. You also tell her that Johnny thinks the puppy is under the piano. If Alicia is now asked where Johnny will look, she will sensibly say that he will look under the piano (Wellman & Bartsch, 1988). Like an adult, a three-year-old understands that a person's actions depend not just on what she sees and desires, but also on what she believes.

But does the three-year-old truly understand the concept of belief? In fact, it is easy to find striking limitations on the child's understanding. Some limitations concern the child's understanding of how beliefs come to be. If asked what color an object is, for example, three-year-olds believe they can find out just as easily by touching an object as they can by looking at it (O'Neill, Astington, & Flavell, 1992). Four-year-olds will confidently assert that they have always known something even if they first learned it from the experimenter just moments earlier (Taylor, Esbensen, and Bennett, 1994).

Other limitations in the child's understanding concern false beliefs, and, according to many authors, a three-year-old does not understand the simple facts that beliefs can be true or false and that different people can have different beliefs. This suggests that there is something seriously lacking in the three-year-old's theory of mind.

Evidence for this comes from studies using false-belief tests (Dennett, 1978; Wimmer & Perner, 1983; also Lang & Perner, 2002). In a typical study of this kind, a child and a teddy bear sit in front of two boxes, one red and the other green. The experimenter opens the red box and puts some candy in it. She then opens the green box and shows the child—and the teddy—that this box is empty. The teddy bear is now taken out of the room (to play for a while), and the experimenter and the child move the candy from the red box into the green one. Next comes the crucial step: the teddy bear is brought back into the room, and the child is asked, "Where will the teddy look for the candy?" Virtually all three-year-olds and some four-year-olds will answer, "In the green box." If you ask them why, they will answer, "Because that's where it is." It would appear, then, that these children do not really understand the nature of belief. They seem to assume that their beliefs are inevitably shared by others, and likewise, they seem not to appreciate that others might have beliefs that are false (see Figure 12.17).

However, by age four and a half or so, children get the idea. Now if they are asked, "Where will the teddy look for the candy?" they will answer, "He'll look in the red box because that's where he thinks the candy is" (Wellman, 1990; Wimmer & Perner, 1983). The children have now learned that not all knowledge is shared, that different individuals have different beliefs, and that which beliefs one will have depends on appropriate access to the relevant information.

## OTHER DOMAINS OF COMPETENCE

Apparently, young children do know something about the beliefs and desires of other individuals. But is it sensible to speak of a three- or four-year-old as having a theory of mind? Many authors believe it is. A scientist uses a theory to account for evidence and to predict new findings. The child's theory does the same. In a scientist's theory, the various specific claims are all interrelated, and this, too, is a trait of the child's theory of mind: the child cannot understand how belief influences action unless she also understands what belief is; she cannot truly understand what a belief is without realizing that false beliefs are possible; and so on. Finally, the scientist's theory has a specific domain of application: Einstein's theory of relativity tells us a great deal about space and time but tells us nothing about how to make a really good pizza. Likewise for the child's theory: a theory of mind helps the child understand the behavior of others but is of little use in helping her solve an arithmetic problem or find her way through the mall.

These parallels seem to justify using the term *theory* when describing the child's theory of mind. But, in addition, the notion of a theory's limited domain invites a question: do young children have other theories that help them make sense of other aspects of their experience? The evidence suggests that they do. For example, children seem to have a set of interrelated beliefs about biological functioning that provide the basis for their thinking about sickness and health, birth and death (Wellman & Gelman, 1992). These same beliefs also guide children's thinking about more mundane topics, such as parental instructions concerning good nutrition ("Eat your spinach").

## THE BIOLOGICAL ROOTS OF THEORY OF MIND

Several investigators have argued that the child's theory of mind has a special status. As humans evolved, they argue, it would have been advantageous to be able to predict the actions of other people or, in some settings, to direct the actions of others. As a result, natural selection would have favored anyone with these capacities, leading to the emergence of a "social cognition module" in our brains (Byrne & Whiten, 1988; Cosmides & Tooby, 1992; Hughes & Cutting, 1999; for a broad review, see Gopnik, 1999).

Several pieces of evidence fit well with this perspective, including the fact that certain forms of brain damage seem to cause impairments specifically to someone's theory of mind, suggesting a biological base for this processing module (see, for example, Happé, Brownell, & Winner, 1999; but also see Frith & Frith, 1999; Frye, Zelazo, & Burack, 1998; Hughes & Cutting, 1999; Perner & Lang, 1999; Rowe, Bullock, Polkey, & Morris, 2001).

What might be contained within this biologically rooted module? The content cannot be too specific, since people in different cultures make very different assumptions about the mind and about the forces that drive human behavior (Lillard, 1997). If we are born with a social cognition module, it cannot specify particular beliefs. (If it did, these beliefs would presumably be shared by all in our species.) Perhaps instead the module consists of a sophisticated set of learning strategies, cognitive tools that allow children at a very young age to construct a theory of mind appropriate for the culture

**12.17 The false-belief test** **(A) The child watches as the experimenter makes the teddy bear "hide" the ball in the oatmeal container. (B) While the teddy bear is gone, the experimenter and the child move the ball to the box. (C) When the child is now asked, "Where does the teddy bear think the ball is?" she points to the box.**

in which they are raised. In this way, the module would resemble the innate capacity for language learning (see Chapter 9), a capacity that is shared by all humans but that allows each of us to learn the specific dialect spoken in the community in which we grow up.

## SEQUENCE OR STAGES?

Where does all of this leave us with regard to Piaget's overall theory and, more specifically, with regard to his claim that cognitive development proceeds through a series of discrete stages? The evidence we have considered suggests that the mental growth of children does not proceed as neatly as a simple stage theory might lead one to expect. In case after case, we have seen children displaying competences that—according to Piaget—should not arrive until many months later, when the child enters the next stage of development. We have also seen evidence, in several different arenas, of developmental continuity, with later achievements growing out of earlier precursors. Piaget's theory, in contrast, would have led us to expect discontinuity, with the skills and capacities of, say, the preoperational child markedly different from those of a sensorimotor child.

Does this mean that Piaget's cognitive milestones have no psychological reality? Certainly not. Consider the difference between a preschool child and a seven-year-old. The younger child can tell the difference between two and three mice regardless of how they are spaced on the table, and in this fashion seems to be conserving number. But he has not yet grasped the underlying idea that number and spatial arrangement are entirely independent of each other and that this is so for all numbers and for all spatial arrangements. As a result, the preschooler will fail a slightly more difficult test for conservation of number in which he must recognize that two rows of, say, nine buttons each contain the same number of buttons, regardless of how the rows are expanded or compressed.

The seven-year-old, in contrast, has no such problem. She can count higher, but that is not the issue. She knows that there is no need to count, because she is confidently aware of the fact that a change in the buttons' arrangement will not change their number. As a result, she can conserve number in general.

Similarly, a preschooler can be drawn away from conserving by subtle hints that (misleadingly) suggest his initial answer was mistaken. The seven-year-old is immune to such hints, because she knows securely and confidently what the proper answer is to the experimenter's questions.

Thus, there are both similarities between younger children and older ones and also important differences. On the one side, it is probably a mistake to speak of toddlers as thinking in a fashion completely different from the way infants think, or preschoolers as completely different from toddlers. Of course, children do gain new skills and capacities as they grow, and, with that, they can master at each age tasks that were hopelessly out of their reach a few months earlier. However, this development probably does not involve the abrupt arrival of wholly new ways of dealing with the world. Instead, a close scrutiny of development at early ages shows us precursors and primitive forms of each capacity and then a gradual growth in the sophistication and fluency of that capacity.

At the same time, however, there are times in a child's life when emerging capacities do allow dramatic leaps forward. The child's understanding of number, for example, or the social world grows slowly and steadily, but it eventually reaches a sophistication that allows the child to use her understanding in a much wider range of settings, and allows her to handle a spectrum of challenges that were simply inaccessible at an earlier age. Hand in hand with that, the gradual growth in the child's skills eventually brings the child to a point where she can use her knowledge spontaneously, without an adult's explicit hints, guides, or support. It is these substantial steps forward—in the ability to apply capacities spontaneously and more broadly—that mark the powerful transitions that we can observe roughly at age two, and roughly at age four or five, and then roughly at age eight or nine. In the end, therefore, Piaget may well have been correct in identifying these as crucial transition ages in the life of the child, even if his emphasis on qualitative change was inappropriate as a way of characterizing these transitions.

# THE CAUSES OF COGNITIVE GROWTH

We have now said a lot to describe cognitive development as it proceeds from early infancy into the school years. But what explains these changes? Piaget was surely correct in arguing that cognitive development is massively influenced by the child's experiences, including both what the child sees and what the child does. Piaget's view also reminds us that the child's experiences are "filtered" through the skills and capacities that the child has at that point; in Piaget's terms, the child experiences the world only through his cognitive schemas. Thus, the meaning and importance of an experience can be very different for a two-year-old and for a fourth-grader, and lessons easily learned at one age are inaccessible at other points.

At the same time, it is also clear that Piaget's account leaves a great deal unsaid, and we turn next to some of the elements that must be added to our theorizing if we are to account for the child's development.

## THE ROLE OF BIOLOGICAL INHERITANCE

Piaget believed that the infant begins life with relatively few skills or abilities. The newborn, he argued, has a small set of reflexes (sucking, grasping), and it is from this narrow base that the child develops his full range of cognitive capacities. Evidence collected in the last few decades, however, has made it clear that this view understates the role of biological inheritance, so that, in order to understand cognitive development more fully, we need to pay more attention to the rich interplay between the child's experience and his innate capacities.

In our discussion so far, we have seen three types of evidence supporting this claim. First, we have seen that genetic factors play a large role in shaping one's abilities, so that, for example, people who resemble each other genetically are likely to end up resembling each other in their verbal skills (pp. 472–473, also see Chapter 14). This is, of course, a powerful argument that the development of our intellectual capacities is shaped by our inherited biology.

Second, we have also mentioned the fact that certain cognitive capacities seem tied to particular neural structures, and so damage to those structures causes specific cognitive deficits. These points were prominent in our discussion of language (see Chapter 9) and came up again in our discussion of the child's theory of mind. This, too, strongly indicates that the functioning and development of some of our cognitive skills must be understood with reference to the relevant aspects of the nervous system.

Third and finally, we have seen indications of some cognitive skills in place early enough in the child's life so that it is simply implausible that the child has had enough time and enough experience to learn these skills. This pattern suggests that these capacities are not derived from experience, and so must be innate.

What are the candidates for these innate capacities? This is still a matter of debate (see, for example, Hespos & Baillargeon, 2001; Spelke, 1994; Spelke & Newport, 1998). Even so, the available evidence has persuaded most investigators that future theorizing must do more to consider the interaction between innate capacities and the child's ongoing experience.

# THE CULTURAL CONTEXT OF DEVELOPMENT

Many investigators, therefore, believe that Piaget understated the role for innate capacities and, more broadly, the biological influences that guide who we are and what we become. Other investigators believe that Piaget may have neglected another crucial factor: the cultural environment in which a child grows up.

Piaget intended his theory to apply to all children in all settings. His data collection, though, had a much narrower focus. Many of Piaget's claims were based, in fact, on observations of his own three children. Later research broadened this base considerably, but, even so, most research has considered children growing up in the Western world.

This raises two questions. First, is the pattern of development different in different cultures, or, within a culture, in different social groups? Second, and more important, what role does the social and cultural environment play in shaping development? Piaget focused largely on the child herself—what she did, what she knew, what she learned. To what extent is our view of development altered if we focus instead on the child together with the other people (peers and adults) who provide her social surroundings?

## DIFFERENCES IN COMPETENCE?

In many regards, mental growth seems rather similar in children of different cultures and nationalities. The age at which various abilities emerge does vary somewhat from culture to culture, as does the sequence with which abilities emerge (see, for example, Mwamwenda, 1992). Even with these variations, however, children in diverse cultures seem to pass the major developmental landmarks identified by Piaget in essentially the same order, and make the same errors on route to these landmarks (Greenfield, 1966; Hyde, 1959; Nyiti, 1976).

We can, of course, find differences from one culture to the next, but, even here, there is some uniformity underneath this (apparent) diversity. For example, we have mentioned that children in different cultures have different ideas about why the people around them are behaving as they are; in other words, children in different cultures may have different theories of mind. However, as we noted earlier, this is compatible with arguing that all children share a biologically rooted capacity to acquire a theory of mind, allowing rapid acquisition of this important intellectual tool.

In other regards, though, cultures do seem to differ in their patterns of cognitive development. In the West, for example, most adolescents pass through the stage of concrete operations and into the stage of formal operations. But in some cultures (for example, that of Australian aborigines and of New Guinea tribesfolk), many adults fail the standard tests of formal operations. In fact, evidence of formal operations using standard tests is rare in cultures in which there is no formal schooling (Hollos & Richards, 1993; Segall, Dasen, Berry, & Poortinga, 1999). In such cultures, most adults seem unable to deal with certain abstract problems, including problems of syllogistic reasoning. Thus, unschooled Kpelle farmers in Liberia were informed that "all Kpelle men are rice farmers. Mr. Smith is not a rice farmer." When asked, "Is Mr. Smith a Kpelle man?" they would typically fail to give the simple syllogistic "no." Instead, they would be noncommittal: "If I know him in person, I can answer that question, but since I do not know him in person, I cannot answer that question" (Scribner, 1975, p. 175).

*Navigation skill*  **Master navigator Mau Piailug teaches navigation to his son and grandson with the help of a star compass consisting of a ring of stones, each stone representing a star or a constellation when it rises or sets on the horizon. The pieces of palm leaf represent the swells which travel from set directions, and so provide further navigational information.**

However, other evidence makes it clear that these same preliterate peoples are capable of complex, sophisticated reasoning within the context of their own lives. One example is provided by Polynesian sailors who reveal extraordinary skills of mental calculation in navigating their boats from one island to the next (Gladwin, 1970). Another comes from the !Kung San hunter-gatherers of the Kalahari desert, who perform remarkable feats of inference while hunting game: weighing the chances of tracking down a wounded giraffe against the cost of a drawn-out search, searching for clues in the pattern of crushed grasses, judging whether blood fell on a twig before or after the twig was bent, and evaluating the various interpretations to decide on a course of action (Blurton-Jones & Konner, 1976).

## THE CULTURAL CONTEXT OF TESTING

The data just described create a dilemma. According to our tests, the Kpelle people in Liberia (and many other preliterate peoples) are incapable of formal reasoning. Yet, when we consider what these people do routinely in their daily lives, it is clear that they are capable of sophisticated reasoning. How can we reconcile these observations?

One possibility is that our tests, designed for Western participants, are simply inappropriate in these other cultures. What could make a test inappropriate? For one thing, it should not rely on knowledge or vocabulary available only to one group, and, indeed, this is crucial whether we are testing children in remote areas of the Sahara or in a poor inner-city neighborhood in the United States. (For discussion on how this concern applies to IQ testing in different groups, see Chapter 14.)

Tests can also be inappropriate for a social or cultural group for relatively subtle reasons, including the group's assumptions about what things are important and what are not. For example, one investigator asked unschooled Kpelle participants to sort a collection of objects into groups. Some of the objects were tools and others were foods. Western participants generally use these semantic categories as the basis for their grouping. However, the Kpelle participants sorted the objects by function—a knife with an orange, a hoe with a potato, and so on. Asked why they sorted the objects as they did, they replied, "That is the way a wise man would do it." When the experimenter asked, "How would a fool do it?" he received the response that he had originally looked for—food in one pile and tools in another (Glick, 1975). Thus, the participants obviously were capable of grouping by categories; this simply was not the grouping scheme they deemed most useful.

In addition, it is important to consider what our tests and experiments look like from the point of view of the people being tested. In many tests, it is clear that the investigator already knows the answers to his own questions but is asking the questions anyhow to find out what the person being tested knows. This is a familiar situation for any Western school child—one re-created whenever a teacher gives a test. For people in other cultures, though, this may be an unusual and puzzling situation. The Wolof people of coastal Senegal, for example, rarely ask each other questions to which they already know the answer; when this kind of questioning does occur, it is likely to be understood as "an aggressive challenge, or a riddle with a trick answer" (Irvine, 1978, p. 309). This would obviously put the Wolof at a disadvantage in our tests. (For further discussion of the social relationship between the investigator and the person being tested, see Rogoff, 1998.)

## SOCIAL AND CULTURAL INFLUENCES ON DEVELOPMENT

Clearly, therefore, we must be alert to the cultural backdrop whenever we design our studies and when we are trying to interpret the available evidence. Many investigators, however, believe that our consideration of the sociocultural context needs to go much further than this. Culture is not merely a "filter," coloring how a research participant understands the study and coloring how we should understand the data. More important, culture is an active and powerful influence on development, shaping what and how the child learns.

Some cultural influences on development are obvious. In ancient Rome, educated children learned to represent numbers with Roman numerals; modern children in the West, in contrast, learn to represent numbers with Arabic numerals. Modern children in the Oksapmim culture (in New Guinea) learn yet a different system, counting using parts of the body rather than a number system (Saxe, 1981). In each case, this culturally provided tool guides (and in some cases, limits) how the children think about and work with numerical quantities.

Related examples are easy to find. Some social and cultural settings involve formal schooling, but others do not, and schooling is a powerful influence on the child's development. (For some comparisons of schooled and unschooled children, see Christian, Bachman, & Morrison, 2000; Segall et al., 1999.) Cultures also differ in what activities children are exposed to, in how frequently these activities occur, and in what the children's role is in the activity. These factors play an important part in determining what skills—intellectual and motor—the children will gain, and the level of skill they will attain (M. Cole & Cole, 2001; Laboratory of Comparative Human Cognition, 1983; Rogoff, 1998, 2000). It is no surprise, therefore, that children in Norway often grow up to be good skiers, and that children growing up in the Kalahari become skilled in tracking wildebeest or locating edible desert plants. These differences would, of course, be difficult to understand without a consideration of the social and cultural context in which the child is developing.

## THE CHILD'S ROLE IN SHAPING THE IMPACT OF CULTURE

Other cultural influences on cognition are less obvious and involve social interactions between the child and her caregivers, or interactions with peers. In these interactions, the child learns a great deal about how others perform tasks or solve problems; the child also learns how to collaborate with others in performing intellectual tasks.

In understanding these interactions, though, it is important to remember that the child is not a passive recipient of social and cultural influences. Instead, the child plays a key role in selecting, shaping, and, in some cases, creating the input provided by the social or cultural setting. Part of the child's role is defined by what Lev Vygotsky (1978) called the *zone of proximal development*. This term refers to the range of accomplishments that are beyond what the child could do on her own, but that are possible if the child is given help or guidance. Attentive caregivers or teachers structure their input to keep the child's performance within this zone, and, importantly, the child herself provides feedback to those around her that helps maintain this level of guidance.

The child's active role is especially visible when processes of learning or problem solving involve the shared efforts of two or more people (after Rogoff, 1998). In such cases, it is clear that we cannot understand development if we focus either on the child or on the cultural context; instead, we must understand the interaction of the two and how each shapes the other.

One example is seen in the child's capacity for remembering life events. One might think that this capacity depends entirely on processes and resources inside of the individual, with little room for social influence. Evidence suggests, however, that the capacity for remembering events grows in part out of conversations in which adults help children to report on events they have experienced. When the child is quite young, these conversations tend to be one-sided, with the parent doing most of the work of describing the remembered event, with little input from the child. ("Remember when we went to see Grandma, and she gave you a teddy bear?") As the child's capacities grow, however, the parent retreats to a narrower role, first asking specific questions to guide the child's report ("Did you see any elephants at the zoo?"), then, at a later age, asking only broader questions ("What happened in school today?"), and, eventually, merely becoming a listener as the child narrates the earlier episode. Across this process, the specific questions asked, the sequence of questions, and the level of detail all provide enormously useful guidance to the child as she figures out what is worth reporting in an event and, for that matter, what is worth paying attention to while the event is unfolding (Fivush, 1998; Nelson & Fivush, 2000; Peterson & McCabe, 1994).

The specific questions a child hears can also have another consequence: these often-detailed questions make it relatively easy for an adult questioner to shape the child's report, inadvertently leading the child in some cases to "remember" events that never occurred. For this reason, considerable care is needed to obtain a full and accurate memory report from a young child. Questions that are too general may elicit no information at all; questions that are too specific can shape (or distort) the child's report. These facts are obviously of great importance in many settings, but especially so in court cases involving child testimony, and, for that reason, the topic of child memory has been an area of intense research in recent years (Bruck & Ceci, 1999; Bruck, Ceci, & Hembrooke, 1998; Fivush & Sales, 2003; Goodman & Schaaf, 1997; for more on the effects of leading questions, see Chapter 7).

Of course, not all parents talk to their children in the same way. Some parents tend to elaborate on what their children have said; some simply repeat the child's comments (Reese & Fivush, 1993). Parents also talk about events differently with their daughters than they do with their sons (see, for example, Fivush, Brotman, Buckner, & Goodman, 2000). Similarly, Mexican Americans and Anglo-Americans differ in how they converse with their children and in what they converse about; there are also differences in adult-child conversations if we compare working-class and middle-class parents (see, for example, Eisenberg, 1999).

*The impact of culture*   *A young child watches as a man prepares meat to be boiled on a campfire in Etengwa, Namibia.*

In each case, these differences in conversational pattern have an impact on what the child remembers and how the child structures his or her memory. As one example, evidence suggests that American mothers talk with their children about past events much more than Asian mothers do (Mullen & Yi, 1995). These conversations may help American children to start organizing their autobiographical recall at an earlier age than Asian children, and, consistent with this suggestion, when Caucasian adults are asked to report their earliest childhood memories, they tend to remember events earlier in life than do Asian adults (Mullen, 1994).

These conversational patterns, then, provide a clear example of how the cultural and social surround can shape the child's developing capacities. It is important to remember, though, that these conversations about past events are conversations, with the child participating as one of the conversational partners. Therefore, how the conversation unfolds depends on the child's contribution just as it does on the parent. This makes it clear that we cannot focus on the culture alone, asking how culture shapes cognition. Instead, we need to understand how the influence of culture shapes and is shaped by the child, understanding the child as a full collaborator in the learning process.

## THE INFORMATION-PROCESSING APPROACH

Thanks to the joint impact of cultural influences, biological predispositions, and the child's own activity and experience, the child develops, gaining skills and capabilities at each age that move him well beyond what he could do at any earlier age. Piaget described this development in terms of a gradual refinement and differentiation of schemas, but most contemporary psychologists prefer a different formulation.

In Chapters 7 and 8, we discussed adult thinking and reasoning in terms of certain cognitive resources: the ability to pay attention, the capacity to remember, to reason, to make judgments, and so on. These are the capacities one would emphasize in taking an *information-processing approach*, an approach that broadly compares human cognitive functioning to the complex ways that a computer functions. Can this approach be useful in understanding cognitive development? Many investigators think it is.

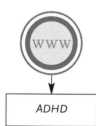

Investigators inclined toward this perspective have examined many aspects of children's information-processing capacities, including the young child's ability to pay attention (see, for example, Colombo, 2001) and the development of the ability to solve problems (see, for example, Case & Okamoto, 1996; Siegler, 1996). Let us look briefly at a sample of this work, focusing on the young children's ability to remember and their capacities at using strategies.

### THE DEVELOPMENT OF MEMORY

*Memory in Infancy*  We have already mentioned some of the social influences on what and how a child remembers, but it is clear that these social influences must build on the child's initial capacities. What are these capacities, and how do they develop? As one step toward addressing this question, we might ask about very young children, including infants. How well, and for how long, can infants remember? In one series of experiments, a string was loosely tied to the leg of a three-month-old; whenever the infant kicked, this tugged on the string and set off the movement of an overhead mobile. The infant quickly learned this contingency and happily kicked at every opportunity. Two weeks later, the infant returned to the laboratory, and the mere sight of the mobile was enough to make him kick. Even after two months, the infant still remembered this earlier experience, especially if the experimenter provided a small reminder, by jiggling the mobile just a bit (Rovee-Collier, 1990, 1999; Rovee-Collier & Gerhardstein, 1997; Rovee-Collier & Hayne, 1987).

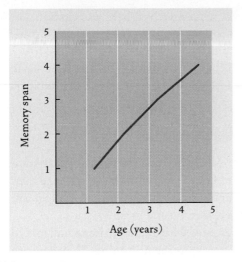

*12.18 Memory span in young children*

Memory span (y-axis), Age (years) (x-axis)

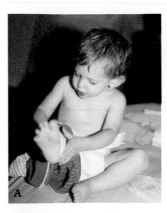

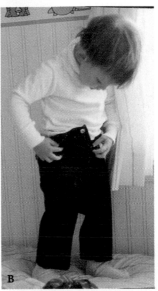

Such findings show that infants can retain experiences over time. The remembering may be of a simple sort, but it serves as the foundation on which later development builds.

*Memory in Early Childhood* By the time the child becomes a toddler, her memory prowess is much increased but still limited in comparison to an adult's. For example, the capacity of the child's working memory seems relatively small. Often, this capacity is measured with a memory-span task, which determines how many items the participant can remember after just one presentation. This number is roughly one item at eighteen months, three at three and a half years, and four at four and a half years, compared to a span of seven (plus or minus two) in adulthood (see Figure 12.18).

## THE CHILD AS NOVICE

The increase in the child's working-memory span is, to a large extent, a matter of maturation: as children's brains grow, so does their memory capacity. But the inability of children to report what they remember also reflects the fact that children know relatively little about the world. For them, everything is new, and so they have no way of knowing which aspects of an event are unusual and which are quite common, which are worthy of notice and which can be taken for granted.

As we have discussed, conversations with adults help the child to overcome this limitation; in these conversations, parents provide guidance, in essence, on how and what the child should remember. Even with this guidance, though, children simply need to gain experience with the world, in order to remember well. It is this experience that will tell the child (for example) that restaurants have menus, doctors' offices have waiting rooms, and pigs have curly tails. Once this experience is gained, the child knows that there is little point in attending to these common aspects of the world, and similarly little gain in reporting on these aspects when describing a restaurant visit or a doctor's appointment. Conversely, until this experience is gained, the child is at a considerable disadvantage in her intellectual performance.

How much does experience, and the knowledge it provides, actually contribute? One way to find out is to examine the capacities of children who happen to be experienced in a particular domain. There are, after all, nine-year-old *Star Wars* experts and eight-year-olds who are fascinated by dinosaurs and who therefore have learned a great deal about dinosaurs. In such domains of expertise, do these children benefit from their experience, and so end up reasoning and remembering just like adults?

One investigator studied the ability of ten-year-old chess experts (recruited from local chess clubs) to remember chess positions. Just like adult chess experts, these children had excellent memories for chess positions, far outperforming adults who hap-

*From apprentice to master* **(A) At two, getting the right body part through the right hole of a shirt is still a major problem. (B) Only six months later, dressing is well on the way to becoming automatic, (C) though complete mastery is not quite there yet.**

The child as expert    Ten-year-old chess champion Etienne Bacrot plays an adult opponent. To make the competition a bit more even, he wears a blindfold.

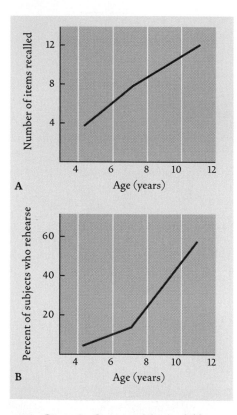

**12.19    Strategies for memorizing in children** (A) Nursery-school children, first graders, and fifth graders were shown a number of pictures and were asked to try to remember them. The figure shows recall as a function of age. (B) While the participants watched the stimuli, the experimenters observed them for signs of rehearsal—naming the pictures, and so on. In the older children, there was quite a bit of rehearsal, but there was very little for the first graders and virtually none for the nursery-school children. (Data from Appel et al., 1972)

pened to be chess novices. Clearly, what mattered here was expertise in the specific domain, not overall level of cognitive development (Chi, 1978; W. Schneider, Gruber, Gold, & Opwis, 1993). Similar results have been obtained with children remembering facts about dinosaurs (Chi & Koeske, 1983) and baseball (Recht & Leslie, 1988). In each case, child experts perform as well as, or sometimes better than, adults, underscoring the importance of expertise, not age, in shaping memory.

## THE CHILD AS A POOR STRATEGIST

*Strategies for Remembering*    It seems, then, that one important factor in intellectual development is the accumulation of knowledge, with this knowledge then serving as a guide to further intellectual functioning. Still another factor is the acquisition of strategies that can broadly improve both reasoning and memory.

For example, when adults are presented with a series of items and told to repeat them a moment later, they do their best to keep them in mind. They *rehearse*, perhaps by repeating the items mentally, perhaps by organizing them in various ways. What about young children? By age three or so, children do show signs of deliberate memory strategies, but the strategies are relatively primitive. In one study, three-year-olds watched while an experimenter placed a toy dog in one of two containers. The experimenter told the children that he would leave the room for a little while, but that they should tell him where the dog was hidden as soon as he came back. During the interval, some children kept looking at the hiding place and nodding yes; others kept their eyes on the wrong container while shaking their heads no; yet others kept their hands on the correct container. They all had found a way of building a bridge between past and present by performing an overt action—keeping the toy dog in their minds by marking its location with their bodies (Wellman, Ritter, & Flavell, 1975).

Keeping one's hand on the to-be-remembered object may be a forerunner of rehearsal, but genuine rehearsal does not occur spontaneously until around age five or six. In one experiment, participants who were five, seven, and ten years old were shown pictures of seven familiar objects (for example, a pipe, a flag, an owl). The experimenter slowly pointed at three of them in turn. The children's job was to point at the same three pictures in the same order after a fifteen-second interval. During this interval their eyes were covered (by a specially designed space helmet), so they could not bridge the interval by looking at the pictures or by surreptitiously pointing at them.

Not surprisingly, the older children did better on the recall test than the younger ones did (Figure 12.19). And, without question, part of their advantage derived from using memory strategies. One of the experimenters was a trained lip-reader who observed that almost all of the ten-year-olds silently mouthed the names of the to-be-remembered pictures—that is, they used rehearsal—during the retention interval, compared to only 10 percent of the five-year-olds. The older children remembered more than the younger ones, not because they had more memory "space," but because they used their memories more effectively (Flavell, Beach, & Chinsky, 1966).

## METACOGNITION

In several studies young nonrehearsers were trained to rehearse, and they easily mastered (and benefited from) the use of this simple strategy. But when later presented with another memory task, most of these participants abandoned the rehearsal method they had just been taught. This was especially likely if the new task was somewhat different from the old. A child taught to remember a set of names by reciting it aloud probably will not apply the same strategy to a shopping list (Flavell, 1970, 1977).

What these children seem to lack, therefore, is a master plan for dealing with memory tasks in general, a strategy for using strategies. To put this more generally, the children seem to lack an understanding of their own mental processes and with it an understanding of when a strategy would be useful and, likewise, which strategies should be applied to which tasks. Their shortcoming, therefore, lies in their *metacognition*—their thinking about their own mental functioning.

Human adults know that rehearsal is useful, know that it helps to pay attention when trying to learn, and can even assess the state of their own knowledge: Have they studied a to-be-remembered item sufficiently? Or is further study still needed? Likewise, adults have a fairly realistic idea of what they can and cannot recall. If briefly shown pictures of four common objects, adults will (correctly) predict that they will be able to recall them after one presentation. If shown ten pictures, they will predict (again correctly) that this set exceeds their capacity. In children, all of these metacognitive skills are less well developed. Thus, for example, first- and second-graders are much less realistic in predicting their own memory performance (Yussen & Levy, 1975).

Metacognition is not limited to memory. Adults also know a great deal, for example, about their own perception—they recognize the role of perspective and know the difference between reality and illusion (Flavell, Flavell, & Green, 1983). Adults also have metacognitive understanding about language, so that they can do more than talk and understand—they can also play with language, as in puns or poems, recognize that some sentences are ill-formed, and become poets or linguists (L. R. Gleitman, Gleitman, & Shipley, 1972). Adults also manifest metacognition in thinking and problem solving. Of course, they think and solve problems, but they can do more—they can use general strategies for reaching solutions, and know when they need more information. In contrast, the young child is rather limited in all of these domains, and so this is an arena of extraordinary growth over the first decade or so of life. The importance of this growth cannot be overstated, since it may well be that these metacognitive processes are one of the distinguishing hallmarks of adult human intelligence (H. Gleitman, 1985).

# COGNITIVE DEVELOPMENT IN OLD AGE

We have now said a great deal about how children develop—in the uterus, during the months of infancy, through the preschool and school years. But development does not cease when the child reaches adulthood. Each of us continues to grow and change across our entire lifetime, a pattern of change often studied under the rubric of *life-span development*. Much of this change involves our emotional and social existence, and we will turn to these points in Chapter 13. But some of the change also involves our cognitive capacities. Let us close the chapter with a brief look at these changes late in life.

## AGING AND INTELLIGENCE

To understand how intellectual functioning changes across the life span, we must distinguish between *fluid* and *crystallized intelligence* (see Chapter 14). *Fluid intelligence* refers to the efficiency and speed of intellectual functioning, usually in arenas that are new to the individual, and so require some strategy choice, some decisions about how to proceed, and so on. *Crystallized intelligence* refers to a person's accumulated knowledge, including their vocabulary, the facts they know, and the strategies they have learned.

Crystallized intelligence remains relatively stable across the life span and, in some studies, seems to grow as the individual gains more and more life experience. Fluid intelligence shows a very different pattern, starting to decline when the person is in their thirties, and with the decline continuing as the years go by. However, the decline is far from

*New skills, new knowledge   Fluid intelligence declines across the lifespan, but crystallized intelligence—including new skills and new knowledge—continues to grow with each new experience.*

precipitous, and many individuals maintain much of their intellectual capacity into their sixties and seventies. In addition, the extent of the decline varies enormously from one person to the next, with some people dropping markedly in their cognitive ability as they age and other people holding on to their capacities quite well (F. I. M. Craik & Salthouse, 2000; Salthouse, 2000; Schaie, 1996; Verhaeghen & Salthouse, 1997).

What accounts for these differences among individuals? There are many theories, but no consensus has yet emerged. Some investigators propose biological explanations: age-related changes in blood flow or neuroanatomy, or the gradual death of neurons across the life span (but see Stern & Carstensen, 2000). Others focus on education level, or the degree of stimulation in the individual's life (see, for example, Schaie & Willis, 1996). Still others have suggested that the key lies in an age-related decline in working memory, or the capacity for paying attention. Research has not yet allowed us to specify the exact role of each of these factors, but, in truth, all are likely to play some part in governing how an individual ages.

In addition, how someone ages is certainly influenced by a variety of medical factors. This reflects the fact that the cells making up the central nervous system can function well only if they receive an ample supply of oxygen and glucose. (In fact, we mentioned in Chapter 2 that the brain consumes about 15 percent of the body's metabolic energy, even though it accounts for only about 2 percent of the overall body weight.) As a result, brain functioning can be impaired by a wide range of bodily changes that diminish the availability of these resources. For example, a decline in kidney function will have an impact throughout the body, but, because of the brain's metabolic needs, it may lead to a loss in mental functioning that is detected well before other symptoms appear. Likewise, circulatory problems (including problems with the heart itself or arteriosclerosis) will obviously diminish the quantity and quality of the brain's blood supply, and so can contribute to a cognitive decline (see, for example, Albert et al., 1995). This is one of the reasons why a program of physical exercise can, in many cases, help preserve mental functioning in the elderly (see, for example, Cotman & Neeper, 1996). Finally, cognitive functioning in the aging is also affected by a number of age-related diseases, including *Alzheimer's disease*, a disorder characterized by a progressive and widespread loss of nerve cells, leading to memory problems, disorientation, and, eventually, total helplessness. Evidence has made it clear that genetic factors can put someone at increased risk for Alzheimer's disease (see, for example, Vickers, Dickson, Allard, & Saunders, 2000), but the exact causes of the disease remain uncertain. (For more on Alzheimer's disease, see Chapter 2.)

## AGING AND MEMORY

Failing memory has long been considered one of the obvious facts of aging. However, some aspects of memory—implicit memory, for one, and some measures of semantic memory—show little or no decline with aging; age-related declines are instead limited to measures of working memory and episodic memory (see, for example, Earles, Connor, Smith, & Park, 1998). And as with intelligence, the extent of decline varies markedly from one person to the next, and the declines that are observed are far from calamitous, with good memory performance often observed in sixty-, seventy- and eighty-year-olds.

What causes the declines? Again, multiple hypotheses are possible. Some researchers have proposed biological explanations, often focusing on anatomical or physiological changes in the hippocampus (see, for example, Ivy, MacLeod, Petit, & Markus, 1992). Others have focused on strategy changes that seem to take place in the elderly, with older adults less likely to use such strategies as organization and elaboration, perhaps because they are less aware that these strategies are needed (see F. I. M. Craik & Jennings, 1992; Salthouse, 1991).

Of course, as the world population ages, all of these issues take on a greater importance and interest. Not surprisingly, then, investigators have turned more and more to questions about interventions, steps that can be taken to halt or even reverse the cognitive decline often associated with aging. Some early efforts in this regard have been quite encouraging, with a number of studies suggesting predictors of "successful aging" and other studies offering interventions (see Freund & Baltes, 1998; Baltes, Staudinger, & Lindenberger, 1999), and this is an issue receiving enormous research scrutiny.

## SOME FINAL THOUGHTS: MATURATION AND ENVIRONMENT

Cognitive development, like so many human processes, is the joint outcome of maturational and environmental factors. Certain aspects of cognitive growth, such as the child's earliest understanding of the perceptual world or the acquisition of language, do seem to be driven largely by maturation. These achievements will unfold in a broad range of environments (though, if the environment is hostile enough, they may be impaired). The situation is different for other aspects of cognitive development that clearly depend on learning. This is certainly true for the abstract skills often identified with Piaget's formal operations; it is also true for the various cultural influences we have discussed.

In short, here, as always, we can emphasize neither maturation alone nor learning alone; development depends on both in a full and rich interaction. A similar message applies to development at the end of the lifespan: as we have seen, there is reason to think that the decline in cognitive functioning in the elderly is influenced heavily by medical factors, such as age-related changes in blood flow; there is also reason to believe the decline is influenced by psychological factors, such as the degree of stimulation in the individual's life. In no regard, then, can humans be understood as biological entities alone, with no attention to our environment, experiences, and learning. Likewise, in no regard can humans be understood as creatures wholly created through experience, with no attention to our biological inheritance and functioning.

## SUMMARY

### WHAT IS DEVELOPMENT?

1. Embryological development involves progressive anatomical differentiation. According to many theorists, differentiation also occurs in the development of behavior. An example is the development of grasping during the infant's first year.

2. The most obvious aspect of physical development is *growth*. Organisms grow as they change from a *fertilized egg* to an *embryo*, and then to a *fetus*. Growth continues, of course, after birth as well, and this is especially visible in humans. A human baby is extraordinarily helpless at birth and remains so for many months. Its brain is far

from mature at birth, continuing to grow in sheer size and number of neural interconnections. After the age of two, the *pruning of synapses* exceeds the formation of new ones, ultimately leaving the adult with only half the number of synapses the child had at two. This lengthy period of development, and the long period of dependency that it entails, have great advantage for a species whose major specialization is its capacity for learning and whose basic invention is culture.

3. Infants have a number of reflexes that help them through their initial period of helplessness. Examples are the *grasp reflex* and the *rooting reflex*. Newborns also have reasonably mature sensory capacities, and can discriminate

tones of different pitch and loudness; they can also discriminate brightness and color, and they can visually track moving stimuli.

## THE PHYSICAL BASIS OF DEVELOPMENT

4. The changes that constitute development are produced by an interaction of genetic endowment and environmental factors. In humans, the genetic commands are contained in twenty-three pairs of chromosomes. One of these pairs determines the sex of the organism. If female, it is an XX pair; if male, an XY pair.

5. Every chromosome contains thousands of genes, some *dominant* and some *recessive*. In most cases, though, it is not a single gene pair that determines an organism's traits. Instead, most of an organism's attributes are influenced by *polygenic inheritance*.

6. The expression of the genes is shaped by the environment, but what is meant by the term "environment" changes as development proceeds. In early embryonic development, the environment of a given cell is the other cells with which it makes contact. Somewhat later, the embryonic environment includes hormonal conditions. An example is the formation of external genitals, which differentiate into those of a male in the presence of *androgens,* but remain those of a female when androgens are absent. That the same physical environment exerts different effects at different ages is shown by *sensitive periods.*

## COGNITIVE DEVELOPMENT

7. All humans go through a process of cognitive development. According to Jean Piaget, they do so by passing through the same sequence of *developmental stages.*

8. In Piaget's account, the first stage is the period of *sensorimotor intelligence,* which lasts until about two years of age. During this period, the infant develops the concept of *object permanence,* builds up coordinated *sensorimotor schemas,* becomes capable of *deferred imitation,* and acquires increasingly complex mental *representations.*

9. The next period lasts until around age six or seven. It is the *preoperational period,* during which children are capable of representational thought but lack *mental operations* that order and organize these thoughts. Characteristic deficits include an *inability to conserve number and quantity,* and *egocentrism,* an inability to take another person's perspective.

10. Piaget believed that at about age seven, children begin to acquire a system of mental operations that allows them to manipulate mental representations with consequent success in conservation tasks and similar tests. But in his view, they remain in the *period of concrete operations,* which lacks an element of abstractness, until they are about

eleven. After eleven, they enter the *period of formal operations.* As a result, they can consider hypothetical possibilities and are capable of scientific thought.

## WHAT IS THE COGNITIVE STARTING POINT?

11. One critical challenge to Piaget's views concerns his beliefs of what capacities are present by the time of birth. A number of critics deny that the infant's mind is the mere jumble of unrelated sensory impressions and motor reactions that Piaget declared it to be, for they believe that some of the major categories by which adults organize the world—such as the concepts of *space, objects, number,* and the *existence of other minds*—have primitive precursors in early life.

12. Studies of visual perception in infancy using *habituation procedures* suggest that humans come equipped with some built-in understanding of space and objects. Infants show appropriate reactions to *perceptual occlusion* and have some notions of the principles that govern objects in space. Piaget to the contrary, they have object permanence. But while they evidently believe that objects do exist, they are rather inept in searching for them. One reason is that the infant has difficulty in overriding the tendency to reach for an object at a place she had previously seen it, as shown by the *A-not-B effect.* Other evidence indicates that an infant's perceptual competence must be understood in the context of the infant not understanding certain other facts about the way the physical world functions, and an example comes from the infant's growing understanding, over the first months of life, of how support works.

13. Further studies show that infants can perceive numerical equivalence if the number of objects in the set is small enough, and also that they have some rudiments of numerical reasoning.

14. Other criticisms suggest that Piaget also underestimated infants' capacity for social cognition. Infants seem to come into the world with the recognition that others see and hear more or less what they do. They respond to the sight of faces shortly after birth. They also seem to understand others' actions in terms of their goals, and not the specific movements themselves.

## COGNITIVE DEVELOPMENT IN PRESCHOOLERS

15. When considering preschoolers, modern research efforts show more precursors of adult cognitive achievements than Piaget had given them credit for. Some of these concern *numerical skills.* There is evidence that preschoolers have begun to master some of the key ideas on which

counting and *numerical reasoning* rest. Other investigations concern *social cognition*. It turns out that preschoolers' thought is not quite as egocentric as Piaget had asserted. They evidently have the rudiments of a *theory of mind*, indicating relatively early competence. Here, too, though, the competence sits side by side with limitations, and the child's growing understanding of *false belief* provides an example of how the young child's competence, impressive as it is, still needs to grow in sophistication across the preschool years.

## THE CAUSES OF COGNITIVE GROWTH

16. Piaget understood cognitive development in terms of the growing differentiation of schemas, with this development driven by the dual mechanisms of *assimilation* and *accommodation*. More recent investigators, however, have argued that Piaget understated the role of biological inheritance, and also the broad impact of culture.

17. The role of culture is obvious when we consider the need to interpret test results in a fashion guided by the cultural context. For example, in some cultures it is unusual and perhaps even rude to ask a question if you already know the answer. However, this situation—common enough in most experimental tests—is entirely familiar to any Western school child. In addition, cultures also differ in the specific content of the information transmitted to children—the finding of edible desert plants for children growing up in the Kalihari, or learning to ski for children growing up in Norway. Most important, the role of culture is visible in cultural influences that are not merely "given" to the child, but in influences that emerge from interactions in which the child is an active participant. An example comes from learning to remember, and to report on one's memories, a skill that grows out of conversations the child has had, with the pattern of those conversations varying from culture to culture.

18. Many modern investigators have sought to understand cognitive development as a change in *information processing*, and have examined the ways in which the child learns to attend, to solve problems, and to remember. One result of research in this vein has been that much of the child's mental growth is based largely on the acquisition of new knowledge. A number of studies have pointed out that in many ways the child is a *novice* at most of the cognitive tasks adults confront, but may do unusually well in certain realms in which he or she has special *expertise*. These studies also emphasize the important role of various *strategies* for thinking and remembering that depend on the development of *metacognition*.

## COGNITIVE DEVELOPMENT IN OLD AGE

19. To understand how intellectual functioning changes across the life span, investigators have found it useful to distinguish between *fluid* and *crystallized intelligence*. The first refers to the efficiency and speed of intellectual functioning, usually in areas that are new to the person. The second refers to an individual's accumulated knowledge, including his or her vocabulary, known facts, and learned strategies. *Fluid intelligence* tends to decline in later years, though the rate of decline is far from precipitous and varies enormously from one person to the next. *Crystallized intelligence* remains relatively stable over the life span and may even grow as the person gains more and more experience. Many hypotheses have been offered for what lies behind the variation, from one individual to the next, in the extent of the changes in intelligence and in memory. Some of the hypotheses emphasize the individual's biological and/or medical status, and others emphasize the individual's mental life, so that people who are mentally more active might preserve their memory more fully as they age.

# SOCIAL DEVELOPMENT

 *I*n the preceding chapter we discussed physical and cognitive development: the ways in which we progress from embryos to full-grown adults. But we humans do not just grow bigger and smarter; we also develop in our relations with other people. We learn to notice the nuances in another's behavior and to communicate our own needs and wishes. We learn to be friendly to allies and wary with adversaries. And we learn all of this within society's rules about what is good and proper conduct. Finding out how we accomplish such complex learning is the task of psychologists who study *social development*.

Physical, cognitive, and social development are all areas in which our abilities change as we move through the human journey from birth to senescence. Physically, we grow in sheer size and strength, letting us move more freely within our environment. Cognitively, we learn to inhabit not only the physical world but also the world of concepts and ideas.

Socially, our horizons expand just as much. In the first weeks of life, our social world is limited to just one person, usually the mother. In time, this social sphere enlarges to include both parents, then the rest of the family, then young peers in the neighborhood, nursery, and school. With the onset of adolescence, a small number of special friends assume more importance as roles change and sexuality blossoms. Before long, many of us become parents and start the reproductive cycle all over again. Of course, social development continues even here, as we move into midlife and then old age, at each stage growing and changing in important ways.

# ATTACHMENT

*Attachment*

The course of social development begins with the very first human bond—that between infants and their primary caregiver, usually the mother.* This bond—the attachment of infants to the person who takes care of them—is sometimes said to lay the foundations for all later relationships. Just what does this attachment entail?

At the outset, human newborns want to be near their mothers, and when distressed, they are comforted by their mother's face, voice, and touch. In this regard, human children have much in common with the young of many other species. Rhesus monkey infants cling to their mother's body, chicks follow the hen, and lambs run after the ewe. As the young mature, they begin to venture away from the mother, but for quite a while they consider her a secure home base, a safe retreat from unmanageable threats.

## THE ROOTS OF ATTACHMENT

What accounts for the infant's attachment to the mother? Until some forty years ago, it was widely believed that love for the mother grew directly out of the fact that she satisfied the infant's basic biological needs by providing food, warmth, physical protection, and relief from pain. The most influential version of this approach was probably that of Sigmund Freud, who believed that the terror of infants at their mother's absence is based on the prospect of going unfed (Chapter 15). Because mothers were seen primarily as food repositories (whether through breast or bottle), Freud's view became known as the *cupboard theory* of mother love (Bowlby, 1969, 1973).

## BOWLBY'S THEORY OF ATTACHMENT

The cupboard theory has been criticized on several grounds, one being the fact that babies often show great interest in people other than those who feed them. For example, infants seem to enjoy being cuddled, smiled at, and played with, and there is not one shred of evidence to indicate that babies enjoy peek-a-boo, say, only because it is associated with food.

Such criticisms led British psychiatrist John Bowlby to argue that infants find this social interaction intrinsically rewarding. For Bowlby, infants do not form attachments

---

* Since the primary caregiver is typically the child's mother (she almost always was in earlier eras), we will refer to the child's caregiver by that traditional term. Of course, the actual caregiver may well be another person, such as the father, grandparent or a nanny; moreover, many children have multiple caregivers, as when mother and father are joint and equally involved caregivers.

because they are seeking food or warmth. Instead, they enter the world predisposed to seek direct contact with an adult (usually the mother).

In many ways, this social contact is pleasing for infants. They enjoy interacting with their mother and quickly learn to recognize and prefer their mother's voice and even her smell (DeCasper & Fifer, 1980; MacFarlane, 1975). When contented, they peacefully gaze and gurgle at her and, by the age of about six weeks, produce a full-blown social smile. Mothers and other important adults happily reciprocate; when babies smile, adults smile back. As infants get older and acquire some ability to move around, they do whatever they can to be in the adults' company—smiling beseechingly toward their mother and father, reaching for them, and crawling toward them (Campos, Barrett, Lamb, Goldsmith, & Sternberg, 1983).

For Bowlby, such behavior is motivated not only by the pleasures of contact but also by a built-in fear of the unknown and unfamiliar, a fear that drives the young of most mammals and birds to huddle with a very familiar object, most likely the ever-present mother (Waters & Cummings, 2000).

Bowlby suggests that this built-in fear of the unfamiliar has a simple survival value. Infants who lack it will stray from their mothers and are more likely to get lost and perish. In particular, they may fall victim to predators, who tend to attack weak animals that are separated from their flock.

Of course, the infants of most species cannot identify likely predators, so their built-in fear is initially quite general. In the absence of the mother, therefore, even mild external threats become overwhelming for the child; this heightened need for reassurance may lead to desperate whining and clinging in the dark or during a thunderstorm.

So powerful is this need to cling to the parents that it may occur even when the fearful stimulus comes from the parents themselves. Children who are severely punished by their parents may become even more clinging and dependent on them. The parents caused the fear, but they are the ones who are approached for reassurance. Similar phenomena may be observed in the Stockholm Syndrome, in which hostages grow fond of and even romantically attached to their captors (Ochberg & Soskis, 1982), and in domestic abuse, where victims often defend their partners, refusing to press charges or testify against them (Auerbach et al., 1994; D. L. R. Graham, Rawlings, & Rigsby, 1994).

## THE ESSENCE OF MOTHERING: COMFORT

According to Bowlby, fear of the unfamiliar is what produces attachment. Of course, the mother provides food and warmth, but for purposes of attachment what really matters is the sense of safety, comfort, and refuge that she provides.

Evidence consistent with Bowlby's view comes from some landmark studies conducted by Harry Harlow (1905–1981). Harlow (1958) raised newborn rhesus monkeys without their mothers. Each rhesus infant lived alone in a cage that contained two stationary figures, one built of wire and the other of soft terry cloth. The wire figure was equipped with a nipple that yielded milk, but the terry-cloth model had none. Even so, the monkey infants spent much more time on the terry-cloth "mother" than on the wire figure. This was especially clear when the infants were frightened. When approached by a clanking mechanical toy, they invariably rushed to the terry-cloth mother and clung tightly. The terry-cloth figure seemed to provide what Harlow called "contact comfort" (Figure 13.1). In contrast, the infants never sought solace from the wire mothers, even though they provided food.

These results stand in complete opposition to the cupboard theory and suggest that the monkey infant loves its mother (whether real or terry cloth) not because she feeds it, but because she provides "comfort." Rhesus infants in the wild grasp and cling to their mother's fur at any threat; presumably, in Harlow's laboratory the terry cloth felt more like fur than the wire did.

*Free-floating anxiety*

**13.1  The need for contact comfort  A frightened rhesus monkey baby clings to its terry-cloth mother for comfort.**

Contact comfort is also important to human infants. Frightened young humans run to their mothers and cling to them just like rhesus infants (Figure 13.2). Human infants even have the same grasping and clinging reflexes shown by rhesus infants, although human mothers do not have the fur for clinging. Children also like stuffed, cuddly toys like teddy bears and hug them tightly when threatened. Could these toys be the human analog to the terry-cloth mother? Perhaps they are, but—contrary to the cupboard theory—not because they are a surrogate breast or bottle.

13.2    *Contact comfort in humans*

## IMPRINTING AND ATTACHMENT

Many other species show this biological programming to seek what is familiar. Evidence is provided by *imprinting*, which was studied extensively by the European ethologist Konrad Lorenz. Imprinting is a kind of learning that occurs very early in life and, in many species, provides the basis for an infant's attachment to its mother. For example, as soon as a duckling can walk (about twelve hours after hatching), it will approach and follow virtually any moving stimulus. If the duckling follows this moving object for about ten minutes, an attachment is formed. The bird has now imprinted on this object and, from this point forward, will continue to follow it, show distress if separated from it, and run to it under threat.

This simple kind of learning is usually quite effective, since the first moving stimulus a duckling sees is generally its mother. But imprinting can occur to other objects, by accident or through an experimenter's manipulations. In some studies, ducklings have been exposed to a moving toy duck on wheels or to a rectangle sliding back and forth behind a glass window, or even to Konrad Lorenz's booted legs (Figure 13.3). In each case, the ducklings follow these objects as if following their mother, uttering plaintive distress calls whenever the attachment object is not nearby (E. H. Hess, 1959, 1973).

A remarkable case of mistaken imprinting put to good use is the wildlife-conservation work undertaken by Operation Migration (Lishman, 1992), which helps young orphaned waterfowl migrate successfully by having them imprint on ultralight airplanes and their pilots. The birds are imprinted in stages. Before hatching, the eggs are exposed to the sound of the airplane motor. A few days after hatching, the birds are handled by the trainer and herded behind the airplane as it taxis up and down a short runway. Finally, at migration time, the plane takes to the air, and the birds obediently flock behind it in their natural V-formation, with the plane in the lead-bird position.

Imprinting occurs most readily during a specific period in the animal's life that can last from hours to days. Subsequent to this period, imprinting is difficult to achieve (see Figure 13.4). For many years, this period of time was referred to as the **critical period** for imprinting. Contemporary investigators, however, prefer the term **sensitive period**, to highlight the fact that imprinting, although far less likely, is still possible after this period has ended (Bateson & Hinde, 1987; see Chapters 9 and 12 for other examples of critical or sensitive periods).

Do humans show imprinting to their mothers? Animal findings such as Lorenz's led some investigators to believe so, suggesting that human infants also have a sensitive period just after birth during which they form attachments to their mothers (Klaus and Kennell, 1976; Klaus, Kennell, Plumb, & Zuehlke, 1970). If so, then this would call into question the standard hospital practice of separating newborns from their mothers

13.3    *Imprinting in ducklings    Imprinted ducklings following Konrad Lorenz.*

*Mistaken imprinting for a good cause* **The movie, Fly Away Home,** *presents a fictionalized version of a procedure actually used in real life: orphaned geese are imprinted on an ultralight airplane, and then led by the plane in their annual migration.*

and moving them to a separate nursery (once done routinely but now reserved for premature and other high-risk babies). However, this concern appears not to be well founded. Studies comparing infants who had after-birth contact with their mothers to those who did not (usually due to medical complications in either mother or baby) show little evidence for such a sensitive period. Instead, normal attachments in humans form gradually, as soon as circumstances allow (Eyer, 1992). *

## SEXUAL IMPRINTING AND SEXUAL ATTRACTION

Perhaps we should not expect imprinting to mothers in humans, since there is little evidence for it in any primate. Unlike birds, primates take a long time to mature, and a quick, one-shot attachment process would ill serve animals who may remain juveniles for years. On the other hand, sexual imprinting is common in mammals and may occur in humans, and one of the main properties that animals may imprint on, and use later as a mating cue, is body odor.

Body odor is like a chemical fingerprint, and some of its important ingredients are coded by the genes of the body's *major histocompatibility complex (MHC)*, part of the genome involved in the immune system's ability to target invading cells and leave one's own cells alone. Several pieces of evidence show the MHC's importance in mate preference. Mice, for example, tend to mate with mice who carry MHC genes dissimilar from their own, as if they were following the rule "don't mate with him if he smells like family"

Strong evidence that this preference for dissimilar smells derives from imprinting comes from a study of female mice who early on were placed with foster mouse parents, a state of affairs never found in normal mouse life. When mature, these mice show a reverse mating preference: they prefer males with similar MHC genes over members of their foster families, who have dissimilar MHC genes (Penn & Potts, 1998).

All this leads to the obvious question of whether humans show similar sexual imprinting. Are we sexually attracted to certain people because they smell different than we do? If

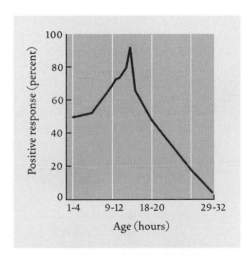

**13.4  Imprinting and the sensitive period**  **The curve shows the relation between imprinting and the age at which a duckling was exposed to a male moving model. The imprinting score represents the percentage of trials on which the duckling followed the model on a later test.**

* Moreover, when infants must spend their initial days with a nurse, or in an incubator, they do not form a lasting attachment to either. Instead, they form a normal attachment to their mother some days later. Clearly, the pattern of imprint-to-object-of-first-exposure, common in many species, is not found in humans.

so, then olfaction may be one basis for the universal avoidance of incest. At least some evidence hints that there may not be much of a difference between mice and men. We humans, just like mice, appear to mate less with individuals who have similar MHC genes than with MHC-dissimilar individuals (Ober et al., 1997). We also prefer the body odors of people (as smelled on preworn T-shirts) who have dissimilar MHC genes to those of MHC-similar individuals (Wedekind & Furi, 1997). Whether our preference is a matter of early olfactory imprinting, as it appears to be in mice, has yet to be determined.

# PATTERNS OF ATTACHMENT

During the first few months of life, human infants will accept substitute mothers, drawing comfort from some other female just as readily as they do from their own mother, perhaps because they have not yet clearly differentiated their own mothers from other people. But from about the ages of six to eight months, infants learn who "mother" is, and they now cry and fuss when she departs. The age at which children begin to protest this separation—that is, the age at which children start to show separation anxiety—is pretty much the same for African bushmen in Botswana, U.S. city dwellers, Indians in a Guatemalan village, and members of an Israeli kibbutz (Kagan, 1976).

## ASSESSING ATTACHMENT

Mother as "secure base"

An infant's reaction to separation and reunion provides a means for examining the attachment infants have to their mothers. A procedure widely used for children about one year old is the Strange Situation devised by Bowlby's frequent collaborator, Mary Ainsworth, and her colleagues (Ainsworth & Bell, 1970; Ainsworth, Blehar, Waters, & Wall 1978). A child is first brought into an unfamiliar room that contains many toys, and then is allowed to explore and play with the mother present. After a while, an unfamiliar woman enters, talks to the mother, and then approaches the child. The next step is a brief separation—the mother leaves the child alone with the stranger. After a few minutes, though, a reunion follows—the mother returns and the stranger leaves.

According to Ainsworth and her colleagues, it is upon reunion with the mother that one-year-old infants reveal their quality of attachment with their mothers, a quality that falls into one of three major categories. Children described as "securely attached" explore, play with the toys, and even make wary overtures to the stranger, so long as the mother is present, and when she leaves, they show minor distress. When she returns, however, they greet her with great enthusiasm. The remaining children show behavior patterns that Ainsworth and her colleagues regard as signs of insecure attachment. Some of these children are described as "anxious/resistant." They do not explore, even in the mother's presence, and become upset and panicky when she leaves. Upon reunion, they act ambivalent, crying and running to her to be picked up, but then kicking or slapping her and struggling to get down. Still other children show a pattern called "anxious/avoidant." They are distant and aloof while the mother is present, and, although they sometimes search for her in her absence, they typically snub her when she returns.

## STABILITY OF ATTACHMENT

Ainsworth and others believe that behavior in the Strange Situation reflects characteristics that are fairly stable, at least for the first few years of life, and so they suggest that we can use the children's behavior in this situation as a basis for predicting how the children will act in other settings and at other times.

Is this correct? Are infants' patterns of attachment relatively stable across situations? The evidence is decidedly mixed. In one study using the Strange Situation to measure attachment, about half of all infants changed their pattern of attachment within a six-month period (Belsky, Campbell, Cohn, & Moore, 1996). In contrast, other, longer-term studies reached the opposite conclusion and found stability. One study, for example, found that infants' attachment style at twelve months predicted other attachment measures at age six, at a rate of agreement of 82 percent (Wartner, Grossman, Fremmer-Bombik, & Suess, 1994). This inconsistent pattern of results led one reviewer to comment sardonically that our best understanding of the data is simply that "sometimes early attachment relationships remain consistent over time, and sometimes they change" (R. A. Thompson, 2000).

Why would an infant's early pattern of attachment change? Attachment researchers now recognize that powerful environmental circumstances can readily alter these patterns (Sroufe et al., 1990, 1999). This is suggested by studies of securely attached infants (at age one or so) who subsequently endured a period of severe family stress, such as serious illness in the family, marital conflict, or unemployment of a parent. In one study of ten disadvantaged infants observed at twelve months, over one-third showed a change to less secure attachment six months later, and the infants most likely to show the changed pattern were those whose mothers reported the most domestic stress (Vaughn, Egelund, Sroufer, & Waters, 1979).

Especially disruptive is the birth of a sibling. This was shown in a study of firstborn preschoolers who had secure attachments to their mothers; they become ambivalently attached when the sibling was born, especially if the mother became depressed or anxious after the delivery (Teti, Sakin, Kucera, Corns, & Das Eiden, 1996). Yet another profound influence on attachment is the intactness of the parents' relationship. Children whose parents separate become less attached to both parents as adolescents, with the loss of attachment more severe the earlier in the child's life the parents separated (L. Woodward, Fergusson, & Belsky, 2000). Taken together, these studies lead to one safe conclusion: the child's pattern of attachment can remain stable only if the major features of his environment also do.

## ATTACHMENT AND LATER ADJUSTMENT

Does early attachment affect social adjustment later in life? According to Ainsworth and her colleagues, the child's early attachments provide the foundation for later social and emotional adjustment. Some theorists even suggest that this early pattern of attachment predicts the pattern of romantic relationships in adolescence and adulthood (Feeney & Collins, 2001; Hazan & Shaver, 1987; Rothbard & Shaver, 1994).

However, the evidence on whether early attachments actually have long-term consequences is mixed. Although some observers find only a weak relationship (see Belsky & Cassidy, 1994), other studies suggest a stronger link. In one study, children rated as securely attached at the age of fifteen months were likely to be more outgoing, popular, and well adjusted in nursery school at age three and a half (Waters, Wippman, & Sroufe, 1979). Moreover, secure infant attachment predicts a lower incidence of anxiety disorders in childhood and adolescence (Warren, Huston, Egeland, & Sroufe, 1997).

Other studies have shown different patterns, but, even in the studies that tie attachment to adjustment, does this mean (as Ainsworth contended) that a child's pattern of early attachment *causes* her later adjustment or maladjustment? The answer is no. After all, if behavior in the Strange Situation is correlated with subsequent behavior, perhaps this merely reflects the relative constancy of factors like the child's physical and emotional health, family members, and nutrition. If the child is healthy at age one, for example, that is a decent predictor that the child will continue to be healthy at age three or four. If so, then the benefits of this good health will be visible both in early attach-

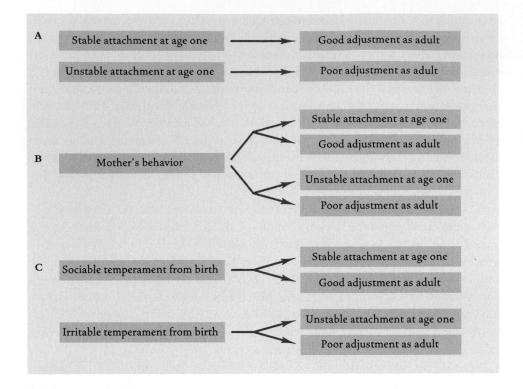

*13.5   Ambiguity in interpreting developmental correlations* **Studies demonstrate a correlation between the stability of attachment at age one and the quality of adjustment as an adult. (Infants who show stable attachment are likely to be well adjusted years later; infants who show unstable attachment are likely to be poorly adjusted years later.) But what is the cause and effect relationship linking these observations? Panels A, B, and C show three different possibilities, all of which could lead to the observed correlation.**

ment and in later tests of adjustment—hence, the child will appear secure in the Strange Situation and also well adjusted later. In this case, early attachment and later adjustment are but the consequences of other, unappreciated influences.

One important influence other than physical health may be the child's own temperament—whether she is constitutionally irritable or sociable. This temperament may underlie both her early attachment behavior and her adjustment years and even decades later. If so, the correlation between attachment as an infant and later behavior may be due more to the invariant qualities of the child than to the attachments she forms along the way (Kagan, 1984).

*Cause and Effect in Attachment and Adjustment*   These various alternatives serve to highlight a crucial point: cause-and-effect relations in child development are difficult to disentangle. It is often easy to observe correlations—for example, the fact that the children who show the most stable attachments at one age are also the best adjusted at a later age. The trick comes in interpreting this correlation: what is causing what? We illustrate some of the possibilities just discussed in Figure 13.5. Since each of these possibilities is consistent with the correlation, we cannot use the correlation itself as a means of choosing among these different hypotheses.

There are various ways in which investigators have tried to address these ambiguities. Some of the techniques are statistical. Others involve experimental manipulation of the key variables, although we often cannot conduct definitive experiments because of ethical prohibitions: we obviously cannot—and should not—try to manipulate the mother's parenting style, the child's health, or the family environment, even if these manipulations would provide us with clean scientific data. As a result, direct tests of developmental hypotheses are often difficult to arrange.

## ATTACHMENT TO THE FATHER

In most of the world's cultures—whether agrarian or technological—young children spend the vast majority of their time with their mothers (M. E. Lamb, 1987, 1997), and we have concentrated on mothers in our discussion.

Are fathers left out in the cold? Not at all. Studies using the Strange Situation with fathers as well as mothers have found similar signs of distress when the father left, and clinging and touching when he returned. Moreover, infants develop attachments to their fathers and their mothers at about the same time (Pipp, Easterbrooks, & Brown, 1993). It thus appears that young children become strongly attached, and attached early on, to both parental figures.

Although attachments to both parents are deep and formed early, they nonetheless differ in kind. The chief difference, observed across numerous studies, is one of playing versus comforting. Fathers are more likely than mothers to play with their children. Fathers also tend to be physical and vigorous in their play, lifting or bouncing their children or tossing them in the air. In contrast to such roughhousing, mothers generally play more quietly with their children, telling them stories or reciting nursery rhymes and providing hugs and caresses rather than tumbles and bounces. The children act accordingly, tending to run to the mother for care and comfort but to the father for active play (Clarke-Stewart, 1978; Parke, 1981; M. E. Lamb, 1997).

What accounts for these differences in interaction with mothers and fathers? In most cultures, fathers tend to be the breadwinners in the household and are correspondingly less involved in daytime caregiving, so they condense their caregiving into episodes of concentrated, intense play (Roopnarine, Johnson, & Hooper, 1994).

Such social factors may not be the whole story, however. Evidence comes from a comparison of fathers who were the infants' secondary caregivers (the usual role in our culture) and fathers who were the primary caregivers. The behavior of these two groups of fathers was quite similar. Both groups engaged in much more physical play with the infants than the mothers did (Field, 1978).

These findings suggest that the fathers' behavior does not merely reflect day-to-day circumstances, so there must be another explanation. One may simply be the father's muscle strength; since fathers are typically stronger than mothers, they can better manage being rambunctious with their growing children. No doubt deeply embedded cultural gender roles come into play here as well. Nor can one discount the likelihood of an innate predisposition. After all, rough-and-tumble play is much more common in male than female primates, whether monkeys, apes, or humans (see Chapter 11).

*Father as a partner in active play*

## THE IMPORTANCE OF FATHERS

Even though the child's attachment to his father is different from that to his mother, it seems equally important. Children whose fathers are active participants in their lives tend to do better in school, show better conduct, have fewer emotional problems, and are less likely to become pregnant or delinquent at adolescence. Once again, though, the cause-and-effect relationship is difficult to determine, and more than father-child attachment may be involved. Involved fathers contribute not only time and parenting but also income and emotional support for the mother; conversely, single mothers are often socially isolated, overstressed, and, if she works, underpaid (Cabrera, Tamis-LeMonde, Bradley, Hofferth, & Lamb, 2000). Any of these factors could account for the apparent relationship between paternal involvement and children's behavior.

Whatever the reasons, though, involved fathers are somehow important, and this fact makes current social trends disturbing. One is that the number of families in the United States with absent fathers has quadrupled compared to just forty years ago, and fully half of all children are reared by only one parent at some point in their childhood (Demo, Allen, & Fine, 2000; Garcia Coll, Meyer, & Brillion, 1995; Harkness & Super, 1995).

On a brighter note, fathers who remain on the scene now spend more time with their children than forty years ago (Yeung, Sandberg, Davis-Kean, & Hofferth, 2001) and are assuming more of the child-rearing duties that used to be the mother's province: going to school conferences, taking the child to the doctor, and doing domestic chores like cooking and laundry. Part of the reason for this increasing equality of parental roles lies in the increased opportunities for women to be gainfully employed; another is the greater cultural diversity in the United States, which brings with it a variety of conceptions of masculinity, fatherhood, and child rearing (Cabrera et al., 2000; Good & Sherrod, 2001).

## EARLY MATERNAL SEPARATION AND DAY CARE

A number of authors believe that early separation from the mother may lead to lasting psychological damage. Thus, John Bowlby (1973), in keeping with the views already described, asserts that any disturbance of a child's initial attachment to the mother will render that child less secure in later life. In this view, separation is psychologically dangerous, and the continuity of a child's first attachment relationship is vital for his ultimate mental health.

This view is both pervasive and influential in the United States, with various social consequences. It has affected legal policies in cases of child placement, with the courts biased toward keeping children in the home, even when there is evidence of parental neglect or abuse (Maccoby, 1980). It has also made many women uneasy about leaving their children with another caretaker for any part of the day. This issue is of special concern given that, according to the U.S. Department of Labor, the majority of mothers are now employed outside the home. Increasingly, child care is provided in out-of-home day-care centers, staffed only with females, and the children often stay so long each day that they spend more time with the day-care staff than with members of their own families (Hofferth, 1996).

Is such surrogate child care damaging to the psychological welfare of our children? Some evidence suggests that it is. A few studies, for example, have examined children who spent extensive amounts of time in the care of others (more than twenty hours per week) during their first year of life. These children are more likely to show insecure patterns of attachment in the Strange Situation and show greater aggression, are less compliant, and have worse relationships with their parents (Barglow, Vaughn, & Molitor, 1987; Belsky, 1988, 2001; Belsky & Braungart, 1991).

*Attachment and day care   While some contend that any early separation from the primary caregiver may adversely affect the child, others contend that it is not the fact of day care that is important so much as it is the quality of day care.*

However, many authors disagree that the results of these studies condemn day care. They argue that the added insecurity detected in these studies is minimal and that certain kinds of behavior in the Strange Situation test have been misinterpreted. For example, the "noncompliance" observed in these studies may not indicate rebelliousness or disobedience; instead, it may indicate that the day-care children had become more independent and self-reliant! Other evidence indicates that day-care children may even outstrip their non-day-care peers on measures of sociability, persistence, and achievement (Clarke-Stewart, 1989, 1993). Perhaps this is unsurprising, if we bear in mind that a day-care child interacts continually with children his own age, and this enriched social experience may compensate for what is lost in the diminished contact with one's own family.

How do the pros and cons of day care add up? The question is not so simply answered. Overall, when the day care is of reasonable quality, children do not seem to suffer (Howes & Hamilton, 1993; NICHD Early Child Care Research Network, 1997), and children from disadvantaged home environments are most likely to benefit, rather than be hurt, by day care (Peisner-Feinberg et al., 2001).

When the quality of care is poor, however, the picture looks different. For example, one study indicated that infants enrolled in poor day-care centers end up inattentive and unsociable in preschool, compared to children who spent the same amount of time in good day-care centers (Howes, 1990). In a similar study, four-year-olds who attended higher-quality day-care centers showed better social and emotional development at age eight than did children who had attended poorer-quality centers, even when factors such as social class and income were equated (Vandell, Henderson, & Wilson, 1988).

The issue would be moot if all day care were of high quality, but by any standard—whether the adult-child ratio; how well the teachers are selected, trained, and paid; the rate of staff turnover; or the quality of the physical facilities—most institutional day care in the United States is deficient. In one large study, 86 percent of day-care centers qualified as poor or mediocre, with only 14 percent qualifying as good (Cost, Quality, and Outcomes Study Team, 1995). Additionally, day care is poorest for those children who are most vulnerable—infants and toddlers, especially those from low-income families who may only be able to afford the least-expensive care (Helburn & Howes, 1996).

One consoling finding is that the effects of poor day care may be impermanent. One study found that they dissipate by four years after children have left day care, leaving the qualities of the parents as the major predictor of their children's academic achievement and social competence (Scarr, 1997, 1998). However, follow-up studies are surely needed to corroborate this important finding.

## DISRUPTED ATTACHMENT: DOMESTIC CONFLICT AND DIVORCE

Day care outside the home involves one sort of early separation routinely experienced by young children. A different and often more distressing disruption of attachment is endured by children whose parents divorce—a situation faced by roughtly a third of the children in the United States. When there is sole custody by one parent, the children often lose or suffer reduced contact with the other parent; in shared custody, there is diminished contact with both. In addition, children of divorced parents often must change residences, schools, and churches or synagogues, experience strained relationships with siblings, and break contact with many peers and adult figures in the process. Parents (usually mothers) who were able to stay at home with their children before the divorce often need to join the workforce after the divorce to support themselves (especially when child support from the other parent is insufficient or delinquent).

As a result of all these changes, children previously raised at home with full-time parenting may now find themselves in some sort of institutional child care. On top of this, many of these children must weather intense domestic strife before the divorce, as well as an atmosphere filled with anger, guilt, and recrimination during the divorce itself (C. M. Buchanan, Maccoby, & Dornbusch, 1996; Wallerstein & Corbin, 1999).

There is some evidence that children of divorced parents may suffer a variety of emotional difficulties in later years. They tend to show conduct problems, become depressed and withdrawn, and are more likely to drop out of high school (Forgatch, Patterson, & Ray, 1996; Hetherington, Stanley-Hagen, & Anderson, 1989; Hetherington, Bridges, & Insabella, 1998; Wallerstein & Lewis, 1998).

Of course, it may not be the divorce itself that produces these unhappy consequences, but living in the stressful home environment that existed prior to the divorce—for example, dealing with parents who fight constantly. Consistent with this suggestion, retrospective studies of children whose parents divorced show that the children manifested many of the same problems before the divorce as they did after (Cherlin et al., 1991).

# WHEN THERE IS NO ATTACHMENT AT ALL

We have seen that deleterious effects on children tend to occur with the impoverished attachments associated with poor day care and the disrupted attachments of acrimonious divorce. Although the damage suffered from poor attachments is bad enough, what happens when no attachment is formed at all? The results are tragic.

## MOTHERLESS MONKEYS

We previously considered some of Harlow's experiments with rhesus monkeys and, in particular, the fate of monkeys raised with substitute mothers made of terry cloth. But suppose the monkey infants were reared without any contact at all. In one study, the infants were isolated for periods that ranged from three months to one year. During this time, they lived in empty steel chambers and saw no living creature.

After their period of solitary confinement, the animals' reactions were observed in various test situations. Although a three-month isolation had comparatively little effect, longer periods had drastic consequences. The animals huddled in a corner of the cage, clasped themselves, and rocked back and forth. When they were brought together with normally reared agemates, the results were clear-cut. Far from exhibiting the active chasing and playful romping that are characteristic of monkeys at that age, the monkeys reared in isolation simply withdrew, huddled, rocked, and bit themselves (Figure 13.6).

This social inadequacy persisted into adolescence and adulthood. One manifestation was a pitiful incompetence in sexual and parental matters. Formerly isolated males were inept at courtship and mating: if they approached other animals at all, they would, in Harlow's words (1962), "grasp other monkeys of either sex by the head and throat aimlessly, a semi-erotic exercise without amorous achievements." Formerly isolated females were no better off and resisted the sexual overtures of normal males. How were these females as mothers? Some of them were eventually impregnated, and Harlow artificially inseminated a few as well. When these motherless monkeys became mothers themselves, they seemed to have no trace of love for their offspring. In a few cases, they grotesquely abused their offspring, chewing off their toes or fingers, or worse. The early social deprivation experienced by these animals had evidently derailed their subsequent social and emotional development (Harlow & Harlow, 1972; Harlow & Novak, 1973; Suomi & Harlow, 1971).

## HUMANS REARED IN INADEQUATE INSTITUTIONS

Can we generalize from monkey infants to human children? To some degree, it seems that we can, because just like monkeys, human infants reared in isolation suffer both socially and emotionally.

13.6 Motherless monkeys (A) A monkey reared in isolation, huddling in terror in a corner of its cage. (B) An isolated monkey biting itself at the approach of a stranger.

The effects of early psychosocial deprivation attained monumentally tragic proportions in the orphanages of Romania, whose residents have been the subject of both intense study and worldwide rescue and adoption efforts. The orphanages began with dictator Nicolae Ceausescu's drive in the 1960s to double the Romanian population within one generation and thereby create abundant cheap labor. Romanian women were ordered to have five children each, and families too poor to rear all these children had to relinquish them to the state-run orphanages, which by 1989, when Ceausescu was deposed and executed, contained up to 150,000 children. The orphanages, when first opened for inspection, told a sad story of massive malnutrition, poor sanitation, two- and three-year-olds who could not yet walk or talk, and rampant AIDS infections due to tainted blood transfusions.

Compared to normally reared children, the orphaned Romanian children show numerous deficits that persist years after foster placement. First, they show markedly higher cortisol levels, indicating chronically elevated responses to stress (Gunnar, Morison, Chisholm, & Schuder, 2001). Second, they are more likely to show disturbed attachments to their current caretakers, with the disturbances proportional to the severity and duration of their early deprivation (Chisholm, 1998; Croft et al., 2001; O'Connor et al., 2000). They are also likely to show cognitive deficits on a wide range of measures including IQ (Castle et al., 1999).

These problems do not arise because the children were in orphanages, but because they were in bad orphanages—a point that parallels the findings on institutional day care. When children are raised in orphanages of adequate quality, they seem to emerge without serious harm. For example, one study examined children who were raised in decent-quality orphanages until they were two years or older. When assessed at age four or eight, after they were adopted or placed in foster homes, these children had better emotional and social adjustment than did those who had been returned to their biological parents (Tizard & Hodges, 1978).

## ARE THE EFFECTS OF EARLY SOCIAL DEPRIVATION REVERSIBLE?

It should be amply clear that social deprivation in early childhood has tragic effects. Can anything be done to reverse its effects? This question of resilience is of paramount importance to those who study or care for children. To Freud—and many others—there was no question that "the events of [the child's] first years are of paramount importance for his whole subsequent life," with the die being cast by the age of five or six. Fortunately, the evidence suggests that the dead hand of the past may not be quite so unyielding, and the odds of some recovery from early damage may not be so bleak.

### UNDOING THE PAST IN ANIMALS

Some evidence suggests that, with concentrated effort, many of the effects of early isolation in monkeys are reversible. In one study, young rhesus monkeys were rehabilitated for social life after six months of isolation by being placed together with carefully chosen monkey "therapists," monkeys who had been reared normally and were three months younger than their "patients." The therapist monkeys were thus too young to display physical aggression but old enough to initiate social contact.

When first introduced to these younger monkeys, the previously isolated monkeys withdrew and huddled in a corner. But they had not counted on the persistence of their little therapists, who followed them and clung to them. After a while, the isolates clung back, and within a few weeks, patients and therapists were playing vigorously with each other (Figure 13.7). Six months later, the patients seemed to have recovered. Later studies showed that this kind of therapy was beneficial even for monkeys isolated for an

*13.7 Therapy to undo the effects of early isolation* (A) A young, would-be therapist tenaciously clings to an unwilling isolate. (B) Some weeks later, there are strong signs of recovery as both patient and therapist engage in vigorous play.

entire year. After the therapy, the treated ex-isolates were admittedly less resilient, appearing more susceptible to stress than control animals. But they usually played and fought and copulated in much the manner of normal monkeys and were often indistinguishable from them (Novak & Harlow, 1975; Suomi, 1989; Suomi and Harlow, 1972).

## UNDOING THE PAST IN HUMANS

With appropriate intervention, animals can recover from early trauma, at least to some extent. Is the same true for humans? In a few instances, isolated or horribly neglected children have been studied after they were rescued and placed in more benign care. The outcomes are quite variable and depend on the case: some children improve substantially, while others remain severely socially and intellectually impaired (M. Cole & Cole, 1996). In the case of the Romanian orphans, the news is mixed. On the bright side, nearly all the adoptees showed appreciable developmental catch-up, but on assessment from four to six years after placement, they still did not equal their nondeprived peers either cognitively or emotionally. How much they caught up was mainly a function of how long they were in the orphanage before placement (O'Connor et al., 2000). Whether the Romanian children will ever catch up fully will be determined in subsequent follow-up studies.

So far, the findings from the Romanian studies parallel other findings about the effects of early deprivation in humans, and these, in turn, echo Harlow's results. Simply put, infants exposed to severe early neglect and abuse differ widely in how much they will be affected. Most will display a remarkable degree of cognitive and emotional catch-up after placement in a normal environment, but may never recover completely.

## REASSESSING THE ROLE OF EARLY EXPERIENCE

In light of all this, we must evidently reassess the once common view that early social experience is all important. Early experience certainly provides a vital foundation on which further social relationships are built. But experiences in infancy or childhood do not affect adult behavior directly. What happens instead is that each step in a sequence of social developments paves the way for the next. The early years are crucial in the sense that certain social patterns, such as the capacity to form attachments to other people, are much more likely to be acquired then. These early attachments provide a basis for developing later relationships, and so children who have never been loved by their parents will be frightened by their peers and hampered in their further social development. But while the earlier attachments (to mother and father) lay the foundation for later ones (to friends, lovers, and their own children), the two are nevertheless quite different. As a result, there may be ways—as with Harlow's monkey therapists—of acquiring the social tools for dealing with later relationships that circumvent the handicaps produced by earlier deprivation. For while the past affects the present, it does not determine it.

To sum up, the easiest way of getting to the second floor of a house is by way of the first floor. But in a pinch one can bring a ladder and climb in through a second-floor window.

*Socialization* **Most authors agree that parents exert some effect on the personality development of their children. What is at issue is what effects they have and how they achieve them.**

# CHILDHOOD SOCIALIZATION

Having healthy attachments to their caregivers is vital for infants, because it marks their entrance into the social world. But infants—and later, children—still have much to learn about this world: how to behave and how not to behave, how to understand others' intentions and convey their own. Children learn all these things through *socialization*, the process by which they acquire the patterns of thought and behavior typical of their culture.

## CULTURAL VALUES AND CHILD REARING

Some of the goals of socialization are similar all over the world and probably were so throughout human history. No matter If the child is an African bushman or a resident of urban America, she still must learn to control bodily functions like excretion (through toilet training) and impulses like physical aggression, and to live with others whose desires take precedence over her own.

Although these universal tasks imply some important similarities in how all children are reared, human societies are diverse, and it matters whether the child is to become a member of a band of nomadic herders, a rural village, or a tribe of Polynesian fishermen (Garcia Coll et al., 1995; Webb, 2001). Each of these societies must instill different characteristics in its young members-to-be. This point is especially clear when we consider the economy on which the society is based. Cultures based on agriculture or animal husbandry tend to stress compliance, conformity, and responsibility in child rearing. These attributes fit the adult role that the child must eventually assume—the patient, cooperative life of a farmer who must plow his soil or milk his cows at specified times so as to protect and augment the family's (or the village's) food supply. In contrast, hunting and fishing societies emphasize self-reliance and initiative—reasonable values for people who have to wrest their food from nature in day-to-day individual encounters (Barry, Child, & Bacon, 1959). Economic factors also affect the sexes differently. In some cultures, child rearing is strictly a job for females, and males are resource-getters and protectors; in others, child rearing is more egalitarian, and so is the working world. In this way, economic roles influence gender roles.

## MECHANISMS OF SOCIALIZATION

If each society leads children to embrace certain values, how is this accomplished? Some theorists stress the role of reward and the fear of punishment. Others point to the importance of imitation. Still others argue for the importance of the child's growing understanding of what she is supposed to do and why. The best guess is that all three of these mechanisms contribute to the child's socialization.

### REINFORCEMENT THEORY

According to both operant conditioning and psychoanalytic theory (see Chapters 4 and 15), children are socialized by a calculus of pain and pleasure. They will continue to do (or wish or think or remember) whatever previously brought them gratification and will refrain from whatever led to punishment and anxiety.

*Social Learning Theory* Although reward and punishment play a large part in socialization, many psychologists argue that these two mechanisms cannot account fully for socialization. They note that we are animals with a culture, which makes us altogether unlike any of the animals studied in the learning laboratory. Thorndike's cats had to discover how to get out of the puzzle box by themselves (see Chapter 4); no other cat told them how to do it, no other cat could. Humans, on the other hand, learn a multitude of solutions that were discovered by those who came before them. They do not have to invent clothes, spoken language, or the alphabet; they do not have to discover fire or the wheel or even how to eat baby food with a spoon. Other people show them.

These observations have led some psychologists to endorse a view known as *social learning theory*, in which one of the prime mechanisms of socialization is *observational learning*. Children observe another person who serves as a model and then imitate what the model does, thus learning how to do something they did not know before

*Modeling in real life*

*13.8   Learning by imitation   Performing a traditional tea ceremony is learned by imitating an accomplished model.*

*Imitating an absent model   The child may dress up to feel like an adult out of a desire for competence and mastery of the universe.*

(Figure 13.8). The ability to imitate starts early. As we noted in Chapter 12, very young human infants can imitate the facial expressions of the people they view; some studies have documented this skill even in newborns (Meltzoff & Moore, 1977). Of course, as the child grows and matures, the capacity for imitation grows as well (Flanders, 1968).

Many cultures explicitly encourage such imitation as a way of inducting the child into adult ways. In one Central American society, young girls are presented with miniature replicas of a water jar, a broom, and a grinding stone. They observe how their mothers use the real objects and through constant imitation acquire the relevant skills themselves (Bandura & Walters, 1963). The modern West has a similar practice: department stores are full of kid-sized tools and vacuum cleaners, toy cooking sets, and dolls that need feeding and diaper changing.

## COGNITIVE DEVELOPMENTAL THEORY

A different perspective on socialization is offered by the *cognitive approach*, which emphasizes the role of understanding in interpersonal thought and action. In this view, children know that some things they do are "bad" and some are "good." Children can also comprehend how they should relate to others and why they should act this way, and their comprehension deepens as their mental development unfolds.

Like social learning theorists, cognitive theorists perceive a crucial role for observational learning. However, the cognitive theorists emphasize the intellectual operations needed to make this learning possible. In important ways, therefore, they view social development as dependent on cognitive development. (For more on children's cognitive development, see Chapter 12.)

Consistent with this emphasis, let us note that even simple imitation requires considerable cognitive complexity. To see this, suppose a child imitates his father pulling up his trousers. In order to pull up his own pants, the boy must physically transpose the various steps. The father is facing one way, the child another way. These absolute positions, however, must be ignored; what matters instead are the relative positions. ("My foot, in relation to my trousers, must be in the same position as my father's foot, in relation to his trousers.") Similarly, the child must ignore many peripheral details ("My father is standing on the rug; I'm on the bare floor") but must be alert to other details ("My father started with his zipper unzipped and so must I"). Given all these complexities, it is no wonder that children are able to imitate more accurately as they get older (Yando, Seitz, & Zigler, 1978).

# THE FIRST AGENTS OF SOCIALIZATION: THE PARENTS

Up to this point, we have looked at socialization from the standpoint of the children who are being socialized, and we have explored how they are socialized—whether by reinforcement, by modeling, by understanding, or by all three. We now shift our focus to those who serve as society's first teachers: children's parents. Does the way parents rear their children really affect their children's behavior? If so, how lasting is the parents' influence?

## FEEDING AND TOILET TRAINING

Just what aspects of parenting are crucial? Until fifty years ago or so, developmental psychologists concerned themselves with aspects of child rearing that had been deemed especially important by Sigmund Freud and his followers, such as breast feeding and toilet training. In psychoanalytic theory, how parents managed both of these steps was pivotal in influencing whether their children became healthy and happy. As it turns out, the emphasis was misplaced, because these child-rearing particulars have little or no effect on the long-term social, emotional, or intellectual development of the child (Orlansky, 1949; Torrey, 1992; E. F. Zigler & Child, 1969; E. F. Zigler, Lamb, & Child, 1982).

## DIFFERENT PARENTING STYLES

Other developmental psychologists have taken a different approach, concentrating not on specific child-rearing practices but on the general home atmosphere in which children are reared (Baumrind, 1967, 1971; Maccoby & Martin, 1983).

In a number of studies, parents were asked to describe how they dealt with their children, and were also observed interacting with them. Several patterns of child rearing emerged. One is the *autocratic pattern*, in which the parents adhere to strict standards about how children should and should not speak and act, and attempt to mold their children's behavior accordingly. Such parents set down firm rules and greet any infractions with stern and sometimes severe punishment (sometimes including spanking). Autocratic parents do not believe it necessary to explain the rules to their children, but expect their children to submit to them by virtue of parental authority: "It's because I say so, that's why."

At the opposite extreme is the *permissive pattern*, in which children encounter few explicit do's and don'ts. The parents try not to assert their authority, impose few restrictions and controls, tend not to have set schedules (for, say, bedtime or watching TV), and rarely use punishment. They also make few demands on their children—such as putting toys away, doing schoolwork, or helping with chores.

Autocratic parents brandish parental power; permissive parents abdicate it. But there is a third approach that is in some ways in between. It is called the *authoritative-reciprocal pattern* because the parents both exercise their power and accept the reciprocal obligation to respond to their children's opinions and reasonable demands. Such parents set down rules of conduct and enforce them, assign chores, and expect mature behavior. But they also spend a good deal of time teaching their children how to act appropriately, encourage independence, and allow a good deal of verbal give and take. Unlike the permissive parents, they govern; but unlike the autocratic ones, they try to govern with the consent of the governed.

These parenting styles were formulated from observations of mostly middle-class children in the United States. But they may not fit all cultures. For example, in Chinese

"They never pushed me. If I wanted to retrieve, shake hands, or roll over, it was entirely up to me."

families children are expected to act very obediently, but such obedience is encouraged through parental warmth, trust, and close involvement rather than through bullying or emotionally distant rule enforcement (Chao, 1994).

Do these different parenting styles make any difference in the children? One investigator who observed U.S. preschoolers found that children raised autocratically were more withdrawn, lacked independence, and were more angry and defiant (especially the boys)—but so were the children raised permissively! In contrast, the children raised in the authoritative-reciprocal mode were more independent, competent, and socially responsible.

The way children are parented may also be related to how they behave in later years. When observed at the age of eight or nine, children whose parents had been judged to be either autocratic or permissive five years earlier seemed to be relatively low in intellectual self-reliance and originality. Once again, the children raised in the authoritative-reciprocal style fared best. They were more self-reliant when facing intellectual challenges, strove for achievement, and were more interpersonally adept and self-confident (Baumrind, 1977, 1991). Later studies have shown that the benefits of the authoritative-reciprocal style extend into the high-school years, where this parental pattern is associated with better grades and SAT scores as well as better social adjustment (Dornbusch et al., 1987; Steinberg, Elkman, & Mounts, 1989; Weiss & Schwarz, 1996).

Although these results seem to offer a ringing endorsement of the authoritative-reciprocal parenting style, this conclusion is far from foregone. Again, we confront the same cause-and-effect ambiguity that we faced with attachment styles. Although autocratic parenting may produce sullen, defiant children, it is equally possible that parents faced with sullen, defiant children must resort to autocratic parenting as their only recourse. Similarly, parents of good-natured, peaceable children may find that permissive parenting works fine. Likewise, parents of independent, responsible children may develop more peerlike, reciprocal relations early on with their children, and their children may be more intelligent, not because of child rearing but because of shared genetics or a number of other factors (see Chapter 14). This theme has larger implications, as we will discuss next.

*Lessons in social behavior* **Not all parent-child interactions are sweetness and light.**

## THE CHILD'S EFFECT ON THE PARENTS

Our asking whether parenting styles are a cause or consequence of children's behavior reflects the increasing awareness that socialization is a two-way street, and children are more than lumps of psychological clay molded by their social environment. Instead, children actively participate in their own rearing. The end result is that parents do not just socialize their children; they are also socialized by them (R. Q. Bell, 1968; R. Q. Bell & Harper, 1977).

For example, parents respond quite differently to infants with different temperaments. As a consequence, there will be a correlation between the parents' behavior and their children's, but this is not because the parents are shaping their children's behavior; instead, the parents' behavior is shaped by the children's (W. P. Collins, Maccoby, Steinberg, Hetherington, & Bornstein, 2000; P. J. Marshall, Fox, and Henderson, 2000; Olweus, 1980; Osofsky & Danzger, 1974; Thomas, Chess, & Birch, 1970; see Figure 13.5). Besides temperament, children also differ in ability, so a child who learns to crawl, walk, speak, or read precociously will be treated differently than a child who does not. To the extent that children differ in either temperament or ability (or in any of several other ways), their parents, siblings, and eventually their peers cannot help but treat them differently (Scarr & McCartney, 1983).

# THE DEVELOPMENT OF MORALITY

Initially, the children's experiences are largely confined to the family, and their first lessons in social behavior are taught within it—pick up your toys, don't push your baby brother, use your fork not your fingers—all circumscribed commands that apply to a very narrow social setting. But their social sphere soon expands to include young peers: at home, in kindergarten or day care, still later in school. These peers grow in importance, and children come to seek their approval as much as that of their parents (and by adolescence, often more eagerly).

As children's social universe expands, so does the set of commands they are expected to obey. While the first rules came directly from their parents, the rules later encountered come from people they have never met and probably never will. These are the rules of the society at large, and among the most important are those of moral conduct.

## NOT DOING WRONG

All societies have prohibitions that its members must obey. In many cases, these prohibitions are enforced by a watchful authority, and so children rarely steal from the cookie jar when their parents are present, just as adults rarely steal automobiles when the police are watching. But civil societies require that their citizens resist temptation even when they are not being watched, and so one aim of socialization is to inculcate moral values that are abided by not only to avoid punishment, but also because people believe that they are right.

### INTERNALIZATION AND SELF-PUNISHMENT

What leads to the internalization of right and wrong? Freud believed that internalization is produced by self-punishment in the form of guilt and anxiety. A child kicks her little brother, and her parents punish her. As a result, the forbidden act becomes associated with anxiety, and so to avoid this anxiety, the child avoids repeating the act. Indeed, to avoid the anxiety, the child must avoid even wanting to repeat the forbidden act. She has internalized the sanction, and so she is her own monitor and her own enforcer. It does not matter, therefore, that the external authorities who once punished her childhood transgressions have long stopped watching the cookie jar. Instead, the authorities now inhabit her mind, where she can no longer hide from them.

### INTERNALIZATION AND MINIMAL SUFFICIENCY

If conscience is in this fashion a vestige of past punishments, one might predict that the nature or degree of internalization should be related to the manner of child rearing. Imagine, for example, a pair of parents who rely on powerful sanctions in disciplining their children—strong punishments or harsh withdrawals of privileges. In this case, the anxiety associated with these punishments should be strong and, on the account just sketched, should lead to a strongly established internal sense of right and wrong.

This prediction turns out not only to be false but exactly backward. A number of studies suggest instead that prohibitions are less effectively internalized by children whose parents relied primarily on power in its various forms to discipline their children. The children of power-asserting (autocratic) parents were more likely to cheat for a prize when they thought no one was looking, and they were less likely to feel guilt about their misdeeds or to confess them when confronted. In contrast, prohibitions are most internalized by children whose parents took them aside to explain just how they had misbehaved and why they should behave differently (Hoffman, 1970).

What can explain these results? One proposal uses the *principle of minimal sufficiency*. This principle states that children will internalize a certain way of acting if they feel just enough pressure to get them to behave in this new way, but not so much pressure that they feel forced to do so.

This principle can explain a number of experimental findings, such as a study in which children were kept from playing with a particularly attractive toy. Some of the children were dissuaded only mildly ("I will be a little bit annoyed with you"), but others were threatened severely ("I will be very upset and very angry with you"). When the children were tested later in a different situation while thinking they were unobserved, the mildly dissuaded children resisted temptation more than the severely threatened ones did. Punishment led to internalization, but only if the punishment was mild. Well-tempered punishments seem to characterize authoritative-reciprocal parents, who somehow manage to strike the proper balance between acting forcefully enough to get their children to behave and mildly enough so that the children come to believe that they behaved morally of their own free will (Lepper, 1983).*

## DOING GOOD

Although the inhibition of forbidden acts is an important part of morality, moral action pertains to do's just as much as don'ts, to doing good as well as committing no evil. In a previous chapter, we noted how humans are capable of positive moral actions that require personal sacrifice (see Chapter 11). We now ask how this capacity develops in children.

Early on, children show positive, *prosocial* behavior, trying to aid and benefit others. Even very young children try to help and comfort others, and occasionally share with them (Radke-Yarrow, Zahn-Waxler, & Chapman, 1983; Rheingold, Hay, & West, 1976), and so one might conclude that children were congenital altruists. But as someone with a more skeptical view of human nature would counter, such apparently altruistic acts are actually quite selfish. Parents and teachers constantly hector children about the importance of sharing, so perhaps children share their toys in order to obtain or maintain parental approval. In the same fashion, perhaps children learn to share and to help others in order to preserve the esteem and support of their friends.

### EMPATHY

Is such a starkly cynical rejoinder justified? Some findings argue against the position that humans are by nature wholly self-centered, indicating instead that we often show *empathy*—a direct emotional response to another person's circumstances, even when we stand to gain nothing from such a reaction. We see a stranger writhe in pain in a hospital bed, and we ourselves experience vicarious distress (Aronfreed, 1968). This sort of empathic response is quite common: it is found in most people and is triggered by a wide range of situations.

Simple precursors to these empathic reactions can even be found in very young infants, in the first two or three days of life. On hearing another newborn's cry, for example, one-day-old infants cry, too, and their hearts beat faster (Sagi & Hoffman, 1976; Simner, 1971). Such infants are less likely to cry in response to nonhuman noises of comparable loudness, including a computer simulation of another infant's crying.

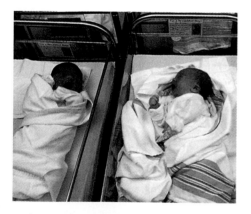

**Early empathy**  *Even very young infants cry in response to the sound of another infant crying. The same infants do not cry in response to other loud sounds, including a computer simulation of an infant's crying.*

* This is reminiscent of the effects of forced compliance on attitudes. As we saw in Chapter 10, participants who are pressured into performing some action that runs counter to their own attitudes will tend to change their attitude if the pressure (the threat or the bribe) is relatively small, but will not change the attitude if the pressure is large (Festinger and Carlsmith, 1959; Aronson and Carlsmith, 1963).

## FROM EMPATHIC DISTRESS TO UNSELFISH ACTION

*Empathy* just means feeling for another, but it does not imply helping the other. Helping requires more than just feeling; it requires action and knowing how to help. And learning what constitutes help is also part of socialization.

Consider a two-year-old boy who sees an adult in pain—say, his mother has cut her finger. In all likelihood, the child will be empathic and become distressed himself. But what will his empathic distress make him do? A number of anecdotes suggest that he will give his mother whatever he finds most comforting himself—for example, his teddy bear. While appreciating his kindly sentiments, the mother would probably have preferred a Band-Aid. But the child is as yet too young to take Mommy's perspective and does not realize that his mother's needs are not the same as his own (Hoffman, 1977a, 1979, 1984).*

As we develop, we become more able to discern what other people are likely to feel in a given situation and how to help if help is needed. Even that may not be enough to guarantee that we will act, because helping is only one means of allaying one's own empathic distress. A more direct but callous method is simply to look away. This often occurs in urban environments, where passers-by grow inured to sights of the homeless and impoverished. It can also occur in war and other situations wherein both adults and children "harden their hearts" to the suffering of others.

Thus, empathy does not guarantee altruism. In fact, there may be some circumstances in which empathic distress interferes with appropriate action. Good soldiers must not experience the enemy's wounds, nor should dentists feel their patients' pain. This point was made in a study of nursing staff on a hospital ward for the severely ill. The nurses who appeared to be the most empathic to their patients were the least effective. The reason was simple: they could not bear their patients' pain, and so they tried to have as little contact with them as possible (Stotland et al., 1978).

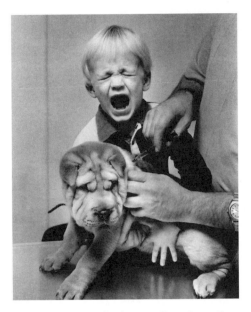

*Feeling distress at the distress of another* **The young boy cries as the veterinarian gives an injection to his puppy.**

## MORAL REASONING

Although we have concentrated on moral behavior, the growing child also develops an internal moral compass, a set of guiding principles by which he regulates and accounts for his actions. A compelling and socially important question concerns how children develop and refine these moral principles.

### KOHLBERG'S STAGES OF MORAL REASONING

An influential account of moral development was devised by Lawrence Kohlberg (1969). His basic method was to confront participants with stories that pose moral dilemmas. An example is a story about a man whose wife will die unless treated with a very expensive drug, a drug that costs $2,000. The husband scraped together all the money he could, but it was not enough, so he promised to pay the balance later. The pharmacist still refused to give him the drug. In desperation, the husband broke into the pharmacy and stole the drug. The participants were asked whether the husband's act was right or wrong and why.

Kohlberg analyzed the participants' answers and concluded that moral reasoning develops in a series of stages. The progression, roughly speaking, begins with a primi-

---

* Some authors make a distinction between *empathic distress*, in which the primary focus is on the unpleasant feelings the victim's plight arouses in us, and *sympathetic distress*, in which there is a desire to help the other person—not merely to relieve one's own empathic distress but to relieve the victim's. According to this view, empathic distress is a more primitive forerunner of sympathetic distress, which does not occur until children are about two years old (Hoffman, 1984).

## TABLE 13.1   KOHLBERG'S STAGES OF MORAL REASONING

| STAGE OF MORAL REASONING | MORAL BEHAVIOR IS THAT WHICH: |
|---|---|
| Preconventional morality | |
|    Level 1 | Avoids punishment |
|    Level 2 | Gains reward |
| Conventional morality | |
|    Level 3 | Gains approval and avoids disapproval of others |
|    Level 4 | Is defined by rigid codes of "law and order" |
| Postconventional morality | |
|    Level 5 | Is defined by a "social contract" generally agreed upon for the public good |
|    Level 6 | Is based on abstract ethical principles that determine one's own moral code |

SOURCE: Adapted from Kohlberg, 1969.

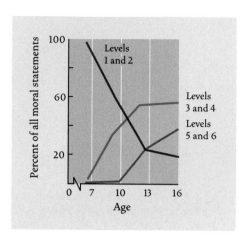

**13.9   Level of moral reasoning as a function of age**   *With increasing age, the level of moral reasoning changes. In this figure, the percent of all moral judgments made by children at various ages falls into one of three general categories defined by Kohlberg. At seven, virtually all moral judgments are in terms of avoiding punishment or gaining reward (Kohlberg's levels 1 and 2). At ten, about half the judgments are based on criteria of social approval and disapproval or of a rigid code of laws (Kohlberg's levels 3 and 4). From thirteen on, some of the children refer to more abstract rules—a generally agreed-upon social contract or a set of abstract ethical principles (Kohlberg's levels 5 and 6).*

tive morality guided by fear of punishment or desire for gain ("If you let your wife die, you'll get in trouble"). This stage is superseded by one in which right and wrong are defined by convention and by what people will say ("Your family will think you're inhuman if you don't help your wife"). Finally, moral development culminates with the internalization of personal moral principles ("If you didn't steal the drug, you wouldn't have lived up to your own standards of conscience").

People advance from stage to stage as they age, but only a few attain Kohlberg's highest level (Kurtines & Gewirtz, 1995). Considering that this final stage characterizes such individuals as Mahatma Gandhi and Mother Teresa, the failure of Kohlberg's participants (and no doubt, most of us) to attain it is probably not too surprising (Figure 13.9, Table 13.1).

### IS KOHLBERG'S FRAMEWORK UNIVERSAL?

There are many questions to be asked about Kohlberg's framework. For one thing, Kohlberg intended his conception to describe all people—both men and women, and people in all cultures. Does it?

*Moral Reasoning in Men and Women*   An influential discussion by Carol Gilligan (1982, 1986) suggests that it may not. In her view, men tend to see morality as a matter of justice, ultimately based on abstract, rational principles by which all individuals will end up being treated fairly. As one eleven-year-old boy put it in describing the moral dilemmas posed by Kohlberg, "It's sort of like a math problem with humans." Women, in contrast, see morality more in terms of compassion, human relationships, and special responsibilities to those with whom one is intimately connected.

Gilligan's view certainly does not imply that one gender is more or less moral than the other. In fact, studies of moral reasoning reveal no reliable sex differences on Kohlberg's test; of 108 studies, only 8 showed a superiority of males over females, while 4 or 5 went in the opposite direction (Brabeck, 1983; Walker, 1984, 1995; but see Baumrind, 1986, Walker, 1989).

Even with these demonstrations of gender equality, the possibility remains that men and women do emphasize different values in their moral reasoning—an abstract conception of justice on the one side, and principles of compassion and human responsibility on the other. That such a difference in emphases exists is suggested by various findings, including the fact that girls seem to place a greater value on going out of one's way to help other people and show more emotional empathy than do boys (Hoffman, 1977b). Just why women emphasize the perspective of care rather than that of abstract justice is still unsettled. The best guess is that it is a result of gendered patterns of socialization that stress different values for boys and girls (Hoffman, 1984).

*Moral Reasoning in Other Cultures*   Moral perspectives and values may also differ from one cultural group to the next. A number of studies have shown that when members of less technological societies are asked to reason about moral dilemmas, they generally attain comparatively low scores on Kohlberg's scale. They justify acts on the basis of concrete issues, such as what neighbors will say or concern over one's wife, rather than on more abstract conceptions of justice and morality (Kohlberg, 1969; Tietjen & Walker, 1985; Walker & Moran, 1991; also see Rozin, 1999).

How should we interpret this evidence? Does it mean that the inhabitants of, say, a small Turkish village are less moral than the residents of Paris or New York City? A more plausible interpretation is that Turkish villagers spend their lives in a small community in continual face-to-face encounters with all the community's members. Under the circumstances, the most likely outcome is a more concrete morality that gives the greatest weight to care, responsibility, and loyalty (Kaminsky, 1984; Simpson, 1974).

## MORAL REASONING AND MORAL CONDUCT

Kohlberg's test focuses on moral reasoning—how people think about and talk about a situation involving some moral dilemma. But can we predict how people will act if we know how they reason morally?

To some extent, we can make such predictions. A number of studies have found that delinquents show lower scores on Kohlberg's tests than do comparable nondelinquents. Other studies suggest that individuals at higher, principled levels of moral reasoning are less likely to cheat in an ambiguous situation and are more likely to remain intransigent in the face of other people's views.

Other results, however, suggest that the relation between moral reasoning and moral conduct is far from perfect (Blasi, 1980; Gibbs et al., 1986; Rest, 1983): often, people with high scores on Kohlberg's tests fail to do the right thing, whereas people with lower scores often behave in ways that seem moral and honorable. Kohlberg's stages, it appears, tell us more about what people will say than what they will do. In other words, espousing moral principles does not mean abiding by them (for discussion, see Blasi, 1984; Kohlberg, Levine, & Hewer, 1984; Rest, 1984). What creates this gap between moral beliefs and moral actions? Here as always, a variety of factors play a role, including whether or not the person identifies himself as a moral person, whether his moral beliefs are cast in specific terms or only in generalities, and more (see, for example, Damon, 1999).

# THE DEVELOPMENT OF SEX AND GENDER

We have been considering social development as a process of growth and expansion, and socialization as the effort to fit the developing person to her culture. But like physical and cognitive development, social development has a flip side—that of differentia-

*Moral reasoning in men and women*
**The belief that men and women focus on different aspects of morality has ancient roots. A classical example is Sophocles' tragedy** Antigone, **which revolves around the irreconcilable conflict between Antigone, who insists on burying her slain brother, and her uncle Creon, the king, who issues a decree forbidding anyone from doing so on pain of death. To Antigone, the ultimate moral obligation is to the family; to Creon, it is to the state and its laws. (From a 1982 production at the New York Shakespeare Festival, with F. Murray Abraham and Lisa Banes.)**

*Learning gender roles* **Some of the cues signaling a child's gender roles are subtle; others are far from it.**

tion. Even as she becomes socialized, the child becomes increasingly aware that people are all different, and the ways that others differ from her. This awareness leads the child to a clearer conception of her own "self" and her own personality—what she is really like, in her own eyes and in others' eyes as well.

Seen in this light, social development goes hand in hand with the development of personal identity. Central to this is one's sex. Biologically, one's sex seems simple enough, but it can refer either to *genetic sex*, possessing XX or XY chromosome pairs, or to *morphological* (that is, structural) *sex*, the possession of a clitoris, vagina, and ovaries or penis, scrotum, and testes.

One's sexuality, though, is far more than body parts. It also embraces three psychological issues. One is *gender role*—a whole host of behavior patterns that a given culture deems appropriate for each sex. Fundamental to gender roles is the second issue, *gender identity*—our inner sense that we are male or female. A third issue is *sexual orientation*—our inclination toward a sexual partner of the same or opposite sex. Gender identity, gender role, and sexual orientation are among the most important aspects of a person's experience.* How do they come about?

## GENDER ROLES

Gender roles pervade all of social life. The induction into one or the other of these roles begins with the first question typically asked of new parents: "Is it a boy or a girl?" As soon as the answer is supplied—which, thanks to fetal ultrasound, may be months before birth—the process of gender typing begins, and the infant is ushered onto one of two quite different social trajectories. Many of the patterns of gender typing have probably changed in the wake of modern feminism, but powerful differences in child rearing persist. In our culture, infants are still dressed in either pink or blue; children play with either dolls or toy airplanes.

Besides this inculcation, children can easily observe gender roles in the adult world and discern further clues about how boys and girls are "supposed" to act. While these gender roles are now blurred a bit, children are still likely to observe that adult women (like Mom) often work at home as unpaid housekeepers, cooks, and child-care workers, while adult men (like Dad) go out into the workplace and bring home a paycheck. If both parents work outside the home, children will observe that men and women generally have different kinds of jobs: Mom is unlikely to be a truck driver, or Dad a secretary. And children are also likely to realize that men's jobs are more highly valued by society than are women's—truck drivers generally earn more than secretaries.

Children may observe, too, that society has different expectations about how the two sexes should act. Typically, men are expected to be tough, aggressive, stoical, and interested more in things than in people. In contrast, women are expected to be submissive, emotionally expressive, and more interested in people than in things (Good & Sherrod, 2001).

Such a "gender belief system" (Deaux & Kite, 1993) indelibly shapes the world that children perceive and also how others interact with them. For example, parents talk to their male and female children differently (M. E. Lamb, 1997; Crowley, Callanan, Tenenbaum, & Allen, 2001). They also play with their children differently, with rough-and-tumble play far more common with boys (O'Brien & Nagle, 1987). This difference in

---

* It has become customary to distinguish between *sex* and *gender*. Sex generally refers to aspects of male-female differences that pertain to reproductive functions (for example, having ovaries versus testes, vagina versus penis) or genetically related factors (for example, differences in height or muscular strength). It is also used to designate erotic feelings, inclinations, or practices (for example, heterosexuality and homosexuality). Gender, on the other hand, refers to social or psychological aspects of being seen as a man or woman or regarding oneself to be so.

styles of play was demonstrated in a study in which mothers of young infants were asked to participate in an experiment on how children play. They were then introduced to a six-month-old baby, little "Joey" or "Janie," and asked to play with him or her for a few minutes. In fact, the same six-month-old was used in both roles, and dressed up either as a boy or as a girl. Even so, the mothers' behavior depended on whether they thought they were playing with "Joey" or "Janie." To "Joey" the mothers offered toys such as hammers or rattles, while "Janie" was invariably given a doll. They also handled "Joey" and "Janie" differently: they often bounced "Joey" about, thus stimulating the whole body. In contrast, their response to "Janie" was gentler and less vigorous (C. Smith & Lloyd, 1978).

Many of these gender stereotypes are explicitly enforced by parents and peers, and violations are correspondingly punished. When young children play with toys that are deemed inappropriate—as when a boy plays with a dollhouse, or a girl with a toy electric drill—their parents are likely to express disapproval (Fagot, 1995). This is especially so for fathers, who sternly object to any female-typical behavior in their sons. By and large, girls are allowed more latitude. A girl can be a "tomboy" and be seen as well adjusted; a boy who is a "sissy" is mocked, taunted, or marginalized (Langlois & Downs, 1980; McCreary, 1994).

## SEX DIFFERENCES IN GENDER ROLES

What makes gender roles so different? We must consider both constitution and enculturation to understand how biology and society conspire to make boys into men and girls into women.

It is self-evident that gender roles are influenced by anatomical and physiological differences. Some of these differences pertain in obvious ways to reproduction, but there are also differences between the sexes in average size, strength, and physical endurance. On many dimensions, girls mature more quickly than boys, as evidenced by a host of measures that includes speaking, toilet training, developing fine-motor skills (such as drawing), getting permanent teeth, reaching puberty, and attaining one's adult body size; boys excel only in basic activity level and at skills requiring power and force (Eaton & Yu, 1989; J. A. Martin, King, Maccoby, & Jacklin, 1984; Tanner, 1990). There are also certain sexually dimorphic areas of the brain—that is, areas that reliably differ in men and women (L. S. Allen, Hines, Shryne, & Gorski, 1989). These areas, many of which lie in and around the hypothalamus, are involved in sexual behavior and, as we shall see, sexual orientation.

*Imitation and gender roles* **Some aspects of "learning to be a girl" or "learning to be a boy" come directly from observation and imitation.**

What about the psychological differences between the sexes? Before we proceed, we need to heed two cautions. First, any psychological difference between the sexes is one of averages. The average three-year-old girl seems to be more dependent than her male counterpart—she is more likely to cling, ask for help, and seek affection (Emmerich, 1966). But this generalization does not apply to every boy and girl, because there are certainly many three-year-old girls who are less dependent, or more physically aggressive, than many three-year-old boys. Thus, we must be careful not to overstate any differences. There is variability within virtually any group, and so findings that describe the average of an entire group cannot and should not be used to characterize each individual within the group.

The second caution is about interpretation, particularly about the relationship between psychological traits and the underlying biology. No trait—whether an individual's hair color or his level of physical aggression—results directly from one's biology. As we have noted in many other contexts, biology and environment interact in rich and complex ways, so that traits that are genetically programmed can often be altered by environmental variation, and traits apparently shaped by culture often depend on some

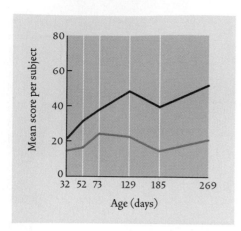

**13.10** *The development of rough-and-tumble play in male and female rhesus monkeys* Roughhouse play in rhesus monkeys during the first year of life. The scores are based on both frequency and vigor of this activity, in which monkeys wrestle, roll, or sham bite—all presumably in play, since no one ever gets hurt. Roughhouse play is considerably more pronounced in males (red) than in females (green), a difference that increases during the first year of life.

"Carolyn Dolnick said my dress is a knockoff!"

*Aggression in girls* **Boys are more physically aggressive than girls, but girls often engage in social aggression.**

sort of biological support. Hand in hand with this, if we find that a trait is shaped by biology, this does not mean that the trait is fixed and immutable. After all, our hair color is strongly governed by genetic factors, but we can easily change it by going out in the sun or using a five-minute chemical rinse. The same is true for almost any other trait one can name. (We return to this issue in Chapter 14.)

## AGGRESSION

The one sex difference that seems to occur across all cultures concerns physical aggression. Males are on average more active and physically more assertive than females. This difference is apparent from the very start. Male infants are more irritable and physically active than female infants, and mothers even report that their boys were more active than their girls *in utero*. At age two or three, boys are much more likely to engage in rough-and-tumble play and mock fighting than are girls (a difference also seen in apes and monkeys; see Figure 13.10). By four or five, they are more ready to exchange insults and to greet aggression with bodily retaliation than are girls (Legault & Strayer, 1990; Crick & Grotpeter, 1995).

The sex difference in physical aggression continues into adulthood. Acts of violence are relatively rare among both sexes, but they are much more common among men than women. Adolescent males are arrested for violent crimes five times more often than are adolescent females (R. E. Johnson, 1979). A similar pattern holds in such widely different cultural settings as Ethiopia, India, Kenya, Mexico, Okinawa, and Switzerland (Maccoby & Jacklin, 1974, 1980; Parke & Slaby, 1983; Whiting & Whiting, 1975).

How can we explain the sex difference in physical aggression? It is found early in life, apparently in all cultures, and is also seen in our primate relatives. All of this suggests a strong biological predisposition.

Even if boys are already predisposed toward physical aggression, though, enculturation seems to maintain and even magnify it. Boys are encouraged to be tough and are given toy swords and guns, while girls are expected to be well behaved and receive cooking sets and Barbie dolls. Parents will generally tolerate and even foster a degree of physical aggressiveness in a boy that they would never countenance in a girl, such as when fathers encourage their sons to fight back when another boy attacks them (Sears, Maccoby, & Levin, 1957).

This process continues in adolescence, where aggressive behavior in boys is tolerated or indulgently winked at, while the same behavior in girls is discouraged in favor of peacekeeping and approval seeking. Despite the advent of the female superhero, the media usually perpetuate sex stereotypes by featuring strong, silent heroes and charming, adoring heroines. Thus, while males and females may start life with different predispositions toward physical aggression, by the time they are adults, society has amplified and encouraged this initial difference (Parke & Slaby, 1983).

Let us note, though, that all of these differences involve physical aggression. This is not because girls are less aggressive overall; rather, it is because girls are less likely to be aggressive in physical ways (Underwood, Galen, & Paquette, 2001; also see Chapter 11). They tend to engage, instead, in *relational aggression*, which is focused on altering social alliances. Relational aggression can take many forms—disdainfully pretending not to know another person, befriending someone else as revenge against another ("You're my new best friend"), excluding someone from one's group (openly not inviting someone to one's birthday party), or trying to harm another's friendships ("Kristen thinks you're dumb") (Crick, Casas, & Mosher, 1997; Crick & Grotpeter, 1995; Feshbach, 1969; Galen & Underwood, 1997; Lagerspetz, Bjorkqvist, & Peltonen, 1988; but see Tomada & Schneider, 1997).

What explains the female preference for relational aggression? We can only offer conjectures. Compared to males, females' lesser stature and physical strength do not lend themselves readily to shows of brute force. Moreover, cultural injunctions that little girls are "made of sugar and spice and everything nice" and must act "ladylike" no doubt discourage frank physical aggression. Finally, some observers have suggested that the subordinate social ranking accorded females in many cultures leaves them little recourse but to negotiate conflicts subtly (see J. W. White, Donat, & Bondurant, 2001).

## PATTERNS OF INTELLECTUAL APTITUDES

One other psychological difference between the sexes is often said to be biologically predisposed—a difference in intellectual abilities. It is not that one sex is any more intelligent than the other: studies comparing males' and females' IQ scores, for example, have reported only small differences, and the direction of the differences (which sex has the higher IQ) has varied from study to study (Held, Alderton, Foley, & Segall, 1993; Lynn, 1994). Where the sexes differ is on more specific tests. On average, boys and men do better on some tests of spatial and mathematical ability (Figure 13.11), whereas girls and women do better on many verbal tasks (Halpern, 1992, 1997; Hines, 1990; Maccoby & Jacklin, 1974, 1980; Masters & Sanders, 1993; J. Stanley, 1993)—although the size of the difference on verbal tasks is contested and, according to some authors, has decreased over the years (Halpern, 1992; J. S. Hyde & Linn, 1988).

This sex difference in specific intellectual abilities is obvious in school performance, especially if we focus on just the children who do particularly well or particularly poorly. For example, a large-scale, thirty-two-year retrospective study looked at children who had scored in the top 10 percent on various tests, and found that three times as many boys as girls scored in the top 10 percent of math and science tests but twice as many girls as boys excelled on writing tests (Hedges & Nowell, 1995).

The difference between boys and girls in mathematics is striking, and a number of authors believe that it reflects a basic sex difference in certain spatial abilities. An example is the ability to visualize objects in space, often assessed by having participants imagine rotating a three-dimensional object in space and then answer questions about the object's shape. (See Chapter 8 for further discussion of this mental rotation task.) This is a task on which men reliably outperform women, and since a number of branches of mathematics seem to rely on such visualization, it is not far-fetched to assume that the sex difference in this ability underlies those in quantitative aptitude and achievement (Burnett, Lane, & Dratt, 1979; Halpern, 1992; E. Hunt, 1985a). Women should not be counted out in the visuospatial realm, however, because on certain tasks that require memory for shapes and perceptual speed (for example, quickly matching shapes to numbers), they excel reliably (Kolb & Whishaw, 1996).

What accounts for these sex differences in cognitive aptitudes? Perhaps they reflect a difference in the way boys and girls are reared. Boys are more often led to take classes in science and math, while girls are shunted elsewhere (toward English or typing classes), and it would be natural to end up more skilled in the ways that were encouraged. But various lines of evidence suggest that early career direction may only be part of the story. An example is a study of SAT scores in 40,000 adolescents. The investigators found the usual sex differences on spatial and mathematical tasks, even when they limited their comparison to boys and girls who had taken the exact same high-school math courses and had expressed the same degree of interest in mathematics (Benbow, 1988; Benbow, Lubinski, Shea, & Eftekhari-Sanjani, 2000; Benbow & Stanley, 1983; Stumpf & Stanley, 1998).

Other investigators have searched for a direct biological basis for the male-female differences in cognitive performance and have focused on differences in the brain. Indeed, post-mortem studies of individuals with aphasia and studies of conscious participants using both PET scans and functional MRI (see Chapter 2) have revealed considerable differences between the brains of males and females, including regions critical

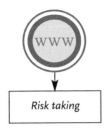

Risk taking

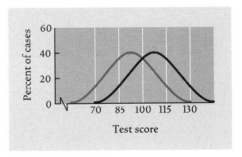

13.11 *Sex differences in spatial ability* **Results on a spatial-mathematical test, which included questions such as "How many times between three and four o'clock do the hands of a clock make a straight line?" The curve plots the percentage of participants who receive a particular score (with men in red and women in green). As the curve shows, the men perform better than the women, though the two curves overlap considerably. (Data from Very, 1967, with test scores adjusted by a method called "normalization.")**

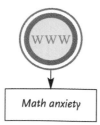

Math anxiety

for verbal and visuospatial tasks (Kolb & Whishaw, 1996; Shaywitz et al., 1995). If the brains of males and females differ in ways that can account for the intellectual differences, then what accounts for the different brains? Various hypotheses have been advanced, including direct genetic programming (McGee, 1979) and the quicker maturation of females' brains (Boles, 1980; Kolb & Whishaw, 1996; Waber, 1977, 1979).

*Testosterone and Spatial Abilities*    One widely endorsed hypothesis about the male-female difference in visuospatial abilities focuses on the influence of the sex hormone testosterone. Males who produce abnormally low levels of testosterone show impairments in visuospatial abilities (Hier & Crowley, 1982), while older males (aged 60–75), whose testosterone levels fall with age, show dramatic improvements in spatial cognition after receiving testosterone supplements (Cherrier et al., 2001; Janowsky, Oviatt, & Orwoll, 1994). Moreover, girls born with adrenal-gland tumors that secrete abnormally high levels of testosterone show enhanced spatial abilities (Resnick, Berenbaum, Gottesman, & Bouchard, 1986), and testosterone fluctuations during the menstrual cycle produce corresponding fluctuations in females' spatial abilities (Hausmann, Slabbekoorn, Van Goozen, Cohen-Kettenis, & Guentuerkuen, 2000).

*Culture and Cognitive Abilities*    Just as with physical aggression, however, we must not overstate the power of these biological effects. Culture unquestionably plays a role in creating and sustaining these cognitive differences. In American society, for example, girls are generally expected to do better in English than in math. This belief is shared by teachers, parents, and the pupils themselves, and all conspire to make it come true. Thus, even girls who could do well on spatial and mathematical tests may nonetheless fail—perhaps because they receive no encouragement in mathematics or perhaps because they are told directly that they should spend their efforts elsewhere.

Unfortunately, these socal influences are often internalized by the students themselves. They begin to believe that math-related careers are the province of males and that a women who is good at math is unfeminine. A female mathematics professor has aptly described the stereotype:

> Many people on hearing the words "female mathematician" conjure up an image of a six-foot, gray-haired, tweed-suited, oxford-clad woman. This image, of course, doesn't attract the young woman who is continually bombarded with messages, both direct and indirect, to be beautiful, "feminine" and catch a man. (Quoted in Halpern, 1992, p. 216)

Consistent with this stereotype, studies indicate that women perform less well on tests of mathematical ability if they are asked, at the start of the test, simply to record their gender on the test form. Presumably, this serves to prime the relevant stereotype and undermine performance (Ambady, Shih, Kim, & Pittinsky, 2001; for more on this sort of "stereotype threat," see Chapter 14). Similarly, sex differences in test scores are clearly influenced by small changes in instructions or context, confirming the role of the expectations and attitudes that are shaped by these situational factors (see, for example, R. P. Brown & Josephs, 1999; Crawford & Chaffin, 1997).

## GENDER IDENTITY

Boys are boys and girls are girls. Or are they? We assume that children all have a fixed gender identity—they know they are boys or girls, as do their parents, peers, doctors, and teachers. Indeed, by about the age of three, most children can report accurately who is male and who is female, and they also know their own sex (Fagot, Leinbach, & Hagen, 1986). But initially their classifications are flexible. For example, when shown a picture of a girl, even four-year-olds say that she could be a boy if she wanted to or if she wore a

*Social factors and sex differences    Social effects augment constitutional differences.*

boy's haircut or wore a boy's clothes (D. E. Marcus & Overton, 1978; and see Kohlberg, 1966).

Nor do preschoolers take anatomy into account. For example, when given dolls that have either male or female genitals and varying hair length, preschoolers generally decide which are boys and which are girls on the basis of hair length (McConaghy, 1979; but see S. L. Bem, 1989). It takes children until the age of five or so to achieve the concept of *gender constancy*—the recognition that being male or female is irrevocable and not dependent on what one wears or does.

## INTERSEXUALITY AND SEX REASSIGNMENT

Of course, all this assumes that the child is actually either a boy or a girl. The situation is not so simple for *intersexuals*, children who are not clearly either. Studies of these individuals, who comprise nearly 2 percent of live births (Fausto-Sterling, 2000), have provided great insights about the influence of biology and culture on gender identity and gender roles.

Intersexuality has various causes. Some cases result from sex chromosomes that depart from the usual XX or XY complements. Others are due to drugs taken during pregnancy or specific hormonal or genetic disorders.

Intersexuality also varies considerably in its manifestations. One kind of intersexuality is *true hermaphroditism*, which occurs when an individual has functioning reproductive tissue from both sexes, such as a testicle on one side and an ovary on the other. In contrast with true hermaphroditism is *pseudohermaphroditism*. Individuals born with this disorder (perhaps one in two thousand births) have external genitals, and sometimes internal organs, that are anatomically ambiguous—that is, not clearly male or female (Fausto-Sterling, 1993).

*Ambiguous Genitalia and Sex Reassignment* In cases of intersexuality, parents and physicians sometimes decide to use plastic surgery to make the external genitalia unambiguous and then give the child a lengthy course of hormone therapy, often with the view that an ambiguously sexed child will become a socially dysfunctional adult. The child's sex is then officially reassigned in both medical records and legal documents, and the child is reared accordingly. By one estimate, in the United States five intersexed children undergo sex reassignment every day (Fausto-Sterling, 2000).

Because of the difficulty of constructing functioning male organs, and the core belief that no male could ever grow up well adjusted without a normal penis, the surgical rule for most cases has been "when in doubt, make it female." The end result in these cases is a person who looks female and can participate sexually as a female (the remnant of the penis becomes the clitoris, and the scrotum is fashioned to make a vagina). But since the newly constructed female has had a great deal of sensitive sexual tissue removed, she is vulnerable to painful genital scarring, infection, and reduced sexual feeling, and since she lacks ovaries and a uterus, she cannot have children. These facts make it easy to understand why some intersexed individuals regard this outcome as a very bad bargain, consider the reassignment to be mutilating rather than "corrective," and believe it should be banned until the intersex child reaches the age of consent (C. Chase, 1998; M. Diamond, 1997).

*The Effects of Reassignment* It is also unclear how well surgical reassignment works to make the person identify with the new sex. Early studies suggested that if the reassignment occurred early enough—according to some investigators, the upper limit was eighteen months; for others, three or four years—the child would adjust well, becoming a he or a she, in part because of other people's expectations (Money & Ehrhardt, 1972).

One influential case study involved "John," born in 1963 as a genetic XY male with normal genitals, but whose penis was burned beyond repair during minor surgery. The doctors urged the parents to allow sex reassignment, and at the age of seventeen months, John had "corrective" surgery. John became "Joan," and Joan's parents, doctors, and teachers all accepted the child as a girl, giving her a life of dolls, dresses, and "girl things." The first assessment of Joan's case considered the reassignment a success (Money & Ehrhardt, 1972), and the story was widely reported in texts and the mass media as showing the power of socialization over biology in determining gender identity and gender roles.

But Joan's life was far from happy. Her mother reports that from the start Joan tore off her dresses, preferred climbing trees to playing house, and, when her brother refused to share his toys, saved her allowance to buy her own toy truck. As she neared puberty, Joan was given the sex hormone estrogen to help her appear more feminine, but she nonetheless came to believe that she was a boy and kept trying to urinate standing up. By age fourteen, Joan was depressed and suicidal. She finally revealed her suspicions to her endocrinologist, and—without being apprised of her unique history—she agreed to plastic surgery to construct a penis, along with treatments of male hormones. Only after the surgery did her (now his) father finally reveal—to an upset and bewildered John—the original accident and surgery (Colapinto, 2000).

John became an attractive male interested romantically in women, and he married at the age of twenty-five and adopted his wife's children from her previous marriage. Today, he has revealed his true identity and discussed his life story with the media (see Figure 13.12). He is happy overall and reasonably well adjusted, but resentful about what happened to him and concerned that no one else be treated similarly (Colapinto, 2000; M. Diamond & Sigmundson, 1997; also see Bradley, Oliver, Chernick, & Zucker, 1998).

In some respects, this case is quite atypical. "John" developed normally in the uterus and for some months afterward, and in this sense was a normal boy, with a normal masculine brain and body. In contrast, most infants given sex reassignment are generally pseudohermaphrodites, whose development is abnormal both prenatally and thereafter. This leaves us cautious about generalizing too much from the "John/Joan" case, and the anecdotal evidence from other case reports clarifies little. Comprehensive follow-up studies of sex-reassignment patients are underway and should allow a better estimate of the surgery's success.

One thing that the "John/Joan" case does make clear is that biological factors early on play a crucial role in sexual interests and behavior. Additional evidence on this point comes from a series of studies of girls who were exposed as fetuses to abnormally high levels of androgens, which masculinized both their brains and their bodies. At birth, many of these girls were pseudohermaphrodites, with ambiguous external genitals (typically, incomplete vaginas and enlarged clitorises). Although the girls received appropriate plastic surgery and were raised as females, follow-up studies showed that the excess androgen during pregnancy had long-term psychological effects. When compared to a control group, the androgenized girls were much more likely to be tomboys during childhood: they chose trucks over dolls, loved to participate in energetic team sports, preferred slacks to dresses, and had little interest in jewelry or perfume. As adolescents, they looked forward to a future in which marriage and maternity were subordinated to a career (Ehrhardt, 1984; Money, 1980; Money & Ehrhardt, 1972). They also had higher rates of lesbianism and lesbian sexual fantasies (Dittmann, Kappes, & Kappes, 1992; Zucker et al., 1996).

What about the gender identity of these women? Most still believed they were female, albeit with typically masculine interests. In other cases, though, the outcome is different, and, in one study of four cases of abnormally androgenized women, gender identity changed gradually, beginning in childhood with the belief that they were "girls" but coming to the conclusion by early adulthood that they were men (Meyer-Bahlburg et al., 1996). These cases show that, unlike "John/Joan," gender identity is not fixed and immutable in everyone.

**13.12  John/Joan**  *To protect his privacy, David Reimer's name was kept a secret when his case was first described; he was instead called "John/Joan." As an adult, though, Reimer has revealed his identity, and has discussed his life story with the media.*

*The Guevedoces Syndrome* Other evidence that gender identity is not always set in stone in early development comes from the discovery of a number of male children with a rare genetic disorder, called *guevedoces syndrome*, in three rural villages in the Dominican Republic. In the fetal stage this disorder makes these children relatively insensitive to many of the effects of androgens. As a result, their external genitals at birth look much like a female's, and so they often are thought to be girls and raised as such. But puberty, with its sudden upsurge in male hormone levels, brings a dramatic change. The misidentified "girls" develop male genitals, their voices deepen, and their torsos become muscular (although they never develop beards).

If gender identity were always established by early childhood, then a natural reassignment at puberty (around age eleven or twelve) ought to result in psychological catastrophe. In actuality, the majority of these adolescents come to adopt their new male identity fairly easily. They change their name and take up male occupations. While they are initially anxious about sex, they ultimately seem to adjust and form normal relationships. In one study, fifteen out of sixteen men with this syndrome eventually married or lived in common-law relationships (Imperato-McGinley, Guerrero, Gautier, & Peterson, 1974; Imperato-McGinley, Peterson, Gautier, & Sturla, 1979).

Thus, the evidence is mixed on when gender identity forms and whether—and in whom—it becomes fixed for life. Despite the clear-cut evidence provided by "John/Joan," findings from highly androgenized women and men with the guevedoces syndrome suggest that, even though gender identity usually jells early in childhood, it is potentially changeable. What is uncertain is how often late changes in gender identity occur, and the hormonal and psychosocial circumstances sufficient to change it.

## SEXUAL ORIENTATION

The majority of men and women are *heterosexual*; they almost exclusively seek a partner of the opposite sex. But for a significant minority, the sexual orientation is otherwise. Some of these individuals experience erotic and romantic feelings almost exclusively toward members of their own sex; such people are *homosexual*. Others commonly experience such feelings for both their own and the opposite sex; such people are *bisexual*.

Importantly, though, virtually all gay and bisexual men think of themselves as men and are so regarded by others; the analogous point holds for lesbians (Marmor, 1975).* Their gender identity is thus not in question. This clearly illustrates the fact that sexual orientation, gender identity, and gender role are in principle independent.

### THE PREVALENCE OF HETEROSEXUALITY AND HOMOSEXUALITY

Perhaps the most comprehensive study of sexual patterns among Americans was an anonymous survey conducted in the 1940s by a research team led by biologist Alfred Kinsey. Kinsey and his associates found that 4 percent of American men are exclusively homosexual during their lifetime (Kinsey, Pomeroy, & Martin, 1948). The comparable prevalence of exclusive homosexuality among women seems to be lower—about 2 percent (Kinsey, Pomeroy, Martin, & Gebhard, 1953). A substantially larger group is predominantly homosexual but has also had some heterosexual experience. According to Kinsey's data, this category includes about 13 percent of American men and 7 percent of women.

*A lesbian couple Rosie O'Donnell and her partner Kelli Carpenter.*

* A small percentage of individuals forms the exception to this rule. Transsexuals are genetically and physiologically entirely male or female but believe that they were born the wrong sex; complete surgical and hormonal sex reassignment is the usual treatment. Transsexuals should not be confused with transvestites, individuals who enjoy and are aroused by dressing like the opposite sex. Transvestites are typically heterosexual males.

Some believe that these estimates are too high, arguing that Kinsey's criteria for homosexual experience were not sufficiently stringent and his survey sample not adequately representative (Hamer et al., 1993a, 1993b; Reisman & Eichel, 1990). Still, more recent surveys of both men and women basically confirm Kinsey's estimates, both in the United States and in other Western cultures (see, for example, ACSF Investigators, 1992; A. M. Johnson, Wadsworth, Wellings, Bradshaw, & Field, 1992). These studies also indicate that despite the sexual revolution of the 1960s and the increasing social acceptance of gays and lesbians, the prevalence of homosexuality has remained about the same since Kinsey's first survey roughly fifty years ago (Pillard, 1996).

Thus, a substantial number of men and women are erotically and romantically oriented toward partners of their own sex. And this orientation persists despite the fact that, while our society is changing, the combined forces of parenting, peers, religion, and the mass media still typically endorse heterosexuality and stigmatize homosexuality. These forces are formidable and prevalent. Until recently, even consenting adult homosexual acts were outlawed in nearly half of the United States and are still illegal in seventy countries, where they are punished by prison, beatings, and executions (Kitzinger, 2001).

We should mention, however, that the cultural taboo against homosexual behavior is by no means universal. According to one cross-cultural survey, two-thirds of the world's societies regard homosexuality as normal and acceptable, at least for some people or for some age groups (Ford & Beach, 1951). In certain historical periods, the practice was glorified and extolled, as in classical Greece, where men commonly had young same-sex lovers and Pericles, the great Athenian statesman, was considered odd because he was not attracted to beautiful boys.

It is also important to realize that much of the sexual behavior of gays and lesbians revolves around feelings of romance and love just as does that of heterosexual people. In other words, dating and love and (often) long-lasting relationships occur within the homosexual community in a manner virtually identical to that observed in the heterosexual community. The only difference, of course, is the obvious one—the gender of the romantic "other" (G. D. Green & Clunis, 1988; Mattison & McWhirter, 1987).

**Homosexual behavior in antiquity**    *Among the ancient Greeks homosexual relations between men were widely practiced and accepted, as the mural from the* Tomb of the Diver *(c. 480 B.C.–470 B.C.), found in what was a Greek settlement in southern Italy, suggests.*

## BISEXUALITY: DUAL ATTRACTION

The statistics from Kinsey's study cited earlier focused exclusively on those whose sexual orientation was solely toward the same sex or toward the opposite sex. But one need not be categorically heterosexual or homosexual. As Kinsey and others discovered, a sizable number of people do not fit easily or exclusively into either of these two categories. Many individuals are predominantly but not exclusively homosexual; likewise, some individuals are predominantly but not exclusively heterosexual. And these categories are blurred still further when we consider those who consider themselves "bisexual."

Bisexuality has many forms, and for that reason an exact definition is elusive (C. E. Hansen & Evans, 1985). Some bisexuals actively seek out romantic and sexual relationships with members of both sexes. Others are romantically attracted to one sex but sexually attracted to the other. Still others live mostly heterosexual lives—and may identify themselves as heterosexual, or "straight"—but seek out occasional, sometimes furtive, same-sex contacts. Even so, bisexuals are probably not more promiscuous than heterosexuals, and many recognize their attractions to both sexes but choose to live monogamously with either same-sex or opposite-sex partners. The overriding distinction is that, in finding and building a relationship, bisexuals attest that whether a prospective partner is male or female does not have the importance it does for either heterosexual or homosexual individuals.

How many people are bisexual? Good estimates are scarce, not only because of the ambiguity of the term, but also because bisexuals are especially reluctant to disclose their orientation (Weinberg, Williams, & Pryor, 1994). Estimating the prevalence of bisexuality is also complicated by the fact that, with few exceptions (which we note below), research on sexual orientation has lumped bisexual with homosexual individuals (Chung & Katayama, 1996; Garber, 1995). Generally, however, investigators agree that bisexuality is probably rarer than homosexuality, and more common in women than in men (Pattatucci & Hamer, 1995; Pillard, 1996).

## DETERMINANTS OF SEXUAL ORIENTATION: ENVIRONMENTAL FACTORS?

*Experience in Early Life* Some of the attempts to explain homosexuality focus on early childhood experience. According to Freud, for example, homosexuality for many men is a response to fears aroused during the Oedipal conflict. The little boy is too terrified to compete with his father for his mother's affections, and his terror generalizes to other women. He, therefore, tries to ingratiate himself with his father by identifying with the mother instead (after all, Father loves her). There is, however, very little evidence to support Freud's theory. Gays and lesbians have been shown to have worse relationships with their parents than heterosexuals, as Freud proposed, but these relationships did not appear to influence the children's sexual orientation. Instead, the poor relationships seem to be a consequence rather than a cause of the children's sexual orientation, a finding that testifies to the difficulty many gays and lesbians have in trying to "come out" to their parents, and the difficulty many parents have in accepting that their children are homosexual (A. P. Bell, Weinberg, & Hammersmith, 1981).

*Experience in Later Childhood or Adolescence* Further evidence undermines the widely held stereotype that homosexuality results when a boy is "seduced" by an older man or a girl by an older woman. The main predictor of eventual homosexuality is the way people felt about sexuality when they were younger. Homosexual feelings and erotic fantasies usually emerge before biological puberty, sometimes as early as age three or four, and they clearly precede any actual homosexual encounters (A. P. Bell et al., 1981). Indeed, many individuals report that "I've been that way all my life" (Saghir & Robins, 1973), and just as future heterosexuals imagine star-struck romances with members of the opposite sex, so do those who will become homosexual imagine same-sex love and romance (R. Green 1979; Zuger, 1984).

Yet another bit of evidence that early sexual experience does not determine sexual orientation comes from other cultures. In a number of cultures, there are socially prescribed periods of homosexual behavior, usually between boys and older men, which begin in childhood and last through adolescence. Despite this intensive homosexual experience, which occurs amid the boys' puberty and sexual awakening, at adulthood most of the young men show the expected heterosexual orientation and pursue marriage and fatherhood (Herdt, 1990; Stoller & Herdt, 1985).*

---

* One recent theory about early environment and sexual orientation relies on the principle of heterogamy, that is, the idea that opposites attract. In this theory, males typically become romantically and sexually attracted to females, and females to males, because they seek union with their gender opposites (A.P. Bell, 1983). According to this view, early childhood experiences with same-sex peers build a sense of familiarity with one's own gender, and a distant, apprehensive fascination with the opposite sex. At puberty, this apprehension becomes eroticized as lust, and "exotic" becomes "erotic" (D. J. Bem, 1996). Homosexuality should be more likely, then, among boys who have typically female interests and with girls who have typically male interests. This view receives some support from findings that children who share more interests early on with members of the opposite sex are more likely to become gay, lesbian, or bisexual (R. Green, 1987). But it cannot explain those children who conform fully to gender stereotypes and yet become homosexual, or those who do not conform but nevertheless become heterosexual. Nor can it explain how children in large families, who grow up quite familiar with both sexes and find neither "exotic," still become overwhelmingly heterosexual.

## DETERMINANTS OF SEXUAL ORIENTATION: BIOLOGICAL FACTORS?

It seems, therefore, that none of the theories emphasizing childhood experience provides the answer to what determines sexual orientation. As an alternative, a number of investigators have looked to biology.

*Genetics and Inheritance Patterns*   One line of research using twin studies considers genetic dispositions. Recall that identical twins share all their nuclear DNA, while fraternal twins (like other siblings) share only about half their nuclear genetic material. Given this information, it is striking that, if a man's identical twin is gay, then the chances that he will also be gay are 52 percent; if the gay twin is fraternal, the chances drop to 22 percent (Bailey & Pillard, 1991). Likewise, a woman's chance of having a homosexual orientation is 48 percent if she has a lesbian identical twin, whereas if her gay twin is fraternal, the chances drop to 16 percent (Bailey, Pillard, Neale, & Agyei, 1993). Clearly, then, the greater the similarity in genetic makeup, the greater the likelihood of having the same sexual orientation. The obvious implication is that one's genotype carries a predisposition toward homosexuality.

One study indicated that the gene or genes involved in the predisposition fell in a certain area on the X chromosome, although the results are controversial (Hamer, Hur, Magnuson, & Hu, 1993a, 1993b). Even if they hold up, the question remains of just what the X-linked genes do to produce the homosexual orientation. Perhaps these genes code for an individual's hormonal makeup, and it is this hormonal pattern that governs sexual orientation. Alternatively, these genes may directly govern the development of certain structures in the brain.

*Hormones in Adulthood*   The idea that homosexuality might be influenced by hormonal levels has been widely discussed, and a number of early investigators proposed that male sexuality is governed by the levels of certain androgens in the bloodstream. If these levels were too low, homosexuality would result. But their results on this issue were quite inconsistent. Some authors found that androgen levels tend to be lower in gay men than in heterosexuals; others found no such difference (see, for example, Kolodny, Masters, Hendryx, & Toro, 1971; Brodie, Gartrell, Doering, & Rhue, 1974). In addition, many studies have shown that administration of androgens to gay men enhances their sexual vigor but does not change its direction—their renewed interest is still toward same-sex partners (see Chapter 11; Kinsey et al., 1948). This and other evidence makes it clear that male homosexuality is not caused by an insufficiency of male hormones. It seems reasonable to assume that the same is true for lesbians, with no straightforward link between hormone levels and orientation. (For another discussion of the relation between homosexual orientation and neuroendocrine effects, see Gladue, Green, & Hellman, 1984.)

*Hormones in the Prenatal Environment*   A different hypothesis maintains that hormones are indeed critical to sexual orientation but that their influence is exerted not during adulthood, but in the months prior to birth (L. Ellis & Ames, 1987). According to this view, certain neural circuits in and around the hypothalamus become sexually differentiated between the second and fifth months of pregnancy, with the nature of this differentiation governed by the hormones circulating in the fetal bloodstream. Ordinarily, these hormones ensure that a male fetus will have a masculinized brain and a female fetus will have a feminized brain. But if the normal hormonal condition is disrupted, then this brain development will be atypical or incomplete. What can cause this sort of hormonal disruption? There are several possibilities, including unusual stress during pregnancy and various genetically produced effects.

One such effect has already been mentioned: prenatal overexposure of females to testosterone. As we discussed earlier, such exposure not only produces a pronounced tomboy pattern in childhood but also has lasting effects, producing higher rates of lesbian behavior and lesbian sexual fantasies (Dittmann et al., 1992), Moreover, a hodge podge of other traits are statistically associated with homosexuality (a greater tendency toward being left-handed, for example, or specific acoustic responses in the inner ear), and these other traits are all, in various ways, made more likely by varying levels of prenatal testosterone (Zucker, 2001).

*Differences in Brain Structure* In addition to hormonal differences, investigators have also reported differences in brain structure between individuals with heterosexual and those with homosexual orientations. One study by Simon Le Vay (1991) examined a sexually dimorphic area in the anterior hypothalamus that affects sexual behavior in animals; this structure had previously been found to be twice as large in the brains of men as in those of women (L. S. Allen et al., 1989). When Le Vay looked at the brains of gay men, he found that this area of the hypothalamus was about the size typical for heterosexual women and therefore only half that typical for heterosexual men. How this difference arises is currently unknown, as is the question of whether it influences sexual orientation or merely reflects one aspect of it.

## TWO SIDES OF THE COIN

So what leads to homosexuality? A biological, perhaps genetically based predisposition is very likely a factor in determining the direction of the child's emerging sexual desire; this is indicated, for example, in the twin data. Cultural conditions are also likely to contribute heavily to whether a child or adolescent is able to accept and then act in accordance with his sexual orientation, and eventually identify himself as "straight," lesbian, gay, or bisexual.

Whatever the answer, though, we should note that the question of "what causes homosexuality" simply represents the flip side of the question, "What leads to heterosexuality?" This second question is rarely asked because most people take the heterosexual orientation for granted. Yet we are no better equipped to answer this question about heterosexuality than we are to answer it for homosexuality. In truth, we know precious little about what causes either.

## CAN SEXUAL ORIENTATION BE CHANGED?

People sometimes ask whether gay men and lesbians can somehow be transformed into heterosexual men and women. The question has become politically charged, because some clinicians claim that psychotherapy can change sexual orientation. For many gays and lesbians, such reparative therapy (or conversion therapy) is objectionable, because it treats their sexual orientation as a "disorder" in need of "cure," and in so doing perpetuates the oppression of sexual minorities (Drescher, 1998; Halpert, 2000). In response, advocates of reparative therapy argue that, whether rightly or wrongly, many people who are gay or lesbian wish they were not, and it would be wrong to deprive these people of treatment.

Is there indeed such a treatment? In other words, does reparative therapy accomplish what it is designed to accomplish? To date, the published evidence is anecdotal and the arguments are polemical. Critics argue that successes are rare, and those who do change their sexual orientation are probably bisexuals who, by act of will, simply suppress their homosexual side. Advocates of reparative therapy acknowledge that treatment often fails, but they cast homosexual behavior as a kind of compulsion that, like all compulsions, is difficult to control with any kind of treatment (Nicolosi, 1991). Both sides may, in fact, underestimate the fluidity of sexual orientation experienced by many people who call themselves gay or lesbian but find themselves attracted to someone of the opposite sex, or vice versa (see L. M. Diamond, 1998, 2000; Weinberg et al., 1994).

Whatever the causes of a homosexual or bisexual orientation, and however change-able it may be, one thing is clear: such an orientation is not a psychological disorder or defect. It is only abnormal in the sense of being the orientation of a minority, say, of some 10 percent or so of the population. But many other traits are "abnormal" in exactly the same sense—being left-handed, for example, is also a characteristic of 10 percent of the population. Gays, lesbians, and bisexuals are neither better nor worse than heterosexuals. While their number includes great painters (Leonardo da Vinci), athletes (Martina Navratilova), musicians (Leonard Bernstein, Aaron Copland), writ-ers (Oscar Wilde, Gertrude Stein), mathematicians and scientists (Alan Turing, Alfred Kinsey himself), philosophers (Wittgenstein), and warriors (Alexander the Great), the great majority are ordinary people whose names will not be recorded in history books. The same no doubt holds for left-handers—and for heterosexuals.

# DEVELOPMENT AFTER CHILDHOOD

So far, our focus in describing human development has been on infancy and childhood. This emphasis reflects the orientation of the major figures in the history of the field, including Piaget, whose work we met in Chapter 12, and Freud, whose work we will con-sider in Chapter 15. In recent years, however, a number of authors have argued that this interpretation of development is too narrow. In their view, humans continue to change as they pass through the life cycle. The problems faced by adolescents are not the same as those of young adults about to get married or become parents, let alone those of the middle aged at the peak of parenthood or their careers, or of the elderly at the sunset of their lives. And just as the problems change, so do the strategies, responses, and resources used in dealing with these problems. It thus seems reasonable to ask how individuals continue to develop, in adolescence and throughout the life span (Baltes, Reese, & Lipsitt, 1980).

Are there any regularities to development over the life span? On this issue, many investigators have been strongly influenced by the psychoanalyst Erik Erikson's "eight ages of man" (see Table 13.2). According to Erikson (1963), all human beings endure a series of major crises as they go through the life cycle. At each stage, there is a critical confrontation between the self the individual has achieved thus far and the various demands posed by social and personal settings. The first few of these crises occur in early childhood and roughly correspond to stages identified within Freud's theory (see Chapter 15). These are followed by adolescence, early adulthood, middle age, and the final years. These crises (and their resolution) define Erikson's "eight ages" (Erikson & Coles, 2000).

This developmental scheme has influenced many investigators of adult develop-ment. We will continue to refer to Erikson's organization as we briefly discuss some issues in the study of adolescence and adulthood.

## ADOLESCENCE

The term *adolescence* is derived from the Latin for "growing up." It is a period of transi-tion in which children become adults. There are biological changes: a growth spurt, a change in bodily proportions, and the attainment of sexual maturity. These physical changes contribute to a deeper socioeconomic transition: from dependence on one's family, to a legally and morally sanctioned independence. And, of course, there are the numerous psychological changes as well. These include the progressive maturing of sexual attitudes and behaviors that will ultimately allow adolescents to form romantic attachments and possibly start their own families. At the same time, adolescents are

**Erik Erikson** *A pioneer in the study of development after childhood.*

## TABLE 13.2 ERIKSON'S EIGHT AGES OF MAN

| APPROXIMATE AGE | DEVELOPMENTAL TASK OF THAT STAGE | PSYCHOSOCIAL CRISIS OF THAT STAGE |
|---|---|---|
| 0–1½ years | Attachment to mother, which lays foundation for later trust in others | Trust versus mistrust |
| 1½–3 years | Gaining some basic control of self and environment (e.g., toilet training, exploration) | Autonomy versus shame and doubt |
| 3–6 years | Becoming purposeful and directive | Initiative versus guilt |
| 6 years–puberty | Developing social, physical, and school skills | Competence versus inferiority |
| Adolescence | Making transition from childhood to adulthood; developing a sense of identity | Identity versus role confusion |
| Early adulthood | Establishing intimate bonds of love and friendship | Intimacy versus isolation |
| Middle age | Fulfilling life goals that involve family, career, and society; developing concerns that embrace future generations | Productivity versus stagnation |
| Later years | Looking back over one's life and accepting its meaning | Integrity versus despair |

SOURCE: Based on Erikson, 1963.

also acquiring many social skills that will eventually enable them to become well-socialized adults. In effect, adolescence for humans is simply a protracted form of what in many animals is rather abrupt—the transition point at which pups or fledglings must leave or are ejected from the nest to make their own way.

## THE NATURE OF THE TRANSITION

Compared to other animals, humans attain adult status rather late in their development, and the transition from childhood to adulthood is itself stretched out over several years. This is, as we mentioned in Chapter 12, an important difference between ourselves and our animal cousins, for it provides time for each generation to learn from the one before. When is this period over?

If we only consider biology, girls can reach their physical adulthood by age fifteen or so and boys by age seventeen. Thus, by the midteens, physical growth is nearly complete. But societies often define different boundaries for the beginning of adulthood. As an example, a study of New England families shows that the age at which sons become autonomous has changed over the course of generations. The sons of the first settlers stayed on their parents' farms until their late twenties before they married and became economically independent. As farmland became scarcer and other opportunities opened in the surrounding villages and towns, the sons left home, learned a trade, married, and became autonomous at a younger age (Greven, 1970). With the onset of mass education in the mid-nineteenth century, this pattern was reversed again. Instead of leaving to become an apprentice or take a job, more and more youths remained with their families and stayed in school through their late teens. This allowed them to acquire the skills required for membership in a complex, technological society, but it postponed their social and economic independence and their full entry into the adult world (Elder, 1980).

Culture evidently has an important say in the when and how of the transition period. It also sets up special occasions that mark the end of this transition period or that highlight certain points along the way. These initiation rites and rites of passage are found in many human societies (Figure 13.13). In some preliterate cultures, these rites can be violent, prolonged, and painful. Examples include certain puberty rites for boys that involve ceremonial beatings and circumcision. According to some anthropologists, these initiation rites are especially severe in cultures that try to emphasize the dramatic distinction between the roles of children and adults, as well as between those of men and women. In our own society, the transition to full adulthood is much more gradual, with milestones that refer not just to biological changes but also to various educational and vocational attainments. We have not one initiation rite but many (none of which would ever be regarded as especially severe): confirmations and bar (or bas) mitzvahs, "sweet sixteen" parties, high-school and college graduations, and so on. Each of these marks an important event, but each represents just one more step on a protracted road to adulthood (Burton & Whiting, 1961; Muuss, 1970).

Cultural factors also determine the time at which other benchmarks of development are reached. An example is the average age at which virginity is lost, which has steadily decreased in our own society during the past few decades, reflecting a change in sexual mores for both men and women. This change is undoubtedly caused by many factors. One is the worldwide increase in obesity, which has made preteen puberties common (for hormonal reasons, females with more body fat have earlier puberties). Another is the existence of increasingly effective methods of birth control that allow the separation of the emotional and recreational aspects of sexuality from its reproductive function.

**13.13 Initiation rites** *These rites signify induction into adulthood, as in (A) preparation for a bar mitzvah, or (B) an Apache girl sitting on a ceremonial rug during a puberty rite.*

## IS ADOLESCENCE ALWAYS TURBULENT?

Traditionally, adolescence has been considered a period of great emotional stress. This notion goes back to the romantic movement of the early nineteenth century, when major writers such as the German poet Johann Wolfgang von Goethe (1749–1832) wrote influential works that featured youths in desperate conflict with a cynical, adult world that drove them to despair, suicide, or violent rebellion. This view was later endorsed by a number of psychological theorists, including Sigmund Freud and many of his followers. To Freud, adolescence was necessarily a period of conflict, since this is the time when the sexual urges repressed by the close of the Oedipal period resurge, only to clash violently with one's unconscious prohibitions. Further conflicts center on struggles with the older generation, especially the same-sex parent, that were repressed in childhood but now come to the fore (see Chapter 15).

Certainly the neuroendocrine events of puberty force all adolescents in all cultures to come to terms with a new, more adultlike physical appearance. This change itself can cause others to treat them more as adults and to expect adult behavior in return. One consequence may be strain at adjusting to these new reactions and expectations, especially in our technological societies. Because of the complexities of our modern world, adult routines are often very different from childhood routines, with no easily located way stations in between. Accordingly, one might expect a fair level of disturbance during adolescence in our own society.

Indeed, such emotional disturbance is a theme often sounded by the mass media and much twentieth-century American literature (for example, J. D. Salinger's *Catcher in the Rye*). But in fact, a number of studies suggest that such turbulence is by no means universal among modern American adolescents. Several investigators find that for many adolescents "development . . . is slow, gradual, and unremarkable" (Josselson, 1980, p. 189; also see Arnett, 1999).

## TRYING TO FIND A PERSONAL IDENTITY

Adolescence may not necessarily be a time of troubles. Even so, it does pose a number of serious challenges for adolescents as they prepare to become autonomous individuals. A number of writers have tried to understand some characteristic adolescent behavior patterns in light of this ultimate goal.

*Establishing a Separate World*  Unlike fledgling birds, adolescents in our society remain in the nest for quite a while after they can fly (or more aptly, after they get their driver's licenses). Thus, living in the world of their parents, adolescents are likely to seek special means of identifying themselves as separate and different from their parents. As one means to this end, many adolescents form small cliques that become like second families, identify themselves as part of a crowd (such as the "brains," "jocks," or "nerds" in a school), and adopt all kinds of external trappings of what's "cool," "rad," or "in," such as adopting new clothing, hair styles, and speech idioms (Figure 13.14; B. B. Brown, 1990; Dunphy, 1963). These often change with bewildering rapidity, as yesterday's adolescent fads diffuse into the broader social world and become today's adult fashions (witness the music of the Beatles, once considered subversive but now played as background music in shopping malls). When this happens, new adolescent fads quickly spring up to maintain the differentiation (Douvan & Adelson, 1958).

*The Identity Crisis of Adolescence*  According to Erikson, differentiating themselves from the adult world is only part of what adolescents really want to achieve. Their major goal throughout adolescence is to discover who and what they really are, as they go through what he calls an *identity crisis*. In our complex culture, there are many social roles, and adolescence is a time to try them on to see which one fits best—which vocation, which ideology, which group membership. The adolescent reaches a fuller appreciation of his race, ethnicity, and religion, and all that they imply. Sexuality blooms and

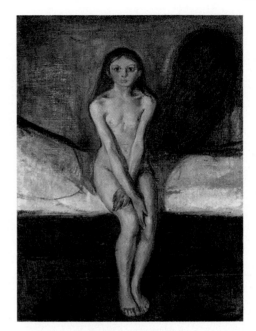

**Puberty**  *By Edward Munch, 1895.*

**13.14  Adolescent fads**  *New adolescent fads spring up to maintain the differentiation between the adolescents' own world and that of the adults around them. They then disappear rather quickly to be replaced by yet newer fads. These photos show some such fads prominent at various times: (A) eighties—punk fashions, (B) nineties—rap singers' styles, (C) 2000—raves.*

there may be "coming out crises" among youth who discover that they are gay, lesbian, or bisexual (D'Augelli & Patterson, 1995).

The primary question adolescents ask themselves is, "Who am I?" and to answer it, they strike a succession of postures, in part for the benefit of others, who then serve as a mirror in which they see themselves. Each role, each human relationship, each world-view is adopted totally, uncompromisingly, and sometimes defiantly, but only for awhile. Like costumes, they are tried on for size, and when adolescents find that some fit, they retain them as part of their adult identity (Erikson, 1963).

## ADULTHOOD

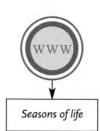

Seasons of life

Erikson describes a number of stages of personality development after adolescence. In young adulthood, healthy individuals must develop a capacity for closeness and intimacy through love, or else suffer from a personal isolation that permits only shallow human relationships. Those in early middle age must develop a sense of personal creativity toward the wider world, toward others, toward their trade or profession, and toward their communities. And near the end of life, the elderly must come to terms with their own lives, accepting them with a sense of integrity rather than despair (Erikson, Erikson, & Kivnick, 1989). Erikson (1963) eloquently sums up this final reckoning: "It is the acceptance of one's own and only life cycle as something that had to be and that, by necessity, permitted of no substitutes. . . . Healthy children will not fear life if their elders have integrity enough not to fear death" (pp. 268–269).

### RECENT ATTEMPTS TO FIND COMMON STAGES

Erikson's developmental scheme is a literary and moving account of the human odyssey through life, but is it accurate? Are the crises he listed universal and as he described them? A number of modern investigators have studied adults at various stages of their lives to find out what, if any, patterns characterize a given time of life. By and large, most of them have described a number of developmental periods that resemble some of Erikson's "ages of man" (Gould, 1978; Levinson, 1978).

A stage of adult development that has received considerable attention from both Erikson and later authors is the *midlife transition* (which sometimes amounts to the "midlife crisis"), in which individuals reappraise what they have done with their lives thus far and may reevaluate their marriage and career (Wethington, 2000; Willis & Reid, 1999). It is a period when individuals begin to see physical changes that show that the summer of life is over and its autumn has begun, a recognition that may occur earlier in women than in men (in part, because of the psychological and physiological impact of menopause). There is a shift in the way one thinks about time, from "How long have I lived?" to "How much time do I have left?" Some investigators point out that the middle aged are in the middle in more than one sense, as they observe their children grow up and their own parents age and die:

> It is as if there are two mirrors before me, each held at a partial angle. I see part of myself in my mother who is growing old, and part of her in me. In the other mirror I see part of myself in my daughter. . . . (Neugarten & Datan, quoted in Colarusso & Nemiroff, 1981, p. 124)

### HOW UNIVERSAL ARE THE STAGES OF ADULT DEVELOPMENT?

The results obtained by various investigators of adult development are consistent enough to suggest that the stages and transitions they describe apply fairly widely to people in our time and place. But are they universal? When we considered various stage theories of child development, we asked whether these stages occur in all cultures. The

*The ages of man* **Jacob Blessing the Sons of Joseph** *by Rembrandt, 1656.*

same question can be asked about adult development. Is there a midlife transition among the natives of Papua New Guinea? Do Eskimo villagers of fifty agonizingly reappraise what they have done with their lives? If the answer is no, then we have to ask ourselves what the various stages described by Erikson and other students of the adult life span really are.

Thus far there is little concrete evidence one way or the other, so we can only guess. Certain adult milestones are clearly biological. In all cultures, humans reach puberty, mate, have children, go through (female) menopause or (male) andropause, endure the discomfitures and diseases of old age, and finally die. But the kinds of crises that confront persons at different points of the life cycle surely depend on the society in which they live.

An example of the effect of social conditions on adult crises is the transition into old age. Over a century ago in the United States, different generations often lived close together as part of an extended family, and there was much less segregation by age. Nursing homes and retirement communities were unheard of. Older people contributed to the family even when they were too old to work outside the home by caring for the children, helping with the housekeeping, and so on. Older people were also sought out for advice on matters of child rearing and housekeeping. But today, the elderly have no such recognized family role. They usually live apart, are effectively segregated from the rest of society, are excluded from the workforce, and have lost their role as esteemed advisers. Given these changes, it follows that the transition into senescence is quite different from what it was 150 years ago. People still age as they did then—although many more people than ever now live into their seventies, eighties, and even their nineties—but they view aging differently and face different life circumstances (Hareven, 1978).

## SOME FINAL THOUGHTS: WHAT IS ADULTHOOD?

The stages of adult development probably vary in their specifics. But Erikson (1974) may still have provided some truths that transcend our own time and place. Perhaps the best suggestion comes from one of his lectures in which he tried to define adulthood:

... In youth you find out what you care to do and who you care to be.... In young adulthood you learn whom you care to be with.... In adulthood, however, you learn what and whom you can take care of.... (p. 124)

Seen in this light, the later phases of the life cycle represent a final expansion in which our concern turns from ourselves to others and from the present to the future. This may or may not be a good description of what genuine adulthood is. But it seems like an admirable prescription for what it ought to be.

# SUMMARY

## ATTACHMENT

1. The social development of infants begins with their first human bond—their attachment to their mothers, fathers, or other caregivers. Studies of infant humans and monkeys indicate that this attachment does not arise because the mother feeds the infants, but because she gives them comfort. According to John Bowlby, attachment is in part rooted in a built-in fear of the unfamiliar, which has a simple survival value since young birds and mammals that lack it are more likely to get lost or fall victim to predators.

2. Many other species show some biological tendency to seek what is familiar. An important example is *imprinting* in birds, based on a kind of learning that occurs in early life.

## PATTERNS OF ATTACHMENT

3. Developmental psychologists have tried to assess the quality of the child's attachment to the caregivers by observing the behavior of infants and young children in the *Strange Situation*. There is some evidence that the quality of attachment at about fifteen months of age predicts behavior two years later, but there is controversy as to whether this reflects a long-term effect of the early caregiver-child relationship or is based on other factors, such as persistent patterns in that relationship or some continuity of childhood temperament.

4. Some theorists have proposed that the attachment to the caregiver can only be formed during a sensitive period in early life. Consistent with this claim, motherless monkeys and children reared in deprivation demonstrate various cognitive and emotional deficits. However, later work on monkey isolates and adopted children suggests that these impairments are not necessarily irrevocable.

## CHILDHOOD SOCIALIZATION

5. The process of *socialization* continues with child-rearing by the parents. Some important differences in the way children are reared depend on the dominant values of their culture. Modern attempts to explain the mechanisms that underlie socialization include *social learning theory*, which emphasizes *modeling*, and *cognitive developmental theory*, which emphasizes the role of understanding.

6. Psychoanalytic theories notwithstanding, the evidence indicates that different modes of weaning or toilet training have little or no long-term effects. What seems to matter instead is the general home atmosphere, as shown by the effects of *autocratic, permissive,* and *authoritative-reciprocal patterns* of child rearing. On the other hand, how the parents treat the child is partially determined by the child's own characteristics, as suggested by studies on *infant temperament*.

## THE DEVELOPMENT OF MORALITY

7. One aspect of moral conduct concerns the *internalization* of prohibitions. According to some theorists, punishment is more likely to lead to such internalization if the threatened punishment fits the *principle of minimal sufficiency*. Another aspect of moral conduct involves *altruistic acts*. Studies of *empathy* and *empathic distress* suggest that some precursors of altruism may be present in early infancy.

8. The study of moral development has been strongly

affected by Kohlberg's analysis of progressive stages in *moral reasoning*. According to a later critique by Carol Gilligan, there are some important sex differences in moral orientation, with men emphasizing justice and women stressing human relationships and compassion. Further differences have been found between different cultural groups.

## THE DEVELOPMENT OF SEX AND GENDER

9. Both socialization and constitutional factors play roles in determining various senses of being male or female, including *gender role, gender identity*, and *sexual orientation*.

10. Certain psychological differences between the sexes may be based on biological predisposition. One is *physical aggression*, which tends to be more pronounced in males. Another is *relational aggression*, the manipulation of social alliances, which is more pronounced in females. Still another is a male advantage on *spatial tests* of mental ability. To whatever extent such differences are based on bio-logical predisposition, they are undoubtedly maintained or magnified by socially imposed gender roles.

11. The causes of *sexual orientation* are not yet clear. There is little evidence to support the view that sexual orientation is determined either by a particular pattern of relations with parents in early childhood or by childhood sexual experiences. Current evidence points to such determinants as differences in hormonal makeup, brain structure, and genetics. But whatever its causes, sexual orientation can be changed only with difficulty, if at all.

## DEVELOPMENT AFTER CHILDHOOD

12. Development continues after childhood. Some theorists, notably Erik Erikson, have tried to map later stages of development. One such stage is *adolescence*, which marks the transition into adulthood. While adolescence is sometimes turbulent, it is not always so. Whether the stages of adulthood described by Erickson and other theorists—for example, a *mid-life crisis*—are universal to all cultures is debatable.

# INDIVIDUAL
# DIFFERENCES

*How do we differ from each other?*

# PART 5

PEOPLE DIFFER FROM ONE ANOTHER. THEY vary in height, weight, and strength, eye color and hair color. They also vary along many psychological dimensions. Some are proud; others are humble. Some are adventurous; others timid. Some are clever; others slow.

So far, differences from one person to the next have not been our main concern. Our emphasis has, instead, been on the attempt to find general psychological laws—whether in physiological function, memory, or social behavior—that apply to all people. To be sure, we have occasionally dealt with individual differences, but our focus was not on these differences as such; rather, it was on what they could tell us about people in general—how color blindness could help to explain the underlying mechanisms of color vision or how variations in child rearing might help us understand some aspects of socialization.

It is time, though, to change this emphasis and to consider individual differences as a topic in its own right. We will start, in this chapter, with one regard in which humans differ: their intelligence. In subsequent chapters, we will turn to a discussion of personality traits and then to the more extreme variation that carries us outside the "normal" range and into the domain of mental disorder.

# INTELLIGENCE: ITS NATURE AND MEASUREMENT

*I*n modern society, particularly in the United States, there is a flourishing enterprise of mental testing or psychological assessment. This enterprise has produced a huge number of psychological tests, measuring many different characteristics, including various aspects of intellectual aptitude. This interest in individual differences is fueled by several factors, but one large influence derives from the social climate of our time: in the modern world, most of us can make choices about the career we will pursue—carpenter or lawyer, physician or politician—the choices are many. Of course, employers also have choices to make—about which candidate to hire and which not to. All of this creates a real need for the systematic assessment of human characteristics, one that can help guide employers as they seek the appropriate person to occupy each niche, and can guide employees as they look for the niche that best

suits them. And, crucially, different jobs require different sorts of training, and training is often expensive. This creates another level of need—for tests that might help us decide, prior to the investment in education, which candidates are most likely to gain from training.

From the beginning, mental tests were designed to fill these pragmatic needs and, in particular, were designed to help in decisions about schooling. IQ tests, for example, were originally created to identify students who would gain from special instruction; the Scholastic Aptitude Test (SAT) taken by most American high-school students was designed from the start as a predictor of performance in college. It is probably inevitable, therefore, that questions about mental testing are linked to a number of social and political issues. Who will get a good job? Who will receive the benefits of the finest education? Should disadvantaged students be denied college admission because of low SAT scores? It is hardly surprising that these questions, especially when they concern intelligence testing, are debated in an emotionally charged atmosphere.

Any reasonable discussion of these questions, however, must be informed by the relevant science, including an understanding of what the tests measure, how they measure it, and why we should (or should not) take these tests seriously. Only against this background can the political and social issues be evaluated.

# MENTAL TESTS

Some mental tests are used to assess achievement. They measure what an individual has learned and what skills she has mastered. These tests, therefore, tell us about the test taker's current status. The results will change as soon as the test taker learns more or gains new skills.

Other tests are used to assess aptitude. They are designed to predict what an individual will be able to do, given the proper training and the right motivation. An example is a test of mechanical aptitude devised to determine the likelihood that an individual will do well as an engineer after an appropriate education. The Scholastic Aptitude Test (SAT), as the name implies, is an aptitude test designed to predict how well students will do in educational settings after high school. Most scholars also consider intelligence tests to be measures of aptitude, although critics of intelligence testing regard such tests as measures of achievement, not measures of potential.

Still other tests have other purposes. Neuropsychological tests, for example, are tools for diagnosing certain learning disabilities as well as the effects of brain damage. Personality tests assess an individual's dispositions, for example, whether the test taker is optimistic or pessimistic, outgoing or withdrawn, confident or insecure, even-tempered or moody, and so on.

We will review many types of these tests, but we first need to explain the reasoning underlying the construction and use of all such tests.

## THE STUDY OF VARIATION

To understand the tests used to assess individual differences, we need to know a bit about measurement, and the ways in which psychologists summarize measurements, using the concepts and the vocabulary of statistics.* In fact, the study of how individuals differ from one another has grown up in close association with the development of

---

* For a fuller description of these and other statistical matters, see the Appendix, "Statistics: The Collection, Organization, and Interpretation of Data."

## TABLE 14.1 HEIGHTS (IN INCHES) FOR A GROUP OF FIFTY WOMEN

| NAME | HEIGHT (IN INCHES) | NAME | HEIGHT (IN INCHES) |
|------|--------------------|------|--------------------|
| Ann | 54.00 | Tracey | 65.50 |
| Michelle | 55.50 | Jenny | 65.75 |
| Abigail | 57.00 | Rachel | 66.00 |
| Patricia | 57.50 | Brianna | 66.25 |
| Marie | 58.25 | Amanda | 66.75 |
| Erica | 58.50 | Enriqueta | 67.00 |
| Kathryn | 59.25 | Gretchen | 67.00 |
| Angela | 60.25 | Jeanette | 67.25 |
| Allison | 60.50 | Jessica | 67.75 |
| Dina | 60.75 | Elena | 68.00 |
| Jane | 61.00 | Lynn | 68.25 |
| Kelly | 61.00 | Anna | 69.50 |
| Joanna | 61.25 | Sylvia | 69.50 |
| Gena | 62.50 | Kristina | 69.75 |
| Sarah | 62.75 | Kirsten | 70.00 |
| Ingrid | 63.00 | Chris | 70.75 |
| Heather | 63.50 | Alicia | 71.25 |
| Lynn | 63.75 | Laura | 71.50 |
| Deborah | 64.00 | Eve | 71.50 |
| Caitlin | 64.00 | Jennifer | 72.25 |
| Alisha | 64.50 | Britney | 73.50 |
| Elizabeth | 64.75 | Susan | 74.75 |
| Melanie | 65.00 | Carolyn | 76.00 |
| Muriel | 65.00 | Miriam | 77.50 |
| Lois | 65.25 | Chelsea | 79.00 |

## TABLE 14.2 FREQUENCY DISTRIBUTION OF HEIGHTS IN TABLE 14.1

| CATEGORY | NUMBER OF CASES |
|----------|-----------------|
| 0–54 | 1 |
| 54.25–56.00 | 1 |
| 56.25–58.00 | 2 |
| 58.25–60.00 | 3 |
| 60.25–62.00 | 6 |
| 62.25–64.00 | 7 |
| 64.25–66.00 | 8 |
| 66.25–68.00 | 7 |
| 68.25–70.00 | 5 |
| 70.25–72.00 | 4 |
| 72.25–74.00 | 2 |
| 74.25–76.00 | 2 |
| 76.25–78.00 | 1 |
| 78.25–80.00 | 1 |

statistical methods, with these methods serving as powerful tools for interpreting and theorizing about these differences.

Two hundred years ago, **statistics** meant little more than the systematic collection of various state records, such as birth and death rates. In poring over such figures, the Belgian scientist Adolphe Quetelet (1796–1874) began to see patterns in these numbers, and this led him to chart the **frequency distribution** of various observations—that is, how often individual cases fall into different categories, with those categories systematically subdividing the full range of measurements.

For example, Table 14.1 merely lists the (fictional) heights of fifty women. In this format, it is difficult to see any pattern at all. If we summarize these data in terms of a frequency distribution (Table 14.2) and then graph this distribution (Figure 14.1), the pattern becomes obvious. The women in this particular group range in height from 54 inches to 79 inches, but most have heights close to 65 inches. Eight women are exactly this height, and as we move further and further from this middle value, the number of women at each height interval gradually drops.

### THE NORMAL CURVE

Quetelet made graphs of frequency distributions for many human attributes—height, weight, waist size, and so on—and realized that, if the sample was large enough, then most of these distributions were bell shaped, like the curve in Figure 14.1. To describe

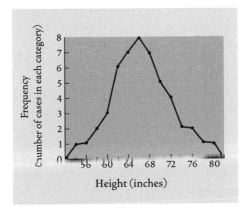

**14.1 Graphic display of a frequency distribution** *This figure shows the data from Table 14.2 in graphic form. In this format, the pattern is easily visible: most women in this sample have heights close to 65 inches. Values further and further from this middle value are less and less frequent. Each dot represents the frequency of each height (i.e., a row in Table 14.2).*

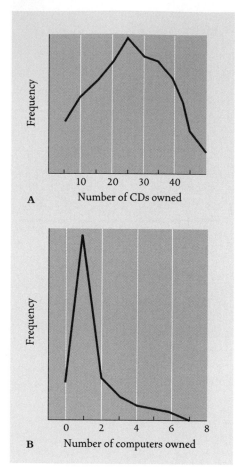

**14.2 Frequency distributions with high variability or low** *(A) People vary enormously in how many CDs they own, ranging from those who own only one or two to those who own hundreds. The frequency distribution (showing fictional data) reflects this high degree of variability. (B) There is relatively little variability in how many computers a family owns. Many families own one computer; some own none; a few own two or three. The (fictional) frequency distribution reflects this narrow variability.*

such bell-shaped curves, it is usually sufficient to specify just two things. First, where is the curve's center? This gives us a measure of the "average case"—in Figure 14.1, the average height for women in this group. The most common way of determining this average is to add up all the scores and then divide the sum by the number of scores; this process yields the *mean*. But there are other ways of determining the average as well. For example, it is sometimes convenient to refer to the *median*, which is the score that separates the top 50 percent of the scores from the bottom 50 percent. (In Figure 14.1, the mean and the median are the same, but often this is not the case.)

A second important aspect of a bell-shaped curve is its *variability*. How much do the individual cases differ from one to the next? A highly variable group will have a frequency distribution that is wide and relatively flat, like the one shown in Figure 14.2A; a group with little variability will be narrow and steep, like the one shown in Figure 14.2B.

Highly variable or not, these curves all tend to have the same bell shape. Sometimes the bell is distorted (Figure 14.2A looks more like a mountain than a bell), and sometimes it is asymmetrical (as in Figure 14.2B). Even with this diversity, though, the curves generally resemble the shape called a *normal curve*, and this resemblance to a normal curve is quite important. Mathematically, normal curves describe the frequency pattern that emerges when an event is being influenced by random accidents. For example, suppose that someone threw six coins in the air and counted how many of the coins landed heads up. Now suppose that this person had the patience to repeat this procedure a thousand times. How often, in these thousand tosses, would the coins fall with all six heads up? How often with five or four or three? So long as the coins have not been tampered with, it is a matter of pure chance how each coin will land, so the number of heads or tails that come up in each toss will also be a matter of chance. Still, a pattern emerges. Figure 14.3 shows what happens if six coins are actually thrown over and over. With each throw, the distribution approaches that of the normal curve.

Quetelet realized that the distributions of many human characteristics—height, weight, chest or shoe size—resemble that of the normal curve. Since the normal curve is the pattern of chance events, perhaps the distributions of these human characteristics are also the product of chance events. More precisely, Quetelet proposed that nature aims at an ideal value for each of these attributes, but a host of little accidents pull most of us away from this ideal. Sometimes the accidents cause us to fall short of the ideal: perhaps a child happened to catch the flu when he was four years old, and this interrupted a growth spurt so that he ended up, as an adult, a few millimeters shorter than he otherwise would have been. Sometimes the accidents cause us to overshoot: perhaps the child happened to like vegetables when he was nine, and this led him to be better nourished, adding a millimeter or two. These and many other accidents accumulate, some adding height, some subtracting it, and in the end produce a distribution just

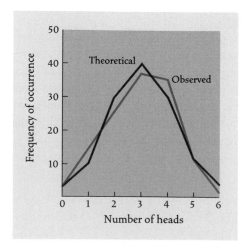

**14.3** *Theoretical and observed distribution of number of heads in 128 throws of 6 coins*

like the distribution of heads shown in Figure 14.3. For most people, the height-promoting or height-detracting accidents more or less balance each other, leaving the individual with a height close to Quetelet's "ideal." Only occasionally will height-promoting or height-detracting accidents dominate, and that is why extremely tall or extremely short people are correspondingly rare.

## VARIABILITY AND DARWIN

For Quetelet, variability was something unfortunate—a departure from the ideal. But after Darwin published *On The Origin of Species*, variability was considered in a new light. For Darwin, variability provided the raw material on which natural selection could work, and so, without variation, there would be no evolution.

Why is variation so important for evolution? In any species, Darwin noted, some individuals have more of a characteristic and some have less (some have longer legs, some have shorter; some are more resistant to a particular virus, some are less). In many environments, these differences will be inconsequential. (If the virus is rare, it does not matter whether an individual is resistant to it or not.) But, if the environment changes, individuals who have the advantageous characteristic are more likely to survive long enough to have offspring. As a result, the characteristic will be more widespread in the subsequent generation.

In essence, then, variation within a species provides the set of options from which natural selection selects. This process can go forward, however, only if an organism's descendants inherit the relevant traits. Otherwise, the effects of selection in one generation will have no impact on the next generation. For Darwin, therefore, variation within a species was crucial and the sources of that variation had to be inherited, so that traits could be preserved from one generation to the next. Of course, Darwin knew that many traits in animals are inherited, but what about humans? Are our traits—not just our appearance, but our personality and intellectual faculties—the result of inheritance?

## CORRELATION

Francis Galton (1822–1911), a half-cousin of Darwin's, spent much of his life trying to prove that heredity does play a crucial role in many human characteristics—including both physical and mental traits. Galton pursued these issues in a number of ways, but one part of his research called for the assessment of similarity among relatives. If an individual is tall, how likely is it that her siblings are also tall? If someone is smart or friendly, how likely is it that her children will share these traits?

Galton knew from the start that children do resemble their parents to some extent. But resemblance is not an all-or-none proposition: seldom is one person a carbon copy of another or, conversely, entirely unlike another. So Galton needed a more precise measure of resemblance, a means of measuring how much people resembled each other.

What Galton was seeking was a measure of *covariation* or *correlation*. To see how these measures work, consider the relationship between height and weight. If we know how tall someone is, does this give us any information about what his weight is likely to be? Data for fifty undergraduate men are graphed in Figure 14.4, a *scatter plot*. Each point in this diagram represents one person, with his height determining the horizontal position of the point and his weight determining the vertical position.

The pattern in this scatter plot—an ellipse running from the lower left to the upper right of the graph—suggests that these two measurements are related: taller people (points to the right on the scatter plot) also tend to weigh more (points higher up on the diagram). But the relationship is not perfect. If it were, all the points would fall on the diagonal line. Nonetheless, the overall pattern of the scatter plot does indicate a relationship: if we know someone's height, we can make a reasonable prediction about what that person's weight is likely to be, and if we know the weight, we can predict the height.

*Francis Galton    A pioneer in the study of individual differences.*

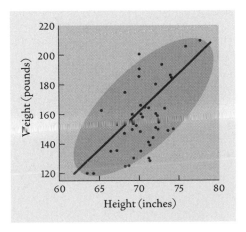

*14.4    Correlation    A scatter diagram of the heights and weights of fifty male undergraduates. Note that the points fall within an ellipse, which indicates that the data are correlated. The correlation for these data was +.70.*

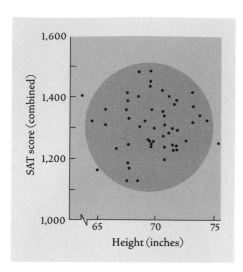

**14.5  A correlation of zero**  *A scatter diagram of Scholastic Aptitude Test scores and the heights of fifty undergraduate males. Not surprisingly, there was no relation, as shown by the fact that the points fall within a circle. The correlation was +.05, which for all essential purposes is equivalent to zero.*

Figure 14.5 shows a different scatter plot, this time examining the relationship between students' heights and their SAT scores. Again, each point on the scatter plot represents one person, with height determining the point's horizontal position and SAT score determining its vertical position. Here there is no relationship: the dots do not cluster to form an elliptical pattern; instead, they are more or less evenly dispersed, and so we can readily find tall people with both high and low SAT scores, and short people with both high and low scores.

Galton and his students developed a mathematical expression that summarized these sorts of relationships. This measure is called the *correlation coefficient*, symbolized by the letter *r*, and it can take any value between +1.00 and −1.00. When *r* = +1.00 or −1.00, the correlation is perfect. For the data depicted graphically in Figure 14.4, which shows the relationship between height and weight, *r* = +.70. This is a strongly positive correlation, but it is also considerably less than *r* = +1.00. In other words, the correlation between height and weight is not perfect. For the data used to draw Figure 14.5, showing the relationship between height and SAT score, *r* = +.05, close to zero, reflecting the fact that there is no relationship here.

When *r* is positive, higher scores on one measure (say, height) are associated with higher scores on the other (say, weight). When it is negative, higher scores on one measure are associated with lower scores on the other. For example, consider the correlation between an individual's verbal SAT score and the time needed for that same individual to read *Hamlet*: students with higher scores generally need less time, so as the SAT verbal score goes up, reading time goes down and vice versa. We should emphasize, though, that the strength of a correlation is reflected by its absolute value—its value regardless of sign: *r* = −.70 is just as strong as *r* = +.70.

As we saw in Chapter 13, correlations provide a useful measure of the degree to which two variables are related, but they also have an important limitation: they cannot, by themselves, tell us whether there is any cause-and-effect relationship between the variables. Sometimes there is: there is a negative correlation between the number of cigarettes smoked per day and life expectancy (the more cigarettes smoked, the shorter the life expectancy), and the causal link here is well known. But often this is not the case. For example, there is also a negative correlation between life expectancy and the number of ashtrays an individual owns, but this is not because owning ashtrays is bad for your health. Instead, owning ashtrays is itself correlated with cigarette smoking (positively: the more ashtrays, the more cigarettes smoked), and smoking is the health risk.

## EVALUATING MENTAL TESTS

The notions of variability and correlation are important in evaluating the tests psychologists have designed to assess individual differences. How can we determine whether a given test adequately assesses the traits on which people differ? Do tests of artistic aptitude, for example, or intelligence actually measure what they are designed to measure?

### RELIABILITY

One criterion of a test's adequacy is its *reliability*—that is, the consistency with which it measures what it measures. Consider a bathroom scale. Imagine that you step onto the scale, and it shows your weight to be 120 pounds. You step off the scale, surprised by the good news. But then you ask, Could this be? What about the large pizza you had yesterday? You step back onto the scale, and it reports your weight as 115 pounds. Puzzled by this change, you step off the scale and quickly back on, and now the scale says you weigh 125 pounds. You would surely conclude that it is time to buy a new scale—this one is not reliable.

This example suggests that one way to assess reliability is by administering the test more than once. The correlation between scores would seem to be a good index of the test's reliability. However, this *test–retest method* is not always suitable. Sometimes the quality to be assessed is itself not stable. The bathroom scale might not register the same weight before and after Thanksgiving dinner, but that would not be the scale's fault. The same might be true of a test to assess mood: the score on the test taken today might not correlate with the score if the test was taken yesterday. But that may not mean a problem with the test, since people's moods change from one day to the next. Tests of knowledge face a similar problem; test takers may well learn more between the test and the retest, and this will reduce the correlation between their two scores.

One solution to this problem is to assess reliability on a single occasion by dividing a test into parts—say, the even-numbered questions versus the odd-numbered ones. If the test consistently measures the same trait, then the test taker's score on one half of the test should correlate with her score on the other half of the test.

Most psychological tests now in use have *reliability coefficients* (that is, test-retest correlations or correlations between the test's halves) in the .90s or in the high .80s. These are high values (recall that $r = +1.00$ or $-1.00$ is a perfect correlation), but reliability is crucial if we hope to interpret these tests as revealing stable and enduring characteristics of the individual.

## VALIDITY

Even more critical than reliability is a test's *validity*, defined simply as the extent to which the test measures what it is supposed to measure. Imagine a psychology professor who assigns final grades in a course based largely on penmanship on exams. This assessment procedure might be reliable (assuming the professor is consistent in his assessment of handwriting), but it is surely not valid, since handwriting has nothing to do with mastery of a course's content.

*Predictive Validity*   How can we assess a test's validity? One approach is to consider the test's *predictive validity*, that is, its ability to predict future performance. If a test claims, for example, to measure scholastic aptitude, then we would probably expect that students who do well on the test will do well in school later on. Similarly, a test of vocational aptitude ought to predict how well people will do on the job. One index of a test's validity, therefore, is its ability to make these predictions. This is usually measured by the correlation between the initial test score and some appropriate criterion.

As it turns out, tests of scholastic aptitude can be used to predict subsequent academic performance, so that there is a correlation of about +.50 between a high-school student's SAT scores and her grade-point average in college, a year or two later. Similarly, tests of vocational aptitude can be used to predict subsequent job performance, with correlations in the same range.

Such correlations are strong enough to indicate that these tests have predictive validity. But their predictions are far from perfect (that is, the correlation is well below 1.00). There are many reasons for this, among them the simple fact that school grades depend on many factors in addition to ability—motivation, for example. The aptitude test, in other words, is measuring just one "ingredient" of the "target" we are making predictions about, and, indeed, in light of this point, we should be impressed that the validity scores are as high as they are.

## STANDARDIZATION

Suppose we learn that a student's verbal aptitude score is 130. By itself, this number tells us very little, even if the aptitude test is both reliable and valid. To interpret this score, we need to know more about the scores obtained by other people who took the same test. These other scores provide the *norms* against which our student's test results can be evaluated. If we knew, for example, that an average performance on this test was 82, then 130 is impressive indeed. If we instead knew that the average test score is 200 or more, then 130 looks very different.

To obtain these norms, a test is first administered to a large sample of the population on which the test is to be used. This initial group is the *standardization sample*. Of course, this sample must be chosen with care. In interpreting an adult's score, it may be of little use to know how children generally perform on the test; in interpreting an American's score, it may (for many tests, and for many purposes) not be relevant to know how a group of Ghanaians did, and so on.

# INTELLIGENCE TESTING

Now that we have the relevant concepts in place, we can turn, at last, to the actual enterprise of intelligence testing.

The first question we need to ask is, What is *intelligence*? We all have some notion of what this term refers to, and our vocabularies are filled with words that describe different levels and types of intellectual functioning—*smart*, *bright*, and *clever*; *slow*, *stupid*, and *dim-witted*. But it is difficult to specify exactly what these terms mean, and attempts at specification often lead to disagreements.

Even experts disagree on exactly how *intelligence* should be defined (Sternberg & Detterman, 1986). Some researchers emphasize the capacity for abstract thinking. Others focus on the ability to acquire new abilities or new knowledge. Still others highlight the ability to adapt to new situations. No single definition of intelligence has been accepted by all. Remarkably, though, this has not been an obstacle to progress in intelligence testing, and so even without an agreed-upon definition, we do have intelligence tests. These tests were developed to fill certain practical needs, and, as we will see, for many purposes these tests work quite well.

## MEASURING INTELLIGENCE

While people plainly disagree about the definition of intelligence, there is a reasonable consensus on the sorts of tasks that require intelligence. For example, it seems obvious that little intelligence is needed to dig a hole with a shovel—Einstein would have been no better at this task (and might have been worse) than someone with far less intellectual prowess. Alternatively, intelligence does seem necessary for learning calculus—for this complex task, someone like Einstein has a considerable advantage.

A century ago, these relatively straightforward intuitions served as the basis for intelligence testing. We can find out how smart people are by looking at their performance on tasks that seem, on the face of things, to require intelligence.

### TESTING INTELLIGENCE IN CHILDREN

In 1904, the French minister of public instruction appointed a committee with the task of identifying children who were performing badly in school and, crucially, children who would benefit from remedial education. The committee concluded that an objective diagnostic test was needed to assess each child, and much of what we know about the measurement of intelligence grows out of this pioneering work.

One member of this committee, Alfred Binet (1857–1911), played a pivotal role. His project was, from the start, entirely pragmatic in its goals and quite optimistic in its tone,

*Alfred Binet*

*Variations on the IQ test*   *In addition to the WAIS, the most widely used intelligence test (discussed on pp. 559—560), many other tests have been developed, each specialized for one purpose or another. For example, the Bayley Scales are used to measure the mental and motor development of very young children (from one to forty-two months of age).*

as he sought both to identify the weaker students and then to improve their performance through special training. As his work developed, Binet prescribed courses in "mental orthopedics" for students with low scores, and, in one book, his chapter on the "training of intelligence" began with an ambitious phrase: "After the illness, the remedy."

*Intelligence as a General Cognitive Capacity*   Binet and his collaborator, Théophile Simon, believed that intelligence was a general attribute that manifested itself in many different spheres of cognitive functioning. This belief led them to construct a test that included many subtasks varying in both content and difficulty: copying a drawing, repeating a string of digits, understanding a story, and so on. Their idea was that a person might do well on one or two of these tasks just by luck or by virtue of some specific prior experience, but only a truly intelligent person would do well on all the tasks in the test. Therefore, intelligence could be measured by a composite score that took all the tasks into account, with the diversity of the tasks ensuring that the test was not measuring some specialized talent but was instead a measure of ability in general. As Binet (1911) put it, "It matters very little what the tests are so long as they are numerous" (p. 329).

Binet found that this composite measure did correlate reasonably well with a child's school grades and also with the teacher's evaluation of the child's intelligence. Thus, the test did have predictive validity.*

## TESTING INTELLIGENCE IN ADULTS

The Binet-Simon test was originally meant for children, but demand soon arose for the assessment of adults' intelligence. This led to the development of a test standardized on an adult population—the Wechsler Adult Intelligence Scale, or WAIS (Wechsler, 1958). This scale was divided into various verbal and performance subtests. The verbal

---

* Originally, the IQ test was evaluated in a fashion that compared the child's actual age and her "mental age"—an estimate of how developed the child was intellectually. The IQ score itself was computed as a ratio between mental and chronological age, and the ratio was then multiplied by 100. It is this ratio, or quotient, that gives the IQ test its name—it is a measure of someone's intelligence quotient. Modern IQ tests are scored differently and no longer compare mental and chronological age. Even so, the name, IQ, remains in place.

COMPREHENSION

1. Why should we obey traffic laws and speed limits?
2. Why are antitrust laws necessary?
3. Why should we lock the doors and take the keys to our car when leaving the car parked?
4. What does this saying mean: "Kill two birds with one stone."

INFORMATION

1. Who wrote *Huckleberry Finn?*
2. Where is Finland?
3. At what temperature does paper burn?
4. What is entomology?

ARITHMETIC

1. How many 15¢ stamps can you buy for a dollar?
2. How many hours will it take a cyclist to travel 60 miles if he is going 12 miles an hour?

**A.** Verbal tests

3. A man bought a used stereo system for 3/4 of what it cost new. He paid $225 dollars for it. How much did it cost new?
4. Six men can finish a job in ten days. How many men will be needed to finish the job in two and a half days?

**B.** Picture completion

**C.** Block design

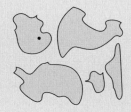 

**D.** Object assembly

**14.6** *Test items similar to some in the Wechsler Adult Intelligence Scale* **The items shown here are not identical to those on the actual Wechsler Test. Those items are kept out of public view, in part to make sure that test-takers are not familiar with the items before being tested.**

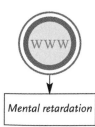

Mental retardation

tests include items that assess general knowledge, vocabulary, comprehension, and arithmetic skills. The performance test includes tasks that require the test taker to assemble the cut-up parts of a familiar object to form the appropriate whole, to complete an incomplete drawing, and to rearrange a series of pictures so that they are in the proper sequence (Figure 14.6).

The revised version of the WAIS is widely used, but other tests are also common. Many of these other tests use a multiple-choice format that allows the simultaneous testing of large groups of people. Some examples are the SAT, taken by most college applicants, and the Graduate Record Examination (GRE), a more difficult version of the SAT designed for applicants to graduate schools (Figure 14.7). A test that emphasizes nonverbal intellectual ability is the Progressive Matrices Test (Figure 14.8). (For still other tests, see, for example, Daniel, 1997.)

# WHAT IS INTELLIGENCE? THE PSYCHOMETRIC APPROACH

The scores people obtain on intelligence tests are remarkably stable, and so, if we know someone's IQ at, say, age six, we can predict accurately what their IQ score will be at age eighteen; if we know their IQ at age eleven, we can predict what their IQ will be at age

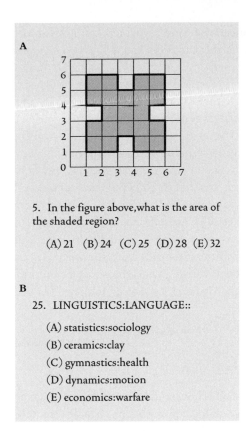

A

5. In the figure above, what is the area of the shaded region?

(A) 21   (B) 24   (C) 25   (D) 28   (E) 32

B

25. LINGUISTICS:LANGUAGE::

(A) statistics:sociology
(B) ceramics:clay
(C) gymnastics:health
(D) dynamics:motion
(E) economics:warfare

14.8   *A sample item from the Progressive Matrices Test*   **The task is to select the alternative that fits into the empty slot above.**

14.7   *Two items from the Scholastic Aptitude Test (SAT) 1: Reasoning Test*

seventy-seven (see, for example, Deary, 2001a, 2001b; Moffitt, Caspi, Harkness, & Silva, 1993). This tells us both that the IQ tests are reliable and that they are measuring something that—at least in part—seems to be an enduring, perhaps even permanent, trait of the individual.

But are the intelligence tests valid? One way to answer this is by looking at the tests' effectiveness in predicting school success. As we mentioned earlier, the tests do reasonably well, with correlations of around +.50 between test scores and subsequent measures of academic performance (for example, grade-point average). The same is true for job performance. One survey examined thousands of studies collected across a span of eighty-five years, and, across all of these studies, tests of general mental ability emerged as among the strongest predictors of success in the workplace (Schmidt & Hunter, 1998). Thus, with impressive consistency, intelligence tests can predict who will do well on the job. (For more on the tests' validity, see Neisser, Boodoo, Bouchard, & Boykin, 1996.)

These results, though straightforward, have been quite controversial (see, for example, Sternberg, 1997, 2000; Wagner, 1997). What is the nature of the controversy? Let us remember that predictive validity is measured by correlations (for example, the correlation between IQ scores and some measure of job performance), but correlations—here as elsewhere—are ambiguous with regard to cause-and-effect relationships. For example, the correlation between IQ and job success might suggest that above-average intelligence enables people to perform more effectively in the workplace. But other interpretations are also possible. Perhaps the IQ tests are grueling to take, and so only people with a lot of patience and motivation do well. If so, it may be these latter traits that are predictive in the long run. Seen in this light, high IQ might not be the cause of better performance at work. Instead, both the IQ score and the performance might be the results of some other factor, but, since they are both effects of the same cause, they would end up correlated with each other. This would be analogous to the correlation

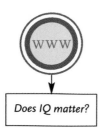

*Does IQ matter?*

between owning ashtrays and dying from cancer; these are correlated, but not because one causes the other. Instead, both derive from the same root cause (being a cigarette smoker), and so end up correlated with each other.

In the case of cigarette smoking, owning ashtrays, and cancer, we are able to specify the cause-and-effect relationships because we understand the mechanism through which cigarette smoking affects health. To specify this mechanism, though, we needed to know more about cigarette smoking, including what exactly it does to the body. The same logic applies to intelligence: if we are to understand how (or whether) intelligence influences performance, we need to know more about what intelligence is—or, to be more precise, we need to know more about what it is that intelligence tests are measuring. One line of attack on this issue has been to scrutinize the test data themselves, in order to sharpen our understanding of what these data actually mean. This idea is at the heart of the ***psychometric*** (literally, "mind-measuring") ***approach to intelligence***. This approach does not begin with theory or definitions. Instead, it begins with the test scores themselves, and the belief that the patterns within these scores may be our best guide in deciding what intelligence is and what it includes. Let us look at how this approach proceeds.

## THE STRUCTURE OF MENTAL ABILITIES

To understand the psychometric approach, consider how it addresses a crucial question about intelligence: Is intelligence one singular ability, applicable to virtually any content? If so, then someone who is intelligent would have an advantage on virtually any mental task—whether it is solving a puzzle, writing a paper, or learning a new mathematical technique.

Or, alternatively, is there really no such thing as being intelligent in a general sort of way? Instead, perhaps each of us has our own collection of talents, with each talent relevant to some mental tasks but not to others. On this view, we probably should not expect to find people who are successful in every sort of intellectual endeavor, or (conversely) people who are inept in every mental task. On the contrary, each of us would be strong on some tasks (for which we had the talents) and somewhat weaker on others (which relied on talents that we lack)—our own individualized profile of strengths and weaknesses.

As we will see, the evidence on this point is somewhat complicated. It turns out that people do have specialized abilities, with each ability applicable to just a certain type of test. It also turns out that there is some factor that does look truly general and does seem pertinent to all sorts of tests. But, before we get to the particulars, let us look at an example that illustrates how the psychometric approach tackles these issues.

A number of investigators have hypothesized that mathematical aptitude helps people in understanding music. Others, in contrast, suggest that mathematical skill has little to do with musical comprehension. How can the psychometric approach lead us to an answer? We might give a test of mathematical skill to a number of people and also give them a test of musical comprehension. If mathematical skill is pertinent to musical understanding, then someone who has a lot of this skill should do well on both tests, and someone without the skill should do poorly on both. Of course, other skills and other capacities are also relevant to these tests, and so we would not expect a perfect correlation between the math scores and the music scores. But, if the tests do overlap in their intellectual requirements, we would expect a positive correlation between the tests' scores.

The idea, then, is that we can use the presence or absence of a correlation as a way of asking whether these two tests overlap in the capacities they require—and the stronger the correlation, the greater the overlap. We could then use the same logic, in turn, to ask whether mathematics tests and reading tests rely on overlapping sets of abilities, whether reading tests and the ability to learn a foreign language do, and so on. And if, in the end, we found that all intellectual tests overlapped in this fashion, this would indicate that there is, in fact, something shared by all of them. That would be our evidence for something that we might call intelligence in general, a capacity that is applicable to all tests.

As a different way of conveying this logic, imagine someone looking at a lake and seeing what appear to be serpentlike parts:

**A**

The parts that the viewer can actually see—the bits of serpent that are above the water—correspond to someone's test scores, scores that, once obtained, are out in the open for any suitably placed observer to see. What we want to ask, though, is how the scores are connected to each other, or, in the case of the serpent, we want to know what lies underneath the water's surface. One hypothesis that the viewer can entertain is that all the visible parts belong to one huge sea monster. This would be analogous to the hypothesis that there is just one unitary intellectual ability, tying together the various test scores, so that all of our test scores are just different measurements of the same underlying skill:

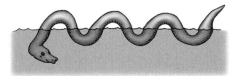

**B**

But, as a different hypothesis, there might also be several such beasts. This would be analogous to the idea that there are five or six different kinds of intelligence, with each kind influencing its own set of tasks:

**C**

Or finally, there might be as many sea animals as there are visible parts, analogous to the hypothesis that every test measures a totally different ability:

**D**

How might our sea-serpent viewer choose among these alternatives, given that he has no way of peering below the waters? His best bet would be to wait and watch how the serpentine parts change over time and space. If he does this, he can find out which parts go together. If all parts move jointly (B), the most reasonable interpretation is that they all belong to one huge sea monster. (For the purposes of our example, we will assume that sea serpents are severely arthritic and so unable to move their body portions separately.) If the first part goes with the second, while the third goes with the fourth (C), there are presumably two smaller creatures. If all parts move separately (D), the best bet is that there are as many sea serpents as there are visible parts.

In effect, our sea-serpent watcher has studied a correlation pattern. Some parts of the sea serpent are directly visible, just as test scores are directly visible. But what is interesting is how these parts (or test scores) are linked to each other, and the links are not visible—they are hidden below the surface. However, we can infer the (invisible) structure by seeing how the visible parts move: if they rise and fall together, we conclude they are linked (different tests all depend on a single ability); if they rise and fall independently, we conclude the opposite—each test depends on a different sort of skill.

## SPEARMAN AND THE CONCEPT OF GENERAL INTELLIGENCE

To address the question of whether intelligence is unitary or multiple, let us consider the WAIS-R. This is one of the most widely used intelligence tests, and it includes four subtests: information or general knowledge (I), comprehension (C), arithmetic (A), and vocabulary (V). As it turns out, the scores on each of these subtests are quite highly correlated with scores on the other subtests. The correlation between I and C is .70, that between I and A is .66, and so on. These results are presented in the form of a *correlation matrix* in Table 14.3.

This pattern certainly suggests that some common factor runs through all of these subtests, since individuals who perform well do so across the board; individuals who do poorly are consistent in their poor performance. Perhaps, therefore, all these tasks draw on the same basic skill. Individuals who are well endowed with this skill do well on all the tests; individuals with less of this skill do poorly across the board.*

To assess this sort of pattern, psychologists rely on a statistical technique known as *factor analysis*, developed by Charles Spearman (1863–1945). Factor analysis allows us to extract a measurement of the common factor that seems to be shared among all of these tasks; Spearman argued that this factor is best described as **general intelligence**, or **g**. He proposed that *g* is a mental attribute called on for any intellectual task, and so individuals with a lot of *g* have an advantage in every intellectual endeavor. If *g* is in short supply, the individual will do poorly on a wide range of tasks.

Spearman realized, though, that this cannot be our entire account of intelligence. If test performance were determined entirely by *g*, then the correlations between any two

---

* Many students are surprised by this pattern of results, since they think of themselves as strong in verbal scores and weak in math, or perhaps strong in math and weak verbally. However, these self-assessments are often misleading, because they are typically made in comparison to other college students, and this, by itself, makes the comparison a relatively narrow one. If we broaden our comparison to include the whole population, and not just college students, then we do find the correlations described here, not only with each person having his or her own profile but also with there usually being a consistency to the profile, with a student strong in general, or weak in general, or in the middle in general.

---

### TABLE 14.3    CORRELATION MATRIX OF FOUR SUBTESTS ON THE WECHSLER ADULT INTELLIGENCE SCALE

|  | I | C | A | V |
|---|---|---|---|---|
| I (Information) | — | .70 | .66 | .81 |
| C (Comprehension) |  | — | .49 | .73 |
| A (Arithmetic) |  |  | — | .59 |
| V (Vocabulary) |  |  |  | — |

NOTE: The matrix shows the correlation of each subtest with each of the other three. Note that the left-to-right diagonal (which is here indicated by the dashes) cannot have any entries because it is made up of the cells that describe the correlation of each subtest with itself. The cells below the dashes are left blank because they would be redundant.
SOURCE: From Wechsler, 1958.

subtests should be perfect (that is, $r = 1.00$). But the correlations, while strongly positive, fall short of this. Spearman proposed, therefore, that each test depends both on $g$ and on some other ability that is specific to the particular subtest. Thus, performance on an arithmetic subtest depends on $g$ and on numerical skills; performance on vocabulary tests depends on $g$ and its own specialized (verbal) skill. People differ from each other both in general intelligence and in these different specialized skills, and this is why the correlations among different subtests are not perfect (Spearman, 1927).

## FLUID AND CRYSTALLIZED INTELLIGENCE

Many investigators since Spearman have endorsed the idea that there is some factor that influences virtually all mental tasks (the factor that Spearman called $g$), and also a set of more specific skills, each applicable just to a particular type of mental task. But what exactly is $g$? This is a complicated question, because $g$ may in fact be composed of several different ingredients, including a component called *fluid intelligence* and another called *crystallized intelligence*.

Fluid intelligence refers to the ability to deal with new and unusual problems; it is an ability heavily influenced by mental speed and flexibility. Crystallized intelligence, on the other hand, refers to the individual's repertoire of previously acquired skills and information, a repertoire that is useful for dealing with familiar problems or problems similar to those already encountered (Cattell, 1963, 1971; J. L. Horn, 1985). As it turns out, there is a substantial correlation ($r = +.60$) between an individual's fluid intelligence and her crystallized intelligence, and so someone who has a lot of one is likely to have a lot of the other; someone short on one is likely to be short on both. This is why these two forms of intelligence can be described with a single number, $g$.

Even with this correlation, however, the evidence suggests that fluid and crystallized intelligence are truly different from each other. For example, crystallized intelligence seems to increase with age, so long as the individual remains in an intellectually stimulating environment (see Chapter 12). Fluid intelligence, on the other hand, reaches its height in early adulthood and declines steadily with age (J. L. Horn, 1985; J. L. Horn & Noll, 1994). Similarly, many factors, including alcohol consumption, fatigue, depression, and some forms of brain damage, cause more impairment in tasks requiring fluid intelligence than in those dependent on crystallized intelligence (Duncan, 1994; E. Hunt, 1995). To put this concretely, someone who is tired (or drunk, or depressed) will probably perform adequately on tests involving familiar routines and familiar facts, since these tests draw heavily on crystallized intelligence. That same individual, however, may be markedly impaired if the test requires quick thinking or a novel approach—both earmarks of fluid intelligence.

Notice, therefore, that a great deal depends here on one's perspective. For purposes of statistical summary, we can usefully describe an individual's fluid and crystallized intelligence with a single number. This is guaranteed by the fact that these two measures are, as we noted, strongly correlated, and so, if we know either one of these measures, we can predict the other with reasonable accuracy. But if our aim is to refine our theories of intelligence, then we cannot collapse fluid and crystallized intelligence into a single theoretical entity. Instead, we need to understand them as separate and distinct capacities—each relevant to different tasks and subject to different influences.

## WHAT IS $G$?

Many people own a toolbox that contains both some all-purpose tools, like a hammer or a pair of pliers, useful for many different jobs, and also some more specialized tools, like a spark-plug socket or a spoke-wrench, designed for particular applications. Intelligence is like that toolbox—containing both general-use components, useful across the board, and more specialized elements, useful for just some tasks. In the case of the toolbox, though, we can examine the individual tools and find out what they are. That is not so easy for intelligence, and, as a result, there remains some debate about what the components are—particularly, the general-use component, $g$.

As we have just seen, $g$ contains at least two elements—fluid and crystallized intelligence. Crystallized intelligence is relatively easy to understand: it contains the facts, procedures, and skills that someone has learned over their lifetime, all ready for use when needed. But what exactly is fluid intelligence? In addition, we might well ask, Are these two constituents all there is to $g$? Or might $g$ have other components as well?

In addressing these questions, it is important to remember that the claim that $g$ exists is, in the end, a claim that rests entirely on a correlation pattern, a pattern that tells us that people who do well on one mental test are likely to have some advantage on every other test we give them. Conversely, people who do poorly on one mental test are likely to have a corresponding across-the-board disadvantage. These correlations are far from perfect, and it is easy to find people who are relatively stronger in some areas than others. (As we have mentioned, this reflects, in large part, the role of other, more specialized forms of intelligence.) Even so, the fact remains that there is a broad pattern of correlations across tasks, and these correlations tell us that all of these tasks have something in common, some mental "ingredient" that contributes to all of them. But the correlations by themselves do not tell us what that ingredient is, and, in fact, this is a point about which investigators continue to disagree.

Some have proposed that $g$ is a measure of the overall neural efficiency of the brain—perhaps, literally, the speed with which the individual neurons communicate (Eysenck, 1986; Vernon, 1987). Others have suggested that $g$ reflects the workings of specific neural circuits in the frontal cortex, circuits closely associated with working memory (Duncan et al., 2000). Holding biological claims to the side, still others propose that $g$ reflects "the ability to keep a (mental) representation active, particularly in the face of interference and distraction" (Engle, Tuholski, Laughlin, & Conway, 1999, p. 309).

But other researchers read the data rather differently (see, for example, Ceci, 1990; E. Hunt, 1995; Sternberg, 2000; see Thomson, 1916, for an early expression of this issue). They suggest that $g$ may provide a useful statistical summary of the data but argue that that $g$ is not a single identifiable capacity. More precisely, $g$ may reflect a *collection* of different elements. That collection includes fluid and crystallized intelligence. It may also contain other elements, including a number of factors that we might not think of as "intellectual capacities," but that are nonetheless pertinent to performance on intellectual tasks. These include one's motivation, one's attitudes toward testing, one's willingness to persevere when a problem becomes frustratingly difficult, and on and on. If all of these attributes happen to be correlated with each other (and they may well be), then a single number (such as $g$) could be used to measure them all. But in this case, the measurement would not refer to a single capacity; it would instead refer to a somewhat heterogeneous package of attributes, all of which together contribute to intellectual performance.

Once again, therefore, a great deal depends on one's perspective. If our purpose is to summarize the data or to predict performance, then there is no question that measures of $g$ are quite useful. These measures do provide broad summaries of an individual's abilities, telling us how well that individual will perform in a wide range of intellectual tasks. But if, in contrast, our purpose is to define intelligence, things remain uncertain. Perhaps $g$ is actually a measure of a specific intellectual capacity that all of us have to some degree, and we have mentioned a few proposals for what this capacity might turn out to be. Perhaps $g$ is simply a measure of a package of diverse capacities, each different from the others, but all correlated (and so measurable with a single number). The debate between these two positions is certain to continue. In the meantime the practical value of $g$ measures remains strong—these measures are powerful predictors!—at the same time that the theoretical meaning of $g$ remains open.

# THE INFORMATION-PROCESSING APPROACH

The tests devised by Binet and his successors have, as we have described, been of considerable practical importance, and they have also, in a variety of ways, spurred theory development. But, as we have also seen, there are many questions that these tests by themselves cannot answer. For example, what is $g$? The psychometric approach, and, more precisely, the pattern of correlations among tests, tell us only that a broad range of mental tasks have something in common, and that this something, whatever it is, varies from individual to individual: some of us have a lot of this something, and others have less. But the psychometric approach cannot by itself tell us what this something is. Our measures of $g$ might reflect some aspect of neural efficiency, or some sort of problem-solving skill, or perhaps something else we have not yet thought of.

For these reasons, some psychologists have turned to a different approach to the study of intelligence, one that is based on an analysis of the cognitive operations needed for intellectual performance, including performance on intelligence tests. The basic idea is to link differences in overall test performance to more fine-grained differences in the way individuals perceive, attend, learn, remember, and think.

## SIMPLE COGNITIVE CORRELATES

Some investigators have proposed that large-scale differences in intellectual capacity actually derive from some remarkably low-level cognitive operations. Skill in carrying out these simple operations is far from what we typically think of as intelligence. But these low-level operations are used again and again in intelligent performance, and so they may well be the building blocks of this performance.

*Reaction Time* One idea we have already mentioned is that differences in mental ability are related to speed of mental processing. As a relatively direct test of this notion, a number of investigators have tried to correlate reaction time with intelligence-test performance. Some studies have measured *simple reaction time*, in which the participant merely responds as quickly as he can when a stimulus appears. Others have measured *choice reaction time*, in which the participant must again respond as quickly as possible but now has to choose among several responses, depending on the stimulus presented. In such tasks, short reaction times do correlate with higher intelligence-test scores. There is also some suggestion that these correlations are weaker for simple reaction time than they are for choice reaction time, and that the correlations go up as the number of choices increases (Jensen, 1987).

According to some investigators, these reaction-time measures are a way of getting at rock-bottom differences in neurological functioning, differences that may be the underpinning of Spearman's $g$. (As we noted earlier, some researchers have literally interpreted $g$ as a measure of "neural efficiency.") But is this right? Reaction time is affected by many variables, including the ability to understand the experimenter's instructions, the ability to keep one's attention focused, and so on. It is possible, therefore, that short reaction times are simply one more achievement made possible by intelligence, rather than the underlying cause of intelligence (Brody, 1992; Deary, 2001b; Detterman, 1987). In addition, we should note that the correlations between IQ and reaction time are not large—around −.35. (The correlation is negative because higher reaction times go with lower intelligence-test scores.) Therefore, even if reaction time does reflect some basic process underlying mental ability, it can only account for a small portion of the variability in the population.

*Verbal Ability and Lexical Access Time*  Perhaps intelligence is not associated with mental speed in general. Perhaps intelligence depends instead on the speed of some specific process or some particular mental event. For example, in order to understand a sentence, one needs to think about the meanings of the individual words within the sentence. Presumably, one retrieves these meanings from some sort of mental dictionary, and this process of "looking up" each word is swift but not instantaneous. Moreover, one must do this look-up again and again, for each of the words encountered. Therefore, being slightly quicker at this task might add up to a considerable benefit, and being slightly slower, to a considerable cost (E. Hunt, 1976, 1985b).

One plausible hypothesis, then, is that speed at this mental look-up is an important contributor to performance on tests of verbal intelligence. To test this hypothesis, investigators have used the ***lexical decision task***, which was designed to provide a direct measure of how quickly words can be accessed in long-term memory. A participant is presented with strings of letters, such as *bread* or *blead,* and asked to decide whether the string is a word or not. Her speed of lexical access is measured by the time it takes her to make this decision.* Several studies show that these memory look-up times are shorter for people who do well on tests of verbal intelligence, exactly as predicted. The difference is seen, for example, between college students with high and low scores on the verbal portion of the SAT or on tests of reading comprehension (E. Hunt, Lunneborg, & Lewis, 1975; M. Jackson & McClelland, 1975, 1979).

## COMPLEX COGNITIVE COMPONENTS

Simple cognitive operations such as choice reaction time and memory look-up are clearly correlated with intelligence-test performance, presumably because intelligence depends on the smooth operation of these simple, rock-bottom cognitive processes. But surely there is more to intelligence than this. To reason about a problem in arithmetic, for example, one has to recognize the numbers (for example, 1 means "one"), and one may have to retrieve the multiplication table from memory (for example, $2 \times 3 = 6$). But recognizing numbers and retrieving the multiplication table are not the same as reasoning arithmetically.

These considerations have led researchers to study some of the higher-level processes that might constitute intelligence, in contrast to the lower-level processes we have considered so far. One such undertaking was Robert Sternberg's analysis (1977) of analogical reasoning. Analogy problems are a staple of many intelligence tests, and since analogy tests are highly correlated with other intelligence subtests, they may provide a particularly good measure of Spearman's *g* factor. For example:

*Hand is to foot as finger is to (arm, leg, thumb, toe).*

Or to give a more difficult item:

*Washington is to one as Lincoln is to (five, ten, twenty).*

What mental processes, or ***cognitive components***, are needed to solve these problems? Sternberg proposed that the problem is solved in separate stages. First, one identifies attributes of each term that might be relevant (for example, both Washington and Lincoln were presidents; Washington was the first president and Lincoln the sixteenth). After this, one tries to discover relationships between the first and second terms of the analogy (for example, Washington was the first president, hence Washington–president one) and then between the first and third terms (for example, Washington–

---

* Strictly speaking, it is the time she takes to make this yes-no decision minus the time it takes her to react to the letter strings when no decision is asked for.

president and Lincoln–president). Finally, one takes the relationships inferred for the Washington–president one pair and tries to apply them to create an appropriate match for Lincoln. For example, applying the relationship Washington–president one to Lincoln would yield Lincoln–president sixteen. But this does not work, since sixteen is not one of the options available. A different relationship links Washington's portrait to the one-dollar bill, and this does work, since Lincoln's portrait is on the five-dollar bill, and "five" is one of the options (Sternberg, 1977; see Figure 14.9).

Perhaps it is skill in these component stages that characterizes intelligence, so that someone better at discovering these relationships, or in applying them to new terms, will do better on intelligence tests (or any other task requiring intelligence). Results consistent with this suggestion come from a study in which participants were presented with various tests of reasoning (Sternberg & Gardner, 1983). Some of the tests involved analogies, others involved classification tasks (for example, which pair of words does *Italy* go with, *Germany/France* or *Vietnam/Korea*?). There was a remarkable correspondence between decision times on these tasks and the participants' scores on several psychometric tests of abstract reasoning. The average correlation was –.65, a very encouraging result for the theory of complex cognitive components. (As before, the correlation was negative because higher decision times correspond to lower reasoning scores.)

**14.9** *Washington is to one as Lincoln is to five*

## THE ROLE OF WORKING MEMORY AND ATTENTION

Other investigators have focused on the role of working memory and attention in intelligence (see Chapters 7 and 8). In solving an analogy problem, for example, one must keep track of the various terms and of their attributes. One must also remember which relationships have already been examined and found unsatisfactory, so that one does not keep examining the same relationships over and over. All of this requires memory storage as well as attention, as one focuses on different aspects of the problem and develops new interpretations of it.

Again, this leads to an obvious proposal: individuals with better working memory and attention should do better on analogy tests and a wide range of other tasks; individuals without these capacities will perform worse. To test this suggestion, researchers have developed *active-span tasks*, procedures designed to assess the ability to store and manipulate different pieces of information simultaneously. One such test is illustrated in Figure 14.10. In this procedure, the participant must first decide whether each equation is true, and then read the word out loud. For the first item, therefore, the subject would say, "true; dog." Then the subject sees another item and another. After a series of these items, a cue appears, and the subject must write down as many of the words as he can recall ("dog, gas, nose . . .").

This seems a peculiar task, but it does require the subject to remember materials while simultaneously working with other materials—exactly the combination we hope to measure. And, as hypothesized, scores on such tasks do correlate with a variety of other intelligence-test scores, including the verbal SAT score, measures of reading comprehension and of reasoning, and some versions of the IQ test (Carpenter, Just, & Shell, 1990; Engle, Cantor, & Carullo, 1992; Just & Carpenter, 1992; Kyllonen & Cristal, 1990).

$$
\begin{aligned}
(7 \times 7) \quad &+ 1 = 50; \text{ dog} \\
(10 / 2) \quad &+ 6 = 10; \text{ gas} \\
(4 \times 2) \quad &+ 1 = 9; \text{ nose} \\
(3 / 1) \quad &+ 1 = 4; \text{ beat} \\
(5 / 5) \quad &+ 1 = 2; \text{ tree} \\
(8 \times 2) \quad &- 4 = 13; \text{ help} \\
(6 / 2) \quad &- 3 = 2; \text{ stay}
\end{aligned}
$$

**14.10** *Test items for an active-span task* **For each item, the person being tested must say aloud whether the answer to the math problem is true or false and then must read the associated word. For the first item the person would say, "true, dog"; for the second, "false, gas," and so forth. After a series of these items, the person must write down as many of the words as he can ("dog, gas, nose . . ."). The number of words correctly recalled is the person's active span.**

## STRATEGIES AND INTELLECTUAL FUNCTIONING

Still another approach to the study of intelligence focuses on the strategies that participants use for solving problems, for learning, and for remembering. We discussed such strategies earlier in our discussion of cognitive development (see Chapter 12). As we saw there, a normal adult can master memory tasks that are generally beyond the reach of a six-year-old, and an important reason for this lies in the strategies the adult uses. Suppose she is asked to memorize unrelated materials, such as the words

*tulip plumber tiger sweater lily tailor daisy
raincoat monkey butcher zebra jacket.*

An adult will do her best to rehearse this list of items by organizing it in some way. For example, she might try rhythmic grouping by, say, repeating the items in threes: "tulip, plumber, tiger, ... sweater, lily, tailor, ... daisy, raincoat, monkey...." Or she might try to organize the list of items into categories, thinking first about the flowers, then the occupations, then the animals. Any of these organizational devices will help her in later tests of recall. A six-year-old, in contrast, is unlikely to have such organizational tricks in her repertoire and so will be less successful at such intellectual tasks (Flavell & Wellman, 1977).

The use of such strategies also accounts for some of the intellectual differences among adults, with the best evidence coming from extreme differences in ability, such as the differences between normal adults and those with mental retardation. Retarded examinees typically attack memory tasks with little or no resort to organization. They are less likely to rehearse, to group items in a list, or to show recall clustering by semantic categories (A. L. Brown, 1974; Campione & Brown, 1977; Campione, Brown, & Ferrara, 1982). Strategy use also provides part of the reason why the elderly often have trouble in remembering—they fail to use strategies when they first encounter the to-be-remembered materials and so are at a disadvantage later on, when the time comes to remember this material (F. Craik & Byrd, 1982; F. Craik & Jennings, 1992). The same is true for individuals who are depressed; they engage poorly with the to-be-remembered materials during learning, and so have difficulty retrieving them later on.

# WHAT IS INTELLIGENCE?
# BEYOND IQ

*Practical intelligence   Betters at a race track rely on sophisticated and complex strategies in deciding which horses will win—but these strategies seem to depend on a form of intelligence separate from that which is assessed by the IQ test.*

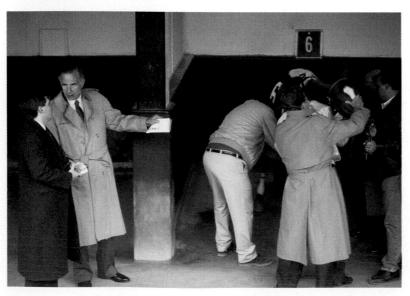

We have now filled in many of the blanks in our portrait of intelligence. Intelligence appears to have multiple ingredients, some specialized and some general use. One might well ask, however, what is left out of this portrait. Unmistakably, the tests we have covered do tap many aspects of what we ordinarily mean by "intelligence." But there are other aspects that we have not yet covered. Consider someone's competence in dealing with the world of practical affairs. Nothing in the intelligence tests will assess someone's common sense, or street smarts, or know-how. A related aptitude is social competence: the ability to persuade others and to judge their moods and desires. Shrewd salespeople have this ability as do successful politicians, quite independent of whether they are "smart" according to IQ tests or not.

A clear illustration of these nonacademic forms of intelligence comes from a study of experienced racetrack handicappers who were asked to predict the outcomes and payoffs in upcoming horse races. This is a tricky mental task that involves highly complex reasoning. Factors like track records, jockeys, and track conditions all have to be remembered and weighed against each other. On the face of it, the ability to perform such mental calculations is just what intelligence tests should measure. But the results prove otherwise, for the handicappers' success turned out to be completely unrelated to their IQs (Ceci & Liker, 1986).

## PRACTICAL INTELLIGENCE

These (and other) findings have persuaded researchers that we need to broaden our conception of intelligence and consider some forms of intelligence simply not measured by IQ tests. For example, a number of researchers, particularly Robert Sternberg, have emphasized the importance of *practical intelligence*. We have already mentioned Sternberg's "componential" approach to intelligence; this approach provides key insights into what Sternberg calls *analytic intelligence*, the sort of intelligence typically measured by intelligence tests. However, other forms of intelligence, Sternberg argues, are just as important, including practical intelligence and *creative intelligence* (Sternberg, 1985; also see Sternberg, 1997; Sternberg & Kaufman, 1998; Sternberg, Wagner, Williams, & Horvath, 1995).

In one study of practical intelligence, business executives were asked to rate the relative importance of various skills needed to head a company department, such as the ability to delegate authority or to promote communication. It turned out that the skills these executives rated as most important were excellent predictors of business success: those who had these skills tended to perform particularly well and to earn the highest salaries. Interestingly, there was virtually no correlation, in this study, between these measures of business success and IQ (Sternberg & Wagner, 1993; R. K. Wagner, 1987; R. K. Wagner & Sternberg, 1987).

Practical and analytic intelligence differ in many ways. Problems demanding practical intelligence tend to be poorly defined initially and usually require some amount of information gathering before they can be tackled. Problems requiring analytic intelligence typically have neither of these properties (Neisser et al., 1996). Sternberg et al. (1995) have also argued that practical intelligence relies heavily on what they call *tacit knowledge*—practical know-how gleaned from everyday experience. This knowledge is in some cases quite sophisticated (think about those racetrack handicappers), but is, in any case, knowledge that is specialized for use in a particular domain. The business executive acquires tacit knowledge about running a company but not pertinent to navigating a ship or handicapping horses. The highly talented handicapper has no advantage in tasks away from the racetrack.

## THE NOTION OF MULTIPLE INTELLIGENCES

A different attempt to expand the notion of intelligence is Howard Gardner's (1983) concept of *multiple intelligences*. Gardner's claims are based, in part, on a consideration of individuals with special talents or special deficits. He notes, for example, that some individuals are exquisitely talented in music but quite ordinary otherwise. This suggests to Gardner that musical intelligence is separate and distinct from other forms of intelligence. Similar considerations led him to propose six specialized "intelligences": linguistic, logical-mathematical, spatial, musical, bodily-kinesthetic, and personal intelligence.

The first three of these are familiar enough and are assessed by most standard intelligence scales. Musical ability includes skill in composition and in performance. By bodily-kinesthetic intelligence, Gardner refers to the ability to learn and create complex motor patterns, as seen in dancers and skilled athletes. By personal intelligence, he refers to the ability to understand oneself and others.

One line of evidence for Gardner's claim comes from studies of patients with brain lesions that devastate some abilities while sparing others. Thus, certain lesions will

*Bodily-kinesthetic intelligence* **Wang Xinyi (a member of the Incredible Acrobats of China troupe) displays what Howard Gardner calls kinesthetic intelligence.**

**14.11   Drawing ability in a retarded savant   A drawing by Nadia, a severely retarded child with remarkable drawing ability. This horse was drawn when Nadia was four years old.**

**14.12   Unusual numerical achievements in an autistic savant   A scene from the 1988 film Rain Man, which depicted an autistic person with extraordinary numerical gifts that enabled him to note the exact number of matches remaining in a matchbox after the box was dropped and some were spilled on the floor, to keep track of all the cards in a casino blackjack game, and so forth. (From Rain Man, with Dustin Hoffman and Tom Cruise.)**

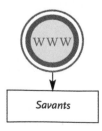

WWW

Savants

make a person unable to recognize drawings (spatial intelligence), while others will make her unable to perform a sequence of movements (bodily-kinesthetic intelligence) or will produce major changes in personality (personal intelligence).

Another argument for Gardner's theory comes from the study of people with so-called *savant syndrome.* These individuals have a single extraordinary talent, even though they are otherwise developmentally disabled (either autistic or mentally retarded) to a profound degree. Some display unusual artistic talent (see Figure 14.11). Others are "calendar calculators," able to answer immediately (and correctly!) when asked questions such as, "What day of the week was March 17 in the year 1682?" (see Figure 14.12). Still others have unusual mechanical talents or unusual musical skills, for example, effortlessly memorizing lengthy and complex musical works (A. J. Hill, 1978; L. K. Miller, 1999).

Gardner's claims are controversial, however, with some of the controversy focusing on the evidence he uses in support of his ideas. For example, he argues that some savants have "preserved mathematical intelligence" even if they are profoundly retarded in other domains; on the face of things, this seems powerful evidence that mathematical intelligence is distinguishable (both functionally and biologically) from other forms of intelligence. But is this really an accurate description of the savants? The answer is probably no. Savants who are calendar calculators can, without question, do extraordinary things with dates, but many of them are unable to calculate 8 + 9 or 7 − 6. It would appear, then, that they do not have something we would call "mathematical intelligence." Instead, what they have is far more specialized, and so cannot be taken as evidence for the existence of mathematical intelligence as a separate and independent sort of mental capacity. Similar claims can be made about other savants, with there sometimes being only a loose congruence between the abilities they have and the sorts of intelligence Gardner has described (L. M. Miller, 1999).

In addition, other investigators have raised questions about Gardner's basic conceptualization. There is no question, they agree, that some individuals—whether savants or otherwise—have special talents and that these talents are immensely impressive. However, is it appropriate to think of these talents as forms of intelligence? Or might we be better served by a distinction between *intelligence* and *talent*? It does seem peculiar to use the same term, *intelligence,* to describe both the capacity that Einstein displayed in developing his theories and the capacity that Brett Favre displays on the football field. Similarly, we might celebrate the vocal talent of Whitney Houston, but is this the same type of talent—and therefore sensibly described by the same term, *intelligence*—that a skilled debater relies on in rapidly thinking through the implications of an argument?

Whatever the ultimate verdict on Gardner's theory, however, he has undoubtedly performed a valuable service by drawing our attention to a set of abilities that is often ignored and undervalued. Both Gardner and Sternberg are surely correct in noting that we tend to focus too much on the skills and capacities that help people succeed in

*There are some aptitudes for which no tests have been developed thus far. (© The New Yorker Collection, 1983 S. Gross from The Cartoon Bank. All rights reserved.)*

"Son, your mother is a remarkable woman."

school, and do too little to celebrate the talents displayed by an artist at her canvas, a skilled dancer in the ballet, or a clergyman's empathy in a hospital room. Whether these other abilities are forms of "intelligence," though, is surely open to debate. But no matter how that debate turns out, these other talents are abilities to be highly esteemed and, if at all possible, nurtured and developed.

## THE CULTURAL CONTEXT OF INTELLIGENCE

Sternberg's work on practical intelligence and Gardner's on multiple intelligences point up certain limitations of standard intelligence tests. These limitations become more glaring when trying to assess intelligence in members of other cultures. To begin with, many standard intelligence tests put a premium on quick and decisive responses. But not all cultures share our Western preoccupation with speed. Indians and Native Americans, for example, place a higher value on being deliberate; in effect, they would rather be right than quick. In addition, they prefer to qualify, or to say, "I don't know" or "I'm not sure," unless they are absolutely certain of their answer. Such deliberations and hedging will not help their test scores; on standard intelligence tests, you get more points if you guess (Sinha, 1983; Triandis, 1989).

Further factors have to do with formal Western schooling, which teaches the students the kinds of questions teachers (and tests) tend to ask. We saw previously that the unschooled in Liberia group objects not according to an abstract semantic category (for example, tools versus foods), but rather on the basis of the concrete situation in which the objects would be used together (for example, a knife with an orange; see Chapter 12). A similar concreteness is seen in the response of an unschooled Russian peasant who was asked, "From Shakhimardan to Vuadil it takes three hours on foot, while to Fergana it is six hours. How much time does it take to go on foot from Vuadil to Fergana?" The reply was, "No, it's six hours from Vuadil to Shakhimardan. You're wrong. . . . It's far and you wouldn't get there in three hours" (Luria, 1976, quoted in Sternberg, 1990, p. 229). If this had been a question on a standard intelligence test, the poor peasant would have scored poorly—not because he was unintelligent, but because he did not regard the question as a test of arithmetical reasoning. It turned out that he was quite able to perform the relevant calculation but could not accept the form in which the question was presented.

All of this makes it clear that we have to be very careful in applying intelligence measures. Intelligence tests do capture important aspects of intellectual functioning, but they do not capture all aspects or all mental abilities. These tests may be useful instruments for predicting school success in Western cultures, but they do much less well in other contexts and on other forms of success. In the end, it seems clear that intelligence tests do measure something of considerable interest, but the meaning and utility of these tests must be understood in the appropriate environmental and cultural context. (For further discussion, see Greenfield, 1997; Sternberg, 1985, 1990.)

"You can't build a hut, you don't know how to find edible roots, and you know nothing about predicting the weather. In other words, you do *terribly* on our I.Q. test."

(© Sidney Harris)

# NATURE, NURTURE, AND INTELLIGENCE

Despite their limitations, it is undeniable that intelligence test scores are widely used— by educators deciding whom to admit to a program and by employers deciding whom to hire. Perhaps it is no surprise, therefore, that these test scores have been the focus of a fierce debate, with important political and social implications (see Block & Dworkin, 1976; Eysenck vs. Kamin, 1981; Fancher, 1987).

## SOME POLITICAL ISSUES

Intelligence testing has been mired in political controversy from the very beginning. Recall that Binet intended his test as a means of identifying schoolchildren who would benefit from extra training. In the early years of the twentieth century, however, a number of people—scientists and politicians—put the test to a different use. They noted the fact (still true today) that there was a correlation between IQ and socioeconomic status: people with lower IQ scores usually end up with lower-paid, lower-status jobs; they are also more likely to end up as criminals than are people with higher IQs. Why therefore should we try to educate these low-IQ individuals? Why waste educational resources, the politicians asked, on people who, because of their low IQ, will never amount to anything anyway?

In contrast, advocates for the disadvantaged took a different view. To begin with, they often disparaged the tests themselves, arguing that they were biased to favor some cultures and some intellectual styles over others. In addition, they argued that the connection between IQ and socioeconomic status was far from inevitable. Good education, they suggested, can lift the status of almost anyone, and perhaps lift their IQ scores as well. Therefore, spending educational resources on the poor is far from a waste of time; instead, it may be the poor who need and benefit from these resources the most.

These contrasting views obviously lead to different prescriptions for social policy, and for many years, those biased toward the first of these positions dominated the debate. An example is the rationale behind the United States' immigration policy between the First and Second World War. The Immigration Act of 1924 set rigid quotas to minimize the influx of what were thought to be biologically "weaker stocks," specifically those from southern and eastern Europe, Asia, and Africa. To "prove" the genetic intellectual inferiority of these immigrants, a congressional committee pointed to the scores of these groups on the U.S. Army's intelligence test, which were indeed substantially below those attained by Americans of northern European ancestry.

In actual fact, these differences were primarily related to the length of time that the immigrants had been in the United States prior to the test. When they first arrived, the immigrants lacked fluency in English as well as knowledge of certain cultural facts important for the tests; it is no surprise, then, that their test scores were low. After some years of residence in the United States, their cultural knowledge and language skills improved and their scores became indistinguishable from those of native-born Americans. Although this observation plainly undermined the hypothesis of a hereditary difference in intelligence between, say, northern and eastern Europeans, the proponents of immigration quotas did not analyze the results so closely. They had their own reasons for restricting immigration, such as fears of competition from cheap labor. The theory that the excluded groups were innately inferior provided a convenient justification for their policies (Kamin, 1974).

A more contemporary example of the relation between psychological theory and social policy is the argument over alleged racial differences in intelligence-test scores. A highly controversial book by Herrnstein and Murray (1994) argued that these differences must be taken seriously and are largely attributable to genetic factors. Herrnstein and Murray noted a number of policy implications that follow from their view, including a reevaluation of many special education programs, such as Head Start, designed to improve the scholastic performance of disadvantaged preschool children.

Herrnstein and Murray's claims have been criticized on many counts. There has been considerable debate, for example, about their interpretation of the test scores and even about whether race is a meaningful biological category. We will return to these points later in the chapter; for now, we simply highlight the fact that these questions have profound political importance, making it imperative that we ensure that policy debates are informed by good science.

*Anti-immigration sentiment in the United States*   *"Immigration Restriction. Prop Wanted." A cartoon that appeared in the January 23, 1903, issue of the* Philadelphia Inquirer *calling for more restrictive immigration laws.*

# GENETIC FACTORS

Plainly, people differ from each other in their intelligence and talents. But what causes these differences? Is it mostly their heredity or their environment? And, in either case, are these differences something that can be altered? Specifically, can people with low intelligence be helped by education or other remediation, or is their intelligence immune to any intervention?

## GENETIC TRANSMISSION

Before turning to the relationship between intelligence-test performance and genetic endowment, let us review a few points about the nature of genetic transmission (also see Chapter 12).

*Phenotype and Genotype*   For most purposes, what we care about is an organism's structure, its observable traits and its actual behavior. But these traits are not what are specified by the genes. Instead, the genes specify a series of commands that constitute something like an architectural blueprint—a set of plans for how the organism should develop. And, of course, it is easy to find cases in which the observable traits, or *phenotype*, depart from the traits specified in the genes, or *genotype*. Thus, an individual born with blonde hair cannot change his genotype, but he can, with a bottle of hair dye, change his phenotype.

The key idea, then, is that the traits one ends up with may be quite different from the traits specified in one's genetic material. In some cases, this is because the genetically specified pattern can be altered after the fact (as hair color can be changed with dye). In other cases, environmental circumstances can block the genetically specified pattern from ever being expressed in the first place. Consider the dark markings on the paws, tail, and ear tips of a Siamese cat. These markings are not present at birth but appear gradually as the kitten matures, and the genealogical records kept by cat breeders leave no doubt that these markings in the mature animal are almost entirely determined by heredity. But this does not mean that they emerge independently of the environment. The dark markings will only appear if the kitten's extremities are kept at their normal temperature during the relevant developmental episodes. If the extremities are too warm during early kittenhood (and cat breeders often arrange for this, by such devices as leggings or earmuffs), they will not darken—in apparent defiance of the creature's genotype (Ilyin & Ilyin, 1930). Similar findings have been obtained with some other animals (see Figure 14.13).

Clearly, then, genes do not operate in a vacuum. They are instructions to the developing organism, specifying how and when certain processes should unfold. But these instructions will be followed only within a given range of environmental conditions, so that, in important ways, the expression of the genetic plan depends on an interaction between the genotype and the environment. Thus, it makes no sense to talk about a trait—any trait—as being a result of either heredity or environment alone. All traits depend on both. There can be no organism without a genotype, and this genotype cannot express itself independently of the environment.

*Heredity and Changeability*   Many people believe that if a trait is inherited, it is unchangeable. The fallacy of this belief, however, lies in confusing phenotype with genotype. Even if we do not change a person's genotype, we can certainly take steps that will markedly change his phenotype. An important illustration involves a severe form of mental retardation associated with *phenylketonuria* or *PKU*. In the United States, about one baby in every fifteen thousand is born with this defect, caused by a problem with a single gene. This gene ordinarily governs the production of an enzyme needed to transform *phenylalanine*, one of the *amino acids* (the building blocks of proteins), into

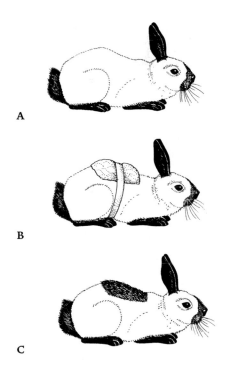

A

B

C

**14.13**   *The effect of temperature on coat color* Normally only the feet, tail, ears, and nose of the Himalayan rabbit are black (A). But when an ice pack is applied to a region of the back (B), the new fur grown at an artificially low temperature also comes in black (C).

a different amino acid. A defect in this gene, however, leads to a deficiency in the enzyme, and as a result, phenylalanine is instead converted into a toxic agent that accumulates in the infant's bloodstream and damages her developing nervous system.

Although PKU is unmistakably of genetic origin, it can be dealt with by a simple intervention—a special diet that contains very little phenylalanine. If this diet is introduced at an early-enough age, retardation can be minimized or avoided altogether. In this case, the genotype for PKU is present but with no phenotypic expression.

Clearly, then, heredity does not imply immutability. Our earlier example of fur color in Siamese cats made this point for a physical characteristic; the example of PKU makes the same point for a psychological pattern. In both cases, the influence of the genes is undeniable, but in no sense inevitable. In the case of fur color, we know how to alter the environment so that the genetic pattern simply is not expressed. In the case of PKU, we know how to change the environment in a fashion that renders the genetic problem largely irrelevant; as a result, this disorder is not merely treatable; it is entirely avoidable (McClearn & DeFries, 1973).

## GENETICS AND IQ

Even with these complications, though, it is plain that some traits (some of them physical, some of them psychological) are heavily influenced by genetics. What about IQ? One way to pursue this issue is to examine the similarities among relatives, an approach that dates back to Galton (1869). For example, the correlation between the IQs of children and the IQs of their parents is about +.47; the correlation between the IQs of siblings is in the same neighborhood (Bouchard & McGue, 1981). Such a correlation might suggest inheritance of mental ability, since family members are highly similar genetically. But parents and children also live in similar social and financial circumstances, and they are likely to receive a similar education. So their similar IQs might be attributable to the effects of their shared environment, rather than their overlapping sets of genes.

Apparently, we need better evidence if we are to disentangle the hereditary and environmental contributions to intelligence. In the last few decades, that evidence has become available. We will consider two important sources of this evidence: the study of twins and the study of adopted children.

*Twin Studies* **Identical twins** originate from a single fertilized egg. Early in development, that egg splits into two exact replicas, and these develop into two genetically identical individuals (see Figure 14.14).* In contrast, *fraternal twins* arise from two different eggs, each fertilized by a different sperm cell. Therefore, the genetic similarity between fraternal twins is the same as that between ordinary siblings.

It is interesting, therefore, that the IQs of identical twins tend to be highly correlated (.86); the correlation for fraternal twins is strongly positive, but appreciably lower, around .60 (Bouchard & McGue, 1981); some further findings on similarity in IQ scores of family members are presented in Table 14.4. On the face of it, this suggests a strong genetic component in the determination of IQ. After all, one might argue, a pair of twins (of either type) grows up in a single environment, so that the twins are matched with regard to factors such as nutrition, education, and social setting. Even within these matched environments, though, greater genetic similarity (as in identical twins) leads to greater IQ similarity.

The impact of genetic factors is even clearly visible in the results obtained for identical twins reared apart. A research center in Minnesota has studied over fifty such twins

**14.14** *Identical twins* Tiki Barber (left) plays professional football as a running back for the New York Giants. His twin brother Ronde Barber (right) is also a football player. He is the cornerback for the Tampa Bay Buccaneers.

---

* In recent years, research has demonstrated that identical twins are not actually identical. They have identical DNA in the nuclei of their bodies' cells, but they differ somewhat in their nonnuclear DNA (for example, in their mitochondria). This detail, however, leaves intact the broad argument we are making here.

## TABLE 14.4  CORRELATION BETWEEN THE IQS OF FAMILY MEMBERS

| | |
|---|---|
| Identical twins reared together | +.86 |
| Fraternal twins reared together | +.60 |
| Siblings reared together | +.47 |
| Child and biological parent by whom child is reared | +.42 |
| Child and biological mother separated from the child by adoption | +.31 |
| Child and unrelated adoptive mother | +.17 |

SOURCE: Data on twins, siblings, and children reared with biological parents from Bouchard and McGue, 1981; data on adopted children from Horn, Loehlin, and Willerman, 1979.

who were separated in early life, reared apart during their formative years, and reunited as adults. Aptitude tests showed a correlation for these twins of about +.75, which is not substantially less than the correlation for identical twins reared together (Bouchard, Lykken, McGue, Segal, & Tellegen, 1990; McGue, Bouchard, Iacono, & Lykken, 1993). It appears, then, that identical genotypes lead to highly similar IQs even when the individuals grow up in markedly different environments.

*Adopted Children* Another line of evidence comes from studies of adopted children. One study was based on three hundred children who were adopted immediately after birth (J. M. Horn, 1983; J. M. Horn, Loehlin, & Willerman, 1979, 1982). When these children were later tested, the correlation between their IQs and those of their biological mothers (whom they had never seen) was greater than the corresponding correlation between their IQs and those of their adoptive mothers (+.28 versus +.15).

Other investigators have shown that this pattern persists into adolescence, and, indeed the effects of genetic relatedness increase as the child moves into adolescence, a point we first mentioned in Chapter 12. Impressive support for this idea comes from the Colorado Adoption Project (CAP), launched in 1975. The CAP has been tracking 245 adopted children, with a variety of measures available for the children themselves, their adoptive parents, and their biological mothers (Plomin, Fulker, Corley, & DeFries, 1997).

What should we expect here if the child's intellect is shaped largely by the environment—that is, the influences the child is exposed to, the instructions he receives? In this case, we should observe correlations between the capacities of the adopted children and those of their adoptive parents. After all, much of the child's knowledge comes either from direct parental instruction or from exposure to the parents' views and conversations. It is the parents who choose what to read to the child or whether to read at all. On all these grounds, if the adoptive parents are intellectually lively, they can help the child to become the same; if the adoptive parents are intellectually dull, odds are good that they would lead their children to the same status. All of this would lead us to expect resemblance between the capacities of the adopted children and the capacities of the parents who raise them.

What should we expect if the child's intellect is shaped largely by genetics? If genes do play a large role here, then two people with similar genetic patterns should end up with similar capacities. Of course, genetically, each of us closely resembles our biological parents, and so, if genes shape intelligence, we should expect resemblance between the capacities of the adopted children and those of their biological parents, not their adoptive parents.

As we mentioned in Chapter 12, the data on these points are clear. There is relatively little correspondence between the intellectual capacities of the child and those of the adoptive parents. Moreover, what correspondence there is decreases as the child matures, and so the correlations between child and adopted parents essentially drop to zero by the time the child enters the teenage years. This pattern emerges if we look at overall intelligence scores; it also emerges if we look at more specific capacities, such as the child's verbal ability, or tests of memory accuracy. The pattern is entirely different, though, if we compare the capacities of adopted children with those of their biological mothers (whom the children have never met). Here there is a reasonable correspondence, and the correspondence increases as the children enter their teenage years. (For more on the genetics of intelligence, including a discussion of new and more powerful techniques used to assess genetic influences, see Plomin & Spinath, 2002.)

## ENVIRONMENTAL FACTORS

It seems clear, therefore, that genetic relatedness does, to a substantial extent, allow us to predict IQ, with the clear implication that our genes do govern, in important ways, the development of our intellectual capacities. But, as we have emphasized, genes do not and cannot operate in a vacuum, and so environmental factors are also crucial.

Some of the evidence comes from the same data that demonstrate the importance of heredity: similarities between family members. For example, the correlation between the IQ scores of fraternal twins is slightly higher than the correlation of scores between ordinary siblings (.60 versus .47). This cannot be readily explained in genetic terms, since, as we noted, the genetic similarity between fraternal twins is nearly the same as that of ordinary siblings. But it can be explained environmentally. If, for example, there were any changes in the family circumstances (changed economic circumstances or an improvement in school district), these changes would hit both twins at the same age.

### IMPOVERISHED ENVIRONMENTS

Further evidence for the importance of environmental factors comes from studies of the effects of impoverished environments. For example, researchers studied children who worked on canal boats in England during the 1920s and rarely attended school, and children who lived in rural Kentucky mountains, where little or no schooling was available. These certainly seem like poor conditions for the development of intellectual skills, and it seems likely that exposure to these conditions would have a cumulative effect: the longer the child remains in such an environment, the lower his IQ should be. This is precisely what the data show. There was a sizable negative correlation between IQ and age. The older the child (the longer he had been in the impoverished environment), the lower his IQ (Asher, 1935; Gordon, 1923).

Similar effects have been observed in communities where schools have closed. These closings typically lead to a decline in intelligence-test scores—in one study, a drop of about six points for every year of school missed (R. L. Green, Hoffman, Morse, Hayes, & Morgan, 1964; see also Neisser et al., 1996).

### ENRICHED ENVIRONMENTS

If impoverished environments are harmful, then enriched ones should be beneficial, and this does seem to be the case. An example is a community in East Tennessee that was quite isolated from the U.S. mainstream in 1930 but became less and less so during the following decade, with the introduction of schools, roads, and radios. Between 1930 and 1940, the average IQ of individuals in this community rose by 10 points, from 82 to 92 (L. R. Wheeler, 1942).

A related effect, produced by explicit training, has been observed by the Venezuelan Intelligence Project, which provides underprivileged adolescents in Venezuela with extensive training in various thinking skills (Herrnstein, Nickerson, de Sanchez, & Swets, 1986). Assessments after training showed substantial benefits on a wide range

*IQ and poverty   IQ is clearly influenced both by genes and by environment, and the longer a child lives under conditions of poverty, the lower her IQ will be.*

of tests. A similar benefit was observed for American preschool children in the Carolina Abecedarian Project (F. A. Campbell & Ramey, 1994). These programs leave no doubt that suitable enrichment and education can provide substantial improvement in intelligence-test scores. (For still other evidence that schooling lifts intelligence scores, see Ceci & Williams, 1997; Grotzer & Perkins, 2000; Perkins & Grotzer, 1997.)

## WORLDWIDE IMPROVEMENT IN IQ SCORES

Another dramatic demonstration of environmental influences comes from the fact that scores on intelligence tests have been gradually increasing over the last few decades, at a rate of approximately three points per decade. This pattern is generally known as the *Flynn effect*, after James R. Flynn (1984, 1987, 1999), one of the first researchers to document this effect systematically. This improvement seems to be occurring worldwide, with clear IQ gains documented both in the West and in many Third World countries.

This effect cannot be explained genetically. While the human genome does change gradually (this is, of course, a prerequisite for human evolution), it does not change at a pace commensurate with the Flynn effect. So how should the effect be explained? Some have proposed that this worldwide improvement reflects the increasing complexity and sophistication of our shared culture: each of us is exposed to more information and a wider set of perspectives than were our grandparents, and this may lead to an improvement in intelligence-test scores. A different possibility is that the Flynn effect is attributable to widespread improvements in nutrition (for broad discussion, see Dickens & Flynn, 2001; Neisser, 1997, 1998). Whatever the explanation, though, this effect is a compelling reminder that intelligence can be measurably improved by suitable environmental conditions.

## HERITABILITY

When we consider the evidence as a whole, we must conclude that both genetic and environmental factors play a part in determining intelligence. The adoption evidence, for example, is an undeniable indication that genetics are important; the Flynn effect is an equally compelling indication that the environment is crucial. What is not clear, though, is the relative weight exerted by each of these factors.

To address this question, investigators usually refer to a technical expression developed by geneticists, the *heritability ratio (H)*. For any trait, this ratio begins with an assessment of the total phenotypic variability: how much do individuals differ in their phenotype from each other? We then seek to ask what proportion of this variability can be attributed to genetic variation.

Researchers estimate that the value of H for IQ falls between .40 and .70; often a figure of .50 is quoted (Neisser et al., 1996). This can be understood as the assertion that, of the variability we observe in IQ, approximately 50 percent is attributable to variations in genetic material. Let us be clear, though, that by definition, heritability is a measure that applies only to trait variations within a population; it does not apply to individuals. Thus, it would be a mistake (for example) to read this heritability estimate is implying that half of an individual's IQ points come from his genes, and half from his environment. Instead, as we have emphasized throughout, the influence of genes and environment are, for any individual, fully intertwined and interdependent, both shaping all aspects of whatever the person becomes.

Moreover, heritability is not a fixed number; instead, it is measured for a particular population at a particular point in time—and so heritability estimates can change as circumstances change. For example, consider a case we have already discussed: the mental retardation caused by PKU. Many years ago, we had no way to remedy this condition, and so the heritability was extremely high. The phenotypic variation (whether someone did or did not have this type of retardation) was almost entirely attributable to whether or not they had the relevant genetic pattern. But we now know that a simple environmental manipulation can minimize the impact of PKU, and, as a result, the heritability estimate for PKU is currently quite low. Whether retardation is observed depends largely on the individual's diet, and so most of the phenotypic variation we observe is due to this environmental factor, not genes.

This example reminds us that heritability estimates are quite fluid. In the world today, the heritability of intelligence is approximately .50, but this estimate could change dramatically if the environment were to change in some relevant fashion (as it did in the case of PKU). Similarly, a very high heritability estimate tells us little about the prospects for changing a trait. Even if a trait's heritability is 1.00, we may be able to alter that trait enormously, once a suitable intervention is found. *

## GROUP DIFFERENCES IN IQ

So far, we have focused on intelligence differences within groups—the group of (mostly) white, middle-class children studied by the Colorado Adoption Project, or the huge (and rather heterogeneous) populations who have provided data relevant to the Flynn effect. These within-group comparisons, however, are not the focus of the real controversy over the genetic roots of intelligence. The real fury is over another issue—the differences in average IQ that are found between groups, specifically the difference between the American white population and American blacks.

Numerous studies have shown that the average score of American blacks is ten to fifteen IQ points below the average of the American white population (Jensen, 1985; Loehlin, Lindzey, & Spuhler, 1975; Reynolds, Chastain, Kaufman, & McLean, 1987). Other group differences can also be documented. Asian Americans, for example, show an achievement level slightly above the level achieved by American whites, although it is unclear whether this reflects an IQ difference or differences in other factors, beyond IQ, contributing to intellectual performance (see, for example, Flynn, 1991). In any case, the fact that these differences exist is not in dispute. What is at issue is what the differences mean and how they come about.

Before proceeding, though, we should emphasize that these differences are between averages. The scores of European-American test takers vary enormously, as do the scores of African-American and Asian-American test takers; indeed, these within-group variations are much greater than the between-group variations, and as a consequence, there is huge overlap among these three populations. We therefore learn relatively little about any individual's IQ simply by knowing her group membership. Nonetheless, the average differences between groups remain. How should we think about these differences?

### BETWEEN-GROUP DIFFERENCES: ARE THE TESTS CULTURE-FAIR?

Some psychologists have argued that the between-group difference in IQ scores—particularly that between African Americans and American whites—is artificial, a by-product of a cultural bias built into the tests themselves (Sarason, 1973). According to

---

* It is useful here to note that the heritability of hair color regularly rises and falls, as a function of changes in fashion. The genetic contribution to hair color does not change, of course, but the relative importance of the genes—and so the heritability—drops whenever dying one's hair is in style (because then the phenotype may bear little resemblance to the color specified in the genotype). Heritability rises again when the style changes so that people return to a preference for their "natural" color. This cyclic rise and fall underscores the way in which heritability is fluid, and reflects a particular setting at a particular time.

this view, the intelligence tests were designed to assess the cognitive skills of the European-American middle class. When these tests are administered to another group with different customs or values—such as inner-city African-American children—the pattern of cultural bias underlying the tests makes the yardstick no longer applicable.

Cultural bias can take many forms. Cultural groups differ in the vocabulary that they routinely use, and so a test phrased using one group's vocabulary will give that group an advantage on the test. Likewise, groups may differ in their day-to-day experience and exposure, so the test will be biased if it relies on the experiences common to only one group. In addition, intelligence tests are usually administered in standard English—a familiar dialect for some test takers but not all. According to some linguists, many American blacks speak a different dialect, sometimes called black English, with a syntax, phonology, and lexicon different from standard English (see, for example, Labov, 1970; Ogbu, 1999; Seymour, Abdulkarim, & Johnson, 1999). This may put some African-American test takers at a linguistic disadvantage.

Some versions of the IQ test probably are biased in these ways. However, these biases can be removed by ensuring that the test uses only vocabulary familiar to all test takers or by rephrasing test questions to make them fully accessible. Still, once these and other similar steps are taken, the contrast between the test scores of European Americans and African Americans remains. For example, in one study, the Stanford-Binet test was translated into black English and then administered orally to black children by black examiners. The performance of these children was virtually identical to that of a group tested with the test's regular version (L. C. Quay, 1971; also Jensen, 1980; Suzuki & Valencia, 1997). Apparently, the contrast between whites' and blacks' test scores cannot be attributed to dialect differences or to these other forms of test bias.

## BETWEEN-GROUP DIFFERENCES: HEREDITY OR ENVIRONMENT?

The between-group difference in average IQ is evidently not an artifact of test bias. So what accounts for it? In the thirty years before 1965, the consensus among social scientists in the United States was that the lower scores often observed for African Americans resulted from the massively inferior environmental conditions that were (and in many ways, still are) the lot of most blacks—systematic discrimination, poorer living conditions, lower life expectancies, inadequate diets and housing, and inferior schooling. But the issue was reopened in the sixties and early seventies by, among others, Arthur Jensen (1969, 1973, 1985), who felt that the hypothesis of a genetic contribution to the between-group difference had been dismissed prematurely. Similar arguments have been offered more recently by Herrnstein and Murray (1994).

As currently conceived, human racial groups (some authors prefer the term *racial-ethnic groups*) are populations whose members are more likely to mate with other members of the group than with outsiders. This restriction on the gene flow between different subgroups may be imposed by geographical barriers, such as oceans and mountains, or by social taboos, such as prohibitions on intermarriage. The restrictions are not complete, but if they last long enough, they may result in a population that differs from other groups in the statistical frequency of various genes.

In the case of white Americans and African Americans, there are undeniably some genetic differences, and these are reflected in such obvious characteristics as skin color and pattern of hair growth. But are genetic differences also relevant to the two groups' performance on intelligence tests? More specifically, is the difference in average black and white IQs partially attributable to different frequencies of IQ-determining genes in the two populations?

*Within-Group Heritability*  One argument sometimes offered in this domain begins with the undeniable finding that IQ has a substantial within-group heritability. The adoption studies, for example, tell us that, within the group of European Americans, differences in intelligence can be traced largely to genetic factors. Doesn't this imply that IQ, in general, is heavily influenced by genetics, so that we should also interpret the between-group difference (that is, the difference between the black and white averages) in these terms?

It turns out that this is simply a bad argument, and, in fact, the within-group heritability of IQ actually tells us nothing about whether there is a genetic contribution to the difference between groups (see, for example, Layzer, 1972). To see the point, imagine a bag of grass seed that contains several genetically different varieties. Some of the seeds from this bag are planted in barren soil and given inadequate care. These will grow poorly, but, even so, some will grow better than others. We cannot attribute these differences to environmental factors, because, in the situation we have described, all the seeds are growing in the exact same (barren) environment, and so differences among individual seeds cannot be attributed to some having a better environment. Instead, this within-group variation must be attributed entirely to genetic factors, with some seeds genetically better prepared than others for these poor conditions.

Other seeds from this same bag are planted in uniformly rich soil and given excellent care. These will grow well, but again, some will grow taller than others. As before, in this completely uniform environment, any variations we observe cannot be attributed to one seed having better nutrients, or better light, than the others—all have the same nutrients and light. Instead, the observed variation must be attributed entirely to genetic sources, with some seeds more prepared to flourish in this rich environment.

Notice, then, that in both cases the within-group variation is of genetic origin. Nonetheless, the contrast between groups is attributable entirely to the environment—the quality of soil, sunlight, and care (after Lewontin, 1976; see Figure 14.15). The moral is simple: variations within a group may be produced by factors very different from those producing variation between groups. This holds for plants and the heights they attain at maturity. And it applies just as strongly to human racial-ethnic groups and the average IQ scores of these groups.

*Matching for Environment*  It seems, then, that the within-group heritability of IQ simply tells us nothing about between-group comparisons. Clearly, therefore, we need more data if we are to understand the between-group difference. What data should we turn to? One line of evidence starts with the hypothesis that African Americans perform more poorly on IQ tests because of the environment in which many African Americans are raised. In the United States, blacks have (on average) lower incomes than whites, and a higher proportion of blacks live in poverty. This means that a higher proportion of blacks are exposed to poor nutrition, fewer (or lower-quality) educational

14.15  *Between-group and within-group differences*  **Between-group differences may be caused by very different factors than within-group differences. Here, the between-group difference reflects an environmental factor (soil) while the within-group difference reflects genetic variation (seed).**

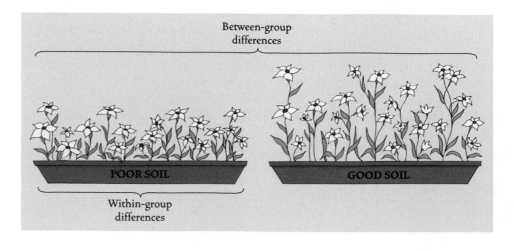

resources, and poorer health care (in childhood and prenatally), all factors that could easily compromise intellectual growth.

This hypothesis suggests that the black-white difference in IQs should disappear if we focus our attention on black and white groups that have been equated with regard to the factors we have just mentioned—a comparison, for example, between blacks and whites who have been matched with regard to such socioeconomic variables as parents' education, income, health care, and so on. And, indeed, some studies confirm this suggestion, finding a markedly reduced black-white difference when comparing the IQ averages of groups that have been matched in this way (Loehlin et al., 1975).

Other investigators have taken a different approach. Rather than trying to match environments, they have asked what happens when the environment is changed. A widely cited example is a study of black children who were adopted at an early age by white middle-class parents, most of whom were college educated (Scarr & Weinberg, 1976). The mean IQ of these children was 110—a value exceeding the national average for black children by about 25 points. (For further discussion, see Scarr & Carter-Saltzman, 1982; Scarr & Weinberg, 1983.)

On the face of it, these results seem to vindicate the environmentalists' view: equate the soil, and the two sets of seeds will grow up alike; move the seeds into more nourishing soil, and the plants will flourish all the more. But the hereditarians have a response to these results: equalizing socioeconomic variables certainly diminishes the black-white difference but does not abolish it (see, for example, Loehlin et al., 1975). In their view, the residual difference that has been observed in several studies—even after matching for environment—makes a genetic hypothesis even more plausible.

But the argument does not stop there. The question at issue here is whether blacks' and whites' IQ scores would be the same if we could match their environments. To address this question, it may not be enough to match for factors like parental education, income, and occupational level. This is because black children, after all, grow up knowing that they are black; white children, that they are white. More, each group is treated differently by the people in their social environment because of the color of their skin. In these ways, their environments and experiences are not matched.

Evidence suggesting that these subtler factors really do matter comes from studies that have used blood-group methods to estimate the degree of African ancestry for each test taker. It turns out that this measure of the genotype is unrelated to IQ, in contradiction to what we might expect if genetic influences (and, specifically, African ancestry) are relevant here (Loehlin, Vendenberg, & Osborne, 1973; Scarr, Pakstis, Katz, & Barker, 1977). What matters instead is the phenotype of having dark skin, just as we would expect if the IQ difference is based on cultural or environmental factors.

*Stereotype Threat*  How could skin color and the social environment influence IQ? Intelligence-test performance (and many aspects of school achievement) depends on a number of factors in addition to intelligence itself: motivation, expectations of success or failure, attitudes about how hard to strive in the face of frustration, and so on. We are only beginning to understand how these factors influence test performance, but they certainly are important ways in which racial groups might differ—especially if one of the groups has been told, over and over, that they are less intelligent and likely to do more poorly on intelligence tests!

As one indication of how these factors matter, consider recent studies of *stereotype threat*, a term that describes the impact that social stereotypes have on task performance. Concretely, imagine an African American taking an intelligence test. That person might well become anxious, because he believes this is a test on which he is expected to do poorly, and the anxiety might then be compounded by the thought that his poor performance will only serve to confirm others' prejudices. This anxiety, of course, could easily erode performance, by making it more difficult to pay attention and so on. Moreover, given the discouraging thought that poor performance is inevitable, the person might well decide not to expend enormous effort—if he is likely to do poorly, why struggle against the tide?

Evidence for these effects comes from a variety of studies, including some in which two groups of African Americans are given the exact same test. One group is told, at the start, that the test is designed to assess their intelligence; the other group is led to believe that the test is simply composed of challenges and is not designed to assess them in any way. The first group, for which the instructions trigger stereotype threat, does markedly worse (Steele, 1998; Steele & Aronson, 1995).

Related results have been shown in many other circumstances. Children, for example, seem to react to stereotype threat just as college-age students do (Ambady, Shih, Kim, & Pittinsky, 2001). Similarly, women reminded of the stereotype that "women can't do math" do worse on math tests than women not reminded of the stereotype, but taking the exact same test (Inzlicht & Ben-Zeev, 2000). In still other circumstances, a reminder about the stereotype can *improve* performance. Many surveys, for example, indicate that Asian Americans have better math skills than European Americans. In one study, a group of Asian-American women were (subtly) reminded of their ethnic background, and they ended up doing slightly better on a math test they were given. In the same study, a different group of Asian-American women were reminded of their gender, and this group performed slightly less well than control subjects! In each case, the group was responding to (and apparently influenced by) the expectations that society had for them and, indeed that they had for themselves (Ambady et al., 2001; for more on stereotype threat, see Blascovich, Spencer, Quinn, & Steele, 2001; Cheryan & Bodenhausen, 2000).

## SOME FINAL THOUGHTS: SCIENTIFIC EVIDENCE AND DEMOCRATIC VALUES

Where does all of this leave us with regard to the black-white difference in intelligence scores and, indeed, with the sources of intelligence overall? Undeniably, individuals do differ in their intellectual capacities, and, undeniably, genetic factors play a large role in shaping these capacities. But, as we have repeatedly noted, these genetic influences do not mean that intelligence is immutable, fixed for each individual by his or her genetic heritage. The example of PKU serves as a powerful reminder that patterns that are unambiguously rooted in the genome can be changed entirely by suitable environmental intervention. And, in the case of intelligence itself, we have ample evidence that environmental changes (most prominently, schooling) can increase IQ scores and, with this, can markedly improve life circumstances.

In a sense, then, it may not matter what the origins of the black-white difference are. As citizens, surely we want to celebrate the talents—perhaps in academic affairs, perhaps in other realms—that each of us possesses. And surely we want to maximize the potential that each individual possesses. Whatever the sources of IQ scores, the data tell us that training and enriched environments can improve IQ, and the implications for policy seem clear.

As scientists, though, we still seek to explain the differences that do exist, and here the evidence is complex. The overall pattern of the evidence does point to an environmental account of the black-white difference in test scores. African Americans in the United States are more likely to be poor than European Americans, and more likely to receive inferior schooling, and this unmistakably has an impact on their test scores. In addition, we have noted that test scores are better predicted by the phenotype of having dark skin than they are by the genotype of having African ancestors, pointing to an environmental, not genetic, account. It is also striking that the black-white difference is in some circumstances influenced by the expectations that are manifest in stereotype threat—again, as we would expect on environmental grounds.

The power of these environmental factors should not be surprising, since the mechanisms in play are likely to reflect the profound impact of three hundred years of slavery and racism. As one recent report put it, "Only a single generation has passed since the Civil Rights movement opened new doors for African Americans, and many forms of discrimination are still all too familiar in their experience today. Hard enough to bear in its own right, discrimination is also a sharp reminder of a still more intolerable past. It would be rash indeed to assume that those experiences, and that historical legacy, have no impact on intellectual development" (Neisser et al., 1996, p. 95).

With all of this said, though, let us again emphasize the considerable variation within each of these groups. And we should also emphasize that in a democratic society, the focus is, and should be, on each individual's merits, abilities, and attributes. A given individual may be a member of a group that, on average, has a particular quality; that individual's group may also have a greater or smaller average gene frequency for this or the other trait. But these facts should have no bearing on how that particular person is judged. When people are assessed according to the average characteristics of the group to which they belong, rather than according to the characteristics they themselves possess, one of the most essential premises of a democratic society is violated.

What about the IQ tests themselves? There is no denying the practical significance of these tests, but, remarkably, many questions remain about what exactly it is that the tests measure. As we have seen, investigators still disagree about what $g$ is, and also what the cognitive or neural capacities are that lead to the observed differences in intelligent performance. Yet other questions are raised by the fact that the tests may assess abilities that only make sense within a given environmental and cultural context, and also the fact that some capacities that seem to involve "intelligence" are not reflected in the standard intelligence tests.

Having emphasized these areas of uncertainty, let us place equal emphasis on the power and sophistication of the IQ test. There is no question that this test is predictive of a broad range of important and consequential life outcomes, and there is also no question that the test measures mental capacities that, to an impressive extent, are stable across the entire lifespan.

Can we do as well in measuring the other dimensions in which people differ? So far, our discussion has been concerned with differences among individuals that have to do with abilities. But people differ not only in what they can do, but also in what they want to do, how they do it, and how they feel about it. These and many other differences among people—whether they are usually sociable or solitary, anxious or self-confident—belong to the topic of human personality, which is the subject we turn to next.

# SUMMARY

## MENTAL TESTS

1. Many physical and psychological characteristics vary from one individual to another. This pattern of variation is often displayed by *frequency distributions*. The scores in a frequency distribution tend to cluster around some average case, usually measured by either the *mean* or the *median*. The graphed frequency distributions of many physical and psychological characteristics have a shape approximating that of the *normal curve*, which describes the pattern of chance events.

2. The extent to which two characteristics vary together is measured by the *correlation coefficient*, or *r*. Perfect correlation is indicated by an *r* of +1.00 or −1.00, no correlation by an *r* of 0.

3. One criterion of a mental test's adequacy is its *reliability*, the consistency with which it measures what it measures, as given by *test-retest correlations* and similar indices. An even more important criterion is a test's *validity*, the extent to which it measures what it is supposed to measure. *Predictive validity* is assessed by determining the correlation between the test and an appropriate criterion.

## INTELLIGENCE TESTING

4. Alfred Binet, the originator of *intelligence tests*, was primarily interested in assessing children, and, in particular, in identifying children who would benefit from remedial education. Binet understood intelligence to be a general attribute, applicable to a very wide range of mental tasks.

5. Different intelligence tests have been developed for various uses. Some are meant to test children, others to test adults; some can be administered individually, others in groups. Specialized tests have also been developed either to evaluate specific capacities, or for specific purposes (i.e., the SAT was developed explicitly for the purpose of predicting performance in college).

## WHAT IS INTELLIGENCE? THE PSYCHOMETRIC APPROACH

6. A number of studies have shown that IQ scores are correlated with other important life outcomes, including school success and job performance. However, this leaves uncertainty about the cause-and-effect relationship underlying these correlations, and this has led investigators to more detailed examinations of what it is the intelligence tests are actually measuring.

7. Investigators using the *psychometric approach* try to discover something about the underlying nature of intelligence by studying the pattern of results provided by the intelligence tests themselves. One issue is the structure of mental abilities. To determine whether intelligence is one unitary ability or is composed of several unrelated abilities, investigators have looked at the correlations among different subtests. *Factor analysis* of these correlations has confirmed that all of the subtests do share some common element, often referred to as *g*, a term proposed by Charles Spearman and intended as an abbreviation for *general intelligence*.

8. There has been debate, however, over what *g* actually measures. Some investigators have proposed that *g* measures neural efficiency. Others have proposed that *g* is a summary measure reflecting the joint contribution of several different capacities. This list of constituents is likely to include both fluid and crystallized intelligence, correlated with each other well enough to be summarized by a single number (such as *g*), but different enough to be worth distinguishing for many purposes.

## THE INFORMATION-PROCESSING APPROACH

9. In the *information-processing approach*, individual differences in intellectual performance are seen as derived from differences in the cognitive processes that underlie remembering, problem solving, and thinking. One line of inquiry tries to relate Spearman's *g* to differences in reaction time. Another approach focuses on a subfactor, such as verbal intelligence, and relates it to simple cognitive operations, such as memory look-up times. A third approach emphasizes the more complex cognitive components of the tasks posed by standard intelligence tests, as exemplified in studies of analogical reasoning. A fourth line of inquiry investigates the role of working memory and attention. A fifth tries to relate intellectual differences to success or failure in the acquisition and use of various cognitive strategies.

## WHAT IS INTELLIGENCE?
### BEYOND IQ

10. Some investigators have concerned themselves with some aspects of the term intelligence that go beyond IQ, such as *practical* and *creative intelligence*. A related approach has led to the notion of *multiple intelligences*, buttressed by evidence from studies of brain lesions and of retarded *savants*.

11. Our understanding of intelligence may also need to take into account the cultural context. People in different cultures have different abilities, and also have a different understanding of the test-taking situation.

## NATURE, NURTURE, AND INTELLIGENCE

12. Intelligence-test performance seems to be determined by both environmental and genetic factors. Evidence for the role of genetic factors comes from the fact that the correlation between IQs of *identical twins* is higher than that for *fraternal twins* and that this correlation is remarkably high even when identical twins are reared apart. Further evidence for a hereditary contribution comes from adopted children whose IQs correlate more highly with those of their biological parents than their adoptive parents. At the same time, however, evidence for environmental effects is provided by increases and decreases in the mean IQ of populations whose cultural or educational level has risen or fallen. Environmental effects are also clearly implicated by the worldwide improvement in IQ scores observed over the last few decades.

13. The relative weight of genetic and environmental factors in determining the variation of a given characteristic is given by the *heritability ratio*, or H. The value of H depends in part upon the given population, for H only describes the degree to which the variability within this particular population can be attributed to genetic variance.

14. In recent years, much interest (and polemic) has focused on IQ differences among racial-ethnic groups. The mean IQ of American blacks is about 10 to 15 points lower than that of American whites. Some authors have argued that this is in part a consequence of a genetic difference between the two groups. But other authors reply that the difference is markedly reduced by various environmental changes such as interracial adoption. In addition, evidence suggests that the "race difference" is more closely tied to the *phenotype* of having dark skin than it is to the *genotype* of having a large number of African ancestors; this too points to an environmental account rather than a genetic one.

15. Whatever the sources of IQ differences (either within-groups or between-groups), IQ may still be changed through appropriate environmental intervention. This remains true even if IQ turns out to be massively influenced by genetics, a point reflected in the changeability of hair color or the avoidability of retardation associated with *phenylketonuria* (PKU). In addition, IQ averages for a large population tell us little about the IQ (or any other trait) of a specific individual.

# PERSONALITY

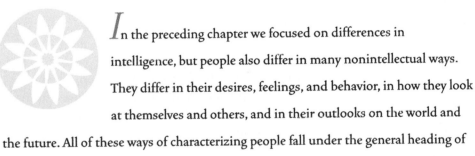In the preceding chapter we focused on differences in intelligence, but people also differ in many nonintellectual ways. They differ in their desires, feelings, and behavior, in how they look at themselves and others, and in their outlooks on the world and the future. All of these ways of characterizing people fall under the general heading of personality.

The fact that people have distinct personalities is hardly a recent discovery. Cro-Magnons surely knew that all Cro-Magnons were not the same; they probably liked some, disliked others, and gossiped about the Cro-Magnons in the cave next door. We obviously do not know, however, whether they had any explicit ideas about the ways in which one person differs from another. Such formulations, or "theories of personality," probably came later. In the main, they were the work of

Masks used by actors in Roman comic drama

A

B

Characters in sixteenth- and seventeenth-century Italy's commedia dell' arte
(A) Pantalone, the rich, stingy, old merchant, who is invariably deceived by his servants, his children, and his young wife. (B) Pulcinella, a sly and boisterous comic.

various writers concerned with the representation of character. An example is a series of sketches entitled "The Characters," written in the fourth century B.C. by the Greek philosopher Theophrastus. These sketches featured such diverse types as the Coward, the Flatterer, the Boor, and so on. Even more influential than Theophrastus's literary efforts were those of the ancient playwrights, and, in fact, the word *personality* comes from *persona*, the name for the mask that Greek and Roman actors wore to indicate the character that they played (Allport, 1937; and see Monte, 1995).

In their comic drama, the Greeks and the Romans tended to think of people as types, a tradition that has continued in various forms to the present day. Their comedy was populated by a large cast of stock characters: the handsome hero, the pretty maiden, the restless wife, the kind-hearted prostitute. Many of these types were resurrected in later times and other countries, including the movies and television shows of our own time. The hero and villain of the Hollywood Western, the busybody and the conniving schemer of the soap opera are only a few of such instantly recognizable types.

Over the ages, dramatists have differed in how they think these characters should be understood, and their arguments are mirrored in current psychological theories of personality. Many questions are at issue in this debate: How much is someone's personality shaped from within, and how much is shaped by the circumstances the person is in? How much does each of us understand about who we are, and why we are as we are? Are the patterns of personality universal, and so the same from one culture to the next or one historical period to the next? Or are the patterns only understandable in relationship to the culture in which each of us resides? We will pursue all these issues in this chapter.

# METHODS OF ASSESSMENT

In studying personality, our first task is descriptive. How do we describe an individual's personality, and, with that, how do we describe both the differences and the commonality between one person and the next? Or, to put this same point more ambitiously, what should our classification scheme for personality look like? How many types of personality are there, and on what dimensions do these types differ? Let us begin our examination of these questions by looking at the personality tests that psychologists use.

## STRUCTURED PERSONALITY TESTS

As in the case of intelligence measurement, personality tests came from the world of practical affairs. The first personality test was designed to identify emotionally disturbed U.S. Army recruits during World War I, and consisted of a list of questions that dealt with various symptoms or problem areas (for instance, "Do you daydream frequently?" and "Do you wet your bed?"). If the recruit reported many such symptoms, he was singled out for further psychiatric examination (Cronbach, 1970). Such tests, because they ask specific questions and require specific answers, are called **structured personality tests** (or sometimes, objective personality tests).

### THE MMPI: CRITERION GROUPS FROM THE CLINIC

Later personality tests were more ambitious and sought to assess how similar someone was to people who had already been diagnosed as paranoid, for example, or depressed, or schizophrenic. The best-known test of this sort is the *Minnesota Multiphasic Personality Inventory*, or *MMPI*, which first appeared in 1940 (Hathaway & McKinley, 1940). The original MMPI, together with its new revision, the MMPI 2, and a version for adolescents, the MMPI-A (Butcher, Dahlstrom, Graham, Tellegen, & Kaemmer, 2001; Butcher et al., 1992), are still widely used in both clinical practice and research (Butcher, Dahlstrom, Graham, Tellegen, & Kaemmer, 1989; Greene, 1991; Lanyon & Goldstein, 1982) and are the psychological tests most frequently administered in professional settings (Butcher & Rouse, 1996; Lubin, Larsen, Matarazzo, & Seever, 1985).

*Constructing the MMPI* The MMPI was constructed using a technique known as empirical criterion keying. The authors began with a large pool of preexisting test questions and administered them to patients with different mental disorders, as well as to a group of nonpatients. The next step was to find and keep all the items that discriminated between the patients and the nonpatient controls and to discard all those that did not. The result was the MMPI—an inventory of 566 items, the responses to which are collated and tallied to form ten major scales. The score on each of these scales indicates how the examinee's answers compare with those of the relevant criterion group (Table 15.1). For example, items on the Pa (Paranoia) scale are the ones that were endorsed by the paranoid patients but not by the nonpatients. Thus, a person's score on this scale reflects how closely she resembles the paranoid patients.

*Character types in the Nō drama of Japan* In the traditional Nō drama of Japan, character is indicated by a mask. The mask shown in the figure is that of a mystical old man with godlike powers. Before donning the mask, the actor who performs this part must go through various rituals of purification, because after he puts it on, the actor "becomes" the god.

**TABLE 15.1 SOME MMPI SCALES WITH REPRESENTATIVE EXAMPLE ITEMS***

| Scale | Criterion Group | Example Items |
|---|---|---|
| Depression | Patients with intense unhappiness and feelings of guilt and hopelessness | "I often feel that life is not worth the trouble." |
| Paranoia | Patients with unusual degree of suspiciousness, together with feelings of persecution and delusions of grandeur | "Several people are following me everywhere." |
| Schizophrenia | Patients with a diagnosis of schizophrenia, characterized by bizarre or highly unusual thoughts or behavior, by withdrawal, and in many cases by delusions and hallucinations | "I seem to hear things that other people cannot hear." |
| Psychopathic deviance | Patients with marked difficulties in social adjustment, with histories of delinquency and other antisocial behavior | "I often was in trouble in school, although I do not understand for what reasons." |

* In the example items here shown, the response appropriate to the scale is "true." For many other items, the reverse is true. Thus, answering "false" to the item "I liked school" would contribute to the person's score on the Psychopathic Deviance scale.

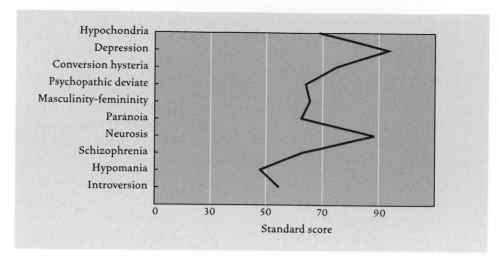

**15.1  MMPI profile**   *The profile is of an adult male seeking help in a community mental health center. The scales are those described in Table 15.1. The scores are based on the performance of the standardization group. Scores above 70 will occur in about 2.5 percent of the cases; scores above 80 in about .1 percent. The profile strongly suggests considerable depression and anxiety. (After Lanyon & Goldstein, 1971)*

*Using the MMPI*   In interpreting the MMPI, clinicians do not look at the scales individually. Instead, they inspect the score profiles, which graph the examinee's scores (Figure 15.1). For example, a clinician may find that a patient has a high score on the D (Depression) scale but a low score on the Si (Social Introversion) scale. This might lead the clinician to conclude that the patient is depressed, but his depression is uncomplicated by excessive shame, shyness, or social withdrawal.

*Validity Scales*   One trouble with self-administered personality inventories is that participants can easily misrepresent themselves. Some may want to avoid the stigma of a mental-disorder diagnosis and try to "look good" on the test. Others may try to "fake bad" in order to claim disability benefits, obtain desired medications, or attain a paid-for stay in the hospital. To cope with this and related problems, the originators of the MMPI added a set of further items that comprise several so-called *validity scales*, scales designed to assess whether the examinee is faking illness, trying to look healthy, or denying serious problems. If the scores on these and similar validity scales are too high, the test record is considered invalid (see Greene, 1988).

## THE CPI: CRITERION GROUPS FROM NORMAL LIFE

The MMPI was intended chiefly as an aid in diagnosing mental disorders and is of limited use with normal examinees. This prompted the development of several new tests constructed according to the same logic that led to the MMPI, but with normal rather than with pathological criterion groups. One of the best known of these is the *California Psychological Inventory*, or *CPI*.

Unlike the MMPI, the CPI's focus is nonclinical and is aimed especially at high-school and college students. It tests for various personality traits such as dominance, sociability, responsibility, a sense of well-being, and so on.

As an example of how scales for these and other traits were derived, consider dominance. High-school and college students were asked to name the most and the least dominant people within their social circles. The people who comprised these two extremes were then used as the criterion groups that defined the dominance-submission dimension. An individual's score on this dimension, therefore, reflects how much she resembles members of these criterion groups. Other traits were defined in a similar manner (Gough, 1975, 1990; Gough & Bradley, 1996). The CPI is widely used in personal and vocational counseling, and employee recruitment and selection.

## THE VALIDITY OF PERSONALITY INVENTORIES

The originators of the MMPI and the CPI took considerable pains to ground their tests on a solid, empirical foundation. But are their tests valid? As we described in Chapter 14, one of the best ways to find out is to look at a test's *predictive validity*, the degree to which it can predict outcomes or behaviors that should be correlated with the trait being measured. By this assessment, personality tests do have some validity. For instance, among college women during the fifties and sixties, the sociability scale of the CPI correlated somewhat with how often the examinee went out on dates and whether she joined a sorority. Other scales correlate with how examinees are rated by their peers (Hase & Goldberg, 1967). Generally, though, the predictive validity of personality tests is not terribly high, with correlations between test scores and various validity criteria in the neighborhood of +.30, indicating a low-to-moderate association. In contrast, intelligence test scores correlate about +.5 with criteria such as academic performance.

The contrast is even sharper if we compare the predictive power of personality tests to that of commonsense measures such as past behavior in related situations. The result is plain. In most cases, the best predictor of future performance (for example, of mental disorder or delinquency) is past performance. A dramatic example is provided by a finding that the thickness of a psychiatric patient's medical chart (a rough index of how many problems there have been in the past, how many doctors' visits, and so on) correlates +.61 with the probability of rehospitalization following discharge (Lasky et al., 1959)—and so the thickness of the chart is an appreciably better predictor than the available personality tests!

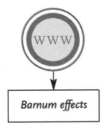

Barnum effects

## PROJECTIVE PERSONALITY TESTS

The 1940s and 1950s saw the increasing popularity of a new approach to personality assessment—the use of *projective techniques*. These tests present the examinee with a relatively unstructured task, such as making up a story to fit a picture or describing what he sees in an inkblot. The purpose is to bypass the direct questioning in the MMPI and related tests, under the assumption that the deeper layers of any individual's personality contain repressed wishes and unconscious conflicts that are not accessible by ordinary means. According to the advocates of this approach, exposing these repressed elements requires techniques that can circumvent the examinee's defenses against these threatening impulses and ideas. This is accomplished by presenting her with stimuli that are essentially unstructured or ambiguous. The assumption is that the examinee cannot help but impose a structure of her own when trying to describe such stimuli, and, in the process, she unveils deeper facets of her personality. In essence, the test materials become a kind of screen on which the examinee "projects" her inner feelings, wishes, conflicts, and ideas.

The number and variety of projective techniques are remarkable. Some require the examinee to give word associations or complete unfinished sentences, others to draw a person or to copy designs, and others to arrange toy figures in a sandbox or give three wishes. We will consider only the two that are used most widely—the *Rorschach inkblot technique* and the *Thematic Apperception Test (TAT)*.

## THE RORSCHACH INKBLOTS

Hermann Rorschach (1921), a Swiss psychiatrist, used the perception of unstructured forms as a diagnostic tool. In the test that now bears Rorschach's name, the examinee is shown ten cards, one at a time, with each card showing a symmetrical inkblot, some colored and some black and white. For each card, the examinee is asked what he sees (see Figure 15.2 for an example of a card similar to those used in the test). After all ten cards have been presented, the examiner questions the examinee about each response to find out which part of the blot was used and which of its attributes were most important (Exner, 1974, 1978, 1993; Klopfer Ainsworth, Klopfer, & Holt, 1954).

The responses are scored according to various categories, such as the portion of the blot that is used in the response (for example, the whole blot, a large detail, a small detail), the attributes of the stimulus that are the basis of the response (for example, form, shading, color), and the content of the response (for example, human figures, parts of human figures, animals or parts of animals, inanimate objects, blood). All these scores still must be interpreted. Rorschach experts stipulate that the interpretation of a Rorschach record is not a simple cookbook affair but must rely on the interrelations among all of the record's features. Nonetheless, Rorschach interpreters do use some general guidelines. For example, responses that use the entire inkblot are said to indicate integrative, conceptual thinking, whereas those that use small details suggest compulsive rigidity. Using the white space as the foreground of a response is supposed to imply rebelliousness and negativism, and responses that are dominated by color suggest emotionality and impulsivity.

## THE THEMATIC APPERCEPTION TEST (TAT)

To Rorschach, the content of the examinee's responses—whether an examinee interpreted the inkblot as a giant moth or a human face or a splotch of blood—mattered much less than the features of the card that were used—the whole card or just a part, the form, color or shading, and so on. In contrast, the originators of the other major projective test in current use, the Thematic Apperception Test (TAT), made content primary, with the aim of uncovering the person's major motives and preoccupations, defenses, conflicts, and ways of interpreting the world (C. D. Morgan & Murray, 1935).

The TAT consists of thirty pictures of scenes involving interpersonal relationships (Figure 15.3), along with one blank card for which the examinee must imagine her own scene. The examiner chooses some relevant subset of the thirty pictures and then asks the examinee to tell a story about each, including the identity of the characters, what is happening in the scene, what led up to the scene, and what the outcome will be. The examiner copies down or takes notes on the stories as they are presented. The examiner then interprets her notes, in a way that is usually rather free-wheeling and impressionistic. Each of the cards depicts some interpersonal theme or conflict, and the examiner tries to piece together the examinee's responses to all of them in order to provide a picture of the person's major motives and conflicts.

The interpretation of TAT responses can be exemplified with a story elicited by one of the cards, which shows a boy looking at a violin that lies on a table in front of him. A forty-five-year-old businessman, who was an important up-and-coming executive in his firm, gave this story:

> This is a child prodigy dreaming over his violin, thinking more of the music than anything else. But of wonderment that so much music can be in the instrument and in the fingers of his own hand.... I would say that possibly he is in reverie about what he can be or what he can do with his music in the times that lie ahead. He is dreaming of concert halls, tours, and ... the beauty he will be able to express and even now can express with his own talents.

*Young girl taking a Rorschach test*

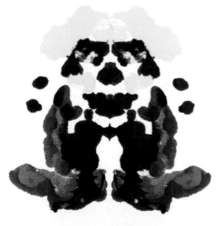

*15.2   An inkblot of the type used in the Rorschach test   Because familiarity with the cards makes it difficult to evaluate a person's first reaction, most psychologists prefer not to print the actual inkblots used in the test. Five of the actual cards are in black and white; five others are colored.*

*TAT   Photographs like Marion Post Wolcott's "Old mountain cabin made of hand-hewn logs near Jackson, Breathitt County, Kentucky," shown here, are used on the TAT.*

According to an interpreter of the response, this story reflects the executive's emphasis on the work to be accomplished (the music), and the executive visualizes eventual success (the concert halls) and sees himself as part of it (the fingers of his own hand). The examiner might reasonably conclude from this that the executive was in general very much concerned with achieving power, success, and recognition (Henry, 1973).

Interpretations of this sort are beguiling, but are the facets of personality suggested by the test interpretation actually there? Or is the examiner's interpretation just a kind of projective test itself? This speaks to the issue of test validity, a property just as critical for projective tests as structured ones.

## THE VALIDITY OF PROJECTIVE TECHNIQUES

By now, there are many thousands of journal articles devoted explicitly to the Rorschach or TAT. Considering all this effort, the gain has been disappointing. According to some experts, these techniques have some limited validity; according to others, they have little or none (Holt, 1978; Kleinmuntz, 1982; Kline, 1995; Rorer, 1990).

Individual Rorschach indices—especially those that refer to features of the card used, rather than content—show only small relationships to external validity criteria. In one study of psychiatric patients, over thirty different scores from the Rorschach records (for instance, whether the examinee's responses included the whole inkblot or just a part) were evaluated for any relationship to later diagnosis. There was none. Similar results apply to nonpsychiatric populations. For example, responses involving human movement supposedly indicate creativity, but the number of such responses did not differ when eminent artists were compared to ordinary persons (Zubin, Eron, & Shumer, 1965).

Some efforts by John Exner (1974, 1978, 1995; Exner & Clark, 1978) suggest that the clinical usefulness of the Rorschach may be increased by using a more rigorous system of administration, scoring, and interpretation. The system he developed to accomplish this, which includes numerous numerical indices of the examinee's responses to the blots, has led to a considerable improvement in the test's reliability, as shown by a large increase in its test-retest stability. Whether it will also increase the test's diagnostic power (that is, its validity) is unclear, although the data so far are still controversial and,

*Astrology (and beyond)* **People have tried a wide range of techniques for assessing their own personalities—and those of their pets. Unlike the techniques used by psychologists, these other procedures (including cat astrology) have little or no validity. (The cat in the photo, by the way, is a Pisces.)**

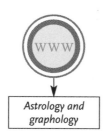

Astrology and graphology

in the view of many, not very promising (Garb, Florio, & Grove, 1998, 1999; Lilienfield, Wood, & Garb, 2000; Parker, Hunsley, & Hanson, 1999).

The TAT has fared no better than the Rorschach in studies of its ability to predict psychiatric diagnosis. One early study demonstrated that the TAT results showed no difference between normals and patients, let alone among different psychiatric groups (Eron, 1950). As a result, the TAT is rarely used for diagnosis, but many clinicians find it useful for breaking the ice with new patients and surmising the interpersonal themes that preoccupy them.

# THE TRAIT APPROACH

Personality tests have a very practical purpose: to aid in diagnosis, counseling, and even job placement. But psychologists who study personality go beyond such day-to-day applications to ask deeper questions about the nature of personality itself. How do people differ from one another? Where do these differences come from? How do the specific qualities on which people differ somehow add together to form an integral personality? In their efforts to answer these questions, psychologists have formulated various kinds of personality theories.

Many theories of personality are not really scientific theories in the conventional sense. They are not specific enough to make the clear-cut predictions that would help us either validate or disqualify them. What they are instead are different orientations from which the subject of personality is approached. We begin with the *trait approach*, which is based on the idea that the proper way to study differences among individuals is by developing a standard set of qualities, or attributes, and then describing people in those terms.

In essence, the proposal here is that traits are the ingredients out of which personality is created. The personality that each of us displays is the result of a distinctive recipe, one that includes a large quantity of this ingredient, less of that one, none at all of some other ingredient. Importantly, though, the huge variety of personalities that one encounters are created from the same limited stock of ingredients, and identifying those ingredients—that is, the traits—must be our first step toward describing how humans differ from each other.

# THE SEARCH FOR THE RIGHT TAXONOMY OF TRAITS

People can be described in a multitude of ways. In fact, an unabridged English dictionary lists 18,000 words referring to personality traits (Allport & Odbert, 1936). Do we need all of these terms? Or can we reduce the list, to reveal some (much smaller) set of basic personality traits?

## CLASSIFICATION THROUGH LANGUAGE

A number of investigators have suggested that the adjectives we use to describe people (for example, *trustworthy*, *loyal*, *helpful*, *friendly*, and so on) embody the accumulated observations of many previous generations (Allport & Odbert, 1936). Their argument, based on a kind of linguistic natural selection, is that these terms have remained in the language for decade after decade for a reason: perhaps these are the most useful terms for describing the individuals around us. In contrast, terms that were superfluous or uninformative have presumably "become extinct," dropping out of common usage. Thus, a systematic sifting of the trait adjectives actually in use might give us clues about individual differences whose description has been important enough to withstand the test of time (Goldberg, 1982).

This logic led to the development of a widely used personality inventory by Raymond Cattell (1957). Cattell's starting point was the set of 18,000 trait words in the unabridged dictionary. This list was reduced by eliminating synonyms, slang, and difficult or uncommon words, leaving Catell with just 171 trait names. Using these terms, a group of judges was asked to rate a group of people they knew well, and their ratings were then subjected to a factor analysis to find out which terms were used in an overlapping fashion (indicating some redundancy in the terms) and which seemed to identify distinctive qualities. (For more on factor analysis, see Chapter 14.) This process yielded what Cattell (1966) thought were some sixteen primary personality dimensions that reasonably encompassed the 171 trait names. Each of these dimensions was defined by a pair of adjectives th.at describe the opposite poles of the dimension, such as *outgoing* versus *reserved*, *suspicious* versus *trusting*, *tense* versus *relaxed*, *happy-go-lucky* versus *sober*, and so on.

## DIMENSIONS OF PERSONALITY: THE BIG FIVE

Other investigators believed that sixteen basic personality factors was too many, and they found evidence (again, from factor analysis) that there was still some degree of overlap among Cattell's dimensions. For example, someone who is described as *talkative* is very likely to be described as *gregarious* as well, and not at all likely to be described as *secretive*. Therefore, there is little point in counting these terms as separate traits; instead, we can regard them as reflections of a single trait, with *talkative* and *gregarious* indicating the presence of that trait, and *secretive* reflecting its absence.

This sort of logic led many researchers to reduce the number of primary dimensions. Currently, the trait system supported by the most evidence is known as the *Big Five*, which originated in work by several investigators who found that Cattell's sixteen personality factors could be readily compacted to five (Fiske, 1949; Norman, 1963; Tupes & Cristal, 1961). The Big Five are most often presented as *extroversion* (sometimes called extraversion), *neuroticism* (sometimes reversed in direction and labeled emotional stability), *agreeableness*, *conscientiousness*, and *openness to experience* (Norman, 1963; see also T. J. Bouchard, 1995; Goldberg, 1993). It is testimony to the current influence of the Big Five in personality research that the MMPI, the most frequently administered personality test, includes Big Five scales in its latest revision (Butcher et al., 2001).

## DIMENSIONS OF PERSONALITY: NEUROTICISM/EMOTIONAL STABILITY AND EXTROVERSION/INTROVERSION

The logic of the Big Five system is that human personalities can be fully described in terms of five dimensions, just as physical size can be fully described in three (height, depth, and width). This still allows an infinite variety in the types of personalities we will encounter, but each of these personalities can be described in an economical way.

Many studies have produced data patterns that point toward five-factor descriptions of personality (see Brody, 1988; P. T. Costa & McCrae, 1992; Goldberg, 1990, 1993; John, 1990). A number of investigators, however, suggest that the underlying dimensions may be even fewer (see, for example, Boyle, Stankov, & Cattell, 1995; H. Livneh & Livneh, 1989). Digman (1997), for example, reanalyzed many of the key Big Five studies and suggested that they were themselves aggregated into two superfactors, which he named Alpha and Beta. Alpha contained agreeableness, conscientiousness, and emotional stability (reverse neuroticism), and Digman believed that it reflects the degree to which socialization has normalized one's personality. Beta is a countervailing dimension that consists of extroversion and openness to experience, and it represents the capacity for personal growth (Yik & Russell, 2001).

The most influential alternative to the Big Five, however, is that proposed by Hans Eysenck (1916–1997), who also tried to encompass the whole spectrum of personality differences in a space defined by just two main dimensions: neuroticism versus emotional stability, and extroversion versus introversion.

Neuroticism, as we mentioned, is equivalent to emotional instability. It is assessed by affirmative answers to questions like "Do you ever feel just miserable for no good reason at all?" and "Do you often feel disgruntled?" Extroversion and introversion refer to the main direction of a person's energies, toward the outer world of other people and material objects or toward the inner world of one's own thoughts and feelings. The extrovert is sociable, impulsive, and enjoys new experiences, while the introvert tends to be more solitary, cautious, and slow to change. Extroversion is indicated by affirmative answers to questions such as "Do you like to have many social engagements?" and "Would you rate yourself as a happy-go-lucky individual?"

As Eysenck conceived it, neuroticism/emotional stability and extroversion/introversion are independent of each other. This leaves us with a two-dimensional classification scheme into which many trait terms can be fitted (see Figure 15.4).

## IS FACTOR ANALYSIS THE ROYAL ROAD TO A TAXONOMY?

As we have seen, Cattell's factor analysis yielded sixteen dimensions of personality; others found five dimensions; still others, three or even two. Why is it that the same kinds of data can lead to such different results? A big part of the problem is factor analysis itself. Factor analysis does provide a powerful way of summarizing a data set, but the results of the analysis depend heavily on the exact contents of that set. In the cases we have been describing, the factor analysis describes clusters of items (for example, someone described as jealous is also likely to be described as irritable and not cooperative). But if the items included in the analysis are changed, with some added or subtracted, the clusters observed—as well as the resulting factors—may well be different. Moreover, the results of a factor analysis still need some interpretation, with a possibility for differences of view with regard to how many factors emerged and what each factor means. (For other complications, see Boyle et al., 1995.)

Despite these concerns, there is no denying the fact that some personality dimensions emerge from the analysis again and again, even when different tests and different kinds of factor analysis are used. This is especially true for the twin pillars of Eysenck's

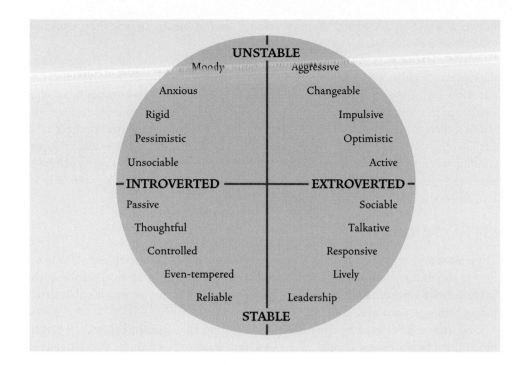

UNSTABLE

Moody          Aggressive
Anxious          Changeable
Rigid              Impulsive
Pessimistic        Optimistic
Unsociable          Active

— INTROVERTED ——————— EXTROVERTED —

Passive            Sociable
Thoughtful          Talkative
Controlled          Responsive
Even-tempered      Lively
Reliable        Leadership

STABLE

15.4 *Eysenck's two-dimensional classification of personality* **Two dimensions of personality—neuroticism/emotional stability and extroversion/inversion—define a space into which various trait terms may be fitted. (After Eysenck & Rachman, 1965)**

classification system, extroversion/introversion and neuroticism/emotional stability. In fact, there is some evidence that these two dimensions apply not just to our own culture but to others, since much the same factor pattern was obtained in such diverse societies as Bangladesh, Brazil, Hong Kong, and Japan (H. J. Eysenck & Eysenck, 1983; Lynn, 1995; Triandis & Suh, 2002; for a further discussion of personality differences and similarities in different cultures, see pp. 632–635). But this should not drive us away from other classification schemes because these too emerge over and over in very different data sets. For example, some researchers have found evidence for Big Five-like traits even in the personalities of other species, including zoo-reared chimpanzees (Weiss, King, & Figueredo, 2000; also see Gosling & John, 1999).

# Traits versus Situations: The Consistency Controversy

Although trait theorists debate among themselves about the kind and number of trait dimensions needed to describe personality, they all still agree on one proposition: individuals' personalities can be described in terms of traits. This in turn rests on a key assumption, namely, that personalities are stable and enduring. After all, when we say that someone is (for example) friendly and warm, we are doing more than describing how he acted on a particular occasion. Instead, we are describing the person and, with that, providing some expectations about how he will act on other occasions, in other settings. But is this right? Is personality stable in this way?

## THE ATTACK ON TRAIT THEORY

The most direct challenge to the trait concept was launched over thirty years ago by Walter Mischel (1968), whose survey of the research literature led him to conclude that people behave much less consistently than a trait theory would predict. He pointed, for example, to a study which showed that a child who was dishonest in one situation (say, cheating on a test) was not necessarily dishonest in another setting (for example, cheating in an athletic contest). The data showed some consistency in behavior across situations, but the degree of consistency was quite low, with a correlation of just .30

between honesty measured in one setting and honesty in another situation (Hartshorne & May, 1928; also Burton, 1963).

Mischel argued that the data were similar for many other traits, such as aggression, dependency, rigidity, and reactions to authority. Measures for any of these, taken in one situation, are only weakly correlated with measures of the same traits taken in another situation. In most studies, the correlations do not rise above +.30 to +.40; in many studies, there is no correlation at all (Mischel, 1968; Nisbett, 1980). In Mischel's view, this inconsistency also explains why personality tests have unimpressive validity. A personality test taps behavior in one setting, while the criterion by which a test is validated assesses behavior in another context. Since cross-situational consistency tends to be low, so are the measures of test validity.

## SITUATIONISM

These results seem to suggest that it is not someone's personality that leads him to act in one way rather than another. If it were, we would expect some consistency in the person's behavior from one situation to the next. But if it is not personality that determines behavior, then what does?

One answer is offered by *situationism*, the notion that human behavior is largely determined by the characteristics of the situation itself rather than by the characteristics of the person. This is obviously true in some cases. Given a red light, most drivers stop; given a green light, most go—regardless of whether they are friendly or unfriendly, stingy or generous, dominant or submissive. Similar control of behavior comes from social roles, which often define what an actor must do with little regard to who the actor is (see Chapter 10). To predict how someone will act in a courtroom, for example, there is little point in asking whether she is sociable, careless with money, or good to her mother. What we really want to know is the role that she will play—judge, prosecutor, defense attorney, or defendant. Seen in this light, what we do depends not on who we are but on where and with whom we are situated.

## IN DEFENSE OF TRAITS

Situationism provides a useful reminder that often our behavior is controlled by our circumstances, rather than by who we are. But, of course, who we are also matters. Even if situations do influence us (and surely they do), each of us is likely to react to a situation

Trait or situation    Do these professional wrestlers fight as they do because they are truly aggressive, or because the situation, and their role within it, demand aggressive behavior?

Consistency over time?    In 1964, a group of English seven-year-olds were interviewed for a British TV project called Seven Up, and then were re-interviewed at seven-year intervals for subsequent documentaries (the latest film is Michael Apted's 42 Up). Some of the interviewees betrayed early promise or rejected the goals they had embraced as children. But does this suggest that consistency of personality is illusory? Such case studies are difficult to interpret.

*Summer camp* *Children in summer camp may act one way in one situation, and differently in some other situation. Even so, they are probably consistent in how they act in situations of a given type.*

in a slightly different way, so that our behavior ends up being a function of both the circumstances and who we are. Said differently, our theories of personality need to consider the interaction between person and situation (see, for example, Magnuson & Endler, 1977).

We have already commented on the fact that people seem inconsistent in how they act, so that someone might be aggressive in a classroom setting but shy when they are meeting strangers. However, once we acknowledge the interaction between person and situation, we need to revisit this issue of inconsistency. Perhaps each of us acts differently in different settings, but we are nonetheless consistent in how we act within a certain type of situation, so that (for example) someone might be reliably aggressive in familiar surrounding but reliably shy with strangers, and so on. (And, of course, other people would each show their own profile, their own pattern for how they reliably behave in each type of situation.)

Several lines of evidence support this more refined notion of consistency. For example, in one study, a large number of children in a summer camp were observed in a variety of situations—settings, for example, in which they were teased or provoked by a peer, or settings in which they were approached in a friendly way by a peer, or settings in which they were scolded by an adult, and so on (Cervone & Shoda, 1999; Mischel, Shoda, & Mendoza-Denton, 2002).

As we would expect from earlier studies, each child's behavior varied from one situation to the next. For example, one child was not at all aggressive when provoked by a friend, but responded aggressively when scolded by an adult. Another child showed the reverse pattern. Thus, the trait label *aggressive* would do a poor job of describing either child—sometimes they were aggressive and sometimes they were not.

In addition, note that the situation itself was a poor basis for predicting how the children would behave. A scolding by an adult evoked aggression in some children, but not in others; the same was true for all the other situations studied.

Even so, there was a clear pattern to the children's behavior, but it is a pattern that emerges only when we simultaneously consider the person and the situation. As the investigators described it, the data suggest that each of the children had a reliable "if...then..." profile: "if in this setting, act in this fashion; if in that setting, act in that fashion" (Mischel et al., 2002). Because of these "if...then..." patterns, each of the children was, in fact, reasonably consistent in how they acted, but with the specific behaviors that they showed "tuned" to the situations they found themselves in. We therefore should not describe any of these children as being "friendly," or "aggressive," or "helpful," relying only on global trait labels. Sometimes the children showed the qualities, and sometimes they did not. If we want to describe the children, therefore, we need to be more specific, saying things like "likely to be friendly in this sort of setting, likely to be helpful in that sort of setting," and so on.

In addition, it should be said that these "if...then..." patterns have more influence in some settings than in others, owing to the simple fact that some situations guide our behavior more than others do. At a traffic light, for example, or on a tennis court or in an exam, there are clear rules for how we are supposed to behave. In these situations, therefore, there will be relatively little correspondence between traits and behavior—it is the surrounding, not the person, that governs action. Other situations, however, are far less constrained and so provide more of an opportunity for our individuality—for our individual "if...then..." profile—to reveal itself. Thus, in situations that are novel, or ambiguous, or stressful, we are much more likely to show our "true colors," and, consistent with this suggestion, the data show greater correspondence between traits and behavior in these less constrained settings (Caspi & Moffitt, 1991, 1993).

## SOME PEOPLE ARE MORE CONSISTENT THAN OTHERS

A final complication comes from the fact that consistency itself—the degree to which people do much the same thing in different situations—varies from person to person, and so it may comprise a trait in its own right.

*Self-Monitoring*  Some individuals, it turns out, are particularly sensitive to their surroundings and adjust their behavior to fit in, no matter what the social context or occasion. The tendency to do this is assessed by the **Self-Monitoring Scale**, developed by Mark Snyder. (For some representative items, see Table 15.2.) High self-monitors care a great deal about how they appear to others, and so, at a cocktail party, they are charming and sophisticated; in a street basketball game they "trash talk." In contrast, low self-monitors are less interested in how they appear to others. They are who they are regardless of the momentary situation, making their behavior much more consistent across situations (Gangestad & Snyder, 2000; M. Snyder, 1987, 1995).

On the face of it, the often-inconsistent high self-monitor seems less admirable than her rock-steady low self-monitoring counterpart. Snyder notes, however, that such value judgments are unfair, because both kinds of people have good qualities. The high self-monitor has diplomatic skills and an adaptability that make him sociable and help him navigate complex social situations. On the other hand, the low self-monitor is steady and reliable, a person of integrity with a set of core values that can anchor others amid ambiguity or chaos.

Although both high and low self-monitors have their virtues, when taken to an

*The extremes of the self-monitoring scale*
*(A) Woody Allen as the high self-monitor, Zelig, the man who can fit in with anybody, anywhere, anytime. (B) As the hero of most of his movies, Woody Allen is the ultimate low self-monitor, who stays true to himself regardless of the situation. (Pictured with Calvin Coolidge and Herbert Hoover in* Zelig, 1983: *with Mira Sorvino in* Mighty Aphrodite, 1995)

| TABLE 15.2    SOME REPRESENTATIVE ITEMS FROM THE SELF-MONITORING SCALE* |
|---|
| 1. I can look anyone in the eye and tell a lie with a straight face (if for a right end). (True) |
| 2. In different situations and with different people, I often act like very different persons. (True) |
| 3. I have trouble changing my behavior to suit different people and different situations. (False) |
| 4. I can only argue for ideas which I already believe. (False) |
| * In the items shown, the key after each question is in the direction of self-monitoring. Thus, high self-monitors would presumably answer "true" to questions 1 and 2, and "false" to questions 3 and 4. |
| SOURCE: Snyder, 1987. |

extreme, neither predisposition is particularly appealing. An extremely high self-monitor is a shallow, unprincipled poseur. An extremely low self-monitor, in her consistent adherence to principle, can become blindly rigid (M. Snyder, 1987, 1995).

## TRAITS AND BIOLOGY

Where does all of this leave us? Plainly, situations do matter in shaping how we act, and, as a result, we can easily document inconsistencies in how someone behaves: they might be honest in one setting but treacherous in another, friendly in one situation but hostile otherwise, with their behavior in each case governed more by where they are than by who they are. At the same time, though, we can also document ways in which each of us is consistent in who we are (although some of us, it seems, are more so than others). We are consistent across time, especially if we understand trait labels as descriptions of how someone acts in a certain sort of situation, rather than a description of what they are like at all times and in all places.

All of this leads to a new question: given that people differ in their predispositions, how do such variations—personality traits—arise? So far, we have talked about traits as if they were merely descriptive labels for broad groups of behavior patterns. But some trait theorists go further. In their view, traits are general predispositions to behave in one way or another that are ultimately rooted in the individual's biological makeup.

## PERSONALITY AND TEMPERAMENT

Many investigators believe that personality traits grow out of the individual's *temperament*, a characteristic reaction pattern that is evident from a rather early age (Rothbart & Ahadi, 1994). In fact, they believe that such temperamental patterns are largely genetic.

Evidence for a genetic basis for personality comes from the same methods used to study hereditary effects in determining intelligence—chiefly, studies of twins and adoptees—and, in just about all cases, identical twins turn out to be more alike than fraternal twins on various personality attributes (see, for example, A. H. Buss & Plomin, 1984; Zuckerman, 1987a). For example, several studies suggest sizable genetic factors underlying the Big Five personality traits, and one study of 123 pairs of identical twins and 127 pairs of fraternal twins found that estimates of genetic influence for the Big Five traits ranged from 40 to 60 percent (Borkenau, Riemann, Angleitner, & Spinath, 2001; Jang, Livesley, & Vernon, 1996; Loehlin, 1992).

In a twin study of Eysenck's traits, a personality questionnaire was administered to over 12,000 pairs of twins in Sweden. The correlations between identical twins averaged +.50 for extroversion/introversion and neuroticism/emotional stability, whereas

"It isn't only that Fenwik is incompetent, but he seems to be a *carrier* of incompetence."

*Biology and behavior* **Different breeds of dogs have been carefully developed so that each breed has its own temperament. This is surely consistent with the claim that personality can be shaped through breeding, and is therefore influenced to some extent by biology.**

for fraternal twins they averaged +.21 and +.23 (Floderus-Myrhed, Pedersen, & Rasmuson, 1980). Given all these findings, there is a strong suspicion that heredity contributes substantially to differences in personality.

Peculiarly, though, genetic influences have been identified for traits such as television watching, traditionalism, and the willingness to divorce (T. J. Bouchard et al., 1990; McGue & Lykken, 1992; Plomin, Corley, DeFries, & Fulker, 1990). In each case, there is a greater resemblance between identical twins with regard to these traits than there is for fraternal twins. But, of course, these traits simply could not be directly coded by the genes: natural selection typically unfolds at a very slow pace, but television has existed for only a few decades. Therefore, it is absurd to think that television watching is a trait shaped directly by genetic influences, and likewise for the other traits just mentioned.

Instead, the genetic influence on each of these specific traits may reflect the operation of more general traits. For example, television watching may be associated with extroversion, and traditionalism with conscientiousness. In fact, the case of willingness to divorce demonstrates just this point: in a study of adult twins, those twins who divorced were likely to score higher on measures related to extroversion and neuroticism, and lower in impulse control (Jockin, McGue, & Lykken, 1996).

This reanalysis is consistent with a proposal, offered by several authors, that there may be a few primary personality dimensions from which other, more specific traits are derived. The most likely candidates for primary traits are extroversion/introversion and neuroticism/emotional stability. It is too early to judge whether this conception will hold up, but it is worth noting that a number of different approaches to the study of traits—including, as we have seen, factor analysis of personality inventories and research on the hereditary basis of personality traits—appear to aim toward the same conclusion.

## THE INTERACTION BETWEEN GENES AND ENVIRONMENT

As we have repeatedly noted, genes do not operate in a vacuum. Instead, any genetic influence will emerge only if certain environmental supports are in place. In addition, virtually any characteristic shaped by the genes is also likely to be shaped by environmental factors. What are the environmental factors relevant to personality? Many of them stem from two sources: differences between families, and differences among members within the same family.

*Between-Family Differences*  Families differ from each other in many ways. They differ in socioeconomic status, nutrition and health, religion, and attitudes about child rearing, and so on. Conceivably, then, the variations people show in personality may reflect differences among their families of origin.

The evidence suggests, however, that between-family differences of this sort are relatively unimportant in determining such personality traits as extroversion, emotionality, conscientiousness, and the like. If the family environment did matter, then, as one implication, we would expect a resemblance between the personalities of adoptive children and those of their adoptive siblings. (This is, of course, a case of shared environment, not shared biology.) The data, however, show no such resemblance, and, in one series of studies, the average correlation between various personality measures for adopted children and the same measures for their adoptive siblings was +.04; that between those children and their adoptive parents was +.05 (Plomin & Daniels, 1987; for corroborative data, see Loehlin, 1992).

This conclusion is buttressed by a University of Minnesota study that compared the personality traits of pairs of adult twins. Some of the twins had been reared within the same family; others had been reared apart and had been separated for an average of over thirty years. The results for the twins that were reared together were just as expected. As

*The similarity of twins?*  *Identical twins Fred and Don Lamb are both astrophysicists (although with different specialties), and both have been enormously successful in their careers. This sort of similarity between twins suggests to many that personality, ability, and interests are all shaped by inheritance (since, after all, twins have the same genetic pattern).*

usual, the personality scores for identical twins were more highly correlated than the scores of fraternal twins, with correlations of +.51 and +.23, respectively. Amazingly, the results were nearly identical for twins that were reared apart and had been separated for many years. Here the median correlations were +.50 and +.21 for identical and fraternal twins, respectively. Similar results were found in a study of the twins' vocational interests (Moloney, Bouchard, & Segal, 1991). On the face of it, one might have expected the correlations between the personality traits and vocational interests of the identical twins to be considerably lower, since the twins were reared in different family environments. That the results were nearly identical argues strongly against granting much importance to between-family environmental factors (T. J. Bouchard, 1984; T. J. Bouchard et al., 1990; Tellegen et al., 1988; also see Turkheimer & Waldron, 2000).

Do between-family environmental differences ever matter? Surely they do, and, if this has not shown up in our studies, it may simply reflect an important limitation of these studies—namely, the restricted range of environments sampled in most of the published research. All of the evidence we have summarized so far is based on children of families whose socioeconomic level was working class or above. Within this range, between-family differences do not seem to affect personality traits very much, but this range constitutes a rather limited sample of environments. It tends not to include the environments provided by parents who are unemployed or that of parents who abuse or neglect their children. Nor does it include families that belong to another culture entirely, such as a family of Masai cattle herders in East Africa or a group of villagers in New Guinea. If the range had been broadened to include all these, between-family environmental differences would almost surely have been demonstrated to be more important (Scarr, 1987, 1992).

"Separated at birth, the Mallifert twins meet accidentally."

*Within-Family Differences* If—within the range of environments studied—between-family environmental differences are relatively unimportant, then what environmental factors do matter? According to Plomin and Daniels (1987), the key lies in how the environments vary for different children within the same family. Although at first blush it seems that all children within a family share the same environment, this is not the case at all. The children in a family are likely to have different friends, teachers, and peer groups, and these can play an important role in shaping how they behave. Moreover, various accidents and illnesses can befall one child but not another, with potentially large effects on their subsequent personalities. Another difference concerns the birth order of each child, since the family dynamic is different for the first-born than it is for later-born children. Some authors have suggested that birth order may have a powerful influence on personality, with later-borns more rebellious, more open to new experiences, than first-borns (Sulloway, 1996).

Still other factors also contribute to within-family personality differences, potentially making siblings quite different from each other despite their shared parents and shared home environment. As one factor, parents often do what they can to encourage differences between their children; some authors have suggested that this is a useful strategy for diminishing sibling rivalry (Schachter, 1982). The gender of the child may also play a role. A brother and sister grow up in the same household, but with different social expectations for how they will behave, different types of interaction with their friends, and so on. This—combined with the biological differences between the sexes (Chapter 11)—helps us understand why women score higher on the "agreeableness" dimension of the Big Five, and why women are less likely to be sensation seekers (Chapter 3; Zuckerman, 1994). The sexes also differ in their vulnerability to some forms of psychopathology, with women, for example, far more vulnerable to depression than men (see Chapter 16). In this context, though, we should also note that many of the popularized gender differences in personality are probably overstated, and, in fact, women and men appear remarkably similar, on average, on many aspects of personality (Feingold, 1994).

## PERSONALITY AND PHYSIOLOGICAL AROUSAL

With these environmental effects acknowledged, the fact remains that personality traits are in part inherited, and so they do have some physical basis, ultimately coded for by genes. Just what is this physical basis? Here the search for an answer has just begun.

*Extroversion/Introversion*   Some investigators have tried to link certain personality traits to aspects of neurophysiological arousal. The pioneer in this area was Hans Eysenck, who tried to relate the extroversion/introversion dimension to many phenomena outside of personality.

As Eysenck conceived it, introverts show a higher level of central nervous system reactivity than do extroverts—in other words, they simply react more strongly to external stimuli. This difference shows up in many contexts. Introverts have lower pain tolerance, for example (Bartol & Costello, 1976), and, when they are studying, they prefer a lower noise level and fewer opportunities for socializing (J. B. Campbell & Hawley, 1982). In general, introverts seem to guard themselves against stimulation from the outside, which to them amounts to overstimulation.

More, these findings have been linked directly to cerebral functioning. In one study, investigators measured the electrical reaction to auditory clicks in several areas of the brain stem that are thought to help activate the cortex. In line with Eysenck's theory, introverts showed a faster response than extroverts, indicating greater reactivity (Bullock & Gilliland, 1993).

*Sensation Seeking*   A related topic concerns **sensation seeking**—the tendency to seek varied and novel experiences, to look for thrills and adventure, and to be highly susceptible to boredom, as shown by affirmative answers to items such as "I would like to try parachute jumping," or "I sometimes like to do crazy things just to see the effect on others," and "I wish I didn't have to waste so much of a day sleeping" (Zuckerman, 1979).

Marvin Zuckerman (1994) has shown that answers to items like these do capture an important element of personality. People who score at the high end of these scales are more likely to participate in risky sports such as sky diving, get more restless in a monotonous, confined situation, are less likely to be afraid of snakes, and are more likely to drive at faster speeds than are people at the lower end (Zuckerman, 1983). A final bit of validation comes from a study on streaking, a popular fad of the 1970s whose practitioners took off their clothes and then ran, walked, or bicycled naked through some public area. When students were asked whether they had ever considered streaking (or had in fact streaked), their answer showed a substantial correlation with the sensation-seeking scales (Bacon, 1974, quoted in Zuckerman, 1979).

According to Zuckerman, the biological basis of sensation seeking is similar to that which Eysenck suggested for extroversion. In Zuckerman's view, sensation seekers are people who show greater responses to novelty in certain systems of the brain, specifically those whose neurotransmitter systems contain the enzyme monoamine oxidase (MAO). This includes systems that rely on norepinephrine (NE) and dopamine as their transmitters (Zuckerman, 1987b, 1990). One of his lines of evidence comes from a study in which the level of NE in the spinal fluid was correlated with various measures on personality scales. The results showed a negative correlation: the greater the sensation-seeking tendency, the lower the NE level (Zuckerman, 1983). This fits in with the general hypothesis that people whose NE level is low presumably have underreactive NE systems. In effect, they are underaroused, which makes them seek thrills and take risks to jog their sluggish NE systems into greater activity (Zuckerman, 1994). Other investigators have focused on dopamine, a transmitter that is chemically related to NE (see Chapters 2 and 3). They found that drug abusers are likely to rate highly as sensation seekers, and they suggest that the biological underpinnings for both involve

*Extroversion/Introversion*   **Many traits, including extroversion and introversion, have a biological basis.**

the dopamine-mediated reward systems of the brain (Bardo, Donohew, & Harrington, 1996; see Chapter 3).

*Arousal seeking* **Some people actively seek thrills and arousal; others seek quiet activities. This difference in personality may derive from the responsiveness of the person's nervous system.**

# THE SOCIAL-COGNITIVE APPROACH

Trait theorists explain the differences in what people do by reference to stable, internal personality predispositions (that is, traits). According to this approach, people do what they do because of who they are: the jovial backslapper is the life of the party because he is an extreme extrovert.

An important alternative to both the trait approach and its extreme opposite, situationism, is the *social-cognitive approach*. According to its proponents, trying to account for personality by reference to traits or situations can provide only superficial explanations. In their view, traits are static entities that cannot do justice to the dynamic way we explore situations and then tailor our ways of acting in them. Nor are situations static and easily definable. They are always in flux, changing from moment to moment as people interact in them. An interview can begin well and go sour instantly if the interviewee flubs a question. A hospice room can instantly become cheerier if the terminally ill patient starts joking about his mortality. How can situations explain behavior if they change fluidly with behavior?

## BEHAVIORAL ROOTS OF SOCIAL-COGNITIVE THEORIES

Social-cognitive theories vary in their specifics, but all derive from two long-standing traditions. The first is the behavioral tradition, set in the vocabulary of reward, punishment, instrumental responses, and observational learning (see Chapter 4). Central to this position is a worldview that, in its extreme form, asserts that virtually anyone can become anything given proper training. This American "can-do" view was distilled in a well-known pronouncement by the founder of American behaviorism, John B. Watson (1925):

> Give me a dozen healthy infants, well-formed, and my own specified world to bring them up in and I'll guarantee to take any one at random and train him to become any type of specialist I might select—doctor, lawyer, artist, merchant-chief, and, yes even beggarman thief, regardless of his talents, penchants, tendencies, abilities, vocations, and race of his ancestors. (p. 82)

The behaviorist lineage of social-cognitive theories is exemplified by Albert Bandura, but Bandura's view of personality goes considerably beyond Watson's and emphasizes the role we play as agents in fashioning our own lives. According to Bandura (2001), we observe relationships between certain actions (whether ours or others) and their real-world consequences (rewards or punishments), and, based on these observations, we develop a set of internalized *outcome expectations*, which then come to govern our actions. In addition, we gradually become aware of ourselves as agents able to produce certain outcomes, marking the emergence of a "self," one with a sense of *self-efficacy*. Once these elements are in place, our actions depend increasingly on a totally internalized system of self-rewards and self-punishments—our values and moral sensibilities—and less on the immediate environment. This reliance on internal standards makes our behavior more consistent than if we were guided simply by the exigencies of the moment, and this consistency is what we know as personality. Note, though, that the personality, in this view, is not just a reflection of who the individual is, with a substantial contribution from biology. Instead, in Bandura's perspective, personality is a reflection of the situations the person has been in in the past, and the expectations that have been gleaned from those situations.

## COGNITIVE ROOTS OF SOCIAL-COGNITIVE THEORIES

A second tradition underlying social-cognitive theories of personality was the cognitive view, first detailed by George Kelly (1955). Kelly believed that most personality theories had people either being pushed around by internal forces (trait theories, or "pitchfork theories" in Kelly's words) or being pulled around by external ones (situational and behavioral theories, which Kelly called "carrot theories"). He argued instead that people were always moving on their own accord and did not need to be pushed or pulled. How they moved depends not just on the situation itself but, crucially, on their interpretations of the situation, which Kelly called their construals. Thus, for Kelly, some people construe the proverbial water glass as half-empty, while others see it as half-full. Kelly proposed that when times are hard, the former people are much more likely to give up and be despondent, but the latter people will persevere and be challenged. According to Kelly, therefore, we will not understand personality unless we consider both the behavior and the construals that explain it.

The influence of Kelly's view on social-cognitive theories of personality today is exemplified by Kelly's student, Walter Mischel—the same Mischel who led the attack on trait theory. For Mischel, the study of personality must consider neither fixed traits nor static situations, but should focus instead on how people dynamically process various aspects of their ever-changing world. Like Kelly, he contends that the personal qualities that form personality are essentially cognitive: different ways of seeing the world, thinking about it, and interacting with it, all acquired over the course of an individual's life.

Mischel details five key cognitive qualities on which people can differ, qualities that form each person's cognitive-affective personality system (CAPS). The first is the individual's encodings, the set of construals by which he interprets inner and outer experiences. Second, individuals also develop expectancies and beliefs about the world, which include the outcome expectations and sense of self-efficacy stressed by Bandura. Third, people differ in their affects, their emotional responses to situations. Fourth, they also differ in their goals and values, the set of outcomes that are considered desirable. Finally, CAPS includes the individual's competencies and self-regulatory plans, the way an individual regulates his own behavior by various self-imposed goals and plans (Mischel, 1973, 1984; Mischel & Shoda, 1998, 2000).

## CONTROL

Both Bandura and Mischel emphasize the fact that each of us believes we have a certain degree of control over the events in our lives. For Bandura, this belief is tied to our sense of self-efficacy; for Mischel, it is part of the expectancies and beliefs that each of us carries about the world. In either formulation, this emphasis turns out to be appropriate, because the evidence shows that people do indeed desire control and benefit from feeling they have control (Peterson, 1999; Rodin, 1990).

A widely cited illustration of the importance of control involved elderly people in a nursing home. Patients on one floor of the nursing home were given small houseplants to care for, and they were also asked to choose the time at which they wanted to participate in some of the nursing-home activities (for example, visiting friends, watching television, planning social events). Patients on another floor were also given plants but with the understanding that the plants would be tended by the staff. They participated in the same activities as the first group of patients, but at times chosen by the staff. The results were clear-cut. According to both nurses' and the patients' own reports, the patients who tended their own houseplants and scheduled their own activities were more active and felt better than the patients who lacked this control, a difference that was still apparent a year later (Langer & Rodin, 1976; Rodin & Langer, 1977).

Related to our desire for control is our belief that we can make things go our way. Bandura (2001) has stressed the importance of this sense of self-efficacy and believes that it underlies several key personality factors, such as whether we are optimistic or pessimistic, undertake challenges, take full advantage of lucky opportunities, persevere in the face of adversity, and react toward frustration with heightened motivation or utter demoralization. Numerous studies show, in fact, that the belief in one's efficacy is associated with better relationship, work, and health outcomes (Bandura, 1997; Maddux, 1995; Schwarzer, 1992). Likewise, self-efficacy beliefs about a particular task ("I'm sure I can do this!") are associated with success in that task. This attitude leads to more persistence and a greater tolerance of frustration, both of which contribute to better performance (Schunk, 1984, 1985).

**Control**   *A person's well-being as they age may be strongly influenced by the degree of control the person has over their routine and their environment.*

## EXPLANATORY STYLE

Objectively, some people have less control over their lives, and some have more. In addition to these objective differences, believing that one has control turns out to be one more way in which people reliably differ from each other, with this belief linked to a fairly stable predisposition known as *explanatory style*. This style can be measured by a specially constructed *attributional-style questionnaire (ASQ)* in which a participant is asked to imagine herself in a number of situations (for example, failing a test) and to indicate what would have caused those events if they had happened to her (Dykema, Bergbower, Doctora, & Peterson, 1996; C. Peterson & Park, 1998; C. Peterson et al., 1982). Her responses on the ASQ reveal how she explains her failure. She may think she did not study enough (an internal cause) or that the teacher misled her about what to study (an external cause). She may think she is generally stupid (a global explanation) or is stupid on just that test material (a specific explanation). Finally, she may believe she is always bound to fail (a stable explanation) or that with a little extra studying she can recover nicely (an unstable explanation).

Much of the interest in explanatory style comes from its use in predicting whether a person is likely to suffer from depression (for a description of depression, see Chapter 16). Being prone to depression is correlated with a particular attributional style—a tendency to attribute unfortunate events to causes that are internal, global, and stable. Thus, a person who is prone to depression is likely to attribute life events to causes related to something within her that applies to many other situations and will continue indefinitely (Buchanan & Seligman, 1995; C. Peterson & Seligman, 1984; C. Peterson & Vaidya, 2001; Seligman & Gillham, 2000).

*Self control* **These children may or may not be able to delay the gratification of gobbling up the birthday cake. Evidence suggests that those who can are likely to experience a number of benefits from this self-control in years to come.**

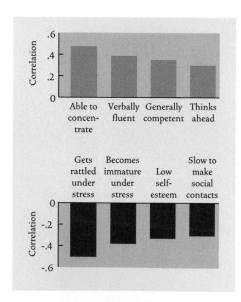

**15.5** *Childhood delay and adolescent competence* **The figure indicates the relation between the ability to delay gratification at age four or five and personality traits at about age sixteen; it depicts correlations between various personality traits of adolescents as rated by their parents and the length of time they delayed gratification as preschoolers. Bars in green show positive correlations; bars in red show negative correlations. (Data from Mischel, 1984)**

# SELF-CONTROL

For social-cognitive theorists, people differ both in their beliefs about control (and with that, their attributional style) and in their capacity for maintaining control, including control over themselves. These differences in *self-control* are visible in various ways. People differ in their ability to overcome internal forces and obstacles; they also differ in how successfully they can refrain from doing what they want to do but should not. People also differ from each other in their capacity to do things they dislike in order to get what they want eventually.*

All of these abilities are relevant to what is often called *will power*, and, according to popular wisdom, some people have more will power than others. But do they really? That is, is "having a lot of will power" a trait that is consistent over time and across situations?

*Delay of Gratification in Young Children* Walter Mischel (1974, 1984) and his associates (Mischel, Shoda, & Rodriguez, 1992) studied this issue in children and showed that self-control, as he measured it, is a stable trait and is related to a number of personality attributes in later life. The participants in his studies were children between four and five years old who were shown two snacks, one preferable to the other (for example, two marshmallows or pretzels versus one). To obtain the snack they preferred, they had to wait about fifteen minutes. If they did not want to wait, or grew tired of waiting, they immediately received the less desirable treat but had to forgo the more desirable one.

Whether the children could manage the wait was powerfully influenced by what the children did and thought while they waited. If they looked at the marshmallow, or worse, thought about eating it, they usually succumbed and grabbed the lesser reward. But they were able to wait for the preferred snack if they found (or were shown) some way of distracting their attention from it, for example, by thinking of something fun, such as Mommy pushing them on a swing. They could also wait for the preferred snack if they thought about the snack in some way other than eating it, for example, by focusing on the pretzels' shape and color rather than on their crunchiness and taste. By mentally transforming their goals, the children managed ultimately to have their cake (or pretzel) and eat it too (Mischel, 1984; Mischel & Baker, 1975; Mischel & Mischel, 1983; Mischel & Moore, 1980; Rodriguez, Mischel, & Shoda, 1989).

## CHILDHOOD DELAY AND ADOLESCENT COMPETENCE

These various findings show that whether a child delays gratification depends in part on how she construes the situation. But it apparently also depends on some qualities of the child herself. The best evidence comes from follow-up studies that show remarkable correlations between children's ability to delay at the age of four years (for example, the ability to wait for the two pretzels) and some of their personality characteristics ten years later. Being able to tolerate lengthy delays of gratification in early childhood predicts both academic and social competence in adolescence (as rated by the child's parents), and also general coping ability. When compared to the children who could not delay gratification, those who could were judged to be more articulate, attentive, self-reliant, able to plan and think ahead, academically competent, and resilient under stress (Mischel, Shoda, & Peake, 1988; Shoda, Mischel, & Peake, 1990; see Figure 15.5).

Why should a four-year-old's ability to wait fifteen minutes to get two pretzels rather than one predict such important qualities as academic and social competence a decade later? Perhaps some of the cognitive processes that underlie this deceptively simple

---

* Some manifestations of self-control involve forgoing a particular gratification altogether for the sake of some other reward or to avoid some aversive state of affairs. An example is quitting smoking.

waiting task in childhood are the same ones needed for success in adolescence and adulthood. After all, success in school often requires that short-term goals (partying during the week) be subordinated to long-term purposes (good grades). The same holds for social relations, because someone who gives in to every momentary impulse will be hard-pressed to keep friends, sustain commitments, or participate in team sports. In both academic and social domains, reaching any long-term goal inevitably means renouncing lesser goals that beckon in the interim.

If there is some general capacity for delaying gratification, useful for child and adult alike, where does it originate? There may be some built-in disposition, but the ability to delay may also be learned. Children may acquire certain cognitive skills (self-distraction, reevaluating rewards, and sustaining attention to distant goals) that they continue to apply and improve upon as they get older. However they originate, though, these attention-diverting strategies appear to emerge in the first two years of life and can be seen in the child's attachment behavior with the mother. In one study, toddlers were observed during a brief separation from their mothers. Some of the toddlers showed immediate distress, while others distracted themselves with other activities. Those who engaged in self-distraction as toddlers were able to delay gratification longer when they reached the age of five (Sethi, Mischel, Aber, Shoda, & Rodriguez, 2000).

## TRAITS AND SOCIAL-COGNITIVE THEORY

Looking back over our discussion, it is clear that social-cognitive theorists have taken a considerable interest in relatively stable and generalized personality traits, as revealed by studies of explanatory style and delay of gratification. How, then, do they differ from trait theorists? There are two answers. One has to do with the role of the situation. By now, everyone agrees that both traits and situations matter, but even so, social-cognitive theorists are more likely than trait theorists to stress the role of the situation and how the individual understands and deals with it. Thus, Mischel found that delay of gratification is an index of a surprisingly stable personal attribute, but he was quick to point out that this index is strongly affected by the way the situation was set up (was the reward visible?) and how it was construed (did the child think about eating the reward?).

The second answer concerns the origins of personality. Unlike trait theorists, who are generally inclined to believe that the major personality traits have a built-in, genetic basis, social-cognitive theorists are more likely to assume that these dispositions are learned.

All of this echoes another dichotomy we have encountered over and over—that between nature and nurture. As we have seen, nature and nurture cannot be disentangled, and both play important roles in shaping who we are and how we behave. In the same way, traits and situations are forever intertwined, and both play a part in shaping the behaviors that those around us perceive as our personality.

*Self-control?* (© *The* New Yorker *Collection 1963 W. Miller from Cartoonbank.com. All rights reserved.)*

# THE PSYCHODYNAMIC APPROACH: FREUD AND PSYCHOANALYSIS

Trait theory and the social-cognitive approach are important and powerful conceptions of personality and have led to much interesting research. But they are by no means the only approaches to this topic, and, in the remainder of this chapter, we turn to three further perspectives from which personality can be viewed: the psychodynamic, the humanistic, and the sociocultural.

Adherents of the *psychodynamic approach* do not deny the assertion that some people are more sociable than others, or that some are more impulsive, or emotionally unstable, or whatever. But they contend that it is far too superficial to try explaining such tendencies either as the expression of a personality trait or as the product of situation factors. In their view, what people do and say—and even what they consciously think—is only the tip of the iceberg. As they see it, human acts and thoughts are just the outer expression of a whole host of motives and desires that are often derived from early childhood experiences, that are generally pitted against each other, and that are for the most part unknown to the person himself. They believe that to understand a person is to understand these hidden psychological forces (often called *dynamics*) that make him an individual divided against himself.

We saw previously that the trait approach bears a certain similarity to dramatic forms that employ stock characters, such as the comedies of the classical and Renaissance ages. In such plays, everything was exactly what it appeared to be. Once the character entered, the audience knew what to expect. If the actor wore the mask of the cowardly soldier, he would brag and run away; if he wore the mask of the miserly old man, he would jealously guard his money.

The psychodynamic perspective, in contrast, is related to a more modern approach to drama in which nothing is quite what it seems. In playing a character, actors who follow this approach pay attention to the subtext, the unspoken thoughts that go through the character's head while she speaks her lines. And many actors are interested in a still deeper subtext, the thoughts and wishes of which the character is unaware. According to the psychodynamic approach, this most basic subtext is the wellspring of all human personality.

## THE ORIGINS OF PSYCHOANALYTIC THOUGHT

Sigmund Freud (1856–1939), a Viennese physician and the founder of psychoanalysis, began with a view of humanity that in many ways is deeply negative—a view that resembles the grim portrait that the philosopher Thomas Hobbes had painted three centuries earlier. Hobbes had insisted that at bottom humans are savage brutes whose natural impulses, if left unchecked, would inevitably lead to murder, rape, and pillage. To curb this beast within, they entered into a social contract and subordinated themselves to a larger social unit, the state.

Unlike Hobbes, however, Freud did not believe that the subjugation of the brute in humankind was a onetime event in political history. Instead, he argued that it occurs in every lifetime, for the social contract is renewed in the childhood of every generation. Freud also differed with Hobbes on the nature of the taming process. According to Hobbes, people's baser instincts are curbed by external social sanctions; they want to rob their neighbors but do not do so because they are afraid of the king's men. According to Freud, the restraints of society are internal, incorporated into each person's thoughts during the first few years of childhood. The earliest curbs on behavior are based on a simple (and quite Hobbesian) fear of direct social consequences—of a scolding or spanking. But eventually the child inhibits his misdeeds because he feels that they are bad and not just because he fears that he will be caught and punished. At this point, the taming force of society has become internalized. The king's men are now within, internalized embodiments of society's dictates whose weapons—the pangs of conscience—are no less powerful for being mental.

### HYSTERIA AND HYPNOSIS

Some of Freud's patients suffered from a disorder then called *hysteria* (now called *conversion disorder*; see Chapter 16). The symptoms of hysteria presented an apparently helter-skelter catalogue of physical and mental complaints—total or partial blindness or deafness, paralysis or anesthesia of various parts of the body, uncontrollable trembling or convulsive attacks, and gaps in memory. Was there any underlying pattern that could make sense of this confusing array of complaints?

The first clue came with the suspicion that hysterical symptoms are *psychogenic*, the results of some unknown psychological cause rather than the product of organic damage to the nervous system. This hypothesis grew out of the work of Jean Charcot (1825–1893), a French neurologist who noticed that many of the bodily symptoms of hysteria made no anatomical sense. For example, some patients suffered from anesthesia of the hand but retained sensation above the wrist. This *glove anesthesia* (so called because of the shape of the affected region) could not possibly be caused by any nerve injury, since an injury to any of the relevant nerve trunks would also affect a portion of the arm above the wrist (Figure 15.6). This ruled out a simple organic interpretation and suggested that glove anesthesia has some psychological basis instead.

In collaboration with another physician, Josef Breuer (1842–1925), Freud came to believe that hysterical symptoms are a disguised means of keeping certain emotionally charged memories under mental lock and key (S. Freud & Breuer, 1895). Originally, Freud and Breuer tried to uncover these memories while the patients were in a hypnotic trance, but Freud eventually abandoned this method, in part because not all patients were readily hypnotized. He decided that crucial memories could instead be recovered in the normal, waking state through the method of *free association*. In this method, his patients were told to say anything that entered their mind, no matter how trivial and unrelated it seemed, or how embarrassing, disagreeable, or indiscreet. Since Freud presumed that all ideas were linked by association, he concluded that the emotionally charged "forgotten" memories would be evoked sooner or later. But a difficulty arose, for it seemed that the patients did not readily comply with Freud's request: there was a *resistance* of which the patient was often unaware.

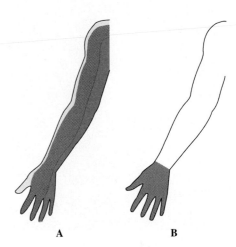

15.6  *Glove anesthesia*  *(A) Areas of the arm's skin that send sensory information to the brain by way of different nerves. (B) A typical region of anesthesia in a patient with hysteria. If there were a nerve injury (in the spinal cord), the anesthesia would extend over the length of the arm, following the nerve distribution shown in (A).*

> The patient attempts to escape . . . by every possible means. First he says nothing comes into his head, then that so much comes into his head that he can't grasp any of it. Then we observe that . . . he is giving in to his critical objections, first to this, then to that; he betrays it by the long pauses which occur in his talk. At last he admits that he really cannot say something, he is ashamed to. . . . Or else, he has thought of something but it concerns someone else and not himself. . . . Or else, what he has just thought of is really too unimportant, too stupid, and too absurd. . . . So it goes on, with untold variations, to which one continually replies that telling everything really means telling everything. (S. Freud, 1917, p. 289)

Freud believed that the intensity of the patient's resistance to certain ideas was an important clue to what was really important. When a patient seemed to struggle especially hard to change a topic, to break off a train of thought, he was probably close to the recovery of an emotionally charged memory. Eventually it would come, often to the patient's great surprise. But if this was so, and if the recovery of these memories helped the patient to get better (as both Freud and his patients believed), why then did the patients resist the retrieval of these memories and obstruct their own cure? Freud concluded that the resistance was the overt manifestation of some powerful force that opposed the bringing of the critical memories into consciousness. Certain experiences in the patient's life—certain acts, impulses, thoughts, or memories—that were especially painful or anxiety provoking had been forcefully pushed out of consciousness, in Freud's term *repressed*, and the same repressive forces that led to their original expulsion were mobilized to oppose their reentry into consciousness when the patient later talked to the psychoanalyst.

The task Freud set for himself was the analysis (as he called it, the *psychoanalysis*) of these ideas and memories, and the conflicts that gave rise to them. Freud was convinced

*Sigmund Freud*

that these conflicts were at the root of most symptoms of psychopathology, but he also came to believe that the same mechanisms operate in normal persons, so that his discoveries were not just a contribution to psychopathology but also laid the foundation for a general theory of human personality. Thus, Freud's psychoanalytic enterprise contained three interlocking parts: a theory of normal personality, a theory of mental disorder, and a set of techniques for alleviating mental suffering. Here, we will take up his theory of personality and, by extension, his theory of mental disorder. His techniques for treating such disorders will be taken up in Chapter 16.

## UNCONSCIOUS CONFLICT

Freud's theory is complex, and he revised and modified it over the course of his long career, so we can cover only the highlights, starting with Freud's conception of personality as an amalgam of separate (and often antagonistic) elements and his mechanisms of unconscious conflict.

### THE ANTAGONISTS OF INNER CONFLICT

When conflict is external, the antagonists are easily identified: David and Goliath, Dorothy and the Wicked Witch of the West, and so on. But what, according to Freud, are the warring forces when the conflict is within the individual? In essence, they are different wishes or motives, such as a patient's desire to go dancing together with her guilt at leaving an ailing father. Freud eventually devised a concept of personality that encapsulated these forces within three distinct subsystems: the *id*, the *ego*, and the *superego*. In some of his writings, Freud treated these three mental systems as if they were separate persons inhabiting the mind. But this is only a metaphor that must not be taken literally; id, ego, and superego are just the names he gave to three sets of very different reaction patterns, and not persons in their own right (S. Freud, 1923).

*The Id*  The id is the most primitive portion of the personality, the portion from which the other two emerge. It consists of all of the basic biological urges: to eat, drink, eliminate, and, most of all, to gain sexual pleasure.* The id abides entirely by the pleasure principle—satisfaction now and not later, regardless of the circumstances and whatever the cost.

*The Ego*  At birth, the infant is all id. But the id's heated striving is soon met by cold reality, because some gratifications take time. The breast or the bottle, for example, is not always present; the infant has to cry to get it. The confrontations between desire and reality lead to a whole set of new reactions that are meant to reconcile the two. Sometimes the result is appropriate action (saying "please"), and sometimes suppression of a forbidden impulse (in Freud's time, not touching one's genitals). All of these reconciliations become organized into a new subsystem of the personality—the ego.

The ego grows out of the id and is essentially still in its service, but as it emerges, it begins to obey a new principle, the reality principle. It tries to satisfy the id (that is, to gain pleasure), but it does so pragmatically, finding strategies that work but also accord with the real world and its real demands.

*The Superego*  The id is not the ego's only master. As the child matures, a new reaction pattern develops that acts as a kind of judge and decides whether the ego has been good or bad. This new mental agency is the superego, which represents the internalized rules and admonitions of the parents and, through them, of society.

---

* These urges are sometimes called *instincts*, but that is a misnomer caused by an unfortunate translation of Freud's original term.

Initially, the ego only has to worry about the outer world. If the ego inhibits some id-inspired action, it is for some immediate reason—for example, the prospect of punishment: you don't steal cookies, because you might be caught and sent to your room. But, as the child gets older, forbidden acts may be suppressed even when there is no chance of being caught. This change occurs because the child starts to act and think as if he himself were the parent who administers praise and reproof. This self-reproach is, in essence, the voice of the superego, and, if the ego lives up to the superego's dictates, then pride is the reward. But if one of the superego's rules is broken, the superego metes out punishment—feelings of guilt or shame—just as the parents scolded or spanked or withdrew their love.

## THE MECHANISMS OF UNCONSCIOUS CONFLICT: REPRESSION AND ANXIETY

Freud's threefold division of the personality was just a way of saying that our thoughts and actions are determined by the interplay of three major factors: our biological drives (the id), the commands and prohibitions of society (the superego), and the various ways we have learned to satisfy the former while respecting the latter (the ego).

How are the conflicts among these forces waged? According to Freud, the conflict starts with the child's performing some forbidden act and then being scolded or disciplined by his parents. The parents may resort to physical punishment, or they may merely register their disapproval with a frown or reprimand; in either case, the child feels threatened with the loss of their love and becomes intensely anxious about this. This anxiety leaves its mark, and the next time the child is about to perform the same act—say, touch his penis or pinch his baby brother—he will feel a twinge of *anxiety*, an internal reminder of the prospect that his parents may castigate him and that he will be abandoned and alone.

Since anxiety is intensely unpleasant, the child will do everything she can to remove it or to ward it off. If the cause of the anxiety is a real-world event or object, the child can simply run away and remove herself from it. But how can she cope with a danger lurking within—a threatening fantasy, a forbidden wish? To quell this anxiety, the child must suppress the thoughts that triggered it, must push the thoughts from conscious view. In short, the thought must be repressed.

Notice, then, that Freud viewed repression as applying to the thought no less than the deed. Almost everyone (both before Freud and after) believes that, say, a four-year-old boy who is punished for pinching his baby brother will refrain from such combative acts in the future. What is crucial for Freud, though, is that the boy not only stops performing these acts; he will probably also stop thinking about them and even fail to remember doing them! Why might this happen? One answer is that thinking about an act is rather similar to performing it, especially for children, who have limited cognitive abilities and have not as yet fully mastered the distinction between thought and action. The inhibition will therefore apply not just to overt action, but to related thoughts, memories, and wishes as well.

## THE MECHANISMS OF UNCONSCIOUS CONFLICT: SUPPLEMENTARY DEFENSE MECHANISMS

Repression can be regarded as the primary *defense mechanism* that protects the individual against anxiety. But repression is often incomplete. The thoughts and urges that were pushed underground may refuse to stay buried and resurge instead. But as they do, so does the anxiety with which they are associated. As a result, various further mechanisms of defense are brought into play to reinforce the original dam against the forbidden impulses.

One such mechanism is *displacement*—a process in which repressed urges find new and often disguised outlets, outlets that are more acceptable to the ego and superego. An example is a child who is disciplined by her parents and who then vents her anger on a doll.

In displacement, the forbidden impulse is rechanneled into a safer course. Other defense mechanisms are attempts to supplement the original repression by blocking the impulse altogether. An example is *reaction formation*, in which the repressed wish is warded off by its diametrical opposite. The young boy who hated his sister and was punished for acts against her may turn his feelings into the very opposite; he now bombards her with exaggerated love and tenderness, a desperate bulwark against aggressive wishes that he cannot accept. But the repressed hostility can still be detected underneath the loving exterior; his love is overly solicitous, and the sister probably feels smothered by it.

In other defense mechanisms, the repressed thoughts do break through but are reinterpreted or unacknowledged. One example of this is *rationalization*, in which the person interprets her own feelings or actions in more acceptable terms. The cruel father beats his child mercilessly but is sure that he does so "for the child's own good."

Another defense mechanism in which cognitive reorganization plays a major role is *projection*. Here, the forbidden urges well up and are recognized as such. But the person does not realize that these wishes are his own; instead, he attributes them to others. "I desire you" becomes "You desire me" and "I hate you" becomes "You hate me"— desperate defenses against repressed sexual or hostile wishes that can no longer be banished from consciousness (S. Freud, 1911; and see Lewis, Bates, & Lawrence, 1994; Schul & Vinokur, 2000).

## UNCONSCIOUS CONFLICT AND THE FORMATION OF PERSONALITY

Freud (1905) believed that the unconscious conflicts he uncovered derived from critical events in early childhood, events that are remarkably similar from person to person and that are pivotal to shaping our personality. Perhaps the most important events were those that involved the child's budding sexuality.

### STAGES OF PSYCHOSEXUAL DEVELOPMENT

In Freud's view, the child starts life as a bundle of instincts to seek pleasure, with the pleasure readily found in the stimulation of certain sensitive zones of the body: the mouth, the anus, and the genitals. Initially, most of the child's pleasure seeking is through the mouth, a period of life that Freud termed the *oral stage*. As the infant attains bowel control, the emphasis shifts to the anus (the *anal stage*). Still later, the child shows increased interest in pleasure from genital stimulation (the *phallic stage*). The culmination of psychosexual development is attained in adult sexuality when pleasure involves not just one's own gratification but also the social and bodily satisfaction brought to another person (the *genital stage*).

The child's progression from one stage to the next is partly a matter of physical maturation. For example, bowel control is simply impossible at birth, because the infant lacks the necessary neuromuscular readiness. But there is another element. As the child's body matures, there is an inevitable change in what the parents allow, prohibit, or demand. Initially, the child nurses but then must be weaned and taught to drink from a cup. She is diapered at first and then toilet trained and expected to retain her feces until she reaches the toilet. When she is old enough, she learns about her "private parts" and is told that they are to be touched only in private, if at all. At each stage, the child is expected to give up her major pleasure and supplant it by the next one in the developmental sequence.

## ORAL AND ANAL CHARACTERS

As Freud saw it, shifting from stage to stage within this sequence is usually frustrating to the infant, and how he handles the frustration lays the groundwork for the personality traits he will develop as he matures. One reaction can be *fixation*, which refers to some degree of lingering attachment to an earlier stage of pleasure seeking even after a new stage has been attained. When fixation occurs, some remnants of the earlier pattern, such as thumb sucking in weaned infants, may hang on for a while. A different response to frustration is reaction formation (discussed earlier), in which a forbidden impulse is pushed out of consciousness and replaced by its very opposite. Thus, during toilet training, the child's forbidden urge—to relax the anal sphincter and defecate whenever he feels like it—leads to anxiety. One means of dealing with the conflict is for the child to do the exact opposite of what he really wants. This reaction formation may manifest itself as constipation.

The child's way of coping with these early stages, Freud thought, leaves its mark on the child's developing personality. An example is the adult personality pattern that Freud called the *oral character*, which he believed was grounded in an oral fixation. During the oral stage, Freud argued, the infant feels warm, well fed, and protected, leading an idyllic existence in which all is given and nothing is asked for in return. According to Freud and his student Karl Abraham, fixation at this stage can leave the adult to relate to others as he once did the breast, usually as passive dependency. Thus, the adult "please love me" derives from the infantile "feed me" (Abraham, 1927).

Freud and Abraham also proposed an *anal character*, which derives from severe conflicts during toilet training. As we mentioned, these conflicts may lead to various forms of reaction formation in which the child inhibits rather than relaxes her bowels (Abraham, 1927; S. Freud, 1908). This refusal to defecate then broadens. The child becomes compulsively clean and orderly ("I must not go in my pants" becomes "I shouldn't make a mess"). Another effect is obstinacy and defiance. The child asserts herself by holding back on the potty ("You can't make me go if I don't want to"), a stubbornness that may soon become a more generalized defiant "no." Other characteristics are stinginess and hoarding, which, for Freud, were nothing but symbolic withholding (the infantile "I will never defecate" becomes the adult "I'm keeping this all to myself").

## THE OEDIPUS COMPLEX

Although he considered the conflicts of the oral and anal stages important in shaping adult personality, Freud believed that their influence paled compared to how the child handled the frustration associated with the phallic stage. Freud called this pivotal point in the child's psychosexual development the *Oedipus complex*, after the mythical king of Thebes who unwittingly committed two awful crimes—killing his father and marrying his mother. According to Freud, an analogous family drama is reenacted in the childhoods of all men and women. Because Freud (1905) came to believe that the sequence of steps is somewhat different in the two sexes, we will take them up separately.

At about the age of three or four years the phallic stage begins. The young boy becomes increasingly interested in his penis, and he seeks an external object for his sexual urges. The inevitable choice, in Freud's view, is the most important woman in the boy's young life—his mother. But there is an obstacle—the boy's father. The little boy wants to have his mother all to himself, as a comforter as well as an erotic partner, but this sexual utopia is out of the question. His father is a rival, and he is bigger. The little boy wants his father to go away and not come back—in short, to die.

At this point, a new element enters into the family drama. The little boy begins to fear the father he is jealous of. According to Freud, this is because the boy is sure that the father knows of his son's hostility and will surely answer hate with hate. With childish

*Oral stage?* **Virtually all children go through a state of exploring objects in the world by putting the objects into their mouths. According to Freud, if a child becomes fixated in this stage, the child will develp an oral character as an adult.**

*Anal personality* **Ebenezer Scrooge (a character in Charles Dickens' A Christmas Carol) exemplifies what Freud envisioned as an anal personality.**

*Oedipus*   *The Oedipal drama crucial to Freud's developmental theory was named after the mythical king of Thebes who killed his father and married his mother. Here Alan Howard, Clare Swinburne, and Tanya Moodie appear in a National Theatre (Britain) production of* The Oedipus Plays. *Howard (in the middle) plays Oedipus.*

logic, the little boy becomes convinced the punishment his father will mete out will be catastrophic. This leads to intolerable anxiety, and so the boy tries to push his hostile feelings out of consciousness, but they refuse to stay underground. They return, and the only defense left is projection—I hate father because father hates me. This naturally increases the boy's fear, which increases his hostility, which is again pushed out of consciousness, resurges, and leads to further projection. This process snowballs, until the father is seen as an overwhelming ogre who threatens to annihilate his little son.

As the little boy grows, so does his rivalry with his father and its accompanying terror. Eventually, though, he hits on a solution. He throws in the towel, relinquishes his mother as an erotic object, and renounces genital pleasure, at least for a while.

Freud believed that, once this resolution has been achieved, the tumult of the Oedipal conflict dies down, and the boy enters a period of comparative sexual quiescence that lasts until the age of twelve years. This is the latency period during which boys play only with boys and want nothing to do with the opposite sex. But as hormone levels rise and the sex organs mature, the repressed sexual impulses can no longer be denied. As these impulses surge to the fore, parts of the Oedipal family skeleton come out as well, dragging along many of the fears and conflicts that had been comfortably hidden away for all these years.

### THE ELECTRA COMPLEX

In Freud's view, females go through essentially identical oral and anal phases as does the male. And in many ways, the development of her phallic interests (Freud used the same term for both sexes) corresponds to the male's. As he focuses his erotic interests on the mother, so she focuses hers on the father. As he resents and eventually fears his father, so does she her mother. In short, there is a female version of the Oedipus complex (sometimes called the *Electra complex* after the Greek tragic heroine who goaded her brother into slaying their mother).

Like young boys, young girl's first attachment is to their mother. Why, according to Freud, does a girl switch love objects and come to desire her father? To answer this question, Freud elaborated a far-fetched scheme that is widely regarded as one of the weakest aspects of his whole theory. He proposed that the shift of attachment begins as the little girl discovers that she does not have a penis. According to Freud, she regards this lack as a catastrophe, considers herself unworthy, and develops *penis envy*. One consequence is that she withdraws her love from the mother, whom she regards as equally unworthy. Freud argued that, painfully, she turns to her father, who has the desirable organ and who she believes can help her obtain a penis substitute—a child. (Why child equals penis requires even more far-fetched arguments.) From here on, the rest of the process unfolds more or less like its counterpart in the boy: love of father, jealousy of mother, increasing fear of mother, eventual repression of the entire complex, and identification with the mother (S. Freud, 1925, 1933a; LaFarge, 1993).

## WINDOWS INTO THE UNCONSCIOUS

Why did Freud think this theory—which many regard as incredibly far-fetched—should be taken seriously? In fact, Freud believed firmly that his theory was demanded by the evidence he collected. Some of the phenomena that he pointed to include lapses of memory, slips of the tongue in everyday life, and the nature of dreams.

### ERRORS OF MEMORY AND SPEECH

Freud continually drew attention to what he called the "psychopathology of everyday life." For example, we might forget a name that reminds us of an embarrassing moment, or suffer a slip of the tongue that unwittingly reveals an underlying motive ("Freudian slips"), or "absent-mindedly" not finish something we did not want to do anyway (see S. Freud, 1901).

Freud did not believe that all slips of the tongue or lapses of memory reveal unconscious motives. The husband who calls a female coworker by his wife's name may not be having unconscious adulterous urges; instead, he may simply be speaking out of habit. Other slips probably reveal nothing more than simple, and quite unmotivated, inattention and memory interference (Baars, 1992; Reason, 2000; see Chapter 7). But some slips, he argued, were revealing, and, if properly interpreted in the context of other evidence about the person, they could provide important insights into an individual's unconscious thoughts and fears.

## DREAMS

Much of Freud's evidence involved the interpretation of dreams (Fosshage, 1983; Freud, 1900). He argued that dreams arise from within the unconscious and, like many day-to-day slips, have a meaning that can be deciphered if one looks deeply enough.

Freud believed that all dreams are at bottom attempts at wish fulfillment. While one is awake, a wish is usually not acted on right away, for there are considerations of both reality (the ego) and morality (the superego) that must be taken into account: Is it possible? Is it allowed? But during sleep these restraining forces are drastically weakened, and the wish then leads to immediate thoughts and images of gratification. In some cases the wish fulfillment is simple and direct. Starving explorers dream of sumptuous meals; people stranded in the desert dream of cool mountain streams. According to a Hungarian proverb quoted by Freud, "Pigs dream of acorns, and geese dream of maize."

What about our more fantastic dreams, the ones with illogical plots, bizarre characters, and opaque symbolism? These are also attempts at wish fulfillment, Freud believed, but with a key difference: they touch on some forbidden, anxiety-laden ideas that cannot be entertained directly. As a result, various mechanisms of defense prohibit the literal expression of the idea but allow it to slip through in disguised, symbolic form (for example, a penis may be symbolized as a sword, a vagina as a cave). Because of this disguise, the dreamer may never experience the underlying *latent content* of the dream—the actual wishes and concerns that the dream is constructed to express. What she experiences instead is the carefully laundered version that emerges after the defense mechanisms have done their work—the dream's *manifest content*. This self-protection takes mental effort, but, according to Freud, the alternative—facing our impulses unadulterated—would let very few of us sleep for long.

## PSYCHOANALYTIC THEORY OF MYTHS

Yet another form of evidence that Freud pointed to are the myths, legends, and fairy tales shared within a culture. He contended that just as dreams are a window into the individual's unconscious, these (often unwritten) forms of literature allow us a glimpse into the hidden concerns shared by whole cultural groups, if not all of humanity. Indeed, one of Freud's earliest colleagues, the Swiss psychiatrist Carl Jung (1875–1961), argued for a *collective unconscious* consisting of primordial stories and images—he called these *archetypes*—that shape our perceptions and desires just as much as Freud's psychodynamics (Monte, 1995).

Psychoanalysts who have delved into such tales have found, for example, an ample supply of Oedipal themes. There are numerous ogres, dragons, and monsters to be slain before the prize can be won. The villain is often a cruel stepparent, a fairly transparent symbol, in their view, of Oedipal hostilities.

As an illustration of a psychoanalytic interpretation of a fairy tale, consider "Snow White and the Seven Dwarfs" (J. F. Brown, 1940). Snow White is a child princess who

"Your wife said you left your briefcase on the front lawn."

*Action slips    For Freud, action slips have meaning, and can be interpreted if one has enough other information about the case. Other scholars disagree.*

*The Dream    By Franz Marc*

*Freud and mythology   Many myths, legends, and stories can be interpreted in psychoanalytic terms.*

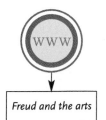

*Freud and the arts*

is persecuted by her stepmother, the wicked queen. The queen is envious of Snow White's beauty and tries to have her killed. The child escapes and lives with seven dwarfs who work in an underground mine. The queen finally discovers Snow White and persuades her to eat part of a poisoned apple. Snow White falls as if dead. The dwarfs place her in a beautiful casket in which she lies motionless for seven years. At this point, a handsome prince appears, opens the casket with his sword, awakens Snow White from her long sleep, and the two live happily ever after.

According to psychoanalytic authors, this fairy tale is a veiled allegory of the Oedipal sequence. The wicked queen is the mother on whom the child projects her own hate and sexual jealousy. The Oedipal—or more precisely, Electra—conflict is temporarily resolved as the child's erotic urges go underground and remain dormant for the seven years of the latency period, symbolized both by Snow White's long sleep and by the seven dwarfs. At the end of this period, her sexuality is reawakened in adult form by the young prince. (The meaning of the sword is left as an exercise for the reader.)

Is this interpretation valid? It is hard to know by what ground rules validity can be judged. There are undoubtedly many alternative (and perhaps more plausible) interpretations of this fairy tale. The same holds for many other legends that psychoanalysts have tried to squeeze into their scheme. Death and resurrection are old themes in mythology that probably refer to many important natural cycles, such as the daily succession of darkness and light and the yearly alternation of winter's desolation and spring's green rebirth; it is not obvious, therefore, why we should prefer an interpretation of these cycles in terms of psychosexual development. In addition, myths may also embody dim folk memories of long-past wars, dynastic conflicts, ancient religions, and various catastrophes. The psychoanalytic view may throw some light on an aspect of our cultural heritage, but it is just one light among many. (For a critique, see Darnton, 1984.)

## A CRITICAL LOOK AT FREUDIAN THEORY

Many of Freud's ideas caught on rather early. In the early part of the twentieth century, the lay public—especially in the United States—was fascinated by the bearded Viennese doctor who spoke so frankly about sex. Scholars in the social sciences, literature, and the arts flocked to read his writings because they were so far-reaching in scope, so profound in their implications. Freud's theories offered nothing less than a new way to understand human nature, and Freudian insights are still influential in many academic pursuits (for example, the interpretation of literature) and in popular culture.

But was Freud right? Was he correct in his account of how personality develops, or the interpretation of dreams? Was the therapy Freud proposed, as a natural outgrowth of his theory, actually effective? Many psychologists have grave doubts about these issues and are deeply skeptical about many of Freud's proposals. What is the nature of their concerns?

## TECHNICAL AND CONCEPTUAL ISSUES

Perhaps the most trenchant criticism of Freud's theory concerns the issue of evidence. Freud's own evidence was drawn from the analytic couch. He considered his patients' free associations, their resistances, their slips of the tongue, and their dreams and then tried to weave them into a coherent pattern that somehow made sense of all the parts. But can one really draw conclusions from this kind of clinical evidence alone? It is striking that some of Freud's followers (for example, the "neo-Freudians," described on pp. 621–622) were able to draw very different conclusions from the same clinical cases—a powerful indicator that the interpretations Freud offered were in no sense demanded by the evidence. Freud's account may have provided a cohesive way to talk about the clinical facts, but other accounts apparently do just as well. On that basis, the clinical facts cannot be taken as powerful support for Freud's claims.

How could it be that more than one interpretation fits fully with the evidence? A large part of the problem rests in the flexibility of Freud's claims. Suppose, for example, that a woman insists that she hates her mother. An analyst might take this at face value, and so be led to one account of the woman's unconscious beliefs and fears. But the analyst might instead take this as an example of reaction formation, in which case the truth would be that the woman loves her mother, leading to a very different account. For that matter, the analyst might interpret the woman's statement in still another way—as projection, with the conclusion, this time, that the woman is convinced that she is hated by her mother—leading, once again, to yet a different account of the woman's psyche.

In these ways, it is not surprising that different analysts are able to draw rather different stories from the same clinical data—leaving us, of course, with no way to count any of these stories as proven correct by the evidence. More broadly, these same concerns have led many to question whether claims like Freud's are scientific claims in any sense. As we argued in Chapter 1, scientific claims are testable, so that we can specify, in advance of any data collection, what evidence would speak in favor of the claim and what would speak against it. But Freud's claims are not testable in this fashion: there is so much leeway in how we interpret the evidence that almost any fact can be accommodated by a suitably flexible analyst (Grünbaum, 1996).

Because of arguments like these, many scholars have reasoned that Freud's theories cannot be considered scientific, cannot be tested, and surely cannot be shown to be correct—by Freud's evidence or by any evidence. More strongly, some have suggested that, for similar reasons, Freud's theory is not very useful. The theory can make no predictions about the future (since, in any scenario, we might plausibly expect a particular outcome, or its opposite), nor can it really explain why something happened in the past (since, again, we could easily well explain the opposite of what happened). In this setting, it is no wonder that many psychologists believe the theory—no matter how influential it has been in our culture—should be set aside in favor of other, more powerful conceptions.

## BIOLOGY OR CULTURE?

The criticisms just offered come from those who disagree with Freud's entire approach—his methods, his assumptions, his arguments. In addition, it is striking that related criticisms came from some of Freud's own followers, many of whom interpreted the clinical evidence differently than Freud did. Specifically, they took strong exception to Freud's insistence that the pattern of unconscious conflicts is biologically based and therefore universal. Their emphasis instead was on social factors, and the relationship betweeen the person and others in his or her social surroundings.

For example, Alfred Adler (1870–1937) argued that a well-adjusted life wasn't just a matter of psychic harmony but required involvement in one's social community. Other criticisms came from a group of like-minded psychoanalysts, situated mostly in America, who are often grouped together under the loose label, **neo-Freudians**, including Erich Fromm (1900–1980), Karen Horney (1885–1952), and H. S. Sullivan (1892–1949). For these neo-Freudians, the important question was not about psychic conflict, but about how humans relate, or try to relate, to others—whether by dominating, or submitting, or becoming dependent, or whatever. Their description of our inner conflicts is therefore in social terms. For example, if they see a mother who toilet trains her child very severely, they are likely to interpret her behavior as part of an overall pattern whereby she tries to push the child to early achievement; the specific frustrations of the anal stage as such are of lesser concern to them. Similarly for the sexual sphere. According to Freud, much psychological conflict centers on the repression of erotic impulses. According to the neo-Freudian critics, the real difficulty is in the area of interpersonal relationships. Inner conflicts often lead to sexual symptoms, not because sex is a powerful biological motive that is shoved out of consciousness, but rather because it is one of the most sensitive barometers of interpersonal attitudes. The man who can only relate to other people by competing with them may well be unable to find sexual pleasure in his marriage bed, but his sexual dysfunction is an effect of his disturbed social pattern rather than its cause.

The same emphasis on social factors highlights the neo-Freudian explanation of how these conflicts arise in the first place. In contrast to Freud, the neo-Feudians deny that these conflicts are biologically ordained; they contend, rather, that these conflicts depend upon the specific cultural conditions in which the child is reared. According to the neo-Freudians, the conflicts that Freud observed may have characterized his turn-of-the-century, mostly upper-middle-class Viennese patients, but this does not mean that these same patterns will be found in people who live at other times and in other places.

These neo-Freudian criticisms highlight the need for objective evaluation of any psychoanalytic interpretation. Freud examined his case studies and saw unconscious conflict growing out of sexual urges. Later analysts examined the same case studies and found a different pattern. Obviously, therefore, the case studies are amenable to more than one interpretation, and it is precisely this ambiguity that makes it impossible to draw strong conclusions from the case studies by themselves. To choose among these interpretations, we need some means of *testing* these interpretations. It won't be enough to ask whether the interpretation fits the analyst's view of the patient's thoughts and feelings, since all the interpretations seem to pass this test.

## CRITIQUE OF FREUD'S THEORIES OF DEVELOPMENT

What about Freud's developmental theories? One of Freud's central arguments was that the pattern of adult personality (whether healthy or not) grew out of the individual's childhood experiences. How has this aspect of the theory fared?

*Oral and Anal Characters* The verdict on the oral character is simple. There is little or no evidence to support the claim that differences in the way the infant was fed have much of an effect on later personality (assuming adequate nutrition). Later adjustment and development appear to be much the same whether the infant was fed by breast or bottle, or weaned early or late. (For an overview, see Zigler & Child, 1969, 1973.)

Some who study childhood development contend that the concept of the anal character may have more validity. They cite evidence that the critical anal traits—neatness, obstinacy, and frugality—do in fact correlate to a significant extent (S. Fisher & Greenberg, 1977). In one study, a number of undergraduates were asked to rate their own and their friends' characteristics. Their ratings showed that the three critical traits do indeed form a coherent cluster: those students who were judged to be obstinate were also those who tended to be orderly and a bit stingy. The convergence of these traits is as Freud predicted, but other evidence suggests we cannot think about this pattern in Freudian terms, for the simple reason that there is no relationship between these traits and either the timing or the severity of a child's toilet training (Beloff, 1957; Y. A. Cohen, 1953; Orlansky, 1949). Why, then, do these traits cluster together? One proposal is that they each reflect a certain type of temperament, which may be partly inherited (Torrey, 1992; see p. 603). Another is that they may be transmitted as part of a general pattern of middle-class values and attitudes, communicated by the general social atmosphere in which the child is raised. Either way, such traits are not by-products of getting the child out of diapers.

*The Oedipus Complex* Within Freud's developmental theory, of special importance were his claims about the Oedipus complex and that this mother-son-father triangle was universal, occurring in all cultures and in all time periods. However, this claim of universality was challenged by a famous case study of the Trobriand Islanders of the western Pacific, a group whose family pattern is quite different from our own (Malinoski, 1926, 1927). Among the Trobrianders, the biological father is not the head of the household. He spends time with his children and plays with them, but he exerts no authority. This role is reserved for the mother's brother, from whom the male children inherit property and status and who acts as disciplinarian to all the children. The Trobriand Islanders thus separate the roles that in Freud's Vienna were played by one and the same person.

According to Freud, this different family pattern should make no difference. There should still be an Oedipus complex in which the father is the hated villain, for after all, it is he who is the little boy's sexual rival. But anthropologists report a different state of affairs, with the child's hostility directed at the maternal uncle, not the father. Similarly, dreams among the Trobriand Islanders often depict the death of the maternal uncle, and rarely the father. Overall, the child has fears and fantasies about the authoritarian figure in his life, and not about his mother's lover—not at all the state of affairs postulated by Freud. (For some alternative interpretations, including ones that may partly salvage Freud's view, see D. E. Brown, 1991; Kurtz, 1991; Powell, 1969; Spiro, 1982, 1992.)

## FREUD'S THEORIES OF DREAMS, REPRESSION, AND DEFENSE

Still other critics of Freud challenge his theory of dreams and his theory of repression and defense. These are key elements of Freud's conception, and so attacks on these ideas strike at the base of the entire psychoanalytic enterprise.

*Freud's Theory of Dreams* Despite Freud's claims, it is doubtful whether many dreams, if any, are attempts at wish fulfillment. In one study, participants were made extremely thirsty before they went to sleep. Since thirst is hardly a forbidden urge, there is no reason to suppose an internal censorship. However, none of the participants reported dreams of drinking. Since they were so thirsty, why didn't they gratify themselves in their dreams (Dement & Wolpert, 1958)?

Another problem is the fact that the same urge can be freely expressed in some dreams but heavily disguised in others. Tonight, the sleeper dreams of unabashed sexual intercourse; tomorrow night, she dreams of riding a team of wild horses. For the sake of argument, let us say that horseback riding is a symbol for intercourse. Why should the censor disguise tomorrow what is so freely allowed tonight? This, too, invites skepticism about Freud's conception of dreams.

Where does all this leave Freud's account of dreams? Dreams do reflect ongoing emotional concerns, but rarely do they seem to be attempts at wish fulfillment. When dreams involve symbols, the symbols are most often transparent and direct representations of emotional content, instead of attempts to disguise it. Indeed, as we saw in Chapter 3, contemporary dream-recall studies suggest that most dreams are not symbol laden or rife with hidden meanings, but instead are mundane and transparently reflective of current life preoccupations (see Domhoff, 1996, 2001).

*Studies of Anxiety and Recall* The concept of repression is the cornerstone of psychoanalytic thought. According to Freud, painful (or anxiety-provoking) material is intolerable to the conscious mind and therefore repressed—not thought about (at least consciously) and not remembered. But whatever Freud claimed, studies seeking to document repression's effects have been largely unsuccessful.

Some studies have yielded data consistent with Freud's view, showing that people are somewhat less likely to recall materials associated with anxiety (see, for example, A. Jacobs, 1955; but, for a methodological critique, see Holmes, 1990). Other studies have shown that participants are more likely to recall events that put them in a good light, in comparison to those that are less flattering (Erdelyi & Goldberg, 1979; Kunda, 1990). Clearly, then, self-service plays a role in memory, whether one is remembering an experimenter's stimuli or the events in one's own life.

There is, however, no reason to cast these results in Freudian terms. As we saw in Chapter 7, information will become established in memory only if it is suitably rehearsed, and a person may simply elect not to mull over unpleasant experiences, making him less likely to remember them later. Likewise, memory retrieval is a process that requires both effort and strategy; for unpleasant memories, someone might choose neither to spend the effort nor to engage an effective strategy. In these ways, we can explain a self-serving bias in memory with no appeal to the sort of imperious censor envisioned by Freud. In addition, the self-serving bias in memory is certainly not strong, and people often remember episodes in which they were anxious, or embarrassed, or suffered some loss (see, for example, Gilovich, 1991)—results seemingly in conflict with the proposal of repression.

Even in cases involving genuine trauma, the data provide little indication of repression. A few studies do show poor memory for traumas, but a variety of problems makes these studies difficult to interpret (see, for example, L. Williams, 1994; and then, for a critique, Shobe & Kihlstrom, 1997). More typically the results indicate the opposite of repression—with people fully able to remember, in vivid and horrifying detail, the horrible traumas they have endured. Women who have been raped, for example, are typically plagued by too many memories about their violators and the setting of their violation; children who have witnessed violent crimes are often long haunted by nightmares about them; survivors of Nazi death camps can recall minutiae about the death chambers, the killings, and the carnage fully half a century later; and so on (see, for example, Terr, 1991, 1994). In all such cases, these deeply painful memories would surely be eligible for repression—and for the victims, repression would be merciful. The fact that these memories are not repressed creates a serious problem for Freud's conception. (For further discussion, see Kihlstrom, 1997; Nadel & Jacobs, 1998; D. L. Schacter, 1996; Shobe & Kihlstrom, 1997; see also Chapter 7.)

Another line of evidence, sometimes cited as a demonstration of repression, is at best ambiguous. This evidence comes from cases in which people have "recovered" long-forgotten memories of painful events; from a Freudian perspective, this "recovery" shows that the memories were present in the person's mind but unconscious for many

*A picture of Freud's consultation room    In classical psychoanalysis, the patient reclines on the couch while the analyst sits behind her, out of sight. Freud adopted this method to avoid influencing the patient's flow of associations by his own facial expressions. He also had a personal motive: "I cannot bear to be gazed at for eight hours a day."*

years—just the pattern we would expect for a repressed memory. As we saw in Chapter 7, though, these reports of memory recovery are highly controversial and open to multiple interpretations. According to one interpretation, these are not memories at all, they are instead sincere, painful, but mistaken beliefs about the past. To be sure, others disagree with this interpretation, but, until these issues are resolved, these "recovered" memories cannot be taken as evidence for Freud's repression theory.

### FREUD'S CONTRIBUTIONS IN RETROSPECT

We have now seen that many of Freud's beliefs have not been confirmed. There is little support for his conception of dreams, or his theory of psychosexual development, even less for his male-centered—and some would say misogynistic—conception of feminine psychology (Chodorow, 1989). When the evidence does go Freud's way (for example, the fact that people who are obstinate tend also to be neat, or the fact that memory is sometimes biased in a self-serving way), there is, as we have seen, no reason at all to interpret these results in Freudian terms.

We have also noted that Freud's work was seriously flawed as science. His claims are sufficiently flexible, and the proposals sufficiently vague, that it is unclear how they can ever be tested.

All in all, this is a formidable set of criticisms. Even so, despite these problems, Sigmund Freud must be regarded as one of the major figures in the history of psychology. Why? One reason is his conception that we are creatures riddled by internal conflicts of which we are often oblivious. Of course, Freud was far from the first to recognize that we are often torn psychologically and do not really know what we want and why (Ellenberger, 1970; Sulloway, 1979), but he was the first to make this insight the cornerstone of an entire theory. Freud saw clearly that we do not know ourselves and that we are often not masters of our own souls.

Freud also deserves a lasting place among the greats of intellectual history because, whatever the difficulties for his theoretical conception, it offered a view of human nature that was virtually all-embracing. It tried to encompass both rational thought and emotional urges. It conceived of psychological ailments as a consequence of the same forces that operate in everyday life. It saw humans as biological organisms as well as social beings, as creatures whose present is rooted in their past. The range of psychological phenomena that Freud encompassed within his theory is staggering—symptoms of mental disorder, personality patterns, social groupings, family relations, humor, slips of the tongue, dreams, artistic production, religious sentiment. Freud's theory has many faults, but this litany highlights some of its virtues: it dealt with matters of genuine human significance; it concerned both human beings and their works; it was an account of the whole of humanity.

Many of Freud's views have now been refuted, but there is no doubt that they have influenced virtually all thinkers in these areas who have come after him. And right or wrong, he showed us the kinds of questions we must answer before we can claim to have a full theory of human personality.

# THE PSYCHODYNAMIC APPROACH: PERSONALITY DIFFERENCES

While the primary focus of psychodynamic theory (and of Freud's theory in particular) is about human personality in general, it does offer some proposals about the way in which people (especially "normal" people) differ from each other and how those differences come about. Freud's theory of oral and anal personalities is one example. More recent attempts at theorizing by various neo-Freudians classify and analyze personality differences in terms of the person's dominant patterns of defense. The neo-Freudians, like Freud himself, believe that anxiety is an inevitable part of human existence and that some defenses against anxiety will therefore be found in everyone. What makes people different, they claim, is the pattern of defenses each of us has erected.

## PATTERNS OF CONFLICT

A major figure in the analysis of these patterns of defenses was Karen Horney (1937), who argued that many people in our society suffer from basic anxiety—an "all-pervading feeling of being alone and helpless in a hostile world" (p. 89). Unlike Freud, Horney believed that this anxiety should not be traced to childhood struggles with infantile sexual conflicts. She felt, instead, that its roots are in our culture, which often makes incompatible demands on the individual.

According to Horney (1937, 1945, 1950), basic anxiety leads some to the frantic pursuit of various goals, sought less for themselves than as a way to deaden this anxiety. They try to assuage their anxiety by seeking love, by seeking prestige or possessions, by withdrawing from any genuine emotional involvements, or by deadening the anxiety with alcohol or drugs. Such efforts often fail, but they generally persist and harden into enduring patterns of personality. The question is why. Horney's answer is that such pursuits create a self-perpetuating vicious circle.

For example, a vicious circle can develop in an unhealthy search for love. If a man needs a woman's love to deaden his sense of basic anxiety, his demands for affection will be unconditional and excessive. But if so, they cannot possibly be fulfilled. The slightest failure to accede to his wishes will be interpreted as a rebuff and rejection. This will increase his feelings of anxiety, which will make him even more desperate for affectionate reassurance, which will further increase the chances of rebuff, and so on.

While vicious circles of this kind are a characteristic of deeply disturbed and unhappy persons, minor versions of such circular mechanisms are found in everyday life. A student has to write an important paper. The paper worries her, so she puts it off. This makes her feel guilty, which makes her more anxious, which makes her put it off yet further, and so on (C. S. Hall, Lindzey, Loehlin, & Manosevitz, 1985). But as Horney points out, there are occasional "lucky circles." Some fortunate encounters in work or love may reverse the circle by increasing self-confidence, which leads to appropriate further efforts and further successes. But all too often, the person's own conflicts make her unable to recognize whatever luck may come her way. Put another way, such conflicts tend to perpetuate themselves, which is one reason why at least some people try to break the pattern by seeking some form of psychotherapeutic help.

*Karen Horney*

## COPING PATTERNS AND MENTAL HEALTH

The patterns we have just described characterize people with emotional conflicts that in some cases are quite serious. But can they help us understand normal people? Contemporary psychodynamically oriented theorists would say that they can. In their view, unconscious conflict and defense mechanisms are found in the well adjusted as well as in people with disabling mental disorders; what distinguishes the two is the extent to which those conflicts are appropriately resolved.

Adherents of this position share the neo-Freudian concern with cultural and interpersonal factors. But they add a further element by stressing the healthy aspects of the self as it tries to cope with the world—to deal with reality as it is rather than to distort it or hide from it. Seen in this light, the ego is not just an arbiter between id and superego, but a clever strategist with intrinsic competencies (A. Freud, 1946; Hartmann, 1964).

## LONGITUDINAL STUDIES OF COPING PATTERNS

This perspective has led a number of investigators to explore how coping patterns are employed over the course of the life span, and some of the data derive from longitudinal studies covering a span of twenty to thirty years. An example is George Vaillant's analysis of the case reports of ninety-four male Harvard College graduates studied at different points in their life span. They were extensively interviewed at age nineteen, then again at thirty-one, and yet again at forty-seven. Vaillant studied the predominant patterns of defense—that is, ways of coping—each man used at these three ages. He classified these coping patterns according to their level of psychological maturity. At the bottom of the hierarchy were mechanisms that are often found in early childhood and during serious mental disorder, such as denial or gross distortions of external reality. Further up the ladder were patterns often seen in adolescence and in disturbed adults, such as projection, hypochondria, and irrational, emotional outbursts. Still higher were the mechanisms studied by Freud and seen in many adults—repression, reaction formation, and the like. At the top of the hierarchy were coping patterns that Vaillant considered healthy (in adolescents and adults)—such as humor, suppression (a conscious effort to push anxiety-provoking thoughts out of mind, at least for the time being, as opposed to repression, which is an unconscious process), and altruism (in which one tries to give to others what one might wish to receive oneself).

Vaillant's findings indicated considerable continuity. Men whose coping patterns were better integrated at age nineteen were somewhat more likely to have mature patterns in their forties, which then predicted the results on various objective indices—satisfaction in marriage, rewarding friendships, gratifying jobs, and good physical health (see Figure 15.7). As so often, it is by no means clear just what in those men's lives was cause and what was effect, but regardless of whether the mature coping defenses produced success in marriage and career or vice versa, it is worth knowing that the two tend to be correlated (Vaillant, 1974, 1976, 1977, 1994). This correlation of coping mechanisms with good late-life outcomes is not restricted to Harvard males; it was also observed in a study of 131 inner-city males interviewed in junior high school and then surveyed thirty years later (G. E. Vaillant, Bond, & Vaillant, 1986).

Similar results were obtained by Jack Block (1971), who studied some 250 men and women in junior high school, in senior high school, and in their thirties. Like Vaillant, Block found considerable continuity in characteristics such as enjoyment of social activities, self-assurance, and desire for achievement. In addition, he found a relation between the participants' adjustment as adults and their family background. By and large, the well-adjusted adults were those who grew up in a (psychologically) benign family atmosphere. Their mothers and fathers were active, self-assured, and warm and took their parenting tasks seriously; they provided firm guidelines but were affectionate in the process. In contrast, the participants judged to be more poorly adjusted as adults came from less favorable family backgrounds. The parents were often at odds with each other, and they were either overinvolved with their child, or rejecting, dictatorial, or indifferent. As Block saw it, the parents provided a familial atmosphere that ultimately helped shape their children for good or ill by inducing healthy or unhealthy coping patterns.

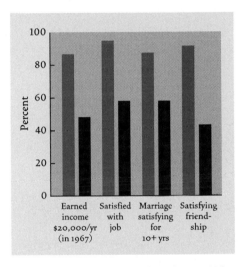

**15.7 Maturity of defense mechanisms and life adjustment** *Adult success at work and love, as shown by men with predominantly mature (green) and immature (red) adaptive styles. (After Vaillant, 1971)*

## COPING AND THE UNCONSCIOUS

On the face of it, the preceding discussion of adaptive patterns may appear rather distant from the orientation of psychodynamic theorists, especially as represented by Freud. After all, Freud emphasized unconscious processes that operated in a murky underground of which we are unaware. In contrast, the coping responses of normal people seem much more ordinary, and they are at least sometimes in plain view. Is there any relation between these two?

Many modern psychologists would answer yes. For whatever their many differences, the defense mechanisms of the anxiety-ridden adult and the "What, me worry?" shrug of the carefree adult have one thing in common—they are both ways of trying to cope with and adapt to the strains and stresses of existence.

The fact that some of these adaptive reactions are fully conscious while others are not does not necessarily mean that there is a sharp break between them. A number of psychologists have pointed out that what Freud called *unconscious mechanisms* may be regarded as ways of not attending, in line with the "kinder, gentler, and more rational" unconscious we discussed previously (see Chapter 8; Bowers, 1984; Erdelyi, 1985; Kihlstrom, 1987). The person who is in favor of a particular political candidate is much more likely to attend to arguments on his behalf than to arguments that favor his opponent. The first he will tend to remember; the second he is likely to forget. Similarly, the man who has just suffered a painful divorce may prefer not to think about his ex-wife. When some topic comes up that starts to remind him about her, he will deliberately try to think about something else and may forget what it was that started the new train of thought. This method of turning away from one's own pain may not be as exotic as the complicated repressive maneuvers that Freud thought he saw in his patients, but it belongs to the same family.

Most of us physically avoid some situations we would rather not face; by the same token, some of us mentally avoid (that is, do not attend to) sights or thoughts or memories we find unpleasant or frightening. Seen in this light, the so-called unconscious mechanisms lose some of their mystery. They are just one more way of dealing with the world.

# THE HUMANISTIC APPROACH

Some forty years ago, a new perspective on human motivation and personality—the *humanistic approach*—gained prominence. According to its adherents, neither trait theorists nor psychodynamic theorists have much to say about healthy, striving human beings. In their view, psychoanalysts look at people as if they are all conflict-ridden emotional cripples, and trait theorists see them as no more than grab bags of descriptors to file in sterile pigeon holes.

Humanistic psychologists believe that these views have lost sight of what is truly human about human beings. Healthy humans want to feel free to choose and determine their own lives rather than to exist as mere pawns either driven by demons from within or pushed around by stimuli from without. They seek more than food and sex and safety, strive for more than mere adjustment—they want to grow, to develop their potential, to become self-actualized.

## THE MAJOR FEATURES OF THE HUMANISTIC MOVEMENT

A major feature of humanistic psychology is its conception of human motivation. As Abraham Maslow (1908–1970) noted early on, behaviorists and psychoanalysts see human beings as engaged in a never-ending struggle to remove some internal tension or make up for some deficit. Seen in this light, people always want to get away from something (pain, hunger, sexual tension) rather than to gain something positive.

But as Maslow pointed out, release from pain and tension does not account for everything we strive for. We sometimes seek things for their own sake, as positive goals in themselves. There is the satisfaction at solving a puzzle, the exhilaration of windsurfing or horseback riding, the ecstasy of fulfilled love, the quiet rapture in contemplating a beautiful sunrise, the grandeur of Beethoven's *Ninth Symphony*. Maslow (1968, 1996)

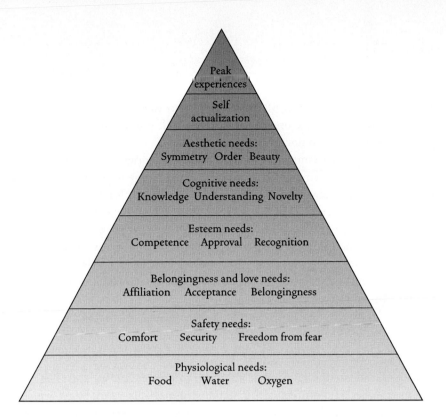

Peak
experiences

Self
actualization

Aesthetic needs:
Symmetry Order Beauty

Cognitive needs:
Knowledge Understanding Novelty

Esteem needs:
Competence Approval Recognition

Belongingness and love needs:
Affiliation Acceptance Belongingness

Safety needs:
Comfort Security Freedom from fear

Physiological needs:
Food Water Oxygen

*15.8 Maslow's hierarchy of needs People will strive for higher-order needs (such as esteem or artistic achievement) generally after lower-order needs (hunger, safety) have been satisfied. (After Maslow, 1954)*

insisted that to understand what is truly human, psychologists must consider all our motives, including ones that transcend mere deficiency needs.

These concerns led Maslow to propose a *hierarchy of needs* in which the lower-order physiological needs are at the bottom, safety needs are further up, the need for attachment and love is still higher, and the desire for esteem is higher yet. At the very top of the hierarchy is the striving for *self-actualization*—the desire to realize oneself to the fullest (of which more later) (see Figure 15.8).

Maslow believed that people will only strive for higher-order needs (say, self-esteem or artistic achievement) when lower-order needs (such as hunger) are satisfied. By and large this is plausible enough; the urge to write poetry generally takes a back seat if one has not eaten for days. But as Maslow pointed out, there are exceptions. Some artists starve rather than give up their poetry or their painting, and some martyrs proclaim their faith regardless of pain or suffering. But to the extent that Maslow's assumption holds, the motive at the very top of his hierarchy—that is, the drive toward self-actualization—will become primary only when all other needs beneath are satisfied.

## THE SELF IN HUMANISTIC PSYCHOLOGY

Before trying to describe what Maslow and other humanistic psychologists mean by self-actualization, we should say a word about the self that is (or is not) being actualized. To humanistic psychologists, the self is enormously important, because one of their primary concerns is with subjective experience—with what the individual thinks and feels right here and now. According to Carl Rogers (1902–1987), a major figure in the humanistic movement, a crucial facet of this subjective experience is the self or *self-concept*. This self-concept develops in early childhood and eventually comes to include one's sense of oneself—the "I"—as an agent who takes (or does not take) actions and makes (or does not make) decisions. It also includes one's sense of oneself as a kind of object—the "me"—that is seen and thought about, liked or disliked (Rogers, 1959, 1961). Ideally, one will develop an abiding, positive sense of self-worth, and this requires that, as a child, the person experienced *unconditional positive regard*—the sense of being accepted and loved without condition or reservation.

## SELF-ACTUALIZATION

Given a reasonable sense of self-worth and the satisfaction of the lower-level needs, the stage is set for the motive at the very top of Maslow's hierarchy of needs, the desire for self-actualization. Maslow (1968, 1970) and other humanistic psychologists describe this as the desire to realize one's potential, to fulfill oneself, to become what one can become. But exactly what does this mean?

Maslow gave some examples by presenting case histories of a number of people who he and his collaborators regarded as self-actualized. Some of them were individuals he had personally interviewed; others were historical figures (for example, Thomas Jefferson and Eleanor Roosevelt) whose lives were studied by means of historical documents. As Maslow (1968, 1970, 1996) saw it, these self-actualizers were all realistically oriented, accepted themselves and others, were spontaneous, cared more about the problems they were working on than about themselves, had intimate relationships with a few people rather than superficial relationships with many, and had democratic values —all in all, an admirable list of human qualities.

## EVALUATING THE HUMANISTIC APPROACH

In trying to evaluate the humanistic approach to personality, we must begin by asking about its empirical and conceptual foundations. Just what is meant by *self-actualization*, or by *letting yourself go* and *being yourself*, or by *unconditional positive regard*? Since these terms are only vaguely defined, it is difficult to know how to evaluate any assertions about them.

Similar qualifications apply to the interpretation of some of Maslow's or Rogers's empirical assertions. How do we know that self-actualizers are in fact as Maslow described them—for example, realistically oriented, accepting of themselves and others, spontaneous, problem centered, democratic, and so on? As yet, there is no real evidence that would allow us to draw such conclusions. Consider Maslow's study of self-actualizers. He picked some examples of people who fulfilled their potential and "actualized" themselves, including a number of prominent and historical figures such as Thomas Jefferson, Abraham Lincoln (in his later years), and Eleanor Roosevelt. Most of us would have little problem with this list, but then why can't the term *self-actualizer* be applied to many other individuals, some of whom are far from admirable and may be veritable monsters? What about Josef Stalin or Adolf Hitler? Why shouldn't we regard

*Self-actualizers   According to Maslow, Thomas Jefferson, Abraham Lincoln, and Eleanor Roosevelt are clear examples of people who self-actualized.*

them as self-actualized? Rogers and Maslow both believed that human growth has an inherent tendency toward good rather than evil, and so they would presumably exclude—by definition—such moral monsters. But this line of reasoning obviously begs the question.

Some critics contend that, despite their noble aspirations, the humanists' concepts are too vague and their assertions too unproven (and maybe too unprovable) to count as serious scientific accomplishments (see, for example, M. B. Smith, 1950). In their view, the humanists serve as moral advocates rather than dispassionate scientists. They tell us what personality should be rather than what it is.

Nonetheless, the humanists have made one certain accomplishment. They have reminded us of many phenomena that other approaches to the study of personality have largely bypassed. People do strive for more than food and sex and prestige; they read poetry, listen to music, fall in love, and try to actualize themselves. Whether the humanistic psychologists have really helped us understand these phenomena is debatable, but their insistence on these phenomena ensures that we cannot forget a vital aspect of what makes us human.

"I'm quite fulfilled. I always wanted to be a chicken."

## POSITIVE PSYCHOLOGY

As we have seen, Maslow enjoined psychologists not to cast their work in terms of deficiency and pathology, because doing so leads us to ignore our higher-level needs and leaves us with a myopic view of human nature. Many of the same themes underlie a recent movement called *positive psychology*.

Advocates of positive psychology note just how many psychology books, courses, and research programs focus on "fixing" what is wrong with the individual, his brain, his hormones, or his social adjustment, but devote comparatively little effort to defining *well-being* and how it is attained. The positive-psychology movement is an attempt to redress this deficiency by defining the "good life" and discerning methods for promoting it. Unlike the humanistic psychology of Maslow and Rogers, however, positive psychology is intended to move past biographical studies and philosophizing about the human condition, to experiments that determine what defines and engenders optimal human functioning (Seligman & Csikszentmihalyi, 2000). It asks such questions as "What is it that makes people healthy?" (see, for example, Salovey et al., 2000) and "What is it that makes us happy?" (see Kahneman, Diener, & Schwarz, 1999).

What are the ingredients of happiness? Various research efforts now underway point to the importance of unvarnished optimism, as well as religious faith, close personal relationships, and a sense of self-determination (Myers, 2000; Peterson, 2000; Ryan & Deci, 2000; Schwartz, 2000; Vaillant, 2000). These qualities appear to influence not only one's mental life but also one's physical health (Salovey et al., 2000). For example, evidence indicates that people who are generally optimistic also have a better functioning immune system, with potential consequences for their physical health (Segerstrom, 2000).

Another crucial factor in determining someone's happiness is the phenomenon of *adaptation*—the fact that humans quickly grow accustomed to (and cease paying attention to) any stimulus or state to which they are continually exposed. One remarkable demonstration of this point comes from a study that compared the sense of well-being among a group of people who had won the lottery and a group of paraplegics (Brickman, Coates, & Janoff-Bullman, 1978). Not surprisingly, these two groups were quite different soon after the winning of the lottery or the loss of their limbs. When surveyed a few months after these events, however, these two groups were extremely similar in their sense of contentment with their lives—an extraordinary testimony to the power of adaptation and to the human capacity for adjusting to extreme circumstances.

*The capacity for adaptation*    *Lottery winners are initially thrilled by their good fortune, but soon adapt to their new status and end up no happier than other people.*

This movement within psychology has also led to a renewed emphasis on positive personal development across the life span; this emphasis leads to questions about how creativity is stimulated, how wisdom is acquired, and how the intellectually gifted can be nourished (Baltes & Staudinger, 2000; Lubinsky & Benbow, 2000; Simonton, 2000; Winner, 2000).

Some argue that positive psychology only recasts old issues into more sanguine and contemporary terms. Is studying psychological resilience different from studying vulnerability? Is research on what keeps people well different from research on the risk factors for disease? The claim and the promise of positive psychology is that these differences are more than semantic, and that the positive approach will lead to new insights and findings. It is too early to weigh its impact, but positive psychology has led researchers in new directions, and it certainly carries on Maslow's vision of a psychology concerned not only with what is basic about human nature, but also what is good and admirable about us.

We should also note, though, that the worldview of some within the positive-psychology movement is rather parochial, and this may limit its impact from the start. Many aspects of positive psychology, like the humanistic movement's focus on personal growth, assume a distinctly Western—even American—perspective on human nature, in which the route to happiness, fulfillment, and self-worth is couched in terms of optimism, accomplishment, strength, and resilience. Not all cultures share this view, and many non-Western cultures eschew it. For them, happiness is not an individual achievement or a reflection of personal strength. Rather, it flows from feelings of belonging and social harmony—from blending in instead of standing out, helping instead of achieving, being "good enough" instead of "better than." These differences come into relief when one studies personality from the sociocultural perspective, which we discuss next.

# THE SOCIOCULTURAL PERSPECTIVE

Whatever their many differences, all of the approaches to personality we have discussed have one thing in common: a focus on the individual. Of course, all individuals exist in a social and cultural context that is critical in shaping and defining them. Yet, by and large, personality theorists have ignored that context and focused almost entirely on the individual, whether by categorizing her (trait theory), by studying how different situations shape her (social-cognitive theory), by trying to uncover her hidden motives (psychodynamic theory), or by celebrating her uniqueness (humanistic psychology). None of these approaches concerns itself particularly with the person's culture.

This may be a serious deficiency. Virtually all of the data on which modern personality theory is based come from the study of middle-class Western Europeans or North Americans. Can we really be sure that what holds true for these people can be generalized to people in different times, different places, and different cultures?

As we might expect, the answer is both yes and no, because it turns out that in some ways people around the world are very different from each other, while in other respects they are much the same.

## PERSONALITY AND HUMAN DIVERSITY

A great deal of the evidence on this issue comes from cultural anthropology, a discipline that studies ways of living among different societies throughout the world. An early pioneer in this enterprise was Franz Boas (1858–1942), who convinced many anthropologists to study the preliterate cultures of the world before they disappeared altogether. Among his students were two of the most influential figures in cultural anthropology, Ruth Benedict (1887–1948) and Margaret Mead (1901–1978).

Ruth Benedict's *Patterns of Culture* (1934) described personality patterns that she believed characterized three very different preliterate societies. Among the Kwakiutl Indians of the Canadian Northwest, the dominant theme seemed to be rivalry and self-glorification. Among the Pueblo Indians of the American Southwest, the primary theme appeared to be self-control, cooperation, and very little aggression within the community. And among the Dobu Islanders, there was apparently considerable enmity and distrust, and a near-universal conviction that everyone practices sorcery against everyone else.

Other accounts pointed to variations in the way different cultures define gender roles. Margaret Mead (1935, 1937) compared the personality traits of men and women in three preliterate New Guinea tribes that lived within a hundred-mile radius of one another. Among the Arapesh, she described both men and women as mild, cooperative, and, so to speak, "maternal" toward each other and especially toward children. Among the neighboring Mundugomor, Mead reported that both sexes were ferociously aggressive and quarrelsome. In Mead's account of yet another tribe, the Tchambuli, the usual sex roles seemed reversed: the women were breadwinners who fished and went to market unadorned, while the men gossiped, adjusted elaborate hairdos, carved and painted, and practiced intricate dance steps.

Of course, neither Benedict nor Mead suggested that every member of a given culture exhibits the pattern they described. Not every Kwakiutl was boastful; not every Arapesh was gentle and cooperative. What they tried to describe is a typical and common personality pattern that characterizes a given cultural group. And the fact that different cultures could show such different patterns seemed to demonstrate that the ways of modern Western society are not necessarily universal characteristics of human nature.

*Margaret Mead in Samoa, 1925*

## HUMAN SAMENESS

Other anthropologists, however, have challenged Benedict's and Mead's accounts, suggesting that their descriptions are in some regards inaccurate and oversimplified. For example, they assert—against Mead—that there are probably some universal sex roles after all; for example, warfare is generally conducted by the men, even among the Tchambuli. They argue that this may very well be due to biological factors (Lynn, 1995; Reinisch, Ziemba-Davis, & Sanders, 1991; and see Chapters 11 and 13). From this biological standpoint, humans are predisposed to physical aggression regardless of their culture, and what culture does is determine how this physical aggression is channeled and against whom, whether it is valued, and how much of it is allowed. (For commentaries and reevaluations of Mead's work, see Brady, 1983, D. E. Brown, 1991; D. Freeman, 1983, 1986; Patience & Smith, 1986; Torrey, 1992; and Chapter 13.)

## THE CROSS-CULTURAL METHOD: STUDIES OF THE EFFECTS OF CHILDHOOD

Anthropological data can provide an informative portrait of another culture, one that we can usefully contrast with our own. In addition, anthropological data sometimes allow a systematic and quantitative comparison of cultures, useful for testing specific hypotheses. Let us look at how this *cross-cultural method* illuminates some claims about personality.

We have repeatedly encountered the notion that what happens in early childhood determines later personality. Those who embrace the cross-cultural method examine this view by studying the relation between a culture's beliefs and practices—family structures, child-rearing patterns, rituals, and religious beliefs—and the typical personality characteristics of its members. In effect, they take advantage of cultural differences to ask how—or, for that matter, whether—certain cultural variations, especially in the area of child rearing, shape personality.

We saw an interesting application of the cross-cultural method in Chapter 13, where we discussed the effect of cultural and socioeconomic factors on child rearing. One study demonstrated a relationship between the economy on which a society is based and its methods of child rearing: cultures that make their living through agriculture tend to stress compliance, conformity, and responsibility in raising their children, whereas hunting and fishing societies tend to stress self-reliance and initiative (Barry, Child, & Bacon, 1959).

## COLLECTIVISM AND INDIVIDUALISM

The relation between child-rearing patterns and cultural factors seems clear enough. But does either cause the other? Most likely there is no direct cause-and-effect link. Instead, they are probably both strands in a complex web of patterns of thought and action handed down from one generation to the next. It is this web that constitutes the culture, and according to many anthropologists, its strands cannot be studied in isolation. From this perspective, the best way to compare cultures would be along some dimension that considers the culture as a whole.

What dimension might we use? As we discussed in Chapter 10, many authors believe that cultures and ethnic subgroups can be distinguished according to their position on the dimension of collectivism-individualism (Triandis, 1989, 1994; Triandis & Suh, 2002). As well as offering a different perspective on some of the social-psychological studies we reviewed in Chapter 10, differences in the collectivism-individualism dimension help to clarify the notions of individuality and the self as they are conceived by members of Western and non-Western cultures.

### INDIVIDUALISM AND SELF-EXPRESSION

Individualism was, and is, a formative concept in Western cultures. Indeed, deindividuation is sometimes demonized in individualistic cultures as a cause of riots, orgies, and torture (see Chapter 11). In contrast, members of collectivist cultures regard a deindividuated society as optimal and see individuation as the source of mayhem and social turmoil (see Markus & Kitayama, 1994, 1999).

John Sabini (1995) has argued that Western individualism has much in common with the value we place on artistic creativity. We celebrate personal uniqueness, appreciate sincerity, approve of spontaneity, and applaud individual accomplishment. The unique self is regarded as a thing of value in itself, for we prize self-expression, regardless of what is expressed. In this regard, we are quite different from collectivists. Americans try to excel and are asked to "be the best that you can be." In contrast, collectivists like the Japanese try to become "so identified with their in-group that [their] individuality is not noticed." Where American children are urged to stand out, Japanese children are taught to blend in (Barlund, 1975; Weisz, Rothbaum, & Blackburn, 1984).

Just how well these different values are inculcated in each culture is revealed in what people say makes them happy. Among Japanese college students, happiness is greatest with positive social engagement: feeling friendly, connected to others, and filled with respect. But for American students, happiness is associated with achievement: feeling proud, superior, and masterful (Kitayama, Marcus, & Kurokawa, 2000; see also Sheldon, Elliot, Kim, & Kasser, 2001). These emotional differences have real consequences for behavior, as shown by comparing how Americans and Japanese each react to failure.

**Collectivist cultures**  *In a collectivist culture, shared activities and blending in with the crowd are highly prized.*

In one study, college students of both cultures were presented with a difficult word-generation task. The Americans tended to give up sooner and considered their performance an unredeemable failure. The Japanese, however, persisted, regarding their failure as an opportunity for self-improvement and taking advantage of corrective feedback along the way (Heine et al., 2001).

## CULTURAL DIFFERENCES IN THE CONCEPT OF THE SELF

Some psychologists believe that our Western conception of the self and human personality has only limited application to cultures other than our own. In their view, many other cultures do not see the individual as we do—as ultimately separate and independent from the social framework in which she lives. They neither see nor value this socially abstracted personal independence, but rather define the self through its interdependence with others (see, for example, Markus & Kitayama, 1991, 1994, 1999).

Thus, cultures often tend to differ on their views of *agency*, a concept used to explain the origins of personal actions. Members of Western cultures tend to see themselves as the originators of their actions ("Why did he do that? Because he *wanted* to."). On the other hand, members of non-Western cultures are more likely to see their actions as arising from collective circumstances ("Why did he do that? Because his family needed it.") (see Hernandez & Iyengar, 2001). This difference in agency runs deep, as shown by one study in which Japanese and American students were shown an image of a school of fish, with one fish swimming ahead of all the others. The Americans saw the lone fish as leading the school; the Japanese saw the school as having dispatched the loner (Morris & Peng, 1994).

One upshot of this difference is that, while members of Western cultures tend to focus on personal rights, those of non-Western cultures focus on social duties (Hong, Ip, Chiu, Morris, & Menon, 2001). Richard Shweder and his collaborators also observed such a personal-versus-social-cultural difference by comparing the responses of Western and non-Western participants who were asked to describe a close acquaintance. Americans were likely to use abstract trait terms, such as "She is friendly." In contrast, participants in India were inclined to describe what a person does in a particular social context, as in "She brings cakes to my family on festival days," or "He has trouble giving to his family" (Shweder & Sullivan, 1993).

In closing, let us suppose that the sociocultural critique is valid in all regards (and this is by no means undisputed; see, for example, Sabini, 1995). If this were so, then our various personality theories would only make sense for people in Western societies, who believe that there is a separate and separable self to explain. Although continued Westernization of the planet seems a foregone conclusion, the sociocultural critique has provided a valuable corrective. It reminds us that we are not the only society in an ever-shrinking world and that others have different perspectives, a reminder that is all the more valuable as the United States becomes increasingly aware of its own multicultural nature.

# SOME FINAL THOUGHTS: THE NEED FOR MULTIPLE APPROACHES

In this chapter, we have considered a number of approaches to personality. One is the trait approach, in which personality is described by reference to a few basic characteristics, many of which have a built-in basis. Another is the social cognitive approach, which stresses the individual's interpretations of situations and the cognitive processes engaged in them. Yet another is the psychodynamic approach, which centers on submerged feelings, unconscious conflicts, and desires. Still another is the humanistic approach, which asks how people achieve selfhood and realize their potential. And we concluded with a discussion of the sociocultural perspective, which suggests that certain conceptions of human individuality and the self may be a product of our Western culture and may not apply to cultures other than our own.

Today, there are relatively few theorists who would espouse any of these approaches in their most extreme form. By now most adherents of the behavioral approach have shifted to a more social-cognitive conception of personality, most psychodynamic theorists see unconscious defenses and conscious coping mechanisms as parts of a continuum, virtually everyone grants that what people do depends on both traits and situations, and many theorists recognize that there are both cultural differences and universals.

Even so, some important differences in approach clearly remain. This is actually fortunate, because these orientations offer different perspectives on the same subject matter. Some aspects of personality are clearly built in (trait theory); others are learned (social-cognitive theory); some reflect conflicts of which we are not aware (psychodynamic theory); others reveal the need for self-actualization (the humanistic approach); and yet others point out that some of these approaches may depend on a particular cultural worldview (the sociocultural perspective). We cannot envisage what a complete theory of personality will ultimately look like, but it will surely have to describe all of these aspects of human functioning.

In this regard, the different perspectives on personality are again similar to different approaches to the presentation of character in literature or on the stage. Is the human drama best described by the use of a number of stock types, perhaps designated by a few well-chosen masks, or by well-rounded characters that are like themselves alone and no one else? The answer cannot be a simple yes or no, for people are both similar to and different from each other. We—especially those of us in individualist cultures—see ourselves as pulled by outer and inner forces, but we also share the conviction that we are free to make our own choices.

We are rational, but we are also impelled by feeling. We are both the masks we wear and something else beneath. We are members of a particular culture, but we are also members of the human race. Each of the approaches to personality—and to dramatic character—focuses on one or another of these aspects of our nature. Each of these aspects exists. And to that extent, each of these approaches is valid.

# SUMMARY

People differ in their predominant desires, in their characteristic feelings, and in their typical modes of expressing these desires and feelings. All of these distinctions fall under the general heading of personality differences.

## METHODS OF ASSESSMENT

1. In studying personality, our first task is descriptive. How do we describe and assess the differences between one person and the next? One approach to personality assessment is by means of objective personality tests, such as the *Minnesota Multiphasic Personality Inventory*, or *MMPI*. The MMPI assesses traits by means of a number of different scales, each of which measures the extent to which a person's answers approximate those of a particular psychiatric criterion group. In actual practice, MMPI records are interpreted by inspecting the person's score profile, including his response to various validity scales. The same is true of its new revision, the *MMPI-2*. A number of other personality inventories, such as the *California Psychological Inventory or CPI*, were constructed in an analogous manner but using normal rather than pathological criterion groups.

2. The validity of personality inventories has been evaluated by using indices of *predictive validity*. The results show that while these tests predict, they don't predict very well, for their validity coefficients are relatively low, about +.30.

3. A very different way of assessing personality is by means of *projective techniques*. Two prominent examples are the *Rorschach inkblot technique* and the *Thematic Apperception Test*, or *TAT*. While these tests are often used in clinical practice, they have been criticized because of their relatively low predictive validity.

## THE TRAIT APPROACH

4. Personality *traits* are attributes that define distinctions in a person's predominating desires and feelings, and also the typical modes of expressing these that are characteristic of different persons. The underlying assumption of *trait theory* is that such traits are fundamentally consistent over time and situations.

5. One of the first aims of the trait approach is to find an appropriate *taxonomy* for personality attributes. Many investigators have tried to develop such a taxonomy by the method of *factor analysis*. This method has led to the identification of five major dimensions, often called the *Big Five*: *extroversion*, *neuroticism*, *agreeableness*, *conscientiousness*, and *openness to experience*. An alternative scheme proposed by Eysenck has just two main dimensions: *neuroticism/emotional stability* and *extroversion/introversion*.

6. The concept of stable personality traits has been challenged by critics who argue that people behave much less consistently than a trait theory would lead one to predict. One alternative is *situationism*, which claims that human behavior is largely determined by the situation in which the individual finds herself.

7. Contemporary theorists acknowledge that both personality and the situation contribute to how someone acts. One way to conceptualize this is in terms of "if . . . then" profiles that describe how a particular person will behave in a particular type of situation. Thus, what defines personality may not be patterns of behavior (being helpful, or being honest) that show up in all situations. Instead, what defines personality may be patterns that show up in certain types of situations (being helpful when with friends, being honest with authority figures, and so on).

8. Consistency of behavior can be regarded as a trait in its own right. Some people tend to be more consistent than others. To the extent that people monitor their behavior and make adjustments so that they will better fit into the social situation they are in, they will behave inconsistently. The tendency to do so is assessed by the *Self-Monitoring Scale*.

9. While some trait theorists view traits as merely descriptive categories, others see them as predispositions to behave in certain ways that are ultimately rooted in the individual's biological makeup. Some evidence for this view grows out of studies of *temperament*, a characteristic reaction pattern of an individual that is present from early childhood on.

10. There is evidence that some personality traits have a genetic basis. Twin studies, for example, show that the correlations between traits such as dominance, sociability, self-acceptance, and self-control are considerably higher in identical than in fraternal twins. Some theorists believe that these effects are based on the high heritability of Eysenck's two super traits, neuroticism/emotional stability and extroversion/introversion.

11. Environmental differences also contribute to the variability on traits such as extroversion and neuroticism. But contrary to expectations, what matters are not *between-*

*family differences* (at least for samples that are limited to this culture), but *within-family differences*. Evidence comes from the fact that the correlation between the personality traits of adopted children and their adoptive siblings is essentially zero and that the correlations between the traits of identical twins reared together are virtually identical to those of identical twins reared apart.

12. Some investigators have tried to link certain personality traits to aspects of neurophysiological arousal. Some believe that introversion corresponds to a higher level of central nervous system arousal than does extroversion. In this view, introverts prefer lower levels of physical and social stimulation, while extroverts prefer to enhance their level of stimulation. Much the same may hold for the trait of *sensation seeking*, which is thought to relate to under arousal of certain regions of the brain.

## THE SOCIAL-COGNITIVE APPROACH

13. An important alternative to trait theory is the *social-cognitive approach*. Social-cognitive theorists, such as Albert Bandura and Walter Mischel, are interested in various cognitive characteristics along which personalities may differ. One example is their *explanatory style*—how they explain the causes of events that happen to them. Some of the interest in explanatory style comes from its use in predicting depression, which is correlated with a tendency to attribute unfortunate events to internal, global, and stable causes. Social-cognitive theorists also emphasize the notion of *control*—a person's ability to do what he wants to do—and also *self-control*, his ability to refrain from doing what he wants to do in order to get something he wants even more. The importance of self-control is reflected in evidence that four-year-olds who are able to tolerate *delay of gratification* for the sake of a more desirable reward show more social and academic competence in adolescence.

## THE PSYCODYNAMIC APPROACH: FREUD AND PSYCHOANALYSIS

14. The *psychodynamic approach* to personality is derived from Sigmund Freud's psychoanalytic theory. Freud asserted that all people experience *unconscious conflicts* originating in childhood. His theories grew out of studies of a *psychogenic* mental disorder then called *hysteria*. Freud proposed that *hysterical symptoms* are a means of keeping repressed thoughts or wishes unconscious. He believed that the symptoms would be eliminated once the repressed materials were recovered, and he devised a procedure, *psychoanalysis*, directed toward this end.

15. Freud distinguished three subsystems of the human personality. One is the *id*, a blind striving toward biological satisfaction that follows the *pleasure principle*. The second is the *ego*, a system of reactions that tries to reconcile id-derived needs with the actualities of the world, in accordance with the *reality principle*. A third is the *superego*, which represents the internalized rules of the parents and punishes deviations through feelings of guilt. morality p.

16. According to Freud, internal conflict is initially prompted by *anxiety*, which becomes associated with forbidden thoughts and wishes, usually in childhood. To ward off this anxiety, the child resorts to repression and pushes the forbidden materials out of consciousness. *Repression* is the primary defense mechanism against anxiety. But the repressed materials generally surface again, together with their associated anxiety. To push these thoughts and wishes down again, further, supplementary *defense mechanisms* come into play, including *displacement, reaction formation, rationalization, projection,* and *isolation*.

17. Freud believed that most adult unconscious conflicts are ultimately sexual in nature and refer to events during childhood psychosexual development. According to Freud, the child passes through three main stages that are characterized by the erogenous zones through which gratification is obtained: *oral, anal,* and *phallic*. In Freud's view, differences in adult personality can be understood as residues of early *fixations* and *reaction formations* that occurred during psychosexual development. An example is the *oral character*, whose nature he believed goes back to a powerful oral fixation. Another example is the *anal character*, whose attributes include compulsive neatness, obstinacy, and stinginess.

18. According to Freud, during the phallic stage, the male child develops the *Oedipus complex*. He directs his sexual urges toward his mother, hates his father as a rival, and comes to dread him as he suffers increasing castration anxiety. He finally renounces his sexual urges, identifies with his father, and represses all relevant memories. At adolescence, repressed sexual urges surface, are redirected toward adult partners, and the person generally achieves genital sexuality. In female children, the *Electra complex* develops, with love toward the father and rivalry toward the mother.

19. Freud tried to apply his theory of unconscious conflict to many areas of everyday life, including slips of the tongue, memory lapses, and dreams. He believed that most dreams are, at bottom, wish fulfillments. Since many of these wishes prompt anxiety, their full expression is censored. The underlying latent dream is transformed into the manifest dream in which the forbidden urges emerge in a disguised, sometimes symbolic form. A similar approach led to the psychoanalytic interpretation of myths and literature that, in Freud's view, provide a glimpse into the hidden concerns shared by whole groups of people.

20. Many of Freud's theories have been seriously challenged

by later critics. Some of the criticisms focused on methodological issues, arguing that some of Freud's claims are in principle untestable. Others concerned the empirical status of Freud's theories of dreams and repression. Thus, while dreams have been shown to be often relevant to personal preoccupations and may feature symbolism, there is little evidence that they are disguised representations of hidden urges. Laboratory studies of repression suggest that when motivated forgetting occurs, it may be a special case of retrieval failure. There are clearly non-conscious mental activities, but they are not necessarily a defense against anxiety, nor do they have the sexual and aggressive quality that Freud attributed to them, prompting some critics to hypothesize a "kinder, gentler ... unconscious."

21. Further problems concern Freud's theories of psychosexual development. To begin with, there is no evidence for the long-term effects of variations in the patterns of weaning and toilet training. In addition, cross-cultural studies have thrown serious doubt on Freud's conception of the Oedipus complex.

22. Some early critiques of Freudian theory came from within the psychoanalytic movement. Among the most influential of these were the *neo-Freudians*, who disputed many of Freud's theories about the nature and origins of unconscious conflict. They focus on interpersonal rather than biological forces in the individual and are generally more interested in the individual's present situation than his childhood past. Their emphasis is on *coping patterns* of defense and coping in normal persons, which show considerable consistency over an individual's lifetime.

## THE HUMANISTIC APPROACH

23. Another major orientation to personality is the *humanistic approach*, which maintains that what is most important about people is how they achieve their own selfhood and actualize their human potential. This approach emphasizes what it considers positive human motives, such as *self-actualization*, and certain positive personal events, such as *peak experiences*, rather than what it calls *deficiency needs*. According to Abraham Maslow, people only strive for higher-order needs when lower-order needs are satis-

fied. A related concern of humanistic psychologists is the *self*. According to Carl Rogers, its development is essentially based on growth. Rogers believed that children will only achieve a solid sense of personal self-worth if they have experienced a sense of *unconditional positive regard*.

24. Many of the themes stressed by humanistic psychologists underlie a more recent movement called *positive psychology*. It has led to a number of empirical investigations, including experiments and questionnaire studies, that try to answer such questions as "what is it that make people healthy?" and "what makes them happy?"

## THE SOCIOCULTURAL PERSPECTIVE

25. A number of authors have argued that much of modern personality theory is based on the study of middle-class Western Europeans and North Americans and may not be applicable to cultures other than our own. The *sociocultural approach* is an attempt to provide a corrective. Testimony to the remarkable diversity of human beings has come from observations by cultural anthropologists. Considerable diversity has been shown in characteristic personality patterns and in gender roles. But as cross-cultural methods demonstrate, there is also evidence for some sameness across cultures, including similar personality dimensions.

26. A number of investigators have tried to use the *cross-cultural method* as a tool to discover the effects of child rearing on adult personality. Evidence suggests that socioeconomic factors affect child-rearing styles in hunting and agricultural societies, and in different socioeconomic classes in our own culture.

27. According to many psychologists and anthropologists, an important psychological dimension along which different cultures can be classified is *collectivism-individualism*. In collectivist societies the emphasis is on the members' interdependence. In individualist societies, including our own, the focus is on the person's private aims and aspirations, and special value is placed on self-expression. Some authors interpret these and other differences as demonstrations that different cultures have different conceptions of the self.

CHAPTER

*16*

# PSYCHOPATHOLOGY

*I*n the previous chapter, we considered normal variations in human personality—the fact that one person tends to be cheerful while another tends to be serious, or the fact that one person tends to be selfish while another is helpful. We turn now to a different sort of variation, one that is a departure from normal functioning and that carries us into the realm of mental illness. The study of such conditions is the province of *psychopathology*, or, as it is sometimes called, *abnormal psychology*.

We should say at the start, though, that there is considerable debate about how psychopathology should be defined. Some observers believe that what we call "psychopathology" merely reflects statistical deviance, consisting of everyday states or behaviors that depart from the norm in either frequency or intensity. For example, all of us are sad some of the time, but, in the statistical deviance view, being sad becomes a diagnosable state when it becomes so frequent as to dominate our lives. Likewise, most of us have occasionally heard someone call our names, only to discover, when we turned around, that no one was there. In the statistical deviance view, hearing voices once a year might be normal, but hearing them three times a day might be a basis for a diagnosis.

For other observers, the different kinds of psychopathology are more than statistical deviations. They are instead qualitatively different from the norm, and not just more intense or more frequent versions of naturally occurring patterns. In this view, being depressed is more than just stronger-than-normal, more-frequent-than-normal sadness; it is an entirely different state, with its own profile and its own consequences.

Which view is correct? As we will see, there is no one answer to this question. The conditions that comprise psychopathology are a mixed lot. In any case, there is little doubt that many of the conditions that come to the attention of the psychopathologist—the psychiatrist, clinical psychologist, social worker, or other mental health specialist—often cause considerable anguish and disability, and so the task of the psychopathologist, in understanding and diagnosing these states (the topic of this chapter) and in treating them (the topic of the next chapter), is one of some urgency.

# DIFFERENT CONCEPTIONS OF MENTAL DISORDER

Mental disorders existed long before there were mental health professions. One of the earliest-known medical documents, the Eber Papyrus (written about 1900 B.C.), refers to mental disorders such as depression (Andreasen & Black, 1996). Other ancient cases include the Greek hero Ajax, who slew a flock of sheep that he mistook for his enemies; King Saul of Judea, who alternated between bouts of homicidal frenzy and suicidal depression; and the Babylonian King Nebuchadnezzar, who walked on all fours in the belief that he was a wolf. Such phenomena were evidently not isolated instances.

## PSYCHOPATHOLOGY AS DEMONIC POSSESSION

What leads to a mental disorder? One of the earliest theories held that the afflicted person was possessed by evil spirits. It followed that the cure for such a malady was to drive the devils out, and so one of the earliest approaches was merely to provide them with a

*An early example of mental disorder* **King Nebuchadnezzar as depicted by William Blake (1795).**

physical escape route. According to some anthropologists, this may explain why Stone-Age people sometimes cut large holes into their fellows' skulls; many such trephined skulls have been found, often with signs that the patient managed to survive the operation. Among some preliterate tribes this practice extended well into the twentieth century (T. D. Stewart, 1977, Figure 16.1).

Later treatment regimens attempted to calm the unruly demons by music, to chase them away with prayers or exorcisms, or even to purge them with emetics (potions that induce vomiting) or laxatives. An alternative was to make the evil spirit so uncomfortable in the patient's body that it would be induced to flee. Accordingly, patients were variously chained, starved, flogged, or immersed in icy or boiling water. None of the treatments was particularly effective, and patients were often driven into worse and worse derangement.

## THE DECLINE OF DEMONOLOGY

This demonological theory of mental abnormality is largely a thing of the past. Even in its heyday, during the plague-ridden Middle Ages, there was an alternative view that such conditions were actually kinds of diseases (Alldderidge, 1979; Neugebauer, 1979). Regrettably, this belief usually did not lead to more humane treatment of the afflicted. The diseased "madmen" were treated with little sympathy, and the interests of society were deemed best served by "putting them away."

To this end, a number of special hospitals were established throughout Europe. Sadly, until the beginning of the nineteenth century (and in some cases, even later), most of these were hospitals in name only. Their real function was to confine all kinds of social undesirables and isolate them from the rest of humankind. Criminals, beggars, the elderly, epileptics, incurables of all sorts, were institutionalized and treated the same way as the mentally disturbed (Rosen, 1966). And the treatments were barbaric. One author described conditions in the major mental hospital for Parisian women at the end of the eighteenth century: "madwomen seized by fits of violence are chained like dogs at their cell doors, and separated from keepers and visitors alike by a long corridor protected by an iron grille; through this grille is passed their food and the straw on which they sleep; by means of rakes, part of the filth that surrounds them is cleaned out" (Foucault, 1965, p. 72).

At the time, this treatment seemed only natural. After all, "madmen" were like dangerous animals and had to be caged. But since caged animals are interesting to watch, some of the hospitals took on another function—they became zoos. At London's Bethlehem hospital (known as "Bedlam," as it sounds when pronounced with a Cockney accent), the patients were exhibited to anyone curious enough to pay the required penny per visit. In 1814, there were 96,000 such visits (Figure 16.2).

A number of reformers gradually succeeded in eliminating the worst of these practices. Historians have given much of the credit to the French physician Philippe Pinel (1745–1826), who was put in charge of the Parisian hospital system in 1793 when the French Revolution was at its height. Pinel wanted to remove the inmates' chains and fetters (albeit treating inmates from upper-class families preferentially) and give them exercise and fresh air, but the government gave its permission only grudgingly. One official argued with Pinel, "Citizen, are you mad

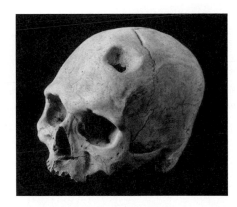

**16.1 Trephining** *A trephined prehistoric skull found in Peru. The patient apparently survived the operation for a while, for there is some evidence of bone healing.*

**16.2 The mentally disturbed on exhibit** *An eighteenth century depiction of a tour of Bethlehem asylum. (The Rake's Progress: The Rake in Bedlam, 1735, William Hogarth)*

*16.3    Pinel ordering the removal of the inmates' fetters*

yourself that you want to unchain these animals?" (Zilboorg & Henry, 1941, p. 322; Figure 16.3). This concern about the prospect of the inmates running free is echoed even today, among people who argue that mental hospitals are a good idea, just so long as neither the hospitals nor the patients come into their neighborhoods.

## MENTAL DISORDER AS AN ORGANIC ILLNESS

Pinel and other reformers sounded one clear theme: "madness" was a disease, and the inmates were patients needing treatment rather than animals deserving confinement. But if these patients had a disease (or, rather, diseases, since it was already known that there were several varieties of mental disorder), then what was the cause? More than two hundred years after Pinel, we are still searching for the causes of most mental disorders.

At first, the notion of mental disorder as an illness suggested an organic or bodily cause, most likely from within the brain. Proponents of this **somatogenic hypothesis** (from the Greek *soma*, meaning "body") could point to the obvious impairing effects of strokes on speech (see Chapter 2), clear evidence that a disorder in the brain could impair psychological functioning. But the somatogenic position gained its greatest impetus at the end of the nineteenth century, thanks to the discovery of the cause of a once commonplace, severe, and debilitating disorder, **general paresis**. This disorder is characterized by a general decline in physical and psychological functions, culminating in a grossly disturbed gait and marked personality aberrations that may include grandiose delusions ("I am the King of England") or profound hypochondriacal depressions ("My heart has stopped beating"). Without treatment, the cognitive deterioration progresses, paralysis ensues, and death occurs within a few years (Dale, 1975).

The breakthrough in understanding general paresis came in 1897 when the Viennese physician Richard von Krafft-Ebing found that it was actually a consequence of earlier infection with syphilis. Once the cause of the disease was known, developing ways to prevent and cure it was just a matter of time. The preferred modern treatment is an antibiotic like penicillin, and such treatment is highly effective if the infection is caught early. While general paresis at one time accounted for more than 10 percent of all admissions to mental hospitals, by 1970 it accounted for less than 1 percent (Dale, 1975).

The discovery of the cause of general paresis was a triumph for the somatogenic view and led many clinicians to believe that all mental disorders would ultimately be shown

ably a virus. (Of course, viral influences are not easily separated from genetic ones, since viruses insinuate themselves within hospitable genes and influence those genes' expression, which may turn still other genes on and off.) The influenza virus has attracted special attention based on the finding that when mothers are in the second trimester of pregnancy during influenza epidemics, the children are somewhat more likely to develop schizophrenia (Adams, Kendell, Hare, & Munk-Jorgensen, 1993; Mednick, Huttunen, & Macho'n, 1994; Sham et al., 1992). Other viruses, such as the viruses for measles, polio, and feline distemper, are also under investigation. Any of these viruses has the potential to cross the placental barrier and damage vulnerable fetal brain cells and neuronal connections.

Still other evidence for an infectious agent comes from epidemiology. First, children who will become schizophrenic are disproportionately likely to have been born during the winter (the months of November to February in the Northern Hemisphere, May to August in the Southern Hemisphere), the season during which people stay inside more and thus share more viral infections. In geographical areas where there are no seasons—that is, areas near the earth's equator—there is no seasonal effect (Battle, Martin, Dorfman, & Miller, 1999; McGrath, Welham, & Pemberton, 1995; Parker, Mehandran, Koh, & Machin, 2000).

The possibility of viral involvement also helps us to understand another fact about schizophrenia and identical twins. It turns out that there are actually two kinds of identical twins. For about two-thirds of identical twins, only one placenta develops, and thus the twins share one prenatal blood supply. In the other third of identical twins, each twin has its own placenta and so its own blood supply from the mother. These two types of twins are difficult to distinguish—they are, after all, both identical twins (that is, virtually identical in their genes)—but they can be told apart on the basis of various biological markers.

If genes were the only prebirth factor that mattered for schizophrenia, then this distinction, separating the two types of twins, should be irrelevant. But the prediction is different when we consider the effect of viruses. A mother's virus is carried to her fetus via the blood supply, and so, if twins share a blood supply, then the odds are good that if one gets the virus, the other will too. If the twins do not share a blood supply, then it is possible that one will get the virus, but the other will not. This explains why the concordance rate for schizophrenia is much higher for single-placenta twins than it is for twoplacenta twins—60 percent versus 11 percent. This difference in concordance rates is a powerful argument that some factor in the blood supply matters for producing the disease, and viral infection is our best candidate (J. Davis & Phelps, 1995; J. Davis, Phelps, & Bracha, 1995).

In short, then, the evidence does seem persuasive that both genetics and prenatal conditions contribute to schizophrenia, and this has led some investigators to argue that schizophrenia is a **neurodevelopmental disorder** (Sawa & Snyder, 2002; Waddington, Torrey, Crow, & Hirsch, 1991), with the child's brain (in its structure and its chemistry) failing to develop as it should from a fairly early age. One line of evidence for this view comes from the fact that many cases of schizophrenia do show preludes in childhood. Affected children are less active and "cuddly," and show delayed motor behavior; by adolescence, they have a host of subtle cognitive and perceptual deficits (Marcus, Hans, Auerbach, & Auerbach, 1993). Additionally, children who will later develop the negative symptoms of schizophrenia also tend to seek isolation and be passive and socially unresponsive, whereas those who will later develop the positive symptoms tend to be irritable, distractible, and aggressive (T. D. Cannon, Mednick, & Parnas, 1990; Parnas & Jorgensen, 1989).

All these findings help us understand the sources of schizophrenia, but they also point to the possibility of a happy conclusion, because in the last few decades, better maternal care, more widespread vaccinations, and better delivery procedures have resulted in fewer prenatal infections and fewer birth risks. The expected (and hopeful) result might be fewer cases of schizophrenia. There indeed is some evidence that the incidence of schizophrenia is on the decline, but it is too soon to be certain (Warner, 1995).

## SOCIAL AND PSYCHOLOGICAL ENVIRONMENT

What about stressors later in life? Can these precipitate schizophrenic reactions? Some investigators have suggested that genetic and prenatal factors are not by themselves enough to produce schizophrenia; in addition, psychological stressors may play a role, triggering the pathology that a person was inclined to develop all along (Gottesman & Shields, 1982; Meehl, 1962). What sources of psychological stress were held responsible? The usual suspects were social class and family of origin.

*Social Class*  Early on, epidemiological studies of schizophrenia revealed an undeniable fact. Compared to an individual at the top of the socioeconomic hierarchy, someone at the bottom is far more likely to be schizophrenic—nine times as likely, according to one study (Hollingshead & Redlich, 1958). The same point can be made geographically, since the prevalence of schizophrenia is highest in the poorest and most dilapidated areas of a city and diminishes as one progresses toward higher-income regions (Figure 16.7; and M. L. Kohn, 1968).

The original interpretation of these findings was that poverty, inferior status, and low occupational rank lead to increased psychological stress, which led vulnerable individuals to become schizophrenic. But most researchers now favor an alternative view, that of **downward drift**, which holds simply that schizophrenics fall to the bottom of the socioeconomic ladder because they cannot hold down a job or sustain a personal relationship. As a result, most investigators are now skeptical about the claim that the stresses of poverty—while certainly damaging on many dimensions—play a large part in producing schizophrenia.

*Family Environment*  Some psychodynamically oriented investigators have looked to the personality of the schizophrenic's parents as a precipitating stressor. Schizophrenics' mothers, they argued, were rejecting, cold, dominating, and prudish, while their fathers were detached, humorless, weak, and passive (Arieti, 1959). However, the evidence for this claim is weak. First, it is not clear that these traits are commonly found in the parents of schizophrenics. And, even if these traits are found, this is far from proof that the family environment caused or triggered the patient's disorder. As an alternative, it is possible that the family pattern is a consequence of the disorder, rather than a cause. Having a family member who suffers from schizophrenia can be tragic for the family. Parents often blame themselves and each other for their disturbed child—and their guilty agony may be redoubled if their therapist is psychogenically inclined and believes the parents did precipitate the schizophrenia. Such parents also become frustrated and despondent in their attempts to reach their child (Mishler & Waxler, 1968; Torrey, 1983).

In addition, schizophrenic children may have difficult parents for another reason: given the linkage between schizophrenia and genetics, a schizophrenic child is likely to have at least one parent with the same pathological genes that eventuated in schizophrenia in the child. In fact, there is some evidence that even the nonschizophrenic parents and siblings of schizophrenics manifest biological markers for the propensity (Holtzman et al., 1988; Reveley, Reveley, & Clifford, 1982; Tsuang et al., 1991).

Thus, there is no compelling evidence that poor familial relations cause the patient's illness. But the family context surely does matter in other ways, including how well the schizophrenic person copes with the disorder. This is reflected in the fact that patients, once treated and released from a hospital, are rehospitalized more often if their parents are hostile and critical toward them (Hooley, 1985). This makes sense. Such reactions

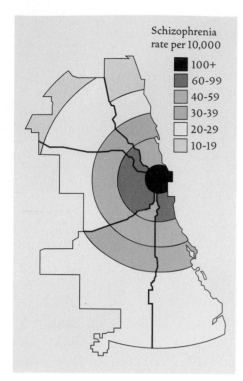

Schizophrenia
rate per 10,000

- 100+
- 60-99
- 40-59
- 30-39
- 20-29
- 10-19

**16.7**  *The prevalence of schizophrenia in different regions of a city*  A map of Chicago (1922–1934) represented by a series of concentric zones. The center zone is the business and amusement area, which is without residents except for some transients and vagabonds. Surrounding this center is a slum region inhabited largely by unskilled laborers. Further out are more stable regions: a zone largely populated by skilled workers, followed by zones of middle- and upper-middle-class apartment dwellers, and, furthest out, the upper-middle-class commuters. The map shows clearly that the incidence of schizophrenia increases the closer one gets to the city's center. (After Faris & Dunham, 1939) by family members are unlikely to ease the patient's adjustment to his illness, and make the hospital look inviting by comparison.

## IS SCHIZOPHRENIA A LIFELONG DISORDER?

What is the outlook for schizophrenic patients? Although the incidence of the disease may be declining, for those afflicted the prospects are not encouraging. One study tracked down two hundred people who had been diagnosed with schizophrenia some thirty years previously. Of these patients, 20 percent were doing well at the time of this thirty-year follow-up, while 45 percent were incapacitated. Sixty-seven percent had never married, and 58 percent had never worked (Andreasen & Black, 1996; Cutting, 1986).

Clearly schizophrenia is devastating in its overall impact, but we hasten to note that about one in five schizophrenics do well. We can hope that the odds will improve as researchers converge on the etiology of the disease and perfect new treatments. Indeed, some new treatments for schizophrenia give grounds for optimism, as we will discuss in the next chapter.

# MOOD DISORDERS

In schizophrenia, the primary symptoms involve disorders in thinking. In the *mood disorders*, in contrast, the predominant disturbances lie in mood and motivation. These disorders (which are sometimes called *affective disorders*) are characterized by emotional and energetic extremes—the maelstrom of mania, the despair of depression, or both.

## BIPOLAR AND UNIPOLAR SYNDROMES

An initial distinction is that between *bipolar disorder* (formerly called manic-depressive illness) and *major depression*. In bipolar disorder, the patient endures episodes at both manic and depressive extremes (with normal periods interspersed). These manic and depressive episodes may be as short as a few hours or as long as several months or more, and they need not alternate: some bipolar patients suffer mainly from mania and have few depressions, and vice versa. Moreover, although depression and mania were once regarded as opposite and mutually exclusive, they are now known to co-occur. In such *mixed states*, patients exhibit signs of both (for example, tearfulness and pessimism combined with grandiosity and racing thoughts).

Bipolar disorder occurs in about 0.5 to 1 percent of the population and is diagnosed more often in women by a ratio of three to two (Andreasen & Black, 1996). Much more frequent are cases of major depression (sometimes called *unipolar depression*, since the mood extreme is of one kind only). According to several estimates, about 10 percent of all men and 20 percent of all women in the United States will suffer from a diagnosable major depressive episode at some time during their lives (Hirschfeld & Cross, 1981; Weissman & Boyd, 1985).

### MANIA

In their milder form, manic states are often hard to distinguish from buoyant spirits. At this point, the person is said to show *hypomania*. She seems to have shifted into high gear. She is infectiously happy, extremely talkative, charming, utterly self-confident, and indefatigable. It is hard to see that something is amiss unless one notices that she jumps

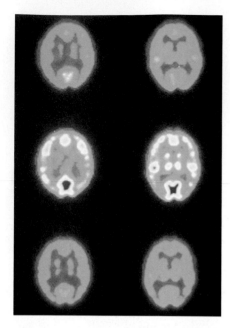

*PET scan of a rapid-cycling bipolar disorder patient* **The top and bottom row are scans obtained on days in which the patient was depressed; the middle row on a day in which he was hypomanic. Reds and yellows indicate a high rate of metabolic activity; blues and greens indicate low rates.**

from one plan to another, seems unable to sit still for a moment, and quickly shifts from unbounded elation to brittle irritation if she meets even the smallest frustration. Kay Redfield Jamison (1995), a psychologist and expert on bipolar disorder—and a sufferer of it as well—provided a lyrical and frank account of the ecstatic allure of hypomania:

> When you're high it's tremendous. The ideas and feelings are fast and frequent like shooting stars, and you follow them until you find better and brighter ones. Shyness goes, the right words and gestures are suddenly there, the power to captivate others a felt certainty. There are interests found in uninteresting people. Sensuality is pervasive and the desire to seduce and be seduced irresistible. Feelings of ease, intensity, power, well-being, financial omnipotence, and euphoria pervade one's marrow. (p. 67)

These signs become greatly intensified as the hypomania escalates into full-blown *mania*. Now the motor is racing and all brakes are off, and in her perceived invincibility the person will likely quit all her antimanic medication. She may begin to stay up all night, engage in an endless stream of talk that runs from one topic to another and knows no inhibitions of social or personal propriety.

These feelings of omnipotence are short-lived, however. They recede as acute or psychotic mania sets in, and invincibility is replaced by terror as the patient loses her tenuous grip on reality:

> The fast ideas are too fast, and there are far too many; overwhelming confusion replaces clarity. Memory goes. Humor and absorption on friends' faces are replaced by fear and concern. Everything previously moving with the grain is now against—you are irritable, angry, frightened, uncontrollable, and enmeshed totally in the blackest caves of the mind. (p. 67)

Patients in the acute manic state may burst into shouts of song, smash furniture, exercise endlessly, sleep only rarely, engage in reckless sexual escapades, spend all their money on gambling, conceive grandiose plans for redirecting the nation's foreign policy or making millions in the stock market, and go on drinking or drug-abuse bouts (nearly 60 percent of people with bipolar disorder are alcohol or drug abusers; Feinman & Dunner, 1996). As Jamison (1995) described this chaotic state:

> I kept on with my life at a frightening pace. I worked ridiculously long hours and slept next to not at all. When I went home at night it was a place of increasing chaos: Books, many of them newly purchased, were strewn everywhere. . . . There were hundreds of scraps of paper as well. . . . One scrap contained an incoherent and rambling poem; I found it weeks later, apparently triggered by my spice collection, which, needless to say, had grown by leaps and bounds during my mania. I had titled it, for reasons that I am sure made sense at the time, "God is an Herbivore." (p. 79)

This torrent of activity can continue unabated over many days and sleepless nights and will eventually sap the patients' health (and that of those around them) if the disorder goes untreated. Although we have focused only on adults, children can also have bipolar disorder, and over 90 percent of these children will be plagued by it throughout adulthood (Kessler, Avenevoli, & Ries Merikangas, 2001).

## DEPRESSION

Depression is the opposite of mania. The patient's mood may be dejected, his outlook hopeless. He has lost interest in other people and believes he is unredeemably sinful or worthless. In describing the depths of his own depression, the novelist William Styron (1990) wrote:

> All sense of hope vanished, along with the idea of a futurity; my brain, in thrall to its outlaw hormones, had become less an organ of thought than an instrument registering,

*Depression* **In his book, Darkness Visible, writer William Styron describes his battles with depression.**

minute by minute, varying degrees of its own suffering. The mornings themselves were becoming bad now as I wandered about lethargic . . . but afternoons were still the worst, when I'd feel the horror, like some poisonous fogbank, roll in upon my mind, forcing me into bed. There I would lie for as long as six hours, stuporous and virtually paralyzed, gazing at the ceiling and waiting for that moment of evening when, mysteriously, the crucifixion would ease up just enough to allow me to force down some food and then, like an automaton, seek an hour or two of sleep again. (pp. 58–59)

Both thought and action can slow to a crawl:

> The patient . . . speaks only in response to questions and even then answers in a word, not a sentence. . . . He speaks in such a low tone that one finds oneself moving close to him and speaking more loudly as if he were the one who could not hear. (R. A. Cohen, 1975, p. 1019)

About 20 percent of depressions have psychotic features; that is, they are accompanied by delusions or hallucinations. Some of these are variations on the theme of worthlessness: "it would be better if I had not been born. . . . I am the most inferior person in the world. . . ." (Beck, 1967, p. 38). Others concern guilt about some unspeakable, unpardonable sin, and patients report hearing the devil tell them that they will surely burn in hell for eternity (Andreasen & Black, 1996). Whatever the manifestation, depressions with psychotic features are more severe, less responsive to treatment, and more likely to recur (Coryell, 1996). The extreme of depression is a *depressive stupor*, in which the person may become entirely unresponsive, rock back and forth, urinate or defecate on herself, and mutter incoherently.

Specific cognitive deficits, including disrupted attention and working memory, often accompany severe depression, and these deficits can be so severe that the patient may be mistakenly diagnosed with Alzheimer's disease. Moreover, depressed patients often exhibit various physical manifestations that are called *vegetative signs*. These can include a loss of appetite and weight loss, weakness, fatigue, poor bowel functioning, sleep disorders (most often insomnia from early-morning awakenings), and loss of interest in sex. It is as if both bodily and psychic batteries have run down completely.

In contrast to earlier views, childhood depression certainly exists and is quite common, with up to 25 percent of the population having been diagnosably depressed at some time by the end of adolescence (Cicchetti & Toth, 1998; Kessler, Keller, & Wittchen, 2001). Although depressed adolescents resemble depressed adults, some of their symptoms come in distinctly teenage form: despair can be seen in substance abuse, apathy in missed classes, irritability in belligerence and defiance, insomnia in too many all-nighters, and suicidal thoughts sometimes linked to a preoccupation with nihilistic books and music and a stark, black style of dress. To be sure, each of these traits can occur without depression—and so not everyone who misses classes, and not everyone who dresses in black, is depressed! But the package, together with other symptoms of depression, can be an indication of profound emotional problems. In younger children, depression takes other forms and often masquerades as "school phobia" ("I hate school"), aggressive outbursts, and somatic complaints like frequent stomachaches (Lamarine, 1995).

*Hamlet on depression* Probably no patient in real life has described his preoccupation with death, suicide, and dissolution as eloquently as that greatest depressive in all of English literature, Prince Hamlet:
"O that this too too sullied flesh would melt,
Thaw, and resolve itself into a dew,
Or that the Everlasting had not fixed
His canon 'gainst self-slaughter! O God, O God,
How weary, stale, flat, and unprofitable
Seem to me all the uses of this world!
Fie on't, ah fie, fie! 'Tis an unweeded garden
That grows to seed; . . ."
(Hamlet I: ii, photograph from the 1948 film version of the play starring Sir Laurence Olivier)

## DEPRESSION AND SUICIDE

Given the depressed individual's bottomless despair, it is not surprising that suicide is a very real risk. Here is Kay Jamison's description (1995) of an episode of depression:

> Each day I awoke deeply tired, a feeling as foreign to my natural self as being bored or indifferent to life. Those were next. Then a gray, bleak preoccupation with death, dying, decaying, that everything was born but to die, best to die now and save the pain while waiting. (p. 38)

Both those with major depression and those in a depressive phase of bipolar disorder can become suicidal. Some actually attempt suicide, and more than a few succeed. The risk of suicide is greater among those with bipolar disorder than among those with major depression. In fact, up to 20 percent of individuals with bipolar disorder commit suicide. As might be expected, people with bipolar disorder rarely commit suicide during manic episodes (Andreasen & Black, 1996), but surprisingly, suicide risk is also relatively low for those in the depths of depression. At that point, gloom is deepest, but so is inertia, and although the patient may have decided to kill himself, he will have neither the energy nor the tenacity to complete the act. He will be more likely to follow through on his resolution as he begins to recover from depression and emerge from closely supervised care. Times of greatest risk, therefore, include weekend leaves from the hospital and the period immediately after discharge (Beck, 1967).

Women are three times as likely to attempt suicide as men are, but when men make the attempt, they are much more likely to succeed; in fact, four times as many men as women kill themselves. One reason for the difference is in the choice of methods. Women are more likely than men to cut their wrists or swallow a bottle of sleeping pills, whereas men tend to use methods that are irreversible, such as shooting themselves or jumping off a rooftop (Fremouw, Perczel, & Ellis, 1990).

## SEASONAL AFFECTIVE DISORDER

Many people who live in cold climates have experienced the phenomenon of "cabin fever," a lethargy that ensues as the days grow short with precious few hours of sunlight. This phenomenon often reaches serious proportions, with depressions that start in late fall when the days become shorter, and then remit—or even switch to mania—when the days lengthen in March or April. Such *seasonal affective disorders* (or *SADs*) are evidently linked to the amount of sunlight the patients receive (see Figure 16.8). When they travel south in the winter, their depression lifts within a few days; when they travel north, their depression gets worse.

What might account for this effect of light on mood? A strong possibility is that it is connected both with the sleeping-waking cycle and with the pineal gland's secretion of the hormone *melatonin*, both of which are sensitive to daylight. Indeed, there is some evidence that all depression, not just the seasonal variety, may involve a disturbance in sleep rhythms, including an overly quick onset of REM sleep during the night (Nofzinger, Buysse, Reynolds, & Kupfer, 1993; Wehr & Goodwin, 1981). The close link between depression and sleep is underscored by the fact that sleep deprivation is a powerful antidepressant, although it works for only a few days (Riemann et al., 1996).

**16.8** *Seasonal affective disorder and day length* *(A) Percentage of patients with seasonal affective disorder who report being depressed in any given month. (B) Mean minutes of daylight per month. (From Rosenthal et al., 1984)*

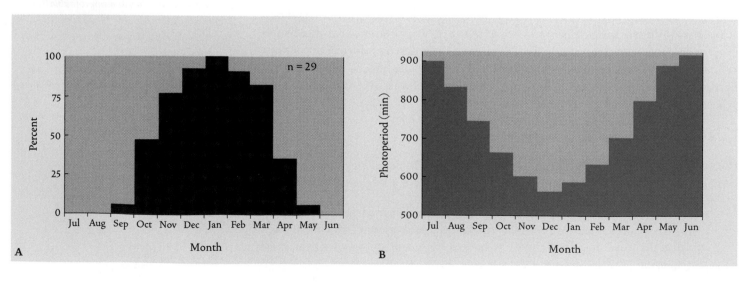

# ORGANIC RISK FACTORS

What produces mood disorders, the extremes of bipolar disorder, major depression, and SADs? Like schizophrenia, depression is thought to result from multiple contributing factors, factors that may be neurochemical, genetic, psychological, and even viral.

## NEUROCHEMICAL MALFUNCTION

The major hypotheses about the physiological disruptions that occur in depression are neurochemical, and they build on the fact that various neurotransmitters seem to be manufactured, released, or used at abnormal levels in the brain of someone suffering from depression. The list of neurotransmitters known to be disrupted in depression is quite long and includes dopamine, norepinephrine and epinephrine, serotonin, GABA, melatonin, and neuropeptide Y (also involved in appetite; see Chapter 3), not to mention neurally active hormones such as glucocorticoids from the adrenal glands, corticotrophin releasing factor (CRF) from the hypothalamus, and immune system chemicals such as interleukin-2 (Leonard, 2001).

How these neurochemical abnormalities lead to depression is not yet known, but one clue comes from the effects of antidepressant medications. These medications are known to increase the activity of three key neurotransmitter systems: norepinephrine, serotonin, and dopamine. Furthermore, drugs that decrease the activity of these systems can produce depression. What goes awry in these neurotransmitter systems? Disruptions appear to occur at many points in neurotransmission: synthesis of the transmitters, release from the axon terminals, the formation of postsynaptic receptors, and the sensitivity of those receptors once they are built. Of the three neurotransmitters, serotonin has received the most attention, spurred by the development of antidepressants that act predominantly on serotonin systems (medications like Prozac and Zoloft; see Chapter 17).

What of bipolar disorder? Many of the same neurotransmitter systems involved in major depression are also disturbed in bipolar disorder, and neuroimaging shows both anatomical and functional changes in the norepinephrine and serotonin systems in the brainstem, in areas responsible for cognitive and behavioral arousal (Baumann & Bogerts, 2001). Other studies indicate deficient activation in areas of the frontal lobes that normally regulate behavior (Bearden, Hoffman, & Cannon, 2001). But in bipolar disorder there is something else to explain. In patients with the disorder, the onset and subsiding of manic and depressive episodes is often quite rapid and seemingly divorced from external circumstances. This suggests the operation of some internal biological switch. The nature of this switch is uncertain. Some investigators believe that it is related to neuronal membranes that do not adequately dampen fluctuations in the levels of certain neurotransmitters (Hirschfeld & Goodwin, 1988; Meltzer, 1986). Others believe that bipolar disorder represents a mitochondrial dysfunction (the mitochondria are involved in cellular energy production), especially given findings that bipolar patients often show abnormalities in mitochondrial DNA (Kato & Kato, 2000).

## GENETIC COMPONENTS

The mood disorders have important hereditary components, reflected in the fact that, overall, concordance rates for mood disorders are some four times higher in identical than in fraternal twins (Andreasen & Black, 1996; Siever, Davis, & Gorman, 1991). Further evidence, specifically for bipolar disorder, comes from detailed genetic studies of extended families with numerous cases of this disorder. In these families, the individuals with bipolar disorder tend also to have a particular enzyme deficiency as well as a type of color blindness. The fact that both of these latter anomalies are due to defective

*Depression and despair    Edward Adamson, a professional artist, founded a studio in a British mental hospital for the use of the institutionalized patients. Many of their works forcefully express these patients' depression and despair, as in the case of this painting entitled* Cri de Coeur *or* Cry from the heart. *(Cri de Coeur, by Martha Smith)*

genes on the X chromosome strongly suggests that the gene(s) causing bipolar disorder may be nearby (Hodgkinson, Mullan, & Gurling, 1990).

Adoption and twin studies also indicate that genetics plays a role in major depression, though probably a less powerful one than in bipolar disorder. Such genetic evidence also indicates that, despite the similarity of their symptoms, the depression that occurs with major depression is quite different from that which occurs as one phase of bipolar disorder. For example, people with one of these disorders tend to have relatives with the one condition but not the other. This suggests that there are separate inheritance pathways for each and makes it likely that they are largely separate disorders (Gershon, Nurnberger, Berrettini, & Golding, 1985; Torgersen, 1986; Wender, Kety, Rosenthal, Schulsinger, & Ortmann, 1986).

## PSYCHOLOGICAL RISK FACTORS

Can the the mechanisms we have described so far fully explain affective disorders? Although it is easy to imagine how neurochemical imbalances might explain changes in a patient's energy level, can they explain why the manic person believes he is Jesus reincarnate, why the psychotically depressed person believes that the Devil is putting worms in his bones? How do changes in neurotransmitter levels lead to beliefs that one is omnipotent and righteous or helpless and morally wretched? The symptoms, in the eyes of many investigators, call for an additional, psychological account. These investigators argue that our psychological states—our beliefs, feelings, attitudes—comprise another important factor that predisposes someone toward depression and shapes the content of the illness when it arises. These investigators also note that many major depressions are often preceded by some stressful event, whether it involves marital or professional difficulties, serious physical illness, or a death in the family (Leff, Roatsch, & Bunney, 1970; Paykel, 1982). We therefore need to ask what the chain of events might be that leads from such bad events to depression?

### BECK'S COGNITIVE THEORY OF DEPRESSION

Many depressed individuals believe that both they and the world are hopeless and wretched. According to the major cognitive view of depression, these beliefs are not derived from the patient's mood. Instead, the beliefs come first and produce the depression. This cognitive view underlies a very influential approach to the understanding and treatment of depression developed by psychiatrist Aaron Beck (1967, 1976). For Beck, depression stems from a set of intensely negative and irrational beliefs that the person holds about herself, her future, and the world around her. The individual believes that she is worthless, that her future is bleak, and that whatever happens around her is sure to turn out for the worst. These beliefs form the core of a *negative cognitive schema* by which the patient interprets whatever happens to her, and leaves her mood nowhere to go but down.

To overcome depression, then, this system of beliefs must be counteracted. For this purpose, Beck developed a psychological treatment called *cognitive therapy* during which the patients confront their defeatist beliefs and replace them with more positive ones (we will discuss this in a later section—see Chapter 17; Beck, 1967; Beck, Rush, Shaw, & Emery, 1979).

The cognitive theory, although prevalent, does not explain several facts about depression. First, most depressions subside by themselves without treatment in three to four months; does the person's way of thinking spontaneously change this fast, when cognitive therapy usually takes much longer? Second, depression is much, much more than mood: it is also insomnia, loss of appetite, memory loss, and broken concentration. Moreover, depressives do not always feel bad; in depressive apathy they may not feel anything at all. Finally, how would the theory account for mixed states, in which the patient is both depressed and manic? In its favor, though, the cognitive theory led to the formulation of a type of psychotherapy that is effective with many depressed individuals, and its causal model may indeed apply to some cases of depression.

## LEARNED HELPLESSNESS AND DEPRESSIVE EXPLANATIONS

Beck's cognitive theory grew out of clinical work with depressed patients. A related cognitive account, proposed by Martin Seligman (1975), began instead with studies of animal learning. We first met this line of research in Chapter 4, and it is a line that has led to the *learned helplessness theory* of depression.

*Learned Helplessness and Depression* As we discussed in Chapter 4, learned helplessness was first observed in dogs. The dogs were placed in a shuttle box containing two compartments and had to learn to jump from one compartment to another in order to escape an electric shock. For one group of dogs, this was the first step in the procedure; these animals learned easily how to escape the shock and, after a bit of practice, how to jump early enough so that they avoided the shock altogether. Things were different, though, for a second group of dogs. Before encountering the shuttle box, they had first been exposed to a series of painful shocks about which they could do absolutely nothing. They were, in other words, objectively helpless in this initial situation, and all they could do was endure the shocks. When this second group was then placed in the shuttle box, their performance was drastically different from that of the dogs in the first group. They did not look for some means of escape. Nor did they ever find the correct response—jumping over the hurdle separating the chambers. Instead, they simply gave up; they lay down, whimpered, and passively accepted their fate. Having once been made helpless, they seemed to have learned that they were generally helpless and so, accordingly, did nothing (Seligman, Maier, & Solomon, 1971).

Seligman argued that this learned helplessness pattern is similar to at least some forms of depression, and indeed depressed humans and helpless animals respond to the same medications: the helplessness disappears, and the animals behave much like normal (nonhelpless) animals (Porsolt, LePichon, & Jalfre, 1977).

One important problem for this conception, though, is that not everyone who has experienced helplessness—not every cancer victim, not every widower—becomes depressed. Some additional factor must be involved, and an additional proposal by Seligman and his colleagues suggests what this factor might be. Perhaps bad events are not by themselves what makes us helpless; in addition, it matters how we think about these events, and how we try to explain them. Do we think that that bad event happened because of something we did, so that, in some direct way, we caused the bad event? Do we believe that similar bad events will arise in other aspects of our life? And do we think that bad events will continue to happen to us, perhaps for the rest of our life? Seligman proposes that much depends on how we answer these questions, and, moreover, suggests that each of us has a consistent style in how we tend to answer such questions—what he and his collaborators call an *explanatory style*. In their view, someone is vulnerable to depression if their explanatory style tends to be internal ("I caused the event, and not some external factor"), global ("This sort of event will also happen in other areas of my life"), and stable ("This is going to keep happening"). With this explanatory style, this person is very likely to end up depressed if something bad happens to them (Abramson, Seligman, & Teasdale, 1978).

There is good evidence that this pessimistic explanatory style is indeed characteristic of depressed persons (as shown by results with the attributional-style questionnaire described in Chapter 15; C. Peterson & Seligman, 1984). These studies, however, invite a crucial question: which of these is the cause and which is the effect? Critics have pointed out that hopelessness, helplessness, and unmitigated self-blame are among the symptoms of the condition we call "depression." To say they are the cause is, in the critics' view, a bit like saying that sneezing and nose blowing cause colds (Coyne & Gotlib, 1983; Lewinsohn, Hoberman, Teri, & Hautzinger, 1985). But in truth the evidence is mixed on the issue. It does appear that the explanatory style predates depression in some instances, with the clear implication that certain habitual ways of interpreting the world are not caused by depression, but instead (as Seligman and his colleagues propose) constitute a factor predisposing an individual toward depression (Alloy, Abramson, & Francis, 1999; C. Peterson & Seligman, 1984; for some contrary evidence, see Lewinsohn et al., 1985).

## SEX DIFFERENCES IN THE PREVALENCE OF MAJOR DEPRESSION

Whatever theories of depression prove correct, one striking fact about major depression needs to be explained. Across most Western cultures, both major depression and bipolar disorder are diagnosed far more often in women than in men (twice as often for major depression and, as we mentioned, in a ratio of three to two for bipolar disorder). These differences persist even after accounting for income and socioeconomic level. What accounts for them? We cannot know for certain, but there are several possibilities. For one, some evidence suggests that some of the susceptibility genes for affective disorders lie on the X chromosome. Women, after all, have two X chromosomes but men have only one; this may double the risk for women. A related explanation is hormonal. Women must endure cyclic hormonal changes, such as significant drops in estrogen and progesterone levels during the premenstrual period, the postpartum period, and menopause, that are themselves associated with depressed moods (Seeman, 1997).

Another hypothesis proposes important differences in how women and men cope with the early stages of depression. In this view, women who are depressed dwell on their despondency, mulling over their problems and discussing them with friends, a process that may backfire and make an initial depression more likely to escalate and last longer. What do men do when they are depressed? They try to distract themselves by fixating on their work or exercising unrelentingly, thus "acting out" their distress rather than manifesting it in depression (Nolen-Hoeksema, 1987).

This escapist strategy is hardly trouble free, because a major way that men act out distress is through alcohol and drug consumption; when depressed, they are much more likely to get drunk or get "high" than get therapy. In fact, men are diagnosed as alcoholic four times as often as women (Andreasen & Black, 1996). Might the male-female difference in depression, then, simply reflect the fact that much male depression is masked by drug and alcohol abuse? Such is the implication of a study of the Old Order Amish of Lancaster County, Pennsylvania. The Amish prohibit illegal drugs and alcohol and openly acknowledge mental disorder, and the rates of major depression among men and women are equal (Egeland & Hostetter, 1983). The same pattern also occurs among Americans of Jewish heritage, who exhibit very low rates of substance abuse (Levav, Kohn, Golding, & Weissman, 1997).

## MOOD DISORDERS AND MULTICAUSALITY

Just as with schizophrenia, the search for a single cause of affective disorders has been abandoned in favor of a multiple-factor causal model. For the affective disorders, the likely contributing factors include a susceptible genotype, psychosocial misfortunes, various neurotransmitter-system anomalies, and a pessimistic explanatory style. More, these factors interact with each other, so that (for example) negative cognitions and learned helplessness may produce neurotransmitter anomalies, and these same anom-

*Sorrow* (Vincent Van Gogh, 1882)

alies may help to perpetuate the negative cognitions. Similarly, the neurochemical changes may affect the expression of certain genes, which will in turn alter the neurochemistry. Fortunately, all this complexity has not prevented the development of ways to treat affective disorders. Many can be treated quickly and effectively, as we discuss in Chapter 17.

*Psychopathology and creativity*

# ANXIETY DISORDERS

In each of the affective disorders, a primary symptom is a profoundly altered mood: the highs of mania, the lows of depression. In the *anxiety disorders*, the main problem is still one of mood, but the primary symptoms include both an intense experience of anxiety, and a series of efforts (sometimes disruptive, and often unsuccessful) to deal with this anxiety. A patient with one of these disorders is chronically apprehensive, fears the worst, and must guard vigilantly against anticipated disasters. Although we all experience anxiety in normal life, we are not usually disabled by it; it is only when there is some serious disability to cope with normal life that the diagnosis of anxiety disorder is warranted.

## PHOBIAS

A relatively common anxiety disorder is *phobia*, which is an intense and irrational fear. Notice the inclusion here of *irrational*. Someone living in the middle of a swamp and constantly worried about snakes is not manifesting a phobia; instead, his fear is perfectly reasonable. However, someone living in a San Francisco apartment and incapacitated by the same fear probably does have a phobia. And it does not help that the person with the phobia probably knows the fear is groundless; for someone with a phobia, this knowledge does not in any way diminish the fear.

### SOCIAL PHOBIA

One example of a general and wide-ranging phobia is *social phobia*, in which the problem is fear of embarrassment or humiliation in front of others (Juster & Heimberg, 1995; Rapaport, Paniccia, & Judd, 1995). People with social phobia will desperately try to avoid situations in which they must expose themselves to public scrutiny. They will avoid public speaking or performing because they think others will think they are stupid; will not eat in restaurants for fear they will choke on their food; and will not go to parties or professional meetings because they may stutter and stammer when trying to make small talk. When forced into situations of this sort, they may try to "fortify" themselves with alcohol or drugs, making substance abuse or dependence a constant risk (Pollack, 2001).

### SPECIFIC PHOBIAS

Unlike the pervasive fear seen in social phobia, the specific phobias concern particular objects or events. During the nineteenth century, some of these irrational fears were catalogued and assigned exotic-sounding Greek or Latin names. Examples are fear of high places (acrophobia), enclosed places (claustrophobia), crowds (ocholophobia), germs (mysophobia), cats (ailurophobia), and even the number 13 (triskaidekophobia)—the list is large.

Some of these phobias seem quirky and curious, but others can be life-changing. An executive must travel to keep her job but has a fear of flying, or a student wants to be a physician but faints at the sight of blood. Such phobias can also expand in scope, coming to exert an enormous effect on every aspect of the sufferer's life. The fear of leopards, say, can grow to become a fear of the locale where the zoo is located, of all cats and things catlike, of all spotted objects, and so on.

Among the specific phobias, one is unique: the blood-injury-injection phobia. What makes it unique is that for all other phobias, facing the phobic stimulus produces panic responses: quick pulse, elevated blood pressure, sweating, and tremor. These are all emergency reactions produced by the sympathetic branch of the autonomic nervous system (Lang, Davis, & Ohman, 2000; and see Chapter 3). For the blood-injury-injection phobia, in contrast, the reaction is produced by the parasympathetic branch. In this *vasovagal reaction*, the pulse slows, blood pressure drops, the muscles go slack, and the person can fall to the ground in a dead faint. As we discuss in Chapter 17, the treatment runs exactly opposite to that for other phobias. For a flying phobia, the treatment involves teaching the phobic person to relax. For a blood-injury-injection phobia, the sufferer must keep up his blood pressure, and so on, and must learn, on cue, to become tense (Hellstrom, Fellenius, & Ost, 1996).

*The Conditioning Account of Specific Phobias*  What is the mechanism that creates and maintains the specific phobias? One notion goes back to John Locke (1690), who believed that such fears were produced by the chance association of ideas, as when a child is told stories about goblins that come by night and is forever after terrified of the dark. Several modern authors express much the same idea in the language of conditioning theory (see Chapter 4). In their view, phobias result from classical conditioning; the conditioned stimulus is the feared object (for example, cats), and the response is the autonomic upheaval (increased heart rate, cold sweats, and so on) characteristic of fear (Wolpe, 1958).

A number of phobias may indeed develop in just this fashion. Examples include fear of dogs after dog bites, fear of heights after falling off a ladder, and fear of cars or driving after a serious automobile accident (Marks, 1969).

*Prepared Learning and Specific Phobias*  The conditioning account of phobias seems plausible, and it seems entirely sensible that a child who was bitten by a dog will become dog phobic for life. Even with this plausibility, though, the conditioning account by itself cannot explain why some phobias seem rare while others seem quite common. For example, automobiles, bathtubs, hammers, and electrical outlets are all rather dangerous and frequently associated with painful accidents. In contrast, rather few people have actually been bitten by a snake or spider. If it is associations with pain or trauma that produce phobias, then we should expect to see many hammer phobias and bathtub phobias, but relatively few snake or spider phobias. But the opposite is the case, and snake and spider phobias are much more common than phobias for these other objects.

A solution to this puzzle, though, is suggested by a more refined version of the conditioning account, often called the *preparedness theory of phobias*. This theory begins with the fact that not all learning proceeds at the same pace; instead, organisms seem "prepared" to learn certain associations (and so learn them quickly), but "unprepared" for other associations (and so learn them more slowly if at all; see Chapter 4). Different species seem prepared for different types of learning, and, in each case, this preparedness is usually understandable in evolutionary terms. How does this apply to phobias? Snakes, spiders, and a small number of other stimuli were relatively common dangers for our primate ancestors; natural selection may therefore have favored animals who were innately predisposed (that is, prepared) to learn to fear these stimuli very quickly, after just one or two experiences with the fearful object (Ohman & Mineka, 2001; Seligman, 1971). On this basis, it is not a problem if painful encounters with these stimuli are rare; this limited experience might still be enough to create and sustain a substantial number

*Specific phobias*  *Phobias about spiders and snakes are very common, even though other objects in our world pose a much greater threat. Falls in bathtubs, for example, are more frequent than snakebites, but this seems not to give rise to bathtub phobias!*

of phobias. And, of course, a few centuries of industrialization has not given natural selection sufficient time to favor those of us prepared to fear more modern hazards; hence painful encounters with these hazards are not enough to produce phobias.

This modification helps, but, even with this refinement, conditioning accounts still cannot explain all the facts about phobias. One difficulty is that specific phobias affect females more than males, and because most originate in childhood, it is hard to argue that girls are exposed more than boys to snakes, spiders, and heights, or even to stories and books about them.

An additional point is the fact that phobias, and phobias of the same type, tend to run in families (Andreasen & Black, 1996). The reason for this is uncertain. Perhaps parents genetically transmit either their phobias or a temperament conducive to developing phobias (Kendler, Myers, Prescott, & Neale, 2001). It may also be that phobias can be transmitted through social learning. For example, observing one's parents shake and sweat and then fortify themselves with alcohol before a flight may lead to a phobia about flying.

## OBSESSIVE-COMPULSIVE DISORDER

In phobias, anxiety is aroused by external objects or situations. In contrast, anxiety in *obsessive-compulsive disorder (OCD)* seems internal in its origins—the sufferer feels invaded by unwanted, unrelenting thoughts or wishes. The most common obsessions concern dirt and contamination, aggression and violence, religion, sex, bodily functions like elimination, and the need for balance and symmetry. For example, an otherwise loving parent may have recurrent thoughts of strangling his children; a salesperson may worry constantly about whether she might have hit someone with her automobile and not noticed it. A seemingly normal businessman may spend hours each night straightening the paintings on his apartment walls; a college student may be unable to concentrate in class because the professor's coffee cup is on one side of the lectern with nothing on the other to "balance" it.

Obsessive thoughts can produce considerable anxiety, and many *compulsions* may be understood as attempts to counteract this anxiety. An obsession with dirt may lead to compulsions like ritualistic cleaning or continual hand washing. An obsession over loss might lead to compulsive counting. In all of these cases, the sufferers know that their behavior is irrational, but they are helpless to stop the thoughts and urges and are all the more tormented by them. Lady Macbeth knew that "what's done cannot be undone," but she kept washing invisible blood off her hands nonetheless.

*Compulsive hand washing in literature*
A scene from the Old Vic's 1956 production of Macbeth with Coral Browne. It shows Lady Macbeth walking in her sleep and scrubbing imaginary blood off her hands, as she relives the night in which she and her husband murdered the king.

Minor and momentary obsessional thoughts and compulsions are commonplace. After all, most people on occasion have checked and rechecked the alarm clock to make certain it is properly set. But in OCD, such thoughts and acts so preoccupy the patient that they become crippling. The patient may check and recheck the stove to be certain it is turned off and as a result may take hours to leave the house for even a simple errand. Someone may wash their hands so often, to ward off germs, that they end up with painful skin problems.

OCD often begins in childhood and afflicts as much as 2 to 3 percent of the population sometime in their lives (March, Leonard, & Swedo, 1995). It is also quite serious: if untreated, most cases worsen over time and are accompanied by recurrent bouts of major depression (Barlow, 1988).

As with many other disorders, there are several factors that predispose an individual to develop OCD. To begin with, there seems to be some genetic basis, as shown by the fact that the concordance rate is higher for identical than for fraternal twins (Black & Noyes, 1990; S. A. Rasmussen, 1993). In fact, different aspects of OCD (for example, cleaning or hoarding compulsions) may have separate inheritance paths (Leckman,

Zhang, Alsobrook, & Pauls, 2001). And as with major depression, the neurological mechanism apparently involves the neurotransmitter serotonin. Medications that increase serotonin activity in certain brain areas reduce the manifestations of OCD, with portions of the basal ganglia and frontal cortex implicated the most (Insel, 1990, 1992; Piccinelli, Pini, Bellantuono, & Wilkinson, 1995; Saxena et al., 1999; Swedo et al., 1992; Winslow and Insel, 1990; Zohar, Insel, Zohar-Kadouch, Hill, & Murphy, 1988). Indeed, an array of evidence suggests that the basal ganglia play a role in instigating many kinds of repetitive behavior, with the frontal lobe acting to regulate and terminate it (Gehring, Himle, & Nisenson, 2000; and see Bradshaw & Sheppard, 2000).

Finally, like the affective disorders and schizophrenia, a pathogen (such as a virus or bacterium) may be involved in some cases of OCD. Here, the pathogen is the common bacterium known as streptococcus (which causes "strep throat"). The link was first proposed after it was discovered in the late 1980s that a high percentage of children who had had rheumatic fever suddenly developed the signs and symptoms of OCD and related disorders, and in those with preexisting OCD, the symptoms worsened. Treating these children with blood filtration and injections of immunoglobulin reduced their symptoms dramatically. The term for this strep-related OCD-spectrum-disorder flareup, *pediatric autoimmune neuropsychiatric disorders associated with streptococcal infections* (abbreviated as *PANDAS*), hints at what the findings show: in these children, the strep infection targeted cells in the basal ganglia, and the body's immunological efforts to kill the bacterium ended up inflaming and destroying many of the basal ganglia cells instead. While PANDAS explains only a small portion of these disorders, it points to the possibility that other pathogen-related processes may be involved in OCD disorders (Leonard & Swedo, 2001; Swedo et al., 1998).

Investigators have also discovered that OCD sufferers are disproportionately likely to suffer from other disorders as well. These disorders, together with OCD, may be manifestations of what is now called the **OCD spectrum**. The existing evidence suggests that many of the **OCD spectrum disorders** share a common inheritance, involvement of the basal ganglia and frontal lobes, and obsessive and compulsive symptoms, and all benefit from treatment with the same kinds of medications and therapies (see Chapter 17). Table 16.1 lists the major OCD spectrum disorders.

## GENERALIZED ANXIETY DISORDER

In a phobia, anxiety is aroused by the phobic stimulus. In obsessive-compulsive disorder, the sufferer is besieged and tormented by intrusive, uncontrollable thoughts and urges, typically focused on anxiety about some particular topic—germs, or loss, for example. In *generalized anxiety disorder (GAD)*, in contrast, the anxiety is not related to anything in particular; instead, it is all-pervasive, or free floating. Still, it can be just as disabling. Patients with this disorder are visibly worried and fretful. They feel inadequate, are oversensitive, cannot concentrate or make decisions, and suffer from insomnia. This state of affairs is generally accompanied by any number of physiological concomitants—rapid heart rate, irregular breathing, excessive sweating, and chronic diarrhea (Rickels & Rynn, 2001).

GAD is probably the most common of the anxiety disorders, occurring in as much as 6 percent of the population in any one year (Weissman, 1985). However, there is uncertainty about its cause. Some have suggested that there may be genetic roots, but the evidence is uncertain. We do know that GAD involves neurochemical abnormalities (for example, in norepinephrine and serotonin systems, and especially in the secretion of the neurotransmitter GABA), but it is unclear whether these abnormalities are the cause of the disorder or one of its effects (Nutt, 2001). For the psychoanalyst, GAD represents the breakdown of ego defenses; for the conditioning theorist, GAD is much like

*The Scream    (Edward Munch, 1893)*

## TABLE 16.1    MAJOR OCD SPECTRUM DISORDERS

| | |
|---|---|
| **"Neurologic" disorders** | |
| Tourette's syndrome | Severe tic disorder with uncontrollable head movements and vocalizations (sniffs, barks, yelps, and sometimes, profanity) |
| Autism | Attention to things, not people; repetitive rocking and hand flapping; echoing others word for word |
| **Disorders of somatic preoccupation** | |
| Anorexia nervosa | Preoccupation with thinness; compulsive starvation, dieting, and exercising |
| Bulimia nervosa | Preoccupation with weight; repeated binging or binge-purge cycles |
| Body dysmorphic disorder | Preoccupation with a body part that the sufferer believes is ugly or deformed (e.g., face, nose, hair), with compulsive checking in the mirror |
| Hypochondriasis | Repeated obsessions about disease with compulsive visits to doctors for diagnosis or reassurance |
| **Impulse control disorders** | |
| Shopping addiction | Compulsive buying |
| Kleptomania | Compulsive stealing |
| Pathological gambling | Compulsive betting, risking ("Next time I'll win!") |
| Paraphilias (sexual compulsions) | Fetishism (need for contact with body part or object—feet, high heels, undergarments—to become aroused), exhibitionism (exposing one's genitals to others), voyeurism ("Peeping Tom"), transvestism (cross-dressing) |
| Trichotillomania | Compulsive hair pulling, resulting in noticeable hair loss |

a phobia, except that the anxiety is conditioned to a very broad range of stimuli so that avoidance is impossible (Wolpe, 1958). Both of these interpretations are difficult to evaluate: the psychoanalytic one because it relies on unobservable processes, and the conditioning one because the supposed stimuli are not easily specified.

## PANIC DISORDER

A related disorder is *panic disorder*. Patients with this disorder do not suffer from the nagging, chronic worries that beset people with generalized anxiety disorder. Instead, their anxiety is intermittent. But when the anxiety strikes, it strikes with a vengeance.

*Panic*    (Hoy by Rufino Tamayo, 1988)

At the heart of panic disorder are **panic attacks**, sudden episodes of terrifying bodily symptoms such as labored breathing, choking, dizziness, tingling in the hands and feet, sweating, trembling, heart palpitations, and chest pain. These bodily sensations are accompanied by feelings of intense apprehension, terror, and a sense of impending doom.

Panic attacks occur in almost all anxiety disorders. The snake-phobia sufferer may have one at the sight of a snake; the patient with obsessive-compulsive disorder may experience one if a compulsion goes unperformed for too long. But the hallmark of panic disorder is that the panic attacks seem to come out of the blue. As a result, the patient often has an intense experience of unreality and fears that he is losing control, is going insane, or is about to die. Panic disorder is diagnosed when there are recurrent unexpected attacks and when either behavioral or psychological troubles follow the attacks. Based on that criterion, it is found in about 2 to 3 percent of women and 1 percent of men (American Psychiatric Association, 1994; Robins et al., 1984).

Panic disorders can be frightening enough, but in addition, sufferers often develop a profound fear of having panic attacks, especially in places such as shopping malls, where they might be embarrassing, or in circumstances that might prove dangerous, such as while driving. As a result, people with the condition can rarely venture outside their designated "safe" places—their houses or even just their bedrooms. A common result is *agoraphobia*, a fear of being alone and outside the home, especially in a public place.

What accounts for panic disorder? Many theorists stress its neurobiological underpinnings and suggest that the main problem is one of autonomic nervous system instability (Andreasen & Black, 1996; Wilhelm, Trabert, & Roth, 2001). Other researchers highlight the role that cognition may play. They believe that panic disorder is produced by a vicious cycle that begins with an overreaction to one's own normal autonomic responses to threat, such as quicker heartbeats and faster and shallower breathing. The person with the panic disorder believes that these reactions indicate an impending heart attack. This makes her fearful, which intensifies the bodily reactions, spiraling upward toward the full-blown attack. This pattern becomes even worse after the patient has her first panic attack, for now every normal anxiety reaction becomes a potential signal of a further panic (D. M. Clark, 1986). In all likelihood, the neurobiological and cognitive aspects of panic disorder interrelate. Thus, the person's tendency to overreact in his interpretation of his bodily reaction may reflect preexisting temperament, and his autonomic overreactivity may be the result of a learned history of catastrophic interpretation.

# REACTIONS TO EXTREME STRESS: ACUTE AND POST-TRAUMATIC STRESS DISORDERS

Human beings sometimes undergo unspeakably traumatic events. For women, the most common such devastation is rape or physical assault; for men, it is military combat. Other calamities can also bring humans to this extreme—being in a serious automobile accident, witnessing a homicide, encountering the carnage following a natural disaster or terrorist attack, and other horrors (Andreasen & Black, 1996; Wolf & Mosnaim, 1990).

The psychological effects of such stress have long been known to medics who treated combat soldiers, and these effects reached wide public attention because of their prevalence among Vietnam War veterans (Figley, 1978). Regardless of what the traumatic event was, the reactions are similar. Immediately after the trauma, there is usually a period of numbness during which the sufferer feels wholly estranged, socially unresponsive, and oddly unaffected by the event, a reaction technically known as ***dissociation***. During this ***acute stress disorder***, there are often recurrent nightmares and waking flashbacks of the traumatic event. These can be so intense and intrusive that the sufferer may momentarily believe that he is back in the situation. Below is a description of the flashbacks experienced by soldiers who served as body handlers:

> ...A dental X-ray technician reported seeing skulls when he saw the teeth of smiling people. A young lieutenant could not enter a local fast food establishment because the smell of burning food elicited a vomiting response.... Soldiers reported seeing bodies when they closed their eyes. Their dream content consisted of nightmarish horror shows where zombie-like bodies were coming to kill the dreamer. One soldier reported seeing himself in a dream where he searched through human body parts and found his own ID tag. (Garrigan, 1987, p. 8)

For many individuals the reactions to such traumas are enduring, and if they persist one month after the stressor, the diagnosis technically becomes one of ***post-traumatic stress disorder (PTSD)***. Gradually, the psychological numbness subsides, but other consequences remain. These can include sleep disturbances, outbursts of anger, difficulties in concentration, and exaggerated responses to being startled. Still another effect may

*Post-traumatic stress disorder* **War-time horrors are a frequent cause of PTSD.**

be "survival guilt" if friends or relatives were harmed or killed by the same traumatic event (M. J. Friedman & Marsella, 1996). The individual with PTSD stays emotionally raw and socially estranged. Drug and alcohol abuse are common among PTSD sufferers, as are bouts of major depression and diminished physical health. If the trauma is severe enough, the manifestations of PTSD may remain for years and even decades, even with the best-available treatments (see Zatzick et al., 1997).

Why do some individuals experience a trauma and develop PTSD, while others endure comparable horrors but seem not to suffer permanent harm? One factor that may predispose to PTSD is genetic, as suggested by twin and family studies. PTSD runs in families: the odds of developing PTSD increase fivefold if a parent has had it (Radant, Tsuang, Peskind, McFall, & Raskind, 2001; True et al., 1993). Studies also suggest that early adverse experiences, such as child abuse or neglect, may predispose an individual to PTSD, which will become an actual PTSD if she is sufficiently stressed as an adult (Bremner, Southwick, Johnson, Yehuda, & Charney, 1993; McCranie, Hyer, Boudewyns, & Woods, 1992; Zaidi & Foy, 1994).

How might early life events create a vulnerability to PTSD? Some investigators believe that early traumatic experience leaves the individual with a distinct weakness in their physiological response to stress. In particular, sufferers of PTSD show abnormally low levels of the substance known as *cortisol*, which is secreted by the adrenal glands during stress. These low cortisol levels may be a marker of both early adversity and later vulnerability (Heim, Owens, Plotsky, & Nemeroff, 1997; Yehuda, 1997).

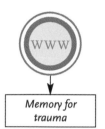

Memory for trauma

# DISSOCIATIVE DISORDERS

Acute and post-traumatic stress disorders show that people can distance themselves psychologically, or dissociate, from ongoing events. They establish this distance by saying things like, "This can't be happening," or "This is all a dream," or "This isn't happening to me." During a calamity we may even experience ourselves as eerily calm, floating outside our bodies as we watch ourselves react.

These adjustments are often adaptive, a way of coping with extraordinary events. But such adjustments can also go too far and thus, in their extreme form, are the defining feature of a number of syndromes now called *dissociative disorders*. An example is *dissociative amnesia*,* in which the individual is suddenly unable to remember some period of his life, or even his entire past, including his own identity. Such episodes usually last less than one week (Andreasen & Black, 1996). In other cases, the dissociation produces *dissociative fugue*, in which the person wanders away from home and then, days or even months thereafter, suddenly realizes that he is in a strange place, does not know how he got there, and has total amnesia for the entire period.

Still more drastic are cases of *dissociative identity disorder* (formerly known as multiple personality disorder). Here the dissociation is so massive that it results in two or more distinct personalities. The "auxiliary" personalities, which can number from just a few to several dozen, seem to be built on a nucleus of memories or fantasies. An example is a shy and inhibited person who has had fantasies of being carefree and outgoing from childhood on. These fantasies eventually take on the characteristics of a separate

---

* These amnesias are distinct from the pattern sometimes alleged for "repressed" memories. Dissociative amnesias typically lift within a few days, unlike the decades-long memory loss claimed for repressed memory. Dissociative amnesias also tend to involve the loss of an entire period in the person's life, unlike repressed memory, which is generally understood as removing only some (painful) elements from the remembered time, leaving most other memories untouched.

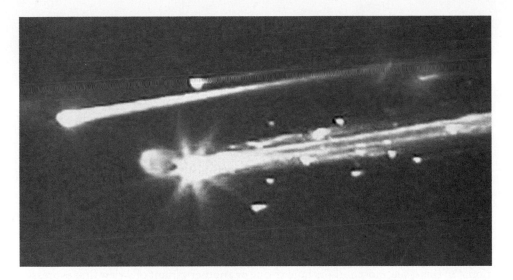

*Dealing with disaster* **Many people responded to the space shuttle** Columbia **disaster with remarks like: "I can't believe this is real. It's like something out of a horrible movie." Such comments can be viewed as an attempt to distance the speaker from the disaster—a coping strategy known as dissociation.**

self. Once formed, the new self may appear quite suddenly, as in the famous case of Eve White, loosely depicted in the movie *The Three Faces of Eve*:

> After a tense moment of silence, her hands dropped. There was a quick, reckless smile and, in a bright voice that sparkled, she said, "Hi there, Doc.".... There was in the new-comer a childishly daredevil air, an erotically mischievous glance, a face marvelously free from the habitual signs of care, seriousness, and underlying distress, so long familiar in her predecessor. This new and apparently carefree girl spoke casually of Eve White and her problems, always using she or her in every reference, always respecting the strict bounds of a separate identity. When asked her own name she immediately replied, "Oh, I'm Eve Black." (Thigpen & Cleckley, 1957, as described in Coleman, 1972, p. 246)

Some twenty years later, Eve White wrote an autobiography in which she described herself more fully. It turned out that at one time in her life she had as many as twenty-two subpersonalities rather than just three (Sizemore & Huber, 1988). The various personalities seen in such cases are not confined to differences in mood and attitudes. Sometimes the individual segregates different skills to different personalities, such that one plays the piano, another cooks, and yet a third speaks French. The personalities can know of each other, be completely oblivious to each other, or exhibit any other pattern of acquaintanceship.

Until twenty years ago, dissociative identity disorder was considered very rare, with fewer than two hundred cases reported before 1975. Now cases number in the thousands; the large majority are females (Kluft, 1987). The rash of reported cases began with the publication of *Sybil*, a popular book about one case of dissociative identity disorder, subsequently made into a television movie (Schreiber, 1973).

This disorder has always been controversial. The diagnosis may well suit some patients (Gleaves, 1996), but critics argue that the flood of diagnoses reflects a fad among therapists who inadvertently lead their suggestible and therefore fad-prone patients—many of whom know the many books and movies on the subject—to develop the signs and symptoms of dissociative identity disorder (Lalonde, Hudson, Gigante, & Pope, 2001; Spanos, 1994). Even the diagnosis of "Sybil" herself has been called into question by an expert therapist who examined her (Borch-Jacobsen, 1997). The controversy extends to the legal realm, now that defendants in some celebrated criminal cases have claimed that "I didn't do it, my other personality did" (Slovenko, 1995).

As yet, it is unclear whether dissociative identity disorder is a "real" phenomenon, one that will outlive its popularity in the media and survive scrutiny among investigators of psychopathology. (For further discussion of this heated issue, see Lilienfeld et al., 1999.)

# PSYCHOLOGICAL FACTORS UNDERLYING DISSOCIATIVE DISORDERS

The mechanisms that underlie the dissociative disorders are still obscure. Some authors suggest that phenomena like the development of auxiliary personalities may represent an attempt to gain attention by using an unusual form of self-dramatization (Sarbin & Allen, 1968; Ziegler, Imboden, & Rodgers, 1963). Others try to understand dissociation in the context of human information processing and stress its similarity to phenomena like encoding specificity and implicit memory (Kihlstrom, 1992; see Chapter 7). In cases of encoding specificity, for example, knowledge acquired in one context may not be recalled if the context changes. Likewise, implicit memories can influence behavior even without any conscious recollection of the relevant events. Both parallel some of the phenomena of dissociation.

There is less debate, however, about the psychological function played by dissociation. On this issue, most authors hold to one or another variant of a view first expressed by Freud. He believed that dissociation was a defense against something too psychologically painful to confront. Dissociation does create a sense of distance from a catastrophe, thus providing a means of diminishing an otherwise intolerable experience and of keeping it from poisoning other aspects of one's life. Sometimes dissociation has tragic consequences, though, as when mothers kill their newborns on the day of birth. In most of these cases, such "neonaticide" occurs with a mother who is dissociating and even denying her own pregnancy (Spinelli, 2001).

# RISK FACTORS FOR DISSOCIATIVE DISORDERS

Not every person who reacts to a catastrophe develops a dissociative disorder. What determines who does? Some investigators have sought a genetic basis, but research has yielded mixed results (Jang, Paris, Zweig-Frank, & Livesly, 1998; Waller & Ross, 1997). Perhaps the best clue is that, apart from traumatic circumstances, people naturally seem to differ in how much they dissociate and in the intensity of the circumstances required to make them do so. Much of the relevant evidence comes from work on hypnosis, which some investigators regard as a form of guided dissociation (Hilgard, 1986). If this is so, one might suspect that people with dissociative disorders should be more hypnotizable than others, which indeed turns out to be the case (Ganaway, 1989). This seems to be especially so for patients with dissociative identity disorder. According to one investigator, such patients were unusually adept at self-hypnosis during childhood and created their new personality (and often more than just one) during a self-induced hypnotic trance. Presumably, this allowed these children a form of escape from threatening traumatic events (Bliss, 1980).

Thus, a preexisting readiness to dissociate in everyday life may predispose individuals toward dissociative disorder. To precipitate a full-fledged disorder, however, there also has to be some unusual stress. In fact, most cases of dissociative amnesia occur after the same kinds of cataclysmic events that may lead to post-traumatic stress disorder. The same holds for dissociative fugues, which can also develop suddenly after personal misfortunes or financial pressures (Andreasen & Black, 1996).

There is reason to believe that the most serious and disabling of the dissociative conditions, dissociative identity disorder, results from the most harrowing stresses in early life. In a large percentage of the case histories, there are terrifying stories of repeated brutal physical and sexual abuse in childhood, often including incest (Putnam, Guroff, Silberman, Barban, & Post, 1986). These findings have led many psychotherapists to believe that child abuse, and especially sexual abuse, is a likely antecedent of dissociative identity disorder.

Others urge caution in accepting this interpretation. Although one report does show a higher incidence of verified early child abuse (Coons, 1994), nearly all the remaining studies are based on the patients' uncorroborated memories of early childhood, and it is unclear how much faith we can place in these reports (Frankel, 1993; see also Chapter 7 for a broader discussion of why we cannot assume the veracity of these, or any, memories). In addition, individuals who are likely to dissociate also may be more prone to developing false memories (Hyman & Billings, 1998; Porter, Birt, Yuille, & Lehman, 2000). Hence, if dissociative symptoms and memories of childhood abuse go together, this may indicate that the incidents of abuse lead to dissociation, or the cause-effect relationship may be the reverse: dissociation may predispose toward memories of childhood abuse. Because of ambiguities like these, conclusions about early child abuse and dissociative identity disorder cannot yet be drawn with confidence.

# SOMATOFORM DISORDERS

Finally, we turn to a set of disorders of a rather different type, disorders in which the predominant symptoms are not mental or emotional, but bodily. These are the *somatoform disorders*.

Some people experience anxiety directly and others dissociate from it. It appears that still others turn it into bodily complaints. At least this is the most common interpretation of the somatoform disorders (disorders that take bodily form). There are several kinds of such disorders, but in each the patient exhibits or describes concerns about his bodily functions in the absence of any known physical illness. The best known of the somatoform disorders is *hypochondriasis*, in which the sufferer believes she has a specific disease and goes to doctor after doctor to be evaluated for it. Somewhat similar is the person with *somatization disorder*. She brings to the doctor a host of miscellaneous aches and pains in various bodily systems that do not add up to any known syndrome in physical medicine. And then there is *somatoform pain disorder*, in which the sufferer describes chronic pain for which no sufficient physical basis can be found.

The most dramatic of the somatoform disorders is *conversion disorder*.* This disorder, which we mentioned early in the chapter, represented the first and most dramatic argument for psychological contributors to mental disorders and was also the foundation on which psychoanalytic theory was built. According to Freud, people with these disorders resolve some intolerable conflict by developing a hysterical ailment, such as being unable to see or hear or move an arm, even though there seems to be nothing organically wrong (see Chapter 15). The soldier who is terrified of going into battle, for example, may become hysterically paralyzed. This allows him to yield to his impulse of refusing to march. But it also lets him do so without guilt or shame—he is not marching because he cannot march.

A century ago, such cases were fairly common, but today they account for a much smaller fraction of mental disorders. One historian has suggested that disorders such as chronic fatigue syndrome and somatoform pain disorder have become the conversion hysterias of the late twentieth century (Shorter, 1992), serving the same function but in a more plausible fashion, given our current understanding of medicine. So maybe what neurologists term "nonepileptic seizures," those that occur in the absence of

* The term *conversion* was coined by Freud, who believed that the repressed energies that fueled the patient's unconscious conflict were converted into a somatic symptom much as a steam engine converts thermal energy into mechanical energy. Until recently, this condition was called *conversion hysteria*. The authors of *DSM-III* dropped the term *hysteria* because of its erroneous implication that conversion disorders were found only in women. (*Hysteria* is derived from the Greek *hystera*, for "womb").

the abnormal brain waves that are usually diagnostic of genuine epilepsy. Conversion disorder is the most common explanation for these otherwise puzzling "seizures" (Alper, Devinsky, Perrine, Vazquez, & Luciano, 1995; Bowman & Markand, 1996).

A final problem is inherent in the diagnosis of conversion disorder itself, because it must necessarily be a diagnosis by exclusion. Before conversion can be diagnosed, all conceivable physical conditions must be ruled out. In this regard, diagnoses of conversion disorder may be declining owing to medical advances in identifying subtler illnesses that might otherwise have been diagnosed as conversion disorders. Support for this notion comes from follow-up studies of patients whose symptoms were diagnosed as conversions. A fair proportion of these patients were later found to have had organic disorders after all, many of which involved neurological damage (Slater & Glithero, 1965; Watson & Buranen, 1979). And in today's litigious medical malpractice climate, a physician diagnoses conversion disorder at her own risk.

# MENTAL DISORDER AND SOCIAL DEVIANCE

All the disorders we have considered are clearly "disorders." Something goes wrong and a person is no longer capable of living as happily and efficiently as before. The task, somehow, is to bring the person back to normal life.

But not all the diagnostic categories within the *DSM-IV* fit this framework so tidily. Some disorders are diagnosed based not only on the suffering of the person with the disorder, but also on the suffering that person causes others. Examples here include heroin abuse, exhibitionism, and kleptomania (compulsive stealing).

These "disorders" fall into a gray area that is sometimes considered "pathology" and treated by the mental health system, and sometimes labeled "criminal" and considered the bailiwick of the judicial system. In actual fact, these classifications surely do overlap. Some people can, of course, be classified unambiguously: you and I (definitely "normal," or so we hope), a professional criminal ("bad"), and someone with a severe case of schizophrenia ("ill"). But many other people seem arguably to be both ill and criminals. The clearest case is someone who is the sort of remorseless, amoral lawbreaker known as a psychopath, or (as they are described in *DSM-IV*) someone with *antisocial personality disorder*.

## THE PSYCHOPATH

The clinical picture of the psychopath is of an individual who gets into continual trouble with others and with society. He is grossly selfish, callous, impulsive, and irresponsible. His—or, somewhat less frequently, her—difficulties generally start with truancy from school, runaway episodes, and a wild adolescence marked by belligerence and precocious sexual promiscuity (L. R. Robins, 1966). There may also be blatant infractions like fire setting and cruelty to animals. Later on there are various minor scrapes with the law, and these often escalate into increasingly serious legal offenses.

But the distinguishing characteristics of psychopaths run deeper, because they lack any genuine feeling of love or loyalty for any person or any group. They also exhibit relatively little guilt or anxiety. As a result, psychopaths are creatures of the present who act to gratify only the impulses they feel now, with little concern for the future and even less remorse about the past.

Psychopaths tend to be genuine loners. But they are often quite adept at the machinations and strategies of personal interaction, manifesting a superficial charm and a greater-than-average intelligence. In this regard, psychopaths are quite different from ordinary criminals and delinquents. Those individuals also violate society's laws and norms, but unlike psychopaths, they generally have a society of their own, such as a juvenile gang or a crime syndicate, whose code they try to honor and to which they have some sense of loyalty. The psychopath, on the other hand, abides by no code of conduct and readily yields to the desire of the moment (McCord & McCord, 1964). An illustration is the case of a forty-four-year-old man:

> [Roger] was reared in a well-to-do family, the only child of a doting mother. In the past ten years, Roger squandered a substantial inheritance and was beginning to "fall on hard times." Handsome, well-educated and suave in manner, he had always been skillful in charming and exploiting others, especially women. Faced with economic adversity, Roger allied himself with a group of stock promoters involved in selling essentially worthless shares of "sure-bet" Canadian mining stock. This led to other "shady deals"; and in time Roger became a full-fledged "love swindler" who intrigued, lived off, and "borrowed" thousands of dollars from a succession of wealthy and "lonely" mistresses. (Millon, 1969, p. 434)

Psychopaths are particularly susceptible to other maladies. Up to one-fourth develop major depressions, and nearly 75 percent are alcoholics or drug abusers. Psychopathy is a lifelong condition, and although the psychopath's crimes and legal entanglements lessen as she ages, her unstable lifestyle, spotty work behavior, and tendency to alcohol and drug abuse persist. About 5 percent of psychopaths commit suicide (Andreasen & Black, 1996).

## SOME POSSIBLE CAUSES OF PSYCHOPATHY

What accounts for antisocial personality disorder? A central feature may be the psychopath's lack of concern for the consequences of his actions. Psychopaths are comparatively fearless, especially when the danger is far off. One investigator told psychopaths and normals that they would receive a shock at the end of a ten-minute period, and the participants' apprehensiveness was assessed by their galvanic skin response (GSR). As the time grew closer, the control participants grew increasingly nervous. In contrast, the psychopaths showed little anticipatory fear (Lippert & Senter, 1966). If impending pain had just as little import when the psychopath was young, his inadequate socialization becomes partially comprehensible. Whoever tried to teach him the don'ts of childhood found that no deterrents had lasting value (Figure 16.9).

The disquieting fearlessness of psychopaths has been observed by several writers who have noted their "extraordinary poise," their "smooth sense of physical being," and their "relative serenity" under conditions that would produce agitation in most of us (Cleckley, 1976). How does this difference between psychopaths and normals come about? Several investigators believe that psychopaths are different physiologically. One line of evidence concerns the EEG (electrical recordings from the brain; see Chapter 3). It appears that a fairly high proportion of psychopaths have abnormal EEGs, with patterns that resemble those of children. One possible interpretation is that this cortical immaturity of psychopaths is the physiological counterpart of their behavioral and psychological childishness—their desire for instant gratification and their belligerent tantrums when thwarted.

A different hypothesis is that psychopaths are cortically underaroused, as if they were not fully awake under normal conditions. Proponents of this hypothesis argue that because of this underarousal, psychopaths actively seek stimulation—they are easily bored and court thrills and danger to rouse themselves to some optimal level of stimulation, much like the rest of us might pinch or shake ourselves to keep from dozing off

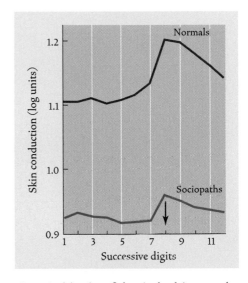

16.9 *Anticipation of electric shock in normals and sociopaths* **Normals and sociopaths were repeatedly presented with a series of twelve consecutive digits from 1 to 12. Whenever the digit 8 appeared, the subjects suffered an electric shock. To determine whether there were any differences in anticipatory anxiety prior to the advent of shock, the galvanic skin response (GSR) was measured. The results are shown in units of log conductance (a measure of GSR activity) for each of the 12 digits in the series. The sociopaths showed a much lower base-response level. In addition, they showed less anticipatory reaction to the digits just prior to the critical digit. (After Hare, 1965)**

(Hare, 1978; H.C. Quay, 1965; for a somewhat different biological view of psychopaths, see Bernstein, Newman, Wallace, & Luh, 2000).*

Both the EEG data and evidence concerning arousal indicate a biological condition underlying psychopathy, and this in turn raises the possibility of a constitutional predisposition toward this disorder. This predisposition may well be genetic, as shown by the fact that identical twins have higher concordance rates for psychopathy than fraternal twins (Slutske, 2001; Taylor, Iacono, & McGue, 2000). Early environment also plays a role. There is considerable evidence that psychopaths are more likely to have a psychopathic or alcoholic father than are normals. An additional factor is discipline; inconsistent discipline in childhood or no discipline at all correlates with psychopathy in adulthood (L. R. Robins, 1966). Indeed, one theory of psychopathy holds that the primary cause is incompetent parenting leading to poor socialization (Lykken, 1995).

## PSYCHOPATHY AND THE DISORDER CONCEPT

We now have some understanding of how psychopathy might arise. But does that justify our calling it a mental disorder? Psychopaths often come to grief, admittedly, but when they do, it is for the same mundane reason as ordinary criminals do: they get caught. Why should we call the psychopath ill and the criminal bad? Why should one be the province of the mental health system while the other is the business of the courts? It is often difficult to distinguish psychopathic criminals from ordinary ones, making it equally difficult to determine who should go to prison and who should go for treatment. Furthermore, most mental health practitioners are pessimistic about the possibility of therapy for psychopaths, making moot any treatment alternative to prison.

A more insidious problem is that not all psychopathic individuals are "disabled" or obviously disordered. Some—especially the very intelligent ones—may be charismatic and become successful politicians, businesspeople, and religious leaders (see Hare, 1993; Lykken, 1995). Under the circumstances, it is not obvious what is gained by classifying psychopathy as a mental disorder.

# THE SCOPE OF PSYCHOPATHOLOGY

Psychopathy is only one of the questionable categories in the psychiatric catalogue. Similar questions can be raised about drug addiction or alcoholism or a number of other deviant or counterproductive patterns of behavior. Are these really mental disorders in the same sense as schizophrenia or obsessive-compulsive disorder? The term *mental disorder* becomes unwieldy when it can be stretched to suit virtually any form of human behavior that causes social harm or personal unhappiness. For example, does the upset caused by losing a spouse merit a clinical diagnosis? How about losing a job? Or the lottery?

Some believe that modern psychopathology is guilty of a sort of imperialism in which it tries to subsume ever more conditions. If this complaint is warranted, this is not solely the fault of an ambitious mental health establishment. Instead, it arises within a society that insists on quick and simple labels, ready diagnoses, and with them, simple solutions. We seem to believe that by designating a problem a mental disorder, we have somehow taken a stride toward its solution. But we have really done nothing of the sort. Calling a problem—alcoholism, sexual exhibitionism, drug addiction, or even

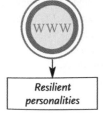

Resilient
personalities

---

* This suggests a relation to sensation seeking, which shows a similar pattern (see Chapter 15).

shoplifting or premenstrual syndrome—a mental disorder does not necessarily make it so. Nor does it mean that we therefore know what to do about it.

Moreover, making the term *mental disorder* too inclusive can have awful consequences. It can effectively make immorality synonymous with illness, with the upshot that some people are referred to treatment when they should be in prison (and vice versa). It can also be harmful to the "innocent," because a diagnosis can be used not only to label and treat, but to brand and ostracize.

# SOME FINAL THOUGHTS: PSYCHOPATHOLOGY AND PHYSICAL MEDICINE

We have now examined many different mental disorders. As we have seen, mental illness is diagnosed using not one sign or symptom but rather a pattern of indications that can include problems in action, motivation, perception, and judgment.

We wish that we could present some kind of simplifying framework for the range of mental disorders. The old "neurotic-psychotic-organic" distinction was such a framework, but it broke down under the weight of findings that these supercategories were not homogeneous, only grab bags of different disorders that defied such large-scale consolidation. In this sense, the science of psychopathology has become more like the practice of physical medicine. Physicians treat broken legs and cancer, backaches and constipation, diaper rash and dandruff, as well as a thousand other ailments, and no one would seriously propose that these be brought together into some kind of unified diagnostic system. From our current vantage point, the mental disorders may be just as heterogeneous.

It also appears that none of the disorders has a simple cause. The old pathology model that assumed a single underlying cause has given way to a multicausal model that presupposes and finds many risk factors—genetics, prenatal environment, neurobiology, socialization, even pathogens—conspiring to produce mental disorders. The evidence is incomplete on how, and how much, each aspect applies to each disorder, and the disorders probably differ considerably in their pattern of causality.

Evidence is also lacking on what interplay of these various influences produces the different disorders. For example, what leads one person under stress to become depressed, another to develop generalized anxiety, and still another to develop an acute stress disorder?

All told, the current status of psychopathology resembles the stage of physical medicine in which diseases were diagnosed by signs such as the pattern of a fever, or the appearance of a rash. In today's physical medicine, criteria like these—requiring some element of judgment—are useful, but are often supplemented with (or replaced by) much more precise and objective laboratory tests. Mental disorders, in contrast, are rarely diagnosed by lab test or biopsy, and so the element of judgment remains in clinical diagnosis. This makes it all the more impressive that we have achieved an excellent degree of diagnostic reliability and consistency, and, more important, that we have treatments for many mental disorders that offer genuine relief and a chance for a normal life. It is to these treatments that we turn next.

# SUMMARY

The field of *psychopathology*, which is sometimes called *abnormal psychology*, deals with a wide assortment of disorders that generally cause considerable anguish and seriously impair the person's functioning.

## DIFFERENT CONCEPTIONS OF MENTAL DISORDER

1. In certain periods of history, mental disorder was seen as a form of demonic possession. More recently, it is regarded as a form of illness. Some of these disorders have traditionally been regarded as *somatogenic*, being the result of a bodily malfunction. An example is *general paresis*, which was discovered to result from a syphilitic infection contracted years before. Other mental disorders are often considered to be *psychogenic*, resulting from psychological rather than organic causes, a view which seemed to apply to many cases once called *hysteria* (now called *conversion disorder*).

## THE MODERN CONCEPTION OF MENTAL DISORDER

2. A very general conception of psychopathology is the *pathology model*, which makes it analogous to physical disorders. A given disorder has various *signs* and *symptoms* that form a pattern or *syndrome*; these, plus the course of the illness, are the bases for diagnosis and classification. The classification system now in use is set out in *DSM-IV*, the current diagnostic manual of psychiatry. In this manual, a greater stress is placed on the description of the disorders rather than on theories about their origin.

3. One approach to mental disorders relies on *single-pathology models*. These include the *biomedical model*, which emphasizes biological malfunctions, the *psychodynamic model*, which regards mental disorders as the result of intra-personal or inter-personal conflicts, and the *learning model*, which considers these disorders as the results of maladaptive learning. More recently, investigators have turned to *multicausal models*, which regard the disorder as the result of an accumulation of factors rather than produced by just one underlying problem.

## SCHIZOPHRENIA

4. Probably the most serious condition in psychopathology is *schizophrenia*. Its main symptoms are disorders of thought and attention, social withdrawal, disruption of emotional responses, and in many cases, the construction of a private world accompanied by *delusions* and *hallucinations*. Subcategories of schizophrenia used in current classification include the *paranoid*, *catatonic*, and *disorganized* subtypes.

5. One question about the pathology of schizophrenia is how best to characterize the schizophrenic's underlying psychological malfunction. Many authors believe that it is fundamentally a disorder of thought, based on an inability to retain the context of one's thoughts and actions. This conception fits some patients but not all.

6. The search for the biological basis of schizophrenia has focused on two possible kinds of pathology. One involves a malfunctioning of neurotransmitters, specifically an oversensitivity to *dopamine*. Evidence comes from the therapeutic effect of *antipsychotic medications*, which are known to block dopamine at neuron synapses. Another organic pathology involves an atrophy of brain tissue found in some schizophrenics. According to the *two-syndrome hypothesis*, schizophrenia is really a composite of two underlying pathologies. According to this hypothesis, one type of shizophrenia is caused by a neurotransmitter malfunction and produces so-called *positive symptoms,* such as delusions and hallucinations. A second type is caused by cerebral atrophy and leads to so-called *negative symptoms,* such as withdrawal and apathy. Support for this view comes from the fact that patients with mostly positive symptoms respond well to standard antipsychotic medications and show little cerebral damage, while patients with mostly negative symptoms are not improved by standard antipsychotics and are more likely to show brain damage.

7. More distal causes of schizophrenia include a genetic factor. The evidence is provided by *concordance* studies of identical and fraternal twins and by studies of children of schizophrenic mothers adopted shortly after birth. But this genetic factor is only a predisposition; its conversion into the actual schizophrenic disorder depends on some precipitating environmental stress. Some investigators believe that the critical environmental factors include socioeconomic class and pathological interactions within the family; however, concerns have been raised about both of these claims. The most influential current model of schizophrenia considers it a *neurodevelopmental disorder*, in which a genetic predisposition produces abnormal fetal brain development, which leaves the individual vulnerable to later stress.

## MOOD DISORDERS

0. In another group of conditions, the *mood disorders*, the dominant disturbance is one of mood, as in the frenzied energy of *mania* or the despair and lethargy of *depression*. One form of mood disorder is *bipolar disorder*, with recurrent swings from one emotional extreme to the other. Another is *major depression*, in which the mood extreme is generally depression. Still another is *seasonal affective disorder*, which seems to be related to the amount of light patients are exposed to, with depressions that start in the fall and end in the spring.

9. According to one view, mood disorders, especially bipolar disorder, are produced by an organic pathology, a belief bolstered by evidence that such conditions have a genetic component. Bipolar disorder may arise from instabilities of neuronal membranes. For major depression, one hypothesis proposes a defect in the supply of certain neurotransmitters, in particular, *norepinephrine* and *serotonin*. Other investigators stress the role of psychogenic factors, such as cognitive outlook. An influential example of such a psychogenic view is the *learned helplessness theory of depression*. Some of its more recent extensions stress the role of *explanatory style* and of *hopelessness*.

10. One striking fact about major depression and bipolar disorder among Western countries is that it seems to occur much more often in women than in men. Some investigators suggest that this is because some of the susceptibility genes for affective disorders lie on the X chromosome (of which women have two, thus incurring twice the risk). Others believe that women try to cope with the early stages of depression by dwelling on their problems while men are more likely to "act out" their distress.

## ANXIETY DISORDERS

11. In another group of conditions, *anxiety disorders*, both the main symptoms and the underlying pathology are primarily psychological. One such disorder is *phobia*, in which there is an intense and irrational fear of some object or situation. According to the *preparedness theory*, these phobias are based on built-in predispositions to fear certain stimuli that were dangerous to our primate ancestors. Other phobias are more pervasive, such as *social phobia*, a general fear of humiliation and avoidance of relevant situations. In *generalized anxiety disorder* (GAD), the anxiety is all-pervasive and free floating. In *panic disorder*, there are sudden, vehement anxiety attacks that strike out of the blue.

12. Another anxiety disorder is *obsessive-compulsive disorder* (OCD), in which anxiety is produced by internal wishes or events, such as *obsessions* that cannot be stopped. This is typically accompanied by *compulsions*, which are attempts to counteract the anxiety. As so often in psychopathology, the disorder has multiple causes. Some are organic, including a genetic predisposition or a viral or bacterial involvement. In addition, OCD patients are more likely to suffer other disorders as well. These, together with OCD, may be manifestations of the *OCD spectrum*.

## REACTIONS TO EXTREME STRESS: ACUTE AND POST-TRAUMATIC STRESS DISORDERS

13. Some disorders are the result of especially stressful events such as fires, war experiences, and rape. For many people the reactions to such events are enduring, and if they persist, it will be diagnosed as *post-traumatic stress disorder* (PTSD), whose symptoms include sleep disturbances, exaggerated startled responses, and sometimes "survival guilt."

## DISSOCIATIVE DISORDERS

14. In another group of disorders, the primary characteristic is *dissociation*. One example of a *dissociative disorder* is *dissociative amnesia*, in which an individual is unable to remember some period of his life, sometimes including his entire past. An extreme form of a dissociative disorder is *dissociative identity disorder*, whose existence has been questioned by some practitioners. According to some investigators, a possible precursor of this is childhood abuse, but this interpretation is controversial.

## SOMATOFORM DISORDERS

15. Another group of disorders are the *somatoform disorders*, characterized by the presence of bodily signs and symptoms that have no apparent organic basis. The somatoform disorders include the classic but now-rare disorder that inspired psychoanalysis, *conversion disorder*.

## MENTAL DISORDER AND SOCIAL DEVIANCE

16. In some conditions such as *antisocial personality disorder* (or *sociopathy*) deviance overlaps mental disorder and criminality. The causes of the disorder are still unknown; hypotheses include cortical immaturity, a chronic state of underarousal that leads to attempts to seek continued stimulation, and a genetic predisposition.

# TREATMENT OF PSYCHOPATHOLOGY

*I*n the previous chapter, we catalogued a variety of illnesses, each of which causes considerable misery both for the person who has the illness and for those around her. In addition, each of these illnesses can cause substantial disruption in people's lives, making it difficult for them to hold a job, sustain social relationships, or, in some cases, even manage the minimal requirements of day-to-day living. All of this makes it imperative to ask what can be done to help those who suffer from mental disorders. There is no scarcity of therapeutic methods, and each has its own adherents. Some practitioners rely on biological interventions such as medications. Others approach the condition psychologically, through various kinds of psychotherapy. For many years, the proven benefits of either kind of treatment were relatively modest, but the outlook is now much more optimistic. There are still no miracle cures, but at least some disorders respond well to the appropriate treatments. In this chapter, we will examine the options available for therapy, and also the evidence suggesting that therapy can, in many cases, be genuinely helpful.

# BIOLOGICAL THERAPIES

One approach to treatment is to regard mental disorders as just another kind of disease, which means treating them using the standard tools of the physician's trade: the administration of medication, and sometimes surgery or other medical interventions.

Initially, these attempts were only marginally successful, and the would-be cures were often far worse than the disease. We already mentioned a very early example in Chapter 16: trephining, the removal of pieces of skull bone, a prehistoric practice that persisted into the twentieth century. Other early procedures involved a relentless succession of bloodlettings and purgatives, all intended somehow to restore harmony among the bodily humors. Later developments were hardly milder. For example, Benjamin Rush (1745–1813), one of the signers of the Declaration of Independence and the acknowledged father of American psychiatry, submersed patients in hot or cold water until they were just short of drowning, or twirled them on special devices at speeds that rendered them unconscious (Figure 17.1). Such methods were said to reestablish balance between bodily and mental functions. They almost certainly had no such salutary effects, although they were probably welcomed by hospital attendants, since such methods undoubtedly terrified the inmates and thus helped to "keep order" (Mora, 1975).

## PHARMACOTHERAPIES

The bleak outlook for such biological therapies did not brighten until the turn of the twentieth century. The first step was the conquest of the progressive disabling syndrome of general paresis, accomplished by attacking the syphilitic infection that caused it (see Chapter 16). But the major advances have come only during the last fifty years or so with the development of a number of *psychotropic drugs*, medications that seem to control, or at least moderate, the manifestations of mental disorder. These medications have had an enormous impact on mental health care and have allowed patients with many disorders to be treated successfully, and often without hospitalization (Olfson & Klerman, 1993).

**17.1** *Early methods for treating mental disorder*   *(A) A crib for violent patients. (B) A centrifugal-force bed. (C) A swinging device.*

A

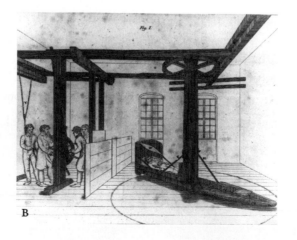

B

C

# DRUG TREATMENT OF SCHIZOPHRENIA: ANTIPSYCHOTICS

The development of psychotropic drugs has gone hand in hand with advances in our understanding of the causes of mental illness. As we have learned more about causes, this has often pointed the way toward new drug treatments, and new drug treatments have often allowed us to test claims about what the causes might be. For example, we saw in the last chapter that a major argument for a neurochemical abnormality in schizophrenia was the effectiveness of certain drugs called antipsychotics. The classical antipsychotics reduce the major positive symptoms of schizophrenia (such as thought disorder and hallucination—see Chapter 16) apparently by blocking dopamine receptors in certain key brain pathways. The most common classical antipsychotics include Thorazine, Haldol, and Stelazine (here we cite only the drugs' trade names; their technical names, drug type, and other common members of each drug class are shown in Table 17.1). Unfortunately, though, these drugs are ineffective in patients with negative symptoms (see Chapter 16).

This shortcoming was remedied by a newer set of medications, the atypical antipsychotics such as Clozaril, Risperdal, Zyprexa, and Seroquel. These medications have revolutionized the treatment of schizophrenia, because not only do they reduce the major positive symptoms (such as delusions and hallucinations), but they reduce the major

**TABLE 17.1    SOME COMMONLY USED PSYCHOTROPIC MEDICATIONS**

| PRIMARY FUNCTION | DRUG CLASS | CHEMICAL NAME | TRADE (COMMERCIAL) NAME |
|---|---|---|---|
| Antidepressants | MAO inhibitors (MAOIs) | Phenelzine | Nardil |
| | | Tranylcypromine | Parnate |
| | Tricyclics (TCAs) | Clomipramine | Anafranil |
| | | Nortriptyline | Pamelor |
| | | Imipramine | Tofranil |
| | Selective serotonin reuptake inhibitors (SSRIs) | Paroxetine | Paxil |
| | | Fluoxetine | Prozac |
| | | Sertaline | Zoloft |
| | Atypical antidepressants | Venlafaxine | Effexor |
| | | Nefazodone | Serzone |
| | | Bupropion | Wellbutrin |
| Antipsychotics | Classic | Haloperidol | Haldol |
| | | Trifluoperazine | Stelazine |
| | | Chlorpromazine | Thorazine |
| | Atypical antipsychotics | Clozapine | Clozaril |
| | | Resperidone | Risperdal |
| | | Quetiapine | Seroquel |
| | | Olanzapine | Zyprexa |
| Antimanic medications ("mood stabilizers") | | Lithium carbonate | Eskalith |
| | | Sodium valproate | Depakote |
| | | Carbamazepine | Tegretol |
| | | Topiramate | Topamax |
| Anxiety-reducing medications (anxiolytics) | Benzodiazepines | Clonazepam | Klonopin |
| | | Diazepam | Valium |
| | | Alprazolam | Xanax |
| | Atypical anxiolytics | Buspirone | Buspar |

*Some adverse effects of deinstitutionalization*
**Some of the homeless in American cities are people discharged from mental hospitals who are unable to adjust to the world outside.**

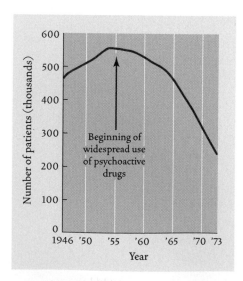

**17.2   *Number of residents in state and local government mental hospitals in the United States, 1946–1973* (Based on data from U.S. Public Health Service)**

negative symptoms as well (such as emotional blunting; Glick, Murray, Vasudevan, Marder, & Hu, 2001). Like the classical antipsychotics, the atypical antipsychotics block the neurotransmission of dopamine, but their enhanced benefits, especially with negative symptoms, are probably due to other mechanisms. These may include alterations in serotonin neurotransmission or a more selective effect on only particular subsets of dopamine neurons (Bantick, Deakin, & Grasby, 2001; Kapur & Remington, 2001; Tandon & Kane, 1993; Wirshing, Marder, Van Putten, & Ames, 1995).

It is sometimes said that these medications are not really antipsychotic agents at all but are only fancy sedatives—"chemical straitjackets"—that merely tranquilize patients. This argument does not square with the facts. While antipsychotic medications alleviate schizophrenic symptoms, powerful sedatives such as phenobarbital have no such effect. They put the patient to sleep, but when he wakes up, his delusions and hallucinations are unabated.

*The Social Reality of Treating Schizophrenia*   Because they allowed many schizophrenic patients to be managed outside of mental hospitals, the classical antipsychotic medications lent impetus to a movement called ***deinstitutionalization***, which was intended to allow for better and less expensive care for patients in their own communities, at local community mental health centers rather than at large centralized hospitals. In part, this movement worked. In the 1950s, mental hospitals housed about 600,000 patients, but by the 1980s this number had dropped to 125,000. These medications also made it possible to discharge schizophrenic patients more quickly than ever. Prior to introduction of the antipsychotic medications, two out of three schizophrenic patients spent most of their lives in the state asylum. In the 1980s, their average stay was about two months (J. M. Davis, 1985a; Lamb, 1984; Lamb & Bachrach, 2001; see Figure 17.2).

The high hopes created by these medications were soon tempered, however, because even given their moderate effectiveness, they still leave much to be desired as treatments. They only hold the schizophrenic symptoms in check so long as they are taken; they neither cure the disease nor alter its progress. Moreover, the antipsychotics—especially the classical antipsychotics—also have potent side effects that can include dramatic weight gain (sometimes twenty to thirty pounds), sedation, constipation, dry mouth, blurred vision, difficulty in urination, cardiac irregularities, tremors and muscle spasms, restlessness, a shuffling gait, and a curiously inexpressive, masklike face. Some patients who take them over the long term eventually develop permanent motor disorders (Caligiuri, Jeste, & Lacro, 2000; Csernansky & Newcomer, 1995; Kurzthaler & Fleischhacker, 2001).

One result of all these risks and side effects is that many schizophrenic patients refuse to take their medication reliably, leading to flare-ups of their signs and symptoms and causing repeated hospitalizations—they become "revolving-door patients."

Even when they do take their medication regularly, 30 to 50 percent of patients have recurrent outbreaks of the illness and need further hospitalization or a change of dosage or type of medication (Andreasen & Black, 1996). As a consequence, although fewer schizophrenics remain in psychiatric hospitals and do not stay in the hospital as long (J. M. Davis, 1985a; Lamb, 1984), the number of times they are readmitted for short stays has increased by 80 percent since the 1960s (Rosenstein, Milazzo-Sayre, & Manderscheid, 1989).

What do schizophrenic patients do when they are discharged from the hospital? Some stay at home with their aging parents. Others live in less-than-ideal board-and-care homes, while still others become drifters and join the swelling ranks of the homeless. According to one report, some 40 percent of New York City's homeless people suffer persistent mental disorder or have a history of mental illness (Golden, 1990). It is thus clear that while the antipsychotic drugs help to alleviate the symptoms of schizophrenia, they do not provide a cure. Given the current inadequacy—and in many cases, the complete lack—of appropriate community services, this represents, at least for now, a failure to achieve the intentions of deinstitutionalization (R. E. Jones, 1983; Lamb, 1984, 1998; Westermeyer, 1987).

## DRUG TREATMENT OF DEPRESSION: ANTIDEPRESSANTS

Shortly after the introduction of antipsychotics as treatments for schizophrenia, other drugs were found that seemed to act specifically on depression. These antidepressants were of two major classes, the monoamine oxidase (MAO) inhibitors such as Nardil and the tricyclic antidepressants such as Tofranil (see Table 17.1). Of these, the tricyclics became the most widely used, mostly because patients taking MAO inhibitors must conform to difficult dietary restrictions (Burke & Preskhorn, 1995).

Both the MAO inhibitors and the tricyclics appear to work in part by increasing the amount of norepinephrine and serotonin available for synaptic transmission (Blier & Abbott, 2001). The mechanisms whereby they accomplish this mission are different (for details, see Figure 17.3). These medications are very effective in counteracting depression, producing marked improvement in up to 65 percent of the patients who take them (Hollister & Csernansky, 1990). Not all of the medications work for all patients, however. Some patients appear to have somewhat different neurochemical deficits and thus do better with one drug than another, with the choice left to the physician's judgment.

These early drug treatments for depression were considered relatively successful, but, even so, the use of medication for treating depression changed dramatically in 1988 with the introduction of the first "designer drug" for depression, Prozac (Kramer, 1993). Prozac was engineered in the laboratory to act minimally on norepinephrine and dopamine and maximally on serotonin, thus marking the introduction of a new class of antidepressants known as *selective serotonin reuptake inhibitors (SSRIs)* (see Table 17.1). For most patients, Prozac and the other SSRIs ameliorate depression as quickly and as completely as their predecessors (Mulrow et al., 2000), but they have far fewer side effects and are thus safer to prescribe—so safe that most are now prescribed not only by psychiatrists but also by primary care physicians (Olfson & Klerman, 1993). Still, while these antidepressants have been touted by some as panaceas, like all medications they too have their side effects, which can include nausea, diarrhea, anxiety, and—in upward of 30 percent of patients—insomnia, as well as a loss of sexual desire or response (Clayton, 2001; Ferguson, 2001; Gursky & Krahn, 2000; Hollander & McCarley, 1992; Jacobsen, 1992; Montgomery, 1995).

If patients are plagued by undue side effects from SSRIs and cannot take the tricyclics or MAO inhibitors, a separate array of antidepressants is available. These *atypical antidepressants* work in varied ways on serotonin, norepinephrine, and dopamine systems, and include Wellbutrin, Effexor, and Serzone. Of these, Wellbutrin is of special interest.

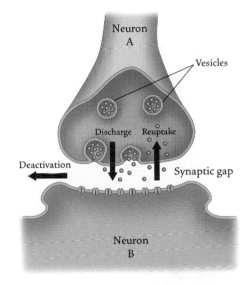

**17.3** *A schematic presentation of two ways in which a drug may increase the available supply of a neurotransmitter* A neurotransmitter, norepinephrine (NE), is discharged by Neuron A into the synaptic gap and diffuses across the gap to stimulate Neuron B. The more NE accumulates at the membrane of Neuron B, the more that neuron will fire. NE at the synapse can be diminished through reuptake, in which NE is pumped back into Neuron A, or through deactivation, whereby certain enzymes (such as MAO) break down the neurotransmitter and render it ineffective. Tricyclics (like Tofranil) and MAO inhibitors (like Nardil) increase the amount of available NE (and serotonin) at the synaptic junction but in different ways. Tricyclics interfere with neurotransmitter reuptake; MAO inhibitors prevent MAO from breaking the transmitters down. Second-generation antidepressants like SSRIs (such as Prozac) block reuptake but act selectively upon serotonin neurons.

It seems to have little effect on serotonin and probably operates on dopamine and nor-epinephrine systems instead. However it works, Wellbutrin has no negative sexual side effects, and many patients report heightened sexual interest and response. It also is generally stimulating, and in addition to curbing nicotine cravings (for which it is also sold as Zyban), it finds wide use as a treatment for adults with attention deficit disorder.

Just as the antipsychotics are not mere sedatives, so the antidepressants do not generate euphoria. Indeed, they have little effect on mood if there is no depression to begin with (J. O. Cole & Davis, 1975). But it is also true that these drugs are more than "just" antidepressants, because they are also quite useful in alleviating the distress of many other conditions, including panic disorder, migraine headache, school phobia, eating disorders like bulimia, premenstrual symptoms, and chronic pain (Barkin & Fawcett, 2000; Hollister & Csernansky, 1990; Olfson & Klerman, 1993; Sheean, 1985; Steiner, 2000). Some serotonin-centered antidepressants such as the tricyclic Anafranil and several SSRIs are also the preferred treatment in most cases of obsessive-compulsive disorder (Ananth, 1985; Dominguez, 1992; Heninger, 1995; Rapoport 1991).

## DRUG TREATMENT OF BIPOLAR DISORDER: ANTIMANICS

Medications are also available to treat bipolar disorder, and these are called *antimanics*, even though they also help forestall the depressive episodes in the disorder. The first medication used specifically for its antimanic action was lithium carbonate (one example is Eskalith; see Table 17.1), and patients who begin taking lithium can generally expect that their manic episodes will subside within five to ten days.

Despite lithium's effectiveness, it only works in 60 to 80 percent of patients with bipolar disorder (Calabrese & Woyshville, 1995). Taking it is also problematic for many patients, most of whom must endure unpleasant side effects such as weight gain, dry mouth, and tremors. Moreover, lithium is toxic at higher doses, requiring patients to have their blood levels tested frequently and making it a risky treatment for patients who are potentially suicidal and might overdose. Nor can lithium be taken during pregnancy or when the patient has kidney disease.

Fortunately, other drugs are now available that achieve some of lithium's gains but without many of its drawbacks. The main contenders are Tegretol, Depakote, and Topamax, which were once used strictly as anticonvulsants to treat epilepsy. Like lithium, they also have side effects (some potentially serious), but they are better tolerated by many patients. In most cases, they are just as effective as lithium and may even be superior when the patient's mood cycles are frequent and rapid (Andreasen & Black, 1996; West, McElroy, & Keck, 1996).

Just what accounts for the antimanic effects of lithium and the anticonvulsants? According to one hypothesis, lithium carbonate may reregulate neurotransmission by stabilizing the influence of calcium on neuronal membranes (Meltzer, 1986; Wood & Goodwin, 1987). Some evidence also suggests that, like depression, mania may involve a serotonin deficit, and that both lithium and the anticonvulsants augment serotonin neurotransmission (Shiah & Yatham, 2000).

## DRUG TREATMENT OF ANXIETY: ANXIOLYTICS

When patients suffer from disabling anxiety, they are often treated with medications that are popularly called tranquilizers and technically known as *anxiolytics* (see Table 17.1). Most anxiolytics apparently work by increasing neurotransmission at synapses containing the neurotransmitter GABA (Brailowsky & Garcia, 1999; Shader & Greenblatt, 1995). Probably the most commonly used anxiolytic is alcohol. Many people, patients or otherwise, medicate themselves for their anxiety as part of their lifestyle, and it would be an excellent medication were it not such a socially destructive drug of abuse. Instead, physicians prescribe what is essentially alcohol in a pill, a class of medications called the *benzodiazepines*. Some of these medications, such as Valium, Xanax, and Klonopin, are prescribed so often that their names have almost become household words. They are useful as short-term treatments for generalized anxiety disorder, panic disorder, post-traumatic stress disorder, alcohol withdrawal, insomnia, muscle spasms, tension headaches, and various other stress-related disorders. They are rarely used for long-term treatment because, unlike the medications we have reviewed so far, they are highly addictive and interact dangerously with alcohol, and like alcohol, can cause profound fetal damage if the patient is pregnant. Some newer anxiolytics such as Buspar are not addictive and have become popular substitutes for the older anxiolytics, especially for patients who are prone to alcohol or drug abuse or who will have to take the medications over a long period of time (Lydiard, Brawman-Mintzer, & Ballenger, 1996; Schweitzer, Rickels, & Uhlenhuth, 1995).

## EVALUATING A MEDICATION

We have now mentioned a number of medications and their effectiveness as treatments for many mental disorders. But we have also noted their liabilities, which (depending on the medication) can include unpleasant side effects, the risk of addiction, and risk to a fetus. Given these risks, it is doubly important that the medications be used only with the patients and the disorders for which they have documented effectiveness. Just how do we assess the effectiveness of a medication? We will discuss this issue in detail, because the issues raised in evaluating medications not only apply to the prescription of medications, but also extend to the evaluation of any therapeutic procedure, including psychotherapy.

Suppose we want to find out whether a given drug, say, Zyprexa, reduces the manifestations of schizophrenia. Obviously, we would need to administer Zyprexa to a group of schizophrenic patients for some period, assessing how well the patients do before and after receiving the medication. In fact, many studies of treatment effectiveness are of just this kind. But a little reflection shows that relying only on this procedure would be a mistake.

*Is the medication effective?* **Many steps are needed to find out if a medication has the desired effect, and, if it does, whether it is more effective than a mere placebo or other medications already in use.**

### CONTROLLING FOR SPONTANEOUS IMPROVEMENT

One problem with a simple before-and-after assessment is that it ignores the possibility that the patient's condition might have improved without any treatment. Such spontaneous improvements occur in many disorders (though not often in schizophrenia). Moreover, many disorders fluctuate in their severity over time; patients are more likely to seek treatment when they are at their worst, and when they improve, it would be wrong to give automatic credit to the treatment.

Controlling for these factors is a bit complex, though. One has to compare two groups of patients drawn from the same population, one of which received Zyprexa for, say, six weeks, while the other group did not receive the drug. Both groups would be assessed at the beginning of the study and after the first group received the treatment (and perhaps at intervals in between). Initially, the groups ought to be equivalent. The question is whether they will be different during or after the treatment.

### CONTROLLING FOR PLACEBO EFFECTS

Suppose that after six weeks the patients who were given Zyprexa seem to be less bothered by hallucinations and delusions than the untreated controls. This result makes it unlikely that the change in the Zyprexa group was due to spontaneous improvement or a natural fluctuation of the illness, since these factors should affect both groups equally. Does this prove that the benefits of treatment were indeed caused by the drug? Unfortunately, no, because we have not yet ruled out the possibility that the result was due to the *placebo effect*.

In medicine, the term *placebo* refers to some inert (that is, medically neutral) substance that is administered to a patient who believes that it has therapeutic power. Such placebo effects probably account for many of the cures of ancient physicians, whose medications included such items as crocodile dung, swine teeth, and moss scraped from the skull of a man who died a violent death (A. K. Shapiro, 1971).

How powerful are placebo effects? The evidence is mixed. Some studies have shown that up to 70 percent of patients suffering from diseases ranging from asthma to coronary heart disease will make some kind of real improvement after taking placebos, be they disguised sugar pills or injections of harmless solutions (Benson & Friedman, 1996). A different conclusion, however, was suggested by a recent review of 130 clinical studies that had compared placebo effects to the effects of medications, physical manipulations, or psychotherapy (Hrobjartsson & Gotzsche, 2001). The researchers found that placebo effects, where they existed, tended to be weak and were found largely in smaller studies that may have had biased outcomes.

Whatever the power of the placebo effect, we do need to make sure that the improvement in the drug-treated group of our example is caused by the properties of the drug itself. Perhaps a sugar pill—or a bit of crocodile dung or a magnet attached to the head or the latest health-food fad—would have done as well. To exclude this possibility, we must administer a placebo to the control patients. They will thus no longer be "untreated." On the contrary, they will receive the same attention from the investigators and the treatment staff, will be told the same things about their treatment, and will be given the same number of pills at the same time as the patients in the true drug group. There will be only one difference between the two groups: the control patients will swallow pills that, unbeknownst to them, contain only inert materials. As a result of this stratagem, we can simultaneously control for two factors, spontaneous improvement and placebo effects, whether those effects are large or small. Now that these two factors are controlled, a difference in the way the two groups appear after treatment can finally be attributed to the effect of the drug itself.

## CONTROLLING FOR EXPECTATIONS

By definition, a placebo control implies that all of the patients in the study (including, of course, the ones receiving the placebo) think that they are being treated with the real medicine. But to guarantee this desired state of ignorance, the treating physicians—and the psychologists and social workers and nurses and attendants who may be part of the research staff—must also be kept in the dark about which patients are receiving the medication and which ones are taking the placebo, because, if they knew which patients were in which group, this information could affect their assessment of the patients' progress.

The staff's knowledge can have further effects. Staff members may unwittingly communicate their beliefs and expectations to the patients, perhaps by observing the medicated patients more closely or by being less concerned if a placebo-treated patient fails to take her morning pill. By such signals, the patients may figure out whether the physicians expect them to get better or not, and their progress may be influenced by these expectations. To guard against this, modern medical evaluators use the *double-blind technique*. In this technique, the patients are "blind" as to whether they are in the medication or placebo group, and the same holds for the staff members who work with and evaluate these patients. With both sides kept in the dark, there is no chance for expectations or beliefs to compromise the data. The only ones who know who is in which group are the investigators who are masterminding the study and who have no direct contact with the patients.

There are still problems with using placebos in studies of medication effectiveness, even when the studies are double-blind. First, in many cases it is unethical to give a placebo and thereby withhold an accepted treatment. Second, it is often easy to discern who is taking medication versus placebo, because many medications have characteristic side effects that are hard for either the patient or the treatment staff to ignore.

Finally, researchers seldom want to know if a new medication is better than nothing; they want to know whether it is better than the standard treatment. For all of these reasons, the most common research practice is to assess a new medication's *incremental effectiveness* against the best current treatment. In this case, the baseline for the comparison is not a placebo group at all. Instead, the comparison is to the "standard medication," the most commonly given treatment. If the group receiving the experimental treatment does better than this baseline, we know that the new treatment is not just effective, it is also an improvement on currently accepted treatments.

## ASSESSING IMPROVEMENT

In even the best-designed investigations of drug effectiveness, success hinges on one question: how do we measure whether the medication works and the patients improve? Typically, outcome measures in drug evaluation studies have consisted of patients' opinions about how they feel while taking the medicine and ratings from the treatment staff about how well the patients function while observed in the hospital or clinic. Occasionally, the results from psychological or medical tests are also used as evidence of effectiveness.

These kinds of outcome measures might seem sufficient, but in today's economically pressured medical climate, they are being challenged by critics who want to know not just whether the treatments are effective, but also whether they are cost-effective. Are the gains provided by the medication commensurate with the cost of the drug? Does taking the medication shorten costly hospital stays (or visits to expensive psychotherapists)? Will the medication make the patient a more reliable wage earner and reduce the financial costs (sick leave pay, worker's compensation, Social Security) associated with illness? Will it restore the patient's ability to parent and reduce the costs of children's care? Increasingly, the money spent on treatment is being weighed against the money saved with treatment, and whether a medication "works" is a question whose answer is poised precariously on this balance sheet (Zarkin, Grabowski, Mauskopf, Bannerman, & Weisler, 1995). The same issue of cost-effectiveness will reemerge in our discussion of psychotherapy.

## LIMITATIONS OF PHARMACOTHERAPY

With drug evaluations designed as we have just described—with controls for spontaneous improvements, placebo effects, expectations, and so on—many drug therapies appear to be extremely effective for many forms of mental disorder. Even excluding the wider issue of cost-effectiveness, though, medications for mental disorders do have their limitations. We have already noted two, that they do not help everyone and that many of them have unpleasant (or dangerous) side effects. But how beneficial are these medications? Critics of pharmacotherapy contend that the beneficial results of drug therapy are still quite limited (S. Fisher & Greenberg, 1989; Moncrieff, 2001). This is especially so for patients taking the classic antipsychotics and antimanic medications, who must remain on a maintenance dose to minimize their disability but who often quit taking their medicine because they find the side effects so unpleasant.

This criticism is less compelling in the case of antidepressants and anxiolytics, which sometimes do for patients with mood and anxiety disorders what insulin does for patients with diabetes: they do not cure the disease, but they can do a fine job of controlling it.

Whatever these limitations, the modern drug therapies are clearly a major step forward. They have restored many patients to normal functioning. They have lifted many others out of misery and distress and returned them to a reasonably normal life. They have allowed still others to remain, however imperfectly, in a family or community setting, when they would have otherwise been relegated to long-term hospital stays. As a result, the modern mental hospital can function more as a therapeutic center than a warehouse. It can provide important social and psychological services, including vocational counseling and psychotherapy, all of which would have been unthinkable in former times. These are, by any measure, enormous gains, and, even acknowledging the limits of drug therapies, there is no question that they have been a boon to many who suffer from a variety of forms of mental illness.

## PSYCHOSURGERY

Until the advent of the major psychotropic drugs, physicians relied on several other biological therapies, all of which involved drastic assaults on the nervous system. Some of these consisted of *psychosurgery*, or brain surgery, to alter thinking or behavior. In prefrontal lobotomy, for example, the neurological connections between the thalamus and the frontal lobes are severed, in whole or in part. This operation was meant to liberate the patient's thoughts from the pathological influence of his emotions, on the simplistic neurological assumption that thought and emotion were localized in the frontal lobes and the thalamus, respectively. Many patients were helped by lobotomy, but the technique was used indiscriminately, and later evaluations often showed that these surgical procedures had deleterious effects on cognitive functions (Maher, 1966; Robbin, 1958; Tierney, 2000; Valenstein, 1986).

In recent years, psychosurgery has reemerged as a useful technique, but the psychosurgery of today has been refined considerably, both in the surgical procedures used and in the patients judged suitable for them (Hurley, Black, Stip, & Taber, 2000; Z. H. Rappaport, 1992). Neurosurgeons now create very precise lesions in very specific brain areas instead of disconnecting or destroying whole lobes or regions. And in the vast majority of cases, such surgery is reserved for patients who are severely disabled and show no improvement after all other medical or psychotherapeutic alternatives have been exhausted. This surgery-as-last-resort has been used in patients with intractable depression or epilepsy, severe obsessive-compulsive disorder, and chronic pain, and the surgery is often beneficial. There are clearly risks inherent in these surgeries, but the risks may be acceptable compared to the severe level of the patients' ongoing disability (Baer et al., 1995; Bridges, 1987; Davies & Weeks, 1993; Hay et al., 1993; Jenike, 2001; Mahli & Bartlett, 2000).

## ELECTROCONVULSIVE THERAPY

Another form of biological therapy is *electroconvulsive therapy (ECT)*, sometimes colloquially called "shock treatment." For about half a second, a current of moderate intensity is passed between two electrodes attached to the patient's head. The result is a 30- to 60-second convulsive seizure similar to that seen in epilepsy (Figure 17.4), with the usual course of ECT consisting of six to ten treatments over a period of a week or two.

When ECT first came into use, patients were conscious and thrashed about during their convulsions, often suffering serious bruises or bone fractures. In clear contrast, modern ECT actually looks very mild. Patients are given short-acting anesthetics to render them temporarily unconscious and muscle relaxants to reduce the manifestations of the seizure to a few slight twitches (Andreasen & Black, 1996).

ECT was originally meant as a treatment for schizophrenia but was soon established as particularly effective for depression. Here, its efficacy is considerable. It works for as

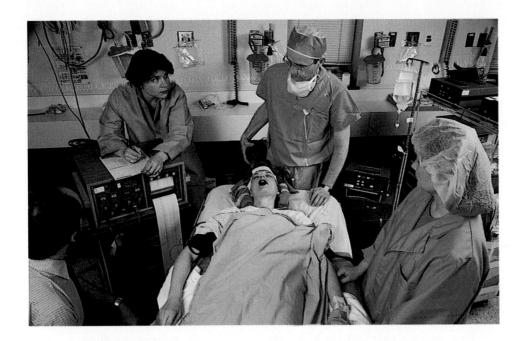

17.4 *Patient about to undergo ECT*

many as 70 to 80 percent of patients who have not responded to any antidepressant medication (Andreasen & Black, 1996; Janicak et al., 1985) or who cannot take such medications because of overdose potential or other medical problems. In addition, ECT seems to act more quickly than antidepressant medications usually do (R. D. Weiner, 1984b, 1985). ECT also seems quite effective in treating acute mania as well as various psychotic states associated with drug intoxication (Gitlin, 2001; Sackeim, Devanand, & Nobler, 1995).

Despite these advantages, the use of ECT remains controversial, partly because in some cases it can produce memory impairment (Rami-Gonzalez et al., 2001; Squire, 1977). Under the circumstances, ECT is generally reserved for use only after medication has failed or when there seems to be a serious chance of suicide. In the latter case, the fast-acting quality of ECT may be an overriding advantage (Andreasen & Black, 1996).

What accounts for the therapeutic effects of ECT? The exact mechanism is uncertain, but ECT is known to produce widespread effects in many neural pathways and neurotransmitter systems. It also affects gene expression, brain protein synthesis, and the secretion of endocrine hormones (Fink, 2001).

# PSYCHOTHERAPY

Biological treatments are but one approach to the treatment of psychopathology. The alternative approach forgoes direct changes to the patient's body and instead relies on psychological means. Such attempts are known collectively as *psychotherapy*.

Many different kinds, or modes, of psychotherapy are in wide use for the treatment of mental disorders,* and they differ in both how psychopathology is conceived and how the actual therapy is practiced. Some approaches are based on psychoanalysis and so emphasize unconscious conflicts and encourage introspection and insight. Others rely on behavioral findings from animal and human experimentation; these seek to identify maladaptive responses and then promote the learning of new responses. Still

*Early forms of therapy?* **This nineteenth century painting shows David playing the harp before Saul.**

---

* There are other kinds of psychotherapy, but they are used more as a modes of self-discovery rather than treatments for psychopathology. These include humanistic therapies such as client-centered therapy (Rogers, 1951, 1970) and existential psychotherapy (e.g., Frankl, 1966; May, 1958).

*Psychoanalysis    In traditional forms of psychoanalysis, the client lies down on a couch or sits in a comfortable chair, and the therapist is positioned in a way that ensures the client receives no signals or cues about what she is saying.*

others take a cognitive approach, focusing on the disabling role of faulty thinking, while teaching more rational thought. Finally, one type is based on establishing and maintaining rewarding social relationships.

In what follows, we will discuss five common modes of individual psychotherapy (therapy conducted with a single patient) that grow out of these approaches: (1) classical psychoanalysis, (2) psychodynamic therapy (a modern offshoot of psychoanalysis), (3) behavior therapy, (4) cognitive therapy, and (5) interpersonal therapy. Later we will discuss extensions of psychotherapy that treat groups and families.

## CLASSICAL PSYCHOANALYSIS

*Classical psychoanalysis* is the method Sigmund Freud developed at the turn of the twentieth century, and according to some writers, it is the ancestor of virtually all modern modes of psychotherapy (London, 1964). Freud's basic assumption was that a patient's ills (in Freud's terms, his neuroses) stemmed from unconscious defenses against unacceptable urges that date back to early childhood. By adulthood, many of these defenses are relics that, though they protect the patient from anxiety, also shield him from seeing clearly both the outer world and his own inner world. These defenses become manifest as psychological symptoms, bodily malfunctions, or tendencies to repeat outdated and by now utterly maladaptive patterns of behavior (see Chapter 15).

Freud believed that for a patient to overcome her neurosis, she must lower her mental shield in order to glimpse her buried thoughts and wishes, and gain insight into why she buried them. Only then can she master the internal conflicts that crippled her for so long. Once these conflicts are resolved, her symptoms will presumably wither away by themselves. In effect, Freud's prescription for the neuroses is the triumph of reason over passion: "where Id was, there shall Ego be."

### THE RECOVERY OF UNCONSCIOUS MEMORIES

Psychoanalytic technique originated in Freud's attempts to treat hysteria (now called conversion disorder) by helping patients recover emotionally charged memories (see Chapter 15). Freud and his then collaborator, Josef Breuer, initially hypnotized patients to facilitate this recovery. Freud later came to believe, however, that such memories could be exhumed even in the normal waking state by the method of *free association*, in which the patient was instructed to say whatever came into his mind, with the expectation that sooner or later the relevant memory would emerge. Freud noted, though, that patients almost invariably tried to derail a given train of thought—by changing the topic, forgetting what they were about to say, and so on. He believed that these behaviors were indications of *resistance* to the task, a resistance motivated by the fact that the train of thought was coming too close to material that the patient found in some fashion threatening. Indeed, Freud interpreted the resistance as an indication that the patient was on the verge of recalling very painful, buried memories and had to work against the forces of repression. As a result, signs of resistance provided important clues for the psychoanalyst, indicating that the associations were nearing a memory of some interest.*

In addition to free association, Freud later asked his patients to tell him their dreams, and he interpreted these as clues to the character of their neurotic conflicts.

---

* That the patient's recollections under the circumstances would invariably be accurate, and of therapeutic value, is now under serious challenge (see Chapter 7).

Freud also tried to interpret many of the patients' behaviors in the same way, whether the behavior was a slip of the tongue, the wiggling of a foot on the couch, a particular choice of words, or whether the patient was late or early for the sessions.

## EMOTIONAL INSIGHT

For Freud, the end result of therapy is not the achievement of blissful happiness, because human life is rarely euphoric and often strife ridden. Instead, the goal and usual result are more modest: as Freud put it, to "turn neurosis into everyday unhappiness." To achieve this goal, the patients needed to attain insights into their long-lost, repressed motives, but these insights could not merely be intellectual. Instead, Freud also wanted his patients to gain access to the feelings that accompany the repressed thoughts. For Freud, this necessary emotional component arose mainly as a function of *transference*, the patient's tendency to respond to the analyst in ways that re-created her responses to the major figures in her own life. Thus, the patient would end up loving or hating the analyst just as she loved or hated her mother, father, siblings, and, more recently, her lovers and friends. All of these feelings are "transferred" to the analyst, as a kind of repetition of the unresolved problems of the patient's childhood.

Freud argued that this transference-charged relationship with the analyst could be a powerful therapeutic tool. It lets the analyst hold up a mirror to the patient to show her how she really feels and acts toward the important people in her life. For example, take a person who expresses violent anger at his psychoanalyst and then is immediately seized by unspeakable terror. How would his analyst interpret this? Perhaps the patient had equated the analyst with his own tyrannical father, and having acted with flagrant disrespect, was now expecting some horrible retribution. Needless to say, the analyst will not act like Daddy, but instead might say something mildly reassuring, such as "That was hard to get out, wasn't it?" The analyst might then point out how the patient's traumatic memories of Daddy distort the ongoing therapeutic relationship.

Through many such experiences, the patient's anxieties gradually abate. The determinedly neutral analyst allows herself temporarily to stand in for the significant characters in the patient's early family drama but will not let herself be drawn into the play. She lets the patient say the same old lines and go through the same old motions, but she will not respond to them as the cast of characters from childhood did. Her job is to let the patient see what he is really doing, what is really happening on his private stage. The effect of all this emotional reeducation is to create a new life script with better lines and a happier ending.

## PSYCHODYNAMIC THERAPY

Many present-day psychotherapists still use techniques that bear Freud's imprint. A few still practice psychoanalysis just as Freud did, but most practitioners have modified Freud's theories and procedures in various ways. Most of them—known variously as psychoanalytic, ego-analytic, or psychodynamic psychotherapists—subscribe to neo-Freudian views or to related approaches such as ego psychology. Like Freud, they believe that what underlies "neurosis" is unconscious conflict, but they differ by emphasizing current interpersonal and cultural factors rather than the psychological traumas of early childhood. If early development is discussed in these modern therapies, it is not to discover decades-past episodes but, instead, to identify how the patterns of interaction in one's childhood influence current choices (Eagle & Wolitsky, 1992; Liff, 1992).

(Cartoon by Sidney Harris)

Psychoanalytically oriented therapists have also revised Freud's doctrines about women, such as Freud's belief that women are passive by nature and have underdeveloped superegos that render them less moral (S. Freud, 1933). Today, such therapists are more likely to consider women different but equivalent to men and recognize that any therapy based on doctrines of sexual inferiority is both intellectually and morally misguided—based on false assumptions and by its very nature oppressive (Auld & Hyman, 1991; Bernstein & Lenhart, 1993; Strouse, 1974).

Other modifications concern the relation between what goes on in the therapist's office and what happens in the patient's "real" life. For Freud, the crucial theater of operations was the analysis itself, and to ensure that the patient's unconscious conflicts could be contained there, the patient's outside life had to remain stable. He therefore insisted that his patients make no major life decisions, such as getting married or divorced or changing careers, while they were in analysis. In contrast, later psychoanalytic psychotherapists came to regard the sessions as a microcosm of the patient's entire life and recommend that the patient actively attempt to apply the lessons learned in therapy to his life outside of therapy (Alexander & French, 1946).

## BEHAVIOR THERAPY

Not all psychotherapists derive their techniques from psychoanalysis. In fact, two major therapeutic approaches are reactions against psychoanalysis, although for opposite reasons. The first is behavior therapy, which maintains that the theoretical notions underlying psychoanalysis are vague and untestable, and that its therapeutic effectiveness is dubious. The second consists of various humanistic therapies (see Chapter 15), which regard psychoanalysis as too mechanistic in focus and concerned more with basic urges like sex and aggression than with the search for higher truths and meanings. Freud, who had a fine sense of irony, would have been wryly amused to find himself accused by one faction of being too scientific and by the other of not being scientific enough.

Behavior therapists hold that the various conditions Freud called "neuroses" are simply caused by maladaptive learning; the remedy, therefore, involves new learning, replacing or overriding the old habits. These therapists see themselves as applied scientists whose techniques for reeducating troubled people are adapted from the principles of classical and instrumental conditioning discovered in the laboratories of Pavlov, Thorndike, and Skinner (see Chapter 4). As befits this line of descent, behavior therapists are basically pragmatic. They emphasize overt, observable behavior rather than hypothetical underlying causes such as unconscious thoughts and wishes, which they regard as hard to define and impossible to observe. Their concern instead is with what a person does that is causing her distress. It is these specific behaviors that are the behavior therapist's target for intervention. These behaviors are not regarded as "symptoms" through which one can identify and then cure the underlying illness. Instead, the maladaptive behaviors themselves are the problem, and it is they that must be removed.

Toward this end, behavior therapists employ various techniques for learning and unlearning, relying on deliberate exposure to anxiety-producing stimuli, conditioning of incompatible reactions, or whatever. These treatments do not include any attempt to have the patient gain insight into the origin of these symptoms. As behavioral therapists see it, such insights, however valid, have no therapeutic value. What is wrong and must be fixed is the patient's behavior in the here and now.

## EXPOSURE TECHNIQUES

One set of techniques often used in behavior therapy derives from classical conditioning and is used to treat the specific phobias (Wolpe & Plaud, 1997). Behavior therapists frequently suggest that the irrational fears that characterize these phobias are simply classically conditioned responses, evoked by particular stimuli, such as storms, elevators, or finding a spider in one's bed (see Chapters 4 and 16). The way to treat these phobias, according to this formulation, is to break the connections between the phobic stimuli and the associated fears.

The most widely used exposure technique is *systematic desensitization*, developed by the psychiatrist Joseph Wolpe (1958). Here, the therapist seeks not only to break the connection between the phobic stimulus and the fear response; she simultaneously seeks to create a new connection between this stimulus and a different response, one that is incompatible with fear and that will therefore displace it. The competing response is usually deep muscular relaxation, and the patient is taught a relaxation technique, typically through meditation-like exercises, before the formal therapy begins. Then, once the patient can relax deeply on cue, the goal is to condition this relaxation response to the stimuli that have been evoking-fear in the past (see Figure 17.5).

In Wolpe's technique, the fear-evoking stimulus is usually not physically present in the clinic room during the therapy sessions. Instead, the patient is asked to imagine the

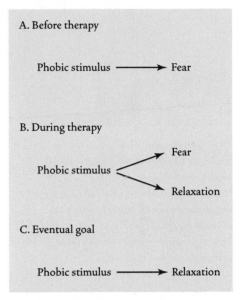

17.5 Systematic desensitization (A) The state of affairs in phobia. Various phobic stimuli arouse fear. (B) These stimuli are conditioned to relaxation. As this connection becomes stronger, the connection between the stimuli and the fear is weakened. (C) The outcome when counterconditioning is complete: relaxation has completely displaced fear.

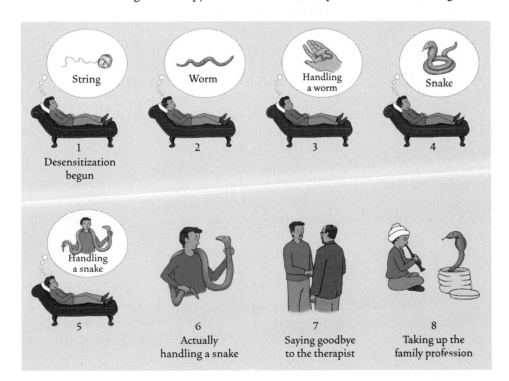

Desensitization (Courtesy of Henry Gleitman and Mary Bullock)

*High tech therapy*   *A common way to combat anxiety is to expose patients gradually to the anxiety-provoking stimulus. Virtual reality displays are sometimes used to make these exposures more and more realistic as the therapy progresses, as for example in this case, in which a virtual reality display helps people overcome the fear of flying.*

*Desensitization*   *As therapy for phobias progresses, the person learns to relax even when exposed directly to the phobic stimulus-, in this case, a spider.*

fearful stimulus as vividly as possible—to imagine standing next to a snake, or standing on the roof of a very tall building. It turns out these imagined situations have enough reality for most patients to evoke a reasonable amount of anxiety (Wolpe & Lazarus, 1966). However, it is important that the therapist does not ask the patient to imagine these scary situations at the very start of therapy. Instead, the therapist works his way toward these situations very gradually, one small step at a time.

To make this possible, the patient is asked, at the very start of therapy, to construct an *anxiety hierarchy*, in which feared situations are arranged from least to most anxiety provoking, and this hierarchy is then used to set the sequence for therapy. The patient starts out by imagining the first scene in the hierarchy (for example, being on the first floor of a tall building) while in a state of deep relaxation. She will stay with this scene—imagining and relaxing—until she no longer feels any qualms. After this, the next scene is imagined (perhaps, looking out of a fourth-floor window in the building), and this scene, too, is thoroughly counterconditioned. The process continues, climbing up the anxiety hierarchy until the patient finally can imagine the most frightening scene of all (leaning over the railing of the building's observation tower, more than a hundred floors above the ground) and still be able to relax. Sometimes this imagined exposure is sufficient to treat the phobia, but often patients need to extend the graduated exposure to instances in the real world—for example, actually visiting a tall building, rather than merely thinking about one. This process is called *in vivo desensitization*, whether with the therapist present or by using guided homework assignments (Goldfried & Davison, 1994).

The design of these desensitization techniques was clearly guided by the view that phobias are classically conditioned responses, and, as we have discussed, many now consider this view of phobias to be problematic (see Chapters 4 and 16). However, this does not invalidate the therapies, and, in fact, exposure techniques are quite effective for specific phobias—suggesting that even if classical conditioning cannot fully explain phobias, it may nonetheless be quite useful in their treatment (Wolpe & Plaud, 1997).

## AVERSION THERAPY

Another behavior therapy technique, *aversion therapy*, uses a different strategy. It attempts to eliminate problematic behavior by attaching negative feelings to it. The basic procedure of aversion therapy is very simple and merely involves pairing the stimulus that one wants to render unpleasant with some obnoxious unconditioned stimulus.

One common use is in treating alcoholism. For example, an individual who wants to quit drinking is made nauseous with a special medication. He is then asked to smell, taste, and swallow his favorite alcoholic beverages, all the while desperately wanting to vomit. After a few such exposures, the person will come to associate the nausea with the alcoholic beverage and should, as a result, be far less likely to reach for or accept a drink (for more on learned taste aversions, see Chapter 4). Several studies have reported the effectiveness of aversive treatment in producing abstinence for at least one year in about two-thirds of alcoholic patients studied (Elkins, 1991; Wiens & Menustik, 1983; Wilson, 1991), but it is not a panacea and is best considered a supplement to conventional approaches such as abstinence and Alcoholics Anonymous (Fuller & Hiller-Sturmhofel, 1999).

This technique has been applied to behaviors that range from overeating and cigarette smoking to certain sexual deviations such as exhibitionism. But perhaps the most common—and most controversial—use of aversion therapy is with the developmentally disabled and mentally retarded. It is sometimes used with individuals who are sexually disinhibited or frankly aggressive, or who bite themselves or bang their heads repeatedly (Matson & Sevin, 1994). For example, an individual who habitually bangs her head against a brick wall may be given brief electrical shocks every time she performs this self-destructive behavior. In obvious ways, this treatment seems inhumane, but this must be weighed against the likelihood of permanent brain damage if the behavior continues. For these uses, the treatment is usually quite effective (Duker & Seys, 1996; Gerhardt, Holmes, Alessandri, & Goodman, 1991). Even given this benefit to the patient, however, the technique presents moral and legal quandaries (Herr, 1990; Matson & Sevin, 1994; Mulick, 1990).

## OPERANT TECHNIQUES

A different set of behavioral therapies is derived from the principles of instrumental conditioning and emphasizes the relation between acts and consequences (see Chapter 4). Its theme is the same as that which underlies the entire operant approach—the control of behavior through reinforcement.

An example of this approach is the use of token economies in certain hospital psychiatric wards. In these settings, tokens function much as money does in our economy; they can be exchanged for desirable items such as snacks or the opportunity to watch TV. Like money, the tokens must be earned by the patient, perhaps by making his own bed, or being neatly dressed, or performing various ward chores. In this fashion, the patient can be systematically rewarded for producing desirable behaviors and not rewarded for producing undesirable ones.

As in the learning laboratory, the reinforcement contingencies can then be gradually adjusted, using the process known as shaping (see Chapter 4). Early on, the patient might be reinforced merely for getting out of bed; later on, tokens might be delivered only for getting out of bed and walking to the dining hall. In this fashion, the patient can be led, step by step, to a fuller, more acceptable level of functioning. The overall effects of this technique are that the patients become less apathetic and the general ward atmosphere is much improved (Ayllon & Azrin, 1968). The problem is that the effects of token economies do not generalize well out of the hospital or even off the ward. Thus, they are probably best seen not as therapy but as ward-management techniques.

But other reinforcement techniques can be useful in individual behavior therapy as part of *contingency management*. In contingency management, the person learns that certain behaviors will be followed by strict consequences (Craighead, Craighead, Kazdin, & Mahoney, 1994). For example, a child who is oppositional and defiant can be presented with a menu of "good behaviors" and "bad behaviors," with an associated reward and penalty for each. Being a "good listener" can earn the child the chance to watch a video, cleaning up her room everyday can get her a dessert after dinner, and so forth, whereas talking back to Mom or making a mess may result in an early bedtime or a time-out in her room. The idea is ultimately not to bribe or coerce the child but to show her that her actions can change how people react to her. Ideally, her changed behavior will result in a more positive social environment that can supplant the "goodies" that initially established the change.

## COGNITIVE THERAPY

Exposure, aversion, and reinforcement therapies focus on fairly obvious observable behaviors and try to modify them using simple classical and operant conditioning techniques. But what if the patient's problems do not involve clear-cut responses or easily identifiable problematic behaviors? Suppose a sufferer of obsessive-compulsive disorder is crippled by anxiety because of a constant obsession that he has poisoned his children. He finds temporary peace of mind only by counting his children over and over again, reassuring himself that each is indeed well. The critical features of this case seem to be internal thoughts and feelings rather than public actions or visible reactions. How does a behavior-oriented therapist handle cases such as this?

In these kinds of cases, a number of therapists attempt to confront directly the way the patient thinks. They try to replace the patient's irrational and disabling beliefs and attitudes with a more realistic way of thinking. This general mode of therapy goes under various labels. A relatively recent version is *cognitive therapy*, originally developed by the psychiatrist Aaron Beck as a treatment for depression (Beck, 1967), and eventually applied to disorders ranging from phobias and other anxiety disorders to obesity and chronic pain (Beck, 1976, 1985; A. Freeman, Simon, Beutler, & Arkowitz, 1989; Cooper & Fairburn, 2001; see Chapter 16 for a discussion of some of Beck's views).

The basic technique of cognitive therapy is to confront patients—actively and often quite directly—with the contradictions inherent in their maladaptive beliefs. Like many modern behavior therapists, a cognitive therapist may also give the patient homework assignments. One such task might be to pinpoint irrational thoughts that come in the form of certain phrases the patient regularly says to herself, such as "It's all my fault," or "If no one loves me, I'm worthless." For example, consider a patient who felt a wave of anxiety when he saw an old friend across the street, but was clueless as to why he was so anxious until he realized that seeing the friend triggered an automatic thought that would provoke anxiety:

> The anxiety seemed incomprehensible until [the patient] "played back" his thoughts: "If I greet Bob, he may not remember me. He may snub me, it has been so long, he may not know who I am...." (Ellis, 1962, quoted in Beck, 1985, p. 1436)

After helping the patient identify the automatic thought, the next task is to reveal its irrationality. After all, Bob may very well remember him. And if he does not, maybe Bob's memory is faulty or he is preoccupied at the moment with his own problems. Here, the cognitive therapist takes the role of a sympathetic Socrates who asks one question after another until the truth is attained. But suppose the patient's original thought is right, and Bob never liked him in the first place and might well have snubbed him. Is that the end of the world? Is it really necessary to be liked by everybody? Once these irrational thoughts are exposed, the patient can eventually refrain from thinking them and substitute more rational thoughts. This will lead him both to feel and to function better.

## INTERPERSONAL THERAPY

*Interpersonal therapy* (**IPT**; Klerman & Weissman, 1993) was originally intended as a brief therapy to counter depression but has been extended to long-term therapy and disorders other than depression (Weissman & Markowitz, 1994). Although its roots are in psychodynamic therapy, IPT resembles cognitive therapy in being a fairly structured approach focused on the patient's present life circumstances, with the therapist being an active and directive participant. Unlike cognitive therapy, however, IPT's axiom is that depression is maintained by a self-imposed social isolation that cuts off the emotional sustenance available from healthy relationships. The focus is on the patient's gaining an understanding of how she interacts with others, and then learning new and more beneficial ways of interacting and communicating.

A course of IPT begins with an assessment of what factors changed in the person's life at the time depression ensued. These factors tend to fall into one or more major areas, which then become the focus of treatment. The first area concerns grieving, and, in these cases, the therapist guides the patient in mourning recent interpersonal losses such as deaths or the loss of a friend or confidant. In the second area, interpersonal disputes, the therapist helps the patient review ongoing conflicts she is having with family members, friends, or coworkers. The work of therapy here is to formulate ways to

Writing for health

*Therapy as social education (© 1950, 1952 United Features Syndicate Inc.)*

resolve these conflicts, or to decide that a relationship is untenable and the patient must move on. The third area is interpersonal role transitions, such as the graduation from college, beginning of a new love affair, getting married, or retiring. People in the midst of such role transitions must learn to act the part and fill other's expectations of the new role (for example, a single man must learn to be a husband), and here the therapist helps that patient to understand the advantages and disadvantages of both the old and the new roles. The final area focuses on interpersonal deficits and addresses interpersonal skills the patient never learned. For example, a thirty-year-old woman who took care of her ailing mother for fifteen years may need to learn flirtation, dating, and relationship skills in order to meet and keep a partner.

How does IPT fare in treating depression? Several studies show that it is more effective than a placebo, and equal to or better than cognitive therapy for the treatment of mild to moderate depression. One might wonder how two therapies predicated on such different assumptions about the nature and causes of depression could have roughly equal effectiveness against it. Many researchers believe the explanation lies in the fact that, despite their theoretical underpinnings, these therapies—actually, all kinds of therapies—have much in common.

## SOME COMMON THEMES

Regardless of their views on mental disorders, there are some important underlying themes that run through the beliefs and practices of all the various psychotherapies, and these may be in large part responsible for their effectiveness.

*Nonspecific Benefits of Therapy* Several benefits of therapy are nonspecific—that is, not due to any specific therapeutic techniques. One is that the patient gains an ally against his problem; this therapeutic alliance helps most patients believe that they really can conquer their problems and achieve better lives (Barber, Connolly, Crits-Christoph, Gladis, & Siqueland, 2000; Horvath & Luborsky, 1993). In fact, some researchers believe that the therapeutic alliance is the most important single ingredient in the effectiveness of psychotherapy and is indispensable even when medication is the primary treatment (Krupnick et al., 1996). A related benefit is that being in therapy fuels the hope that the patient will finally get better, and this hope can itself promote successes in the outside world. Finally, therapy provides the patient with an intimate, confiding relationship with another person, a kind of secular confessional. This alone may be a boon to some people who have no close bonds to anyone and for whom psychotherapy may amount to "the purchase of friendship" (Schofield, 1964).

*The advantages of talk If many different forms of therapy are all equally effective, then we might ask what the forms of therapy have in common. One common feature is the presence of serious, sympathetic, earnest talk, helping someone to work through a problem. Of course, this sort of helpful talk can also happen outside of therapy, but that does not remove the fact that this talk, in therapy, is likely to be part of why therapy is helpful.*

*Alienation in the modern world* (*Government Bureau* by *George Tooker, 1956*)

*Emotional Defusing* People usually enter psychotherapy of whatever stripe with many anxieties: "What's wrong with me?" "Am I normal?" These kinds of questions are commonplace. New patients are often worried that their problems are weird or shameful and either too trivial to warrant therapy or so severe that no treatment will work. They may hope for, and dread, the opportunity to reveal things they have kept secret, often for years. All psychotherapists, regardless of their approach, spend a great deal of time in therapy hearing these concerns and secrets, and responding to them in an accepting and nonjudgmental manner. With some reassurance and a little education, patients' anxieties abate as they learn that their problems are understandable, rather common, not shameful, and quite treatable.

*Interpersonal Learning* All major schools of psychotherapy stress the importance of interpersonal learning and believe that the therapeutic relationship is an important tool for bringing this about. This relationship shows the patient how she generally reacts to others, and it provides a testing ground for trying new and better ways of reacting. These concerns are, of course, front-stage center in interpersonal therapy, but they are visible in all the other therapies as well.

*Self-Knowledge* Most psychotherapists try to help their patients achieve greater self-knowledge, although the various therapeutic schools differ in what kind of self-knowledge they try to bring about. For psychoanalysts, the crucial emotional insights the patient must acquire refer to his own past; for behavior therapists, the relevant self-understanding is the correct identification of the eliciting stimuli or consequences that maintain problematic behavior; for interpersonal therapists, the most important insights concern how one mismanaged but can now manage social relationships. In each case, patients can use this self-knowledge to guide their future actions and interactions.

*Therapy as an Incremental Process* There is also general agreement that psychotherapy is a gradual affair and that this is so regardless of whether the therapy emphasizes insight, emotion, or overt action. There are few sudden flashes of insight or emotional understanding that change a patient overnight. Instead, each new skill or newfound insight must be laboriously applied in one life situation after another before the patient can call it her own.

In addition to these elements that all psychotherapies have in common, recent years have seen some rapprochement among the different schools of psychotherapy. Some psychoanalytically oriented practitioners have come to use techniques that were formerly the province of behavior therapists, such as modeling and homework assignments (Wachtel, 1977, 1982). From the opposite vantage point, many behavior therapists have come to realize that the client-therapist relationship is a crucial part of treatment, that something like Freud's "transference" comes into play even in mechanistic conditioning therapies such as desensitization (Lazarus, 1971, 1981). The endpoint of this integration is seen in a survey of influential psychotherapists who strongly advocated what they call technical eclecticism—basically, doing whatever works—as the trend in therapy (Beitman, Goldfried, & Norcross, 1989; Norcross & Freedheim, 1992). This eclectic orientation dovetails with recent changes in the practice of psychotherapy that were prompted by economic considerations, as we will see below (see pp. 712–713).

## EXTENSIONS OF PSYCHOTHERAPY

As we have just seen, various forms of therapy actually have a lot in common with each other and have evolved in recent years in ways that emphasize these commonalities, with each form of therapy adopting techniques and perspectives that used to be unique to some other form of therapy. Another recent development is just as important. In Freud's time, psychotherapy was considered an arcane art, practiced by a few initiates (mostly physicians) and available only to a selected group of well-educated adult patients. Since then, psychotherapy has been extended to cover increasingly broader terrain. The individuals now receiving therapy include children, the developmentally disabled, sociopaths, substance abusers, and sufferers of schizophrenia. This broadening of the definition of who can be a "patient" has been accelerated by the advent of psychotherapy and counseling sessions over the Internet—a development that poses unprecedented challenges to the practice and evaluation of therapy, and tests the limits of therapist-patient communication and confidentiality (see Huang & Alessi, 1996).

Another extension was a shift from the original one therapist–one patient formula to various modes of group therapy that feature all conceivable permutations: one therapist and several patients, several therapists and several patients, several patients and no therapist, and so on. Treating patients in groups had two initial advantages: more patients could be accommodated by a limited number of therapists, and patients could be provided with care at a lower cost than individual sessions. But it was appealing for other reasons as well. It often allowed therapists to observe and work with problems that emerged more readily in group settings. More profoundly, group treatment also seemed to fill a void, at least temporarily, left by the weakening of family and religious ties of modern urbanized society.

*Extensions of therapy*    **In the movie,** Good Will Hunting, *the therapist helps his client through a difficult life transition—leaving behind his friends and blue collar neighborhood—to pursue the opportunities made possible by his gift for mathematics.*

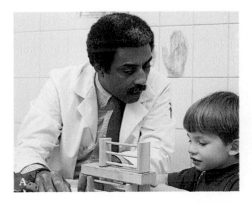

*Play therapy, an extension of psychotherapy adapted for children*    (A) *In play therapy, the therapist tries to help the child understand and express his feelings about his parents and other family members through play with various toys.* (B) *Puppets are sometimes used to act out problems, as in this example of a therapy session with victims of child abuse.*

## GROUP AND RELATIONSHIP THERAPIES

*Shared-Problem Groups*　One approach is to organize a group of people all of whom
have the same problem. They may all be alcoholics, or abuse victims, or ex-convicts. The
members meet, share relevant advice and information, help newcomers along, exhort
and support each other in their resolve to overcome their difficulties. The classic example
is Alcoholics Anonymous (AA), which provides the alcoholic with a sense that he is not
alone and helps him weather crises without suffering a relapse. Another is Toastmasters,
a social club for people with public speaking phobias. In such we-are-all-in-the-same-
boat groups, the primary aim is to manage the problem that all members share. No specific attention is paid to emotional problems that are unique to any one individual.

*Therapy Groups*　The rules of the game are very different in groups explicitly organized for the purpose of group therapy. Here, a group of selected patients, usually
around eight to ten, is treated together under the guidance of a trained therapist. This
form of therapy may have some advantages that individual treatment lacks. According
to its proponents, in group therapy the therapist does not really treat the members of
the group; instead, she helps them to treat each other. The specific techniques of the
therapist may vary from psychoanalytically oriented insight therapy to interpersonal
therapy to various forms of behavior therapy.

　　Whatever techniques the therapist favors, the treatment of each group member really
begins as he realizes that he is not all that different from the others. He learns that there

*A group therapy session*

are other people who are painfully afraid of rejection, are desperately lonely, have hostile fantasies about their parents, or whatever. Further benefits come from a sense of group belongingness, of support, and of encouragement. Most important of all is the fact that the group provides a ready-made laboratory in interpersonal relations. The patient can discover just what he does that rubs others the wrong way, how he can relate to certain kinds of people more effectively, and so on (Sadock, 1975).

*Couples Therapy and Family Therapy*   In the therapy groups we have considered thus far, the members are almost always strangers before the sessions begin. This is in marked contrast to what happens in couples and family therapy. Here, the people seeking help know each other very well (sometimes all too well) before they enter therapy.

Couples therapy (including marriage counseling) and family therapy have become major therapeutic movements (Kerr & Bowen, 1988; Minuchin, 1974; Satir, 1967). It is probably no coincidence that this growth has occurred during a time of turmoil in American families, evidenced by spiraling divorce rates and reports of child and spousal abuse, and by the increasing numbers of single-parent households.

Family and couples therapists regard the family as an emotional unit that can influence the onset and continuing manifestation of many mental disorders and social problems. Seen from this perspective, the key to relationship and family distress is not necessarily found in pinpointing the "identified patient" in the couple or family. Rather, the interlocking relationships that constitute a family operate in a delicate balance, and any strain will ricochet throughout the family and affect all its members (Dadds, 1995). The situation is rather like the joints of the body: a sprained ankle causes an immediate limp, but the imbalance in posture the sufferer must maintain while healing can cause back strain, headaches, and pain in the other leg. Many couples and family therapists feel that their task is like that of the orthopedist who is treating the sprained ankle: they try to restore full function both to the ankle and to all the affected parts as well.

## THE EXPANSION OF THERAPEUTIC GOALS

All of these extensions of psychotherapy have made therapy available to a much larger number of people. But did all of them really need it? The answer depends on the goals of therapy.

For Freud, the matter was simple. Most of his patients were disabled by persistent phobias or all-consuming compulsions and were rendered unable to work and love. Freud wanted to heal these patients so that they could once again live normally. As we

*Extensions of psychotherapy   Even pets can benefit from a good therapist.*

noted earlier, he never believed that his treatment would automatically produce happiness or fulfillment or the discovery of personal meaning. These the patients had to find for themselves, and they might very well fail to do so even when they are no longer saddled with undue inner conflict.

Later therapists broadened the goals of treatment. As we mentioned in the previous chapter, there has been a tendency over the years to group more and more behavior patterns under the broad rubric of "mental disorder" and thus make them fodder for psychotherapy. We have reached the point that people who overspend are called "shopping addicts" and are urged to join a self-help program; women who have had several unrewarding relationships are diagnosed as suffering from an excessive need to love and are referred to groups for "women who love too much"; and so on.

Even with this expansion, some observers have suggested that mental health professionals are still too conservative in diagnosing even the standard set of disorders (that is, the disorders catalogued in the *DSM-IV*). They argue that many individuals fall just short of the criteria for formal diagnosis, yet they are still hobbled by "shadow syndromes" that are mild versions of mental disorders (Ratey & Johnson, 1997). For example, take the man who worries constantly about whether his car's engine needs work and takes his car to the repair shop at least once a week just to make sure that everything is okay. Is he just showing an everyday kind of eccentricity, or is he in fact suffering from a mild form of obsessive-compulsive disorder that should be treated?

One study surveyed over 2,000 individuals for the presence of major depression. Based on their signs and symptoms, these individuals were classified into three groups: normal, diagnosable for major depression, or having subsyndromal depression—that is, they had some of the signs and symptoms of major depression but not enough to be diagnosed as having the disorder. Compared to the normal subjects, both the subsyndromal depressives and the fully diagnosable ones had suffered more financial losses, had poorer health, spent more days in bed because they felt unable to go to work, showed impaired functioning on the job, and reported more stress in the home. On most measures, in fact, the subsyndromal and the major depressives were equally impaired (Judd, Paulus, Wells, & Rapaport, 1996). Later research showed that antidepressant medication was quite effective in reversing the impairments associated with subsyndromal depression (Rapaport & Judd, 1998).

Given such evidence, should those with subsyndromal conditions be treated? Some critics believe that they should, but others argue that this would be a first step down a dangerous path, eventually leading to a "cosmetic psychopharmacology" in which people take medication to adjust their personalities just as they now seek nose jobs, liposuction, and face-lifts. Indeed, this view might lead to a world in which nearly any human eccentricity is regarded as problematic and a candidate for treatment, with the term *normal* reserved for the relatively few who are sufficiently bland to survive labeling. Moreover, such indiscriminate diagnosis might also lead people to use their subsyndromal conditions to excuse bad social conduct or poor job performance (see Olson, 1997; J. Q. Wilson, 1997). There are obvious dangers here, but let us note just as well that diagnostic criteria that are too stringent and rigid may exclude from treatment people who might reasonably benefit from it. Clearly, these issues allow no easy resolution.

## CULTURAL COMPETENCE IN PSYCHOTHERAPY

The originators of the theories and techniques we have discussed throughout this chapter were all Europeans and North Americans. Did this affect their proposals? Are their proposals suited only for people in the developed West? Some have suggested, in fact, that psychotherapy may ill serve patients from other cultures. This has led many authors to stress the importance of cultural competence in psychotherapy (Sue, 1998).

They argue that the therapist must understand the patient's culture well enough to modify the goals of therapy so as to conform to the values appropriate for that patient.

For example, many Asian cultures place considerable emphasis on formality in all their affairs. Social roles within these cultures are often clearly defined and tend to be structured largely by age and sex, with a father's authority rarely challenged within the family (Sue & Kirk, 1973). Growing up in such a culture may play an important part in shaping the values a patient brings to therapy. A therapist insensitive to these values risks offending the patient and endangering the therapy. Similarly, a therapy that emphasizes individual autonomy over family loyalties might inadvertently run afoul of the patient's cultural traditions and so be counterproductive.

Likewise, therapists who expect their patients to take responsibility for making changes in their lives may be ineffective with clients whose cultural worldview stipulates that important events are due to fate, chance, or powerful others (Pedersen, Fukuyama, & Heath, 1989). And therapies that solely emphasize personal growth and self-exploration may create rather than reduce a patient's problems of daily living, if the individual happens to belong to a group that is regularly discriminated against (Wohl, 1989). Finally, practitioners who consider psychotherapy a secular endeavor would do well to remember that, for non-Western cultures and many Western ones, any kind of healing must fully acknowledge the patient's spirituality.

*Therapy and cultural values* **Different cultural groups differ in their views of family roles, in their views of the elderly, and also in their views of what it is that causes our behavior in the first place. A therapist not sensitive to these cultural differences could easily do more harm to a client than good.**

# EVALUATING THERAPEUTIC OUTCOME

We have just surveyed what different kinds of therapists believe and do. But do these practices do any good? Does therapy actually help patients? We have already said that drug therapies seem in many ways successful, but certainly have their limitations. What about psychotherapy?

These questions often arouse indignant protests from therapists, who see the question as akin to asking the clergy to prove its success in saving souls. The members of the clergy believe that their success is self-evident; many therapists believe the same. And these beliefs seem to be shared by patients: most patients feel utterly certain that they have been helped, and therefore see no point in doubting the obvious (see Seligman, 1995). But testimonials alone are not convincing.* For one thing, both patients and therapists have a serious stake in believing that psychotherapy works. If it does not, the patient has wasted his money, and the therapist has perpetrated a sham (Dawes, 1994; Torrey, 1992). Under the circumstances, neither patient nor therapist may be objective in judging whether there was beneficial change.

Even if change does occur during the weeks (or months) of therapy, what caused it? Our previous explanation of how medications are evaluated should now raise some obvious questions. Was the change produced by the psychotherapy itself, or would it

---

* In the widely touted *Consumer Reports* survey (1995) to evaluate whether psychotherapy is beneficial, 184,000 of the magazine's readers were asked whether they had received help for a mental health problem since 1991. Those who did were further asked to state the problems for which they sought treatment and to rate their satisfaction with it. Of those who received psychotherapy (2,900, or 1.6 percent of the original sample), 54 percent believed that therapy had helped "a great deal," with 90 percent reporting that it helped at least "somewhat." Despite an enthusiastic commentary by the survey's psychologist consultant (Seligman, 1995; and see description of survey by Kotkin, Daviet, & Gurin, 1996), the survey has been controversial and has, for example, been criticized for many of the reasons we discuss in the contexts of evaluating the effectiveness of medication and psychotherapy: no control group, subjective outcome measures, and so on (see Brock, Green, Reich, & Evans, 1996; Hollon, 1996; Jacobson & Christenson, 1996). For more on this issue, see the Web supplement "Does therapy work?"

have occurred anyway? People naturally have ups and downs in their lives and often seek out therapy when they are at their worst. This makes it likely that they will improve somewhat during therapy, thanks simply to the passage of time. And even if we can rule out this concern, other problems remain. If the patient improves, is this attributable to the specific therapeutic intervention? Perhaps, instead, the patient was helped merely by the sense of having an ally during her time of trouble—what we referred to earlier as the therapeutic alliance. Or did the improvement simply come from the decision to turn over a new leaf or from the mere expectation of a cure?

## DOES PSYCHOTHERAPY WORK?

Does therapy work?

An early impetus for research in this domain came from a sharp attack launched by the British psychologist Hans Eysenck. Eysenck (1961) was particularly concerned with the efficacy of psychoanalysis and similar "insight" therapies. To assess these therapies, Eysenck surveyed some two-dozen articles that reported the number of "neurotic" patients (mostly, patients with depression or anxiety disorders in today's nomenclature) who improved or failed to improve after psychotherapy. Overall, about 60 percent improved, a result that might be considered fairly encouraging. But Eysenck argued that this was really nothing to cheer about. According to Eysenck's analysis, the spontaneous recovery rate in so-called neurotics—the number of neurotics who got better with no treatment—was, if anything, even higher, about 70 percent. If so, psychotherapy apparently has no curative effects.

In retrospect, it appears that Eysenck's attack was unduly harsh, and today his study is widely discredited (Jacobson & Christenson, 1996). In particular, he evidently overestimated the rate of spontaneous improvement. According to one review, the median rate of patients who get better without therapy is, depending on the diagnostic composition of the group of patients, around 30 percent. This compares to an average improvement rate of 60 percent for patients who received psychotherapy, a difference that constitutes what the author called "some modest evidence that psychotherapy 'works'" (Bergin, 1971, p. 229; see also Luborsky, Singer, & Luborsky, 1975).

### META-ANALYSES OF THERAPY OUTCOME

Several recent analyses of the effectiveness of psychotherapy provide a more optimistic picture. For the most part, they are based on a statistical technique called *meta-analysis*, by means of which the results of many different studies can be combined. In the most comprehensive analysis of this kind, 475 different studies, comprising 25,000 patients in all, were reviewed (M. L. Smith, Glass, & Miller, 1980). In each of these studies, patients who received some kind of psychotherapy were compared to a similar group of patients who did not. The studies differed in many respects. One factor that varied was the kind of psychotherapy used, whether psychodynamic, humanistic, behavioral, or cognitive. Another factor that varied was the criterion of improvement. In some cases, the criterion was the level of a symptom: the amount of avoidance that snake phobics eventually showed toward snakes, the number of washing episodes shown by compulsive washers, and so on. In others, it was based on an improvement in functioning, such as a rise in a disturbed student's grade-point average (GPA). In still others, such as studies on depressed patients, it was an improvement in mood, as rated by scales completed by the patient himself or by knowledgeable outsiders such as his spouse and children. Given all these differences among the studies, combining the results seemed problematic, but meta-analysis provided a method.

Consider two hypothetical studies, *A* and *B*. Let us say that Study *A* shows that, after treatment, the average snake phobic can move closer to a snake than the average patient who received no treatment. Let us also assume that Study *B* found that depressed students who received psychotherapy show a greater increase in GPA than do equivalent students in an untreated control group. On the face of it, there is no way to average the results of the two studies, because they are presented using completely different units. In the first case, the average effect of therapy— that is, the difference between the group that received treatment and the one that did not—is measured in feet (how near to the snake the patient will go); in the second, it is counted in GPA points. But here is the trick provided by meta-analysis. Let us suppose we find that in Study A, 85 percent of the patients are able to move closer to the snake than the average untreated patient. Let us further suppose that in Study B, 75 percent of the students who received psychotherapy earn a GPA higher than the average GPA of the untreated students. Now we can average the scores. To be sure, feet and GPA points are like apples and oranges and cannot be compared. But the percentage relationships—in our case, 85 and 75—are comparable. Since this is so, they can be averaged across different studies.

The conclusion drawn by averaging across the 475 studies reviewed was that the "average person who receives therapy is better off at the end of it than 80 percent of the persons who do not" (M. L. Smith et al., 1980, p. 87). Later analyses used somewhat more stringent criteria in selecting studies for inclusion within the meta-analysis, but these yielded similar results (see, for example, Andrews & Harvey, 1981; D. A. Shapiro & Shapiro, 1982). Further studies showed that these improvements are still found when patients are studied months or years after treatment (Nicholson & Berman, 1983).

## DETERIORATION EFFECTS

Overall, it appears that patients who receive psychotherapy are better off than patients who do not. But this statement applies to averages. When we look at individuals, we find that while psychotherapy has an effect, this effect is not always for the better. A certain proportion of patients seem to get worse. Some evidence that this is so came from an inspection of the variability of post-treatment test scores (for example, self-ratings). After psychotherapy, the scores on such tests are more divergent than the scores of an untreated control group. This suggests that while some patients improve, some others— fortunately, a smaller number, between 5 and 10 percent of patients—become worse (Bergin, 1967; M. L. Smith et al., 1980).

Many cases of deterioration in psychotherapy seem to be due to a bad therapist-patient relationship at the outset or to outright incompetence or even pathology in the therapist (Hadley & Strupp, 1976; M. L. Smith et al., 1980). Other cases of deterioration may have a subtler cause. Psychotherapy sometimes disrupts what is stable in the patient's life and provides no substitute (Bergin, 1967; Hadley & Strupp, 1976). Sometimes the original problems worsen, or the patient begins to show new ones. For example, the therapy may lead a patient to regard her marriage as unsatisfactory, but as she takes steps toward separation or divorce, she may become severely depressed at the prospect of being alone. Good psychotherapists are alert to such dangers and attempt to avert such deterioration whenever possible.

## COMPARING DIFFERENT THERAPIES

Even given these risks, the majority of patients who receive psychotherapy will end up better off than patients who do not. To the extent that this is so, psychotherapy works. But as we have seen, there are many different types of psychotherapy. Do any of them work better than the others? This question is hotly debated among psychotherapists. Psychodynamically oriented therapists tend to believe that their behavioral and cognitive colleagues are doing mere "patch-up" work. Behavioral and cognitive therapists, in turn, believe that their psychoanalytic associates are using unproven techniques based on pseudoscientific theory. Who is right?

*"Everyone has won and all must have prizes."*
*(From Lewis Carroll, Alice in Wonderland,*
*1865/1963)*

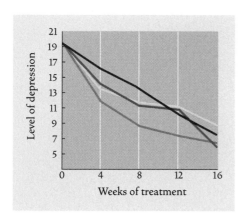

**17.6    The dodo bird verdict    The figure shows**
*the results of a study of 279 depressed patients*
*receiving either cognitive therapy (red line),*
*interpersonal therapy (green line) (Klerman et al.,*
*1984), the antidepressant medication Tofranil*
*(blue line), or a placebo (yellow line). The results*
*after four months show that, while all treated*
*patients were better off than the placebo*
*controls, the particular treatment they received*
*made little difference (Gibbons et al., 1993).*

## THE DODO BIRD VERDICT

The answer, which comes from many comparisons of psychotherapeutic outcomes, is unlikely to provide comfort for the adherents of any one school of psychotherapy. Most of these studies suggest that the various psychotherapies are all about equally effective. This view is sometimes called the **dodo bird verdict** after the dodo bird in *Alice in Wonderland* who organized a race among various Wonderland creatures and concluded, "Everyone has won and all must have prizes" (see Figure 17.6; Luborsky et al., 1975). While a few reviewers feel that the behavioral and cognitive therapies have a slight advantage (see, for example, D. A. Shapiro & Shapiro, 1982), many others judge that the outcome similarities far outweigh the differences (see, for example, Elkin et al., 1989; Shear, Pilkonis, Cloitre, & Leon, 1994; Sloane, Staples, Cristol, Yorkston, & Whipple, 1975; M. L. Smith et al., 1980; Wampold et al., 1997).

## PLACEBO EFFECTS

How could therapies so different from each other all be roughly equivalent in their effectiveness? Several factors contribute. One, simply, is a placebo effect. According to this view, the patients got better because they expected to get better. This is analogous to what happens when patients ingest little blue sugar pills in the belief that they are swallowing a potent medicine (see pp. 691–693). All that matters is the patients' belief in the therapy and hope for help through it.

Placebo effects are important, but other evidence indicates that there is more to therapy than this. Specifically, several meta-analytic studies have compared the effect of placebo treatments to the effect of genuine psychotherapies and found genuine psychotherapy clearly superior (Andrews & Harvey, 1981; Robinson, Berman, & Neimeyer, 1990; M. L. Smith et al., 1980; for a contrary view and discussion, see Prioleau, Murdock, & Brody, 1983).

## COMMON FACTORS

Placebo effects are one factor contributing to the dodo bird verdict, but apparently they are not the whole story. Another factor centers on the shared themes that underlie many of the beliefs and practices of the various modes of psychotherapy. These include therapeutic efforts to defuse emotional situations, provide interpersonal learning, and offer an empathic relationship with another person (see pp. 703–705). To the extent that these features are indeed beneficial and are common to the various schools, we would expect that they (together with some, perhaps small, contribution from placebo effects) exert similar beneficial effects.

## SPECIFIC FACTORS

There may also be some effects that are not so readily detected by the outcome studies (for the most part, meta-analytic) we have discussed thus far. These studies suggested that all psychotherapies are equally effective, regardless of the type. But the real issue may not be which therapy is most effective, but rather which treatment is most effective for which patient under which set of circumstances (Paul, 1967). The meta-analyses we have considered so far may not be the best way to answer this question, because they tend to lump different disorders together. And if the meta-analyses indicate that the various therapies are all equally effective (that is, the dodo bird result), this may be because each of the therapies has its own strengths—perhaps a particular set of disorders for which the therapy is effective, or a particular type of patient with whom the therapy is successful. In this case, the dodo bird result may be akin to comparing weight-lifters, marathon runners, and tennis players and concluding that they are all equally physically fit. This verdict would be true, but it would miss the fact that each of these groups has its own distinctive qualities. Concretely, the verdict would miss the fact that a weight-lifter will not do well if asked to run twenty miles, and a marathon runner will fail if asked to lift two hundred pounds. Is the situation with therapies the same?

According to some practitioners, the analogy is plausible, because some treatments are more effective for some patients and some conditions than for others. They believe that psychotherapy works best, therefore, if specific therapies are matched to the disorder and the patient (Beutler & Clarkin, 1990; Fisher, Beutler, & Williams, 1999; Norcross, 1991; Norcross & Freedheim, 1992). This position is sometimes called *prescriptionism*, for it argues that specific therapies should be prescribed for patients suffering from particular mental disorders just as specific medications are prescribed for particular physical illnesses.

A number of such "prescriptions" are in current use today. For example, it is widely believed that phobias and related anxiety conditions are best treated by any of the behavior therapies that try to eliminate fear, such as systematic desensitization (Emmelkamp, 1986). Panic disorder responds well to cognitive therapy or reflective listening, and such psychotherapy is often accompanied by antidepressant medication to block panic attacks (D. M. Clark, 1988; Shear et al., 1994). Schizophrenia responds to the antipsychotics, with medication by Risperdal, Zyprexa, or Seroquel preferable if possible and medically permissible. Depression seems to be effectively treated by antidepressant medications, cognitive therapy, or interpersonal therapy, and ECT usually works well if these do not. Eskalith (lithium carbonate) or the anticonvulsants Depakote, Tegretol, Neurontin, and Topamax are the favored medications for bipolar disorder, with psychotherapy of no direct use. These are just a few examples of what amounts to an emerging cookbook of therapeutic prescriptions for mental disorders.

## ACCOUNTABILITY FOR PSYCHOTHERAPY

While attacks such as Eysenck's provoked the initial studies of therapeutic effectiveness, a more recent impetus has been the demand for economic accountability. Beginning in the 1970s, private insurance companies that for years had reimbursed patients for both inpatient care and outpatient psychotherapy began to question the costs and benefits of each. As health maintenance organizations (HMOs) began to provide group health care, they too began to require that psychotherapists account for themselves by showing that the time they spent with patients was worth the cost. Finally, tax-funded government programs like Medicare debated whether even to finance psychotherapy (Garfield, 1992).

These issues have forced drastic changes in the practice of psychotherapy. Instead of justifying psychotherapy based on theories about psychopathology or commentaries about meaning and existence, practitioners suddenly had to show that what they practiced improved patients using the most concrete of dependent variables: How fast could the patient be discharged from therapy? How rapidly could she return to work? How long was the patient able to function without further use of professional services? If the costs of therapy were to be paid or reimbursed by an HMO or private insurer, the insurer began to require that the therapy be the most cost-effective kind. And if a patient was making no progress in therapy, the solution was not to conduct more therapy but to discontinue it entirely.

Similar questions have arisen in legal contexts. Could a therapist be guilty of malpractice for not offering a patient the best treatment or at least a proven treatment? Indeed, this was the question behind a widely cited court case that pitted biological against psychoanalytic approaches to the treatment of depression. The case concerned a patient who was severely depressed and was admitted to a psychoanalytically oriented private hospital where he received no antidepressant medication, only intensive psychoanalytically based psychotherapy. During his hospital stay his condition worsened: he lost forty pounds, and his overall physical condition deteriorated. Even so, the therapy was continued, and the patient's deterioration was interpreted as reflecting the patient's difficulties in "working through his defenses." After seven months, the patient's family became alarmed, removed him from this hospital, and placed him in another in which he was immediately treated with antidepressant medication. He recovered within three months and began initiating the lawsuit against the first hospital (*Osheroff v. Chestnut Lodge*; see Klerman, 1990). The lawsuit was settled out of court, but the result stirred the medical community to form a set of standards for effective treatment of many kinds of mental disorders.

Given these economic and legal factors, most psychotherapists today rarely engage patients in therapy oriented toward long-term insight or self-discovery. Instead, they try to provide therapies that have a better-documented chance of working and working quickly. Likewise, the content of psychotherapy today, and not just its theoretical framework, also reflects this pragmatic concern with expense and expediency (Barlow, 1996). Often, therapy consists of brief problem-solving sessions, various psychoeducational interventions such as stress-management classes, and time-limited behavioral therapy (Vandenbos, Cummings, & DeLeon, 1992).

## PARITY FOR MENTAL DISORDERS

The same health insurance cost controls that mandated that all psychotherapy be quick and demonstrably effective also led to a dire situation for many with mental disorders. They discovered that their health care plans would cover the entire costs of treatment for their heart attack or their children's broken legs. But if they or their children were disabled by a mental disorder, the insurance would pay—if any at all—for only a very short hospital stay, a little bit of medication, a few sessions of psychotherapy. For mental health advocates, this amounted to the refusal to consider mental disorders to be real illnesses whose consequences can be as devastating as diseases like cancer or emphysema.

These advocates launched a push for **mental health parity**, arguing that insurance plans should reimburse for the costs of treating mental disorders on the same terms as they do other medical disorders (National Advisory Mental Health Council, 1997). In the United States, one initial result was the Mental Health Parity Act of 1996, which mandated mental health parity by insurers but was weakened by numerous exemptions (for example, employers who could show that parity would cost too much were exempted). More comprehensive parity legislation has now been passed by the majority of states, but even here, parity is extended only to disorders said to be "biologically based," like schizophrenia, major depression, bipolar disorder, and obsessive-compulsive disorder. Critics of parity legislation are justifiably concerned that such coverage will drive up insurance costs, perhaps so much that many employers will no longer be able to provide any health insurance for their employees—even despite the known costs of mental illness in lowered productivity, absenteeism, and other areas. The years ahead will determine the costs and benefits of mental health parity and determine its reasonable limits.

Career paths in mental health

## SOME FINAL THOUGHTS: FAR, BUT NOT YET FAR ENOUGH

Where does all of this leave us? It has been more than a hundred years since Krafft-Ebing's discovery that general paresis is caused by syphilis and since Freud and Breuer's classic studies of hysteria. What can we say today about the treatment of mental disorder?

All in all, there has been considerable progress. Let us begin with psychotherapy. There is little doubt that psychotherapy produces some nonspecific benefits. It helps people by providing someone in whom they can confide, who lends advice about troubling matters, who listens to them, and who instills hope that they will get better. The critic may reply that such gains merely reflect placebo effects and similar matters. According to this view, the benefits are not produced by any specific psychotherapeutic technique but might just as easily have been provided by a wise aunt, the understanding family doctor, or the local clergy.

Even if this were true—and it is certainly not the whole story—it may be irrelevant. Wise aunts are in short supply today; the extended family in which aunts and uncles, nieces, nephews, and grandparents lived nearby is largely a thing of the past. The same is true of the family doctor, who has virtually vanished from the scene, together with his house calls and bedside manner. Nor do many people today have a member of the clergy as a lifelong confidant. All of this suggests that psychotherapy has come to fill a social vacuum. Some of its effect may well be placebo-like, but a placebo is better than nothing.

But this is by no means all. Over and above placebo effects, there are clearly some genuine, specific psychotherapeutic benefits that produce improvement, though rarely a complete cure. The specific ingredients that bring these effects about have not been pinpointed, but they probably include emotional defusing, interpersonal learning, and some insight—all acquired within the therapeutic situation and somehow transferred to the patient's life beyond.

How about biological therapies? Here the progress has been dramatic. Antipsychotic medications control some of the worst manifestations of schizophrenia. The antidepressants and antimanic medications (and where appropriate, ECT) do the same for the mood swings of depression and mania, as do the anxiolytics for disabling anxiety. These advances are far from what one might wish—the medicines do not cure, they just keep symptoms in check, and all have side effects.

But we have come far from where we started more than a century ago. This is especially clear when we look back and compare our current practices with those at the time of the American Revolution, when Benjamin Rush dunked his patients into ice-cold water or whirled them around until they were unconscious. Good treatments are now available for a number of mental disorders, and they enable many people to rebound from complete disability to normal function. Although we have much further to go, there is much to celebrate.

# SUMMARY

## BIOLOGICAL THERAPIES

1. *Biological therapies* constitute one major form of treatment of mental disorder. Of these, the most widely used are the *psychotropic medications*. The classic *antipsychotics* like *Thorazine* are helpful in holding in check the major *positive symptoms* of schizophrenia, and new antipsychotics like *Clozaril* show promise in treating *negative symptoms* as well. These new antipsychotics have fewer motor side effects, and can often produce beneficial results in schizophrenics who have not responded to classic antipsychotics.

2. Classic *antidepressants* such as the *MAO inhibitors* and *tricyclics* counteract depressions, and one particular tricyclic, *Anafranil*, is effective in many cases of obsessive-compulsive disorder. However, these antidepressants all have many undesirable side effects, and this has led to a search for better medications. The last few decades have seen the advent of the so-called "designer drugs," engineered to specifically enhance—or inhibit—certain neurotransmitters but not others. Of these the best known is *Prozac*, which is of the group of *selective serotonin reuptake inhibitors (SSRIs)*. These newer drugs have fewer side effects and are equally effective for depressions and obsessive-compulsive disorder.

3. *Lithium carbonate* is useful in cases of bipolar disorder, especially in forestalling or reducing the intensity of manic episodes.

4. Evaluating the effectiveness of psychotropic medications—as indeed of all therapies—requires careful evaluations that control for *spontaneous improvement* and *placebo effects*, and that also guard against both the physicians' and the patients' expectations by use of *double-blind techniques*. Such studies have demonstrated genuine effects of certain psychotropic medications, some of which are quite specific to a particular disorder. These medications reduce the signs and symptoms of a disorder but do not cure it. Without maintenance doses, patients discharged from care may relapse (as may patients who choose on their own to stop taking their medication).

5. The effectiveness of antipsychotic medications lent impetus to the *deinstitutionalization* movement. This led to a major decrease in the number of patients housed in U.S. mental institutions. The high hopes of this movement have been tempered by the fact that while the antipsychotic drugs alleviate the symptoms of schizophrenia, they do not provide a cure. As a result many of the discharged persons have to be readmitted, becoming "revolving door" patients.

6. Other biological therapies include *psychosurgery*, a procedure that was once done promiscuously and to the detriment of the recipients but is now conducted much more selectively and precisely. *Electroconvulsive therapy (ECT)* is markedly effective in cases of severe and potentially suicidal depression, and for cases of bipolar disorder that resist antimanic medications.

## PSYCHOTHERAPY

7. A very different approach to the treatment of mental disorder, *psychotherapy*, relies on psychological means alone. It derived from *classical psychoanalysis* but in modern practice has generally expanded and diversified in both guiding principles and techniques.

8. *Psychoanalysts* try to help their patients to recover repressed memories and wishes so that they can overcome crippling internal conflicts. Their tools include *free association* and the *interpretation* of the patient's *resistance* to their own associations. The goal is emotional rather than mere intellectual *insight*, an achievement made possible by an analysis of the *transference* relationship between analyst and patient.

9. In *psychodynamic therapy*, therapists follow Freud's basic principles but generally place greater emphasis on current interpersonal and social problems rather than on psychosexual matters in the patient's past. They also tend to take a more active role in helping the patient extend the therapeutic experience to the world outside.

10. A different approach is taken by *behavior therapists* whose concern is with unwanted, overt behaviors rather than with hypothetical underlying causes. Many of the behavior therapists' techniques are derived from the principles of classical and instrumental conditioning. Therapies based on classical conditioning include *systematic desensitization*, which tries to *countercondition* the patient's fear by a policy of gradual exposure. Another is *aversion therapy*, in which undesirable behaviors, thoughts, and desires are coupled with unpleasant stimuli. Therapies based on operant conditioning principles include the use of *token economies*, in which patients are systematically reinforced for desirable behaviors.

11. Some recent offshoots of behavior therapy share its concrete and directive orientation but not its emphasis on conditioning. One example is *cognitive therapy*, which tries to change the way the patient thinks about his situation. Others include various attempts to advance the patient's social education, using techniques such as *graded task assignments, modeling,* and *role playing.* A related approach is *interpersonal therapy (IPT)*, whose focus is on the patient's current life situation.

12. Despite their differences, the various forms of psychotherapy have some important similarities. They include various non-specific benefits such as the *therapeutic alliance, emotional defusing, interpersonal learning,* and greater *self-knowledge,* and they agree that the therapeutic process is incremental.

13. The last few decades have seen an enormous extension of psychotherapy. One extension is of method. An example is *group therapy*, in which patients are treated in groups rather than individually. Another example is *family (and marital) therapy,* whose practitioners believe that family distress is not in the pathology of any one individual, but in the relationships within the family system, and who therefore try to rectify these faulty relationships. Another extension concerns the therapeutic goals. While the original purpose of psychotherapy was to cure pathology, some practitioners gradually broadened this goal to include personal growth. In addition, therapists are now encouraged to develop *cultural competence,* so that they can adapt their therapies to the patient's specific cultural values and customs.

14. In recent years, investigators have begun to assess the effectiveness of psychotherapies through a statistical technique called *meta-analysis,* by means of which the results of many different studies can be combined. The results of such analyses indicate that the various psychotherapies are more effective than placebo treatments, which in turn are better than no treatment at all. Comparing the effect of different psychotherapies is enormously difficult, but the main finding is that therapies tend to be fairly effective, and that they are effective to about the same extent (the *dodo bird verdict*).

15. The dodo-bird verdict comes from studies that combine many types of patients and disorders. Work is underway to determine the extent to which therapy can be matched to the patient and the disorder. Practitioners who adopt the *prescriptionist* position believe that in addition to placebo effects and the various common factors such as *interpersonal learning*, particular therapies have some specific effects on particular conditions.

16. Legal issues and health insurance costs have forced psychotherapists to reexamine their own efforts and provide only those services that have demonstrated effectiveness. This is leading to the development of generally accepted professional standards of care for specific mental disorders and standards of *accountability.* Mental health advocates have pushed for *mental health parity,* arguing that insurance plans should reimburse treatment costs for mental disorders on the same terms as other medical disorders.

# EPILOGUE

We have come to the end of our journey. We have traveled through the sprawling fields of psychology, a loosely federated intellectual empire that stretches from the domains of the biological sciences on one border to those of the social sciences on the other. We have gone from one end of psychology to another. What have we learned?

In looking back over our journey, it is clear that, today, we know vastly more about mind and behavior than we did in the days of, say, Thorndike and Köhler, let alone those of Descartes, Locke, and Kant. Indeed, psychology is by now a science of considerable accomplishments. We know an enormous amount about how the mind functions, and what the biological basis is for this functioning. We know a lot about how people view each other and how they treat each other. We know a great deal about how people differ from one another—whether within a culture or between cultures—and we also know much about what it is that people have in common. In many cases, our knowledge is of considerable theoretical interest, and this has led (among other benefits) to rich discussions between psychologists and philosophers about the nature of the mind, the nature of knowledge, and the nature of being human. Indeed, as psychology's power and breadth have grown, the dialog between our field and other disciplines has become rich, sophisticated, and beneficial both to psychology and to our intellectual neighbors—in linguistics, sociology, anthropology, biology, neuroscience, political science, and computer science.

In still other cases, the knowledge psychology has gained is of great practical importance, and this is evident in psychological clinics around the globe, and equally visible whenever a psychologist appears in the courtroom to evaluate eyewitness testimony or whenever a member of our profession works with an organization to improve the functioning and well-being of the organization's members. And, throughout, psychology can also look with pride on a powerful set of technical, methodological, and statistical tools that have been developed, all of which provide strong assurance that the knowledge we have gained is well established and that our prospects for learning even more are extremely bright.

As impressive as this picture is, though, we should not ignore the fact that what we know today still remains only a small clearing in a vast unknown jungle. We have learned more and more over the years, and so the clearing in the jungle has expanded mightily, but so has the circumference that borders on the uncharted wilderness.

What can we say? We can point at what we know and congratulate ourselves. Or we can consider what we do not know and bemoan our ignorance. Perhaps a wiser course is one recommended by Sigmund Freud, among others, on thinking about some aspects of human intellectual history (Freud, 1917).

Freud suggested a parallel between the psychological growth of each human child and the intellectual progress of humanity as a whole. As he saw it, the infant is initially possessed by a pervasive sense of his own power and importance. He cries and his parents come to change or feed or rock him, and so he comes to believe that he is the cause of whatever happens around him, the center of a world that revolves around him alone. But this happy delusion of omnipotence cannot last forever. Eventually the growing infant discovers that he is not the hub of the universe. This recognition may come as a cruel blow, but he will ultimately be the better for it. For the child cannot become strong and capable without some awareness that he is not so as yet, without first accepting the fact that he can't have his way just by wishing. His first achievements will be slight—as he lifts his own cup or says his first word—but they are real enough, and they lay the foundation for his later mastery of his environment.

Freud thought that a similar theme underlies the growth of humankind's awareness of the world in which we live. On two crucial occasions in our history, we had to relinquish some cherished beliefs in our own power and importance. With Copernicus, we had to cede our place in the center of the physical universe: the sun does not circle us, but we the sun. With Darwin, we had to forfeit our presumption of centrality in the biological sphere: we are not specially created but are descended from other animals. Each of these intellectual revolutions ran into vehement opposition, in large part because each represented a gigantic blow to humanity's self-love and pride. They made us contemplate our own ignorance and reassess our relative significance. But however painful it may have been initially, each recognition of our weakness ultimately helped us gain strength, each confession of ignorance eventually led to deeper understanding. The Copernican revolution forced us to admit our minute place in the celestial scheme of things, but this admission was the first step in a journey of ever-increasing physical horizons, a journey which in our own time brought us to the moon. The Darwinian revolution made us aware that we are just one biological species among millions, the product of the same evolutionary process that brought forth sea urchins and penguins. But this awareness opened the way for continually expanding explorations of the biological universe, explorations that have already given us much greater control of our own bodily condition and of the fragile environment in which we and other species exist.

In the last hundred years we have had to suffer yet another blow to our self-pride. We learned that we cannot be sure of what goes on in our own minds. Modern psychology, for all its accomplishments, has made it utterly clear that thus far we know even less about our own mental processes and behavior than we know about the physical and biological world around us. Here, too, we have to confess our ignorance. We can only hope that this confession will have some of the effects of our previous ones, that here again strength will grow out of weakness and knowledge out of folly and ignorance. If so, we may finally understand why we think and do what we think and do, so that we may improve our capacity to control, and perhaps even change, our inner selves, just as we have learned to change many aspects of the world around us.

There are few goals in science that are worthier than this.

# APPENDIX

# STATISTICS:
# THE DESCRIPTION,
# ORGANIZATION, AND
# INTERPRETATION OF DATA

In Chapter 1, we considered how psychologists gather data—how they design a study or an experiment, how they ensure external and internal validity, and so on. But what do they do once the data are gathered? In this appendix, we will focus on the statistical methods investigators use to organize and interpret numerical data.

Let us begin with an example. Suppose some investigators want to find out whether three-year-old boys are more physically aggressive than three-year-old girls. To find out, the investigators will first have to come up with some appropriate measure of physical aggression. They will then have to select the participants for the study. Since the investigators presumably want to say something about three-year-olds in general, not just the particular three-year-olds in their study, they must select their participants appropriately. Even more important, they must select boys and girls who are well matched to each other in all regards except gender, so that the investigators can be reasonably sure that any differences between the two groups are attributable to the difference in sex rather than to other factors (such as intellectual development, social class, and so on).

We discussed in Chapter 1 how investigators design studies and collect data. So we'll start here with what investigators do once their data have been collected. Their first task is to organize these data in a meaningful way. Suppose the study used two groups of 50 boys and 50 girls, each observed on 10 separate occasions. This means that the investigators will end up with at least 1,000 separate numerical entries, 500 for the boys and 500 for the girls. Something has to be done to reduce this mass of numbers into some manageable form. This is usually accomplished by some process of averaging scores.

The next step involves statistical interpretation. Suppose the investigators find that the average score for physical aggression is greater for the boys than for the girls. (It probably will be.) How should this fact be interpreted? Should it be taken seriously, or might it just be a fluke, some sort of accident? For it is just about certain that the data contain *variability*: the children within each group will not perform identically to each other; furthermore, the same child may very well behave differently on one occasion than on another. Thus, the number of aggressive acts for the boys might be, say, 5.8 on average, but might vary from a low of 1.3 (the score from completely calm Calvin) to a high of 11.4 (the score from awfully aggressive Albert). The average number of aggressive acts for the girls might be 3.9 (and so lower than the boys' average), but this derives from a range of scores that include 0 (from serene Sarah) and 6.2 (from aggressive Agnes).

Is it possible that this difference between boys and girls is just a matter of chance, an accidental by-product of this variability? For example, what if boys and girls are, in fact, rather similar in their levels of aggression, but—just by chance—the study happened to include four or five extremely aggressive boys and a comparable number of extremely unaggressive girls? After all, we know that our results would have been different if Albert had been absent on the day of our testing; the boys' average, without his contribution, would have been lower. Likewise, Agnes's twin sister was not included in our test group because of the random process through which we selected our research participants. If she had been included, and if she was as aggressive as her twin, then the girls' average would have been higher. Is it possible that accidents like these are the real source of the apparent difference between the groups? If so, then another study, without these same accidents, might yield a different result. One of the main reasons for using statistical methods is to deal with questions of this sort, to help us draw useful conclusions about behavior despite the unavoidable variability, and, specifically, allowing us to ask in a systematic way whether our data pattern is reliable (and so would emerge in subsequent studies) or just the product of accidents.

## DESCRIBING THE DATA

In the example above, we assumed that the investigators would be collecting numerical data. We made this assumption because much of the power of statistics results from the fact that numbers can be manipulated using the rules of arithmetic, unlike open-ended responses in an interview, videotapes of social interactions, or lists of words recalled in a memory experiment. (How could you average together one participant's response of "Yes, I like them" with another's response of "Only on weekends"?) As a result, scientists prefer to use numerical response measures whenever possible. Consider our hypothetical study of physical aggression. The investigators who watched the research participants might rate their physical aggression in various situations from 1 to 5, with 1 being "extremely docile" and 5 being "extremely aggressive," or they might count the number of aggressive acts (say, hitting or kicking another child). This operation of assigning numbers to observed events is called *scaling*.

There are several types of scales that will concern us. They differ by the arithmetical operations that can be performed on them.

## CATEGORICAL AND ORDINAL SCALES

Sometimes the scores assigned to individuals are merely *categorical* (also called *nominal*). For example, when respondents to a poll are asked to name the television channel they watch most frequently, they might respond "4," "2," or "13." These numbers serve only to group the responses into categories. They can obviously not be subjected to any arithmetic operations. (If a respondent watches channels 2 and 4 equally often, we can't summarize this by claiming that, on average, she watches channel 3!)

*Ordinal* scales convey more information, in that the relative magnitude of each number is meaningful—not arbitrary, as in the case of categorical scales. If individuals are asked to list the ten people they most admire, the number 1 can be assigned to the most admired person, 2 to the runner-up, and so on. The smaller the number assigned, the more the person is admired. Notice that no such statement can be made of television channels: channel 4 is not more anything than channel 2, just different from it.

Scores that are ordinally scaled cannot, however, be added or subtracted. The first two persons on the most-admired list differ in admirability by 1; so do the last two. Yet the individual who has done the ranking may admire the first person far more than the other nine, all of whom might be very similar in admirability. Imagine, for example, a child who, given this task, lists his mother first, followed by the starting lineup of the Chicago Cubs. In this case, the difference between rank 1 and rank 2 is enormous; the difference between rank 2 and rank 3 (or any other pair of adjacent ranks) is appreciably smaller. Or, to put it another way, the difference of eight between person 2 and person 10 probably represents a smaller difference in judged admirability than the difference of one obtained between persons 1 and 2 (at least so the mother hopes).

## INTERVAL SCALES

Scales in which equal differences between scores, or intervals, can be treated as equal units are called *interval scales*. Response time is a common psychological variable that is usually treated as an interval scale. In some memory experiments, for example, the participant must respond as quickly as possible to each of several words, some of which she has seen earlier in the experiment; the task is to indicate, by pressing the appropriate button, whether each word had appeared earlier or not.

Suppose that someone requires an average of 2 seconds to respond to nouns, 3 seconds to verbs, and 4 seconds to adjectives. The difference in decision time between verbs and nouns (3 − 2 = 1 second) is the same as the difference in decision time between adjectives and verbs (4 − 3 = 1 second). We can make this statement—which in turn suggests various hypotheses about the factors that underlie such differences—precisely because response time can be regarded as an interval scale.

## RATIO SCALES

Scores based on an interval scale allow subtraction and addition. But they do not allow multiplication and division. Consider the Celsius scale of temperature. The difference between 10 and 20 degrees Celsius is equal to that between 30 and 40 degrees Celsius. But can one say that 20 degrees Celsius is twice as high a temperature as 10 degrees Celsius? The answer is no, for the Celsius scale of temperature is only an interval scale. It is not a *ratio scale*, which allows statements such as 10 feet is one-fifth as long as 50 feet, or 15 pounds is three times as heavy as 5 pounds. To make such statements, one needs a true zero point. Such a ratio scale with a zero point does exist for temperature—the Kelvin absolute temperature scale, whose zero point (*absolute zero* to chemists and physicists) is about −273 degrees Celsius.

Some psychological variables can be described by a ratio scale. For example, it does make sense to say that the rock music emanating from your neighbor's dorm room is four times as loud as your roommate singing in the shower. But there are many psychological variables that cannot be described in ratio terms. For example, let us say that we assemble a list of behaviors commonly associated with clinical depression, and we find that, say, Person 1 displays 8 of these behaviors, while Person 2 displays 16 of them. We could legitimately say that there is a difference of 8 behaviors here—this is an interval scale. But we should not say that Person 2's score is twice as worrisome as that of Person 1, because we really don't know the zero point for this scale. More specifically, what we need to know is how many of these behaviors can be observed in people who do not suffer from depression. If we knew that people without depression showed none of these behaviors, then zero would be the true starting point for our scale (and so, in this scenario, it would appear that Person 2 does have twice as many of the relevant behaviors as Person 1). But if we found that people without depression showed 7 of these behaviors, then that would be the starting point for our scale (and so Person 1, with only 1 behavior more than this starting point, would appear to be vastly better off than Person 2, with 9 behaviors beyond the starting point).

# ORGANIZING THE DATA

We have considered the ways in which psychologists describe the data provided by their studies by assigning numbers to them (scaling). Our next task is to see how these data are organized.

## THE FREQUENCY DISTRIBUTION

Suppose that an investigator wanted to determine whether visual imagery aids memory. (See Chapter 7 for some actual research on this topic.) To find out he designed an experiment that required participants to memorize a list of words and later to recall as many of these words as possible. Members of the experimental group were instructed to form visual images connecting each word to the preceding word. Members of the control group were not given any imagery instructions. Let us say that there are ten people in each group, and so the scores from the control group might have been

$$8, 11, 6, 7, 5, 9, 5, 9, 9, 11.$$

A first step in organizing these data is to list all the possible scores and the frequencies with which they occurred, as shown in Table A.1. Such an arrangement is called a *frequency distribution* because it shows the frequency with which each number of words was recalled (e.g., how many of the participants recalled 11 words, how many recalled 10 words, and so on).

The frequency distribution can also be expressed graphically. A common means for doing this is a *histogram*, which uses a series of rectangles to depict the frequency distribution (Figure A.1). The values of the dependent variable (the number of words recalled) are shown by the location of each rectangle on the x-axis. The frequency of each score is shown by the height of each rectangle, as measured on the y-axis. This is simple enough for our example, but in practice graphic presentation

**TABLE A.1 FREQUENCY DISTRIBUTION**

| SCORE | FREQUENCY |
| --- | --- |
| 11 | 2 |
| 10 | 0 |
| 9 | 3 |
| 8 | 1 |
| 7 | 1 |
| 6 | 1 |
| 5 | 2 |

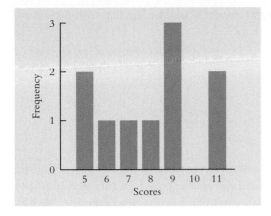

A.1 Histogram    In a histogram, a frequency distribution is graphically represented by a series of rectangles. The location of each rectangle on the x-axis indicates a score, while its height shows how often that score occurred.

often requires a further step. The number of possible values the dependent variable can assume is often very large. As a result, it is possible that every specific score in the data list appears just once! For example, in a response-time study, there might be only one response in the entire data set that took exactly 224.01 milliseconds, just one that took exactly 224.02 milliseconds, and so on. If the investigator created a frequency distribution showing how often each score occurred, the resulting histogram would be very wide (with many rectangles), very flat (since all rectangles would have the same height), and not at all informative. To get around this, it is common for investigators to group together similar observations, and this is usually done by dividing the data into "bins." Thus, the histogram might plot the frequency of observing a response time between, say, 200 and 225 milliseconds (that would be one bin), the frequency of observing a time between 225.01 and 250 milliseconds, and so on.

## MEASURES OF CENTRAL TENDENCY

For many purposes we want a description of an experiment's result that is more concise than a frequency distribution. We might, for example, wish to describe how a typical or average participant behaved. This sort of data summary is provided by a *measure of central tendency*, which locates the center of the distribution. Three measures of central tendency are commonly used: the *mode*, the *median*, and the *mean*.

The mode is simply the score that occurs most frequently. In our example, the mode for the control group is 9. More people (to be exact, 3) recalled 9 words than recalled any other number of words.

The median is the point that divides the distribution into two equal halves, when the scores are arranged in increasing order. To find the median in our example, we first list the scores.

5, 5, 6, 7, 8, 9, 9, 9, 11, 11
↑

Since there are ten scores, the median lies between the fifth and sixth scores, that is, between 8 and 9, as indicated by the arrow. Any score between 8 and 9 would divide the distribution into two equal halves, but it is conventional to choose the number in the center of the interval between them, that is, 8.5. When there is an odd number of scores this problem does not arise, and the middle number is used.

The third measure of central tendency, the mean (M), is the familiar arithmetic average. If $N$ stands for the number of scores, then

$$M = \frac{\text{sum of scores}}{N}$$

$$= \frac{5+5+6+7+8+9+9+9+11+11}{10} = \frac{80}{10} = 8.0$$

The mean is the measure of central tendency most commonly used by psychologists, in part because a number of further calculations can be based on this measure. It is common, therefore, for the results of experiments like our imagery example to be displayed as shown in Figure A.2. The values of the independent variable (in this case, getting imagery instructions) are indicated on the $x$-axis, and the values of the dependent variable (mean number of words recalled) on the $y$-axis.

Despite the common use of the mean, each of these measures of central tendency has its own advantages. The mode is used relatively rarely, because the modes of two samples can differ greatly even if the samples have very similar distributions. If one of the 3 participants who recalled 9 words recalled only 5 instead, the mode would have been 5 rather than 9. But the mode does have its uses. For example, a home builder might decide to include a two-car garage on a new house because 2 is the mode for the number of cars owned by American families; more people will be content with a two-car garage than with any other size.

The median and the mean differ most in the degree to which they are affected by extreme scores. If the highest score in our sample were changed from 11 to 111, the median would be unaffected, whereas the mean would jump from 8.0 to 18.0. Most people would find the median (which remains 8.5) a more compelling "average" than the mean in such a situation, since most of the scores in the distribution are close to the median but are not close to the mean (18.0). This is why medians are often preferred when the data become highly variable, even though the mean has computational advantages.

The advantages of the median become particularly clear with distributions of scores that contain a few extreme values. Such distributions are said to be *skewed*, and a classic example is income distribution, since there are only a few very high incomes but many low ones. Suppose we sample ten individuals from a neighborhood and find their yearly incomes (in thousands of dollars) to be

$$10, 12, 20, 20, 40, 40, 40, 80, 80, 4,000$$

The median income for this sample is 40 ($40,000), since both the fifth and sixth scores are 40. This value reflects the income of the typical individual. The mean income for this sample, however, is (10 + 12 + 20 + 20 + 40 + 40 + 40 + 80 + 80 + 4,000)/ 10 = 418, or $418,000. A politician who wants to demonstrate that her neighborhood has prospered might—quite accurately—use these data to claim that the average (mean) income is $418,000. If, on the other hand, she wished to plead for financial relief, she might say—with equal accuracy—that the average (median) income is only $40,000. There is no single "correct" way to find an "average" in this situation, but it is obviously important to know which average (that is, which measure of central tendency) is being used.

When deviations in either direction from the mean are equally frequent, the distribution is said to be *symmetrical*. In such distributions, the mean and the median are likely to be close to each other in actual value, and so either can be used in describing the data. Many psychological variables have symmetrical distributions, but for variables with skewed distributions, like income, measures of central tendency must be chosen with care.

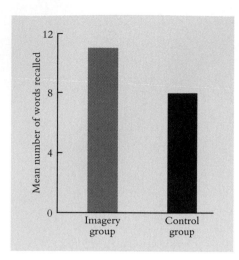

**A.2    The results of an experiment on memorizing**    *Participants in the imagery group, who were asked to form visual images of the words they were to memorize, recalled an average of 11 words. Participants in the control group, who received no special instructions, recalled an average of 8 words.*

# MEASURES OF VARIABILITY

In reducing an entire frequency distribution to an average score, we have discarded a lot of very useful information. Suppose the National Weather Service measures the temperature every day for a year in various cities and calculates a mean for each city. This tells us something about the city's climate, but certainly does not tell us everything. This is shown by the fact that the mean temperature in both San Francisco and Albuquerque is 56 degrees Fahrenheit. But the climates of the two cities differ considerably, as indicated in Table A.2.

The weather displays much more variability in the course of a year in Albuquerque than in San Francisco, but, of course, this variability is not reflected in the mean. One way to measure this variability is the *range*, the highest score minus the lowest. The range of temperatures in San Francisco is 15, while in Albuquerque it is 42.

A shortcoming of the range as a measure of variability is that it reflects the values of only two scores in the entire sample. As an example, consider the following distributions of ages in two college classes:

Distribution *A*: 19, 19, 19, 19, 19, 20, 25

Distribution *B*: 17, 17, 17, 20, 23, 23, 23

Intuitively, distribution *A* has less variability, since all scores but one are very close to the mean. Yet the range of scores is the same (6) in both distributions. The problem arises because the range is determined by only two of the seven scores in each distribution.

A better measure of variability would incorporate every score in the distribution rather than just two. One might think that the variability could be measured by asking how far each individual score is away from the mean, and then taking the average of these distances. This would give us a measure that we could interpret (roughly) as "on average, all the data points are only two units from the mean" (or "... three units ..." or whatever it turned out to be). The most straightforward way to measure this would be to find the arithmetic difference (by subtraction) between each score and the mean (that is, computing [score − M] for each score), and then to take the average of these differences (that is, add up all of these differences, and divide by the number of observations):

$$\frac{\text{sum of (score} - \text{M)}}{N}$$

This hypothetical measure is unworkable, however, because some of the scores are greater than the mean and some are smaller, so that the numerator is a sum of both positive and negative terms. (In fact, it turns out that the sum of the positive terms equals

| TABLE A.2   TEMPERATURE DATA FOR TWO CITIES (DEGREES FAHRENHEIT) | | | | |
|---|---|---|---|---|
| CITY | LOWEST MONTH | MEAN | HIGHEST MONTH | RANGE |
| Albuquerque, New Mexico | 35 | 56 | 77 | 42 |
| San Francisco, California | 48 | 56 | 63 | 15 |

the sum of the negative terms, so that the expression shown above always equals zero.) The solution to this problem is simply to square all the terms in the numerator, thus making them all positive.* The resulting measure of variability is called the *variance (V)*:

$$V = \frac{\text{sum of (score} - M)^2}{N} \tag{1}$$

The calculation of the variance for the control group in the word-imagery experiment is shown in Table A.3. As the table shows, the variance is obtained by subtracting the mean (M, which equals 8) from each score, squaring each result, adding all the squared terms, and dividing the resulting sum by the total number of scores (N, which equals 10), yielding a value of 4.4.

Because deviations from the mean are squared, the variance is expressed in units different from the scores themselves. If our dependent variable were a distance, measured in centimeters, the variance would be expressed in square centimeters. As we will see in the next section, it is convenient to have a measure of variability that can be added to or subtracted from the mean; such a measure ought to be expressed in the same units as the original scores. To accomplish this end, we employ another measure of variability, the *standard deviation*, or *SD*. The standard deviation is derived from the variance by taking the square root of the variance. Thus

$$SD = \sqrt{V}$$

In our example, the standard deviation is about 2.1, the square root of the variance which is 4.4.

---

* An alternative solution would be to sum the *absolute value* of these differences, that is, to consider only the magnitude of this difference for each score, not the sign. The resulting statistic, called the average deviation, is little used, however, primarily because absolute values are not easily dealt with in certain mathematical terms that underlie statistical theory. As a result, statisticians prefer to transform negative into positive numbers by squaring them.

---

## TABLE A.3    CALCULATING VARIANCE

| SCORE | SCORE − MEAN | (SCORE − MEAN)$^2$ |
|---|---|---|
| 8 | $8 - 8 = 0$ | $0^2 = 0$ |
| 11 | $11 - 8 = 3$ | $3^2 = 9$ |
| 6 | $6 - 8 = -2$ | $(-2)^2 = 4$ |
| 7 | $7 - 8 = -1$ | $(-1)^2 = 1$ |
| 5 | $5 - 8 = -3$ | $(-3)^2 = 9$ |
| 9 | $9 - 8 = 1$ | $1^2 = 1$ |
| 5 | $5 - 8 = -3$ | $(-3)^2 = 9$ |
| 9 | $9 - 8 = 1$ | $1^2 = 1$ |
| 9 | $9 - 8 = 1$ | $1^2 = 1$ |
| 11 | $11 - 8 = 3$ | $3^2 = 9$ |
| | | sum $= 44$ |

$$V = \frac{\text{sum of (score} - \text{mean})^2}{N} = \frac{44}{10} = 4.4$$

# CONVERTING SCORES TO COMPARE THEM

Suppose a person takes two tests. One measures his memory span—how many digits he can remember after one presentation. The other test measures his reading speed—how quickly he can read a 200-word essay. It turns out that he can remember 8 digits and needs 140 seconds for the essay. Is there any way to compare these two numbers, to decide whether he can remember digits as well (or worse or equally well ) as he can read? On the face of it, the question seems absurd; it seems like comparing apples and oranges. But for some purposes, we would want to compare these numbers. For example, a first step toward identifying people with dyslexia is documenting that their reading ability is markedly lower than we would expect, based on their intellectual performance in other areas. For this purpose, a comparison much like the one just sketched might be useful. But how do we compare digits-remembered to number-of-seconds-needed-for-reading?

In fact, there is a way to make this comparison, starting with an assessment of how each of these two scores compares to the scores of other persons who have been given the same two tests.

## PERCENTILE RANKS

One way of doing this is by transforming each of the two scores into a **percentile rank**. The percentile rank of a score indicates the percentage of all scores that lie below that given score. Let us assume that 8 digits is the 78th percentile. This means that 78 percent of the relevant comparison group remembers fewer digits. Let us further assume that a score of 140 seconds in the reading task is the 53rd percentile of the same comparison group. We can now answer the question with which we started. This person can remember digits more effectively than he can read. By converting into percentile ranks we have rendered incompatible scores compatible, allowing us to compare the two.

## STANDARD SCORES

For many statistical purposes there is an even better method of comparing scores or of interpreting the meaning of individual scores. This is to express them by reference to the mean and standard deviation of the frequency distribution of which they are a part. This is done by converting the individual scores into **standard scores** (often called *z-scores*). The formula for calculating a *z*-score is:

$$z = \frac{(\text{score} - \text{M})}{\text{SD}} \tag{2}$$

Suppose you take a test that measures aptitude for accounting and are told your score is 36. In itself, this number cannot help you decide whether to pursue or avoid a career in accounting. To interpret your score you need to know both the average score and how variable the scores are. If the mean is 30, you know you are above average, but how far above average is 6 points? This might be an extreme score or one attained by many, depending on the variability of the distribution.

Let us suppose that the standard deviation of the distribution is 3. Your *z*-score on the accounting test is (36 - 30)/3 = +2. That is, your score is 2 SDs above the mean.

But how to use this information? Let us say that you are still unsure whether to become an accountant, and so you take a screen test to help you decide whether to become an actor instead. Here, your score is 100. This is a larger number than the 36 you scored on the earlier test, but it may not reveal much acting aptitude. Suppose the mean score on the screen test is 80, and the standard deviation is 20; then your *z*-score is (100 − 80)/20 = +1. In acting aptitude, you are 1 SD above the mean (that is, *z* = +1)—above average but not by much. In accounting aptitude, you are 2 SDs above the mean (that is, $z = +2$), and so the use of $z$-scores makes your relative abilities clear.

Percentile rank and a $z$-score give similar information, but, to convert one into the other, we need a bit more information.

## THE NORMAL DISTRIBUTION

Frequency histograms can have a wide variety of shapes, but many variables that interest psychologists have a ***normal distribution*** (often called a ***normal curve***), which is a symmetrical distribution of the shape shown in Figure A.3. (For more on normal curves, see Chapter 14.) The graph is smooth, unlike the histogram in Figure A.1, because it describes the distribution of scores from a very large sample. The normal curve is bell shaped, with most of its scores near the mean; the farther a score is from the mean, the less likely it is to occur. Among the many variables whose distributions are approximately normal are IQ, scholastic aptitude test (SAT) scores, and women's heights (see Table A.4).*

These three variables—IQ, SAT score, and height—obviously cannot literally have the same distribution, since their means and standard deviations are different (Table A.4 gives plausible values for them). In what sense, then, can they all be said to be normally distributed? The answer is that the shape of the distributions for all these variables is the same. For example, an IQ of 115 is 15 points, or 1 SD, above the IQ mean of 100; a height of 165 centimeters is 5 centimeters, or 1 SD, above the height mean of 160 centimeters. Both scores, therefore, have $z$-scores of 1. And crucially, the percentage of heights between 160 and 165 centimeters is the same as the percentage of IQ scores between 100 and 115, that is, 34 percent. This is true not just for these two variables, but in general: it is the percentage of scores that lie between the mean and 1 SD above the mean for any normally distributed variable.

### THE PERCENTILE RANK OF A Z-SCORE

In fact, this point can be put more generally: each normal curve has its own mean and its own standard deviation. But all normal curves have the same shape, and, as a result, the percentage of scores that fall between the mean and +1 standard deviation (and so have $z$-scores between 0 and 1.0) is always the same: 34 percent. Likewise, for all normal curves, the percentage of the scores that fall between +1 standard deviation and +2

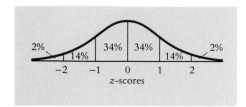

**A.3   Normal distribution   Values taken from any normally distributed variable (such as those presented in Table A.4) can be converted to z-scores by the formula z = (score − M)/(SD). The figure shows graphically the proportions that fall between various values of z.**

---

* Men's heights are also normally distributed, but the distribution of the heights of *all* adults is not. Such a distribution would have two peaks, one for the modal height of each sex, and would thus be shaped quite differently from the normal curve. Distributions with two modes are called *bimodal*.

| TABLE A.4 | NORMALLY DISTRIBUTED VARIABLES | | | | | | | |
|---|---|---|---|---|---|---|---|---|
| | | | VALUES CORRESPOINDING TO SPECIFIC $z$-SCORES | | | | | |
| VARIABLE | MEAN | STANDARD DEVIATION | | −2 | −1 | 0 | 1 | 2 |
| IQ | 100 | 15 | | 70 | 85 | 100 | 115 | 130 |
| SAT | 500 | 100 | | 300 | 400 | 500 | 600 | 700 |
| Height (women) | 160 cm | 5 cm | | 150 | 155 | 160 | 165 | 170 |

standard deviations (and so have z-scores between 1.0 and 2.0) is always the same: 14 percent. And, since normal curves are symmetrical, the same proportions hold for below the mean (and so 34 percent of the scores have z-scores between 0 and −1, and so on). These relationships are illustrated in Figure A.3.

These facts allow us to convert any z-score directly into a percentile rank. A z-score of 1 has a percentile rank of 84. That is, 84 percent of all the scores are below this particular score. (This is true because 34 percent of the scores lie between the mean and $z = 1$, and 50 percent of the scores lie below the mean). Likewise, a z-score of −1 (1 SD below the mean) corresponds, in a normal distribution, to a percentile rank of 16: only 16 percent of the scores are lower. And so on.

## HOW THE NORMAL CURVE ARISES

Why should variables such as height or IQ (and many others) form distributions that have this particular shape? Mathematicians have shown that whenever a given variable is the sum of many smaller variables, its distribution will be close to that of the normal curve. One example is lifetime earnings—obviously the sum of what one has earned on many prior occasions. A different example is height. Height can be thought of as the sum of the contributions of the many genes and the many environmental factors that influence this trait; it, therefore, satisfies the general condition. The basic idea is that the many different factors that influence a given measure (such as the genes for height) operate independently of the others, and, for each of these factors, it is a matter of chance whether the factor applies to a particular individual or not. Thus, if someone's father had a certain height-promoting gene on one chromosome but not on the other chromosome in the pair, then it would literally be a matter of chance whether the person inherited this gene or not (and likewise for each of the other genes—and surely there are many—that determine height). The person's height would also depend on accidents in his experience—for example, whether, just by bad luck, he happened to catch the flu at an age that interrupted what would have otherwise been a strong growth spurt.

In essence, then, we can think of each person's height as dependent on a succession of coin tosses, with each toss describing whether that person received the height-promoting factor or not—inherited the gene or not, got the flu at just the wrong time or not, and so on. Of course, each factor contributes its own increment to the person's height, and so his ultimate height depends on how many of these factors fell the right way. Thus, if we want to predict the person's height, we need to explore the (relatively simple) mathematics that describe how these chance events unfold.

Let us imagine that someone literally does toss a coin over and over, with each head corresponding to a factor that tends to increase height and each tail to a factor that tends to diminish it. Predicting the person's height, therefore, would be equivalent to predicting how many heads, in total, the person will obtain after a certain number of tosses. If the coin is tossed only once, then there will be either 0 heads or 1 head, and these are equally likely. The resulting distribution is shown in the top panel of Figure A.4.

If the number of tosses (which we will call $N$) is 2, then 0, 1, or 2 heads can arise. However, not all these outcomes are equally likely: 0 heads come up only if the sequence tail-tail (TT) occurs; 2 heads only if head-head (HH) occurs; but 1 head results from either HT or TH. The distribution of heads for $N = 2$ is shown in the second panel of Figure A.4. The area above 1 head has been subdivided into two equal parts, one for each possible sequence containing a single head.*

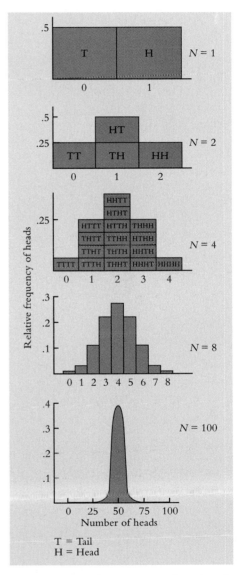

**A.4** *Histograms showing expected number of heads in tossing a fair coin N times* **In successive panels, N = 1, 2, 4, and 8. The bottom panel illustrates the case when N = 100 and shows a smoothed curve.**

---

* The distribution of the number of heads is called the *binomial distribution*, because of its relation to the binomial theorem: the number of head-tail sequences that can lead to $k$ heads is the $(k + 1)$st coefficient of $(a + b)^N$.

As *N* increases, the distribution of the number of heads looks more and more like the normal distribution, as the subsequent panels of Figure A.4 show. When *N* becomes as large as the number of factors that determine height, the distribution of the number of heads is virtually identical to the normal distribution, and this gives us just the claim we were after: as we have described, this logic of coin tossing corresponds reasonably well to the logic of the factors governing height, and so, just as the distribution of coin tosses will (with enough tosses) be normally distributed, so will height. The same logic applies to many other measures of interest to psychologists—the distribution of people's intelligence or personality traits, the distribution of response times in an experimental procedure, the distribution of students' scores on a mid-term exam. These, too, are influenced by a succession of chance factors, and so, just like the coin tosses, they will be normally distributed.

# DESCRIBING THE RELATION BETWEEN TWO VARIABLES: CORRELATION

So far, we have focused on how psychologists measure a single variable—what scales they use, how they measure the variable's average or its variability. In general, though, investigators want to do more than this—they want to ask how two (or more) variables are related to each other. Is there a relationship between the sex of a child (the independent variable) and how physically aggressive (the dependent variable) that child is? Is there a relationship between using visual imagery (the independent variable) and memory (the dependent variable)? One way to measure this relationship is by examining the *correlation* between the two variables.*

## POSITIVE AND NEGATIVE CORRELATION

Imagine that a manager of a taxicab company wants to identify drivers who will earn relatively large amounts of money (for themselves and, of course, for the company). The manager makes the plausible guess that one relevant factor is the driver's knowledge of the local geography, so she devises an appropriate test of street names, routes from place to place, and so on, and administers the test to each driver. The question is whether this test score is related to the driver's job performance as measured by his weekly earnings. To decide, the manager has to find out whether there is a correlation between the test score and the earnings—that is, whether they tend to vary together.

In the taxicab example, the two variables will probably be positively correlated—as the independent variable (test score) increases, the dependent variable (earnings) will generally increase too. But other variables may be negatively correlated—when one increases, the other will tend to decrease. An example is a phenomenon called Zipf's law, which states that words that occur frequently in a language tend to be relatively short. The two variables—word length and word frequency—are negatively correlated, since one variable tends to increase as the other decreases.

---

* In Chapter 1, we contrasted experimental and correlational designs; correlational designs are those which exploit differences that exist independently of the investigator's manipulations. Thus a comparison between boys and girls is a correlational design (because the sex difference certainly exists independently of the investigator's procedures), and so is a comparison between, say, young children and old children. All of this is different from the *statistical technique* that computes correlations. The statistic is just a specific means of exploring the relationship between two variables. Correlational designs often use correlational statistics, but often do not.

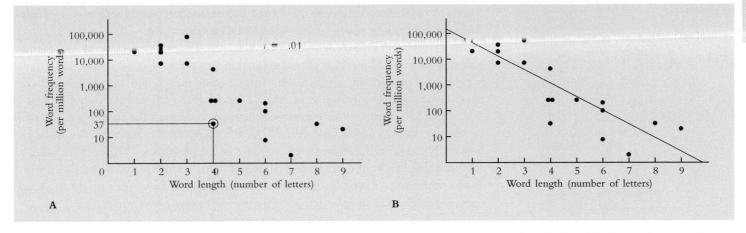

A

B

**A.5   Scatter plot of a negative correlation between word length and word frequency**

Correlational data are often displayed in a *scatter plot* (or *scatter diagram*) in which values of one variable are shown on the *x*-axis and variables of the other on the *y*-axis. Figure A.5A is a scatter plot of word frequency versus word length for the words in this sentence.* Each word is represented by a single point. An example is provided by the word *plot*, which is four letters long and occurs with a frequency of 37 times per million words of English text (and is represented by the circled dot). The points on the graph display a tendency to decrease on one variable as they increase on the other, although the relation is by no means perfect.

It is helpful to draw a line through the various points in a scatter plot that comes as close as possible to all of them (Figure A.5B). The line is called a *line of best fit*, and it indicates the general trend of the data. Here, the line slopes downward because the correlation between the variables is negative.

The three panels of Figure A.6 are scatter plots showing the relations between other pairs of variables. In Figure A.6A hypothetical data from the taxicab example show that there is a positive correlation between test score and earnings (since the line of best fit slopes upward). Test score is not a perfect predictor of on-the-job performance, however, since the points are fairly widely scattered around the line. Points above the line

**A.6   Scatter plots of various correlations**
**(A) The scatter plot and line of best fit show a positive correlation between a taxi-driving test and earnings. (B) A perfect positive correlation. The line of best fit passes through all the points. (C) A correlation of zero. The line of best fit is horizontal.**

*There is no point for the "word" A.5A in this sentence. The frequencies of the other words are taken from H. Kucera and W. N. Francis, *Computational Analysis of Present-Day American English* (Providence, R. I.: Brown University Press, 1967).

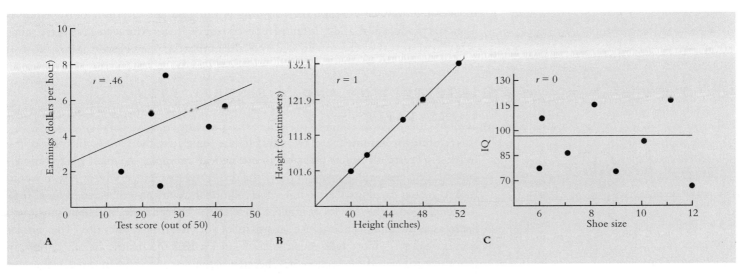

A

B

C

represent individuals who earn more than their test score would lead one to predict; points below the line represent individuals who earn less.

The examples in Figures A.5 and A.6A illustrate moderate correlations; in contrast, panels B and C of Figure A.6 illustrate extreme cases. Figure A.6B shows data from a hypothetical experiment conducted in a fourth-grade class to illustrate the relation between metric and English units of length. The heights of five children are measured twice, once in inches and once in centimeters; each point on the scatter plot gives the two height measurements for one child. All the points in the figure fall on the line of best fit, because height in centimeters always equals 2.54 times height in inches. The two variables, height in centimeters and height in inches, are perfectly correlated—one can be perfectly predicted from the other. Thus, once you know your height in inches, there is no information to be gained by measuring yourself in centimeters.

Figure A.6C presents a relation between IQ and shoe size. These variables are unrelated to each other; people with big feet have neither a higher nor a lower IQ than people with small feet. The line of best fit is therefore horizontal: The best guess of an individual's IQ is the same no matter what his or her shoe size—it is the mean IQ of the population.

## THE CORRELATION COEFFICIENT

Correlations are usually described by a *correlation coefficient*, denoted $r$, a number that expresses the strength and the direction of the correlation. For positive correlations, $r$ is positive; for negative correlations, it is negative; for variables that are completely uncorrelated, $r$ equals 0. The largest positive value $r$ can have is +1.00, which represents a perfect correlation (as in Figure A.6B); the largest possible negative value is −1.00, which is also a perfect correlation. The closer the points in a scatter plot come to falling on the line of best fit, the nearer $r$ will be to +1.00 or −1.00 and the more confident we can be in predicting scores on one variable from scores on the other. The values of $r$ for the scatter plots in Figures A.5 and A.6A are given on the figures.

The method for calculating $r$ between two variables, $X$ and $Y$, is shown in Table A.5 (on the next page). The formula is:

$$r = \frac{\text{sum}(z_x z_y)}{N} \tag{3}$$

The variable $z_x$ is the $z$-score corresponding to $X$; $z_y$ is the $z$-score corresponding to $Y$. To find $r$, each $X$ and $Y$ score must first be converted to a $z$-score by subtracting the mean for that variable and then dividing by the standard deviation for the variable. Then the product of $z_x$ and $z_y$ is found for each pair of scores. The average of these products (the sum of the products divided by $N$, the number of pairs of scores) is $r$.

## INTERPRETING AND MISINTERPRETING CORRELATIONS

It is tempting to assume that if two variables are correlated, then one is the cause of the other. This certainly seems plausible in our taxicab example, in which greater knowledge of local geography would improve the driver's performance, which in turn would lead to greater earnings. Cause-and-effect relationships are also reflected in other real-life correlations. There is, for example, a correlation between how much loud music you listen to as an adolescent and the sensitivity of your hearing in later life. (The correlation is negative—more loud music is associated with less sensitive hearing.) And, in fact, there is a causal connection here, because listening to loud music can damage your

## TABLE A.5    CALCULATION OF THE CORRELATION COEFFICIENT

1. Data (from Figure A.6A).

| Test score (X) | Earnings (Y) |
|---|---|
| 45 | 6 |
| 25 | 2 |
| 15 | 3 |
| 40 | 5 |
| 25 | 6 |
| 30 | 8 |

2. Find the mean and standard deviation for $X$ and $Y$.

For $X$, mean $= 30$, standard deviation $= 10$
For $Y$, mean $= 5$, standard deviation $= 2$

3. Convert each $X$ and each $Y$ to a $z$-score, using $z = \dfrac{(\text{score} - M)}{SD}$

| X | Y | z-score for X $(z_x)$ | z-score for Y $(z_y)$ | $z_x z_y$ |
|---|---|---|---|---|
| 45 | 6 | 1.5 | 0.5 | 0.75 |
| 25 | 2 | −0.5 | −1.5 | 0.75 |
| 15 | 3 | −1.5 | −1.0 | 1.50 |
| 40 | 5 | 1.0 | 0.0 | 0.00 |
| 25 | 6 | −0.5 | 0.5 | −0.25 |
| 30 | 8 | 0.0 | 1.5 | 0.00 |
|   |   |   |   | 2.75 |

4. Find the product $z_x z_y$ for each pair of scores.

5. $r = \dfrac{\text{sum } (z_x z_y)}{N} = \dfrac{2.75}{6} = .46$

hearing. Similarly, there is a correlation between the vividness of your visual imagery while awake and how often you remember your dreams on awakening (Cory, Ormiston, Simmel, & Dainoff, 1975). This correlation is positive—greater vividness is associated with more frequent dream recall. And here, too, there may be a causal connection: vivid waking imagery creates a mental perspective similar to the nighttime experience of dreaming, and this similarity of perspective facilitates recall.

However, as we emphasized in Chapter 1 and again in many other contexts in this book, often a correlation does *not* indicate a cause-and-effect relationship, or, if it does, the direction of causation is ambiguous. For example, consider the negative correlation between obesity and life expectancy: people who are overweight tend to die younger than people who are not overweight. For many years, this was interpreted as a cause-and-effect relationship: being overweight caused early death. Newer evidence, however, suggests that this is incorrect. Instead, it turns out that obesity is often associated with inactivity, and inactivity is what causes the problems. Overweight people who are active actually have lower mortality rates than normal-weight people who are sedentary (Kampert, Blair, Barlow, & Kohl, 1996; see Chapter 3).

Thus, a correlation, by itself, cannot indicate a cause-and-effect relationship. Some correlations do indicate causation, but many do not. As a result, correlational results are important and instructive but must be interpreted with care.

# INTERPRETING THE DATA

Any data collected in the real world contain variability, and data in psychology are no exception. In memory experiments, for example, different research participants recall different numbers of items, and the same participant is likely to perform differently if tested again later. But investigators nonetheless hope to draw general conclusions from data despite this variability. Nor is variability necessarily the enemy, because as we shall see, understanding the sources of variability in one's data can provide insights into the factors that influence the data.

Let us first consider how the pattern of variability can be used as a source of information concerning why the data are as they are. From this base, we will turn to the specific procedures that researchers use in implementing this logic, as they seek to ask whether their data are reliable or not and whether their data will support their conclusions or not. (Some readers may prefer to focus just on the procedures necessary for statistical analysis, rather than the underlying conceptualization; those readers can skip ahead to the heading, "Hypothesis testing.")

## ACCOUNTING FOR VARIABILITY

As an example of how variability may be explained, consider a person shooting a pistol at a target. Although she always aims at the bull's-eye, the shots scatter around it (Figure A.7A). Assuming that the mean is the bull's-eye, the variance of these shots is the average squared deviation of the shots from the center. Suppose we find this variance to be 100; we next must explain it.

If the shooting was done outdoors, the wind may have increased the spread; moving the shooter to an indoor shooting range produces the tighter grouping shown in Figure A.7B. The new variance is 80, a reduction of 20 percent. This means that the wind accounts for 20 percent of the original variance.

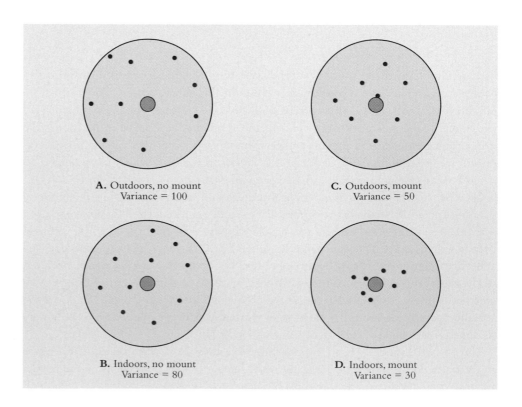

A.7  *Results of target shooting under several conditions*  *In each case, the bull's-eye is the mean, and the variance is the average squared deviation of the shots from the bull's-eye.*

**A.** Outdoors, no mount
Variance = 100

**C.** Outdoors, mount
Variance = 50

**B.** Indoors, no mount
Variance = 80

**D.** Indoors, mount
Variance = 30

In addition, some of the initial variance may have resulted from the unsteady hand of the shooter, so we now mount the gun (although still leaving it outdoors). This yields a variance of 50 (Figure A.7C), a reduction of 50 percent. So 50 percent of the variance can be attributed to the shaky hand of the shooter. To find out how much of the variance can be explained by both the wind and the shaking, we mount the gun and move it indoors; now we may find a variance of only 30 (Figure A.7D). This means we have explained 70 percent of the variance, leaving 30 percent unaccounted for.*

But not all changes in the situation will reduce the variance. For example, if we find that providing the shooter with earmuffs leaves the variance unchanged, we know that none of the original variance was due to the noise of the pistol.

## VARIANCE AND EXPERIMENTS

Figure A.8 shows how this approach can be applied to the experiment on visual imagery described earlier (see pp. A4–A5). Figure A.8A shows the distribution of scores for all twenty people in the experiment lumped together; the total variance of this overall distribution is 6.25. But as we saw, the ten members of the experimental group had been instructed to use visual imagery in memorizing, whereas the ten members of the control group were given no special instructions. How much of the overall variance can be explained by the difference in these instructions? In

*We are grateful to Paul Rozin for suggesting this example.

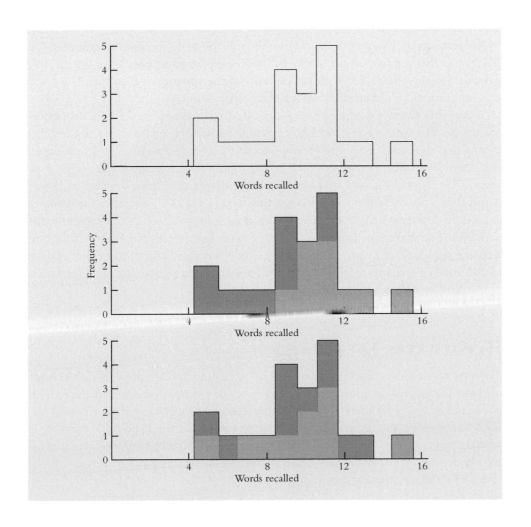

A.8  *Accounting for variance in an experiment on memorizing*    **(A) The distribution of number of words recalled is shown for all twenty participants lumped together; the variance of this distribution is 6.25. (B) The distributions of the experimental and control groups are displayed separately. The number of words recalled by the group that received imagery instructions is shown in blue; the number recalled by the control group that received no special instructions is shown in red. Within each of these groups, the variance is about 4.00. (C) The distribution of words recalled is plotted separately for men and women regardless of how they were instructed. Blue indicates the number of words recalled by women, red the number recalled by men. The variance is 6.25.**

Figure A.8B, the distributions are no longer lumped together. They are instead presented as two separate histograms; the people who received imagery instructions are shown in blue, while those who did not are indicated in red. As the figure shows, there is less variability within either the imagery group or the control group than within the overall distribution that lumped both kinds of participants together. While the variance in the overall distribution is 6.25, the variance within the two subgroups averages to only 4.0. We conclude that the difference between the two sets of instructions accounted for 36 percent of the variance and that 64 percent $(4 \div 6.25)$ still remains unexplained.

Figure A.8C shows a situation in which an independent variable (in this case, sex) accounts for little or none of the variance. In this figure, the participants' scores are again presented as two histograms—separately depicting the scores of the men and the women (regardless of whether they were instructed to use imagery or not). The men's scores are shown in red, the women's in blue. Now the variance of the two subgroups (that is, men versus women) averages to 6.25, a value identical to that found for the overall distribution. We conclude that the participant's sex accounts for none of the overall variance in recall.

## VARIANCE AND CORRELATION

The technique of explaining the variance in one variable by attributing it to the effect of another variable can also be applied to correlational studies. Here, the values of one variable are explained (that is, accounted for) when the values of the other variable are known. Recall the taxicab example, in which a correlation of +.46 was found between taxi drivers' earnings and their scores on an aptitude test. Since the correlation is neither +1.00 nor 0, some but not all of the variance in job performance can be explained by the test scores. The greater the magnitude of $r$, the more variance is accounted for. The rule is that the proportion of variance that is explained equals $r^2$. If $r = +.46$, one variable accounts for $(.46)^2 = .21$ (21 percent) of the variance of the other. (Just why this proportion is $r^2$ is beyond the scope of this discussion.)

To put this another way, suppose all the cab drivers were identical in their performance on the aptitude test, which measured knowledge of local geography. This means that the variance on that variable would be zero. As a result, the variability on the second variable, earnings, would be reduced, and the formula tells us by how much. The original variance on earnings can be determined from the data in Figure A.6A. It is 4. Its correlation with the aptitude test is +.46. If we remove the variance caused by differences in how much the cab drivers know about local geography, the variability on earnings will be $4 - (.46)^2 \times 4 = 3.16$. The drop in the variance from 4 to 3.16 is a reduction of 21 percent. So the aptitude test does help us to predict taxicab earnings, for it accounts for 21 percent of the variance. But a good deal of the variance, 79 percent, is still unexplained.

## HYPOTHESIS TESTING

The logic we have described—cast in terms of explaining the variance—lies at the heart of many techniques used for statistical analysis. For example, we saw that the participant's sex accounts for none of the overall variance in recall in our (hypothetical) imagery experiment; this is what tells us that we can reject the hypothesis that sex is relevant to performance in this task. Conversely, we saw that the variance is reduced if we divide the data according to experimental group (imagery group versus control group); this tells us that imagery is relevant here.

But how exactly is this logic put into practice? In this section, we tackle this question by means of some simple examples.*

Much behavioral research attempts to answer questions such as: Does the amount of food a person eats depend on the effort required to eat it? Can people learn while they are sleeping? Is drug *X* more effective than drug *Y*? Each of these questions suggests an experiment.

## TESTING HYPOTHESES ABOUT SINGLE SCORES

We will begin by testing a hypothesis about single scores. Consider the problem in identifying people with dyslexia (see Chapter 2). As one step in identifying such people, we might give each person a test of reading comprehension. If the person's score was unusually low, this might be an indication of dyslexia (although several other tests would be needed to confirm this possibility). The question, though, is how low a score must be before it is "unusually low."

We know from the start that reading scores among nondyslexic readers vary—some read rather well, others read at some middle level, and some read rather poorly. As a result, it is possible that a poor reader is not dyslexic at all; he is simply at the low end of the normal range for reading skills. How can we evaluate this possibility?

Suppose we tested a large number of nondyslexic readers and found that the average reading score is 50, that the standard deviation of these scores is 10, and that the scores are normally distributed. We now look at the reading score from an individual we are concerned about. Let us say that her score is 40. How likely is it that she has dyslexia? This is equivalent to asking: How *unlikely* is a score of 40 within the distribution of scores obtained by the general population (that is, a population of people who we believe are *not* dyslexic)? To answer these questions, we can convert her score to a *z*-score by computing its distance from the mean and dividing this difference by the standard deviation. The resulting *z*-score is $(40 - 50)/10$ or $-1$ SD. Since the distribution is normal, Figure A.3 tells us that 16 percent of the general population would score as low or even lower than this. Under the circumstances, it's plausible that a score of 40 does not indicate dyslexia; this score is common enough even among people without dyslexia. Our conclusion might be different, though, if the score were 30 or below. For then the *z*-score would be $(30 - 50)/10$ or $-2$, 2 SDs below the mean for the general population. Only 2 percent of the population obtain scores this low, and so we might now feel more comfortable concluding that a person with this particular score is likely not to be drawn from the general population. Instead, we might conclude that this score is likely to have been drawn from a *different* population—the population of people who do in fact suffer from dyslexia.

In this example we have to decide between two hypotheses about this individual's score. One hypothesis is that the score was drawn from the population of nondyslexic readers. True, a score of 40 or even 30 might seem atypical, but, on this view, this is

---

* The logic of explaining variance is crucial for most statistical procedures, but this logic turns out to be most visible with more complicated cases—for example, cases involving the comparison of two different groups (as in the example illustrated in Figure A.8), or the analysis of experiments in which two variables are manipulated. (For example, an experimenter might ask whether imagery instructions are as helpful for children as they are for adults; in this case, the experiment's design would have four groups: children and adults, and, then, within each of these groups, some participants given imagery instructions and some not). In the following pages, however, we have chosen to use simpler examples. This makes the underlying logic, in terms of explaining the variance, a bit less obvious, but it also makes the statistical procedures themselves much easier to grasp!

merely a reflection of the ordinary variability around the mean of the broader population. This is the **null hypothesis**, the hypothesis that there really is no systematic difference between the particular observation we are interested in and other observations we have made on other occasions and with other individuals. The alternative hypothesis is that the null hypothesis is *false* and that the score now before us is far enough away from the other scores for us to conclude that it did not arise by chance and is instead in a different category (in our example, the category of scores obtained by people with dyslexia).

As we have already suggested, the choice between these two hypotheses turns out to be a matter of probabilities. In essence, we start by adopting the working assumption that the null hypothesis is correct, and ask, within this assumption, what the probability would be of obtaining the score we have before us. If this probability—computed from the *z*-score—is relatively high (that is, if this score would be observed relatively often if the null hypothesis were correct), we conclude that the score poses no challenge to the null hypothesis, and so we accept the null hypothesis as probably correct. If, on the other hand, we start by assuming the null hypothesis, but then calculate that the score would be extremely rare under the null hypothesis, then we have two choices: either we have just observed an extremely rare event or the null hypothesis is false. Since the first of these choices is, by definition, very unlikely, we opt for the second choice.

With this logic, all depends on the *z*-score associated with our observation, and so, in the context of hypothesis testing, the *z*-score is referred to as the **critical ratio**. Behavioral scientists generally stipulate a critical ratio of 2 as the cutoff point. If it is 2 or more, they generally reject the null hypothesis and conclude that the test observation is systematically different from the control observations. Critical ratios of 2 or more are considered **statistically reliable**, which is just another way of saying that the null hypothesis can be rejected. Critical ratios of less than 2 are considered too small to allow the rejection of the null hypothesis.*

This general procedure is not foolproof. It is certainly possible for an individual to have a reading score of 30 (a critical ratio of 2) or even lower without being dyslexic. According to Figure A.3, this will happen about 2 percent of the time. Raising the cutoff value to a critical ratio of 3 or 4 would make such errors less common but would not eliminate them entirely; furthermore, raising the critical value might mean failure to detect some individuals with dyslexia. One of the important consequences of the variability in psychological data can be seen here: the investigator who has to decide between two interpretations of the data (the null hypothesis and the alternative hypothesis) cannot be correct all the time. Using statistics, in other words, is a matter of playing the odds.

## TESTING HYPOTHESES ABOUT MEANS

In the preceding discussion, our concern was with hypotheses about single scores. We now turn to the more commonly encountered problems in which the hypotheses involve means.

In many experiments, the investigator compares two or more groups—participants tested with or without a drug, with or without imagery instructions, and so on. Suppose we get a difference between the groups. How do we decide whether the difference is genuine rather than due merely to chance?

---

* Many authors use the term *statistically significant* instead of *statistically reliable*, and the decision process we are describing is sometimes referred to as *significance testing*. However, the term we are using, *reliability*, seems preferable for two reasons. First, what the statistics are measuring really is a matter of reliability—that is, whether the observation before us is likely to be an accident (and so probably would not reappear if we ran the test again), or whether it is reliable (and so would reappear if we retested). Second, the term *significance* implies that a result is important, consequential, worth publicizing. The statistical tests tell us none of those things, and so a "statistically significant" result might, in truth, be entirely insignificant in the eyes of the world! Hence the label of *statistical significance* seems a misnomer.

## TABLE A.6    NUMBER OF ITEMS RECALLED WITH AND WITHOUT IMAGERY INSTRUCTION, FOR TEN PARTICIPANTS

| SUBJECT | SCORE WITH IMAGERY | SCORE WITHOUT IMAGERY | IMPROVEMENT |
|---|---|---|---|
| Alphonse | 11 | 5 | 6 |
| Betsy | 15 | 9 | 6 |
| Cheryl | 11 | 5 | 6 |
| Davis | 9 | 9 | 0 |
| Earl | 13 | 6 | 7 |
| Fred | 10 | 11 | −1 |
| Germaine | 11 | 8 | 3 |
| Hortense | 10 | 11 | −1 |
| Imogene | 8 | 7 | 1 |
| Jerry | 12 | 9 | 3 |
| Mean | 11 | 8 | 3 |

$$\text{Variance of improvement scores} = \frac{\text{sum of } (\text{score} - 3)^2}{10} = 8.8$$

$$\text{Standard deviation of improvement scores} = \sqrt{8.8} = 2.97$$

Let us return to the experiment in which memory for words was tested with and without instructions to imagine the items. To simplify, we will here consider a modified version of the experiment in which the same participants serve in both the imagery and the nonimagery conditions. Each participant memorizes a list of 20 words without instructions, then memorizes a second list of 20 words under instructions to visualize. What we want to know is whether the participants show any improvement with the imagery instructions. There is no separate control group in this experiment. Because each person's score while using imagery can be compared with his score without using imagery, each provides his own control.*

Table A.6 gives data for the ten participants in the experiment. For each one, the table lists the number of words recalled without imagery instructions, the number recalled with such instructions, and the improvement (the difference between the two scores). The mean improvement overall is 3 words, from a mean of 8 words recalled without imagery to a mean of 11 words with imagery. But note that this does not hold for all participants. For example, for Fred and Hortense, the "improvement" is negative: they both do better without imagery instructions. But is there an imagery facilitation effect overall? Put in other words, is the difference between the two conditions statistically reliable?

* This sort of design, in which participants serve in more than one condition, is called a *within-subjects design*, in contrast to a *between-subjects design* in which different people serve in the different conditions. Within-subjects designs have certain advantages; among them, we can obviously be certain that the participants in one group are identical to the participants in the other group. But within-subjects designs also introduce their own complications. For example, if the participants serve in one condition first, then in the other condition, then this creates a confound: any differences observed might be due to the effects of practice, which obviously benefits the second condition. For present purposes, we ignore these complications (and also the steps needed to control for this confound). For more on this issue, though, see Chapter 1. In any case, the logic of the statistics here is very similar to the logic relevant to between-subjects designs, and so we will use this (simpler) case as a way to convey this logic.

As one way to approach this question, note that, ultimately, we are not trying to draw conclusions about the specific ten people we ran in the experiment. Instead, we want to draw broader conclusions, about the population at large. One way to make sure our data justify such broad conclusions would be to test the entire population in our study—every adult in North America, justifying claims about North America, or every adult in Europe, justifying claims about Europe, and so on.

Of course, we could not run these huge studies—they would require absurd amounts of time and effort. What we do instead is test a sample of individuals, and so we observe a mean *for this sample*. But can we extrapolate from this sample? It is useful to keep in mind here that we might easily have run a different sample, and it would have produced its own mean, or some other sample, with its own mean, and on and on and on for the vast number of samples we could have tested. Each sample would produce a mean (called, for obvious reasons, a *sample mean*), and, if we did in fact run sample after sample, we would end up with a set of sample means. From that set—from the distribution of sample means—we could compute a mean of all the means, and this would tell us something about the broader population (and so this mean of means, averaging together all the samples we might gather, is called the *population mean*). We could also ask how variable this set is—by computing a standard deviation for the distribution of sample means.

What we really want to ask, therefore, is whether the sample mean we actually obtained (based on the data in Table A.6) is representative of the population mean—the average that we would observe if we ran sample after sample after sample and averaged them all together. The possibility that we hope for is that our sample mean *is* representative of this larger group, which is equivalent to claiming that we would get roughly the same result if we were to do the experiment a second, third, or fourth time. A different possibility, though, is that our sample mean is just a lucky accident—showing an apparent difference between the conditions that would not show up reliably if we performed the experiment again and again. This latter possibility is, in this context, the null hypothesis. As we mentioned, the null hypothesis is, in general, a claim that there is no systematic difference between the observations we are comparing. In the dyslexia case, this was a claim that the person we had tested was not systematically different from the broader population. In the present case, it is a claim that there is no systematic difference between memory with imagery and memory without. It is, therefore, the claim that, if we conducted the memory experiment again and again, we would not observe a difference, and therefore the difference that has emerged in our data is just a fluke.

We test the null hypothesis in the memory experiment in the same way that we did in our dyslexia example. In that example, we computed a critical ratio (that is, a z-score) based on the difference between the score we had actually observed and the mean that was predicted by the null hypothesis. The null hypothesis claimed that the individual we tested was not dyslexic, and so the relevant mean was the mean for the broad population of nondyslexics. In the present example, we follow the same logic. The null hypothesis claims that, if we run the test over and over, we will not observe a difference, and so the mean we should expect, on this hypothesis, is zero. (In other words, the null hypothesis claims that the population mean, in this case the mean difference between the imagery and control conditions, is zero.)

The formula we will use for the present case is the standard one:

$$Z = \frac{(\text{score} - M)}{\text{SD}}$$

The score we will use in this calculation will be the sample mean we actually obtained—a value of 3 (see Table A.6). The mean (M) will be the mean assumed by the null hypothesis—in this case, zero. But what is the denominator? It is the standard deviation from the set of all the sample means, a measure of how variable the data would be as we move from one sample to another. This value—the standard deviation of a distribution of sample means—is called the *standard error (SE)* of the mean. Its value is determined by two factors: the standard deviation of the sample and the size of that sample. Specifically,

$$SE = \frac{SD}{\sqrt{N-1}} \tag{4}$$

Why this formula takes this particular form is beyond the scope of our discussion. Two elements of the formula should, however, seem sensible. First, in calculating the standard error, all we have to go on in most cases is information about the actual sample we have observed. We have no information about all those other samples that we might have tested (but actually did not!). Therefore, it is plausible that our estimate of how variable the data would be in general (and this is, of course, exactly what the standard error measures) depends heavily on how variable our original sample is (that is, what the standard deviation of the sample measures). It should, in other words, be no surprise that the standard error is proportional to the standard deviation.

Second, it should also seem right that the standard error goes down as the size of our particular sample goes up. If our sample included only two or three observations, then it is entirely likely that our sample mean has been drawn off by one or more atypical scores. If our sample was larger, then the impact of these atypical scores would be diluted within the larger data set. In that case, our sample would more likely be reflective of the population at large, and our estimate of the standard error is correspondingly lowered.

In any case, with the standard error now defined, we can conclude our analysis of the results of our memorization experiment. The critical ratio to be evaluated is

$$\text{Critical ratio} = \frac{\text{obtained sample mean} - \text{population mean}}{SE}$$

Since the population mean is assumed to be zero (by the null hypothesis), this expression becomes

$$\text{Critical ratio} = \frac{\text{obtained sample mean}}{SE} \tag{5}$$

To compute the standard error, we first find the standard deviation of the imagery scores; this turns out to be 2.97, as shown in Table A.6. Then equation (4) tells us

$$SE = \frac{SD}{\sqrt{N-1}} = \frac{2.97}{\sqrt{10-1}} = .99$$

The critical ratio is now the obtained mean difference divided by the standard error, or 3/.99 = 3.03. This is clearly larger than 2.0, so we conclude that the observed difference in memory between the imagery and control conditions probably should not be attributed to chance. Said differently, the sample we have run (which does show a difference between conditions) is probably representative of the data we would get if we ran the experiment again, with a new group of participants and a new set of stimuli. Thus the pattern is deemed reliable, and so we can conclude that giving visual imagery instructions does improve recall.*

## CONFIDENCE INTERVALS

In using statistics to test hypotheses, we ask whether a certain sample mean could have been drawn by chance from a set of sample means distributed around some assumed population mean. (When testing the null hypothesis, this assumed population mean is zero.) But there is another way of phrasing the entire issue: given a sample of data with its own sample mean, can we extrapolate from this in a fashion that allows us to specify, with reasonable confidence, what the possible range of values might be for the population mean? If we know the standard error of the mean, the answer is yes. We have already seen that about 2 percent of the scores in a normal distribution are more than 2 SDs above the distribution's mean (see Figure A.3). Similarly, about 2 percent of the scores have values lower than 2 SDs below the mean. Since this is so, we can conclude that the chances are roughly 96 in 100 that the population mean is within an interval whose largest value is 2 SEs above the sample mean and whose lowest value is 2 SEs below. Because we can be fairly (96 percent) confident that the actual population mean will fall within this specified range, it is often called the *confidence interval*.

As an example, consider the prediction of elections. During election campaigns, polling organizations report the current standing of various candidates by statements such as the following: "In a poll of 1,000 registered voters, 57 percent favored candidate Smith; the margin of error was 3 percent." This margin of error is the confidence interval around the proportion (that is, ±3 percent).

To determine this confidence interval, the pollsters compute the standard error of the proportion they found (in this case, .57). This standard error is analogous to the standard error of a mean we discussed in the previous section. Given an N of 1,000,

---

\* There are several simplifications in this account. One is that the critical ratio described here does not have an exactly normal distribution. When the sample size is large, this effect is unimportant, but for small samples (like the one in the example) they can be material. To deal with these and related problems, statisticians often use measures that refer to distributions other than the normal one. An example is the *t*-test, a kind of critical ratio based on what is called the *t*-distribution.

**A.9   A candidate's poll results and her confidence intervals** *The results of a mythical poll conducted for a no-less-mythical candidate Smith by randomly sampling 200 people in each of five regions of the United States. The figure shows the pro-Smith proportions in each region, together with the confidence intervals around them, and indicates that she is ahead in all five samples. But there are two regions where she cannot be confident that she is ahead in the population—the South and the Southwest, where the confidence intervals of the pro-Smith proportion dip below 50 percent.*

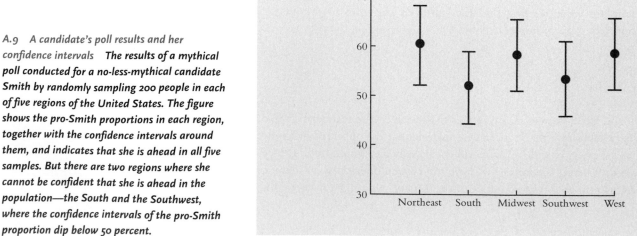

this standard error happens to be .015.* Since 2 × .015 is .03 or 3 percent, the appropriate confidence interval for our example is the interval from 54 to 60 percent. Under the circumstances, candidate Smith can be fairly confident that she has the support of at least 50 percent of the electorate, since 50 percent is well below the poll's confidence interval (see Figure A.9).

## SOME IMPLICATIONS OF STATISTICAL INFERENCE

The methods of testing hypotheses and estimating confidence intervals that we just described are routinely employed in evaluating the results of psychological research. But they have several characteristics that necessarily affect the interpretation of all such results.

### THE PROBABILISTIC NATURE OF HYPOTHESIS TESTING AND CONFIDENCE INTERVALS

As we have already noted, the nature of statistical testing always leaves the possibility of error. In our dyslexia case, we discussed the fact that it is unlikely that someone with a score 2 SDs below the population mean is, in truth, drawn from that population, but it is still possible. (In fact we know exactly how often this sort of unusual occurrence would occur: 2 percent of the time.) Likewise, if we use a confidence interval of ± 2 SEs, the chance that the population mean (or proportion, or whatever) falls outside of that interval is less than 4 or 5 in 100. This is a small chance for error, but it is still a chance.

Do we want to be more confident than this? If so, we might use a confidence interval of ± 3 SEs, where the equivalent chance is only 1 in 1,000. The same holds for critical ratios. If we want to be cautious, we might insist that the critical ratio be larger than the usually assumed value of 2—perhaps 3 (a chance factor of 1 in 2,000) or 4 (1 in 20,000), and so on. But the likelihood of these chance occurrences is never zero, and so, as long as there is some unexplained variance, there is some possibility of error.

The probabilistic nature of statistical reasoning has another consequence. Even if we can come to a correct conclusion about the mean of a population (or a proportion, as in polls), we cannot generalize to individuals. The variability within the population (or within our sample) simply prohibits us from applying claims, true for the population, to each individual within the population. Thus, a study which shows that men have higher scores than women on spatial relations tests does not preclude the existence of brilliant female artists or architects.

### THE ROLE OF SAMPLE SIZE

A last point concerns the role of sample size in affecting how the results are interpreted. The larger the sample, the smaller the standard error and the smaller the confidence interval around the mean or the proportion. This can have major effects on hypothesis testing. Suppose that, in the population, a certain independent variable produces a very small difference. As an example, suppose that the population difference between men and

---

* The standard error of a proportion (e.g., the proportion of polled voters who express pro-$X$ sentiments) is analogous to the standard error of the mean and measures the precision with which our sample proportion estimates the population proportion. The formula for the standard error of a proportion $p$ is:

$$SE_p = \sqrt{\frac{p \times (1 - p)}{N}}$$

In our example, $p = .57$ and $N = 1,000$, so $SE_p = .015$.

women on a certain test of spatial relations is 1 percent. We would probably be unable to reject the null hypothesis (that is, the hypothesis that there is no sex difference on the test) with samples of moderate size. But if the sample size were sufficiently large, we could reject the null hypothesis. For an *N* of such magnitude would lead to a decrease in the standard errors of the sample means, which in turn would lead to an increase in the critical ratio. Someone who read a report of this experiment would now learn that, by using thousands of participants, we discovered a reliable difference of 1 percent. A fair reaction to this bit of intelligence would be that the null hypothesis can indeed be rejected, but that the psychological significance of this finding is rather slight. The moral is simple: Statistical reliability does indicate a difference and, moreover, indicates that the difference is unlikely to be a fluke or chance occurrence. But statistical reliability, by itself, does not indicate whether the effect discovered is of psychological significance or of any practical importance.

# SUMMARY

1. Statistical methods concern the ways in which investigators describe, organize, and interpret collections of numerical data. A crucial concern of statistical endeavors is to interpret the *variability* that is encountered in all research.

2. An early step in processing numerical data is *scaling*, a procedure for assigning numbers to psychological responses. Scales can be *categorical, ordinal, interval,* or *ratio scales*. These differ in the degree to which they can be subjected to arithmetical operations.

3. An important step in organizing the data is to arrange them in a *frequency distribution*, often displayed in graphic form, as in a *histogram*. Frequency distributions are summarized by a *measure of central tendency*. The common measure of central tendency is the *mean (M)*, though sometimes another measure, the *median*, may be preferable, as in cases when the distribution is *skewed*. Important measures of variability are the *variance (V)* and the *standard deviation (SD)*.

4. One way of comparing two scores drawn from different distributions is to convert both into *percentile ranks*. Another is to transform them into *z*-scores, which express the distance of a score from its mean in standard deviations. The percentile rank of a *z*-score can be computed if the shape of that score's distribution is known. An important example is the *normal distribution*, graphically displayed by the *normal curve*, which describes the distribution of many psychological variables and is basic to much of statistical reasoning.

5. In some studies, the relation between variables is expressed in the form of a *correlation*, which may be positive or negative. It is measured by *r*, the correlation coefficient, a number that can vary from +1.00 to −1.00. Correlations reflect the extent to which two variables vary together, but they do not necessarily indicate that one of them causes the other.

6. One of the main functions of statistical methods is to help test hypotheses about a population given information about the sample. An important example is the difference between mean scores obtained under two different conditions. Here, the investigator has to decide between the *null hypothesis*, which asserts that the difference was obtained by chance, and the *alternative hypothesis*, which asserts that the difference is genuine and exists in the population. The decision is made by dividing the obtained mean difference by the *standard error (SE)*, a measure of the variability of that mean difference. If the resulting ratio, called the *critical ratio*, is large enough, the null hypothesis is rejected, the alternative hypothesis is accepted, and the difference is said to be *statistically reliable*. A related way of making statistical decisions is by using a *confidence interval*, or margin of error. This is based on the variability of the scores from a sample and determines the interval within which the population mean or proportion probably falls.

# GLOSSARY

**abnormal psychology**   *See* psychopathology.

**above-average effect**   A data pattern, commonly observed in individualist cultures, in which people rate themselves as being above average on many dimensions, for example, a better driver than the average, more likeable than the average, and so on.

**accommodation**   (1) The process by which the lens is thickened or flattened to focus on an object. (2) In Piaget's theory of development, one of the twin processes that underlies cognitive development. Accommodation is the way the child changes his schemas as he continues to interact with the environment. *See* assimilation.

**acetylcholine (Ach)**   A neurotransmitter found in many parts of the nervous system. Among many other functions, it serves as an excitatory transmitter at the synaptic junctions between muscle fibers and motor neurons.

**ACh**   *See* acetylcholine.

**achromatic colors**   Colors, such as black, white, and the neutral grays, that do not have the property of hue.

**acquisition**   The initial step toward remembering in which new information is taken in.

**action potential**   A brief change in the electrical potential of an axon, which is the physical basis of the nervous impulse.

**activation-synthesis hypothesis**   An account which holds that dreams may reflect the brain's aroused state during REM sleep, when the cerebral cortex is active but shut off from sensory input. This helps explain the content and often disjointed form of REM dreams.

**active-span tasks**   Tasks in which research participants are asked to remember materials while simultaneously working on some other task; such tasks are an effective means of measuring working memory's capacity.

**activity dependence**   A property of neuronal plasticity such that changes in a neuron's functioning will occur only if that neuron is active (i.e., firing) at the same time as another neuron.

**actor-observer difference**   The difference in attributions made by actors who describe their own actions and observers who describe another person's. The former emphasizes external, situational causes; the latter, internal, dispositional factors. *See also* fundamental attribution error.

**act-outcome representation**   A type of association hypothesized by Edward Tolman to be the product of instrumental learning; an organism that has acquired this sort of association has acquired the knowledge that a certain type of act leads to a particular outcome.

**acuity**   The ability to distinguish between separate points projected on the retina. Acuity is greatest in the fovea, where the receptors are closely bunched together.

**acute stress disorder**   A reaction sometimes observed in individuals who have experienced a traumatic event, characterized by recurrent nightmares and waking flashbacks of the traumatic event.

**adaptation**   The process by which the sensitivity to a stimulus declines if the stimulus is continually presented.

**addiction**   The result of repeated use of some drugs. The consequences are increased tolerance and also withdrawal symptoms if the drug is unavailable, usually causing the addiction to be self-perpetuating.

**adipose cells**   The cells within the body that provide long-term storage of energy resources, usually in the form of fatty acids that can be converted to glucose when needed.

**afferent nerves**   Nerves that carry messages to the brain.

**agency**   A term referring to the view that a person has about the origins of her behaviors. People in individualist cultures often have a sense of agency in which the person herself is regarded as the source of the actions; people in collectivist cultures have a sense of agency that emphasizes the role of the situation.

**aggression**   Hostile action directed against another member of one's species, usually intended to do physical or social harm or, for hostile intent, to limit the target's actions. Aggression must be distinguished from the behaviors involved in predation.

**agnosia**   A disturbance in the organization of sensory information produced by lesions in certain cortical areas. An example is visual agnosia in which the patient can see but often does not recognize what he sees.

**agonists**   Drugs that enhance the activity of a neurotransmitter, often by increasing the amount of transmitter substance available (e.g., by blocking reuptake or by increasing the availability of precursors).

**agoraphobia**   The fear of being alone and outside of the home, especially in a public place; often observed in those with panic disorder. *See also* phobia.

**algorithm**   In problem solving, a procedure in which all of the steps toward the solution are specified. *See also* heuristics.

**all-or-none law**   A law that describes the fact that all action potentials have the same amplitude regardless of the stimulus that triggered them.

**alpha rhythm**   A pattern of regular pulses, between eight and twelve per second, visible in the EEG waves of a person who is relaxed but awake, and typically with eyes closed.

**Alzheimer's disease**   A degenerative brain disorder characterized by memory loss followed by increasing disorientation and culminating in total physical and mental helplessness. One of the major sites of the destruction is a pathway of acetylcholine-releasing cells leading from the base of the forebrain to the cortex and hippocampus. *See also* acetylcholine.

**American Sign Language (ASL)**   The manual-visual language system of deaf persons in America.

**amino acid**　The building blocks of proteins.

**amplitude**　The height of a wave crest, used as a measure of intensity of a sound or light wave.

**amygdala**　An almond-shaped structure in the temporal lobe that plays a central role in emotion and in the evaluation of stimuli.

**amyloid plaques**　Large blobs of amyloid protein created in the development of Alzheimer's disease; these plaques seem to trigger an immune response in the brain, resulting in the death of many neurons.

**amyloid protein**　A protein normally created by neurons; abnormal forms contribute to the development of Alzheimer's disease.

**anal character**　An adult personality pattern allegedly produced (according to psychoanalysts) by a fixation on the anal stage. This character includes traits like orderliness and stinginess.

**analgesic**　A pain reliever.

**analogical representation**　A representation that shares some of the physical characteristics of an object; for example, a picture of a mouse is an analogical representation because it looks like the small rodent it represents.

**anal stage**　In psychoanalytic theory, the stage of psychosexual development during which the focus of pleasure is on activities related to elimination.

**analytic intelligence**　According to some investigators, the type of intelligence typically measured by intelligence tests and crucial for success in academic pursuits.

**androgen**　Any male sex hormone (e.g., testosterone).

**anecdotal evidence**　Evidence (usually just a few cases) collected informally, as in anecdotes told from one person to another.

**anomia**　A difficulty in finding words that is often experienced by people with brain injuries.

**anorexia nervosa**　An eating disorder that primarily afflicts young women and that is characterized by an exaggerated concern with being overweight and by compulsive dieting, sometimes to the point of self-starvation and death. *See also* bulimia.

**A-not-B effect**　The tendency of infants around nine months of age to search for a hidden object by reaching for place *A*, where it was previously hidden, rather than a new place *B*, where it was hidden most recently while the child was watching.

**ANS**　*See* autonomic nervous system.

**antagonists**　Drugs that impede the activity of a neurotransmitter, often by decreasing the amount available (e.g., by speeding reuptake and decreasing availability of precursors).

**anterograde amnesia**　A memory deficit suffered after some brain damage. It is an inability to learn and remember any information encountered after the injury, with little effect on memory for information acquired before the injury. *See also* retrograde amnesia.

**antimanics**　Drugs that alleviate the symptoms of mania, the energetic phase of bipolar disorder.

**antisocial personality disorder**　Also called psychopathy or sociopathy. The term describes persons who get into continual trouble with society, are indifferent to others, are impulsive, and have little concern for the future or remorse about the past.

**anxiety**　A global apprehensiveness related to uncertainty.

**anxiety disorders**　*See* acute stress disorder, dissociative disorders, generalized anxiety disorder, obsessive-compulsive disorder, panic disorder, phobia, post-traumatic stress disorder (PTSD), social phobia.

**anxiety hierarchy**　*See* systematic desensitization.

**anxiolytics**　Drugs that alleviate the symptoms of anxiety.

**aphasia**　A disorder of language produced by lesions in certain areas of the cortex. A lesion in Broca's area leads to nonfluent aphasia, one in Wernicke's area to fluent aphasia.

**apparent movement**　The perception of movement produced by stimuli that are stationary but flash on and off at appropriate positions and at appropriate time intervals.

**apraxia**　A serious disturbance in the organization of voluntary action produced by lesions in certain cortical areas, often in the frontal lobes.

**archetypes**　According to Carl Jung, the stories and images that constitute our collective unconscious.

**arousal**　Activation in any of the body's systems (e.g., activation of the sympathetic nervous system or the cerebral cortex). Arousal as a general term has resisted definition, because sometimes one system is activated while another is not.

**ASL**　*See* American Sign Language.

**ASQ**　*See* attributional-style questionnaire.

**assimilation**　In Piaget's theory, one of the twin processes by means of which cognitive development proceeds. Assimilation is the process whereby the environment is interpreted in terms of the schemas the child has at the time. *See* accomodation.

**association**　A linkage between two psychological processes or representations as a result of past experience in which the two have occurred together.

**associative links**　Connections in memory that tie one memory, or one concept, to another.

**associative retrieval**　A type of memory retrieval that seems swift and effortless: the sought-after information simply "pops" into mind.

**attitude**　A fairly stable, evaluative disposition that makes a person think, feel, or behave positively or negatively about some person, group, or social issue.

**attributional-style questionnaire (ASQ)**　A questionnaire designed to assess a person's habitual pattern of attributing events in a certain way (e.g., to internal forces or external ones, to forces that influence just that event or to broader forces).

**attribution-of-arousal theory**　An approach that combines the James-Lange emphasis on bodily feedback with a cognitive approach to emotion. Various stimuli can trigger a general state of arousal, which is then interpreted in light of the subject's present situation and shaped into a specific emotional experience.

**atypical antidepressants**　A recently developed group of medications that work in varied ways on serotonin, norepinephrine, and dopamine systems to combat the symptoms of depression.

**atypical antipsychotics**　Drugs (such as Clozaril, Risperdal, and Zyprexa) that operate by blocking receptors for both dopamine and serotonin; these drugs seem to be effective in treating schizophrenic patients' positive symptoms, such as thought disorders and hallucinations, as well as their negative symptoms, such as apathy and emotional blunting.

**auditory canal**　The tube that carries sound from the outer ear to the eardrum.

**auditory ossicles**　The three bones of the middle ear that transmit vibrations from the eardrum to the oval window.

**authoritarian personality**　A cluster of personal attributes (e.g., submission to persons above and harshness to those below) and social attitudes (e.g., prejudice against minority groups) that is sometimes held to constitute a distinct personality.

**authoritative-reciprocal pattern**　A pattern of child rearing in which parents exercise considerable power but also respond to the child's point of view and reasonable demands. Parents following this pattern set rules of conduct and are fairly demanding but also encourage the child's independence and self-expression.

**autocratic pattern**　A pattern of child rearing in which the parents control the child strictly, setting stern and usually unexplained rules whose infraction leads to severe, often physical, punishment.

**automaticity**   The state that is achieved when an action has gone through the process of automatization.

**autonomic division**   *See* autonomic nervous system.

**autonomic nervous system (ANS)**   A part of the nervous system that controls the internal organs, usually not under voluntary control.

**availability heuristic**   A rule of thumb often used to make probability estimates, which depends on the frequency with which certain events readily come to mind. This can lead to errors, since, for example, very vivid events will be remembered out of proportion to their actual frequency of occurrence.

**aversion therapy**   A form of behavior therapy in which the undesirable response leads to an aversive stimulus (e.g., the patient shocks herself every time she reaches for a cigarette).

**avoidance responses**   Responses that allow an organism to avoid contact with an aversive stimulus.

**axon**   Part of a neuron that transmits impulses to other neurons or effectors.

**axonal branches**   A structure in many neurons in which the axon forks into several branches, with the neuronal impulse propagated to all branches.

**axon terminals**   The knoblike swellings on the ends of an axon. The terminals contain the synaptic vesicles that are filled with neurotransmitters.

**basal ganglia**   In the extrapyramidal motor system, a set of subcortical structures in the cerebrum that send messages to the spinal cord through the midbrain to modulate various motor functions.

**basal metabolic rate**   The speed at which organisms ordinarily "burn" food to maintain themselves; this rate is higher for endotherms than for ectotherms.

**basic emotions**   According to some theorists, a small set of elemental, built-in emotions revealed by distinctive patterns of physiological reaction and facial expression.

**basilar membrane**   *See* cochlea.

**behavioral contrast**   A pattern of responding in which an organism seems to evaluate a reward relative to other rewards that are available or that have been available recently. For example, an animal might respond only weakly to a reward of two pellets if it recently received a reward of five pellets for some other response.

**belongingness in learning**   The fact that the ease with which associations are formed depends on the items to be associated. This holds for classical conditioning in which some conditioned stimulus-unconditioned stimulus combinations are more effective than others (e.g., learned taste aversions) and for instrumental conditioning in which some response-reinforcer combinations work more easily than others (e.g., specific defense reactions in avoidance conditioning of species). *See also* biological constraints, equipotentiality.

**benzodiazepines**   A class of medications used to combat anxiety; the class includes Valium, Xanax, and Klonopin.

**beta rhythm**   A rhythmic pattern in the electrical activity of the brain, often observed when one is engaged in active thought.

**between-subject comparisons**   Within an experiment, comparing one group of individuals to a different group; usually contrasted with within-subject comparisons.

**Big Five**   A nickname often used to refer to five apparently crucial dimensions of personality: extroversion, neuroticism (or emotional instability), agreeableness, conscientiousness, and openness to experience. These five traits often emerge from factor analyses of trait terms.

**binding problem**   The problem confronted by the brain of recombining the elements of a stimulus, once these elements have been separately analyzed by different neural systems.

**binocular disparity**   An important cue for depth perception. Each eye obtains a different view of an object, the disparity becoming less pronounced the farther the object is from the observer.

**biological constraints**   Principles governing what each species can learn easily and what it cannot learn at all. *See also* belongingness in learning.

**biomedical model**   An approach to mental disorders that emphasizes somatogenic causes.

**bipolar cells**   The intermediate neural cells in the eye that are stimulated by the receptors and excite the ganglion cells.

**bipolar disorder**   A mood disorder in which the patient swings from one emotional extreme to another, experiencing both manic and depressive episodes. Formerly called manic-depressive psychosis.

**bisexuality**   A sexual orientation in which a person has erotic and romantic feelings for both their own and the opposite sex.

**blindsight**   The ability of a person with a lesion in the visual cortex to reach toward or guess at the orientation of objects projected on the part of the visual field that corresponds to this lesion, even though they report that they can see absolutely nothing in that part of their visual field.

**blind spot**   The region of the retina that contains no visual receptors and therefore cannot produce visual sensations.

**blocking effect**   An effect produced when two conditioned stimuli, *A* and *B*, are both presented together with the unconditioned stimulus (US). If stimulus *A* has previously been associated with the unconditioned stimulus while *B* has not, the formation of an association between stimulus *B* and the US will be impaired (i.e., blocked).

**blood-brain barrier**   Specialized membranes that surround the blood vessels within the brain and that filter toxins and other harmful chemicals, ensuring brain cells a relatively pure blood supply.

**bottom-up processes**   *See* top-down processes.

**brightness**   A perceived dimension of visual stimuli—the extent to which they appear light or dark.

**brightness contrast**   The perceiver's tendency to exaggerate the physical difference in the light intensities of two adjacent regions. As a result, a gray patch looks brighter on a black background, darker on a white background.

**Broca's area**   A brain area in the frontal lobe crucial for language production. *See also* aphasia.

**bulimia**   An eating disorder characterized by repeated binge-and-purge bouts. In contrast to anorexics, bulimics tend to be of roughly normal weight. *See also* anorexia nervosa.

**bystander effect**   The phenomenon that underlies many examples of failing to help strangers in distress: the larger the group a person is in (or thinks he is in), the less likely he is to come to a stranger's assistance. One reason is diffusion of responsibility (no one thinks it is his responsibility to act).

**California Psychological Inventory (CPI)**   A commonly used personality test, aimed especially at high-school and college students, that tests for traits such as dominance, sociability, responsibility, and so on.

**cannabinoid (CB) receptors**   Receptors in the midbrain which are sensitive to endogenously produced substances that chemically resemble the active ingredient in marijuana.

**case markers**   Indicators used by a language to relate a word and the "action" in the sentence, for example, whether the word identifies the source of the action, the receiver of the action, and so on. In most languages, case markers occur as function morphemes; very often they serve as suffixes at the ends of noun content morphemes.

**case study**   An observational study in which one person is studied intensively. *See also* single-case experiment.

**catatonic schizophrenia**   A subcategory of schizophrenia. Its main symptoms are peculiar motor patterns, such as periods in which the patient is immobile and maintains strange positions for hours on end.

**catch trials** Trials in a signal detection experiment in which no signal is presented. These trials ensure that the observer is taking the task seriously and truly trying to determine whether a signal is present or not.

**categorical scale** A scale that divides responses into categories that are not numerically related. *See also* interval scale, nominal scale, ordinal scale, ratio scale.

**causal ambiguity** A status in which there is no way to determine which of several causes actually produced an observation. In circumstances of causal ambiguity, no conclusions about causes can be drawn.

**causal attribution** A step of inferring or concluding what the cause of an observation was.

**CB receptors** *See* cannabinoid (CB) receptors.

**CCK** *See* cholecystokinin.

**cell body** The portion of the cell that contains the metabolic machinery which keeps the cell alive and able to function.

**central nervous system (CNS)** The brain and spinal cord.

**central route to persuasion** The processes involved in attitude change when someone cares about an issue and devotes resources to thinking about the issue. This route depends on evidence and good arguments, and is contrasted with the *peripheral route*.

**central trait** A trait that is associated with many other attributes of the person who is being judged. Warmth and coldness are central because they are important in determining overall impressions.

**CER** *See* conditioned emotional response.

**cerebellum** Two small hemispheres that form part of the hindbrain and control muscular coordination and equilibrium.

**cerebral cortex** The outermost layer of the gray matter of the cerebral hemispheres.

**childhood amnesia** The failure to remember the events of our very early childhood. This is sometimes ascribed to massive change in retrieval cues, sometimes to different ways of encoding memories in early childhood.

**choice reaction time** A measure of the speed of mental processing in which the subject has to choose between one of several responses depending on which stimulus is presented.

**cholecystokinin (CCK)** A hormone released by the duodenum that appears to send a "stop eating" message to the brain.

**chromatic colors** Colors that have a discernible hue. These are in contrast to the achromatic colors, which include black, the various shades of gray, and white.

**chromosomes** Structures in the nucleus of each cell that contain the genes, the units of hereditary transmission. A human cell has forty-six chromosomes, arranged in twenty-three pairs. One of these pairs consists of the sex chromosomes. In males, one member of the pair is an X chromosome, the other a Y chromosome. In females, both members are X chromosomes. *See also* gene, X chromosome.

**chunking** A process of reorganizing (or recoding) materials in memory that permits a number of items to be packed into a larger unit.

**circadian rhythm** A rhythm that spans about a twenty-four-hour day, such as that of the sleep-waking cycle. Circadian rhythms in humans originate from a clock circuit in the hypothalamus that is set by information from the optic nerve about whether it is day or night.

**classical antipsychotics** Drugs (such as Thorazine and Haldol) that operate by blocking receptors for dopamine; these drugs seem to be effective in treating many schizophrenic patients' positive symptoms, such as thought disorders and hallucinations. Also called major tranquillizers and neuroleptics.

**classical conditioning** A form of learning in which a previously neutral stimulus, the conditioned stimulus (CS), is paired with an unconditioned stimulus

(US) regardless of what the animal does. In effect, what has to be learned is the relation between these two stimuli. *See also* instrumental conditioning.

**classical psychoanalysis** The method developed by Sigmund Freud which assumes that a patient's ills stem from unconscious defenses against unacceptable urges that date back to early childhood.

**clinical observation** A source of data in which one observes patients with some biological or psychological problem and seeks to draw conclusions from this about normal brain or mental functioning.

**CNS** *See* central nervous system.

**cochlea** A coiled structure in the inner ear that contains the basilar membrane whose deformation by sound-produced pressure stimulates the auditory receptors.

**cocktail-party effect** The effect one experiences in settings such as noisy parties, where one tunes in to the voice of the person one is talking to and filters out the other voices as background noise. This phenomenon is often taken as the model for studying selective attention.

**cognitive components** Capacities or skills regarded as the building blocks of more complex intellectual performance. A cognitive component approach to intelligence proposes that differences among individuals can best be understood in terms of each individual's level of skill, fluency, or efficiency in these various cognitive components.

**cognitive dissonance** An inconsistency among some experiences, beliefs, attitudes, or feelings. According to dissonance theory, this sets up an unpleasant state that people try to reduce by reinterpreting some part of their experiences to make them consistent with the others.

**cognitive rehabilitation** Techniques involving new strategies that enable a person to function normally despite mental problems or biological damage.

**cognitive science** A multidisciplinary attempt to address questions about the mind by integrating what we know from psychology, linguistics, philosophy, anthropology, and computer science.

**cognitive therapy** An approach to therapy that tries to change some of the patient's habitual modes of thinking about herself, her situation, and her future. It is related to behavioral therapy because it regards such thought patterns as a form of behavior.

**collateral sprouts** New branches grown on previously damaged axons, allowing some recovery of function.

**collective unconscious** A set of primordial stories and images, hypothesized by Carl Jung to be shared by all of humanity, and which he proposed underlie and shape our perceptions and desires.

**collectivism** A cultural pattern in which people are considered to be fundamentally interdependent and obligations within one's family and immediate community are emphasized. Many of the societies of Latin America, and most of the cultures of Asia and Africa, are collectivist. *See also* individualism.

**color circle** A means of representing the visible hues, arranged in a circle according to perceptual similarity.

**color disk** A two-dimensional object allowing one to display two of the dimensions of color: saturation and hue. Saturation is represented by radius (with achromatic colors at the center of the disk and fully saturated colors at the periphery), and hue is represented by angular position around the disk.

**color solid** A three-dimensional object allowing one to display all three dimensions of color: brightness, saturation, and hue. Brightness is represented by height (with black at the bottom and white at the top), saturation by radius (with achromatic colors at the center of the solid and fully saturated colors at the periphery), and hue by angular position around the solid.

**communal relationships** Relationships in which another's gains are seen as our own, and so there is no "keeping track" of who owes what to whom.

**companionate love**   A state of emotion (usually contrasted with romantic love) characterized by the affection we feel for those whose lives are deeply intertwined with our own.

**comparative approach**   *See* comparative method.

**comparative method**   A research method in which one makes systematic comparisons among different species in order to gain insights into the function of a particular structure or behavior, or the evolutionary origins of that structure or behavior.

**compensatory reaction**   An internally produced response through which the body seeks to reduce the effects of some external influence by producing a reaction opposite in its characteristics to those of the external influence. For example, the body produces an increase in pain sensitivity in response to the decrease in pain sensitivity caused by morphine, thereby canceling out morphine's reaction and so producing drug tolerance.

**complementary colors**   Two colors that, when additively mixed with each other in the right proportions, produce the sensation of gray.

**compulsions**   *See* obsessive-compulsive disorder.

**computerized tomography scan**   *See* CT scan.

**concept**   A class or category that subsumes a number of individual instances. An important way of relating concepts is through propositions, which make some assertion that relates a subject (e.g., *chickens*) and a predicate (e.g., *lay eggs*).

**concordance**   The probability that a person who stands in a particular familial relationship to a patient (e.g., an identical twin) has the same disorder as the patient.

**concrete operations period**   In Piaget's theory, the period from ages six or seven to about eleven. At this time, the child has acquired mental operations that allow him to abstract some essential attributes of reality, such as number and substance, but these operations are as yet applicable only to concrete events and cannot be considered entirely in the abstract.

**conditional statements**   Statements of the format "if…then…," such as "If he calls me, then we can go to the movies." Called conditional because the "if" clause states the condition under which the "then" clause is guaranteed to be true.

**conditioned emotional response (CER)**   A type of conditioned response that involves a complex set of behaviors characterizing fear. In many cases, the CER is measured by its capacity to interrupt other ongoing behaviors.

**conditioned reflex**   *See* conditioned response.

**conditioned reinforcer**   An initially neutral stimulus that acquires reinforcing properties through pairing with another stimulus that is already reinforcing.

**conditioned response (CR)**   A response elicited by some initially neutral stimulus, the conditioned stimulus (CS), as a result of pairings between that CS and an unconditioned stimulus (US). This CR is typically not identical with the unconditioned response though it often is similar to it. *See also* conditioned stimulus (CS), unconditioned response (UR), unconditioned stimulus (US).

**conditioned stimulus (CS)**   In classical conditioning, the stimulus which comes to elicit a new response by virtue of pairings with the unconditioned stimulus. *See also* conditioned response (CR), unconditioned response (UR), unconditioned stimulus (US).

**cones**   Visual receptors that respond to greater light intensities and give rise to chromatic (color) sensations.

**confabulation**   Sincere but false recollections, usually produced when one encounters a gap in the memory record and (unwittingly) tries to fill this gap.

**confidence interval**   An interval around a sample mean within which the population mean is likely to fall. In common practice, the largest value of the interval is 2 standard errors above the mean and the smallest value is 2 standard errors below it.

**confirmation bias**   The tendency to seek evidence to support one's hypothesis rather than to look for evidence that will undermine the hypothesis.

**confirmed hypothesis**   A hypothesis that has been tested many times and each time has made successful predictions.

**confounds**   Variables within a study that might influence the pattern of results and thereby introduce ambiguity regarding why the results are as they are.

**connectionist model**   A model of how information in memory is retrieved that relies on distributed representations. In a distributed representation, a concept is conveyed by a pattern of activation across an entire network, rather than by the activation of a single node. In such models, processing depends on having just the right links between concepts, at just the right strengths.

**content morphemes**   Morphemes that carry the main burden of meaning (e.g., *strange*). This is in contrast to function morphemes that add details to the meaning but also serve various grammatical purposes (e.g., the suffixes *s* and *er*, the connecting words *and*, *or*, *if*, and so on).

**context reinstatement**   A step aimed at improving someone's ability to remember, by putting her back into the same mental and physical state that she was in during the initial learning.

**contingency management**   A form of behavior therapy in which the environment is structured such that certain behaviors are reliably followed by well-defined consequences.

**contralateral control**   The pattern in which movements on the right side of the body are controlled by the left half of the brain, while movements on the left side of the body are controlled by the right half of the brain. Contralateral control is seen in nearly all vertebrate nervous systems.

**control group**   A group to which the experimental manipulation is not applied.

**control system**   A mechanism that can change the operation of some process or machine in response to feedback.

**conversion disorder**   Formerly called conversion hysteria. A condition in which there are physical symptoms that seem to have no physical basis. They instead appear to be linked to psychological factors and are often believed to serve as a means of reducing anxiety. *See also* hysteria.

**convolutions**   The wrinkles visible in the cortex that allow the enormous surface area of the human cortex to be stuffed into the relatively small space of the skull.

**cornea**   The eye's transparent outer coating.

**corpus callosum**   A bundle of fibers that connects the two cerebral hemispheres.

**correct negative**   One of the four possible outcomes in a detection task. If the signal is *not* present and the person says so, this is a correct negative. *See* miss.

**correlation**   The tendency of two variables to vary together. If one goes up as the other goes up, the correlation is positive; if one goes up as the other goes down, the correlation is negative.

**correlational studies**   Studies in which the investigator is seeking to observe the relationship among variables that were in place prior to the study (as opposed to factors that the investigator creates or manipulates).

**correlation coefficient ($r$)**   A number that expresses both the size and the direction of a correlation, varying from $+1.00$ (perfect positive correlation) through $0.00$ (absence of any correlation) to $-1.00$ (perfect negative correlation).

**correlation matrix**   A data table reporting the correlations among multiple variables.

**correspondence problem**   In a moving display, the difficulty in determining which aspects of the display now visible correspond to which aspects of the display visible a moment ago.

**cortex**   The outermost layer of an organ in the body.

**cortisol**   A substance secreted by the adrenal glands in response to stress.

**counterbalance**   A procedural step through which an experiment is arranged so that possible confounds will have an equal effect on all conditions, and thus cannot influence the comparison between conditions.

**courtship rituals** Particular behaviors that announce an organism's reproductive availability and intentions.

**covariation** *See* correlation.

**CPI** *See* California Psychological Inventory.

**cranial nerves** The twelve pairs of nerves that enter and exit directly from the hindbrain. These nerves control movements of the head and neck, carry sensations from them including vision, olfaction, and audition, and regulate the various glandular secretions in the head.

**creative intelligence** The form of intelligence alleged by some authors as essential for devising new ideas or new strategies. Often contrasted with analytic intelligence or practical intelligence.

**critical period** A period in the development of an organism when it is particularly sensitive to certain environmental influences. Outside of this period, the same environmental influences have little effect (e.g., the period during which a duckling can be imprinted). After embryonic development, this phenomenon is rarely all-or-none. As a result, most developmental psychologists prefer the term *sensitive period*.

**critical period hypothesis** The proposal that certain skills must be gained or ideas acquired at a particular age or developmental stage. A related, but less rigid proposal is the *sensitive* period hypothesis, which suggests that the skills are just more likely to be gained during that stage.

**critical ratio** A score, usually a *z*-score, that determines whether an investigator will accept or reject the null hypothesis. If a test score exceeds the critical ratio, the null hypothesis is rejected.

**cross-cultural method** The study of the relation between a culture's beliefs and practices and the typical personality characteristics of its members. *See also* sociocultural approach.

**crystallized intelligence** The repertoire of information, cognitive skills, and strategies acquired by the application of fluid intelligence to various fields. This is said to increase with age, in some cases into old age. *See also* fluid intelligence.

**CT (computerized tomography) scan** A technique for examining brain structure in living humans by constructing a composite X-ray picture based on views from all different angles. Also called CAT (computerized axial tomography) scan.

**cultural display rules** Learned but deeply ingrained conventions that govern what facial expressions of emotion may or may not be shown in what contexts.

**cupboard theory** A hypothesis about the infant's attachment to the primary caregiver; according to this theory, the attachment is motivated largely by the fact that the mother is a source of nourishment (whether through breast or bottle).

**DA** *See* dopamine.

**data driven** A process determined by the input received (often, the sensory information) rather than being determined by pre-existing ideas or expectations.

**debriefing** A step at the end of a procedure in which participants are told what the procedure involved and why it was designed as it was, and in which any manipulations to the participants' beliefs or state are undone.

**decibels** The logarithmic units used to describe sound intensity (or amplitude).

**declarative knowledge** Knowing "that" (e.g., knowing someone's name), as contrasted with procedural knowledge, which is knowing "how" (e.g., knowing how to ride a bicycle).

**deductive reasoning** Reasoning in which one tries to determine whether some statement follows logically from certain premises, as in the analysis of syllogisms. This is in contrast with inductive reasoning in which one observes a number of particular instances and tries to determine a general rule that covers them all.

**deep processing** *See* depth-of-processing hypothesis.

**defense mechanism** In psychoanalytic theory, a collective term for a number of reactions that try to ward off or lessen anxiety by various unconscious means. *See also* displacement, projection, rationalization, reaction formation, repression.

**definitional theory of word meaning** The theory that our mental representation of word meaning is made up of a small number of simpler concepts. The representation of bachelor, for example, is made up of "adult," "unmarried," and "male."

**dehumanization of the victim** Steps often taken to make a potential victim seem not human (labeling him as vermin, for example, or treating him as a mere number); these steps make aggression toward the victim more likely and less troubling to the aggressor.

**deindividuation** A weakened sense of personal identity in which self-awareness is diminished and one's own goals are merged in the collective goals of a group.

**deinstitutionalization** A movement intended to obtain better and less expensive care for chronically mentally ill patients in their own communities rather than at large, centralized hospitals.

**delusions** Systematized false beliefs, often of grandeur or persecution.

**delusions of persecution** A delusion in which the person believes that other people are seeking to harm him.

**demand characteristics** The cues that tell a research participant what the experimenter expects.

**dendrites** A typically highly branched part of a neuron that receives impulses from receptors or other neurons and conducts them toward the cell body and axon.

**dendritic spines** Little knobs that are attached to the surface of the dendrites and serve as the "receiving stations" for most synapses.

**dependent variable** The thing that is measured or recorded in an experiment, called the dependent variable because the experiment seeks to ask whether this variable *depends on* (is caused by or predicted by) another variable (the independent variable). Typically, experiments are done to find out if the independent variable does have an influence on the dependent variable.

**depressants** Drugs that have the effect of diminishing activity levels.

**depressive stupor** An extreme state of depression in which the person may become entirely unresponsive, rock back and forth, urinate or defecate on herself, and mutter incoherently.

**depth cues** Sources of information that signal the distance from the observer to the distal stimulus. Some depth cues are present in a single retinal image (the pictorial cues), some require a comparison of the information received from the two eyes (binocular cues), some involve the pattern of motion in the retinal image (parallax and optic flow), and some arise from the positions of the eyes in viewing (e.g., convergence angle).

**depth-of-processing hypothesis** A theory of memory that stresses the nature of encoding at the time of acquisition. It argues that deeper levels of processing (e.g., attending to a word's meaning) lead to better retention and retrieval than shallower levels of processing (e.g., attending to the word's sound). Thus, maintenance rehearsal leads to much poorer retrieval than elaborative rehearsal. *See also* elaborative rehearsal, maintenance rehearsal.

**diagnosis** A practitioner's best opinion, based on a patient's signs and symptoms, as to the patient's specific disorder.

***Diagnostic and Statistical Manual for Mental Disorders (DSM)*** *See* DSM-IV.

**dichotic presentation** An experimental procedure in which the participant hears two simultaneous messages, one presented to each ear. Typically, one of these is to be attended to and the other ignored.

**difference threshold** The amount by which a given stimulus must be increased or decreased so that the research participant can perceive a just-noticeable difference (jnd).

**diffusion of responsibility** *See* bystander effect.

**directed thinking** Thinking that is aimed at the solution of a problem.

**direction specific** Responding to motion in just one direction.

**disconfirmed hypothesis** A hypothesis that has been tested but for which the data do not conform to the pattern it predicted.

**discrimination** A process of learning to respond to certain stimuli that are reinforced and not to others that are unreinforced.

**discriminative stimuli** In instrumental conditioning, the external stimuli that signal a particular relationship between the instrumental response and the reinforcer. For example, a green light is a positive discriminative stimulus when it signals to a pigeon that it will now get food if it hops on a treadle; the reverse is true of a red light, or the negative discriminative stimulus, which indicates that this action will not now lead to a food reward.

**disorganized schizophrenia** A subtype of schizophrenia in which the predominant symptoms are extreme incoherence of thought and marked inappropriateness of behavior and affect.

**displacement** In psychoanalytic theory, a redirection of an impulse from a channel that is blocked into another, more available outlet (e.g., displaced aggression, as in a child who hits a sibling when punished by her parents).

**dissociation** (1) A term used for symptoms when a patient is impaired in one function but relatively unaffected in another. (2) In post-traumatic stress disorder (PTSD), the period of numbness immediately after the trauma in which the sufferer feels estranged, socially unresponsive, and oddly unaffected by the traumatizing event. (3) A defense mechanism in which one seeks to create a sense of physical or psychological distance from the threatening event, person, or stimulus.

**dissociative amnesia** A form of memory loss in which an individual seems unable to remember some period of her life, or even her entire past, including her own identity. This memory loss is often understood as a means of coping with extraordinarily painful events.

**dissociative disorders** Disorders in which a whole set of mental events seems to be stored out of ordinary consciousness. These include dissociative amnesia, fugue states, and, very rarely, cases of dissociative identity disorder.

**dissociative fugue** A state in which the person wanders away from home, and then, days or even months later, suddenly realizes that he is in a strange place and does not know how he got there; this pattern is often understood as a means of coping with (and escaping from) extraordinarily painful events.

**dissociative identity disorder** Formerly multiple personality disorder. A dissociative disorder that results in a person developing two or more distinct personalities.

**distal stimulus** An object or event outside (e.g., a tree) as contrasted to the proximal stimulus (e.g., the retinal image of the tree), which is the pattern of physical energies that originates from the distal stimulus and impinges on a sense organ.

**distance cues** *See* depth cues.

**distributed representations** A model of cognitive organization, especially semantic memory, in which each concept is represented, not by a designated node or group of nodes, but by a widespread pattern of activation across the entire network. *See also* connectionist model, local representations, network model, node.

**doctrine of specific nerve energies** The law formulated by Johannes Müller which holds that differences in sensory quality are not caused by differences in the stimuli themselves but by the different nervous structures that these stimuli excite. Thus, stimulating the retina will produce sensations of light, whether the retina is stimulated by a beam of light or pressure to the eyeball.

**dodo bird verdict** An expression often used to summarize the comparison of the effectiveness of different forms of psychotherapy. According to the dodo bird in *Alice in Wonderland*, "Everyone has won and all must have prizes." Regarding psychotherapy, this statement is understood to mean that all the major forms of psychotherapy are equally effective.

**dominance hierarchy** A social order developed by animals that live in groups by which certain individuals are understood to have a certain status or rank, and this determines their access to resources and how they exert power over others.

**dominant** A relationship among genes such that if the gene on one chromosome specifies one developmental path, and the corresponding gene on the other chromosome specifies a different path, a gene that is dominant will govern the outcome. If a gene is recessive, it will govern the outcome only if the corresponding gene on the other chromosome redundantly specifies the same (recessive) trait.

**dopamine (DA)** A neurotransmitter involved in various brain structures, including those that control motor action.

**dopamine hypothesis** Asserts that schizophrenics are oversensitive to the neurotransmitter dopamine. Evidence for this view comes from the fact that the classical antipsychotics, which alleviate positive schizophrenic symptoms, block dopamine transmission. *See also* classical antipsychotics.

**dopamine-serotonin interaction hypothesis** Asserts that schizophrenics are oversensitive to both dopamine and serotonin. Evidence for this view comes from the fact that atypical antipsychotics, which relieve both positive and negative symptoms, block receptors for both dopamine and serotonin. *See also* atypical antipsychotics.

**double-blind design** *See* double-blind technique.

**double-blind technique** A technique for evaluating a manipulation independent of the effects produced by the expectations of research participants (placebo effects) or the experimenters. This is done by assigning participants to the experimental group or a placebo group with both the participants and the researchers in ignorance of who is assigned to which group. *See also* placebo effect.

**downward drift** The proposed process through which schizophrenics fall to the bottom of the socioeconomic ladder because they cannot hold down a job or sustain a personal relationship.

**dream condensation** The idea that events in a dream flash by in a very fast sequence, taking much less time than the dreamed-about events would ordinarily require.

**drive** A term used by Hull (among others) to refer to a state of internal bodily tension, such as hunger or thirst or the need for sleep.

**drive-reduction theory** A theory that claims that all built-in rewards are at bottom reductions of some noxious bodily state. The theory has difficulty in explaining motives in which one seeks stimulation, such as sex and curiosity.

**DSM-IV** The current diagnostic manual of the American Psychiatric Association (adopted in 1994), a substantial revision of its predecessor, *DSM-III-R*.

**dual-center theory** A hypothesis about the hypothalamic control of eating. One center (in the lateral hypothalamus) was hypothesized as the "on" center, the initiator of eating; another center (in the ventromedial region) was hypothesized as the "off" center, the terminator of eating. Current evidence indicates, however, that these brain regions, while crucial for eating, are only a part of the circuits controlling eating.

**duplex theory of vision** The theory that rods and cones handle different aspects of vision. The rods are the receptors for night vision; they operate at low light intensities and lead to achromatic (colorless) sensations. The cones are used in day vision; they respond at higher illumination levels, have greater acuity, and are responsible for sensations of color.

**dyslexia** Any difficulty in reading not associated with obvious problems like bad eyesight.

**eardrum** The taut membrane that transmits vibrations caused by sound waves across the middle ear to the inner ear.

**ECT** *See* electroconvulsive therapy.

**ectotherms** Organisms that control their body temperature by using mechanisms that are mostly external (such as choosing a sunny or shady environment). Previously called *cold blooded*.

**EEG** *See* electroencephalography, electroencephalogram.

**effectors** Organs of action; in humans, muscles and glands.

**efferent nerves** Nerves that carry messages to the effectors.

**ego** In Freud's theory, a set of reactions that try to reconcile the id's blind pleasure strivings with the demands of reality. These lead to the emergence of various skills and capacities that eventually become a system that can look at itself—an "I." *See also* id and superego.

**egocentrism** In Piaget's theory, a characteristic of preoperational children, an inability to see another person's point of view.

**elaborative rehearsal** Rehearsal in which material is actively reorganized and elaborated while in working memory. In contrast to maintenance rehearsal, this confers considerable benefit for subsequent memory. *See also* maintenance rehearsal.

**Electra complex** *See* Oedipus complex.

**electrical synapses** Synapses in which the electrical signal of one axon potential directly influences another axon, without the chemical intermediates involved at most other synapses.

**electroconvulsive therapy (ECT)** A somatic treatment, mostly used for cases of severe depression, in which a brief electric current is passed through the brain to produce a convulsive seizure.

**electroencephalogram (EEG)** A record of the summed activity of cortical cells picked up by wires placed on the skull.

**electroencephalography** The procedure through which one records an electroencephalogram.

**embryo** The earliest stage in a developing animal. In humans, up to about eight weeks after conception.

**empathy** A direct emotional response to another person's emotions.

**empiricism** A school of thought that holds that all knowledge comes by way of empirical experience, that is, through the senses.

**encoding specificity** The hypothesis that retrieval is most likely if the context at the time of recall approximates that during the original encoding.

**endocrine glands** *See* endocrine system.

**endocrine system** The system of ductless glands whose secretions are released directly into the bloodstream and affect organs elsewhere in the body (e.g., adrenal gland, pancreas, pituitary gland).

**endorphin** A drug produced within the brain itself whose effects and chemical composition are similar to such pain-relieving opiates as morphine.

**endotherms** Organisms that control their body temperature by using mechanisms that are mostly internal or physiological. Previously called *warm blooded.*

**epinephrine (adrenaline)** A neurotransmitter released into the bloodstream by the adrenal medulla as part of sympathetic activation leading to a diverse set of effects (e.g., racing heart).

**equipotentiality principle** The claim (contradicted by much evidence) that organisms can learn to associate any response with any reward or to associate any pair of stimuli.

**escape responses** Responses that allow an organism to end an aversive state, for example, to gain warmth while cold, or to terminate an electric shock.

**estrogen** A female sex hormone that dominates the first half of the female cycle through ovulation.

**estrus** In mammals, the period in the cycle when the female is sexually receptive (in heat).

**exchange relationship** A hypothesized type of social relationship in which the relationship depends on reciprocity; if goods (or esteem or loyalty) are given by one of the partners in the relationship, then the other must respond in kind.

**excitation threshold** The voltage difference between a neuron's interior and exterior that, if exceeded, causes the neuron to fire. This voltage is about −55 millivolts in mammals. If the voltage reaches this threshold (from a "resting" voltage of −70 millivolts), the neuron's membrane destabilizes, leading to an action potential.

**excitation transfer** The transfer of autonomic arousal from one situation to another, as when strenuous exercise leads to an increased arousal when presented with aggression-arousing or erotic stimuli.

**excitement** According to some authors, one of the four stages of sexual arousal.

**experimental group** The group within an experimental design that receives the (potential) effects of the independent variable.

**experimental manipulation** The thing that is deliberately altered in an experiment in order to learn about its effects. The experimental manipulation defines the *independent variable* (e.g., presence or absence of an instruction, or a happy or sad story).

**explanatory style** The characteristic manner in which a person explains good or bad fortunes that befall him. An explanatory style in which bad fortunes are generally attributed to internal, global, and stable causes may create a predisposition that makes a person vulnerable to depression.

**explicit attitude** An attitude that a person acknowledges having and can be expressed; often contrasted with an implicit attitude. *See also* implicit attitude.

**explicit memory** Memory retrieval in which there is awareness of remembering at the time of retrieval. *See also* implicit memory.

**external validity** The degree to which a study's participants, stimuli, and procedures adequately reflect the world as it actually is.

**extinction** In classical conditioning, the weakening of the tendency of the conditioned stimulus (CS) to elicit the conditioned response (CR) by unreinforced presentations of the CS. In instrumental conditioning, a decline in the tendency to perform the instrumental response brought about by unreinforced occurrences of that response.

**eyewitness identification** A selection, usually from a group of people or photographs, made by someone who observed a crime (or a simulation of a crime, in a research study), picking the person who was the perpetrator of that crime.

**factor analysis** A statistical method for studying the interrelations among various tests, the object of which is to discover what the tests have in common and whether these communalities can be ascribed to one or several factors that run through all or some of these tests.

**false alarm** A response indicating that a signal is present when it is not. Cases include hearing tones that are not presented, or concluding that a suspect is guilty when she is in fact innocent.

**family resemblance structure** Overlap of features among members of a category such that no members of the category have all of the features but all members have some of them.

**feature detectors** Neurons in the retina or brain that respond to specific features of the stimulus, such as movement, orientation, and so on.

**feature net** A model of pattern recognition in which there is a network of detectors, with feature detectors at the bottom.

**Fechner's law** The assertion that the strength of a sensation is proportional to the logarithm of physical stimulus intensity.

**feedback** A system in which an action produces some consequence that affects (feeds back on) the action. In negative feedback, the consequence stops or reverses the action (e.g., thermostat-controlled furnace). In positive feedback, the consequence strengthens the action (e.g., rocket that homes in on airplanes).

**fetus** The stage in gestation following the embryonic stage. In humans, from about eight weeks until birth.

**FI schedule** *See* fixed-interval (FI) schedule.

**figure** The object focused on, with the rest of the stimulus input considered merely as "background" (*see* ground). By virtue of being focused on, the figure gains certain other attributes: it is seen as having distinct edges, for example, while the same edges merely mark places that the ground drops from view. *See* figure-ground organization.

**figure-ground organization** The segregation of the visual field into a part (the figure) that stands out against the rest (the ground).

**file-drawer problem** A tendency for disappointing or negative results not to be reported (and so merely dumped into a file drawer). This tendency can cause a bias in the pattern of evidence available.

**fissures** Deep grooves in the brain, between convolutions, or in some cases marking the boundaries between large structures.

**5HT** *See* serotonin.

**5-hydroxy-tryptamine** *See* serotonin.

**fixation** (1) In problem solving, the result of rigid mental sets that makes it difficult for people to approach a problem in new and different ways. (2) In Freud's theory of personality, the lingering attachment to an earlier stage of pleasure seeking, even after a new stage has been attained.

**fixed-interval (FI) schedule** A pattern of rewards in which an organism can earn some reinforcement only after a certain time period (the interval) has elapsed. After that time period, the very next response will be rewarded. In a fixed-interval one-minute schedule, for example, any responses during the initial minute will not be rewarded. The very first response after the minute will be rewarded.

**fixed-ratio (FR) schedule** A pattern of rewards in which an organism can earn some reinforcement only by producing a certain number of responses. In a fixed-ratio 5 schedule, for example, the animal must respond five times in order to be rewarded.

**flashbulb memories** Vivid, detailed memories said to be produced by unexpected and emotionally important events.

**fluent aphasias** A syndrome derived from a specific form of brain damage, in which the person seems able to produce speech but is unable to understand what is said to her. In most cases, the sentences produced by the person make little sense, consisting instead of "word salad."

**fluid intelligence** The ability, which is said to decline with age, to deal with essentially new problems. *See also* crystallized intelligence.

**Flynn effect** An effect observed worldwide over the last several decades in which IQ scores seem to be rising.

**fMRI scan** *See* functional MRI (fMRI) scan.

**follicles** Ova-containing sacs in the mammalian ovary.

**foot-in-the-door technique** A technique of persuasion, initially used by door-to-door salespeople, in which one first obtains a small concession that then makes it easier to persuade the target to make a subsequent, larger concession.

**forebrain** In mammals, the bulk of the brain. Its foremost region includes the cerebral hemispheres; its rear includes the thalamus and hypothalamus.

**forgetting curve** A curve showing the inverse relationship between memory and the retention interval.

**formal operations period** In Piaget's theory, the period from about age eleven on, when genuinely abstract mental operations (e.g., the ability to entertain hypothetical possibilities) can be undertaken.

**fovea** The area of the retina on which an image falls when the viewer is looking directly at the source of the image. Acuity is greater when the image falls on the fovea than it is when it falls on any other portion of the retina.

**framing** A heuristic that affects the subjective desirability of an event by changing the standard of reference for judging the desirability (e.g., by comparing all outcomes to the worst-possible result, rather than comparing them to the best-possible result).

**fraternal twins** Twins that arise from two different eggs that are (simultaneously) fertilized by different sperm cells. Their genetic similarity is no greater than that between ordinary siblings. *See also* identical twins.

**free association** Method used in psychoanalytic therapy in which the patient is to say anything that comes to her mind, no matter how apparently trivial, unrelated, or embarrassing.

**free recall** A test of memory that asks for as many items in a list as a research participant can recall regardless of order.

**frequency** (1) In sound waves or light waves, the number of wave peaks per second. In sound, frequency governs the perceived pitch of the sound; in light, frequency governs the perceived hue of the light. (2) In statistical analysis, the number of occurrences of a particular observation.

**frequency distribution** An arrangement in which scores are tabulated by how often they occur.

**frequency theory** The proposal that the perception of a tone's pitch is coded by the rate of firing of neurons in the auditory system. This proposal is probably correct for the perception of lower pitches, but certainly false for higher pitches.

**frontal lobe** The lobe in each cerebral hemisphere that includes the prefrontal area and the motor projection areas.

**FR schedule** *See* fixed-ration (FR) schedule.

**functional MRI (fMRI) scan** An adaptation of the standard MRI procedures that can measure fast-changing physiology (mostly blood flow and oxygen use) within the brain.

**function morphemes** Words or parts of words that help specify the relations among words. Examples include the *–s* morpheme in English used to mark plurals, the *–ed* morpheme which marks the past tense, or the word *will*, used to mark future tense. *See also* content morphemes.

**fundamental attribution error** The tendency to attribute behaviors to dispositional qualities while underrating the role of the situation. *See also* actor-observer difference.

**g** *See* general intelligence.

**GABA (gamma-amino butyric acid)** The most widely distributed inhibitory transmitter of the central nervous system.

**GAD** *See* generalized anxiety disorder.

**gamma-amino butyric acid** *See* GABA.

**gamma-band oscillation** A particular rhythm of about forty pulses per second; different neurons in different parts of the brain all fire at this rate and in synchrony when they are responding to (different aspects of) the same stimulus.

**ganglion** A neural control center that integrates messages from different receptor cells and coordinates the activity of different muscle fibers; plural: ganglia.

**ganglion cells** In the retina, one of the intermediate links between the receptor cells and the brain. The axons of the ganglion cells converge into a bundle of fibers that leave the eyeball as the optic nerve. *See also* bipolar cells.

**garden path** A term used to describe sentences that initially lead the listener toward one interpretation but then demand a different interpretation, for example, "Fat people eat accumulates."

**gender constancy** The recognition that being male or female is to all intents and purposes irrevocable.

**gender identity** The inner sense of being male or female. *See also* gender role, sexual orientation.

**gender role** The set of external behavior patterns a given culture deems appropriate for each sex. *See also* gender identity, sexual orientation.

**gene** The unit of hereditary transmission, located at a particular place in a given chromosome. Both members of each chromosome pair have corresponding locations at which there are genes that carry instructions about the same characteristic (e.g., eye color). If one member of a gene pair is dominant and the other is recessive, the dominant gene will exert its effect regardless of what the recessive gene calls for. The characteristic called for by the recessive gene will only be expressed if the other member of the gene pair is also recessive. *See also* chromosomes.

**general intelligence** (*g*) A mental attribute that is hypothesized as being called on in any intellectual task a person has to perform.

**generalization gradient** The curve that shows the relationship between the tendency to respond to a new stimulus and its similarity to the original conditioned stimulus (CS).

**generalized anxiety disorder** (**GAD**) A mental disorder whose primary characteristic is an all-pervasive, "free-floating" anxiety. A member of the diagnostic category "anxiety disorders," which also includes phobias and obsessive-compulsive disorders. *See also* anxiety disorders.

**general paresis** A psychosis characterized by progressive decline in cognitive and motor function culminating in death, reflecting a deteriorating brain condition produced by syphilitic infection.

**generic memory** Memory for items of knowledge as such (e.g., The capital of France is Paris), independent of the occasion on which they are learned.

**genetic sex** A designation of an organism's sex based entirely on the genetic pattern, whether XY (male) or XX (female). Often contrasted with morphological sex, which is based on anatomical features.

**geniculate nucleus** *See* lateral geniculate nucleus.

**genital stage** In psychoanalytic theory, the stage of psychosexual development reached in adult sexuality in which sexual pleasure involves not only one's own gratification but also the social and bodily satisfaction brought to another person.

**genotype** The genetic blueprint of an organism which may or may not be overtly expressed by its phenotype. *See also* phenotype.

**geons** Primitive geometric figures, such as cubes, cylinders, and pyramids, from which all other shapes are created through combination. In many models of pattern recognition, the organism must first determine which geons are present and then determine what the objects are.

**Gestalt** An organized whole such as a visual form or a melody.

**Gestalt psychology** A theoretical approach that emphasizes the role of organized wholes (Gestalten) in perception and other psychological processes.

**glands** Bodily organs that produce hormones. *See also* endocrine system.

**glial cells** Cells in the brain that act as guidewires for growing neurons, provide a supportive scaffolding for mature neurons, and form the myelin sheath and blood-brain barrier.

**glove anesthesia** A condition sometimes seen in conversion disorders, in which there is an anesthesia of the entire hand with no loss of feeling above the wrist. This symptom makes no organic sense given the anatomical arrangement of the nerve trunks and indicates that the condition has a psychological basis.

**glucoreceptors** Receptors in the brain (in the area of the hypothalamus) that detect the amount of glucose in the bloodstream.

**glucose** The form of sugar that is the major source of energy for most bodily tissues. If plentiful, much of it is converted into glycogen and stored.

**glutamate** The most critical neurotransmitter in the retina, it also appears to be important for long-term memory and the perception of pain.

**glycogen** A stored form of metabolic energy derived from glucose. To be used, it must first be converted back into glucose.

**goal state** The situation one is trying to reach or set up when solving a problem.

**gonads** The body's primary sexual organs—ovaries in the female, testes in the male.

**good continuation** A factor in visual grouping. Contours tend to be seen in such a way that their direction is altered as little as possible.

**gray matter** That portion of the brain that appears gray. The color reflects the absence of myelination (which makes neural tissue appear white). The gray matter consists of the cell bodies, dendrites, and unmyelinated axons that comprise the nervous system's microcircuitry.

**great-person theory** The notion that significant events in history are caused by specific and exceptional individuals, rather than being precipitated largely by surrounding events.

**ground** The backdrop against which a figure is viewed. *See* figure-ground organization.

**grouping** The step in perception in which one determines which elements of the display belong together, as parts of a larger unit, and which do not.

**group polarization** A pattern often observed in group discussions in which the attitudes of each member of the group become more extreme as a result of the discussion, even though the discussion drew their attention to arguments on the other side of the issue, arguments that plausibly might have moderated their views.

**groupthink** A pattern of thinking that occurs when a group works on a problem, especially if the group is highly cohesive, faced by some external threat, and closed to outside information or opinions.

**guevedoces syndrome** A genetic disorder in which the external genitals appear to be female, but, at puberty, develop into normal male genitals.

**H** *See* heritability ratio.

**habituation** A decline in the tendency to respond to stimuli that have become familiar. While short-term habituation dissipates in a matter of minutes, long-term habituation may persist for days or weeks.

**habituation procedure** A widely used method for studying infant perception. After some exposure to a visual stimulus, an infant becomes habituated and stops looking at it. The extent to which a new stimulus leads to renewed interest and resumption of looking is taken as a measure of the extent to which the infant regards this new stimulus as different from the old one to which he became habituated.

**hair cells** The auditory receptors in the cochlea, lodged between the basilar membrane and other membranes above.

**hallucinations** Perceived experiences that occur in the absence of actual sensory stimulation.

**heritability ratio** (*H*) This refers to the relative importance of heredity and environment in determining the observed variation of a particular trait. More specifically, *H* is the proportion of the variance of the trait in a given population that is attributable to genetic factors.

**hertz** (**Hz**) A measure of frequency in number of cycles per second.

**heterosexuality** A sexual orientation leading to a choice of sexual partners of the opposite sex.

**heuristics** In problem solving, a procedure that has often worked in the past and is likely, but not certain, to work again. Heuristics typically sacrifice accuracy or guarantee of success in order to gain efficiency. *See also* algorithm.

**hierarchy of needs** According to Maslow and other adherents of the humanistic approach, human needs are arranged in a hierarchy with physiological needs such as hunger at the bottom, safety needs further up, the need for attachment and love still higher, and the desire for esteem yet higher. At the very top of the hierarchy is the striving for self-actualization. By and large, people will only strive for the higher order needs when the lower ones are fulfilled. *See also* self-actualization.

**higher-order invariants** Aspects of the stimulus input, usually involving ratios or relationships, that remain unchanged despite changes in viewing circumstances. For example, if a viewer walks toward a car, the retinal image cast by that car grows larger as the viewing distance shrinks. Even so, there is no change in the relationship between the car's image size and, say, the image size of the person standing next to the car. Some have hypothesized that by attending to this unchanging ratio, the viewer can gain a more accurate perception of the car's size.

**hindbrain** The rearmost portion of the brain just above the spinal cord, which includes the pons, medulla, and cerebellum.

**histogram** A graphic rendering of a frequency distribution which depicts the distribution by a series of contiguous rectangles. *See also* frequency distribution.

**hit** A response indicating that a signal is present when it is in fact present. *See* false alarm.

**homeostasis** The body's tendency to maintain the conditions of its internal environment by various forms of self-regulation.

**homogamy** The tendency of like to mate with like.

**homosexuality** A sexual orientation leading to a choice of partners of the same sex.

**hormone** A chemical released by one of the glands. Hormones travel through the bloodstream and control a number of bodily functions, including metabolic rate, arousal level, sugar output of the liver, and so on.

**hue** A perceived dimension of visual stimuli whose meaning is close to the term color (e.g., red, blue).

**humanistic approach** Asserts that what is most important about people is how they achieve their selfhood and actualize their potentialities. *See also* psychodynamic approach, situationism, sociocultural approach.

**Huntington's disease** A progressive hereditary disorder that involves degeneration of the basal ganglia and that results in jerky limb movements, facial twitches, and uncontrolled writhing of the body.

**hypnosis** A temporary, trancelike state that can be induced in normal persons. During hypnosis, various hypnotic or posthypnotic suggestions sometimes produce effects that resemble some of the symptoms of conversion disorders. *See also* conversion disorder.

**hypochondriasis** A disorder in which the sufferer believes he has a specific disease and typically goes from doctor to doctor to be evaluated for it.

**hypomania** A mild manic state in which the individual seems infectiously merry, extremely talkative, charming, and indefatigable.

**hypothalamus** A small structure at the base of the forebrain that plays a vital role in the control of the autonomic nervous system, of the endocrine system, and of the major biological drives.

**hysteria** An older term for a group of presumably psychogenic disorders including conversion disorders and dissociative disorders. Since DSM-III, it is no longer used as a diagnostic category, in part because of an erroneous implication that the condition is more prevalent in women (Greek *hystera*—womb). *See also* conversion disorder, dissociative disorders, glove anesthesia.

**id** In Freud's theory, a term for the most primitive reactions of human personality, consisting of blind strivings for immediate biological satisfaction regardless of cost. *See also* ego, superego.

**ideas of reference** A characteristic of some mental disorders, notably schizophrenia, in which the patient begins to think that external events are specially related to her personally (e.g., "People walk by and follow me").

**identical twins** Twins that originate from a single fertilized egg that then splits into two exact replicas that develop into two genetically identical individuals. *See also* fraternal twins.

**identity crisis** A hypothesized period of adolescence in which the individual must discover who and what he really is.

**ill-defined problems** Problems for which the goal state is defined only in general terms, and for which the available steps in reaching that goal state are not specified.

**illusory conjunction** A pattern of errors found, for example, in visual search tasks, in which observers correctly perceive the features present (redness, greenness, roundness, angularity) but misperceive how these were combined in the display (and so they might see a green *O* and a red *X* when, in fact, a green *X* and red *O* were presented).

**illusory correlation** A perception that two facts or observations tend to occur together, even though they do not, such as the erroneous belief that all accountants are introverted.

**implicit attitude** An attitude that a person does not realize she holds, but which nonetheless influences her actions and other beliefs.

**implicit memory** Memory retrieval in which there is no awareness of remembering at the time of retrieval. *See also* explicit memory.

**implicit theories of personality** Beliefs about the way in which different patterns of behavior of people hang together and why they do so.

**impression management** The steps that people take to influence or guide how other people perceive them.

**imprinting** A learned attachment that is formed at a particular period in life (the critical, or sensitive, period) and is difficult to reverse (e.g., the duckling's acquired tendency to follow whatever moving stimulus it encounters twelve to twenty-four hours after hatching).

**incidental learning** Learning without trying to learn (e.g., as in a study in which participants judge a speaker's vocal quality when she recites a list of words and are later asked to produce as many of the words as they can recall).

**incubation** The hypothetical process of continuing to work on a problem unconsciously after one has ceased to work on that problem consciously. Most contemporary investigators are skeptical about whether such a process truly exists.

**independent variable** The variable used within a study as a possible basis for making predictions. In an actual experiment, the independent variable is manipulated by the experimenter; in a correlational study, the independent variable is observed and then used as a (potential) basis for predicting other data.

**individualism** A cultural pattern in which people are considered to be fundamentally independent and in which the emphasis is on the ways a person can stand out through achieving private goals. Individualist societies include the dominant cultures of the United States, Western Europe, Canada, and Australia. *See also* collectivism.

**induced motion** Perceived movement of an objectively stationary stimulus that is enclosed by a moving framework.

**induced motion of the self** A pattern in which surrounding objects are in fact moving but are perceived as stationary, and in which the self is therefore (falsely) perceived as moving. An example occurs in traffic, when the next car rolls forward but is misperceived as stationary and one's own car is misperceived as rolling backward.

**inductive reasoning** Reasoning in which one observes a number of particular instances and tries to determine a general rule that covers them all.

**information-processing approach** A perspective that seeks to explain some aspect of behavior by referring to the underlying capacities to remember, pay attention, solve problems, and so on.

**informed consent**   A procedural step, conducted before an experiment begins, in which the research participants are asked to give their agreement to participate, based on full information about what the experiment will involve.

**in-group**   The social group that one is a member of, usually perceived as more homogeneous than other groups of which one is not a member.

**inhibitor**   A stimulus which signals that an event is not coming, and which thereby produces a response opposite to that ordinarily produced by the stimulus that is now signaled as not coming.

**initial state**   The status a person is in at the start of her attempts toward solving a problem. In solving the problem she hopes to move from this initial state to the problem's goal state.

**inner ear**   The portion of the ear in which the actual transduction of sound takes place.

**instrumental conditioning**   Also called operant conditioning. A form of learning in which a reinforcer (e.g., food) is given only if the animal performs the instrumental response (e.g., pressing a lever). In effect, what has to be learned is the relationship between the response and the reinforcer. *See also* classical conditioning.

**internal validity**   The degree to which a study is successful at measuring what it purports to measure, with all confounds removed and the dependent variable sensibly measured.

**interneurons**   Neurons that carry information from one neuron to another (rather than to a gland or muscle fiber or from a sensory receptor).

**interpersonal therapy (IPT)**   A mode of therapy originally intended as a brief method to counter depression, but now extended to other disorders. In this therapy, the focus is on the patient's gaining an understanding of how she interacts with others, and then learning new and more beneficial ways of interacting and communicating.

**interposition**   A monocular depth cue in which objects that are farther away are blocked from view by any other opaque object obstructing their optical path to the eye.

**interrater reliability**   A measure of the agreement among several independent observers of an event or stimulus.

**intersexual**   A child who is not clearly male or female, in some cases because of genetic factors, in others because of morphology.

**interval scale**   A scale in which equal differences between scores can be treated as equal so that the scores can be added or subtracted. *See also* categorical scale, nominal scale, ordinal scale, ratio scale.

**intrinsic motivation**   Motivation that seems inherent in an activity itself, as when we engage in an activity for its own sake or merely because it is fun.

**introspection**   The process of "looking within" through which a person might try to observe (and perhaps report) the contents of his own mind – his thoughts, beliefs, and feelings, and in some cases the processes through which he came to those current thoughts, beliefs, or feelings.

**in vivo desensitization**   A step used in treating phobias in which the person, at the end of therapy, is gradually exposed to instances of the phobic stimulus or situation in the real world.

**ion channels**   Biochemical "windows" in a cell wall that allow ions to flow in or out of the cell.

**ion pumps**   Biochemical mechanisms that use energy to move ions either into or out of the cell.

**iris**   The smooth circular muscle in the eye that surrounds the pupil and contracts or dilates under reflex control in order to govern the amount of light entering.

**ITP**   *See* interpersonal therapy.

**James-Lange theory of emotions**   A theory that asserts that the subjective experience of emotion is the awareness of one's own bodily reactions in the presence of certain arousing stimuli.

**jnd**   *See* just-noticeable difference.

**just-noticeable difference (jnd)**   The smallest possible difference between two stimuli that an organism can reliably detect.

**kinesthesis**   A general term for sensory information generated by receptors in the muscles, tendons, and joints which informs us of our skeletal movement.

**kin-selection hypothesis**   The proposal that helpful or altruistic behavior is more likely among organisms that are genetically related to each other than it is among unrelated organisms; the logic of the proposal is that helpful behavior among related organisms promotes the survival of their shared genes.

**knowledge-driven processes**   Processes that are influenced by the person's knowledge and prior beliefs; usually contrasted with data-driven processes.

**Korsakoff's syndrome**   A brain disorder characterized by serious memory disturbances. The most common cause is extreme and chronic alcohol use.

**latent content**   In psychoanalytic interpretation, the actual wishes and concerns that a dream or behavior is intended to express; usually contrasted with manifest content.

**latent learning**   Learning that occurs without being manifested by performance.

**lateral geniculate nucleus**   An important neural waystation on the path from the eye to the brain; ganglion neurons on the retina send their signals to the lateral geniculate nucleus; from there, other neurons carry the signal to the visual cortex in the occipital lobe.

**lateral inhibition**   The tendency of adjacent neural elements of the visual system to inhibit each other; it underlies brightness contrast and the accentuation of contours. *See also* brightness contrast.

**lateralization**   An asymmetry of function of the two cerebral hemispheres. In most right-handers, the left hemisphere is specialized for language functions, while the right hemisphere is better at various visual and spatial tasks.

**law of effect**   A theory that the tendency of a stimulus to evoke a response is strengthened if the response is followed by reward and is weakened if the response is not followed by reward. Applied to instrumental learning, this theory states that as trials proceed, incorrect bonds will weaken while the correct bond will be strengthened.

**learned helplessness**   A condition created by exposure to inescapable aversive events. This retards or prevents learning in subsequent situations in which escape or avoidance is possible.

**learned helplessness theory**   The theory that depression is analogous to learned helplessness effects produced in the laboratory. *See also* learned helplessness.

**learned taste aversion**   A specialized form of learning in which an organism learns to avoid a taste after just one pairing of that taste with illness. For example, an animal will avoid a food that on an earlier occasion made it sick.

**learning curve**   A curve in which some index of learning (e.g., the number of drops of saliva in Pavlov's classical conditioning experiment) is plotted against trials or sessions.

**learning model**   As defined in the text, a subcategory of the pathology model that (1) views mental disorders as the result of some form of faulty learning, and (2) believes that these should be treated by behavior therapists according to the laws of classical and instrumental conditioning or by cognitive therapists who try to affect faulty modes of thinking. *See also* cognitive therapy.

**learning theorists**   A group of theorists who argued that most learning can be understood in terms of a small number of principles that apply to all organisms and all situations.

**lens**   The portion of the eye that bends light rays and thus can focus an image on the retina.

**leptin**    A chemical produced by the adipose cells that seems to signal that plenty of fat is stored and that no more fat is needed. This signal may diminish eating.

**lesions**    The damage incurred by an area of the brain.

**lexical decision task**    A task in which the participant must decide as quickly as possible whether a stimulus (*book, trup, filt*) is or is not a word.

**life-span development**    The process of change and development that can be observed across the entire span of life, from prenatal development to death.

**limbic system**    A group of interconnected subcortical structures crucial for many emotional and motivaton activities, and many aspects of learning and memory. The limbic system includes the hypothalamus, the amygdala, and other structures.

**linear perspective**    A cue for distance that can be portrayed on a flat surface, exploiting the fact that objects appear smaller if viewed from a distance, and that parallel lines seem to converge as they recede into depth.

**line of best fit**    A line drawn through the points in a scatter diagram. It yields the best prediction of one variable when given the value of the other variable.

**lobes**    Rounded substructures within a larger organ. The brain, for example, contains four major lobes—the frontal, parietal, temporal, and occipital.

**localization of function**    The process of determining what each region of the brain contributes to which aspects of thinking and behavior.

**local representations**    A model of cognitive organization, especially semantic memory, in which each concept is represented by a single node or, more plausibly, a group of nodes. *See also* distributed representations, node.

**lock-and-key model**    The theory that neurotransmitter molecules will only affect the postsynaptic membrane if their shape fits into that of certain synaptic receptor molecules.

**longitudinal fissure**    The front-to-back cleavage that divides the left and right hemispheres of the brain.

**long-term memory**    Those parts of the memory system that are currently dormant and inactive, but have enormous storage capacity. *See also* stage theory of memory, working memory.

**long-term potentiation (LTP)**    A form of cellular plasticity in which a postsynaptic neuron becomes more sensitive (potentiated) to the signal received from the presynaptic neuron. This potentiation is usually produced by a rapid and sustained burst of firing by the presynaptic neuron. The potentiation can then spread to other presynaptic neurons provided that they have fired in the past at the same time as the presynaptic cell that produced the potentiation in the first place. *See also* activity dependence.

**loss aversion**    A strong tendency to regard losses as considerably more important than gains of comparable magnitude, and, with this, a tendency to take steps to avoid possible loss.

**LTP**    *See* long-term potentiation.

**Mach bands**    The accentuated edges between two adjacent regions that differ in brightness. This sharpening is maximal at the borders where the distance between the two regions is smallest and the contrast most striking.

**magic number**    According to George Miller, the number (seven plus or minus two) that represents the holding capacity of the working memory system.

**magnetic resonance imaging (MRI)**    *See* MRI.

**magno cells**    Ganglion cells found largely in the periphery of the retina that, because of their sensitivity to brightness changes, are particularly suited to the perception of motion and depth. *See also* parvo cells.

**maintenance rehearsal**    Repetition to keep material in working memory for a while. In contrast to elaborative rehearsal, this confers little long-term benefit for longer-term retention. *See also* elaborative rehearsal.

**major depression**    A mood disorder in which patients are disabled by guilt or sadness (especially in Western cultures), experience a loss of energy, pleasure and motivation, and disturbances of sleep, diet, and other bodily functions.

**major histocompatibility complex (MHC)**    Part of the genome involved in the immune system's ability to target invading cells and leave one's own cells alone.

**mania**    A mood disorder characterized by racing thoughts, pressured speech, irritability or euphoria, and marked impairments in judgment. *See also* bipolar disorder.

**manifest content**    In psychoanalytic interpretation, the immediately visible, surface content of a dream or behavior. This content is hypothesized to be a means of representing the latent content in disguised form, to protect the person from the anxiety associated with the latent content.

**matching hypothesis**    The hypothesis that persons seek romantic or sexual partners who possess a similar level of physical attractiveness.

**mean (M)**    *See* measure of central tendency.

**means-end analysis**    An important strategy for problem solving in which one's current position and resources are continually evaluated with respect to one's goal.

**measure of central tendency**    A single number intended to summarize an entire distribution of experimental results. Three commonly used measures of central tendency are: (1) the mode, or the score that occurs most frequently; (2) the median, or the point that divides the distribution into two equal halves; and (3) the mean, or the arithmetic average.

**medial forebrain bundle (MFB)**    A tract of fibers that runs through the base of the forebrain and parts of the hypothalamus. Electric stimulation of this bundle is usually experienced as rewarding.

**median**    *See* measure of central tendency.

**medulla**    Part of the hindbrain and the rearmost portion of the brain, just adjacent to the spinal cord. It is involved in the control of respiration, circulation, balance, and protective reflexes such as coughing and sneezing.

**melatonin**    A neurohormone secreted by the pineal gland that is involved in regulating the sleep-waking cycle.

**memory acquisition**    The processes of gaining new knowledge, that is, of establishing new memories in long-term storage.

**memory encoding**    The process of "translating" information into a format in which it can be stored for later use.

**memory span**    The number of items that can be recalled after a single presentation. *See also* magic number.

**memory trace**    The record in the nervous system that actually preserves a memory of a past experience.

**menstrual flow**    The discharge consisting of the sloughed-off uterine lining that was built up in preparation for a fertilized ovum, that signals the onset of menstruation.

**mental disorders**    A clinically-significant problem in thinking, behavior, or emotion that is associated with distress, disability, or significantly increased risk of suffering.

**mental health parity**    The policy position that insurance plans should reimburse for the costs of treating mental disorders on the same terms that they do for other medical disorders.

**mental images**    Analogical representations that reserve some of the characteristic attributes of our senses.

**mental maps**    A mental representation of the spatial layout of a scene, whether a small scene (so that the representation might show, say, the locations of various objects on a table top) or a larger scene (e.g., a representation of an entire city).

**mental representations**    Internal symbols that stand for something but are not equivalent to it, such as internalized actions, images, or words.

**mental rotation**   A task in which participants are presented with a rotated figure and must discern whether the figure is normal or, say, mirror-reversed. Participants apparently must visualize the figure rotated to an upright position before responding.

**mental set**   The predisposition to perceive, remember, or think of one thing rather than another.

**meta-analysis**   A statistical technique for combining the results of many studies even when the studies used different methods to collect the data. This technique has been useful in many areas, including studies on the outcome of psychotherapy.

**metacognition**   A general term for knowledge about knowledge, as in knowing that we do or do not remember something.

**method of loci**   A mnemonic technique that requires the learner to visualize each of the items she wants to remember in a different spatial location (locus). Recall requires that each location be mentally inspected for the item placed there.

**MFB**   *See* medial forebrain bundle.

**MHC**   *See* major histocompatibility complex.

**microcircuitry**   Networks of interneurons within which most of the brain's information processing occurs.

**midbrain**   The portion of the brain between hindbrain and forebrain that is involved in arousal, the sleep-waking cycle, and auditory and visual targeting.

**middle ear**   An antechamber to the inner ear which amplifies the sound-produced vibrations of the eardrum and transfers them to the cochlea. *See also* cochlea.

**midlife transition**   A period of time proposed by many authors in which individuals reappraise what they have done with their lives thus far and may reevaluate their marriage and career.

**Minnesota Multiphasic Personality Inventory (MMPI)**   A structured (objective) test of personality; the most widely used personality test.

**miss**   One of the four possible outcomes in a detection task. If the signal is present and the person says it is not, this is a miss. *See* correct negative.

**mixed states**   A pattern sometimes observed with bipolar disorder in which the person displays a combination of mania and depression, for example, tearfulness and pessimism combined with grandiosity and racing thoughts.

**MMPI**   *See* Minnesota Multiphasic Personality Inventory.

**mnemonics**   Deliberate strategies for helping memory, many of which use imagery.

**mode**   *See* measure of central tendency.

**monocular depth cues**   Features of the visual stimulus (e.g., linear perspective and motion parallax) that indicate depth even when it is viewed with one eye.

**monogamy**   A mating pattern in which a reproductive partnership is based on a special, more or less permanent tie between one male and one female.

**mood disorders**   A group of disorders distinguished primarily by changes in mood and motivation; these include bipolar disorder and major depression. *See also* bipolar disorder, major depression, mania.

**morpheme**   The smallest significant unit of meaning in a language (e.g., the word boys has two morphemes, *boy* and *s*). *See also* content morpheme, function morpheme.

**morphological sex**   Classification as male or female based on one's sex organs and bodily appearance (e.g., ovaries, vagina, and smooth facial skin versus testes, penis, and facial hair).

**Motherese**   A whimsical term for the singsong speech pattern that mothers and other adults generally employ when talking to infants.

**motion detectors**   Cells in the visual cortex that are sensitive to an image moving across the retina.

**motion parallax**   A depth cue provided by the fact that, as an observer moves, the images cast by nearby objects move more rapidly on the retina than the images cast by objects farther away.

**motoneurons**   Neurons whose cell bodies are in the brain or spinal cord and whose axons terminate on muscle fibers.

**MRI (magnetic resonance imaging)**   A noninvasive neurodiagnostic technique that relies on nuclear magnetic resonance. An MRI scan passes a high frequency alternating magnetic field through the brain to detect the different resonant frequencies of its nuclei. A computer then assembles this information to form a picture of brain structure. *See also* functional MRI (fMRI) scan.

**MS**   *See* multiple sclerosis.

**multicausal models**   A conception of a particular effect that emphasizes the role of many factors in leading to that effect.

**multiple intelligences**   In Howard Gardner's theory, the six essential, independent mental capacities, some of which are outside the traditional academic notions of intelligence, i.e., linguistic, logical-mathematical, spatial, musical, bodily-kinesthetic, and personal intelligence.

**multiple sclerosis (MS)**   A progressive neurological disease wherein the immune system mistakenly destroys the myelin sheaths that comprise the brain's white matter, producing manifestations such as numbness, blindness, and paralysis.

**myelin sheath**   The series of fatty wrappers, formed by special glial cells, that surround the axons of those neurons that must communicate over long distances in the nervous system and that allow for fast propagation of action potentials along those axons. *See also* nodes of Ranvier.

**nativism**   The view that some important aspects of perception and of other cognitive processes are innate.

**natural selection**   The explanatory principle by which Darwin accounted for biological evolution. It refers to the greater likelihood of successful reproduction for those organisms possessing attributes that are advantageous in a given environment. If these attributes are hereditary, then they will be well represented in the next generation, and, if the process continues over many generations, it can result in wholesale changes in bodily form and behavior.

**NE**   *See* norepinephrine.

**negative afterimage**   In color vision, the persistence of an image that possesses the hue complementary to that of the stimulus (e.g., seeing a yellow afterimage after staring at a blue lamp), resulting from the operation of opponent processes.

**negative cognitive schema**   For Aaron Beck, the core cognitive component of depression, consisting of an individual's automatic negative interpretations concerning himself, his future, and the world. *See also* explanatory style.

**negative feedback**   *See* feedback.

**negative symptoms of schizophrenia**   Symptoms that involve deficits in normal functioning, such as apathy, impoverished speech, and emotional blunting. *See also* positive symptoms of schizophrenia.

**neglect syndrome**   The result of certain lesions of the right parietal lobe that leave a patient inattentive to stimuli to her left (e.g., not eating food on the left side of the plate) and result in her ignoring the left side of her body (e.g., putting makeup on only the right side of her face).

**neocortex**   The outermost, convoluted layer of the forebrain, often referred to merely as the cortex.

**neo-Freudians**   A group of theorists who accept the psychoanalytic conception of unconscious conflicts but who differ with Freud in ways that can include (1) describing these conflicts in social terms rather than in terms of bodily pleasures or frustrations, (2) maintaining that many of these conflicts arise from specific cultural conditions instead of being biologically preordained.

**nerve growth factor**   A neurochemical that promotes the sprouting of new neuronal connections.

**nerve impulse** *See* action potential.

**network models** Theories of cognitive organization, especially of semantic memory, which hold that items of information are represented by a system of nodes linked through associative connections. *See also* connectionist model, distributed representations, local representations, node.

**neural correlates** The events in the nervous system that happen at the same time as (and are thus correlated with) the mental or behavioral events we hope to explain.

**neural plasticity** The capacity for neurons to alter their functioning as a result of experience.

**neural plate** A small thickening, running the length of the embryo, from which the neural tube and, eventually, the nervous system, develop.

**neural stem cells** Cells within the fetus that are the developmental precursors of neurons.

**neural tube** The tubular structure, formed by the fusion of the edges of the neural plate, from which the central nervous system (forebrain, midbrain, hindbrain, and spinal cord) develops.

**neurodevelopmental disorder** A disorder that stems from early brain abnormalities. Many researchers believe that schizophrenia is one such disorder and may originate in abnormal fetal brain development.

**neurofibrillary tangles** Stringy debris observed in the brain as a consequence of the neuron degeneration in Alzheimer's disease.

**neurogenesis** The process through which the nervous system grows and develops, a process including cellular signaling, differentiation, migration and proliferation.

**neuroimaging techniques** Methods that permit noninvasive study and depiction of brain structure or function. *See also* CT scan, MRI, functional MRI scan, and PET scan.

**neuromuscular junction** The location where a motoneuron meets a muscle fiber; activation of this neuron causes the muscle fiber to contract.

**neuron** A nerve cell.

**neuropeptide Y (NPY)** A chemical found widely in the brain and periphery. In the brain, it acts as a neurotransmitter; when administered at sites in and near the hypothalamus, it is a potent elicitor of eating.

**neuropsychologists** Investigators who draw claims about brain-behavior relationships, using evidence from cases of brain damage, plus close observation of the changes in function associated with that damage.

**neurosis** A broad term once used for mental disorders whose primary symptoms are anxiety or what seem to be defenses against anxiety. Since the adoption of DSM-III, the term has been dropped as a broad diagnostic label, and what were once considered the various subcategories of neurosis (e.g., phobia, anxiety, conversion and dissociative disorders) are now classified as separate disorders.

**neurotoxin** Any chemical poisonous to neurons.

**neurotrophic factors** Chemicals that influence developing neural cells.

**NGF** *See* nerve growth factor.

**node** A point in a network at which a number of connections converge.

**nodes of Ranvier** The gaps occurring between the glial-cell wrappers that form the myelin sheath surrounding many kinds of axons. The nodes are crucial to the rapidity at which neural impulses travel along myelinated axons.

**nominal scale** A scale in which responses are ordered only into different categories. *See also* categorical scale, interval scale, ordinal scale, ratio scale.

**nonfluent aphasia** Speech disorder in which the main difficulty is in speech production, often involving damage to Broca's area in the frontal lobe.

**norepinephrine (NE)** The neurotransmitter found in the nerves of the sympathetic branch of the autonomic nervous system. It is also one of the neurotransmitters involved in various arousal systems in the brain.

**normal curve** A symmetrical, bell-shaped curve that describes the probability of obtaining various combinations of chance events. It depicts the normal distribution, the frequency distribution of many physical and psychological attributes of humans and animals.

**normal distribution** A frequency distribution whose graphic representation has a symmetrical, bell-shaped form—the normal curve. Its characteristics are often referred to when investigators test statistical hypotheses and make inferences about the population from a given sample.

**norms** In intelligence testing, the scores taken from a large sample of the population against which an individual's test scores are evaluated.

**NPY** *See* neuropeptide Y.

**nucleus accumbens** A dopamine-rich area in the forebrain that is critical in the physiology of reward.

**null hypothesis** The hypothesis that an obtained difference is merely a chance fluctuation from a population in which the true mean difference is zero.

**object permanence** The conviction that an object remains perceptually constant over time and exists even when it is out of sight. According to Piaget, this does not develop until infants are eight months old or more.

**observational learning** A mechanism of socialization whereby a child observes another person who serves as a model and then proceeds to imitate what that model does.

**observational study** A study in which the investigator does not manipulate any of the variables but simply observes their relationship as they occur naturally.

**obsessive-compulsive disorder (OCD)** A disorder whose symptoms are obsessions (persistent and irrational thoughts or wishes) and compulsions (uncontrollable, repetitive acts), which seem to be defenses against anxiety. A member of a diagnostic category called anxiety disorders, which also includes generalized anxiety disorder and phobias.

**occipital lobe** The rearmost lobe in each cerebral hemisphere, which includes the primary visual projection area.

**OCD** *See* obsessive-compulsive disorder.

**OCD spectrum disorders** A family of disorders believed to derive from the same genetic inheritance, and involving the basal ganglia and frontal lobes. All involve some form of obsessive and compulsive symptoms and may benefit from the same kinds of medications as OCD.

**Oedipus complex** In psychoanalytic theory, a general term for the cluster of impulses and conflicts hypothesized to occur during the phallic phase, at around age five. In boys, a fantasized form of intense, possessive sexual love is directed at the mother, which is soon followed by hatred for and fear of the father. As the fear mounts, the sexual feelings are pushed underground and the boy identifies with the father. An equivalent process is hypothesized in girls and is called the Electra complex.

**one-trial learning** In classical conditioning, the establishment of a conditioned response (CR) after only one pairing of conditioned stimulus (CS) and unconditioned stimulus (US).

**operant** In Skinner's system, an instrumental response, defined by the effect it has (the way it "operates") on the environment. *See also* instrumental conditioning.

**operant conditioning** *See* instrumental conditioning.

**operations** According to Piaget, the mental transformations and relationships that underlie logical thought.

**opponent-process theory** (1) A theory of color vision that proposes three pairs of color antagonists: red-green, blue-yellow, and white-black. Excitation of one member of a pair automatically inhibits the other member. (2) A theory of motivation that asserts that the nervous system tends to counteract any deviation from the neutral point on the pain-pleasure dimension. If the original stimulus is maintained, there is an attenuation of the emotional state one is in; if it is withdrawn, the opponent process reveals itself, and the emotional state swings sharply in the opposite direction.

**optic flow**    The phenomenon wherein an object's retinal image enlarges as we approach the object and shrinks as we retreat from it. It is used as a depth cue by the visual system.

**optic nerve**    The bundle of fibers that proceeds from each eyeball to the brain, made up of axons whose cell bodies are retinal ganglion cells.

**oral character**    According to Freud, a personality type based on a fixation at the oral stage of development and whose manifestations can include passive dependency or "biting" hostility. *See also* oral stage.

**oral stage**    In psychoanalytic theory, the earliest stage of psychosexual development during which the primary source of bodily pleasure is stimulation of the mouth and lips, as in sucking at the breast.

**ordinal scale**    A scale in which responses are rank-ordered by relative magnitude but in which the intervals between successive ranks are not necessarily equal. *See also* categorical scale, interval scale, nominal scale, ratio scale.

**orexins**    Hormones synthesized in the lateral hypothalamus that are potent elicitors of eating.

**organic brain syndromes**    Mental disorders that are reliably associated with definitive brain damage (e.g., Alzheimer's disease).

**orgasm**    A brief episode during sexual activity when the organism experiences involuntary muscle contractions throughout the body. In males, rhythmic contractions of the urethra expel semen during orgasm.

**orienting**    The tendency of an organism to shift its attention and sensory surfaces (e.g., by moving the eyes or turning the ears) to inspect a novel or unexpected stimulus.

**oscilloscope**    An electronic monitoring device that uses a cathode ray tube (CRT) to display electrical signals such as electrocardiograph signals or action potentials.

**outcome expectations**    A set of beliefs, drawn from experience, about what the consequences (rewards or punishments) of certain actions are likely to be.

**outer ear**    The portion of the structures of the ear that includes the earflap, the auditory canal, and the outer surface of the eardrum.

**out-group**    A social group with which one does not identify or to which one does not belong.

**out-group homogeneity effect**    A phenomenon related to stereotyping in which a member of a group (the in-group) tends to view members of another group (the out-group) as more alike (less varied) than are members of his or her own group.

**oval window**    The membrane separating the middle ear from the inner ear.

**overregularization errors**    A pattern of mistakes in which a person treats irregular cases as though they followed the rules, for example, saying "goed" instead of "went," or "foots" instead of "feet."

**oxytocin**    A hormone manufactured mostly in the hypothalamus that plays an important role in regulating sexual activity, nesting, and breast-feeding.

**PANDAS**    *See* pediatric autoimmune neuropsychiatric disorders associated with streptococcal infections.

**panic attack**    A sudden episode consisting of terrifying bodily symptoms such as labored breathing, choking, dizziness, tingling in the hands and feet, sweating, trembling, heart palpitations, and chest pain. Panic attacks occur in a number of mental disorders and are common in phobias, panic disorder, and post-traumatic stress disorder (PTSD).

**panic disorder**    An anxiety disorder characterized by repeated or disabling panic attacks. *See also* anxiety disorders, panic attack.

**parallel distributed processing (PDP)**    Models of cognitive processing in which the relevant symbolic representations do not correspond to any one unit of the network but to the state of the network as a whole. *See also* connectionist model, distributed representation.

**paranoid schizophrenia**    A subcategory of schizophrenia. Its dominant symptom is a set of delusions that are often elaborately systematized, usually of grandeur or persecution.

**parasympathetic branch**    A division of the autonomic nervous system that serves vegetative functions and conserves bodily energies (e.g., slowing heart rate). Its action is often antagonistic to that of the sympathetic branch.

**parietal lobe**    The lobe in each cerebral hemisphere that lies between the occipital and frontal lobes, and that includes the primary sensory projection area.

**Parkinson's disease**    A degenerative neurological disorder characterized by various motor difficulties that include tremor, muscular rigidity, and slowed movement. This disease involves degeneration of dopamine-releasing neurons in the basal ganglia of the forebrain, which are crucial for motor control.

**partial reinforcement**    A condition in which repeated responses are reinforced only some of the time.

**parvo cells**    Ganglion cells found throughout the retina that, because of their sensitivity to differences in hue, are particularly suited to the perception of color and form. *See also* magno cells.

**pattern recognition**    The process by which the perceptual system identifies the forms it encounters.

**pattern theory**    The theory that a stimulus attribute is not coded by being sent along specific sensory fibers, but rather by a specific pattern of firing of all the relevant sensory fibers.

**PDP**    *See* parallel distributed processing.

**pediatric autoimmune neuropsychiatric disorders associated with streptococcal infections (PANDAS)**    A medical condition related to streptococcus, commonly producing one or more of the OCD spectrum disorders.

**penis envy**    In psychoanalytic theory, the wish for a penis that is assumed to ensue normally in females as part of the Electra complex.

**percentile rank**    The percentage of all the scores in a distribution that lie below a given score.

**perceptual constancies**    Constant attributes of a distal object, such as its shape and size, that we are able to perceive despite vagaries of the proximal stimulus.

**perceptual organization**    A step of interpretation, provided by the perceiver, in which decisions are made about which elements of the display belong together, as parts of a larger whole, and which elements belong to different objects.

**perceptual parsing**    The process of grouping various visual elements of a scene appropriately, deciding which elements go together and which do not.

**peripheral nervous system**    The parts of the nervous system outside the central nervous system, including the cranial and spinal nerves that exit the skull and spinal column, respectively.

**peripheral route to persuasion**    The processes involved in attitude change when someone does not care particularly about an issue or devotes few resources to thinking about the issue. This route depends on superficial considerations, such as the appearance of the person giving the persuasive information, and is contrasted with the *central route*.

**permastore**    Near-permanent retention of some kinds of items in memory, mostly involving semantic or general knowledge (e.g., multiplication tables, names of family members).

**permissive pattern**    A parental style in which parents try not to assert their authority and impose few restrictions or demands on their children.

**perseveration**    The tendency to repeat the same response inappropriately, typically accompanying the defects in strategy formation often observed with prefrontal lesions.

**personal space**    The physical region all around us whose intrusion we guard against. This aspect of human behavior has been likened to territoriality in animals.

**persuasive communications** Messages that openly try to convince us to act a certain way or to hold a particular belief.

**PET (positron emission tomography) scan** A technique for examining brain function by observing the degree of metabolic activity of different regions of the brain.

**phallic stage** In psychoanalytic theory, the stage of psychosexual development during which the child begins to regard his or her genitals as a major source of gratification.

**phenotype** The overt appearance and behavior of an organism, regardless of its genetic blueprint. *See also* genotype.

**phenylalanine** An amino acid that cannot be transformed due to an enzyme deficiency in those with phenylketonuria (PKU). In an infant with PKU, phenylalanine is converted into a toxic agent that accumulates in an infant's bloodstream and damages the developing nervous system.

**phenylketonuria (PKU)** A condition in which one lacks the gene that enables one to metabolize phenylalanine. If detected early enough, this condition can be treated by means of a special diet. If not detected early, this disorder can cause a severe form of retardation. *See also* phenylalanine.

**phobia** An anxiety disorder that is characterized by an intense and, at least on the surface, irrational fear. *See also* anxiety disorders, social phobia.

**phoneme** The smallest significant unit of sound in a language. In English, it corresponds roughly to a letter of the alphabet (e.g., apt, tap, and pat are all made up of the same phonemes).

**photoreceptor** One of the visual-pigment-filled light-sensitive cells at the back of the retina, whether rods or cones. These are the cells that transduce light energy into neural impulses, launching the processes of vision.

**phrase** An organized sequence of words within a sentence that functions as a unit.

**phrase structure description** A tree diagram that shows the hierarchical structure of a sentence. The descending branches of the tree correspond to smaller and smaller units of sentence structure.

**pictorial cues** The monocular depth cues (such as interposition, linear perspective, and relative size) that the eye exploits as depth cues; these cues are an optical consequence of the projection of a three-dimensional world onto a flat surface.

**pitch** The psychological dimension of sound that corresponds to frequency; as frequency increases, pitch appears to rise.

**pituitary gland** An endocrine gland that is actually a functional extension of the hypothalamus. The pituitary gland is often called the master gland because many of its secretions trigger hormone secretions in other glands.

**PKU** *See* phenylketonuria.

**placebo** In medical practice, a term for a chemically inert substance that produces real medical benefits because the patient believes it will help her.

**placebo effect** The medical or psychological benefits of a treatment produced simply because a patient believes the treatment has therapeutic powers.

**place theory** A theory of pitch proposed by Hermann von Helmholtz which states that different regions of the basilar membrane respond to different sound frequencies. The nervous system interprets the excitation from different basilar regions as different pitches.

**plasticity** The changeability of a trait or behavior with experience (e.g., eye color shows little plasticity, while hair color shows considerably more).

**plateau** According to some authors, one of the four stages of sexual arousal, and the stage during which orgasm occurs.

**pluralistic ignorance** A situation in which individuals in a group don't know that there are others in the group who share their perception (and often, their confusion), and interpret the others' inaction as reflecting knowledge that in truth is not there.

**polyandry** A type of mating system in which one female monopolizes the reproductive efforts of several males.

**polygamy** Any mating system, including polyandry and polygymy, in which one member of a sex monopolizes the reproductive efforts of several members of the other sex.

**polygenic inheritance** Inheritance of an attribute whose expression is controlled not by one but by many gene pairs.

**polygyny** A type of polygamous mating system in which one male monopolizes the reproductive efforts of several females.

**pons** The topmost portion of the hindbrain just above the medulla and in front of the cerebellum; it is involved in coordinating facial sensations and muscular actions, and in regulating sleep and arousal.

**population** The entire group of research participants (or test trials) about which the investigator wants to draw conclusions. *See also* sample.

**positive psychology** A movement within the field of psychology that seeks to emphasize in its research the factors that make people healthy, happy, able to cope, or well adjusted to their life circumstances.

**positive symptoms of schizophrenia** Symptoms that involve behavior or thinking that is either less pronounced or nonexistent in normal individuals, such as hallucinations, delusions, or bizarre behavior. *See also* negative symptoms of schizophrenia.

**positron emission tomography (PET) scan** *See* PET scan.

**postsynaptic membrane** The membrane of the receiving cell across the synaptic gap that contains specialized receptor sites.

**postsynaptic neuron** The cell receiving a neural message at the synapse.

**post-traumatic stress disorder (PTSD)** A chronic, sometimes lifelong disorder that has its onset some time after an especially stressful traumatic event. Symptoms include dissociation, recurrent nightmares, flashbacks, and sleep disturbances. *See also* acute stress disorder, anxiety disorders, dissociation.

**potentiation** In motivation, the tendency to make some behaviors, perceptions, and feelings more probable than others. *See also* long-term potentiation.

**practical intelligence** The intelligence required to solve everyday problems.

**precursor** A substance required for the chemical manufacture of some other substance.

**predicate** *See* concept.

**predictive validity** An assessment of whether a test measures what it is intended to measure; the assessment hinges on the correlation between the test score and some external criterion (e.g., a correlation between a scholastic aptitude test score and college grades).

**prefrontal area** The frontmost portion of the frontal lobes, which is involved in working memory, strategy formation, and response inhibition.

**prefrontal lobotomy** A neurosurgical treatment that surgically cuts the connections between the prefrontal areas of the frontal lobes and the rest of the brain. Once used widely (and mostly unsuccessfully) for many mental disorders but now performed very rarely.

**preoperational period** In Piaget's theory, the period from about ages two to six during which children come to represent actions and objects internally but cannot systematically manipulate these representations or relate them to each other. The child is therefore unable to conserve quantity across perceptual transformations and also is unable to take points of view other than his own.

**preparedness theory of phobias** The theory that phobias grow out of a built-in predisposition (preparedness) to learn to fear certain stimuli (e.g., snakes and spiders) that may have posed serious dangers to our primate ancestors.

**prescriptionism** The view that psychotherapeutic treatments for mental disorders may ultimately be like prescriptions for medications: tailored to both the disorder and the individual patient.

**presynaptic facilitation** A process that underlies many kinds of learning, documented in studies of *Aplysia*. It occurs when learning results in the increased readiness of presynaptic neurons to fire.

**presynaptic neuron** The cell that shoots a neurotransmitter across the synaptic gap.

**primacy effect** (1) In free recall, the tendency to recall the first items on a list more readily than those in the middle. (2) In forming an impression of another person, the tendency to give greater weight to attributes noted at the outset than to those noted later. *See also* recency effect.

**primary messengers** The neurochemicals responsible for neuron-to-neuron communication in chemical synapses, i.e., neurotransmitters. Primary messengers are contrasted with second messengers, those neurochemicals responsible for communication within neurons.

**primary motor projection area** A strip of cortex located at the back of the frontal lobe just ahead of the primary sensory projection area in the parietal lobe. This region is the primary projection area for muscular movements.

**primary projection areas** Regions of the cortex that serve as receiving stations for sensory information or as dispatching stations for motor commands.

**primary sensory projection area** Areas of the cortex that are the initial "receiving stations" for sensory information.

**priming effect** Phenomenon wherein giving a participant advance knowledge about or exposure to a stimulus can increase the ease of its subsequent recall or recognition.

**primitive features** Attributes of an object (such as its location, contour, color, and shape) that are first detected separately and then coordinated to enable identification of the object.

**prisoner's dilemma** A particular arrangement of payoffs in a two-person situation in which each individual has to choose between two alternatives without knowing the other's choice. The payoff structure is arranged such that the optimal strategy for each person depends upon whether she can trust the other or not. If trust is possible, the payoffs for each will be considerably higher than if there is no trust.

**probability of response** A common measure of the strength of conditioning, assessing the likelihood that a response will be produced.

**procedural knowledge** *See* declarative knowledge.

**progesterone** A female sex hormone that dominates the latter phase of the female cycle during which the uterine walls thicken to receive the embryo.

**projection** In psychoanalytic theory, a mechanism of defense in which various forbidden thoughts and impulses are attributed to another person rather than the self, thus warding off some anxiety (e.g., "I hate you" becomes "You hate me").

**projective techniques** Sometimes called unstructured personality tests. Methods of assessing personality that use relatively ambiguous stimuli in order to elicit responses that are unguarded and authentic. The most common projective techniques are the TAT and the Rorschach inkblot test.

**propagation** The spread of the action potential down an axon, caused by successive destabilizations of the neuronal membrane.

**proposition** *See* concept.

**prosopagnosia** The inability to recognize faces, usually produced by lesions in the parietal lobes.

**prototype** The typical example of a category of (e.g., a robin is a prototypical bird for many Americans).

**prototype theory** The theory that concepts are formed around average or typical exemplars rather than lists of single attributes.

**proximal stimulus** The stimulus information that actually reaches the sensory receptors. *See also* distal stimulus.

**proximity** (1) In perception, the closeness of two figures. The closer together they are, the more they will tend to be grouped together perceptually. (2) The nearness of people, which is one of the most important determinants of attraction and liking.

**pseudohermaphroditism** The most common kind of intersexuality, in which individuals have ambiguous genitalia. *See also* intersexual.

**psychoanalysis** (1) A theory of both normal and abnormal human personality development, formulated by Freud, whose key assertions include unconscious conflict and early psychosexual development. (2) A method of therapy that draws heavily on this theory of personality. Its main aim is to have the patient gain insight into her own unconscious thoughts and feelings. Therapeutic tools employed toward this end include free association, interpretation, and the appropriate use of the transference relationship between patient and analyst. *See also* free association, transference.

**psychodynamic approach** An approach to personality originally derived from psychoanalytic theory that asserts that personality differences are based on unconscious (dynamic) conflicts within the individual. *See also* humanistic approach, situationism, sociocultural approach, trait approach.

**psychodynamic model** An approach to mental disorders which holds that they are the end-products of internal psychological conflicts that generally originate in one's childhood experiences. *See also* learning model.

**psychogenic disorders** Disorders whose origins are psychological rather than organic (e.g., phobias).

**psychogenic symptoms** Symptoms believed to result from some psychological cause rather than from actual tissue damage.

**psychological intensity** The magnitude of a stimulus as it is perceived, not in terms of its physical attributes.

**psychometric approach to intelligence** An attempt to understand the nature of intelligence by studying the pattern of results obtained on intelligence tests.

**psychopathology** (1) The study of mental disorders, or (2) the mental disorder itself.

**psychophysics** An approach to understanding perception that relates the characteristics of physical stimuli to attributes of the sensory experience they produce.

**psychosis** Loss of contact with reality (most often evidenced as delusions or hallucinations), as can occur in severe cases of many kinds of mental disorders such as mania, major depression, or schizophrenia.

**psychosurgery** Neurosurgery performed to alleviate manifestations of mental disorders that cannot be brought under control using psychotherapy, medication, or other standard treatments. Psychosurgery can be helpful in severe cases of, for example, obsessive-compulsive disorder.

**psychotherapy** As used here, a collective term for all forms of treatment that use psychological rather than somatic methods.

**psychotropic drugs** Medications that seem to control, or at least moderate, the manifestations of mental disorder.

**PTSD** *See* post-traumatic stress disorder.

**punishment** A way to suppress a response by having its occurrence followed by an aversive event.

**puzzle box** An apparatus used by Edward Thorndike to demonstrate trial-and-error learning in cats. Animals were required to perform a simple action in order to escape the puzzle box and obtain food.

***r*** *See* correlation coefficient.

**random assignment** In experimental design, the random placement of participants in experimental versus control groups in order to insure that all groups are matched at the outset of the experiment.

**random sample**    *See* sample.

**range**    A measure of the variability contained in a set of scores, calculated by subtracting the lowest score from the highest.

**rationalization**    In psychoanalytic theory, a mechanism of defense by means of which unacceptable thoughts or impulses are reinterpreted in more acceptable and, thus, less anxiety-arousing terms (e.g., the jilted lover who convinces herself that she never loved her fiancé anyway).

**ratio scale**    An interval scale in which there is a true zero point, thus allowing statements about proportions (e.g., this sound is twice as loud as the other). *See also* categorical scale, interval scale, nominal scale, ordinal scale.

**reaction formation**    In psychoanalytic theory, a mechanism of defense in which a forbidden impulse is turned into its opposite (e.g., hate toward a sibling becomes exaggerated love).

**reasoning**    The determination of the conclusions that can be drawn from certain premises.

**reasoning schemas**    A series of rules, derived from ordinary practical experience, used to guide reasoning about problems involving conditions.

**recall**    A task in which some item must be produced from memory. *See also* recognition.

**recency effect**    In free recall, the tendency to recall items at the end of the list more readily than those in the middle. *See also* primacy effect (in free recall).

**receptive field**    The retinal area in which visual stimulation affects a particular cell's firing rate.

**recessive gene**    *See* gene.

**reciprocal altruism**    A pattern of helpful behavior in which one organism does something for another, and so gains the benefit that the second organism will do something for the first.

**reciprocal inhibition**    The arrangement by which excitation of some neural system is accompanied by inhibition of that system's antagonist (as in antagonistic muscles).

**reciprocity principle**    A basic rule of many social interactions that decrees that one must repay whatever one has been given.

**recoding**    Changing the form in which information is stored.

**recognition**    A task in which a participant must judge whether he has encountered a stimulus previously. *See also* recall.

**reconditioning**    In classical conditioning, the presentation of further reinforced conditioning trials after a conditioned response (CR) has been extinguished.

**reflex**    A simple, stereotyped reaction in response to some stimulus (e.g., limb flexion in withdrawal from pain).

**rehearsal**    *See* elaborative rehearsal, maintenance rehearsal.

**relational aggression**    A strategy for attaining social advantage by manipulating others' social alliances. Females are apparently more relationally aggressive, whereas males are apparently more physically aggressive.

**relative size**    A monocular depth cue in which far-off objects produce a smaller retinal image than nearby objects of the same size.

**reliability**    The degree of consistency with which a test measures a trait or attribute. Assuming that a trait or attribute remains constant, a perfectly reliable test of that measure will produce the same score each time it is given.

**reliability coefficient**    The coefficient used in determining the consistency of mental tests, that is, the repeatability of their results. It is usually derived from test-retest correlations or from correlations between alternative forms of a test. *See also* test-retest method.

**REM rebound**    The tendency to spend more time in REM sleep if deprived of it on previous nights. REM rebound often occurs during withdrawal from medications that suppress REM sleep (e.g., barbiturates or alcohol).

**REM sleep**    The type of sleep characterized by rapid eye movements, an EEG indicative of high cortical arousal, speeded heart rate and respiration, near-paralysis of limb muscles, and recall of highly visual dreams.

**repetition priming**    An increase in the likelihood that an item will be identified, recognized, or recalled caused by recent exposure to that item, which may occur without explicit awareness.

**replication**    A repetition of an experiment that yields the same results.

**report bias**    A tendency to announce some outcomes more often than others. For example, gamblers might suffer from a report bias, boasting about their wins but keeping quiet about their losses.

**representative heuristic**    A rule of thumb by means of which we estimate the probability that an object (or event) belongs to a certain category based on how prototypical it is of that category, regardless of how common it actually is. *See also* prototype.

**repressed memory**    In psychoanalytic theory, a memory that is so anxiety-laden that it has been pushed out of consciousness where it may fester until it is "recovered."

**repression**    In psychoanalytic theory, a mechanism of defense by means of which thoughts, impulses, or memories that give rise to anxiety are pushed out of consciousness.

**resistance**    In psychoanalysis, a term describing the patient's failure to associate freely and say whatever enters her head.

**resolution**    According to some authors, one of the four stages of sexual arousal.

**response amplitude**    The size of a response, used commonly as a sign of response strength in classical and operant conditioning.

**response rate**    The number of responses per unit of time. This is one measure of the strength of an operant response.

**response suppression**    The inhibition of a response by conditioned fear.

**resting potential**    The difference in voltage across a neuronal membrane when the neuron is not firing.

**restitutional symptoms**    For Eugen Bleuler, symptoms such as delusions and hallucinations that originated in the schizophrenic patient's attempt to compensate for his increasing isolation from the world.

**restructuring**    A reorganization of a problem that can facilitate its solution; a characteristic of creative thought.

**retention interval**    In memory experiments, the time that elapses between the original learning and a later test.

**retina**    The tissue-thin structure at the back of the interior of the eye that contains the photoreceptors, several layers of intermediate neurons, and the cell bodies of the axons that form the optic nerve.

**retinal image**    The image of an object that is projected on the retina. Its size increases with the size of that object and decreases with the object's distance from the eye.

**retrieval**    The process of searching for some item in memory and of finding it. If retrieval fails, this may or may not mean that the relevant memory trace is missing. The trace may simply be inaccessible.

**retrieval cue**    A stimulus that helps one to recall a memory.

**retrieval failure**    The inability to access a memory, often due to poor encoding; an alternative to erasure as an explanation for forgetting.

**retrieval paths**    The mental connections, linking one idea to the next, that one uses in locating a bit of information in memory.

**retrograde amnesia**    A memory deficit, often suffered after a head injury, in which the patient loses memory of some period prior to the injury. *See also* anterograde amnesia.

**reversible figures**    Visual patterns that easily allow more than one interpretation, including figures that allow parsing such that what is initially figure becomes ground and vice versa.

**rhodopsin**    The photopigment used in the rods within the retina.

**rhythm**    The pattern of timing in the delivery of a stimulus, such as music or speech.

**risky shift**    A pattern in which a group appears more willing to take chances, or more willing to take an extreme stance, than the individual group members would have been on their own.

**rods**    Photoreceptors in the retina that respond to lower light intensities and give rise to achromatic (colorless) sensations. *See also* cones.

**romantic love**    A state of emotion characterized by idealization of the beloved, turbulent emotions, and obsessive thoughts. *See also* companionate love.

**Romeo-and-Juliet effect**    The intensification of romantic love that can occur with parental opposition.

**rooting reflex**    In the infant, the sucking elicited by stroking applied on or around the lips; aids breast-feeding.

**Rorschach inkblot technique**    A projective (unstructured) personality assessment that requires the examinee to look at a series of inkblots and report everything she sees in them.

**rules of syntax**    The regular principles governing how words can be assembled into sentences, and also describing the structure of those sentences.

**SAD**    *See* seasonal affective disorders.

**sample**    A subset of a population selected by the investigator for study. A random sample is constructed such that each member of the population has an equal chance of being picked. A stratified sample is constructed such that every relevant subgroup of the population is randomly sampled in proportion to its size. *See also* population.

**sample mean**    The mean for a particular group of observations; often contrasted with the population mean, which is the mean of every possible observation. The population mean can also be obtained by obtaining the sample mean for sample after sample after sample, and then taking the mean of these means.

**saturation**    A perceived dimension of visual stimuli that describes the "strength" of a color—the extent to which it appears rich or pale (e.g., light pink vs. hot pink).

**savant syndrome**    A syndrome in a mentally retarded person who has some remarkable talent that seems out of keeping with his low level of general intelligence. Previously idiot savant, a term now abandoned as derogatory.

**scaling**    A procedure for assigning numbers to a subject's responses. *See also* categorical scale, interval scale, nominal scale, ordinal scale, ratio scale.

**scatter diagram**    *See* scatter plot.

**scatter plot**    A graph depicting the relationship between two interval- or ratio-scale variables, with each axis representing one variable; often used to graph correlation data.

**schedule of reinforcement**    The pattern of occasions on which responses are to be reinforced. Commonly, reinforcement is scheduled after a stipulated number of responses occurs or when a response occurs after a preset time interval has elapsed. *See also* fixed-ratio schedule, fixed-interval schedule.

**schema**    (1) In theories of memory and thinking, a term that refers to a general cognitive structure in which information is organized. (2) In Piaget's theory of development, a mental pattern.

**schizophrenia**    A group of severe mental disorders characterized by at least some of the following: marked disturbance of thought, withdrawal, inappropriate or flat emotions, delusions, and hallucinations. See also catatonic schizophrenia, disorganized schizophrenia, negative symptoms of schizophrenia, paranoid schizophrenia, positive symptoms of schizophrenia.

**SD**    *See* standard deviation.

**seasonal affective disorder (SAD)**    A mood disorder that shows reliable fluctuations with the time of year. One example is a depression that ensues in the fall when the days become shorter and ends in the spring when the days lengthen.

**second messengers**    Neurochemicals within the neuron that regulate such mechanisms as the creation of receptor sites for specific neurotransmitters and the synthesis of the neuron's own neurotransmitter, thus determining the neuron's overall responsiveness. *See also* primary messengers.

**second-order conditioning**    A form of learning in which a stimulus is first made meaningful or consequential for an organism through an initial step of learning, and then that stimulus is used as a basis for learning about some new stimulus. For example, an animal might first learn to associate a bell with food (first-order conditioning), but then learn to associate a light with the bell (second-order conditioning).

**selection task**    A commonly used research task in which participants must decide which cards to turn over in order to determine if a rule has been followed or not.

**selective serotonin reuptake inhibitors (SSRIs)**    Medications such as Prozac, Zoloft, and Paxil that increase serotonin turnover in the brain and find wide use as treatments for depression, obsessive-compulsive disorder, panic disorder, and many other disorders.

**self-actualization**    According to Abraham Maslow and some other adherents of the humanistic approach to personality, the full realization of one's potential. *See also* hierarchy of needs.

**self-concept**    Generally, the sum of one's beliefs about and attitudes toward oneself. For Carl Rogers, the sense of oneself as both agent and object.

**self-control**    The ability to pursue a goal while adequately managing internal conflicts about it, or to delay pursuing a goal because of other considerations or constraints.

**self-disclosure**    The act of revealing personal information; usually occurs reciprocally and facilitates intimacy.

**self-efficacy**    The sense a person has about what things he can plausibly accomplish.

**self-handicapping**    A self-protective strategy in which one arranges for an obvious and nonthreatening obstacle to one's own performance, such that any failure can be attributed to the obstacle and not to one's own limitations.

**Self-Monitoring Scale**    A personality measure that seeks to determine the degree to which a person alters or adjusts their behavior in order to act appropriately in new circumstances.

**self-perception theory**    The theory that we know our own attitudes and feelings only indirectly, by observing our own behavior and then performing much the same processes of attribution that we employ when trying to understand others.

**self-report data**    Data supplied by the research participant describing herself (usually, ratings of attitudes or moods, or tallies of behavior), rather than that collected by the experimenter.

**semantic feature**    The smallest significant unit of meaning within a word (e.g., male, human, and adult are semantic features of the word man).

**semantic memory**    The component of generic memory that concerns the meaning of words and concepts.

**semantic priming**    The enhanced performance on verbal tasks that occurs when the items being considered have similar meanings.

**semantic role**   The part that each word plays in the "who did what to whom" drama described by a sentence; one word takes the role of being the cause of the action, another, the source of the action, and so on.

**sensations**   According to the empiricists, the primitive experiences that emanate from the senses (e.g., greenness, bitterness).

**sensation seeking**   A predisposition to seek novel experiences, look for thrills and adventure, and be highly susceptible to boredom.

**sensitive period**   *See* critical period.

**sensorimotor intelligence**   In Piaget's theory, intelligence during the first two years of life, consisting mainly of sensations and motor impulses, with little in the way of internalized representations.

**sensory coding**   The process through which the nervous system represents the qualities of the incoming stimulus—whether auditory or visual, for example, or whether a red light or a green one, a sour taste or a sweet taste.

**sensory neurons**   Neurons that convey information from sense organs to other portions of the nervous system.

**sensory quality**   A distinguishing attribute of a stimulus (e.g., brightness or hue or pitch).

**sentence**   A sequence of words constructed in accord with the rules of syntax. "The boy hit the ball" is a sentence, but "Ball the hit boy the," is not. Sentences do not have to be meaningful: "The green idea tripped" is a sentence, although "Tripped idea green the" is not.

**serotonin (5HT)**   A neurotransmitter involved in many of the mechanisms of sleep, arousal, aggression, and mood.

**setpoint**   A general term for the level at which negative feedback tries to maintain stability. An example is the setting of a thermostat.

**sex flush**   One of the bodily states achieved during the plateau stage of sexual activity; in this stage, changes in blood flow can cause the skin on many surfaces to redden.

**sexual dimorphism**   The state of affairs, observed in many species, in which the sexes differ in form (such as deer antlers or peacock tail feathers) or size. Sexual dimorphism is minimal among monogamous animals and maximal among polygamous ones.

**sexual orientation**   A person's predisposition to choose members of the same or the opposite sex as romantic and sexual partners. *See also* bisexuality, heterosexuality, and homosexuality.

**shadowing**   The procedure, often used in dichotic presentations, in which a participant is asked to repeat aloud, word for word, only what she hears through one earphone.

**shallow processing**   The encoding of a stimulus using its superficial characteristics, such as the way a word sounds or the typeface in which it is printed.

**shape constancy**   The tendency to perceive objects as retaining their shapes despite changes in our angle of regard that produce changes in the image projected on the retina.

**shaping**   An instrumental learning procedure in which an animal (or human) learns a rather difficult response through the reinforcement of successive approximations to that response. *See also* successive approximations.

**short-term memory**   *See* stage theory of memory.

**signal-detection theory**   The theory that the act of perceiving or not perceiving a stimulus is actually a judgment about whether a momentary sensory experience is due to background noise alone or to the background noise plus a signal. The theory also includes a procedure for measuring sensory sensitivity.

**signs**   In psychopathology, what the diagnostician observes about a patient's physical or mental condition (e.g., tremor, inattentiveness). *See also* symptoms, syndrome.

**similarity**   In perception, a principle by which we tend to group like figures, especially by color and orientation.

**simple reaction time**   A measurement of the speed with which a research participant can respond to a stimulus.

**simultaneous color contrast**   The effect produced by the fact that any region in the visual field tends to induce its complementary color in adjoining areas. For example, a gray patch will tend to look bluish if surrounded by yellow and yellowish if surrounded by blue.

**sine waves**   Waves (e.g., sound waves or light waves) that correspond to the plot of the trigonometric sine function.

**single-case experiment**   A study in which the investigator manipulates the values of some independent variable, just as she would in an experiment with many participants, and then assesses the effects of this variable by recording a single participant's responses. *See also* case study.

**situationism**   The view that human behavior is largely determined by the characteristics of the situation rather than personal predispositions. *See also* humanistic approach, psychodynamic approach, sociocultural perspective, trait approach.

**size constancy**   The tendency to perceive objects as retaining their size, despite the increase or decrease in the size of the image projected on the retina caused by moving closer to or farther from the objects.

**skewed**   A term used to describe distributions of experimental results that are asymmetrical (tending to have outlying values at one end).

**skin senses**   The group of senses, including pressure, warmth, cold, and pain, through which an organism gains information about its immediate surround.

**sleep paralysis**   The phenomenon of waking up unable to move for several seconds, due to the persistence of the loss of muscle tone that occurs during REM sleep. While sleep paralysis is sometimes frightening, it is harmless.

**sleep-wake cycle**   A daily rhythm in which the body moves from alert vigilance to sleep and back again.

**slow-wave sleep**   Type of sleep characterized by slow, rolling eye movements, an EEG indicative of low cortical arousal, slowed heart rate and respiration, and recall of "boring," mostly verbal dreams.

**smooth muscles**   The nonstriated muscles controlled by the autonomic nervous system that constrict the blood vessels to help regulate blood pressure and that line many internal organs such as those that produce peristalsis in the digestive tract.

**social cognition**   The way in which we interpret and try to comprehend social events.

**social-cognitive approach**   A perspective on personality which argues that in explaining behavior, we should emphasize neither the person's traits by themselves nor the situation by itself. Instead, we should examine how people and situations change, moment by moment, in their interactions.

**social comparison**   A process of reducing uncertainty about one's own beliefs and attitudes by comparing them to those of others.

**social development**   A child's growth in his or her relations with other people.

**social exchange**   A theory that asserts that each partner in a social relationship gives something to the other and expects to get something in return.

**social facilitation**   The tendency to perform better in the presence of others than when alone. This facilitating effect works primarily for simple or well-practiced tasks.

**social impact theory**   The theory that the influence others exert on an individual increases with their number, their immediacy, and their strength (e.g., status).

**socialization**   The process whereby the child acquires the patterns of behavior characteristic of his or her society.

**social learning theory**   A theoretical approach to socialization and personality that is midway between radical behaviorism and cognitive approaches to learning. It stresses learning by observing others who serve as models and who show the child whether a response he already knows should or should not be performed.

**social loafing**   An example of the diffusion of social impact in which people working collectively on a task generate less total effort than they would had they worked alone.

**social phobia**   A fear of embarrassment or humiliation that causes people to avoid situations that might expose them to public scrutiny. *See also* anxiety disorders, phobia.

**sociocultural perspective**   Within social psychology and personality psychology, the view that many psychological phenomena, some of which have been presumed to be universal, result from or are affected substantially by cultural norms. *See also* humanistic approach, psychodynamic approach, trait approach, situationism.

**sociopathy**   *See* antisocial personality disorder.

**soma**   *See* cell body.

**somatic division**   A division of the peripheral nervous system primarily concerned with the control of the skeletal musculature and the transmission of information from the sense organs.

**somatization disorder**   A mental disorder in which the patient reports miscellaneous aches and pains in various bodily systems that do not add up to any known syndrome in physical medicine.

**somatoform disorders**   The generic term for mental disorders in which bodily symptoms predominate despite the absence of any known physical cause; included are conversion disorder, hypochondriasis, somatization disorder, and somatoform pain disorder.

**somatoform pain disorder**   A mental disorder in which the sufferer describes chronic pain for which there is no discernible physical basis.

**somatogenic hypothesis**   The hypothesis that mental disorders result from organic (bodily) causes.

**somatosensory area**   *See* primary sensory projection area.

**sound waves**   Successive pressure variations in the air that vary in amplitude and wavelength.

**source confusion**   A type of memory error in which information acquired in one context is remembered as having been encountered in another (e.g., a person's recalling that she had chocolate cake on her last birthday when she actually had it two birthdays ago).

**spatial summation**   The process whereby two or more stimuli that are individually below threshold will elicit a reflex if they occur simultaneously at different points on the body.

**spatial thinking**   The mental computations engaged in when we must locate objects and discern the spatial relationships among them.

**specificity theory**   An approach to sensory experience which asserts that different sensory qualities are signaled by different neurons. These neurons are somehow labeled with their quality, so that whenever they fire, the nervous system interprets their activation as that particular sensory quality.

**specific language impairment**   A syndrome in which individuals are very slow to learn language and throughout their lives have difficulty in understanding and producing many sentences, even though these individuals seem normal on most other measures, including measurements of intelligence.

**spectral sensitivity**   The pattern of a receptor's (or pigment's) reactions to different wavelengths of light.

**spectral sensitivity curve**   A graphical representation of a receptor's spectral sensitivity.

**spontaneous recovery**   The reappearance of a previously extinguished response after a time interval in which neither the conditioned stimulus (CS) nor the unconditioned stimulus (US) is presented.

**SSRIs**   *See* selective serotonin reuptake inhibitors.

**stage theory of memory**   An approach to memory that proposes several memory stores. One is short-term (or working) memory, which holds a small amount of information for fairly short intervals; another is long-term memory, which can hold vast amounts of information for extended periods. According to the theory, information can only be transferred to long-term memory if it has first been in short-term memory.

**standard deviation (SD)**   A measure of the variability of a frequency distribution, calculated as the square root of the variance (V) — SD = $\sqrt{\text{V}}$. *See also* variance (V).

**standardization sample**   The group of individuals to which a test is given to decide what "normal" performance on the test looks like.

**standard score (*z*-score)**   A score that is expressed as a deviation from the mean in standard deviations (SDs), which allows a comparison of scores drawn from different distributions; if M is the mean, then $z = (\text{score} - \text{M})/\text{SD}$.

**statistical reliability**   The degree to which an observed difference in sample means reflects a real difference in population means and is not attributable to chance.

**statistics**   The process of quantitatively describing, analyzing, and making inferences about numerical data.

**stereotypes**   Schemas by which people try to categorize complex groups. Group stereotypes are often negative, especially when applied to minority groups. *See also* out-group homogeneity effect.

**stereotype threat**   A hypothesized mechanism through which a person's performance on a test (e.g., a test of intelligence) is influenced by her perception that the test results may confirm others' stereotypes about her.

**stimulant**   An influence (typically, a drug) that has activating or excitatory effects on brain or bodily functions (e.g., amphetamines, Ritalin, cocaine).

**stimulus generalization**   In classical conditioning, the tendency to respond to stimuli other than the original conditioned stimulus (CS). The greater the similarity between the CS and the new stimulus (CS$^+$), the greater generalization will be. An analogous phenomenon in instrumental conditioning is a response to stimuli other than the original discriminative stimulus.

**storage capacity**   The amount of information that can be retained in memory. *See also* magic number.

**strategic retrieval**   A deliberate effort to recall information by supplying one's own retrieval cues (e.g., "Let's *see*, the last time I remember seeing my wallet was …").

**stratified sampling**   An experimental procedure in which each subgroup of the population is sampled in proportion to its size.

**stress**   In psychopathology, the psychological or physical wear-and-tear that, together with a preexisting vulnerability, may lead to mental disorder.

**Stroop effect**   A marked decrease in the speed of naming the colors in which various color names (such as green, red, etc.) are printed when the colors and the names are different. An important example of automatization.

**structured personality test**   A personality test (e.g., the MMPI or CPI) that asks specific questions and requires specific answers.

**subcortical structures**   Usually the forebrain structures, such as those comprising the limbic system and extrapyramidal motor system, that lie beneath the cortex.

**subjective contours**   Perceived contours that do not exist physically. We tend to complete figures that have gaps in them by perceiving a contour as continuing along its original path.

**subroutines**   In a hierarchical organization, lower-level operations that function semiautonomously but are supervised by higher-level ones.

**successive approximations**   The process of shaping a response by rewarding closer and closer versions of the desired response. *See also* shaping.

**superego**   In Freud's theory, reaction patterns that emerge from within the ego, represent the internalized rules of society, and come to control the ego by punishment with guilt. *See also* ego, id.

**syllogism**   A logic problem containing two premises and a conclusion that may or may not follow from them.

**symbolic representation**   A type of mental representation that does not correspond to the physical characteristics of that which it represents. Thus, the word *mouse* does not resemble the small rodent it represents. *See also* analogical representation.

**symmetrical distribution**   A distribution of numerical data in which deviations in either direction from the mean are equally frequent.

**sympathetic branch**   The division of the autonomic nervous system that mobilizes the body's energies for physical activity (e.g., increasing heart rate, sweating, and respiration). Its action is typically antagonistic to that of the parasympathetic branch.

**symptoms**   In psychopathology, what the patient reports about his physical or mental condition (e.g., nervousness, hearing voices). *See also* signs, syndrome.

**synapse**   The juncture of two neurons, consisting of the presynaptic and postsynaptic membranes, and—in nonelectrical synapses—the synaptic gap between them.

**synaptic gap**   The space between two communicating neurons; neurotransmitters are released by the presynaptic neuron, cross the synaptic gap, and trigger a response in the postsynaptic neuron.

**synaptic reuptake**   The process through which neurotransmitters are reabsorbed by the presynaptic neuron, so that they can be released again, sending a new signal, the next time that axon fires.

**synaptic vesicles**   Tiny sacs within a presynaptic membrane that contain the neurotransmitter; when the presynaptic neuron fires, some of these vesicles burst and eject their contents into the synaptic gap.

**syndrome**   A pattern of signs and symptoms that tend to co-occur.

**systematic desensitization**   A behavior therapy that tries to remove anxiety connected to various stimuli by gradually counterconditioning to them a response incompatible with fear, usually muscular relaxation. The stimuli are usually evoked as mental images according to an anxiety hierarchy, whereby relaxation is conditioned to the less frightening stimuli before the more frightening ones.

**tabula rasa**   The notion that each person is born as a "blank slate," that is, without innate knowledge, so that all knowledge must be gained from experience.

**tacit knowledge**   Practical "how to" knowledge that is unwittingly accumulated from everyday experience.

**tape-recorder theory of memory**   The erroneous view that the brain contains an indelible record of everything one experiences.

**TAT**   *See* Thematic Apperception Test.

**tau protein**   A protein that normally helps sustain the internal structure of the brain's axons. Its metabolism somehow goes awry, however, in the development of Alzheimer's disease.

**temperament**   In modern usage, a characteristic level of reactivity and energy, often thought to be constitutional.

**temporal contiguity**   Co-occurrence of stimuli. A condition Pavlov thought would be favorable for forming associations; actually forward pairing is most favorable.

**temporal lobe**   The lobe of the cortex lying below the temples in each cerebral hemisphere, which includes the primary auditory projection area, Wernicke's area, and subcortically, the amygdala and hippocampus.

**temporal summation**   The process whereby a stimulus that is below threshold will elicit a reflex if the stimulus occurs repeatedly.

**territory**   A term used by ethologists to describe a region a particular animal stakes out as its own. The territory holder is usually a male, but in some species the territory is held by a mating pair or by a group.

**testable hypothesis**   A hypothesis that has been formulated specifically enough so that it is clear what observations would confirm the hypothesis and what observations would challenge it.

**testosterone**   The principal male sex hormone in mammals. *See also* androgen.

**test profile**   A graphical indication of an individual's performance on several components of a test. This is often useful for guidance or clinical evaluation because it indicates that person's pattern of abilities or traits.

**test-retest method**   A way of ascertaining the reliability of a test. It involves administering the same test to the same group of subjects after a certain time lag and assessing the correlation of scores. *See also* reliability coefficient.

**texture gradient**   A distance cue based on changes in surface texture that depend on how far away the observer is.

**thalamus**   A part of the lower portion of the forebrain that serves as a major relay and integration center for sensory information.

**Thematic Apperception Test (TAT)**   A projective technique in which persons are shown a set of pictures and asked to make up a story about each one.

**theory of mind**   A set of interrelated concepts used to try to make sense of our own mental processes and those of others, including the variation in beliefs and desires from one person to another.

**thermoregulation**   The process by which organisms maintain a constant body temperature. For ectotherms, it is matter of external behavior such as seeking sun or shade, while for endotherms it also involves numerous internal adjustments such as sweating.

**third-variable problem**   The major obstacle to discerning causation from correlation, because two variables may be correlated only because of the operation of a third variable. For example, sales of ice cream are correlated with rates of violent crime, but only because both increase during hot weather and decrease during cold weather.

**tip-of-the-tongue phenomenon**   The condition in which one remains on the verge of retrieving a word or name but continues to be unsuccessful.

**TMS**   *See* transcranial magnetic stimulation.

**tolerance**   *See* opponent-process theory of motivation.

**tone**   A difference in pitch used in some languages (such as Mandarin Chinese) to signal differences in meaning.

**top-down processes**   Processes in form recognition that begin with larger units and then proceed to smaller units (e.g., from phrases to words to letters). This contrasts with bottom-up processes, which start with smaller component parts and gradually build up to the larger units (e.g., from letters to words to phrases). One demonstration of top-down processing is provided by context effects in which knowledge or expectations affect what one sees.

**trace consolidation**   A hypothesis that newly acquired memory traces undergo a gradual change that makes them more and more resistant to any disturbance.

**trait**   *See* trait approach.

**trait approach**   The view that differences in personality are best characterized in terms of underlying, possibly innate, attributes (traits) that predispose one toward patterns of thinking and behavior that are essentially consistent over time and across situations. *See also* humanistic approach, psychodynamic approach, situationism, sociocultural perspective.

**transcranial magnetic stimulation (TMS)** A technique through which repeated magnetic stimulation at the surface of the skull is used (at some strengths) to stimulate a region of the brain or (at other strengths) to cause a temporary lesion of a region of the brain.

**transduction** The process by which a receptor reacts to some physical stimulus (e.g., light or pressure) and creates action potentials in another neuron.

**transection** Surgical cutting of a nerve tract or brain region, performed to isolate functionally the regions on either side.

**transference** In therapy, a patient's tendency to respond to the analyst in ways that re-create her responses to the major figures in her own life.

**transfer of training tests** Procedures used to ascertain whether skills learned in one setting generalize to other settings.

**transposition** The phenomenon whereby visual and auditory patterns (i.e., figures and melodies) remain essentially the same even though the parts of which they are composed change.

**trichromatic color vision** The principle underlying human color vision. Color vision occurs through the operation of three sets of cones, each maximally sensitive to a different wavelength of light.

**true hermaphroditism** Rare type of intersexuality in which an individual possesses reproductive tissue of both sexes (e.g., testes and ovaries).

**ultimatum task** A task commonly used to measure people's tendency toward fairness or selfishness in dividing some resource.

**ultradian rhythm** The 90- to 100-minute biological rhythm that characterizes the alternation of REM and slow-wave periods during sleep and attentiveness while awake. *See also* circadian rhythm.

**unconditional positive regard** For Carl Rogers, the belief that one is accepted and loved without reservation; an essential component of Rogerian psychotherapy.

**unconditioned reflex** *See* unconditioned response.

**unconditioned response (UR)** In classical conditioning, the response that is elicited without prior training by the unconditioned stimulus (US). *See also* conditioned response (CR), conditioned stimulus (CS), unconditioned stimulus (US).

**unconditioned stimulus (US)** In classical conditioning, the stimulus that elicits the unconditioned response (UR) and the presentation of which acts as reinforcement. See conditioned response (CR), conditioned stimulus (CS), unconditioned response (UR).

**unconscious inference** A process postulated by Hermann von Helmholtz to explain certain perceptual phenomena such as size constancy. For example, an object is perceived to be at a certain distance and this is unconsciously taken into account in assessing its retinal image size, with the result that size constancy is maintained. *See also* size constancy.

**unipolar depression** *See* major depression.

**unique blue** The hue corresponding to a wavelength of 445 nanometers, which is perceived as containing no red or green.

**unique green** The hue corresponding to a wavelength of 500 nanometers, which is perceived as containing no blue or yellow.

**unique yellow** The hue corresponding to a wavelength of 570 nanometers, which is perceived as containing no red or green.

**validity** The extent to which a test measures what it is supposed to measure. *See also* predictive validity.

**validity scales** Scales used within a measure (e.g., a personality test) designed to assess whether the examinee is trying to disguise their traits or their attitudes.

**variability** The degree to which scores in a frequency distribution depart from the central value. See also central tendency, measure of central tendency, standard deviation (SD), variance (V).

**variable-interval (VI) schedule** A pattern of rewards similar to a fixed-interval schedule, but with the interval used varying from reward to reward. Thus, on a variable-interval 1 schedule, reward will be available *on average* after one minute has gone by, but for some rewards the actual interval might be shorter or longer.

**variable-ratio (VR) schedule** A pattern of rewards similar to a fixed-ratio schedule, but with the ratio used varying from reward to reward. Thus, on a variable-ratio 5 schedule, reward will be available *on average* after five responses, but for some rewards the number of required responses might be fewer, and for others more.

**variance (V)** A measure of the variability of a frequency distribution. It is computed by finding the difference between each score and the mean (M), squaring the result, adding all these squared deviations, and dividing the sum by the number of cases. If N is the number of scores, then $V = $ sum of $(\text{score} - M)^2 / N$.

**vasocongestion** A contraction of the capillaries that squeezes blood away from that area. *See also* vasoconstriction.

**vasoconstriction** The constriction of blood vessels brought on by activation of the sympathetic branch of the autonomic nervous system. Vasoconstriction occurs in emergencies, when blood is diverted from the skin and internal organs to the muscles. It is also crucial in mammalian thermoregulation; in response to excessive cold, blood is diverted from the skin to reduce heat loss. *See also* vasodilatation.

**vasodilatation** The dilating of blood vessels brought on by activation of the parasympathetic division of the autonomic nervous system. Vasodilatation is one component of mammalian thermoregulation; in response to excessive heat, warm blood flows to the body's surface and results in heat loss by radiation. *See also* vasoconstriction.

**vasovagal reaction** A reaction from the parasympathetic branch of the nervous system in which the pulse slows, blood pressure drops, the muscles go slack, and the person can fall to the ground in a dead faint.

**vegetative signs** Physical manifestations that often accompany major depression, such as loss of appetite and weight loss, weakness, fatigue, poor bowel functioning, sleep disorders (most often early-morning awakenings), and loss of interest in sex.

**ventral tegmental area (VTA)** A region in the midbrain containing dopamine-releasing pathways thought to be involved in reward.

**vestibular senses** A set of receptors that provide information about the orientation and movements of the head, located in the semicircular canals and the vestibular sacs of the inner ear.

**VI schedule** *See* variable-interval (VI) schedule.

**visible spectrum** The range of wavelengths to which our visual system can respond, extending from about 400 (the wavelength usually perceived as the color violet) to 750 nanometers (the wavelength usually perceived as the color reddish orange).

**visual imagery** The capacity to form and use quasi-perceptual representations, often referred to as mental pictures, in the absence of the relevant visual input.

**visual pigment** The chemical inside a photoreceptor that, when exposed to light, changes form, thus releasing some energy and triggering a neural impulse. The chemical is then restored to its original form so that it becomes ready to respond to the next bit of incoming light.

**visual search task** A task in which observers are asked to hunt for a specified target within a field of stimuli. The identity of the target can be defined in various ways ("look for the red item," or "look for the green letter *H*"), and the background items can vary both in number and in identity.

**visual segregation** The step in perception that involves locating an object's boundary, so that the perceiver can discern where one object stops and the next begins.

**VR schedule** *See* variable-ratio (VR) schedule

**VTA** *See* ventral tegmental area.

**wavelength** The distance between the crests of two successive waves and the major determinant of pitch (for sound) and hue (for light).

**Weber fraction** In Weber's law, the fraction given by the change in stimulus intensity ($\Delta I$) divided by the standard intensity ($I$) required to produce a just-noticeable difference: $\Delta I/I = C$.

**Weber's law** The observation that the size of the difference threshold is proportional to the intensity of the standard stimulus.

**well-defined problems** Problems for which there is a clear-cut way of deciding whether a proposed solution is correct. This contrasts with ill-defined problems, for which it is unclear what a correct solution might be.

**Wernicke's area** A brain area adjacent to the auditory projection area, damage to which leads to deficits in understanding word meaning.

**"what" system** The system of visual circuits and pathways leading from the visual cortex to the temporal lobe, especially involved in object identification.

**"where" system** The system of visual circuits and pathways leading from the visual cortex to the parietal lobe, especially involved in the spatial localization of objects and in the coordination of movements.

**white matter** Whitish-appearing patches and paths in the brain composed of myelinated axons.

**withdrawal symptoms** A consequence of drug addiction that occurs when the drug is withheld. These effects tend to be the opposite of those produced by the drug itself.

**within-subject comparisons** Within the same study, comparing each participant's behavior in one situation to the same participant's behavior in another situation; usually contrasted with between-subject comparisons.

**working memory** A part of the memory system that is currently activated but has relatively little cognitive capacity.

**X chromosome** One of the two sex chromosomes containing the genes that determine whether a given animal will be male or female. In mammalian females, both sex chromosomes are X chromosomes; in mammalian males, there is one X chromosome and one Y chromosome.

**Y chromosome** *See* X chromosome.

**Young-Helmholtz theory** A theory of color vision which holds that each of the three receptor types (short-wave, medium-wave, and long-wave) gives rise to the experience of one basic color (blue, green, or red).

**zone of proximal development** The range of accomplishments that are beyond what the child could do on his or her own, but are possible if the child is given help or guidance.

# REFERENCES

ABRAHAM, K. (1927). The influence of oral eroticism on character formation. In K. Abraham, *Selected papers* (pp. 393–406). London: Hogarth Press.

ABRAMSON, L. Y., SELIGMAN, M. E. P., & TEASDALE, J. D. (1978). Learned helplessness in humans: Critique and reformulation. *Journal of Abnormal Psychology, 87,* 49–74.

ACSF INVESTIGATORS. (1992). AIDS and sexual behaviour in France. *Nature, 360,* 407–409.

ADAMS, W., KENDELL, R. E., HARE, E. H., & MUNK-JORGENSEN, P. (1993). Epidemiological evidence that maternal influenza contributes to the aetiology of schizophrenia: An analysis of Scottish, English, and Danish data. *British Journal of Psychiatry, 163,* 522–524.

ADLER, N. T. (1979). On the physiological organization of social behavior: Sex and aggression. In P. Marler & J. G. Vandenbergh (Eds.), *Handbook of behavioral neurobiology: Vol. 3. Social behavior and communication* (pp. 29–71). New York: Plenum.

ADOLPH, E. F. (1947). Urges to eat and drink in rats. *American Journal of Physiology, 151,* 110–125.

ADORNO, T. W., ADORNO, F. F.-B., LEVINSON, D. J., SANFORD, R. N., IN COLLABORATION WITH ARON, B., LEVINSON, M. H., & MORROW, W. (1950). *The authoritarian personality.* New York: Harper.

AHN, W.-K, & GRAHAM, L. M. (1999). The impact of necessity and sufficiency in the Wason four-card task. *Psychological Science, 10,* 237–242.

AINSWORTH, M. D. S., & BELL, S. M. (1970). Attachment, exploration, and separation: Illustrated by the behavior of one-year-olds in a strange situation. *Child Development, 41,* 49–67.

AINSWORTH, M. D. S., BLEHAR, M. C., WATERS, E., & WALL, S. (1978). *Patterns of attachment.* Hillsdale, NJ: Erlbaum.

AJZEN, I. (2001). Nature and operation of attitudes. *Annual Review of Psychology, 52,* 27–58.

AKIYAMA, Y., HONMOU, O., KATO, T., UEDE, T., HASHI, K., & KOCSIS, J. D. (2001). Transplantation of clonal neural precursor cells derived from adult human brain establishes functional peripheral myelin in the rat spinal cord. *Experimental Neurology, 167,* 27–39.

ALBA, J. W., & HASHER, W. (1983). Is memory schematic? *Psychological Bulletin, 93,* 203–231.

ALBERT, M. S., JONES, K., SAVAGE, C. R., BERKMAN, L., SEEMAN, T., BLAZER, D., ET AL. (1995). Predictors of cognitive change in older persons: MacArthur studies of successful aging. *Psychology and Aging, 10,* 578–589.

ALDAG, R. J., & FULLER, S. R. (1993). Beyond fiasco: A reappraisal of the groupthink phenomenon and a new model of group decision processes. *Psychological Bulletin, 113*(3), 533–552.

ALEXANDER, F., & FRENCH, T. (1946). *Psychoanalytic theory.* New York: Ronald Press.

ALLARD, F., GRAHAM, S., & PAARSALU, M. E. (1980). Perception in sport: Basketball. *Journal of Sport Psychology, 2,* 14–21.

ALLDERIDGE, P. (1979). Hospitals, mad houses, and asylums: Cycles in the care of the insane. *British Journal of Psychiatry, 134,* 321–324.

ALLEN, J., & SEIDENBERG, M. S. (1999) The emergence of grammaticality in connectionist networks. In B. MacWhinney (Ed.) *The emergence of language* (pp. 115–151). Hillsdale, NJ: Erlbaum.

ALLEN, L. S., HINES, Z. M., SHRYNE, J. E., & GORSKI, R. A. (1989). Two sexually dimorphic cell groups in the human brain. *Journal of Neuroscience, 9,* 497–506.

ALLEN, V. L. (1975). Social support for non-conformity. In L. Berkowitz (Ed.), *Advances in experimental social psychology: Vol. 8.* New York: Academic Press.

ALLEN, V. L., & LEVINE, J. M. (1971). Social support and conformity: The role of independent assessment. *Journal of Experimental Social Psychology, 7,* 48–58.

ALLOY, L. B., ABRAMSOM, L. Y., & FRANCIS, E. L. (1999). Do negative cognitive styles confer vulnerability to depression? *Current Directions in Psychological Science, 8,* 128–132.

ALLPORT, G. W. (1937). *Personality: A psychological interpretation.* New York: Henry Holt.

ALLPORT, G. W., & ODBERT, H. S. (1936). Trait-names: A psychological study. *Psychological Monographs, 47*(Whole No. 211).

ALPER, K., DEVINSKY, O., PERRINE, K., VAZQUEZ, B., & LUCIANO, D. (1995). Psychiatric classification of nonconversion nonepileptic seizures. *Archives of Neurology, 52,* 199–201.

ALTMAN, I. (1973). Reciprocity of interpersonal exchange. *Journal for Theory of Social Behavior, 3,* 249–261.

ALTMANN G., & STEEDMAN, M. (1988). Interaction with context during human sentence processing. *Cognition, 30,* 191–238.

ALTMANN, G. T. M., & KAMIDE, Y. (1999). Incremental interpretation at verbs: Restricting the domain of subsequent reference. *Cognition, 73,* 247–264.

AMBADY, N., SHIH, M., KIM, A., & PITTINSKY, T. L. (2001). Stereotype susceptibility in children: Effects of identity activation on quantitative performance. *Psychological Science, 12,* 385–390.

AMERICAN PSYCHIATRIC ASSOCIATION. (1968). *Diagnostic and statistical manual for mental disorders* (2nd ed.). Washington, DC: Author.

AMERICAN PSYCHIATRIC ASSOCIATION. (1980). *Diagnostic and statistical manual for mental disorders* (3rd ed.). Washington, DC: Author.

AMERICAN PSYCHIATRIC ASSOCIATION. (1987). *Diagnostic and statistical manual for mental disorders* (3rd ed., rev.). Washington, DC: Author.

AMERICAN PSYCHIATRIC ASSOCIATION. (1994). *Diagnostic and statistical manual for mental disorders* (4th ed.). Washington, DC: Author.

AMERICAN PSYCHOLOGICAL ASSOCIATION. (1981). Ethical principles of psychologists. *American Psychologist, 36,* 633–638.

AMERICAN PSYCHOLOGICAL ASSOCIATION. (1982). *Ethical principles in the conduct of research with human participants.* Washington, DC: Author.

ANANTH, J. (1985). Pharmaco-therapy of obsessive-compulsive disorder. In M. Mavissakalian, S. M. Turner, & L. Michelson (Eds.), *Obsessive-compulsive disorder: Psychological and pharmacological treatment* (pp. 167–205). New York: Plenum.

ANDERSEN, E., DUNLEA, A., & KEKELIS L (1993). The impact of input: language acquisition in the visually impaired. *First Language, 13,* 23–49.

ANDERSON, A. K., & PHELPS, E. A. (2000). Expression without recognition: Contribution of the human amygdala to emotional communication. *Psychological Science, 11,* 106–111.

ANDERSON, C. A., & BUSHMAN, B. J. (2001). Effects of violent video games on aggressive behavior, aggressive cognition, aggressive affect, physiological arousal, and prosocial behavior: A meta-analytic review of the scientific literature. *Psychological Science, 12,* 353–360.

ANDERSON, C. A., & BUSHMAN, B. J. (2002). Human aggression. *Annual Review of Psychology, 53,* 27–51.

ANDERSON, J. (1993). *Rules of the mind.* Hillsdale, NJ: Erlbaum.

ANDERSON, J. R. (1990). *Cognitive psychology and its implications* (3rd ed.). San Francisco: Freeman.

ANDERSON, J. R. (1996). ACT: A simple theory of complex cognition. *American Psychologist, 51,* 355–365.

ANDERSSON, M. (1982). Female choice selects for extreme tail length in a widowbird. *Nature, 299,* 818–820.

ANDREASEN, N. C., ARNDT, S., ALLIGER, R., MILLER, D., & FLAUM, M. (1995). Symptoms of schizophrenia. *Archives of General Psychiatry, 52,* 341–351.

ANDREASEN, N. C., & BLACK, D. W. (1996). *Introductory textbook of psychiatry* (2nd ed.). Washington, DC: American Psychiatric Press.

ANDREASEN, N. C., NASRALLAH, H. A., DUNN, V., OLSEN, S. C., GROVE, W. M., EHRHARDT, J., ET AL. (1986). Structural abnormalities in the frontal system in schizophrenia: A magnetic resonance imaging study. *Archives of General Psychiatry, 43,* 136–144.

ANDREASEN, N. C, NOPOULOS, P., O'LEARY, D. S., MILLER, D. D., WASSINK, T., FLAUM, M. (1999). Defining the phenotype of schizophrenia: Cognitive dysmetria and its neural mechanisms [Review]. *Biological Psychiatry, 46(7),* 908–920.

ANDREWS, G., & HARVEY, R. (1981). Does psychotherapy benefit neurotic patients? A reanalysis of the Smith, Glass, and Miller data. *Archives of General Psychiatry, 38,* 1203–1208.

ANGRIST, B., SATHANANTHAN, G., WILK, S., & GERSHON, S. (1974). Amphetamine psychosis: Behavioral and biochemical aspects. *Journal of Psychiatric Research, 11,* 13–24.

ANTHONY, L. (2000). Naturalizing radical translation. In A. Orenstein & P. Kotatko (Eds.), *Knowledge, language, and logic* (pp. 141–150). Dordrecht: Kluwer.

APPEL, L. F., COOPER, R. G., McCARRELL, N., SIMS-KNIGHT, J., YUSSEN, S. R., & FLAVELL, J. H. (1972). The development of the distinction between perceiving and memorizing. *Child Development, 43,* 1365–1381.

ARENDT, H. (1965). *Eichmann in Jerusalem: A report on the banality of evil.* New York: Viking Press.

ARIETI, S. (1959). Schizophrenia: The manifest symptomatology, the psychodynamic and formal mechanisms. In S. Arieti (Ed.), *American handbook of psychiatry: Vol. 1* (pp. 455–484). New York: Basic Books.

ARMITAGE, R., HOFFMANN, R., & MOFFITT, A. (1992). Interhemispheric EEG activity in sleep and wakefulness: Individual differences in the basic rest-activity cycle (BRAC). In J. S. Antrobus & M. Bertini (Eds.), *The neuropsychology of sleep and dreaming* (pp. 17–45). Hillsdale, NJ: Erlbaum.

ARMSTRONG, S. L., GLEITMAN, L. R., & GLEITMAN, H. (1983). What some concepts might not be. *Cognition, 13,* 263–308.

ARNDT, S., ANDREASEN, N. C., FLAUM, M., MILLER, D., & NOPOULOS, P. (1995). A longitudinal study of symptom dimensions in schizophrenia. Prediction and patterns of change. *Archives of General Psychiatry, 52,* 352–360.

ARNETT, J. J. (1999). Adolescent storm and stress, reconsidered. *American Psychologist, 54,* 317–326.

ARONFREED, J. (1968). *Conduct and conscience.* New York: Academic Press.

ARONSON, E. (1969). The theory of cognitive dissonance: A current perspective. In L. Berkowitz (Ed.), *Advances in experimental social psychology: Vol. 4* (pp. 1–34). New York: Academic Press.

ARONSON, E., & CARLSMITH, J. M. (1963). The effect of the severity of threat on the devaluation of forbidden behavior. *Journal of Abnormal and Social Psychology, 66,* 584–588.

ARONSON, E., & MILLS, J. (1959). The effect of severity of initiation on liking for a group. *Journal of Abnormal and Social Psychology, 59,* 177–181.

ARONSON, E., TURNER, J. A., & CARLSMITH, J. M. (1963). Communicator credibility and communication discrepancy as determinants of opinion change. *Journal of Abnormal and Social Psychology, 67,* 31–36.

ASCH, S. E. (1946). Forming impressions of personality. *Journal of Abnormal and Social Psychology, 41,* 258–290.

ASCH, S. E. (1952). *Social psychology.* New York: Prentice-Hall.

ASCH, S. E. (1956). Studies of independence and conformity: A minority of one against a unanimous majority. *Psychological Monographs, 70(9, Whole No. 416).*

ASCH, S. E., & GLEITMAN, H. (1953). Yielding to social pressure as a function of public or private commitment. Unpublished manuscript.

ASERINSKY, E., LYNCH, J. A., MACK, M. E., TZANKOFF, S. P., & HURN, E. (1985). Comparison of eye motion in wakefulness and REM sleep. *Psychophysiology, 22,* 1–10.

ASHER, E. J. (1935). The inadequacy of current intelligence tests for testing Kentucky Mountain children. *Journal of Genetic Psychology, 46,* 480–486.

ASLIN, R. N. (1987). Visual and auditory development in infancy. In J. D. Osofksy (Ed.), *Handbook of infant development* (2nd ed., pp. 5–97). New York: Wiley.

ASLIN, R. N., SAFFRAN, J. R., & NEWPORT, E. L. (1998). Computation of conditional probability statistics by 8-month-old infants. *Psychological Science, 9,* 321–324.

ASTON-JONES, G. (1985). Behavioral functions of locus coeruleus derived from cellular attributes. *Physiological Psychology, 13,* 118–126.

ASTRUP, A. (2000). Thermogenic drugs as a strategy for treatment of obesity. *Endocrine, 13,* 207–212.

ATKINS, C. M., SELCHER, J. C., PETRAITIS, J. J., TRZASKOS, J. M., & SWEATT, J. D. (1998). The MAPK cascade is required for mammalian associative learning. *Nature Neuroscience, 1,* 602–609.

ATKINSON, A., THOMAS, M. S. C., & CLEEREMANS, A. (2000). Consciousness: Mapping the theoretical landscape. *Trends in Cognitive Science, 4,* 372–382.

ATKINSON, R. C., & SHIFFRIN, R. M. (1968). Human memory: A proposed system and its control. In K. W. Spence & J. T. Spence (Eds.), *The psychology of learning and motivation: Vol. 2* (pp. 89–105). New York: Academic Press.

AUERBACH, S. M., KIESLER, D. J., STRENTZ, T., SCHMIDT, J. A., & OTHERS. (1994). Interpersonal impacts and adjustment to the stress of simulated captivity: An empirical test of the Stockholm syndrome. *Journal of Social and Clinical Psychology, 13,* 207–221.

AULD, F., & HYMAN, M. (1991). *Resolution of inner conflict: An introduction to psychoanalytic therapy.* Washington, DC: American Psychiatric Press.

AVERILL, J. R. (1978). Anger. In H. Howe & Dienstbier (Eds.), *Nebraska Symposium on Motivation*. Lincoln, NE: University of Nebraska Press.

AX, A. F. (1953). The physiological differentiation of fear and anger in humans. *Psychosomatic Medicine, 15*, 433–442.

AYLLON, T., & AZRIN, N. H. (1968). *The token economy: A motivational system for therapy and rehabilitation*. New York: Appleton-Century-Crofts.

AZRIN, N. H., & HOLZ, W. C. (1966). Punishment. In W. K. Honig (Ed.), *Operant behavior: Areas of research and application*. New York: Appleton-Century-Crofts.

BAARS, B. J. (ED.). (1992). *Experimental slips and human error: Exploring the architecture of volition*. New York: Plenum.

BABIGIAN, H. M. (1975). Schizophrenia: Epidemiology. In A. M. Freedman, H. I. Kaplan, & B. J. Saddock (Eds.), *Comprehensive textbook of psychiatry–I: Vol. 1* (pp. 860–866). Baltimore: Williams & Wilkins.

BADDELEY, A. D. (1976). *The psychology of human memory*. New York: Basic Books.

BADDELEY, A. D. (1978). The trouble with levels: A reexamination of Craik and Lockhart's framework for memory research. *Psychological Review, 85*, 139–152.

BADDELEY, A. D. (1986). *Working memory*. Oxford: Clarendon Press.

BAER, L., RAUCH, S. L., BALLANTINE, H. T., MARTUZA, R., COSGROVE, R., CASSEM, E., ET AL. (1995). Cingulotomy for intractable obsessive-compulsive disorder. Prospective long-term follow-up of 18 patients. *Archives of General Psychiatry, 52*, 384–392.

BAHRICK, H. (1984). Semantic memory content in permastore: 50 years of memory for Spanish learned in school. *Journal of Experimental Psychology: General, 113*, 1–29.

BAHRICK, H., HALL, L. K., & BERGER, S. A. (1996). Accuracy and distortion in memory for high school grades. *Psychological Science, 7*, 265–271.

BAHRICK, H., & HALL, L. (1991). Lifetime maintenance of high school mathematics content. *Journal of Experimental Psychology: General, 120*, 20–33.

BAHRICK, H., HALL, L., GOGGIN, J., BAHRICK, L. & BERGER, S. (1994). Fifty years of language maintenance and language dominance in bilingual Hispanic immigrants. *Journal of Experimental Psychology: General, 123*, 264–283.

BAILEY, J. M., & PILLARD, R. C. (1991). A genetic study of male sexual orientation. *Archives of General Psychiatry, 48*, 1089-1096.

BAILEY, J. M., PILLARD, R. C., NEALE, M. C., & AGYEI, Y. (1993). Heritable factors influence sexual orientation in women. *Archives of General Psychiatry, 50*, 217–223.

BAILLARGEON, R. (1987). Object permanence in 3 1/2- and 4 1/2-month-old infants. *Developmental Psychology, 23*, 655–664.

BAILLARGEON, R. (1994). How do infants learn about the physical world? *Current Directions in Psychological Science, 3*(5), 133–140.

BAILLARGEON, R., & GRABER, M. (1987). Where is the rabbit? 5 1/2-Month-old infants' representation of the height of hidden objects. *Cognitive Development, 2*, 375–392.

BAILLARGEON, R., SPELKE, E. S., & WASSERMAN, S. (1985). Object permanence in five-month-old infants. *Cognition, 20*, 191–208.

BAILLARGEON, R., & WANG, S.-H. (2002). Event categorization in infancy. *Trends in Cognitive Science, 6*, 85–93.

BAKER, M. (1988). *Incorporation: A theory of grammatical function changing*. Chicago: University of Chicago Press.

BAKER, R. R., & BELLIS, M. A. (1993). Human sperm competition: Ejaculate manipulation by females and a function for the female orgasm. *Animal Behaviour, 46*, 887–909.

BAKER, R. R., & BELLIS, M. A. (1995). *Human sperm competition*. London: Chapman & Hall.

BAKER, T. B., & TIFFANY, S. T. (1985). Morphine tolerance as habituation. *Psychological Review, 92*, 78–108.

BALDWIN, D. A. (1991). Infants' contribution to the achievement of joint reference. *Child Development, 62*, 875–890.

BALTES, P. B., REESE, H. W., & LIPSITT, L. P. (1980). Life-span developmental psychology. In M. R. Rosenzweig & L. W. Porter (Eds.), *Annual Review of Psychology, 31, 65–110.*

BALTES, P. B., & STAUDINGER, U. M. (2000). Wisdom: A metaheuristic (pragmatic) to orchestrate mind and virtue toward excellence. *American Psychologist, 55*(1), 122–136.

BALTES, P. B., STAUDINGER, U. M., & LINDENBERGER, U. (1999). Lifespan psychology: Theory and application to intellectual functioning. *Annual Review of Psychology, 50*, 471–507.

BANAJI, M. R., & GREENWALD, A. G. (1995). Implicit gender stereotyping in judgments of fame. *Journal of Personality and Social Psychology, 68*(2), 181–198.

BANAJI, M. R., & HARDIN, C. D. (1996). Automatic stereotyping. *Psychological Science, 7*(3), 136–141.

BANCROFT, J. (1986). The roles of hormones in female sexuality. In Dennerstein & Fraser (Eds.), *Hormones and behavior* (pp. 551–560). Amsterdam: International Society of Psychosomatic Obstetrics and Gynecology, Elsevier.

BANDURA, A. (1997). *Self-efficacy: The exercise of control*. New York: Freeman.

BANDURA, A. (2001). Social cognitive theory: An agentic perspective. *Annual Review of Psychology, 52*, 1–26.

BANDURA, A., & WALTERS, R. H. (1963). *Social learning and personality development*. New York: Holt, Rinehart & Winston.

BANTICK, R. A., DEAKIN, J. F., & GRASBY, P. M. (2001). The 5–HT1A receptor in schizophrenia: A promising target for novel atypical neuroleptics? *Journal of Psychopharmacology, 15*, 37–46.

BARBER, J. P., CONNOLLY, M. B., CRITS-CHRISTOPH, P., GLADIS, L., & SIQUELAND, L. (2000). Alliance predicts patients' outcome beyond in-treatment change in symptoms. *Journal of Consulting and Clinical Psychology, 68*, 1027–1032.

BARBER, T. X. (1969). *Hypnosis: A scientific approach*. New York: Van Nostrand Reinhold.

BARDO, M. T., DONOHEW, R. L., & HARRINGTON, N. G. (1996). Psychobiology of novelty seeking and drug seeking behavior. *Behavioural Brain Research, 77*, 23–43.

BARGH, J. A., & CHARTRAND, T. L. (1999). The unbearable automaticity of being. *American Psychologist, 54*(7), 462 479.

BARCH, J. A., & FERGUSON, M. J. (2000). Beyond behaviorism: On the automaticity of higher mental processes. *Psychological Bulletin, 126*(6), 925 945.

BARGLOW, P., VAUGHN, B. E., & MOLITOR, N. (1987). Effects of maternal absence due to employment on the quality of infant-mother attachment in a low-risk sample. *Child Development, 58*(4), 945–954.

BARKIN, R. L., & FAWCETT, J. (2000). The management challenges of chronic pain: The role of antidepressants. *American Journal of Therapeutics, 7*, 31–47.

BARLOW, D. H. (1988). *Anxiety and its disorders*. New York: Guilford Press.

BARLOW, D. H. (1996). Health care policy, psychotherapy research, and the future of psychotherapy. *American Psychologist, 51*, 1050–1058.

BARLOW, D. H., & HERSON, M. (1984). *Single case experimental designs: Strategies for studying behavior change* (2nd ed.). New York: Pergamon Press.

BARLUND, D. C. (1975). *Public and private self in Japan and the United States*. Tokyo: Simul Press.

BARNETT, S. A. (1963). *The rat: A study in behavior*. Chicago: Aldine.

BARRETT, L. F., & RUSSELL, J. A. (1999). The structure of current affect: Controversies and emerging consensus. *Current Directions in Psychological Science, 8*(1), 10–14.

BARRY, H., III, CHILD, I. L., & BACON, M. K. (1959). Relation of child training to subsistence economy. *American Anthropologist, 61*, 51–63.

BARTLETT, F. C. (1932). *Remembering: A study in experimental and social psychology*. Cambridge: Cambridge University Press.

BARTOL, C. R., & COSTELLO, N. (1976). Extraversion as a function of temporal duration of electric shock: An exploratory study. *Perceptual and Motor Skills, 42*, 1174.

BASS, B. M. (1990). *Bass and Stogdill's handbook of leadership: Theory, research, and managerial applications* (3rd ed.). New York: Free Press.

BASS, E., & DAVIS, L. (1988). *The courage to heal.* New York: Harper and Row.

BASSILI, J. N. (1993). Response latency versus certainty as indexes of the strength of voting intentions in a CATI survey. *Public Opinion Quarterly, 57*(1), 54–61.

BASSILI, J. N. (1995). Response latency and the accessibility of voting intentions: What contributes to accessibility and how it affects vote choice. *Personality and Social Psychology Bulletin, 21*(7), 686–695.

BATES, E. (1976). *Language and context: The acquisition of pragmatics.* New York: Academic Press.

BATES, E., CHEN, S., TZENG, O., LI, P. & OPIE, M. (1991). The noun-verb problem in Chinese aphasia. *Brain and Language, 41*, 203–233.

BATTLE, Y. L., MARTIN, B., C., DORFMAN, J. H., & MILLER, L. S. (1999). Seasonality and infectious disease in schizophrenia: The birth hypothesis revisited. *Journal of Psychiatric Research, 33*, 501–509.

BAUMANN, B., & BOGERTS, B. (2001). Neuroanatomical studies on bipolar disorder [Suppl.]. *British Journal of Psychiatry, 41*, 142–147.

BAUMEISTER, R. F. (2001). Violent pride. *Scientific American, 284*, 96–101.

BAUMEISTER, R. F., SMART, L., & BODEN, J.M. (1996). Relation of threatened egotism to violence and aggression: The dark side of high self-esteem. *Psychological Review, 103*, 5–33.

BAUMRIND, D. (1964). Some thoughts on the ethics of research: After reading Milgram's behavioral study of obedience. *American Psychologist, 19*, 421–423.

BAUMRIND, D. (1967). Child care practices anteceding three patterns of preschool behavior. *Genetic Psychology Monographs, 75*, 43–88.

BAUMRIND, D. (1971). Current patterns of parental authority. *Genetic Psychology Monographs, 1.*

BAUMRIND, D. (1977). Socialization determinants of personal agency. Paper presented at the biennial meetings of the Society for Research in Child Development, New Orleans. Cited in Maccoby, E. E. (1980). *Social development.* New York: Harcourt Brace Jovanovich.

BAUMRIND, D. (1986). Sex differences in moral reasoning: Response to Walker's (1984) conclusion that there are none. *Child Development, 57*, 511–521.

BAUMRIND, D. (1991). The influence of parenting style on adolescent competence and substance use. *Journal of Early Adolescence, 11*(1), 56–95.

BAYER, E. (1929). Beitrage zur Zweikomponententheorie des Hungers. *Zeitschrift der Psychologie, 112*, 1–54.

BAZERMAN, M. H. (1998). *Judgment in managerial decision making* (4th ed.). New York: Wiley.

BEACH, C. M. (1991). The interpretation of prosodic patterns at points of syntactic structure ambiguity: Evidence for cue trading relations. *Journal of Memory and Language, 30*, 644–663.

BEAR, M. F., CONNORS, B. W., & PARADISO, M. A. (1996). *Neuroscience: Exploring the brain.* Baltimore: Williams & Wilkins.

BEARDEN, C. E., HOFFMAN, K. M., & CANNON, T. D. (2001). The neuropsychology and neuroanatomy of bipolar affective disorder: A critical review. *Bipolar Disorder, 3*, 106–150.

BECHARA, A., DAMASIO, H., TRANEL, D., & DAMASIO, A. R. (1997). Deciding advantageously before knowing the advantageous strategy. *Science, 275*, 1293–1295.

BECHARA, A., TRANEL, D., DAMASIO, H., ADOLPHS, R., ROCKLAND, C., & DAMASIO, A. (1995). Double dissociation of conditioning and declarative knowledge relative to the amygdala and hippocampus in humans. *Science, 269*, 1115–1118.

BECK, A. T. (1967). *Depression: Causes and treatment.* Philadelphia: University of Pennsylvania Press.

BECK, A. T. (1976). *Cognitive therapy and the emotional disorders.* New York: International Universities Press.

BECK, A. T. (1985). Cognitive therapy. In H. I. Kaplan & J. Sadock (Eds.), *Comprehensive textbook of psychiatry* (4th ed.). Baltimore: Williams & Wilkins.

BECK, A. T., RUSH, A. J., SHAW, B. F., & EMERY, G. (1979). Cognitive therapy of depression. New York: Guilford Press.

BECK, J. (1966). Effect of orientation and of shape similarity on perceptual grouping. *Perception and Psychophysics, 1*, 300–302.

BECK, J. (1982). Textural segmentation. In J. Beck (Ed.), *Organization and representation in perception* (pp. 285–317). Hillsdale, NJ: Erlbaum.

BÉDARD, J., & CHI, M. (1992). Expertise. *Current Directions in Psychological Science, 1*, 135–139.

BEGG, I., ANAS, A., & FARINACCI, S. (1992). Dissociation of processes in belief: Source recollection, statement familiarity, and the illusion of truth. *Journal of Experimental Psychology: General, 121*, 446–458.

BEHRMANN, M. (2000). The mind's eye mapped onto the brain's matter. *Current Directions in Psychological Science, 9*, 50–54.

BEITMAN, B. D., GOLDFRIED, M. R., & NORCROSS, J. C. (1989). The movement toward integrating the psychotherapies: An overview. *American Journal of Psychiatry, 146*, 138–147.

BÉKÉSY, G. VON. (1957). The ear. *Scientific American, 197*, 66–78.

BELL, A. P. (1983). Sexual preference: An addendum. In M. F. Schwartz, A. S. Moracsewski, & J. A. Monteleone (Eds.), *Sex and gender: A theological and scientific inquiry* (pp. 235–245). St. Louis, MO: The Pope John Center.

BELL, A. P., WEINBERG, M. S., & HAMMERSMITH, S. K. (1981). *Sexual preference: Its development in men and women.* Bloomington, IN: Indiana University Press.

BELL, R. Q. (1968). A reinterpretation of the direction of effects in studies of socialization. *Psychological Review, 75*, 81–95.

BELL, R. Q., & HARPER, L. V. (1977). *Child effects on adults.* Hillsdale, NJ: Erlbaum.

BELLODI, L., CAVALLINI, M. C., BERTELLI, S., CHIAPPARINO, D., RIBOLDI, C., & SMERALDI, E. (2001). Morbidity risk for obsessive-compulsive spectrum disorders in first-degree relatives of patients with eating disorders. *American Journal of Psychiatry, 158*, 563–569.

BELLUGI, U. (1971). Simplification in children's language. In R. Huxley & E. Ingram (Eds.), *Language acquisition: Models and methods.* New York: Academic Press.

BELLUGI, U., MARKS, S., BIHRLE, A., & SABO, H. (1991). Dissociation between language and cognitive function in Williams syndrome. In D. Bishop & K. Mogford (Eds.), *Language development in exceptional circumstances.* Hillsdale, NJ: Erlbaum.

BELLUGI, U., POIZNER, H., & KLIMA, E. S. (1983). Brain organization for language: Clues from sign aphasia. *Human Neurobiology, 2*, 155–171.

BELOFF, H. (1957). The structure and origin of the anal character. *Genetic Psychology Monographs, 55*, 141–172.

BELSKY, J. (1988). The "effects" of infant day care reconsidered [Special Issue]. *Infant Day Care, Early Childhood Research Quarterly, 3*, 235–272.

BELSKY, J. (2001). Emanuel Miller Lecture: Developmental risks (still) associated with early child care. *Journal of Child Psychology and Psychiatry and Allied Disciplines, 42*, 845–859.

BELSKY, J., & BRAUNGART, J. M. (1991). Are insecure-avoidant infants with extensive day-care experience less stressed by and more independent in the Strange Situation? *Child Development, 62*, 657–671.

BELSKY, J., CAMPBELL, S. B., COHN, J. F., & MOORE, G. (1996). Instability of infant-parent attachment security. *Developmental Psychology, 32*(5), 921–924.

BELSKY, J., & CASSIDY, J. (1994). Attachment and close relationships: An individual-difference perspective. *Psychological Inquiry, 5*(1), 27–30.

BELSON, W. A. (1978). *Television violence and the adolescent boy.* Westmead, England: Saxon House, Teakfield Ltd.

BEM, D. J. (1967). Self-perception: An alternative interpretation of cognitive dissonance phenomena. *Psychological Review, 74*, 183–200.

BEM, D. J. (1972). Self-perception theory. In L. Berkowitz (Ed.), *Advances in experimental social psychology: Vol. 6* (pp. 2–62). New York: Academic Press.

BEM, D. J. (1996). Exotic becomes erotic: A developmental theory of sexual orientation. *Psychological Review, 103*(2), 320–335.

BEM, S. L. (1989). Genital knowledge and gender constancy in preschool children. *Child Development, 60,* 649–662.

BENBOW, C. P. (1988). Sex differences in mathematical reasoning ability in intellectually talented preadolescents: Their nature, effects, and possible causes. *Behavior and Brain Sciences, 11,* 169–232.

BENBOW, C. P., LUBINSKI, D., SHEA, D. L., & EFTEKHARI-SANJANI, H. (2000). Sex differences in mathematical reasoning ability at age 13: Their status 20 years later. *Psychological Science, 11,* 474–480.

BENBOW, C. P., & STANLEY, J. C. (1983). Sex differences in mathematical reasoning: More facts. *Science, 222,* 1029–1031.

BENEDICT, R. (1934). *Patterns of culture.* New York: Houghton Mifflin.

BENNETT, C., LINDSKOLD, S., & BENNETT, R. (1973). The effects of group size and discussion time on the risky shift. *Journal of Social Psychology, 91*(1), 137–147.

BENSON, H., & FRIEDMAN, R. (1996). Harnessing the power of the placebo effect and renaming it "remembered wellness." *Annual Review of Medicine, 47,* 193–199.

BERCOVITCH, F. B. (1988). Coalitions, cooperation and reproductive tactics among adult male baboons. *Animal Behaviour, 36*(4), 1198–1209.

BERGIN, A. E. (1967). An empirical analysis of therapeutic issues. In D. Arbuckle (Ed.), *Counseling and psychotherapy: An overview* (pp. 175–208). New York: McGraw-Hill.

BERGIN, A. E. (1971). The evaluation of therapeutic outcomes. In A. E. Bergin & S. L. Garfield (Eds.), *Handbook of psychotherapy and behavior change: An empirical analysis.* New York: Wiley.

BERKOWITZ, L., & MACAULEY, J. (1971). The contagion of criminal violence. *Sociometry, 34,* 238–260.

BERLIN, B., & KAY, P. (1969). *Basic color terms: Their universality and evolution.* Berkeley and Los Angeles, CA: University of California Press.

BERMANT, G., & DAVIDSON, J. M. (1974). *Biological bases of sexual behavior.* New York: Harper & Row.

BERNARD, V. W., OTTENBERG, P., & REDL, F. (1965). Dehumanization: A composite psychological defense in relation to modern war. In M. Schwebel (Ed.), *Behavioral science and human survival* (pp. 64–82). Palo Alto, CA: Science and Behavior Books.

BERNSTEIN, A., NEWMAN, J. P., WALLACE, J. F., & LUH, K. E. (2000). Left-hemisphere activation and deficient response modulation in psychopaths. *Psychological Science, 11,* 414–418.

BERNSTEIN, A. E., & LENHART, S. A. (1993). *The psychodynamic treatment of women.* Washington, DC: American Psychiatric Press.

BERSCHEID, E., DION, K., WALSTER, E., & WALSTER, G. W. (1971). Physical attractiveness and dating choice: A test of the matching hypothesis. *Journal of Experimental Social Psychology, 7,* 173–189.

BERSCHEID, E., & WALSTER, E. (1974). Physical attractiveness. In L. Berkowitz (Ed.), *Advances in experimental social psychology: Vol. 7.* New York: Academic Press.

BERSCHEID, E., & WALSTER, E. H. (1978). *Interpersonal attraction* (2nd ed.). Reading, MA: Addison-Wesley.

BEUTLER, L. E., & CLARKIN, J. (1990). *Systematic treatment selection: Toward targeted treatment interventions.* New York: Brunner-Maazel.

BEVER, T. G. (1970). The cognitive basis for linguistic structures. In J. R. Hayes (Ed.), *Cognition and the development of language* (pp. 279–362). New York: Wiley.

BHASKAR, R., & SIMON, H. A. (1977). Problem solving in semantically rich domains: An example from engineering thermodynamics. *Cognitive Science, 1*(2), 193–215.

BIANCHI, L. (1922). *The mechanism of the brain and the function of the frontal lobes.* Edinburgh: Livingstone.

BIEDERMAN, I. (1987). Recognition-by-components: A theory of human image understanding. *Psychological Review, 94,* 115–147.

BIGELOW, A. (1987). Early words of blind children. *Journal of Child Language, 14*(1), 1–22.

BINET, A. (1911). *Les idées modernes sur les enfants.* Paris, Flammarion. Republished by Flammarion in 1973 with a Preface by Jean Piaget. [Published in English as: *Modern Ideas about Children.* Menlo Park, CA: Suzanne Heisler, 1984.]

BJÖRKLUND, A., & STENEVI, U. (1984). Intracerebral implants: Neuronal replacement and reconstruction of damaged circuitries. *Annual Review of Neuroscience, 7,* 279–308.

BJORKLUND, D. F., & SHACKELFORD, T. K. (1999). Differences in parental investment contribute to important differences between men and women. *Current Directions in Psychological Science, 8*(3), 86–89.

BLACK, D. W., & ANDREASEN, N. C. (1994). Schizophrenia, schizophreniform disorder, and delusional paranoid disorder. In J. A. Talbott, R. E. Hales, & S. C. Yudofsky (Eds.), *American Psychiatric Press textbook of psychiatry* (pp. 411–463). Washington, DC: American Psychiatric Press.

BLACK, D. W., & NOYES, R. (1990). Comorbidity in obsessive-compulsive disorder. In J. D. Maser & C. D. Cloninger (Eds.), *Comorbidity in anxiety and mood disorders* (pp. 305–316). Washington, DC: American Psychiatric Press.

BLAIR, I. V., & BANAJI, M. R. (1996). Automatic and controlled processes in stereotype priming. *Journal of Personality and Social Psychology, 70.*

BLANCHETTE, I., & DUNBAR, K. (2000). How analogies are generated: The roles of structural and superficial similarity. *Memory and Cognition, 28*(1), 108–124.

BLASCOVICH, J., SPENCER, S. J., QUINN, D., & STEELE, C. (2001). African Americans and high blood pressure: The role of stereotype threat. *Psychological Science, 12,* 225–229.

BLASI, A. (1980). Bridging moral cognition and moral action: A critical review of the literature. *Psychological Bulletin, 88,* 1–45.

BLASI, A. (1984). Moral identity: Its role in moral functioning. In W. M. Kurtines & L. Gewirtz (Eds.), *Morality, moral behavior, and moral development* (pp. 128–139). New York: Wiley.

BLASS, T. (ED.). (2000). *Obedience to authority: Current perspectives on the Milgram paradigm.* Mahwah, NJ: Erlbaum.

BLEULER, E. (1911). *Dementia praecox, or the group of schizophrenias* (J. Zinkin & N. D. C. Lewis, Trans.). New York: International Universities Press, 1950.

BLIER, P., & ABBOTT, F. V. (2001). Putative mechanisms of action of antidepressant drugs in affective and anxiety disorders and pain. *Journal of Psychiatry and Neuroscience, 26,* 37–43.

BLISS, E. L. (1980). Multiple personalities: Report of fourteen cases with implications for schizophrenia and hysteria. *Archives of General Psychiatry, 37,* 1388–1397.

BLISS, T. V. P., & LOMO, T. (1973). Long-term potentiation of synaptic transmission in the dentate area of the anesthetized rabbit following stimulation of the perforant path. *Journal of Physiology, 232,* 331–356.

BLOCK, J. (1971). *Lives through time.* Berkeley, CA: Bancroft Books.

BLOCK, N., FLANAGAN, O., & GUZELDERE, G. (1997). *The nature of consciousness: Philosophical debates.* Cambridge: MIT Press.

BLOCK, N. J., & DWORKIN, G. (1976). *The IQ controversy: Critical readings.* New York: Pantheon.

BLOOM, F. E. (1983). The endorphins: A growing family of pharmacologically pertinent peptides. *Annual Review of Pharmacology and Toxicology, 23,* 151–170.

BLOOM, F. E. (1993). Advancing a neurodevelopmental origin for schizophrenia. *Archives of General Psychiatry, 50,* 224–227.

BLOOM, F. E., LAZERSON, A., & HOFSTADTER, L. (1988). *Brain, mind, and behavior.* New York: Freeman.

BLOOM, L. (1993). *The transition from infancy to language: Acquiring the power of expression.* New York: Cambridge University Press.

BLOOM, L., & MUDD, S. (1991). Depth of processing approach to face recognition: A test of two theories. *Journal of Experimental Psychology: Learning, Memory and Cognition, 17,* 556–565.

BLOOM, P. (1996). Intention, history, and artifact concepts. *Cognition, 60,* 1–29.

BLOOM, P. (2000). *How children learn the meanings of words.* Cambridge, MA: MIT Press.

BLUMSTEIN, D. T. (1999). Selfish sentinels. *Science, 284,* 1633–1634.

BLURTON-JONES, N., & KONNER, M. J. (1976). !Kung knowledge of animal behavior. In B. Lee & I. DeVore (Eds.), *Kalahari hunter-gatherers.* Cambridge, MA: Harvard University Press.

BODNAR, R. J., KELLY, D. D., BRUTUS, M., & GLUSMAN, M. (1980). Stress-induced analgesia: Neural and hormonal determinants. *Neuroscience and Biobehavioral Reviews, 4,* 87–100.

BOGEN, J. E. (1969). The other side of the brain II: An appositional mind. *Bulletin of the Los Angeles Neurological Societies, 34,* 135–162.

BOGEN, J. E. (1995). On the neurophysiology of consciousness: Part I: An overview. *Consciousness and Cognition, 4,* 52–62.

BOGEN, J. E., FISHER, E. D., & VOGEL, P. J. (1965). Cerebral commissurotomy: A second case report. *Journal of the American Medical Association, 194,* 1328–1329.

BOLES, D. B. (1980). X-linkage of spatial ability: A critical review. *Child Development, 51,* 625–635.

BOLLES, R. C. (1970). Species-specific defense reactions and avoidance learning. *Psychological Review, 77,* 32–48.

BOLLES, R. C., & BEECHER, M. D. (EDS.). (1988). *Evolution and learning.* Hillsdale, NJ: Erlbaum.

BOLLES, R. C., & FANSELOW, M. S. (1982). Endorphins and behavior. *Annual Review of Psychology, 33,* 87–102.

BOND, C. F., & TITUS, L. J. (1983). Social facilitation: A meta-analysis of 241 studies. *Psychological Bulletin, 94*(2), 265–292.

BOND, R., & SMITH, P. B. (1996). Culture and conformity: A meta-analysis of studies using Asch's (1952, 1956) line judgment task. *Psychological Bulletin, 119*(1), 111–137.

BOOK, A. S., STARZYK, K. B., & QUNISEY, V. L (2001). The relationship between testosterone and aggression: A meta-analysis. *Aggression and Violent Behavior, 6,* 579–599.

BOOTH, A. E., & WAXMAN, S. R. (2002). Word learning is "smart": evidence that conceptual information affects preschoolers' extension of novel words. *Cognition, 84,* B11–B22.

BORCH-JACOBSEN, M. (1997). Sybil—The making of a disease: An interview with Dr. Herbert Spiegel. *New York Review of Books, 44,* 60–64.

BORDEN, R. J. (1980). Audience influence. In P. B. Paulus (Ed.), *Psychology of group influence* (pp. 99–132). Hillsdale, NJ: Erlbaum.

BORDEN, V. M. H., & LEVINGER, G. (1991). Interpersonal transformations in intimate relationships. In W. H. Jones & D. Perlman (Eds.), *Advances in personal relationships: Vol. 2* (pp. 35–56). London: Jessica Kingsley Publishers.

BORKENAU, P., RIEMANN, R., ANGLEITNER, A., & SPINATH, F. M. (2001). Genetic and environmental influences on observed personality: Evidence from the German Observational Study of Adult Twins. *Journal of Personality and Social Psychology, 80*(4), 655–668.

BORNSTEIN, M. H. (1973). Color vision and color naming: A psychophysiological hypothesis of cultural difference. *Psychological Bulletin, 80,* 257–285.

BORNSTEIN, M. H. (1985). Human infant color vision and color perception. *Infant Behavior and Development, 8*(1), 109–113.

BORODITSKY, L. (2001). Does language shape thought? Mandarin and English speakers' conceptions of time, *Cognitive Psychology, 43,* 1–22.

BORONAT, C. B., & LOGAN, G. D. (1997). The role of attention in automatization: Does attention operate at encoding, or retrieval, or both? *Memory and Cognition, 25,* 36–46.

BOTHWELL, M. (1995). Functional interactions of neurotrophins and neurotrophin receptors. *Annual Review of Neuroscience, 18,* 223–253.

BOTTGER, P. C. (1984). Expertise and air time as bases of actual and perceived influence in problem-solving groups. *Journal of Applied Psychology, 69,* 214–222.

BOUCHARD, T. J. (1995). Longitudinal studies of personality and intelligence: A behavior genetic and evolutionary perspective. In D. H. Saklofske & M. Zeidner (Eds.), *International handbook of personality and intelligence* (pp. 81–106). New York: Plenum.

BOUCHARD, T. J., JR. (1984). Twins reared apart and together: What they tell us about human diversity. In S. Fox (Ed.), *The chemical and biological bases of individuality* (pp. 147–184). New York: Plenum.

BOUCHARD, T. J., JR., LYKKEN, D. T., MCGUE, M., SEGAL, N. L., & TELLEGEN, A. (1990). Sources of human psychological differences: The Minnesota study of twins reared apart. *Science, 250,* 223–250.

BOUCHARD, T. J., JR., & MCGUE, M. (1981). Familial studies of intelligence: A review. *Science, 212,* 1055–1059.

BOWER, G. H. (1970). Analysis of a mnemonic device. *American Scientist, 58,* 496–510.

BOWER, G. H. (1972). Analysis of a mnemonic device. In M. Coltheart (Ed.), *Readings in cognitive psychology.* Toronto: Holt, Rinehart & Winston, Inc.

BOWER, G. H., BLACK, J. B., & TURNER, T. J. (1979). Scripts in memory for text. *Cognitive Psychology, 11,* 177–220.

BOWER, G. H., MCLEAN, J., & MEACHEM, J. (1966). Value of knowing when reinforcement is due. *Journal of Comparative and Physiological Psychology, 62,* 184–192.

BOWERMAN, M. (1982). Reorganizational processes in language development. In E. Wanner & L. R. Gleitman (Eds.), *Language development: State of the art.* New York: Cambridge University Press.

BOWERS, K. S. (1984). On being unconsciously influenced and informed. In K. S. Bowers & D. Meichenbaum, D. (Eds.), *The unconscious reconsidered.* New York: Wiley.

BOWLBY, J. (1969). *Attachment and loss: Vol. 1. Attachment.* New York: Basic Books.

BOWLBY, J. (1973). *Separation and loss.* New York: Basic Books.

BOWMAKER, J. K., & DARTNALL, H. J. A. (1980). Visual pigments and rods and cones in a human retina. *Journal of Physiology, 298,* 501–511.

BOWMAN, E. S., & MARKAND, O. N. (1996). Psychodynamics and psychiatric diagnoses of pseudoseizure subjects. *American Journal of Psychiatry, 153,* 57–63.

BOYD, R., & SILK, J. (1997). *How humans evolved.* New York: Norton.

BOYLE, G. J., STANKOV, L., & CATTELL, R. B. (1995). Measurement and statistical models in the study of personality and intelligence. In D. H. Saklofske & M. Zeidner, M. (Eds.), *International handbook of personality and intelligence* (pp. 417–446). New York: Plenum.

BRABECK, M. (1983). Moral judgement: Theory and research on differences between males and females. *Developmental Review, 3,* 274–291.

BRADLEY, S. J., OLIVER, G. D., CHERNICK, A. B., & ZUCKER, K. J. (1998). Experiment of nurture: Ablatio penis at 2 months, sex reassignment at 7 months, and a psychosexual follow-up in young adulthood. *Pediatrics, 102,* e9 (electronic article available at http://www.pediatrics.org/cgi/content/full/102/1/e9).

BRADSHAW, J. L. (2001). *Developmental disorders of the frontostrial system: Neuropsychological, neuropsychiatric, and evolutionary perspectives.* Philadelphia: Psychology Press/Taylor & Francis.

BRADSHAW, J. L., & SHEPPARD, D. M. (2000). The neurodevelopmental frontostriatal disorders: Evolutionary adaptiveness and anomalous lateralization. *Brain and Language, 73,* 297–320.

BRADY, I. (1983). Speaking in the name of the real: Freeman and Mead on Samoa [Special section]. *American Anthropologist, 85,* 908–947.

BRAILOWSKY, S., & GARCIA, O. (1999). Ethanol, GABA and epilepsy. *Archives of Medical Research, 30,* 3–9.

BRAIN, L. (1965). *Speech disorders: Aphasia, apraxia, and agnosia*. London: Butterworth.

BRAINERD, C. J., REYNA, V. F., & MOJARDIN, A. H. (1999). Conjoint recognition *Psychological Review*, 106, 160–179.

BRAMMER, G. L., RALEIGH, M. J., & McGUIRE, M. T. (1994). Neurotransmitters and social status. In L. Ellis (Ed.), *Social stratification and socioeconomic inequality: Vol. 2. Reproductive and interpersonal aspects of dominance and status* (pp. 75–91). Westport, CT: Praeger/Greenwood.

BRANSFORD, J. D., & JOHNSON, M. K. (1972). Contextual prerequisites for understanding. *Journal of Verbal Learning and Verbal Behavior*, 11, 717–726.

BRAUER, M., JUDD, C. M., & GLINER, M. D. (1995). The effects of repeated expressions on attitude polarization during group discussions. *Journal of Personality and Social Psychology*, 68(6), 1014–1029.

BREMNER, J. D., SOUTHWICK, S. M., JOHNSON, D. R., YEHUDA, R., & CHARNEY, D. S. (1993). Childhood physical abuse and combat-related posttraumatic stress disorder in Vietnam veterans. *American Journal of Psychiatry*, 150, 235–239.

BREWER, W. F., & TREYENS, J. C. (1981). Role of schemata in memory for places. *Cognitive Psychology*, 13, 207–230.

BRICKMAN, J. C., & D'AMATO, B. (1975). Exposure effects in a free-choice situation. *Journal of Personality and Social Psychology*, 32, 415–420.

BRICKMAN, P., COATES, D. & JANOFF-BULLMAN, R. (1978). Lottery winners and accident victims: Is happiness relative? *Journal of Personality and Social Psychology*, 36, 917–927.

BRIDGEMAN, B., & STARK, L. (1991). Ocular proprioception and efference copy in registering visual direction. *Vision Research*, 31, 1903–1913.

BRIDGES, P. (1987). Psychosurgery for resistant depression. In J. Zohar & R. H. Belmaker, (Eds.), *Treating resistant depression* (pp. 397–411). New York: PMA Publishing.

BROADBENT, D. E. (1958). *Perception and communication*. London: Pergamon Press.

BROCK, T. C., GREEN, M. C., REICH, D. A., & EVANS, L. M. (1996). The Consumer Reports study of psychotherapy: Invalid is invalid. *American Psychologist*, 51, 1083.

BRODIE, H. K. H., GARTRELL, N., DOERING, C., & RHUE, T. (1974). Plasma testosterone levels in heterosexual and homosexual men. *American Journal of Psychiatry*, 131, 82–83.

BRODY, N. (1988). *Personality*. New York: Academic Press.

BRODY, N. (1992). *Intelligence* (2nd ed.). New York: Academic Press.

BROWN, A., & MITCHELL, D. (1994). A reevaluation of semantic versus nonsemantic processing in implicit memory. *Memory and Cognition*, 22, 533–541.

BROWN, A. L. (1974). The role of strategic memory in retardate-memory. In N. R. Ellis (Ed.), *International review of research in mental retardation: Vol. 7* (pp. 55–108). New York: Academic Press.

BROWN, A. S., & HALLIDAY, H. E. (1990). *Cryptomnesia and source memory difficulties*. Southwestern Psychological Association Convention.

BROWN, B. B. (1990). Peer groups and peer cultures. In S. S. Feldman & G. R. Elliott (Eds.), *At the threshold: The developing adolescent*. Cambridge, MA: Harvard University Press.

BROWN, C. M., HAGOORT, P., & TER KEURS M. (1999) Electrophysiological signatures of visual lexical processing of open- and closed-class words. *Journal of Cognitive Neuroscience*, 11, 261–281.

BROWN, D. E. (1991). *Human universals*. New York: McGraw-Hill.

BROWN, J. F. (1940). *The psychodynamics of abnormal behavior*. New York: McGraw-Hill.

BROWN, R. (1957). Linguistic determinism and parts of speech. *Journal of Abnormal and Social Psychology*, 55, 1–5.

BROWN, R. (1958). *Words and things*. New York: Free Press, Macmillan.

BROWN, R. (1965). *Social psychology*. New York: Free Press, Macmillan.

BROWN, R., & BELLUGI, U. (1964). Three processes in the child's acquisition of syntax. *Harvard Educational Review*, 34, 133–151.

BROWN, R., & KULIK, J. (1977). Flashbulb memories. *Cognition*, 5, 73–99.

BROWN, R., & McNEILL, D. (1966). The tip of the tongue phenomenon. *Journal of Verbal Learning and Verbal Behavior*, 5, 325–327.

BROWN, R. P., & JOSEPHS, R. A. (1999). A burden of proof: Stereotype relevance and gender differences in math performance. *Journal of Personality and Social Psychology*, 76, 246–257.

BROWN, R. W., & LENNEBERG, E. H. (1954). A study of language and cognition. *Journal of Abnormal and Social Psychology*, 49, 454–462.

BROWNELL, K. D., GREENWOOD, M. R. C., STELLAR, E., & SHRAGER, E. E. (1986). The effects of repeated cycles of weight loss and regain in rats. *Physiology and Behavior*, 38, 459–464.

BRUCE, V., & GREEN, P. (1985). *Visual perception: Physiology, psychology, and ecology*. Hillsdale, NJ: Erlbaum.

BRUCH, H. (1973). *Eating disorders*. New York: Basic Books.

BRUCH, H. (1978). *The golden cage*. Cambridge, MA: Harvard University Press.

BRUCK, M., & CECI, S. J. (1999). The suggestibility of children's memory. *Annual Review of Psychology*, 50.

BRUCK, M., CECI, S. J., & HEMBROOKE, H. (1998). Reliability and credibility of young children's reports: From research to policy and practice. *American Psychologist*, 53(2), 136–151.

BRUNER, J. S. (1973). *Beyond the Information given*. New York: Norton.

BRUNER, J. S., & TAGIURI, R. (1954). The perception of people. In G. Lindzey (Ed.), *Handbook of social psychology: Vol. 2*. Reading, MA: Addison-Wesley.

BUCHANAN, C. M., MACCOBY, E. E., & DORNBUSCH, S. M. (1996). *Adolescents after divorce*. Cambridge, MA: Harvard University Press.

BUCHANAN, G. M., & SELIGMAN, M. E. P. (EDS.). (1995). *Explanatory style*. Hillsdale, NJ: Erlbaum.

BUCHANAN, T. W. & ADOLPHS, R. (2003). The neuroanatomy of emotional memory in humans. In D. Reisberg & P. Hertel (Eds.), *Emotion and Memory*. New York: Oxford University Press.

BULLOCK, W. A., & GILLILAND, K. (1993). Eysenck's arousal theory of introversion-extraversion: A covergent measures investigation. *Journal of Personality and Social Psychology*, 64, 113–123.

BURGESS, E. W., & WALLIN, P. (1943). Homogamy in social characteristics. *American Journal of Sociology*, 49, 109–124.

BURKE, M. J., & PRESKHORN, S. H. (1995). Short-term treatment of mood disorders with standard antidepressants. In F. E. Bloom & D. Kupfer (Eds.), *Psychopharmacology: The fourth generation of progress* (pp. 1053–1065). New York: Raven.

BURNETT, S. A., LANE, D. M., & DRATT, L. M. (1979). Spatial differences and sex differences in quantitative ability. *Intelligence*, 3, 345–354.

BURNS, J. M. (1978). *Leadership*. New York: Harper and Row.

BURTON, R. V. (1963) Generality of honesty reconsidered. *Psychological Review*, 70, 481–499.

BURTON, R. V., & WHITING, J. W. M. (1961). The absent father and cross-sex identity. *Merrill-Palmer Quarterly*, 7, 85–95.

BUSS, A. H., & PLOMIN, R. (1984). *Temperament: Early developing personality traits*. Hillsdale, NJ: Erlbaum.

BUSS, D. M. (1989). Sex differences in human mate preferences: Evolutionary hypotheses tested in 37 cultures. *Behavioral and Brain Sciences*, 12, 1–50.

BUSS, D. M. (1992). Mate preference mechanisms: Consequences for partner choice and intrasexual competition. In J. H. Barkow, L. Cosmides, & J. Tooby (Eds.), *The adapted mind* (pp. 249–266). New York: Oxford University Press.

BUSS, D. M., & BARNES, M. F. (1986). Preferences in human mate selection. *Journal of Personality and Social Psychology*, 50, 559–570.

Buss, D. M., Larsen, R. J., Westen, D., & Semmelroth, J. (2001). Sex differences in jealousy: Evolution, physiology, and psychology. In W. Parrott (Ed.), *Emotions in Social Psychology: Essential readings.* Philadelphia: Psychology Press.

Butcher, J. N., Dahlstrom, W. G., Graham, J. R., Tellegen, A. M., & Kaemmer, B. (1989). *MMPI-2: Manual for administration and scoring.* Minneapolis, MN: University of Minnesota Press.

Butcher, J. N., Dahlstrom, W. G., Graham, J. R., Tellegen, A., & Kaemmer, B. (2001). *MMPI-2 (Minnesota Multiphasic Personality Inventory-2) manual for administration and scoring* (2nd ed.). Minneapolis, MN: University of Minnesota Press.

Butcher, J. N., & Rouse, S. V. (1996). Personality: Individual differences and clinical assessment. *Annual Review of Psychology, 47,* 87–111.

Butcher, J. N., Williams, C. L., Graham, J. R., Archer, R. P., Tellegen, A., Ben-Porath, Y. S., et al. (1992). *MMPI-A (Minnesota Multiphasic Personality Inventory—Adolescent) manual for administration, scoring, and interpretation.* Minneapolis, MN: University of Minnesota Press.

Butler, R. A. (1954). Incentive conditions which influence visual exploration. *Journal of Experimental Psychology, 48,* 19–23.

Butterworth, B. (1999). A head for figures. *Science, 284,* 928–929.

Butterworth, G., & Cochran, E. (1980). Towards a mechanism of joint visual attention in human infancy. *International Journal of Behavioral Development, 3,* 253–272.

Butterworth, G., & Jarrett, N. (1991). What minds have in common is space: Spatial mechanisms serving joint visual attention in infancy. Perspectives on the child's theory of mind [Special issue]. *British Journal of Developmental Psychology, 9,* 55–72.

Byrne, R. W., & Whiten, A. (Eds.). (1988). *Machiavellian intelligence: Social expertise and the evolution of intellect in monkeys, apes, and humans.* New York: Oxford University Press.

Cabeza, R. & Nyberg, L. (2000). Imaging cognition II: An empirical review of 275 PET and fMRI studies. *Journal of Cognitive Neuroscience, 12,* 1–47.

Cabrera, N. J., Tamis-LeMonda, C. S., Bradley, R. H., Hofferth, S., & Lamb, M. E. (2000). Fatherhood in the twenty-first century. *Child Development, 71,* 127–136.

Cacioppo, J. T., & Berntson, G. G. (1994). Relationship between attitudes and evaluative space: A critical review, with emphasis on the separability of positive and negative substrates. *Psychological Bulletin, 115*(3), 401–423.

Cacioppo, J. T., Crites, S. L., Berntson, G. G., & Coles, M. G. (1993). If attitudes affect how stimuli are processed, should they not affect the event related brain potential? *Psychological Science, 4*(2), 108–112.

Calabrese, J. R., & Woyshville, M. J. (1995). Lithium therapy: Limitations and alternatives in the treatment of bipolar disorders. *Annals of Clinical Psychiatry, 7,* 103–112.

Caligiuri, M. R., Jeste, D. V., & Lacro, J. P. (2000). Antipsychotic-induced movement disorders in the elderly: Epidemiology and treatment recommendations. *Drugs and Aging, 17,* 363–384.

Cammalleri, J. A., Hendrick, H. W., Pittman, W. C., Jr., Bout, H. D., & Prather, D. C. (1973). Effects of different styles of leadership on group accuracy. *Journal of Applied Psychology, 57,* 32–37.

Campbell, F. A., & Ramey, C. T. (1994). Effects of early intervention on intellectual and academic achievement: A follow up study of children from low income families. *Child Development, 65*(2), 684–698.

Campbell, J. B., & Hawley, C. W. (1982). Study habits and Eysenck's theory of extraversion-introversion. *Journal of Research in Personality, 16,* 139–146.

Campbell, J. D., Tesser, A., & Fairey, P. J. (1986). Conformity and attention to the stimulus: Some temporal and contextual dynamics. *Journal of Personality and Social Psychology, 51,* 315–324.

Campbell, R., & Conway, M. A. (Eds.). (1995). *Broken memories: Case studies in memory impairment.* Cambridge, MA: Blackwell.

Campbell, W. K., Sedikides, C., Reeder, G. D., & Elliott, A. J. (2000). Among friends? An examination of friendship and the self-serving bias. *British Journal of Social Psychology, 39,* 229–239.

Campfield, L. A., & Rosenbaum, M. (1992). Human hunger. Is there a role for blood glucose dynamics? *Appetite, 18,* 244.

Campfield, L. A., & Smith, F. J. (1990a). Systemic factors in the control of food intake. In E. M. Stricker (Ed.), *Handbook of behavioral neurobiology: Vol. 10. Neurobiology of food and fluid intake* (pp. 183–206). New York: Plenum.

Campfield, L. A., & Smith, F. J. (1990b). Transient declines in blood glucose signal meal initiation. *International Journal of Obesity, 14,* 15–33.

Campione, J. C., & Brown, A. L. (1977). Memory and metamemory development in educable retarded children. In R. V. Kail, Jr. & J. W. Hagen (Eds.), *Perspectives on the development of memory and cognition.* Hillsdale, NJ: Erlbaum.

Campione, J. C., Brown, A. L., & Ferrara, R. A. (1982). Mental retardation and intelligence. In R. J. Sternberg (Ed.), *Handbook of human intelligence* (pp. 392–492). New York: Cambridge University Press.

Campos, J. J., Barrett, K. C., Lamb, M. E., Goldsmith, H. H., & Sternberg, C. (1983). Socioemotional development. In P. E. Mussen (Ed.), M. M. Haith, & J. J. Campos (Vol. Eds.) *Carmichael's manual of child psychology: Vol. 2. Infancy and developmental psychobiology* (pp. 783–916). New York: Wiley.

Candland, D. K. (1993). *Feral children and clever animals: Reflections on human nature.* New York: Oxford University Press.

Cannon, T. D. (1991). Genetic and prenatal sources of structural brain abnormalities in schizophrenia. In S. A. Mednick, T. D. Cannon, C. E. Barr, & M. Lyon (Eds.), *Fetal neural development and adult schizophrenia.* Cambridge: Cambridge University Press.

Cannon, T. D., Mednick, S. A., & Parnas, J. (1990). Antecedents of predominantly negative- and predominantly positive-symptom schizophrenia in a high-risk population. *Archives of General Psychiatry, 47,* 622–632.

Cannon, W. B. (1927). The James-Lange theory of emotions: A critical examination and an alternative theory. *American Journal of Psychology, 39,* 106–124.

Cannon, W. B. (1929). *Bodily changes in pain, hunger, fear and rage* (rev. ed.). New York: Appleton-Century.

Cannon, W. B. (1932 and 1960). *The wisdom of the body* (revised and enlarged). New York: Norton.

Cantor, J. R., Zillman, D., & Bryant, J. (1975). Enhancement of experienced sexual arousal in response to erotic stimuli through misattribution of unrelated residual excitation. *Journal of Personality and Social Psychology, 32,* 69–75.

Cantor, N., & Mischel, W. (1979). Prototypes in person perception. In L. Berkowitz (Ed.), *Advances in experimental social psychology: Vol. 12.* New York: Academic Press.

Caramazza, A., & Hillis, A. (1991). Lexical organization of nouns and verbs in the brain, *Nature, 349,* 788–790.

Carey, D. B. (2001). Do action systems resist visual illusions. *Trends in Cognitive Science, 5,* 109–113.

Carey, S. (1978). The child as word learner. In M. Halle, J. Bresnan, & G. A. Miller (Eds.), *Linguistic theory and psychological reality* (pp. 264–293). Cambridge, MA: MIT Press.

Carey, S. (1985). *Conceptual change in childhood.* Cambridge, MA: MIT Press.

Carlson, G., & Tanenhaus, M. (1988). Thematic roles and language comprehension. In W. Wilkins (Ed.), *Syntax and semantics: Vol. 21. Thematic relations.* San Diego, CA: Academic Press.

Carlson, N. R. (1986). *Physiology of behavior* (3rd ed). Boston: Allyn and Bacon.

Carlson, N. R. (1991). *Physiology of behavior.* Boston: Allyn and Bacon.

Carlyle, T. (1841). *On heroes, hero-worship, and the heroic in history.* Berkeley, CA: University of California Press, 1992.

CARPENTER, P. A., JUST, M. A., & SHELL, P. (1990). What one intelligence test measures. A theoretical account of processing in the Raven Progressive Matrix Test. *Psychological Review, 97*(3), 404–431.

CARPENTER, P. A., MIYAKE, A., & JUST, M. A. (1995). Language comprehension: Sentence and discourse processing. *Annual Review of Psychology, 46*, 91–120.

CARROLL, L. (1969). *Alice in wonderland.* Abridged by J. Frank and illustrated by M. M. Torrey. New York: Random House, (originally published 1865).

CARSON, B. S. (2000). Indications and outcomes for lobectomy, corpus callosotomy, and hemispherectomy in pediatric neurosurgical patients. *Clinical Neurosurgery, 47*, 385–399.

CARTER, C. S. (1992). Oxytocin and sexual behavior. *Neuroscience and Biobehavioral Research, 16*, 131–144.

CARTER, C. S., MINTUN, M., NICHOLS, T., & COHEN, J. D. (1997). Anterior cingulate gyrus dysfunction and selective attention deficits in schizophrenia: $^{15}OH_2O$ PET study during single-trial Stroop task performance. *American Journal of Psychiatry, 154*, 1670–1675.

CARTWRIGHT, R. D. (1977). *Night life: Explorations in dreaming.* Englewood Cliffs, NJ: Prentice-Hall.

CASE, R., & OKAMOTO, Y. (1996). The role of central conceptual structures in the development of children's thought. *Monographs of the Society for Research in Child Development, 61*(1–2), v–265.

CASELLI, M.-C., BATES, E., CASADIO, P., & FENSON, J. (1995). A cross-linguistic study of early lexical development. *Cognitive Development, 10*(2), 159–199.

CASPI, A., & HERBENER, E. (1990). Continuity and change: Assortative marriage and the consistency of personality in adulthood. *Journal of Personality and Social Psychology, 58*, 250–258.

CASPI, A., HERBENER, E. S., & OZER, D. J. (1992). Shared experiences and the similarity of personalities: A longitudinal study of married couples. *Journal of Personality and Social Psychology, 62*(2), 281–291.

CASPI, A., & MOFFITT, T. E. (1991). Individual differences are accentuated during periods of social change: The sample case of girls at puberty. *Journal of Personality and Social Psychology, 61*(1), 157–168.

CASPI, A., & MOFFITT, T. E. (1993). When do individual differences matter? A paradoxical theory of personality coherence. *Psychological Inquiry, 4*(4), 247–271.

CASTLE, J., GROOTHUES, C., BREDENKAMP, D., BECKETT, C., O'CONNOR, T., RUTTER, M., ET AL. (1999). Effects of qualities of early institutional care on cognitive attainment. *American Journal of Orthopsychiatry, 69*, 424–437.

CATEL, J. (1953). Ein Beitrag zur Frage von Hirnenentwicklung unter Menschwerdung. *Klinische Weisschriften, 31*, 473–475.

CATRAMBONE, R. (1998). The subgoal learning model: Creating better examples so that students can solve novel problems. *Journal of Experimental Psychology: General, 127*(4), 355–376.

CATTELL, R. B. (1957). *Personality and motivation structure and measurement.* New York: Harcourt, Brace and World.

CATTELL, R. B. (1963). Theory of fluid and crystallized intelligence: A critical experiment. *Journal of Educational Psychology, 54*, 1–22.

CATTELL, R. B. (1966). *The scientific analysis of personality.* Chicago: Aldine.

CATTELL, R. B. (1971). *Abilities: Their structure, growth, and action.* Boston: Houghton Mifflin.

CECI, S. (1990a). A sideway glance at this thing called LD: A context X process X person framework. In H. L. Swanson & B. K. Keogh (Eds.), *Learning disabilities: Theoretical and research issues* (pp. 59–73). Hillsdale, NJ: Lawrence Erlbaum.

CECI, S. (1990b). *On intelligence . . . more or less: A bioecological treatise on intellectual development.* Englewood Cliffs, NJ: Prentice Hall.

CECI, S., & LIKER, J. (1986). Academic and nonacademic intelligence: An experimental separation. In R. J. Sternberg & R. K. Wagner (Eds.), *Practical intelligence: Nature and origins of competence in everyday life* (pp. 119–142). New York: Cambridge University Press.

CECI, S. J., & WILLIAMS, W. M. (1997). Schooling, intelligence, and income. *American Psychologist, 52*, 1051–1058.

CECI, S., & BRUCK, M. (1995). *Jeopardy in the courtroom: A scientific analysis of children's testimony.* Washington, DC: American Psychological Association.

CECI, S., HUFFMAN, M., & SMITH, E. (1994). Repeatedly thinking about a non-event: Source misattributions among preschoolers. *Consciousness and Cognition, 3*, 388–407.

CENTERS FOR DISEASE CONTROL (1994, September). *HIV/AIDS surveillance.* Atlanta: U.S. Department of Health and Human Services, Public Health Service.

CENTERWALL, B. S. (1989). Exposure to television as a risk factor for violence. *American Journal of Epidemiology, 129*, 643–652.

CERVONE, D., & SHODA, Y. (1999). Beyond traits in the study of personality coherence. *Current Directions in Psychological Science, 8*, 27–32.

CHAIKEN, S. (1987). The heuristic model of persuasion. In M. P. Zanna, J. M. Olson, & C. P. Herman (Eds.), *Social influence: The Ontario symposium: Vol. 5* (pp. 3–40). Hillsdale, NJ: Erlbaum.

CHAIKEN, S., LIBERMAN, A., & EAGLY, A. H. (1989). Heuristic and systematic information processing within and beyond the persuasion context. In J. S. Uleman, & J. A. Bargh (Eds.), *Unintended thought* (pp. 212–252). New York: Guilford Press.

CHAIKEN, S., WOOD, W., & EAGLY, A. H. (1996). Principles of persuasion. In E. T. Higgins & A. W. Kruglanski (Eds.), *Social psychology: Handbook of basic principles* (pp. 702–742). New York: The Guilford Press.

CHALMERS, D. (1996). *The conscious mind: In search of a fundamental theory.* New York: Oxford University Press.

CHALMERS, D. (1998). On the search for the neural correlate of consciousness. In S. Hameroff (Ed.), *Toward a science of consciousness II: The 1996 Tucson discussions and debates.* Cambridge, MA: MIT Press.

CHAMBERS, D., & REISBERG, D. (1985). Can mental images be ambiguous? *Journal of Experimental Psychology: Human Perception and Performance, 11*, 317–328.

CHAO, R. K. (1994). Beyond parental control and authoritarian parenting style: Understanding Chinese parenting through the cultural notion of training. *Child Development, 65*, 1111–1119.

CHAPMAN, L. J., & CHAPMAN, J. P. (1973). *Disordered thought in schizophrenia.* New York: Appleton-Century-Crofts.

CHARNESS, N. (1981). Search in chess: Age and skill differences. *Journal of General Psychology: General, 110*, 21–38.

CHARTRAND, T., PINCKERT, S., & BURGER, J. M. (1999). When manipulation backfires: The effects of time delay and requester on the foot-in-the-door technique. *Journal of Applied Social Psychology, 29*(1), 211–221.

CHASE, C. (1998). Hermaphrodites with attitude: Mapping the emergence of intersex political activism. *Gay and Lesbian Quarterly, 4*, 189–211.

CHASE, W. G., & SIMON, H. A. (1973a). Perception in chess. *Cognitive Psychology, 4*, 55–81.

CHASE, W. G., & SIMON, H. A. (1973b). The mind's eye in chess. In W. G. Chase (Ed.), *Visual information processing.* New York: Academic Press.

CHEN, D. Y., DEUTSCH, J. A., GONZALEZ, M. F., & GU, Y. (1993). The induction and suppression of c-fos expression in the rat brain by cholecystokinin and its antagonist L364,718. *Neuroscience Letters, 149*, 91–94.

CHEN, M., & BARGH, J. A. (1997). Nonconscious behavioral confirmation processes: The self-fulfilling consequences of automatic stereotype activation. *Journal of Experimental Social Psychology, 33*(5), 541–560.

CHENEY, D. L., & SEYFARTH, R. M. (1982). Recognition of individuals within and between groups of free-ranging vervet monkeys. *American Zoologist, 22*, 519–529.

CHENEY, D. L., & SEYFARTH, R. M. (1990). *How monkeys see the world.* Chicago: University of Chicago Press.

CHENG, H., CAO, Y., & OLSON, L. (1996). Spinal cord repair of adult paraplegic rats: Partial restoration of hind limb function. *Science, 273*, 510–513.

CHENG, P. W., & HOLYOAK, K. J. (1985). Pragmatic reasoning schemas. *Cognitive Psychology, 17*, 391–416.

CHENG, P. W., HOLYOAK, K. J., NISBETT, R. E., & OLIVER, L. M. (1985). Pragmatic versus syntactic approaches to training deductive reasoning. *Cognitive Psychology, 18*, 293–328.

CHERLIN, A. J., FURSTENBERG, F. F., CHASE-LANSDALE, P. L., KIERNAN, K. E., ROBINS, P. K., MORRISON, D. R., ET AL. (1991). Longitudinal studies of effects of divorce on children in Great Britain and the United States. *Science, 252*, 1386–1389.

CHERRIER, M. M., ASTHANA, S., PLYMATE, S., BAKER, L., MATSUMOTO, A. M., PESKIND, E., ET AL. (2001). Testosterone supplementation improves spatial and verbal memory in healthy older men. *Neurology, 57*, 80–88.

CHERRY, E. C. (1953). Some experiments upon the recognition of speech, with one and with two ears. *Journal of the Acoustical Society of America, 25*, 975–979.

CHERYAN, S., & BODENHAUSEN, G. V. (2000). When positive stereotypes threaten intellectual performance: The psychological hazards of "model minority" status. *Psychological Science, 11*, 399–402.

CHEVRIER, J., & DELORME, A. (1983). Depth perception in Pandora's box and size illusion: Evolution with age. *Perception, 12*, 177–185.

CHI, M. T., & KOESKE, R. D. (1983). Network representation of a child's dinosaur knowledge. *Developmental Psychology, 19*(1), 29–39.

CHI, M. T. H. (1978). Knowledge structures and memory development. In R. S. Siegler (Ed.), *Children's thinking: What develops?* (pp. 73–96). Hillsdale, NJ: Erlbaum.

CHI, M. T. H., FELTOVICH, P. J., & GLASER, R. (1981). Categorization and representation of physics problems by experts and novices. *Cognitive Science, 5*, 121–152.

CHISHOLM, K. (1998). A three year follow-up of attachment and indiscriminate friendliness in children adopted from Romanian orphanages. *Child Development, 69*, 1090–1104.

CHODOROW, N. (1989). *Feminism and psychoanalytic theory.* New Haven, CT: Yale University Press.

CHOI, I., NISBETT, R. E., & NORENZAYAN, A. (1999). Causal attribution across cultures: Variation and universality. *Psychological Bulletin, 125*(1), 47–63.

CHOI, S., & BOWERMAN, M. (1991). Learning to express motion events in English and Korean: The influence of language-specific lexicalization patterns. *Cognition, 41*, 83–121.

CHOMSKY, N. (1959). Review of B. F. Skinner "Verbal Behavior." *Language, 35*, 26–58.

CHOMSKY, N. (1965). *Aspects of the theory of syntax.* Cambridge, MA: MIT Press.

CHOMSKY, N. (1981a). Knowledge of language: Its elements and origins. *Philosophical Transactions of the Royal Society of London, 295*(1077, Series B), 223–234.

CHOMSKY, N. (1981b). *Lectures on government and binding.* Dordrecht: Foris.

CHOMSKY, N. (1995). *The minimalist program.* Cambridge, MA: MIT Press.

CHOVIL, N. (1991). Social determinants of facial displays. *Journal of Nonverbal Behavior, 15*(3), 141–154.

CHRISTIAN, K., BACHMAN, H. J., & MORRISON, F. J. (2000). Schooling and cognitive development. In R. J. Sternberg & R. L. Grigorenko (Eds.), *Environmental effects on cognitive abilities.* Mahwah, NJ: Erlbaum.

CHRISTIANSEN, M. H., & CHATER, N. (2001). Connectionist psycholinguistics: capturing the empirical data. *Trends in Cognitive Science, 5*(2), 82–88.

CHRISTIANSEN, M. H., CHATER, N., & SEIDENBERG, M. S. (1999). Connectionist models of human language processing: Progress and prospects [Special Issue]. *Cognitive Science, 23.*

CHUA, S. E., & MCKENNA, P. J. (1995). Schizophrenia: A brain disease? *British Journal of Psychiatry, 166*, 563–582.

CHUNG, Y. B., & KATAYAMA, M. (1996). Assessment of sexual orientation in lesbian/gay/bisexual studies. *Journal of Homosexuality, 30*, 49–62.

CHURCH, R. M. (1969). Response suppression. In B. A. Campbell & R. M. Church (Eds.), *Punishment and aversive behavior.* New York: Appleton-Century-Crofts.

CHURCHLAND, P. S., & SEJNOWSKI, T. J. (1992). *The computational brain.* Cambridge, MA: MIT Press.

CIALDINI, R. B. (1984). *Influence: How and why people agree to do things.* New York: Quill.

CIALDINI, R. B. (1993). *Influence: Science and practice* (3rd ed.). New York: HarperCollins.

CIALDINI, R. B., PETTY, R. E., & CACIOPPO, J. T. (1981). Attitude and attitude change. In M. R. Rosenzweig & L. W. Porter (Eds.), *Annual Review of Psychology, 32*, 357–404.

CIALDINI, R. B., TROST, M. R., & NEWSOM, J. T. (1995). Preference for consistency: The development of a valid measure and the discovery of surprising behavioral implications. *Journal of Personality and Social Psychology, 69*(2), 318–328.

CIALDINI, R. R., VINCENT, J. E., LEWIS, S. K., CATALAN, J., WHEELER, D., & DARBY, L. (1975). Reciprocal concession procedure for inducing compliance: The door-in-the-face technique. *Journal of Personality and Social Psychology, 31*, 206–215.

CICCHETTI, D., & TOTH, S. L. (1998). Twins with schizophrenia: Genes or germs? *Schizophrenia Bulletin, 21*, 13–18.

CIPOLOTTI, L. (2001). Long-term retrograde amnesia . . . The crucial role of the hippocampus. *Neuropsychologia, 39*, 151–172.

CLARK, D. M. (1986). A cognitive approach to panic. *Behavior Research and Therapy, 24*, 461–470.

CLARK, D. M. (1988). A cognitive model of panic attacks. In S. Rachman & J. D. Maser (Eds.), *Panic: Psychological perspectives.* Hillsdale, NJ: Erlbaum.

CLARK, E. V. (1987). The principle of contrast: A constraint on acquisition. In B. MacWhinney (Ed.), *Mechanisms of language acquisition.* Hillsdale, NJ: Erlbaum.

CLARK, E. V., GELMAN, S. A., & LANE, N. M. (1985). Compound nouns and category structure in young children. *Child Development, 56*, 84–94.

CLARK, H. H. (1978). Inferring what is meant. In W. Levelt & G. Flores d'Arcais (Eds.), *Studies in the perception of language.* Chichester, England: Wiley.

CLARK, M. S., & MILLS, J. (1979). Interpersonal attraction in exchange and communal relationships. *Journal of Personality and Social Psychology, 37*, 12–24.

CLARK, M. S., & MILLS, J. (1993). The difference between communal and exchange relationships: What it is and is not. *Personality and Social Psychology Bulletin, 19*, 684–691.

CLARKE, A. C. (1952). An examination of the operation of residual propinquity as a factor in mate selection. *American Sociological Review, 27*, 17–22.

CLARKE-STEWART, A. (1978). And daddy makes three: The father's impact on mother and young child. *Child Development, 49*, 466–478.

CLARKE-STEWART, A. (1989). Infant day care: Malignant or maligned. *American Psychologist, 44*, 266–273.

CLARKE-STEWART, A. (1993). *Daycare* (rev. ed.). Cambridge, MA: Harvard University Press.

CLAYTON, A. H. (2001). Recognition and assessment of sexual dysfunction associated with depression [Suppl.]. *Journal of Clinical Psychiatry, 62*(3), 5–9.

CLEARFIELD, M. W., & MIX, K. S. (1999). Number versus contour length in infants' discrimination of small visual sets. *Psychological Science, 10*, 408–412.

CLECKLEY, J. (1976). *The mask of sanity* (5th ed.). St. Louis, MO: Mosby.

CLUTTON-BROCK, T. H., O'RIAIN, M. J., BROTHERTON, P. N. M., GAYNOR, D., KANSKY, R., GRIFFIN, A. S., & MANSER, M. (1999). Selfish sentinels in cooperative mammals. *Science, 284*, 1640–1644.

COBB, S. (1941). *Foundations of neuropsychiatry.* Baltimore: Williams & Wilkins.

COHEN, A., & RAFAL, R. D. (1991). Attention and feature integration: Illusory conjunctions in a patient with a parietal lobe lesion. *Psychological Science, 2*, 106–110.

COHEN, D., NISBETT, R. E., BOWDLE, B. F., & SCHWARZ, N. (1996). Insult, aggression, and the Southern culture of honor: An "experimental ethnography." *Journal of Personality and Social Psychology, 70*, 945–960.

COHEN, J. D., PERLSTEIN, W. M., BRAVER, T. S., NYSTROM, L. E., NOLL, D. C., JONIDES, J., ET AL. (1997). Temporal dynamics of brain activation during a working memory task. *Nature, 386,* 604–698,

COHEN, N. J., & SQUIRE, L. R. (1980). Preserved learning and retention of pattern-analyzing skill in amnesia: Dissociation of knowing how and knowing what. *Science, 210,* 207–210.

COHEN, R. A. (1975). Manic-depressive illness. In A. M. Freedman, H. I. Kaplan, & B. J. Sadock (Eds.), *Comprehensive textbook of psychiatry–II: Vol. 1* (pp. 1012–1024). Baltimore: Williams & Wilkins.

COHEN, Y. A. (1953). A study of interpersonal relations in a Jamaican community. Unpublished doctoral dissertation, Yale University.

COLAPINTO, J. (2000). *As nature made him: The boy who was raised as a girl.* New York: HarperCollins.

COLARUSSO, C. A., & NEMIROFF, R. A. (1981). *Adult development: A new dimension in psychodynamic theory and practice.* New York: Plenum Press.

COLE, J. O., & DAVIS, J. M. (1975). Antidepressant drugs. In A. M. Freedman, H. I. Kaplan, & B. J. Sadock (Eds.), *Comprehensive textbook of psychiatry: Vol. 2* (pp. 1941–1956). Baltimore: Williams & Wilkins.

COLE, M., & COLE, S. R. (1996). *The development of children* (3rd ed.). New York: Freeman.

COLE, M., & COLE, S. R. (2001). *The development of children* (4th ed.). New York: Worth.

COLEMAN, J. C. (1972). *Abnormal psychology and modern life* (4th ed.). Glenview, IL: Scott, Foresman.

COLLINS, A. M., & LOFTUS, E. F. (1975). A spreading activation theory of semantic processing. *Psychological Review, 82,* 407–428.

COLLINS, N. L., & MILLER, L. C. (1994). Self-disclosure and liking: A meta-analytic review. *Psychological Bulletin, 116,* 457–475.

COLLINS, W. A., MACCOBY, E. E., STEINBERG, L., HETHERINGTON, E. M., & BORNSTEIN, M. H. (2000). Contemporary research on parenting: The case for nature and nurture. *American Psychologist, 55*(2), 218–232.

COLOMBO, J. (2001). The development of visual attention in infancy. *Annual Review of Psychology, 52,* 337–367.

COLWILL, R. M., & RESCORLA, R. A. (1985). Postconditioning devaluation of a reinforcer affects instrumental responding. *Journal of Experimental Psychology: Animal Behavior Processes, 11,* 120–132.

CONEL, J. L. (1939). *The postnatal development of the human cortex: Vol. 1.* Cambridge, MA: Harvard University Press.

CONEL, J. L. (1947). *The postnatal development of the human cortex: Vol. 3.* Cambridge, MA: Harvard University Press.

CONEL, J. L. (1955). *The postnatal development of the human cortex: Vol. 5.* Cambridge, MA: Harvard University Press.

*CONSUMER REPORTS.* (1995). Mental health: Does therapy work? November, 734–739.

CONWAY, M., ANDERSON, S., LARSEN, S., DONNELLY, C., McDANIEL, M., McCLELLAND, A. G. R., ET AL. (1994). The formation of flashbulb memories. *Memory and Cognition, 22,* 326–343.

CONWAY, M. A. (1996). Autobiographical memories and autobiographical knowledge. In D. C. Rubin (Ed.), *Remembering our past: Studies in autobiographical memory* (pp. 67–93). Cambridge: Cambridge University Press.

CONWAY, M. A. (ED.). (1997). *Recovered memories and false memories.* New York: Oxford University Press.

CONWAY, M. A., COHEN, G., & STANHOPE, N. (1991). On the very long-term retention of knowledge acquired through formal education: Twelve years of cognitive psychology. *Journal of Experimental Psychology (General), 120,* 395–409.

CONWAY, M. A., & FTHENAKI, K. (1999). Disruption and loss of autobiographical memory. In L. S. Cermak (Ed.), *Handbook of neuropsychology: Memory.* Amsterdam: Elsevier.

CONWAY, M. A., & PLEYDELL-PEARCE, C. W. (2000). The construction of autobiographical memories in the self-memory system. *Psychological Review, 107*(2), 261–288.

COOK, R. G., CAVOTO, K. K., & CAVOTO, B. R. (1995). Same-different texture discrimination and concept learning by pigeons. *Journal of Experimental Psychology: Animal Behavior Processes, 21*(3), 253–260.

COONS, P. M. (1994). Confirmation of childhood abuse in child and adolescent cases of multiple personality disorder and dissociative disorder not otherwise specified. *Journal of Nervous and Mental Disease, 182,* 461–464.

COOLEY, C. H. (1902). *Human nature and the social order.* New York: Scribner's.

COOPER, J., & FAZIO, R. H. (1984). A new look at dissonance theory. In L. Berkowitz (Ed.), *Advances in experimental social psychology: Vol. 17.* New York: Academic Press.

COOPER, J., ZANNA, M. P., & GOETHALS, G. R. (1974). Mistreatment of an esteemed other as a consequence affecting dissonance reduction. *Journal of Experimental Social Psychology, 10,* 224–233.

COOPER, L. A., & SHEPARD, R. N. (1973). The time required to prepare for a rotated stimulus. *Memory and Cognition, 1,* 246–250.

COOPER, Z., & FAIRBURN, C. G. (2001). A new cognitive behavioural approach to the treatment of obesity. *Behavior Research and Therapy, 39,* 499–511.

COPPOLA, M., SENGHAS A., NEWPORT, E. L., & SUPALLA, T. (1998). Evidence for verb agreement in the gesture systems of older Nicaraguan home signers. Boston University Conference on Language Development, Boston, MA.

COREN, S., PORAC, C., & WARD, L. M. (1978 and 1984). *Sensation and perception* (1st and 2nd eds.). New York: Academic Press.

COREN, S., & WARD, L. M. (1989). *Sensation and perception* (3rd ed.). San Diego, CA: Harcourt Brace Jovanovich.

CORKIN, S. (1965). Tactually-guided maze-learning in man: Effects of unilateral cortical excisions and bilateral hippocampal lesions. *Neuropsychologia, 3,* 339–351.

CORKIN, S. (1984). Lasting consequences of bilateral medial temporal lobectomy: Clinical course and experimental findings in H.M. *Seminar in Neurology, 4,* 249–259.

CORNSWEET, T. M. (1970). *Visual perception.* New York: Academic Press.

CORY, T. L., ORMISTON, D. W., SIMMEL, E., & DAINOFF, M. (1975). Predicting the frequency of dream recall. *Journal of Abnormal Psychology, 84,* 261–266.

CORYELL, W. (1996). Psychotic depression. *Journal of Clinical Psychiatry, 57*[suppl.](3), 27–31.

COSMIDES, L. (1989). The logic of social exchange. Has natural selection shaped how humans reason? Studies with the Wason selection task. *Cognition, 31,* 187–276.

COSMIDES, L., & TOOBY, J. (1992). Cognitive adaptations for social exchange. In J. H. Barkow, L. Cosmides, & J. Tooby (Eds.), *The adapted mind: Evolutionary psychology and the generation of culture* (pp. 163–228). New York: Oxford University Press.

COST, QUALITY, AND OUTCOMES STUDY TEAM. (1995). *Cost, quality and child outcomes in child care centers, executive summary* (2nd ed.). Denver, CO: Economics Department, University of Colorado at Denver.

COSTA, P. T., & McCRAE, R. R. (1992). Four ways five factors are basic. *Personality and Individual Differences, 13,* 653–665.

COTMAN, C. W., & NEEPER, S. (1996). Activity-dependent plasticity and the aging brain. In E. L. Schneider & J. W. Rose (Eds.), *Handbook of the biology of aging* (4th ed.). San Diego: Academic Press.

COURTNEY, S. M., UNGERLEIDER, L. G., KEIL, K., & HAXBY, J. V. (1997). Transient and sustained activity in a distributed neural system for human working memory. *Nature, 38,* 608–611.

COUVILLON, P., & BITTERMAN, M. E. (1980). Some phenomena of associative conditioning in honeybees. *Journal of Comparative and Physiological Psychology, 94,* 878–885.

COWAN, G., & HODGE, C. (1996). Judgments of hate speech: The effects of target group, publicness, and behavioral responses of the target. *Journal of Applied Social Psychology, 26*(4), 355–374.

COWEY, A., & STOERIG, P. (1992). Reflections on blindsight. In A. D. Milner & M. D. Rugg, (Eds.), *The neuropsychology of consciousness* (pp. 11–38). San Diego, CA: Academic Press.

COWLES, J. T. (1937). Food-tokens as incentives for learning by chimpanzees. *Comparative Psychology Monographs, 14*(5, Serial No. 71).

COYNE, J. C., & GOTLIB, I. H. (1983). The role of cognition in depression: A critical appraisal. *Psychological Bulletin, 94,* 472–505.

CRAIGHEAD, L. W., CRAIGHEAD, W. E., KAZDIN, A. E., & MAHONEY, M. J. (EDS.). (1994). *Cognitive and behavioral interventions: An empirical approach to mental health problems.* Boston: Allyn and Bacon.

CRAIK, F., & BYRD, M. (1982). Aging and cognitive deficits: The role of attentional resources. In F. Craik & S. Trehub (Eds.), *Age and cognitive processes* (pp. 191–221). New York: Plenum.

CRAIK, F., & JENNINGS, J. M. (1992). Human memory. In F. Craik & T. Salthouse (Eds.), *Handbook of aging and cognition* (pp. 51–110). Hillsdale, NJ: Erlbaum.

CRAIK, F. I. M., & LOCKHART, R. S. (1972). Levels of processing. A framework for memory research. *Journal of Verbal Learning and Verbal Behavior, 11,* 671–684.

CRAIK, F. I. M., & TULVING, E. (1975). Depth of processing and the retention of words in episodic memory. *Journal of Experimental Psychology: General, 104,* 268–294.

CRAIK, F. I. M., & SALTHOUSE, T. A. (EDS.). (2000). *The handbook of aging and cognition* (2nd ed.). Hillsdale, NJ: Erlbaum.

CRAIK, F. I. M., & WATKINS, M. J. (1973). The role of rehearsal in short-term memory. *Journal of Verbal Learning and Verbal Behavior, 12,* 599–607.

CRAIN, S., & STEEDMAN, M. (1985). On not being led up the garden path: The use of context by the psychological syntax parser. In D. Dowty, L. Kartunnen, & A. Zwicky (Eds.), *Natural language parsing.* Cambridge: Cambridge University Press.

CRAWFORD, M., & CHAFFIN, R. (1997). The meanings of difference: Cognition in social and cultural context. In P. J. Caplan, M. Crawford, J. S. Hyde, & J. T. E. Richardson (Eds.), *Gender differences in human cognition* (pp. 81–130). New York: Oxford University Press.

CRESPI, L. (1942). Quantitative variation in incentive and performance in the white rat. *American Journal of Psychology, 55,* 467–517.

CRICK, N. R., CASAS, J. F., & MOSHER, M. (1997). Relational and overt aggression in preschool. *Developmental Psychology, 33,* 579–588.

CRICK, N. R., & GROTPETER, N. (1995). Relational aggression, gender and social psychological adjustment. *Child Development, 66,* 710–722.

CRICK, R., & KOCH, C. (1995). Are we aware of neural activity in primary visual cortex? *Nature, 375,* 121–123.

CROFT, C., O'CONNOR, T. G., KEAVENEY, L., GROOTHUES, C., RUTTER, M., & ENGLISH AND ROMANIAN ADOPTION STUDY TEAM (2001). Longitudinal change in parenting associated with developmental delay and catch-up. *Journal of Child Psychology and Psychiatry and Allied Disciplines, 42,* 649–659.

CRONBACH, L. J. (1970). *Essentials of psychology testing* (3rd ed). New York: Harper & Row.

CROOK, C. (1987). Taste and olfaction. In P. Salapateck & L. Cohen (Eds.), *Handbook of infant perception: From perception to cognition: Vol. 2* (pp. 237–264). Orlando, FL: Academic Press.

CROW, T. J. (1980). Molecular pathology of schizophrenia: More than one disease process? *British Medical Journal, 280,* 66–68.

CROW, T. J. (1982). Two dimensions of pathology in schizophrenia: Dopaminergic and non-dopaminergic. *Psychopharmacology Bulletin, 18,* 22–29.

CROW, T. J. (1985). The two-syndrome concept: Origins and current status. *Schizophrenia Bulletin, 11,* 471–486.

CROWDER, R. G. (1976). *Principles of learning and memory.* Hillsdale, NJ: Erlbaum.

CROWDER, R. G. (1982). The demise of short-term memory. *Acta Psychologica, 50,* 291–323.

CROWDER, R. G. (1985). Basic theoretical concepts in human learning and cognition. In L.-G. Nillson & T. Archer (Eds.), *Perspectives on learning and memory.* Hillsdale, NJ: Erlbaum.

CROWLEY, K., CALLANAN, M. A., TENENBAUM, H. R., & ALLEN, E. (2001). Parents explain more often to boys than to girls during shared scientific thinking. *Psychological Science, 12,* 258–261.

CRUTCHFIELD, R. S. (1955). Conformity and character. *American Psychologist, 10,* 191–199.

CSERNANSKY, J. G., & NEWCOMER, J. G. (1995). Maintenance drug treatment for schizophrenia. In F. E. Bloom & D. Kupfer (Eds.), *Psychopharmacology: The fourth generation of progress* (pp. 1267–1275). New York: Raven.

CSIBRA, G., DAVIS, G., SPRATLING, M. W., & JOHNSON, M. H. (2000). Gamma oscillations and object processing in the infant brain. *Science, 290,* 1582–1585.

CUMMINS, D. (1992). Role of analogical reasoning in induction of problem categories. *Journal of Experimental Psychology: Learning, Memory and Cognition, 18,* 1103–1124.

CUMMINS, D. D., & ALLEN, C. (EDS.) (1998). *The evolution of mind.* New York: Oxford University Press.

CUNNINGHAM, M. R., ROBERTS, A. R., BARBEE, A. P., DRUEN, P. B., & WU, C.-H. (1998). "Their ideas of beauty are, on the whole, the same as ours": Consistency and variability in the cross-cultural perception of female physical attractiveness. *Journal of Personality and Social Psychology, 68,* 261–279.

CUNNINGHAM, W. A., PREACHER, K. J., & BANAJI, M. R. (2001). Implicit attitude measures: Consistency, stability, and convergent validity. *Psychological Science, 121*(2), 163–170.

CURTISS, S. (1977). *Genie: A linguistic study of a modern-day "wild child."* New York: Academic Press.

CUTLER, A. (1994). Segmentation problems, rhythmic solutions. In L. R. Gleitman & B. Landau (Eds.), Lexical acquisition [Special Issue]. *Lingua, 92,* 81–104.

CUTLER, A., & BUTTERFIELD, S. (1992). Rhythmic cues to speech segmentation. *Journal of Memory and Language, 31,* 218–236.

CUTLER, A., MEHLER, J., NORRIS, D., & SEGUI, J. (1986). The syllable's differing role in the segmentation of French and English. *Journal of Memory and Language, 25.*

CUTLER, A., & OTAKE, T. (1994). Mora or phneme? Further evidence for language-specific listening. *Journal of Memory and Language, 33,* 824–844.

CUTTING, J. (1986). Outcome in schizophrenia: Overview. In T. A. Kerr & R. P. Snaith (Eds.), *Contemporary issues in schizophrenia* (pp. 436–440). Washington, DC: American Psychiatric Press.

DA COSTA, D. (1997). The role of psychosurgery in the treatment of selected cases of refractory schizophrenia: A reappraisal. *Schizophrenia Research, 28,* 223–230.

DABBS, J. M. (1992). Testosterone measurements in social and clinical psychology. *Journal of Social and Clinical Psychology, 11,* 302–321.

DADDS, M. R. (1995). *Families, children, and the development of dysfunction.* Thousand Oaks, CA: Sage.

DALE, A. J. D. (1975). Organic brain syndromes associated with infections. In A. M. Freedman, H. I. Kaplan, & B. J. Sadock (Eds.), *Comprehensive textbook of psychiatry—II: Vol. 1* (pp. 1121–1130). Baltimore: Williams & Wilkins.

DAMASIO, A. R. (1994). *Descartes' error: emotion, reason, and the human brain.* New York: G.P. Putnam.

DAMASIO, A. R., TRANEL, D., & DAMASIO, H. (1989). Disorders of visual recognition. In H. Goodglass & A. R. Damasio (Eds.), *Handbook of neuropsychology: Vol. 2.* New York: Elsevier.

DAMON, W. (1999). The moral development of children. *Scientific American, 281,* 72–78.

DANIEL, M. H. (1997). Intelligence testing: Status and trends. *American Psychologist, 52,* 1038–1045.

DARLEY, J., & LATANÉ, B. (1968). Bystander intervention in emergencies: Diffusion of responsibility. *Journal of Personality and Social Psychology, 10,* 202–214.

DARLEY, J. M., & BATSON, C. D. (1973). "From Jerusalem to Jericho": A study of situational and dispositional variables in helping behavior. *Journal of Personality and Social Psychology, 27,* 100–108.

DARNTON, R. (1984). The meaning of Mother Goose. *New York Review of Books,* February 2, 41–47.

DARWIN, C. (1871). *The descent of man, and selection in relation to sex.* London: Murray.

DARWIN, C. (1872a). *The origin of species.* New York: Macmillan, 6th ed., 1962.

DARWIN, C. (1872b). *The expression of the emotions in man and animals.* London: Appleton.

D'AUGELLI, A. R., & PATTERSON, C. J. (EDS.). (1995). *Lesbian, gay, and bisexual identities over the lifespan: Psychological perspectives.* New York: Oxford University Press.

DAVIDSON, A. R., & JACCARD, J. J. (1979). Variables that moderate the attitude-behavior relation: Results of a longitudinal survey. *Journal of Personality and Social Psychology, 37,* 1364–1376.

DAVIDSON, J. M. (1969). Hormonal control of sexual behavior in adult rats. In G. Rasp (Ed.), *Advances in bioscience: Vol. 1* (pp. 119–169). New York: Pergamon.

DAVIDSON, J. M. (1986). Androgen replacement therapy in a wider context: Clinical and basic aspects. In L. Dennerstein & I. Fraser (Eds.), *Hormones and behavior* (pp. 433–440). Amsterdam: International Society of Psychosomatic Obstetrics and Gynecology, Elsevier.

DAVIES, I. R. L. (1998). A study of color grouping in three languages: A test of linguistic relativity hypothesis. *British Journal of Psychology 89*(3), 433–452.

DAVIES, K. G., & WEEKS, R. D. (1993). Temporal lobectomy for intractable epilepsy: Experience with 58 cases over 21 years. *British Journal of Neurosurgery, 7,* 23–33.

DAVIS, D. E. (1964). The physiological analysis of aggressive behavior. In W. Etkin (Ed.), *Social behavior and organization among vertebrates.* Chicago: University of Chicago Press.

DAVIS, J. M. (1985a). Antipsychotic drugs. In H. I. Kaplan & J. Sadock (Eds.), *Comprehensive textbook of psychiatry* (4th ed., pp. 1481–1513). Baltimore: Williams & Wilkins.

DAVIS, J. M. (1985b). Antidepressant drugs. In H. I. Kaplan & J. Sadock (Eds.), *Comprehensive textbook of psychiatry* (4th ed., pp. 1513–1537), Baltimore: Williams & Wilkins.

DAVIS, J. O., & PHELPS, J. A. (1995). Twins with schizophrenia: Genes or germs? *Schizophrenia Bulletin, 21,* 13–18.

DAVIS, J. O., PHELPS, J. A., & BRACHA, H. S. (1995). Prenatal development of monozygotic twins and concordance for schizophrenia [erratum appears in Schizophrenia Bulletin 1995;214:539]. *Schizophrenia Bulletin, 21,* 357–366.

DAVIS, K. (1947). Final note on a case of extreme social isolation. *American Journal of Sociology, 52,* 432–437.

DAVIS, M. (1992). The role of the amygdala in conditioned fear. In J. P. Aggleton (Ed.), *The amygdala: Neurobiological aspects of emotion, memory, and mental dysfunction* (pp. 255–306). New York: Wiley Liss.

DAVIS, M. (1997). The neurophysiological basis of acoustic startle modulation: Research on fear motivation and sensory gating. In P. J. Lang, R. F. Simons, & M. T. Balaban (Eds.), *Attention and orienting: Sensory and motivational processes* (pp. 69–96). Mahwah, NJ: Erlbaum.

DAWES, R. M. (1994). *House of cards: Psychology and psychotherapy built on myth.* New York: Free Press.

DAWES, R. W. (1980). Social dilemmas. *Annual Review of Psychology, 31,* 169–193.

DE BODE, S., & CURTISS, S. (2000). Language after hemispherectomy. *Brain and Cognition, 43,* 135–138.

DE GROOT, A. D. (1965). *Thought and choice in chess.* The Hague: Mouton.

DE RENZI, E. (2000). Prosopagnosia. In M. J. Farah & T. E. Feinberg, (Eds.), *Patient-based approaches to cognitive neuroscience* (pp. 85–95). Cambridge, MA. MIT Press.

DE ROUGEMONT, D. (1940). *Love in the western world.* New York: Harcourt Brace Jovanovich.

DE VALOIS, R. L. (1965). Behavioral and electrophysiological studies of primate vision. In W. D. Neff (Ed.), *Contributions of sensory physiology: Vol. 1.* New York: Academic Press.

DE VALOIS, R. L., & DE VALOIS, K. K. (1975). Neural coding of color. In E. C. Carterette & M. P. Friedman (Eds.), *Handbook of perception: Vol. 5* (pp. 117–162). New York: Academic Press.

DE WAAL, F. (1982). *Chimpanzee politics.* New York: Harper & Row.

DEARY, I. J. (2001a). Human intelligence differences: A recent history. *Trends in Cognitive Science, 5,* 127–130.

DEARY, I. J. (2001b). Human intelligence differences: Toward a combined experimental-differential approach. *Trends in Cognitive Science, 5,* 164–170.

DEAUX, K., & KITE, M. E. (1993). Gender stereotypes. In F. L. Denmark & M. A. Paludi (Eds.), *Psychology of women: A handbook of issues and theories* (pp. 107–139). Westport, CT: Greenwood Press.

DECASPER, A. J., & FIFER, W. P. (1980). Of human bonding: Newborns prefer their mothers' voices. *Science, 208,* 1174–1176.

DECI, E. L., KOESTNER, R., & RYAN, R. M. (1999a). A meta-analytic review of experiments examining the effects of extrinsic reward. *Psychological Bulletin, 125,* 627–668.

DECI, E. L., KOESTNER, R., & RYAN, R. M. (1999b). The undermining effect is a reality after all—Extrinsic rewards, task interest, and self-determination: Reply to Eisenberger, Pierce, and Cameron (1999) and Lepper, Henderlong, and Gingras (1999). *Psychological Bulletin, 125,* 692–700.

DEECKE, L., SCHEID, P., & KORNHUBER, H. H. (1968). Distribution of readiness potential, pre-motion positivity, and motor potential of the human cerebral cortex preceding voluntary finger movements. *Experimental Brain Research, 7,* 158–68.

DEHAENE, S., & NACCACHE, L. (2001). Toward a cognitive neuroscience of consciousness: Basic evidence and workspace framework. *Cognition, 79,* 1–37.

DEHAENE-LAMBERTZ, G., DEHAENE, S., & HERTZ-PANNIER, L. (2002). Functional neuroimaging of speech perception in infants, *Science, 298,* 2013–2015.

DELL, G. S., ET AL. (1999). Connectionist models of language production: Lexical access and grammatical encoding. *Cognitive Science, 23,* 517–542.

DEMENT, W. C., & KLEITMAN, N. (1957). The relation of eye movements during sleep to dream activity: An objective method for the study of dreaming. *Journal of Experimental Psychology, 53,* 339–346.

DEMENT, W. C., & MITNER, M. M. (1993). It's time to wake up to the importance of sleep disorders [Commentary]. *Journal of the American Medical Association, 269,* 1548–1549.

DEMENT, W. C., & VAUGHAN, C. (1999). *The promise of sleep.* New York: Delacorte.

DEMENT, W. C., & WOLPERT, E. A. (1958). The relationship of eye-movements, body motility, and external stimuli to dream content. *Journal of Experimental Psychology, 55,* 543–553.

DEMO, D. H., ALLEN, K. R., & FINE, M. A. (EDS.). (2000). *Handbook of family diversity.* New York: Oxford University Press.

DEMONET, J. F., WISE, R., & FRACKOWIAK, R. S. J. (1993). Language functions explored in normal subjects by positron emission tomography: A critical review. *Human Brain Mapping, 1,* 39–47.

DENNETT, D. (1978). *Brainstorms: Philosophical essays on mind and psychology.* Montgomery, VT: Bradford Books.

DENNETT, D. C. (1991). *Consciousness explained.* Boston: Little, Brown.

DESIMONE, R., ALBRIGHT, T. D., GROSS, C. G., & BRUCE, C. (1984). Stimulus-selective properties of inferior temporal neurons in the macaque. *Journal of Neuroscience, 4,* 2051–2062.

DESTENO, D., BARTLETT, M. Y., & SALOVEY, P. (2002). Sex differences in jealousy: Evolutionary mechanism or artifact of measurement. *Journal of Personality and Social Psychology, 83,* 1103–1116.

DETTERMAN, D. K. (1987). What does reaction time tell us about intelligence? In P. A. Vernon (Ed.), *Speed of information processing and intelligence.* Norwood, NJ: Ablex.

DEUTSCH, J. A., PUERTO, A., & WANG, M. L. (1978). The stomach signals satiety. *Science, 201,* 165–167.

DEVANE, W. A., DYSARZ, F. A., JOHNSON, M. R., MELVIN, L. S., & HOWLETT, A. C. (1988). Determination and characterization of a cannabinoid receptor in rat brain. *Molecular Pharmacology, 34,* 605–613.

DEVANE, W. A., HANUS, L., BREUER, A., PERTWEE, R. G., STEVENSON, L. A., GRIFFIN, ET AL. (1992). Isolation and structure of a brain constituent that binds the cannabinoid receptor. *Science, 258,* 1946–1949.

DIAMOND, A. (1988). The abilities and neural mechanisms underlying A-not-B performance. *Child Development, 59,* 523–527.

DIAMOND, A. (1989). Developmental progression in human infants and infant monkeys, and the neural bases of A-not-B and delayed response performance. Paper presented at a meeting on "The development and neural bases of higher cognitive functions," Philadelphia, PA, May 20–24, 1989.

DIAMOND, A., & GOLDMAN-RAKIC, P. S. (1989). Comparative development of human infants and rhesus monkeys on Piaget's A-not-B task: Evidence for dependence on dorsolateral prefrontal cortex. *Experimental Brain Research, 74,* 24–40.

DIAMOND, L. M. (1998). Development of sexual orientation among adolescent and young adult women. *Developmental Psychology, 34,* 1085–1095.

DIAMOND, L. M. (2000). Sexual identity, attractions, and behavior among young sexual-minority women over a 2-year period. *Developmental Psychology, 36,* 241–250.

DIAMOND, M. (1997). Sexual identity and sexual orientation in children with traumatized or ambiguous genitalia. *The Journal of Sex Research, 34,* 199–211.

DIAMOND, M., & SIGMUNDSON, K. (1997). Sex reassignment at birth: A long-term review and clinical implications. *Archives of Pediatric and Adolescent Medicine, 151,* 298–304.

DIAMOND, R., & ROZIN, P. (1984). Activation of existing memories in the amnesic syndrome. *Journal of Abnormal Psychology, 93,* 98–105.

DICKENS, W. T., & FLYNN, J. R. (2001). Heritability estimates versus large environmental effects: The IQ paradox resolved. *Psychological Review, 108*(2), 346–369.

DICKINSON, A. (1987). Animal conditioning and learning theory. In H. J. Eysenck & I. Martin (Eds.), *Theoretical foundations of behavior theory.* New York: Plenum.

DICKS, H. V. (1972). *Licensed mass murder: A sociopsychological study of some S. S. killers.* New York: Basic Books.

DIENER, E. (1979). Deindividuation: The absence of self-awareness and self-regulation in group members. In P. Paulus (Ed.), *The psychology of group influence* (pp. 209–242). Hillsdale, NJ: Erlbaum.

DIGMAN, J. (1997). Higher-order factors of the Big Five. *Journal of Personality and Social Psychology, 73,* 1246–1256.

DION, K., BERSCHEID, E., & WALSTER, E. (1972). What is beautiful is good. *Journal of Personality and Social Psychology, 24,* 285–290.

DITTMAN, R. W., KAPPES, M. W. E., & KAPPES, M. H. (1992). Sexual behavior in adolescent and adult females with congenital adrenal hyperplasia. *Psychoneuroendocrinology, 17,* 153–170.

DOI, T. (1973). *The anatomy of dependence.* Tokyo: Kodansha.

DOLAN, M., ANDERSON, I. M., & DEAKIN, J. F. W. (2001). Relationship between 5–HT function and impulsivity and aggression in male offenders with personality disorders. *British Journal of Psychiatry, 178,* 352–359.

DOMHOFF, G. W. (1996). Finding meaning in dreams: A quantitative approach. New York: Plenum.

DOMHOFF, G. W. (2000). The problems with activation-synthesis theory. *Behavioral and Brain Sciences, 23,* 543–548.

DOMHOFF, G. W. (2001). A new neurocognitive theory of dreams. *Dreaming, 11,* 13–33.

DOMINGUEZ, R. A. (1992). Serotonergic antidepressants and their efficacy in obsessive-compulsive disorder. *Journal of Clinical Psychiatry, 53,* 56–59.

DOMJAN, M. (1983). Biological constraints on instrumental and classical conditioning: Implications for general process theory. In G. H. Bower (Ed.), *The psychology of learning and motivation: Vol. 17.* New York: Academic Press.

DORNBUSCH, S. M., RITTER, P. L., LIEDERMAN, P. H., ROBERTS, D. F., & FRALEIGH, M. J. (1987). The relation of parenting style to adolescent school performance Schools and development [Special Issue]. *Child Development, 58,* 1244–1257.

DOUVAN, E., & ADELSON, J. (1958). The psychodynamics of social mobility in adolescent boys. *Journal of Abnormal and Social Psychology, 56,* 31–44.

DOVIDIO, J. F., & GAERTNER, S. L. (1999). Reducing prejudice: Combating intergroup biases. *Current Directions in Psychological Science, 8*(4), 101–105.

DOWTY, D. (1991). Thematic proto-roles and argument selection. *Language, 67,* 547–619.

DRESCHER, J. (1998). I'm your handyman: A history of reparative therapies. *Journal of Homosexuality, 36,* 19–42.

DRISCOLL, R., DAVIS, K. E., & LIPETZ, M. E. (1972). Parental interference and romantic love: The Romeo and Juliet effect. *Journal of Personality and Social Psychology, 24,* 1–10.

DUKER, P. C, & SEYS, D. M. (1996). Long-term use of electrical aversion treatment with self-injurious behavior. *Research in Developmental Disabilities, 17,* 293–301.

DUNBAR, K., & BLANCHETTE, I. (2001). The in vivo/in vitro approach to cognition: The case of analogy. *Trends in Cognitive Sciences, 5*(8), 334–339.

DUNCAN, J. (1994). Attention, intelligence, and the frontal lobes. In M. Gazzaniga (Ed.), *The cognitive neurosciences.* Cambridge, MA: MIT Press.

DUNCAN, J., & OWEN, A. M. (2000). Common regions of the human frontal lobe recruited by diverse cognitive demands. *Trends in Neurosciences, 23*(10), 475–483.

DUNCAN, J., RUDIGER, J. S., KOLODNY, J., BOR, D., HERZOG, H., AHMED, A., ET AL. (2000). A neural basis for general intelligence. *Science, 289,* 457–460.

DUNCKER, K. (1929). Über induzierte Bewegung. *Psychologische Forschung, 12,* 180–259.

DUNCKER, K. (1945). On problem solving. *Psychological Monographs,* (Whole No. 270), 1–113.

DUNNING, D., & COHEN, G. L. (1992). Egocentric definitions of traits and abilities in social judgment. *Journal of Personality and Social Psychology, 63,* 341–355.

DUNNING, D., MEYEROWITZ, J. A., & HOLZBERG, A. D. (1989). Ambiguity and self-evaluation: The role of idiosyncratic trait definitions in self-serving assessments of ability. *Journal of Personality and Social Psychology, 57,* 1082–1090.

DUNPHY, D. C. (1963). The social structure of urban adolescent peer groups. *Sociometry, 26,* 230–246.

DUPOUX, E., ET AL (1997). A distressing "deafness" in French? *Journal of Memory and Language, 36,* 406–421.

DUTTON, D. G., & ARON, A. P. (1974). Some evidence for heightened sexual attraction under conditions of high anxiety. *Journal of Personality and Social Psychology, 30,* 510–517.

DYKEMA, J., BERGBOWER, K., DOCTORA, J. D., & PETERSON, C. (1996). An attributional style questionnaire for general use. *Journal of Psychoeducational Assessment, 14,* 100–108.

EAGLE, M. N., & WOLITSKY, D. L. (1992). Psychoanalytic theories of psychotherapy. In D. K. Freedheim (Ed.), *History of psychotherapy.* Washington, DC: American Psychological Association.

EAGLY, A. H., & CHAIKEN, S. (1984). Cognitive theories of persuasion. In L. Berkowitz (Ed.), *Advances in experimental social psychology: Vol. 17.* New York: Academic Press.

EAGLY, A. H., & CHAIKEN, S. (1993). *The psychology of attitudes.* Fort Worth, TX: Harcourt Brace Jovanovich.

EAGLY, A. H., & CROWLEY, M. (1986). Gender and helping behavior: A meta-analytic review of the social psychological literature. *Psychological Bulletin, 100,* 283–308.

EAGLY, A. H., & WOOD, W. (1999). The origins of sex differences in human behavior: Evolved dispositions versus social roles. *American Psychologist, 54*(6), 408–423.

EAGLY, A. H., ASHMORE, R. D., MAKHIJANI, M. G., & LONGO, L. C. (1991). What is beautiful is good, but . . . : A meta-analytic review of research on the physical attractiveness stereotype. *Psychological Bulletin, 110,* 109–128.

EARLES, J. L., CONNOR, L. T., SMITH, A. D., & PARK, D. C. (1998). Interrelations of age, self-reported health, speed, and memory. *Psychology and Aging, 12,* 675–683.

EATON, W. O., & YU, A. P. (1989). Are sex differences in child motor activity a function of sex differences in maturational status? *Child Development, 60,* 1005–1011.

EBBESEN, E. B., KJOS, G. L., & KONECNI, V. J. (1976). Spatial ecology: Its effects on the choice of friends and enemies. *Journal of Experimental Social Psychology, 12*(6), 505–518.

EBBINGHAUS, H. (1885). *Memory.* New York: Teacher's College, Columbia University, 1913. Reprint edition, New York: Dover, 1964.

ECCLES, J. C. (1973). *The understanding of the brain.* New York: McGraw-Hill.

EDELMAN, G. M., MURRAY, B. A., MEGE, R. M., CUNNINGHAM, B. A., & GALLIN, W. J. (1987) Cellular expression of liver and neural cell adhesion molecules after transfection with their cDNAs results in specific cell-cell binding. *Proceedings of the National Academy of Science USA. December, 84*(23), 8502–8506.

EFRON, R. (1990). *The decline and fall of hemispheric specialization.* Hillsdale, NJ: Erlbaum.

EGELAND, J. A., & HOSTETTER, A. M. (1983). Amish study, 1: Affective disorders among the Amish. *American Journal of Psychiatry, 140,* 56–71.

EGETH, H., JONIDES, J., & WALL, S. (1972). Parallel processing of multielement displays. *Cognitive Psychology, 3,* 674–698.

EGLIN, M., ROBERTSON, L. C., & KNIGHT, R. T. (1989). Visual search performance in the neglect syndrome. *Journal of Cognitive Neuroscience, 1,* 372–385.

EHRHARDT, A. A. (1984). Gender differences: A biological perspective. In R. A. Dienstbier & T. B. Sonderegger (Eds.), *Nebraska Symposium on Motivation* (pp. 37–58). Lincoln, NE: University of Nebraska.

EIMAS, P. D., SIQUELAND, E. R., JUSCZYK, P., & VIGORITO, J. (1971). Speech perception in infants. *Science, 171,* 303–306.

EISENBERG, A. R. (1999). Emotion talk among Mexican American and Anglo American mothers and children from two social classes. *Merrill-Palmer Quarterly, 45*(2), 267–284.

EISENBERGER, R., PIERCE, W. D., & CAMERON, J. (1999). Effects of reward on intrinsic motivation—negative, neutral, and positive: Comment on Deci, Koestner, and Ryan (1999). *Psychological Bulletin, 125,* 677–691.

EKMAN, P. (1972). Universals and cultural differences in facial expressions of emotion. In J. Cole (Ed.), *Nebraska Symposium on Motivation, 1971: Vol. 19* (pp. 207–283). Lincoln, NE: University of Nebraska Press.

EKMAN, P. (1973). Cross-cultural studies of facial expression. In P. Ekman (Ed.), *Darwin and facial expression* (pp. 169–222). New York: Academic Press.

EKMAN, P. (1977). Biological and cultural contributions to body and facial movement. In J. Blacking (Ed.), *The anthropology of the body* (A. S. A. Monograph 15). London: Academic Press.

EKMAN, P. (1980). *The face of man: Expression of universal emotions in a New Guinea village.* New York: Garland STPM Press.

EKMAN, P. (1984). Expression and the nature of emotion. In P. Ekman & K. Scherer (Eds.), *Approaches to emotion* (pp. 319–343). Hillsdale, NJ: Erlbaum.

EKMAN, P. (1985). *Telling lies.* New York: Norton.

EKMAN, P. (1992). An argument for basic emotions. *Cognition and Emotion, 6,* 169–200.

EKMAN, P. (1994). Strong evidence for universals in facial expression: A reply to Russell's mistaken critique. *Psychological Bulletin, 115,* 268–287.

EKMAN, P., & FRIESEN, W. V. (1971). Constants across cultures in the face and emotion. *Journal of Personality and Social Psychology, 17*(2), 124–129.

EKMAN, P., & FRIESEN, W. V. (1975). *Unmasking the face.* Englewood Cliffs, NJ: Prentice-Hall.

EKMAN, P., & FRIESEN, W. V. (1986). A new pan-cultural facial expression of emotion. *Motivation and Emotion, 10,* 159–168.

EKMAN, P., FRIESEN, W. V., & O'SULLIVAN, M. (1988). Smiles when lying. *Journal of Personality and Social Psychology, 54,* 414–420.

EKMAN, P., LEVENSON, R. W., & FRIESEN, W. V. (1983). Autonomic nervous system activity distinguishes among emotions. *Science, 221,* 1208–1210.

EKMAN, P., & OSTER, H. (1979). Facial expression of emotion. *Annual Review of Psychology, 30,* 527–554.

ELDER, G. H., JR. (1980). Adolescence in historical perspective. In J. Adelson (Ed.), *Handbook of adolescent psychology.* New York: Wiley.

ELKIN, I., SHEA, M. T., WATKINS, J. T., IMBER, S. D., SOTSKY, S. M., COLLINS, J. S., ET AL. (1989). National Institute of Mental Health treatment of depression collaborative research program: General effectiveness of treatments. *Archives of General Psychiatry, 46,* 971–982.

ELKIN, R. A., & LEIPPE, M. R. (1986). Physiological arousal, dissonance, and attitude change: Evidence for a dissonance-arousal link and a "don't remind me" effect. *Journal of Personality and Social Psychology, 51,* 55–65.

ELKINS, R. L. (1991). An appraisal of chemical aversion emetic therapy approaches to alcoholism treatment. *Behaviour Research and Therapy, 29,* 387–413.

ELLEMERS, N., SPEARS, R., & DOOSJE, B. (2002). Self and social identity. *Annual Review of Psychology, 53,* 161–186.

ELLENBERGER, H. F. (1970). *The discovery of the unconscious.* New York: Basic Books.

ELLIOT, A. J., & DEVINE, P. G. (1994). On the motivational nature of cognitive dissonance: Dissonance as psychological discomfort. *Journal of Personality and Social Psychology, 67*(3), 382–394.

ELLIOT, M. A., & MULLER, H. J. (2000). Evidence for 40–Hz oscillatory short-term visual memory revealed by human reaction-time measurements. *Journal of Experimental Psychology: Learning, Memory, and Cognition, 26,* 7093–7718.

ELLIS, A. (1962). *Reason and emotion in psychotherapy.* Secaucus, NJ: Lyle Stuart.

ELLIS, L., & AMES, M. A. (1987). Neurohormonal functioning and sexual orientation: A theory of homosexuality-heterosexuality. *Psychological Bulletin, 101,* 233–258.

ELLSWORTH, P. C. (1994). Sense, culture, and sensibility. In S. Kitayama & H. R. Markus (Eds.), *Emotion and culture* (pp. 23–50). Washington, DC: American Psychological Association.

ELMAN, J. L. (1991). Distributed representation, simple recurrent networks, and grammatical structure. *Machine Learning, 7,* 195–225.

ELMS, A. C., & MILGRAM, S. (1966). Personality characteristics associated with obedience and defiance toward authoritative command. *Journal of Experimental Research in Personality, 1,* 282–289.

ELPHICK, M. R., & EGERTOVA, M. (2001). The neurobiology and evolution of cannabinoid signalling. *Philosophical Transactions: Biological Sciences, 356,* 381–408.

EMMELKAMP, P. M. G. (1986). Behavior therapy with adults. In S. L. Garfield & A. E. Bergin (Eds.), *Handbook of psychotherapy and behavior change* (3rd ed.). New York: Wiley.

EMMERICH, W. (1966). Continuity and stability in early social development, II. Teacher ratings. *Child Development, 37,* 17–27.

ENGLE, R. W., CANTOR, J., & CARULLO, J. J. (1992). Individual differences in working memory and comprehension: A test of four hypotheses. *Journal of Experimental Psychology Learning, Memory, and Cognition, 18*(5), 972–992.

ENGLE, R. W., TUHOLSKI, S. W., LAUGHLIN, J. E., & CONWAY, A. R. A. (1999). Working memory, short-term memory, and general fluid intelligence: A latent variable approach. *Journal of Experimental Psychology: General, 128,* 309–331.

ENQUIST, M., & LEIMAR, O. (1990). The evolution of fatal fighting. *Animal Behaviour, 39,* 1–9.

EPSTEIN, H. T. (1978). Growth spurts during brain development: Implications for educational policy and practice. In J. S. Chard & A. F. Mirsky (Eds.), *Education and the brain.* Chicago: University of Chicago Press.

EPSTEIN, W. (1961). The influence of syntactical structure on learning. *American Journal of Psychology, 74,* 80–85.

ERDELYI, M., & GOLDBERG, B. (1979). Let's not sweep repression under the rug: Toward a cognitive psychology of repression. In J. F. Kihlstrom, & F. J. Evans (Eds.), *Functional disorders of memory.* Hillsdale, NJ: Erlbaum.

ERDELYI, M. H. (1985). *Psychoanalysis: Freud's cognitive psychology.* New York: Freeman.

ERIKSEN, C. W., & HOFFMAN, J. E. (1972). Temporal and spatial characteristics of selective encoding from multielement displays. *Perception and Psychophysics, 12,* 201–204.

ERIKSON, E. H. (1963). *Childhood and society.* New York: Norton.

ERIKSON, E. H. (1974). *Dimensions of a new identity: The Jefferson lectures in the humanities.* New York: Norton.

ERIKSON, E. H., & COLES, R. (EDS.). (2000). *The Erik Erikson reader.* New York: Norton.

ERIKSON, E. H., ERIKSON, J. M., & KIVNICK, H. Q. (1989). *Vital involvement in old age.* New York: Norton.

ERON, L. D. (1950). A normative study of the thematic apperception test. *Psychological Monographs, 64*(whole No. 315).

ERON, L. D., & HUESMANN, L. R. (1980). Adolescent aggression and television. *Annals of the New York Academy of Sciences, 347,* 319–331.

ERON, L. D., & HUESMANN, L. R. (1985). The role of television in the development of prosocial and antisocial behavior. In D. Olweus, M. Radke-Yarrow & J. Block (Eds.), *Development of antisocial and prosocial behavior.* Orlando, FL: Academic Press.

ESSER, J. K. (1998). Alive and well after 25 years: A review of groupthink research. *Organizational Behavior and Human Decision Processes, 73*(2–3), 116–141.

ESTES, W. K., & SKINNER, B. F. (1941). Some quantitative properties of anxiety. *Journal of Experimental Psychology, 29,* 390–400.

EVANS, G. W., LEPORE, S. J., & ALLEN, K. M. (2000). Cross-cultural differences in tolerance for crowding: Fact or fiction? *Journal of Personality and Social Psychology, 79,* 204–210.

EVANS, J. S. B. T., NEWSTEAD, S. E., & BYRNE, R. M. J. (1993). *Human reasoning: The psychology of deduction.* London: Erlbaum.

EVERSON, C. A., & TOTH, L. A. (2000). Systematic bacterial invasion induced by sleep deprivation. *American Journal of Physiology: Regulator, Integrative and Comparative Physiology, 278,* R905–R916.

EXNER, J. E. (1974). *The Rorschach system.* New York: Grune and Stratton.

EXNER, J. E. (1978). *A comprehensive system: Current research and advanced interpretation: Vol. 2.* New York: Wiley Interscience.

EXNER, J. E. (ED.). (1995). *Issues and methods in Rorschach research.* Mahwah, NJ: Erlbaum.

EXNER, J. E., & CLARK, B. (1978). The Rorschach. In B. B. Wolman (Ed.), *Clinical diagnosis of mental disorders.* New York: Plenum.

EXNER, J. E., JR. (1993). *The Rorschach: A comprehensive system: Vol. 1. Basic foundations* (3rd ed). New York: Wiley.

EYER, D. E. (1992). *Mother-infant bonding: A scientific fiction.* New Haven, CT: Yale University Press.

EYSENCK, H. J. (1961). The effects of psychotherapy. In H. J. Eysenck (Ed.), *Handbook of abnormal psychology* (pp. 697–725). New York: Basic Books.

EYSENCK, H. J. (1986). Toward a new model of intelligence. *Personality and Individual Differences, 7*(5), 731–736.

EYSENCK, H. J., & EYSENCK, S. B. G. (1983). Recent advances: The cross-cultural study of personality. In J. N. Butcher, & C. D. Spielberger (Eds.), *Advances in personality assessment: Vol. 2* (pp. 41–72). Hillsdale, NJ: Erlbaum.

EYSENCK, H. J. VERSUS KAMIN, L. (1981). *The intelligence controversy.* New York: Wiley.

EYSENCK, H. J., & RACHMAN, S. (1965). *The causes and cures of neurosis.* San Diego, CA: Robert E. Knapp.

FAGOT, B. I. (1995). Psychosocial and cognitive determinants of early gender-role development. *Annual Review of Sex Research, 6,* 1–31.

FAGOT, B. I., LEINBACH, M. D., & HAGEN, R. (1986). Gender labeling and adoption of same-sex behaviors. *Developmental Psychology, 22,* 440–443.

FALLON, A. E., & ROZIN, P. (1985). Sex differences in perceptions of desirable body shape. *Journal of Abnormal Psychology, 94,* 102–105.

FANCHER, R. E. (1987). *The intelligence men: Makers of the IQ controversy.* New York: Norton.

FANT, L. G. (1972). *Ameslan: An introduction to American Sign Language.* Silver Springs, MD: National Association of the Deaf.

FARAH, M. (1988). Is visual imagery really visual? Overlooked evidence from neuropsychology. *Psychological Review, 95,* 307–317.

FARAH, M. (1990). *Visual agnosia.* Cambridge, MA: MIT Press.

FARAH, M. J., & FEINBERG, T. E. (2000). Disorders of perception and awareness. In M. J. Farah & T. E. Feinberg, (Eds.), *Patient-based approaches to cognitive neuroscience* (pp. 143–154). Cambridge, MA: MIT Press.

FARIS, R. E. L., & DUNHAM, H. W. (1939). *Mental disorders in urban areas.* Chicago: University of Chicago Press.

FAUSTO-STERLING, A. (1993). The five sexes: Why male and female are not enough. *The Sciences,* March/April, 20–24.

FAUSTO-STERLING, A. (2000). *Sexing the body: Gender politics and the construction of sexuality.* New York: Basic Books.

FEDER, H. H. (1984). Hormones and sexual behavior. *Annual Review of Psychology, 35,* 165–200.

FEENEY, B. C., & COLLINS, N. L. (2001). Predictors of caregiving in adult intimate relationships: An attachment theoretical perspective. *Journal of Personality and Social Psychology, 80*(6), 972–994.

FEINGOLD, A. (1988). Matching for attractiveness in romantic partners and same-sex friends: A meta-analysis and theoretical critique. *Psychological Bulletin, 104,* 226–232.

FEINGOLD, A. (1992). Good-looking people are not what we think. *Psychological Bulletin, 111,* 304–341.

FEINGOLD, A. (1994). Gender differences in personality: A meta-analysis. *Psychological Bulletin, 116,* 429–456.

FEINMAN, J. A., & DUNNER, D. L. (1996). The effect of alcohol and substance abuse on the course of bipolar affective disorder. *Journal of Affective Disorders, 37,* 43–49.

FELDMAN, H., GOLDIN-MEADOW, S., & GLEITMAN, L. R. (1978). Beyond Herodotus: The creation of language by linguistically deprived deaf children. In A. Lock (Ed.), *Action, gesture, and symbol: The emergence of language* (pp. 351–414). New York: Academic Press.

FERGUSON, J. M. (2001). The effects of antidepressants on sexual functioning in depressed patients: A review [Suppl.]. *Journal of Clinical Psychiatry, 62*(3), 22–34.

FERNALD, A. (1985). Four-month-old infants prefer to listen to motherese. *Infant Behavior and Development, 8*, 181–195.

FERNALD, A. (1992). Human maternal vocalizations to infants as biologically relevant signals: An evolutionary perspective. In J. H. Barkow, L. Cosmides, & J. Tooby (Eds.), *The adapted mind* (pp. 391–428). New York: Oxford.

FERNALD, A., & MORIKAWA, H. (1993). Common themes and cultural variations in Japanese and American mothers' speech to infants. *Child Development, 64*, 637–656.

FERNANDEZ-DOLS, J. M., & RUIZ-BELDA, M.-A. (1995). Are smiles a sign of happiness? Gold medal winners at the Olympic Games. *Journal of Personality and Social Psychology, 69*, 1113–1119.

FESHBACH, N. (1969). Sex differences in children's mode of aggressive responses toward outsiders. *Merrill-Palmer Quarterly, 15*, 249–258.

FESHBACH, S. (1970). Aggression. In P. H. Mussen (Ed.), *Carmichael's manual of child psychology* (3rd ed., pp. 159–260). New York: Wiley.

FESTINGER, L. (1954). A theory of social comparison processes. *Human Relations, 7*, 117–140.

FESTINGER, L., & CARLSMITH, J. M. (1959). Cognitive consequences of forced compliance. *Journal of Abnormal and Social Psychology, 58*, 203–210.

FESTINGER, L., PEPITONE, A., & NEWCOMB, T. (1952). Some consequences of deindividuation in a group. *Journal of Abnormal and Social Psychology, 47*, 387–389.

FIEDLER, F. E. (1978). Recent developments in research on the contingency model. In L. Berkowitz (Ed.), *Group processes.* New York: Academic Press.

FIELD, T. (1978). Interaction behaviors of primary versus secondary caretaker fathers. *Developmental Psychology, 14*, 183–184.

FIGLEY, C. R. (1978). Symptoms of delayed combat stress among a college sample of Vietnam veterans. *Military Medicine, 143*, 107–110.

FILLMORE, C. (1968). The case for case. In E. Bach & R. Harms (Eds.), *Universals in linguistic theory.* New York: Holt, Rinehart and Winston.

FILLMORE, C. (1982). Towards a descriptive framework for spatial deixis. In R. J. Jarvella & W. Klein (Eds.), *Speech, place, and action: Studies in deixis and related topics.* Chichester, England: Wiley.

FINE, A. (1986). Transplantation in the central nervous system. *Scientific American, August*, 52–58.

FINK, B., & PENTON-VOAK, I. (2002). Evolutionary psychology of facial attractiveness. *Current directions in Psychological Science, 11*, 154–158.

FINK, M. (2001). Convulsive therapy: A review of the first 55 years. *Journal of Affective Disorders, 63*, 1–15.

FINKE, R. (1993). Mental imagery and creative discovery. In B. Roskos-Ewoldsen, M. J. Intons-Peterson, & R. Anderson (Eds.), *Imagery, creativity, and discovery* (pp. 255–285). New York: North-Holland.

FINKE, R., WARD, T., & SMITH, S. (1992). *Creative cognition: Theory, research and applications.* Cambridge, MA: MIT Press.

FISHER, C., GLEITMAN, H., & GLEITMAN, L. (1991). On the semantic content of subcategorization frames. *Cognitive Psychology, 23*(3), 331–392.

FISHER, C., HALL, G., RAKOWITZ, S., & GLEITMAN, L. R. (1994). When it is better to receive than to give. In L. R. Gleitman & B. Landau (Eds.), *Lexical acquisition, Lingua* [Special Issue], *92*, 333–375.

FISHER, D., BEUTLER, L. E., & WILLIAMS, O. B. (1999). Making assessment relevant to treatment planning: The STS Clinician Rating Form. Systemic Treatment Selection. *Journal of Clinical Psychology, 55*, 825–842.

FISHER, R. P., & CRAIK, F. I. M. (1977). The interaction between encoding and retrieval operations in cued recall. *Journal of Experimental Psychology: Human Learning and Memory, 3*, 701–711.

FISHER, S., & GREENBERG, R. P. (1977). *The scientific credibility of Freud's theory and therapy.* New York: Basic Books.

FISHER, S., & GREENBERG, R. P. (1996). *Freud scientifically appraised.* New York: Wiley.

FISHER, S., & GREENBERG, R. P. (EDS.). (1989). *The limits of biological treatments for psychological distress.* Hillsdale, NJ: Erlbam.

FISKE, A. P., KITAYAMA, S., MARKUS, H. R., & NISBETT, R. E. (1998). The cultural matrix of social psychology. In D. T. Gilbert, S. T. Fiske, & G. Lindzey, G. (Eds.), *The handbook of social psychology* (4th ed., pp. 915–981). New York: McGraw-Hill.

FISKE, A. P., & TETLOCK, P. E. (1997). Taboo trade-offs: Reactions to transactions that transgress the spheres of justice. *Political Psychology, 18*(2), 255–297.

FISKE, D. W. (1949). Consistency of the factorial structures of personality ratings from different sources. *Journal of Abnormal Social Psychology, 44*, 329–344.

FISKE, S. T. (1998). Stereotyping, prejudice, and discrimination. In D. T. Gilbert, S. T. Fiske, & G. Lindzey (Eds.), *The handbook of social psychology* (4th ed., pp. 357–411). New York: McGraw-Hill.

FITZGERALD, F. T. (1981). The problem of obesity. *Annual Review of Medicine, 32*, 221–231.

FIVUSH, R. (1998). The stories we tell: How language shapes autobiography. *Applied Cognitive Psychology, 12*(5), 483–487.

FIVUSH, R., BROTMAN, M. A., BUCKNER, J. P., & GOODMAN, S. H. (2000). Gender differences in parent-child emotion narratives. *Sex Roles, 42*(3–4), 233–253.

FIVUSH, R. & SALES, J. (2003). Children's memories of emotional events. In D. Reisberg & P. Hertel (Eds.), *Memory and emotion.* New York: Oxford University Press.

FIVUSH, R., & SCHWARZMUELLER, A. (1998). Children remember childhood: Implications for childhood amnesia. *Applied Cognitive Psychology, 12*, 455–474.

FLANAGAN, O. (1994). *Consciousness reconsidered.* Cambridge, MA: Bradford Books.

FLANAGAN, O. (2000). *Dreaming souls: Sleep, dreams, and the evolution of the conscious mind.* New York: Oxford University Press.

FLANDERS, J. P. (1968). A review of research on imitative behavior. *Psychological Bulletin, 69*, 316–337.

FLAVELL, J. H. (1970). Developmental studies of mediated memory. In H. W. Reese, & L. P. Lipsitt (Eds.), *Advances in child development and behavior: Vol. 5.* New York: Academic Press.

FLAVELL, J. H. (1977). *Cognitive development.* Englewood Cliffs, NJ: Prentice-Hall.

FLAVELL, J. H. (1985). *Cognitive development* (2nd ed.). Englewood Cliffs, NJ: Prentice-Hall.

FLAVELL, J. H., & WELLMAN, H. M. (1977). Metamemory. In R. V. Kail, Jr. & J. W. Hagen (Eds.), *Perspectives on the development of memory and cognition* (pp. 3–34). Hillsdale, NJ: Erlbaum.

FLAVELL, J. H., BEACH, D. H., & CHINSKY, J. M. (1966). Spontaneous verbal rehearsal in a memory task as a function of age. *Child Development, 37*, 283–299.

FLAVELL, J. H., FLAVELL, E. R., & GREEN, F. L. (1983). Development of the appearance-reality distinction. *Cognitive Psychology, 15*, 95–120.

FLEMING, J. H., & RUDMAN, L. A. (1993). Between a rock and a hard place: Self concept regulating and communicative properties of distancing behaviors. *Journal of Personality and Social Psychology, 64*(1), 44–59.

FLODERUS-MYRHED, B., PEDERSEN, N., & RASMUSON, L. (1980). Assessment of heritability for personality, based on a short form of the Eysenck Personality Inventory: A study of 12,898 twin pairs. *Behavior Genetics, 10*, 153–162.

FLUOXETINE BULIMIA NERVOSA COLLABORATIVE STUDY GROUP. (1992). Fluoxetine in the treatment of bulimia nervosa: A multicenter, placebo-controlled, double-blind trial. *Archives of General Psychiatry, 49*, 139–147.

FLYNN, J. R. (1984). The mean IQ of Americans: Massive gains 1932 to 1978. *Psychological Bulletin, 95*(1), 29–51.

FLYNN, J. R. (1987). Massive IQ gains in 14 nations: What IQ tests really measure. *Psychological Bulletin, 101*(2), 171–191.

FLYNN, J. R. (1991). *Asian Americans: Achievement beyond IQ.* Hillsdale, NJ: Erlbaum.

FLYNN, J. R. (1999). Searching for justice: The discovery of IQ gains over time. *American Psychologist, 54*, 5–20.

FOARD, C. F. (1975). Recall subsequent to tip-of-the-tongue experience. Unpublished first-year graduate research paper, University of Pennsylvania, Philadelphia.

FOCH, T. T., & McCLEARN, G. E. (1980). Genetics, body weight, and obesity. In A. J. Stunkard (Ed.), *Obesity* (pp. 48–71). Philadelphia: Saunders.

FODOR, J. (1997). connectionism and the problem of systematicity (continued): Why Smolensky's solution still doesn't work. *Cognition, 62*(1), 109–119.

FODOR, J. A. (1983). *The modularity of mind.* Cambridge, MA: MIT Press, Bradford Books.

FODOR, J. A. (1992). A theory of the child's theory of mind. *Cognition, 44,* 283–296.

FONG, G., & NISBETT, R. (1991). Immediate and delayed transfer of training effects in statistical reasoning. *Journal of Experimental Psychology: General, 120,* 34–45.

FONG, G., KRANTZ, D., & NISBETT, R. (1986). The effects of statistical training on thinking about everyday problems. *Cognitive Psychology, 18,* 253–292.

FORD, C. S., & BEACH, F. A. (1951). *Patterns of sexual behavior.* New York: Harper & Row.

FORGATCH, M. S., PATTERSON, G. R., & RAY, J. A. (1996). Divorce and boys' adjustment problems: Two paths with a single model. In E. M. Hetherington, & E. A. Blechmen (Eds.), *Stress, coping, and resiliency in children and families. Family research consortium: Advances in family research* (pp. 67–105). Mahwah, NJ: Erlbaum.

FOSSHAGE, J. L. (1983). The psychological function of dreams: A revised psychoanalytic perspective. *Psychoanalysis and Contemporary Thought, 6,* 641–669.

FOUCAULT, M. (1965). *Madness and civilization.* New York: Random House.

FOULKES, D. (1983). Cognitive processes during sleep: Evolutionary aspects. In A. Mayes (Ed.), *Sleep mechanisms and functions in humans and animals: An evolutionary perspective* (pp. 313–337). Wokington, UK: Van Nostrand Reinhold.

FOULKES, D. (1999). *Children's dreaming and the development of consciousness.* Cambridge, MA: Harvard University Press.

FOUTS, R. S. (1972). Use of guidance in teaching sign language to a chimpanzee (Pantroglodytes). *Journal of Comparative and Physiological Psychology, 80,* 515–522.

FOUTS, R. S., HIRSCH, A. D., & FOUTS, D. H. (1982). Cultural transmission of a human language in a chimpanzee mother-infant relationship. In H. E. Fitzgerald, J. A. Mullins, & P. Gage (Eds.), *Child nurturance: Vol. 3. Studies of development in nonhuman primates* (pp. 159–169). New York: Plenum.

FRANKEL, F. H. (1993). Adult reconstruction of childhood events in the multiple personality disorder literature. *American Journal of Psychiatry, 150,* 954–958.

FRANKL, V. E. (1966). *The doctor and the soul.* New York: Knopf.

FRAZIER, L., & FODOR, J. D. (1978). The sausage machine: A new two-stage parsing model. *Cognition, 6,* 291–325.

FREED, C. R., GREENE, P. E., BREEZE, R. E., TSAI, W. Y., DuMOUCHEL, W., KAO, R., ET AL. (2001). Transplantation of embryonic dopamine neurons for severe Parkinson's disease. *New England Journal of Medicine, 344*(10), 710–719.

FREEDMAN, J. L., & FRASER, S. C. (1966). Compliance without pressure: The foot-in-the-door technique. *Journal of Personality and Social Psychology, 4,* 195–202.

FREEMAN, A., SIMON, K. M., BEUTLER, L. E., & ARKOWITZ, H. (EDS.). (1989). *Comprehensive handbook of cognitive therapy.* New York: Plenum.

FREEMAN, D. (1983). *Margaret Mead and Samoa: The making and unmaking of an anthropological myth.* Cambridge, MA: Harvard University Press.

FREEMAN, D. (1986). Rejoinder to Patience and Smith. *American Anthropologist, 88,* 161–167.

FREMOUW, W. J., PERCZEL, M., & ELLIS, T. E. (1990). *Suicide risk: Assessment and response guidelines.* Elmsford, NY: Pergamon.

FREUD, A. (1946). *The ego and the mechanisms of defense.* London: Hogarth Press.

FREUD, S. (1900). The interpretation of dreams. In J. Strachey (Trans. and Ed.), *The complete psychological works: Vols. 4–5.* New York: Norton, 1976.

FREUD, S. (1901). *The psychopathology of everyday life.* A. Tyson (Trans.). New York: Norton, 1971.

FREUD, S. (1905). Three essays on the theory of sexuality. In J. Strachey (Trans. and Ed.), *The complete psychological works: Vol. 7.* New York: Norton, 1976.

FREUD, S. (1908). Character and anal eroticism. In P. Rieff (Ed.), *Collected papers of Sigmund Freud: Character and culture.* New York: Collier Books, 1963.

FREUD, S. (1911). Psychoanalytic notes upon an autobiographical account of a case of paranoia (dementia paranoides). In J. Strachey (Trans. and Ed.), *The complete psychological works: Vol. 12.* New York: Norton, 1976.

FREUD, S. (1917). *A general introduction to psychoanalysis.* J. Riviere (Trans.). New York: Washington Square Press, 1952.

FREUD, S. (1923). *The ego and the id.* J. Riviere (Trans.). New York: Norton, 1962.

FREUD, S. (1925). Some psychical consequences of the anatomical distinction between the sexes. In J. Strachey (Trans. and Ed.), *The complete psychological works: Vol. 19.* New York: Norton, 1976.

FREUD, S. (1933). Femininity. In J. Strachey (Trans. and Ed.), *The complete psychological works: Vol. 22* (pp. 112–115). New York: Norton, 1976.

FREUD, S., & BREUER, J. (1895). Studies on hysteria. In J. Strachey (Trans. and Ed.), *The complete psychological works: Vol. 2.* New York: Norton, 1976.

FREUND, A. M., & BALTES, P. B. (1998). Selection, optimization, and compensation as strategies of life management: Correlations with subjective indicators of successful aging. *Psychology and Aging, 13,* 531–543.

FREYD, J. (1996). *Betrayal trauma: The logic of forgetting childhood abuse.* Cambridge, MA: Harvard University Press.

FRIDLUND, A. J. (1997). The new ethology of human facial expressions. In J. A. Russell & J. Fernandez-Dols (Eds.), *The psychology of facial expression* (pp. 103–129). Cambridge: Cambridge University Press.

FRIDLUND, A. J. (1991). Evolution and facial action in reflex, social motive, and paralanguage. *Biological Psychology, 32*(1), 3–100.

FRIDLUND, A. J. (1994). *Human facial expression: An evolutionary view.* San Diego: Academic Press.

FRIDLUND, A. J., & DUCHAINE, B. (1996). "Facial Expressions of Emotion" and the delusion of the hermetic self. In R. Harré & W. G. Parrott, *The emotions* (pp. 259–284). Cambridge: Cambridge University Press.

FRIDLUND, A. J., EKMAN, P., & OSTER, H. (1983). Facial expression of emotion: Review of literature, 1970–1983. In A. Siegman (Ed.), *Nonverbal behavior and communication.* Hillsdale, NJ: Erlbaum.

FRIDLUND, A. J., & MacDONALD, M. (1998). Approaches to Goldie: A field study of human approach responses to canine juvenescence. *Anthrozoos, 11*(2), 95–100.

FRIEDERICI, A. D., & WESSELS, J. M. I. (1993). Phonotactic knowledge of word boundaries and its use in infant speech perception. *Perception and Psychophysics, 54,* 287–295.

FRIEDMAN, M. I. (1990a). Body fat and the metabolic control of food intake. *International Journal of Obesity, 14,* 53–67.

FRIEDMAN, M. I. (1990b). Making sense out of calories. In E. M. Stricker (Ed.), *Handbook of behavioral neurobiology: Vol. 10. Neurobiology of food and fluid intake* (pp. 513–529). New York: Plenum.

FRIEDMAN, M. I., & STRICKER, E. M. (1976). The physiological psychology of hunger: A physiological perspective. *Psychological Review, 83,* 409–431.

FRIEDMAN, M. J., & MARSELLA, A. J. (1996). Posttraumatic stress disorder: An overview of the concept. In A. J. Marsella, M. J. Friedman, E. T. Gerrity, & R. M. Scurfield (Eds.), *Ethnocultural aspects of posttraumatic stress disorder: Issues, research, and clinical applications* (pp. 11–32). Washington, DC: American Psychological Association.

FRIES, P., REYNOLDS, J. H., RORIE, A. E., & DESIMONE, R. (2001). Modulation of oscillatory neural synchronization by selective visual attention. *Science, 291,* 1560–1563.

FRIJDA, N. H. (1986). *The emotions*. New York, NY ; Paris, France: Cambridge University Press; Editions de la Maison des Sciences de l'Homme.

FRIJDA, N. H., & MESQUITA, B. (1994). The social roles and functions of emotions. In S. Kitayama & H. R. Markus (Eds.), *Emotion and culture* (pp. 51–87). Washington, DC: American Psychological Association.

FRISHBERG, N. (1975). Arbitrariness and iconicity: Historical change in American Sign Language. *Language, 51,* 696–719.

FRITH, C. D., & FRITH, U. (1999). Interacting minds—a biological basis. *Science, 286,* 1692–1695.

FROMKIN, V., KRASHEN, S., CURTISS, S., RIGLER, D., & RIGLER, M. (1974). The development of language in Genie: A case of language acquisition beyond the "critical period." *Brain and Language, 1,* 81–107.

FRYE, D., ZELAZO, P. D., & BURACK, J. A. (1998). Cognitive complexity and control: I. Theory of mind in typical and atypical development. *Current Directions in Psychological Science, 7,* 116–120.

FUJIMOTO, W. Y., BERGSTROM, R. W., BOYKO, E. J., LEONETTI, D. L., NEWELL-MORRIS, L. L., & WAHL, P. W. (1995). Susceptibility to development of central adiposity among populations. *Obesity Research, 3*(suppl. 2), 179S–186S.

FULLER, R. K., & HILLER-STURMHÖFEL, S. (1999). Alcoholism treatment in the United States. An overview. *Alcohol Research and Health, 23,* 69–77.

FUNKENSTEIN, D. H. (1956). Norepinephrine-like and epinephrine-like substances in relation to human behavior. *Journal of Mental Diseases, 124,* 58–68.

FURNHAM, A., TAN, T., & MCMANUS, C. (1997). Waist-to-hip ratio preferences for body shape: A replication and extension. *Personality and Individual Differences, 22,* 539–549.

GAGE, F. H., & BJÖRKLUND, A. (1986). Cholinergic septal grafts into the hippocampal formation improve spatial learning and memory in aged rats by an atropine-sensitive mechanism. *Journal of Neuroscience, 6,* 2837–2847.

GALABURDA, A. M. (1994). Developmental dyslexia and animal studies: At the interface between cognition and neurology. *Cognition, 56,* 833–839.

GALEN, B. R., & UNDERWOOD, M. K. (1997). A developmental investigation of social aggression in children. *Developmental Psychology, 33,* 589–600.

GALLISTEL, C. R. (1990). *The organization of learning.* Cambridge, MA: MIT Press (Bradford).

GALLISTEL, C. R. (1994). Space and time. In N. J. Mackintosh (Ed.), *Animal learning and cognition* (pp. 221–253). New York: Academic Press.

GALLISTEL, C. R. (2002). Language and spatial frames of reference in mind and brai. *Trends in Cognitive Science, 6*(8), 321–322.

GALLISTEL, C. R., & GELMAN, R. (2000). Non-verbal numerical cognition: From reals to integers. *Trends in Cognitive Science, 4,* 59–65.

GALLISTEL, C. R., SHIZGAL, P., & YEOMANS, J. (1981). A portrait of the substrate for self stimulation. *Psychological Review, 88,* 228–273.

GALLISTEL, R. (1995). Is long-term potentiation a plausible basis for memory? In J. L. McGaugh, N. M. Weinberger, & G. Lynch, (Eds.), *Brain and memory: Modulation and mediation of plasticity.* New York: Oxford University Press.

GALLO, V., & CHITAJALLU, R. (2001). Unwrapping glial cells from the synapse: what lies inside? *Science, 292,* 872–873.

GALTON, F. (1869). *Hereditary genius: An inquiry into its laws and consequences.* London: Macmillan.

GALTON, F. (1883). *Inquiries into human faculty and its development.* London: Macmillan.

GANAWAY, G. K. (1989). Historical versus narrative truth: Clarifying the role of exogenous trauma in the etiology of MPD and its variants. *Dissociation, 2,* 205–220.

GANGESTAD, S., & SNYDER, M. (2000). Self-monitoring: Appraisal and reappraisal. *Psychological Bulletin, 126,* 530–555.

GARB, H. N., FLORIO, C. M., & GROVE, W. M. (1998). The validity of the Rorschach and the Minnesota Multiphasic Personality Inventory: Results from meta-analyses. *Psychological Science, 9*(5), 402–404.

GARB, H. N., FLORIO, C. M., & GROVE, W. M. (1999). The Rorschach controversy: Reply to Parker, Hunsley, and Hanson. *Psychological Science, 10*(3), 293–294.

GARBER, M. (1995). *Vice versa: Bisexuality and the eroticism of everyday life.* New York: Simon & Schuster.

GARCIA, J., & KOELLING, R. A. (1966). The relation of cue to consequence in avoidance learning. *Psychonomic Science, 4,* 123–124.

GARCIA COLL, C. T., MEYER, E. C., & BRILLON, L. (1995). Ethnic and minority parenting. In M. H. Bornstein (Ed.), *Handbook of parenting: Vol. 2. Biology and ecology of parenting* (pp. 189–209). Hillsdale, NJ: Erlbaum.

GARDNER, H. (1983). *Frames of mind: The theory of multiple intelligences.* New York: Basic Books.

GARDNER, R. A., & GARDNER, B. T. (1969). Teaching sign language to a chimpanzee. *Science, 165,* 664–672.

GARDNER, R. A., & GARDNER, B. T. (1978). Comparative psychology and language acquisition. *Annals of the New York Academy of Science, 309,* 37–76.

GARFIELD, S. L. (1992). Major issues in psychotherapy research. In D. K. Freedheim (Ed.), *History of psychotherapy.* Washington, DC: American Psychological Association.

GARRIGAN, J. L. (1987). Post-traumatic stress disorder in military disaster workers. In *The human response to the Gander military air disaster: A summary report* (Division of Neuropsychiatry Report No. 88–12). Washington, DC: Walter Reed Army Institute of Research.

GARRIS, P. A., KILPATRICK, M., BUNIN, M. A., MICHAEL, D., WALKER, Q. D., & WIGHTMAN, R. M. (1999). Dissociation of dopamine release in the nucleus accumbens from intracranial self-stimulation. *Nature, 398,* 67–69.

GAZZANIGA, M. S. (1967). The split brain in man. *Scientific American, 217,* 24–29.

GAZZANIGA, M. S. (1983). Right hemisphere language following brain bisection: A 20-year perspective. *American Psychologist, 38,* 525–537.

GEARY, D. C., & BJORKLUND, D. F. (2000). Evolutionary developmental psychology. *Child Development, 71,* 57–65.

GEEN, R. G. (2001). *Human Aggression* (2nd ed.). London: Taylor & Francis.

GEHRING, W. J., HIMLE, J., & NISENSON, L. G. (2000). Action-monitoring dysfunction in obsessive-compulsive disorder. *Psychological Science, 11,* 1–6.

GELDARD, F. A. (1962). *Fundamentals of psychology.* New York: Wiley.

GELDARD, F. A. (1972). *The human senses.* New York: Wiley.

GELMAN, R. (1978). Cognitive development. *Annual Review of Psychology, 29,* 297–332.

GELMAN, R. (1982). Basic numerical abilities. In R. J. Sternberg (Ed.), *Advances in the psychology of human intelligence: Vol. 1* (pp. 181–205). Hillsdale, NJ: Erlbaum.

GELMAN, R., & BAILLARGEON, R. (1983). A review of some Piagetian concepts. In P. Mussen (Ed.), E. M. Markman, & J. H. Flavell (Vol. Eds.), *Carmichael's manual of child psychology: Vol 3. Cognitive development* (pp. 167–230). New York: Wiley.

GELMAN, R., & GALLISTEL, R. C. (1978). *The child's understanding of number.* Cambridge, MA: Harvard University Press.

GELMAN, R., & LUCARIELLO, J. (2002). Role of learning in cognitive development. In C. R. Gallistel (Ed.), *Stevens' handbook of experimental psychology: Vol 3. Learning, motivation, and emotion* (3rd ed., pp. 395–444). New York: Wiley.

GELMAN, S., & WELLMAN, H. (1991). Insides and essences: early understanding of the nonobvious. *Cognition 38,* 213–244.

GENTNER, D. (1983). Structure-mapping: A theoretical framework for analogy. *Cognitive Science 7,* 155–170.

GENTNER, D., & BORODITSKY, L. (2001). Individuation, relativity and early word learning. In M. Bowerman & S. C. Levinson (Eds.), *Language acquisition and conceptual development* (pp. 215–256). New York: Cambridge University Press.

GENTNER, D., & JEZIORSKI, M. (1989). Historical shifts in the use of analogy in science. In B. Gholson, W. Shadish, R. Neimeyer, & A. Houts (Eds.), *Psychology of science: Contributions to metascience.* Cambridge: Cambridge University Press.

GERARD, H. B., & MATHEWSON, G. C. (1966). The effects of severity of initiation on liking for a group: A replication. *Journal of Experimental Social Psychology, 2,* 278–287.

GERHARDT, P. F., HOLMES, D. L., ALESSANDRI, M., & GOODMAN, M. (1991). Social policy on the use of aversive interventions: Empirical, ethical, and legal considerations. *Journal of Autism and Developmental Disorders, 21,* 265–277.

GERKEN, L. (1996). Prosody's role in language acquisition and adult parsing. *Journal of Psycholinguistic Research, 25(2),* 345–356.

GERKEN, L., LANDAU, B., & REMEZ, R. (1990). Function morphemes in young children's speech perception and production. *Developmental Psychology, 26(2),* 204–216.

GERSHON, E. S., NURNBERGER, J. I., JR., BERRETTINI, W. H., & GOLDIN, L. R. (1985). Affective disorders: Genetics. In H. I. Kaplan & J. Sadock (Eds.), *Modern synopsis of comprehensive textbook of psychiatry* (4th ed.). Baltimore: Williams & Wilkins.

GESCHWIND, N., & GALABURDA, A. M. (1985). Cerebral lateralization: Biological mechanisms, associations and pathology. *Archives of Neurology, 42,* 428–459, 521–554.

GESCHWIND, N., & LEVITSKY, W. (1968). Human brain: Left-right asymmetries in temporal speech region. *Science, 161(3837),* 186–187.

GHAZANFAR, A. A., & HAUSER, M.D. (1999). The neuroethology of primate vocal communication: substrates for the evolution of speech. *Trends in Cognitive Sciences, 3,(10),* 377–381.

GIBBS, J., & SMITH, G. P. (1984). The neuroendocrinology of postprandial satiety. In L. Martini & W. F. Ganong (Eds.), *Frontiers in neuroendocrinology: Vol. 8.* New York: Raven.

GIBBS, J. C., CLARK, P. M., JOSEPH, J. A., GREEN, J. L., GOODRICK, T. S., & MAKOWSKI, D. G. (1986). Relations between moral judgment, moral courage, and filed independence. *Child Development, 57,* 1040–1043.

GIBBS, W. W. (1996). Gaining on fat. *Scientific American, 275,* 88–94.

GIBSON, J. J. (1950). *The perception of the visual world.* Boston: Houghton Mifflin.

GIBSON, J. J. (1966). *The senses considered as perceptual systems.* Boston: Houghton Mifflin.

GIBSON, J. J. (1979). *The ecological approach to visual perception.* Boston: Houghton Mifflin.

GICK, M. L. (1986). Problem-solving strategies. *Educational Psychologist, 21(1–2),* 99–120.

GICK, M. L., & HOLYOAK, K. J. (1980). Analogical problem solving. *Cognitive Psychology, 12,* 306–355.

GICK, M. L., & HOLYOAK, K. J. (1983). Schema induction and analogical transfer. *Cognitive Psychology, 15,* 1–38.

GIGERENZER, G., & HOFFRAGE, U. (1995). How to improve Bayesian reasoning without instruction: Frequency formats. *Psychological Review, 102,* 684–704.

GIGERENZER, G., & HOFFRAGE, U. (1999). Overcoming difficulties in Bayesian reasoning: A reply to Lewis and Keren (1999) and Mellers and McGraw (1999). *Psychological Review, 106,* 425–430.

GIGERENZER, G., & HUG, K. (1992). Domain-specific reasoning: Social contracts, cheating and perspective change. *Cognition, 43,* 127–172.

GILES, J. W., GOPNIK, A., & HEYMAN, G. D. (2002). Source monitoring reduces the suggestibility of preschool children. *Psychological Science, 13,* 288–291.

GILHOOLY, K. (1988). *Thinking: Direct, undirected and creative* (2nd ed.). New York: Academic Press.

GILLETTE, J., GLEITMAN, H., GLEITMAN, L. R., & LEDERER, A. (1999). Human simulations of vocabulary learning. *Cognition, 73,* 135–176.

GILLIGAN, C. (1982). *In a different voice: Psychological theory and women's development.* Cambridge, MA: Harvard University Press.

GILLIGAN, C. (1986). Profile of Carol Gilligan. In S. Scarr, R. A. Weinberg, & A. Levine, (1986) *Understanding development* (pp. 488–491). New York: Harcourt Brace Jovanovich.

GILOVICH, T. (1991). *How we know what isn't so.* New York: Free Press.

GILOVICH, T., & MEDVEC, V. H. (1995). The experience of regret: What, when, and why. *Psychological Review, 102,* 379–395.

GILOVICH, T., MEDVEC, V. H., & KAHNEMAN, D. (1998). Varieties of regret: A debate and partial resolution. *Psychological Review, 105,* 602–605.

GITLIN, M. J. (2001). Treatment-resistant bipolar disorder. *Bulletin of the Menninger Clinic, 65,* 26–40.

GIURFA, M., ZHANG, S., JENETT, A., MENZEL, R., & SRINIVASAN, M. V. (2001). The concepts of "sameness" and "difference" in an insect. *Nature, 410(6831),* 930–933.

GLADUE, B. A., GREEN, R., & HELLMAN, R. E. (1984). Neuroendocrine responses to estrogen and sexual orientation. *Science, 225,* 1496–1498.

GLADWIN, T. (1970). *East is a Big Bird.* Cambridge, MA: Belknap Press.

GLANZER, M., & CUNITZ, A. (1966). Two storage mechanisms in free recall. *Journal of Verbal Learning and Verbal Behavior 5:*531–560.

GLEAVES, D. H. (1996). The sociocognitive model of dissociative identity disorder: A reexamination of the evidence. *Psychological Bulletin, 120,* 42–59.

GLEITMAN, H. (1963). Place-learning. *Scientific American, 209,* 116–122.

GLEITMAN, H. (1971). Forgetting of long-term memories in animals. In W. K. Honig & P. H. R. James (Eds.), *Animal memory* (pp. 2–46). New York: Academic Press.

GLEITMAN, H. (1985). Some trends in the study of cognition. In S. Koch, & D. E. Leary (Eds.), *A century of psychology as science* (pp. 420–436). New York: McGraw-Hill.

GLEITMAN, H. (1990). Some reflections on drama and the dramatic experience. In I. Rock (Ed.), *The legacy of Solomon Asch: Essays in cognition and social psychology.* Hillsdale, NJ: Erlbaum.

GLEITMAN, H., & JONIDES, J. (1976). The cost of categorization in visual search: Incomplete processing of targets and field items. *Perception and Psychophysics, 20(4),* 281–288.

GLEITMAN, L. R. (1986). Biological dispositions to learn language. In W. Demopolous & A. Marras (Eds.), *Language learning and concept acquisition.* Norwood, NJ: Ablex.

GLEITMAN, L. R. (1990). The structural sources of verb meanings. *Language Acquisition, 1,* 3–55.

GLEITMAN, L. R., & GLEITMAN, H. (1997), What is a language made out of? *Lingua, 100,* 29–55.

GLEITMAN, L. R., GLEITMAN, H., LANDAU, B., & WANNER, E. (1988). Where learning begins: Initial representations for language learning. In F. J. Newmeyer (Ed.), *Linguistics: The Cambridge survey, Vol. 3. Language: Psychological and biological aspects* (pp. 150–193). New York: Cambridge University Press.

GLEITMAN, L. R., GLEITMAN, H., & SHIPLEY, E. F. (1972). The emergence of the child as grammarian. *Cognition, 1(2),* 137–164.

GLEITMAN, L. R., & NEWPORT, E.L. (1995). The invention of language by children: Environmental and biological influences on the acquisition of language. In L.R. Gleitman & M.Y. Liberman (Eds.), *Invitation to Cognitive Science: Vol. 1. Language.* Cambridge, MA: MIT Press.

GLEITMAN, L. R., & WANNER, E. (1982). Language acquisition: The state of the state of the art. In E. Wanner & L. R. Gleitman (Eds.), *Language acquisition: State of the art* (pp. 3–48). New York: Cambridge University Press.

GLICK, I. D., MURRAY, S. R., VASUDEVAN, P., MARDER, S. R., & HU, R. J. (2001). Treatment with atypical antipsychotics: New indications and new populations. *Journal of Psychiatric Research, 35,* 187–191.

GLICK, J. (1975). Cognitive development in cross-cultural perspective. In F. G. Horowitz, (Ed.), *Review of child development research: Vol. 4.* Chicago: University of Chicago Press.

GLISKY, E., SCHACTER, D., & TULVING, E. (1986). Computer learning by memory impaired patients: Acquisition and retention of complex knowledge. *Neuropsychologia, 24,* 313–328.

GOBET, F., LANE, P. C. R., CROKER, S., CHENG, P. C.-H., JONES, G., OLIVER, I., ET AL. (2001). Chunking mechanisms in human learning. Trends in *Cognitive Science, 5,* 236–243.

GOBET, F., & SIMON, H. A. (1996a). Recall of random and distorted chess positions: Implications for the theory of expertise. *Memory and Cognition, 24,* 493–503.

GOBET, F., & SIMON, H. A. (1996b). The roles of recognition processes and look-ahead search in time-constrained expert problem solving: Evidence from grand-master-level chess. *Psychological Science, 7,* 52–55.

GOBET, F., & SIMON, H. A. (2000). The relative contributions of recognition and search-evaluation processes to high-level chess performance: Reply to Lassiter. *Psychological Science, 11*(2), 174.

GODDEN, D. R., & BADDELEY, A. D. (1975). Context-dependent memory in two natural environments: On land and underwater. *British Journal of Psychology, 66,* 325–331.

GOEBEL, R., KHORRAM-SEFAT, D., MUCKLI, L., HACKER, H., & SINGER, W. (1998). The constructive nature of vision: Direct evidence from functional magnetic resonance imaging studies of apparent motion and motion imagery. *European Journal of Neuroscience, 10*(5), 1563–1573.

GOFFMAN, E. (1959). *The presentation of self in everyday life.* Garden City, New York: Anchor Books, Doubleday.

GOLDBERG, L. R. (1982). From ace to zombie: Some explorations in the language of personality. In C. Spielberger & J. N. Butcher (Eds.), *Advances in personality assessment: Vol. 1.* Hillsdale, NJ: Erlbaum.

GOLDBERG, L. R. (1990). An alternative "description of personality": The Big-Five factor structure. *Journal of Personality and Social Psychology, 59,* 1216–1229.

GOLDBERG, L. R. (1993). The structure of phenotypic personality traits. *American Psychologist, 48,* 26–34.

GOLDEN, T. (1990, April 2). Ill, possibly violent, and no place to go. *New York Times,* pp. A1, B4.

GOLDFRIED, M. R., & DAVISON, G. C. (EDS.). (1994). *Clinical behavior therapy.* New York: Wiley.

GOLDIN-MEADOW, S. (1982). The resilience of recursion: A study of a communication system developed without a conventional language model. In E. Wanner & L. R. Gleitman (Eds.), *Language acquisition: The state of the art* (pp. 51–77). New York: Cambridge University Press.

GOLDIN-MEADOW, S. (2000). Learning with and without a helping hand. In B. Landau, J. Sabini, J. Jonides, & E. L. Newport (Eds.), *Perception, cognition, and language: Essays in honor of Henry and Lila Gleitman* (pp. 121–138). Cambridge, MA: MIT Press.

GOLDIN-MEADOW, S., & FELDMAN, H. (1977). The development of language-like communication without a language model. *Science, 197,* 401–403.

GOLDSTEIN, E. B. (1989). *Sensation and perception* (3rd ed.). Belmont, CA: Wadsworth.

GOLDSTEIN, J. M., & TSUANG, M. T. (1990). Gender and schizophrenia: An introduction and synthesis of findings. *Schizophrenia Bulletin, 16,* 179–183.

GOLDSTONE, R. L., LIPPA, Y., & SHIFFRIN, R. M. (2001). Altering object representations through category learning. *Cognition, 78,* 27–43.

GOMBRICH, E. H. (1961). *Art and illusion.* Princeton, NJ: Bollingen Series, Princeton University Press.

GOOD, G. E., & SHERROD, N. B. (2001). The psychology of men and masculinity: Research status and future directions. In R. K. Unger (Ed.), *Handbook of the psychology of women and gender* (pp. 201–214). New York: Wiley.

GOODALE, M. A. (1995). The cortical organization of visual perception and visuo-motor control. In S. M. Kosslyn & D. Osherson (Eds.), *Visual cognition: An invitation to cognitive science (2nd ed.).* Cambridge, MA: MIT Press.

GOODMAN, G. S., & SCHAAF, J. M. (1997). Over a decade of research on children's eyewitness testimony: What have we learned? Where do we go from here? [Special Issue] *Applied Cognitive Psychology, 11,* S5–S20.

GOPNIK, A. (1999). Theory of mind. In R. A. Wilson & F. C. Keil (Eds.), *The MIT encyclopedia of the cognitive sciences* (pp. 838–841). Cambridge, MA: MIT Press.

GOPNIK, A., & MELTZOFF A. N. (1997). *Words, thoughts and theories.* Cambridge, MA: MIT Press.

GOPNIK, M., & CRAGO, M. B. (1990). Familial aggregation of a developmental language disorder. *Cognition, 39,* 1–50.

GORDON H. (1923). Mental and scholastic tests among retarded children. *Educational pamphlet,* no. 44. London: Board of Education.

GOREN, C. C., SARTY, M., & WU, P. Y. K. (1975). Visual following and pattern discrimination of face-like stimuli by newborn infants. *Pediatrics, 56,* 544–559.

GOSLING, S. D., & JOHN, O. P. (1999). Personality dimensions in nonhuman animals: A cross-species review. *Current Directions in Psychological Science, 8,* 69–75.

GOTTESMAN, I. I., McGUFFIN, P., & FARMER, A. (1987). Clinical genetics as clues to the "real" genetics of schizophrenia (a decade of modest gains while playing for time). *Schizophrenia Bulletin, 13,* 23–47.

GOTTESMAN, I. I., & SHIELDS, J. (1972). *Schizophrenia and genetics: A twin study vantage point.* New York: Academic Press.

GOTTESMAN, I. I., & SHIELDS, J. (1982). *Schizophrenia: The epigenetic puzzle.* New York: Cambridge University Press.

GOUGH, H. G. (1975). *California psychological inventory: Manual* (rev. ed.). Palo Alto, CA: Consulting Psychologists Press (original edition, 1957).

GOUGH, H. G. (1990). The California Psychological Inventory. In C. E. Watkins, Jr. & V. L. Campbell (Eds.), *Testing in counseling practice. Vocational* (pp. 37–62). Hillsdale, NJ: Erlbaum.

GOUGH, H. G., & BRADLEY, P. (1996). CPI manual (3rd ed.). Palo Alto, CA: Consulting Psychologists Press.

GOULD, J. L. (1990). Honey bee cognition. *Cognition, 37,* 83–103.

GOULD, S. J. (1977). *Ontogeny and phylogeny.* Cambridge, MA: Harvard University Press.

GOULD, S. J. (1978). Sociobiology: The art of storytelling. *New Scientist, 80,* 530–533.

GOULDNER, A. W. (1960). The norm of reciprocity: A preliminary statement. *American Sociological Review, 25,* 161–179.

GRAF, P., & MANDLER, G. (1984). Activation makes words more accessible, but not necessarily more retrievable. *Journal of Verbal Learning and Verbal Behavior, 23,* 553–568.

GRAF, P., MANDLER, G., & HADEN, P. (1982). Simulating amnesic symptoms in normal subjects. *Science, 218,* 1243–1244.

GRAF, P., MANDLER, G., & SQUIRE, L. R. (1984). The information that amnesic patients don't forget. *Journal of Experimental Psychology: Learning, Memory, and Cognition, 10,* 164–178.

GRAHAM, C. H., & HSIA, Y. (1954). Luminosity curves for normal and dichromatic subjects including a case of unilateral color blindness. *Science, 120,* 780.

GRAHAM, D. L. R., RAWLINGS, E. I., & RIGSBY, R. K. (1994). *Loving to survive: Sexual terror, men's violence, and women's lives.* New York: New York University Press.

GRAMMER, K., & THORNHILL, R. (1994). Human homo sapiens facial attractiveness and sexual selection: The role of symmetry and averageness. *Journal of Comparative Psychology, 108,* 233–242.

GRANT, H. M., BREDAHL, L. C., CLAY, J., FERRIE, J., GROVES, J. E., McDORMAN, T. A., ET AL. (1998). Context-dependent memory for meaningful material: Information for students. *Applied Cognitive Psychology, 12,* 617–623.

GRANT, V. W. (1976). *Falling in love*. New York: Springer.

GRAY, C. M., KOENIG, P., ENGEL, A. K., & SINGER, W. (1989). Oscillatory responses in cat visual cortex exhibit inter-columnar synchronization which reflects global stimulus properties. *Nature, 338*,(6213), 334–337.

GRAY, S. (1977). Social aspects of body image: Perception of normalcy of weight and affect of college undergraduates. *Perceptual and Motor Skills, 45,* 1035–1040.

GRAZIANO, M. S., TAYLOR, C. S., & MOORE, T. (2002). Complex movements evoked by microstimulation of precentral cortex. *Neuron, 34,* 841–851.

GREEN, D. M. (1976). *An introduction to hearing*. New York: Academic Press.

GREEN, G. D., & CLUNIS, D. M. (1988). Married lesbians. Lesbianism: Affirming Nontraditional Roles [Special Issue]. *Women and Therapy, 8,* 41–49.

GREEN, R. (1979). Childhood cross-gender behavior and subsequent sexual preference. *American Journal of Psychiatry, 136,* 106–108.

GREEN, R. (1987). *The sissy-boy syndrome and the development of homosexuality*. New Haven, CT: Yale University Press.

GREEN, R. G. (1998). Aggression and Antisocial behavior. In D. T. Gilbert, S. T. Fiske, & G. Lindzey, G. (Eds.), *The Handbook of Social Psycology: Vol. 2* (4th ed., pp. 317–356). New York: McGraw Hill.

GREEN, R. L., HOFFMAN, L. T., MORSE, R., HAYES, M. E. B., & MORGAN, R. F. (1964). *The educational status of children in a district without public schools*. Cooperative Research Project No. 23211. Washington, DC: Office of Education. U.S. Department of Health, Education, and Welfare.

GREEN, S. (1975). Variation of vocal pattern with social situation in the Japanese monkey (Macaca fuscata): A field study. In L. A. Rosenblum (Ed.), *Primate Behavior* (pp. 1 –102). New York: Academic Press.

GREEN, S. K., BUCHANAN, D. R., & HEUER, S. K. (1984). Winners, losers, and choosers: A field investigation of dating initiation. *Personality and Social Psychology Bulletin, 10,* 502–511.

GREENE, R. L. (1988). Assessment of malingering and defensiveness by objective personality inventories. In R. Rogers (Ed.), *Clinical assessment of malingering and deception* (pp. 123–158). New York: Guilford Press.

GREENE, R. L. (1991). *The MMPI-2/MMPI: An interpretative manual*. Needham Heights, MA: Allyn and Bacon.

GREENFIELD, P. M. (1966). On culture and conservation. In J. R. Bruner, R. R. Olver, & P. M. Greenfield (Eds.), *Studies in cognitive growth*. New York: Wiley.

GREENFIELD, P. M. (1997). You can't take it with you: Why ability assessments don't cross cultures. *American Psychologist, 52,* 1115–1124.

GREENWALD, A., SPANGENBERG, E., PRATKANIS, A., & ESKENAZI, J. (1991). Double-blind tests of subliminal self-help audiotapes. *Psychological Science, 2,* 119–122.

GREENWALD, A. G., & BANAJI, M. R. (1995). Implicit social cognition: Attitudes, self-esteem, and stereotypes. *Psychological Review, 102*(1), 4–27.

GREENWALD, A. G., BANAJI, M. R., RUDMAN, L. A., FARNHAM, S. D., NOSEK, B. A., & MELLOTT, D. S. (2002). A unified theory of implicit attitudes, stereotypes, self-esteem, and self-concept. *Psychological Review, 109*(1), 3–25.

GREENWALD, A. G., McGHEE, D. E., & SCHWARTZ, J. L. K. (1998). Measuring individual differences in implicit cognition: The implicit association test. *Journal of Personality and Social Psychology, 74*(6), 1464–1480.

GREENWALD, A. G., & NOSEK, B. A. (2001). Health of the Implicit Association Test at age 3. *Zeitschrift Fuer Experimentelle Psychologie, 48*(2), 85–93.

GREVEN, P. J., JR. (1970). *Four generations: Population, land, and family in colonial Andover, Massachusetts*. Ithaca, NY: Cornell University Press.

GRICE, H. P. (1975). Logic and conversation. In P. Cole & J. L. Morgan (Eds.), *Syntax and semantics 3: Speech acts*. New York: Academic Press.

GRIGGS, R.A., & COX, J.R. (1982). The elusive thematic-materials effect in Wason's selection task. *British Journal of Psychology, 73,* 407–420.

GRIGORENKO, E. L. (2001). Developmental dyslexia: An update on genes, brains, and environments. *Journal of Child Psychology and Psychiatry, 42,* 91–125.

GRIGORENKO, E. L., WOOD, F. B., MEYER, M. S., HART, I., SPEED, W. K., SHUSTER, A., ET AL. (1997). Susceptibility loci for distinct components of developmental dyslexia on chromosomes 6 and 15. *American Journal of Human Genetics, 60,* 27–39.

GRIGORENKO, E. L., WOOD, F. B., MEYER, M. S., & PAULS, D. L. (2000). Chromosome 6p influences on different dyslexia-related cognitive processes: Further confirmation. *American Journal of Human Genetics, 66,* 715–723.

GRIMSHAW, J. (1990). *Argument structure*. Cambridge, MA: MIT Press.

GRIMSHAW, J. (1981). Form, function, and the language acquisition device. In C. L. Baker & J. J. McCarthy (Ed.), *The logical problem of language acquisition* (pp. 165–182). Cambridge, MA: MIT Press.

GRIMSHAW, J. (1994). Lexical reconciliation. *Lingua, 92,* 411–430.

GROOP, L. C., & TUOMI, T. (1997). Non-insulin-dependent diabetes mellitus—a collision between thrifty genes and an affluent society. *Annals of Medicine, 29,* 37–53.

GROTZER, T. A., & PERKINS, D. N. (2000). Teaching intelligence: A performance conception. In R. J. Sternberg (Ed.), *Handbook of intelligence*. Cambridge: Cambridge University Press.

GRUBER-BALDINI, A. L., SCHAIE, K. W., & WILLIS, S. L. (1995). Similarity in married couples: A longitudinal study of mental abilities and rigidity-flexibility. *Journal of Personality and Social Psychology, 69,* 191–203.

GRÜNBAUM, A. (1996). Is psychoanalysis viable? In W. O'Donohue & R. F. Kitchener, (Eds.), *The philosophy of psychology* (pp. 281–290). London: Sage.

GUENTHER, F. H., & GJAJA, M. N. (1996). The perceptual magnet effect as an emergent property of neural map formation. *Journal of the Acoustical Society of America, 100,* 1111–1121.

GUESBECK, N. R., HICKEY, M. S., MacDONALD, K. G., PORIES, W. J., HARPER, I., RAVUSSIN, E., ET AL. (2001). Substrate utilization during exercise in formerly morbidly obese women. *Journal of Applied Physiology, 90,* 1007–1012.

GUNNAR, M. R., MORISON, S. J., CHISHOLM, K., & SCHUDER, M. (2001). Salivary cortisol levels in children adopted from Romanian orphanages. *Development and Psychopathology, 13,* 611–628.

GURSKY, J. T., & KRAHN, L.E. (2000). The effects of antidepressants on sleep: A review. *Harvard Review of Psychiatry, 8,* 298–306.

GUTH, W., SCHMITTBERGER, R., & SCHWARZE, B. (1982). An experimental analysis of ultimatum bargaining. *Journal of Economic Behavior and Organizations, 3,* 367–388.

GUTTMANN, N., & KALISH, H. I. (1956). Discriminability and stimulus generalization. *Journal of Experimental Psychology, 51,* 79–88.

HADLEY, S. W., & STRUPP, H. H. (1976). Contemporary accounts of negative effects in psychotherapy: An integrated account. *Archives of General Psychiatry, 33,* 1291–1302.

HALBERSTADT, J., & RHODES, G. (2000). The attractiveness of nonface averages: Implications for an evolutionary explanation of the attractiveness of average faces. *Psychological Science, 11,* 285–289.

HALL, C. S. (1966). *The meaning of dreams*. New York: McGraw-Hill.

HALL, C. S., LINDZEY, G., LOEHLIN, J. C., & MANOSEVITZ, M. (1985). *Introduction to theories of personality*. New York: Wiley.

HALL, C. S., & VAN DE CASTLE, R. (1966). *The content analysis of dreams*. New York: Appleton-Century-Crofts.

HALL, D. G., QUANTZ, D. H., & PERSONAGE, K. A., ET AL. (2000). Preschoolers' use of form class cues in word learning. *Developmental Psychology, 36*(4), 449–462.

HALL, J. A., & TAYLOR, S. E. (1976). When love is blind: Maintaining idealized images of one's spouse. *Human Relations, 29,* 751–761.

HALPERN, D. (1992). *Sex differences in cognitive abilities* (2nd ed.). Hillsdale, NJ: Erlbaum.

HALPERN, D. (1998). Teaching critical thinking for transfer across domains. *American Psychologist, 53,* 449–455.

HALPERN, D. F. (1997). Sex differences in intelligence: Implications for education. *American Psychologist, 52,* 1091–1102.

HALPERT, S. C. (2000). "If it ain't broke, don't fix it": Ethical considerations regarding conversion therapies. *International Journal of Sexuality and Gender Studies, 5,* 19–35.

HAMBURG, D. A., MOOS, R. H., & YALOM, I. D. (1968). Studies of distress in the menstrual cycle and the postpartum period. In R. P. Michael (Ed.), *Endocrinology and human behavior* (pp. 94–116). London: Oxford University Press.

HAMER, D., HUR, S., MAGNUSON, V., & HU, N. (1993a). A linkage between DNA markers on the X-chromosome and male sexual orientation. *Science, 261*(5119), 321–327.

HAMER, D., HUR, S., MAGNUSON, V., & HU, N. (1993b). Genetics and male sexual orientation [Response]. *Science, 261*(5126), 1259.

HAMILL, R., WILSON, T. D., & NISBETT, R. E. (1980). Insensitivity to sample bias: Generalizing from atypical cases. *Journal of Personality and Social Psychology, 39,* 578–589.

HAMILTON, D. L., & ROSE, T. L. (1980). Illusory correlation and the maintenance of stereotypic beliefs. *Journal of Personality and Social Psychology, 39,* 832–845.

HAMILTON, W. D. (1964). The genetical evolution of social behavior. *Journal of Theoretical Biology, 7,* 1–51.

HANEY, C., BANKS, C., & ZIMBARDO, P. (1973). Interpersonal dynamics in a simulated prison. *International Journal of Criminology and Penology, 1*(1), 69–97.

HANEY, C., & ZIMBARDO, P. (1998). The past and future of U.S. prison policy: Twenty-five years after the Stanford Prison Experiment. *American Psychologist, 53*(7), 709–727.

HANSEN, C. E., & EVANS, A. (1985). Bisexuality reconsidered: An idea in pursuit of a definition. In F. Klein & T. J. Wolf (Eds.), *Bisexualities: Theory and research* (pp. 1–6). New York: Haworth Press.

HANSEN, J. T., & SCHULDT, W. J. (1984). Marital self-disclosure and marital satisfaction. *Journal of Marriage and the Family, 46,* 923–926.

HAPPÉ, F., BROWNELL, H., & WINNER, E. (1999). Acquired "theory of mind" impairments following stroke. *Cognition, 70,* 211–240.

HARE, R. D. (1965). Temporal gradients of fear arousal in psychopaths. *Journal of Abnormal Psychology, 70,* 422–445.

HARE, R. D. (1978). A research scale for the assessment of psychopathy in criminal populations. *Personality and Individual Differences, 1,* 111–119.

HARE, R. D. (1993). *Without conscience: The disturbing world of the psychopaths among us.* New York: Pocket Books.

HAREVEN, T. K. (1978). The last stage: Historical adulthood and old age. In E. H. Erikson (Ed.), *Adulthood* (pp. 201–216). New York: Norton.

HARKNESS, S., & SUPER, C. M. (1995). Culture and parenting. In M. H. Bornstein (Ed.), *Handbook of parenting, Vol. 2: Biology and ecology of parenting* (pp. 211–234). Hillsdale, NJ: Erlbaum.

HARLOW, H. F. (1958). The nature of love. *American Psychologist, 13,* 673–685.

HARLOW, H. F. (1962). The heterosexual affectional system in monkeys. *American Psychologist, 17,* 1–9.

HARLOW, H. F., & HARLOW, M. K. (1972). The young monkeys. In *Readings in Psychology Today* (2nd ed.). Del Mar, CA: CRM Books.

HARLOW, H. F., & NOVAK, M. A. (1973). Psychopathological perspectives. *Perspectives in Biology and Medicine, 16,* 461–478.

HARRIS, C. R. (2002). Sexual and romantic jealousy in heterosexual and homosexual adults. *Psychological Science, 13,* 7–12.

HARRIS, G. W., & MICHAEL, R. P. (1964). The activation of sexual behavior by hypothalamic implants of estrogen. *Journal of Physiology, 171,* :275–301.

HARRIS, P. L. (1987). The development of search. In P. Salapatek & L. Cohen (Eds.), *Handbook of infant perception* (pp. 155–208). New York: Academic Press.

HARRIS, Z. (1951). *Methods in structural linguistics.* Chicago: Chicago University Press.

HARRIS, Z. S. (1952). Discourse analysis: A sample text. *Language, 28,* 474–494.

HARTER, S. (1990). Causes, correlates and the functional role of global self-worth: A life span perspective. In R. J. Sternberg & J. Kolligan (Eds.), *Competence considered* (pp. 67–97). New Haven, CT: Yale University Press.

HARTMANN, H. (1964). *Essays on ego psychology: Selected problems in psychoanalytic theory.* New York: International Universities Press.

HARTSHORNE, H., & MAY, M. A. (1928). *Studies in the nature of character: Vol. 1.* New York: Macmillan.

HARVEY, L. O., JR., & LEIBOWITZ, H. (1967). Effects of exposure duration, cue reduction, and temporary monocularity on size matching at short distances. *Journal of the Optical Society of America, 57,* 249–253.

HASE, H. D., & GOLDBERG, L. R. (1967). Comparative validities of different strategies of constructing personality inventory scales. *Psychological Bulletin, 67,* 231–248.

HASSELMO, M. E. (1999). Neuromodulation: Acetylcholine and memory consolidation. *Trends in Cognitive Science, 6,* 351–359.

HATFIELD, E. (1988). Passionate and companionate love. In R. J. Sternberg & M. L. Barnes (Eds.), *The psychology of love.* New Haven, CT: Yale University Press.

HATHAWAY, S. R., & MCKINLEY, J. C. (1940). A multiphasic personality schedule (Minnesota): I. Construction of the schedule. *Journal of Psychology, 10,* 249–254.

HAURI, P. (1977). *The sleep disorders.* Kalamazoo, MI: Upjohn Pharmaceuticals.

HAURI, P., & LINDE, S. (1991). *No more sleepless nights.* New York: Wiley.

HAUSER, M. (1996). *The evolution of communication.* Cambridge, MA: MIT Press.

HAUSMANN, M., SLABBEKOORN, D., VAN GOOZEN, S. H. M., COHEN-KETTENIS, P. T., & GUENTUERKUEN, O. (2000). Sex hormones affect spatial abilities during the menstrual cycle. *Behavioral Neuroscience, 114,* 1245–1250.

HAY, P., SACHDEV, P., CUMMING, S., SMITH, J. S., LEE, T., KITCHENER, P., ET AL. (1993). Treatment of obsessive-compulsive disorder by psychosurgery. *Acta Psychiatrica Scandinavica, 87,* 197–207.

HAYES, J. (1985). Three problems in teaching general skills. In S. Chipman, J. Segal, & R. Glaser (Eds.), *Thinking and learning skills* (pp. 391–406). Hillsdale, NJ: Erlbaum.

HAYWARD, W. G., & TARR, M. J. (1995). Spatial language and spatial representation. *Cognition, 55,* 39–84.

HAZAN, C., & SHAVER, P. (1987). Romantic love conceptualized as an attachment process. *Journal of Personality and Social Psychology, 52,* 511–524.

HAZELTINE, E., & IVRY, R. B. (2002). Can we teach the cerebellum new tricks? *Science, 296,* 1979–1980.

HEALY, A. F., & MILLER, G. A. (1970). The verb as the main determinant of sentence meaning. *Psychonomic Science, 20,* 372.

HEARST, E. (1972). Psychology across the chessboard. In *Readings in Psychology Today* (2nd ed.). Albany, New York: Delmar Publishers, CRM Books.

HECKERS S. (1997). Neuropathology of schizophrenia: Cortex, thalamus, basal ganglia, and neurotransmitter-specific projection systems. *Schizophrenia Bulletin, 23,* 403–421.

HEDGES, L. V., & NOWELL, A. (1995). Sex differences in mental test scores, variability, and numbers of high-scoring individuals. *Science, 269,* 41–45.

HEIDER, E. R. (1972). Universals in color naming and memory. *Journal of Experimental Psychology, 93,* 1–20.

HEIDER, F. (1958). *The psychology of interpersonal relationships.* New York: Wiley.

HEILMAN, K. M., & WATSON, R. T. (1977). Mechanisms underlying the unilateral neglect syndrome. In E. A. Weinstein & R. P. Friedland (Eds.), *Hemi-inattention and hemisphere specialization.* New York: Raven Press.

HEIM, C., OWENS, M. J., PLOTSKY, P. M., & NEMEROFF, C. B. (1997). Endocrine factors in the pathophysiology of mental disorders. *Psychopharmacology Bulletin, 33,* 185–192.

HEINE, S. J., KITAYAMA, S., LEHMAN, D. R., TAKATA, T., IDE, E., LEUNG, C., ET AL. (2001). Divergent consequences of success and failure in Japan and North America: An investigation of self-improving motivations and malleable selves. *Journal of Personality and Social Psychology, 81,* 599–615.

HELBURN, S. W., & HOWES, C. (1996). Child care cost and quality. *The Future of Children, 6,* 62–82.

HELD, J. D., ALDERTON, D. L., FOLEY, P. P., & SEGALL, D. O. (1993). Arithmetic reasoning gender differences: Explanations found in the Armed Services Vocational Aptitude Battery (ASVAB). *Learning and Individual Differences, 5,* 171–186.

HELLSTROM, K., FELLENIUS, J., & OST, L. G. (1996). One versus five sessions of applied tension in the treatment of blood phobia. *Behavior Research and Therapy, 34,* 101–112.

HELMHOLTZ, H. (1909). *Wissenschaftliche Abhandlungen, II* (pp. 764–843).

HELMUTH, L. (2001). Boosting brain activity from the outside in. *Science, 292,* 1284–1286.

HENDRY, D. P. (ED.). (1969). *Conditioned reinforcement.* Homeward, IL: Dorsey Press.

HENINGER, G. R. (1995). Indoleamines: The role of serotonin in clinical disorders. In F. E. Bloom & D. Kupfer (Eds.), *Psychopharmacology: The fourth generation of progress* (pp. 471–482). New York: Raven.

HENRY, W. E. (1973). *The analysis of fantasy.* Huntington, NY: Robert E. Krieger.

HENSS, R. (2000). Waist-to-hip ratio and female attractiveness. Evidence from photographic stimuli and methodological considerations. *Personality and Individual Differences, 28,* 501–513.

HERDT, G. (1990). Developmental discontinuities and sexual orientation across cultures. In D. P. McWhirter, S. A. Sanders, & J. M. Reinisch (Eds.), *Homosexuality/heterosexuality: Concepts of sexual orientation.* New York: Oxford University Press.

HERING, E. (1920). *Outlines of a theory of the light sense* (pp. 150–151). L. M. Hurvich & D. Jameson (Eds.). Cambridge, MA: Harvard University Press.

HERMANN, D., & YODER, C. (1998). The potential effects of the implanted memory paradigm on child subjects. *Applied Cognitive Psychology, 12*(3), 198–206.

HERNANDEZ, M., & IYENGAR, S. S. (2001). What drives whom? A cultural perspective on human agency. *Social Cognition, 19,* 269–294.

HERR, S. S. (1990). The law on aversive and nonaversive behavioral intervention. In S. L. Harris & J. S. Handleman (Eds.), *Aversive and nonaversive interventions: Controlling life-threatening behavior by the developmentally disabled* (pp. 80–118). New York: Springer.

HERRNSTEIN, R. J. (1979). Acquisition, generalization, and discrimination reversal of a natural concept. *Journal of Experimental Psychology: Animal Behavior Processes, 5,* 118–129.

HERRNSTEIN, R. J., LOVELAND, D. H., & CABLE, C. (1976). Natural concepts in pigeons. *Journal of Experimental Psychology: Animal Behavior Processes, 2,* 285–311.

HERRNSTEIN, R. J., & MURRAY, C. A. (1994). *The bell curve: Intelligence and class structure in American life.* Cambridge, MA: Free Press.

HERRNSTEIN, R. J., NICKERSON, R. S., DE SANCHEZ, M., & SWETS, J. A. (1986). Teaching thinking skills. *American Psychologist, 41,* 1279–1289.

HESPOS, S. J., & BAILLARGEON, R. (2001a). Infants' knowledge about occlusion and containment events: A surprising discrepancy. *Psychological Science, 12,* 141–147.

HESPOS, S. J., & BAILLARGEON, R. (2001b). Reasoning about containment events in very young infants. *Cognition, 78,* 207–245.

HESS, E. H. (1959). Imprinting. *Science, 130,* 133–141.

HESS, E. H. (1973). *Imprinting: Early experience and the developmental psychobiology of attachment.* New York: Van Nostrand.

HESS, U., BANSE, R., & KAPPAS, A. (1995). The intensity of facial expression is determined by underlying affective state and social situation. *Journal of Personality and Social Psychology, 69,* 280–288.

HETHERINGTON, E. M., BRIDGES, M., & INSABELLA, G. M. (1998). What matters? What does not? Five perspectives on the association between marital transitions and children's adjustment. *American Psychologist, 53*(2), 167–184.

HETHERINGTON, E. M., STANLEY-HAGEN, M., & ANDERSON, E. R. (1989). Marital transitions: A child's perspective. *American Psychologist, 41,* 303–312.

HEWSTONE, M., RUBIN, M., & WILLIS, H. (2002). Intergroup bias. *Annual Review of Psychology, 53,* 575–604.

HIER, D. B., & CROWLEY, W. F. (1982). Spatial ability in androgen-deficient men. *New England Journal of Medicine, 306,* 1202–1205.

HIGBEE, K. L., (1977). *Your memory: How it works and how to improve it.* Englewood Cliffs, NJ: Prentice-Hall.

HIGGINS, R., SNYDER, C. R., & BERGLAS, S. (1990). (Eds.). *Self-handicapping: The paradox that isn't.* New York: Plenum Press.

HIGLEY, J. D., SUOMI, S. J., & LINNOILA, M. (1990). Parallels in aggression and serotonin: Consideration of development, rearing history, and sex differences. In H. M. Van Praag, R. Plutchik, & A. Apter (Eds.), *Violence and suicidality: Perspectives in clinical and psychobiological research: Vol 3. Clinical and experimental psychiatry* (pp. 245–256). New York: Brunner/Mazel.

HILGARD, E. R. (1977). *Divided consciousness: Multiple controls in human thought and action.* New York: Wiley.

HILGARD, E. R. (1986). *Divided consciousness: Multiple controls in human thought and action* (rev. ed.). New York: Wiley.

HILL, A. L. (1978). Savants: Mentally retarded individuals with specific skills. In N. R. Ellis (Ed.), *International review of research in mental retardation: Vol. 9.* New York: Academic Press.

HILL, C. T., RUBIN, L., & PEPLAU, L. A. (1976). Breakups before marriage: The end of 103 affairs. *Journal of Social Issues, 32,* 147–168.

HILTS, P. J. (1995). *Memory's ghost: The strange tale of Mr. M and the nature of memory.* New York: Simon and Schuster.

HINDE, R. A. (1985). Expression and negotiation. In G. Zivin (Ed.), *The development of expressive behavior* (pp. 103–116). Orlando, FL: Academic Press.

HINELINE, P. N., & RACHLIN, H. (1969). Escape and avoidance of shock by pigeons pecking a key. *Journal of the Experimental Analysis of Behavior, 12,* 533–538.

HINES, M. (1990). Gonadal hormones and human cognitive development. In J. Balthazar, (ED.), *Hormones, brains, and behaviors in vertebrates 1. Sexual differentiation neuroanatomical aspects, neurotransmitters, and neuropeptides l.* Basel: Karger.

HINTZMAN, D. L. (1990). Human learning and memory: Connections and dissociations. *Annual Review of Psychology, 41,* 109–139.

HIRSCHFELD, R. M. A., & CROSS, C. K. (1981). Epidemiology of affective disorders. *Archives of General Psychiatry, 39,* 3546.

HIRSCHFELD, R. M., & GOODWIN, F. K. (1988). Mood disorders. In J. A. Talbott, R. E. Hales, & S. C. Yudofsky (Eds.), *The American Psychiatric Press textbook of psychiatry: Vol. 7.* Washington, DC: American Psychiatric Press.

HIRSH-PASEK, K., & GOLINKOFF, R. (1996). *The origins of grammar: Evidence from early language comprehension.* Cambridge, MA: MIT Press.

HIRSH-PASEK, K., & TREIMAN, R. (1982). Doggerel: Motherese in a new context. *Journal of Child Language, 9*(1), 229–237.

HIRSH-PASEK, K., GOLINKOFF, R., FLETCHER, DEGASPE-BEAUBIEN, & CAULEY. (1985). In the beginning: One-word speakers comprehend word order. Paper presented at Boston Child Language Conference, October, 1985.

HIRTH, D. H., & MCCULLOUGH, D. R. (1977). Evolution of alarm signals in ungulates with special reference to white-tailed deer. *American Naturalist, 111,* 31–42.

HOBSON, J. A. (1988). *The dreaming brain.* New York: Basic Books.

HOBSON, J. A., & McCARLEY, R. W. (1977). The brain as a dream-state generator: An activation-synthesis hypothesis of the dream process. *American Journal of Psychiatry, 134,* 1335–1368.

HOBSON, J. A., PACE-SCHOTT, E., & STICKGOLD, R. (2000). Dreaming and the brain: Towards a cognitive neuroscience of conscious states. *Behavioral and Brain Sciences, 23.*

HOCHBERG, J. (1981). On cognition in perception: Perceptual coupling and unconscious inference. *Cognition, 10,* 127–134.

HOCHBERG, J. (1988). Visual perception. In R. C. Atkinson, R. J. Herrnstein, G. Lindzey, & R. D. Luce (Eds.), *Stevens' handbook of experimental psychology: Vol. 1. Perception and motivation* (rev. ed., pp. 195–276). New York: Wiley.

HOCHBERG, J. E. (1978a). *Perception* (2nd ed.). Englewood Cliffs, NJ: Prentice-Hall.

HOCHBERG, J. E. (1978b). Art and perception. In E. C. Carterette & M. P. Friedman (Eds.), *Handbook of perception: Vol. 10* (pp. 225–255). New York: Academic Press.

HODGKIN, A. L., & HUXLEY, A. F. (1939). Action potentials recorded from inside nerve fiber. *Nature, 144,* 710–711.

HODGKINSON, S., MULLAN, M. J., & GURLING, H. M. (1990). The role of genetic factors in the etiology of the affective disorders. *Behavior Genetics, 20,* 235–250.

HOEBEL, B. G., & TEITELBAUM, P. (1976). Weight regulation in normal and hyperphagic rats. *Journal of Physiological and Comparative Psychology, 61,* 189–193.

HOFFERTH, S. L. (1996). Child care in the United States today. *The Future of Children, 6,* 41–61.

HOFFMAN, M. L. (1970). Moral development. In P. H. Mussen (Ed.), *Carmichael's manual of child psychology* (3rd. ed., vol. 2, pp. 457–558). New York: Wiley.

HOFFMAN, M. L. (1977a). Empathy, its development and prosocial implications. In C. B. Keasey (Ed.), *Nebraska Symposium on Motivation, 25,* 169–217.

HOFFMAN, M. L. (1977b). Sex differences in empathy and related behaviors. *Psychological Bulletin, 84,* 712–722.

HOFFMAN, M. L. (1979). Development of moral thought, feeling, and behavior. *American Psychologist, 34,* 295–318.

HOFFMAN, M. L. (1984). Empathy, its limitations, and its role in a comprehensive moral theory. In W. M. Kurtines & L. Gewirtz (Eds.), *Morality, moral behavior, and moral development* (pp. 283–302). New York: Wiley.

HOLDING, D. H. (1985). *The psychology of chess skill.* Hillsdale, NJ: Erlbaum.

HOLDING, D. H., & REYNOLDS, R. I. (1982). Recall or evaluation of chess positions as determinants of chess skill. *Memory and Cognition, 10,* 237–242.

HOLLAND, P. (1984). Origins of behavior in Pavlovian conditioning. *Psychology of Learning and Motivation, 18,* 129–174.

HOLLANDER, E. P. (1985.) Leadership and power. In G. Lindzey & E. Aronson (Eds.), *Handbook of social psychology: Vol 2* (3rd ed.). New York: Random House.

HOLLANDER, E., & McCARLEY, A. (1992). Yohimbine treatment of sexual side effects induced by serotonin reuptake blockers. *Journal of Clinical Psychiatry, 53,* 197–199.

HOLLINGSHEAD, A. B., & REDLICH, F. C. (1958). *Social class and mental illness: A community study.* New York: Wiley.

HOLLIS, K. L. (1984). The biological function of Pavlovian conditioning: The best defense is a good offense. *Journal of Experimental Psychology: Animal Learning and Behavior, 10,* 413–425.

HOLLISTER, L. E., & CSERNANSKY, J. G. (1990). *Clinical pharmacology of psychotherapeutic drugs* (3rd. ed.). New York: Churchill-Livingstone.

HOLLON, S. D. (1996). The efficacy and effectiveness of psychotherapy relative to medications. *American Psychologist, 51,* 1025–1030.

HOLLOS, M., & RICHARDS, F. A. (1993). Gender-associated development of formal operations in Nigerian adolescents. *Ethos, 21*(1), 24–52.

HOLM, K. H., CICCHETTI, F., BJÖRKLUND, L., BOONMAN, Z., TANDON, P., COSTANTINI, L. C., ET AL. (2001). Enhanced axonal growth from fetal human bcl-2 transgenic mouse dopamine neurons transplanted to the adult rat striatum. *Neuroscience 104,* 397–405.

HOLMES, D. (1990). The evidence for repression: An examination of sixty years of research. In J. Singer (Ed.), *Repression and dissociation: Implications for personality theory, psychopathology and health* (pp. 85–102). Chicago: University of Chicago Press.

HOLT, R. R. (1978). *Methods in clinical psychology: Vol. 1. Projective assessment.* New York: Plenum.

HOLTZMAN, P. S., KRINGLEN, E., MALTHYSSE, S., FLANAGAN, S. D., LIPTON, R. B., CRAMER, G., ET AL. (1988). A single dominant gene can account for eye tracking dysfunctions and schizophrenia in offspring of discordant twins. *Archives of General Psychiatry, 45,* 641–647.

HOLTZWORTH-MUNROE, A., & JACOBSON, N. S. (1985). Causal attributions of married couples: When do they search for causes? What do they conclude when they do? *Journal of Personality and Social Psychology, 48,* 1398–1412.

HOLWAY, A. F., & BORING, E. G. (1947). Determinants of apparent visual size with distance variant. *American Journal of Psychology, 54,* 21–37.

HONG, Y., IP, G., CHIU, C., MORRIS, M. W., & MENON, T. (2001). Cultural identity and dynamic construction of the self: collective duties and individual rights in Chinese and American cultures. *Social Cognition, 19,* 251–268.

HOOK, S. (1955). *The hero in history.* Boston: Beacon Press.

HOOLEY, J. M. (1985). Expressed emotion: A review of the critical literature. *Clinical Psychology Review, 5,* 119–139.

HORN, J. L. (1985). Remodeling old models of intelligence. In B. B. Wolman (Ed.), *Handbook of intelligence: Theories, measurements, and applications* (pp. 267–300). New York: Wiley.

HORN, J. L., & NOLL, J. (1994). A system for understanding cognitive capabilities: A theory and the evidence on which it is based. In D. K. Detterman (Ed.), *Current topics in human intelligence: Vol. 4. Theories of intelligence.* Norwood, NJ: Ablex.

HORN, J. M. (1983). The Texas Adoption Project: Adopted children and their biological and adoptive parents. *Child Development, 54,* 268–275.

HORN, J. M., LOEHLIN, J. C., & WILLERMAN, L. (1979). Intellectual resemblance among adoptive and biological relatives: The Texas Adoption Project. *Behavior Genetics, 13,* 459–471.

HORN, J. M., LOEHLIN, J. C., & WILLERMAN, L. (1982). Aspects of the inheritance of intellectual abilities. *Behavior Genetics, 12,* 479–516.

HORNE, J. A. (1988). *Why we sleep: The functions of sleep in humans and other mammals.* New York: Oxford University Press.

HORNEY, K. (1937). *The neurotic personality of our time.* New York: Norton.

HORNEY, K. (1945). *Our inner conflicts.* New York: Norton.

HORNEY, K. (1950). *New ways in psychoanalysis.* New York: Norton.

HORVATH, A. O., & LUBORSKY, L. (1993). The role of the therapeutic alliance in psychotherapy. *Journal of Consulting and Clinical Psychology, 61,* 561–573.

HOSKEN, D. J. (2001). Size and fluctuating asymmetry in sexually selected traits. *Animal Behaviour. 62,* 603–605.

HOVLAND, C. I., & WEISS, W. (1952). The influence of source credibility on communication effectiveness. *Public Opinion Quarterly, 15,* 635–650.

HOWES, C. (1990). Can the age of entry into child care and the quality of child care predict adjustment in kindergarten? *Developmental Psychology, 26,* 292–303.

HOWES, C., & HAMILTON, C. E. (1993). Child care for young children. In B. Spodek (Ed.), *Handbook of research on the education of young children.* New York: Macmillan.

HRDY, S. B., & WILLIAMS, G. C. (1983). Behavioral biology and the double standard. In S. K. Wasser (Ed.), *The social behavior of female vertebrates* (pp. 3–17). New York: Academic Press.

HROBJARTSSON, A., & GOTZSCHE, P. C. (2001). Is the placebo powerless? An analysis of clinical trials comparing placebo with no treatment. *New England Journal of Medicine, 344,* 1594–1602.

HUANG, M. P., & ALESSI, N. E. (1996). The Internet and the future of psychiatry. *American Journal of Psychiatry, 153,* 861–869.

HUBEL, D. H. (1963). The visual cortex of the brain. *Scientific American, 209,* 54–62.

HUBEL, D. H., & WIESEL, T. N. (1959). Receptive fields of single neurons in the cat's visual cortex. *Journal of Physiology, 148,* 574–591.

HUBEL, D. H., & WIESEL, T. N. (1968). Receptive fields and functional architecture of monkey striate cortex. *Journal of Physiology, 195,* 215–243.

HUDSPETH, A. J. (1989). How the ear's works work. *Nature, 341,* 397–404.

HUESMANN, L. R. (1986). Psychological processes promoting the relation between exposure to media violence and aggressive behavior by the viewer. *Journal of Social Issues, 42,* 125–139.

HUESMANN, L. R., LAGERSPETZ, K., & ERON, L. D. (1984). Intervening variables in the TV violence-aggression relation: Evidence from two countries. *Developmental Psychobiology, 20,* 1120–1134.

HUESMANN, L. R., & MILLER, L. S. (1994). Long-term effects of repeated exposure to media violence in childhood. In L. R. Huesmann (Ed.), *Aggressive behavior: Current perspectives.* New York: Plenum.

HUGHES, C., & CUTTING, A. L. (1999). Nature, nurture, and individual differences in early understanding of mind. *Psychological Science, 10*(5), 429–432.

HUME, D. (1739/1978). *A treatise on human nature.* Oxford: Clarendon.

HUMPHREYS, L. G. (1939). The effect of random alternation of reinforcement on the acquisition and extinction of conditioned eyelid reactions. *Journal of Experimental Psychology, 25,* 141–158.

HUNT, E. (1976). Varieties of cognitive power. In L. B. Resnick (Ed.), *The nature of intelligence.* Hillsdale, NJ: Erlbaum.

HUNT, E. (1985a). The correlates of intelligence. In D. K. Detterman (Ed.), *Current topics in human intelligence: Vol. 1.* Norwood, NJ: Ablex.

HUNT, E. (1985b). Verbal ability. In R. J. Sternberg (Ed.), *Human abilities: An information processing approach* (pp. 31–58). New York: Freeman.

HUNT, E. (1995). *Will we be smart enough? A cognitive analysis of the coming workforce.* New York: Russell Sage Foundation.

HUNT, E., LUNNEBORG, C., & LEWIS, J. (1975). What does it mean to be high verbal? *Cognitive Psychology, 7,* 194–227.

HUNT, M. M. (1959). *The natural history of love.* New York: Knopf.

HURLEY, R. A., BLACK, D. N., STIP, E., & TABER, K. H. (2000). Surgical treatment of mental illness: Impact of imaging. *Journal of Neuropsychiatry and Clinical Neuroscience, 12,* 421–424.

HURVICH, L. M. (1981). *Color vision.* Sunderland, MA: Sinauer Assoc.

HURVICH, L. M., & JAMESON, D. (1957). An opponent-process theory of color vision. *Psychological Review, 64,* 384–404.

HUSTON, T. L., RUGGIERO, M., CONNER, R., & GEIS, G. (1981). Bystander intervention into crime: A study based on naturally occurring episodes. *Social Psychology Quarterly, 44,* 14–23.

HUTCHINSON, R. R., & RENFREW, J. W. (1966). Stalking attack and eating behaviors elicited from the same sites in the hypothalamus. *Journal of Comparative and Physiological Psychology, 61,* 360–367.

HUTTENLOCHER, J. (1974). The origins of language comprehension. In R. L. Solso (Ed.), *Theories in cognitive psychology: The Loyola symposium* (pp. 331–368). Potomac, MD: Erlbaum.

HUTTENLOCHER, J., SMILEY, P., & CHARNEY, R. (1983). Emergence of action categories in the child: Evidence from verb meanings. *Psychological Review, 90,* 72–93.

HUTTENLOCHER, J. E., & HEDGES, L. V. (1994). Combining graded categories: Membership and typicality. *Psychological Review, 101,* 157–165.

HUTTENLOCHER, P. R. (1979). Synaptic density in human frontal cortex—developmental changes and effects of aging. *Brain Research, 163,* 195–205.

HYDE, D. M. (1959). An investigation of Piaget's theories of the development of the concept of number. Unpublished doctoral dissertation. University of London. Quoted in J. H. Flavell (Ed.), *The developmental psychology of Jean Piaget* (p. 383). New York: Van Nostrand Reinhold.

HYDE, J. S., & LINN, M. C. (1988). Gender differences in verbal ability: A meta-analysis. *Psychological Bulletin, 104,* 53–69.

HYMAN, I., & BILLINGS, F. J. (1998). Individual differences and the creation of false childhood memories. *Memory, 6,* 1–20.

HYMAN, I., HUSBAND, T., & BILLINGS, F. (1995). False memories of childhood experiences. *Applied Cognitive Psychology, 9,* 181–198.

IINO, M., GOTO, K., KAKEGAWA, W., OKADO, H., SUDO, M., ISHIUCHI, S., ET AL. (2001). Glia-synapse interaction through Ca2+-permeable AMPA receptors in Bergmann glia. *Science, 292,* 926–929.

ILYIN, N. A., & ILYIN, V. N. (1930). Temperature effects on the color of the Siamese cat. *Journal of Heredity, 21,* 309–318.

IMPERATO-MCGINLEY, J., GUERRERO, L., GAUTIER, T., & PETERSON, R. E. (1974). Steroid 5–alpha reductase deficiency in man: An inherited form of male pseudohermaphroditism. *Science, 186,* 1213–1215.

IMPERATO-MCGINLEY, J., PETERSON, R. E., GAUTIER, T., & STURLA, E. (1979). Androgens and the evolution of male-gender identity among male pseudohermaphrodites with 5–alpha reductase deficiency. *New England Journal of Medicine, 300,* 1233–1237.

INSEL, T. R. (1990). New pharmacologic approaches to obsessive compulsive disorder [Supplement]. *Journal of Clinical Psychiatry, 51,* 47–51.

INSEL, T. R. (1992). Toward a neuroanatomy of obsessive-compulsive disorder. *Archives of General Psychiatry, 49,* 739–740.

INTERNATIONAL HUMAN GENOME SEQUENCING COSORTIUM (IHGSC) (2001). *Nature, 409,* 860.

INZLICHT, M., & BEN-ZEEV, T. (2000). A threatening intellectual environment: Why females are susceptible to experiencing problem-solving deficits in the presence of males. *Psychological Science, 11,* 365–371.

IRVINE, J. T. (1978). Wolof "magical thinking": Culture and conservation revisited. *Journal of Cross-cultural Psychology, 9,* 300–310.

ISACSON, O. (1999). The neurobiology and neurogenetics of stem cells. *Brain Pathology, 9,* 495–498.

ISHA, A., & SAGI, D. (1995). Common mechanisms of visual imagery and perception. *Science, 268,* 1772–1774.

IVY, G. O., MacLEOD, C. M., PETIT, T. L., & MARKUS, E. J. (1992). A physiological framework for perceptual and cognitive changes in aging. In F. I. M. Craik & T. A. Salthouse (Eds.), *The handbook of aging and cognition.* Hillsdale, NJ: Erlbaum.

IZARD, C. E. (1971). *The face of emotion.* New York: Appleton-Century-Crofts.

IZARD, C. E. (1977). *Human emotions.* New York: Plenum.

IZARD, C. E. (1991). *The psychology of emotions.* New York: Plenum.

IZARD, C. E. (1994). Innate and universal facial expressions: Evidence from developmental cross-cultural research. *Psychological Bulletin, 115,* 288–299.

IZZETT, R. (1971). Authoritarianism and attitudes toward the Vietnam War as reflected in behavioral and self-report measures. *Journal of Personality and Social Psychology, 17,* 145–148.

JACKENDOFF, R. (1972). *Semantic interpretation in generative grammar.* Cambridge MA: MIT Press.

JACKENDOFF, R. (2002). *Foundations of language: Brain, meaning, grammar, evolution.* Oxford: Oxford University Press.

JACKSON, J. M., & LATANÉ, B. (1981). All alone in front of all those people: Stage fright as a function of the number and type of coperformers and audience. *Journal of Personality and Social Psychology, 40,* 73–85.

JACKSON, L. A., HUNTER, J. E., & HODGE, C. N. (1995). Physical attractiveness and intellectual competence: A meta-analytic review. *Social Psychology Quarterly, 58,* 108–122.

JACKSON, M., & McCLELLAND, J. L. (1975). Sensory and cognitive determinants of reading speed. *Journal of Verbal Learning and Verbal Behavior, 14,* 565–574.

JACKSON, M. D., & MCCLELLAND, J. L. (1979). Processing determinants of reading speed. *Journal of Experimental Psychology: Experimental, 108,* 151–158.

JACOBS, A. (1955). Formation of new associations to words selected on the basis of reaction-time-GSR combinations. *Journal of Abnormal and Social Psychology, 51,* 371–377.

JACOBS, G. H. (1993). The distribution and nature of colour vision among the mammals. *Biological Reviews of the Cambridge Philosophical Society, 68,* 413–471.

JACOBSEN, F. M. (1992). Fluoxetine-induced sexual dysfunction and an open trial of yohimbine. *Journal of Clinical Psychiatry, 53,* 119–122.

JACOBSEN, L. K., GIEDD, J. N., BERQUIN, P. C., KRAIN, A. L., HAMBURGER, S. D., KUMRA, S., ET AL. (1997). Quantitative morphology of the cerebellum and fourth ventricle in childhood-onset schizophrenia. *American Journal of Psychiatry, 154,* 1663–1669.

JACOBSON, N. S., & CHRISTENSON, A. (1996). Studying the effectiveness of psychotherapy. *American Psychologist, 51,* 1031–1039.

JACOBY, L. L., & DALLAS, M. (1981). On the relationship between autobiographical memory and perceptual learning. *Journal of Experimental Psychology: General, 3,* 306–340.

JACOBY, L. L., KELLEY, C., BROWN, J., & JASECHKO, J. (1989). Becoming famous overnight: Limits on the ability to avoid unconscious influences of the past. *Journal of Personality and Social Psychology: General, 56,* 326–338.

JACOBY, L. L., & WITHERSPOON, D. (1982). Remembering without awareness. *Canadian Journal of Psychology, 36,* 300–324.

JAKOBS, E., FISCHER, A. H., & MANSTEAD, A. S. R. (1997). Emotional experience as a function of social context: The role of the other. *Journal of Nonverbal Behavior, 21,* 103–130.

JAKOBS, E., MANSTEAD, A. S. R., & FISCHER, A. H. (1996). Social context and the experience of emotion. *Journal of Nonverbal Behavior, 20,* 123–142.

JAKOBS, E., MANSTEAD, A. S. R., & FISCHER, A. H. (2001). Social context effects on facial activity in a negative emotional setting. *Emotion, 1,* 51–69.

JAMES, L. E., & BURKE, D. M. (2000). Phonological priming effects on word retrieval and tip-of-the-tongue experiences in young and older adults. *Journal of Experimental Psychology: Learning, Memory and Cognition, 26,* 1378–1391.

JAMES, W. (1890). *Principles of psychology.* New York: Henry Holt.

JAMESON, D., & HURVICH, L. M. (1975). From contrast to assimilation: In art and in the eye. *Leonardo, 8,* 125–131.

JAMISON, K. R. (1995). Manic-depressive illness and creativity. *Scientific American, 272,* 62–67.

JANG, K. L., LIVESLEY, W. J., & VERNON, P. A. (1996). Heritability of the big five personality dimensions and their facets: A twin study. *Journal of Personality, 64,* 577–591.

JANG, K. L., PARIS, J., ZWEIG-FRANK, H., & LIVESLEY, W. J. (1998). Twin study of dissociative experience. *Journal of Nervous and Mental Disease, 186,* 345–351.

JANICAK, P. G., DAVIS, J. M., GIBBONS, R. D., ERICKSEN, S., CHANG, S., & GALLAGHER, P. (1985). Efficacy of ECT: A meta-analysis. *American Journal of Psychiatry, 142,* 297–302.

JANIS, I. (1982). *Groupthink: Psychological studies of policy decisions and fiascoes* (2nd ed.). Boston: Houghton Mifflin.

JANOWSKY, J. S., OVIATT, S. K., & ORWOLL, E. S. (1994). Testosterone influence spatial cognition in men. *Behavioral Neuroscience, 108,* 325–332.

JASPER, H. H. (1995). A historical perspective: The rise and fall of prefrontal lobotomy. In H. H. Jasper, R. et al. (Eds.), *Epilepsy and the functional anatomy of the frontal lobe* (pp. 97–114). New York: Raven Press.

JENIKE, M. A. (2001). An update on obsessive-compulsive disorder. *Bulletin of the Menninger Clinic, 65,* 4–25.

JENKINS, J. G., & DALLENBACH, K. M. (1924). Oblivescence during sleep and waking. *American Journal of Psychology, 35,* 605–612.

JENNINGS, E. E. (1972). *An anatomy of leadership: Princes, heroes, and supermen.* New York: McGraw-Hill.

JENSEN, A. R. (1969). How much can we boost I.Q. and scholastic achievement? *Harvard Educational Review, 39,* 1–123.

JENSEN, A. R. (1973). *Educability and group differences.* New York: Harper & Row.

JENSEN, A. R. (1980). Chronometric analysis of intelligence. *Journal of Social and Biological Structures, 3,* 103–122.

JENSEN, A. R. (1985). The nature of the black-white difference on various psychometric tests: Spearman's hypothesis. *Behavioral and Brain Sciences, 8,* 193–263.

JENSEN, A. R. (1987). Individual differences in the Hick paradigm. In P. A. Vernon (Ed.), *Speed of information processing and intelligence.* Norwood, NJ: Ablex.

JOBE, J., TOURANGEAU, R., & SMITH, A. (1993). Contributions of survey research to the understanding of memory. *Applied Cognitive Psychology, 7,* 567–584.

JOCKIN, V., McGUE, M., & LYKKEN, D. T. (1996). Personality and divorce: A genetic analysis. *Journal of Personality and Social Psychology, 71,* 288–299.

JOHN, O. P. (1990). The "Big Five" taxonomy: Dimensions of personality in the natural language and in questionnaires. In L. A. Pervin (Ed.), *Handbook of personality: Theory and research* (pp. 676–1000). New York: Guilford Press.

JOHNSON, A. M., WADSWORTH, J., WELLINGS, K., BRADSHAW, S., & FIELD, J. (1992). Sexual lifestyles and HIV risk. *Nature, 360,* 410–412.

JOHNSON, J., & NEWPORT, E. (1989). Critical period efforts in second-language learning: The influence of maturational state on the acquisition of English as a second language. *Cognitive Psychology, 21,* 60–99.

JOHNSON, M. H. (1993). Cortical maturation and the development of visual attention in early infancy. In M. H. Johnson (Ed.), *Brain Development and Cognition.* Cambridge, MA: Blackwell.

JOHNSON, R. D., & DOWNING, L. L. (1979). Deindividuation and valence of cues: Effects on prosocial and antisocial behavior. *Journal of Personality and Social Psychology, 37(9),* 1532–1538.

JOHNSON, R. E. (1979). *Juvenile delinquency and its origins.* New York: Cambridge University Press.

JOINT STATEMENT ON THE IMPACT OF ENTERTAINMENT VIOLENCE ON CHILDREN: CONGRESSIONAL PUBLIC HEALTH SUMMIT. (2000. July 26). Retrieved October 22, 2002 from the World Wide Web: http://www.aap.org/advocacy/releases/jstmtevc.htm.

JONES, E. E., & BERGLAS, S. (1978). Control of attributions about the self through self handicapping strategies: The appeal of alcohol and the role of underachievement. *Personality and Social Psychology Bulletin, 4(2),* 200–206.

JONES, E. E., & NISBETT, R. E. (1972). The actor and the observer: Divergent perceptions of the cause of behavior. In E. E. Jones, D. E. Karouse, H. H. Kelley, R. E. Nisbett, S. Valins, & B. Weiner (Eds.), *Attribution perceiving the causes of behavior.* Morristown, NJ: General Learning Press.

JONES, R. E. (1983). Street people and psychiatry: An introduction. *Hospital Community Psychiatry, 34,* 807–811.

JONES, S. S. (1996). Imitation or exploration? Young infants' matching of adults' oral gestures. *Child Development, 67,* 1952–1969.

JONES, S., COLLINS, K., & HONG, H. (1991). An audience effect on smile production in 10-month-old infants. *Psychological Science, 2(1),* 45–49.

JONIDES, J. (1980). Toward a model of the mind's eye's movement. *Canadian Journal of Psychology, 34,* 103–112.

JONIDES, J. (1983). Further toward a model of the mind's eye's movement. *Bulletin of the Psychonomic Society, 21,* 247–250.

JONIDES, J., & BAUM, D. R. (1978). Cognitive maps as revealed by distance estimates. Paper presented at the 18th annual meeting of the Psychonomic Society. Washington, DC.

JORGENSEN, B. W., & CERVONE, J. C. (1978). Affect enhancement in the pseudo recognition task. *Personality and Social Psychology Bulletin, 4,* 285–288.

JOSHI, A.K. (2002) Tree adjoining grammar. In R. Mitkov (Ed.), *Handbook of Computational Linguistics* (pp. 483–498). New York: Oxford University Press.

JOSSELSON, R. (1980). Ego development in adolescence. In J. Adelson (Ed.), *Handbook of adolescent psychology* (pp. 188–211). New York: Wiley.

JOURARD, S. M. (1964). *The transparent self.* New York: Van Nostrand.

JOUVET, M. (1967). The stages of sleep. *Scientific American, 216,* 62–72.

JOY, L. A., KIMBALL, M. M., & ZABRACK, M. L. (1986). Television and aggressive behavior. In T. M. Williams (Ed.), *The impact of television: A natural experiment involving three towns.* New York: Academic Press.

JUDD, L. L., PAULUS, M. P., WELLS, K. B., & RAPAPORT, M. H. (1996). Socioeconomic burden of subsyndromal depressive symptoms and major depression in a sample of the general population. *American Journal of Psychiatry, 153,* 1411–1417.

JULESZ, B. (1978). Perceptual limits of texture discrimination and their implications to figure-ground separation. In E. Leeuwenberg & H. Buffart (Eds.), *Formal theories of perception* (pp. 205–216). New York: Wiley.

JULIEN, R. M. (1985). *A primer of drug action* (4th ed.). New York: Freeman.

JUSCZYK, P. (1985). On characterizing the development of speech perception. In J. Mehler & R. Fox (Eds.), *Neonate cognition: Beyond the blooming buzzing confusion.* Hillsdale, NJ: Erlbaum.

JUSCZYK, P. W., CUTLER, A., & REDANZ, N. J. (1993) Infants' preference for the predominant stress patterns of English words. *Child Development, 64,* 675–687.

JUSCZYK, P. W., FRIEDERICI, A. D., WESSELS, J. M., SVENKERUD, V. Y., & JUSCZYK, A. M. (1993). Infants' sensitivity to the sound patterns of native language words. *Journal of Memory and Language, 32,* 402–420.

JUSCZYK, P. W., HIRSH-PASEK, K., KEMLER-NELSON, D. G., KENNEDY, L. J., WOODWARD, A., & PIWOZ, J. (1992). Perception of acoustic correlates of major phrasal units by young infants. *Cognitive Psychology, 24,* 252–293.

JUSCZYK, P. W., JOHNSON, S. P., SPELKE, E. S., & KENNEDY, L. J. (1999). Synchronous change and perception of object unity: Evidence from adults and infants. *Cognition, 71,* 257–288.

JUSCZYK, P. W., LUCE, P. A., & CHRLES-LUCE, J. (1994). Infants' sensitivity to phonotactic patterns in the native language. *Journal of Memory and Language, 33,* 630–645.

JUST, M. A., & CARPENTER, P. A. (1992). A capacity theory of comprehension: Individual differences in working memory. *Psychological Review, 99*(1), 122–149.

JUSTER, H. R., & HEIMBERG, R. G. (1995). Social phobia. Longitudinal course and long-term outcome of cognitive-behavioral treatment. *Psychiatric Clinics of North America, 18,* 821–842.

KAGAN, J. (1976). Emergent themes in human development. *American Scientist, 64,*186–196.

KAGAN, J. (1984). *The nature of the child.* New York: Basic Books.

KAHNEMAN, D., DIENER, E., & SCHWARZ, N. (EDS.). (1999). *Well-being: The foundations of hedonic psychology.* New York: Russell Sage Foundation.

KAHNEMAN, D., & MILLER, D. T. (1986). Norm theory: Comparing reality to its alternatives. *Psychological Review, 93,* 136–153.

KAHNEMAN, D., & TVERSKY, A. (1972). Subjective probability: A judgment of representativeness. *Cognitive Psychology, 3,* 430–454.

KAHNEMAN, D., & TVERSKY, A. (1973). On the psychology of prediction. *Psychological Review, 80,* 237–251.

KAHNEMAN, D., & TVERSKY, A. (1982). The simulation heuristic. In D. Kahneman, P. Slovic, & A. Tversky (Eds.), *Judgment under uncertainty.* New York: Cambridge University Press.

KAHNEMAN, D., & TVERSKY, A. (1984). Choices, values and frames. *American Psychologist, 39,* 341–350.

KAHNEMAN, D., & TVERSKY, A. (1996). On the reality of cognitive illusions. *Psychological Review, 103,* 582–591.

KAISER, E., & TRUESWELL, J. C. (2002). A new "look" in the processing of non-canonical word orders. Paper presented at the 15th Annual CUNY Conference on Human Sentence Processing, New York, March 2002.

KALICHMAN, S. C., HECKMAN, T., & KELLY, J. A. (1996). Sensation seeking as an explanation for the association between substance abuse and HIV-related risky sexual behavior. *Archives of Sexual Behavior, 25,* 141–154.

KALICK, S. M., ZEBROWITZ, L. A., LANGLOIS, J. H., & JOHNSON, R. M. (1998). Does human facial attractiveness honestly advertise health? Longitudinal data on an evolutional question. *Psychological Science, 9,* 8–13.

KAMIN, L. J. (1965). Temporal and intensity characteristics of the conditioned stimulus. In W. F. Prokasy (Ed.), *Classical conditioning.* New York: Appleton-Century-Crofts.

KAMIN, L. J. (1968). "Attention-like" processes in classical conditioning. In M. R. Jones (Ed.), *Miami symposium on the prediction of behavior: Aversive stimuli.* Miami: University of Miami Press.

KAMIN, L. J. (1974). *The science and politics of I.Q.* New York: Wiley.

KAMINSKY, H. (1984). Moral development in historical perspective. In W. M. Kurtines & J. L. Gerwitz (Eds.), *Morality, moral behavior, and moral development.* New York: Wiley.

KAMPERT, J. B., BLAIR, S. N., BARLOW, C. E., & KOHL, H. W. III. (1996). Physical activity, physical fitness, and all-cause and cancer mortality: A prospective study of men and women. *Annals of Epidemiology, 6,* 452–457.

KANDEL, E. R., & HAWKINS, R. D. (1992). The biological basis of learning and individuality. *Scientific American, 267,* 78–87.

KANIZSA, G. (1976). Subjective contours. *Scientific American, 234,* 48–52.

KAPUR, N. (1999). Syndromes of retrograde amnesia. *Psychological Bulletin, 125,* 800–825.

KAPUR, S., & REMINGTON, G. (1996). Serotonin-dopamine interaction and its relevance to schizophrenia. *American Journal of Psychiatry, 153,* 466–476.

KAPUR, S., & REMINGTON, G. (2001). Atypical antipsychotics: New directions and new challenges in the treatment of schizophrenia. *Annual Review of Medicine, 52,* 503–517.

KARAU, S. J., & WILLIAMS, K. D. (1995). Social loafing: Research findings, implications, and future directions. *Current Directions in Psychological Science, 4,* 134–140.

KASSER, T., & SHARMA, Y. S. (1999). Reproductive freedom, educational equality, and females' preference for resource-acquisition characteristics in mates. *Psychological Science, 10*(4), 374–377.

KASTRUP, O., LEONHARDT, G., KURTHEN, M., & HUFNAGEL, A. (2000). Cortical motor reorganization following early brain damage and hemispherectomy demonstrated by transcranial magnetic stimulation. *Clinical Neurophysiology, 111,* 1346–1352.

KATO, T., & KATO, N. (2000). Mitochondrial dysfunction in bipolar disorder. *Bipolar Disorders, 2*(3 Pt 1), 180–190.

KATZ, J. J. (1972). *Semantic theory.* New York: Harper & Row.

KATZ, J. J., & FODOR, J. A. (1963). The structure of a semantic theory. *Language, 39,* 170–210.

KATZ, N., BAKER, E., & MACNAMARA, J. (1974). What's in a name? A study of how children learn common and proper names. *Child Development, 45,* 469–473.

KAWAKAMI, K., DION, K. L., & DOVIDIO, J. F. (1998). Racial prejudice and stereotype activation. *Personality and Social Psychology Bulletin, 24*(4), 407–416.

KAY, P. (1996). Intra-speaker relativity. In J. J. Gumperz & S. C. Levinson (Eds.), *Rethinking linguistic relativity. Studies in the social and cultural foundations of language.* Cambridge: Cambridge University Press.

KAYUMOV, L., BROWN, G., JINDAL, R., BUTTOO, K., & SHAPIRO, C. M. (2001). A randomized, double-blind, placebo-controlled crossover study of the effect of exogenous melatonin on delayed sleep phase syndrome. *Psychosomatic Medicine, 63,* 40–48.

KEESEY, R. E., & POWLEY, T. L. (1986). The regulation of body weight. *Annual Review of Psychology, 37,* 109–134.

KEETON, W. T. (1972 and 1988). *Biological science* (2nd and 3rd eds.). New York: Norton.

KEGL, J., SENGHAS, A. & COPPOLA, M. (1999). Creation through contact: Sign language emergence and sign language change in Nicaragua. In Degraff, M., (Ed.), *Language creation and language change: Creolization, diachrony, and development* (pp. 179–237). Cambridge, MA: The MIT Press.

KEIL, F. L. (1989). *Concepts, kinds, and cognitive development.* Cambridge, MA: MIT Press.

KELLEY, H., & THIBAUT, J. W. (1978). *Interpersonal relations: A theory of interdependence.* New York: Wiley-Interscience.

KELLEY, H. H. (1967). Attribution theory in social psychology. In D. Levine (Ed.), *Nebraska Symposium on Motivation* (pp. 192–238). Lincoln, NE: University of Nebraska Press.

KELLEY, H. H., & MICHELA, J. L. (1980). Attribution theory and research. *Annual Review of Psychology, 31,* 457–501.

KELLEY, S., & MIRER, T. W. (1974). The simple act of voting. *American Political Science Review, 68,* 572–591.

KELLMAN, P. J., & SHIPLEY, T. F. (1991). A theory of visual interpolation in object perception. *Cognitive Psychology, 23,* 141–221.

KELLMAN, P. J., & SPELKE, E. S. (1983). Perception of partially occluded objects in infancy. *Cognitive Psychology, 15,* 483–524.

KELLMAN, P. J., SPELKE, E. S., & SHORT, K. R. (1986). Infant perception of object unity from translatory motion in depth and vertical translation. *Child Development, 57,* 72–86.

KELLY, G. A. (1955). *The psychology of personal constructs.* New York: Norton.

KELLY, J. A., & OTTO-SALAJ, L. L., SIKKEMA, K. J., PINKERTON, S. D., & OTHERS. (1998). Implications of HIV treatment advances for behavioral research on AIDS: Protease inhibitors and new challenges in HIV secondary prevention. *Health Psychology, 17,* 310–319.

KELLY, M. H., & MARTIN, S. (1994). Domain-general abilities applied to domain-specific tasks: Sensitivity to probabilities in perception, cognition, and language. In L. R. Gleitman & B. Landau (Eds.), Lexical acquisition [Special Issue]. *Lingua, 92,* 108–140.

KEMENY, M. E. (1994). Psychoneuroimmunology of HIV infection. *Psychiatric Clinics of North America, 17,* 55–68.

KENDALL-TACKETT, K. A., WILLIAMS, L. M., & FINKELHOR, D. (1993). Impact of sexual abuse on children: A review and synthesis of recent empirical studies. *Psychological Bulletin, 113,* 164–180.

KENDLER, K. S., & GRUENBERG, A. M. (1984). An independent analysis of the Danish adoption study of schizophrenia: VI. The relationship between psychiatric disorders as defined by DSM-III in the relatives and adoptees. *Archives of General Psychiatry, 41,* 555–564.

KENDLER, K. S., MYERS, J., PRESCOTT, C. A., & NEALE, M. C. (2001). The genetic epidemiology of irrational fears and phobias in men. *Archives of General Psychiatry, 58,* 257–265.

KENNY, D., & ZACCARO, S. J. (1983). An estimate of variance due to traits in leadership. *Journal of Applied Psychology, 68,* 678–685.

KENRICK, D. T., & CIALDINI, R. B. (1977). Romantic attraction: Misattribution versus reinforcement explanations. *Journal of Personality and Social Psychology, 35,* 381–391.

KENRICK, D. T., CIALDINI, R. B., & LINDER, D. E. (1979). Misattribution under fear-producing circumstances: Four failures to replicate. *Personality and Social Psychology Bulletin, 5,* 329–334.

KERR, M. E., & BOWEN, M. (1988). *Family evaluation.* New York: Norton.

KERR, N. L., & KAUFMANN-GILLILAND, C. M. (1994). Communication, commitment, and cooperation. *Journal of Personality and Social Psychology, 66,* 513–529.

KESSLER, R. C., AVENEVOLI, S., & RIES MERIKANGAS, K. (2001). Mood disorders in children and adolescents: An epidemiologic perspective. *Biological Psychiatry, 49,* 1002–1014.

KESSLER, R. C., KELLER, M. B., & WITTCHEN, H.-U. (2001). The epidemiology of generalized anxiety disorder. *Psychiatric Clinics of North America, 24,* 19–39.

KETY, S. S. (1983). Mental illness in the biological and adoptive relatives of schizophrenic adoptees: Findings relevant to genetic and environmental factors in etiology. *Journal of American Psychiatry, 140,* 720–727.

KHANNA, S. M., & LEONARD, D. G. B. (1982). Basilar membrane tuning in the cat cochlea. *Science, 215,* 305–306.

KIHLSTROM, J. F. (1987). The cognitive unconscious. *Science, 237,* 1445–1452.

KIHLSTROM, J. F. (1992). Dissociation and dissociations: A comment on consciousness and cognition. *Consciousness and Cognition: An International Journal, 1,* 47–53.

KIHLSTROM, J. F. (1993). The recovery of memory in the laboratory and the clinic. Paper presented at the 1993 conventions of the Rocky Mountain and the Western Psychological Associations. Phoenix, Arizona.

KIHLSTROM, J. F. (1997). Suffering from reminiscences: Exhumed memory, implicit memory, and the return of the repressed. In M. Conway (Ed.), *Recovered memories and false memories* (pp. 100–117). New York: Oxford University Press.

KIHLSTROM, J. F., MULVANEY, S., TOBIAS, B. A., & TOBIS, I. P. (2000). The emotional unconscious. In E. Eich & J. Kihlstrom (Eds.), *Cognition and emotion* (pp. 30–86). New York: Oxford University Press.

KILHAM, W., & MANN, L. (1974). Level of destructive obedience as a function of transmitter and executant roles in the Milgram obedience paradigm. *Journal of Personality and Social Psychology, 29,* 696–702.

KIMBLE, G. A. (1961). *Hilgard and Marquis' conditioning and learning.* New York: Appleton-Century-Crofts.

KIMURA, D., & WATSON, N. (1989). The relation between oral movement and speech. *Brain and Language, 37,* 565–590.

KINSEY, A., POMEROY, W. B., & MARTIN, C. E. (1948). *Sexual behavior in the human male.* Philadelphia: Saunders.

KINSEY, A., POMEROY, W., MARTIN, C., & GEBHARD, P. (1953). *Sexual behavior in the human female.* Philadelphia: Saunders.

KITAYAMA, S., MARKUS, H. R., & KUROKAWA, M. (2000). Culture, emotion, and well-being: Good feelings in Japan and the United States. *Cognition and Emotion, 14,* 93–124.

KITAYAMA, S., MARKUS, H. R., & MATSUMOTO, H. (1995). Culture, self and emotion: A cultural perspective on "self-conscious" emotions. In J. P. Tangney & K. W. Fischer (Eds.), *Self-conscious emotions* (pp. 439–487). New York: Guilford.

KITZINGER, C. (2001). Sexualities. In R. K. Unger (Ed.), *Handbook of the psychology of women and gender* (pp. 272–285). New York: Wiley.

KLAUER, K. C., MUSCH, J., & NAUMER, B. (2000). On belief bias in syllogistic reasoning. *Psychological Review, 107,* 852–884.

KLAUS, M. H., & KENNELL, J. H. (1976). *Maternal-infant bonding: The impact of early separation or loss on family development.* St. Louis, MO: Mosby.

KLAUS, M. H., KENNELL, J. H., PLUMB, N., & ZUEHLKE, S. (1970). Human maternal behavior at the first contact with her young. *Pediatrics, 46,* 187.

KLEIN, D. F. (1989). Repeated observations of yawning, clitoral engorgement, and orgasm associated with fluoxetine administration. *Journal of Clinical Psychopharmacology, 9,* 384.

KLEINMUNTZ, B. (1982). *Personality and psychological assessment.* New York: St. Martin's Press.

KLERMAN, G., & WEISSMAN, M. (1993). Interpersonal psychotherapy for depression: Background and concepts. In *New applications of interpersonal therapy.* Washington DC: American Psychological Association Press.

KLERMAN, G. L. (1990). The psychiatric patient's right to effective treatment: Implications of Osheroff v. Chestnut Lodge. *American Journal of Psychiatry, 147,* 409–418.

KLIMA, E., & BELLUGI, U., WITH BATTISON, R., BOYES-BRAEM, P., FISCHER, S., FRISHBERG, N., ET AL. (1979). *The signs of language.* Cambridge, MA: Harvard University Press.

KLINE, P. (1995). A critical review of the measurement of personality and intelligence. In D. H. Saklofske & M. Zeidner (Eds.), *International handbook of personality and intelligence* (pp. 505–524). New York: Plenum.

KLOPFER, B., AINSWORTH, M., KLOPFER, W. G., & HOLT, R. R. (1954). *Developments in the Rorschach technique.* Yonkers, NY: World Book.

KLUFT, R. P. (1987). An update on multiple-personality disorder. *Journal of Hospital and Community Psychiatry, 38,* 363–373.

KOHLBERG, L. (1966). A cognitive developmental analysis of children's sex-role concepts and attitudes. In E. E. Maccoby (Ed.), *The development of sex differences* (pp. 82–171). Stanford, CA: Stanford University Press.

KOHLBERG, L. (1969). Stage and sequence: The cognitive developmental approach to socialization. In D. A. Goslin (Ed.), *Handbook of socialization theory of research* (pp. 347–480). Chicago: Rand McNally.

KOHLBERG, L., LEVINE, C., & HEWER, A. (1984). Synopses and detailed replies to critics. In L. Kohlberg (Ed.), *The psychology of moral development: The nature and validity of moral stages* (pp. 320–386). San Francisco: Harper & Row.

KÖHLER, W. (1925). *The mentality of apes.* New York: Harcourt Brace and World.

KÖHLER, W. (1947). *Gestalt psychology.* New York: Liveright.

KOHN, A. (1993). *Punished by rewards.* New York: Houghton Mifflin.

KOHN, M. L. (1968). Social class and schizophrenia: A critical review. In D. Rosenthal & S. S. Kety (Eds.), *The transmission of schizophrenia* (pp. 155–174). London: Pergamon.

KOHUT, H. (1978). *The psychology of the self: A case book.* New York: International Universities Press.

KOLATA, G., & PETERSON, I. (2001 July 21). New way to insure eyewitnesses can ID the right bad guy. *New York Times,* p. 1.

KOLB, B., & WHISHAW, I. Q. (1996). *Fundamentals of human neuropsychology* (4th ed.). New York: Freeman.

KOLB, I., & WHISHAW, I. Q. (2001). *An Introduction to brain and behavior.* New York: Worth.

KOLODNY, R., MASTERS, W., HENDRYX, J., & TORO, G. (1971). Plasma testosterone and semen analysis in male homosexuals. *New England Journal of Medicine, 285,* 1170–1174.

KOMORITA, S. S, & PARKS, C. D. (1999). Reciprocity and cooperation in social dilemmas: Review and future directions. In D. V. Budescu, I. Erev et al. (Eds.), *Games and human behavior: Essays in honor of Amnon Rapoport* (pp. 315–330). Mahwah, NJ: Erlbaum.

KONDRO, W. (1998). New rules on human subjects could end debate in Canada. *Science, 280,* 1521.

KONDZIOLKA, D., WECHSLER, L., GOLDSTEIN, S., MELTZER, C., THULBORN, K. R., GEBEL, J., ET AL. (2000). Transplantation of cultured human neuronal cells for patients with stroke. *Neurology, 55*(4), 565–569.

KORDOWER, J. H., FREEMAN, T. B., SNOW, B. J., VINGERHOETS, F. J. G., MUFSON, E. J., SANBERG, P. R., ET AL. (1995). Neuropathological evidence of graft survival and striatal reinnervation after the transplantation of fetal mesencephalic tissue in a patient with Parkinson's disease. *New England Journal of Medicine, 332,* 1118–1124.

KORDOWER, J. H., WINN, S. R., LIU, Y. T., MUFSON, E. J., SLADEK, J. R., JR., HAMMANG, J. R., ET AL. (1994). The aged monkey basal forebrain: Rescue and sprouting of axotomotized basal forebrain neurons after grafts of encapsulated cells secreting human nerve growth factor. *Proceedings of the National Academy of Sciences of the United States, 91,* 10898–10902.

KORIAT, A., & LIEBLICH, I. (1974). What does a person in a TOT state know that a person in a "Don't Know" state doesn't know? *Memory and Cognition, 2,* 647–655.

KORN, J. H. (1997). *Illusions of reality: A history of deception in social psychology.* Albany, NY: State University of New York Press.

KOSONEN, P., & WINNE, P. H. (1995). Effects of teaching statistical laws on reasoning about everyday problems. *Journal of Educational Psychology, 87,* 33–56.

KOSSLYN, S. M., & PASCUAL-LEONE, A., ET AL. (1999). The role of area 17 in visual imagery: Convergent evidence from PET and rTMS. *Science, 284,* 167–170.

KOSSLYN, S. M., BALL, T. M., & REISSER, B. J. (1978). Visual images preserve metric spatial information: Evidence from studies of image scanning. *Journal of Experimental Psychology: Human Perception and Performance, 4,* 1–20.

KOTKIN, M., DAVIET, C., & GURIN, J. (1996). The Consumer Reports mental health survey. *American Psychologist, 51,* 1080–1082.

KRAMER, P. D. (1993). *Listening to Prozac.* New York: Viking.

KRASNE, F. B., & GLANZMAN, D. L. (1995). What we can learn from invertebrate learning. *Annual Review of Psychology, 45,* 585–624.

KRAUS, S. J. (1995). Attitudes and the prediction of behavior: A meta analysis of the empirical literature. *Personality and Social Psychology Bulletin, 21*(1), 58–75.

KRAUT, R. E., & JOHNSTON, R. E. (1979). Social and emotional messages of smiling: An ethological approach. *Journal of Personality and Social Psychology, 37*(9), 1539–1553.

KREBS, J. R. (1982). Territorial defence in the great tit (Parus Major L.). *Ecology, 52,* 2–22.

KRIPKE, D. (1982). Ultradian rhythms in behavior and physiology. In F. M. Brown & R. C. Graeber (Eds.), *Rhythmic aspects of behavior* (pp. 313–343). Hillsdale, NJ: Erlbaum.

KRUGER, J. (1999). Lake Wobegon be gone! The "below-average effect" and the egocentric nature of comparative ability judgments. *Journal of Personality and Social Psychology, 77,* 221–232.

KRUPNICK, J. L., SOTSKY, S. M., SIMMENS, S., MOYER, J., ELKIN, I., WATKINS, J., ET AL. (1996). The role of the therapeutic alliance in psychotherapy and pharmacotherapy outcome: Findings in the National Institute of Mental Health Treatment of Depression Collaborative Research Program. *Journal of Consulting and Clinical Psychology, 64,* 532–539.

KRUSCHKE, J. K., & BLAIR, N. J. (2000). Blocking and backward blocking involve learned inattention. *Psychonomics Bulletin and Review, 7,* 636–645.

KUAN, D. Y., ROTH, K. A., FLAVELL, R. A., & RAKIC, P. (2000). Mechanisms of programmed cell death in the developing brain. *Trends in Neuroscience, 23,* 291–297.

KUFFLER, S. W. (1953). Discharge pattern and functional organization of mammalian retina. *Journal of Neurophysiology, 16,* 37–68.

KUHL, P., WILLIAMS, K., LACERDA, F., STEVENS, K., & LINDBLOM, B. (1992). Linguistic experience alters phonetic perception in infants by six months of age. *Science, 255,* 606–608.

KUNDA, Z. (1990). The case for motivated reasoning. *Psychological Bulletin, 108,* 480–498.

KUNDA, Z., FONG, G. T., SANITIOSO, R., & REBER, E. (1993). Directional questions direct self conceptions. *Journal of Experimental Social Psychology, 29*(1), 63–86.

KUPFER, D. J., & REYNOLDS, C. F., III. (1997). Management of insomnia. *New England Journal of Medicine, 336,* 341–346.

KURTINES, W. M., & GEWIRTZ, J. L. (EDS.). (1995). *Moral development: An introduction.* Boston: Allyn and Bacon.

KURTZ, S. N. (1991). Polysexualization: A new approach to Oedipus in the Trobriands. *Ethos, 19,* 68–101.

KURZBAN, R., AND LEARY, M. R. (2001). Evolutionary origins of stigmatization: The functions of social exclusion. *Psychological Bulletin, 127,* 187–208.

KURZTHALER, I., & FLEISCHHACKER, W. W. (2001). The clinical implications of weight gain in schizophrenia [Suppl.]. *Journal of Clinical Psychiatry, 62*(7), 32–37.

KYLLONEN, P. C., & CHRISTAL, R. E. (1990). Reasoning ability is (little more than) working memory capacity? *Intelligence, 14*(4), 389–433.

LABORATORY OF COMPARATIVE HUMAN COGNITION (1983). Culture and cognitive development. In P. Mussen (Ed.), *Handbook of child psychology: Vol. 1. History, theory and methods* (4th ed.). New York: Wiley.

LABOV, W. (1970). The logic of nonstandard English. In F. Williams (Ed.), *Language and poverty: Perspectives on a theme* (pp. 153–189). Chicago: Markham.

LADEFOGED, P. (1975) *A course in phonetics.* New York: Harcourt, Brace Jovanovich.

LAFARGE, L. (1993). The early determinants of penis envy. In R. A. Glick & S. P. Roose, (Eds.), *Rage, power, and aggression. The role of affect in motivation, development, and adaptation: Vol. 2* (pp. 80–101). New Haven, CT: Yale University Press.

LAGERSPETZ, K. M. J., BJORKQVIST, K., & PELTONEN, T. (1988). Is indirect aggression typical of females? Gender differences in aggressiveness in 11- to 12-year-old girls. *Aggressive Behavior, 14,* 403–414.

LAKOFF, G., & JOHNSON, M. (1980). *Metaphors we live by.* Chicago: University of Chicago Press.

LALONDE, J. K., HUDSON, J. I., GIGANTE, R. A., & POPE, H. G., JR. (2001). Canadian and American psychiatrists' attitudes toward dissociative disorders diagnoses. *Canadian Journal of Psychiatry, 46,* 407–412.

LAMARINE, R. (1995). Child and adolescent depression. *Journal of School Health, 65,* 390–394.

LAMB, H. R. (1984). Deinstitutionalization and the homeless mentally ill. *Hospital Community Psychiatry, 35,* 899–907.

LAMB, H. R. (1998). Deinstitutionalization at the beginning of the new millennium. *Harvard Review of Psychiatry, 6,* 1–10.

LAMB, H. R., & BACHRACH, L. L. (2001). Some perspectives on deinstitutionalization. *Psychiatric Services, 52,* 1039–1045.

LAMB, M. E. (ED.). (1987). *The father's role: Cross-cultural perspectives.* Hillsdale, NJ: Erlbaum.

LAMB, M. E. (ED.). (1997). *The role of the father in child development* (3rd ed.). New York: Wiley.

LAMBERT, A. J., CRONEN, S., CHASTEEN, A. L., & LICKEL, B. (1996). Private vs public expressions of racial prejudice. *Journal of Experimental Social Psychology, 32*(5), 437–459.

LANDAU, B. (1982). Will the real grandmother please stand up? The psychological reality of dual meaning representations. *Journal of Psycholinguistic Research, 11,* 47–62.

LANDAU, B., & GLEITMAN, L. R. (1985). *Language and experience: Evidence from the blind child.* Cambridge, MA: Harvard University Press.

LANDAU, B., & MUNNICH, E. (1998). The representation of space of spatial language: Challenges for cognitive science. In P. Olivier & K. Gapp (Eds.), *Representation and processing of spatial expressions* (pp. 263–272). Mahwah, NJ: Lawrence Erlbaum.

LANDAU, B., SMITH, L., & JONES, S. (1988). The importance of shape in early lexical learning. *Cognitive Development, 3,* 299–321.

LANDAU, B., & STECKER, D. (1990). Objects and places: Geometric and syntactic representations in early lexical learning. *Cognitive Development, 5,* 287–312.

LANDAU, B., & ZUKOWSKI, A. (2002). Objects, motions, and paths: Spatial language of children with Williams Syndrome. Developmental Neuropsychology [Special Issue, C. B. Mervis (Ed.)]., in press.

LANDIS, C., & HUNT, W. A. (1932). Adrenalin and emotion. *Psychological Review, 39,* 467–485.

LANG, B., & PERNER, J. (2002). Understanding of intention and false belief and the development of self-control. *British Journal of Developmental Psychology, 20*(1), 67–76.

LANG, P. J., DAVIS, M., & OHMAN, A. (2000). Fear and anxiety: Animal models and human cognitive psychophysiology. *Journal of Affective Disorders, 61,* 137–159.

LANGER, E. J., & RODIN, J. (1976). The effects of choice and enhanced personal responsibility for the aged: A field experiment in an institutional setting. *Journal of Personality and Social Psychology, 34,* 191–198.

LANGLOIS, J. H., & DOWNS, A. C. (1980). Mothers, fathers, and peers as socialization agents of sex-typed play behaviors in young children. *Child Development, 51,* 1237–1347.

LANGLOIS, J. H., ROGGMAN, L. A., CASEY, R. J., RITTER, J. M., RIESER-DANNER, L. A., & JENKINS, V. Y. (1987). Infant preferences for attractive faces: Rudiments of a stereotype. *Developmental Psychobiology, 23,* 363–369.

LANYON, R. I., & GOLDSTEIN, L. D. (1971). *Personality assessment.* New York: Wiley.

LANYON, R. I., & GOLDSTEIN, L. D. (1982). *Personality assessment* (2nd ed.). New York: Wiley.

LAPIERE, R. (1934). Attitudes versus actions. *Social Forces, 13,* 230–237.

LARRICK, R. P., & BLOUNT, S. (1997). The claiming effect: Why players are more generous in social dilemmas than in ultimatum games. *Journal of Personality and Social Psychology, 72*(4), 810–825.

LASKY, J. J., HOVER, G. L., SMITH, P. A., BOSTIAN, D. W., DUFFENDECK, S. C.. & NORD, C. L. (1959). Post-hospital adjustment as predicted by psychiatric patients and by their staff. *Journal of Consulting Psychology, 23,* 213–218.

LASSEN, N. A., INGVAR, D. H., & SKINHOJ, E. (1978). Brain function and blood flow. *Scientific American, 239,* 62–71.

LASSITER, G. D. (2000). The relative contributions of recognition and search-evaluation processes to high-level chess performance: Comment on Gobet and Simon. *Psychological Science, 11*(2), 172–173.

LATANÉ, B. (1981). The psychology of social impact. *American Psychologist, 36,* 343–356.

LATANÉ, B. (1997). Dynamic social impact: The societal consequences of human interaction. In C. McGarty & S. A. Haslam (Eds.) *The message of social psychology: Perspectives on mind in society* (pp. 200–220). Oxford: Blackwell.

LATANÉ, B., & HARKINS, S. (1976). Cross-modality matches suggest anticipated stage fright as a multiplicative power function of audience size and status. *Perception and Psychophysics, 20,* 482–488.

LATANÉ, B., & NIDA, S. (1981). Group size and helping. *Psychological Bulletin, 89,* 308–324.

LATANÉ, B., NIDA, S. A., & WILSON, D. W. (1981). The effects of group size on helping behavior. In J. P. Rushton & R. M. Sorrentino (Eds.), *Altruism and helping behavior: Social, personality, and developmental perspectives.* Hillsdale, NJ: Erlbaum.

LATANÉ, B., & RODIN, J. (1969). A lady in distress: Inhibiting effects of friends and strangers on bystander intervention. *Journal of Experimental Social Psychology, 5,* 189–202.

LATANÉ, B., WILLIAMS, K., & HARKINS, S. (1979). Many hands make light the work: The causes and consequences of social loafing. *Journal of Personality and Social Psychology, 37,* 822–332.

LAYZER, D. (1972). Science or superstition: A physical scientist looks at the I.Q. controversy. *Cognition, 1,* 265–300.

LAZARUS, A. A. (1971). *Behavior therapy and beyond.* New York: McGraw-Hill.

LAZARUS, A. A. (1981). *The practice of multi-modal therapy.* New York: McGraw-Hill.

LE BON, G. (1895). *The crowd.* New York: Viking Press, 1960.

LE VAY, S. (1991). A difference in hypothalamic structure between heterosexual and homosexual men. *Science, 253,* 1034–1037.

LEA, S. E. G., & RYAN, C. M. E. (1990). Unnatural concepts and the theory of concept discrimination in birds. In M. L. Commons, R. J. Herrnstein, S. Kosslyn, & D. Mumford (Eds.), *Quantitative analysis of behavior, vol. VIII: Behavioral approaches to pattern recognition and concept formation* (pp. 165–185). Hillsdale, NJ: Erlbaum.

LEARY, M. R., & KOWALSKI, R. M. (1990). Impression management: A literature review and two-component model. *Psychological Bulletin, 107,* 34–47.

LECKMAN, J. F., ZHANG, H., ALSOBROOK, J. P., & PAULS, D. L. (2001). Symptom dimensions in obsessive-compulsive disorder: Toward quantitative phenotypes. *American Journal of Medical Genetics, 105,* 28–30.

LEDOUX, J. E. (1994). Emotion, memory, and the brain. *Scientific American, 270,* 50–57.

LEFF, M. J., ROATSCH, J. F., & BUNNEY, W. E., JR. (1970). Environmental factors preceding the onset of severe depressions. *Psychiatry, 33,* 298–311.

LEGAULT, F., & STRAYER, F. F. (1990). The emergence of sex-segregation in preschool peer groups. In F. F. Strayer, (Ed.), *Social interaction and behavioral development during early childhood.* Montreal: La Maison D'Ethologie de Montréal.

LEHMAN, D., LEMPERT, R. O., & NISBETT, R. E. (1988). The effects of graduate training on reasoning: Formal discipline and thinking about everyday-life events. *American Psychologist, 43,* 431–442.

LEHMAN, D., & NISBETT, R. (1990). A longitudinal study of the effects of undergraduate education on reasoning. *Developmental Psychology, 26,* 952–960.

LEIBOWITZ, S. F. (1991). Brain neuropeptide Y: An integrator of endocrine, metabolic and behavioral processes. *Brain Research Bulletin, 27,* 333–337.

LENNEBERG, E. H. (1967). *Biological foundations of language.* New York: Wiley.

LEON, M., COOPERSMITH, R., BEASLEY, L. J., & SULLIVAN, R. M. (1990). Thermal aspects of parenting. In N. A. Krasnegor & R. S. Bridges (Eds.), *Mammalian parenting: Biochemical, neurobiological, and behavioral determinants* (pp. 400–415). New York: Oxford University Press.

LEONARD, B. E. (2001). The immune system, depression and the action of antidepressants. *Progress in Neuropsychopharmacology and Biological Psychiatry, 25,* 767–780.

LEONARD, H. L., & SWEDO, S. E. (2001). Paediatric autoimmune neuropsychiatric disorders associated with streptococcal infection (PANDAS). *International Journal of Neuropsychopharmacology, 4,* 191–198.

LEPPER, L., HENDERLONG, J., & GINGRAS, I. (1999). Understanding the effects of extrinsic rewards on intrinsic motivation—uses and abuses of meta-analysis: Comment on Deci, Koestner, and Ryan (1999). *Psychological Bulletin, 125,* 669–676.

LEPPER, M. R. (1983). Social control processes, attributions of motivation, and the internalization of social values. In E. T. Higgins, D. N. Ruble, & W. W. Hartup (Eds.), *Social cognition and social behavior: Developmental perspectives.* New York: Cambridge University Press.

LEPPER, M. R., GREENE, D., & NISBETT, R. E. (1973). Undermining children's intrinsic interest with extrinsic rewards: A test of the "overjustification" hypothesis. *Journal of Personality and Social Psychology, 28,* 129–137.

LEROITH, D., SHILOACH, J., & ROTH, J. (1982). Is there an earlier phylogenetic precursor that is common to both the nervous and endocrine systems? *Peptides, 3,* 211–215.

LESLIE, A. M. (1992). Pretense, autism, and the theory of mind module. *Current Directions in Psychological Science, 1,* 18–21.

LETTVIN, J. Y., MATURAN, H. R., McCULLOCH, W. S., & PITTS, W. H. (1959). What the frog's eye tells the frog's brain. *Proceedings of the Institute of Radio Engineers, 47,* 1940–1951.

LEVAV, I., KOHN, R., GOLDING, J. M., & WEISSMAN, M. M. (1997). Vulnerability of Jews to affective disorders. *American Journal of Psychiatry, 154*(7), 941–947.

LEVELT, W. (1970). A scaling approach to the study of syntactic relations. In G. Flores d'Arcais & W. Levelt (Eds.), *Advances in psycholinguistics* (pp. 109–121). Amsterdam: North-Holland.

LEVIN, B. (1993). *English verb classes and alternations.* Chicago: University of Chicago Press.

LEVINE, J. M., & MORELAND, R. L. (1998). Small groups. In D. Gilbert, S. Fiske, & G. Lindzey (Eds.), *The handbook of social psychology* (4th ed., pp. 415–469). Boston: McGraw-Hill.

LEVINSON, D. J. (1978). *The seasons of a man's life.* New York: Knopf.

LEVINSON, S. (1983). *Pragmatics.* Cambridge: Cambridge University Press.

LEVINSON, S. C., KITA, S., HAUN, D. B. M., & RASCH, B. H. (2002). Returning the tables: Language affects spatial reasoning. *Cognition, 84*(2), 155–188.

LEVY, J. (1974). Psychobiological implications of bilateral asymmetry. In S. J. Dimond & J. G. Beaumont (Eds.), *Hemisphere function in the human brain* (pp. 121–183). New York: Wiley.

LEVY, J. (1983). Language, cognition, and the right hemisphere: A response to Gazzaniga. *American Psychologist, 38,* 538–541.

LEVY, J. (1985). Right brain, left brain: Facts and fiction. *Psychology Today, 19,* 38–44.

LEVY, W. B., & STEWARD, O. (1979). Synapses as associative memory elements in the hippocampal formation. *Brain Research, 175,* 233–245.

LEWINSOHN, P. M., & ROSENBAUM, M. (1987). Recall of parental behavior by acute depressives, remitted depressives, and nondepressives. *Journal of Personality and Social Psychology, 52,* 611–619.

LEWINSOHN, P. M., HOBERMAN, H., TERI, L., & HAUTZINGER, M. (1985). An integrative theory of depression. In S. Reiss & R. Bootzin (Eds.), *Theoretical issues in behavior therapy.* Orlando, FL: Academic Press.

LEWIS, C., & KEREN, G. (1999). On the difficulties underlying Bayesian reasoning: A comment on Gigerenzer and Hoffrage. *Psychological Review, 106,* 411–416.

LEWIS, J. R., BATES, B. C., & LAWRENCE, S. (1994). Empirical studies of projection: A critical review. *Human Relations, 47*(11), 1295–1319.

LEWONTIN, R. C. (1976). Race and intelligence. In N. J. Block & G. Dworkin (Eds.), *The IQ controversy* (pp. 78–92). New York: Pantheon.

LI, P. (1994). *Subcategorization as a predictor of verb meaning: Cross-language study in Mandarin.* Unpublished manuscript, University of Pennsylvania.

LI, P., & GLEITMAN, L. R. (2002). Turning the tables: Language and spatial reasoning. *Cognition, 83,* 265–294.

LIBERMAN, A. M., COOPER, F. S., SHANKWEILER, D. P., & STUDDERT-KENNEDY, M. (1967). Perception of the speech code. *Psychological Review, 74,* 431–461.

LIBET, B. (1993). The neural time factor in conscious and unconscious events. *Ciba Foundation Symposium, 174,* 123–137; discussion 137–146.

LIBET, B. (2000). Time factors in conscious processes: Reply to Gilberto Gomes. *Consciousness and Cognition, 9*(1), 1–12.

LICHTER, D. G., & CUMMINGS, J. L. (EDS.). (2001). *Frontal-subcortical circuits in psychiatric and neurological disorders.* New York: Guilford Press.

LIEBERMAN, J. A. (1995). Signs and symptoms. Commentary. *Archives of General Psychiatry, 52,* 361–363.

LIEBERMAN, P. L. (1975). *On the origins of language.* New York: Macmillan.

LIFF, Z. A. (1992). Psychoanalysis and dynamic techniques. In D. K. Freedheim (Ed.), *History of psychotherapy.* Washington, DC: American Psychological Association.

LILIENFELD, S. O., KIRSCH, I., SARBIN, T. R., LYNN, S. J., CHAVES, J. F., GANAWAY, G. K., ET AL. (1999). Dissociative identity disorder and the sociocognitive model: Recalling the lessons of the past. *Psychological Bulletin, 125,* 507–523.

LILIENFIELD, S. O., WOOD, J. M., & GARB, H. N. (2000). The scientific status of projective techniques. *Psychological Science in the Public Interest, 1,* 27–66.

LILLARD, A. S. (1997). Other folks' theories of mind and behavior. *Psychological Science, 8,* 268–274.

LINDSAY, P. H., & NORMAN, D. A. (1977). *Human information processing* (2nd ed.). New York: Academic Press.

LIPPERT, W. W., & SENTER, R. J. (1966). Electrodermal responses in the sociopath. *Psychonomic Science, 4,* 25–26.

LISHMAN, B. (1992). *Father Goose and his goslings.* Seattle: Storytellers Ink.

LIVNEH, H., & LIVNEH, C. (1989). The five-factor model of personality: Is evidence of its cross-measure validity premature? *Personality and Individual Differences, 10,* 75–80.

LOCKE, J. (1690). *An essay concerning human understanding.* A. D. Woozley (Ed.). Cleveland: Meridian Books, 1964.

LOEHLIN, J. C. (1992). *Genes and environment in personality development.* Newbury Park, CA: Sage.

LOEHLIN, J. C., LINDZEY, G., & SPUHLER, J. N. (1975). *Race difference in intelligence.* San Francisco: Freeman.

LOEHLIN, J. C., VANDENBERG, S. G., & OSBORNE, R. T. (1973). Blood group genes and Negro-White ability differences. *Behavior Genetics, 3,* 263–270.

LOFTUS, E. F. (1975). Leading questions and the eyewitness report. *Cognitive Psychology, 7,* 560–572.

LOFTUS, E. F. (1993). The reality of repressed memories. *American Psychologist, 48,* 518–537.

LOFTUS, E. F. (1997). Creating false memories. *Scientific American, 277*(3), 70–75.

LOFTUS, E. F., & LOFTUS, G. R. (1980). On the permanence of stored information in the human brain. *American Psychologist, 35,* 409–420.

LOFTUS, E. F., & ZANNI, G. (1975). Eyewitness testimony: The influence of the wording of a question. *Bulletin of the Psychonomic Society, 5,* 86–88.

LOGAN, G. D. (1988). Toward an instance theory of automatization. *Psychological Review, 95,* 492–527.

LOGAN, G. D., TAYLOR, S. E., & ETHERTON, J. L. (1996). Attention in the acquisition and expression of automaticity. *Journal of Experimental Psychology: Learning, Memory and Cognition, 22,* 620–638.

LOGUE, A. W. (1986). *The psychology of eating and drinking.* New York: Freeman.

LONDON, P. (1964). *The modes and morals of psychotherapy.* New York: Holt, Rinehart & Winston.

LORD, C. G., ROSS, L., & LEPPER, M. R. (1979). Biased assimilation and attitude polarization: The effects of prior theories on subsequently considered evidence. *Journal of Personality and Social Psychology, 37*(11), 2098–2109.

LORD, R. G., DeVADER, C. L., & ALLIGER, G. M. (1986). A meta-analysis of the relationship between personality traits and leadership perceptions: An application of validity generalization procedures. *Journal of Applied Psychology, 7,* 401–410.

LORENZ, K. (1950). Part and parcel in animal and human societies. In *Studies in animal and human behavio: Vol. II* (pp. 115–195). London: Methuen.

LORENZ, K. Z. (1966). *On aggression.* London: Methuen.

LUBIN, B., LARSEN, R. M., MATARAZZO, J. D., & SEEVER, M. (1985). Psychological test usage patterns in five professional settings. *American Psychologist, 40,* 857–861.

LUBINSKI, D., & BENBOW, C. P. (2000). States of excellence. *American Psychologist, 55*(1), 137–150.

LUBORSKY, L. I., SINGER, B., & LUBORSKY, L. (1975). Comparative studies of psychotherapies. *Archives of General Psychiatry, 20,* 84–88.

LUCE, R. D., & RAIFFA, H. (1957). *Games and decisions.* New York: Wiley.

LUCHINS, A. S. (1942). Mechanization in problem-solving: The effect of Einstellung. *Psychological Monographs, 54*(Whole No. 248).

LUGINBUHL, J. E. R., CROWE, D. H., & KAHAN, J. P. (1975). Causal attributions for success and failure. *Journal of Personality and Social Psychology, 31,* 86–93.

LURIA, A. R. (1966). *Higher cortical functions in man.* New York: Basic Books.

LURIA, A. R. (1976). *Cognitive development: Its cultural and social foundations.* Cambridge, MA: Harvard University Press.

LUTZ, C. (1986). The domain of emotion words on Ifaluk. In R. Harr (Ed.), *The social construction of emotions* (pp. 267–288). Oxford, Blackwell.

LUTZ, C. (1988). *Unnatural emotions.* Chicago: University of Chicago Press.

LUZZATTI, C., RAGGI, R., ZONCA, G., PISTARINI C., CONTARDI A., & PINNA G. (2001). Verb-noun double dissociation in aphasic lexical impairments: The role of word frequency and imageability. *Brain and Language,* 1–13.

LYDIARD, R. B., BRAWMAN-MINTZER, O., & BALLENGER, J. C. (1996). Recent developments in the psychopharmacology of anxiety disorders. *Journal of Consulting and Clinical Psychology, 64,* 660–668.

LYKKEN, D. T. (1995). *The antisocial personalities.* Hillsdale, NJ: Erlbaum.

LYNN, R. (1994). Sex differences in intelligence and brain size: A paradox resolved. *Personality and Individual Differences, 17*(2), 257–271.

LYNN, R. (1995). Cross-cultural differences in intelligence and personality. In D. H. Saklofske & M. Zeidner (Eds.), *International handbook of personality and intelligence,* (pp. 107–121). New York: Plenum.

LYNN, S. J., LOCK, T. G., MYERS, B., & PAYNE, D. G. (1997). Recalling the unrecallable: Should hypnosis be used to recover memories in psychotherapy. *Current Directions in Psychological Science, 6,* 79–83.

MACCOBY, E. E. (1980). *Social development.* New York: Harcourt Brace Jovanovich.

MACCOBY, E. E. (2002). Gender and group process: A developmental perspective. *Current Directions in Psychological Science, 11,* 54–58.

MACCOBY, E. E., & JACKLIN, C. N. (1974). *The psychology of sex differences.* Stanford, CA: Stanford University Press.

MACCOBY, E. E., & JACKLIN, C. N. (1980). Sex differences in aggression: A rejoinder and reprise. *Child Development, 51,* 964–980.

MACCOBY, E. E., & MARTIN, J. A. (1983). Socialization in the context of the family: Parent-child interaction. In P. H. Mussen (Ed.) & M. E. Hetherington (Vol. Ed.). *Carmichael's manual of child psychology: Vol. 4. Socialization, personality and social development* (pp. 1–102). New York: Wiley.

MACDONALD, M. C. (1993). The interaction of lexical and syntactic ambiguity. *Journal of Memory and Language, 32,* 692–715.

MACDONALD, M. C., PEARLMUTTER, N. J., & SEIDENBERG, M. S. (1994). The lexical nature of syntactic ambiguity resolution. *Psychological Review, 101*(4), 676–703.

MACDONALD, S., UESILIANA, K., & HAYNE, H. (2000). Cross-cultural and gender differences in childhood amnesia. *Memory, 8*(6), 365–376.

MACFARLANE, A. (1975). Olfaction in the development of social preferences in the human neonate. *Parent-infant interaction.* Amsterdam: CIBA Foundation Symposium.

MACK, A., & ROCK, I. (1998). *Inattentional blindness.* Cambridge, MA: MIT Press.

MACNAMARA, J. (1982). *Names for things.* Cambridge, MA: MIT Press.

MACNICHOL, E. F., JR. (1964). Three-pigment color vision. *Scientific American, 211,* 48–56.

MACNICHOL, E. F., JR. (1986). A unifying presentation of photopigment spectra. *Vision Research, 29,* 543–546.

MACPHAIL, E. M. (1996). Cognitive function in mammals: the evolutionary perspective. *Cognitive Brain Research, 3,* 279–290.

MADDUX, J. E. (1995). *Self-efficacy, adaptation, and adjustment: Theory, research, and application.* Englewood Cliffs, NJ: Prentice-Hall.

MAFFEI, M., HALAAS, J., RAVUSSIN, E., PRATLEY, R. E., LEE, G. H., ZHANG, Y., ET AL. (1995). Leptin levels in human and rodent: Measurement of plasma leptin and ob RNA in obese and weight-reduced subjects. *Nature Medicine, 1,* 1155–1161.

MAGNUSSON, D., & ENDLER, N. S. (1977). Interactional psychology: Present status and future prospects. In D. Magnusson & N. S. Endler (Eds.), *Personality at the crossroads* (pp. 3–31). New York: Wiley.

MAGOUN, H. W., HARRISON, F., BROBECK, J. R., & RANSON, S. W. (1938). Activation of heat loss mechanisms by local heating of the brain. *Journal of Neurophysiology, 1,* 101–114.

MAHER, B. A. (1966). *Principles of psychopathology.* New York: McGraw-Hill.

MAHONEY, M. J. (1976). *Scientist as subject: The psychological imperative.* Cambridge, MA: Ballinger.

MAHONEY, M. J., & DeMONBREUN, B. G. (1981). Problem-solving bias in scientists. In R. D. Tweney, M. E. Doherty, & C. R. Mynatt (Eds.), *On scientific thinking* (pp. 139–144). New York: Columbia University Press.

MALASPINA, D., HARLAP, S., FENNIG, S., HEIMAN, D., NAHON, D., FELDMAN, D., ET AL. (2001). Advancing paternal age and the risk of schizophrenia. *Archives of General Psychiatry, 58,* 361–367.

MALHI, G. S., & BARTLETT, J. R. (2000). Depression: A role for neurosurgery? *British Journal of Neurosurgery, 14,* 415–422.

MALINOWSKI, B. (1926). *Crime and custom in savage society.* London: Paul, Trench, and Trubner.

MALINOWSKI, B. (1927). *Sex and repression in savage society.* New York: Meridian, 1955.

MALT, B. C., SLOMAN, S. A., GENNARI, S., SHI, M., & WANG, Y. (1999). Knowing versus naming: Similarity and the linguistic categorization of artifacts. *Journal of Memory and Language, 40,* 230–262.

MANDLER, G. (1975). *Mind and emotion.* New York: Wiley.

MANDLER, G. (1984). *Mind and body: Psychology of emotion and stress.* New York: Norton.

MANDLER, G. (1997). *Human nature explored.* New York: Oxford University Press.

MANDLER, G. (1998). Consciousness and mind as philosophical problems and as psychological issues. In J. Hochberg (Ed.), *Perception and cognition at century's end.* San Diego, CA: Academic Press.

MANDLER, J. M. (1992). How to build a baby: II. Conceptual primitives. *Psychological Review, 99,* 587–604.

MANDLER, J. M. (2000). Perceptual and conceptual processes in infancy. *Journal of Cognition and Development, 1,* 3–36.

MANFREDI, M., BINI, G., CRUCCU, G., ACCORNERO, N., BERARDELLI, A., & MEDOLAGO, L. (1981). Congenital absence of pain. *Archives of Neurology, 38,* 507–511.

MANN, F., BOWSHER, D., MUMFORD, J., LIPTON, S., & MILES, J. (1973). Treatment of intractable pain by acupuncture. *Lancet, 2,* 57–60.

MANTELL, D. M., & PANZARELLA, R. (1976). Obedience and responsibility. *British Journal of Social and Child Psychology, 15,* 239–245.

MARAÑON, G. (1924). Review of Fr. *Endocrinology, 2,* 301.

MARCH, J. S., LEONARD, H. L., & SWEDO, S. E. (1995). Obsessive-compulsive disorder. In J. S. March (Ed.), *Anxiety disorders in children and adolescents* (pp. 251–275). New York: Guilford Press.

MARCUS, D. E., & OVERTON, W. F. (1978). The development of cognitive gender constancy and sex-role preferences. *Child Development, 49,* 434–444.

MARCUS, G. F., PINKER, S., ULLMAN, M., HOLLANDER, M., ROSEN, T. J., & XU, F. (1992). Overregularization in language acquisition. *Monographs of the Society for Research in Child Development, 57*(4, Serial No. 228).

MARCUS, G. F., VIJAYAN, S., BANDI RAO, S., & VISHTON, P. M. (1999) Rule learning by seven-month old infants. *Science, 283,* 77–80.

MARCUS, J., HANS, S. L., AUERBACH, J. G., & AUERBACH, A. G. (1993). Children at risk for schizophrenia: The Jerusalem Infant Development Study. II. Neurobehavioral deficits at school age. *Archives of General Psychiatry, 50,* 797–809.

MARESCHAL, D. (2000). Object knowledge in infancy: Current controversies and approaches. *Trends in Cognitive Science, 4,* 408–416.

MARKMAN, E. (1989). *Categorization and naming in children: Problems of induction.* Cambridge, MA: MIT Press.

MARKMAN, E. M. (1994). Constraints children place on word meanings. In P. Bloom (Ed.), *Language acquisition: Core readings.* Cambridge, MA: MIT Press.

MARKMAN, E. M., & HUTCHINSON, J. E. (1984). Children's sensitivity to constraints on word meaning: Taxonomic vs. thematic relations. *Cognitive Psychology, 16,* 1–27.

MARKMAN, E. M., & WACHTEL, G. A. (1988). Children's use of mutual exclusivity to constrain the meaning of words. *Cognitive Psychology, 20,* 121–157.

MARKS, I. M. (1969). *Fears and phobias.* New York: Academic Press.

MARKSON, I. & BLOOM, P. (1997) Evidence against a dedicated system for word learning in children, *Nature, 385,* 813–815.

MARKUS, H. R., & KITAYAMA, S. (1994). The cultural construction of self and emotion: Implications for social behavior. In S. Kitayama & H. R. Markus (Eds.), *Emotion and culture* (pp. 89–130). Washington, DC: American Psychological Association.

MARKUS, H. R., & KITAYAMA, S. (1991). Culture and the self: Implications for cognition, emotion, and motivation. *Psychological Review, 98,* 224–253.

MARKUS, H. R., & KITAYAMA, S. (1999). Culture and the self: Implications for cognition, emotion, and motivation. In R. F. Baumeister (Ed.). *The self in social psychology* (pp. 339–371). Philadelphia: Psychology Press/Taylor & Francis.

MARLER, P. R. (1970). A comparative approach to vocal learning: Song development in white-crowned sparrows. *Journal of Comparative and Physiological Psychology Monographs, 71*(No. 2, Part 2), 1–25.

MARLER, P. R., DUFFY, A., & PICKERT, R. (1986a). Vocal communication in the domestic chicken: I. Does a sender communicate information about the quality of a food referent to a receiver? *Animal Behaviour, 34,* 188–193.

MARLER, P. R., DUFFY, A., & PICKERT, R. (1986b). Vocal communication in the domestic chicken: II. Is a sender sensitive to the presence and nature of a receiver? *Animal Behaviour, 34,* 194–198.

MARMOR, J. (1975). Homosexuality and sexual orientation disturbances. In A. M. Freedman, H. I. Kaplan, & B. J. Sadock (Eds.), *Comprehensive textbook of psychiatry—II: Vol. 2* (pp. 1510–1519). Baltimore: Williams & Wilkins.

MARSHALL, G. D., & ZIMBARDO, P. G. (1979). Affective consequences of inadequately explained physiological arousal. *Journal of Personality and Social Psychology, 37,* 970–988.

MARSHALL, P. J., FOX, N. A., & HENDERSON, H. A. (2000). Temperament as an organizer of development. *Infancy, 1,* 239–244.

MARSLEN-WILSON, W. (1975). Sentence perception as an interactive parallel process. *Science, 189,* 226–228.

MARSLEN-WILSON, W. D., & TEUBER, H. L. (1975). Memory for remote events in anterograde amnesia: Recognition of public figures from news photographs. *Neurobiologia, 13,* 353–364.

MARSLEN-WILSON, W. D. & TYLER, L. K. (1998) Rules, representations, and the English past tense. *Trends in Cognitive Science 2*(11), 428–435.

MARTIN, J. A., KING, D. R., MACCOBY, E. E., & JACKLIN, C. N. (1984). Secular trends and individual differences in toilet-training progress. *Journal of Pediatric Psychology, 9,* 457–467.

MARTIN, P., & ALBERS, P. (1995). Cerebellum and schizophrenia: A review. *Schizophrenia Bulletin, 21,* 241–251.

MARTINEZ, J. L., & DERRICK, B. E. (1996). Long-term potentiation and learning. *Annual Review of Psychology, 47,* 173–203.

MASLACH, C. (1979). Negative emotional biasing of unexplained physiological arousal. *Journal of Personality and Social Psychology, 37,* 953–969.

MASLOW, A. H. (1954). *Motivation and personality.* New York: Harper & Row.

MASLOW, A. H. (1968). *Toward a psychology of being* (2nd ed.). Princeton, NJ: Van Nostrand.

MASLOW, A. H. (1970). *Motivation and personality* (2nd ed.). New York: Harper.

MASLOW, A. H. (1996). *Future visions: The unpublished papers of Abraham Maslow,* (E. Hoffman, Ed.). Thousand Oaks, CA: Sage.

MASSEY, C. & GELMAN, R. (1988) Preschoolers' ability to decide whether a photographed unfamiliar object can move itself. *Developmental Psychology, 24*(3), 307–317.

MASTERS, M. S., & SANDERS, B. (1993). Is the gender difference in mental rotation disappearing? *Behavior Genetics, 23,* 337–341.

MATARAZZO, J. D. (1983). The reliability of psychiatric and psychological diagnosis. *Clinical Psychology Review, 3,*:103–145.

MATHEWS, K. A. (1982). Psychological perspectives on the type A behavior pattern. *Psychological Bulletin, 91,* 293–323.

MATIN, L., PICOULT, E., STEVENS, J., EDWARDS, M., & MACARTHUR, R. (1982). Ocuparalytic illusion: Visual-field dependent spatial mislocations by humans partially paralyzed with curare. *Science, 216*, 198–190.

MATSON, J. L., & SEVIN, J. A. (1994). Issues in the use of aversives: Factors associated with behavior modification for autistic and other developmentally disabled people. In E. Schopler & G. B. Mesibov (Eds.), *Behavioral issues in autism* (pp. 211–225). New York: Plenum.

MATTISON, A., & MCWHIRTER, D. (1987). Male couples: The beginning years. Intimate Relationships: Some Social Work Perspectives on Love [Special Issue]. *Journal of Social Work and Human Sexuality, 5*, 67–78.

MAURICE, D. M. (1998). An ophthalmological explanation of REM sleep. *Experimental Eye Research, 66*, 139–145.

MAY, R. (1958). Contributions of existential psychotherapy. In R. May, E. Angel, & H. F. Ellenberger (Eds.), *Existence* (pp. 37–91). New York: Basic Books.

MAYES, A. R. (1988). *Human organic memory disorders.* New York: Cambridge University Press.

MAYEUX, R., & KANDEL, E. R. (1991). Disorders of language: The aphasias. In E. R. Kandel, J. H. Schwartz, & T. M. Jessell (Eds.), *Principles of neural science* (3rd ed.). New York: Elsevier.

MAYHAN, W. G. (2001). Regulation of blood-brain barrier permeability. *Microcirculation, 8*, 89–104.

MAYNARD-SMITH, J. (1965). The evolution of alarm calls. *American Naturalist, 100*, 637–650.

MAZUKA, R., & FRIEDMAN, R.S. (2000). Linguistic relativity in Japanese and English: Is language the primary determinant in object classification? *Journal of East Asian Linguistics, 9*, 353–377.

MCANDREW, F. T. (2002). New evolutionary perspectives on altruism: Multilevel-selection and costly-signaling theories. *Current Directions in Psychological Science, 11*, 79–82.

MCCLEARN, G. E., & DEFRIES, J. C. (1973). *Introduction to behavioral genetics.* San Francisco: Freeman.

MCCLELLAND, J. L., & PATTERSON, K. (2002). Rules or connections in past-tense inflections: What does the evidence rule out? *Trends in Cognitive Sciences, 6*(11), 465–472.

MCCLELLAND, J. L., & PLAUT, D. C. (1999). Does generalization in infant learning implicate abstract algebra-like rules? *Trends in Cognitive Science, 3*(4), 166–167.

MCCLELLAND, J. L., & RUMELHART, D. E. (EDS.) (1986). *Parallel distributed processing: Explorations in the microstructure of cognition: Vol. 2. Psychological and biological models.* Cambridge, MA: MIT Press.

MCCLELLAND, J. L., RUMELHART, D. E., & HINTON, G. E. (1986). The appeal of parallel distributed processing. In D. E. Rumelhart, J. L. McClelland, and the PDP Research Group, *Parallel distributed processing: Vol. 1. Foundations* (pp. 3–44). Cambridge, MA: MIT Press.

MCCLELLAND, J. L., & SEIDENBERG, M. S. (2000). Why do kids say goed and brang? *Science, 287*, 47–48.

MCCLINTOCK, M. K., & ADLER, N. T. (1978). The role of the female during copulation in wild and domestic Norway rats (*Rattus Norvegicus*). *Behaviour, 67*, 67–96.

MCCLOSKEY, M., & EGETH, H. E. (1983). Eyewitness identification: What can a psychologist tell a jury? *American Psychologist, 38*(5), 550–563.

MCCLOSKEY, M., WIBLE, C. G., & COHEN, N. J. (1988). Is there a special flashbulb-memory mechanism? *Journal of Experimental Psychology: General, 117*, 171–181.

MCCONAGHY, M. J. (1979). Gender constancy and the genital basis of gender: Stages in the development of constancy by gender identity. *Child Development, 50*, 1223–1226.

MCCONNELL, A. R., & LEIBOLD, J. M. (2001). Relations among the Implicit Association Test, discriminatory behavior, and explicit measures of racial attitudes. *Journal of Experimental Social Psychology, 37*(5), 435–442.

MCCORD, W., & MCCORD, J. (1964). *The psychopath: An essay on the criminal mind.* New York: Van Nostrand.

MCCRANIE, E. W., HYER, L. A., BOUDEWYNS, P. A., & WOODS, M. G. (1992). Negative parenting behavior, combat exposure and PTSD symptom severity. Test of a person-event interaction model. *Journal of Nervous and Mental Disease, 180*, 431–438.

MCCREARY, D. R. (1994). The male role and avoiding femininity. *Sex Roles, 31*, 517–531.

MCEWEN, B. S., BIEGON, A., DAVIS, P. G., KREY, L. C., LUINE, V. N., MCGINNIS, M., ET AL. (1982). Steroid hormones: Humoral signals which alter brain cell properties and functions. *Recent Progress in Brain Research, 38*, 41–83.

MCFALL, R. M., & TREAT, T. A. (1999). Quantifying the information value of clinical assessments with signal detection theory. *Annual Review of Psychology, 50*, 215–242.

MCGAUGH, J. L. (2000). Memory—A century of consolidation. *Science, 287*, 248–251.

MCGEE, M. G. (1979). Human spatial abilities: Psychometric studies and environmental, genetic, hormonal and neurological influences. *Psychological Bulletin, 86*, 889–918.

MCGEOCH, J. A., & IRION, A. L. (1952). *The psychology of human learning* (2nd ed.). New York: Longmans, Green, & Co.

MCGHIE, A., & CHAPMAN, J. (1961). Disorders of attention and perception in early schizophrenia. *British Journal of Medical Psychology, 34*, 103–116.

MCGRATH, J., WELHAM, J., & PEMBERTON, M. (1995). Month of birth, hemisphere of birth, and schizophrenia. *British Journal of Psychiatry, 167*, 783–785.

MCGREGOR, G. P., DESAGA, J. F., EHLENZ, K., FISCHER, A., HEESE, F., HEGELE, A., ET AL. (1996). Radiommunological measurement of leptin in plasma of obese and diabetic human subjects. *Endocrinology, 137*, 1501–1504.

MCGUE, M., BOUCHARD, T. J., JR., IACONO, W. G., & LYKKEN, D. T. (1993). Behavioral genetics of cognitive ability: A life span perspective. In R. Plomin & G. E. McClearn (Eds.), *Nature, nurture and psychology* (pp. 59–76). Washington, DC: American Psychological Association.

MCGUE, M., & LYKKEN, D. T. (1992). Genetic influence on risk of divorce. *Psychological Science, 3*, 368–372.

MCGUIRE, W. J. (1985). The nature of attitude and attitude change. In G. Lindzey & E. Aronson (Eds.), *Handbook of social psychology: Vol. 2* (3rd ed.). New York: Random House.

MCNAUGHTON, B. L., DOUGLAS, R. M.. & GODDARD, G. V. (1978). Synaptic enhancement in fascia dentata: Cooperativity among coactive afferents. *Brain Research, 157*, 277–293.

MEAD, M. (1935). *Sex and temperament in three primitive societies.* New York: Morrow.

MEAD, M. (1937). *Cooperation and competition among primitive peoples.* New York: McGraw-Hill.

MEALEY, L., BRIDGSTOCK, R., & TOWNSEND, G. C. (1999). Symmetry and perceived facial attractiveness: A monozygotic co-twin comparison. *Journal of Personality and Social Psychology, 76*, 151–158.

MEDDIS, R. (1977). *The sleep instinct.* London: Routledge and Kegan Paul.

MEDIN, D. L., SCHWARTZ, H., BLOK, S. V., & BIRNBAUM, L. A. (1999). The semantic side of decision making. *Psychonomics Bulletin and Review, 6*, 562–569.

MEDIN, D. L., GOLDSTONE, R. L., & GENTNER, D. (1993). Respects for similarity. *Psychological Review, 100*(2), 254–278.

MEDNICK, S. A., HUTTUNEN, M. O., & MACHO'N, R. A. (1994). Prenatal influenza infections and adult schizophrenia. *Schizophrenia Bulletin, 20*, 263–267.

MEEHL, P. D. (1962). Schizotaxia, schizotypy, schizophrenia. *American Psychologist, 17*, 827–838.

MEGENS, A. A., & KENNIS, L. E. (1996). Risperidone and related 5HT2/D2 antagonists: A new type of antipsychotic agent? *Progress in Medicinal Chemistry, 33*, 185–232.

MEHLER, J., ET AL. (1996) Coping with linguistic diversity: the infant's viewpoint. In J. L. Morgan & K. Demuth (Eds.), *Signal to Syntax: Bootstrapping from speech to grammar in early acquisition* (pp. 101–116). Hillsdale, NJ: Erlbaum.

MEHLER, J., JUSCZYK, P., LAMBERTZ, G., HALSTED, N., BERTONCINI, J., & AMIEL-TISON, C. (1988). A precursor to language acquisition in young infants. *Cognition, 29,* 143–178.

MELLERS, B., HERTWIG, R., & KAHNEMAN, D. (2001). Do frequency representations eliminate conjunction effects? An exercise in advance collaboration. *Psychological Science, 12,* 269–275.

MELLERS, B. A., & MCGRAW, A. P. (1999). How to improve Bayesian reasoning: Comment on Gigerenzer and Hoffrage. *Psychological Review, 106,* 417–424.

MELTZER, H. Y. (1986). Lithium mechanisms in bipolar illness and altered intracellular calcium functions. *Biological Psychiatry, 21,* 492–510.

MELTZER, H. Y. (1987). Biological studies in schizophrenia. *Schizophrenia Bulletin, 13,* 77–111.

MELTZOFF, A. N. (1995). Understanding the intentions of others: Re-enactment of intended acts by 18-month-old children. *Developmental Psychology, 31*(5), 838–850.

MELTZOFF, A. N., GOPNIK, A., & REPACHOLI, B. M. (1999). Toddlers' understanding of intentions, desires and emotions: Explorations of the dark ages. In P. D. Zelazo & J. W. Astington (Eds.), *Developing theories of intention: Social understanding and self-control* (pp. 17–41). Mahwah, NJ: Erlbaum.

MELTZOFF, A. N., & MOORE, M. K. (1977). Imitation of facial and manual gestures by human neonates. *Science, 198,* 75–78.

MELTZOFF, A. N., & MOORE, M. K. (1995). Infants' understanding of people and things: From body imitation to folk psychology. In J. L. Bermudez & A. J. Marcel (Eds.), *The body and the self* (pp. 43–69). Cambridge, MA: MIT Press.

MELTZOFF, A. N., & MOORE, M. K. (1998). Infant intersubjectivity: Broadening the dialogue to include imitation, identity and intention. In S. Braten (Ed.), *Intersubjective communication and emotion in early ontogeny.* Cambridge: Cambridge University Press.

MELZACK, R. (1973). *The puzzle of pain.* New York: Basic Books.

MENYUK, P. (1977). *Language and maturation.* Cambridge, MA: MIT Press.

MENZEL, E. W. (1973). Chimpanzee spatial memory organization. *Science, 182,* 943–945.

MENZEL, E. W. (1978). Cognitive maps in chimpanzees. In S. H. Hulse, H. Fowler, & W. K. Honig (Eds.), *Cognitive processes in animal behavior* (pp. 375–422). Hillsdale, NJ: Erlbaum.

MERVIS, C. B., & CRISAFI, M. (1978). Order acquisition of subordinate, basic, and superordinate level categories. *Child Development, 49,* 988–998.

MESQUITA, B., & FRIJDA, N. H. (1992). Cultural variations in emotion: A review. *Psychological Bulletin, 112,* 179–204.

METCALFE, J. (1986). Premonitions of insight predict impending error. *Journal of Experimental Psychology: Learning, Memory and Cognition, 12,* 623–634.

METCALFE, J., & WEIBE, D. (1987). Intuition in insight and noninsight problem solving. *Memory and Cognition, 15,* 238–246.

MEYER, D. E., & SCHVANEVELDT, R. W. (1971). Facilitation in recognizing pairs of words: Evidence of a dependence between retrieval operations. *Journal of Experimental Psychology, 90,* 227–234.

MEYER-BAHLBURG, H. F. L., GRUEN, R. S., NEW, M. I., BELL, J. J., MORISHIMA, A., SHIMSHI, M., ET AL. (1996). Gender change from female to male in classical congenital adrenal hyperplasia. *Hormones and Behavior, 30,* 319–332.

MIASKIEWICZ, S. L, STRICKER, E. M., & VERBALIS, J. G. (1989). Neurohypophyseal secretion in response to cholecystokinin but not meal-induced gastric distention in humans. *Journal of Clinical Endocrinology and Metabolism, 68,* 837–843.

MILGRAM, S. (1963). Behavioral study of obedience. *Journal of Abnormal and Social Psychology, 67,* 371–378.

MILGRAM, S. (1965). Some conditions of obedience and disobedience to authority. *Human Relations, 18,* 57–76.

MILGRAM, S. (1974). *Obedience to authority.* New York: Harper & Row.

MILGRAM, S., & MURRAY, T. H. (1992). Can deception in research be justified? In B. Slife & J. Rubenstein (Eds.), *Taking sides: Clashing views on controversial psychological issues* (7th ed.). Gilford, CT: Dushkin Publishing Group.

MILLER, A. G. (1986). *The obedience experiments: A case study of controversy in social science.* New York: Praeger.

MILLER, D. T. (1976). Ego involvement and attribution for success and failure. *Journal of Personality and Social Psychology, 34,* 901–906.

MILLER, G., & JOHNSON-LAIRD, P. (1976). *Language and perception.* Cambridge, MA: Harvard University Press.

MILLER, G. A. (1956). The magical number seven plus or minus two: Some limits in our capacity for processing information. *Psychological Review, 63,* 81–97.

MILLER, J. G. (1984). Culture and the development of everyday social explanation. *Journal of Personality and Social Psychology, 46,* 961–978.

MILLER, L. C. (1990). Intimacy and liking: Mutual influence and the role of unique relationships. *Journal of Personality and Social Psychology, 59,* 50–60.

MILLER, L. C., & KENNY, D. A. (1986). Reciprocity of self-disclosure at the individual and dyadic levels: A social relations analysis. *Journal of Personality and Social Psychology, 50,* 713–719.

MILLER, L. C., PUTCHA-BHAGAVATULA, A. D., & PEDERSEN, W. C. (2002). Men's and women's mating preferences: Distinct evolutionary mechanisms? *Current Directions in Psychological Science, 11,* 88–93.

MILLER, L. K. (1999). The Savant Syndrome: Intellectual impairment and exceptional skill. *Psychological Bulletin, 125,* 31–46.

MILLER, N. E., BAILEY, C. J., & STEVENSON, J. A. F. (1950). Decreased "hunger" but increased food intake resulting from hypothalamic lesions. *Science, 112,* 256–259.

MILLER, R. R., BARNET, R. C., & GRAHAME, N. J. (1995). Assessment of the Rescorla-Wagner model. *Psychological Bulletin, 117,* 363–387.

MILLER, R. S. (1987). Empathic embarrassment: Situational and personal determinants of reactions to the embarrassment of another. *Journal of Personality and Social Psychology, 53*(6), 1061–1069.

MILLER, R. S. (1996). *Embarrassment.* New York: Guilford Press.

MILLON, T. (1969). *Modern psychopathology.* Philadelphia: Saunders.

MILLS, J., & CLARK, M. S. (1994). Communal and exchange relationships: Controversies and research. In R. Erber & R. Gilmour (Eds.), *Theoretical frameworks for personal relationships* (pp. 29–42). Hillsdale, NJ: Erlbaum.

MILNER, A. D., & GOODALE, M. A. (1995). *The visual brain in action.* New York: Oxford University Press.

MILNER, B. (1963). Effects of different brain lesions on card sorting. *Archives of Neuropsychology, 9,* 90–100.

MILNER, B. (1966). Amnesia following operation on the temporal lobes. In C. W. M. Whitty & O. L. Zangwill (Eds.), *Amnesia* (pp. 109–133). London: Butterworth.

MILNER, B., CORKIN, S., & TEUBER, H. L. (1968). Further analysis of the hippocampal syndrome: 14-year follow-up study of H. M. *Neuropsychologia, 6,* 215–234.

MILNER, B., & PETRIDES, M. (1984). Behavioural effects of frontal-lobe lesions in man. *Trends in Neurosciences, 7,* 403–407.

MINUCHIN, S. (1974). *Families and family therapy.* Cambridge, MA: Harvard University Press.

MISCHEL, W. (1968). *Personality and assessment.* New York: Wiley.

MISCHEL, W. (1973). Towards a cognitive social learning reconceptualization of personality. *Psychological Review, 80,* 252–283.

MISCHEL, W. (1974). Processes in delay of gratification. In L. Berkowitz (Ed.), *Advances in experimental social psychology: Vol. 7.* New York: Academic Press.

MISCHEL, W. (1984). Convergences and challenges in the search for consistency. *American Psychologist, 39,* 351–364.

MISCHEL, W., & BAKER, N. (1975). Cognitive appraisals and transformations in delay behavior. *Journal of Personality and Social Psychology, 31,* 254–261.

MISCHEL, W., & MISCHEL, H. N. (1983). Development of children's knowledge of self-control strategies. *Child Development, 54,* 603–619.

MISCHEL, W., & MOORE, B. (1980). The role of ideation in voluntary delay for symbolically presented awards. *Cognitive Therapy and Research, 4,* 211–221.

MISCHEL, W., & SHODA, Y. (1998). Reconciling processing dynamics and personality dispositions. *Annual Review of Psychology, 49,* 229–258.

MISCHEL, W., & SHODA, Y. (2000). A cognitive-affective system theory of personality: Reconceptualizing situations, dispositions, dynamics, and invariance in personality structure. In E. T. Higgins & A. W. Kruglanski (Eds.), *Motivational science: Social and personality perspectives* (pp. 150–176). Philadelphia: Psychology Press/Taylor & Francis.

MISCHEL, W., SHODA, Y., & MENDOZA-DENTON, R. (2002). Situation-behavior profiles as a locus of consistency in personality. *Current Directions in Psychological Science, 11,* 50–54.

MISCHEL, W., SHODA, Y., & PEAKE, P. K. (1988). The nature of adolescent competencies predicted by preschool delay of gratification. *Journal of Personality and Social Psychology, 54,* 687–696.

MISCHEL, W., SHODA, Y., & RODRIGUEZ, M. L. (1992). Delay of gratification in children. In G. Loewenstein & J. Elster, (Eds), *Choice over time* (pp. 147–164). New York: Russell Sage Foundation.

MISELIS, R. R., & EPSTEIN, A. N. (1970). Feeding induced by 2-deoxy-D-glucose injections into the lateral ventrical of the rat. *Physiologist, 13,* 262.

MISHKIN, M., & APPENZELLER, T. (1987). The anatomy of memory. *Scientific American, 256,* 80–89.

MISHKIN, M., UNGERLEIDER, L. G., & MACKO, K. (1983). Object vision and spatial vision: Two cortical pathways. *Trends in Neurosciences, 6,* 414–417.

MISHLER, E. G., & WAXLER, N. E. (1968). Family interaction and schizophrenia: Alternative frameworks of interpretation. In D. Rosenthal & S. S. Kety (Eds.), *The transmission of schizophrenia* (pp. 213–222). New York: Pergamon.

MITA, T. H., DERMER, M., & KNIGHT, J. (1977). Reversed facial images and the mere exposure hypothesis. *Journal of Personality and Social Psychology, 35,* 597–601.

MITCHELL, K. J., & JOHNSON, M. K. (2000). Source monitoring: Attributing memories to sources. In E. Tulving & F. I. M. Craik (Eds.), *The Oxford handbook of memory* (pp. 179–195). London: Oxford University Press.

MITROFF, I. I. (1974). *The subjective side of science.* Amsterdam: Elsevier.

MIYASHITA, Y. (1995). How the brain creates imagery: Projection to primary visual cortex. *Science, 268,* 1719–1720.

MODIGLIANI, A. (1971). Embarrassment, face work and eye contact: Testing a theory of embarrassment. *Journal of Personality and Social Psychology, 17,* 15–24.

MOFFITT, T. E., CASPI, A., HARKNESS, A. R., & SILVA, P. A. (1993). The natural history of change in intellectual performance: Who changes? How much? Is it meaningful? *Journal of Child Psychology and Psychiatry and Allied Disciplines, 34*(4), 455–506.

MOLONEY, D. P., BOUCHARD, T. J., JR., & SEGAL, N. L. (1991). A genetic and environmental analysis of the vocational interests of monozygotic and dizygotic twins reared apart. *Journal of Vocational Behavior, 39,* 76–109.

MONCRIEFF, J. (2001). Are antidepressants overrated? A review of methodological problems in antidepressant trials. *Journal of Nervous and Mental Disease, 189,* 288–295.

MONEY, J. (1980). *Love and love sickness.* Baltimore: Johns Hopkins University Press.

MONEY, J., & EHRHARDT, A. A. (1972). *Man and woman, boy and girl.* Baltimore: Johns Hopkins University Press.

MONTE, C. F. (1995). *Beneath the mask* (5th ed.). Fort Worth, TX: Harcourt Brace.

MONTGOMERY, S. A. (1995). Selective serotonin reuptake inhibitors in the acute treatment of depression. In F. E. Bloom & D. Kupfer (Eds.), *Psychopharmacology: The fourth generation of progress* (pp. 1043–1051). New York: Raven.

MOORE, C. C., ROMNEY, A. K., & TI-LIEN, HSIA. (2000). Shared cognitive representations of perceptual and semantic structures of basic colors in Chinese and English. *PNAS, 97*(9), 5007–5010.

MOORHEAD, G., FERENCE, R., & NECK, C. P. (1991). Group decision fiascoes continue: Space shuttle Challenger and a revised groupthink framework. *Human Relations, 44*(6), 539–550.

MORA, F., ROLLS, E. T., & BURTON, M. J. (1976). Modulation during learning of the responses of neurons in the lateral hypothalamus to the sight of food. *Experimental Neurology, 53,* 508–519.

MORA, G. (1975). Historical and theoretical trends in psychiatry. In A. M. Freedman, H. I. Kaplan, & B. J. Sadock (Eds.), *Comprehensive textbook of psychiatry: Vol. 1* (pp. 1–75). Baltimore: Williams & Wilkins.

MORAY, N. (1959). Attention in dichotic listening: Affective cues and the influence of instructions. *Quarterly Journal of Experimental Psychology, 11,* 56–60.

MORELAND, R. L., & ZAJONC, R. B. (1982). Exposure effects in person perception: Familiarity, similarity, and attraction. *Journal of Experimental Social Psychology, 18,* 395–415.

MORGAN, C. D., & MURRAY, H. A. (1935). A method for investigating fantasies: The thematic apperception test. *Archives of Neurological Psychiatry, 34,* 289–306.

MORGAN, C. P., & ARAM, J. D. (1975). The preponderance of arguments in the risky shift phenomenon. *Journal of Experimental Social Psychology, 11*(1), 25–34.

MORGAN, I. G., & BOELEN, M. K. (1996). A retinal dark-light switch: A review of the evidence. *Visual Neuroscience, 13,* 399–409.

MORGAN, J. L. (1996). A rhythmic bias in preverbal speech segmentation. *Journal of Memory and Language, 35,* 666–688.

MORRIS, M. W., & PENG, K. (1994). Culture and cause: American and Chinese attributions for social and physical events. *Journal of Personality and Social Psychology, 67,* 949–971.

MORSBACH, H., & TYLER, W. J. (1986). In R. Harr (Ed.), *The social construction of emotions* (pp. 289–307). Oxford: Blackwell.

MORTON, T. U. (1978). Intimacy and reciprocity of exchange: A comparison of spouses and strangers. *Journal of Personality and Social Psychology, 36,* 72–81.

MOSCOVICI, S., & ZAVALLONI, M. (1969). The group as a polarizer of attitudes. *Journal of Personality and Social Psychology, 12*(2), 125–135.

MOSCOVITCH, M. (1994). Memory and working-with-memory. Evaluation of a component process model and comparisons with other models. In D. L. Schacter & E. Tulving (Eds.), *Memory systems 1994* (pp. 269–310). Cambridge, MA: MIT Press.

MOSCOVITCH, M. (1995). Confabulation. In D. L. Schacter, J. T. Coyle, G. D. Fischbach, M.-M. Mesulam, & L. E. Sullivan (Eds.), *Memory distortion: How minds, brains, and societies reconstruct the past* (pp. 226–254). Cambridge, MA: Harvard University Press.

MOSER, M. D. (1999). Making more synapses: A way to store information? Cellular and Molecular Life Sciences, 55, 593–600.

MOWRER, O. H. (1960). *Learning theory and behavior.* New York: Wiley.

MULFORD, R. (1986). First words of the blind child. In M. Smith & J. Locke (Eds.), *The emergent lexicon: The child's development of a linguistic vocabulary.* New York: Academic Press.

MULICK, J. A. (1990). The ideology and science of punishment in mental retardation. *American Journal on Mental Retardation, 95,* 142–156.

MULLEN, M. K. (1994). Earliest recollections of childhood: A demographic analysis. *Cognition, 52*(1), 55–79.

MULLEN, M. K., & YI, S. (1995). The cultural context of talk about the past: Implications for the development of autobiographical memory. *Cognitive Development, 10*(3), 407–419.

MULROW, C. D., WILLIAMS, J. W., JR., CHIQUETTE, E., AGUILAR, C., HITCHCOCK-NOEL, P., LEE, S., ET AL. (2000). Efficacy of newer medications for treating depression in primary care patients. *American Journal of Medicine, 108,* 54–64.

MURDOCK, B. (1962). The serial position effect of free recall. *Journal of Experimental Psychology, 64,* 482–488.

MUUSS, R. E. (1970). Puberty rites in primitive and modern societies. *Adolescence, 5,* 109–128.

MWAMWENDA, T. S. (1992). Cognitive development in African children. *Genetic, Social, and General Psychology Monographs, 118*(1), 5–72.

MYERS, D. G. (2000). The funds, friends, and faith of happy people. *American Psychologist, 55*(1), 56–67.

NADEL, L., & JACOBS, W. J. (1998). Traumatic memory is special. *Current Directions in Psychological Science, 7,* 154–157.

NADEL, L., & MOSCOVITCH, M. (2001). The hippocampal complex and long-term memory revisited. *Trends in Cognitive Science, 5,* 228–230.

NADEL, L., & ZOLA-MORGAN, S. (1984). Infantile amnesia: A neurobiological perspective. In M. Moscovich (Ed.), *Infant memory* (pp. 145–172). New York: Plenum Press.

NAIGLES, L. G. (1990). Children use syntax to learn verb meanings. *Journal of Child Language, 17,* 357–374.

NAIGLES, L. G., & KAKO, E. T. (1993). First contact in verb acquisition: defining a role for syntax. *Child Development, 64,* 1665–1687.

NAKATANI, L. H., & DUKES, K. D. (1977). Locus of segmental cues for word juncture. *Journal of the Acoustical Society of America, 62,* 714–719.

NATHAN, P. W. (1978). Acupuncture analgesia. *Trends in Neurosciences, 1,* 210–223.

NATIONAL ADVISORY MENTAL HEALTH COUNCIL. (1997). *Parity in coverage of mental health services in an era of managed care. An interim report to Congress.* Washington, DC: Department of Health and Human Services.

NATIONAL COMMISSION ON SLEEP DISORDERS. (1993). *Wake up America: A national sleep alert.* Washington, DC.

NAUTA, W. J. H., & FEIRTAG, M. (1986). *Fundamental neuroanatomy.* New York: Freeman.

NAVARRA, P., DELLO RUSSO, C., MANCUSO, C., PREZIOSI, P., & GROSSMAN, A. (2000). Gaseous neuromodulators in the control of neuroendocrine stress axis. *Annals of the New York Academy of Sciences, 917,* 638–646.

NAZZI, T., BERTONCINI, J., & MEHLER, J. (1998). Language discrimination by newborns: Toward an understanding of the role of rhythm. *Journal of Experimental Psychology: Human Perception and Performance, 24,* 756–766.

NEEDHAM, A., & BAILLARGEON, R. (1993). Intuitions about support in 4.5 month old infants. *Cognition, 47,* 121–148.

NEEDHAM, D., & BEGG, I. (1991). Problem-oriented training promotes spontaneous analogical transfer: Memory-oriented training promotes memory for training. *Memory and Cognition, 19,* 543–557.

NEIMEYER, G. J. (1984). Cognitive complexity and marital satisfaction. *Journal of Social and Clinical Psychology, 2,* 258–263.

NEISSER, U. (1967). *Cognitive psychology.* New York: Appleton-Century-Crofts.

NEISSER, U. (1982a). *Memory observed.* San Francisco: Freeman.

NEISSER, U. (1982b). On the trail of the tape-recorder fallacy. Paper presented at a symposium on "The influence of hypnosis and related states on memory: Forensic implications" at the meetings of the American Association for the Advancement of Science, Washington, DC., in January 1982.

NEISSER, U. (1986). Remembering Pearl Harbor: Reply to Thompson and Cowan. *Cognition, 23,* 285–286.

NEISSER, U. (1989). Domains of memory. In P. R. Solomon, G. R. Goethals, C. M. Kelley, & B. R. Stephens (Eds.), *Memory: Interdisciplinary approaches* (pp. 67–83). New York: Springer Verlag.

NEISSER, U. (1997). Rising scores on intelligence tests. *American Scientist, 85,* 440–447.

NEISSER, U. (ED.). (1998). *The rising curve: Long-term gains in IQ and related measures.* Washington, DC: American Psychological Association.

NEISSER, U., & BECKLEN, R. (1975). Selective looking: Attending to visually specified events. *Cognitive Psychology, 7*(4), 480–494.

NEISSER, U., BOODOO, G., BOUCHARD, T. J., JR., & BOYKIN, A. W. (1996). Intelligence: Knowns and unknowns. *American Psychologist, 51*(2), 77–101.

NELSON, K., & FIVUSH, R. (2000). Socialization of memory. In E. Tulving & F. I. M. Craik (Eds.), *The Oxford handbook of memory* (pp. 283–295). London: Oxford University Press.

NEMETH, C., & CHILES, C. (1988). Modeling courage: The role of dissent in fostering independence. *European Journal of Social Psychology, 18,* 275–280.

NEUGEBAUER, R. (1979). Medieval and early modern theories of mental illness. *Archives of General Psychiatry, 36,* 477–484.

NEW, A. S., TRESTMAN, R. L., MITROPOULOU, V., & BENISHAY, D. S. (1997). Serotonergic function and self-injurious behavior in personality disorder patients. *Psychiatry Research, 69*(1), 17–26.

NEWCOMBE, F., RATCLIFF, G., & DAMASIO, H. (1987). Dissociable visual and spatial impairments following right posterior cerebral lesions: Clinical, neuropsychological and anatomical evidence. *Neuropsychologia, 25*(1 B), 149–161.

NEWCOMBE, N. S., DRUMMEY, A. B., FOX, N. A., LIE, E., & OTTINGER-ALBERTS, W. (2000). Remembering early childhood: How much, how, and why (or why not). *Current Directions in Psychological Science, 9,* 55–58.

NEWCOMBE, N. S., & HUTTENLOCHER, J. E. (2000). *Making space: The development of spatial representation and reasoning.* Cambridge, MA: MIT Press.

NEWELL, A., & SIMON, H. A. (1972). *Human problem solving.* Englewood Cliffs, NJ: Prentice-Hall.

NEWMAN, E. A., & ZAHS, K. R. (1998). Modulation of neuronal activity by glial cells in the retina. *Journal of Neuroscience, 18,* 4022–4028.

NEWPORT, E. (1990). Maturational constraints on language learning. *Cognitive Science, 14,* 11–28.

NEWPORT, E. L. (1984). Constraints on learning: Studies in the acquisition of American Sign Language. *Papers and Reports on Child Language Development, 23,* 1–22. Stanford, CA: Stanford University Press.

NEWPORT, E. L. (1999). Reduced input in the acquisition of signed languages: Contributions to the study of creolization. In M. DeGraff (Ed.), *Language creation and language change: Creolization, diachrony, and development.* Cambridge, MA: MIT Press.

NEWPORT, E. L., & ASHBROOK, E. F. (1977). The emergence of semantic relations in American Sign Language. *Papers and Reports in Child Language Development, 13,* 16–21.

NEWPORT, E. L., GLEITMAN, H., & GLEITMAN, L. R. (1977). Mother, I'd rather do it myself: Some effects and non-effects of maternal speech style. In C. E. Snow & C. A. Ferguson (Eds.), *Talking to children: Language input and acquisition* (pp. 109–149). New York: Cambridge University Press.

NEWSOME, W. T., SHADLEN, M. N., ZOHARY, E., BRITTEN, K. H., & MOVSHON, J. A. (1995). Visual motion: Linking neuronal activity to psychophysical performance. In M. S. Gazzaniga (Ed.), *The cognitive neurosciences* (pp. 401–414). Cambridge, MA: MIT Press.

NICHD EARLY CHILD CARE RESEARCH NETWORK. (1997). The effects of infant child care on infant-mother attachment security: Results of the NICHD study of early child care. *Child Development, 68,* 860–879.

NICHOLSON, R. A., & BERMAN, J. S. (1983). Is follow-up necessary in evaluating psychotherapy? *Psychological Bulletin, 93,* 261–278.

NICKERSON, R. A., & ADAMS, M. J. (1979). Long-term memory for a common object. *Cognitive Psychology, 11,* 287–307.

NICOL, S. E., & GOTTESMAN, I. I. (1983). Clues to the genetics and neurobiology of schizophrenia. *American Scientist, 71,* 398–404.

NICOLOSI, J. (1991). *Reparative therapy of male homosexuality.* Northvale, NJ: Jason Aronson.

NISBETT, R., & ROSS, L. (1980). *Human inference: Strategies and shortcomings of social judgment.* Englewood Cliffs, NJ: Prentice-Hall.

NISBETT, R. E. (1980). The trait construct in lay and professional psychology. In L. Festinger (Ed.), *Retrospections on social psychology* (pp. 109–130). New York: Oxford University Press.

NISBETT, R. E. (1993). *Rules for reasoning.* Hillsdale, NJ: Erlbaum.

NISBETT, R. E., CAPUTO, C., LEGANT, P., & MARACEK, J. (1973). Behavior as seen by the actor and as seen by the observer. *Journal of Personality and Social Psychology, 27,* 154–164.

NISBETT, R. E., & COHEN, D. (1996). *Culture of honor: The psychology of violence in the south.* Boulder, CO: Westview Press.

NISBETT, R. E., KRANTZ, D. H., JEPSON, C., & KUNDA, Z. (1983). The use of statistical heuristics in everyday inductive reasoning. *Psychological Review, 90,* 339–363.

NISBETT, R. E., & NORENZAYAN, A. (2002). Culture and cognition. In H. Pashler & D. Medin (Eds.), *Steven's handbook of experimental psychology (3rd ed.), Vol. 2: Memory and cognitive processes* (pp. 561–597). New York: John Wiley & Sons, Inc.

NISBETT, R. E., PENG, K., CHOI, I., & NORENZAYAN, A. (2001). Culture and systems of thought: Holistic versus analytic cognition. *Psychological Review, 108*(2), 291–310.

NISBETT, R. E., & WILSON, T. D. (1977). Telling more than we can know: Verbal reports on mental processes. *Psychological Review, 84,* 231–259.

NOFZINGER, E. A., BUYSSE, D. J., REYNOLDS, C. F., & KUPFER, D. J. (1993). Sleep disorders related to another mental disorder nonsubstance/primary: A DSM-IV literature review. *Journal of Clinical Psychiatry, 54,* 244–255.

NOLEN-HOEKSMA, S. (1987). Sex differences in unipolar depression: Evidence and theory. *Psychological Bulletin, 101,* 259–282.

NOPOULOS, P., FLAUM, M., & ANDREASEN, N. C. (1997). Sex differences and brain morphology in schizophrenia. *American Journal of Psychiatry, 154,* 1648–1654.

NORCROSS, J. C. (1991). Prescriptive matching in psychotherapy: Psychoanalysis for simple phobias? *Psychotherapy, 28,* 439–443.

NORCROSS, J. C., & FREEDHEIM, D. K. (1992). Into the future: Retrospect and prospect in psychotherapy. In D. K. Freedheim (Ed.), *History of psychotherapy.* Washington, DC: American Psychological Association.

NORENZAYAN, A., CHOI, I., & NISBETT, R. E. (2002). Cultural similarities and differences in social inference: Evidence from behavioral predictions and lay theories of behavior. *Personality and Social Psychology Bulletin, 28*(1), 109 120.

NORENZAYAN, A., & NISBETT, R. E. (2000). Culture and causal cognition. *Current Directions in Psychological Science, 9*(4), 132–135.

NORMAN, W. T. (1963). Toward an adequate taxonomy of personality attributes: Replicated factor structure in peer nomination personality ratings. *Journal of Abnormal and Social Psychology, 66,* 574–583.

NOVAK, M. A., & HARLOW, H. F. (1975). Social recovery of monkeys isolated for the first year of life: I. Rehabilitation and therapy. *Developmental Psychology, 11,* 453–465.

NUTT, D. J. (2001). Neurobiological mechanisms in generalized anxiety disorder [Suppl.]. *Journal of Clinical Psychiatry, 62*(11), 22–27.

NYITI, R. M. (1976). The development of conservation in the Meru children of Tanzania. *Child Development, 47*(4), 1122–1129.

OBER C., WEITKAMP, L. R., COX, N., DYTCH, H., KOSTYU, D., & ELIAS, S. (1997). HLA and mate choice in humans. *American Journal of Human Genetics, 61,* 497–504.

O'BRIEN, M., & NAGLE, K. J. (1987). Parents' speech to toddlers: The effect of play context. *Journal of Child Language, 14,* 269–279.

OCHBERG, F. M., & SOSKIS, D. A. (EDS.). (1982). *Victims of terrorism.* Boulder, Colorado: Westview Press.

O'CONNOR, T. G., RUTTER, M., BECKETT, C., KEAVENEY, L., KREPPNER, J. M., & ENGLISH AND ROMANIAN ADOPTION STUDY TEAM (2000). The effects of global severe privation on cognitive competence: Extension and longitudinal follow-up. *Child Development, 71*(2), 376–390.

ODIORNE, J. M. (1957). Color changes. In M. E. Brown (Ed.), *The physiology of fishes: Vol. 2.* New York: Academic Press.

ÖSTERMAN, K., BJÖRKQVIST, K., LAGERSPETZ, K. M. J., KAUKIAINEN, A., LANDAU, S. F., FRACZEK, A., & CAPRARA, G. V. (1998). Cross-cultural evidence of female indirect aggression. *Aggressive Behavior, 24*(1), 1–8.

OFSHE, R. (1992). Inadvertent hypnosis during interrogation: False confession due to dissociative state; mis-identified multiple personality and the Satanic Cult Hypothesis. *International Journal of Clinical and Experimental Hypnosis, 40,* 125–136.

OGBU, J. U. (1999). Beyond language: Ebonics, proper English, and identity in a Black-American speech community. *American Educational Research Journal, 36*(2), 147–184.

OGBURN, W. F., & BOSE, N. K. (1959). On the trail of the wolf-children. *Genetic Psychology Monographs, 60,* 117–193.

OHANIAN, H. C. (1985 and 1993). *Physics* (1st and 2nd eds.). New York: Norton.

OHMAN, A. (2002). Automaticity and the amygdala: Nonconscious responses to emotional faces. *Current Directions in Psychological Science, 11,* 62–66.

OHMAN, A., & MINEKA, S. (2001). Fears, phobias, and preparedness: Toward an evolved module of fear and fear learning. *Psychological Review, 108,* 483–522.

OLDS, J., & MILNER, P. (1954). Positive reinforcement produced by electrical stimulation of septal areas and other regions of rat brains. *Journal of Comparative and Physiological Psychology, 47,* 419–427.

OLFSON, M., & KLERMAN, G. L. (1993). Trends in the prescription of psychotropic medications. The role of physician specialty. *Medical Care, 31,* 559–564.

OLSON, D. J. (1991). Species differences in spatial memory among Clark's nutcrackers, scrub jays, and pigeons. *Journal of Experimental Psychology: Animal Behavior Processes, 17*(4), 363–376.

OLSON, G. A., OLSON, R. D., & KASTIN, A. J. (1995). Endogenous opiates: 1994. *Peptides, 16,* 1517–1555.

OLSON, W. K. (1997). *The excuse factory: How employment law is paralyzing the American workplace.* New York: Free Press.

OLTON, D. S. (1978). Characteristics of spatial memory. In S. H. Hulse, H. Fowler, & W. K. Honig (Eds.), *Cognitive processes in animal behavior* (pp. 341–373). Hillsdale, NJ: Erlbaum.

OLTON, D. S. (1979). Mazes, maps, and memory. *American Psychologist, 34,* 583–596.

OLTON, D. S., & SAMUELSON, R. J. (1976). Remembrance of places passed: Spatial memory in rats. *Journal of Experimental Psychology: Animal Behavior Processes, 2,* 97–116.

OLWEUS, D. (1980). Familial and temperamental determinants of aggressive behavior in adolescent boys: A causal analysis. *Developmental Psychology, 16,* 644–666.

O'NEILL, D. K., ASTINGTON, J. W., & FLAVELL, J. H. (1992). Young children's understanding of the role that sensory experiences play in knowledge acquisition. *Child Development, 63*(2), 474–490.

ORBELL, J. M., VAN DE KRAGT, A. J. C., & DAWES, R. M. (1988). Explaining discussion-induced cooperation. *Journal of Personality and Social Psychology, 54,* 811–819.

ORING, L. W. (1985). Avian polyandry. *Current Ornithology, 3,* 309–351.

ORLANSKY, H. (1949). Infant care and personality. *Psychological Bulletin, 46,* 1–48.

ORNE, M. T. (1951). The mechanisms of hypnotic age regression: An experimental study. *Journal of Abnormal and Social Psychology, 58,* 277–299.

ORNE, M. T. (1979). The use and misuse of hypnosis in court. *The International Journal of Clinical and Experimental Hypnosis, 27,* 311–341.

ORNE, M. T., & HAMMER, A. G. (1974). Hypnosis. In *Encyclopaedia Brittanica* (5th ed., pp. 133–40). Chicago: Encyclopaedia Brittannica.

ORNSTEIN, R. (1977). *The psychology of consciousness* (2nd ed.). New York: Harcourt Brace Jovanovich.

ORTONY, A., & TURNER, T. J. (1990). What's basic about basic emo-tions? *Psychological Review, 97,* 315–331.

OSOFSKY, J. D., & DANZGER, B. (1974). Relationships between neo-natal characteristics and mother-infant characteristics. *Developmental Psychology, 10,* 124–130.

OSTROM, T. M. (1977). Between-theory and within-theory conflict in explaining context effects in impression formation. *Journal of Experimental Social Psychology, 13,* 492–503.

PACKER, C. (1977). Reciprocal altruism in olive baboons. *Nature, 265,* 441–443.

PAEZ, D., & VERGARA, A. I. (1995). Culture differences in emotion knowledge. In J. A. Russell, J.-M. Fernandez-Dols, A. S. R. Manstead, & J. C. Wellenkamp (Eds.), *Everyday conceptions of emotion: An introduction to the psychology, anthropology and linguistics of emotion* (pp. 415–434). Dordrecht, Netherlands: Kluwer Academic Publishers.

PALLIER, C., CHRISTOPHE, A., & MEHLER, J. (1997). Language-specific listening. *Trends In Cognitive Science, 1*(4).

PALMER, S. E. (2002). Perceptual grouping: It's later than you think. *Current Directions in Psychological Science, 11*(3), 101–106.

PAPINI, M. R., & BITTERMAN, M. E. (1990). The role of contingency in classical conditioning. *Psychological Review, 97,* 396–403.

PARKE, R. D. (1981). *Fathers.* Cambridge, MA: Harvard University Press.

PARKE, R. D., & SLABY, R. G. (1983). The development of aggression. In P. H. Mussen (Ed.), M. E. Hetherington (Vol. Ed.), *Carmichael's manual of child psychology: Vol. 4. Socialization, personality and social development* (pp. 547–642). New York: Wiley.

PARKER, G., MAHENDRAN, R., KOH, E. S., & MACHIN, D. (2000). Season of birth in schizophrenia: No latitute at the equator. *British Journal of Psychiatry, 176,* 68–71.

PARKER, K. C. H., HUNSLEY, J., & HANSON, R. K. (1999). Old wine from old skins sometimes tastes like vinegar: A response to Garb, Florio, and Grove. *Psychological Science, 10*(3), 291–292.

PARNAS, J., & JORGENSEN, A. (1989). Premorbid psychopathology in schizophrenia spectrum. *British Journal of Psychiatry, 155,* 623–627.

PARROTT, W. G., SABINI, J., & SILVER, M. (1988). The roles of self-esteem and social interaction in embarrassment. *Personality and Social Psychology Bulletin, 14,* 191–202.

PASHLER, H., JOHNSTON, J. C., & RUTHRUFF, E. (2000). Attention and performance. *Annual Review of Psychology, 52,* 629–651.

PATIENCE, A., & SMITH, J. W. (1986). Derek Freeman and Samoa: The making and unmaking of a biobehavioral myth. *American Anthropologist, 88,* 157–161.

PATTATUCCI, A. M. L., & HAMER, D. H. (1995). Development and familiarity of sexual orientation in females. *Behavior Genetics, 25,* 407–420.

PATTERSON, M. L. (1983). *Nonverbal behavior: A functional perspective.* New York: Springer-Verlag.

PATTERSON, T., SPOHN, H. E., BOGIA, D. P., & HAYES, K. (1986). Thought disorder in schizophrenia: Cognitive and neuroscience approaches. *Schizophrenia Bulletin, 12,* 460–472.

PAUL, G. L. (1967). Insight versus desensitization in psychotherapy two years after termination. *Journal of Consulting Psychology, 31,* 333–348.

PAVLOV, I. (1927). *Conditioned reflexes.* Oxford: Oxford University Press.

PAYKEL, E. S. (1982). Life events and early environment. In E. S. Paykel (Ed.), *Handbook of affective disorders.* New York: Guilford.

PAYNE, B. K. (2001). Prejudice and perception: The role of automatic and controlled processes in misperceiving a weapon. *Journal of Personality & Social Psychology, 81*(2), 181–192.

PEARCE, J. M., & BOUTON, M. E. (2001). Theories of associative learning in animals. *Annual Review of Psychology, 52,* 111–139.

PEDERSEN, P. B., FUKUYAMA, M., & HEATH, A. (1989). Client, counselor, and contextual variables in multicultural counseling. In P. B. Pedersen, J. G. Draguns, W. J. Lonner, & J. E. Trimble (Eds.), *Counseling across cultures* (pp. 23–52). Honolulu: University of Hawaii.

PEDERSEN, W. C., GONZALES, C., AND MILLER, N. (2000). The moderating effect of trivial triggering provocation on displaced aggression. *Journal of Personality and Social Psychology, 78,* 913–927.

PEDERSEN, W. C., MILLER, L. C., PUTCHA-BHAGAVATULA, A. D., & YANG, Y. (2002). Evolved sex differences in the number of partners desired? The long and the short of it. *Psychological Science, 13,* 157–161.

PEDERSON, E., DANZIGER, E., WILKINS, D., LEVINSON, S., KITA, S., & SENFT, G. (1998). Semantic typology and spatial conceptualization. *Language 74*(3), 557–589.

PEISNER-FEINBERG, E. S., BURCHINAL, M. R., CLIFFORD, R. M., CULKIN, M. L., HOWES, C., KAGAN, S. L., AND YAZEJIAN, N. (2001). The relation of preschool child-care quality to children's cognitive and social developmental trajectories through second grade. *Child Development, 72,* 1534–1553.

PEÑA, M., BONATTI, L., NESPOR, M., & MEHLER, J. (2002). Signal driven computations in speech processing. *Science, 298,* 604–607.

PENDERGAST, M. (1995). *Victims of memory: Sex abuse accusations and shattered lives.* Hinesburg, VT: Upper Access Inc.

PENFIELD, W., & RASMUSSEN, T. (1950). *The cerebral cortex of man.* New York: Macmillan.

PENN, D., AND POTTS, W. (1998). MHC-disassortative mating preferences reversed by cross-fostering. *Proceedings of the Royal Society of London B Biological Sciences, 265,* 1299–1306.

PENNEBAKER, J. W. (1997). Writing about emotional experiences as a therapeutic process. *Psychological Science, 8,* 162–166.

PENNEBAKER, J. W., & GRAYBEAL, A. (2001). Patterns of natural language use: Disclosure, personality, and social integration. *Current Directions in Psychological Science, 10,* 90–93.

PERANI, D., PAULESCU, E., SEBASTIAN-GALLES, N., DUPOUX, E., DEHAENE, S., BETTINGARDI, V., ET AL. (1998), The blingual brain: Proficiency and age of acquisition of the second language, *Brain, 121,* 1841–1852.

PERDUE, C. W., DOVIDIO, J. F., GURTMAN, M. B., & TYLER, R. B. (1990). Us and them: Social categorization and the process of intergroup bias. *Journal of Personality and Social Psychology, 59,* 475–486.

PERKINS, D. N., & GROTZER, T. A. (1997). Teaching intelligence. *American Psychologist, 52,* 1125–1133.

PERNER, J., & LANG, B. (1999). Development of theory of mind and executive control. *Trends in Cognitive Science, 6,* 337–344.

PETERSON, C. (1999). Personal control and well-being. In D. Kahneman, E. Diener, & N. Schwarz (Eds.), *Well-being: The foundations of hedonic psychology* (pp. 288–301). New York: Russell Sage Foundation.

PETERSON, C. (2000). The future of optimism. *American Psychologist, 55*(1), 44–55.

PETERSON, C., & MCCABE, A. (1994). A social interactionist account of developing decontextualized narrative skill. *Developmental Psychology, 30*(6), 937–948.

PETERSON, C., & PARK, C. (1998). Learned helplessness and explanatory style. In D. F. Barone, M. Hersen, & V. Van Hasselt (Eds.), *Advanced personality* (pp. 287–310). New York: Plenum.

PETERSON, C., & SELIGMAN, M. E. P. (1984). Causal explanations as a risk factor for depression: Theory and evidence. *Psychological Review, 91,* 341–374.

PETERSON, C., SEMMEL, A., von BAEYER, C., ABRAMSON, L. Y., METALSKY, G. I., & SELIGMAN, M. E. P. (1982). The Attributional Style Questionnaire. *Cognitive Therapy and Research, 6,* 287–299.

PETERSON, C., & VAIDYA, R. S. (2001). Explanatory style, expectations, and depressive symptoms. *Personality and Individual Differences, 31,* 1217–1223.

PETERSON, S. E., FOX, P. T., POSNER, M. I., MINTUN, M., & RAICHLE, M. E. (1988). Positron emission tomographic studies of the processing of single words. *Journal of Cognitive Neuroscience, 1,* 153–170.

PETTIGREW, T. F. (1998). Intergroup contact theory. *Annual Review of Psychology, 49.*

PETTY, R. E., & CACIOPPO, J. T. (1985). The elaboration likelihood model of persuasion. In L. Berkowitz (Ed.), *Advances in experimental social psychology: Vol. 19.* New York: Academic Press.

PETTY, R. E., & WEGENER, D. T. (1998). Matching versus mismatching attitude functions: Implications for scrutiny of persuasive messages. *Personality and Social Psychology Bulletin, 24*(3), 227–240.

PETTY, R. E, WEGENER, D. T., & FABRIGAR, L. R. (1997). Attitudes and attitude change. *Annual Review of Psychology, 48,* 609–647.

PHILIPS, M. F., MATTIASSON, G., WIELOCH, T., BJÖRKLAND, A., JOHANSSON, B. B., TOMASEVIC, G., (2001). Neuroprotective and behavioral efficacy of nerve growth factor-transfected hippocampal progenitor cell transplants after experimental traumatic brain injury. *Journal of Neurosurgery, 94,* 765–774.

PIAGET, J. (1952). *The origins of intelligence in children.* New York: International University Press.

PICCINELLI, M., PINI, S., BELLANTUONO, C., & WILKINSON, G. (1995). Efficacy of drug treatment in obsessive-compulsive disorder: A meta-analytic review. *British Journal of Psychiatry, 166,* 424–443.

PILLARD, R. C. (1996). Homosexuality from a familial and genetic perspective. In R. P. Cabaj & T. S. Stein (Eds.), *Textbook of homosexuality and mental health* (pp. 115–128). Washngton, DC: American Psychiatric Press.

PILLEMER, D. B. (1998). Momentous events, vivid memories. Cambridge, MA: Harvard University Press.

PINKER, S. (1984). *Language learnability and language development.* Cambridge, MA: Harvard University Press.

PINKER, S. (1994). *The language instinct.* New York: William Morrow.

PINKER, S. (1995). Why the child holded the baby rabbits: A case study in language acquisition. In L. R. Gleitman & M. Liberman (Eds.), *Language: An invitation to cognitive science: Vol. 1* (2nd ed., pp. 107–133). Cambridge, MA: MIT Press.

PINKER, S. (1999). *Words and rules: The ingredients of language.* New York: Basic Books.

PINKER, S., & PRINCE, A. (1988). On language and connectionism: Analysis of a parallel distributed processing model of language acquisition. *Cognition, 28*(1), 73–194.

PINKER, S., & ULLMAN, M. T. (2002). The past and future of the past tense. *Trends in Cognitive Sciences, 6*(11), 456–463.

PIPP, S., EASTERBROOKS, M. A., & BROWN, S. R. (1993). Attachment status and complexity of infants' self- and other-knowledge when tested with mother and father. *Social Development, 2,* 1–114.

PLOMIN, R., CORLEY, R., DeFRIES, J. C., & FULKER, D. W. (1990). Individual differences in television viewing in early childhood: Nature as well as nurture. *Psychological Science, 1,* 371–377.

PLOMIN, R., & DANIELS, D. (1987). Why are children from the same family so different from one another? *Behavioral and Brain Sciences, 10,* 1–16.

PLOMIN, R., FULKER, D. W., CORLEY, R., & DeFRIES, J. C. (1997). Nature, nurture, and cognitive development from 1 to 16 years: A parent-offspring adoption study. *Psychological Science, 8,* 442–447.

PLOMIN, R., & SPINATH, F. M. (2002). Genetics and general cognitive ability (g). *Trends in Cognitive Science, 6,* 169–176.

POLEY, W. (1974). Dimensionality in the measurement of authoritarian and political attitudes. *Canadian Journal of Behavioral Science, 6,* 83–94.

POLLACK, M.H. (2001). Comorbidity, neurobiology, and pharmacotherapy of social anxiety disorder [Suppl.]. *Journal of Clinical Psychiatry, 62*(12), 24–29.

PORSOLT, R. D., LePICHON, M., & JALFRE, M. (1977). Depression: A new animal model sensitive to antidepressant treatments. *Nature, 266,* 730–732.

PORTER, S., BIRT, A. R., YUILLE, J. C., & LEHMAN, D. R. (2000). Negotiating false memories: Interviewer and rememberer characteristics relate to memory distortion. *Psychological Science, 11,* 507–510.

POSNER, M., SNYDER, C., & DAVIDSON, B. (1980). Attention and the detection of signals. *Journal of Experimental Psychology: General, 109,* 160–174.

POULOS, C. X., & CAPPELL, H. (1991). Homeostatic theory of drug tolerance: A general model of physiological adaptation. *Psychological Review, 98,* 390–408.

POVINELLI, D.J. (2000). *Folk physics for apes: the chimpanzees theory of how the world works.* Oxford: Oxford University Press.

POVINELLI, D. J., BERING, J. M., & GIAMBRONE S. (2000). Toward a science of other minds: Escaping the argument by analogy. *Cognitive Science, 24,* 509–542.

POWDERLY, W. G., LANDAY, A., & LEDERMAN, M. M. (1998). Recovery of the immune system with antiretroviral therapy: The end of opportunism? *JAMA, 280,* 72–77.

POWELL, H. A. (1969). Genealogy, residence, and kinship in Kiriwina. *Man, 4,* 177–202.

PRASADA, S., & PINKER, S. (1993a). Similarity-based and rule-based generalizations in inflectional morphology. *Language and Cognitive Processes, 8,* 1–56.

PRASADA, S., & PINKER, S. (1993b). Generalizations of regular and irregular morphology. *Language and Cognitive Processes, 8,* 1–56.

PREMACK, A., & PREMACK, D. (1983). *The mind of an ape.* New York: Norton.

PREMACK, D. (1965). Reinforcement theory. In D. Levine (Ed.), *Nebraska Symposium on motivation.* Lincoln, NE: University of Nebraska Press.

PREMACK, D. (1976). *Intelligence in ape and man.* Hillsdale, NJ: Erlbaum.

PREMACK, D. (1978). On the abstractness of human concepts: Why it would be difficult to talk to a pigeon. In S. H. Hulse, H. Fowler, & W. K. Honig (Eds.), *Cognitive processes in animal behavior.* Hillsdale, NJ: Erlbaum.

PREMACK, D., & WOODRUFF, G. (1978). Does the chimpanzee have a theory of mind? *Behavioral and Brain Sciences, 4,* 515–526.

PRICE, R. A., & GOTTESMAN, I. I. (1991). Body fat in identical twins reared apart: Roles for genes and environment *Behavior Genetics, 21*(1), 1–7.

PRINZ, J. J. (2002). *Furnishing the mind: Concepts and their perceptual basis.* Cambridge, MA: MIT Press.

PRIOLEAU, L., MURDOCK, M., & BRODY, N. (1983). An analysis of psychotherapy versus placebo studies. *Behavioral and Brain Sciences, 6,* 275–310.

PRISLIN, R. (1996). Attitude stability and attitude strength: One is enough to make it stable. *European Journal of Social Psychology, 26*(3), 447–477.

PRISLIN, R., & OUELLETTE, J. (1996). When it is embedded, it is potent: Effects of general attitude embeddedness on formation of specific attitudes and behavioral intentions. *Personality & Social Psychology Bulletin, 22*(8), 845–861.

PULLAM, G. (1991). *The great eskimo vocabulary hoax and other essays on the study of language.* Chicago: University of Chicago Press.

PUTNAM, F. W., GUROFF, J. J., SILBERMAN, E. K., BARBAN, L., & POST, R. M. (1986). The clinical phenomenology of multiple personality disorder: Review of 100 recent cases. *Journal of Clinical Psychiatry, 47,* 285–293.

PUTNAM, K. E. (1979). Hypnosis and distortions in eye witness memory. *International Journal of Clinical and Experimental Hypnosis, 27,* 437–448.

QUAY, H. C. (1965). Psychopathic personality as pathological stimulation seeking. *American Journal of Psychiatry, 122,* 180–183.

QUAY, L. C. (1971). Language, dialect, reinforcement, and the intelligence test performance of Negro children. *Child Development, 42,* 5–15.

QUINE, W. (1960). *Word and object.* New York: Wiley.

RADANT, A., TSUANG, D., PESKIND, E. R., McFALL, M., & RASKIND, W. (2001). Biological markers and diagnostic accuracy in the genetics of posttraumatic stress disorder. *Psychiatry Research, 102,* 203–215.

RADKE-YARROW, M., ZAHN-WAXLER, C., & CHAPMAN, M. (1983). Children's prosocial dispositions and behavior. In P. E. Mussen (Ed.), E. M. Hetherington (Vol. Ed.), *Carmichael's manual of child psychology: Vol. 4. Socialization, personality, and social development* (pp. 469–546). New York: Wiley.

RAFAL, R. (1994). Neglect. *Current Opinion in Neurobiology, 4,* 231–236.

RAFAL, R., & ROBERTSON, L. (1995). The neurology of visual attention. In M. Gazzaniga, (Ed.), *The cognitive neurosciences* pp. 625–648. Cambridge, MA: MIT Press.

RAKIC, P. (1995). Corticogenesis in human and nonhuman primates. In M. Gazzaniga (Ed.), *The cognitive neurosciences* (pp. 127–145). Cambridge, MA: MIT Press.

RALEIGH, M. J., BRAMMER, G. L., McGUIRE, M. T., POLLACK, D. B., & OTHERS. (1992). Individual differences in basal cisternal cerebrospinal fluid 5–HIAA and HVA in monkeys: The effects of gender, age, physical characteristics, and matrilineal influences. *Neuropsychopharmacology, 7,* 295–304.

RALEIGH, M. J., McGUIRE, M. T., BRAMMER, G. L., POLLACK, D. B., & OTHERS. (1991). Serotonergic mechanisms promote dominance acquisition in adult male vervet monkeys. *Brain Research, 559,* 181–190.

RAMI-GONZALEZ, L., BERNARDO, M., BOGET, T., SALAMERO, M., GIL-VERONA, J. A., & JUNQUE, C. (2001). Subtypes of memory dysfunction associated with ECT: characteristics and neurobiological bases. *Journal of ECT, 17,* 129–135.

RAMUS, F., NESPOR, M., & MEHLER, J. (1999). Correlates of linguistic rhythm in the speech signal. *Cognition, 73,* 265–292.

RAO, S. C., RAINER, G., & MILLER, E. K. (1997). Integration of what and where in the primate prefrontal cortex. *Science, 276,* 821–824.

RAPAPORT, M. H., & JUDD, L. L. (1998). Minor depressive disorder and subsyndromal depressive symptoms: functional impairment and response to treatment. *Journal of Affective Disorders, 48,* 227–232.

RAPAPORT, M. H., PANICCIA, G., & JUDD, L. L. (1995). A review of social phobia. *Psychopharmacology Bulletin, 31,* 125–129.

RAPER, J. R. (1997). Review of R. E. Nisbett and D. Cohen, *Culture of Honor: The Psychology of Violence in the South. Southern Cultures, 3.*

RAPOPORT, A. (1988). Experiments with N-person social traps. II. Tragedy of the commons. *Journal of Conflict Resolution, 32,* 473–499.

RAPOPORT, J. L. (1991). Recent advances in obsessive-compulsive disorder. *Neuropsychopharmacology, 5,* 1–10.

RAPPAPORT, Z. H. (1992). Psychosurgery in the modern era: Therapeutic and ethical aspects. *Medicine and Law, 11,* 449–453.

RASMUSSEN, S. A. (1993). Genetic studies of obsessive-compulsive disorder. *Annals of Clinical Psychiatry, 5,* 241–247.

RASMUSSEN, T., & MILNER, B. (1977). The role of early left brain injury in determining lateralization of cerebral speech functions. *Annals of the New York Academy of Sciences, 299,* 355–369.

RATEY, J., & JOHNSON, C. (1997). *Shadow syndromes.* New York: Pantheon.

RATTERMANN, M., & GENTNER, D (1998). The effect of language on similarity: The use of relational labels improves young children's performance in a mapping task. In K. Holyoak, D. Gentner, & B. Kokinov (Eds.), *Advances in analogy research* (pp. 274–282). Sphia: New Bulgarian University.

RAVUSSIN, E. (1994). Effects of a traditional lifestyle on obesity in Pima Indians. *Diabetes Care, 17,* 1067–1074.

RAVUSSIN, E., & BOUCHARD, C. (2000). Human genomics and obesity: Finding appropriate drug targets. *European Journal of Pharmacology, 410,* 131–145.

RAYNER, K., CARLSON, M., & FRAZIER, L. (1983). The interaction of syntax and semantics during sentence processing: Eye movements in the analysis of semantically biased sentences. *Journal of Verbal Learning and Verbal Behavior, 22,* 358–374.

REASON, J. (2000). The Freudian slip revisited. *Psychologist, 13,* 610–611.

REBER, A. S. (1985). *The Penguin dictionary of psychology.* New York: Viking Penguin.

REBERG, D., & BLACK, A. H. (1969). Compound testing of individually conditioned stimuli as an index of excitatory and inhibitory properties. *Psychonomic Science, 17,* 3031.

RECHT, D. R., & LESLIE, L. (1988). Effect of prior knowledge on good and poor readers' memory of text. *Journal of Educational Psychology, 80(1),* 16–20.

RECHTSCHAFFEN, A. (1998). Current perspectives on the function of sleep. *Perspectives in Biology and Medicine, 41,* 359–389.

RECHTSCHAFFEN, A.. & BERGMANN, B. (1995). Sleep deprivation in the rat by the disc-over-water method. *Behavioral Brain Research, 69,* 55–63.

REED, D. R., DING, Y., XU, W., CATHER, C., GREEN, E. D., & PRICE, R. A. (1996). Extreme obesity may be linked to markers flanking the human OB gene. *Diabetes, 45,* 691–694.

REESE, E., & FIVUSH, R. (1993). Parental styles of talking about the past. *Developmental Psychology, 29(3),* 596–606.

REEVES, L., & WEISBERG, R. W. (1994). The role of content and abstract information in analogical transfer. *Psychological Bulletin, 115(3),* 381–400.

REINISCH, J. M., ZIEMBA-DAVIS, M., & SANDERS, S. A. (1991). Hormonal contributions to sexually dimorphic behavioral development in humans. *Psychoneuroendocrinology, 16(1–3),* 213–278.

REINITZ, M., MORRISSEY, J., & DEMB, J. (1994). Role of attention in face encoding. *Journal of Experimental Psychology: Learning, Memory and Cognition, 20,* 161–168.

REIS, H. T., & WHEELER, L. (1991). Studying social interaction with the Rochester Interaction Record. In M. P. Zanna (Ed.), *Advances in experimental social psychology: Vol. 24* (pp. 269–318). New York: Academic Press.

REISBERG, D. (2001). *Cognition: Exploring the science of the mind* (2nd ed.). New York: Norton.

REISBERG, D., & HEUER, F. (2002). Visuospatial imagery. In A. Miyake & P. Shah (Eds.), *Handbook of visuospatial thinking.* New York: Cambridge University Press.

REISBERG, D., & HEUER, F. (2003). Remembering emotional events. In D. Reisberg & P. Hertel, (Eds.), *Emotion and memory.* New York: Oxford University Press.

REISENZEIN, R. (1983). The Schachter theory of emotions: Two decades later. *Psychological Bulletin, 94,* 239–264.

REISMAN, J. A., & EICHEL, E. W. (1990). *Kinsey, sex, and fraud.* Lafayette, LA: Huntington House.

REISS, D., McCOWAN, B., & MARINO L. (1997). Communicative and other cognitive characteristics of bottlenose dolphins. *Trends in Cognitive Science, 1(2),* 140–145.

REISS, D., & MARINO, L. (2001). Mirror self-recognition in the bottlenose dolphin: A case of cognitive convergence. *Proceedings of the National Academy of Science, 98(10),* 5937–5942.

REPACHOLI, B. M., & GOPNIK, A. (1997). Early reasoning about desires: Evidence from 14- and 18-month-olds. *Developmental Psychology, 33(1),* 12–21.

RESCORLA, R. A. (1967). Pavlovian conditioning and its proper control procedures. *Psychological Review, 74,* 71–80.

RESCORLA, R. A. (1988). Behavioral studies of Pavlovian conditioning. *Annual Review of Neuroscience, 11,* 329–352.

RESCORLA, R. A. (1991). Associative relations in instrumental learning: The eighteenth Bartlett Memorial lecture. *Quarterly Journal of Experimental Psychology, 43b,* 1–23.

RESCORLA, R. A. (1993a). Inhibitory associations between S and R extinction. *Animal Learning and Behavior, 21,* 327–336.

RESCORLA, R. A. (1993b). Preservation of response-outcome associations through extinction. *Animal Learning and Behavior, 21,* 238–245.

RESCORLA, R. A., & WAGNER, A. R. (1972). A theory of Pavlovian conditioning: Variations in the effectiveness of reinforcement and non-reinforcement. In A. H. Black & W. F. Prokasy (Eds.), *Classical conditioning II.* New York: Appleton-Century-Crofts.

RESNICK, S. M., BERENBAUM, S. A., GOTTESMAN, I. I., & BOUCHARD, T. J. (1986). Early hormonal influences on cognitive functioning in congenital adrenal hyperplasia. *Developmental Psychology, 22,* 191–198.

REST, J. R. (1983). Morality. In P. E. Mussen (Ed.), E. M. Hetherington (Vol. Ed.), *Carmichael's manual of child psychology: Vol. 4. Socialization, personality, and social development.* New York: Wiley.

REST, J. R. (1984). The major components of morality. In W. M. Kurtines & L. Gewirtz (Eds.), *Morality, moral behavior, and moral development.* New York: Wiley.

REVELEY, A. M., REVELEY, M. A., & CLIFFORD, C. A., & OTHERS. (1982). Cerebral ventricular size in twins discordant for schizophrenia. *Lancet, 1,* 540–541.

REY, G. (1996). Concepts and stereotypes. In E. Margolis & S. Laurence (Eds.), *Concepts: Core readings* (pp. 278–299). Cambridge MA: MIT Press.

REYNOLDS, C. R., CHASTAIN, R. L., KAUFMAN, A. S., & MCLEAN, J. E. (1987). Demographic characteristics and IQ among adults: Analysis of the WAIS—R standardization sample as a function of the stratification variables. *Journal of School Psychology, 25*(4), 323–342.

RHEINGOLD, H. L., HAY, D. F., & WEST, M. J. (1976). Sharing in the second year of life. *Child Development, 47,* 1148–1158.

RHODES, G., PROFFITT, F., GRADY, J. M., & SUMICH, A. (1998). Facial symmetry and the perception of beauty. *Psychonomics Bulletin and Review, 5,* 659–669.

RHODES, G., SUMICH, A., & BYATT, G. (1999). Are average facial configurations attractive only because of their symmetry? *Psychological Science, 10,* 52–59.

RICHARDSON-KLAVEHN, A., & GARDINER, J. M. (1998). Depth-of-processing effects on priming in stem completion: Tests of the voluntary-contamination, conceptual-processing, and lexical-processing hypothesis. *Journal of Experimental Psychology: Learning, Memory and Cognition, 24,* 593–609.

RICKELS, K., & RYNN, M.A. (2001). What is generalized anxiety disorder? [Suppl.] *Journal of Clinical Psychiatry, 62*(11), 4–12.

RIEMANN, D., HOHAGEN, F., KONIG, A., SCHWARZ, B., GOMILLE, J., VODERHOLZER, U., ET AL. (1996). Advanced vs. normal sleep timing: Effects on depressed mood after response to sleep deprivation in patients with a major depressive disorder. *Journal of Affective Disorders, 37,* 121–128.

RIGGIO, R. E. & MURPHY, S. E. (EDS.). (2002), *Multiple intelligences and leadership.* Mahwah, NJ: Erlbaum.

RIPS, L. (1990). Reasoning. *Annual Review of Psychology, 41,* 321–353.

RIVANO-FISCHER, M. (1987). Human territoriality: Notes on its definition, classification systems and micro territorial behavior. *Psychological Research Bulletin, 27,* 18.

ROBBIN, A. A. (1958). A controlled study of the effects of leucotomy. *Journal of Neurology, Neurosurgery and Psychiatry, 21,* 262–269.

ROBBINS, S. J. (1990). Mechanisms underlying spontaneous recovery in autoshaping. *Journal of Experimental Psychology: Animal Behavior Processes, 16,* 235–249.

ROBERTSON, I. H., & MANLEY, T. (1999). Sustained attention deficits in time and space. In Humphreys, G. W, & Duncan J. (Eds.), *Attention, space, and action: Studies in cognitive neuroscience* (pp. 297–310). New York: Oxford University Press.

ROBERTSON, L., TREISMAN, A., FRIEDMAN-HILL, S., & GRABOWECKY, M. (1997). The interaction of spatial and object pathways: Evidence from Balint's syndrome. *Journal of Cognitive Neuroscience, 9*(3), 295–317.

ROBINS, L. N., HELZER, J. E., WEISSMAN, M. M., ORVASCHEL, H., GRUENBERG, E., BURKE, J. D., ET AL. (1984). Lifetime prevalence of specific psychiatric disorders in three sites. *Archives of General Psychiatry, 41,* 948–958.

ROBINS, L. R. (1966). *Deviant children grown up: A sociological and psychiatric study of sociopathic personality.* Baltimore: Williams & Wilkins.

ROBINSON, L. A., BERMAN, J. S., & NEIMEYER, R. A. (1990). Psychotherapy for the treatment of depression: A comprehensive review of controlled outcome research. *Psychological Bulletin, 108,* 30–49.

ROCK, I. (1977). In defense of unconscious inference. In W. W. Epstein (Ed.), *Stability and constancy in visual perception: Mechanisms and processes* (pp. 321–374). New York: Wiley

ROCK, I. (1983). *The logic of perception.* Cambridge, MA: MIT Press.

ROCK, I. (1986). The description and analysis of object and event perception. In K. R. Boff, L. Kauffman, & J. P. Thomas (Eds.), *Handbook of perception and human performance: Vol. 2. Cognitive processes and performance* (pp. 1–71). New York: Wiley.

RODIN, J. (1990). Control by any other name: Definitions, concepts, and processes. In J. Rodin, C. Schooler, & K. W. Schaie (Eds.), *Self-directedness: Cause and effects throughout the life course* (pp. 1–17). Hillsdale, NJ: Erlbaum.

RODIN, J., & LANGER, E. J. (1977). Long-term effects of a control-relevant intervention with the institutionalized aged. *Journal of Personality and Social Psychology, 35,* 897–902.

RODMAN, H. R., GROSS, C. G., ALBRIGHT, T. D. (1989). Afferent basis of visual response properties in area MT of the macaque. I. Effects of striate cortex removal. *Journal of Neuroscience, 9,* 2033–2050.

RODRIGUEZ, M. L., MISCHEL, W., & SHODA, Y. (1989). Cognitive person variables in the delay of gratification of older children at risk. *Journal of Personality and Social Psychology, 57,* 358–367.

ROEDIGER, H. L., III. (1980). Memory metaphors in cognitive psychology. *Memory and Cognition, 8,* 231–246.

ROEDIGER, H. L., III. (1990). Implicit memory: Retention without remembering. *American Psychologist, 45,* 1043–1056.

ROGERS, C. R. (1951 and 1970). *Client-centered therapy: Its current practice, implications, and theory* (1st and 2nd eds.). Boston: Houghton Mifflin.

ROGERS, C. R. (1959). A theory of therapy, personality, and interpersonal relationships as developed in the client-centered framework. In S. Koch (Ed.), *Psychology: A study of a science: Vol. 3.* New York: McGraw-Hill.

ROGERS, C. R. (1961). *On becoming a person: A therapist's view of psychotherapy.* Boston: Houghton Mifflin.

ROGOFF, B. (1998). Cognition as a collaborative process. In W. Damon (Ed.), *Handbook of child psychology, Vol. 2* (5th ed., pp. 679–744). New York: Wiley.

ROGOFF, B. (2000). *Culture and development.* New York: Oxford University Press.

ROLAND, P. E., LARSEN, B., LASSEN, N. A., & SKINHØJ, E. (1980). Supplementary motor area and other cortical areas in organization of voluntary movements in man. *Journal of Neurophysiology, 43,* 539–560.

ROLLS, E. J. (1978). Neurophysiology of feeding. *Trends in Neurosciences, 1,* 1–3.

ROMANES, G. J. (1882). *Animal intelligence.* London: Kegan Paul.

ROOPNARINE, J. L., JOHNSON, J. E., & HOOPER, F. H. (1994). *Children's play in diverse cultures.* Albany, NY: SUNY Press.

ROPER, T. J. (1983). Learning as a biological phenomenon. In T. R. Halliday & P. J. B. Slater (Eds.), *Genes, development and behavior: Vol. 3. Animal Behavior,* (pp. 178–212). Oxford: Blackwell.

RORER, L. G. (1990). Personality assessment: A conceptual survey. In L. A. Pervin (Ed.), *Handbook of personality: Theory and research* (pp. 693–722). New York: Guilford Press.

RORSCHACH, H. (1921). *Psychodiagnostik.* Berne: Bircher.

ROSCH, E. (1977). Human categorization. In N. Warren (Ed.), *Studies in cross-cultural psychology* (pp. 3–49). London: Academic Press.

ROSCH, E. H. (1973a). Natural categories. *Cognitive Psychology, 4,* 328–350.

ROSCH, E. H. (1973b). On the internal structure of perceptual and semantic categories. In T. E. Moore (Ed.), *Cognitive development and the acquisition of language.* New York: Academic Press.

ROSCH, E. H. (1978). Principles of categorization. In E. Rosch & B. Lloyd (Eds.), *Cognition and categorization.* Hillsdale, NJ: Erlbaum.

ROSCH, E. H., & MERVIS, C. B. (1975). Family resemblances: Studies in the internal structure of categories. *Cognitive Psychology, 7,* 573–605.

ROSCH, E. H., MERVIS, C. B., GRAY, W. D., JOHNSON, D. M., & BOYES-BRAEM, P. (1976). Basic objects in natural categories. *Cognitive Psychology, 8,* 382–439.

ROSEN, G. (1966). *Madness in society.* Chicago: University of Chicago Press.

ROSEN, W. D., ADAMSON, L. B., & BAKEMAN, R. (1992). An experimental investigation of infant social referencing: Mothers' messages and gender differences. *Developmental Psychology, 28*(6), 1172–1178.

ROSENFELD, P., GIACALONE, R. A., & TEDESCHI, J. T. (1984). Cognitive dissonance and impression management explanations for effort justification. *Personality and Social Psychology Bulletin, 10,* 394–401.

ROSENSTEIN, M. J., MILAZZO-SAYRE. L. J., & MANDERSCHEID, R. W. (1989). Care of persons with schizophrenia: A statistical profile. *Schizophrenia Bulletin, 15,* 45–58.

ROSENTHAL, A. M. (1964). *Thirty-eight witnesses.* New York: McGraw-Hill.

ROSENTHAL, D. (1970). *Genetic theory and abnormal behavior.* New York: McGraw-Hill.

ROSENTHAL, D. M. (1993). Higher-order thoughts and the appendage theory of consciousness. *Philosophical Psychology, 6,* 155–166.

ROSENTHAL, N. E., SACK, D. A., GILLIN, J. C., LEWY, A. J., GOODWIN, F. K., DAVENPORT, Y., ET AL. (1984). Seasonal affective disorder: A description of the syndrome and preliminary findings with light therapy. *Archives of General Psychiatry, 41,* 72–80.

ROSENZWEIG, M. R., & LEIMAN, A. L. (1982). *Physiological psychology.* New York: Random House.

ROSENZWEIG, M. R., & LEIMAN, A. L. (1989). *Physiological psychology* (2nd ed.). New York: Random House.

ROSENZWEIG, M. R., LEIMAN, A. K., & BREEDLOVE, S. M. (1996). *Biological psychology.* Sunderland, MA: Sinauer.

ROSS, D. F., READ, J. D., & TOGLIA, M. P. (EDS). (1994). *Adult eyewitness testimony: Current trends and developments.* New York: Cambridge University Press.

ROSS, J., & LAWRENCE, K. Q. (1968). Some observations on memory artifice. *Psychonomic Science, 13,* 107–108.

ROSS, L. (1977). The intuitive psychologist and his shortcomings: Distortions in the attribution process. In L. Berkowitz (Ed.), *Advances in experimental social psychology: Vol. 10.* New York: Academic Press.

ROSS, L., AMABILE, T. M., & STEINMETZ, J. L. (1977). Social roles, social control, and biases in social perception processes. *Journal of Experimental Social Psychology, 35,* 817–829.

ROTHBARD, J. C., & SHAVER, P. R. (1994). Continuity of attachment across the life span. In M. B. Sperling & W. H. Berman (Eds.), *Attachment in adults: Clinical and developmental perspectives* (pp. 31–71). New York: Guilford Press.

ROTHBART, M. K., & AHADI, S. A. (1994). Temperament and the development of personality. *Journal of Abnormal Psychology, 103,* 55–66.

ROVEE-COLLIER, C. (1999). The development of infant memory. *Current Directions in Psychological Science, 8*(3), 80–85.

ROVEE-COLLIER, C. K. (1990). The "memory system" of prelinguistic infants. In A. Diamond (Ed.), *The development and neural bases of higher cognitive functions.* New York: The New York Academy of Sciences.

ROVEE-COLLIER, C. K., & HAYNE, H. (1987). Reactivation of infant memory: Implications for cognitive development. In H. W. Reese (Ed.), *Advances in child development and behavior: Vol. 20.* New York: Academic Press.

ROVEE-COLLIER, C., & GERHARDSTEIN, P. (1997). The development of infant memory. In N. Cowan (Ed.), *The development of memory in childhood: Studies in developmental psychology.* Hove, England: Psychology Press.

ROWE, A. D., BULLOCK, P. R., POLKEY, C. E., & MORRIS, R. G. (2001). "Theory of mind" impairments and their relationship to executive functioning following frontal lobe excisions. *Brain, 124,* 600–616.

ROZIN, P. (1999). The process of moralization. *Psychological Science, 10,* 218–221.

ROZIN, P., & KALAT, J. W. (1971). Specific hungers and poison avoidance as adaptive specializations of learning. *Psychological Review, 78,* 459–486.

ROZIN, P., & KALAT, J. W. (1972). Learning as a situation-specific adaptation. In, M. E. P. Seligman & J. L. Hager (Eds.), *Biological boundaries of learning* (pp. 66–96). New York: Appleton-Century-Crofts.

ROZIN, P., & SCHULL, J. (1988). The adaptive-evolutionary point of view in experimental psychology. In R. C. Atkinson, R. J. Herrnstein, G. Lindzey, & R. D. Luce (Eds.), *Steven's handbook of experimental psychology: Vol. 1 Perception and motivation* (2nd ed., pp. 503–546). New York: Wiley.

RUBENSTEIN, J. L., & RAKIC, P. (1999). Genetic control of cortical development. *Cerebral Cortex, 9,* 521–523.

RUBIN, Z., HILL, C. T., PEPLAU, L. A., DUNKEL-SCHETTER, C. (1980). Self-disclosure in dating couples: Sex roles and the ethic of openness. *Journal of Marriage and the Family, 42*(2), 305–317.

RUMBAUGH, D. (ED.). (1977). *Language learning by a chimpanzee: The Lana Project.* New York: Academic Press.

RUMELHART, D. E. (1997). The architecture of mind: A connectionist approach. In J. Haugeland (Ed.), *Mind design 2: Philosophy, psychology, artificial intelligence* (2nd ed.). Cambridge, MA: MIT Press.

RUMELHART, D. E., & MCCLELLAND, J. L. (1986) On learning past tenses of English verbs. In J. L. McClelland & D. E. Rumelhart (Eds.), *Parallel Distributed Processing: Vol. 2* (pp. 216–271). Cambridge, MA: MIT Press.

RUSSEK, M. (1971). Hepatic receptors and the neurophysiological mechanisms controlling feeding behavior. In S. Ehrenpreis (Ed.), *Neurosciences research: Vol. 4.* New York: Academic Press.

RUSSELL, J. A. (1994). Is there universal recognition of emotion from facial expressions? A review of the cross-cultural studies. *Psychological Bulletin, 115,* 102–141.

RUSSELL, J. A. (1995). Facial expressions of emotion: What lies beyond minimal universality? *Psychological Bulletin, 118,* 379–391.

RUSSELL, J. A., & FERNANDEZ-DOLS, J. M. (EDS.). (1997). *The psychology of facial expression.* Cambridge: Cambridge University Press.

RYAN, R. M., & DECI, E. L. (2000). Self-determination theory and the facilitation of intrinsic motivation, social development, and well-being. *American Psychologist, 55*(1), 68–78.

SABINI, J. (1995). *Social psychology* (2nd ed.). New York: Norton.

SABINI, J., & SILVER, M. (1982). *Moralities of everyday life.* New York: Oxford University Press.

SABINI, J., SIEPMANN, M., AND STEIN, J. (2001). The really fundamental attribution error in social psychological research. *Psychological Inquiry, 12,* 1–15.

SACKEIM, H., DEVANAND, D. P., & NOBLER, M. S. (1995). Electroconvulsive therapy. In F. E. Bloom & D. Kupfer (Eds.), *Psychopharmacology: The fourth generation of progress* (pp. 1123–1141). New York: Raven.

SACKS, O. (1985). *The man who mistook his wife for a hat.* New York: Harper & Row.

SADOCK, B. J. (1975). Group psychotherapy. In A. M. Freedman, H. I. Kaplan, & B. J. Sadock (Eds.), *Comprehensive textbook of psychiatry: Vol. 2* (pp. 1850–1876). Baltimore: Williams & Wilkins.

SAFFRAN, J. R., ASLIN, R. N., & NEWPORT, E. L. (1996). Statistical learning by 8-month-old infants. *Science, 274,* 1926–1928.

SAFFRAN, J. R., SENGHAS, A., & TRUESWELL, J. C. (2001). The acquisition of language by children. PNAS, *98*(23) 12874–12875.

SAGHIR, M. T., & ROBINS, E. (1973). *Male and female homosexuality.* Baltimore: Williams & Wilkins.

SAGI, A., & HOFFMAN, M. L. (1976). Empathic distress in the newborn. *Developmental Psychology, 12,* 175–176.

SAKURIAM, T., AMEMIYA, A., ISHII, M., & OTHERS. (1998). Orexins and orexin receptors: A family of hypothalamic neuropeptides and G protein-coupled receptors that regulate feeding behavior. *Cell, 92,* 573–585.

SALOVEY, P., ROTHMAN, A. J., DETWEILER, J. B., & STEWARD, W. T. (2000). Emotional states and physical health. *American Psychologist, 55*(1), 110–121.

SALTHOUSE, T. A. (1991). *Theoretical perspectives on cognitive aging.* Hillsdale, NJ: Erlbaum.

SALTHOUSE, T. A. (2000). Steps toward the explanation of adult age differences in cognition. In T. J. Perfect & E. A. Maylor (Eds.), *Models of cognitive aging.* New York: Oxford University Press.

SANTELMANN, L. M., & JUSCZYK, P. W. (1998). Sensitivity to discontinuous dependencies in language learners: evidence for limitations in processing space. *Cognition, 69,* 105–134.

SAPOLSKY, R. M. (1998). *The trouble with testosterone.* New York: Simon & Schuster.

SARASON, S. B. (1973). Jewishness, blackness, and the nature nurture controversy. *American Psychologist, 28,* 926–971.

SARBIN, T. R., & ALLEN, V. L. (1968). Role theory. In G. Lindzey & E. Aronson (Eds.), *The handbook of social psychology:, Vol. 1* (2nd ed., pp. 488–567). Reading, MA: Addison-Wesley.

SATINOFF, E. (1964). Behavioral thermoregulation in response to local cooling of the rat brain. *American Journal of Physiology, 206,* 1389–1394.

SATIR, V. (1967). *Conjoint family therapy* (rev. ed.). Palo Alto, CA: Science and Behavior Books.

SAVAGE-RUMBAUGH, E., McDONALD, D., SEVCIK, R., HOPKINS, W., & RUPERT, E. (1986). Spontaneous symbol acquisition and communicative use by pygmy chimpanzees. *Journal of Experimental Psychology: General, 115,* 211–235.

SAVAGE-RUMBAUGH, E., RUMBAUGH, D., SMITH, S., & LAWSON, J. (1980). Reference: The linguistic essential. *Science, 210,* 922–925.

SAVAGE-RUMBAUGH, S. (1987). A new look at ape language: Comprehension of vocal speech and syntax. *Nebraska Symposium on Motivation, 35,* 201–255.

SAVIN, H. B. (1973). Professors and psychological researchers: Conflicting values in conflicting roles. *Cognition, 2,* 147–149.

SAVITSKY, K., EPLEY, N., & GILOVICH, T. (2001). Do others judge us as harshly as we think? Overestimating the impact of our failures, shortcomings, and mishaps. *Journal of Personality and Social Psychology, 81,* 44–56.

SAWA, A., & SNYDER, S. H. (2002). Schizophrenia: Diverse approaches to a complex disease. *Science, 296,* 692–695.

SAWAMOTO, K., NAKAO, N., KAKISHITA, K., OGAWA, Y., TOYAMA, Y., YAMAMOTO, A., ET AL. (2001). Generation of dopaminergic neurons in the adult brain from mesencephalic precursor cells labeled with a nestin-GFP transgene. *Journal of Neuroscience, 21,* 3895–3903.

SAXE, G. (1981). Body parts as numerals: A developmental analysis of numeration among the Oksapmin in Papua, New Guinea. *Child Development, 52,* 306–316.

SAXENA, S., BRODY, A. L., MAIDMENT, K. M., DUNKIN, J. J., COLGAN, M., ALBORZIAN, S., ET AL. (1999). Localized orbitofrontal and subcortical metabolic changes and predictors of response to paroxetine treatment in obsessive-compulsive disorder. *Neuropsychopharmacology, 21,* 683–693.

SAYWITZ, K. J., & GEISELMAN, R. E. (1998). Interviewing the child witness: Maximizing completeness and minimizing error. In S. J. Lynn & K. M. McConkey (Eds.), *Truth in memory* (pp. 190–223). New York: The Guilford Press.

SCAIFE, M., & BRUNER, J. S. (1975). The capacity for joint visual attention in the infant. *Nature, 253*(5489), 265–266.

SCARR, S. (1987). Distinctive environments depend upon genotypes. *Behavioral and Brain Sciences, 10,* 38–39.

SCARR, S. (1992). Developmental theories for the 1990s: Development and individual differences. *Child Development, 63,* 1–19.

SCARR, S. (1997). Why child care has little impact on most children's development. *Current Directions in Psychological Science, 6,* 143–148.

SCARR, S. (1998). American child care today. *American Psychologist, 53*(2), 95–108.

SCARR, S., & CARTER-SALTZMAN, L. (1982). Genetics and intelligence. In R. J. Sternberg (Ed.), *Handbook of human intelligence* (pp. 792–896). New York: Cambridge University Press.

SCARR, S., & McCARTNEY, K. (1983). How people make their own environments: A theory of genotype-environment effects. *Child Development, 54,* 424–435.

SCARR, S., PAKSTIS, A. J., KATZ, S. H., & BARKER, W. B. (1977). Absence of a relationship between degree of White ancestry and intellectual skills within a Black population. *Human Genetics, 39,* 69–86.

SCARR, S., & WEINBERG, R. A. (1976). IQ test performance of black children adopted by white families. *American Psychologist, 31,* 726–739.

SCARR, S., & WEINBERG, R. A. (1983). The Minnesota adoption studies genetic differences and malleability. *Child Development, 54,* 260–267.

SCHACHER, S. (1981). Determination and differentiation in the development of the nervous system. In E. R. Kandel & J. H. Schwartz (Eds.), *Principles of neural science.* New York: Elsevier North Holland.

SCHACHTEL, E. G. (1947). On memory and childhood amnesia. *Psychiatry, 10,* 1–26.

SCHACHTER, S. (1964). The interaction of cognitive and physiological determinants of emotional state. In L. Berkowitz (Ed.), *Advances in experimental social psychology* (pp. 49–80). New York: Academic Press.

SCHACHTER, S., & SINGER, J. (1962). Cognitive, social and physiological determinants of emotional state. *Psychological Review, 69,* 379–399.

SCHACHTER, S., & SINGER, J. E. (1979). Comments on the Maslach and Marshall-Zimbardo experiments. *Journal of Personality and Social Psychology, 37,* 989–995.

SCHACHTER, F. (1982). Sibling deidentification and split-parent identification: A family tetrad. In M. Lamb and B. Sutton-Smith (eds.), *Sibling relationships: Their nature and significance over the lifespan.* Hillsdale, N.J.: Erlbaum.

SCHACTER, D. (1992). Understanding implicit memory. *American Psychologist, 47,* 559–569.

SCHACTER, D. L. (1987). Implicit memory: History and current status. *Journal of Experimental Psychology: Learning, Memory, and Cognition, 13,* 501–518.

SCHACTER, D. L. (1996). *Searching for memory: The brain, the mind and the past.* New York: Basic Books.

SCHAIE, K. W. (1996). *Intellectual development in adulthood: The Seattle Longitudinal study.* New York: Cambridge University Press.

SCHAIE, K. W., & WILLIS, S. L. (1996). Psychometric intelligence and aging. In F. Blanchard Fields & T. M. Hess (Eds.), *Perspectives on cognitive change in adulthood and aging* (pp. 293–322). New York: McGraw-Hill.

SCHEEPENS, A., SIRIMANNE, E. S., BREIER, B. H., CLARK, R. G., GLUCKMAN, P. D., & WILLIAMS, C. E. (2001). Growth hormone as a neuronal rescue factor during recovery from CNS injury. *Neuroscience, 104,* 677–687.

SCHEERER, M. (1963). Problem solving. *Scientific American, 208,* 118–128.

SCHEERER, M., GOLDSTEIN, K., & BORING, E. G. (1941). A demonstration of insight: The horse-rider puzzle. *American Journal of Psychology, 54,* 437–438.

SCHERER, K. R. (1997). The role of culture in emotion-antecedent appraisal. *Journal of Personality and Social Psychology, 73,* 902–922.

SCHIFFMAN, H. R. (1976). *Sensation and perception: An integrated approach.* New York: Wiley.

SCHLENKER, B. R. (1980). *Impression management: The self-concept, social identity and interpersonal relations.* Monterey, CA: Brooks/Cole.

SCHLENKER, B. R., & WEIGOLD, M. F. (1992). Interpersonal processes involving impression regulation and management. *Annual Review of Psychology, 43,* 133–168.

SCHMIDT, F. L., & HUNTER, J. E. (1998). The validity and utility of selection methods in personnel psychology: Practical and theoretical implications of 85 years of research findings. *Psychological Bulletin, 124*(2), 262–274.

SCHMITT, D. P., & BUSS, D. M. (2001). Human mate poaching: Tactics and temptations for infiltrating existing mateships. *Journal of Personality & Social Psychology, 80*(6), 894–917.

SCHNEIDER, D. J. (1973). Implicit personality theory: A review. *Psychological Bulletin, 79,* 294–309.

SCHNEIDER, D. J., HASTORF, A. H., & ELLSWORTH, P. C. (1979). *Person perception* (2nd ed.) Reading, MA: Addison-Wesley.

SCHNEIDER, K., & JOSEPHS, I. (1991). The expressive and communicative functions of preschool children's smiles in an achievement situation. *Journal of Nonverbal Behavior, 15*, 185–198.

SCHNEIDER, W., GRUBER, H., GOLD, A., & OPWIS, K. (1993). Chess expertise and memory for chess positions in children and adults. *Journal of Experimental Child Psychology, 56*(3), 328–349.

SCHOFIELD, W. (1964). *Psychotherapy: The purchase of friendship.* Englewood Cliffs, NJ: Prentice-Hall.

SCHRAW, G., DUNKLE, M., & BENDIXEN, L. (1995). Cognitive processes in well-defined and ill-defined problem solving. *Applied Cognitive Psychology, 9*, 523–538.

SCHREIBER, F. R. (1973). *Sybil.* New York: Warner Paperback.

SCHROEDER, H. E. (1973). The risky shift as a general choice shift. *Journal of Personality and Social Psychology, 27*(2), 297–300.

SCHUL, Y., & VINOKUR, A. D. (2000). Projection in person perception among spouses as a function of the similarity in their shared experiences. *Personality and Social Psychology Bulletin, 26*(8), 987–1001.

SCHULZ-HARDT, S. FREY, D., LÜTHGENS, C., & MOSCOVICI, S. (2000). Biased information search in group decision making. *Journal of Personality and Social Psychology, 78*, 655–669.

SCHUNK, D. H. (1984). Self-efficacy perspective on achievement behavior. *Educational Psychologist, 19*(1), 48–58.

SCHUNK, D. H. (1985). Self-efficacy and classroom learning. *Psychology in the Schools, 22*(2), 208–223.

SCHWARTZ, B. (2000). Self-determination: The tyranny of freedom. *American Psychologist, 55*(1), 79–88.

SCHWARTZ, B., & ROBBINS, S. (1995). *Psychology of learning and behavior.* New York: Norton.

SCHWARTZ, B., WASSERMAN, E. A., & ROBBINS, S. (2002). Psychology of learning and behavior. New York: Norton.

SCHWARTZ, G. E., WEINBERGER, D. A., & SINGER, J. A. (1981). Cardiovascular differentiation of happiness, sadness, anger, and fear following imagery and exercise. *Psychosomatic Medicine, 43*, 343–364.

SCHWARZ, N. (1999). Self-reports: How the questions shape the answers. *American Psychologist, 54*, 93–105.

SCHWARZER, R. (ED.) (1992). *Self-efficacy: Thought control of action.* Washington, DC: Hemisphere.

SCHWEDER, R. A. (1994). "You're not sick, you're just in love": Emotion as an interpretive system. In P. Ekman & R. J. Davidson (Eds.), *The nature of emotion* (pp. 32–47). New York: Oxford University Press.

SCHWEITZER, E., RICKELS, K., & UHLENHUTH, E. H. (1995). Issues in the long-term treatment of anxiety disorders. In F. E. Bloom & D. Kupfer (Eds.), *Psychopharmacology: The fourth generation of progress* (pp. 1349–1359). New York: Raven.

SCRIBNER, S. (1975). Recall of classical syllogisms: A cross-cultural investigation of error on logical problems. In R. J. Falmagne (Ed.), *Reasoning, representation and process in children and adults* (pp. 153–174). Hillsdale, NJ: Erlbaum.

SEARLE, J., DENNETT, D. C., & CHALMERS, D. J. (1997). *The mystery of consciousness.* New York: New York Review of Books.

SEARS, R. R., MACCOBY, E. E., & LEVIN, H. (1957). *Patterns of child rearing.* Evanston, IL: Row, Peterson.

SEEMAN, M. V. (1997). Psychopathology in women and men: Focus on female hormones. *American Journal of Psychiatry, 154*, 1641–1647.

SEGALL, M. H., DASEN, P. R., BERRY, J. W., & POORTINGA, Y. H. (1999). *Human behavior in global perspective: An introduction to cross-cultural psychology* (2nd ed.). New York: Pergamon Press.

SEGERSTROM, S. C. (2000). Personality and the immune system: Models, methods, and mechanisms. *Annals of Behavioral Medicine, 22*, 180–190.

SEIDENBERG, M. S., & PETITTO, L. A. (1979). Signing behavior in apes: A critical review. *Cognition, 7*, 177–215.

SEIDLER, R. D., PURUSHOTHAM, A., KIM, S.-G., UGURBIL, K., WILLINGHAM, D., & ASHE, J. (2002). Cerebellum activation associated with performance change but not motor learning. *Science, 296*, 2043–2046.

SELFRIDGE, O. G. (1955). Pattern recognition and modern computers. In *Proceedings of Western Joint Computer Conference.* Los Angeles, CA.

SELFRIDGE, O. G. (1959). Pandemonium: A paradigm for learning. In D. V. Blake & A. M. Uttley (Eds.), *Proceedings of the Symposium on the Mechanisation of Thought Processes.* London: HM Stationary Office.

SELIGMAN, M. E. P. (1970). On the generality of the laws of learning. *Psychological Review, 77*, 406–418.

SELIGMAN, M. E. P. (1971). Phobias and preparedness. *Behavior Therapy, 2*, 307–320.

SELIGMAN, M. E. P. (1975). *Helplessness: On depression, development, and death.* San Francisco: Freeman.

SELIGMAN, M. E. P. (1995). The effectiveness of psychotherapy: The Consumer Reports study. *American Psychologist, 50*, 965–974.

SELIGMAN, M. E. P., & CSIKSZENTMIHALYI, M. (2000). Positive psychology: An introduction. *American Psychologist, 55*(1), 5–14.

SELIGMAN, M. E. P., & GILLHAM, J. (2000). *The science of optimism and hope: Research essays in honor of Martin E. P. Seligman.* Philadelphia: Templeton Foundation Press.

SELIGMAN, M. E. P., & HAGER, J. L. (EDS.). (1972). *Biological boundaries of learning.* New York: Appleton-Century-Crofts.

SELIGMAN, M. E. P., KLEIN, D. C., & MILLER, W. R. (1976). Depression. In H. Leitenberg (Ed.), *Handbook of behavior modification and behavior therapy.* Englewood Cliffs, NJ: Prentice-Hall.

SELIGMAN, M. E. P., & MAIER, S. F. (1967). Failure to escape traumatic shock. *Journal of Experimental Psychology, 74*, 1–9.

SELIGMAN, M. E. P., MAIER, S. F., & SOLOMON, R. L. (1971). Unpredictable and uncontrollable aversive events. In F. R. Brush (Ed.), *Aversive conditioning and learning.* New York: Academic Press.

SENGHAS, A. (1995). Conventionalization in the first generation: A community acquires a language. *Journal of Contemporary Legal Issues, 6*, 501–519.

SENGHAS, A. (1995). The development of Nicaraguan Sign Language via the language acquisition process. In D. MacLaughlin & S. McEwen (Eds.), *Proceedings of the Boston University Conference on Language Development, 19*, 543–552.

SENGHAS, A., COPPOLA, M., NEWPORT, E. L., & SUPALLA, T. (1997). Argument structure in Nicaraguan Sign Language: The emergence of grammatical devices. In E. Hughes, M. Hughes, & A. Greenhill (Ed.), *Proceedings of the Boston University Conference on Language Development* (pp. 550–561). Boston: Cascadilla Press.

SERENO, A. B., & MAUNSELL, J. H. R. (1998). Shape selectivity in primate lateral intraparietal cortex. *Nature, 395*, 500–503.

SETHI, A., MISCHEL, W., ABER, J. L., SHODA, Y., & RODRIGUEZ, M. L. (2000). The role of strategic attention deployment in development of self-regulation: Predicting preschoolers' delay of gratification from mother-toddler interactions. *Developmental Psychology, 36*, 767–777.

SEYMOUR, H. N., ABDULKARIM, L., & JOHNSON, V. (1999). The Ebonics controversy: An educational and clinical dilemma. *Topics in Language Disorders, 19*(4) Aug 1999, Inc.

SHADER, R. I., & GREENBLATT, D. J. (1995). The pharmacotherapy of acute anxiety. In F. E. Bloom & D. Kupfer (Eds.), *Psychopharmacology: The fourth generation of progress* (pp. 1341–1348). New York: Raven.

SHALTER, M. D. (1984). Predator-prey behavior and habituation. In H. V. S. Peeke & L. Petrinovich (Eds.), *Habituation, sensitization and behavior* (pp. 423–458). New York: Academic Press.

SHAM, P. V. C., O'CALLAGHAN, E., TAKEI, N., MURRAY, G. K., HARE, E. H., & MURRAY, R. M. (1992). Schizophrenia following pre-natal exposure to influenza epidemics between 1939 and 1960. *British Journal of Psychiatry, 160,* 461–466.

SHANAB, M. E., & YAHYA, K. A. (1977). A behavioral study of obedience in children. *Journal of Personality and Social Psychology, 35,* 530–536.

SHAPIRO, A. K. (1971). Placebo effects in medicine, psychotherapy, and psychoanalysis. In A. E. Bergin & S. L. Garfield (Eds.), *Handbook of psychotherapy and behavior change* (pp. 439–473). New York: Wiley.

SHAPIRO, C. M., BORTZ, R., MITCHELL, D., BARTELL, P., & JOOSTE, P. (1981). Slow wave sleep: A recovery period after exercise. *Science, 214,* 1253–1254.

SHAPIRO, D. A., & SHAPIRO, D. (1982). Meta-analysis of comparative therapy outcome studies: A replication and refinement. *Psychological Bulletin, 92,* 581–604.

SHAPIRO, P. N., & PENROD, S. (1986). Meta-analysis of facial identification studies. *Psychological Bulletin, 100,* 139–156.

SHAVITT, S., SWAN, S., LOWREY, T. M., & WANKE, M. (1994). The interaction of endorser attractiveness and involvement in persuasion depends on the goal that guides message processing. *Journal of Consumer Psychology, 3*(2), 137–162.

SHAYWITZ, B. A., SHAYWITZ, S. E., PUGH, K. R., CONSTABLE, R. T., SKUDLARSKI, P., FULBRIGHT, R. K., ET AL. (1995). Sex differences in the functional organization of the brain for language. *Nature, 373,* 607–609.

SHEAR, M. K., PILKONIS, P. A., CLOITRE, M., & LEON, A. C. (1994). Cognitive behavioral treatment compared with nonprescriptive treatment of panic disorder. *Archives of General Psychiatry, 51,* 395–401.

SHEEAN, D. (1985). Monoamine oxidase inhibitors and alprazolam in the treatment of panic disorder and agoraphobia. *Psychiatric Clinics of North America, 8,* 49–82.

SHEFFIELD, F. D., & ROBY, T. B. (1950). Reward value of a non-nutritive sweet taste. *Journal of Comparative and Physiological Psychology, 43,* 471–481.

SHEINGOLD, K., & TENNEY, Y. J. (1982). Memory for a salient childhood event. In U. Neisser (Ed.), *Memory observed* (pp. 201–212). San Francisco: Freeman.

SHELDON, K. M., ELLIOT, A. J., KIM, Y., & KASSER, T. (2001). What is satisfying about satisfying events? Testing 10 candidate psychological needs. *Journal of Personality and Social Psychology, 80,* 325–339.

SHELLEY, P. B. (1821). To a skylark. As published in A. T. Quiller-Couch (Ed.), *The Oxford book of English verse* (1900). Oxford: Clarendon.

SHEPARD, R. N., & COOPER, L. A. (1982). Mental images and their transformations. Cambridge, MA: MIT Press.

SHEPHERD, G. M. (1994). Discrimination of molecular signals by the olfactory receptor neuron. *Neuron, 13,* 771–790.

SHERMAN, P. W. (1977). Nepotism and the evolution of alarm calls. *Science, 197,* 1246–1254.

SHERMER, M. (1997). *Why people believe weird things: Pseudoscience, superstition, and other confusions of our time.* New York: W. H. Freeman.

SHERROD, D. (1989). The influence of gender on same-sex friendships. In C. Hendrick (Ed.), *Close relationships: Vol. 10. Review of personality and social psychology.* Newbury Park, CA: Sage.

SHETTLEWORTH, S. J. (1972). Constraints on learning. In D. S. Lehrman, R. A. Hinde, & E. Shaw (Eds.), *Advances in the study of behavior: Vol. 4.* New York: Academic Press.

SHETTLEWORTH, S. J. (1983). Memory in food-hoarding birds. *Scientific American, 248,* 102–110.

SHETTLEWORTH, S. J. (1984). Learning and behavioral ecology. In J. R. Krebs & N. B. Davies (Eds.), *Behavioral ecology* (2nd ed., pp. 170–194). Oxford: Blackwell.

SHETTLEWORTH, S. J. (1990). Spatial memory in food-storing birds. *Philosophical Transactions of the Royal Society, Series B, 329,* 143–151.

SHI, R., MORGAN, J. L., & ALLOPENNA, P. (1998). Phonological and acoustic bases for earliest grammatical category assignment: a cross-linguistic perspective. *Journal of Child Language, 25,* 169–201.

SHIAH, I. S., & YATHAM, L. N. (2000). Serotonin in mania and in the mechanism of action of mood stabilizers: A review of clinical studies. *Bipolar Disorders, 2,* 77–92.

SHIFFRIN, R. M. (1997). Attention, automatism, and consciousness. In J. D. Cohen & J. W. Schooler (Eds.), *Scientific approaches to consciousness* (pp. 49–64). Mahwah, NJ: Lawrence Erlbaum Associates.

SHIPLEY, E. F., KUHN, I. F., & MADDEN, E. C. (1983). Mothers' use of superordinate category terms. *Journal of Child Language, 10,* 571–588.

SHIPLEY, E. F., SMITH, C. S., & GLEITMAN, L. R. (1969). A study in the acquisition of language: Free responses to commands. *Language, 45,* 322–342.

SHIVELY, C. A., FONTENOT, M. B., & KAPLAN, J. R. (1995). Social status, behavior, and central serotonergic responsivity in female cynomolgus monkeys. *American Journal of Primatology, 37,* 333–339.

SHOBE, K. K., & KIHLSTROM, J. F. (1997). Is traumatic memory special? *Current Directions in Psychological Science, 6,* 70–74.

SHODA, Y., MISCHEL, W., & PEAKE, P. K. (1990). Predicting adolescent cognitive and self-regulatory competencies from preschool delay of gratification: Identifying diagnostic conditions. *Developmental Psychology, 26,* 978–986.

SHORTER, E. (1992). *From paralysis to fatigue: A history of psychosomatic illness in the modern era.* New York: Macmillan Free Press.

SHWEDER, R. & SULLIVAN, M. (1993). Cultural psychology: Who needs it? *Annual Review of Psychology, 44,* 497–523.

SICOLY, F., & ROSS, M. (1977). Facilitation of ego-biased attributions by means of self-serving observer feedback. *Journal of Personality and Social Psychology, 35,* 734–741.

SIEGAL, M. (1997). *Knowing children: Experiments in conversation and cognition* (2nd ed.). New York: Psychology Press.

SIEGEL, A., & DEMETRIKOPOULOS, M. K. (1993). Hormones and aggression. In J. Schulkin (Ed.), *Hormonally induced changes in mind and brain* (pp. 99–127). San Diego, CA: Academic Press.

SIEGEL, R. K. (1984). Changing patterns of cocaine use: Longitudinal observations, consequences, and treatment. In J. Grabowski (Ed.), *Cocaine: Pharmacology, effects, and treatment of abuse* (pp. 92–110). NIDA Research Monograph 50.

SIEGEL, S. (1977). Morphine tolerance acquisition as an associative process. *Journal of Experimental Psychology: Animal Behavior Processes, 3,* 1–13.

SIEGEL, S. (1983). Classical conditioning, drug tolerance, and drug dependence. In Y. Israel, F. B. Slower, H. Kalant, R. E. Popham, W. Schmidt, & R. G. Smart (Eds.), *Research advances in alcohol and drug abuse: Vol. 7* (pp. 207–246). New York: Plenum.

SIEGEL, S. (1989). Pharmacological conditioning and drug effects. In A. J. Goudie & M. W. Emmett-Oglesby (Eds.), *Psychoactive drugs: Tolerance and sensitization* (pp. 115–180). Clifton, NJ: Humana Press.

SIEGEL, S., & ALLAN, L. G. (1998). Learning and homeostasis: Drug addiction and the McCollough effect. *Psychological Bulletin, 124,* 230–239.

SIEGLER, R. S. (1996). *Emerging minds: The process of change in children's thinking.* New York: Oxford University Press.

SIEVER, L. J., DAVIS, K. L., & GORMAN, L. K. (1991). Pathogenesis of mood disorders. In K. Davis, H. Klar, & J. T. Coyle (Eds.), *Foundations of psychiatry.* Philadelphia: Saunders.

SILK, J. B. (1986). Social behavior in evolutionary perspective. In B. B. Smuts, D. L. Cheney, R. M. Seyfarth, R. W. Wrangham, & T. T. Struhsaker (Eds.), *Primate societies.* Chicago: University of Chicago Press.

SIMNER, M. L. (1971). Newborn's response to the cry of another infant. *Developmental Psychology, 5,* 136–150.

SIMONS, D. J., & CHABRIS, C. F. (1999). Gorillas in our midst: Sustained inattentional blindness for dynamic events. *Perception, 28*(9), 1059–1074.

SIMONTON, D. K. (2000). Creativity: Cognitive, personal, developmental, and social aspects. *American Psychologist, 55*(1), 151–158.

SIMPSON, E. L. (1974). Moral development research: A case of scientific cultural bias. *Human Development, 17,* 81–106.

SIMS, E. A. (1986). Energy balance in human beings: The problems of plentitude. *Vitamins and Hormones: Research and Applications, 43,* 1–101.

SINGER, W. (1996). Neuronal synchronization: A solution to the binding problem? In R. R. Llinas, & P. S. Churchland (Eds.), *The mind-brain continuum: Sensory processes* (pp. 101–130). Cambridge, MA: MIT Press.

SINGH, D. (1993). Adaptive significance of female physical attractiveness: role of waist-to-hip ratio. *Journal of Personality and Social Psychology, 65,* 293–307.

SINGH, D. (1994). Waist-to-hip ratio and judgment of attractiveness and healthiness of female figures by male and female physicians. *International Journal of Obesity and Related Metabolic Disorders, 18,* 731–737.

SINGH, D., & LUIS, S. (1995). Ethnic and gender consensus for the effect of waist-to-hip ratio on judgment of women's attractiveness. *Human Nature, 6,* 51–65.

SINHA, D. (1983). Human assessment in the Indian context. In S. H. Irvine & J. W. Berry, (Eds.), *Human assessment and cultural factors* (pp. 17–34). New York: Plenum.

SINHA, R., & PARSONS, O. A. (1996). Multivariate response patterning of fear and anger. *Cognition and Emotion, 10,* 173–198.

SIZEMORE, C. C., & HUBER, R. J. (1988). The twenty-two faces of Eve. *Individual Psychology: Journal of Adlerian Theory, Research and Practice, 44,* 53–62.

SKINNER, B. F. (1938). *The behavior of organisms.* New York: Appleton-Century-Crofts.

SLATER, E., & GLITHERO, E. (1965). A follow-up of patients diagnosed as suffering from hysteria. *Journal of Psychosomatic Research, 9,* 9–13.

SLOANE, R. B., STAPLES, F. R., CRISTOL, A. H., YORKSTON, N. J., & WHIPPLE, K. (1975). *Psychotherapy vs. behavior therapy.* Cambridge, MA: Harvard University Press.

SLOBIN, D. I. (1982). Universal and particular in the acquisition of language. In E. Wanner & L. R. Gleitman (Eds.), *Language acquisition: The state of the art* (pp. 128–172). New York: Cambridge University Press.

SLOVENKO, R. (1995). Multiple personality: Perplexities about the law. *Medicine and Law, 14,* 623–629.

SLOVIC, P., FISCHOFF, B., & LICHTENSTEIN, S. (1982). Facts versus fears: Understanding perceived risk. In D. Kahneman, P. Slovic, & A. Tversky (Eds.), *Judgment under uncertainty: Heuristics and biases.* New York: Cambridge University Press.

SLUTSKE, W. S. (2001). The genetics of antisocial behavior. *Current Psychiatry Reports, 3,* 158–162.

SMELSER, N. J. (1963). *Theory of collective behavior.* New York: Free Press, Macmillan.

SMITH, C. (1996). Women, weight and body image. In J. C. Chrisler, C. Golden, & P. D. Rozee (Eds.), *Lectures on the psychology of women.* New York: McGraw Hill.

SMITH, C., & LLOYD, B. (1978). Maternal behavior and perceived sex of infant: Revisited. *Child Development, 49,* 1263–1265.

SMITH, D. G. (1981). The association between rank and reproductive success of male rhesus monkeys. *American Journal of Primatology, 1,* 83–90.

SMITH, E. E., & MEDIN, D. L. (1981). *Categories and concepts.* Cambridge, MA: Harvard University Press.

SMITH, L. B., THELEN, E., TITZER, R., & McLIN, D. (1999). Knowing in the context of acting: The task dynamics of the A-Not-B error. *Psychological Review, 106,* 235–260.

SMITH, M. (1983). Hypnotic memory enhancement of witnesses: Does it work? *Psychological Bulletin, 94,* 387–407.

SMITH, M. B. (1950). The phenomenological approach in personality theory: Some critical remarks. *Journal of Abnormal and Social Psychology, 45,* 516–522.

SMITH, M. L., GLASS, G. V., & MILLER, R. L. (1980). *The benefits of psychotherapy.* Baltimore: Johns Hopkins Press.

SMITH, P. B., & BOND, M. B. (1993). *Social psychology across cultures.* New York: Harvester Wheatsheaf.

SMITH, S. M. (1979). Remembering in and out of context. *Journal of Experimental Psychology: Human Learning and Memory, 5,* 460–471.

SMITH, S. M., & BLANKENSHIP, S. E. (1989). Incubation effects. *Bulletin of the Psychonomic Society, 27(4),* 311–314.

SMITH, S. M., & VELA, E. (2001). Environmental context-dependent memory: A review and meta-analysis. *Psychonomics Bulletin and Review, 8,* 203–220.

SMITH, W. J. (1977). *The behavior of communicating.* Cambridge, MA: Harvard University Press.

SMOLENSKY, P. (1999). Grammar-based connectionist approaches to language. *Cognitive Science, 23,* 589–613.

SNEAD, O. C. (2001). Surgical treatment of medically refractory epilepsy in childhood. *Brain Development, 23,* 199–207.

SNEDEKER, J., & GLEITMAN, L. (in press). Why it is hard to label our concepts. To appear in D. G. Hall & S. R. Waxman (Eds.), *Weaving a lexicon.* Cambridge, MA: MIT Press.

SNOW, C., & HOEFNAGEL-HOHLE, M. (1978). The critical period for language acquisition: Evidence from second language learning. *Child Development, 49,* 1114–1128.

SNYDER, M. (1987). *Public appearances/private realities.* New York: Freeman.

SNYDER, M. (1995). Self-monitoring: Public appearances versus private realities. In G. G. Brannigan & M. R. Merrens (Eds.), *The social psychologists: Research adventures* (pp. 35–50). New York: McGraw-Hill.

SNYDER, M., & CUNNINGHAM, M. R. (1975). To comply or not comply: Testing the self-perception explanation of the "foot-in-the-door" phenomenon. *Journal of Personality and Social Psychology, 31,* 64–67.

SNYDER, M., & ICKES, W. (1985). Personality and social behavior. In G. Lindzey & E. Aronson (Eds.), *Handbook of social psychology: Vol. 2* (3rd ed.). New York: Random House.

SNYDER, M. L., STEPHAN, W. G., & ROSENFIELD, D. (1976). Egotism and attribution. *Journal of Personality and Social Psychology, 33,* 435–441.

SNYDER, S. H. (1976). The dopamine hypothesis of schizophrenia. *American Journal of Psychiatry, 133,* 197–202.

SNYDER, S. H., & CHILDERS, S. R. (1979). Opiate receptors and opioid peptides. *Annual Review of Neuroscience, 2,* 35–64.

SOJA, N. N. (1992). Inferences about the meanings of nouns: The relationship between perception and syntax. *Cognitive Development, 7,* 29–45.

SOJA, N. N., CAREY, S., & SPELKE, E. S. (1991). Ontological categories guide young children's inductions of word meaning: Object terms and substance terms. *Cognition, 38,* 179–211.

SOLMS, M. (1997). *The neuropsychology of dreams.* Mahwah, NJ: Erlbaum.

SOLOMON, R. L. (1980). The opponent-process theory of acquired motivation: The costs of pleasure and the benefits of pain. *American Psychologist, 35,* 691–712.

SOLOMON, R. L., & CORBIT, J. D. (1974). An opponent-process theory of motivation: I. Temporal dynamics of affect. *Psychological Review, 81,* 119–145.

SPANOS, N. P. (1994). Multiple identity enactments and multiple personality disorder: A sociocognitive perspective. *Psychological Bulletin, 116,* 143–165.

SPANOS, N. P., BURGESS, C. A., BURGESS, M. F., SAMUELS, C., & BLOIS, W. O. (1999). Creating false memories of infancy with hypnotic and nonhypnotic procedures. *Applied Cognitive Psychology, 13,* 201–218.

SPEARMAN, C. (1927). *The abilities of man.* London: Macmillan.

SPELKE, E. S., & NEWPORT, E. (1998). Nativism, empiricism, and the development of knowledge. In R. Lerner (Ed), *Handbook of Child Psychology: Vol. 1. Theoretical models of human development* (5th ed.). New York: Wiley.

SPELKE, E. S. (1994). Initial knowledge: Six suggestions. *Cognition, 50(1–3),* 431–445.

SPELKE, E. S. (1999). Innateness, learning and the development of object representation. *Developmental Science, 2(2),* 145–148.

SPELKE, E. S. (2000). Core knowledge. *American Psychologist, 55*, 1233–1243.

SPEMANN, H. (1967). *Embryonic development and induction.* New York: Hafner Publishing Company.

SPENCE, J. T., & SPENCE, K. W. (1966). The motivational components of manifest anxiety: Drive and drive stimuli. In C. D. Spielberger (Ed.), *Anxiety and behavior.* New York: Academic Press.

SPERBER, D., & WILSON, D. (1986). *Relevance: Communication and cognition.* Oxford: Blackwell.

SPERLING, G. (1960). The information available in brief visual presentations. *Psychological Monographs, 74*(Whole No. 11).

SPERRY, R. W. (1974). Lateral specialization in the surgically separated hemispheres. In F. O. Schmitt, & F. G. Worden (Eds.), *The Neuroscience Third Study Program.* Cambridge, MA: MIT Press.

SPERRY, R. W. (1982). Some effects of disconnecting the cerebral hemispheres. *Science, 217*, 1223–1226.

SPIES, G. (1965). Food versus intracranial self-stimulation reinforcement in food deprived rats. *Journal of Comparative and Physiological Psychology, 60*, 153–157.

SPINELLI, M. G. (2001). A systematic investigation of 16 cases of neonaticide. *American Journal of Psychiatry, 158*, 811–813.

SPIRO, M. (1982). *Oedipus in the Trobriands.* Chicago: University of Chicago Press.

SPIRO, M. E. (1992). Oedipus redux. *Ethos, 20*, 358–376.

SPORER, S. (1991). Deep-deeper-deepest? Encoding strategies and the recognition of human faces. *Journal of Experimental Psychology: Learning, Memory and Cognition, 17*, 323–333.

SPRINGER, S. P., & DEUTSCH, G. (1998). *Left brain, right brain: Perspectives from cognitive neuroscience* (5th ed.). New York: Freeman.

SQUIRE, L. R. (1977). ECT and memory loss. *American Journal of Psychiatry, 134*, 997–1001.

SQUIRE, L. R. (1986). Mechanisms of memory. *Science, 232*, 1612–1619.

SQUIRE, L. R. (1987). *Memory and brain.* New York: Oxford University.

SQUIRE, L. R., & COHEN, N. J. (1979). Memory and amnesia: Resistance to disruption develops for years after learning. *Behavioral Biology and Neurology, 25*, 115–125.

SQUIRE, L. R., & COHEN, N. J. (1982). Remote memory, retrograde amnesia, and the neuropsychology of memory. In L. S. Cermak (Ed.), *Human memory and amnesia* (pp. 275–304). Hillsdale, NJ: Erlbaum.

SQUIRE, L. R., & COHEN, N. J. (1984). Human memory and amnesia. In J. McGaugh, G. Lynch, & N. Weinberger (Eds.), *Neurobiology of learning and memory.* New York: Guilford.

SQUIRE, L. R., & SHIMAMURA, A. (1996). The neuropsychology of memory dysfunction and its assessment. In I. Grant, K. M. Adams, et al. (Eds.), *Neuropsychological assessment of neuropsychiatric disorders* (2nd ed., pp. 232–262). New York: Oxford University Press.

SROUFE, L. A., CARLSON, E. A., LEVY, A. K., & EGELAND, B. (1999). Implications of attachment theory for developmental psychopathology. *Development and psychopathology, 11*, 1–13.

SROUFE, L. A., EGELAND, B., & KREUTZER, T. (1990). The fate of early experience following developmental change: Longitudinal approaches to individual adaptation in childhood. *Child Development, 61*, 1363–1373.

STACHER, G., BAUER, H., & STEINRINGER, H. (1979). Cholecystokinin decreases appetite and activation evoked by stimuli arising from preparation of a meal in man. *Physiology and Behavior, 23*, 325–331.

STAGER, C. L., & WERKER, J. F. (1997). Infants listen for more phonetic detail in speech perception than in word-learning tasks. *Nature, 388*, 381–382.

STANLEY, B. G., MAGDALIN, W., & LEIBOWITZ, S. F. (1989). A critical site for neuropeptide Y-induced eating lies in the caudolateral paraventricular/perifornical region of the hypothalamus. *Society for Neuroscience Abstracts, 15*, 894.

STANLEY, J. (1993). Boys and girls who reason well mathematically. In G. R. Beck & K. Ackrill (Eds.), *The origins and development of high ability.* Chichester, England: Wiley.

STARKEY, P., SPELKE, E. S., & GELMAN, R. (1983). Detection of intermodal numerical correspondences by human infants. *Science, 222*, 179–181.

STARKEY, P., SPELKE, E. S., & GELMAN, R. (1990). Numerical abstraction by human infants. *Cognition, 36*, 97–127.

STARR, C., & TAGGART, R. (1989). *Biology: The unity and diversity of life* (5th ed.). Belmont, CA: Wadsworth.

STEELE, C. M. (1998). Stereotyping and its threat are real. *American Psychologist, 53*, 680–681.

STEELE, C. M., & ARONSON, J. (1995). Stereotype threat and the intellectual test performance of African Americans. *Journal of Personality and Social Psychology, 69*(5), 797–811.

STEELE, C. M., & LIU, T. J. (1983). Dissonance processes as self-affirmation. *Journal of Personality and Social Psychology, 45*, 5–19.

STEINBERG, L., ELKMAN, J. D., & MOUNTS, N. S. (1989). Authoritative parenting, psychosocial maturity, and academic success among adolescents. *Child Development, 60*(6), 1424–1436.

STEINER, M. (2000). Premenstrual syndrome and premenstrual dysphoric disorder: guidelines for management. *Journal of Psychiatry and Neuroscience, 25*, 459–468.

STEINMETZ, H., VOLKMANN, J., JANCKE, L., & FREUND, H. (1991). Anatomical left-right asymmetry of language-relate temporal cortex. *Annals of Neurology, 29*, 315–319.

STELLAR, J. R., & STELLAR, E. (1985). *The neurobiology of motivation and reward.* New York: Springer Verlag.

STERN, J. S., HIRSCH, J., BLAIR, S. N., FOREYT, J. P., FRANK, A., KUMANYIKA, S. K., ET AL. (1995). Weighing the options: Criteria for evaluating weight-management programs. The Committee to Develop Criteria for Evaluating the Outcomes of Approaches to Prevent and Treat Obesity. *Obesity Research, 3*, 591–604.

STERN, P. C., & CARSTENSEN, L. L. (2000). *The aging mind.* Washington, DC: National Academy Press.

STERNBERG, R. J. (1977). *Intelligence, information processing, and analogical reasoning: The componential analysis of human abilities.* Hillsdale, NJ: Erlbaum.

STERNBERG, R. J. (1985). General intellectual ability. In R. Sternberg, *Human abilities: An information processing approach.* New York: Freeman.

STERNBERG, R. J. (1990). *Metaphors of mind.* New York: Cambridge University Press.

STERNBERG, R. J. (1997). The concept of intelligence and its role in lifelong learning and success. *American Psychologist, 52*, 1030–1037.

STERNBERG, R. J. (2000). The Holey Grail of general intelligence. *Science, 289*, 399–401.

STERNBERG, R. J., & DAVIDSON, J. E. (1983). Insight in the gifted. *Educational Psychologist, 18*, 51–57.

STERNBERG, R. J., & DETTERMAN, D. K. (EDS.). (1986). *What is intelligence? Contemporary viewpoints on its nature and definition.* Norwood, NJ: Ablex.

STERNBERG, R. J., & GARDNER, M. K. (1983). Unities in inductive reasoning. *Journal of Experimental Psychology: General, 112*, 80–116.

STERNBERG, R. J., & KAUFMAN, J. C. (1998). Human abilities. *Annual Review of Psychology, 49*, 479–502.

STERNBERG, R. J., & WAGNER, R. K. (1993). The egocentric view of intelligence and job performance is wrong. *Current Directions in Psychological Science, 2*, 1–5.

STERNBERG, R. J., WAGNER, R. K., WILLIAMS, W. M., & HORVATH, J. A. (1995). Testing common sense. *American Psychologist, 50*, 912–927.

STEVENS, A., & COUPE, P. (1978). Distortions in judged spatial relations. *Cognitive Psychology, 10*, 422–437.

STEVENS, L., & JONES, E. E. (1976). Defensive attributions and the Kelley cube. *Journal of Personality and Social Psychology, 34,* 809–820.

STEVENS, S. S. (1955). The measurement of loudness. *Journal of the Acoustical Society of America, 27,* 815–819.

STEWART, T. D. (1957). Stone age surgery: A general review, with emphasis on the New World. *Annual Review of the Smithsonian Institution.* Washington, DC: Smithsonian Institution.

STOKOE, W. C., JR. (1960). Sign language structure: An outline of the visual communication systems. *Studies in Linguistics,* Occasional Papers 8.

STOLLER, R. J. (1968). *Sex and gender: On the development of masculinity and femininity.* New York: Science House.

STOLLER, R. J., & HERDT, G. H. (1985). Theories of origins of male homosexuality: A cross-cultural look. *Archives of General Psychiatry, 42,* 399–404.

STOLZ, J. A., & BESNER, D. (1999). On the myth of automatic semantic activation in reading. *Current Directions in Psychological Science, 8(2),* 61–65.

STORMS, M. D. (1973). Videotape and the attribution process: Reversing actors' and observers' points of view. *Journal of Personality and Social Psychology, 27,* 165–175.

STOTLAND, E., & OTHERS. (1978). *Empathy, fantasy and helping.* Beverly Hills, CA: Sage.

STOWE, L. (1987). Thematic structures and sentence comprehension. In G. Carlson & M. Tanenhaus (Eds.), *Linguistic structure in language processing.* Dordrecht: Reidel.

STRICKER, E. M., & ZIGMOND, M. J. (1976). Recovery of function after damage to catecholamine-containing neurons: A neurochemical model for the lateral hypothalamic syndrome. In J. M. Sprague & A. N. Epstein (Eds.), *Progress in psychobiology and physiological psychology: Vol. 6* (pp. 121–188). New York: Academic Press.

STROOP, J. R. (1935). Studies of interference in serial verbal reactions. *Journal of Experimental Psychology, 18,* 643–662.

STROUSE, J. (ED.). (1974). *Women and analysis.* New York: Grossman.

STUMPF, H., & STANLEY, J. C. (1998). Stability and change in gender-related differences on the College Board Advanced Placement and Achievement tests. *Current Directions in Psychological Science, 7,* 192–198.

STUNKARD, A. J. (1975). Obesity. In A. M. Freedman, H. I. Kaplan, & B. J. Sadock (Eds.), *Comprehensive textbook of psychiatry–II: Vol. 2* (pp. 1648–1654). Baltimore: Williams & Wilkins.

STYRON, W. (1990). *Darkness visible: A memoir of madness.* New York: Random House.

SUE, D. W., & KIRK, B. A. (1973). Psychological characteristics of Chinese-American college students. *Journal of Counseling Psychology, 19,* 142–148.

SUE S. (1998). In search of cultural competence in psychotherapy and counseling. *American Psychologist, 53,* 440–448.

SULLOWAY, F. (1996). *Born to rebel.* N.Y.: Pantheon Books.

SULLOWAY, F. J. (1979). *Freud, biologist of the mind: Beyond the psychoanalytic legend.* Cambridge, MA: Harvard University Press.

SULS, J. M. (1972). A two-stage model for the appreciation of jokes and cartoons: An information processing analysis. In J. H. Goldstein & P. E. McGhee (Eds.), *The psychology of humor* (pp. 81–100). New York: Academic Press.

SULS, J. M. (1983). Cognitive processes in humor appreciation. In P. E. McGhee & J. H. Goldstein (Eds.), *Handbook of humor research: Vol. 1* (pp. 39–58). New York: Springer.

SULS, J. M., & MILLER, R. L. (EDS.). (1977). *Social comparison processes: Theoretical and empirical perspectives.* New York: Washington Hemisphere Publishing Co.

SUOMI, S., & HARLOW, H. (1972). Social rehabilitation of isolate-reared monkeys. *Developmental Psychology, 6,* 487–496.

SUOMI, S. J. (1989). Personal communication.

SUOMI, S. J., & HARLOW, H. F. (1971). Abnormal social behavior in young monkeys. In J. Helmuth (Ed.), *Exceptional infant: Studies in abnormalities: Vol. 2* (pp. 483–529). New York: Brunner/Mazel.

SUPALLA, I., & NEWPORT, E. L. (1978). How many seats in a chair? The derivation of nouns and verbs in American Sign Language. In P. Siple, (Ed.), *Understanding language through sign language research.* New York: Academic Press.

SUPÈR, H., SPEKREIJSE, H., & LAMME, V. A. F. (2001). A neural correlation of working memory in the monkey primary visual cortex. *Science, 293,* 120–124.

SUZUKI, L. A., & VALENCIA, R. R. (1997). Race-ethnicity and measured intelligence. *American Psychologist, 52,* 1103–1114.

SWEDO, S. E., LEONARD, H. L., GARVEY, M., MITTLEMAN, B., ALLEN, A. J., PERLMUTTER, S., ET AL. (1998). Pediatric autoimmune neuropsychiatric disorders associated with streptococcal infections: Clinical description of the first 50 cases. *American Journal of Psychiatry, 155,* 264–271.

SWEDO, S. E., PIETRINI, P., LEONARD, H. L., SCHAPIRO, M. B., RETTEW, D. C., GOLDBERGER, E. L., ET AL. (1992). Cerebral glucose metabolism in childhood-onset obsessive-compulsive disorder. Revisualization during pharmacotherapy. *Archives of General Psychiatry, 49,* 690–694.

SWETS, J. A., DAWES, R. M., & MONAHAN, J. (2000). Psychological Science can improve diagnostic decisions. *Psychological Science in the Public Interest, 1,* 1–26.

SWINGLEY, D., & FERNALD, A., (2002) Recognition of words referring to present and absent objects by 24-month olds. *Journal of Memory and Language, 46,* 39–56.

SYMONS, D. (1979). *The evolution of human sexuality.* New York: Oxford University Press.

TANDON, R., & KANE, J. M. (1993). Neuropharmacologic basis for clozapine's unique profile [Letter]. *Archives of General Psychiatry, 50,* 158–159.

TANENHAUS, M. K., SPIVEY-KNOWLTON, M. J., EBERHARD, K. M., & SEDIVY, J. C. (1995). Integration of visual and linguistic information in spoken language comprehension. *Science, 268(5217),* 1632–1634.

TANNER, J. M. (1970). Physical growth. In P. H. Mussen (Ed.), *Carmichael's manual of child psychology* (3rd ed., pp. 77–105). New York: Wiley.

TANNER, J. M. (1990). *Fetus into man: Physical growth from conception to maturity* (rev. ed.). Cambridge, MA: Harvard University Press.

TARPY, R. M. (1997). *Contemporary learning theory and research.* New York: McGraw Hill.

TASSINARY, L. G., & HANSEN, K. A. (1998). A critical test of the waist-to-hip-ratio hypothesis of female physical attractiveness. *Psychological Science. 9,* 150–155.

TAYLOR, J. (2002). Paying attention to consciousness. *Trends in Cognitive Science, 6,* 206–210.

TAYLOR, M., ESBENSEN, B. M., & BENNETT, R. T. (1994). Children's understanding of knowledge acquisition: The tendency for children to report that they have always known what they have just learned. *Child Development, 65(6),* 1581–1604.

TAYLOR, J., IACONO, W. G., & McGUE, M. (2000). Evidence for a genetic etiology of early-onset delinquency. *Journal of Abnormal Psychology, 109,* 634–643.

TAYLOR, S. E., & FISKE, S. T. (1975). Point of view and perceptions of causality. *Journal of Personality and Social Psychology, 32,* 439–445.

TECHNICAL WORKING GROUP FOR EYEWITNESS EVIDENCE (1999). *Eyewitness evidence: A guide for law enforcement.* Washington, DC: United States Department of Justice, Office of Justice Programs.

TEITELBAUM, P. (1955). Sensory control of hypothalamic hyperphagia. *Journal of Comparative and Physiological Psychology, 48,* 156–163.

TEITELBAUM, P. (1961). Disturbances in feeding and drinking behavior after hypothalamic lesions. In M. R. Jones (Ed.), *Nebraska Symposium on Motivation* (pp. 39–65). Lincoln, NE: University of Nebraska Press.

TEITELBAUM, P., & EPSTEIN, A. N. (1962). The lateral hypothalamic syndrome: Recovery of feeding and drinking after lateral hypothalamic lesions. *Psychological Review, 69,* 74–90.

TEITELBAUM, P., & STELLAR, E. (1954). Recovery from failure to eat produced by hypothalamic lesions. *Science, 120,* 894–895.

TELLEGEN, A., LYKKEN, D. T., BOUCHARD, T. J., WILCOX, K. J., SEGAL, N. L., & RICH, S. (1988). Personality of twins reared apart and together. *Journal of Personality and Social Psychology, 54,* 1031–1039.

TERR, L. C. (1991). Acute responses to external events and posttraumatic stress disorders. In M. Lewis (Ed.), *Child and adolescent psychiatry: A comprehensive textbook* (pp. 755–763). Baltimore: Williams & Wilkins.

TERR, L. C. (1994). *Unchained memories: True stories of traumatic memories, lost and found.* New York: Basic.

TERRACE, H. S., PETITTO, L. A., SANDERS, R. J., & BEVER, T. G. (1979). Can an ape create a sentence? *Science, 206*(4421), 891–902.

TERVOORT, B. T. (1961). Esoteric symbolism in the communication behavior of young deaf children. *American Annals of the Deaf, 106,* 436–480.

TETI, D. M., SAKIN, W. J., KUCERA, E., CORNS, K. M., & DAS EIDEN, R. (1996). And baby makes four: Predictors of attachment security among preschooler-age firstborns during the transition to siblinghood. *Child Development, 67,* 579–596.

TETLOCK, P. E., PETERSON, R. S., McGUIRE, C., CHANG, S.-J., & ET AL. (1992). Assessing political group dynamics: A test of the groupthink model. *Journal of Personality and Social Psychology, 63*(3), 403–425.

THAPAR, A., & GREENE, R. (1994). Effects of level of processing on implicit and explicit tasks. *Journal of Experimental Psychology: Learning, Memory and Cognition, 20,* 671–679.

THIGPEN, C. H., & CLECKLEY, H. M. (1957). *The three faces of Eve.* New York: McGraw-Hill.

THOMAS, A., CHESS, S., & BIRCH, H. G. (1970). The origin of personality. *Scientific American, 223,* 102–109.

THOMPSON, C. P., & COWAN, T. (1986). Flashbulb memories: A nicer recollection of a Neisser recollection. *Cognition, 22,* 199–200.

THOMPSON, M. M., ZANNA, M. P., & GRIFFIN, D. W. (1995). Let's not be indifferent about (attitudinal) ambivalence. In R. E. Petty & J. A. Krosnick (Eds.), *Attitude strength: Antecedents and consequences: Vol. 4* (pp. 361–386). Mahwah, NJ: Lawrence Erlbaum.

THOMPSON, R. A. (2000). The legacy of early attachments. *Child Development, 71,* 145–152.

THOMPSON, R. F. (1973). *Introduction to biopsychology.* San Francisco: Albion Publishing Co.

THOMPSON, W.L., & KOSSLYN, S.M. (2000). Neural systems activated during visual mental imagery: A review and meta-analyses. In J. Mazziotta, & A. Toga (Eds.), *Brain mapping II: The applications.* New York: Academic Press.

THOMSON, G. H. (1916). A hierarchy without a general factor. *Brain, 49,* 271–281.

THORNHILL, R., & GAGESTAD, S. G. (1999). Facial attractiveness. *Trends in Cognitive Science, 3,* 452–460.

THORNHILL, R., & GANGESTAD, S. W. (1994). Human fluctuating asymmetry and sexual behavior. *Psychological Science, 5,* 297–302.

TIERNEY, A.J. (2000). Egas Moniz and the origins of psychosurgery: A review commemorating the 50th anniversary of Moniz's Nobel Prize. *Journal of the History of Neuroscience, 9,* 22–36.

TIETJEN, A. M., & WALKER, L. J. (1985). Moral reasoning and leadership among men in a Papua New Guinea society. *Developmental Psychology, 21,* 982–989.

TIMBERLAKE, W. (1995). Reconceptualizing reinforcement: A causal system approach to reinforcement and behavior change. In W. O'Donohue & L. Krasner (Eds.), *Theories in behavior therapy* (pp. 59–96). Washington, DC: APA Books.

TIMBERLAKE, W., & ALLISON, J. (1974). Response deprivation: An empirical approach to instrumental performance. *Psychological Review, 81,* 146–164.

TIZARD, B., & HODGES, J. (1978). The effect of early institutional rearing on the development of eight-year-old children. *Journal of Child Psychology and Psychiatry, 19,* 98–118.

TOLMAN, E. C. (1932). *Purposive behavior in animals and men.* New York: Appleton-Century-Crofts.

TOLMAN, E. C. (1948). Cognitive maps in rats and men. *Psychological Review, 55,* 189–208.

TOLMAN, E. C., & HONZIK, C. H. (1930). Introduction and removal of reward, and maze performance in rats. *University of California Publications in Psychology, 4,* 257–275.

TOLSTOY, L. (1868). *War and peace* (second epilogue). H. Gifford (Ed.), L. Maude & A. Maude (Trans.). New York: Oxford University Press, 1922.

TOMADA, G., & SCHNEIDER, B. H. (1997). Relational aggression, gender, and peer acceptance: Invariance across culture, stability over time, and concordance among informants. *Developmental Psychology, 33,* 601–609.

TOMASELLO, M., STROSBERG R., & AKHTAR, N. (1996). Eighteen month old children learn words in non-ostensive contexts. *Journal of Child Language, 23,* 157–176.

TOMASO, E., BELTRAMO, M., & PIOMELLI, D. (1996). Brain cannabinoids in chocolate. *Nature, 382,* 677–678.

TOMKINS, S. S. (1963). *Affect, imagery, consciousness: Vol. 2. The negative affects.* New York: Springer.

TORGERSEN, S. (1986). Genetic factors in moderately severe and mild affective disorders. *Archives of General Psychiatry, 43,* 222–226.

TORREY, E. F. (1983). *Surviving schizophrenia: A family manual.* New York: Harper & Row.

TORREY, E. F. (1987). Prevalence studies in schizophrenia. *British Journal of Psychiatry, 150,* 598–608.

TORREY, E. F. (1992). *Freudian fraud: The malignant effect of Freud's theory on American thought and culture.* New York: HarperCollins.

TREISMAN, A. M. (1986a). Properties, parts, and objects. In K. R. Boff, L. Kaufman, & J. P. Thomas (Eds.), *Handbook of perception and human performance: Vol. II* (Chapter 35). New York: Wiley.

TREISMAN, A. M. (1986b). Features and objects in visual processing. *Scientific American, 255,* 114–125.

TREISMAN, A. M. (1988). Features and objects: The Fourteenth Barlett Memorial Lecture. *Quarterly Journal of Experimental Psychology, 40A,* 201–237.

TREISMAN, A. M., & GELADE, G. (1980). A feature-integration theory of attention. *Cognitive Psychology, 12,* 97–136.

TREISMAN, A. M., & SOUTHER, J. (1985). Search assymetry: A diagnostic for preattentive processing of separable features. *Journal of Experimental Psychology: General, 114,* 285–310.

TRIANDIS, H. (1994). Major cultural syndromes and emotion. In S. Kitayama & H. R. Markus (Eds.), *Emotion and culture* (pp. 285–306). Washington, DC: American Psychological Association.

TRIANDIS, H. C. (1989). Cross-cultural studies of individualism and collectivism. *Nebraska Symposium on Motivation, 37,* 41–134. Lincoln, NE: University of Nebraska Press.

TRIANDIS, H. C., BONTEMBO, R., VILLAREAL, M. J., ASAI, M., & LUCA, N. (1988). Individualism and collectivism: Cross-cultural perspectives on self-group relationships. *Journal of Personality and Social Psychology, 54,* 323–338.

TRIANDIS, H. C., & SUH, E. M. (2002). Cultural influences on personality. *Annual Review of Psychology, 53*(1), 133–160.

TRIMMER, B.A., BEECH, J. S., STROEMER, R. P., WATSON, W. P. & HODGES, H. (2001). Resolution of stroke deficits following contralateral grafts of conditionally immortal neuroepithelial stem cells. *Stroke, 32,* 1012–1019.

TRIVERS, R. L. (1972). Parental investment and sexual selection. In B. Campbell (Ed.), *Sexual selection and the descent of man* (pp. 139–179). Chicago: Aldine. Trubner.

TRUE, W. R., RISE, J., EISEN, S., HEATH, A. C., GOLDBERG, J., LYONS, M., ET AL. (1993). A twin study of genetic and environmental contributions to liability for posttraumatic stress symptoms. *Archives of General Psychiatry, 50,* 257–264.

TRUESWELL, J. C., SEKERINA, I., HILL, N. M., & LOGRIP, M. L. (1999). The kindergarten-path effect: Studying on-line sentence processing in young children. *Cognition, 73,* 89–134.

TRUESWELL, J. C., & TANENHAUS, M. K. (1994). Toward a lexicalist framework of constraint-based syntactic ambiguity resolution. In C. Clifton, Jr. & L. Frazier (Eds.), *Perspectives on sentence processing* (pp. 155–179). Hillsdale, NJ: Erlbaum.

TRUESWELL, J. C., TANENHAUS, M. K., & GARNSEY, S. M. (1994). Semantic influences on parsing: Use of thematic role information in syntactic ambiguity resolution. *Journal of Memory and Language, 33,* 285–318.

TSUANG, M. T., GILBERTSON, M. W., & FARAONE, S. V. (1991). The genetics of schizophrenia. *Schizophrenia Research, 4,* 157–171.

TULVING, E. (2002). Episodic memory: From mind to brain. *Annual Review of Psychology, 53,* 1–25.

TULVING, E., & OSLER, S. (1968). Effectiveness of retrieved cues in memory for words. *Journal of Experimental Psychology, 77,* 593–606.

TULVING, E., & THOMSON, D. M. (1973). Encoding specificity and retrieval processes in episodic memory. *Psychological Review, 80,* 352–373.

TULVING, E., SCHACTER, D. L., & STARK, H. A. (1982). Priming effects in word-fragment completion are independent of recognition memory. *Journal of Experimental Psychology: Learning, Memory, and Cognition, 8,* 336–342.

TULVING, E., SCHACTER, D. L., McLACHLAN, D. R., & MOSCOVITCH, M. (1988). Priming of semantic autobiographical knowledge: A case study of retrograde amnesia. *Brain and Cognition, 8,* 3–20.

TUPES, E. C., & CHRISTAL, R. E. (1961, May). *Recurrent personality factors based on trait ratings (ASD-TR-61–97).* Lackland Air Force Base, TX: Aeronautical Systems Division, Personnel Laboratory.

TURKHEIMER, E., & WALDRON, M. (2000). Nonshared environment: A theoretical, methodological, and quantitative review. *Psychological Bulletin, 126*(1), 78–108.

TVERSKY, A. (1977). Features of similarity. *Psychological Review, 84*(4), 327–352.

TVERSKY, A., & KAHNEMAN, D. (1973). Availability: A heuristic for judging frequency and probability. *Cognitive Psychology, 5,* 207–232.

TVERSKY, A., & KAHNEMAN, D. (1981). The framing of decisions and the psychology of choice. *Science, 211,* 453–458.

TWENEY, R. D. (1998). Toward a cognitive psychology of science: Research research and its implications. *Current Directions in Psychological Science, 7,* 150–154.

TWENEY, R. D., DOHERTY, M. E., & MYNATT, C. R. (1981). *On scientific thinking.* New York: Columbia University Press.

TZENG, O., & WANG, W. Y. S. (1984). Search for a common neurocognitive mechanism for language and movements. *American Journal of Physiology, 246,* 904–911.

U.S. DEPARTMENT OF LABOR. (1995). *Marital and family characteristics of the labor force from the March 1994 Current Population Survey.* Washington, DC: Bureau of Labor Statistics.

UNDERWOOD, M. K., GALEN, B. R., & PAQUETTE, J. A. (2001). Top ten challenges for understanding gender and aggression in children: Why can't we all just get along? *Social Development, 10,* 248–266.

UNGERLEIDER, L. G., & HAXBY, J. V. (1994). "What" and "where" in the human brain. *Current Opinions in Neurobiology, 4,* 157–165.

UNGERLEIDER, L. G., & MISHKIN, M. (1982). Two cortical visual systems. In D. J. Ingle, M. A. Goodale, & R. J. W. Mansfield (Eds.), *Analysis of visual behavior* (pp. 549–586). Cambridge, MA: MIT Press.

URWIN, C. (1983). Dialogue and cognitive functioning in the early language development of three blind children. In A. E. Mills (Ed.), *Language acquisition in the blind child.* London: Croom Helm.

VAILLANT, G. E. (1971). Theoretical hierarchy of adaptive ego mechanisms. *Archives of General Psychiatry, 24,* 107–118.

VAILLANT, G. E. (1974). Natural history of male psychological health. II. Some antecedents of healthy adult adjustment. *Archives of General Psychiatry, 31,* 15–22.

VAILLANT, G. E. (1976). Natural history of male psychological health. V: Relation of choice of ego mechanisms of defense to adult adjustment. *Archives of General Psychiatry, 33,* 535–545.

VAILLANT, G. E. (1977). *Adaptation to life.* Boston: Little, Brown & Co.

VAILLANT, G. E. (1994). "Successful aging" and psychosocial well-being: Evidence from a 45-year study. In E. H. Thompson (Ed.), *Older men's lives: Vol. 6. Research on men and masculinities* (pp. 2–41). Thousand Oaks, CA: Sage.

VAILLANT, G. E. (2000). Adaptive mental mechanisms: Their role in a positive psychology. *American Psychologist, 55*(1), 89–98.

VAILLANT, G. E., BOND, M., & VAILLANT, C. O. (1986). An empirically validated hierarchy of defense mechanisms. *Archives of General Psychiatry, 43,* 786–794.

VALENSTEIN, E. S. (1986). *Great and desperate cures.* New York: Basic Books.

VALINS, S. (1966). Cognitive effects of false heart-rate feedback. *Journal of Personality and Social Psychology, 4,* 400–408.

VAN CANTFORT, E., & RIMPAU, J. (1982). Sign language studies with children and chimpanzees. *Sign Language Studies, 34,* 15–72.

VAN DER LELY, H. K., & CHRISTIAN, V. (2000). Lexical word formation in Grammatical SLI children: A grammar-specific or input processing deficit? *Cognition, 75,* 33–63.

VAN ESSEN, D. C., & DeYOE, E. A. (1995). Concurrent processing in the primate visual cortex. In M. S. Gazzaniga (Ed.), The cognitive neurosciences (pp. 383–400). Cambridge, MA: MIT Press.

VAN HOOFF, J. A. R. A. M. (1972). A comparative approach to the phylogeny of laughter and smiling. In R. A. Hinde (Ed.), *Non-verbal communication.* New York: Cambridge University Press.

VANDELL, D. L., HENDERSON, V. K., & WILSON, K. S. (1988). A longitudinal study of children with day care experiences of varying quality. *Child Development, 59,* 1286–1292.

VANDELLO, J. A., & COHEN, D. (1999). Patterns of individualism and collectivism across the United States. *Journal of Personality and Social Psychology, 77*(2), 279–292.

VANDENBOS, G. R., CUMMINGS, N. A., & DeLEON, P. H. (1992). A century of psychotherapy: Economic and environmental influences. In D. K. Freedheim (Ed.), *History of psychotherapy.* Washington, DC: American Psychological Association.

VAUGHN, B. E., EGELAND, B. R., SROUFE, L. A., & WATERS, E. (1979). Individual differences in infant-mother attachment at twelve and eighteen months: Stability and change in families under stress. *Child Development, 50,* 971–975.

VAULTIN, R. G., & BERKELEY, M. A. (1977). Responses of single cells in cat visual cortex to prolonged stimulus movement: Neural correlates of visual aftereffects. *Journal of Neurophysiology, 40,* 1051–1065.

VEIZOVIC, T., BEECH, J. S., STROEMER, R. P., WATSON, W. P., & HODGES, H. (2001). Resolution of stroke deficits following contralateral grafts of conditionally immortal neuroepithelial stem cells. *Stroke, 32,* 1012–1019.

VENTER, J. C., ADAMS, M. D., MYERS, E. W., LI, P. W., MURAL, R. J., SUTTON, G. G., ET AL. (2001). The sequence of the human genome. *Science, 291,* 1304–1351.

VERHAEGHEN, P., & SALTHOUSE, T. A. (1997). Meta-analyses of age-cognition relations in adulthood: Estimates of linear and nonlinear age effects and structural models. *Psychological Bulletin, 122*(3), 231–249.

VERKHRATSKY, A. (1998). Calcium signalling in glial cells. *Journal of Physiology, 506,* 15.

VERNON, P. A. (ED.). (1987). *Speed of information processing and intelligence.* Canada: Ablex Publishing.

VERTES, R. P., & EASTMAN, K. E. (2000). The case against memory consolidation in REM sleep. *Behavioral and Brain Sciences, 23,* 793–1121.

VICKERS, J. C., DICKSON, T. C., ADLARD, P. A., & SAUNDERS, H. L. (2000). The causes of neural degeneration in Alzheimer's disease. *Neurobiology, 60,* 139–165.

VOLPICELLI, J. (1989). Psychoactive substance use disorders. In D. L. Rosenhan & M. E. P. Seligman, *Abnormal psychology* (2nd ed.). New York: Norton.

VROOMEN, J., VAN DEN BOSCH, A., & DE GELDER, B. (1998). A connectionist model for bootstrap learning of syllabic structure. *Language and Cognitive Processes, 13,* 193–220.

VYGOTSKY, L. S. (1978). *Mind in society.* Cambridge, MA: Harvard University Press.

WABER, D. P. (1977). Sex differences in mental abilities, hemispheric lateralization, and rate of physical growth at adolescence. *Developmental Psychology, 13,* 29–38.

WABER, D. P. (1979). Cognitive abilities and sex-related variations in the maturation of cerebral cortical functions. In M. A. Wittig & A. C. Petersen (Eds.), *Sex-related differences in cognitive functioning* (pp. 161–189). New York: Academic Press.

WACHTEL, P. L. (1977). *Psychoanalysis and behavior therapy: Toward an integration.* New York: Basic Books.

WACHTEL, P. L. (1982). What can dynamic therapies contribute to behavior therapy? *Behavior Therapy, 13,* 594–609.

WADDINGTON, J. L., TORREY, E. F., CROW, T. J., & HIRSCH, S. R. (1991). Schizophrenia, neurodevelopment, and disease. *Archives of General Psychiatry, 48,* 271–273.

WAGNER, H. L., & SMITH, J. (1991). Facial expression in the presence of friends and strangers. *Journal of Nonverbal Behavior, 15,* 201–214.

WAGNER, R. K. (1987). Tacit knowledge in everyday intelligent behavior. *Journal of Personality and Social Psychology, 52,* 1236–1247.

WAGNER, R. K. (1997). Intelligence, training, and employment. *American Psychologist, 52*(10), 1059–1069.

WAGNER, R. K., & STERNBERG, R. J. (1987). Tacit knowledge in managerial success. *Journal of Business and Psychology, 1,* 301–312.

WAKEFIELD, J. C. (1992). The concept of mental disorder: On the boundary between biological facts and social values. *American Psychologist, 47*(3), 373–388.

WALD, G. (1950). Eye and camera. *Scientific American, 183,* 32–41.

WALDEN, T. A., & BAXTER, A. (1989). The effect of context and age on social referencing. *Child Development, 60*(6), 1511–1518.

WALDFOGEL, S. (1948). The frequency and affective character of childhood memories. *Psychological Monographs, 62*(Whole No. 291).

WALKER, L. J. (1984). Sex differences in the development of moral reasoning: A critical review. *Child Development, 55,* 677–691.

WALKER, L. J. (1989). Sex differences in the development of moral reasoning: A reply to Baumrind. *Child Development, 57,* 522–526.

WALKER, L. J. (1995). Sexism in Kohlberg's moral psychology. In W. M. Kurtines & J. L. Gewirtz (Eds.), *Moral development: An introduction.* Boston: Allyn and Bacon.

WALKER, L. J., & MORAN, T. J. (1991). Moral reasoning in a communist Chinese society. *Journal of Moral Education, 20,* 139–155.

WALLACH, H. (1976). *On perception.* New York: Quadrangle.

WALLACH, H., WEISZ, A., & ADAMS, P. A. (1956). Circles and derived figures in rotation. *American Journal of Psychology, 69,* 48–59.

WALLAS, G. (1926). *The art of thought.* New York: Harcourt, Brace.

WALLER, N. G., & ROSS, C. A. (1997). The prevalence and biometric structure of pathological dissociation in the general population: Taxometric and behavior genetic findings. *Journal of Abnormal Psychology, 106,* 499–510.

WALLERSTEIN, J. S., & CORBIN, S. B. (1999). The child and the vicissitudes of divorce. In: R. M. Galatzer-Levy and L. Kraus (Eds.), *The scientific basis of child custody decisions* (pp. 73–95). New York: Wiley.

WALLERSTEIN, J. S., & LEWIS, J. (1998). The long-term impact of divorce on children: A first report from a 25-year study. *Family and Conciliation Courts Review, 36,* 368–383.

WALSTER, E., ARONSON, E., & ABRAHAMS, D. (1966). On increasing the persuasiveness of a low prestige communicator. *Journal of Experimental Social Psychology, 2,* 325–342.

WALSTER, E., ARONSON, E., ABRAHAMS, D., & ROTTMAN, L. (1966). The importance of physical attractiveness in dating behavior. *Journal of Personality and Social Psychology, 4,* 508–516.

WALTERS, J. R., & SEYFARTH, R. M. (1986). Conflict and cooperation. In B. B. Smuts, D. L. Cheney, R. M. Seyfarth, R. W. Wrangham, & T. T. Struhsaker (Eds.), *Primate societies.* Chicago: University of Chicago Press.

WAMPOLD, B. E., MONDIN, G. W., MOODY, M., STICH, F., BENSON, K., & AHN, H. (1997). A meta-analysis of outcome studies comparing bona fide psychotherapies: Empirically, "all must have prizes." *Psychological Bulletin, 122,* 203–216.

WAPNER, W. T., JUDD, T., & GARDNER, H. (1978). Visual agnosia in an artist. *Cortex, 14,* 343–364.

WARNER, R. (1995). Time trends in schizophrenia: Changes in obstetric risk factors with industrialization. *Schizophrenia Bulletin, 21,* 483–500.

WARREN, R. M. (1970). Perceptual restorations of missing speech sounds. *Science, 167,* 392–393.

WARREN, S. L., HUSTON, L., EGELAND, B., AND SROUFE, L. A. (1997). Child and adolescent anxiety disorders and early attachment. *Journal of the American Academy of Child & Adolescent Psychiatry, 36,* 637–644.

WARRINGTON, E. K., & WEISKRANTZ, L. (1978). Further analysis of the prior learning effect in amnesic patients. *Neuropsychologia, 16,* 169–176.

WARTNER, U. G., GROSSMANN, K., FREMMER-BOMBIK, E., & SUESS, G. (1994). Attachment patterns at age six in south Germany: Predictability from infancy and implications for preschool behavior. *Child Development, 65,* 1014–1027.

WASMAN, M., & FLYNN, J. P. (1962). Directed attack elicited from the hypothalamus. *Archives of Neurology, 6,* 220–227.

WASON, P. C. (1960). On the failure to eliminate hypotheses in a conceptual task. *Quarterly Journal of Experimental Psychology, 12,* 129–140.

WASON, P. C. (1966). Reasoning. In Foss, B. (Ed.), *New horizons in psychology* (pp. 135–151). Middlesex, England: Penguin.

WASON, P. C. (1968). On the failure to eliminate hypotheses—A second look. In P. C. Wason & P. N. Johnson-Laird (Eds.), *Thinking and reasoning.* Harmondsworth, England: Penguin Books.

WASSERMAN, E. A., HUGART, J. A., & KIRKPATRICK-STEGER, K. (1995). Pigeons show same-different conceptualization after training with complex visual stimuli. *Journal of Experimental Psychology: Animal Behavior Processes, 21,* 248–252.

WATABE, K., SAKAMOTO, T., OHASHI, T., KAWAZOE, Y., OYANAGI, K., TAKESHIMA, T., ET AL. (2001). Adenoviral gene transfer of glial cell line-derived neurotrophic factor to injured adult motoneurons. *Human Cell, 14,* 7–15.

WATERS, E., & CUMMINGS, E. M. (2000). A secure base from which to explore close relationships. *Child Development, 71*(1), 164–172.

WATERS, E., WIPPMAN, J., & SROUFE, L. A. (1979). Attachment, positive affect, and competence in the peer group: Two studies in construct validation. *Child Development, 50,* 821–829.

WATSON, C. G., & BURANEN, C. (1979). The frequency of conversion reaction. *Journal of Abnormal Psychology, 88,* 209–211.

WATSON, J. B. (1925). *Behaviorism.* New York: Norton.

WATSON, J. S. (1967). Memory and "contingency analysis" in infant learning. *Merrill-Palmer Quarterly, 13,* 55–76.

WAUGH, N. C., & NORMAN, D. A. (1965). Primary memory. *Psychological Review, 72,* 89–104.

WEBB, N. B. (ED.) (2001). *Culturally diverse parent-child and family relationships: A guide for social workers and other practitioners.* New York: Columbia University Press.

WEBB, W. B. (1972). Sleep deprivation: Total, partial, and selective. In M. H. Chase (Ed.), *The sleeping brain* (pp. 323–362). Los Angeles: Brain Information Service, Brain Research Institute.

WEBB, W. B. (1979). Theories of sleep functions and some clinical implications. In R. Drucker-Colin, M. Shkurovich, & M. B. Sterman (Eds.), *The functions of sleep* (pp. 19–36). New York: Academic Press.

WEBB, W. B. (1982). Some theories about sleep and their clinical implications. *Psychiatric Annals, 11*, 415–422.

WECHSLER, D. (1958). *The measurement and appraisal of adult intelligence* (4th ed.). Baltimore: Williams & Wilkins.

WEDEKIND, C., & FURI, S. (1997). Body odour preferences in men and women: do they aim for specific MHC combinations or simply heterozygosity? *Proceedings of the Royal Society of London B Biological Sciences, 264*, 1471–1479.

WEHR, T. A., & GOODWIN, F. K. (1981). Biological rhythms and psychiatry. In S. Arieti & H. K. H. Brodie (Eds.), *American handbook of psychiatry: Vol. 7* (pp. 46–74). New York: Basic Books.

WEIGEL, R. H., VERNON, D. T. A., & TOGNACCI, L. N. (1974). Specificity of the attitude as a determinant of attitude-behavior congruence. *Journal of Personality and Social Psychology, 30*, 724–728.

WEINBERG, M. S., WILLIAMS, C. J., & PRYOR, D. W. (1994). *Dual attraction: Understanding bisexuality.* New York: Oxford University Press.

WEINBERGER, D. R., GOLDBERG, T. E., & TAMMINGA, C. A., (1995). Prefrontal leukotomy. *American Journal of Psychiatry, 152*, 330–331.

WEINER, B. (1982). The emotional consequences of causal attributions. In M. S. Clark & S. T. Fiske (Eds.), *Affect and cognition: The 17th annual Carnegie symposium on cognition.* Hillsdale, NJ: Erlbaum.

WEINER, R. D. (1984a). Does electroconvulsive therapy cause brain damage? [with peer commentary]. *Behavioral and Brain Sciences, 7*, 1–54.

WEINER, R. D. (1984b). Convulsive therapy: 50 years later. *American Journal of Psychiatry, 141*, 1078–1079.

WEINER, R. D. (1985). Convulsive therapies. In H. I. Kaplan & J. Sadock (Eds.), *Comprehensive textbook of psychiatry* (4th ed). Baltimore: Williams & Wilkins.

WEINGARTNER, H., & PARKER, E. S. (EDS.) (1984). *Memory consolidation: Psychobiology of cognition.* Hillsdale, NJ: Erlbaum.

WEISBERG, R. (1986). *Creativity: Genius and other myths.* New York: Freeman.

WEISKRANTZ, L. (1986). *Blindsight: A case study and implications.* Oxford: Clarendon Press.

WEISKRANTZ, L., & WARRINGTON, E. K. (1979). Conditioning in amnesic patients. *Neuropsychologia, 18*, 177–184.

WEISS, A., KING, J. E., & FIGUEREDO, A. J. (2000). The heritability of personality factors in chimpanzees (Pan troglodytes). *Behavior Genetics, 30*, 213–221.

WEISS, B., & LATIES, V. G. (1961). Behavioral thermoregulation. *Science, 133*, 1338–1344.

WEISS, L. H., & SCHWARZ, J. C. (1996). The relationship between parenting types and older adolescents' personality, academic achievement, adjustment, and substance use. *Child Development, 67*, 2101–2114.

WEISSMAN, M. (1985). The epidemiology of anxiety disorders: Rates, risks, and familial patterns. In A. H. Tuma & J. D. Maser (Eds.), *Anxiety and the anxiety disorders* (pp. 275–296). Hillsdale, NJ: Erlbaum.

WEISSMAN, M., & BOYD, J. H. (1985). Affective disorders: Epidemiology. In H. I. Kaplan, & J. Sadock (Eds.), *Modern synopsis of comprehensive textbook of psychiatry* (4th ed.). Baltimore: Williams & Wilkins.

WEISSMAN, M. M., & MARKOWITZ, J. C. (1994). Interpersonal psychotherapy. Current status. *Archives of General Psychiatry, 51*, 599–606.

WEISSTEIN, N., & WONG, E. (1986). Figure-ground organization and the spatial and temporal responses of the visual system. In E. C. Schwab & H. C. Nusbaum (Eds.), *Pattern recognition by humans and machines: Vol. 2.* New York: Academic Press.

WEISZ, J. R., ROTHBAUM, F. M., & BLACKBURN, T. C. (1984). Standing out and standing in: The psychology of control in American and Japan. *American Psychologist, 39*, 955–969.

WELKER, W. I., JOHNSON, J. I., & PUBOLS, B. H. (1964). Some morphological and physiological characteristics of the somatic sensory system in raccoons. *American Zoologist, 4*, 75–94.

WELLER A., BLASS, E., GIBBS, J., & SMITH, G. P. (1995). Odor-induced inhibition of intake after pairing of odor and CCK-8 in neonatal rats. *Physiology and Behavior, 57*, 181–183.

WELLMAN, H., & GELMAN, S. (1992). Cognitive development: Foundational theories of core domains. *Annual Review of Psychology, 43*, 337–375.

WELLMAN, H. M. (1990). *The child's theory of mind.* Cambridge, MA: MIT Press.

WELLMAN, H. M., & BARTSCH, K. (1988). Young children's reasoning about beliefs. *Cognition, 30*, 239–277.

WELLMAN, H. M., & WOOLLEY, J. D. (1990). From simple desires to ordinary beliefs: The early development of everyday psychology. *Cognition, 35*, 245–275.

WELLMAN, H. M., RITTER, K., & FLAVELL, J. H. (1975). Deliberate memory behavior in the delayed reactions of very young children. *Developmental Psychology, 11*, 780–787.

WELLS, G., & OLSON, E. (2002). Eyewitness identification. *Annual Review of Psychology, 54*, 277–295.

WENDER, P. H., KETY, S. S., ROSENTHAL, D., SCHULSINGER, F., & ORTMANN, J. (1986). Psychiatric disorders in the biological relatives of adopted individuals with affective disorders. *Archives of General Psychiatry, 43*, 923–929.

WERKER, J. (1991). The ontogeny of speech perception. In I. G. Mattingly & M. Studdert-Kennedy (Eds.), *Modularity and the motor theory of speech perception: Proceedings of a conference to honor Alvin M. Liberman* (pp. 91–109). Hillsdale, NJ: Erlbaum.

WERKER, J. F. (1995). Exploring developmental changes in cross-language speech perception. In L. R. Gleitman & M. Liberman (Eds.), *An invitation to cognitive science: Vol. 1* (pp. 87–106). Cambridge, MA: MIT Press.

WERKER, J. F., & TEES, R. C. (1984). Cross-language speech perception: Evidence for perceptual reorganization during the first year of life. *Infant Behavior and Development, 7*, 49–63.

WERTHEIMER, M. (1912). Experimentelle Studien über das Gesehen von Bewegung. *Zeitschrift frPsychologie, 61*, 161–265.

WERTHEIMER, M. (1923). Untersuchungen zur Lehre von der Gestalt, II. *Psychologische Forschung, 4*, 301–350.

WEST, S. A., McELROY, S. L., & KECK, P. E. (1996). Valproate. In P. J. Goodnick (Ed.), *Predictors of treatment response in mood disorders.* Washington, DC: American Psychiatric Press.

WESTERMEYER, J. (1987). Public health and chronic mental illness. *American Journal of Public Health, 77*, 667–668.

WETHINGTON, E. (2000). Expecting stress: Americans and the "midlife crisis." *Motivation & Emotion, 24*, 85–103.

WHALEN, P. J. (1998). Fear, vigilance, and ambiguity: Initial neuroimaging studies of the human amygdala. *Current Directions in Psychological Science, 7*, 177–188.

WHEELER, L., REIS, H., & BOND, M. H. (1989). Collectivism-individualism in everyday social life: The middle kingdom and the melting pot. *Journal of Personality and Social Psychology, 57*, 79–86.

WHEELER, L. R. (1942). A comparative study of the intelligence of East Tennessee mountain children. *Journal of Educational Psychology, 33*, 321–334.

WHITE, G. L. (1980). Physical attractiveness and courtship progress. *Journal of Personality and Social Psychology, 39*, 660–668.

WHITE, J. W., DONAT, P. L. N., & BONDURANT, B. (2001). A developmental examination of violence against girls and women. In R. K. Unger (Ed.), *Handbook of the psychology of women and gender* (pp. 343–357). New York: Wiley.

WHITE, S. H., & PILLEMER, D. B. (1979). Childhood amnesia and the development of a functionally accessible memory system. In J. F. Kihlstrom & F. J. Evans (Eds.), *Functional disorders of memory.* Hillsdale, NJ: Erlbaum.

WHITING, J. W. M., & WHITING, B. B. (1975). *Children of six cultures: A psychocultural analysis*. Cambridge, MA: Harvard University Press.

WHORF, B. (1956). *Language, thought, and reality: Selected writings of Benjamin Lee Whorf*. New York: Wiley.

WICKELGREN, I. (1997). Getting a grasp on working memory. *Science, 275*, 1580–1582.

WICKELGREN, W. A. (1974). *How to solve problems*. San Francisco: Freeman.

WICKER, A. W. (1969). Attitudes versus actions: The relationship of verbal and overt behavioral responses to attitude objects. *Journal of Social Issues, 25*(4), 41–78.

WIENS, A. N., & MENUSTIK, C. E. (1983). Treatment outcome and patient characteristics in an aversion therapy program for alcoholism. *American Psychologist, 38*, 1089–1096.

WIESENTHAL, D. L., ENDLER, N. S., COWARD, T. R., & EDWARDS, J. (1976). Reversibility of relative competence as a determinant of conformity across different perceptual tasks. *Representative Research in Social Psychology, 7*, 319–342.

WILCOXIN, H. C., DRAGOIN, W. B., & KRAL, P. A. (1971). Illness-induced aversions in rat and quail: Relative salience of visual and gustatory cues. *Science, 171*, 826–828.

WILHELM, F. H., TRABERT, W., & ROTH, W. T. (2001). Physiologic instability in panic disorder and generalized anxiety disorder. *Biological Psychiatry, 49*, 596–605.

WILLIAMS, E. (1994), Remarks on lexical knowledge. [Special volume on lexical acquisition, L. Gleitman & B. Landau (Eds).] *Lingua 92*(1–4), 7–34.

WILLIAMS, G. C. (1966). *Adaptation and natural selection*. Princeton, NJ: Princeton University Press.

WILLIAMS, H. L, TEPAS, D. I.; & MORLOCK, H. C. (1962). Evoked responses to clicks and electroencephalographic stages of sleep in man. *Science, 138*, 685–686.

WILLIAMS, L. (1994). Recall of childhood trauma: A prospective study of women's memories of child sexual abuse. *Journal of Consulting and Clinical Psychology, 62*, 1167–1176.

WILLIS, S. L., & REID, J. D. (EDS.) (1999). *Life in the middle: Psychological and social development in middle age*. San Diego: Academic Press.

WILSON, D. H., REEVES, A. G., GAZZANIGA, M. S., & CULVER, C. (1977). Cerebral commissurotomy for the control of intractable seizures. *Neurology, 27*, 708–715.

WILSON, E. O. (1975). *Sociobiology*. Cambridge, MA: Harvard University Press.

WILSON, G. T. (1991). Chemical aversion conditioning in the treatment of alcoholism: Further comments. *Behaviour Research and Therapy, 29*, 415–419.

WILSON, J. Q. (1997). *Moral judgment: Does the abuse excuse threaten our legal system?* New York: Basic Books.

WIMMER, H., & PERNER, J. (1983). Beliefs about beliefs: Representation and constraining function of wrong beliefs in young children's understanding of deception. *Cognition, 13*, 103–128.

WINKLER, J., & TAYLOR, S. E. (1979). Preference, expectation, and attributional bias: Two field experiments. *Journal of Applied Social Psychology, 1*, 183–197.

WINNER, E. (2000). The origins and ends of giftedness. *American Psychologist, 55*(1), 159–169.

WINOGRAD, E., & NEISSER, U. (EDS.). (1993). *Affect and accuracy in recall: Studies of "flashbulb" memories*. New York: Cambridge University Press.

WINSLOW, J. T., & INSEL, T. R. (1990). Neurobiology of obsessive-compulsive disorder: A possible role for serotonin [Suppl.]. *Journal of Clinical Psychiatry, 51*, 27–31.

WIRSHING, W. C., MARDER, S. R., VAN PUTTEN, T., & AMES, D. (1995). Acute treatment of schizophrenia. In F. E. Bloom & D. Kupfer (Eds.), *Psychopharmacology: The fourth generation of progress* (pp. 1259–1266). New York: Raven.

WISE, R. A., & ROMPRE, P. P. (1989). Brain dopamine and reward. *Annual Review of Psychology, 40*, 191–226.

WISEMAN, S., & NEISSER, U. (1974). Perceptual organization as a determinant of visual recognition memory. *American Journal of Psychology, 87*, 675–681.

WISHNER, J. (1960). Reanalysis of "impressions of personality." *Psychological Review 67*, 96–112.

WITTENBRINK, B., JUDD, C. M., & PARK, B. (1997). Evidence for racial prejudice at the implicit level and its relationship with questionnaire measures. *Journal of Personality and Social Psychology, 72*(2), 262–274.

WITTGENSTEIN, L. (1953). *Philosophical investigations*. G. E. M. Anscombe (Trans.) Oxford: Blackwell.

WOHL, J. (1989). Cross-cultural psychotherapy. In P. B. Pedersen, J. G. Draguns, W. J. Lonner, & J. E. Trimble (Eds.), *Counseling across cultures* (pp. 79–113). Honolulu: University of Hawaii.

WOICIECHOWSKY, C., VOGEL, S., MEYER, B. U., & LEHMANN, R. (1997). Neuropsychological and neurophysiological consequences of partial callosotomy. *Journal of Neurosurgical Science, 41*, 75–80.

WOLF, M. E., & MOSNAIM, A. D. (1990). *Post-traumatic stress disorder: Etiology, phenomenology, and treatment*. Washington, DC: American Psychiatric Press.

WOLFE, J. M. (1994). Guided search 2.0: A revised model of visual search. *Psychonomics Bulletin and Review, 1*, 202–238.

WOLLEN, K. A., WEBER, A., & LOWRY, D. (1972). Bizarreness versus interaction of mental images as determinants of learning. *Cognitive Psychology, 3*, 518–523.

WOLPE, J. (1958). *Psychotherapy by reciprocal inhibition*. Stanford, CA: Stanford University Press.

WOLPE, J., & LAZARUS, A. A. (1966). *Behavior therapy techniques: A guide to the treatment of neuroses*. Elmsford, NY: Pergamon.

WOLPE, J., & PLAUD, J. J. (1997). Pavlov's contributions to behavior therapy: The obvious and the not so obvious. *American Psychologist, 52*, 966–972.

WOOD, A. J., & GOODWIN, G. M. (1987). A review of the biochemical and neuropharmacological actions of lithium. *Psychological Medicine, 17*, 579–600.

WOOD, W. (2000). Attitude change: Persuasion and social influence. *Annual Review of Psychology, 51*, 539–570.

WOODRUFF, P. W. R., WRIGHT, I. C., BULLMORE, E. T., BRAMMER, M., HOWARD, R. J., WILLIAMS, S. C. R., ET AL. (1997). Auditory hallucinations and the temporal cortical response to speech in schizophrenia: A functional magnetic resonance imaging study. *American Journal of Psychiatry, 154*, 1676–1682.

WOODS, B. T., & TEUBER, H. L. (1978). Changing patterns of childhood aphasia. *Archives of Neurology, 3*, 273–280.

WOODWARD, A. L. (1998). Infants selectively encode the goal object of an actor's reach. *Cognition, 69*, 1–34.

WOODWARD, L., FERGUSSON, D. M., & BELSKY, J. (2000). Timing of parental separation and attachment to parents in adolescence: Results of a prospective study from birth to age 16. *Journal of Marriage and the Family, 62*, 162–174.

WOOLF, N. J. (1998). A structural basis for memory storage in mammals. *Progress in Neurobiology, 55*, 59–77.

WYERS, E. J., PEEKE, H. V. S., & HERZ, M. J. (1973). Behavioral habituation in invertebrates. In H. V. S. Peeke & M. J. Herz (Eds.), *Habituation: Vol. 1. Behavioral studies*. New York: Academic Press.

WYNN, K. (1992). Addition and subtraction by human infants. *Nature, 358*, 749–750.

WYNN, K. (1995). Infants possess a system of numerical knowledge. *Current Directions in Psychological Science, 4*, 172–176.

XIANG, J., WUNSCHMANN, S., DIEKEMA, D. J., KLINZMAN, D., PATRICK, K. D., GEORGE, S. L., ET AL. (2001). Effect of coinfection with GB virus C on survival among patients with HIV infection. [See comments.] *New England Journal of Medicine, 345*, 707–714.

XU, F. (2002). The role of language in acquiring object concepts in infancy. *Cognition, 85*, 223–250.

Xu, F., & Carey, S. (1996). Infants' metaphysics: The case of numerical identity. *Cognitive Psychology, 30*(2), 111–153.

Yando, R., Seitz, V., & Zigler, E. (1978). *Imitation: A developmental perspective.* Hillsdale, NJ: Erlbaum.

Yehuda, R. (1997). Sensitization of the hypothalamic-pituitary-adrenal axis in posttraumatic stress disorder. In R. Yehuda & A. C. (Eds.), Psychobiology of posttraumatic stress disorder. *Annals of the New York Academy of Sciences, 821,* 57–75.

Yeung, W. J., Sandberg, J. F., Davis-Kean, P. E., & Hofferth, S. L. (2001). Children's time with fathers in intact families. *Journal of Marriage & the Family, 63,* 136–154.

Yik, M. S. M., & Russell, J. A. (2001). Predicting the Big Two of affect from the Big Five of personality. *Journal of Research in Personality, 35*(3), 247–277.

Young, W. (1996). Spinal cord regeneration. *Science, 273,* 451.

Yussen, S. R., & Levy, V. M. (1975). Developmental changes in predicting one's own span of memory. *Journal of Experimental Child Psychology, 19,* 502–508.

Zaidel, E. (1976). Auditory vocabulary of the right hemisphere following brain bisection or hemidecortication. *Cortex, 12,* 191–211.

Zaidel, E. (1983). A response to Gazzaniga. Language in the right hemisphere, convergent perspectives. *American Psychologist, 38*(5), 542–546.

Zaidi, L. Y., & Foy, D. W. (1994). Childhood abuse experiences and combat-related PTSD. *Journal of Traumatic Stress, 7,* 33–42.

Zajonc, R. B. (1965). Social facilitation. *Science, 149,* 269–274.

Zajonc, R. B. (1968). Attitudinal effects of mere exposure. *Journal of Personality and Social Psychology, 9*(monograph suppl.), 1–27.

Zajonc, R. B., Adelmann, P. K., Murphy, S. T., Niedenthal, P. M. (1987). Convergence in the physical appearance of spouses. *Motivation and Emotion, 11,* 335–346.

Zajonc, R. B., & Sales, S. M. (1966). Social facilitation of dominant and subordinate responses. *Journal of Experimental Social Psychology, 2*(2), 160–168.

Zaragoza, M. S., & Mitchell, K. J. (1996). Repeated exposure to suggestion and the creation of false memories. *Psychological Science, 7,* 294–300.

Zarkin, G. A., Grabowski, H. G., Mauskopf, J., Bannerman, H. A., & Weisler, R. H. (1995). Economic evaluation of drug treatment for psychiatric disorders. In F. E. Bloom & D. Kupfer (Eds.), *Psychopharmacology: The fourth generation of progress* (pp. 1897–1905). New York: Raven.

Zatzick, D. F., Marmar, C. R., Weiss, D. S., Browner, W. S., Metzler, T. J., Golding, J. M., et al. (1997). Posttraumatic stress disorder and functioning and quality of life outcomes in a nationally representative sample of male Vietnam veterans. *American Journal of Psychiatry, 154,* 1690–1695.

Zelazo, P. D., & Frye, D. (1998). Cognitive complexity and control: II. The development of executive function in childhood. *Current Directions in Psychological Science, 7,* 121–125.

Zener, K. (1937). The significance of behavior accompanying conditioned salivary secretion for theories of the conditioned response. *American Journal of Psychology, 50,* 384–403.

Zentall, T. R. (2000). Symbolic representation by pigeons. *Current Directions in Psychological Science, 9,* 118–123.

Zhou, W., & King, W. M. (1997). Binocular eye movements not coordinated during REM sleep. *Experimental Brian Research, 117,* 153–160.

Ziegler, F. J., Imboden, J. B., & Rodgers, D. A. (1963). Contemporary conversion reactions: III. Diagnostic considerations. *Journal of the American Medical Association, 186,* 307–311.

Zigler, E., & Child, I. L. (1969). Socialization. In G. Lindzey & E. Aronson (Eds.), *The handbook of social psychology: Vol. 3* (pp. 450–589). Reading, MA: Addison-Wesley.

Zigler, E. F. & Child, I. L. (1973). *Socialization and personality development.* Reading, MA: Addison-Wesley.

Zigler, E. F., Lamb, M. E., & Child, I. L. (1982). *Socialization and personality development* (2nd ed.). New York: Oxford University Press.

Zigler, P. (1991). *The black death.* Dover, NH: Sutton.

Zilboorg, G., & Henry, G. W. (1941). *A history of medical psychology.* New York: Norton.

Zillman, D. (1983). Transfer of excitation in emotional behavior. In J. T. Cacioppo & R. E. Petty (Eds.), *Social psychophysiology: A sourcebook* (pp. 215–240). New York: Guilford.

Zillman, D. (1996). Sequential dependencies in emotional experience and behavior. In R. D. Kavanaugh, B. Zimmerberg, and S. Fein (Eds.), *Emotion: interdisciplinary perspectives* (pp. 243–272). Hillsdale, NJ: Erlbaum.

Zillman, D., Katcher, A. H., & Milavsky, B. (1972). Excitation transfer from physical exercise to subsequent aggressive behavior. *Journal of Experimental Social Psychology, 8,* 247–259.

Zimbardo, P. G. (1969). The human choice: Individuation, reason, and order versus deindividuation, impulse and chaos. In W. J. Arnold & E. Levine (Eds.), *Nebraska Symposium on Motivation* (pp. 237–308). Lincoln, NE: University of Nebraska Press.

Zimbardo, P. G. (1970). The human choice: Individuation, reason and order versus deindividuation, impulse and chaos. In W. J. Arnold & D. Levine, (Eds.), *Nebraska Symposium on Motivation: Vol 18.* Lincoln, NE: University of Nebraska Press.

Zimbardo, P. G. (1973). On the ethics of intervention in human psychological research: With special reference to the Stanford prison experiment. *Cognition, 2*(2), 243–256.

Zimbardo, P. G. (1978). The psychology of evil: On the perversion of human potential. In L. Krames, & P. Pliner & T. Alloway (Eds.), *Aggression, Dominance, and Individual Spacing: Vol 4* (pp. 155–169). New York: Plenum Press.

Zohar, J., Insel, T., Zohar-Kadouch, R. C., Hill, J. L., & Murphy, D. (1988). Serotonergic responsivity in obsessive-compulsive disorder. Effects of chronic clomipramine treatment. *Archives of General Psychiatry, 45,* 167–172.

Zorilla, L.T. E., & Cannon, T. D. (1995). Structural brain abnormalities in schizophrenia: Distribution, etiology, and implications. In S. A. Mednick (Ed.), *Neural development in schizophrenia: Theory and research.* New York: Plenum Press.

Zubin, J., Eron, L. D., & Shumer, F. (1965). *An experimental approach to projective techniques.* New York: Wiley.

Zucker, K. J. (2001). Biological influences on psychosexual differentiation. In R. K. Unger (Ed.), *Handbook of the psychology of women and gender.*

Zucker, K. J., Bradley, S. J., Oliver, G., Blake, J., Fleming, S., & Hood, J. (1996). Psychosexual development of women with congenital adrenal hyperplasia. *Hormones and Behavior, 30,* 300–318.

Zuckerman, M. (1979). *Sensation seeking: Beyond the optimum level of arousal.* Hillsdale, NJ: Erlbaum.

Zuckerman, M. (1983). A biological theory of sensation seeking. In M. Zuckerman (Ed.), *Biological bases of sensation seeking, impulsivity, and anxiety.* Hillsdale, NJ: Erlbaum.

Zuckerman, M. (1987a). All parents are environmentalists until they have their second child. Peer commentary on Plomin, R., & Daniels, D. Why are children from the same family so different from one another? *Behavioral and Brain Sciences, 10,* 38–39.

Zuckerman, M. (1987b). A critical look at three arousal constructs in personality theories: Optimal levels of arousal, strength of the nervous system, and sensitivities to signals of reward and punishment. In J. Strelau & H. J. Eysenck (Eds.), *Personality dimensions and arousal: Perspectives on individual differences* (pp. 217–230). New York: Plenum.

Zuckerman, M. (1990). The psychophysiology of sensation seeking [Special Issue]. Biological foundations of personality: Evolution, behavioral genetics, and psychophysiology. *Journal of Personality, 58,* 313–345.

Zuckerman, M. (1994). *Behavioral expressions and biosocial bases of sensation seeking.* NY: Cambridge University Press.

Zuger, B. (1984). Early effeminate behavior in boys. *Journal of Nervous and Mental Disease, 172,* 90–96.

# ACKNOWLEDMENTS AND CREDITS

## FIGURES

Chapter 1: 1.1 Courtesy of Professor Joseph J. Campos, University of California, Berkeley. 1.2A Photograph by Robert Estall/Corbis. 1.2B Photograph by David Gillison/Peter Arnold, Inc. 1.2C Photograph by Wolfgang Kaehler/Corbis. 1.3A Photograph by George H. Harrison/Grant Heilman. 1.3B Photograph by Peter Hendrie/The Image Bank. 1.4 From *Biological Psychology* by Rosenzweig, Leiman, and Breedlove.

Chapter 2: 2.1 From Descartes, R. (1662). *Trait de l'homme*, Haldane, E. S., and Ross, G. R. T. (trans.). Cambridge: Cambridge University Press. 2.2 David Becker/SPL/Photo Researchers, Inc. 2.3B Photograph by Dr. John Mazziotta, UCLA School of Medicine/Science Photo Library/Photo Researchers. 2.4A Courtesy Warren Museum, Harvard Medical School. 2.4B Damasio, H., Grabowski, T., Frank, R., Galaburda, A. M., & Damasio, A. R. (1994), The return of Phineas Gage: Clues about the brain from the skull of a famous patient, *Science*, 264; courtesy Hanna Damasio. 2.5 Zephyr/SPL/Photo Researchers, Inc. 2.6 Photograph © Paul Shambroom. 2.7 NIH/SPL/Photo Researchers. Reprinted with permission from Dr. Krish Singh, Department of Psychology, University of Liverpool. 2.8 From *Brain: A Scientific American Book*, edited by Scientific American. 2.9 From *Biological Science*, Sixth Edition by James Gould and William T. Keeton. 2.10 After Bloom, F. E., Lazerson, A., and Hofstadter, L. *Brain, Mind and Behavior*. New York: Freeman, 1988. 2.11A Children's Hospital & Medical Center/Corbis. 2.14 From *Higher Cortical Functions in Man*, 2nd ed. by A. R. Luria. Copyright © 1979 by Consultants Bureau Enterprises, Inc. and Basic Books, Inc. Reprinted by permission of Basic Books, a member of Perseus Books, L. L. C.; Luria, A.R. "Drawings by a patient with visual agnosia" from *Higher Cortical Functions in Man*. Copyright © 1976. Reprinted by permission of publisher, Kluwer Academic/Plenum Publishers. 2.15 *Physiological Psychology*, 2nd ed., by Mark Rosenzweig and Arnold Leiman. 2.18 Gazzaniga, M. S., The split brain in man, *Scientific American* 217 (August 1967): 25. 2.21A SPL/Photo Researchers Inc. 2.21B CNRI/SPL/Photo Researchers, Inc. 2.21C © Guigoz/Dr. A. Privat/Petit Format/Science Source/Photo Researchers. 2.22 Nancy Kedersha/SPL/Photo Researchers, Inc. 2.25 From *Biology: The Unity and Diversity of Life* 6th edition by Starr/Taffart. © 1992. Reprinted with permission of Brooks/Cole, a division of Thomas Learining: www.thomsonrights.com. Fax 800 730-2215. 2.27 J. C. Eccles, *The Understanding of the Brain*, Copyright The McGraw-Hill Companies. Reproduced with the permission of The McGraw-Hill Companies. 2.29 © Lewis and Everhart and Zeevi/Visuals Unlimited. 2.30 Bloom, *Peripheral nervous system, synaptic transmission and limbic system*. Reprinted with the permission of Thirteen/WNET New York. 2.31 Rosenzweig, Leiman, "Lock and Key Model of Synaptic transmission" from *Physiological Psychology*. Copyright (1989) M.R. Rosenzweig and A.L. Leiman. Reprinted with the permission of the authors.

Chapter 3: 3.4 Reprinted with permission from Weiss, B. and Laties, V.G., Behavioral thermoregulation, *Science* 133 (28 April 1961): 1338–44, Figure 1. Copyright © 1961 by the American Association for the Advancement of Science. 3.6B Courtesy Neal E. Miller, Rockefeller University. 3.7 From Bouchard, Tremblay, et.al, The response to long-term overfeeding in identical twins. *New England Journal of Medicine* 322: pp. 1477–1482. 3.8 Andres, R., Influence of obesity on longevity in the aged, in Borek, C., Fenoglio, C. M., and King, D. W. (Eds.), *Aging, Cancer, and Cell Membranes*, pp. 230–46. New York: Thieme-Stratton, 1980.

3.9 From *Bodily Changes in Pain, Hunger, Fear and Rage* by W. B. Cannon. 3.10 Photograph by Walter Chandoha. 3.11A Blakemore, C., *Mechanics of the Mind*, p. 42. New York: Cambridge University Press, 1977. Reprinted by permission of the publisher. 3.11B Photograph © Dan McCoy, 1994/Rainbow/PNI. 3.17 Dement, William "Sleep and the EEG" from *Some Must Watch While Some Must Sleep*. Reprinted with the permission of the author. 3.18 Adapted from Kleitman, N., Patterns of dreaming, *Scientific American* 203 (November 1960): 82–88. 3.21 Photograph courtesy of the University of Wisconsin Primate Laboratory. 3.22 Courtesy of Dr. M. E. Olds.

Chapter 4: 4.4 Pavlov, I.P. *Lectures on Conditioned Reflexes*, Vol. I. Reprinted by permission of the publisher, International Publishers Company, Inc. 4.5 Stimulus control by Moore, John W. in *Classical Conditioning II: Research and Theory* edited by Black/Prokasy. 1972. Prentice-Hall, Inc., Upper Saddle River, NJ. 4.10A Photograph by Mike Salisbury. 4.10B Photograph by Susan M. Hogue. 4.11 From *A Primer of Operant Conditioning* by G. S. Reynolds. (Scott, Foresman & Co.). 4.12 AP Photo/Richard Vogel. 4.13 Courtesy Yerkes Regional Primate Research Center of Emory University. 4.16 Spooner, A., and Kellogg, W. N., The backward conditioning curve, *American Journal of Psychology* 60 (1947): 321–34. 1947. The University of Illinois Press. 4.18 Colwill, R. M., and Rescorla, R. A., Postconditioning devaluation of a reinforcer affects instrumental responding, *Journal of Experimental Psychology: Animal Behavior Processes* 11 (1985): 120–32. 4.20 Maier, S. F., Seligman, M. E. P., and Solomon, R. L., Pavlovian fear conditioning and learned helplessness: Effects on escape and avoidance behavior of (a) the CS-US contingency and (b) the independence of the US and voluntary responding, in Campbell, B. A., and Church, R. M. (Eds.), *Punishment and Aversive Behavior*, 1969, p. 328. 4.22 Olton, D. S., and Samuelson, R. J., Remembrance of places passed: Spatial memory in rats, *Journal of Experimental Psychology: Animal Behavior Processes* 2 (1976): 97–116. 4.23 and 4.24 From Köhler, W. 1925. *The mentality of apes*. New York: Harcourt Brace and World.

Chapter 5: 5.2 Erich Lessing/Art Resource. 5.3 Gibson, James J. "The Senses Considered As Perceptual Systems." Copyright © 1966 by Houghton Mifflin Company. Reprinted by permission. 5.4 Thompson, Richard, "Sine waves of hertz tones" from *Introduction to Biopsychology*. Reprinted by permission of author. 5.8A Lindsay P. H., and Norman, D. A., *Human Information Processing*, 2nd edition, p. 136. New York: Academic Press, 1977. Adapted by permission of the author and Harcourt Brace Jovanovich. 5.8B Coren, S., and Ward, L. M., *Sensation and Perception*, 3rd ed. San Diego: Harcourt Brace Jovanovich, 1989. Adapted by permission of the author and publisher. 5.9 Mose, Eric, "Eye and Camera" from *Scientific American*. Illustration by Eric Mose, Copyright © 1950 Eric Mose. 5.10 Figure from *Sensation and Perception*, Third Edition, by Stanley Coren and Lawrence M. Ward. 1989. Harcourt Brace & Company. 5.11 and 5.12 Cornsweet, T. M., *Visual Perception*. New York: Academic Press, 1970. 5.13 © Peter Sedgley Courtesy of the Peter Scott Gallery, Lancaster University, UK. 5.15 Hering, E., "The effect of distance between contrasting regions" from *Outlines of a Theory of the Light Sense*. Copyright © Springer-Verlag Gmgh & Co. KG. Reprinted by permission of the publisher. 5.16 Vasarely, Victor, "Contrast" Smithsonian Institution from *Arcturus II*, Hirshorn Museum & Sculpture Garden. Copyright © 1966.

Reprinted with the permission of Michelle Vasarely. 5.17 "Mach Bands," Coren, Porac, Ward from *Sensation and Perception*. Copyright © John Wiley & Sons, Inc. Reprinted by permission of John Wiley & Sons, Inc. 5.21 Hurvich, L. M., *Color Vision*. Sunderland, Mass.: Sinauer Associates, 1981. 5.23 Douglas Downing, "The Color Disk" Reprinted with the permission of the author, Douglas Downing. 5.24 Courtesy of Munsell Color, 2441 N. Calvert Street, Baltimore, Md., 21218. 5.26 Photographs by Fritz Goro/Life Magazine, © Time Warner, Inc. 5.29 Hurvich, L. M., and Jameson, D., An opponent-process theory of color vision, *Psychological Review* 64 (1957): 384–404. 5.31 DeValois, R. L., and DeValois, K. K., Neural Coding of Color, in Carterette, E. C., and Friedman, M. P., (Eds.), *Handbook of Perception*, vol. 5. New York: Academic Press, 1975. 5.33 Figure 11.28 from Schiffman, H. *Sensation and Perception* 2/e. 1982. John Wiley & Sons, Inc. 5.34 Adapted from Kuffler, S. W., Discharge pattern and functional organization of mammalian retina, *Journal of Neurophysiology* 16 (1953): 37–68. 5.35 Hubel, D. H., The visual cortex of the brain, *Scientific American* 209 (November 1963): 54–58.

Chapter 6: 6.1 *Perception*, 2/e by Hochberg, J. © Reprinted by permission of Pearson Education, Inc. Upper Saddle River, NJ. 6.4 Alexander Walter/Stone/Getty Images. 6.6A © Stephen J. Krasemann/Allstock. 6.6B Lee Snider/Corbis. 6.7 Gibson, James J. "The Perception of the Visual World" Copyright © by Houghton Mifflin Company. Reprinted with permission. 6.8 "Motion Parallax" Coren, Porac, Ward from *Sensation and Perception*. Copyright © John Wiley & Sons, Inc. Reprinted by permission of John Wiley & Sons, Inc. 6.12 Duncker, K., Uber induzierte Bewegung, Psychologische Forschung 12 (1929): 180–259. Adapted by permission of Springer-Verlag, Inc., Heidelberg. 6.17A Photograph by Jeffery Grosscup. 6.23 Beck, J., Effect of orientation and shape similarity on perceptual grouping, *Perception and Psychophysics* 1 (1966): 300–302. Psychonomic Society Publications. 6.25 Figure 10 from *Gestalt Psychology* by Dr. Wolfgang Kohler. 1947. Liveright Publishing Corporation. 6.26 Photographs by Michael & Patricia Fogden/Corbis. 6.27 Kanizsa, G. "Subjective Contours" from *Scientific American* 234. Copyright © 1976 Reprinted by permission of Jerome Kuhl. 6.29 Selfridge, Oliver, "Context influences perception (pattern recognition) from *Proceedings of the Western Computer Conference*. Copyright © 1955. Reprinted with the permission of the author. 6.31 Biederman, I., Recognition-by-components: A theory of human image understanding, *Psychological Review* 94 (1987):115–47. 6.32 From Martha Farah, *Visual Agnosia: Disorders of Object Recognition*, Cambridge, MA: The MIT Press, 1990. 6.38 Gibson, James J. "The Perception of the Visual World" Copyright © by Houghton Mifflin Company. Reprinted with permission. 6.41 Courtesy of The Metropolitan Museum of Art.

Chapter 7: 7.1 From *Psychological Review*, Primary memory by N. C. Waugh and D. A. Norman, Vol. 72: pp. 89–108. 7.2 Adapted from Murdock, B., The serial position effect of free recall, *Journal of Experimental Psychology* 64 (1962): 482–88. 7.3 Glanzer, M., and Cunitz, A., Two storage mechanisms in free recall, *Journal of Verbal Learning and Verbal Behavior* 5 (1966): 351–60. 7.5 Adapted from Bower, G. H. "Analysis of mnemonic device" from *American Scientist* 58. Reprinted by American Scientist 1970. 7.6 Baddeley, Alan. "Context-dependent memory in two environments: On land and underwater" from *British Journal of Psychology* 66. Copyright © 1975. Reprinted by permission of publisher. 7.10 Adapted from Bahrick, H. P., Semantic memory content in permastore: Fifty years of memory for Spanish learned in school, *Journal of Experimental Psychology: General* 113 (1984): 1–35. 7.11 Orne, M. T., The mechanisms of hypnotic age regression: An experimental study, *Journal of Abnormal and Social Psychology* 58 (1951): 277–99. Copyright 1951 by the American Psychological Association. 7.12 From *Scientific American* "The Anatomy of Memory" by M. Mishkin and T. Appenzeller, vol. 256, pp. 80–89. 7.13A From *Fundamentals of Human Neuropsychology*, 2nd ed., by B. Kolb and I. Q. Whishaw, Figure 20-5, p. 485. San Francisco: W. H. Freeman and Company. 7.13B Milner, B., Corkin, S., and Teuber, H. L., Further analysis of the hippocampal amnesic syndrome: Fourteen-year follow-up of H.M., *Psychologia* 6 (1968): 215–34.

Chapter 8: 8.2 *Science*, Mental rotation of 3-D objects by R. N. Shepard and J. Metzler, vol. 171, pp. 701–703. 1971 American Association for the Advancement of Science. 8.3 Adapted from Kosslyn, S. M., Ball, T. M., and Reisser, V. J., Visual images preserve metric spatial information: Evidence from studies of image scanning, *Journal of Experimental Psychology: Human Perception and Performance* 4 (1978): 47–60. 8.10 R. Bootzin, *Psychology Today: An Introduction*. Copyright The McGraw-Hill Companies. Reproduced with the permission of The McGraw-Hill Companies. 8.15 Scheerer, M., Goldstein, K., and Boring, E. G., A demonstration of insight: The horse-rider puzzle, *American Journal of Psychology* 54 (1941): 437–38. 8.18 Engraving by Walter H. Ruff; courtesy The Granger Collection. 8.19 Suls, Jerry, "A Two-stage model of the appreciation of jokes and cartoons" from *The Psychology of Humor*. Copyright Jerry Suls. Reprinted with the permission of the author.

Chapter 9: 9.7 By permission. From *Merriam-Webster's Collegiate* © *Dictionary 10th Edition* © 2002, by Merriam-Webster's, Incorporated. 9.8 Courtesy Sharon Armstrong. 9.11 Reprinted from *Cognition*, Vol. 73, Altmann Gerry, "Incremental interpretation at verbs restricting the domain of subsequent reference" pp 247–264 Copyright © 1999 with permission of Elsevier Science. 9.13A Photograph by Philip Morse, University of Wisconsin. 9.13B Eimas et al. "Speech Perception in Infants" from *Science* 171. Copyright © 1971 American Association for the Advancement of Science. 9.16 Adapted from Roberta Golinkoff. 9.20 Brown, R., Cazden, C., and Bellugi-Klima, U., The child's grammar from 1 to 3, in Hill, J. P. (Ed.), *Minnesota Symposium on Child Psychology* by The University of Minnesota Press, Minneapolis. 9.18 Brown et al. "Mean utterance length and age in three children" from The Child's Grammar from I to III from John P. Hill (ed.) *Minnesota Symposia on Child Psychology, Volume 2* (University of Minnesota Press, 1969). 9.19 Photographs courtesy AP/Wide World Photos. 9.20 Frishberg, N., Arbitrariness and iconicity: Historical change in American Sign Language, *Language* 51 (1975): 696–719. Photographs of and by Ted Supalla. 9.21 Yovovich, Noel, "Self-made signs in a deaf boy never exposed to sign language. Copyright © 1982. Reprinted with the permission of the illustrator, Noel Yovovich. 9.22 Drawings courtesy Robert Thacker. 9.23 P. R. Marler, "A Comparative approach to vocal learning" from *Journal of Comparative and Physiological Psychology Monograph* 71. Copyright © by the American Psychological Association. Reprinted with permission. 9.24 Reprinted from *Cognitive Psychology*, Vol. 21 Johnson & Newport, "Critical period effects in second language learning" pp 60–99 Copyright © 1989 with permission of Elsevier Science. 9.25 E. Newport, "Maturational constraints on language learning" from *Cognitive Science*. Reprinted with the permission of the author.

Chapter 10: 10.2 Asch, S. E., Studies of independence and conformity: A minority of one against a unanimous majority, *Psychological Monographs* 70 (9, Whole No. 416), 1956. 10.3 and 10.4 © by Stanley Milgram. From the film *Obedience*, distributed by Penn State Audio-Visual Services.

Chapter 11: 11.1 © 1987 Garry D. McMichael/Photo Researchers. 11.2A Photograph by Philip Green. 11.2B Photograph by Jeff Foott/Bruce Coleman. 11.2C Michael & Patricia Fogden/Corbis. 11.3 Leonardo da Vinci's *La Jaconde* (Mona Lisa), Louvre, Paris; photograph courtesy of Service Photographique de la Reunion des Musées Nationaux. 11.4 Photograph © Rudie H. Kuiter, Oxford Scientific Films. 11.5A Photograph by Francisco J. Erize/Bruce Coleman. 11.5B Photograph © Jim Clare, Partridge Films Ltd./Oxford Scientific Films. 11.6 Cole, Ruth/Animals Animals/Earth Scenes. 11.7B Walt Disney Productions. 11.8 Barnett, S. A., 1963. *The Rat: A Study in Behavior*. Chicago: The University of Chicago Press. Copyright © 1963 by Aldine Publishing Co. Reprinted by permission of the University of Chicago Press. 11.9 *Top* Yann Arthus-Bertrand/Corbis. *Bottom* Caroline Penn/Corbis. 11.10A Photograph by Rod Williams, © Bruce Coleman, Inc., 1991. 11.10B Kevin Schafer, Corbis. 11.11 Photograph by Hans Reinhard, © Bruce Coleman, Inc., 1988. 11.12 Wayne Lankinen/Bruce Coleman. 11.13 Georg D. Lepp/Bio-Tec Images. 11.14 Joe McDonald/Corbis. 11.19 Paul Ekman, "Attempts to porta emotion by New Guinea tribesman" from *Unmasking the Face*. Copyright 1980. Reprinted with the permission of the author, Paul Ekman. 11.20 Russell, James A. "Success at matching facial expression to label six emotions" from *The Psychology of Facial Expression*. Reprinted with the permission of Cambridge University Press. 11.21 AP Photo/Eric Risberg.

Chapter 12: 12.1 Conel, J. L., *The Postnatal Development of the Human Cortex*, vols. 1, 3, 5. Cambridge, Mass.: Harvard University Press, 1939, 1947, 1955. 12.2 Tanner, J.M. "Physical growth" from Carmichael's Manual of *Child Psychology* 3/e. Reprinted by permission of John Wiley & Sons, Inc. 12.3 Photograph courtesy of M. M. Grumbach. 12.6, 12.7, and 12.8 Geri Enberg Photography. 12.10 Kellman, Philip, "Perception of partially occluded objects in infancy" from *Cognitive Psychology*. Copyright © 1983 Reprinted by permission of author, Philip Kellman. 12.11 Adapted from Baillargeon, R., Object permanence in $3^1/_2$- and $4^1/_2$-month-old infants, *Developmental Psychology* 23 (1987): 655–64. 12.13 Courtesy Adele Diamond. 12.15 Johnson & Morton "Rudimentary face recognition in newborns" from *Biology of Cognitive Development: The Case of Face Recognition*. Reprinted by permission of publisher, Blackwell Publishers. 12.16 From A.N. Meltzoff & M.K. Moore, "Imitation of facial and manual gestures by human neonates." *Science*, 1977, 198, 75–78. 12.18 Case, R. "Intellectual development from birth to adulthood: A neoPiagetian interpretation" from *Children's Thinking: What Develops*. 1978.

Chapter 13: **13.1** Photograph by Martin Rogers/Stock Boston. **13.2** Larry Williams/Corbis. **13.3** Photograph by Nina Leen/Life Magazine, © Time Warner, Inc. **13.6 and 13.7** Courtesy Harry Harlow, University of Wisconsin Primate Laboratory. **13.8** Photograph by Michael Heron/Woodfin Camp. **13.9** Kohlberg, L., Development of children's orientation towards a moral order in sequence in the development of moral thought, *Vita Humana* 6 (1963): 11–36. **13.12** © Reuters Newsmedia Inc./Corbis. **13.13A** Courtesy Dan Reisberg. **13.13B** © Bill Gillette/Stock Boston. **13.14A** © Spencer Grant/The Picture Cube. **13.14B** © Timothy Ross/The Image Bank. **13.14C** www.livingart.com.

Chapter 14: **14.6** *Simulated items similar to those in Wechsler Intelligence Scale for Children: Third Edition*. Copyright © 1949, 1974, 1981, 1991 by The Psychological Corporation. Reproduced by permission. All rights reserved. **14.7** SAT materials selected from SAT I: Reasoning Test. Reprinted by permission of the College Entrance Examination Board, the copyright owner. **14.8** Lewis, H.K. "A sample item from the Progressive Matrices Test" from *Standard Progressive Matrices*. Copyright © J. C. Raven Ltd. Reprinted by permission of the publisher. **14.10** Jones, H. E., and Kaplan, O. J., Psychological aspects of mental disorders in later life, in Kaplan, O. J. (Ed.), *Mental Disorders in Later Life*, 72. Stanford, Calif.: Stanford University Press, 1945. **14.11** Selfe, S. *Nadia: A Case of Extraordinary Drawing Ability in an Autistic Child*. New York: Academic Press, 1977. Reproduced by permission of Academic Press and Lorna Selfe. **14.12** Courtesy Photofest. **14.13** Based on Winchester, A. M., *Genetics*, 5th ed. Boston: Houghton Mifflin, 1977. **14.14** Reuters NewMedia Inc./Corbis.

Chapter 15: **15.1** Lanyon, R.I. "MMPI Profile" from *Personality Assessment* 3/e. Reprinted by permission of John Wiley & Sons, Inc. **15.4** Eysnck, H. J., and Rachman, S., *The causes and cures of neurosis*, p. 16. San Diego, Calif.: Robert R. Knapp, 1965. **15.8** *Motivation and Personality* by Maslow © Reprinted by permission of Pearson Education, Inc. Upper Saddle River, NJ.

Chapter 16: **16.1** Negative #31568. Courtesy Department of Library Services, The American Museum of Natural History. **16.2** William Hogarth's *The Madhouse*, 1735/1763; courtesy The Bettmann Archive. **16.3** © Stock Montage, Inc. **16.4** Photograph by Bill Bridges/Globe Photos. **16.6** Nicol, S. E. Clues to the genetics and neurobiology of schizophrenia. *American Scientist* 71. Reprinted by American Scientist 1983. **16.7** Data from Faris, R. E. L., and Dunham, H. W., *Mental Disorders in Urban Areas*. Chicago: University of Chicago Press, 1939. **16.8** Rosenthal et al. "Seasonal affective disorder and day length" from *Archives of General Psychiatry* 41. Reprinted by permission of the publisher, American Medical Association. **16.9** Hare, R. D., Temporal gradient of fear arousal in psychopaths, *Journal of Abnormal Psychology* 70 (1965): 442–45.

Chapter 17: **17.1A** Courtesy Historical Pictures Service. **17.1B** Courtesy National Library of Medicine. **17.1C** Culver Pictures. **17.4** Photograph by James D. Wilson/Woodfin Camp.

## TABLES

**Table 13.1** Adapted from Kohlberg, L., Classification of moral judgment into levels and stages of development, in Sizer, Theodore R., *Religion and Public Education*, pp. 171–73. 1967. Houghton Mifflin Company. **Table 13.2** Erikson, E. H., *Childhood and Society*. New York: W. W. Norton & Company, Inc., 1963. **Table 14.2** Adapted from *Mental Retardation Activities of the U. S. Department of Health, Education, and Welfare*. Washington, DC: United States Government Printing Office, 1963, p. 2. Score interval data from a classificatory system formerly recommended by the American Association for Mental Deficiency. **Table 14.3** Wechsler, D., *The Measurement and Appraisal of Adult Intelligence*, 4th ed. Baltimore, Md.: The Williams & Wilkins Co., 1958. Table adapted from the Manual for the Wechsler Adult Intelligence Scale.

## UNNUMBERED PHOTOS AND ART

**2** (*Chapter 1 Opener*) Picasso. *Studies*. 1920. Musée Picasso, Paris. © 2003 Estate of Pablo Picasso/Artists Rights Society (ARS), New York. Photo: Photos12.com-ARJ. **4** *Top* Courtesy of Dr. Guinevere Eden, Georgetown University. *Bottom* The Kobal Collection/Summit Entertainment. **7** *Top* Photofest. *Bottom* Fabian Cevallos/Corbis Sygma. **8** The Kobal Collection/Paramount. **9** *Bottom left, middle, and right* Reprinted with permission from R. J. Dolan, *Science* 298, p. 1193 (2002) fig. 2, Copyright 2002. **10** Reuters NewMedia Inc./Corbis. **11** Owen Franken/Corbis. **12** *Top* Dex Image, Inc./Corbis. *Bottom* Richard

Abarno/Corbis. **13** *Top* Courtesy of Archives of the History of American Psychology–University of Akron. *Bottom* The Warder Collection. **14** *Bottom* Courtesy of Clarence Brown. **15** Courtesy of Sidney Harris, ScienceCartoonsPlus.com. **16** *Top* Reuters News Picture Service. *Bottom* © 2002 The *New Yorker* Collection from cartoonbank.com. All Rights Reserved. **18** © 2002 The *New Yorker* Collection from cartoonbank.com. All Rights Reserved. **19** Corbis. **20** Courtesy of John Chase http://members.aol.com/chasetoons. **22** Courtesy of Sidney Harris, ScienceCartoonsPlus.com. **24** Dimitri Lundt; TempSport/Corbis. **27** Archives Jean Piaget/Université De Genève. **30** Bettman/Corbis. **31** Photos12-Collection Cinema. **38–39** (*Part 1 Opener*) *Discus Thrower*. Gianni Dagli Orti/Corbis. **40** (*Chapter 2 Opener*) Morris Kyle. *Number 14*. Photo: Burstein Collection/Corbis. **42** *Top* Courtesy National Library of Medicine. **53** The Science Museum/Science & Society Picture Library. **55** *Bottom* Courtesy of The Natural History Museum, London. **70** *Bottom* Photograph by David M. Phillips/Visuals Unlimited. **71** *Top* Courtesy National Library of Medicine. **74** *Top* Photograph by B. Malkin/Anthro-Photo. *Bottom* Buddy Mays/Corbis. **81** AP/Wide World Photos. **86** (*Chapter 3 Opener*) Piotr Konchalovsky. *Alexei Nikolaiyevic, Guest of the Painter*. The State Russian Museum, St. Petersburg. Photo: Scala/Art Resource, NY. **88** AFP/Corbis. **91** *Top* The Image Bank/Getty Images. *Bottom* Photodisc/Getty Images. **92** Drawing by Chas. Addams; © 1987, The *New Yorker* Magazine, Inc. **93** Photos12-Collection Cinema. **95** *Top* Peter Brueghel the Elder, *The Peasants' Wedding*, 1568, Kunsthistorisches Museum. Photograph © Erich Lessing/Art Resource, NY. *Bottom* Associated Press/Rockefeller University. **96** This *Far Side* cartoon by Gary Larson is reprinted by permission of Chronicle Features, San Francisco, California, all rights reserved. **99** Photograph by Jane Carter. **100** *Top* Courtesy Museo del Prado. *Bottom* AFP/Corbis. **109** Photograph by Grant Leduc/Monkmeyer. **115** *Jacob's Ladder*, from the Lambeth Bible; courtesy the Archbishop of Canterbury and the Trustees of Lambeth Palace Library. **117** *Top* Lindsay Hebberd/Corbis. *Bottom* The Kobal Collection/Dimension Films/Goode, Nicola. **122** (*Chapter 4 Opener*) Detail Paul Klee. *Tight Rope Dancer*. © 2003 Artists Rights Society (ARS), New York/VG Bild-Kunst, Bonn. Photo: Burstein Collection/Corbis. **125** Galen Roswell/Corbis. **126** Courtesy of the Bettman Archive. **132** Bob Daemmrich/PictureQuest. **134** Photograph by Nina Leen/Life Magazine, © Time Warner. **143** Courtesy Psychology Department, University of California, Berkeley. **152** Photographs by Lincoln P. Brower. **153** W. Perry Conway/Corbis. **156** Copyright Dennis Kunkel Microscopy, Inc. **157** The Warder Collection. **164–165** (*Part 2 Opener*) Auguste Rodin. *The Thinker*. ca. 1880. Bettmann/Corbis. **166** (*Chapter 5 Opener*) Rene Magritte. *La Condition Humaine*. 1933. Private Collection. © 2003 C. Herscovici, Brussels/Artists Rights Society (ARS), New York. Photo: Giraudon/Art Resource, NY. **168** *Top* Courtesy National Portrait Gallery, London. *Bottom* Detail from *The Bermuda Group* by John Smibert; courtesy Yale University Art Gallery; gift of Isaac Lothrop of Plymouth, Mass. **170** Culver Pictures, Inc., New York. **182** Courtesy National Library of Medicine. **194** Photographs Courtesy of Department of Psychology, University of Pennsylvania. **202** (*Chapter 6 Opener*) Picasso. *Girl Before a Mirror*. 1932. The Museum of Modern Art. Gift of Mrs. Simon Guggenheim (2.1938). © 2003 Estate of Pablo Picasso/Artists Rights Society (ARS), New York. Digital Image © The Museum of Modern Art/Licensed by SCALA/Art Resource, NY. **204** Claude Monet, *Terrace at Sainte-Adresse*, oil on canvas, $38^5/_8 \times 51^1/_8$"; reproduced by permission of the Metropolitan Museum of Art, New York; purchased with special contributions and purchase funds given or bequeathed by friends of the Museum, 1967. **210** © Globus Studios/The Stock Market. **214** Photograph by Paul Haller. **224** Photograph by Ronald James. **225** Penrose, L. S. & Penrose, R. "Impossible objects: A special type of visual illusion" from *British Journal of Psychology* 49, 31–33. Reproduced with permission from the British Journal of Psychology. **229** From Tarbus et al. *Eye-movements and Vision*. Copyright © 1967, Plenum Publishing Corp. Reprinted with the permission of the publisher. **231** Courtesy of Daniel Simons. **232** Anton Vengo/SuperStock. **233** Courtesy E. J. Gibson. **235** Photographs by Jeffrey Grosscup. **240** (*Chapter 7 Opener*) Jacob Lawrence. *The Libraries Are Appreciated*. 1943. © Gwendolyn Knight Lawrence, courtesy of the Jacob and Gwendolyn Lawrence Foundation. Photo: Philadelphia Museum of Art/Corbis. **242** Geri Enberg Photography. **247** Detail of *Netherlandish Proverbs* by Pieter Brueghel, 1559; courtesy of Gemaldegalerie, Staatliche Museen Preuischer Kulturbesitz, Berlin. **248** Strauss/Curtis/Corbis. **249** David Butow/Corbis SABA. **250** Courtesy of Sidney Harris, ScienceCartoonsPlus.com. **253** The Warder Collection. **256** Cartoon by Abner Dean. **258** Photograph by Suzanne Szasz. **261** *Top* AP/Wide World Photos. *Bottom* Chris Collins/Corbis. **262** Bob Rowan; Progressive Image/Corbis. **263** Elizabeth Loftus. **264** © The *New Yorker* Collection 1979 Chas. Addams from Cartoonbank.com. All Rights Reserved. **276** (*Chapter 8 Opener*) Modigliani. *Head of a Woman*, ca. 1917. Photo: Christie's Images/Corbis. **278** *Saint Jerome* by Guido Reni. Alinari/Art Resource, NY. **279** *Left* Photograph by Lee Miller, Lee Miller Archives, Chiddingly, England. *Right* Giraudon/Art Resource, NY. **298** John Caldwell. **299** © 1998 by Sidney Harris. **302** Illustration by Henry

# NAME INDEX

# SUBJECT INDEX

Page numbers in *italics* refer to illustrations, tables, and charts; *n* refers to footnotes.